CHECKLIST OF KEY FIGURES

Chapter 1

E1-3	Net Income, $3,500
E1-4	Total Assets, $19,000
E1-6	Total Equity, $12,250
E1-7	Net Income, $450
E1-8	Cash Balance, $650
E1-9	Cash Outflow from Operating Activities, $1,850
E1-10	Net Income, $2,200; Total Assets, $15,200
P1-1	Net Income, $3,000; Total Assets, $14,000
P1-2	Net Income, $1,000; Total Equity, $12,000
P1-3	Net Income, $2,000; Total Assets, $13,000
P1-4	Cash Balance, $3,900; Net Income, $9,300; Cash Outflow from Operating Activities, $1,100
P1-5	Accounts Payable, $2,600; Net Income, $130; Total Assets, $10,730; Cash Outflow from Operating Activities, $3,220
AP1-1	Net Income, $9,050; Total Assets, $53,050
AP1-2	Net Income, $1,500; Total Assets, $8,700
AP1-3	Net Income, $800; Total Equity, $9,800
AP1-4	Cash Balance, $1,600; Net Income, $1,800; Cash Outflow from Operating Activities, $2,400
AP1-5	Total Assets, $14,730; Net Income, $830; Cash Outflow from Operating Activities, $200

Chapter 2

E2-3	Cash Balance, $650; Accounts Payable, $6,800
E2-4	Total Debits, $15,300
E2-5	Net Income, $450
E2-6	Total Assets, $12,250; Net Cash Outflow from Operating Activities, $1,850
E2-8	Total Debits, $17,300
E2-9	Total Credits, $2,245
P2-1	Total Debits, $36,500; Total Assets, $23,000
P2-2	Total Debits, $14,150
P2-3	Total Debits, $30,625
P2-4	Cash Balance, $3,900; Total Debits, $26,250; Net Income, $9,300; Total Assets, $22,550
P2-5	Cash Balance, $1,600; Total Credits, $12,750; Net Income, $1,800; Total Equity, $9,300; Cash Outflow from Operating Activities, $2,400
AP2-1	Total Credits, $26,850; Net Income, $1,500; Total Equity, $20,000
AP2-2	Total Debits, $15,900
AP2-3	Total Credits, $18,450
AP2-4	Cash Balance, $2,280; Total Debits, $15,700; Net Income, $130; Current Assets, $6,730
AP2-5	Accounts Payable, $7,450; Total Debits, $19,300; Net Income, $830; Total Equity, $14,730; Cash Outflow from Operating Activities, $200

Chapter 3

P3-1	Cash Balance, $14,150; Total Debits, $32,100; Net Loss, $2,100; Total Assets, $20,900; Cash Inflow from Operating Activities, $7,400
P3-2	Cash Balance, $125; Total Credits, $31,590
AP3-1	Cash Balance, $13,900; Total Debits, $58,775; Net Loss, $16,525; Total Equity, $41,025; Cash Outflow from Operating Activities, $11,100
AP3-2	Cash Balance, $350; Total Credits, $29,975

Chapter 4

E4-1	Net Income, $4,550
E4-5	Net Income, $1,950
P4-1	Net Income, $2,000
P4-2	
P4-3	
P4-4	
P4-5	
AP4-1	
AP4-2	Net Loss, $400
AP4-3	Net Income, $850; Total Credits, Post-Closing Trial Balance, $9,200
AP4-4	Net Income, $2,000
AP4-5	Net Income, $2,600; Total Equity, $21,100

Chapter 5

E5-3	Cost of Goods Sold, $2,945
E5-4	Cost of Goods Sold, A, $270; B, $390; C, $500; D, $375; E, $475
E5-5	Corrected Cost of Goods Sold, $5,925
E5-6	Net Income, $26,300
E5-7	Gross Profit, $11,300
E5-8	19X7 Current Ratio, 1.25:1
E5-9	19X7 Quick Current, 63:1
E5-10	19X7 Return on Assets, 5.3
E5-11	19X7 Return on Equity, 5.6
E5-12	19X7 Return on Sales, 6.9
E5-13	19X7 Earnings per Share, $2.50
E5-14	19X7 Price Earnings Ratio, 14:1
P5-1	Gross Profit, $414,160
P5-4	Total Assets, $75,000; Debt-to-Equity Ratio, 6.5:1
P5-5	Net Income, $3,250; Retained Earnings, $3,850; Total Equity, $25,850
AP5-1	Cost of Goods Sold, $360,550
AP5-4	Total Equity, $211,500; Current Ratio, 1.76:1
AP5-5	Net Income, $3,500; Retained Earnings, $4,900; Total Assets, $30,000

Chapter 6

P6-1	Total Debits to Purchases, $8,300; Total Debits to Accounts Payable, $6,500; Total Credits to Cash, $6,452
P6-2	Total Credits to Sales, $5,050; Total Credits to Accounts Receivable, $4,700; Total Debits to Cash, $4,658
P6-3	Total Debits to Cash, $8,042; Total Credits to Cash, $7,676; Ending Accounts Receivable, $6,900; Ending Accounts Payable, $1,950
P6-4	Net Pay, $2,820; Total Payroll Tax Expense, $561
AP6-1	Total Debits to Purchases, $5,600; Total Credits to Accounts Payable, $6,150; Total Debits to Cash, $6,103
AP6-2	Total Credits to Sales, $4,850; Total Credits to Accounts Receivable, $3,900; Total Debits to Cash, $3,878
AP6-3	Total Debits to Cash, $6,538; Total Credits to Cash, $8,050; Ending Accounts Receivable, $4,300; Ending Accounts Payable, $1,950
AP6-4	Net Pay, $1,880; Total Payroll Tax Expense, $369

Chapter 7

E7-1	Adjusted Balance, $18,530
E7-2	Adjusted Balance, $18,515
E7-3	Adjusted Balance, $18,165
E7-4	Adjusted Balance, $20,665
E7-5	Adjusted Balance, $20,665
E7-6	Cash Short and Over, $5
E7-7	Bad Debt Expense, $18,000
E7-8	Bad Debt Expense, $18,000
E7-9	Bad Debt Expense, $7,000
E7-10	Bad Debt Expense, $17,000
E7-11	Bad Debt Expense, $8,890
E7-12	Bad Debt Expense, $18,890
P7-1	Adjusted Balance, $87,978
P7-2	Adjusted Balance, $24,000

FINANCIAL ACCOUNTING

AN INTRODUCTION TO DECISION MAKING

THE HBJ ACCOUNTING SERIES

Bischoff, INTRODUCTION TO COLLEGE ACCOUNTING, Chs. 1–14

Bischoff, INTRODUCTION TO COLLEGE ACCOUNTING, Chs. 1–28

Lee, ACCOUNTING: AN INTRODUCTION, Part I, Revised Edition

Lee and Kelley, ACCOUNTING: AN INTRODUCTION, Part II

Hillman, Kochanek, and Reynolds, PRINCIPLES OF ACCOUNTING, Fifth Edition

Walgenbach, Hanson, and Hamre, PRINCIPLES OF ACCOUNTING, Fifth Edition

Wanlass, COMPUTER RESOURCE GUIDE: PRINCIPLES OF ACCOUNTING, Third Edition

Backers, Elgers, and Asebrook, FINANCIAL ACCOUNTING: PRACTICE AND CASES

Beirne and Dauderis, FINANCIAL ACCOUNTING: AN INTRODUCTION TO DECISION MAKING

Brigham and Knechel, FINANCIAL ACCOUNTING USING LOTUS 1-2-3

Hoskin and Hughes, FINANCIAL ACCOUNTING CASES

Kochanek and Hillman, FINANCIAL ACCOUNTING

Stickney, Weil, and Davidson FINANCIAL ACCOUNTING, Sixth Edition

Walgenbach and Hanson, FINANCIAL ACCOUNTING, Sixth Edition

Ketz, Campbell, and Baxendale, MANAGEMENT ACCOUNTING

Maher, Stickney, Weil, and Davidson, MANAGERIAL ACCOUNTING, Fourth Edition

Williams, Stanga, and Holder, INTERMEDIATE ACCOUNTING, Third Edition

Huefner and Largay, ADVANCED FINANCIAL ACCOUNTING, Second Edition

Pahler and Mori, ADVANCED ACCOUNTING, Fourth Edition

Stickney, FINANCIAL STATEMENT ANALYSIS

Guy, Alderman, and Winters, AUDITING, Second Edition

Douglas, GOVERNMENTAL AND NONPROFIT ACCOUNTING

Ziebell and DeCoster, MANAGEMENT CONTROL SYSTEMS IN NONPROFIT ORGANIZATIONS

Bloom and Elgers, ACCOUNTING THEORY AND POLICY, Second Edition

Everett, Boley, Duncan, and Jamison, HBJ FEDERAL TAX COURSE, Vol. I

Sommerfeld, Madeo, and Milliron, AN INTRODUCTION TO TAXATION

Miller, GAAP GUIDE, College Edition

Miller and Bailey, GAAS GUIDE, College Edition

FINANCIAL ACCOUNTING

AN INTRODUCTION TO DECISION MAKING

THOMAS J. BEIRNE
California State University, Sacramento

HENRY DAUDERIS
Concordia University

HARCOURT BRACE JOVANOVICH, PUBLISHERS
San Diego   New York   Chicago   Austin   Washington, D.C.
London   Sydney   Tokyo   Toronto

THE MARKET

Financial Accounting: An Introduction to Decision Making is designed for use in introductory courses in financial accounting, whether for students who seek a general introduction or for students who plan to specialize in the study of accounting. Students at this level need to be introduced to the ever-changing business environment and its language: accounting. This textbook extends beyond the mechanics of accounting, introducing students to the *use* of accounting data throughout all eighteen chapters. Decision making is emphasized, beginning with Chapter 1, and every attempt is made to avoid overly legalistic or technical jargon.

DECISION MAKING IN ACCOUNTING

This textbook stresses how to use the data in making decisions, rather than how to prepare it, an approach woven into almost all the chapters. In Chapter 1 students are given two income statements and then asked to decide which entity would make the better investment. Some chapters, however, do not lend themselves to the decision-making focus. By its very nature, some material is purely mechanical, such as the descriptions of worksheets in Chapters 4 and 5. Since decision making plays a lesser role in such chapters, the use of accounting data is not emphasized there.

The focus throughout the text is on accounting for the corporate form of business, which is more suitable to the decision-making emphasis. However, in Chapter 12, accounting for sole proprietorships and partnerships is introduced so students can understand the role of such organizations in the business environment.

FEATURES

Each chapter features the following:

Chapter Preview Questions

Every chapter begins with a set of Chapter Preview Questions that are keyed to the chapter material and then answered at the end of the chapter as a form of review. This motivates students to delve into the chapter material covering the various questions, thereby improving their cognitive skills.

Real World Examples, Discussion Cases, and Decision Problems

Each chapter also includes at least one real world example of a particular topic discussed in the chapter, along with at least one discussion case and one decision problem. This enables students to see an immediate application of the material they have just learned to the real world. These three features make the text adaptable to an introductory-level financial accounting course offered in a master of business administration or master of accountancy program. Instructors could use the real world examples to discuss the material on a more mature level to whet the appetite of graduate students taking their first course in accounting.

Complete Set of Real World Financial Statements

The material in the back of the textbook includes a complete set of financial statements from the 1989 annual report of United Telecom, an old-line company that has just acquired the Sprint network. Each part division of the textbook ends with a Financial Statement Analysis Problem utilizing the statements so that students can apply to an actual entity what they had just learned in the previous chapters.

Exhibits

The referenced exhibits, including examples for Saguaro Computers, Inc., a hypothetical computer company used throughout the textbook, are color-coded. Financial statements are blue; tables, charts, and graphs are burgundy; and journal entries, ledgers, worksheets, and similar documents are green.

Key Terms

Key terms are in color in the chapter text, and are listed at the end of each chapter with their corresponding page numbers. A glossary is provided at the end of the textbook for checking definitions at any time.

Parallel Problems and Alternate Problems

The problems and alternate problems at the end of each chapter are parallel, in that the alternate problems present similar situations but with different data. This feature gives students the ability to work additional problems similar to assigned homework problems when preparing for a test. Instructors may also want to use the alternate problems for quizzes or exams to test students with more familiar situations.

Self-Test Questions and Demonstration Problems

Each chapter also ends with multiple-choice questions that are answered and explained on the last page of the chapter. Students acquire immediate feedback after reading the chapter by answering these self-test questions. The answers provide a complete explanation, rather than just the correct answer. This section also includes demonstration problems and solutions. Where chapters cover more than one main topic, the demonstration problems are expanded to include all of the major topics. Students should be encouraged to work through the demonstration problem to determine the extent of their understanding of the chapter material. Instructors also could use the demonstration problems as a basis for their lectures on the material.

Other Features

Other textbook features include the following:

CHART OF ACCOUNTS AND CHECKLIST OF KEY FIGURES

A master Chart of Accounts and a Checklist of Key Figures are provided on the front and back endpapers to integrate useful information for both instructors and students working on assignments.

INDEX OF DISCUSSION CASES AND REAL WORLD EXAMPLES

For easy reference, the Discussion Cases and Real World Examples are listed in a separate index.

TEXTBOOK FORMAT

The subject matter of this textbook is divided into six parts: The Accounting Process, Operating Activities, Financing Activities, Investing Activities, Disclosure and Financial Reporting, and Special Topics. The "activities" format closely follows the content of the statement of cash flows. This approach was taken because of the emphasis being placed on the statement of cash flows in today's business environment. Cash flow information is introduced in the first four chapters, and then is examined in detail again in Chapter 17.

TEXTBOOK ADAPTABILITY

Although it has only eighteen chapters, this textbook is very adaptable. For instance, in a course emphasizing decision making, Chapter 4, which discusses worksheets, can be deleted without hindering students' understanding of later chapters. The material in Chapter 5 could be discussed without applying the worksheet information. Chapter 6, Accounting Systems, could be eliminated if course emphasis is on using accounting data rather than on collecting data. The additional time available to instructors who skip these two chapters could be used for classroom discussion of the Real World Examples found in every chapter.

The material on sole proprietorships and partnerships in Chapter 12 also could be skipped if so desired. Chapter 12 is placed in Part III, Financing Activities, because the two forms of business organization differ mainly from a financing activities point of view.

The information in Part IV, Investing Activities, has a separate chapter (Chapter 15) on business combinations for instructors choosing to take introductory students one step further in the accounting process. Although business combinations are quite complicated, the chapter is written at as elementary a level as possible, given the nature of the material. Chapter 15 also could be skipped with no hardship whatsoever on students.

Chapter 16 gives students a good background for entry into the basic finance courses found in most business programs. As mentioned before, Chapter 17 offers a complete investigation into the statement of cash flows.

Chapter 18, which makes up Part VI, Special Topics, also could be eliminated, in that it addresses two distinct areas of financial reporting. Foreign translations and transactions are introduced in the first part of the chapter, and accounting for inflation is discussed in the second part. The two topics are covered in one chapter because they are tied together mathematically.

Four appendixes provide supplementary information on ethics, governmental and nonprofit accounting, Microstudy + ®, and the *What If?* templates.

The inclusion of many topics in this textbook frees instructors to choose subject matter they consider important at the introductory level. Also, since several of the chapters can be skipped without any continuity problems, *Financial Accounting* can be easily used in a course under the quarter system.

ANCILLARIES

The ancillary package is extensive and includes the following:

For the Instructor

The *Solutions Manual* was prepared by the authors in order to maintain consistency between the text and the solutions. The print is large and well-spaced so that the transparencies taken from the manual project well onto the screen.

The *Instructor's Manual* by Joanne Rockness, North Carolina State University, includes chapter objectives, instructor lecture notes, and an overview of assignment material. These are an invaluable aid to new and less-experienced instructors, and even seasoned instructors could benefit from Rockness's manual. The manual also contains solutions to *Practice Set A.*

The ancillary package includes a testbook by Cheryl Matsumoto of the University of Hawaii at Manoa. Each chapter is covered by 20 true or false questions, 30–40 multiple-choice questions, and 10 problems, all cross-referenced to the Chapter Preview Questions. The testbook is an excellent source manual for quizzes, midterm exams, and comprehensive finals.

SOPH-TEST℠, a computerized test bank by SOPH-WARE Supplements, contains all items in the *Testbook* for instant access on most personal computers. This makes it simple to prepare customized quizzes, tests, and exams. Editing and browsing capabilities are just two of this program's many convenient features.

Transparencies are available for *all* exercises, problems, alternate problems, and cases included in the *Solutions Manual,* plus more than 70 four-color teaching transparencies of selected textbook exhibits. As mentioned before, the *Solutions Manual* is set in large, well-spaced type, resulting in outstanding reproductions for the transparencies.

What If? Electronic Spreadsheet Templates for Decision Making, by Kent Finkle, offers instructor's notes and solutions for the assignments in the student version of this package. These are designed to show students how computers are helpful in making decisions. Finkle has done an exceptional job in fitting the templates to the text material.

The *Solutions Disk to Practice Set A* contains a spreadsheet template that allows the instructor to view and print individualized solutions and check figures.

For the Student

A study guide, by Michael Chase and David Davidson of California State University at Long Beach, includes chapter summaries and self-study questions. Having another viewpoint on the material covered in the text is beneficial to students. Chase and Davidson have provided excellent coverage.

Working papers are available for all exercises, problems, and alternate problems. Key information is preprinted on the working papers.

The *What If? Electronic Spreadsheet Templates for Decision Making* package is keyed to the Demonstration Problems in the text. Brief instructions appear in a textbook appendix. Additional instructions appear on the templates themselves. The templates are designed to improve decision-making skills. These tools will help students improve their computer skills, as well as prepare them for decision-making situations.

Practice Set A, a manual practice set by Sandra H. Pelfry of Oakland University, is also available in a computerized version. The integration of students' social security numbers makes each solution slightly different, but easily reconciled to the solutions that appear in the *Instructor's Manual.* Students therefore are unable to "borrow" a solution from one another. The practice set helps students consolidate their learning. The computerized version, by Carol Asplund of the College of Lake County, is available for most DOS-based microcomputers.

ACKNOWLEDGMENTS

It is always impossible to thank everyone who helped in a project like this. First, the following reviewers offered all the constructive criticisms that made this end product possible:

Karen Adamson, Central Washington University
Jane Campbell, University of Dayton
Gyan Chandra, University of Miami (Ohio)
Virginia Clark, University of Cincinnati
John Corless, California State University at Sacramento
P.E. Dascher, Drexel University
Robert Giacoletti, Eastern Kentucky University
Marcia Halvorsen, University of Cincinnati
David J. Harr, George Mason University
Chor T. Lau, California State University at Los Angeles
Brock Murdoch, California State University at Chico
Charles Neyhart, Oregon State University
Sandra H. Pelfrey, Oakland University (Michigan)
Ralph Spanswick, California State University at Los Angeles
C.A. Srinivasan, Drexel University
T. Sterling Wetzel, Oklahoma State University
Ken Winter, University of Wisconsin at LaCrosse

The HBJ editorial staff made invaluable suggestions. Kenneth W. Rethmeier, Bill Teague, Paul Raymond, and Craig Avery provided great help and assistance in developing the manuscript. Kay Kaylor and Michael Kleist did an outstanding job of editing the manuscript and processing the proofs; they were extremely thorough. For the physical appearance of the book, we thank designers Nancy Simerly, Cheryl Solheid, Steve Lux, and Linda Miller, and for coordinating the various stages of production, production managers Diane Southworth and, for its ancillaries, Alison Howell. We are also grateful to Eleanor Garner for her help with permissions.

Personal thanks deserve a place amid these other acknowledgments. From Tom Beirne: "My wife Norma was a fantastic supporter throughout the creation of the manuscript and the lengthy editing process; without her constant encouragement I could not have completed the project." From Henry Dauderis: "The creation of another book is again a wonderful opportunity to acknowledge the support of family, friends, and colleagues, and to express here a particularly warm gratitude to Anne and Mary."

Thomas J. Beirne

Henry Dauderis

CONTENTS

PREFACE   V

PROLOGUE   XXVI

Part I

THE ACCOUNTING PROCESS

1 FINANCIAL STATEMENTS AND THE ACCOUNTING MODEL   2
Chapter Preview Questions   3
Financial Statements   4
The Entity Concept   4   •   Financial Accounting and Managerial
Accounting   5   •   Required Financial Statements   5   •   The
Income Statement   6   •   The Statement of Retained Earnings   7
•   The Balance Sheet   7   •   Statement of Cash Flows   9
Forms of Business Organization   9
Proprietorship and Partnership Equity   9   •   Corporate
Organization   11
The Accounting Model   12
The Accounting Equation Illustrated   13   •   Financial Structure   14
Transactions Analysis   15
Double-Entry Accounting   16
Real World Example 1-1   Why Are So Many Corporations Incorporated in Delaware?   20
Accounting Time Periods   23   •   The Periodicity Concept   26
Chapter Review   27
Key Terms   29
Self-Test Questions for Review   31
Demonstration Problem   32
Discussion Questions   34
Discussion Case: Rodolph and Marmaduke   35
Exercises   36
Problems   39
Alternate Problems   42
Decision Problem   45
Answers to Self-Test Questions   45

2 GAAP AND THE ACCOUNTING PROCESS   46
Chapter Preview Questions   47
Generally Accepted Accounting Principles   48
Generally Accepted Assumptions   48   •   Characteristics of
Accounting Information   51   •   Limitations on the Disclosure of
Useful Accounting Information   52   •   The Accounting Profession
and the Development of GAAP   53   •   The Auditor's Report   54
Accounts in the Accounting Process   54
Real World Example 2-1   If It's Too Complicated, Forget It   56

Transactions Analysis Using Accounts   59

Preparation of the Trial Balance   64   •   Account Classifications on the Balance Sheet   66   •   Preparation of Financial Statements   68

Using Formal Accounting Records   70

Recording Transactions in the General Journal   70   •   Posting Transactions in the Ledger   71   •   Chart of Accounts   73   •   The Accounting Cycle   73

Chapter Review   74

Key Terms   77

Self-Test Questions for Review   80

Demonstration Problem   81

Discussion Questions   85

Discussion Case: Ivan and Igor, Wheat Growers   86

Exercises   87

Problems   90

Alternate Problems   93

Decision Problem   96

Answers to Self-Test Questions   97

3   GAAP AND THE OPERATING CYCLE: PART ONE   98

Chapter Preview Questions   99

The Operating Cycle   100

Revenue Recognition   101   •   Recording Cost Outlays   102   •   The Need for Consistency   103

Transactions Analysis Involving Cost Outlays and Revenue Recognition   104

The Accounting Cycle—Review of Steps 1–3   108

Accrual Accounting and the Matching Concept   111

Real World Example 3-1   The Matching Principle: Why It's So Hard to Achieve in Practice   114

Adjusting Balance Sheet Accounts   114

The Need for Adjusting Entries   114

Mixed Long-term Accounts   118

Adjusting Income Statement Accounts   122

Accruals   125

Unrecorded Revenues   125   •   Unrecorded Expenses   127   •   Recording Taxes   130

The Accounting Cycle—Steps 4–6   131

Chapter Review   132

Key Terms   136

Self-Test Questions for Review   137

Demonstration Problem   138

Discussion Questions   140

Discussion Case: The Bottom Line   141

Exercises   142

Problems   144

Alternate Problems   150

Decision Problem   155

Answers to Self-Test Questions   156

4   GAAP AND THE OPERATING CYCLE: PART TWO   158

Chapter Preview Questions   159

The Worksheet   160

Recording a Trial Balance in the Worksheet   161   •   Balancing the Worksheet   163

Preparation of Financial Statements from the Worksheet 164

Income Statement Preparation 164 • Statement of Retained
Earnings and Balance Sheet Preparation 165

Closing the Books 166

The Closing Procedure 166

Real World Example 4-1 Closing Entries in Early Forms of Bookkeeping 168

Posting the Closing Entries to the Ledger 170 • The Post-Closing
Trial Balance 170

The Sequence of Steps in the Accounting Process 170

Reversing Entries 172

Accrual Adjustments 173 • Mixed Income Statement Account
Adjustments 176 • Mixed Balance Sheet Account
Adjustments 177 • Review of the Accounting Cycle 177

Chapter Review 178

Key Terms 179

Self-Test Questions for Review 180

Demonstration Problem 181

Discussion Questions 186

Discussion Case: Enormous Successful Corporation 187

Notes 188

Exercises 190

Problems 192

Alternate Problems 196

Decision Problem 200

Answers to Self-Test Questions 202

PART I FINANCIAL STATEMENT ANALYSIS PROBLEM 203

Part II OPERATING ACTIVITIES

5 ACCOUNTING FOR MERCHANDISING OPERATIONS 206

Chapter Preview Questions 207

The Calculation of Gross Profit 208

The Sales and Collection Cycle 208

Sales 209

Real World Example 5-1 The Price Is Right 210

The Purchase and Payment Cycle 212

Purchases 213 • Inventory 218 • Purchase and Payment:
Related Recording 219

Completion of the Worksheet 220

Closing Entries 222

Classified Financial Statements 223

The Classified Income Statement 224 • Other Income Statement
Classifications 225 • The Statement of Retained Earnings 227
• The Classified Balance Sheet 229

Evaluation of the Entity 230

Short-term Solvency Analysis 231

Current Ratio 231 • The Acid-Test Ratio 233

Operations Efficiency Analysis 234

Return on Total Assets Ratio 234 • Return on Stockholders'
Equity Ratio 235 • Return on Sales Ratio 236 • Return on
Each Share/Earnings per Share 237 • Price-Earnings Ratio 237

Chapter Review   238
Key Terms   239
Self-Test Questions for Review   241
Demonstration Problem   242
Discussion Questions   248
Discussion Case: Joe, the Restaurateur   249
Exercises   251
Problems   254
Alternate Problems   259
Decision Problem   263
Answers to Self-Test Questions   264

6   ACCOUNTING SYSTEMS   266
Chapter Preview Questions   267
Special Journals   268
The Sales and Collection Cycle   269 • The Purchase and Payment
Cycle   273 • Other Special Journals   278
The General Ledger and Subsidiary Ledgers   278
Flow through the Sales and Collection Cycle Accounts   279 • Flow
through the Purchase and Payment Accounts   279 • The One-
Write System   282
The Payroll Cycle   284
Required Payroll Deductions   285 • Optional Payroll
Deductions   286 • The Payroll Journal   287 • Flow through the
Control Account   287 • Flow through the Subsidiary Accounts:
Individual Employee Records   290
Computerized Accounting System   290
Payroll System   292 • Sales Order Entry System   292
• Inventory Control System   293
Real World Example 6-1   Computers in the Supermarket   293
Accounts Receivable System   294 • Accounts Payable
System   294 • General Ledger System   294 • Management Uses
of Computerized Accounting Systems   294
Chapter Review   296
Key Terms   298
Self-Test Questions for Review   299
Demonstration Problem   301
Discussion Questions   304
Discussion Case: Making Dough with a PC   305
Exercises   307
Problems   308
Alternate Problems   313
Decision Problem   318
Answers to Self-Test Questions   318

7   CASH AND RECEIVABLES   320
Chapter Preview Questions   321
The Concept of Internal Control   322
Cash Collections and Payments   323
Book Reconciling Items   323
Real World Example 7-1   To Catch a Thief   324
Bank Reconciling Items   325 • Updating the Accounting
Records   331 • Petty Cash Transactions   332

Completion of the Sales and Collections Cycle—Accounts Receivable 333

Estimating Uncollectible Accounts Receivable 334 • Writing Off Bad Debts 337 • Credit Balances in Accounts Receivable 339

Chapter Review 340

Key Terms 342

Self-Test Questions for Review 343

Demonstration Problem 344

Discussion Questions 346

Discussion Case: Cash on the Balance Sheet 347

Exercises 348

Problems 351

Alternate Problems 355

Decision Problems 358

Answers to Self-Test Questions 360

8 INVENTORY 362

Chapter Preview Questions 363

Determining the Cost of Inventory 364

Specific Identification 365 • The Actual Flow of Goods 365 • The Flow of Costs 367

Real World Example 8-1 Surprise! 370

Impact of Different Inventory Cost Flows 370

Impact on the Income Statement 371 • Impact on the Balance Sheet 373

Inventory Systems 375

Periodic Inventory System 375 • Perpetual Inventory System 375 • Inventory Systems Compared 377 • Inventory Errors 379

Estimating Inventory Costs 381

Calculating Gross Profit 381

Other Inventory Valuation Methods 385

Chapter Review 385

Key Terms 387

Self-Test Questions for Review 388

Demonstration Problem 389

Discussion Questions 392

Discussion Cases

Case 1: Control Data's Fall from Grace 393 • Case 2: Surprise! 394

Exercises 395

Problems 397

Alternate Problems 400

Decision Problems 402

Answers to Self-Test Questions 403

9 LONG-TERM ASSETS 406

Chapter Preview Questions 407

Establishing the Cost of Long-term Assets 408

Capital Expenditures 408 • Betterments versus Extraordinary Repairs 410

The Nature of Depreciation 412

Long-term Asset Cost Allocation Methods 413

Depreciation Methods Compared   420
Production   420 • Time-based Straight-Line   420 • Time-based Accelerated   420 • Phantom Profits   421
Other Depreciation Issues   422
Long-term Assets on the Balance Sheet   422 • Revision of Depreciation Charges   424
Disposal of Long-term Assets   425
Sale or Abandonment of Long-term Assets   425 • Disposals Involving Trade-in   426
Depletion of Natural Resources   428
Intangible Assets   429
Patents   430 • Copyrights   430 • Trademarks   431 • Franchises   431 • Secret Processes   431 • Goodwill   431
Real World Example 9-1   The Coca-Cola Secret   432
Organization Costs   432 • Leases   433 • Development of Software   433
Chapter Review   433
Key Terms   435
Self-Test Questions for Review   437
Demonstration Problem   438
Discussion Questions   440
Discussion Cases
Case 1: J.R.'s Ranch   441 • Case 2: Carpar   442
Exercises   442
Problems   445
Alternate Problems   447
Decision Problems   450
Answers to Self-Test Questions   452

PART II   FINANCIAL STATEMENT ANALYSIS PROBLEM   453

Part III

FINANCING ACTIVITIES

10   STOCKHOLDERS' EQUITY   456
Chapter Preview Questions   457
The Corporate Structure   458
Corporate Characteristics   458 • Rights of Stockholders   460 • Board of Directors   460 • Corporate Terminology   461
Real World Example 10-1   Independence of the Board of Directors   462
Paid-in Capital Transactions   464
Recording Stock Transactions   464 • Stock Splits   467
Real World Example 10-2   This Stock Split Is 4799 for 1   469
Retained Earnings Restrictions   470
Other Sources of Stockholders' Equity   472
Components of Stockholders' Equity   473
Book Value per Share   473
Book Value of Preferred Stock   474
Stock Subscriptions   475
Chapter Review   477
Key Terms   479
Self-Test Questions for Review   480
Demonstration Problem   481

Discussion Questions   485
Discussion Case: A Reverse Stock Split   486
Exercises   486
Problems   489
Alternate Problems   491
Decision Problem   493
Answers to Self-Test Questions   494

11   DIVIDEND DISTRIBUTIONS   496
Chapter Preview Questions   497
Dividends   498
Components of Stockholders' Equity   498 • Dividend Policy   499
• Dividend Declaration   499
Real World Example 11-1   A Tough Call: The Dividend   500
Accounting for Dividends   501
Stockholder Preference to Dividends   502
Cumulative Dividend Preferences   502 • Participating Dividend
Preferences   504
Stock Dividend Distributions   506
Accounting for Stock Dividends   508 • Stock Dividend versus
Stock Split   509
Treasury Stock   511
Dividends and Treasury Stock   512
Chapter Review   513
Key Terms   514
Self-Test Questions for Review   515
Demonstration Problem   516
Discussion Questions   519
Discussion Case: Dividend Choices   519
Exercises   520
Problems   522
Alternate Problems   524
Decision Problems   525
Answers to Self-Test Questions   527

12   SOLE PROPRIETORSHIPS AND PARTNERSHIPS   528
Chapter Preview Questions   529
Sole Proprietorships   530
Partnerships   531
Partnership Characteristics   532 • Advantages of a
Partnership   533 • Disadvantages of a Partnership   533
Real World Example 12-1   Why Partnerships Break Up   534
Partnership Accounting   536
Division of Partnership Profits and Losses   538
Division Using a Fixed Ratio   538 • Division Using Capital
Balances   538 • Division Using Salary and Interest
Allocations   539
Admission of a New Partner   541
Purchase of an Existing Partner's Interest   542
Withdrawal of an Existing Partner   545
Sale to a New Partner   546 • Sale to the Remaining Partners   546
• Payment from Partnership Assets   546
Liquidation of a Partnership   547

Gains on Sale of Assets   548   •   Loss on Sale of Assets   548
• Liquidation Statement   551

Chapter Review   551

Key Terms   554

Self-Test Questions for Review   555

Demonstration Problem   556

Discussion Questions   558

Discussion Case: To Incorporate or Not?   559

Exercises   559

Problems   562

Alternate Problems   563

Decision Problems   564

Answers to Self-Test Questions   565

13   FINANCING ACTIVITIES: LONG-TERM DEBT   566

Chapter Preview Questions   567

The Decision to Issue Bonds   568

Rights of Bondholders   568   •   Bond Authorization   568
• Recording the Bond Authorization   568   •   Bond Issues in the
Financial Statements   569   •   The Bond Financing Decision   569

Bond Characteristics and Terminology   571

Classification of Bonds   571

Real World Example 13-1   Assessing Corporate Capital Needs   572

Special Features of Bonds   573   •   Face Value   574   •   Balance
Sheet Presentation   575

The Bond Accounting Process   576

Amortizing Premiums and Discounts Using the Straight-Line
Method   577   •   Interest on a Bond   577   •   Amortization   578
• Operation of a Bond Sinking Fund   581   •   Bond
Redemption   583   •   Sale of Bonds between Interest Dates   584

The Effective Interest Method of Amortization   586

Calculating Interest Payments and Premium Amortization   587
• Calculating Interest Expense and Discount Amortization   589
• Comparison of the Effective Interest Method with the Straight-
Line Method   591   •   Accrual of Bond Interest at Year-End   592

Appendix: Time Value of Money Analysis—Present and Future Values   592

Present Value Calculations   593   •   Future Value Calculations   596

Present Value Tables   598

Future Value Tables   600

Chapter Review   602

Key Terms   604

Self-Test Questions for Review   605

Demonstration Problem   607

Discussion Questions   610

Discussion Case: Jasmine Technologies, Inc.   611

Exercises   613

Problems   616

Alternate Problems   619

Decision Problem   623

Answers to Self-Test Questions   623

PART III   FINANCIAL STATEMENT ANALYSIS PROBLEM   625

Part IV   **INVESTING ACTIVITIES**

14   SHORT-TERM AND LONG-TERM INVESTMENT PORTFOLIOS   628
Chapter Preview Questions   629
The Investment Decision   630
   Valuation of Investments   631
Short-term Portfolio Investments   632
   Short-term Investments in Bonds   632 • Short-term Investments
   in Stock: No Significant Influence   635 • Short-term Investments
   in Stock: Significant Influence   637
Real World Example 14-1   A Different Approach to Stock Splits   638
Long-term Portfolio Investments: Stock   640
   No Significant Influence   640 • Significant Influence   641
   • Actual Control   642
Long-term Portfolio Investments: Bonds   642
   Purchase Cost of Bonds   642 • Amortizing Premiums and
   Discounts   643 • Effective Interest Method: Long-term Bond
   Investments   648
Chapter Review   651
Key Terms   653
Self-Test Questions for Review   654
Demonstration Problem   655
Discussion Questions   660
Discussion Case: Compound Interest   660
Exercises   661
Problems   664
Alternate Problems   666
Decision Problem   667
Answers to Self-Test Questions   668

15   BUSINESS COMBINATIONS   670
Chapter Preview Questions   671
Business Combinations   672
   The Accounting Equation Reviewed   672 • Recording the
   Acquisition   673
Wholly Owned Subsidiaries   674
   Recording the Acquisition   674 • Preparation of Consolidated
   Financial Statements   675
Partially Owned Subsidiaries   680
   Recording the Purchase   680 • Preparation of Consolidated
   Financial Statements   681
Pooling of Interests   686
Application of LCM Where Control Exists   688
Real World Example 15-1   LCM and the October 19, 1987, Decline   688
Financial Statements after Date of Acquisition   689
Chapter Review   690
Key Terms   691
Self-Test Questions for Review   692
Demonstration Problem   693
Discussion Questions   696
Discussion Case: Which Solution?   697

Exercises   698
Problems   700
Alternate Problems   702
Decision Problem   705
Answers to Self-Test Questions   706

PART IV   FINANCIAL STATEMENT ANALYSIS PROBLEM   707

Part V   DISCLOSURE AND FINANCIAL REPORTING

16   ANALYSIS OF FINANCIAL STATEMENTS   710
Chapter Preview Questions   711
Financial Structure: Saguaro Computers, Inc.   712
   Short-term versus Long-term Debt   713
Short-term Solvency Analysis   715
   Working Capital   717 • The Acid-Test Ratio   719 • Management
   Decisions Related to Receivables   720 • Management Decisions
   Related to Inventory   721 • The Revenue Operating Cycle   723
   • What Is Causing Saguaro's Financial Problems?   724
Analysis of Operations Efficiency   724
   Return on Total Assets   725 • Return on Stockholders'
   Equity   725 • Earnings per Share   727 • Return-on-Sales
   Ratio   728 • Management Decisions Related to Long-term
   Assets   729
Saguaro Computers, Inc.'s Performance   730
   Analysis of Operating Efficiencies   730 • Saguaro's Management
   Decisions Related to Long-term Assets   731
Summary of Ratios   735
Real World Example 16-1   Calculating the Z Score   737
Chapter Review   740
Key Terms   742
Self-Test Questions for Review   743
Demonstration Problem   745
Discussion Questions   746
Discussion Cases
   Case 1: Murphy, Inc.   747 • Case 2: Fitz, Inc., and Roy Corp.   748
   • Case 3: Achilles Corp.   749
Exercises   751
Problems   753
Alternate Problems   755
Decision Problems   757
Answers to Self-Test Questions   759

17   STATEMENT OF CASH FLOWS   760
Chapter Preview Questions   761
Financial Statement Reporting   762
The Statement of Cash Flows   762
Analysis of Cash Flows   763
Real World Example 17-1   How Cash Flows Are Classified   764
   Step 1   Calculation of the Increase or Decrease in Cash   764
   • Step 2   Calculation of Cash Flows from Operating Activities   767
   • Step 3   Analysis of Changes in Noncurrent Accounts   773

• Step 4   Analysis of Current Accounts Not Used in the
Measurement of Income 775 • Step 5   Preparation of the Formal
Statement of Cash Flows 776 • Noncash Financing and Investing
Activities 777

The Worksheet Approach to Solving Cash-Flow Problems 777

Appendix: The T-Account Approach to Solving Cash-Flow Problems 791

The Direct Method 791 • The Indirect Method 796

Chapter Review 799

Key Terms 801

Self-Test Questions for Review 802

Demonstration Problem 803

Discussion Questions 806

Discussion Case: Ben & Jerry's 807

Exercises 808

Problems 810

Alternate Problems 813

Decision Problem 816

Answers to Self-Test Questions 817

PART V   FINANCIAL STATEMENT ANALYSIS PROBLEM 819

Part VI   SPECIAL TOPICS

18   INTERNATIONAL AND INFLATION ACCOUNTING 822

Chapter Preview Questions 823

International Issues 824

Foreign Translations 824

Foreign Transactions 827

Accounting for Inflation 831

Constant Dollar Accounting 832

Real World Example 18-1   Inflation Hits 8-Year High 834

Current Cost Accounting 840

Chapter Review 844

Key Terms 846

Self-Test Questions for Review 848

Demonstration Problem 849

Discussion Questions 852

Discussion Case: Saguaro Computers, Inc. 852

Exercises 853

Problems 857

Alternate Problems 860

Decision Problem 863

Answers to Self-Test Questions 863

PART VI   FINANCIAL STATEMENT ANALYSIS PROBLEM 865

APPENDIX A   Ethics   867

APPENDIX B   Governmental and Nonprofit Accounting   877

APPENDIX C   Microstudy + ® Operating Instructions   883

APPENDIX D Student Instructions for *What If? Electronic Spreadsheet Templates for Decision Making*   885

GLOSSARY   889

1989 UNITED TELECOM ANNUAL REPORT   907

INDEX   921

INDEX OF DISCUSSION CASES AND REAL WORLD EXAMPLES   931

**To My Wife Norma
and My Parents Tom, Sr., and Helen**
—Thomas J. Beirne

**To My Wife Margarita
and
James, Andrew, and Dana,
for Many Hours That
Should Have Been Theirs**
—Henry Dauderis

FINANCIAL ACCOUNTING

AN INTRODUCTION TO DECISION MAKING

PROLOGUE

FOR whatever reason, you have decided to take an introductory course in accounting. This prologue puts the field of accounting in perspective and summarizes the process by which economic events are communicated. Transactions are completed in terms of U.S. dollars, which constitute numerical units accountants have accepted as the most appropriate method of measuring transactions and communicating them to interested parties who use the reported amounts to evaluate business organizations.

The accounting process consists of five steps and involves the way in which the dollar amounts of transactions are transformed into financial statement information and then communicated to statement users. These steps are outlined as follows and summarized in Exhibit P-1.

Step 1

An economic event takes place. If you see a car for sale with a card in the window advertising $1,000, this is not an economic event in an accounting sense. If you walk up to the dealer and say that you are willing to pay $800 for the car, this is not an economic event. If the dealer says he will accept $950 for the car, this is still not an economic event. If you then offer $900, and the dealer accepts, now you have an economic event from an accounting point of view.

Step 2

Once an economic event has taken place, it must be recorded. Similar events are recorded in like manner (that is, they are classified), and at the end of a given period of time (one day, week, month, quarter, or year) all the economic events that took place during that period are summarized. This second step is generally referred to as the *bookkeeping cycle*.

Step 3

All of the above information is given to the accountant, who, on a uniform and consistent basis, prepares financial statements.

Step 4

The accountant then analyzes and interprets the information in the accounting statements and communicates this information to the users of accounting information. Some of the possible users of this information are the owners of the business, the managers of the business (who may or may not be the owners), lenders, and the Internal Revenue Service, which is especially interested in how much income was earned during the year.

Step 5   The users analyze and interpret the information in the financial statements and act in a way to try to influence or alter future economic events related to the company. If the focus of the above information is on users outside the business, the process emphasizes *financial accounting*. If the focus is on users inside the business, usually management, the process emphasizes *managerial accounting*. (The difference between these two areas of accounting is discussed further in Chapter 1.)

Graphically, the above relationships appear as shown in Exhibit P-1.

EXHIBIT P-1

THE ACCOUNTING PROCESS

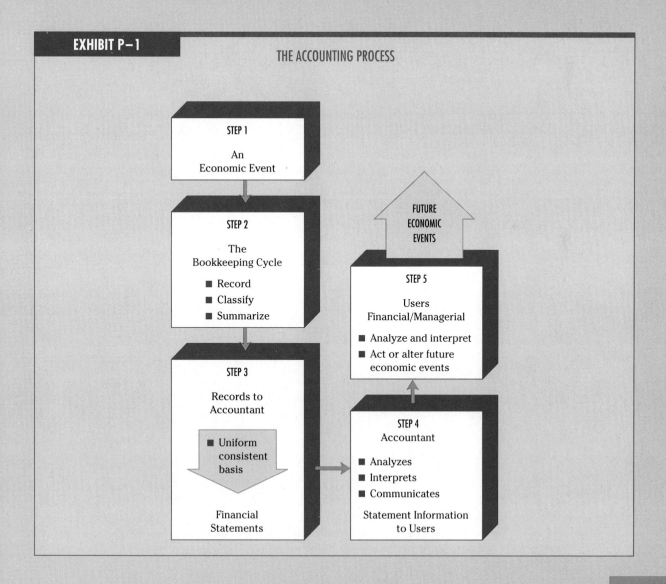

THE ACCOUNTING PROCESS

P ART I focuses on the accounting process in order to familiarize students with the methods underlying the accumulation of financial information, and the bookkeeping methods used to record and summarize this information. Knowing these methods is necessary for making sound interpretations of the information communicated through the financial statements.

Chapter 1 identifies the basic financial statements used to communicate financial information and describes the accounting model used to accumulate this information. Chapter 2 introduces the student to generally accepted accounting principles (GAAP) and to the various organizations that have developed the principles since the early part of the twentieth century. The accounting model is then investigated further, resulting in a more sophisticated means of accumulating accounting information. Chapter 3 explains the operating cycle, its various elements, and the need to adjust accounting data because of the operating cycle assumptions. Part I concludes with Chapter 4, which introduces the student to the tools available to the accountant to prepare financial statements in a complex situation. The text is written so that an instructor could skip Chapter 4 in an accounting course designed solely for decision-making.

1

FINANCIAL STATEMENTS AND THE ACCOUNTING MODEL

C HAPTER 1 introduces financial information, giving students an overview of accounting, particularly financial accounting. The essential financial statements are presented and students are exposed to a multitude of key business terms in the glossary at the end of the chapter. A basic approach to gathering financial information is investigated, enabling students to prepare all of the financial statements of an entity. Fundamental relationships among the elements of financial statements are also described, especially the relationship between debt and equity.

After studying Chapter 1, you should be able to answer the following questions:

1 How do accountants communicate financial information to interested parties? (pp.4–5)

2 From the accountant's point of view, what is a financial transaction? (pp.4, 13)

3 In what way do financial transactions constitute one of the boundaries of accounting? (p.4)

4 What is the entity concept, and how is it also one of the boundaries of accounting? (p.4–5)

5 In what way does financial accounting differ from managerial accounting? (p.5)

6 Which accounting report measures profitability? Which measures financial position? (p.5)

7 What information does the statement of cash flows provide? (p.9)

8 What are the advantages and disadvantages of different forms of business organization? (p.11)

9 How do stockholders participate in day-to-day management? (p.11)

10 Accountants view financial transactions as economic events that change components within the accounting equation. What are these components and how do they change? (pp.13–14)

11 What is the distinction between a calendar year-end and a fiscal year-end? (pp.23, 26)

12 What impact does the periodicity concept have on the reporting of financial information? (pp.26–27)

FINANCIAL STATEMENTS

Q1: Communicating financial information

Accounting has been called the language of business. Just as all language develops out of a need to communicate information, **accounting** has evolved as a means of communicating financial information. Part of this information concerns the financial status of the business itself and is usually presented in the form of financial statements that typically deal with assets and liabilities. **Assets** are probable future economic benefits obtained or controlled by a particular entity as a result of past transactions or events. **Liabilities** are probable future economic sacrifices of economic benefits arising from the present obligations of an entity to transfer assets or provide services to other entities in the future as a result of past transactions or events.

Q2: Accountant's view of a financial transaction

Assets are continually being exchanged, as are obligations; each exchange is referred to as a **transaction.** Any exchange of an asset for another asset is also a transaction. Acceptance of an obligation in return for an asset is also a transaction. Because exchanges usually involve dollar amounts, they are called **financial transactions.** Understanding financial accounting is essentially a matter of understanding financial transactions.

For example, a financial transaction occurs when you buy a car. A transaction occurs whether you pay cash for the car or obtain 100% financing from a bank. The car loan is a liability, a future transfer of assets. The dollar amount is measurable, and the effect of the transaction is determinable.

Q3: Transactions as accounting boundary

Financial transactions represent one of the boundaries of accounting because accountants ignore in their reports many events and activities that do not involve a financially measurable exchange. When you buy a car, your negotiations with the dealer, the market demand (or lack of it) for cars, and your acceptance of a counteroffer fall outside the boundaries of accounting. They stop short of constituting a financial transaction.

The Entity Concept

Q4: Entity concept as accounting boundary

Each transaction always has two or more parties. Accountants view each party as a separate financial unit—that is, as a separate entity. An **entity** can be thought of as a unit of accountability that exists separately from other units of accountability and also separately from those who own the entity. The accountant for the entity focuses only on the transactions of the business, which he or she translates into accounting information. In this way, the entity concept also represents one of the boundaries of accounting.

- **Business transactions are translated into accounting information.**
- **In selecting transactions to be translated into accounting information, the accountant is only interested in those affecting the unit of accountability, or *entity*.**

Entities seek to use their assets in activities that will not only increase the value of those assets but also will increase the total assets of the entity. For example, Macy's operates a chain of department stores where assets, in the form of merchandise, are exchanged for customers' assets, usually in the form of cash but sometimes in the form of credit. Similarly, Standard Oil uses its assets in the exploration of oil so the oil can be exchanged for other assets of its customers. Both of these entities provide *goods* in exchange for assets belonging to others. Other entities provide *services* that they exchange for assets belonging to others. The emphasis in Chapters 1–4 is on companies that provide a service. In Chapter 5, the focus is on companies that provide goods, commonly referred to as merchandisers.

Some entities are more successful than others in the performance of the activities for which they were formed; accounting information is necessary to measure the progress of each entity and to conform to legal requirements. This information is reported in terms of dollars, and the accounting reports that communicate this information are commonly referred to as *financial statements*.

Financial Accounting and Managerial Accounting

Q5: Financial vs.
Managerial

Financial accounting is the process of recording transactions and preparing financial statements for external users of financial information. Users outside the business include investors, owners (such as stockholders), creditors, and the government. In contrast, **managerial accounting** focuses on internal users of financial information. Users inside the business include managers and owners (such as sole proprietors or partners) directly involved with day-to-day business operations.

Because of the **fiduciary relationship** (based on mutual trust) between the outside users and the accountant, many more rules and regulations govern financial accounting than managerial accounting. In fact, in the latter, the accountant can give management almost any type of information desired using a variety of measurement bases—whereas much of financial accounting is governed by historical cost.

Required Financial Statements

Q1: Communicating
financial
information
Q6: Financial
accounting
reports

A standard group of financial statements has become generally accepted and required in the United States and many other countries. These include the following:

1. The **income statement** communicates the inflow of assets (called *revenues*) and the outflow or consumption of assets (called *expenses*) resulting from the entity's activities. Thus it shows the results of operations, measured in terms of profitability. An excess of inflows over outflows is called **net income.** An excess of outflows over inflows is called **net loss.**

2. The **statement of retained earnings** shows the changes in the retained earnings (introduced later) that occurred during the past year due to net income and dividends.

3. The **balance sheet** communicates the balances of what the entity owns (called *assets*), what the entity owes (called *liabilities*), and the difference between the assets and the liabilities, called *equity* or *owners' equity.* The equity amount represents the balance that belongs to the owners of the entity. The balance sheet measures the *financial position* of a business.

4. The **statement of cash flows** shows the inflows and outflows of cash from the entity's three main activities: operating, investing, and financing.

These four statements, together with footnote disclosures, constitute the package of financial information usually given to outside users. These statements are briefly discussed in the following sections and are more fully developed in subsequent chapters. The information in the statement examples is derived from the transactions analysis discussed on pp. 16–25.

The Income Statement

The income statement can be compared to a video camera with a counter that continually records the transactions of an entity; the counter accumulates these transactions while the camera records them. The income statement, however, is very selective in that it accumulates only the revenue and expense transactions of the entity. When the camera stops, the counter shows the accumulated total of all these revenue and expense transactions.

The following income statement is for Saguaro Computers, Inc. (SCI), the company used as an example throughout this textbook. For SCI's statement, the camera was started on November 1 and was stopped at November 30, and the counter shows a net income of $2,000. The expenses of the November period are deducted from the revenue of the same period. Identifying expenses and revenues within a time period is referred to as the **accrual method of accounting.**

Saguaro Computers, Inc.
Income Statement
For the Month Ended November 30, 19X1

Revenue		
Repair Revenue		$7,000
Expenses		
Rent Expense	$ 600	
Salaries Expense	2,500	
Supplies Expense	1,200	
Truck Expense	700	
Total Expenses		5,000
Net Income		$2,000

When the camera begins again in December, the counter continues to accumulate revenue and expense transactions; that is, it adds the December transactions to those of November.

One cartridge is used for each 12-month period. At the end of the year, the exposed cartridge is removed and a new cartridge is inserted for the next 12 months. When the new cartridge is inserted, the counter in the camera is automatically reset to zero; in this way only the transactions of the new year are accumulated. The income statement is therefore referred to as a *period-of-time financial statement.*

WHAT IS REVENUE?

Revenue consists of the inflow of assets to an entity in return for services performed or goods sold during that period. It is expressed in terms of dollars. In the case of Saguaro Computers, Inc., the services performed are computer repairs.

WHAT ARE EXPENSES?

Expenses represent either an outflow or consumption of assets, or the resources belonging to the entity that have been used up, or the obligations incurred in performing the revenue-producing services. Saguaro Computers, Inc. uses parts, for example, to make repairs; these parts are one of the entity's resources used up in performing repairs. These expenses represent the outflow or consumption of assets needed to earn the $7,000 revenue.

WHAT IS NET INCOME?

The difference between revenue and expenses is net income. It is a guide for the reader of the income statement as to how profitably the activities of the entity are being conducted; it is a measure of the success of the entity. The net income calculation is also used in calculating taxes payable to the government, and it is one criterion used to determine the amount of dividends to be paid. (**Dividends** are payments made by a corporation to its owners and are never included in an income statement.) The accumulated net income not paid as dividends is referred to as **retained earnings.** The accounting for dividends is further discussed in Chapters 5 and 11.

The Statement of Retained Earnings

As noted previously, the statement of retained earnings shows the changes in retained earnings during the year caused by net income and the distribution of net income as dividends to the owners. Because no dividends were paid to the owners of SCI during November 19X1, its statement of retained earnings is quite simple:

Saguaro Computers, Inc.
Statement of Retained Earnings
For the Month Ended November 30, 19X1

Retained Earnings, November 1, 19X1	$ –0–
Net Income	2,000
	$2,000
Dividends Paid	–0–
Retained Earnings, November 30, 19X1	$2,000

The Balance Sheet

The balance sheet can be compared to a still camera that produces a picture of the entity at a point in time. In the following balance sheet of Saguaro Computers, Inc. the still was made on November 30. It shows the corporate assets, liabilities, and equity on that date.

Saguaro Computers, Inc.
Balance Sheet
November 30, 19X1

Assets		Liabilities		
Cash	$ 5,000	Bank Loan	$ 5,000	
Accounts Receivable	3,000	Accounts Payable	1,000	
Equipment	2,000	Total Liabilities		$ 6,000
Truck	8,000			
		Equity		
		Common Stock	$10,000	
		Retained Earnings	2,000	12,000
		Total Liabilities		
Total Assets	$18,000	and Equity		$18,000

A balance sheet can be compiled whenever necessary but is *always* prepared at the end of the corporation's business year. The balance sheet is therefore referred to as a *point-in-time financial statement.*

The economic resources owned by the entity are listed as assets on the balance sheet; these assets are individually described and their cost is indicated. Those having a claim against these assets are listed as liabilities and equities. Note that the total amount of assets equals the total claims against those assets. The date of the balance sheet is important because it identifies the date at which the assets owned and the existing claims against the assets are listed. In this format, one of two (see Chapter 2), the right side of the balance sheet represents the **financial structure** of an entity.

The term *balance sheet* is widely used; however, other titles more descriptive of the statement's purpose are also used: *statement of financial position* and *statement of financial condition*.

WHAT IS AN ASSET?

An asset was broadly defined at the beginning of this chapter as probable future economic benefits obtained or controlled by a particular entity as a result of past transactions or events. One could say that an asset was anything of value owned by an entity. However, in the complex world of business the definition must go further. For example, if a business leases an asset for most if not all of its useful life, does the entity "own" the asset? No, but if the entity benefits from the use of that asset for most of its useful life, shouldn't the asset be reported on the entity's balance sheet? Assets include property such as buildings and equipment, as well as claims to cash, such as accounts and notes receivable. Assets also include rights that an entity has from obtaining documents such as patents, copyrights, and trademarks. To be classified as an asset, the item must have some future economic benefit to the entity. This future benefit is usually determined by the asset's ability to produce revenue.

Assets are generally recorded at their original cost, since this is the most objectively determinable amount. Therefore, the balance sheet valuation for an asset *does not* purport to measure the current cost of the asset, the cost of replacing the asset, or how much the asset could be sold for if offered for sale. Accountants have decided to record assets at cost because the amount is generally determined in an **"arm's length" transaction,** making the amount at market value and thus objectively determinable.

WHAT IS A LIABILITY?

A liability was defined at the beginning of this chapter as probable future economic sacrifice of economic benefits arising from the present obligations of an entity to transfer assets or provide services to other entities in the future as a result of past transactions or events. More simply put, a liability is an obligation to pay money, or to provide goods and services in the future. Until that liability or obligation is satisfied, the creditor, the entity to whom the resource is owed, has a claim against the assets of the entity. For example, if you borrowed money to buy a car, the lending institution has a claim against that asset. But if for some reason the car was destroyed, and you had no insurance on the vehicle, the lending institution would have a claim on your other assets, such as a jet ski, stereo, computer, or other property. Some common business liabilities would be **accounts payable** (amounts owed—payables—to suppliers who have given short-term credit); bank loans; and taxes payable for property, income, or payroll.

WHAT IS EQUITY?

Owners' equity represents the amount of net assets accruing to the owners of the entity. In the case of Saguaro Computers, Inc., this equity belongs to stockholders who own a corporation. **Equity** is the balance that remains after liabilities are deducted from assets. In SCI's November 30 balance sheet, equity is calculated as $12,000 ($18,000 assets minus $6,000 liabilities).

WHAT IS COMMON STOCK?

Common stock represents all ownership interest of the stockholders in the *net assets* (assets minus liabilities) of the corporation. A **stock certificate** represents a unit of ownership in the corporation; it is nothing more than an elaborately printed piece of paper indicating a particular investor's right of ownership. A typical stock certificate is illustrated in Exhibit 1-1.

Statement of Cash Flows

Q7: Information in statement of cash flows

As was mentioned earlier, the statement of cash flows shows the inflows and out-flows of cash from an entity's three main activities: operating, investing, and financing. The SCI statement of cash flows for the month of November would appear as in Exhibit 1-2. This statement is a variation of the direct method. The two schedules that would accompany it are explained in Chapter 17. The statement of cash flows is a very important financial statement in that it shows the owners and other inter-ested users just where cash has gone, and where it has come from. The income statement measures inflows and outflows on the "accrual basis" as we will see in Chapter 2, and does not measure cash inflow and outflow.

The statement demonstrates the importance of SCI collecting **accounts receivable** (amounts due—receivables—from customers for goods or services provided) on a timely basis. In the case of SCI, it shows that even though net income was $2,000 (as reported earlier), the net cash outflow from operating activities was $1,000 because $3,000 of accounts receivable were not collected during the month.

FORMS OF BUSINESS ORGANIZATION
Proprietorship and Partnership Equity

The preceding discussion of owners' equity refers to the corporate form of business organization. A business entity can also be a sole-owner **proprietorship** or a mul-tiple-owner **partnership.** The only significant difference between the balance sheet of a proprietorship and of a partnership is the treatment of owners' equity. A capital account is used to record owner contributions to the business. Any owner with-drawals, usually called *drawings,* reduce this account; net income earned by the business increases the account. Unlike the corporate form of organization, no dis-tinction is made in the balance sheet between owner capital contributions and net income earned and retained in the business. It is necessary in the corporate form to maintain the distinction between amounts invested (common stock), and the net income kept in the business (retained earnings) for various reasons, most important of which is that a corporation is considered a legal entity. The topic of common stock will be studied intensively in Chapter 10. The owners' equity of a proprietorship and of a partnership appears on the balance sheets as follows:

Proprietor's Equity		Partners' Equity	
Capital—B. Adams	$12,000	Capital—B. Adams	$ 8,000
		Capital—C. Dill	4,000
		Total	$12,000

EXHIBIT 1–1

A TYPICAL STOCK CERTIFICATE

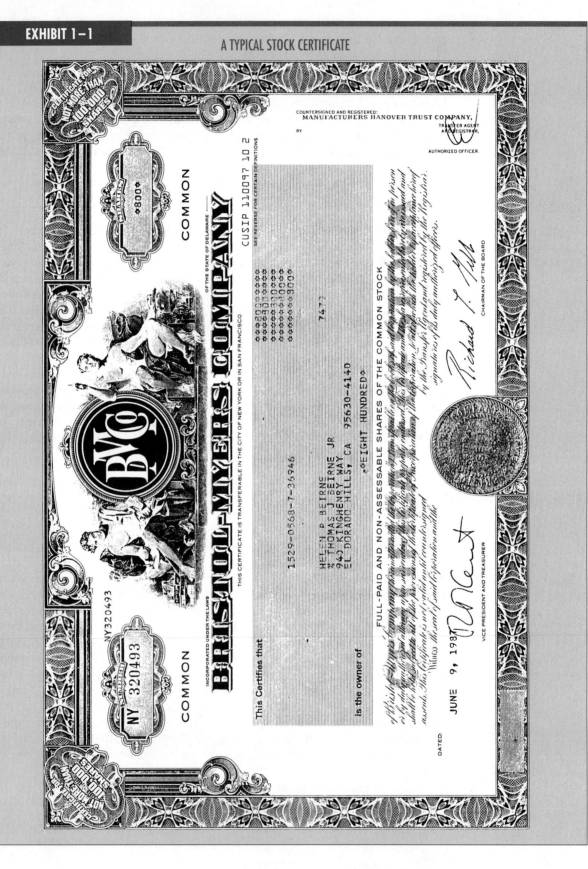

EXHIBIT 1–2

Saguaro Computers, Inc.
Statement of Cash Flows (Direct Method)
For the Month Ended November 30, 19X1

Cash Flows from Operating Activities
Inflows:
Cash Received from Customers $ 4,000
(Outflows):
Cash Paid for Expenses (5,000)
 Net Cash Outflow from Operating Activities $(1,000)

Cash Flows from Investing Activities
Inflows:
Sale of Equipment 1,000
(Outflows):
Purchase of Equipment $(2,000)
Purchase of a Truck (3,000)
 Total Cash Outflows (5,000)
 Net Cash Outflow from Investing Activities $(4,000)

Cash Flows from Financing Activities
Inflows:
Issuance of Common Stock 10,000
 Net Cash Inflow from Financing Activities 10,000
Net Inflow of Cash $ 5,000
Cash Balance, November 1, 19X1 –0–
Cash Balance, November 30, 19X1 $ 5,000

Q8: Advantages of different forms of business

A partnership has the added advantages over a proprietorship of a greater amount of capital contributed by the several partners and the different abilities that they bring to the management of the business. The primary disadvantage of a partnership is that each owner can be held personally responsible for all the debts of the business.

Neither a proprietorship nor a partnership pays income tax itself to the government as does a corporation; rather, the proprietor and each partner personally pay income tax on the net income of the business in addition to his or her other income.

Corporate Organization

Q9: Stockholders and day-to-day management

Stockholders do not usually participate in the day-to-day management of a business. They participate indirectly through the election of a **board of directors,** although a stockholder may become a member of the board, a corporate officer, or both. The board of directors also does not participate in the day-to-day management of the corporation, but delegates this responsibility to the officers of the corporation, the president, secretary, treasurer, and vice-presidents. This delegation of responsibility is illustrated in Exhibit 1-3.

Stockholders usually meet annually to vote for a board of directors—either to reelect the current directors or to elect new directors. The board of directors meets monthly or quarterly to review the operations of the corporation and to set policies

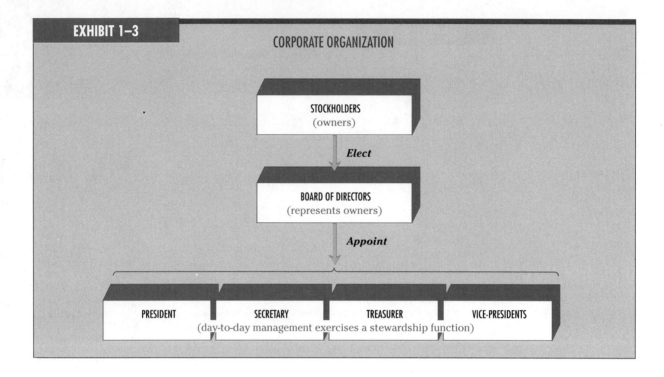

EXHIBIT 1–3

CORPORATE ORGANIZATION

for future operations. Based on the performance of the corporation, the board may decide to distribute some assets, usually in the form of cash, as a dividend to stockholders.

THE ACCOUNTING MODEL

The mechanics used in the accounting process were first published in 1494 by a Franciscan friar living in Italy. In his book *Arithmetic, Geometry and Proportion,* **Luca Pacioli** included a description of a **double-entry bookkeeping system** designed to ensure the accuracy of transactions being recorded. As early as 1200, a more primitive version of this recording system was in use in Venice, and by Pacioli's time the double-entry system was widely used. Although Pacioli is often given credit for its invention, it is doubtful he originated the double-entry model, often referred to as the *accounting equation.* It is more likely he either refined the recording practice of the day or integrated the system into the wider mathematical context of his book.

The **accounting equation** states that the total assets belonging to an entity must always equal the total claims (called equities) against those assets. The equality between assets and equities is shown by an equal sign. The equation is expressed as follows:

ASSETS = EQUITIES

The use of the word *equities* in this expression of the accounting equation includes claims of both **creditors** (anyone to whom the business owes money) and owners against the assets of the entity.

An equally correct way of expressing the relationship between assets and equities is

$$\text{ASSETS} = \text{SOURCES OF ASSETS}$$

Since assets can only be received from two sources—financing activities and operating activities—the accounting equation could be expanded further:

$$\text{ASSETS} = \text{FINANCING ACTIVITIES} + \text{OPERATING ACTIVITIES}$$

Since assets are the result of investing activities, the equation could be expanded even further:

$$\text{INVESTING ACTIVITIES} = \text{FINANCING ACTIVITIES} + \text{OPERATING ACTIVITIES}$$

The above form of the equation is the basis for the statement of cash flows. Although in this form the equation would not balance because of overlapping factors, it is a good indication of what items on the balance sheet would be affected by cash flows. The statement of cash flows is discussed extensively in Chapter 17.

Since creditors' claims to the assets (called liabilities) are primary claims, the owners' claims become residual (called equity). Put in another way, the owners get everything left over after all liabilities have been satisfied. Therefore, the accounting equation could also be restated as follows:

$$\text{ASSETS} - \text{LIABILITIES} = \text{EQUITY}$$

Note: The word *equity,* as used in this expression of the accounting equation, refers only to owners' equity throughout this textbook; this restricted meaning of the word is the more widely accepted in accounting literature.

Q2: Accountant's view of financial accounting

This basic accounting model forms the foundation on which accounting is built. In addition to providing this foundation, it also expresses an equality between the assets and the total claims against those assets. Accountants view financial transactions as economic events that change components within the accounting equation.

The Accounting Equation Illustrated

Q10: Changing components in accounting equation

The following example illustrates the use of the equation. Assume a business owns one asset, a truck, which it purchased for $8,000, and that $3,000 has been paid at the purchase date, with a $5,000 balance due to the bank (a creditor) remaining. The equation now appears in the following form:

$$\begin{array}{ccccc} \text{ASSETS} & = & \text{LIABILITIES} & + & \text{EQUITY} \\ \$8,000 & & \$5,000 & & \$3,000 \end{array}$$

In this situation the business owns $8,000 of assets (truck), a creditor (the bank that lent the money) has a primary claim of $5,000, and the owners have residual claims (the balance remaining) of $3,000. It is clear the *asset* total of $8,000 *equals* the total of the *equity* side of the equation, $5,000 + $3,000.

Since owners are interested in knowing the amount of their equity in an entity, financial statements are designed to show the amount left for them after all other claims have been recognized. Owners' claims are expressed as the difference between total assets and total liabilities. The accounting equation is often stated in the following manner to emphasize owners' claims:

$$\begin{array}{ccccc} \text{ASSETS} & - & \text{LIABILITIES} & = & \text{EQUITY} \\ \$8,000 & & \$5,000 & & \$3,000 \end{array}$$

Since total assets minus total liabilities also equals net assets, it is obvious that net assets is synonymous with the owners' equity interest in total assets. The $3,000 difference between assets and liabilities also can be referred to as net assets.

Financial Structure

The accounting equation therefore expresses a relationship between assets owned by the entity and the claims against those assets. Although stockholders own a corporation, they alone do not finance the corporation; creditors also finance a part of its activities. Creditors and stockholders together are said to form the *financial structure* of a corporation. The financial structure of Saguaro Computers, Inc., is as follows:

$$\text{ASSETS} = \text{LIABILITIES} + \text{EQUITY}$$
$$\$18,000 \qquad \$6,000 \qquad \$12,000$$

SCI has a low reliance on debt in its financial structure; therefore, creditors have only a small claim against its assets. Analysts and investors are concerned with the financial structure of a corporation—that is, with the proportion of stockholders' claims against the assets of a corporation compared with creditors' claims. This proportion is important because the long-term financial strength of the corporation depends on its ability to service its debt (pay the interest and principal when due) and earn profits to be able to pay dividends and keep the stockholders content. The interest on debt must be paid, but dividends on stock are paid at the discretion of the board of directors. Therefore, the higher the amount of debt a business has in relation to the amount of equity, the greater the risk is to the business. A proper mix must be achieved in order for the business to continue in existence in the long run. When the proportion of debt to equity grows too high, and profits are not sufficient to pay the interest, control of the company may be transferred to the creditors, with bankruptcy the result.

The proportion of creditors' claims to stockholders' claims is calculated by dividing total liabilities by total stockholders' equity. The relevant information to calculate the debt/equity ratio for SCI is as follows:

	19X1	
Total Liabilities	(a)	$ 6,000
Equity	(b)	12,000
Debt/Equity	(a) ÷ (b)	$.50

This calculation shows that SCI has received 50 cents from creditors for every dollar invested from stockholders. Owners, therefore, are currently financing the bulk of SCI operations. This fact can be a cause for concern. On one hand, management's reliance on stockholder financing is good. Creditors are usually willing to extend additional financing for business operations when stockholders finance the bulk of a corporation's activities. Stockholders are thereby spared from the purchase of additional shares to finance expansion. On the other hand, management's reliance on stockholder financing is poor policy. Interest does not usually have to be paid to short-term creditors (trade accounts payable) and the corporation thereby has the free use of credit for business operations. Stockholders can invest less in a corporation when it has a greater reliance on creditor financing.

The proportion of stockholders' and creditors' claims is a management decision. In the final analysis, a reasonable balance has to be maintained. Although no fixed rule for an adequate proportion exists, there are ways of designing an optimum balance. This balance involves the weighing of **leverage** (the proportion of debt) against the risk involved and is the subject of studies in finance; it is not usually attempted in an accounting course. What is attempted, however, is an evaluation of an existing financial structure, which is discussed further in Chapters 5 and 15.

This involves an analysis of the corporation's solvency (its ability to pay debts as they become due) and the efficiency with which it conducts its operations. Solvency is analyzed using primarily balance sheet data, whereas net income is the starting point in evaluating the efficiency of operations. These topics also are discussed in Chapters 5 and 15.

TRANSACTIONS ANALYSIS

Accountants view financial transactions as economic events that change components in the accounting equation. These changes are usually measured by reference to **source documents**, which provide objective and verifiable data so anyone can make the same measurements using these documents. Source documents can be prepared internally and externally. An internally prepared document supporting the purchase of supplies is called a *purchase order;* the supplier's *invoice* is the externally prepared document supporting the purchase. The financial transactions resulting in changes in the accounting equation are then recorded. Analysis of financial transactions is illustrated next, using the following expanded accounting equation:

ASSETS	=	**LIABILITIES**	+	**EQUITY**
Accounts		Bank Accounts		Common $\begin{bmatrix} + \text{ Revenue} \\ - \text{ Expenses} \end{bmatrix}$
Cash + Receivable + Equipment + Truck =		Loan + Payable +		Stock +

Remember, the above equation could be restated as follows:

ASSETS	=	**LIABILITIES**	+	**EQUITY**	
				Common Retained	
				Stock + Earnings	
Investing		Financing		Financing Operating	
Activities =		Activities	+	Activities + Activities	

Note that at this point, the operating activity portion of equity is the excess of revenues over expenses (net income), which has not been distributed to the owners as dividends and, therefore, results in retained earnings.

The assets of Saguaro Computers, Inc., consist of the following:

1. Cash, which includes coins, currency, and checks
2. Accounts receivable, which consists of amounts due from customers for services rendered by Saguaro Computers, Inc.
3. Equipment, which is used for repairing computers
4. A truck, which permits the repairperson to conduct business

The liabilities of Saguaro Computers, Inc., consist of a bank loan and accounts payable, amounts owed to creditors resulting from obligations incurred by the corporation in exchange for the acquisition of an asset.

Equity represents assets less liabilities and for Saguaro Computers, Inc., consists of the following:

1. Common stock, which represents the investments of stockholders in the corporation
2. Revenues, which represent the performance of repair services by the corporation in exchange for assets of the customers (asset inflows)
3. Expenses, which represent an outflow or consumption of assets from the corporation incurred in earning the revenue
4. Retained earnings, which is the net of 2 and 3 above reduced by any dividends paid during the accounting period

Notice that this expression of the accounting equation incorporates the different accounting categories discussed in the first two sections of this chapter: assets, liabilities, equity, revenue, and expenses. The transactions analysis illustrated here is in accordance with Pacioli's double-entry system.

Double-Entry Accounting

Pacioli's double-entry model reflects the dual nature of each transaction: each one affects at least two different items within the equation. If one item within the equation is changed, then another item also must be changed to balance it. In this way, the equality of the equation is maintained. For example, if an asset increases, then there must be a decrease in another asset or a corresponding change in a liability or equity. This is the essence of double-entry recordkeeping. The equation itself always remains in balance after each transaction.

The operation of double-entry accounting is illustrated in Exhibit 1-4 (pp. 18–19), which shows seven transactions of Saguaro Computers, Inc. Note the effect of each of the seven transactions on the accounting equation. A change in one item within the equation always results in another change elsewhere within the equation. The equality of the equation is thus maintained. SCI is an entity formed to perform computer repairs for customers and recently incorporated under the laws of the state in which the corporation was chartered (received the authority to do business). A corporation does not have to be chartered by the state in which it is doing business, but it must be registered as a corporation in that state. A corporation only has to be chartered by one state. Many U.S. corporations are chartered in Delaware because of favorable laws within that state. See Real World Example 1-1 (pp. 20–21).

Illustrative Problem   **DOUBLE-ENTRY ACCOUNTING**

The double-entry recording of each of SCI's November transactions (in Exhibit 1-4) is illustrated in the following section.

Transaction 1 (November 1)   Saguaro Computers, Inc., issued 1,000 shares of common stock for a total of $10,000 cash.

Analysis This is the corporation's first transaction. The issuance of common stock results in cash being received by the corporation. The asset Cash is therefore increased by this transaction. The equity Common Stock is also increased by $10,000 from this transaction.

Recording When the amounts are entered into the accounting equation, the transaction appears as follows:

ASSETS					=	LIABILITIES		+	EQUITY		
Cash	+	Accounts Receivable	+ Equipment +	Truck	=	Bank Loan	+ Accounts Payable	+	Common Stock	+	+Revenue −Expenses
+$10,000									+$10,000		

Notice that this transaction does not affect the liabilities component of the equation. *Note:* In this and the following transactions, the plus and minus signs are used to show the direction of change in each item caused by the transaction.

Transaction 2 (November 2) Equipment was purchased for $3,000 on account. The equipment is said to be purchased on account because it will be paid for at a later date.

Analysis An asset is acquired and a liability incurred in this transaction. The asset Equipment is acquired here and is therefore recorded as an increase. By the purchase of equipment, an obligation is incurred; therefore, it is recorded as an increase in the liability Accounts Payable.

Recording When the amounts are entered into the accounting equation, it appears as follows:

ASSETS					=	LIABILITIES		+	EQUITY		
Cash	+	Accounts Receivable	+ Equipment +	Truck	=	Bank Loan	+ Accounts Payable	+	Common Stock	+	+Revenue −Expenses
			+$3,000				+$3,000				

Transaction 3 (November 3) A repair truck to be delivered on November 3 was purchased for $8,000; SCI paid $3,000 cash and incurred a $5,000 loan for the balance.

Analysis One asset is exchanged in this transaction; an obligation to pay an asset in the future is also incurred. The asset Truck is acquired by this purchase and is therefore recorded as an increase. The asset Cash is decreased by the purchase of the truck. A liability is incurred in connection with the truck purchase and is recorded as an increase on the bank loan section.

Recording When the amounts are entered into the accounting equation, it appears as follows:

ASSETS					=	LIABILITIES		+	EQUITY		
Cash	+	Accounts Receivable +	Equipment +	Truck	=	Bank Loan	+ Accounts Payable	+	Common Stock	+	+Revenue −Expenses
−$3,000				+$8,000		+$5,000					

Notice that the equation is in balance after the recording of this transaction.

| EXHIBIT 1-4 | EFFECTS OF TRANSACTONS ON THE ACCOUNTING EQUATION OF SAGUARO COMPUTERS, INC. IN NOVEMBER | | | | |

Transaction/ Date	Description of Transaction	ASSETS	=	LIABILITIES	+	EQUITY
1. Nov. 1	Saguaro Computers, Inc., issued 1,000 shares of common stock for $10,000 cash. *This transaction has a dual nature; the asset Cash is increased while the equity Common Stock is also increased.*	+				+
2. Nov. 2	Purchased $3,000 of equipment on account. This purchase on account represents an obligation for SCI to pay the supplier of the equipment at a later date. *The increase in the asset Equipment is one side of this transaction; the obligation to pay for this asset at a later date is the other side of the transaction. The obligation results in an increase in the liability Accounts Payable.*	+		+		
3. Nov. 3	Purchased a delivery truck for $8,000, paying $3,000 cash and receiving a bank loan for the balance. *In this transaction, the asset Cash is decreased, while the asset Equipment is increased; the liability Bank Loan is also increased.*	− +		+		
4. Nov. 14	Paid $2,000 on account to the creditor for equipment purchased on Nov. 2 (transaction 2). This payment on account represents a part payment of the obligation incurred by the corporation when the equipment was purchased. *The asset Cash is decreased as one side of this transaction; the other side of the transaction decreases the obligation Accounts Payable.*	−		−		

Effect on the Accounting Equation

Transaction 4 (November 14)   The corporation paid $2,000 on account to the creditor for the November 2 equipment purchase (transaction 2).

Analysis   This payment decreases the asset Cash. The creditor's interest in the assets of SCI is satisfied; therefore, their "equity" should also decrease. Note that the liability Accounts Payable decreases by the same amount.

Recording   When the amounts are entered into the accounting equation, it appears as follows:

Transaction/ Date	Description of Transaction	Effect on the Accounting Equation			
		ASSETS	= LIABILITIES	+	EQUITY
5. Nov. 20	Equipment costing $1,000 was sold for $1,000 cash. *In this transaction, the asset Cash is increased and the asset Equipment is decreased.*	+ −			
6. Nov. 27	Computer repairs totaling $7,000 were performed for customers during November. $4,000 was received in cash as soon as the repairs were made; $3,000 of the repairs were made on credit (payment will be received at a later date). *On one side of this transaction, both the asset Cash and the asset Accounts Receivable increase, since the owners have a right to this increase in assets. Equity increases by the sum of Cash and Accounts Receivable.*	+ +			+
7. Nov. 29	Paid operating expenses for the month as follows: $600 for rent; $2,500 for salaries; $1,200 for supplies; and $700 for truck expenses (gas, oil, etc.). *The dual nature of this transaction consists of a decrease in the asset Cash on one side of the transaction, and on the other side, the decrease of computer Repair Revenue recorded on Nov. 27 (transaction 6).*	−			−

	ASSETS				=	LIABILITIES	+		EQUITY	
Cash	+	Accounts Receivable	+ Equipment +	Truck	=	Bank Loan +	Accounts Payable	+	Common Stock +	$\begin{bmatrix} +\text{Revenue} \\ -\text{Expenses} \end{bmatrix}$
− $2,000							− $2,000			

Transaction 5 (November 20)   Unnecessary equipment that had cost $1,000 was sold for $1,000 cash and will be delivered to the purchaser today.

REAL WORLD EXAMPLE 1-1
Why Are So Many Corporations Incorporated in Delaware?

[F]IRST] we noticed that two of the largest New York banks, Citibank and Chase Manhattan, were incorporated in Delaware. Both banks' names betray their New York roots, so surely there must be some practical reasons why they chose to incorporate in another state.

Then we encountered a November 1986 *Forbes* article, which reported that Delaware houses more than thirty out-of-state banks. A call to the Delaware Chamber of Commerce yielded even more startling statistics. More than 170,000 companies are incorporated in Delaware, including more than one-half of all Fortune 500 companies, 42 percent of all New York Stock Exchange listees, and a similar proportion of AMEX companies.

How could Delaware, the home of fewer than 700,000 people, house so many corporations? The answer is a textbook illustration of the ways a small state can attract big business by changing its laws and tax structure to attract outsiders. One of the reasons that Delaware attracted so many banks, for example, is that it abolished usury ceilings, which are set by the state rather than by the federal government. Let's look at the other inducements that Delaware offers corporations seeking a home.

Favorable Tax Laws

1. No state sales tax.

2. No personal property tax.

3. No corporate income tax for corporations maintaining a corporate office in Delaware but not doing business in the state. If Chase Manhattan were incorporated in New York, New York State would demand a share of the income generated beyond its borders.

4. No corporate income tax holding companies handling intangible investments or handling tangible properties located outside Delaware.

5. An extremely low franchise tax, based on authorized capital stock (the minimum is a staggeringly low $30; but there is also a maximum, $130,000 per year, that is very attractive to big corporations). Even with the low rate, the franchise tax generates 14 percent of the state's general fund revenues—Delaware collected over $126 million in 1986.

6. The corporate tax rate itself is a low 8.7 percent and is collected only on money generated inside Delaware. Compare this to the 10 percent New York State tax and the total burden of 19 percent for companies operating within New York City.

Favorable Corporation Law

1. Delaware's court of Chancery sets the nation's standards for sophistication and timeliness in shaping corporate law. Donald E. Schwartz, professor of law at Georgetown Law Center, says: "There is, by an order of several magnitudes, a larger body of case law from Delaware than there is from any other jurisdiction, enabling not only lawyers who practice in Delaware, but lawyers everywhere who counsel Delaware corporations to be able to render opinions with some confidence." By quickly establishing precedents on the issues that confront corporate heads today, Delaware has defined the legal parameters for doing business faster and more comprehensively than any other state. Business leaders feel more secure in making decisions and planning for the future, because the law is set early; as Schwartz puts it, "Corporate managers and their lawyers seek predictability."

2. In Delaware, only a majority of shareholders of a company need agree to incorpo-

rate a company. Many states require a two-thirds majority.

3. Delaware allows mergers to proceed with less intrusion than just about any other state.

4. Once incorporated, a corporation can change its purpose of business without red tape from the state.

5. The corporation's terms of existence is perpetual in Delaware. Some states require renewals, which involve paper work and extra expense.

Favorable Treatment of Corporate Leaders

Delaware has recently enacted several laws designed to make life easier for corporate heads, particularly boards of directors.

1. Delaware law allows corporations to indemnify directors, officers, and agents against expenses and often against judgments, fines, and costs of settlements incurred in suits against them filed by third parties.

2. Delaware law makes it difficult to unseat directors of a corporation.

3. Directors of a Delaware corporation do not necessarily have to meet in Delaware. Decisions can be made by conference call; they can even take an action without any meeting if there is unanimous written consent.

4. Perhaps most important in this category, Delaware passed an enabling act that allowed corporations to limit or eliminate outside directors' personal financial liability for violations of their fiduciary duty (including potential liability for gross negligence). This rule makes it much easier to attract directors to Delaware corporations; would-be directors in many states are forced to pay high liability insurance premiums to protect themselves against just such lawsuits. Although Delaware law does not allow directors to escape unscathed for perpetrating fraud, the knowledge that they won't be held up for making a mistake (even a "gross" one) makes directors happy to work in the state.

Other factors also make Delaware attractive to corporations. Unions are not as entrenched in Delaware as in most areas of the Mid-Atlantic and Northeast. Pay and cost-of-living scales are lower than in surrounding regions.

Perhaps the most enticing nontangible asset of Delaware in attracting business is the accessibility of government officials to business people. State Insurance Commissioner David Levinson was quoted in the *Forbes* article on this subject: "If you have a problem and you're operating a company in Delaware, within 48 hours you can have in one room the governor, the insurance commissioner, the president pro tem of the senate and the speaker of the house."

Delaware's probusiness slant has revived what was once a stagnant economy. But has this infusion of incorporations helped the average citizen of Delaware, when most companies do not relocate there? Evidence suggests that money has trickled down. Although there are pockets of poverty in Delaware, unemployment is now well below the national average.

The secret weapon of Delaware is its small size. A bigger state would need promises of a large number of jobs before offering financial concessions to corporations. But a small state like Delaware can siphon off the gravy and thrive. For example, Delaware offers some tax breaks to out-of-state banks if they incorporate in Delaware and maintain an office with at least one hundred employees. To a multinational bank, one hundred jobs is a drop in the bucket. To a state with fewer than twenty thousand unemployed people, one hundred jobs represents a substantial opportunity.

Analysis   One asset is exchanged for another in this transaction. The asset Cash is increased by $1,000 from the sale of the equipment. The asset Equipment is decreased in this transaction.

Recording   When the amounts are entered into the accounting equation, it appears as follows:

ASSETS				=	LIABILITIES		+	EQUITY	
Cash +	Accounts Receivable +	Equipment +	Truck =		Bank Loan +	Accounts Payable +		Common Stock +	[+Revenue / −Expenses]
+$1,000		−$1,000							

This equipment was sold at cost. If it had been sold at a price above or below cost, equity would have been increased or decreased by the amount of the gain or loss.

Transaction 6 (November 27)   A total of $7,000 of computer repairs was made for customers by the corporation during the first month of business activities.

Analysis   An analysis of these revenue-creating activities reveals that the company earned $4,000 from cash customers and also earned $3,000 for repairs made on account. These activities increase two assets: the asset Cash by $4,000 and the asset Accounts Receivable by $3,000. The total revenue earned during the month is $7,000 and this increases equity.

Recording   When the amounts are entered into the accounting equation, it appears as follows:

ASSETS				=	LIABILITIES		+	EQUITY	
Cash +	Accounts Receivable +	Equipment +	Truck =		Bank Loan +	Accounts Payable +		Common Stock +	[+Revenue / −Expenses]
+$4,000	+$3,000								+$7,000

Equity is only temporarily increased by this transaction, because the expenses incurred to make these repairs must be deducted from revenue so that net income for the month can be calculated. It is the net income that actually increases equity.

Transaction 7 (November 29)   Paid operating expenses incurred during the month to earn the repair revenue described at November 27 (transaction 6). These expenses consist of rent, $600; salaries, $2,500; supplies, $1,200; and truck expenses, $700 (for gas, oil, etc.).

Analysis   These expenses, summarized here as one transaction for illustrative purposes, reduce the assets and equity of the accounting equation.

Recording   When the paid amounts are recorded in the equation, the asset Cash is reduced by $5,000 ($600 + $2,500 + $1,200 + $700) and equity is reduced by the same amount, leaving the accounting equation as follows:

ASSETS				=	LIABILITIES		+	EQUITY	
Cash +	Accounts Receivable +	Equipment +	Truck =		Bank Loan +	Accounts Payable +		Common Stock +	[+Revenue / −Expenses]
−$5,000									−$ 600
									− 2,500
									− 1,200
									− 700

The above expenses reduce repair revenue to determine net income for the month.

The increases and decreases recorded in the preceding transactions of Saguaro Computers, Inc., can now be totaled to show a final amount for each category in the expanded accounting equation. A transactions worksheet, as shown in Exhibit 1-5, is a useful tool for illustrative purposes but is not prepared in practice for reporting information. The exhibit shows how the financial statements are prepared from the worksheet.

Note that with this simple transactions worksheet the cash column can be analyzed at this time and a statement of cash flows prepared. Recall that the statement of cash flows is made up of three sections showing the cash inflow and outflow to and from the three activities an entity performs: operating, investing, and financing.

The following analysis of the cash column at the top of Exhibit 1-5 supplies the information for preparing the cash flow statement appearing in Exhibit 1-2 on p. 11. Trace each change in the cash column to the inflows and outflows given in Exhibit 1-2. However, the analysis here is in chronological order from Exhibit 1-5 rather than in the order of the statement (Exhibit 1-2).

1. The $10,000 increase would be considered the result of a financing activity. The owners chose to finance the entity with stock rather than with debt.

2. This transaction did not involve cash.

3. The $3,000 decrease would be considered the result of an investing activity. The owners chose to invest in a truck at this time.

4. The $2,000 decrease would be considered the result of an investing activity. The owners chose to purchase equipment on account, and when that equipment is paid for, the outflow would be from investing activities.

5. The $1,000 increase would be considered the result of an investing activity. The owners chose to sell some equipment previously purchased. When that equipment was purchased, the purchase was considered the result of an investing activity.

6. The $4,000 increase would be considered the result of an operating activity. The owners' business is providing repair service to computer owners.

7. The $5,000 decrease would be considered the result of an operating activity. In providing the repair service, the owners incur such expenses as rent, salaries, supplies, and upkeep on the truck.

When all these increases and decreases in cash are classified and presented, the statement of cash flows appears as in Exhibit 1-2.

The difference between the change in cash and the net income for the accounting period is of great importance to the owners of the business. However, it is premature to analyze the difference at this point. It is more important to understand the content of the three major financial statements. The income statement matches revenue and expenses during an accounting period, the balance sheet shows the financial position of the business at the end of the accounting period, and the statement of cash flows shows where cash has come from and where it has gone in relation to the entity's three main activities: operating, investing, and financing.

The statement of cash flows will be examined in more detail in Chapter 17.

Accounting Time Periods

Q11: Calendar vs. fiscal year-end

Financial statements are prepared at regular intervals—usually monthly or quarterly—and at the end of each 12-month period. The timing of these statements is determined by the needs of management in running the entity. Financial statements

EXHIBIT 1–5

TRANSACTIONS WORKSHEET AND FINANCIAL STATEMENTS FOR SAGUARO COMPUTERS, INC., FOR NOVEMBER

Transactions	ASSETS				=	LIABILITIES		+	EQUITY	
	Cash	+ Accounts Receivable	+ Equipment	+ Truck	=	Bank Loan	+ Accounts Payable	+	Common Stock	+ Revenue [− Expenses]
1. Common stock issued for cash $10,000	+ $10,000								+ $10,000	
2. Equipment purchased for $3,000 on account			+ $3,000				+ $3,000			
3. Truck purchased for $8,000: paid $3,000 cash and incurred a bank loan for the balance.	− 3,000			+ $8,000		+ $5,000				
4. Paid $2,000 on account to the corporation's creditor	− 2,000						− 2,000			
5. Equipment sold for $1,000 cash	+ 1,000		− 1,000							
6. Repairs performed for $4,000 cash and $3,000 on account	+ 4,000	+ $3,000								+ $7,000
7. Paid operating expenses incurred during the month: Rent $600; Salaries $2,500; Supplies $1,200; Truck expenses $700	− 5,000									− 600 − 2,500 − 1,200 − 700
Balances	$ 5,000 +	$3,000 +	$2,000 +	$8,000 =		$5,000 +	$1,000 +		$10,000 +	$2,000

Used to prepare the statement of cash flows

Used to prepare the balance sheet

Revenue − Expenses

Used to prepare the income statement

Saguaro Computers, Inc.
Income Statement
For the Month Ended November 30, 19X1

Revenue	
Repair Revenue	$7,000
Expenses	
Rent Expense	$ 600
Salaries Expense	2,500
Supplies Expense	1,200
Truck Expense	700
Total Expenses	5,000
Net Income	$2,000

Saguaro Computers, Inc.
Balance Sheet
November 30, 19X1

Assets	
Cash	$ 5,000
Accounts Receivable	3,000
Equipment	2,000
Truck	8,000
	$18,000

Liabilities	
Bank Loan	$ 5,000
Accounts Payable	1,000
	$ 6,000

Equity	
Common Stock	$10,000
Retained Earnings	2,000
	12,000
	$18,000

Since this is the first accounting period for Saguaro Computers, Inc. (the first month of operations) and dividends have not been paid (distributions of net income to the owners), net income equals retained earnings.

also may be required by outside parties, such as bankers, before the granting of loans to the entity can be considered. It is also customary for corporations listed on stock exchanges to prepare quarterly accounting reports for the use of stockholders, investors, and other interested parties in evaluating the progress of these corporations.

CALENDAR YEAR-END

An entity operates on the basis of 12-month time periods. Accounting reports, called the annual financial statements, are prepared at the end of each 12-month period, which is known as the **year-end** of the entity. Companies having a year-end that coincides with the calendar year are said to have a December 31 year-end or *calendar year-end.* Although financial statements also can be prepared quarterly or monthly (these are commonly referred to as **interim financial statements**), they are always prepared at the calendar year-end, December 31.

FISCAL YEAR-END

Companies whose year-end does not coincide with the calendar year are said to operate on a **fiscal year.** For example, some corporations have a June 30 fiscal year-end; others choose a year-end that coincides with their natural year. A *natural year* ends when business operations are at a low point. A ski resort will probably have a year ending in late spring or early summer—for example, April 30—when its business operations are at their lowest point. Although interim financial statements also can be prepared quarterly or monthly, annual financial statements are always prepared at the fiscal year-end, in the case of the ski resort, April 30. The interrelationship of the interim and year-end financial statements is illustrated in Exhibit 1-6.

Note that Saguaro Computers, Inc.'s fiscal year-end coincides with the calendar year ending December 31. Because SCI began operations on November 1, 19X1, its first year-end consists of only two months. Each subsequent fiscal year will comprise 12 months.

The headings of the financial statements shown in this chapter are designed to identify the entity for which the statements are being prepared: Saguaro Computers, Inc.; the name of the statement, either income statement or balance sheet; and the date of the statements, either the month ended November 30, 19X1, or November 30, 19X1.

The *income statement* is dated *For the Month Ended November 30, 19X1,* because it is intended to show the performance of the entity over the November time period.

The *balance sheet* is dated *November 30, 19X1,* because it is designed to show the financial position of the entity at a particular point in time—November 30.

The Periodicity Concept

Q12: Periodicity concept and financial reporting

The time-period assumption requires the preparation of timely and useful financial statements. Underlying this assumption, however, is the concept that the entity's activities can actually be broken into meaningful time periods. Although necessary for financial reporting, this concept—also called the **periodicity concept**—results in accounting measurement problems that require compensation through the use of accrual accounting and the matching concept. As noted earlier, the accrual method of accounting matches expenses and revenues within a particular time period; under this method, the cost of assets transferred to customers or consumed

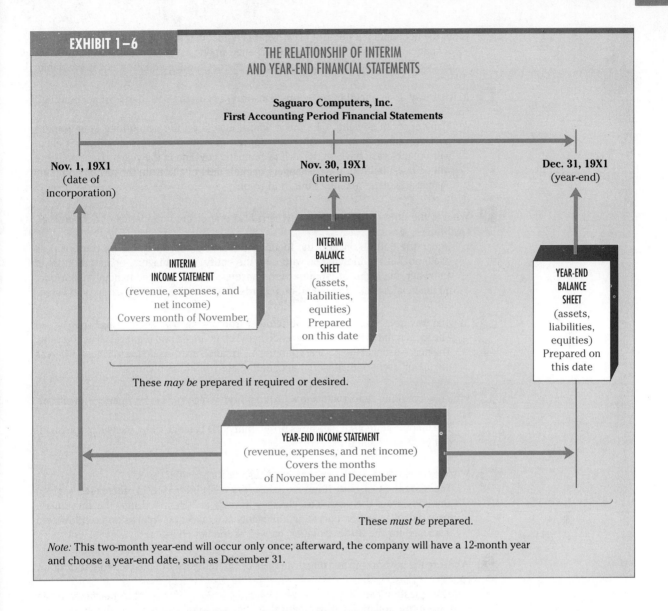

EXHIBIT 1–6

THE RELATIONSHIP OF INTERIM
AND YEAR-END FINANCIAL STATEMENTS

Saguaro Computers, Inc.
First Accounting Period Financial Statements

Nov. 1, 19X1
(date of
incorporation)

Nov. 30, 19X1
(interim)

Dec. 31, 19X1
(year-end)

INTERIM
INCOME STATEMENT
(revenue, expenses, and
net income)
Covers month of November.

INTERIM
BALANCE
SHEET
(assets,
liabilities,
equities)
Prepared
on this date

YEAR-END
BALANCE
SHEET
(assets,
liabilities,
equities)
Prepared on
this date

These *may be* prepared if required or desired.

YEAR-END INCOME STATEMENT
(revenue, expenses, and net income)
Covers the months
of November and December

These *must be* prepared.

Note: This two-month year-end will occur only once; afterward, the company will have a 12-month year
and choose a year-end date, such as December 31.

during the period are considered as expenses; the revenue generated by these
expenses is included in the income statement of the same period. In this way,
expenses incurred are matched with revenue generated. The application of these
concepts is explained and illustrated further in Chapter 3.

CHAPTER REVIEW

1 How do accountants communicate financial information to interested parties? (pp.
4–5)

Accountants communicate financial information through the use of financial statements. The financial position of the business is shown on the balance sheet, the
results of operations is shown on the income statement, and the flow of cash during
the period is shown on the statement of cash flows.

2 From the accountant's point of view, what is a financial transaction? (pp. 4, 13)

A financial transaction involves an exchange among assets and liabilities. The dollar amount is measurable, and the effect on the accounting equation is determinable.

3 In what way do financial transactions constitute one of the boundaries of accounting? (p. 4)

Many economic events take place whose effects on the accounting equation are not determinable, or the dollar amount not measurable. For example, what effect will a plane crash have on the airline company now and in the years to come? There will be lawsuits from the passengers or their next of kin, from the airline company against the plane manufacturer, and so on.

4 What is the entity concept, and how is it also one of the boundaries of accounting? (pp. 4–5)

Under the entity concept, the focus of the accounting model is on the business itself, not on the individuals who own the entity, its managers, or its creditors. If an owner, manager, or creditor of the business suffers a huge financial misfortune, no financial transaction would be recorded—unless the entity is directly affected.

5 In what way does financial accounting differ from managerial accounting? (p. 5)

The focal point is the main difference between financial and managerial accounting. The major users of financial accounting information are outside the business, whereas the major users of managerial accounting are within the business.

6 Which accounting report measures profitability? Which measures financial position? (p. 5)

The income statement measures profitability; the balance sheet measures the financial position of the firm.

7 What information does the statement of cash flows provide? (p. 9)

The statement of cash flows explains why cash increased or decreased a given amount during the year. The changes in cash are classified into the three main activities of an entity; operating, financing, and investing. Inflows and outflows are disclosed for the three activities, as well as the net changes.

8 What are the advantages and disadvantages of different forms of business organization? (p. 11)

This question can only be answered simplistically at this point. A partnership can raise more dollars for investment than can a sole proprietorship, simply because more people are involved. However, the larger the ownership base, the more problems arise. Further, both forms are subject to unlimited liability for losses and debts. The corporate form is subject to only limited liability, for the most part, and can usually raise an unlimited amount of investors' dollars.

9 How do stockholders participate in day-to-day management? (p. 11)

Stockholders participate by electing the board of directors, which then appoints officers of the business who, in turn, manage day-to-day operations. Therefore, the stockholders participate in the everyday operations only indirectly.

10 Accountants view financial transactions as economic events that change components within the accounting equation. What are these components and how do they change? (pp. 13–14)

The components are basically assets and liabilities, with equity a residual of the two—that is, assets minus liabilities equals equity. Within equity can be found elements of both the financing activity of a business (common stock) and the results of operating activity in the form of the excess of revenue over expenses that has not been distributed to the owners of the business (dividends).

11 What is the distinction between a calendar year-end and a fiscal year-end? (pp. 23, 26) A calendar-year operation uses December 31 as the arbitrary end of the business year, whereas a fiscal-year operation will choose a time period (such as the last day of any month) as the end of its year. The major benefit to using a fiscal year is that the entity can choose a point at which business activity (accounts receivable, accounts payable, and inventory) are all at their lowest.

12 What impact does the periodicity concept have on the reporting of financial information? (pp. 26–27) The period-ending information presented to the users of financial information is the result of many estimates. These estimates involve the use of accrual accounting and the matching concept. The only true profit and financial position can be determined at the end of the life of the business.

KEY TERMS

accounting (p. 4)   The process of identifying, measuring, and communicating economic information to permit informed judgments and decisions by the users of the information.

accounting equation (p. 12)   The foundation on which accounting is developed and the basic formula for the balance sheet. It expresses the dollar amounts of assets, liabilities, and equities and can be stated as ASSETS = LIABILITIES + EQUITY.

accounts payable (p. 8)   Amounts due (payables) to suppliers of goods or services for which no cash has been paid.

accounts receivable (p. 9)   Amounts due (receivables) from customers for which goods or services were provided, but no cash has been received.

accrual method of accounting (p. 6)   Method of accounting that recognizes revenues when they are earned and expenses when they are incurred; ignores when cash is received or paid in recognizing revenues or expenses; also referred to as the accrual basis of accounting.

"arm's length" transaction (p. 8)   A business transaction assumed to take place at market value. No secret agreements are included, and the monetary value decided on would be the same for anyone involved in similar transactions. An objectively determined transaction.

assets (p. 4)   Probable future economic benefits obtained or controlled by a particular entity as a result of past transactions or events.

balance sheet (p. 5)   A financial report showing the assets, liabilities, and equities of an entity on a specific date; also referred to as a statement of financial position or a statement of financial condition.

board of directors (p. 11)   Elected representatives of a corporation's stockholders.

common stock (p. 9)   The class of stock that is a basic ownership unit in a corporation. Ownership carries the right to vote and to share in dividends.

creditors (p. 12)   Individuals to whom money is owed by an entity; often referred to as *primary claims*.

dividends (p. 7)   Distributions of the entity's net income to its owners. Since they are distributions of net income, they are not determinants of net income; therefore, they are not subtracted from revenue as are expenses.

double-entry bookkeeping system (p. 12)   The method of accounting that recognizes the dual nature of each transaction—that is, both the property is accounted for (assets) and who has the right to that property (equity).

entity (p. 4)   A unit of accountability that exists separately from its owners; the term *legal entity* is used when referring to a corporation, which has a legal existence separate from its owners.

equity (p. 9)   Claims against assets of the entity; consists of creditor claims and owner claims.

expenses (p. 6)   An outflow of assets or the resources of an entity used up, or obligations incurred during a time period, in the course of performing revenue-producing services.

fiduciary relationship (p. 5)   A relationship based on mutual trust between two or more individuals.

financial accounting (p. 5)   The area of accounting that focuses on users outside the entity, such as owners (stockholders), creditors, and the government.

financial structure (p. 8)   The financial structure of an entity refers to the right side of the balance sheet—the mix between the amount of assets provided by creditors (liabilities) and the amount provided by owners (stockholders).

financial transaction (p. 4)   The financial aspect of a transaction, expressed in terms of dollars.

fiscal year (p. 26)   An arbitrary twelve-month period beginning on the first day of any month. Fiscal years are used many times instead of calendar years, so the year ends when the business activity is at its lowest point.

income statement (p. 5)   A financial report summarizing the entity's progress during a time period; summarizes revenue earned and expenses incurred, and calculates net income for the period.

interim financial statement (p. 26)   A financial report prepared monthly or quarterly, always for a time period of less than 12 months.

leverage (p. 15)   The use of borrowed capital in an attempt to earn more in the business than the rate of interest paid on the borrowed capital.

liabilities (p. 4)   Probable future economic sacrifices of economic benefits arising from the present obligations of an entity to transfer assets or provide services to other entities in the future as a result of past transactions or events.

managerial accounting (p. 5)   The area of accounting that focuses on users inside the entity, such as management and owners (such as sole proprietors or partners) who are closer to the day-to-day operations of the business.

net assets (p. 14)   The excess of assets over liabilities; often referred to as *equity*.

net income (p. 5)   The excess of revenue over expenses for a period of time.

net loss (p. 5)   The excess of expenses over revenue for a period of time.

Luca Pacioli (p. 12)   The first person to publish a description of double-entry record-keeping, designed to ensure the accuracy of transactions being recorded. His book *Arithmetic, Geometry and Proportion* was published in 1494 in Italy.

partnership (p. 9)   An entity owned by two or more persons, each of whom has unlimited liability for the obligations of the entity.

periodicity concept (p. 26)   The assumption that the entire life of a business can be divided into arbitrary periods of 12 months or less. This assumption allows for the issuance of timely financial statements so users can measure the performance and accomplishments of the enterprise. This also has been known as the time-period assumption.

proprietorship (p. 9)   An entity owned by one person who has unlimited liability for the obligations of the entity; often referred to as a *sole proprietorship*.

retained earnings (p. 7)   That portion of net income not distributed but instead kept (retained) in the business.

revenue (p. 6)   An inflow of assets to an entity in return for services performed or goods sold during that period.

source documents (p. 15)   The raw data from which the financial transactions of a business are recorded. They include such items as bank deposit slips, cancelled checks, sales invoices, purchase invoices, insurance policies, and invoices from various service suppliers such as phone, electricity, and natural gas companies.

statement of cash flows (p. 5)   A financial statement that shows the inflows and outflows of cash as a result of the entity's three main activities—operating, investing, and financing—for a period.

statement of retained earnings (p. 5)   A financial statement showing the changes in retained earnings during the past year due to net income and dividends.

stock certificate (p. 9)   The printed form representing a specific number of units of corporate ownership.

transaction (p. 4)   An exchange of assets, obligations, services, or goods.

year-end (p. 26)   The last day of the fiscal year, or of the calendar year.

SELF-TEST QUESTIONS FOR REVIEW   (Answers are at the end of this chapter.)

Q6
1. Net income can be defined as
   (a)   the net increase in cash during a period of time.
   (b)   the increase in retained earnings during a period of time.
   (c)   the excess of revenues over expenses during a period of time.
   (d)   the excess of cash received from customers during a period of time over the amount of cash spent for expenses during that same period of time.

Q6
2. A balance sheet discloses the assets, liabilities, and equities of an entity held
   (a)   at the beginning of the year.
   (b)   during the year.
   (c)   at the end of a period of time.
   (d)   at some other time than stated above.

Q10
3. Which of the following forms of the accounting equation is not correct?
   (a)   Assets − Liabilities = Equity
   (b)   Assets = Liabilities + Equity
   (c)   Investing activities = Financing Activities + Operating Activities
   (d)   Assets = Equities
   (e)   All of the above are correct.

Q7
4. The statement of cash flows contains the same information as the
   (a)   balance sheet.
   (b)   income statement.
   (c)   statement of retained earnings.
   (d)   None of the above

Q10
5. An increase in an asset account could result in
   (a)   a decrease in another asset account.
   (b)   an increase in a liability account.
   (c)   an increase in an equity account.
   (d)   All of the above

Q10

6. A decrease in a liability account could result in
   (a) a decrease in an asset account.
   (b) an increase in another liability account.
   (c) an increase in an equity account.
   (d) All of the above

Q10

7. A decrease in an equity account could result in
   (a) a decrease in an asset account.
   (b) an increase in another equity account.
   (c) an increase in a liability account.
   (d) All of the above

DEMONSTRATION PROBLEM

The following amounts appeared on the transactions worksheet of Meadow Tool Rentals, Inc., on May 1, 19X1.

				ASSETS							=	LIABILITY	+		EQUITY	
		Prepaid										Accounts		Common		[+ Revenue
Cash	+	Insurance	+	Supplies	+	Equipment	+	Truck	=			Payable	+	Stock	+	− Expense]
$1,600				$400		$3,000		$7,000				$4,000		$8,000		

The following transactions occurred during May:

a. Collected $5,000 cash for tool rental during the month (Meadow does not rent tools on account)

b. Paid rent for May in the amount of $500

c. Paid $1,500 on account for purchase of equipment and trucks

d. Paid $600 for a one-year insurance policy effective May 1

e. Purchased a used truck on account for $5,000

f. Paid the following expenses: advertising, $300; salaries, $2,500; telephone, $150; and truck maintenance, $550

g. Transferred the portion of the insurance policy that has expired during the month of May

h. Estimated that $200 of the supplies have been used during May

Required
1. Prepare a transactions worksheet and record the listed events.
2. Determine the total of all the worksheet columns to be sure that the worksheet is in balance.
3. Prepare an income statement.
4. Prepare a balance sheet.
5. Prepare a statement of cash flows.

SOLUTION TO DEMONSTRATION PROBLEM

1., 2.

	Cash	+	Prepaid Insurance	+	Supplies	+	Equipment	+	Truck	=	Accounts Payable	+	Common Stock	+	+ Revenue / − Expense
	$1,600				$400		$3,000		$ 7,000		$4,000		$8,000		
a.	+ 5,000														+ $5,000
b.	− 500														− 500
c.	− 1,500										− 1,500				
d.	− 600		+ 600												
e.									+ 5,000		+ 5,000				
f.	− 3,500														− 300
															− 2,500
															− 150
															− 550
g.			− 50												− 50
h.					− 200										− 200
	$ 500	+	$550	+	$200	+	$3,000	+	$12,000	=	$7,500	+	$8,000	+	$ 750

$16,250 = $16,250

3.

Meadow Tool Rentals, Inc.
Income Statement
For the Month Ended May 31, 19X1

Revenue
  Rent Earned $5,000

Expenses
  Rent Expense .... $ 500
  Advertising Expense   300
  Salaries Expense 2,500
  Truck Expense   550
  Supplies Expense   200
  Insurance Expense   50
  Telephone Expense   150
    Total Expenses   4,250
  Net Income .... $ 750

4.

Meadow Tool Rentals, Inc.
Balance Sheet
May 31, 19X1

Assets		Liabilities	
Cash	$ 500	Accounts Payable	$ 7,500
Prepaid Insurance	550		
Supplies	200	**Equity**	
Equipment	3,000	Common Stock	$ 8,000
Truck	12,000	Net Income	750
		Total Liabilities	
Total Assets	$16,250	and Equity	$16,250

5.

Meadow Tool Rentals, Inc.
Statement of Cash Flows (Direct Method)
For the Month Ended May 31, 19X1

Cash Flows from Operating Activities

Inflows:

Cash Received from Customers	$5,000	
(Outflows):		
Cash Paid for Expenses	(4,600)	
Net Cash Inflow from Operating Activities		$ 400

Cash Flows from Investing Activities

(Outflows):

Payments on Equipment and Trucks	(1,500)	
Net Cash Outflow from Investing Activities		(1,500)

Cash Flows from Financing Activities
[none]

Net Outflow of Cash	($1,100)
Cash Balance, May 1, 19X1	1,600
Cash Balance, May 31, 19X1	$ 500

The above amounts are taken from the cash column of the transactions worksheet of Meadow Tool Rentals, Inc.

DISCUSSION QUESTIONS

Q1-1   Explain, using an example, what is meant by the term *financial transaction.*

Q1-2   What is the entity concept of accounting? Why is it important?

Q1-3   How does an accountant select business transactions that are translated into accounting information applicable to a particular entity?

Q1-4   What are financial statements?

Q1-5   What is the purpose of an income statement? a balance sheet? How do they interrelate?

Q1-6   Define the terms *revenue* and *expense* as they are understood by accountants.

Q1-7   What is net income? Why is it a useful measure for readers of financial statements?

Q1-8   What are assets? Where do they appear in financial statements?

Q1-9   What do the terms *liability* and *equity* refer to? In which way can they both be referred to as equity?

Q1-10   Why are financial statements prepared at regular intervals? Who are the users of these statements?

Q1-11   What is a year-end? How does the timing of year-end financial statements differ from that of interim financial statements?

Q1-12   How does a fiscal year differ from a calendar year?

Q1-13   Define the accounting process. What are the five steps in this accounting process?

Q1-14   Distinguish between financial and managerial accounting.

Q1-15   What is the accounting model? How does it work?

Q1-16   Why is the accounting equation expanded when financial transactions are recorded? Illustrate, using the example of Saguaro Computers, Inc.

Q1-17   The accounting model is often referred to as a double-entry bookkeeping system. Explain how it works.

Q1-18   What is the financial structure of a corporation?

Q1-19   What is the importance of the proportion of stockholders' and of creditors' claims against the assets of the entity?

Q1-20   Is management's reliance on stockholder financing good or bad for the business? Explain.

DISCUSSION CASE

Rodolph and Marmaduke

Q1–Q4

Scene: The great hall of that fine old English castle, Dogsberry Towers. The date is 1291. As the curtain rises, that good, simple-minded old knight, Sir Rodolph the Uninspired, is discovered behind a large table littered with bits of paper, slate, and sharp stones (the recording implements of the time), among which the old fellow is shuffling about, pausing from time to time to scratch a figure laboriously, with much licking of pointed stones. Finally, he gives up in exasperation and bangs loudly on the table with a tankard.

RODOLPH: What ho, without there! Fetch me another double mead—standing up.

VOICE WITHOUT: Coming, sire.

[*A servant shuffles in with a tankard.*]

ROD.: And where is my steward Marmaduke? Is he not yet arrived?

SERVANT: I was on the point of showing him in, sire.

[*He does so. Enter Marmaduke.*]

ROD.: Dear Marmaduke! I am so glad to see you. Something terrible has happened—you see before you a ruined man.

MARMADUKE: [*Incredulously.*] A ruined man? But, my lord, you are one of the wealthiest men in Christendom.

ROD.: I was once, but I am sinking fast. I have it all here.

[*He fumbles about and finally emerges with a piece of slate.*]

Yes, since you made up the last statement of my affairs a few years ago, my wealth has declined. Here, let me see . . . [*reads*] from 812 to 533.

MAR.: From 812 to 533? But what figures are these?

ROD.: [*Excitedly.*] Well, they are my own invention. You see, I listed down everything I owned—just as you showed me. But when I was finished, I wanted to see whether I was going ahead or behind. So [*with an expression of delight at his own cunning*] I added all the things up. Last time, I had 812 things; this time 533. It's as simple as that—bankruptcy in a few more years, at this rate.

Q6

MAR.: But you can't do that. That's like adding barrels of ale and goblets of wine.

ROD.: Well, what's wrong with that? Three barrels and two goblets make five things, right?

MAR.: [*Effort at control*] I am a member of the guild of stewards, after serving the customary 25-year apprenticeship. May I respectfully suggest that you leave these counting matters to me.

ROD.: [*Piteously*] But you had taught me to add . . . and I thought you would be so pleased.

Q10

MAR.: [*Relenting.*] Look, my lord. Would you rather have three horses and one rabbit, or one horse and ten rabbits?

ROD.: Naturally, I would rather have three horses and one rabbit.

MAR.: Quite right. You see, you would be better off with four animals than with eleven [*his voice gradually rises as he loses his control*] because they are not the same kind of animal! [*He continues more calmly.*] You see, the reason you had so many things at the time of the first count was that you had just bought 500 exotic birds.

ROD.: They were a passing fancy of my wife's. I can deny her nothing.

MAR.: Whereas, they are all gone now, my lord.

ROD.: [*Indulgently.*] She changed her mind, the little dear.

MAR.: So you see, if you disregard the birds—which you didn't like anyway—you have actually increased your possessions from 312 to 533.

ROD.: But then, I lost some large items, too. After all, that bastard Guido the Provocative burned down one of my best manor houses.

MAR.: On the other hand, however, in a reprisal raid you took from him half his holdings.

ROD.: I counted that. I added in a half for that.

MAR.: That's just fine: you get half Guido's holdings and you lose 500 birds—so it's a net loss of 499½. As a matter of fact, the guild is very worried about this. There is some nut—from Edinburgh, of course (wouldn't you know it)—who is going about the kingdom advocating a new idea in which you value everything and add it all up to a big total. Our Conduct and Discipline Committee think they can hang a witchcraft charge on him. This whole idea of his involves the introduction of new mathematical techniques, such as long division. And of course the guild believes that long division is too erratic and too subjective a process to be relied on for accounting. Our Research Committee has got out a pronouncement saying that it has considered the use of long division and has concluded that it is inappropriate at this time.

ROD.: [Shyly.] Do you think that your guild members would be interested in my idea of just counting things?

MAR.: I'm afraid not, my lord. At best, they might endorse it as an alternate procedure, which is what they do when they want to go out of their way to be patronizing.

[Curtain.]

Source Adapted from Howard Ross, *Financial Statements: A Crusade for Current Values* (Toronto: Pitman, 1969), pp. 30–33.

For Discussion

1. Rodolph, a separate entity, has been counting his assets. Has he also been accounting for them? Why or why not?

2. The process of valuing assets requires the use of some common denominator so different kinds of assets can be added together. Is the common denominator in use today better than that used by Rodolph? Why or why not?

EXERCISES

Transactions and the accounting equation (Q10)

E1-1   The following list covers all possible transactions that can occur within an entity. Notice that each transaction has a dual effect.

Types of Accounting Transactions

	ASSETS	= LIABILITIES	+ EQUITY
1.	+		+
2.	+	+	
3.	+ −		
4.	−		−
5.	−	−	
6.		+	−
7.		−	+
8.		+ −	
9.			+ −

The dual effect of each transaction illustrated above maintains the equality of the accounting equation.

Required

Study the following transactions and identify, using the accounting equation, the effect of the transaction. Use a plus (+) to denote an increase and a minus (−) to denote a decrease. Some of the transactions may not involve a financial transaction for reporting.

Example

Issued common stock for cash $\dfrac{A = L + E}{+ \quad\quad +}$

1. Paid cash for the purchase of a new truck
2. Received 100% financing from the bank for the purchase of equipment
3. Paid the month's rent
4. Paid the power company a required deposit to begin electric service
5. Signed a new union contract that provides for increased wages
6. Sent invoices to customers for services already performed
7. Made a payment for credit previously extended
8. Received payment from customers who received the above invoices
9. Collected cash from a customer who had just received the services
10. Paid for gas, oil, etc., for the operation of the truck
11. Made the first monthly payment to the bank; this payment included a portion of the amount borrowed and interest charged by the bank. (*Hint:* This transaction affects more than two parts of the equation.)

Transactions and the accounting equation (Q10)

E1-2 Refer to the list of types of accounting transactions in E1-1.

Required

Study the following transactions and identify by number (1 to 9) the type of transaction. Some transactions do not involve accounting.

Example

Issued common stock for cash   1

1. Paid an account payable
2. Borrowed money from a bank and issued a note
3. Collected an account receivable
4. Collected a commission on a sale made today
5. Paid for an advertisement in a newspaper
6. Signed a contract to purchase a computer
7. Received an invoice for supplies used during the month
8. Received a payment on account
9. Sent an invoice for repairs made today
10. Sold equipment for cash
11. Purchased a truck on account
12. Requested payment of an overdue account receivable
13. Settled a union dispute by increasing vacations from one to two weeks
14. Recorded the amount due to the landlord for rent
15. Received the monthly telephone answering-service invoice

Preparation of an income statement (Q1, Q6, Q11)

E1-3   The following information is taken from the records of Jackson Music, Inc., as of April 30, 19X1:

Accounts Payable	$7,000	Insurance Expense	$ 300
Accounts Receivable	6,000	Interest Expense	500
Cash	1,000	Rent Expense	700
Common Stock	8,500	Truck	8,000
Equipment	4,000	Truck Expense	600
Fees Earned	8,100	Wages Expense	2,500

Required
From the information given, prepare an income statement as of April 30, 19X1.

Preparation of a balance sheet (Q1, Q6, Q11)

E1-4

Required
Using the data and your solutions to E1-3, prepare a balance sheet dated April 30, 19X1.

For exercises E1-5 through E1-9, use the following transactions worksheet. This worksheet of Maple Builders, Inc., shows ten (*a* to *j*) recorded transactions during January 19X1.

	ASSETS					=	LIABILITY +		EQUITY		
Cash +	Accounts Receivable +	Supplies +	Equipment +	Truck =			Accounts Payable +		Common Stock +	+ Revenue − Expense	
a.	+ $5,000									+ $5,000	
b.				+ $1,000				+ $1,000			
c.			+ $300					+ 300			
d.		+ $3,500									+ $3,500
e.	− 350										− 350
f.	+ 1,000	− 1,000									
g.	− 500							− 500			
h.	− 2,000				+ $8,000			+ 6,000			
i.	− 2,500										− 500
											− 1,200
											− 800
j.			− 200								− 200

Additional information: transaction *e* involved rent for the month of January and transaction *i* involved advertising, salaries, and truck repairs, in that order.

Identifying transactions from a worksheet (Q10)

E1-5

Required
Using the worksheet, describe what most likely happened in each transaction.

Determining effects of transactions on account balances (Q10)

E1-6

Required
Determine the totals for each column in the transactions worksheet.

Preparation of an income statement (Q1, Q6, Q11)

E1-7

Required
Prepare an income statement for the month of January 19X1.

Preparation of a balance sheet (Q1, Q6, Q11)	**E1-8**

Required

Prepare a balance sheet dated January 31, 19X1, on your solution to E1-7 and the transactions worksheet.

Preparation of a statement of cash flows (Q1, Q6, Q7, Q11)	**E1-9**

Required

Using your solutions to Exercises E1-5 to E1-8 and the transactions worksheet, prepare a statement of cash flows for the month of January 19X1.

Correcting financial statements (Q1, Q6, Q11)

E1-10   The following financial statements have been prepared from the records of No Strings, Inc.

<table>
<tr><td colspan="2" align="center">**No Strings, Inc.**
Income Statement
May 31, 19X1</td><td colspan="2" align="center">**No Strings, Inc.**
Balance Sheet
May 31, 19X1</td></tr>
<tr><td colspan="2">**Revenue**</td><td></td><td></td></tr>
<tr><td>Service Revenue</td><td>$6,500</td><td></td><td></td></tr>
<tr><td></td><td></td><td>Accounts Payable</td><td>$5,000</td></tr>
<tr><td colspan="2">**Expenses**</td><td>Accounts Receivable</td><td>4,000</td></tr>
<tr><td>Advertising Expense</td><td align="right">$ 200</td><td>Cash</td><td>3,000</td></tr>
<tr><td>Equipment</td><td align="right">2,000</td><td>Common Stock</td><td>8,000</td></tr>
<tr><td>Truck Expense</td><td align="right">500</td><td>Equipment Rental Expense</td><td>300</td></tr>
<tr><td>Wages Expense</td><td align="right">3,300</td><td>Truck</td><td>6,200</td></tr>
<tr><td>Total Expenses</td><td align="right">6,000</td><td>Net Income</td><td>500</td></tr>
<tr><td>Net Income</td><td align="right">$ 500</td><td>Total</td><td>$ 0</td></tr>
</table>

Required

Prepare NSI's interim financial statements in the correct format.

PROBLEMS

Preparation of interim statements (Q1, Q6, Q11)

P1-1   The following are the asset, liability, and equity account balances of Drake, Inc., as of January 31, 19X1, its first month of operations.

ASSETS		=	LIABILITIES		+	EQUITY	
Cash	$1,300		Bank Loan	$8,000		Common Stock	$2,000
Accounts Receivable	2,400		Accounts Payable	1,000		Service Revenue	7,500
Prepaid Insurance	550					Advertising Expense	500
Supplies	750					Commissions Expense	720
Truck	9,000					Insurance Expense	50
						Interest Expense	80
						Rent Expense	400
						Supplies Expense	100
						Telephone Expense	150
						Wages Expense	2,500

Required

1. Prepare an interim income statement for the month ended January 31, 19X1, in the correct format. Record the expenses in alphabetical order.

2. Prepare an interim balance sheet as of January 31, 19X1, in the correct format.

Preparation of interim statements (Q1, Q6, Q11)

P1-2 The following is an alphabetical list of data from the records of Financial Services, Inc., at March 31, 19X1.

Accounts Payable	$9,000	Equipment Rental Expense	$ 500
Accounts Receivable	3,900	Fees Earned	4,500
Advertising Expense	300	Insurance Expense	400
Cash	3,100	Interest Expense	100
Common Stock	2,000	Truck Expense	700
Equipment	5,000	Wages Expense	1,500

Required

1. Prepare an interim income statement as of March 31 in the correct format. Record the expenses in alphabetical order.

2. Prepare an interim balance sheet as of March 31 in the correct format.

Preparation of interim statements (Q1, Q6, Q11)

P1-3 The following financial statement was prepared from the records of Annuity Reports, Inc., as of August 31, 19X1.

Annuity Reports, Inc.
Financial Statement
August 31, 19X1

Cash	$ 400	Accounts Payable	$ 7,800
Accounts Receivable	3,800	Common Stock	3,200
Supplies	100	Service Revenue	6,000
Equipment	8,700		
Advertising Expense	300		
Interest Expense	500		
Maintenance Expense	475		
Supplies Expense	125		
Wages Expense	2,600		
	$17,000		$17,000

Required

1. What kind of statement is this?

2. Using the data given, prepare an interim income statement as of August 31, 19X1, in the correct format.

3. Prepare an interim balance sheet as of August 31, 19X1, in the correct format.

Preparation of a work-sheet and statements (Q1, Q6, Q7, Q10, Q11)

P1-4 The following transactions occurred in Brock Accounting, Inc., during August 19X1, its first month of operations.

Aug. 1 Issued common stock for $3,000
     1 Borrowed $10,000 cash from the bank
     1 Paid $8,000 for a used truck
     4 Paid $600 for a one-year truck insurance policy effective August 1 (recorded as Prepaid Insurance since it will benefit more than one month)
     5 Collected $2,000 fees from a client for work performed
     7 Sent invoices totaling $5,000 to clients for services performed to date

9   Paid $250 for supplies used to date

12 Purchased on account supplies costing $500; these supplies will be used in the future

15 Received $1,000 from clients to whom invoices were sent on Aug. 7

16 Paid $200 for advertising in *The News* during the first two weeks of August

20 Paid for one-half of the supplies purchased on August 12

25 Paid the following expenses for August; rent, $350; salaries, $2,150; telephone, $50; and upkeep on the truck, $250.

28 Called clients for payment of the balance due from August 7

29 Sent invoices totaling $6,000 to clients for services performed to date

31 Transferred the amount of August's truck insurance to Insurance Expense

31 Counted $100 of supplies still on hand (recorded the amount used as an expense)

Required

1. Record the Brock transactions on a transactions worksheet, as discussed in this chapter, and calculate the total of each column at the end of August. Use the following headings on your worksheet.

ASSETS					=	LIABILITIES	+		EQUITY	
Cash +	Accounts Receivable +	Prepaid Insurance +	Supplies +	Truck =		Bank Loan +	Accounts Payable +	Common Stock +	+ Revenue	− Expense

2. Prepare an interim income statement as of August 31 in the correct format. Identify the revenue earned as Fees Earned. Record the expenses in alphabetical order.

3. Prepare a statement of cash flows and explain the difference between the net income and the increase in cash for August.

Preparation of a worksheet and statements (Q1, Q6, Q7, Q10, Q11)

P1-5 The following transactions took place in Mason Renovations, Inc., during June 19X1, its first month of operations.

June 1 Issued common stock for $8,000

1 Paid $600 on rent due for June and July

1 Purchased on account equipment costing $5,000

2 Collected $600 cash for repairs completed today

3 Paid $20 for supplies used June 2

4 Purchased on account supplies costing $1,000; these supplies will be used in the future

5 Sent invoices totaling $2,500 for repairs completed to date

8 Received $500 from customers to whom invoices were sent on June 5

10 Paid $2,500 for equipment purchased on account on June 1

15 Sold excess equipment for $1,000 on account (the same amount as the original cost of this equipment)

18 Paid for the supplies purchased June 4

20 Received an invoice for $100 from the power company for electricity consumed to date

23 Signed a union contract

25 Received $1,000 from customers to whom invoices were sent on June 5

27 Paid the following expenses: advertising, $150; telephone, $50; truck expense (rental, gas), $1,000; wages, $2,500

30 Sent invoices totaling $2,000 for repairs completed to date

30 Transferred the amount for June rent to Rent Expense

30 Counted $150 of supplies still on hand (recorded the amount used as an expense)

Required

1. Record the Mason transactions on a transactions worksheet and calculate the total of each column at the end of June. Use the following headings on your worksheet.

		ASSETS			=	LIABILITY	+		EQUITY
Cash	+	Accounts Receivable	+	Prepaid Rent	+ Supplies + Equipment =	Accounts Payable	+	Common Stock	+	+ Revenue − Expense

2. Prepare an income statement and a balance sheet as of June 30 in the correct format. Identify the revenue earned as Repair Revenue. Record the expenses on the income statement in alphabetical order.

3. Prepare a statement of cash flows and explain the difference between the net income and the increase in cash for June.

ALTERNATE PROBLEMS

Preparation of interim statements (Q1, Q6, Q11)

AP1-1   The following are the asset, liability, and equity account balances of Stone, Inc., at December 31, 19X1, its first month of operations.

ASSETS		=	LIABILITIES		+	EQUITY	
Cash	$ 1,000		Accounts Payable	$17,000		Common Stock	$25,000
Accounts Receivable	9,000		Salaries Payable	2,000		Fees Earned	13,600
Prepaid Taxes	2,250					Advertising Expense	1,000
Land	10,000					Insurance Expense	250
Building	25,000					Property Tax Expense	200
Equipment	5,800					Salaries Expense	3,000
						Telephone Expense	100

Required

1. Prepare an interim income statement for the month ended December 31, 19X1, in the correct format. Record the expenses in alphabetical order.

2. Prepare an interim balance sheet as of December 31, 19X1, in the correct format.

Preparation of interim statements (Q1, Q6, Q11)

AP1-2   The following is an alphabetical list of data from the records of Managerial Services, Inc., at September 30, 19X1.

Accounts Payable	$2,200	Repair Revenue	$6,550
Accounts Receivable	6,000	Rent Expense	400
Advertising Expense	50	Salaries Expense	2,350
Cash	700	Supplies Expense	100
Common Stock	5,000	Telephone Expense	75
Equipment	2,000	Truck Expense	325
Maintenance Expense	250	Wages Expense	1,500

Required

1. Prepare an interim income statement as of September 30 in the correct format. Record the expenses in alphabetical order.

2. Prepare an interim balance sheet as of March 31 in the correct format.

Preparation of interim
statements (Q1, Q6,
Q11)

AP1-3 The following financial statement was prepared from the records of Sundown, Inc., as of November 30, 19X1.

Sundown, Inc.
Financial Statement
November 30, 19X1

Cash	$ 750	Bank Loan	$5,000
Accounts Receivable	2,200	Accounts Payable	3,000
Prepaid Insurance	550	Common Stock	1,000
Supplies	300	Repair Revenue	5,000
Equipment	6,000		
Advertising Expense	200		
Commissions Expense	1,500		
Insurance Expense	50		
Rent Expense	450		
Wages Expense	2,000		
	$14,000		$14,000

Required

1. What kind of financial statement is this?

2. Using the data given, prepare an interim income statement as of November 30, 19X1, in the correct format.

3. Prepare an interim balance sheet as of November 30, 19X1, in the correct format.

Preparation of a work-
sheet and statement
(Q1, Q6, Q7, Q10, Q11)

AP1-4 Electrical Contractors, Inc., was incorporated on May 1, 19X1, and had the following transactions during its first month of operations.

May 1	Issued common stock for $5,000
1	Paid $1,500 in advance for three months' rent: May, June, and July
2	Purchased on account supplies costing $1,000
3	Sent an invoice for $1,500 to a customer for repairs already performed
4	Paid $50 for an advertisement in *The News*
5	Received $250 for repairs made today
10	The customer for whom repairs were made on May 3 paid the invoice
15	Paid $500 on account
18	Borrowed $2,000 from the bank
20	Signed a major contract for work to be done in June
22	Purchased for cash equipment costing $3,000
25	Sent invoices totaling $3,500 for repairs completed to date
27	Paid the following expenses: electricity, $75; telephone, $25; and wages, $2,000
31	Transferred a portion of the prepaid rent to Rent Expense
31	Counted $200 of supplies still on hand

Required

1. Record the ECI transactions on a transactions worksheet and calculate the total of each column at the end of May. Use the following headings on your worksheet.

ASSETS					=	LIABILITIES	+	EQUITY	
Cash +	Accounts Receivable +	Prepaid Rent +	Supplies +	Equipment =		Bank Loan +	Accounts Payable +	Common Stock +	+ Revenue − Expense

2. Prepare an interim income statement for the month of May. Identify the revenue earned as Repair Revenue. Record the expenses in alphabetical order.

3. Prepare a statement of cash flows, and explain the difference between the net income and the increase in cash for May.

Preparation of a work-
sheet and statements
(Q1, Q6, Q7, Q10, Q11)

AP1-5   Nick's Snow Removal, Inc., was incorporated on December 1, 19X1, and had the following transactions during its first month of operations.

Dec. 1 Issued common stock for $6,000
       1 Purchased a used truck for $9,000: paid $4,000 cash with the balance due January 15
       2 Purchased on account a $2,000 snowplow to be attached to the truck (recorded as an increase in the cost of the truck)
       3 Sent invoices totaling $5,000 to customers for snow removal services during December. Nick expects to earn the entire $5,000 by the end of December.
       5 Purchased on account salt, sand, and gravel costing $500 (recorded as supplies)
       6 Paid truck expenses of $200
       7 Paid $360 for a one-year truck insurance policy effective December 1
      14 Paid $1,500 for wages incurred during the first half of December
      16 Paid $40 to the municipal court for a parking ticket received yesterday
      20 Received an invoice for truck maintenance items costing $350
      24 Purchased tire chains for $100 on account
      24 Received $3,500 from customers to whom invoices were sent on December 15
      27 Paid for the purchase made on December 5
      28 Collected $400 for snow removal performed today for a new customer
      28 Paid $1,500 for wages incurred during the second half of December
      30 Phoned all the customers who had not paid their account for the first half of December
      31 Transferred the portion of the insurance policy on the truck that expired during December
      31 Estimated that sand, salt, and gravel costing $100 were still on hand at the end of December
      31 Determined that $450 in wages were earned by the employees during the last three days in December. (Enter the amount due to the employees in the Wages Payable column.)

Required

1. Record the NSR transactions on a transactions worksheet and calculate the total of each column at the end of December. Use the following headings on your worksheet.

ASSETS					=	LIABILITIES		+	EQUITY	
Cash +	Accounts Receivable +	Prepaid Insurance +	Supplies +	Truck =		Accounts Payable +	Wages Payable +		Common Stock +	+ Revenue − Expense

2. Prepare an income statement and a balance sheet as of December 31 in the correct format. Identify the revenue as Service Revenue. Record the expenses on the income statement in alphabetical order.

3. Prepare a statement of cash flows and explain the difference between the net income and the increase in cash for December.

DECISION PROBLEM

Q1, Q6, Q11

Drake, Inc., (described in P1-1) and Stone, Inc., (described in AP1-1) are involved in similar, competing business activities. You are considering investing some money in one of these two businesses. While Stone, Inc., is larger, it appears to you that Drake, Inc., has more activity during business hours. Both have provided you with the information contained in P1-1 and AP1-1. While you would want more information if you were actually investing in these corporations, base your responses solely on the information provided.

Required

1. Comment on the financial structure of both Drake, Inc., and Stone, Inc.

2. Which of the two corporations is more efficient in its business activities?

3. What further information would you, as a user of financial information for investment purposes, want to be provided?

ANSWERS TO SELF-TEST QUESTIONS

1. **(c)** Net income is the difference between revenues and expenses for the period. It is not the excess cash received from customers over the cash paid for expenses because sometimes revenue is recorded before it is received in cash (accounts receivable) and sometimes expenses are recorded before they are paid in cash (accounts payable).

2. **(c)** The balance sheet discloses the financial position of an entity as of the *end* of a period of time, which could be the end of a day, week, month, quarter, or year. If a balance sheet is prepared on the first day of a new business year, it reflects the financial position at the *end* of that day. Therefore, *a* is not a correct answer.

3. **(e)** All the equations listed here are derivations of the basic accounting equation stated in *a*.

4. **(d)** Why would an entity want to publish two different statements that contain the same information? The statement of cash flows reports just what the title implies; where did the cash come from, and where did it go?

5. **(d)** All are true statements. An increase in an asset could cause another asset to decrease (a). This would happen when a truck is purchased for cash. If that truck was purchased on credit (accounts payable), assets would increase, and liabilities would also increase (b). If the seller of the truck agreed to take common stock in exchange for the truck, then assets would increase while equity increased (c).

6. **(d)** All are true statements. A decrease in a liability would result in a decrease in an asset when an account payable was paid (a). If one liability was exchanged for another, liabilities would increase and decrease at the same time (b). If one liability was satisfied by issuing common stock, *c* would be true.

7. **(d)** Again, all are true.

Note: Questions 5, 6, and 7 can be answered simply by looking at the effect of each situation on the accounting equation.

2 GAAP AND THE ACCOUNTING PROCESS

ACCOUNTING information is prepared and communicated in accordance with a number of basic assumptions that have been made over time as the nature of the business enterprise changed. The first part of this chapter introduces the concept of "Generally Accepted Accounting Principles" (GAAP) and some of the more general assumptions on which financial information is based. The qualities inherent in accounting information are presented, as well as some limiting factors that affect the information. The next part of the chapter identifies some of the organizations involved in determining GAAP on both a domestic and international basis. The final part of this chapter, and most important at the introductory level, is a description of the accounting process introduced in Chapter 1. The tools used to record financial information are identified and explained. Also described are further classifications on the balance sheet that make the information more useful to interested parties.

CHAPTER PREVIEW QUESTIONS

After studying Chapter 2, you should be able to answer the following questions:

1 What is the framework of principles now generally accepted within the accounting profession? (p.48)

2 Has the accounting profession agreed on a definitive list of fundamentals underlying the accounting process? (p.48)

3 Is the dollar a stable unit of measure? Is it the most appropriate measure for transactions, and for the reporting of accounting information? (p.49)

4 Financial statements are prepared on the basis of historical cost. Why is historical cost used to measure financial transactions? (p.49)

5 In what way does accrual accounting match revenue with expenses? (p.50)

6 When do accountants assume revenue is earned? (p.50)

7 What characteristics is financial information expected to have? (pp.51–52)

8 What are the impacts of conservatism and consistency in situations where a choice is made between equally defensible accounting principles? (p.52)

9 What are the authoritative accounting bodies in the United States? How do they interact in issuing pronouncements related to accounting? (pp.53–54)

10 What is the function of the auditors' report in relation to GAAP? (p.54)

11 How are accounts used in the accounting process? (p.55)

12 What are the meanings of the terms *debit* and *credit*? (p.55)

13 How does the use of debits and credits facilitate and control the accounting process? (pp.55, 57)

14 What is the function of a trial balance? a general journal? a general ledger? (pp.64–66)

15 What classifications are used on the balance sheet? Why are they helpful? (pp.66–68, 70)

16 What are the sequential steps performed by the accountant in converting economic data into financial information? (p.73)

GENERALLY ACCEPTED ACCOUNTING PRINCIPLES

Financial statements are prepared based on a number of assumptions about the entity and about the environment where the entity operates, and according to a number of accounting practices. A consensus has occurred over the years as to how assets, liabilities, and equities should be recorded and communicated. This consensus is necessary because of the wide range of users of financial statements, most of whom are external to the firm; these include stockholders, investors, creditors, customers, unions, governments, and the general public. Within the entity itself, management needs the financial statements for decision making and problem solving.

Q1: Framework of principles

The framework of principles now generally accepted within the business community and accounting profession is referred to as **generally accepted accounting principles** (usually shortened to GAAP). These principles are reviewed in detail in the following sections. Since the word *principles* implies something is based in the sciences, the principles will be referred to as assumptions.

Generally Accepted Assumptions

ASSUMPTION 1: THE ENTITY

Q2: Accounting fundamentals

Under the **entity assumption,** each business is seen as a unit separate from its owner. Therefore, for sole owners of a business, the transactions of that business are accounted for separately from personal transactions. If the owner buys a delivery truck for the business, that transaction is accounted for in the business, but if the owner buys a new suit, that is a personal transaction and is not recorded as a transaction of the business. Separate records are kept for the transactions of each entity and for personal financial activities. This assumption was introduced in Chapter 1.

As noted earlier, a corporation is a legal entity. Except for a few special situations, such as professional corporations, personal guarantees, and bankruptcy laws, the assets of a corporation can not be used to pay the obligations of the owners and vice versa. No *legal* distinction exists, however, between the assets and obligations of a proprietorship and its owner or between those of a partnership and its owners. In these cases, personal assets of the owner(s) may be used to pay the entity's obligations; the assets of the entity may be used to pay personal obligations of the owner(s). Some rules of law govern the order in which partnership assets and personal assets are disbursed. This will be more fully explained in Chapter 12, where partnership accounting is explored. Nevertheless, separate records are still maintained for the entity and for its owner(s).

ASSUMPTION 2: THE GOING CONCERN

Under the **going-concern assumption,** each entity is assumed to have an unlimited life; that is, it is assumed to continue operating indefinitely. This assumption is necessary because it provides the foundation for the periodic accounting reports that measure the entity's performance. Such performance reports cannot wait until the end of the entity's life when it is assumed to be indefinite. This assumption therefore leads to the periodicity assumption and the resulting need for accrual accounting and the matching assumption (introduced in Chapter 1 and further discussed in Chapter 3).

ASSUMPTION 3: THE STABLE UNIT OF MEASURE

Q3: The dollar

Since transactions are recorded in terms of a monetary unit (the U.S. dollar), the unit under the **stable-unit-of-measure assumption** is assumed to have the same purchasing value from one year to the next. In fact, the monetary unit of most countries is *not* stable and never has been. Many countries are plagued with chronic inflation. Henry Rand Hatfield wrote in 1909 that the stable-dollar assumption is one of the most ridiculous assumptions that the accounting profession has ever made.

The accounting profession has considered the effect of inflation on accounting information, and for a brief period of time (1979–1985) required the presentation of supplemental inflation-adjusted information. At present, inflation-adjusted data are not required but are recommended. A brief introduction to inflation accounting is in Chapter 18.

ASSUMPTION 4: HISTORICAL COST

Q4: Historical cost

Under the **historical-cost assumption,** the cost of an asset is measured by the amount paid for that asset, or the fair market value of the asset given in exchange for the new asset if a noncash transaction, or the amount of the liability undertaken if acquired in a credit transaction. Cost is seen as one reasonable basis for valuation because it is objectively determined, usually the result of an *arm's length transaction.* Accountants generally assume that the use of historical cost minimizes the opportunity to manipulate the information in financial statements.

Subsequent to the acquisition of an asset, its recorded cost is not changed even though the measurement unit—the dollar—has become unstable through inflation. Assume that, on a later date, Saguaro Computers, Inc. pays $15,000 for another truck identical to the $8,000 truck it currently owns, and that the difference in price is solely a result of the impact of inflation. Although this example is hypothetical, it illustrates that subsequent financial statements would report two identical assets, each having a different cost. The difference in this case would be attributable to a change in the dollar measurement unit resulting from inflation. This gives rise to the phrase "**adding apples and oranges.**" Within the Truck account, SCI would add the cost of the old truck ($8,000) to the cost of the new truck ($15,000), reporting on the resulting balance sheet that SCI has trucks with a cost of $23,000. In other words, apples, the old truck, are added to oranges, the new truck, coming up with a total of trucks costing $23,000. This is one of the major problems with accounting data, and it is caused by the changing value of the dollar.

The use of historical cost is defendable if the entity is a going concern (Assumption 2). If the prospect of the entity continuing in existence is in doubt, then using **liquidation values** would be more appropriate. The items on the asset side of the balance sheet would be reported at the amount of cash that probably would be received in a forced sale.

ASSUMPTION 5: PERIODICITY

Under the **periodicity assumption,** it is assumed that an entity's business activities can be broken down into meaningful reporting periods so performance reports in the form of financial statements can be prepared. Reports can be prepared monthly, quarterly, or for any other useful time period; they must always be reported annually. The application of the periodicity assumption was introduced in Chapter 1 by the preparation of all the financial statements for SCI for the month of November. Those statements were based entirely on the assumption that SCI would be in business long enough to collect the accounts receivables, to operate the equipment and trucks for their entire useful life, and to pay all debts owed as of the end of November.

ASSUMPTION 6: INCOME DETERMINATION AND MATCHING

Q5: Accrual account-ing and matching

Under the **income determination and matching assumption,** income is measured by recording revenue when it is earned and matching that against expenses incurred to earn that revenue. This matching might be direct, as in the cost of repair supplies used on a repair job, or indirect, as in the allocation of a portion of the cost of an insurance policy to the month of November. Referred to as the *accrual basis of accounting,* this matching is illustrated later in this chapter. Pacioli's methods of matching debits and credits are discussed and illustrated in the next section, and the application of matching in the measurement of net income is detailed in Chapter 3, then discussed in the remainder of the text.

ASSUMPTION 7: REVENUE RECOGNITION

Q6: Revenue earned

Revenue recognition is concerned with establishing the point at which the revenue of the entity is earned. Although revenue has been earned by the time the service is completed or the goods are exchanged and cash is collected, accountants generally assume that revenue is earned at an earlier point—after the service has been performed or the goods have been exchanged but *before* payment has been received. This point can be objectively determined, thereby avoiding the need for subjective estimates. In practice, it is convenient to recognize revenue (that is, record the transaction) at the point when an invoice is prepared and sent to the customer. The application of this assumption is discussed further in Chapter 3.

Exceptions to this assumption exist, however. Revenue is sometimes recognized before it is realized. For example, in the long-term construction industry (large buildings, bridges, dams, and so on), revenue is recorded as earned during the construction process, even though the project might not be completed in the current year or even the following year (some construction projects take three, four, or more years). This area of financial accounting is discussed in more advanced accounting courses. Another exception is to recognize no revenue until the cash has been received. If the cash is to be received over a long period of time, the installment method of accounting may be used. This is discussed in Chapter 7.

Although these seven assumptions are said to be generally accepted, it is important to note that the accounting profession has yet to agree on a definitive list of the fundamentals underlying the accounting process. This lack of agreement exists because of the nature of these assumptions, which:

are not derivable from physical science or natural law; they are, rather, conventions, related to certain necessarily pragmatic postulates, whose existence and validity derive from public exposure, debate, and acceptance. Generally accepted accounting principles, . . . in short, are not discovered, but declared. Their existence cannot forerun their utterance and acceptance by the profession itself.[1]

Because accounting principles are declared rather than discovered, accounting literature and practice include variations and differences, which result in some lack of precision in financial statements.

[1]From an *amicus curiae* brief submitted by the American Institute of Certified Public Accountants in a 1968 legal case. Quoted by Howard Ross, *Financial Statements: A Crusade for Current Values* (Toronto: Pitman, 1969), p. 50.

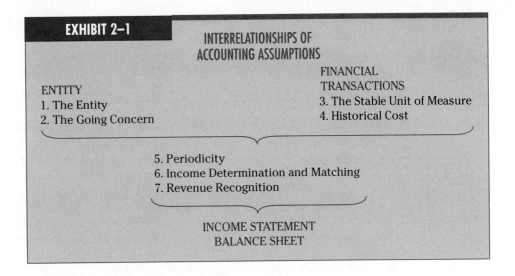

EXHIBIT 2-1

INTERRELATIONSHIPS OF
ACCOUNTING ASSUMPTIONS

ENTITY
1. The Entity
2. The Going Concern

FINANCIAL
TRANSACTIONS
3. The Stable Unit of Measure
4. Historical Cost

5. Periodicity
6. Income Determination and Matching
7. Revenue Recognition

INCOME STATEMENT
BALANCE SHEET

Exhibit 2-1 summarizes the way the seven accounting assumptions relate to the accounting process. All of an entity's economic events are recorded within the confines of these seven assumptions. The recording is also influenced by the concept of the operating cycle. Visually, the operating cycle appears as follows:

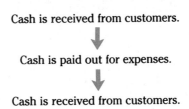

Cash is received from customers.

Cash is paid out for expenses.

Cash is received from customers.

This cash-to-cash sequence is referred to as the **operating cycle.** Chapter 3 discusses the impact of this operating cycle on financial statement disclosure and the identification of revenue with different time periods.

Characteristics of Accounting Information

Q7: Characteristics of financial information

Accounting converts transactions of an entity into financial statement information. The framework of principles involved in the preparation of these statements was discussed in the preceding pages. The subsequent reporting of this financial information is intended to facilitate decision making by its users. Accordingly, it is necessary to understand what characteristics this information is expected to have. One of the characteristics is **relevance.** The information has to be timely and useful; it should reduce uncertainty associated with decision making. Another characteristic is **reliability;** the user should be able to depend on the information and employ it in order to evaluate alternatives. Accountants use **materiality** as a test when deciding to disclose certain relevant information; the disclosure of immaterial information is more likely to hinder than help the user of financial statements. The information also must be comparable to similar information of previous accounting time periods **(consistency)** and to the statements of other entities in the same industry **(uniformity).**

Often, GAAP permits a choice between equally defensible alternate accounting principles in a given business situation. When making a choice, the accountant may often practice conservatism. Once the choice is made, the accounting profession requires consistency to ensure usefulness of the information.

CONSERVATISM

Q8: Impact of conservatism

Conservatism represents the accounting profession's preference for prudence when dealing with conditions involving uncertainty and risk. When making a choice between equally defensible alternatives, the accountant chooses the alternative that will produce the least favorable result for the entity. Therefore, when estimating the useful life of Saguaro's equipment and truck, for example, SCI's accountant should use the lowest estimate if two or more equally defensible estimates are available.

With conservative estimates, the asset cost expires more quickly, producing the least favorable result because it translates into a lower net income figure and a lower unexpired asset balance reported in the balance sheet. More discussion of this issue appears in Chapters 3 and 9. Other examples involving choice between equally defensible estimates are introduced throughout this book.

In the past, an extreme application of conservatism required the selection of an alternative that "anticipates no profit and provides for all possible losses." The intent, then, was for financial statements to avoid favorable exaggeration; understatements of reported net income and balance sheet amounts were intended to protect users making decisions from this information. Today, the emphasis is on the fair presentation of financial statement information. Therefore, the focus is on a choice between only equally defensible alternatives. The choice of a less defensible alternative simply to produce the least favorable result is not in accordance with GAAP.

CONSISTENCY

Q8: Impact of consistency

The usefulness of financial statements is enhanced by the consistent use of accounting principles chosen from among alternatives. *Consistency* requires that these selected accounting principles be used for each accounting time period. In this way, the financial information produced by the entity is uniform; changes between accounting time periods can then be attributed to operations and not to changes in the selection of accounting principles. Comparability of financial statement information from one time period to another of the same entity and among different entities is thereby enhanced.

Changes in accounting principles are discouraged unless such changes improve financial statement reporting or are required because of changed conditions. Such changes must be disclosed in the financial statements; this disclosure is usually made through notes to the financial statements. Accounting for changes is discussed briefly in Chapter 5.

Limitations on the Disclosure of Useful Accounting Information

Financial statements are prepared and distributed at regular accounting time periods so useful information is available for decision making. Useful information is not always reported. The accountant uses materiality to decide whether particular items of information need be disclosed. The accountant, in addition, makes a cost-benefit judgment, which also limits the disclosure of useful information.

MATERIALITY

Some information may not be sufficiently large in amount or importance to affect the judgment of a reasonably knowledgeable user. For example, the cost of a calculator is not *material* when compared to the cost of Saguaro's truck. Although both are theoretically assets until their useful life expires, the calculator cost would never be shown as an asset in an accounting report; rather, it would be expensed when purchased.

In practice, no clear-cut distinction can be drawn between material and immaterial amounts. Each case has to be considered on its own merits. As a matter of expediency, policies are usually established within the entity to facilitate consistent recording of certain transactions. Their subsequent disclosure is influenced by materiality. The application of the concept of materiality is one of the most difficult for a new member of the accounting profession to accept. When he or she was an undergraduate student, $5 was a material amount; on the job that first year out of school, $1,000,000 may not be material in a given situation.

COST–BENEFIT JUDGMENTS

Useful information is not always reported because the costs associated with its preparation exceed the expected benefits. Therefore, the decision to prepare inflation-adjusted financial statements in addition to historical-cost financial statements is influenced by **cost–benefit judgments.** As with materiality, individual, highly subjective judgment is required in the application of cost–benefit decisions. Accountants use consistent guidelines in practice to minimize this subjective element.

The Accounting Profession and the Development of GAAP

Q9: Accounting authorities

As was noted earlier, accounting principles are neither found nor discovered; instead, they evolve, and are ever-changing in response to changes in, among other factors, the nature of the business enterprise, of the economy, and of technology. Over time a number of accounting organizations have helped formulate generally accepted accounting principles that reflect such broad changes.

Not much was officially written until the later part of the 1910s, when the **Federal Reserve Board** issued a number of statements on "uniform accounting." After the stock market crash in 1929, Congress established (in 1933) the **Securities and Exchange Commission (SEC),** which was given the authority to *promulgate* (or establish) accounting rules and regulations for entities whose shares are publicly traded. Almost immediately, the SEC turned the job of establishing accounting guidelines over to the accounting profession itself. The American Institute of Accountants, today called the **American Institute of Certified Public Accountants (AICPA),** took on the role. The AICPA soon established the Committee on Accounting Procedure, which began issuing Accounting Research Bulletins (ARBs). The output from this committee, 51 ARBs, was the basis for GAAP in the United States until 1959, when the AICPA established the Accounting Principles Board, which established GAAP through the issuance of 31 Opinions during the period through mid-1973. At that time, the profession established the Financial Accounting Foundation, which funded the **Financial Accounting Standards Board (FASB).** The FASB is this country's first full-time, paid standard-setting group. Their predecessors had been volunteer committees. Since its founding, the FASB has issued nearly 120 official Statements regarding GAAP.

The SEC has not been completely silent or inactive in the establishment of GAAP for financial reporting, but it has generally left this job to the accounting profession.

The above-mentioned organizations mainly concentrate on GAAP for financial accounting reporting (that is, communicating accounting information to users who need or require the information). Other groups also establish guidelines for reporting accounting information. The **Internal Revenue Service (IRS)** has established rules and regulations for reporting financial information to it so it may determine each entity's responsibility for the payment of income taxes. The **Governmental Accounting Standards Board (GASB)** is responsible for issuing standards of reporting for governmental units.

These are only organizations operating in the United States. Every industrialized country in the world has similar problems (and standard-setting organizations) regarding financial reporting. More than 40 standard-setting groups exist around the world. In fact, in 1977 the **International Federation of Accountants (IFAC)** was founded to promote agreement on accounting issues. Although the entire world will likely never agree on a single set of standards, the fact that the group has more than 50 members today is indication enough that various countries are discussing the issues. Another international group, the **International Accounting Standards Committee (IASC),** has issued a number of international standards that have been translated into many different languages.

Other, broader organizations operating in the United States have their hand in the establishment of accounting rules and regulations. Among others, the **American Accounting Association (AAA)** is made up of accounting educators and focuses on research and theory. The **National Association of Accountants (NAA)** has as members mostly accountants in industry. The **Financial Executives Institute (FEI)** consists of accountants who hold higher management positions in large corporations.

The Auditors' Report

Q10: Auditors' report and GAAP

When year-end financial statements are published, they are usually accompanied by an **auditor's report.** This report indicates that the statements have been examined by a **certified public accountant (CPA),** an independent, professional accountant who is legally permitted to do so. It further indicates that the statements fairly present the financial position of the entity and the results of its operations for a particular time period. The independent, professional accountant, usually referred to as the *auditor,* also indicates whether the financial statements have been prepared in accordance with generally accepted accounting principles. If there is a violation of GAAP in the financial statements, the auditor's report is modified to alert readers to the violation. For an example of an auditor's report, see the extract of United Telecom's annual report for 1989, reproduced after the textbook glossary. For an interesting commentary on the worth of GAAP statements, see Real World Example 2-1 (pp. 56–57).

ACCOUNTS IN THE ACCOUNTING PROCESS

The dual nature of accounting transactions was explained and illustrated in Chapter 1, where the November transactions of Saguaro Computers, Inc., were first analyzed to determine the changes in each item in the accounting equation brought about by each transaction. Increases and decreases in each item were then recorded in a series of expanded accounting equations, using the following headings: Cash, Accounts Receivable, Equipment, Truck, Bank Loan, Accounts Payable, Common Stock, and Revenue less Expenses. Next, the dollar amounts of each transaction were recorded on a transaction worksheet and two financial statements were prepared from the totals calculated on the worksheet. These financial statements can communicate the necessary financial information of SCI, a legal entity, to interested parties.

The recordkeeping and the means for gathering the information for those financial statements were unwieldy. Imagine a business the size of Standard Oil, which has millions of transactions each year, using such a system. The system developed in Chapter 1 would not work in all but the smallest of operations.

Although the widespread use of computers has revolutionized recordkeeping and the calculation process, it is essential for all accounting students to know how these transactions are recorded in a manual system in order to understand the basis of accounting and appreciate what the computer has done for bookkeeping and the recordkeeping function.

Q11: Use of accounts   Each accounting transaction is actually recorded in, and accumulated by, an **account.** A separate account is used for each asset, liability, equity, revenue, and expense. A simplified account, often used graphically, is a **T account** (because it resembles the letter T). The term **debit** is used to describe the left side of the account, the term **credit** the right side.

Debit	Credit
(always the left side)	(always the right side)

Q12: Debit and credit   *Debit* and *credit* may have had meaning in their Latin roots, but the terms today mean nothing more than the location on the left or right side of the account, respectively, where amounts are recorded. Historically, students of accounting have tried to attach such meanings as "good" and "bad" or "increase" and "decrease" to *debit* and *credit.* Remember, however, that the terms refer only to the left or right side of an account. Both in the textbook, and in accounting literature, the left side of the account is often abbreviated "Dr.," while the right side is abbreviated "Cr."

Q13: Use of debits and credits   In the November transactions of SCI, a separate T account would be prepared for each of the following accounts: Cash, Accounts Receivable, Equipment, Truck, Bank Loan, Accounts Payable, Common Stock, Repair Revenue, Rent Expense, Salaries Expense, Supplies Expense, and Truck Expense. Each transaction of the corporation affects more than one of these accounts. In fact, if a transaction affects the left side of one account, it also affects the right side of another account, and vice versa. This matching is *always* true of all accounting transactions. For example, study these three types of transactions:

Type of Transaction	An Asset		A Liability		Equity	
	Debit (increase)	Credit (decrease)	Debit (decrease)	Credit (increase)	Debit (decrease)	Credit (increase)
1. An increase in an asset and an increase in equity.	X					X
2. An increase in an asset and an increase in a liability.	X			X		
3. A decrease in an asset and a decrease in a liability.		X	X			

REAL WORLD EXAMPLE 2-1
If It's Too Complicated, Forget It

I N a letter to *Forbes,* B. Philip Chenok, president of the American Institute of Certified Public Accountants, called my Aug. 8 column a "cheap shot" at auditors. It was not meant to be. The column warned investors to be skeptical when they read annual reports and to pay close attention to footnotes.

Chenok was especially outraged by two statements: "The slimiest managements find the slimiest auditors"; and "Some managements would capitalize hot air if they could, and so would their auditors." As spokesman for the accounting group, Chenok claimed that a recent poll found that auditors have "the highest credibility and trust."

Yes, Mr. Chenok, most company managements and auditors are honest, but like all groups, at one end of the bell curve are folks who are honest to a fault, while at the other are the con merchants. No certification or association—CPA or otherwise—eliminates all con artistry.

The minority of con artists get away with things in auditing because it is specific but imperfect. Imperfect because there is no solidly real number on any financial statement except for the item marked cash. The rest is calculated via assumptions, and the closer you get toward net income per share and shareholders' equity, the more the assumptions and errors compound.

To standardize methodology, accounting has decades of rulings from the Accounting Principles Board (APB) and more recently the Financial Accounting Standards Board (FASB). Auditors are supposed to examine reality and apply correct accounting based on the APBs and the FASBs. But this permits the bad guys to study the rules looking for loopholes and then plan transactions that, by their nature, require accounting that paints the financials in an unreal shade of reality.

So, with due respect to Mr. Chenok and his fellows, I still advise paying careful heed to the often overlooked footnotes.

Will reading the footnotes enable you to spot deliberate misrepresentation? Only rarely. But reading them will help you better understand the financials. It did recently for me. *Sequa Corp.* (63) surfaced on my firm's computer's value screen, and its annual report rippled onto my desk for review. Its footnotes detailed information that modified what anyone could see from the financial statements alone. For example, the financials showed rapid growth, with sales tripling in three years—while earnings from continuing operations rose from $12 million in

---

Notice that in each type of transaction affecting the accounts shown, a change on one side of a T account always results in a change on the other side of another account. This dual feature of the debit–credit mechanism is common to every accounting transaction recorded in accounts; it is part of the double-entry model.

Although the evolution of this mechanism is unknown, a set of rules has gradually developed to record transactions in a manner that results in an equality of debits with credits. These rules are not self-evident truths, but rather a methodology that has become generally accepted. They have to be learned before double-entry bookkeeping as it is practiced today can be mastered.

The *type* of account determines whether a debit represents an increase or a decrease or whether a credit represents an increase or a decrease in a particular transaction.

The pattern of recording increases and decreases is common to accounts representing *assets* and *expenses*.

1985 to $28 million in 1986 to $50 million in 1987. Wow!

Now to the footnotes. Footnote number 3 showed that the growth came mostly from the way in which acquisitions were accounted for. For instance, in December 1987 Sequa bought Atlantic Research for $325 million. It used the "equity method" of "purchase accounting"—as required by 1970's APB number 16—all quite correct, but also confusing. A legally required "pro forma" (in the footnote) shows that if Sequa had accounted for the deal as if Atlantic Research had been owned for both years, the combined operations—what is there now—would have shown an earnings decline, from $64 million to $36 million—almost the exact reverse of what its income statement shows.

Sequa got our computer's attention with a balance sheet that exceeded a formula based partially on "equity." But the financials show that $365 million of its $674 million of equity comes from "goodwill." The footnotes further show that $200 million of the $365 million of goodwill hangs on the Atlantic Research take-over. Sequa paid a fancy price (about 24 times earnings and 2.7 times book value). Maybe the goodwill is worth that much. Maybe it isn't. But my point is that you couldn't begin to figure it out without studying the footnotes.

Read on in this same report. Sequa has 21 major footnotes, more than giants IBM, Exxon, or Sears—including $150 million of unconsolidated subsidiaries, a $21-million nonrecurring pension plan gain, $80 million of unbilled receivables—all proper but also all altering how you perceive Sequa.

Don't get me wrong. I'm not saying Sequa or its auditors engaged in fraud or misrepresentation. Quite the contrary, the annual report includes three pages of unrequired disclosures, and the "President's Message" clearly points you toward the notes. And the company was quite open in speaking with me. This is not a case of sleight of hand, but rather one of such complexity that I, for one, cannot grasp what the numbers really mean. Who could? My point in highlighting Sequa is to show the absolute importance of footnotes.

Precious few individuals will read all those notes, much less understand them. My advice is: Unless you think you're the next Ben Graham or John Templeton, think five times before buying any stock with lots of complicated footnotes. The more of them and the more complicated, the more trouble you will have distinguishing the phony from the merely complex.

Source Kenneth L. Fisher, "If It's Too Complicated, Forget It," *Forbes*, Reprinted by permission of *Forbes* magazine, October 3, 1988. © Forbes Inc., 1988.

This guideline can be explained using the following graphic T account:

Debit (always the left side)	*Credit* (always the right side)
A debit records an increase in assets and expenses.	A credit records a decrease in assets and expenses.

The pattern of recording increases and decreases is also common to accounts representing *liabilities, equity,* and *revenues.*

This guideline can be explained using the following graphic T account:

Debit (always the left side)	*Credit* (always the right side)
A debit records a decrease in liabilities, equity, and revenues.	A credit records an increase in liabilities, equity, and revenues.

Students often have difficulty at first with this debit–credit, increase–decrease methodology. The following summary shows how debits and credits are used to record increases and decreases in various types of accounts:

ASSETS EXPENSES	LIABILITIES EQUITY REVENUES
Increases are **debited.** Decreases are **credited.**	Increases are **credited.** Decreases are **debited.**

Instead of simply memorizing the set of statements just given, keep in mind the accounting equation and its variations, discussed in Chapter 1.

$$\text{ASSETS} = \text{EQUITIES}$$

$$\text{ASSETS} = \text{SOURCES OF ASSETS}$$

$$\text{ASSETS} = \text{LIABILITIES} + \text{OWNERS' EQUITY}$$

$$\text{ASSETS} = \text{FINANCING ACTIVITIES} + \text{OPERATING ACTIVITIES}$$

$$\text{INVESTING ACTIVITIES} = \text{FINANCING ACTIVITIES} + \text{OPERATING ACTIVITIES}$$

$$\text{INVESTING ACTIVITIES} = \text{FINANCING ACTIVITIES} + \text{FINANCING ACTIVITIES} + \text{OPERATING ACTIVITIES}$$

With a little study (and understanding of basic algebra), it should be clear that a change (increase or decrease) on one side of the equation results in a change in the same direction on the other side of the equation. Therefore, if an asset account increases and no other asset account decreases, then an account on the other side of the equal sign also must increase. If an increase in an asset account is recorded as a debit, then an increase on the other side of the equation must be recorded as a credit.

As you use this system over time, you'll find that the debit–credit system used in recording transactions becomes second nature. However, the prior summary is repeated on some of the following pages, where transactions of SCI are recorded to help you become familiar with the process. Refer to it as often as you find necessary.

Accounting converts the transactions of an entity into financial statement informa-tion. In this conversion process, transactions are analyzed and recorded, summa-rized, and subsequently communicated to interested individuals. The equality of debits with credits is used to control the accuracy of this process. The basic account-ing model is used not only to organize the transactions but also to communicate financial statement information. Accounting is essentially an art; it is not a science.

TRANSACTIONS ANALYSIS USING ACCOUNTS

Every business is involved in the analysis and recording of financial transactions. Accountants use the debit and credit system as a shorthand to keep track efficiently of the thousands of different financial events that occur during a time period.

The use of this debit and credit shorthand can be illustrated in the recording of the November transactions of Saguaro Computers, Inc., first examined in Chapter 1 (Exhibit 1-4). The transactions are analyzed and recorded, then are summarized by account.

The analysis and recording process involves use of accounting procedures; the focus, however, is on the entire accounting process and how GAAP is applied in the records of an entity so useful information is made available for decision making.

Illustrative Problem:

THE DEBIT–CREDIT METHODOLOGY AND USE OF ACCOUNTS

The November transactions for Saguaro Computers, Inc., first analyzed in the Illustrative Problem for Chapter 1, are used in Exhibit 2-2 to show the debit–credit methodology and the use of accounts. Where each transaction is discussed, the data are accumulated in the conceptual T accounts to the right of the text.

Refer to the following as you analyze each transaction:

ASSETS	LIABILITIES
	EQUITY
EXPENSES	REVENUES

| Increases are **debited**. | Increases are **credited**. |
| Decreases are **credited**. | Decreases are **debited**. |

Transaction 1 (November 1)   Saguaro Computers, Inc., issued 1,000 shares of common stock for a total of $10,000 cash.

Analysis   This is the corporation's first transaction. The issuance of common stock results in cash being received by the corporation. An asset account, Cash, is therefore increased by this transaction.

Debit   An asset is increased by a debit.

Debit   Cash   10,000

Cash	
Debit	*Credit*
10,000	

An equity account, Common Stock, is also increased by $10,000 from this transaction.

Credit   An equity is increased by a credit.

Credit   Common Stock   10,000

Common Stock	
Debit	*Credit*
	10,000

EXHIBIT 2–2	DEBIT–CREDIT METHODOLOGY AS IT APPLIES TO SCI'S NOVEMBER TRANSACTIONS		
		Application of Debit–Credit Methodology	
Transaction/ Date	Description of Transaction	Debit	Credit
1. Nov. 1	Saguaro Computers, Inc., issued 1,000 shares of common stock for $10,000 cash.	Cash	Common Stock
2. Nov. 2	Purchased $3,000 of equipment on account.	Equipment	Accounts Payable
3. Nov. 3	Purchased a delivery truck for $8,000; paying $3,000 cash and receiving a bank loan for the balance.	Truck	Cash Bank Loan
4. Nov. 14	Paid $2,000 on account to the creditor for equipment purchased on Nov. 2 (transaction 2).	Accounts Payable	Cash
5. Nov. 20	Equipment costing $1,000 was sold for $1,000 cash.	Cash	Equipment
6. Nov. 27	Computer repairs totaling $7,000 were performed for customers during November. $4,000 was received in cash as soon as the repairs were made; however, $3,000 of the repairs were made on credit (payment will be received at a later date).	Cash Accounts Receivable	Repair Revenue
7. Nov. 29	Paid operating expenses for the month as follows: $600 for rent $2,500 for salaries $1,200 for supplies $700 for truck expenses (gas, oil, etc.)	Rent Expense Salaries Expense Supplies Expense Truck Expense	Cash

Transaction 2 (November 2)   Equipment was purchased for $3,000 on account.

Analysis   An asset is acquired and a liability incurred in this transaction. The asset Equipment is acquired here and is therefore recorded as an increase in the Equipment account.

Debit   An asset is increased by a debit.

Debit   Equipment   3,000

	Equipment	
Debit		*Credit*
3,000		

By the purchase of equipment, a liability is incurred and is therefore recorded as an increase in Accounts Payable.

Credit   A liability is increased by a credit.

Credit   Accounts Payable   3,000

	Accounts Payable	
Debit		*Credit*
		3,000

Transaction 3 (November 3)   A repair truck was purchased for $8,000; SCI paid $3,000 cash and was given a $5,000 bank loan for the balance.

Analysis   One asset is exchanged in this transaction; an obligation to pay an asset in the future is also incurred. An asset Truck is acquired from this purchase and is therefore recorded as an increase in the Truck account.

Debit   An asset is increased by a debit.

Debit   Truck   8,000

	Truck	
Debit		*Credit*
8,000		

The asset Cash is decreased by the purchase of the truck.

Credit   An asset is decreased by a credit.

Credit   Cash   3,000

	Cash	
Debit		*Credit*
10,000		
		3,000

A liability, bank loan, is incurred in the acquisition of the asset truck.

Credit   An obligation is increased by a credit.

Credit   Bank Loan   5,000

Bank Loan

Debit	Credit
	5,000

Transaction 4 (November 14)   The corporation paid $2,000 on account to a creditor.

Analysis   This payment decreases Accounts Payable, a liability account, because the $2,000 is due to a creditor of the corporation.

Debit   A liability is decreased by a debit.

Debit   Accounts Payable   2,000

Accounts Payable

Debit	Credit
	3,000
2,000	

The payment also decreases the asset Cash.

Credit   An asset is decreased by a credit.

Credit   Cash   2,000

Cash

Debit	Credit
10,000	3,000
	2,000

Transaction 5 (November 20)   Unnecessary equipment that had cost $1,000 was sold for $1,000 cash.

Analysis   One asset is exchanged for another in this transaction. The asset Cash is increased by $1,000 from the sale of the equipment at its original cost.

Debit   An asset is increased by a debit.

Debit   Cash   1,000

Cash

Debit	Credit
10,000	3,000
	2,000
1,000	

The asset Equipment is decreased in this transaction.

Credit   An asset is decreased by a credit.

Credit   Equipment   1,000

Equipment

Debit	Credit
3,000	
	1,000

Transaction 6 (November 27)   A total of $7,000 in computer repairs was made for customers by the corporation during its first month of business activities.

Analysis   An analysis of these revenue-creating activities reveals that the company earned $4,000 from cash customers and also earned $3,000 for repairs made on account. These revenue activities increase two asset accounts: the asset Cash is increased by $4,000 and the asset Accounts Receivable is increased by $3,000.

Debit   Both of these assets are increased by a debit.

Debit   Cash   4,000
Debit   Accounts Receivable   3,000

Cash

Debit	Credit
10,000	3,000
1,000	2,000
4,000	

Accounts Receivable

Debit	Credit
3,000	

The total revenue earned during the month is $7,000 and this increases revenue of the corporation.

Credit   An increase of revenue is recorded by a credit.

Credit   Repair Revenue   7,000

Repair Revenue

Debit	Credit
	7,000

Transaction 7 (November 29)   Operating expenses were incurred and paid during the month to earn the repair revenue described at November 27 (transaction 6). These consist of rent, $600; salaries, $2,500; supplies, $1,200; and truck expenses, $700 (for gas, oil, etc.).

Analysis   These expenses, summarized here as one transaction for illustrative purposes, are recorded as increases.

Debit   Expenses are increased by a debit.

Debit   Rent Expense   600
Debit   Salaries Expense   2,500
Debit   Supplies Expense   1,200
Debit   Truck Expense   700

Rent Expense			Supplies Expense	
Debit	*Credit*		*Debit*	*Credit*
600			1,200	

Salaries Expense			Truck Expense	
Debit	*Credit*		*Debit*	*Credit*
2,500			700	

Note that each expense is recorded in a separate expense account. Each type of expense is always recorded in its own T account. The total payment of these expenses amounts to $5,000 ($600 + $2,500 + $1,200 + $700) and, since they have been paid in cash, the asset account, Cash, is decreased by $5,000.

Credit   An asset is decreased by a credit.

Credit   Cash   5,000

Cash	
Debit	*Credit*
10,000	3,000
1,000	2,000
4,000	5,000

Because the expenses have been summarized here as one transaction for illustrative purposes, the total payment is also summarized. In practice, each paid expense would be recorded individually by a debit to the appropriate expense account and a credit for each to Cash.

Preparation of the Trial Balance

Q14: Function of trial balance

After the November transactions of Saguaro Computers, Inc., have been analyzed and recorded, the T accounts are totaled in a process called **footing,** as shown in Exhibit 2-3; that is, each account with more than one transaction on the debit or credit side is totaled and the difference between the debit balance and the credit balance is calculated. In the case of the Cash account in the diagram, the balance of $5,000 is called a *debit balance.* In the following T accounts, the numbers in parentheses refer to the transaction numbers used in the preceding pages; the date of the transaction generally would be inserted here.

A **trial balance** lists and totals all the debit and credit account balances in a two-column schedule. It is prepared after all transactions for the accounting period (November, in this case) have been recorded in appropriate accounts. The end of the month is the usual time for preparation of the trial balance although it can be prepared at any time to check the mathematical accuracy of the recording process.

The form and content of a trial balance is illustrated in Exhibit 2-4, using the account labels and account balances of Saguaro Computers, Inc.

Since a double-entry system has been used in recording the transactions of Saguaro Computers, Inc., the total of debit account balances must equal the total of credit account balances. The trial balance establishes that this equality actually

EXHIBIT 2–3

FOOTING OF T ACCOUNTS FOR SCI

ASSETS (Economic resources owned by a business) = **LIABILITIES** (Creditors' claims to assets) + **EQUITY** (Stockholders' claims to assets)

Cash

(1)	10,000	(3)	3,000
(5)	1,000	(4)	2,000
(6)	4,000	(7)	5,000
	15,000		10,000
Bal.	5,000		

Accounts Receivable

(6)	3,000

Equipment

(2)	3,000	(5)	1,000
Bal.	2,000		

Truck

(3)	8,000

Bank Loan

	(3)	5,000

Accounts Payable

(4)	2,000	(2)	3,000
		Bal.	1,000

Common Stock

	(1)	10,000

Repair Revenue

	(6)	7,000

Rent Expense

(7)	600

Salaries Expense

(7)	2,500

Supplies Expense

(7)	1,200

Truck Expense

(7)	700

EXHIBIT 2-4

Saguaro Computers, Inc.
Trial Balance
November 30, 19X1

Account Balances

	Debit	Credit	
Cash	$ 5,000		
Accounts Receivable	3,000		
Equipment	2,000		These accounts are
Truck	8,000		used to prepare the
Bank Loan		$ 5,000	balance sheet
Accounts Payable		1,000	
Common Stock		10,000	
Repair Revenue		7,000	
Rent Expense	600		These accounts are
Salaries Expense	2,500		used to prepare the
Supplies Expense	1,200		income statement.
Truck Expense	700		
	$23,000	$23,000	
	Total Debits	=	Total Credits

exists, but it does not ensure that each item has been entered in the proper account. For example, a transaction that increased Cash (a debit) and increased Common Stock (a credit) could have been recorded erroneously as an increase to Trucks (a debit) and a decrease to Cash (a credit). The transaction would be recorded incorrectly, but the trial balance would still be equal. Nor does the trial balance ensure that all items that should have been entered have in fact been entered. Both of these errors could have occurred and the trial balance would still balance. In addition, a transaction may have been recorded twice. Nevertheless, a trial balance is prepared before the financial statements are begun.

Account Classifications on the Balance Sheet

Q15: Balance sheet classifications

Before the financial statements of SCI are prepared from the trial balance in Exhibit 2-4, some major classifications of the balance sheet should be identified. These classifications make the financial statement easier to interpret, and allow the user to conduct a number of mathematical relationships discussed later in the text. The number of classifications depend on the entity's needs. The classifications used by SCI are described here. Remember that this is not a definitive segregation, and that each entity should develop its own presentation.

CURRENT ASSETS
Current assets are resources the entity expects to convert to cash or to consume during the next year or within the operating cycle of the entity. Included in this category are the following accounts, listed in order of their *liquidity,* or convertibility to cash:

1. **Cash,** the most liquid asset, comprising paper money and coins, deposits at banks, checks, and money orders

2. Temporary Investments, the investment of idle cash

3. Accounts Receivable due to be collected within one year—not as easily converted into cash as temporary investments

4. Notes Receivable, which consist of **notes** due to be collected within one year—not as easily converted into cash as accounts receivable, but can be discounted (covered in Chapter 7)

5. Merchandise Inventory expected to be sold within one year—not as easily converted into cash as accounts or notes receivable (covered in Chapter 5)

Current assets also include accounts whose future benefit is expected to expire in a short period of time. These are not expected to be converted into cash:

6. Prepaid Expenses to expire in the next year, usually consisting of advance payments for insurance, rent, and other similar items

7. Supplies to be used during the next year

For convenience, all prepaid expense and supplies accounts are grouped together into one amount on the balance sheet titled "Prepaid Expenses." This grouping is convenient because the amounts are usually small and their individual disclosure would provide no meaningful information to the reader of financial statements.

LONG-TERM ASSETS

Long-term assets, sometimes known as *fixed assets,* are assets that are useful for more than one year. With the exception of Land, however, they do wear out over time. Long-term assets are customarily listed in the inverse order of their liquidity, with Land shown first.

1. Land on which buildings have been constructed, the least liquid asset

2. Buildings used in the business

3. Equipment used in the business

4. Trucks used in the business

Other long-term assets include:

5. Long-term funds, investments, and receivables that pertain to the long-term commitment of funds

6. Long-term intangible resources or assets, which include items such as patents, goodwill, and trademarks; most of these intangibles are listed as assets only when outsiders have made expenditures to acquire them (covered in Chapter 9)

The cost of depreciable assets is allocated to operations over their useful life. The recording of depreciation expense is explained in Chapters 3 and 9.

CURRENT LIABILITIES

Current liabilities are obligations that must be paid within the next 12 months or the operating cycle of the entity. They are listed in order of their due dates:

1. Bank Loans payable on demand or due within the next fiscal year, the most current obligation

2. Accounts Payable, obligations that must be paid within a relatively short period of time

3. Accruals (often small in amount compared with accounts payable) usually grouped with accounts payable and disclosed as Accounts Payable and Accruals

4. The current portion of long-term debt, such as a partial repayment of a mortgage within the next fiscal year, listed in order of due date in relation to other current liabilities

5. Income tax liabilities, which usually follow the Accounts Payable and Accruals amount

The current-liability category also includes accounts that represent the unearned portion of amounts received from customers or obligations to provide goods or services within the next year.

LONG-TERM LIABILITIES

Long-term liabilities are obligations that do not require payment for one or more years, such as noncurrent loans and mortgages. Where the operating cycle of the entity is longer than one fiscal year—the manufacturing and aging of scotch, for example—exceptions to the one-year rule are permitted.

Preparation of Financial Statements

PREPARING THE INCOME STATEMENT AND THE BALANCE SHEET

An **interim financial statement** is one that is prepared before the end of an entity's business year. The interim income statement for November for SCI, prepared from the revenue and expense accounts found in the trial balance, is shown in Exhibit 2-5. The interim balance sheet is prepared next. The assets, liabilities, and equities are reported on the balance sheet. The income statement must be prepared first, since the determination of net income is used to update part of the equity section of the balance sheet (see Exhibit 2-6). A statement of cash flows will not be shown here since we have already prepared one for November for SCI from the transactions worksheet in Chapter 1. A year-end statement of cash flows will be prepared for the fiscal year ending on December 31 for SCI in Chapter 3.

Note that the actual format of the balance sheet can vary. Two commonly used formats are the *account form* and the *report form,* illustrated next. The same information is conveyed by both formats.

Balance Sheet Formats

Account Form

Assets	$xxx	Liabilities	$ xx
		Equity	x
	$xxx		$xxx

Assets appear on the left side, and liabilities and equity appear on the right side when the **account form balance sheet is used.**

Report Form

Assets	$xxx
	$xxx
Liabilities	$ xx
Equity	x
	$xxx

Assets are presented first, with liabilities and equity following when the **report form balance sheet is used.**

EXHIBIT 2–5

PREPARING THE INCOME STATEMENT
FROM THE TRIAL BALANCE

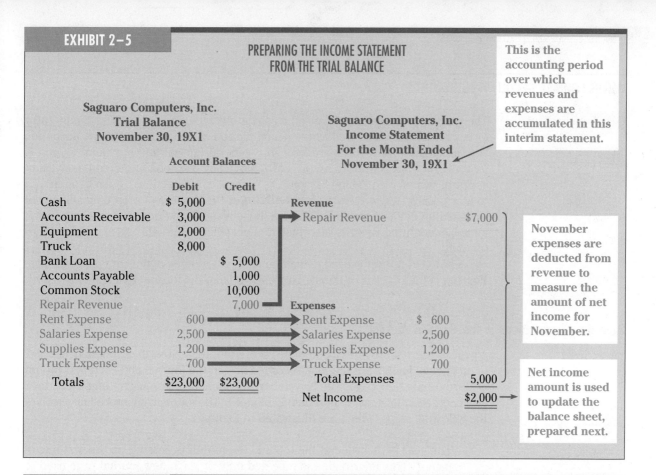

Saguaro Computers, Inc.
Trial Balance
November 30, 19X1

This is the accounting period over which revenues and expenses are accumulated in this interim statement.

Saguaro Computers, Inc.
Income Statement
For the Month Ended
November 30, 19X1

Account Balances		
	Debit	Credit
Cash	$ 5,000	
Accounts Receivable	3,000	
Equipment	2,000	
Truck	8,000	
Bank Loan		$ 5,000
Accounts Payable		1,000
Common Stock		10,000
Repair Revenue		7,000
Rent Expense	600	
Salaries Expense	2,500	
Supplies Expense	1,200	
Truck Expense	700	
Totals	$23,000	$23,000

Revenue
Repair Revenue $7,000

Expenses
Rent Expense .... $ 600
Salaries Expense 2,500
Supplies Expense 1,200
Truck Expense 700
    Total Expenses 5,000
Net Income $2,000

November expenses are deducted from revenue to measure the amount of net income for November.

Net income amount is used to update the balance sheet, prepared next.

EXHIBIT 2–6

PREPARING THE BALANCE SHEET
FROM THE TRIAL BALANCE

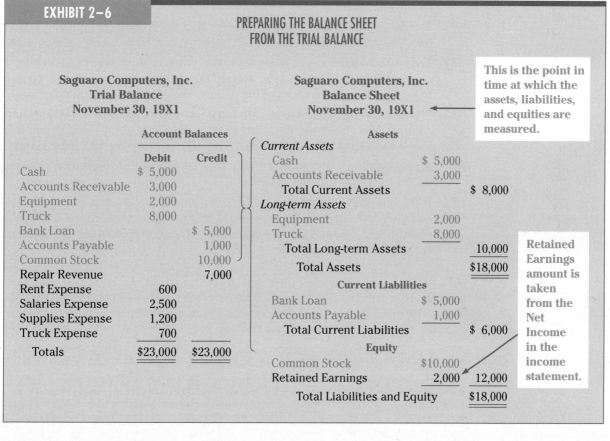

Saguaro Computers, Inc.
Trial Balance
November 30, 19X1

Saguaro Computers, Inc.
Balance Sheet
November 30, 19X1

This is the point in time at which the assets, liabilities, and equities are measured.

Account Balances		
	Debit	Credit
Cash	$ 5,000	
Accounts Receivable	3,000	
Equipment	2,000	
Truck	8,000	
Bank Loan		$ 5,000
Accounts Payable		1,000
Common Stock		10,000
Repair Revenue		7,000
Rent Expense	600	
Salaries Expense	2,500	
Supplies Expense	1,200	
Truck Expense	700	
Totals	$23,000	$23,000

Assets
Current Assets
Cash .... $ 5,000
Accounts Receivable 3,000
    Total Current Assets .... $ 8,000
Long-term Assets
Equipment 2,000
Truck 8,000
    Total Long-term Assets 10,000
    Total Assets $18,000

Current Liabilities
Bank Loan .... $ 5,000
Accounts Payable 1,000
    Total Current Liabilities .... $ 6,000

Equity
Common Stock $10,000
Retained Earnings 2,000   12,000
    Total Liabilities and Equity $18,000

Retained Earnings amount is taken from the Net Income in the income statement.

USING FORMAL ACCOUNTING RECORDS

Q15: Functions of general journal and general ledger

The preceding analysis of financial transactions included a debit and credit entry for each transaction as well as the accumulation of dollar amounts in T accounts. Formal accounting records are kept in a general journal and a general ledger. A **general journal** is used to record chronologically the debit and credit analysis of *each* transaction (see Exhibit 2-7 for SCI's November transactions). It is often referred to as a *book of original entry.* **Journalizing** is the process of recording a financial transaction (called a **journal entry**) in the journal. In addition to a general journal, formal accounting records also include specialized journals, discussed in Chapter 6.

A **general ledger** is used to maintain all the accounts of the entity in one place. **Posting** is the process of transferring entries from the journal to a ledger account.

Recording Transactions in the General Journal

A general journal provides a complete record of transactions in chronological order in one place. Each transaction is recorded first in the journal and each new month is started on a new page. The November transactions of Saguaro Computers, Inc., are recorded in its general journal in Exhibit 2-7. The journalizing procedure involves the following steps, which are illustrated in Exhibit 2-7.

(1)   The year is recorded at the top and the month is entered on the first line of page 1. This information is repeated only on each new journal page used to record transactions.[2]

(2)   The date of the first transaction is entered in the second column, on the first line. The date of each transaction is always recorded in this second column.

(3)   The name of the account to be debited is entered in the description column on the first line. Accounts to be debited are always recorded before accounts to be credited. The amount of the debit is recorded in the debit column.

(4)   The name of the account to be credited is on the second line of the description column and is indented. Accounts to be credited are always indented in this way in the journal. The amount of the credit is recorded in the credit column.

(5)   An explanation of the transaction is entered also in the description column, on the next line. It is not indented.

(6)   A line is usually skipped after each journal entry to separate individual entries and the date of the next entry recorded. It is unnecessary to repeat the month (November here) as long as it is unchanged from that recorded at the top of the page.

SCI's first two journal entries have one debit and credit. An entry can also have more than one debit or credit, in which case it is referred to as a **compound journal entry.** The entries on November 3, 27, and 29 are examples of compound entries.

[2]In this textbook, transactions and their accompanying dates may be simply listed without regard to their (often handwritten) placement on actual journal pages. Thus, transactions may be continued over more than one textbook page. In such cases, the month is repeated at the top of each new book page as a reminder and may not coincide with where the date would be placed in the journal itself.

EXHIBIT 2-7

GENERAL JOURNAL TRANSACTIONS FOR SCI IN NOVEMBER

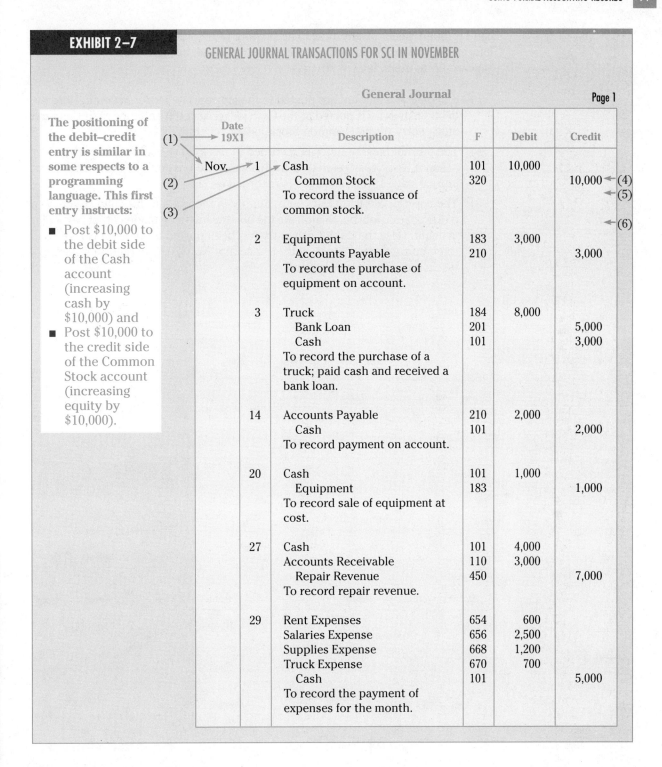

The positioning of the debit–credit entry is similar in some respects to a programming language. This first entry instructs:

- Post $10,000 to the debit side of the Cash account (increasing cash by $10,000) and
- Post $10,000 to the credit side of the Common Stock account (increasing equity by $10,000).

General Journal   Page 1

Date 19X1		Description	F	Debit	Credit
Nov.	1	Cash	101	10,000	
		Common Stock	320		10,000
		To record the issuance of common stock.			
	2	Equipment	183	3,000	
		Accounts Payable	210		3,000
		To record the purchase of equipment on account.			
	3	Truck	184	8,000	
		Bank Loan	201		5,000
		Cash	101		3,000
		To record the purchase of a truck; paid cash and received a bank loan.			
	14	Accounts Payable	210	2,000	
		Cash	101		2,000
		To record payment on account.			
	20	Cash	101	1,000	
		Equipment	183		1,000
		To record sale of equipment at cost.			
	27	Cash	101	4,000	
		Accounts Receivable	110	3,000	
		Repair Revenue	450		7,000
		To record repair revenue.			
	29	Rent Expenses	654	600	
		Salaries Expense	656	2,500	
		Supplies Expense	668	1,200	
		Truck Expense	670	700	
		Cash	101		5,000
		To record the payment of expenses for the month.			

(1) (2) (3) (4) (5) (6)

Posting Transactions in the Ledger

The **ledger account** is a more formal variation of the T account and is used by companies with a manual accounting system. Ledger accounts are kept in the general ledger, often a loose-leaf binder. Debits and credits recorded in the general ledger are posted to appropriate ledger accounts so that the balance of each account can be found easily at any time. The posting of amounts and recording of other information is illustrated in three steps in Exhibit 2-8, using the first transaction of Saguaro Computers, Inc.

(1)   The date and amount are posted to the appropriate ledger account. Here the debit Cash entry is posted to the Cash ledger account and the credit Common Stock entry to the Common Stock ledger account.

(2)   The journal page number is recorded in the folio (F) column of each ledger account as a cross reference. In this case, the posting has been made from journal page 1; the reference is recorded as "J.1."

(3)   The appropriate ledger account number is recorded in the folio (F) column of the general journal to indicate the posting has been made to that particular account. Here the debit Cash entry has been posted to Account No. 101 and the credit Common Stock entry to Account No. 320. (Account numbering is discussed in the next section.)

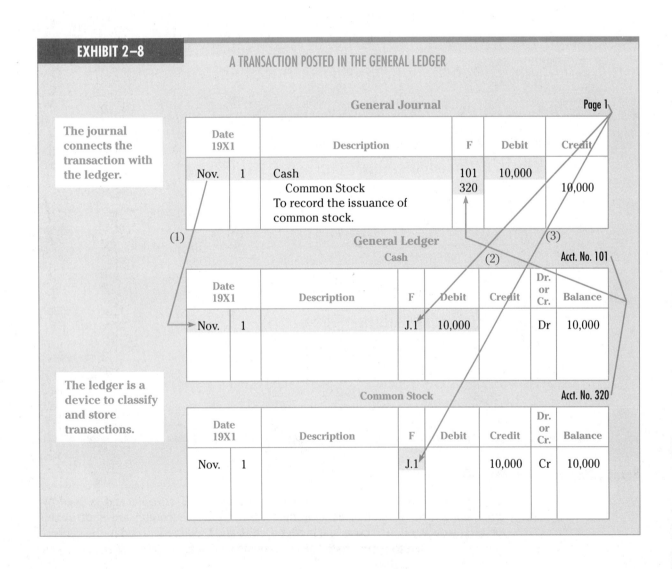

EXHIBIT 2–8

A TRANSACTION POSTED IN THE GENERAL LEDGER

The journal connects the transaction with the ledger.

The ledger is a device to classify and store transactions.

General Journal   Page 1

Date 19X1		Description	F	Debit	Credit
Nov.	1	Cash	101	10,000	
		Common Stock	320		10,000
		To record the issuance of common stock.			

General Ledger

Cash   Acct. No. 101

Date 19X1		Description	F	Debit	Credit	Dr. or Cr.	Balance
Nov.	1		J.1	10,000		Dr	10,000

Common Stock   Acct. No. 320

Date 19X1		Description	F	Debit	Credit	Dr. or Cr.	Balance
Nov.	1		J.1		10,000	Cr	10,000

Following the posting process, a balance is calculated for each ledger account. A notation is recorded in the "Dr./Cr." column, indicating whether the balance in the account is a debit or credit. This manual posting is a slow process. Most businesses, no matter how small or large, have usually used mechanical or electronic devices to help in the recording and posting of transactions. More recently, computers, especially personal computers, have taken the place of manual systems. But it is important to know how transactions were recorded manually to get a full understanding of what is happening to business transactions as they flow through a computer.

In this and several subsequent chapters, the informal T account will be used to analyze transactions, rather than the more formal three-column (Debit, Credit, Balance) ledger account. It is recommended you use the T-account format in completing assignments in order to save time. However, your instructor may require the ledger account format for homework assignments.

Chart of Accounts

The ledger accounts used by an entity are organized using a **chart of accounts.** Typically accounts are grouped within asset, liability, equity, revenue, and expense classifications; a number is assigned to each account to be used by the entity. Flexibility is built into the chart of accounts through the inclusion of gaps in the numerical sequence, so subsequent accounts can be added. Exhibit 2-9 is the chart of accounts for Saguaro Computers, Inc. A broader chart of accounts that combines these and other accounts named throughout the text is printed on the front inside cover of this textbook.

A common practice is to have the accounts arranged in a manner compatible with the order of their use in financial statements. Although it is not a rigid rule to number accounts in this manner, it does have considerable advantage and is recommended in this text. (List accounts in the above sequence when completing assignment material for this text that requires the preparation of financial statements. The above accounts and account numbers are applicable to all the assignment material in this and the following chapters.)

The Accounting Cycle

Q16: Steps to convert economic data

In the preceding pages, the November transactions of Saguaro Computers, Inc., were used to demonstrate the sequential steps performed by the accountant in converting economic data into financial information. This conversion was carried out in accordance with the basic double-entry accounting model established by Luca Pacioli in 1494. These sequential steps can be visually summarized as shown in Exhibit 2-10.

The sequence described in the exhibit, beginning with the journalizing of the transactions and ending with the communication of financial information in financial statements, is commonly referred to as the **accounting cycle.** Although the number of steps is expanded, with some added in-between in Chapters 3 and 4, the basic sequence is not changed. These additional steps are needed because of the large number of transactions facing the modern corporation and the special accounting procedures needed for the artificial time periods within which financial information is communicated.

EXHIBIT 2–9

SAGUARO COMPUTERS, INC.
CHART OF ACCOUNTS

Balance Sheet Accounts

101–179 *Current Asset Accounts*
  101 Cash
  106 Temporary Investments
  110 Accounts Receivable
  116 Interest Receivable
  120 Notes Receivable
  150 Merchandise Inventory
  160 Prepaid Advertising
  161 Prepaid Insurance
  162 Prepaid Rent
  173 Supplies
180–199 *Long-term Asset Accounts*
  180 Land
  181 Building
  182 Furniture
  183 Equipment
  184 Truck
200–299 *Current Liability Accounts*
  201 Bank Loan
  210 Accounts Payable
  214 Loans Payable
  222 Interest Payable
  226 Salaries Payable
  231 Property Taxes Payable
  236 Utilities Payable
  237 Wages Payable
300–399 *Stockholders' Equity Accounts*
  320 Common Stock
  340 Retained Earnings ⎫
  350 Dividends   ⎬
  360 Income Summary   ⎭

Income Statement Accounts

400–499 *Revenue Accounts*
  450 Repair Revenue
  460 Revenue (for other types not
         identified within the operating
         revenue category)
  470 Service Revenue
  480 Subscriptions Revenue
600–699 *Expense Accounts*
  610 Advertising Expense
  615 Commissions Expense
  630 Equipment Rental Expense
  631 Insurance Expense
  632 Interest Expense
  641 Maintenance Expense
  642 Miscellaneous Expense
  650 Office Supplies Expense
  651 Property Tax Expense
  654 Rent Expense
  656 Salaries Expense
  668 Supplies Expense
  669 Telephone Expense
  670 Truck Expense
  676 Utilities Expense
  677 Wages Expense
800–899 *Other Accounts*
  830 Income Tax Expense
           ↑

The use of these accounts is explained in
Chapter 4.

CHAPTER REVIEW

1 What is the framework of principles now generally accepted within the accounting profession? (p. 48)

This framework is what has become known as *generally accepted accounting principles* (GAAP). They are not scientific principles, but assumptions and beliefs that have evolved over the years. GAAP is constantly changing as the needs of business change.

2 Has the accounting profession agreed on a definitive list of fundamentals underlying the accounting process? (p. 48)

If a definitive list exists, it does so only at a point in time. Some of the basic assumptions, such as "historical cost" and "stable dollar," have not changed for some time, but even these assumptions cannot and should not be referred to as a definitive list.

EXHIBIT 2-10

THE ACCOUNTING CYCLE

Step 1: Transactions are analyzed and recorded in the general journal.
Journalizing consists of analyzing transactions as they occur, to see how they affect the accounting equation, and then recording the transactions chronologically in the general journal.

Step 2: Transactions are summarized by account and posted to the general ledger.
Posting consists of transferring debits and credits from the general journal to the appropriate ledger accounts.

Step 3: The equality of debits with credits is established in a trial balance to ensure accuracy.
Preparing a trial balance consists of listing account names and balances to prove the equality of total debit balances with total credit balances.

Step 4: The summarized transactions are communicated in financial statements.
Preparing financial statements at this point consists of using the data listed in the columns of the trial balance to prepare the income statement and the balance sheet.

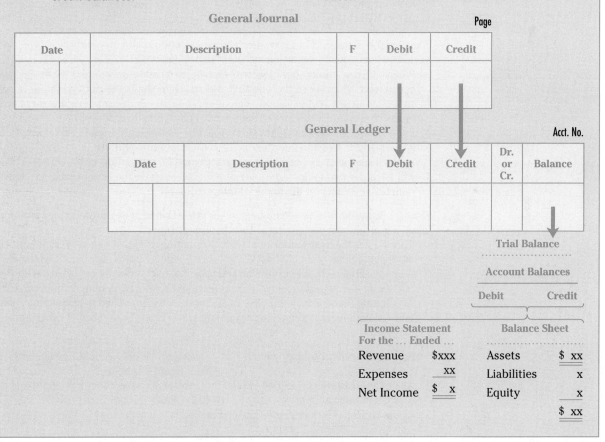

General Journal   Page

Date	Description	F	Debit	Credit

General Ledger   Acct. No.

Date	Description	F	Debit	Credit	Dr. or Cr.	Balance

Trial Balance
....

Account Balances

	Debit	Credit

Income Statement For the ... Ended ...		Balance Sheet	
Revenue	$xxx	Assets	$ xx
Expenses	xx	Liabilities	x
Net Income	$ x	Equity	x
			$ xx

3 Is the dollar a stable unit of measure? Is it the most appropriate measure for transactions, and for the reporting of accounting information? (p. 49)

The U.S. dollar is not stable, nor is any other monetary unit from any other country. However, money does give the accounting profession a common denominator to use as a measurement basis for financial information. Therefore, it is the most appropriate measurement unit.

4   Financial statements are prepared on the basis of historical cost. Why is historical cost used to measure financial transactions? (p. 49)

Historical cost is determinable, objective, and verifiable.

5   In what way does accrual accounting match revenue with expenses? (p. 50)

Under accrual accounting, revenues are recognized when they are earned, and expenses are recognized when they are incurred in the generation of that revenue. Hence we can say that expenses are matched against the corresponding revenues, producing a more accurate measurement of net income.

6   When do accountants assume revenue is earned? (p. 50)

Revenue is assumed to be earned generally at the time the service has been performed or the goods delivered. As later chapters point out, sometimes revenue is recognized before the service has been completely performed, or the goods (or a portion of them) have been delivered.

7   What characteristics is financial information expected to have? (pp. 51–52)

For accounting information to be useful, it must be both relevant and reliable. This sometimes presents the accountant with a dilemma. Information may be highly relevant but not reliable, or highly reliable but not relevant. Consistency and comparability are also important objectives.

8   What are the impacts of conservatism and consistency in situations where a choice is made between equally defensible accounting principles? (p. 52)

When given a choice between two equally defensible accounting methods, the accountant will choose the one that will result in the lower net income or asset valuation, or the higher liability valuation. In doing so, he or she will present the most "conservative" picture of the financial condition. In order for the information to be usable, accounting applications must be consistently applied, so information is comparable to other information for past accounting periods. When the accountant is faced with a choice regarding a change in application of GAAP, he or she will consider two factors: the cost of the change given the benefit, and the materiality of the effect on the financial information.

9   What are the authoritative accounting bodies in the United States? How do they interact in issuing pronouncements related to accounting? (pp. 53–54)

The SEC has the *legal* authority to issue accounting rules and regulations for entities whose shares are publicly traded. No other body has this authority. When the SEC was commissioned, the profession was asked to determine its own rules, with the SEC as an overseer. Currently, the professional rule-making body is the Financial Accounting Standards Board. The FASB is primarily interested in accounting rules and regulations regarding external financial reporting. A number of other bodies explore other areas. Some are:

American Accounting Association (AAA)

American Institute of Certified Public Accountants (AICPA)

Financial Executives Institute (FEI)

Governmental Accounting Standards Board (GASB)

National Association of Accountants (NAA)

This is not to be considered a definitive list.

10   What is the function of the auditors' report in relation to GAAP? (p. 54)

The auditor's report gives credence to the information in the financial statements. The users know that an accountant outside the entity (a CPA) has examined the records and found them to be fairly presented and in conformity with GAAP.

11   How are accounts used in the accounting process? (p. 55)

Accounts are used to classify and summarize a series of economic events.

12 What are the meanings of the terms *debit* and *credit?* (p. 55)

The terms *debit* and *credit,* as they are used in accounting, mean nothing more than the left and right side of an account, depicted as a T account.

Debit	Credit
(left)	(right)

13 How does the use of debits and credits facilitate and control the accounting process? (pp. 55, 57)

Through the use of debits and credits, the accounting equation can always be kept in balance, thereby controlling the efficiency of the accounting process.

14 What is the function of a trial balance? a general journal? a general ledger? (pp. 64–66)

The trial balance simply shows that the accounts are in balance. It does not show whether all transactions were recorded correctly.

The general journal is a book of original entry. All business transactions are recorded first in the journal.

The general ledger is a listing of all the accounts in the accounting system of an entity. After the economic event is recorded in the journal, it is transferred (posted) to the proper accounts in the ledger in order to classify and summarize the economic events for a period of time.

15 What classifications are used on the balance sheet? Why are they helpful? (pp. 66–68, 70)

The asset and liability sections of the balance sheet are classified as either current or long-term. The classifications are helpful when evaluating the financial position of the entity. For example, the relationship between the current assets and the current liabilities is important when evaluating liquidity.

16 What are the sequential steps performed by the accountant in converting economic data into financial information? (p. 73)

At this point, the accounting cycle consists of four steps:

1. Record the event in the general journal.
2. Post the transaction to the general ledger.
3. Prepare a trial balance of the ledger to determine if the accounts are in balance.
4. Prepare financial statements from the trial balance.

KEY TERMS

account   (p. 55) A record designed to classify and summarize the effect of economic events on a particular element in an entity (such as cash, equipment, or accounts payable).

account form balance sheet   (p. 68) A balance sheet in which liabilities and equities are listed to the right of assets.

accounting cycle   (p. 73) The individual steps required to process accounting information during an accounting period.

"adding apples and oranges"   (p. 49) An old cliché in accounting. It is believed or accepted that monetary units (dollars) from different time periods can be added together to get meaningful amounts. Because those dollars have different values caused by inflation, the sum is not meaningful. Just as adding apples and oranges gives us mixed fruit, adding dollars of different values gives us mixed dollars.

American Accounting Association (AAA)   (p. 54) The membership of this group consists mainly of accounting educators, who promote most of the research conducted today in accounting. The group has contributed much of the base for accounting theory.

American Institute of Certified Public Accountants (AICPA)   (p. 53) A national professional accounting association that has been very active in the development of GAAP in this century. This group also develops and grades the national Certified Public Accountants (CPA) Examination.

auditor's report   (p. 54) An opinion of a professional accountant on the financial statements of an entity; states whether the financial statements fairly present the financial position and operating results of the entity and whether these statements have been prepared according to GAAP.

cash   (p. 66) Anything that will be accepted by a bank for a deposit; serves as a unit of account, a medium of exchange, and a store of purchasing power. Includes cash in the bank, cash on hand, and petty cash.

certified management accountant (CMA)   (p. 79) A professional accountant, generally in industry, who has passed the CMA Examination and has satisfied all other professional requirements.

certified public accountant (CPA)   (p. 54) A professional accountant who has passed the CPA Examination and has satisfied all other professional requirements for admittance.

chart of accounts   (p. 73) A list of account names and numbers used in the general ledger; usually found in financial statement presentation order.

compound journal entry   (p. 70) A journal entry that includes more than one account that is debited, or more than one account that is credited.

conservatism   (p. 52) When making a choice between equally defensible alternatives, the accountant will choose the one that will produce the least favorable results for the entity. This presents the most conservative estimate of financial position or net income.

consistency   (p. 51) The consistent application of accounting principles from one accounting period to the next. This makes it possible to compare one year's financial statements with another year, when changes are made in the application of accounting principles.

cost–benefit judgment   (p. 53) The measuring of the cost of providing information with the benefit the users will receive from having access to the information. If the cost exceeds the benefit, the information will not be provided.

credit   (p. 55) The right side of an account.

current assets   (p. 66) Economic resources to be converted to cash or consumed during the next year.

current liabilities   (p. 67) Obligations to be paid within one year or within the normal operating cycle, whichever is longer.

debit   (p. 55) The left side of an account.

entity assumption   (p. 48) The business enterprise is always assumed to be separate from its owners.

Federal Reserve Board   (p. 53) A federal board that oversees much of the banking activity in the United States.

Financial Accounting Standards Board (FASB)   (p. 53) A board funded by the Financial Accounting Foundation to establish accounting rules and regulations. Unlike its predecessors, this is an independent, full-time, paid group of individuals.

Financial Executives Institute (FEI)   (p. 54) A group of accountants who hold higher management positions in the financial hierarchy in large corporations.

footing   (p. 64) A total of a column of figures; the difference between the debit and credit balances is then calculated.

general journal   (p. 70) A chronological record of an entity's financial transactions; often referred to as a book of original entry.

general ledger   (p. 70) A book that contains the asset, liability, equity, revenue, and expense accounts of an entity.

generally accepted accounting principles (GAAP)   (p. 48) A set of constantly changing accounting principles and practices that have become generally accepted and are used by accountants in the preparation of financial statements.

going-concern assumption   (p. 48) The entity will remain in existence indefinitely.

Governmental Accounting Standards Board (GASB)   (p. 54) Another board funded by the Financial Accounting Foundation to establish accounting rules and regulations for governmental units.

historical-cost assumption   (p. 49) The belief that the most objective measure of an asset's worth is the amount paid for the asset. Subsequent changes in the value of the asset are not recorded.

income determination and matching assumption   (p. 50) The determination of income by the accrual basis of accounting, where revenue is recognized when earned and expenses are recognized when incurred. The expenses are then matched against the revenue generated to determine net income.

interim financial statement   (p. 68) A financial statement that does *not* report the activities and financial position for an entire business year. An interim statement could be for *any* period of time, from one day to 11 months. Financial statements for a 12-month period are not referred to as interim statements.

Internal Revenue Service (IRS)   (p. 54) The agency of the federal government that collects various taxes for the U.S. Treasury. The IRS has different rules for determining income for tax purposes than those used to determine income for financial accounting purposes. In many cases, an entity will maintain two sets of records, one for the IRS and one using GAAP for financial reporting.

International Accounting Standards Committee (IASC)   (p. 54) A group that has issued many international accounting standards that have been translated into a number of languages.

International Federation of Accountants (IFAC)   (p. 54) A group made up of professional accounting bodies from more than 50 countries in the world. It was founded primarily to nurture international discussion on accounting issues.

journal entry   (p. 70) An entry recorded in the general journal with at least one debit and one credit.

journalizing   (p. 70) The process of recording a transaction in a journal.

ledger account   (p. 71) An account kept in a book called a ledger.

liquidation value   (p. 49) The valuation of assets at their net realizable value; based on the assumption that the entity will go out of business and will sell its assets.

long-term assets   (p. 67) Assets that will be useful for more than one year; sometimes referred to as *fixed assets.*

long-term liabilities   (p. 68) Obligations that do not require repayment for one or more years.

materiality   (p. 51) The judgment call an accountant must make when deciding to disclose a given piece of information. The more immaterial the item is, the lesser the chance that it will be disclosed, since too much information can cloud the issue.

National Association of Accountants (NAA)   (p. 54) A group made up mostly of accountants in industry. This group develops and grades the **Certified Management Accountants (CMA)** Examination.

note   (p. 67) A written promise by a borrower to repay a specified amount.

operating cycle   (p. 51) The cash-to-cash sequence of events for the revenue-producing operations of an entity.

periodicity assumption   (p. 49) The belief that the life of a business enterprise can be divided into arbitrary units of time, ususally one year, for the purpose of measuring net income and financial position.

posting (p. 70) The process of transferring amounts from the journal to a ledger account.

relevance (p. 51) The usefulness and timeliness of accounting information. Can it be used to reduce the uncertainty associated with decision making?

reliability (p. 51) The dependability of accounting information. Can the user employ the information to evaluate alternative possibilities?

report form balance sheet (p. 68) A balance sheet in which liabilities and equities are listed below the assets.

revenue recognition (p. 50) Revenue is recognized when earned. This is usually at the time the good or service is provided, although in some cases revenue may be recognized before all the goods or services have been provided, or in some other cases, the revenue may not be recorded until the cash has been received.

Securities and Exchange Commission (SEC) (p. 53) An agency of the U.S. government that has the legal power to develop accounting principles and reporting practices for companies whose stock is traded on domestic markets. The commission has asked the accounting profession to regulate its own practices, but it monitors the situation very closely.

stable-unit-of-measure assumption (p. 49) The monetary unit used to measure the value of an economic event has the same value from year to year. In the United States, the monetary unit is the U.S. dollar.

T account (p. 55) A form of a general ledger account that is easy to use as a learning tool in the classroom to illustrate the accumulation of financial data.

trial balance (p. 64) A list of each account together with its individual debit or credit balance; used to establish the equality of debits with credits before the preparation of financial statements.

uniformity (p. 51) GAAP should be applied consistently within an industry so that the financial statements of one firm in the industry can be compared to another firm in the same industry.

SELF-TEST QUESTIONS FOR REVIEW   (Answers are at the end of this chapter.)

Q1, Q2

1. The term *principle,* as used in the phrase "generally accepted accounting principles," means
   (a) the same as a law.
   (b) the same as the term is used in the sciences.
   (c) more of an assumption.
   (d) that they never change.

Q9

2. Which of the following organizations has the authority given to it by law to establish GAAP for financial accounting purposes?
   (a) American Institute of CPAs
   (b) Securities and Exchange Commission
   (c) Financial Accounting Standards Board
   (d) Internal Revenue Service
   (e) All of the above

Q7

3. Which of the following characteristics of financial information means that some information may not be disclosed?
   (a) Materiality
   (b) Cost–benefit
   (c) Conservatism
   (d) Consistency

Q12, Q13

4. A debit to an asset account could result in a
   (a) debit to another asset account.
   (b) debit to a liability account.

(c) debit to an equity account.
(d) credit to another asset account.

Q15

5. All transactions are first recorded in
   (a) the trial balance.
   (b) the general ledger.
   (c) a T account.
   (d) the general journal.

Q14

6. All of the following would be classifications found on a balance sheet except
   (a) short-term liabilities.
   (b) long-term liabilities.
   (c) long-term assets.
   (d) current assets.

Q15

7. The term *post* means to
   (a) record a transaction in the general journal.
   (b) prepare a trial balance.
   (c) record the effect of transactions on the general ledger.
   (d) cross-reference entries in the general ledger.

DEMONSTRATION PROBLEM

The following balances appeared in the general ledger of Meadow Tool Rentals, Inc., on May 1, 19X1.

Cash	$1,600	Accounts Payable	$4,000
Supplies	400	Common Stock	8,000
Equipment	3,000		
Truck	7,000		

The following transactions occurred during May:

a. Collected $5,000 cash for tool rental during the month (Meadow does not rent tools on account).

b. Paid rent for May in the amount of $500.

c. Paid $1,500 on account.

d. Paid $600 for a one-year insurance policy effective May 1.

e. Purchased a used truck for $5,000 on account.

f. Paid the following expenses: advertising, $300; salaries, $2,500; telephone, $150; truck, $550.

g. Transferred the portion of the insurance policy that has expired during the month of May.

h. Estimated $200 of supplies to have been used during May.

Required
1. Open ledger accounts for the following and enter the May 1 balances: Cash, Prepaid Insurance, Supplies, Equipment, Truck, Accounts Payable, Common Stock, Rent Earned, Advertising Expense, Insurance Expense, Rent Expense, Salaries Expense, Supplies Expense, Telephone Expense, Truck Expense.

2. Prepare journal entries to record the May transactions. Post these entries to the ledger accounts.

3. Prepare a trial balance as of May 31.

4. Prepare an interim income statement and interim balance sheet as of May 31.

5. Using the T account for Cash, prepare a statement of cash flows.

1.

Meadow Tool Rentals, Inc.
General Ledger

ASSETS = LIABILITIES + EQUITY

ASSETS

Cash No. 101

	1,600	(b)	500
(a)	5,000	(c)	1,500
		(d)	600
		(f)	3,500
	6,600		6,100
Bal.	500		

Prepaid Insurance No. 161

(d)	600	(g)	50
Bal.	550		

Supplies No. 173

	400	(h)	200
Bal.	200		

Equipment No. 183

	3,000

Truck No. 184

	7,000	
(e)	5,000	
Bal.	12,000	

LIABILITIES

Accounts Payable No. 210

(c)	1,500		4,000
		(e)	5,000
	1,500		9,000
		Bal.	7,500

EQUITY

Common Stock No. 320

8,000

Rent Earned No. 440

(a)	5,000

Advertising Expense No. 610

(f)	300

Insurance Expense No. 631

(g)	50

Rent Expense No. 654

(b)	500

Salaries Expense No. 656

(f)	2,500

Supplies Expense No. 668

(h)	200

Telephone Expense No. 669

(f)	150

Truck Expense No. 670

(f)	550

2.

Meadow Tool Rentals, Inc.
General Journal

Description	F	Debit	Credit
a. Cash	101	5,000	
Rent Earned	440		5,000
To record tool rental revenue collected.			
b. Rent Expense	654	500	
Cash	101		500
To record rent expense for May.			
c. Accounts Payable	210	1,500	
Cash	101		1,500
To record payment made on account.			
d. Prepaid Insurance	161	600	
Cash	101		600
To record payment for insurance policy.			
e. Truck	184	5,000	
Accounts Payable	210		5,000
To record purchase of truck on account.			
f. Advertising Expense	610	300	
Salaries Expense	656	2,500	
Telephone Expense	669	150	
Truck Expense	670	550	
Cash	101		3,500
To record payment of expenses.			
g. Insurance Expense	631	50	
Prepaid Insurance	161		50
To record expired portion of insurance for May.			
h. Supplies Expense	668	200	
Supplies	173		200
To record supplies used in May, based on an inventory.			

3.

Meadow Tool Rentals, Inc.
Trial Balance
May 31, 19X1

	Account Balances	
	Debit	Credit
Cash	$ 500	
Prepaid Insurance	550	
Supplies	200	
Equipment	3,000	
Truck	12,000	
Accounts Payable		$ 7,500
Common Stock		8,000
Rent Earned		5,000
Advertising Expense	300	
Insurance Expense	50	
Rent Expense	500	
Salaries Expense	2,500	
Supplies Expense	200	
Telephone Expense	150	
Truck Expense	550	
	$20,500	$20,500

Total Debits = Total Credits

4.

Meadow Tool Rentals, Inc.
Income Statement
For the Month Ended May 31, 19X1

Revenue		
Rent Earned		$5,000
Expenses		
Advertising Expense	$ 300	
Insurance Expense	50	
Rent Expense	500	
Salaries Expense	2,500	
Supplies Expense	200	
Telephone Expense	150	
Truck Expense	550	
Total Expenses		4,250
Net Income		$ 750

Meadow Tool Rentals, Inc.
Balance Sheet
May 31, 19X1

Assets

Current Assets		
Cash	$ 500	
Prepaid Insurance	550	
Supplies	200	
Total Current Assets		$ 1,250
Long-term Assets		
Equipment	3,000	
Truck	12,000	
Total Long-term Assets		15,000
Total Assets		$16,250

Liabilities

Accounts Payable		$ 7,500

Equity

Common Stock	8,000	
Retained Earnings	750	8,750
Total Liabilities and Equity		$16,250

5.

Meadow Tool Rentals, Inc.
Statement of Cash Flows (Direct Method)
For the Month Ended May 31, 19X1

Cash Flows from Operating Activities		
Inflows:		
Cash Received from Customers		$5,000
(Outflows):		
Cash Paid for Expenses:		
Supplies	$(1,500)	
Advertising	(300)	
Insurance	(600)	
Rent	(500)	
Salaries	(2,500)	
Telephone	(150)	

(continued)

Truck	(550)	
Total Cash Outflows		(6,100)
Net Cash Outflow from Operating Activities		$(1,100)
Cash Flows from Investing Activities		
[none]		
Cash Flows from Financing Activities		
[none]		
Net Outflow of Cash		(1,100)
Cash Balance, May 1, 19X1		1,600
Cash Balance, May 1, 19X1		$ 500

DISCUSSION QUESTIONS

Q2-1 What are generally accepted accounting principles (GAAP)?

Q2-2 The dollar is seen as the most appropriate measure for the analysis and recording of transactions. Is its use valid in these days of rapid inflation? Why or why not?

Q2-3 What is the recognition concept?

Q2-4 How does the matching concept attempt to determine most accurately the income of a business?

Q2-5 What are the characteristics that accounting information is expected to have?

Q2-6 Name the accounting organizations concerned with the formulation of accounting principles.

Q2-7 What is an auditor's report? What does it indicate?

Q2-8 Why is the use of a transactions worksheet impractical in practice?

Q2-9 What is an account? How are debits and credits used to record transactions?

Q2-10 Students tend to associate "good" and "bad" or "increase" and "decrease" with credits and debits. Is this a valid association? Explain.

Q2-11 The pattern of recording increases and decreases is common to asset and expense accounts. Explain, using an example.

Q2-12 The pattern of recording increases and decreases is also common to liabilities, equity, and revenues. Explain, using an example.

Q2-13 Summarize the rules for using debits and credits to record assets, expenses, liabilities, equity, and revenues.

Q2-14 What is a trial balance? Why is it prepared?

Q2-15 How is a trial balance used to prepare financial statements?

Q2-16 A general journal is often called a *book of original entry*. Why?

Q2-17 The positioning of a debit–credit entry in the general journal is similar in some respects to programming methods. Explain, using an example.

Q2-18 What is a ledger? Why is it prepared?

Q2-19 What is a chart of accounts? What is the advantage of arranging the accounts in a manner compatible with the order of their use in financial statements?

Q2-20 List the steps in the accounting cycle.

Q2-21 Define accounting.

Q2-22 Is accounting an art or a science?

Q2-23   Refer to the Discussion Case in Chapter 1. Accountants refer to GAAP when valuing assets shown on a balance sheet. Identify the accounting principles that relate directly to Sir Rodolph and explain the application of each principle in Sir Rodolph's case.

DISCUSSION CASE

Ivan and Igor, Wheat Growers

Q1–Q8   Many, many years ago, there lived a feudal landlord in a small province of Central Europe. The landlord, called the Red-Bearded Baron, lived in a castle high on a hill, and this benevolent fellow was responsible for the well-being of many peasants who occupied the lands surrounding his castle. Each spring, as the snow began to melt and thoughts of other, less influential men turned to matters other than business, the baron would decide how to provide for all his serf-dependents during the coming year.

One spring, the baron was thinking about the wheat crop of the coming growing season. "I believe that 30 acres of my land, being worth 5 bushels of wheat per acre, will produce enough wheat for next winter," he mused, "but who should do the farming? I believe I'll give Ivan the Indefatigable and Igor the Immutable the task of growing the wheat." Whereupon Ivan and Igor, two serfs noted for their hard work and not overly active minds, were summoned for an audience with the landlord.

"Ivan, you will farm on the 20-acre plot of ground, and Igor will farm the 10-acre plot," the baron began. "I will give Ivan 20 bushels of wheat for seed and 20 pounds of fertilizer. (Twenty pounds of fertilizer are worth 2 bushels of wheat.) Igor will get 10 bushels of wheat for seed and 10 pounds of fertilizer. I will give each of you an ox to pull a plough, but you will have to make arrangements with Feyador, the ploughmaker, for a plough. The oxen, incidentally, are only three years old and have never been used for farming, so they should have a good 10 years of farming ahead of them. Take good care of them, because an ox is worth 40 bushels of wheat. Come back next fall and return the oxen and the ploughs along with your harvest."

Ivan and Igor genuflected and withdrew from the Great Hall, taking with them the things provided by the baron.

The summer came and went, and after the harvest Ivan and Igor returned to the Great Hall to account to their master for the things given them in the spring. Ivan, pouring 223 bushels of wheat onto the floor, said, "My lord, I present you with a slightly used ox, a plough broken beyond repair, and 223 bushels of wheat. I, unfortunately, owe Feyador the ploughmaker, 3 bushels of wheat for the plough I got from him last fall. And, as you might expect, I used all the fertilizer and seed you gave me last spring. You will also remember, my lord, that you took 20 bushels of my harvest for your own personal use."

Igor, who had been given 10 acres of land, 10 bushels of wheat, and 10 pounds of fertilizer, spoke next. "Here, my lord, is a partially used ox, the plough for which I gave Feyador the ploughmaker 3 bushels of wheat from my harvest, and 105 bushels of wheat. I, too, used all my seed and fertilizer last spring. Also, my lord, you took 30 bushels of wheat several days ago for your own table. I believe the plough is good for two more seasons."

"Fellows, you did well," said the Red-Bearded Baron. Blessed with this benediction and not wishing to press their luck further, the two serfs departed hastily.

After the servants had taken their leave, the Red-Bearded Baron, watching the two hungry oxen slowly eating the wheat piled on the floor, began to contemplate what had happened. "Yes," he thought, "they did well, but I wonder which one did better?"

Source W. T. Andrews, Jr., "Another Improbable Occurrence," *The Accounting Review*, April 1974.

For Discussion

Assuming that a bushel of wheat is the standard measure in use in this province of Central Europe, prepare:

1. A separate balance sheet at the beginning of the spring season for Ivan and for Igor.
2. A separate income statement for the harvest season for Ivan and for Igor.
3. A separate balance sheet at the end of the fall season for Ivan and for Igor.
4. If the Red-Bearded Baron was willing to give the serf who achieved the greater gain a bonus of one bushel of wheat, which serf would receive the bonus?

    Consider using each of the following measures of efficiency in making your decision:

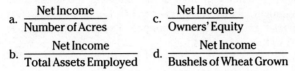

$$a.\ \frac{Net\ Income}{Number\ of\ Acres} \qquad c.\ \frac{Net\ Income}{Owners'\ Equity}$$

$$b.\ \frac{Net\ Income}{Total\ Assets\ Employed} \qquad d.\ \frac{Net\ Income}{Bushels\ of\ Wheat\ Grown}$$

EXERCISES

Debit and credit relationships among the five account categories (Q12, Q13)

E2-1

Required

For each of the accounts listed, show which side of the account would be used for an increase and which for a decrease. Plus (+) and minus (−) symbols may be used.

Asset		Liability		Equity	
Dr.	Cr.	Dr.	Cr.	Dr.	Cr.

Revenue		Expense	
Dr.	Cr.	Dr.	Cr.

E2-2 through E2-4 are based on the transactions worksheet for Maple Builders, Inc., shown here.

		ASSETS				=	LIABILITIES	+		EQUITY	
	Cash	+ Accounts Receivable	+ Supplies	+ Equipment	+ Truck	=	Accounts Payable	+	Common Stock	+	+ Revenue − Expenses
a.	+ $5,000								+ $5,000		
b.				+ $1,000			+ $1,000				
c.			+ $300				+ 300				
d.		+ $3,500									+ $3,500
e.	− 350										− 350
f.	+ 1,000	− 1,000									
g.	− 500						− 500				
h.	− 2,000				+ $8,000		+ 6,000				
i.	− 2,500										− 500
											− 1,200
											− 800
j.		− 200									− 200

Additional information: transaction *e* involved rent and transaction *i* involved advertising, salaries, and truck expenses, in that order.

Preparation of journal entries from a transactions worksheet (Q15, Q16)	**E2-2**

Required

Prepare general journal entries with explanations for each of the transactions shown on the worksheet.

Opening T accounts and posting entries (Q12, Q13, Q15, Q16)	**E2-3**

Required

Open T accounts for each of the following accounts: Cash, Accounts Receivable, Supplies, Equipment, Truck, Accounts Payable, Common Stock, Revenue, Advertising Expense, Rent Expense, Salaries Expense, Supplies Expense, and Truck Expense. Then post the entries in E2-2 to the T accounts.

Preparation of a trial balance (Q12, Q13, Q15, Q16)	**E2-4**

Required

From the T accounts in E2-3, prepare a trial balance for January 31, 19X1.

Preparation of an income statement from a trial balance (Q12, Q13, Q15, Q16)	**E2-5**

Required

From the trial balance in E2-4, prepare an income statement for the month of January 19X1.

Preparation of a balance sheet from a trial balance (Q12, Q13, Q15, Q16)	**E2-6**

Required

From the trial balance in E2-4, prepare a classified balance sheet as of January 31, 19X1.

Preparation of a statement of cash flows (Q12, Q13, Q15, Q16)	**E2-7**

Required

From the T accounts in E2-3, prepare a statement of cash flows for the month of January 19X1.

Preparation of journal entries from T accounts (Q12, Q13, Q15, Q16)	**E2-8** The following accounts are taken from the ledger of Trusty, Inc., at the end of July, its first month of operation.

Cash	No. 101	Bank Loan	No. 201	Insurance Expense	No. 631
1,000	9,000		10,000	1,200	
10,000	900				
1,500	50			Interest	
2,000	75			Expense	No. 632
	600			600	
	2,200				

Accounts Receivable	No. 110		Accounts Payable	No. 210		Rent Expense	No. 654
3,000	1,500			1,200		300	
				100			

Prepaid Rent	No. 162		Common Stock	No. 320		Salaries Expense	No. 656
900	300			1,000		2,200	

Truck	No. 184		Repair Revenue	No. 450		Telephone Expense	No. 669
9,000				3,000		75	
				2,000			

Advertising Expense	No. 610		Utilities Expense	No. 676
50			100	

Required

1. Prepare journal entries for the transactions recorded in the ledger accounts.

2. Prepare a trial balance from the ledger accounts.

Correcting an erroneous trial balance (Q12, Q13, Q15, Q16)

E2-9 The following trial balance has been prepared from the ledger of MacDonald Voyages, Inc.

MacDonald Voyages, Inc.
Trial Balance
January 31, 19X1

	Account Balances	
	Debit	Credit
Cash	$ 60	
Accounts Receivable		$ 140
Supplies	10	
Equipment		300
Bank Loan	100	
Accounts Payable		20
Common Stock	250	
Service Revenue	990	
Fees Earned		885
Advertising Expense	200	
Salary Expense		800
Supplies Expense	20	
Telephone Expense	10	
Utilities Expense	5	
Wages Expense		700
Totals	$1,645	$2,845

Required

Prepare a correct trial balance.

PROBLEMS

Preparation of a trial balance, income statement, and balance sheet (Q11–Q16)

P2-1 The following account balances are taken from the records of Pana-Micro, Inc., as of October 31, 19X1.

Accounts Payable	$9,000	Insurance Expense	$ 500
Accounts Receivable	6,000	Repair Revenue	19,000
Advertising Expense	2,200	Supplies Expense	800
Bank Loan	5,000	Telephone Expense	250
Cash	1,000	Truck	9,000
Common Stock	2,000	Truck Expense	1,250
Commissions Expense	4,500	Wages Expense	4,000
Equipment	7,000	Wages Payable	1,500

Required

1. Prepare a trial balance as of October 31.

2. Prepare an interim income statement as of October 31 in the correct format.

3. Prepare an interim balance sheet as of October 31 in the correct format.

Reconstruction of journal entries from T accounts; preparation of a trial balance (Q11–16)

P2-2 The following ledger accounts were prepared for Bentley Tool Rentals, Inc., during the first month of operations ended May 31, 19X1. No journal entries were prepared in support of the amounts recorded in the ledger accounts.

Cash		Equipment		Commissions Expense	
5,000	1,000	2,000	800	1,100	
2,000	500				
1,500	300				
1,200	600				
800	400				
	3,500				

		Accounts Payable		Rent Expense	
		600	1,000	400	
			150		
			1,100		

Accounts Receivable		Common Stock		Salaries Expense	
3,000	1,500		5,000	3,500	
2,500	1,200				

Prepaid Advertising		Rental Earned		Supplies Expense	
500	250		3,000	100	
			2,000		
			2,500		

Supplies		Advertising Expense		Telephone Expense	
300	100	250		150	

Required

1. Reconstruct the transactions that occurred during the month and prepare journal entries to record these transactions.

2. Calculate the balance in each account and prepare a trial balance as of May 31, 19X1.

Correcting an erro-
neous trial balance
(Q11–Q16)

P2-3   The following trial balance was prepared for Driven Consultants, Inc., as of January 31, 19X1, its first month of operations, by a newly hired bookkeeper who has insufficient training.

Driven Consultants, Inc.
Trial Balance
January 31, 19X1

	Account Balances	
	Debit	**Credit**
Accounts Payable	$ 9,000	
Accounts Receivable		$ 8,000
Advertising Expense	150	
Bank Loan		3,625
Cash	2,000	
Common Stock		7,000
Equipment		4,000
Furniture		1,000
Interest Expense	200	
Maintenance Expense		250
Prepaid Advertising	300	
Repair Revenue	9,500	
Rent Expense		400
Salaries Expense		2,600
Salaries Payable		1,500
Supplies Expense	350	
Telephone Expense	125	
Truck	9,000	
Truck Expense		750
Wages Expense		1,500
Totals	$30,625	$30,625

Required

1. Prepare a correct trial balance as of January 31. List the accounts by the sequence in the chart of accounts in Exhibit 2-9 and record the amounts in their proper debit–credit positions.

2. How is it possible that the debit–credit totals amount to $30,625 in both trial balances? (Assume individual amounts are correct.)

Journal entries, posting,
trial balance, income
statement, and balance
sheet (Q11–Q16)

P2-4   The following transactions occurred in Brock Accounting, Inc., during August 19X1, its first month of operations.

Aug. 1   Issued common stock for $3,000
     1   Borrowed $10,000 from the bank
     1   Paid $8,000 for a used truck
     4   Paid $600 for a one-year insurance policy on the truck, effective August 1
     5   Collected $2,000 cash fees from a client for work performed today
     7   Sent invoices totaling $5,000 to clients for services performed to date
     9   Paid $250 for supplies used to date

12   Purchased supplies costing $500 on account; these supplies will be used in the future

15   Received $1,000 from clients to whom invoices were sent on Aug. 7

16   Paid $200 for advertising in *The News* during the first two weeks of August

20   Paid for one-half of the supplies purchased on August 12

25   Paid the following expenses for August; rent, $350; salaries, $2,150; telephone, $50; and upkeep on the truck, $250

28   Called clients for payment of the balance due from August 7

29   Sent invoices totaling $6,000 to clients for services performed to date

31   Transferred the amount of August's truck insurance to Insurance Expense

31   Counted $100 of supplies still on hand

Required

1. Open ledger accounts for the following: Cash, Accounts Receivable, Prepaid Insurance, Supplies, Truck, Bank Loan, Accounts Payable, Common Stock, Revenue, Advertising Expense, Insurance Expense, Rent Expense, Salaries Expense, Supplies Expense, Telephone Expense, Truck Expense.

2. Prepare journal entries to record the August transactions. Post these entries to the ledger accounts.

3. Prepare a trial balance as of August 31.

4. Prepare an interim income statement and interim balance sheet as of August 31 in the correct format.

Journal entries, posting, trial balance, income statement, balance sheet, and statement of cash flows (Q11–Q16)

P2-5   Electrical Contractors Corp. was incorporated on May 1, 19X1 and had the following transactions during its first month of operations.

May 1   Issued common stock for $5,000

     1   Paid $1,500 for three months' rent in advance: May, June, and July

     2   Purchased supplies costing $1,000 on account

     3   Sent an invoice for $1,500 to a customer for repairs already completed

     4   Paid $50 for an advertisement in *The News*

     5   Received $250 for repairs made today

    10   The customer for whom repairs were made on May 3 paid the invoice

    15   Paid $500 on account

    18   Borrowed $2,000 from the bank

    20   Signed a major contract for work to be done in June

    22   Purchased equipment costing $3,000 with cash

    25   Sent invoices totaling $3,500 for repairs completed to date

    27   Paid the following expenses: electricity, $75; telephone, $25; wages, $2,000

    31   Transferred a portion of the Prepaid Rent to Rent Expense

    31   Counted $200 of supplies still on hand

Required

1. Open ledger accounts for the following: Cash, Accounts Receivable, Prepaid Rent, Supplies, Equipment, Bank Loan, Accounts Payable, Common Stock, Repair Revenue, Advertising Expense, Rent Expense, Supplies Expense, Telephone Expense, Utilities Expense, Wages Expense.

2. Prepare journal entries to record the May transactions. Post these transactions to the ledger accounts.

3. Prepare a trial balance as of May 31.

4. Prepare an interim income statement and interim balance sheet as of May 31 in the correct format.

5. Using the T account for Cash, prepare a statement of cash flows.

ALTERNATE PROBLEMS

Preparation of a trial
balance, income state-
ment, and balance
sheet (Q11–Q16)

AP2-1 The following account balances are taken from the records of Geosign Repairs,
Inc., as of November 30, 19X1:

Accounts Payable	$5,000	Rent Expense	$ 700
Accounts Receivable	6,000	Repair Revenue	8,350
Advertising Expense	500	Salaries Expense	3,000
Bank Loan	4,500	Salaries Payable	1,000
Cash	2,000	Supplies	500
Common Stock	8,000	Supplies Expense	250
Commissions Expense	1,500	Truck	8,000
Equipment	3,500	Truck Expense	900

Required
1. Prepare a trial balance as of November 30.
2. Prepare an interim income statement as of November 30 in the correct format.
3. Prepare an interim balance sheet as of November 30 in the correct format.

Reconstruction of
journal entries from T
accounts; preparation
of a trial balance
(Q11–Q16)

AP2-2 The following accounts were prepared for Kingsley Garage, Inc., during the first
month of operations ended July 31, 19X1. No journal entries were prepared in
support of the amounts recorded in the ledger accounts.

Cash		Truck		Advertising Expense	
3,000	1,000	7,000		100	
1,500	400				
1,200	600				
2,000	300				
	1,100				
	3,200				

Accounts Receivable		Accounts Payable		Insurance Expense	
2,500	1,200	300	6,000	50	
3,500	2,000	1,100	500		
			200		
			100		

Prepaid Insurance		Common Stock		Rent Expense	
600	50		3,000	400	

Supplies		Repair Revenue		Supplies Expense	
500	150		2,500	150	
			1,500		
			3,500		

Salaries Expense	
3,200	

Truck Expense	
200	

Required

1. Reconstruct the transactions that occurred during the month and prepare journal entries to record these transactions.

2. Calculate the balance in each account and prepare a trial balance as of July 31, 19X1.

Correcting an erro-
neous trial balance
(Q11–Q16)

AP2-3   The following trial balance was prepared for Benner Services, Inc., as of March 31, 19X1, its first month of operations, by a part-time bookkeeper who has insufficient training.

Benner Services, Inc.
Trial Balance
March 31, 19X1

	Account Balances	
	Debit	Credit
Accounts Payable	$ 5,000	
Accounts Receivable		$ 3,000
Bank Loan		3,550
Cash	1,500	
Common Stock	3,000	
Equipment	2,000	
Fees Earned	6,900	
Insurance Expense	50	
Interest Expense		100
Rent Expense		600
Truck		8,000
Truck Expense		
Utilities Expense		200
Wages Expense		3,000
Totals	$18,450	$18,450

Required

1. Prepare a correct trial balance as of March 31. List the accounts by the sequence in the chart of accounts in Exhibit 2-9 and record the amounts in their proper debit–credit positions.

2. How is it possible that the debit–credit totals amount to $18,450 in both trial balances? (Assume individual amounts are correct.)

Journal entries, posting,
trial balance, income
statement, and balance
sheet (Q11–Q16)

AP2-4   The following transactions took place in Mason Renovations, Inc., during June 19X1, its first month of operations.

June 1   Issued common stock for $8,000
       1   Paid $600 for rent due for June and July
       1   Purchased equipment costing $5,000 on account
       2   Collected $600 for repairs completed today
       3   Paid $20 for supplies used on June 2
       4   Purchased supplies costing $1,500 on account; these supplies will be used in the future
       5   Sent invoices totaling $2,500 for repairs completed to date
       8   Received $500 from customers to whom invoices were sent on June 5
      10   Paid $2,500 for equipment purchased on account on June 1
      15   Sold on account excess equipment for $1,000 (its original cost)

18 Paid for the supplies purchased on June 4
20 Received an invoice for $100 from the power company for electricity consumed to date
23 Signed a union contract
25 Received $1,000 from customers to whom invoices were sent on June 5
27 Paid the following expenses: advertising, $150; telephone, $50; truck expense (for rental and gas), $1,000; wages, $2,500
30 Sent invoices totaling $2,000 for repairs completed to date
30 Transferred the amount for June's rent to Rent Expense
30 Counted $150 of supplies still on hand (recorded the amount used as an expense).

Required

1. Open ledger accounts for the following: Cash, Accounts Receivable, Prepaid Rent, Supplies, Equipment, Accounts Payable, Common Stock, Repair Revenue, Advertising Expense, Rent Expense, Supplies Expense, Telephone Expense, Truck Expense, Utilities Expense, Wages Expense.

2. Prepare journal entries to record the June transactions. Post these entries to the ledger accounts.

3. Prepare a trial balance as of June 30.

4. Prepare an interim income statement and interim balance sheet as of June 30 in the correct format.

Journal entries, posting, trial balance, income statement, balance sheet, and statement of cash flows (Q11–Q16)

AP2-5   Nick's Snow Removal, Inc., was incorporated on December 1, 19X1, and had the following transactions during its first month of operations.

Dec. 1 Issued common stock for $6,000 cash
      1 Purchased a used truck for $9,000: paid $4,000, with the balance due January 15
      2 Purchased a $2,000 snowplow on account
      3 Sent invoices totaling $5,000 to customers for snow removal services during December
      5 Purchased salt, sand, and gravel for $500 on account
      6 Paid truck expenses of $200
      7 Paid $360 for a one-year insurance policy effective December 1
     14 Paid $1,500 for wages incurred during the first half of December
     16 Paid $40 to municipal court for a parking ticket received yesterday
     20 Received an invoice for truck maintenance items costing $350
     24 Purchased tire chains for $100 on account
     24 Received $3,500 from customers to whom invoices were sent on December 15 3rd
     27 Paid for the purchase made on December 5
     28 Collected $400 for snow removal performed today for a new customer
     28 Paid $1,500 for wages incurred during the second half of December
     30 Phoned all the customers who had not paid their account for the first half of December
     31 Transferred the portion of the insurance policy on the truck that expired during December
     31 Estimated that sand, salt, and gravel costing $100 were still on hand at the end of December
     31 Determined that $450 in wages were earned by the employees during the last three days in December (Enter the amount due to the employees in the Wages Payable account.)

Required

1. Open ledger accounts for the following: Cash, Accounts Receivable, Prepaid Insurance, Supplies, Truck, Accounts Payable, Wages Payable, Common Stock, Service Revenue, Insurance Expense, Supplies Expense, Truck Expense, Wages Expense.

2. Prepare journal entries to record the December transactions. Post transactions to the ledger accounts.

3. Prepare a trial balance as of December 31.

4. Prepare an income statement and a balance sheet as of December 31 in the correct format.

5. Using the T account for Cash, prepare a statement of cash flows.

DECISION PROBLEM

Q11–Q16

Alliene Kennedy, a second-year business student at California State University at Sacramento (CSUS), had a hard time finding an enjoyable summer job that paid well, so she decided to begin her own business for the summer. She and two high school friends met and decided to establish a home-repair business. Alliene said she would run the business side of the operation, while her two friends, Bev Silva and Donna Rain, who are also second-year business students at CSUS, agreed to do a majority of the home repairs with Alliene filling in whenever she could.

A corporate form of organization was chosen for liability reasons, and each of the three contributed $1,000 in exchange for common stock with a total value of $3,000.

The three decided to call their corporation Albedons (ABD). ABD agreed to rent a van from Dr. Sam Burn, one of their accounting professors, for $200 per month. Under this agreement, ABD would be responsible for all fuel and repair costs. The corporation was ready to do business.

The business proved to be successful from the start. Alliene, a marketing major, spent most of her time promoting the business, making sales calls, and writing up estimates. Alliene spent little time developing an accounting system or keeping any kind of formal records. She had not particularly liked her first accounting course at CSUS and was under the impression that ABD could survive with only a checkbook. In order for all transactions to flow through the checkbook, Alliene established accounts at the local Shell Service Station and Lumberjack Supply Co.

On August 31, the students had completed their summer's work and were preparing to return to school. All payments from customers had been received, and all outstanding invoices had been paid. The three agreed that Bev's brother, Steve Silva, a senior in accounting at CSUS, would prepare the financial statements for ABD as of August 31.

From the records, Steve discovered that receipts from customers for the summer totaled $35,542. The materials bought for use by ABD amounted to $24,500, with $2,500 of unused material, such as paint, lumber, nails, and electrical fixtures, remaining. Of these, 80% could be returned for full credit, while 20% had to be considered expenses. Other expenses incurred were $75 for advertising and $375 for fuel and oil for the van. Luckily, the van did not need any repairs. The students paid themselves $1,500 each on August 1. The bank balance for ABD on August 31 showed a total of $8,492.22. The unused supplies had not yet been returned for credit.

Required

1. Prepare two balance sheets: one dated June 1, and one dated August 31.

2. Prepare an income statement for ABD for the three months ended August 31.

3. If each student worked 190 hours per month from June 1 through August 31, how successful have they been?

4. Steve was also asked to make recommendations to Alliene, Bev, and Donna, since they plan to resume the business next summer. What should Steve suggest to these young business people?

ANSWERS TO SELF-TEST QUESTIONS

1. **(c)** Accounting principles are assumptions made about a number of matters that affect the reporting of financial information. Changes in principles are dictated by changes in the business environment, unlike some of the principles in the sciences.

2. **(b)** Only the Securities and Exchange Commission has the authority given to it by "law" to establish accounting principles. All of the organizations mentioned have an effect on the establishment of GAAP. Currently, the Financial Accounting Standards Board is the source of most GAAP for financial reporting.

3. **(a)** and **(b)** Some information may not be disclosed because it is immaterial in nature (a), and the lack of disclosure does not affect the usability of the information. Also, if the cost of supplying the information outweighs the benefit derived from the disclosure (b), the information may not be disclosed.

4. **(d)** Since debits must always equal the credits, a debit to an asset account could only be offset by a *credit* to another account. That account could be another asset account, or a liability, equity, revenue, or expense account.

5. **(d)** The general journal is referred to as the *book of original entry.* All entries are recorded there first, then posted to a T account in the general ledger. Next a trial balance of all the accounts in the general ledger is prepared.

6. **(a)** The term used on the balance sheet is *current liabilities,* not *short-term liabilities,* although their financial meanings could be interchanged.

7. **(c)** *Posting* is the act of recording each entry from the general journal to the general ledger. *Cross-referencing* entries in the general ledger refers to the identification in the ledger of the page number in the journal where the original entry may be found.

3

GAAP AND THE OPERATING CYCLE: PART ONE

CHAPTER 3 introduces the concept of the operating cycle, and the related problems that arise because of it and the arbitrary division of the life of a business into twelve-month periods.

Balance sheet and income statement accounts that have elements of both statements in their balances are investigated, along with alternative ways of recording transactions for such mixed accounts.

The need to adjust mixed accounts at the end of an accounting period is explained, as well as their effect on the adjusting process. Revenue and expense items that must be accrued at the end of an accounting period are identified.

The chapter ends with the presentation of a complete set of financial statements prepared from an adjusted trial balance.

After studying Chapter 3, you should be able to answer the following questions:

1 Describe the operating cycle. What would be the shortest cycle in time? the longest? Explain. (pp.100–101)

2 What operating cycle problems arise at the end of the accounting period? (p.101)

3 When cash is received prior to the time revenue has been earned, is the amount recorded as a liability or as a revenue? Explain. (p.102)

4 When cash is paid out (cost outlay) prior to the time that its benefit has been received, should the amount be recorded as an asset or as an expense? Explain. (pp.102–3)

5 The recording of journal entries both in the journal and in the ledger is just doubling the work. Entries could be made directly into the ledger accounts to eliminate one-half the effort. Comment. (pp.109–11)

6 The matching concept involves both transactions that have already been recorded and transactions that have not been recorded. Explain. (p.113)

7 How can unearned rent be considered a liability? (pp.114–15)

8 Are mixed accounts limited to balance sheet accounts? to income statement accounts? Explain. (p.115)

9 Does the act of recording depreciation result in the establishment of a current value of the asset in the balance sheet? Explain. (pp.118–19)

10 When mixed items are income statement accounts, are adjustments made to other income statement accounts? Explain. (pp.122–24)

11 Why are accrued expenses recorded? Are revenues ever accrued? Explain. (p.125)

12 If interest on a bank loan is not due for a number of months, why is it recorded as a liability on the year-end balance sheet? (p.129)

13 If income taxes are due on April 15, 19X2, why are they recorded as an expense for an entity whose year ends December 31, 19X1? (p.130)

14 Why must an adjusted trial balance be prepared? (p.131)

THE OPERATING CYCLE

Financial transactions that occur continuously during an accounting period are part of a sequence of activities. In Saguaro Computers, Inc., this sequence takes the following form:

Q1: Operating cycle

1. Operations begin with some cash on hand.
2. This cash is used to purchase supplies and to pay expenses incurred while performing computer repairs.
3. Revenue is earned as repair services are performed. (Accounts receivable may result.)
4. Cash is collected.

This cash-to-cash sequence of events is commonly referred to as an operating cycle, as described in Chapter 2. This cycle is illustrated in Exhibit 3-1. The exhibit refers to only one operating cycle. In practice, many cycles of this type are under way simultaneously and overlap. The overlapping of these cycles during an accounting period is illustrated in Exhibit 3-2. Note that because of the nature of the operating cycle and the arbitrary nature of an accounting period, the end of an accounting period falls somewhere in the middle of an operating cycle. In order for the end of an accounting period and the end of an operating cycle to fall at the same time, an entity would have to cease operations days, weeks, or even months before the end of the fiscal year, which would be impossible if the business is to survive. The dashed curve in Exhibit 3-2 reflects the portion of an operating cycle that is completed in the next accounting period.

As some transactions in one cycle are being completed, others are only beginning. For example, while repairs are being completed in one cycle, repair supplies are being purchased for use in another cycle; while expenses are being paid in one

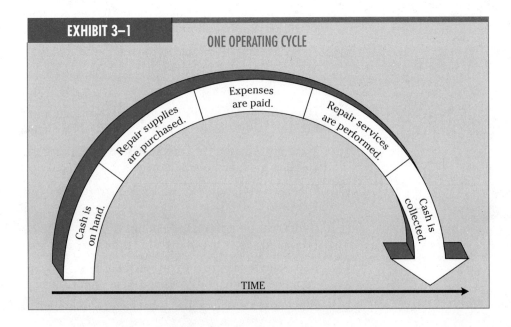

EXHIBIT 3–1   ONE OPERATING CYCLE

Cash is on hand.
Repair supplies are purchased.
Expenses are paid.
Repair services are performed.
Cash is collected.

TIME

EXHIBIT 3–2

OVERLAPPING OPERATING CYCLES

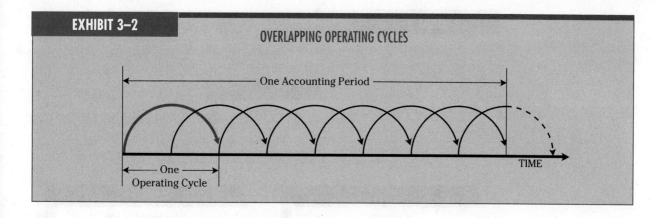

cycle, repairs are beginning in another cycle; and, while all this is going on, cash is being collected and paid out continuously. A similar operating cycle exists for every entity, whether it provides a service, buys and sells merchandise, or manufactures products. Although the cycle of each type of entity may have different components, the basic sequence remains the same.

Under the going-concern assumption, any incomplete cycles, those at the beginning and end of each accounting period, will be completed during the first part of the next accounting period. Accordingly, the use of historical costs to value assets chargeable to future operating cycles can be defended. The cost of the particular item is objectively determined, and can be verified by reference to source documents.

Q2: Operating cycle problems

Accountants are obviously concerned with the accurate recording of all these transactions. However, the recording of some transactions causes more theoretical problems than the recording of others. For example, the choice of a point at which revenue can be said to be earned causes numerous problems for accountants; the point at which an asset becomes an expense is not always clear-cut, either. Later in this chapter, we examine some further transactions of Saguaro Computers, Inc. in order to focus on two major categories of transactions that cause recording problems for accountants. These two categories are:

1. Transactions involving services performed or goods sold by the business and the establishment of *the point at which revenue is earned* from these services

2. Transactions involving cost outlays and expenses incurred to earn those revenues

Revenue Recognition

Revenue recognition is concerned with establishing the point at which the revenue of a business is actually earned.

1. Is revenue earned when cash from the service is collected?

2. Is some revenue earned throughout the complete accounting cycle, while the service is being completed? If so, how is an estimate accurately made?

3. Is revenue earned only when the service has been completed?

Although revenue has been earned by the time the service is completed and the cash is collected, accountants generally assume that revenue is earned at an

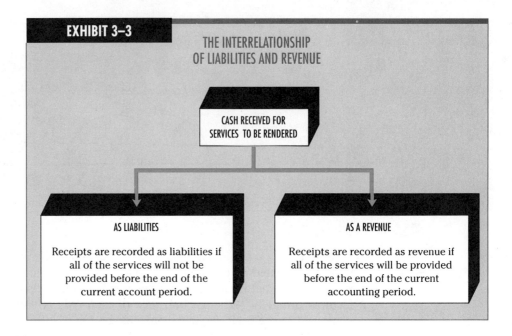

EXHIBIT 3-3

THE INTERRELATIONSHIP
OF LIABILITIES AND REVENUE

CASH RECEIVED FOR
SERVICES TO BE RENDERED

AS LIABILITIES

Receipts are recorded as liabilities if
all of the services will not be
provided before the end of the
current account period.

AS A REVENUE

Receipts are recorded as revenue if
all of the services will be provided
before the end of the current
accounting period.

earlier point—when the service is completed but payment, in the form of cash, has not yet been received. This point can be more objectively determined than subjective estimates. In practice, it is convenient to recognize revenue at the point when an invoice is prepared and sent to the customer. A transaction of this type creates an asset called accounts receivable, which is exchanged for the asset cash when payment is received.

In some cases, a deposit or advance payment is obtained *before* the service is performed. When an advance payment is received, accountants use the following accepted practice to record this type of receipt consistently:

Q3: Recording
receipts before
revenue earned

1. Receipts are recorded as *liabilities* if the services are not expected to be completed before the end of the current accounting period.

2. Receipts are recorded as *revenue* if the services are expected to be completed during the current accounting period.

The interrelationship of liabilities and of revenue when accounting for cash received for services is illustrated in Exhibit 3-3.

Recording Cost Outlays

Q4: Recording cost
outlays before
benefits received

Cost outlays (cash payments) are made continuously during the accounting period and are recorded at cost, that is, at the amount paid. Each cost outlay is recorded either as an *asset,* if it can be used to produce future revenues, or as an *expense,* if it does not have the potential to produce future revenues. Accountants often use the following practice to record cost outlays consistently:

1. Costs are recorded as *assets* if they will be used to produce revenue in current and future accounting time periods.

2. Costs are recorded as *expenses* if they will be used to produce revenue only in the current year.

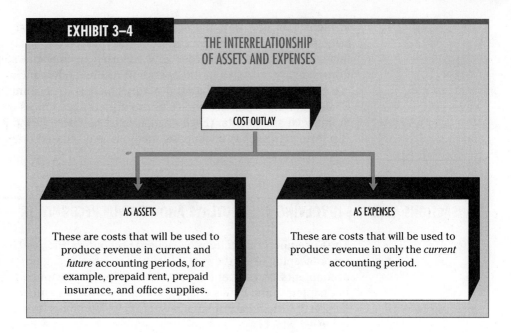

EXHIBIT 3–4

THE INTERRELATIONSHIP
OF ASSETS AND EXPENSES

COST OUTLAY

AS ASSETS

These are costs that will be used to produce revenue in current and *future* accounting periods, for example, prepaid rent, prepaid insurance, and office supplies.

AS EXPENSES

These are costs that will be used to produce revenue in only the *current* accounting period.

This interrelationship of assets and expenses is illustrated in Exhibit 3-4. Theoretically, any cost outlay that has a future value—that is, if it will be used to produce revenue in future accounting periods—should be recorded as an asset. In practice, an arbitrary rule is usually adopted to facilitate the need to keep track of assets that expire in the future:

If the future value of the asset benefits more than the current accounting period, then it is recorded as an *asset*. If the future value of the asset expires during the current accounting period, then it is recorded as an *expense*.

Under this policy, a transaction may be recorded as an asset if the cost outlay benefits more than one accounting period, but at the end of the current accounting period, the portion of the benefit received during the current period must be moved from an asset to an expense. If SCI paid two months' rent on November 1, the cost outlay should be recorded as an asset. But by the end of November, one-half of the amount paid is now an expense, and must be moved from the asset, Prepaid Rent, to the expense, Rent Expense. *Adjusting journal entries* are used to make these modifications; they are discussed on pp. 114–24 of this chapter.

In practice, management policy will govern how cash receipts from customers and cash payments for current and future services are recorded. After adjusting entries are made, the results are the same no matter which way the transaction was first recorded.

The Need for Consistency

An overall concern of the accountant in recording revenues and cost outlays is that the income statement and balance sheet accurately reflect the operating results and financial position of the entity at the end of the period.

One possible manipulation of an entity's operating results and financial position occurs when different accounting policies and rules are used from one accounting period to another. Although many revenues and expenses can be recorded properly in more than one way, the accounting practice of consistency requires that the same policies and rules be used from one time period to another. In this way, the financial information recorded and reported in financial statements is uniform. Consequently, changes in the operating results and financial position of an entity are caused by its operations and not by changes in accounting policies and rules. Changes in these policies and rules are discouraged unless they improve reporting in financial statements. (Each change must be noted in the financial statements.) Disclosing changes in accounting methods is discussed briefly in Chapter 5.

TRANSACTIONS ANALYSIS INVOLVING COST OUTLAYS AND REVENUE RECOGNITION

The December transactions of Saguaro Computers, Inc., will be used to demonstrate recordkeeping using the cost outlay and revenue recognition assumptions made by accountants. November transactions 1 to 7 were previously recorded and discussed in Chapters 1 and 2; this chapter continues with December transactions 8 to 14. In Exhibit 3-5 the adjacent summary of these December transactions appears with a guide to which assumption—cost outlay or revenue recognition—is being discussed in each transaction.

Illustrative Problem:

COST OUTLAY AND REVENUE RECOGNITION ANALYSIS

The analysis and recording of each transaction is described in detail in the following pages. The numbers in parentheses in T accounts refer to the transaction number. The posted ledger accounts appear below the journal entries.

Refer to the following as you analyze each transaction:

Cost Outlay	Revenue Recognition
The cost is recorded as an *asset* if it will be used to produce revenue in future accounting periods.	The receipt is recorded as a *liability* if the provision of the service is not expected to be completed before the end of the current accounting period.
The cost is recorded as an *expense* if it will be used to produce revenue in only the current accounting period.	The receipt is recorded as a *revenue* if the provision of the service is expected to be completed during the current accounting period.

Transaction 8 (December 1)   Saguaro Computers, Inc., paid $1,200 for a comprehensive one-year insurance policy, effective December 1.

Analysis   Since the one-year period will not expire by the time financial statements are prepared at December 31, the insurance cost is considered to be an asset at the payment date.

Journal Entry   The asset account, Prepaid Insurance, is increased by this transaction. (An asset increase is recorded as a debit.) Payment of the insurance results in a decrease in the asset account, Cash. (An asset decrease is recorded as a credit.) The journal entry appears as follows:

EXHIBIT 3–5			
	COST OUTLAY AND REVENUE RECOGNITION AS IT APPLIES TO SCI's DECEMBER TRANSACTIONS		
		Application of Accounting Assumptions	
Transaction/ Date	**Description of Transaction**	**Cost Outlay**	**Revenue Recognition**
8. Dec. 1	Saguaro Computers, Inc. paid $1,200 for a comprehensive one–year insurance policy, effective December 1.	ASSET	
9. Dec. 3	The corporation received $600 as an advance payment for the part–time rental of the corporation truck for three months as follows: $200 for December, $200 for January, $200 for February.		LIABILITY
10. Dec. 5	The corporation purchased on account $900 in repair supplies expected to be used during December.	EXPENSE	
11. Dec. 16	The corporation performed $5,000 in repairs for a customer who signed a 60–day, 12–percent, interest–bearing note as payment.		REVENUE
12. Dec. 26	The corporation received $2,000 from a customer for repairs expected to be performed before the end of December.		REVENUE
13. Dec. 31	Additional computer repairs were performed for customers during December. $9,395 was received in cash at the time the repairs were made, while $500 in repairs were made on account.		REVENUE
14. Dec. 31	Miscellaneous expenses were paid during the month: $600, rent; $2,500, salaries; $700, truck; and $300, utilities.	EXPENSE	

Dec. 1	Prepaid Insurance	161	1,200	
	Cash	101		1,200
	To record payment for one-year policy.			

Prepaid Insurance		Cash	
(8) 1,200		(8) 1,200	

Transaction 9 (December 3)   The corporation realized it did not use its truck on weekends or Wednesdays. Another business in town agreed to rent the truck on those days. An advance payment of $600 was received for the months of December, January, and February. The agreed on rent was $200 per month if paid in advance for three months.

Analysis   The revenue relating to this cash receipt will not be earned by the end of the current accounting period. Therefore, it is considered to be a payment received in advance of its being earned.

Journal Entry   An asset account, Cash, is increased at the time the contract is signed. (An asset increase is recorded as debit.) A liability account, Unearned Rent, is increased by this transaction. (A liability increase is recorded as a credit.) The journal entry appears as follows:

Dec. 3	Cash	101	600	
	Unearned Rent	248		600
	To record advance payment for three months' truck rental.			

Cash		Unearned Rent	
(9) 600		(9) 600	

Transaction 10 (December 5)   The corporation purchased on account $900 in repair supplies expected to be used during December.

Analysis   Since the repair supplies are expected to be used during the current accounting period, the cost of the supplies is considered to be an expense.

Journal Entry   An expense account, Supplies Expense, is increased by this transaction. (An expense increase is recorded as a debit.) A liability account, Accounts Payable, is increased by the transaction. (A liability increase is recorded as a credit.) The journal entry appears as follows:

Dec. 5	Supplies Expense	668	900	
	Accounts Payable	210		900
	To record the purchase of supplies.			

Supplies Expense		Accounts Payable	
(10) 900		(10) 900	

Transaction 11 (December 16)   The corporation performed $5,000 in repairs for a customer who signed a 60-day, 12-percent, interest-bearing note as payment. The $5,000 principal and interest will be paid at the end of 60 days.

Analysis   These repairs were completed before the end of December; revenue has therefore been earned and must be recorded.

Journal Entry   An asset account, Notes Receivable, is increased by this transaction. (An asset increase is recorded as a debit.) A revenue account, Repair Revenue, is increased by this transaction. (A revenue increase is recorded as a credit.) The journal entry appears as follows:

Dec. 16	Notes Receivable	120	5,000	
	Repair Revenue	450		5,000
	To record payment for repairs by note.			

Notes Receivable		Repair Revenue	
(11) 5,000			(11) 5,000

Note: The interest is not accounted for at this time. Interest is money paid for the use of money. Therefore, interest accrues (is earned) as time passes, not at the signing of the note.

Transaction 12 (December 26)   The corporation received $2,000 from a customer for repairs expected to be performed before the end of December.

Analysis   Since the repairs are expected to be performed before the end of the current accounting period, the $2,000 is recorded as a revenue.

Journal Entry   An asset account, Cash, is increased in this transaction. (An asset increase is recorded as a debit.) A revenue account, Repair Revenue, is also increased by the transaction. (A revenue increase is recorded as a credit.) The journal entry appears as follows:

Dec. 26	Cash	101	2,000	
	Repair Revenue	450		2,000
	To record payment for repairs to be made in December.			

Cash		Repair Revenue	
(12) 2,000			(12) 2,000

Transaction 13 (December 31)   Additional computer repairs were performed for customers during December. $9,395 was received in cash at the time the repairs were made, while $500 in repairs were made on account.

Analysis   These revenue activities affect two asset accounts. The asset accounts, Cash and Accounts Receivable, are increased by the revenue earned during the month. Because three accounts are involved in this transaction, a compound journal entry is necessary.

Journal Entry   The asset accounts, Cash and Accounts Receivable, are increased by this transaction. (An asset increase is recorded as a debit.) A revenue account, Repair Revenue, is increased by this transaction. (A revenue increase is recorded as a credit.) The journal entry appears as follows:

Dec. 31	Cash	101	9,395	
	Accounts Receivable	110	500	
	Repair Revenue	450		9,895
	To record repairs made during December.			

Cash		Accounts Receivable		Repair Revenue	
(13) 9,395		(13) 500			(13) 9,895

Transaction 14 (December 31)   Paid expenses incurred during the month to earn the repair revenue. These expenses consist of: Rent Expense for December, $600; Salaries Expense for four weeks in December, $2,500; Truck Expense for gas, oil, etc., $700; and Utility Expense, $300.

Analysis   These expenses, summarized here for demonstration, are applicable to the current accounting period, since their cost has been used up during the month.

Journal Entry   In practice, each paid expense would be recorded individually as the payment was made. Each expense is increased in this transaction. (An expense increase is recorded as a debit to each expense account.) An asset account, Cash, is decreased by these expenses. (An asset decrease is recorded as a credit.) Since the transactions are summarized here, only one credit of $4,100 is made to the Cash account. The journal entry appears as follows:

Dec. 31	Rent Expense	654	600	
	Salaries Expense	656	2,500	
	Truck Expense	670	700	
	Utilities Expense	676	300	
	Cash	101		4,100
	To record December expenses paid in cash.			

Rent Expense	Salaries Expense	Truck Expense
(14) 600	(14) 2,500	(14) 700

Utilities Expense	Cash
(14) 300	(14) 4,100

THE ACCOUNTING CYCLE—REVIEW OF STEPS 1–3

In Chapter 2 the four steps in the accounting cycle were identified on p. 75. The first three of these are reviewed next. Later in the chapter, three more steps that are necessary before the financial information is communicated to the users via the financial statements will be introduced. The first two steps occur continually throughout the time period, while the third step occurs only at the end of a period, and is taken to prove the equality of the debit and credit entries made during the period.

STEP 1: TRANSACTIONS ARE ANALYZED AND RECORDED IN THE JOURNAL.
The general journal provides a complete record of a corporation's transactions, listed in chronological order. Because this journal is the first place a transaction is recorded, the general journal is commonly referred to as a *book of original entry*. Exhibit 3-6 shows the December transactions for Saguaro.

EXHIBIT 3-6

SCI'S GENERAL JOURNAL FOR DECEMBER, 19X1

General Journal

19X1					
Dec. 1	Prepaid Insurance		161	1,200	
	Cash		101		1,200
	To record payment for one–year policy.				
3	Cash		101	600	
	Unearned Rent		248		600
	To record advance payment for three months' truck rental.				
5	Supplies Expense		668	900	
	Accounts Payable		210		900
	To record the purchase of supplies.				
16	Notes Receivable		120	5,000	
	Repair Revenue		450		5,000
	To record payment for repairs by note.				
26	Cash		101	2,000	
	Repair Revenue		450		2,000
	To record payment for repairs to be made in December.				
	Cash		101	9,395	
31	Accounts Receivable		110	500	
	Repair Revenue		450		9,895
	To record repairs made during December.				
31	Rent Expense		654	600	
	Salaries Expense		656	2,500	
	Truck Expense		670	700	
	Utilities Expense		676	300	
	Cash		101		4,100
	To record December expenses paid in cash.				

Q5: Recording in both journal and ledger

STEP 2: THE JOURNAL ENTRIES ARE POSTED TO LEDGER ACCOUNTS.

After the December transactions have been posted to the general ledger accounts, a net debit or credit balance is determined for each account by footing both sides and subtracting the smaller from the larger. Remember that asset and expense accounts should have debit balances, while liability, equity, and revenue accounts should have credit balances. The general ledger accounts for SCI are shown in Exhibit 3-7. The conceptual T-account format is used in place of the more formal

EXHIBIT 3-7

SCI'S GENERAL LEDGER AS OF DECEMBER 31, 19X1

ASSETS = LIABILITIES + EQUITY

ASSETS

Cash No. 101

Debit		Credit	
Bal.	5,000	(8)	1,200
(9)	600	(14)	4,100
(12)	2,000		
(13)	9,395		
	16,995		5,300
*Bal.	11,695		

Accounts Receivable No. 110

Debit		Credit	
Bal.	3,000	(13)	500
Bal.	3,500		

Notes Receivable No. 120

Debit		Credit	
(11)	5,000		

Prepaid Insurance No. 161

Debit		Credit	
(8)	1,200		

Equipment No. 183

Debit		Credit	
Bal.	2,000		

Truck No. 184

Debit		Credit	
Bal.	8,000		

LIABILITIES

Bank Loan No. 201

Debit		Credit	
		Bal.	5,000

Accounts Payable No. 210

Debit		Credit	
		Bal.	1,000
		(10)	900
		Bal.	1,900

Unearned Rent No. 248

Debit		Credit	
		(9)	600

EQUITY

Common Stock No. 320

Debit		Credit	
		Bal.	10,000

Repair Revenue No. 450

Debit		Credit	
		Bal.	7,000
		(11)	5,000
		(12)	2,000
		(13)	9,895
		Bal.	23,895

Rent Expense No. 654

Debit		Credit	
Bal.	600		
(14)	600		
Bal.	1,200		

Salaries Expense No. 656

Debit		Credit	
Bal.	2,500		
(14)	2,500		
Bal.	5,000		

Supplies Expense No. 668

Debit		Credit	
Bal.	1,200		
(10)	900		
Bal.	2,100		

Truck Expense No. 670

Debit		Credit	
Bal.	700		
(14)	700		
Bal.	1,400		

Utilities Expense No. 676

Debit		Credit	
(14)	300		

Note: The highlighted items are the December 31 balances.

EXHIBIT 3–8			

Saguaro Computers, Inc.
Trial Balance
December 31, 19X1

	Account Balances		
	Debit	Credit	
Cash	$11,695		
Accounts Receivable	3,500		
Notes Receivable	5,000		
Prepaid Insurance	1,200		These are
Equipment	2,000		**Balance Sheet**
Truck	8,000		account balances.
Bank Loan		$ 5,000	
Accounts Payable		1,900	
Unearned Rent		600	
Common Stock		10,000	
Repair Revenue		23,895	
Rent Expense	1,200		These are
Salaries Expense	5,000		**Income Statement**
Supplies Expense	2,100		account balances.
Truck Expense	1,400		
Utilities Expense	300		
	$41,395	$41,395	
	Total debit balances	=	Total credit balances

ledger account in order to emphasize the relationship between the accounting equation and the accounts that fall under each component of that equation. Because of space limitations, only the December transactions are posted to December 1 balances that were carried forward from the November 30 trial balance in Chapter 2 (Exhibit 2-4).

STEP 3: THE EQUALITY OF DEBITS WITH CREDITS IS ESTABLISHED BY THE TRIAL BALANCE.

The account balances are listed in the trial balance to establish the equality of total debit balances with total credit balances. Exhibit 3-8 shows the December trial balance for Saguaro Computers, Inc.

ACCRUAL ACCOUNTING AND THE MATCHING CONCEPT

At the beginning of this chapter, the transactions of business entities were shown to comprise a sequence of events, identified as an operating cycle. Each entity's accounting period consists of a series of such cycles. As the transactions in one operating cycle are completed, other cycles are beginning; still others are in progress. Financial statements are prepared on the basis of data originating from both fully completed and partially completed cycles. Accrual accounting, as described in Chapter 1, matches expenses with revenues of a particular time period. The

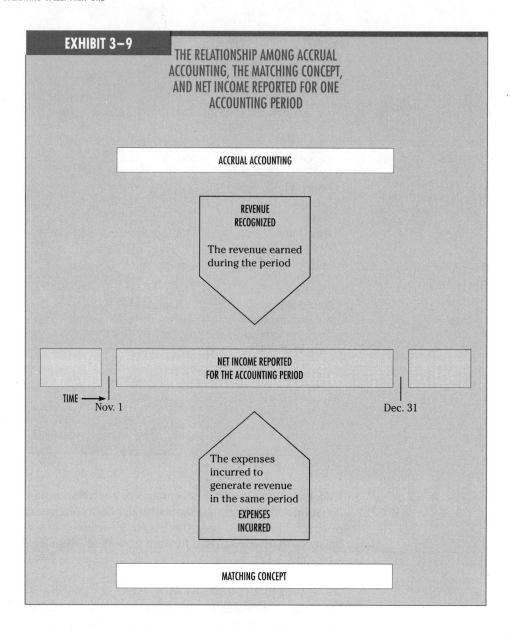

EXHIBIT 3-9

THE RELATIONSHIP AMONG ACCRUAL ACCOUNTING, THE MATCHING CONCEPT, AND NET INCOME REPORTED FOR ONE ACCOUNTING PERIOD

ACCRUAL ACCOUNTING

REVENUE RECOGNIZED

The revenue earned during the period

NET INCOME REPORTED FOR THE ACCOUNTING PERIOD

TIME →
Nov. 1   Dec. 31

The expenses incurred to generate revenue in the same period

EXPENSES INCURRED

MATCHING CONCEPT

matching of revenues with expenses is the objective; the accrual method of accounting is the basis on which accounts are adjusted to reach the objective. Under this method, the cost of assets transferred to customers or consumed during the period are considered expenses; these expenses are matched with the revenues generated by these expenses and are included in the income statement of the same period.

Reported net income, therefore, results from the application of accrual accounting and the matching concept. Their relationship within an accounting period can be illustrated as in Exhibit 3-9.

Since only the cost of assets transferred to customers or consumed during the period are considered expenses, any cost outlay relating to other accounting periods are excluded from the calculation of net income for the current period—except certain extraordinary items that do not occur regularly and are material in amount; these are discussed in Chapter 5.

Q6: Matching
recorded and
unrecorded
transactions

For accrual accounting, three different categories of expenses require matching with revenue. They can be distinguished as follows:

Category 1   The cost of goods (either items sold or services provided) transferred to customers can be easily matched with revenue generated. For example, at Saguaro Computers, Inc., the use of parts in repairing computers (expenses) can be identified with revenue generated by the repairs that required those parts.

Category 2   The cost of assets only partially consumed during the time period is not always easily matched with generated revenue. For example, Saguaro's equipment and truck were used to generate revenue in November and December 19X1 but were not fully used up during its first months of operation; that is, they still have some future benefit. Accordingly, the utilized amount of the useful "life" of the equipment and the truck must be estimated, and this estimate allocated as an expense incurred in generating the revenue of that time period. The estimate is often not easily calculated in practice.

Category 3   The cost of some expenses incurred during the period is also not always identified easily with generated revenue. For example, the president of Saguaro maintains that part of his salary benefits future time periods; for instance, his time spent soliciting future customers in November and December resulted in no generation of revenue during that period. His accountant agrees. However, in this and similar cases, his salary is recorded as a 19X1 expense, the time period in which his services as an employee are performed. This practice is in accordance with GAAP because no future benefit can be identified clearly with salary expense; therefore, the salary does not qualify as an asset, the only other way it could have been recorded. Another example is the expenses incurred with advertising. SCI might have placed a small ad with its phone number in the yellow pages of several surrounding communities. This cost might be several thousand dollars in a large metropolitan area. The total amount paid is considered an expense of the period in which it was paid, even though customers might read the ad as much as one year from the time it was placed, possibly generating revenue at that point. The matching concept is not as easy to accomplish as it appears on the surface.

These categories relate to the accrual method of accounting. An alternate method is referred to as the *cash basis* of accounting. Under this method, cash payments and receipts are matched with a particular time period. The excess of cash receipts over payments indicates a positive cash flow, and an excess of cash payments over receipts, a negative cash flow. However, cash receipts are seldom the same as revenue earned; for example, credit is often extended to customers permitted to pay at a later date. Similarly, cash payments are seldom the same amount as expenses incurred because of the purchase of services and goods on account. As a result, the cash basis of accounting, while it measures cash flow, fails to provide an accurate measurement of net income. Its use, therefore, is not considered GAAP. As was mentioned earlier, a financial statement that reports the inflows and outflows of cash from the three activities of an entity—operating, investing, and financing—is required in addition to the income statement and the balance sheet. This statement has been introduced in Chapter 1 and is more fully explained in Chapter 17.

For a further discussion of the matching principle, see Real World Example 3-1.

REAL WORLD EXAMPLE 3-1
The Matching Principle:
Why It's So Hard to Achieve in Practice

I N an exchange economy, the goal of productive activity is to sell a product or service for more than its cost of production. In accounting, income is the difference between costs (sacrifices) and revenues (benefits). If one visualizes a business in the form of a single venture, income over its entire lifetime will be the difference between cash receipts (excluding capital paid in) and cash disbursements (excluding capital withdrawn or return on capital, such as dividends, paid out). It is natural, therefore, to think of revenue as an inflow of assets—ultimately, cash—in exchange for the product of the enterprise.

This discussion oversimplifies matters. An enterprise may receive cash other than in exchange for product or service, or as a capital contribution. For example, if an asset is destroyed by fire, the insurance proceeds would not represent payment for the productive activity of the enterprise. It is still true that over the lifetime of an enterprise the excess of cash receipts over cash disbursements (excluding cash associated with capital transactions) will equal the net gain. But that net gain will consist of (1) the excess of revenues from productive activity over costs of earning those revenues, together with (2) miscellaneous gains or losses on events or activities that are not part of the main activity of the enterprise.

When speaking of the lifetime of an enterprise from initial cash investment to ultimate cash realization, it is possible to talk solely about movements in cash. Accounting for a period shorter than enterprise lifetime, however, presents a problem. At any given point of time, the enterprise will have delivered product or services for which it has not yet received payment. Conversely, it may have received payment for which it has not yet satisfied its obligation to deliver. It will also have incurred other costs and acquired rights or items that may reasonably be expected to be rewarded by the receipt of cash in a future exchange transaction. Moreover, it may not yet have paid for goods or services it has received. Thus, estimation of income for a period based on transactions is considerably more difficult than determination of income for a completed business lifetime. Such estimation requires that non-capital cash inflows of past, present, and future periods be assigned to periods in which they are "earned." Similarly, non-capital cash outflows of past, present, and future periods must be assigned to the period in which any benefit from them is used up. That is, the goal of income accounting under the transaction-based model is to provide rules for assigning revenues and expenses from operating transactions, and gains and losses from peripheral activities to accounting periods.

ADJUSTING BALANCE SHEET ACCOUNTS

The Need for Adjusting Entries

The trial balance of Saguaro Computers, Inc., at December 31 includes cost outlays recorded as *assets* of the corporation. These are recorded as assets during an accounting period if they can be used to produce future revenue. At the end of the period, an accounting adjustment is required by the matching concept. The amount of the asset that has expired during the period must be calculated and that amount transferred to *expense*. In this way, revenues for the period are matched with expenses incurred to earn that revenue.

Q7: Unearned rent as liability

The December 31 trial balance of SCI also includes cash receipts recorded as *liabilities*. Remember that when revenue has been received but has not been earned (services will be provided after the receipt of cash), the amount should be recorded

Because income accounting associates cash flows with time periods, it automatically results in recognizing assets and liabilities. For example, a cash receipt today that is associated with revenue of a future period must be recorded as unearned revenue—a liability to deliver product or service in the future. A cash disbursement today associated with revenue of future periods must be recorded as an asset—an expectation of future benefit. In other words, asset and liability recognition (and changes in assets and liabilities previously recognized) can result from income accounting conventions as well as the conventions governing initial recognition of asset and liabilities.

It is convenient to summarize here the definitions of elements of financial statements provided by the FASB. These definitions make a useful distinction whereby revenues and expenses are described as the outcome of the primary business operations, and gains and losses are described as the result of incidental or peripheral events or activities.

- Assets are probable future economic benefits obtained or controlled by a particular entity as a result of past transactions or events.
- Liabilities are probable future sacrifices of economic benefits arising from present obligations of a particular entity to transfer assets or provide services to other entities in the future as a result of past transactions or events.

- Revenues are inflows or other enhancements of assets of an entity or settlements of its liabilities (or a combination of both) during a period from delivering or producing goods, rendering services, or other activities that constitute the entity's ongoing major or central operations.
- Expenses are outflows or other using up of assets or incurrences of liabilities (or a combination of both) during a period from delivering or producing goods, rendering services, or carrying out other activities that constitute the entity's ongoing major or central operations.
- Gains are increases in equity (net assets) from peripheral or incidental transactions of an entity and from all other transactions and other events and circumstances affecting the entity during a period, except those that result from revenues or from investments by owners.
- Losses are decreases in equity (net assets) from peripheral or incidental transactions of an entity and from all other transactions and other events and circumstances affecting the entity during a period, except those that result from expenses or from distributions to owners.

Source "Accounting Standards in Evolution" by Ross Skinner. © 1987 by Holt, Rinehart and Winston of Canada, Ltd.

as a liability, such as Unearned Rent in this case. At the end of the accounting period an accounting adjustment is again required. The amount of the revenue earned during the period must be determined and that amount transferred to *revenue*. In this way, revenues for the period are matched with expenses incurred to earn that revenue.

MIXED CURRENT ASSET AND CURRENT LIABILITY ACCOUNTS

Q8: Mixed accounts

The asset and liability accounts just referred to are called **mixed accounts** by accountants. An account is given this name because it includes both a *balance sheet* portion and an *income statement* portion at the end of the accounting period. This allocation of mixed accounts is accomplished by an **adjusting journal entry,** an entry made in the accounts to reflect the correct balance sheet or income valuation of an item.

Illustrative Problem:

UNMIXING CURRENT ASSET AND CURRENT LIABILITY ACCOUNTS

The following balance sheet accounts of Saguaro Computers, Inc., require an adjustment at December 31:

Partial Trial Balance
December 31, 19X1

	Account Balances	
	Debit	**Credit**
Prepaid Insurance	$1,200	
Unearned Rent		$600 ← This is a *liability* account balance.

When these accounts are analyzed, it is determined that adjusting entries for them need to be prepared. Each of the accounts is analyzed in the following manner:

Step 1   At the end of the accounting period, determine which portion of the mixed account belongs in the balance sheet and which belongs in the income statement.

Step 2   The portion that does not belong in the asset or liability account must be transferred to the income statement in an expense or revenue account. To accomplish this transfer, an adjusting entry is recorded in the general journal and then posted to the proper general ledger accounts.

PREPAID INSURANCE AND INSURANCE EXPENSE

In December, the company paid for a 12-month insurance policy, effective December 1 (transaction 8).

The general ledger shows the following Prepaid Insurance account:

This balance resulted from the recording of the following journal entry:

Prepaid Insurance (asset)		No. 161
1,200		

Prepaid Insurance	1,200	
Cash		1,200

At December 31, only one month of the policy has expired.

Step 1:
At the end of the accounting period, Prepaid Insurance is a mixed account; $1,100 is still an asset; $100 has expired and is, therefore, an expense.

Prepaid Insurance (mixed)		No. 161
1,200		

asset $1,100
expense $ 100

Step 2:
The expired amount of $100 does not belong in this account. Therefore, an adjusting journal entry is necessary to transfer the amount out of Prepaid Insurance and into the Insurance Expense account.

Prepaid Insurance (unmixed)		No. 161
1,200		
		100
Bal. 1,100		

This is the adjusting journal entry:

Dec. 31	Insurance Expense	631	100	
	Prepaid Insurance	161		100
	To record insurance expense for			
	December.			

This adjusting entry transfers the expired $100 of prepaid insurance to the Insurance Expense account. The balance remaining in the Prepaid Insurance account after the entry is posted ($1,200 − $100) represents the unexpired asset that will benefit future periods.

When the adjusting entry is posted in the ledger, the expense portion of the mixed account is transferred as follows:

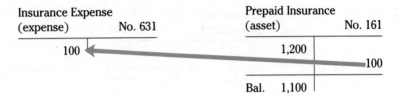

Insurance Expense (expense)   No. 631

100

Prepaid Insurance (asset)   No. 161

1,200

100

Bal.   1,100

An expense account, Insurance Expense, is increased by the expired $100. An expense increase is recorded as a debit.

An asset account, Prepaid Insurance, is decreased by the $100 that has expired during December. An asset decrease is recorded as a credit.

UNEARNED RENT AND RENT EARNED

On December 3, the corporation signed a contract for the use of its truck on a part-time basis and received an advance payment of $600 for use of the truck as follows: $200 for December, $200 for January, and $200 for February (transaction 9).

The Unearned Rent ledger account is reproduced below:

The receipt of this advance payment was recorded as follows:

Unearned Rent (liability)   No. 248

600

Cash	600	
Unearned Rent		600

This advance payment was recorded as unearned, since it was received before it was earned. At December 31, however, one month of the rent has been earned.

Step 1:
At the end of the accounting period, Unearned Rent is a mixed account: $400 remains as a liability because the corporation must provide the use of the truck for January and February; $200 for December has been earned and is a revenue.

Unearned Rent (mixed)   No. 248

600

liability $400
revenue $200

Step 2:
The earned amount of $200 does not belong in this account. Therefore, an adjusting journal entry is necessary to transfer the amount out of Unearned Rent and into the Rent Earned account.

Unearned Rent (unmixed)   No. 248

600

200

Bal.   400

This is the adjusting journal entry:

Dec. 31	Unearned Rent	248	200	
	Rent Earned	440		200
	To record rental earned during			
	December.			

This adjusting entry transfers the $200 of rent earned to revenue. The balance remaining in Unearned Rent after the entry is posted ($600 − $200) represents the unearned amount that will be earned in future periods.

When the adjusting entry is posted, the revenue element is removed from the mixed account as follows:

Unearned Rent (liability) No. 248	Rent Earned (revenue) No. 440
	600	200
200	Bal. 400	200

A liability account, Unearned Rent, is decreased by $200 which has been earned in December. A liability decrease is recorded as a debit.

A revenue account, Rent Earned, is increased by $200. A revenue increase is recorded as a credit.

Mixed Long-term Accounts

As was shown, the mixed portion of SCI's prepaid insurance that had expired was transferred from the asset account to an expense account. The mixed portion of unearned rent that had been earned was transferred from the liability account to a revenue account. The expired portion of a **long-term asset** is handled in a different manner. Accountants still unmix the account, but do so in an indirect manner. Because the original cost of a long-term asset *and* the amount of that cost that has expired over the years are both relevant information items, the expired cost is maintained in a separate account called **Accumulated Depreciation.** The expired portion of the cost of a long-term asset is called **depreciation.** The periodic expired cost is called **depreciation expense.** Although depreciation requires no cash outlay, it is still a continuous expense in operating a business, and therefore is treated the same as any other expense incurred in the generation of revenue.

Q9: Depreciation and current value

The journal entry to record depreciation takes the following form:

| Depreciation Expense | XXX | |
| Accumulated Depreciation | | XXX |

The Depreciation Expense account represents the estimated expense that should be matched to the current accounting period. This account is found on the income statement along with other accounts like Rent Expense, Supplies Expense and Utilities Expense. The amount in the Accumulated Depreciation account is deducted from the original cost in a particular long-term asset account on the balance sheet to arrive at the net **book value** of the asset. For this reason, the account is referred to as a **valuation account** or a *contra-asset account.* The balance in the Accumulated Depreciation account represents the amount of the original cost that has expired.

The amount of depreciation is determined by using an estimate of the **useful life** of the asset and its approximate **scrap value** at the end of its useful life. The calculation is shown in the Illustrative Problem that follows.

Illustrative Problem:

MIXED LONG-TERM-ASSET ACCOUNTS

The following long-term-asset accounts of Saguaro Computers, Inc., consist of mixed balances at the end of the accounting period:

Partial Trial Balance
December 31, 19X1

	Account Balances	
	Debit	Credit
Equipment	$2,000	
Truck	8,000	

Each account is analyzed in the following manner:

Step 1   At the end of the accounting period, determine the amount of depreciation expense.

Step 2   The estimated depreciation is *not* transferred from the asset account; rather, an adjusting journal entry is prepared using two new accounts, one of which is a contra-asset account. Note that a contra-long-term asset account *always has a credit balance*.

EQUIPMENT

SCI owns $2,000 of equipment (transactions 2 and 5).

The Equipment ledger account appears as follows:

This account balance resulted from two journal entries, summarized below for illustrative purposes only:

Equipment (asset)	No. 183		Equipment	2,000	
2,000			Cash		2,000

The equipment is a long-term asset to Saguaro since it has a 5-year (60 month) life, was used in the business during December, and is not held for resale. (Although SCI purchased the equipment in November, it is assumed for the purpose of this illustration that the equipment was not used in the repair process until December 1. The asset has an estimated salvage value of $200. At December 31, therefore, only one month of the asset's cost has expired. The depreciation expense that should be recorded at the end of December is $30, determined by the **straight-line method of depreciation:**

$$\frac{\text{Cost} - \text{Salvage Value}}{\text{Useful Life}} = \text{Depreciation}$$

$$\frac{\$2,000 - \$200}{60\,(\text{months})} = \$30\,\text{per month}$$

The assumption in this method is that an asset is used equally over its useful life, or in a "straight line."

Step 1:
At the end of the accounting period, Equipment is a mixed account: $1,970 is still an asset; $30 has expired and is therefore an expense.

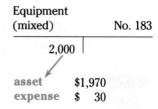

Step 2:
The expired amount of $30 does not belong in an asset account. By accounting convention for long-term assets, the expired portion is *not* removed from the Equipment account.

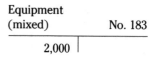

The following adjusting journal entry is made:

Dec. 31	Depreciation Expense—Equipment	623	30	
	Accumulated Depreciation—			
	Equipment	193		30
	To record depreciation for December.			

This adjusting entry records the $30 of depreciation on equipment. The mixed balance remains in the Equipment account.

When the adjusting entry is posted, the accounts appear as follows (the Equipment account remains unchanged):

An expense account, Depreciation Expense, is increased by $30 that has expired. An expense increase is recorded as a debit.

The valuation account, Accumulated Depreciation, is also increased by the $30 that has expired. This valuation account increase is recorded as a credit.

On the balance sheet, this asset will be reported as follows:

Equipment	$2,000	
Less: Accumulated Depreciation	30	
Net Book Value		$1,970

TRUCK

SCI has a truck with a historical cost of $8,000 (transaction 3).

The truck ledger account appears as follows:

```
      Truck
    (asset)        No. 184
    _____
      8,000 |
```

The truck purchase journal entry appears as follows:

Truck	8,000	
Bank Loan		5,000
Cash		3,000

The truck is considered a long-term asset since it has a useful life of more than one year (5 years), was used in the business, and not held for resale. The estimated salvage value is $800. As of December 31, the truck has been used for two months; therefore, $\frac{2}{60}$ of $7,200 ($8,000 − $800), or $240, should be allocated to the income statement.

Step 1:
At the end of the accounting period, Truck is a mixed account: $7,760 is still an asset; $240 has expired and is therefore an expense.

Truck
(mixed)   No. 184

8,000

asset $7,760
expense $ 240

Step 2:
The expired amount of $240 does not belong in an asset account. By accounting convention for long-term assets, the expired portion is *not* removed from the Truck account. This account remains a mixed account.

Truck
(mixed)   No. 184

8,000

The following adjusting journal entry is made:

Dec. 31 Depreciation Expense—Truck   624   240
              Accumulated Depreciation—
         Truck   194   240
         To record depreciation for November
         and December.

This entry records the estimated portion of the original cost to be allocated (matched) to the income statement. Note that the mixed balance remains in the Truck account, and Depreciation Expense is matched on the income statement by being recorded as an expense deducted from revenue that was earned during November and December.

When the adjusting entry is posted, the accounts appear as follows (the Truck account remains unchanged):

Depreciation Expense
(expense)   No. 624

240

Accumulated Depreciation
(asset valuation)   No. 194

240

An expense account, Depreciation Expense, is increased by $240, which has expired. An expense increase is recorded as a debit.

The valuation account, Accumulated Depreciation, is also increased by the $240 that has expired. This valuation account increase is recorded as a credit.

On the balance sheet, this asset will be reported as follows:

Truck $8,000
Less: Accumulated Depreciation   240
Net Book Value $7,760

ADJUSTING INCOME STATEMENT ACCOUNTS

The trial balance of Saguaro Computers, Inc., at December 31 includes a receipt that has been recorded as a revenue of the corporation.

Receipts are recorded as *revenues* during an accounting period if they are expected to be earned during the period. If, in fact, they have not been earned by the end of the period, an accounting adjustment is required. The amount of revenue not earned as of the balance sheet date must be determined and transferred to an unearned revenue account (a *liability*) at the end of the period. This ensures that only revenues earned during the period are matched with the expenses incurred in earning those revenues.

The trial balance of Saguaro also includes a cost outlay recorded as an expense of the corporation.

Cost outlays are recorded as *expenses* during an accounting period if they are expected to be used up (that is, if they are expected to expire) during the period. If, in fact, they have not been completely consumed by the end of the accounting period, an accounting adjustment is required. The amount of the expense that has not expired, or has not been consumed, must be determined and transferred to an *asset* account. Again, this ensures a proper matching of revenue earned and expenses incurred in order to determine a proper net income for the accounting period.

The revenue and expense accounts just referred to are also mixed accounts, since they include both an income statement portion and a balance sheet portion at the end of the period.

Illustrative Problem:

Q10: Adjusting income statement accounts

UNMIXING INCOME STATEMENT ACCOUNTS

The following income statement accounts of Saguaro Computers, Inc., require adjustment at December 31:

Partial Trial Balance
December 31, 19X1

	Account Balances	
	Debit	Credit
Repair Revenue		$23,895 ◄── This is a revenue account.
Supplies Expense	$2,100 ◄─────── This is an expense account.

These accounts are analyzed and adjusted as follows:

Step 1 At the end of the accounting period, determine which portion of the mixed account belongs in the balance sheet and which belongs in the income statement.

Step 2 The portion that does not belong in the revenue or expense account must be transferred to the balance sheet as either a liability or an asset account. This is accomplished by recording an adjusting entry in the general journal and then posting the entry to the proper accounts in the general ledger.

REPAIR REVENUE

SCI received $2,000 on December 26 for repairs to be made in December (transaction 12). According to its best estimates, the company would begin the repairs in January and hopefully have the work completed by mid-February.

The Repair Revenue account appears as follows at December 31:

The revenue had been recorded by a number of different journal entries, summarized below:

Repair Revenue
(revenue)   No. 450
| | 23,895 |

Cash	15,395	
Notes Receivable	5,000	
Accounts Receivable	3,500	
Repair Revenue		23,895

Step 1:
The title Repair Revenue classifies it as a revenue account, but at December 31 it is actually a mixed account: the amount of $2,000 has not been earned during December. The amount of revenue earned during the month is $21,895.

Repair Revenue
(mixed)   No. 450
| | 23,895 |

revenue $21,895
liability $ 2,000

Step 2:
This revenue account must be decreased by $2,000 to leave a balance of $21,895. An adjusting journal entry is prepared.

Repair Revenue
(unmixed)   No. 450
	23,895
2,000	
	Bal. 21,895

This is the adjusting journal entry:

Dec. 31	Repair Revenue	450	2,000	
	Unearned Repair Revenue	247		2,000
	To record unearned repair revenue at			
	December 31.			

The Repair Revenue is decreased by the $2,000 that has not yet been earned. In this way, the mixed revenue account is split into two portions: the unearned amount is transferred to the balance-sheet liability account; what remains in the account is the income statement portion, the amount earned.

When this adjusting entry is posted, the unearned portion is transferred from the mixed account as follows:

Repair Revenue
(revenue)   No. 450
	23,895
2,000	
	Bal. 21,895

Unearned Repair Revenue
(liability)   No. 247
| | 2,000 |

A revenue decrease is recorded as a debit.

A liability increase is recorded as a credit.

SUPPLIES EXPENSE

SCI purchased $2,100 in supplies to be used during November and December (transactions 7 and 10). Since these supplies were expected to be used during that accounting period, their cost was recorded as an expense.

The Supplies Expense account appears as follows at December 31:

This expense had been recorded by a number of different journal entries, summarized below:

Supplies Expense (expense)	No. 668
2,100	

Supplies Expense	2,100	
Cash		1,200
Accounts Payable		900

At December 31, an actual count of the supplies in the storeroom indicated that supplies costing $495 were still on hand.

Step 1:
The title Supplies Expense indicates that it is an income statement account, but it is actually a mixed account: supplies costing $495 have not been consumed during the month; therefore, the amount of expense to match against the revenues should be only $1,605.

Supplies Expense (mixed)	No. 668
2,100	

expense $1,605
asset $ 495

Step 2:
This expense account has to be decreased by $495. An adjusting journal entry is prepared.

Supplies Expense (unmixed)	No. 668
2,100	
	495
Bal. 1,605	

This is the adjusting journal entry:

Dec. 31	Supplies (inventory)	173	495	
	Supplies Expense	668		495
	To record unused supplies at December 31.			

The asset account in usually simply named *Supplies;* the account is really reporting the amount of supplies still on hand, the *supplies inventory.*

When the adjusting entry is posted, the unexpired portion is transferred from the mixed account as follows:

An asset increase is recorded as a debit.

An expense decrease is recorded as a credit.

ACCRUALS

Q11: Accrued expenses and revenues

In the last two sections, mixed balance sheet and income statement accounts were examined, demonstrating the need for adjusting entries to adhere to the matching concept. The mere fact that these accounts are referred to as mixed accounts indicates that the accounts contain existing balances in the general ledger.

Some revenues are earned during a time period that are not reflected in the accounts, and some expenses are incurred during a time period and similarly are not reflected in the accounts. These revenue and expense items are said to *accrue* and are referred to as **accruals. Accrued revenues** are revenues that have been earned as of the end of the accounting period but have not been recorded, while **accrued expenses** are expenses that have been incurred, but have not been recorded. These adjustments must be made in order to achieve a proper matching of revenue and expenses. Some examples of items that accrue on a day-to-day basis are:

Interest expense/interest earned. These two items are usually recorded when the interest is paid or received. Since interest is usually paid or received *after* it is incurred or earned, interest must be accrued during the adjustment process.

Salaries expense. Salaries are usually paid after the benefit has been received by the employer (employees are paid after they have performed the services). Since employees are generally not paid at the end of each day, at the end of an accounting period the employer has incurred the salaries earned by the employees since the last pay period ended. In order for a proper matching, salaries must be accrued during the adjustment process.

Income tax expense. Income tax expense is incurred over the accounting year, but taxes are only due to be paid after the end of the year. Therefore, income taxes would have to be accrued to have a proper matching.

During the accounting period, regular business transactions are recorded as they occur. At the end of the period, the accountant may find that ledger account balances are incomplete. In the case of revenue and expense items that accrue, some new amounts must be brought into the accounts. The adjusting entries to accomplish this balance are referred to as *accruals*.

Illustrative Problem:

RECORDING ACCRUALS

The following accounts of Saguaro Computers, Inc., require an accrual at December 31:

Income Statement Accounts	Balance Sheet Accounts
Interest Earned	Interest Receivable
Salaries Expense	Salaries Payable
Interest Expense	Interest Payable
Income Tax Expense	Income Tax Payable

The accounts are discussed and adjusting entries are shown in the following pages.

Unrecorded Revenues

Unrecorded revenues consist of revenues that have been earned during the accounting period but that are not due to be collected until sometime in the next period.

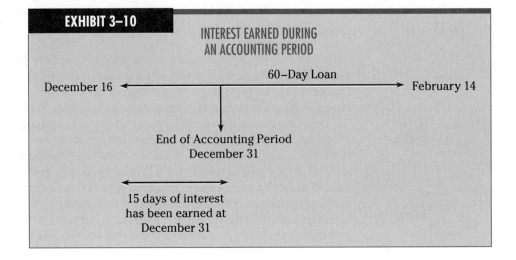

EXHIBIT 3-10

INTEREST EARNED DURING AN ACCOUNTING PERIOD

December 16 ←――――――― 60-Day Loan ―――――――→ February 14

End of Accounting Period
December 31

15 days of interest
has been earned at
December 31

INTEREST EARNED AND INTEREST RECEIVABLE

Saguaro Computers, Inc., performed $5,000 in repairs for one of its customers, who signed a 60-day, 12-percent, interest-bearing note dated December 16.

Although interest accrues daily on the $5,000 loan, the interest is actually received only at the maturity date of the note, February 14, when the amount due (principal plus interest) is paid by the customer. At December 31, the end of the accounting period for SCI, interest has been earned for 15 days in December (December 16–31), as shown in Exhibit 3-10, but this interest earned has not yet been recorded by the company.

The formula for computing interest is:

$$\text{Interest} = \text{Principal} \times \text{Interest Rate} \times \frac{\text{Elapsed Time in Days}}{365}$$

The interest revenue accrued at December 31 is computed as follows:

$$\text{Interest} = \$5{,}000 \times 0.12 \times \frac{15}{365} = \$24.66 \text{ (or \$25 rounded for illustrative purposes)}$$

The principal multiplied by the interest rate equals the total interest for one year ($5,000 × 0.12 = $600); the interest for a year ($600), multiplied by the elapsed fraction of a year (15/365), is the interest revenue for 15 days ($600 × 15/365), or $25. The use of 365 days in the formula, ignoring leap years, is consistent with commercial practice, primarily to simplify calculation. In fact, in the years before the advent of computers, businesses frequently simply assumed that the year consisted of 12, 30-day months, or a business year of 360 days.

Step 1:
At the end of the accounting period, $25 interest has been earned by the corporation from December 16 to 31, a period of 15 days. This interest will be received February 14, when the amount due (principal plus interest) is paid by the customer.

Interest Earned
(revenue)   No. 430

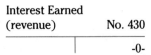

-0-

Step 2:
The $25 interest earned has to be recorded in December in order to match revenues with expenses. An adjusting entry is prepared.

Interest Earned
(revenue)   No. 430
                                25

This is the adjusting journal entry:

Dec. 31	Interest Receivable	116	25	
	Interest Earned	430		25
	To record interest accrued at			
	December 31.			

This adjusting entry enables SCI to include in income of the period the interest earned, even though the payment has not yet been received. The entry created an accrued receivable—that is, a receivable for an income earned during an accounting period but collectible in another accounting period.

When the adjusting entry is posted, the accounts appear as follows:

Interest Receivable		Interest Earned	
(asset)	No. 116	(revenue)	No. 430
25			25

An asset, Interest Receivable, exists at December 31. An asset increase is recorded as a debit.

Interest earned is a revenue that has been earned for 15 days in December. A revenue increase is recorded as a credit.

Other adjusting entries for various revenues that have been earned by the company during the accounting period but have not been received or are not due to be collected until some time in the next period, are recorded in a manner similar to the adjustment for interest earned. The amount earned must be calculated and is recorded in the accounts by the following type of journal entry:

Receivable	XXX	
Earned		XXX
To accrue revenue.		

For instance, if a portion of a building is rented to another business, and that business had not paid the December rent of $650 as of December 31, SCI would prepare the following adjusting journal entry:

Rent Receivable	650	
Rent Earned		650
To accrue the rent for December.		

Unrecorded Expenses

Unrecorded expenses are expenses that have been incurred during the accounting period but have not been paid during the accounting period, or that are not due to be paid until some time in the next period.

SALARIES EXPENSE AND SALARIES PAYABLE

At December 31, the end of the accounting period for Saguaro, salary expense had been incurred for three days in December, as shown in Exhibit 3-11, but this expense had not been recorded.

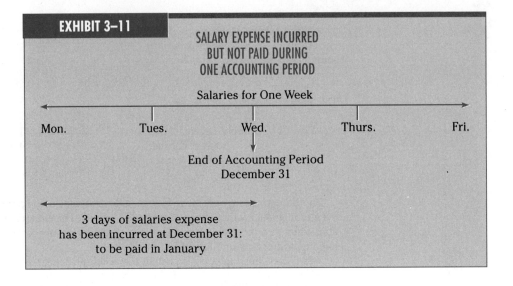

EXHIBIT 3-11

SALARY EXPENSE INCURRED
BUT NOT PAID DURING
ONE ACCOUNTING PERIOD

Salaries for One Week

Mon.   Tues.   Wed.   Thurs.   Fri.

End of Accounting Period
December 31

3 days of salaries expense
has been incurred at December 31:
to be paid in January

Step 1:
During the accounting year, employees have been paid $5,000 in salaries; this amount has been already recorded. At the end of the accounting period, employees have earned additional salaries of $150 for work on December 29, 30, and 31, the last three days of the accounting period. This amount is not yet recorded in the company's books, since it will be paid in January.

Salaries Expense
(expense)   No. 656

5,000	

Step 2:
The matching principle requires the recording of the salary expense at December 31, which is done by the preparation of an adjusting entry.

Salaries Expense
(expense)   No. 656

5,000	
150	
Bal. 5,150	

This is the adjusting entry:

Dec. 31	Salaries Expense	656	150	
	Salaries Payable	226		150
	To record salaries accrued at December 31.			

This entry enables the company to include in expense all salaries earned by employees, even though not all salaries have yet been paid. The entry creates an accrued liability—a liability for an expense incurred during one accounting period (December) but payable in another accounting period (January).

When the adjusting entry is posted, the accounts appear as follows:

Salaries Expense (expense)	No. 656		Salaries Payable (liability)	No. 226
5,000				
150	←	→		150
Bal. 5,150				

Salaries Expense is an expense that has been incurred at December 31. An expense increase is recorded as a debit.	A liability, Salaries Payable, exists at December 31. A liability increase is recorded as a credit.

Q12: Interest as liability

INTEREST EXPENSE AND INTEREST PAYABLE

SCI had borrowed $5,000 from the bank when it purchased a truck in November. The interest rate was 12 percent per year. Since interest is money paid for the use of money, interest accrues daily on the loan, but will not be paid until some time in the next accounting period.

At December 31, the end of the accounting period for SCI, interest has accrued for 58 days to December 31 (November 3 to December 31), but this interest expense has not yet been recorded by the company.

The interest expense accrued at December 31 is computed as follows:

$$\text{Interest} = \$5,000 \times 0.12 \times \frac{58}{365} = \begin{array}{l}\$95.34 \text{ (or }\$95\text{ rounded for}\\ \text{illustrative purposes)}\end{array}$$

Step 1:
At the end of the accounting period, $95 interest expense has accrued for a period of 58 days. This amount is not yet recorded in the company's books, since it will be paid in January.

Interest Expense
(expense)   No. 632
-0-

Step 2:
The matching principle requires the recording of the $95 expense at December 31. This is done by the preparation of an adjusting entry.

Interest Expense
(expense)   No. 632
95

This is the adjusting entry:

Dec. 31	Interest Expense		632	95	
	Interest Payable		222		95
	To record interest accrued at December 31.				

The entry creates an accrued liability—that is, a liability for an expense incurred during the current accounting period but payable in another accounting period (January).

When the adjusting entry is posted, the accounts appear as follows:

Interest Expense (expense)	No. 632		Interest Payable (liability)	No. 222
95	←	→		95

Interest Expense is an expense that has accrued to December 31. An expense increase is recorded as a debit.	A liability, Interest Payable, exists at December 31. A liability increase is recorded as a credit.

Other adjusting entries for expense (such as utilities, telephone, and so on) that have been incurred by the company during the accounting period but are not due to be paid until the next period are recorded in a manner similar to the adjustment for salary and interest expenses. The amount of the expense must be calculated and then recorded in the following type of entry:

Date	Expense	XXX	
	Expense Payable		XXX
	To accrue an expense.		

Recording Taxes

Q13: Income taxes as expense

Another adjustment required of SCI involves the recording of estimated income taxes that may be due to federal, state, and/or local governmental units. Income taxes are incurred at the time income is earned throughout the fiscal year. As expenses, estimated taxes must be matched with revenue. It is estimated that as a corporation, SCI will owe a total of $6,000 to various taxing authorities.

INCOME TAX EXPENSE AND INCOME TAX PAYABLE

Step 1:
An estimate of the current period's income tax has not yet been recorded.

Income Tax Expense
(expense)   No. 830
_____
              -0- |

Step 2:
The corporation's estimate of income taxes at December 31 is $6,000. These income taxes are recorded by an adjusting entry.

Income Tax Expense
(expense)   No. 830
_____
           6,000 |

This is the adjusting entry:

Dec. 31	Income Tax Expense	830	6,000	
	Income Tax Payable	260		6,000
	To record estimated income taxes at December 31.			

When the adjusting entry is posted, the accounts appear as follows:

Income Tax Expense
(expense)   No. 830
_____
        6,000 ◄

Income Tax Payable
(liability)   No. 260
_____
                    ► 6,000

Income Tax Expense is an expense that has been incurred. An expense increase is recorded as a debit.

Income Tax Payable is a liability that has accrued at December 31. A liability increase is recorded as a credit.

This adjusting entry enables the company to show the income taxes applicable to the income earned during the period.

THE ACCOUNTING CYCLE—STEPS 4–6

Six steps in the accounting process prior to the preparation of financial statements can now be identified. The first three of these were summarized on pp. 108–11 of this chapter. Steps 4 through 6 are summarized here:

STEP 4: THE ACCOUNT BALANCES ARE ANALYZED AND ADJUSTING ENTRIES ARE PREPARED.

As is the case with the December transactions (recorded in Exhibit 3-6), the adjusting entries are also recorded in the journal of Saguaro Computers, Inc., at the end of December.

The caption *Adjusting Entries* is written in the journal on the line following the last regular journal entry of the corporation.

STEP 5: THE ADJUSTING ENTRIES ARE POSTED TO LEDGER ACCOUNTS.

When the December adjusting entries have been posted to the ledger accounts, the ledger accounts are footed and debit or credit balances are calculated. For example, the Prepaid Insurance account has a debit balance of $1,100 after it has been footed. During the posting process, the entries in the journal are cross-referenced to the ledger, showing in the journal folio column the account number to which the amount was posted, and the postings in the ledger are cross-referenced to the particular page of the journal where the entry was recorded.

Q14: Adjusted trial balance

STEP 6: AN ADJUSTED TRIAL BALANCE IS PREPARED TO PROVE THE EQUALITY OF DEBITS AND CREDITS.

A trial balance prepared after the posting of adjusting entries to the ledger would contain the accounts and account balances shown in Exhibit 3-12. Note that new accounts have been included as required by the adjusting entries, and that this trial balance is labelled as an **adjusted trial balance** to distinguish it from the *unadjusted* trial balance prepared earlier.

The purpose of any trial balance is to establish the equality of debits and credits to ensure the accuracy of the mechanical process of recording transactions and posting of journal entries to the ledger.

The trial balance, or in this case the adjusted trial balance, is useful to the accountant in the preparation of financial statements. The accountant could prepare these statements directly from the ledger accounts, but the trial balance or adjusted trial balance is a convenient summary of this information. Basic financial statements now can be prepared from the adjusted trial balance at December 31 for Saguaro. It is readily apparent that the transactions worksheet from Chapter 1 and the scattered information from this chapter are not adequate for reporting an accounting system of any magnitude. Chapter 4 describes the worksheet, which is a tool the accountant uses to gather information at the end of a fiscal year to prepare the financial statements. The worksheet is necessary for a full appreciation of the accounting process, but if the focus of a course is strictly the use of accounting information, then an instructor might skip Chapter 4 and have students prepare some financial statements from the assignment material at the end of this chapter. The requirements for Problem 3-1 and Alternate Problem 3-1 have been expanded to accommodate courses with a decision-making focus.

The financial statements in Exhibits 3-13 to 3-15 (pp. 133–35) were prepared from the adjusted trial balance for Saguaro Computers, Inc., in Exhibit 3-12.

EXHIBIT 3–12

Saguaro Computers, Inc.
Adjusted Trial Balance
December 31, 19X1

	Account Balances	
	Debit	Credit
Cash	$11,695	
Accounts Receivable	3,500	
Interest Receivable	25	
Notes Receivable	5,000	
Prepaid Insurance	1,100	
Supplies	495	
Equipment	2,000	
Truck	8,000	
Accumulated Depreciation — Equipment		$ 30
Accumulated Depreciation — Truck		240
Bank Loan		5,000
Accounts Payable		1,900
Interest Payable		95
Salaries Payable		150
Unearned Repair Revenue		2,000
Unearned Rent		400
Income Tax Payable		6,000
Common Stock		10,000
Interest Earned		25
Repair Revenue		21,895
Rent Earned		200
Depreciation Expense — Equipment	30	
Depreciation Expense — Truck	240	
Insurance Expense	100	
Interest Expense	95	
Rent Expense	1,200	
Salaries Expense	5,150	
Supplies Expense	1,605	
Truck Expense	1,400	
Utilities Expense	300	
Income Tax Expense	6,000	
	$47,935	$47,935

The Cash account shows an increase of $6,695 during December, which is a result of operating activities reported in the SCI statement of cash flows, Exhibit 3-15.

CHAPTER REVIEW

1 Describe the operating cycle. What would be the shortest cycle in time? the longest? Explain. (pp. 100–101)

In its simplest form, the operating cycle is "cash to cash," meaning that an entity starts with some cash, whether it comes from operating, financing, or investing activities, and "puts" it into operations. The entity buys goods for resale, provides

EXHIBIT 3–13

Saguaro Computers, Inc.
Income Statement
for the Two Months Ended
December 31, 19X1

Revenue

Interest Earned	$ 25	
Repair Revenue	21,895	
Rent Earned	200	
Total Revenue		$22,120

Expenses

Depreciation Expense — Equipment	30	
Depreciation Expense — Truck	240	
Insurance Expense	100	
Interest Expense	95	
Rent Expense	1,200	
Salaries Expense	5,150	
Supplies Expense	1,605	
Truck Expense	1,400	
Utilities Expense	300	
Total Expenses		10,120
Net Income before Tax		$12,000
Income Tax		6,000
Net Income		$ 6,000

services, or manufactures goods for resale. After the sale of the goods or the provision of services, the entity either receives cash or account receivables that eventually will be converted to cash, and the cycle begins again. In practice, a new cycle may begin daily. The shortest possible operating cycle is one day or less, while the longest possible may be several years. Some scotch whiskeys (goods) may be held for 20 years before being bottled and sold.

2 What operating cycle problems arise at the end of the accounting period? (p. 101)

Since an accounting period is arbitrary, the end falls in the middle of one of the many operating cycles that begin during the accounting period. Thus, activities taking place during the period result in mixed accounts whose balances must be allocated between the balance sheet and income statement, or vice versa.

3 When cash is received prior to the time revenue has been earned, is the amount recorded as a liability or as a revenue? Explain. (p. 102)

When the cash is received, the amount represents a liability. However, if the revenue is fully earned before the end of the accounting period, the cash received may be recorded as revenue at the time it is received. If some of the revenue will not be earned until some time in the next accounting period, the amount of cash received in advance of earning the revenue should be recorded as a liability.

4 When cash is paid out (cost outlay) prior to the time that its benefit has been received, should the amount be recorded as an asset or as an expense? Explain. (pp. 102–3)

When a cost outlay occurs, the amount is recorded as an asset if a future benefit (insurance policy) is involved, or as an expense if no future benefit (salaries paid after employee services have been performed) is involved. However, if the entire

---

EXHIBIT 3–14

Saguaro Computers, Inc.
Balance Sheet
December 31, 19X1

Assets

Current Assets

Cash	$11,695	
Accounts Receivable	3,500	
Interest Receivable	25	
Notes Receivable	5,000	
Prepaid Insurance	1,100	
Supplies	495	
Total Current Assets		$21,815

Long-term Assets

Equipment	$2,000		
Less: Accumulated Depreciation	30	1,970	
Truck	8,000		
Less: Accumulated Depreciation	240	7,760	
Total Long-term Assets			9,730
Total Assets			$31,545

Liabilities

Current Liabilities

Bank Loan	$ 5,000	
Accounts Payable	1,900	
Interest Payable	95	
Salaries Payable	150	
Unearned Repair Revenue	2,000	
Unearned Rent	400	
Income Tax Payable	6,000	
Total Current Liabilities		$15,545

Stockholders' Equity

Common Stock	$10,000	
Retained Earnings	6,000	
Total Stockholders' Equity		16,000
Total Liabilities and Stockholders' Equity		$31,545

---

future benefit will be received during the current accounting period, the amount may be recorded as an expense at the time paid.

5 The recording of journal entries both in the journal and in the ledger is just doubling the work. Entries could be made directly into the ledger accounts to eliminate one-half the effort. Comment. (pp. 109–11)

In a *very* small operation this approach might be possible. However, the recording of the transaction in only one book would still be a problem. Recording each transaction twice results in a chronological record of each transaction (the journal), and the summarization of the effects of those transactions on the company's financial position (the ledger). Both the journal and the ledger serve different purposes, and therefore do not represent doubled work.

EXHIBIT 3–15

Saguaro Computers, Inc.
Statement of Cash Flows (Direct Method)
For the Month Ended December 31, 19X1

Cash Flows from Operating Activities
Inflows:

Cash Received from Customers	$ 11,395	
Cash Received from Truck Rental	600	
Total Cash Inflows	11,995	

(Outflows):
Cash Paid for Expenses:

Insurance	$ (1,200)	
Rent	(600)	
Salaries	(2,500)	
Utilities	(300)	
Truck	(700)	
Total Cash Outflows	(5,300)	
Net Cash Inflow from Operating Activities		$ 6,695

Cash Flows from Investing Activities
[none]

Cash Flows from Financing Activities
[none]

Net Inflow of Cash	$ 6,695
Cash Balance, December 1, 19X1	5,000
Cash Balance, December 31, 19X1	$11,695

6 The matching concept involves both transactions that have already been recorded and transactions that have not been recorded. Explain. (p. 113)

The results of transactions already recorded must be analyzed to determine if any of the accounts contain mixed balances. Those accounts must be adjusted so only the amounts to be carried forward appear on the balance sheet, and the amounts that should be matched with revenue in the current accounting period appear on the income statement. In the process, more transactions are recorded. When transactions have not been recorded, the revenue that has been earned and expenses that have been incurred must be matched with other revenue and expenses on the income statement.

7 How can unearned rent be considered a liability? (pp. 114–15)

When rent is paid in advance, it is considered to be unearned. Since the money has already been received, the landlord has the responsibility (liability) of ensuring that the premises are free of danger to "life and limb." Generally, if the rent received in advance is to be earned before the end of a fiscal year, it may be recorded directly as a revenue.

8 Are mixed accounts limited to balance sheet accounts? to income statement accounts? Explain. (p. 115)

Both balance sheet and income statement accounts may be considered mixed. Income statement accounts may contain a portion that should be on the balance sheet, and vice versa.

9 Does the act of recording depreciation result in the establishment of a current value of the asset in the balance sheet? Explain. (pp. 118–19)

Depreciation is merely the allocation of the cost of an asset over its useful life. Conceptually, there is no difference between a 3-year insurance policy and a truck that has a useful life of 3 years.

10 When mixed items are income statement accounts, are adjustments made to other income statement accounts? Explain. (pp. 122–24)

When an income statement item is referred to as mixed, generally the reference is to a portion that should be included on the balance sheet. A mixed income statement account that affects other income statement accounts is merely a reclassification—an amount recorded as a debit to Insurance Expense when it should have been recorded as a debit to Interest Expense.

11 Why are accrued expenses recorded? Are revenues ever accrued? Explain. (p. 125)

Under the matching concept, if an expense has been incurred, it should be matched against revenue. Some expenses, such as salaries, utilities, and income taxes, are incurred before the liability exists and must be recorded as expenses to achieve a proper matching. If a revenue has been earned but is not yet due to be paid, such as interest on a note receivable, the amount should be recognized as revenue to match it against expenses incurred during the time period.

12 If interest on a bank loan is not due for a number of months, why is it recorded as a liability on the year-end balance sheet? (p. 129)

As stated in the answer to question 11, the expense of a bank loan should be recorded when it is incurred, not when it is due to be paid. Interest is money paid for the use of money and should be recorded during the period of time that the money is being used. Revenue is generated during this time period, and should be matched against any interest expense incurred.

13 If income taxes are due on April 15, 19X2, why are they recorded as an expense for an entity whose year ends December 31, 19X1? (p. 130)

Income taxes are incurred at the time income is earned, which is continuously throughout the fiscal year. Therefore, taxes should be recorded as an expense to be matched against revenue, even if the taxes are not due until the next accounting period.

14 Why must an adjusted trial balance be prepared? (p. 131)

An adjusted trial balance is prepared to test the equality of debits and credits after the adjustment process takes place. If a worksheet is being used (see Chapter 4) to accumulate accounting information, then a formal adjusted trial balance is not necessary. As noted in the text, financial statements may be prepared directly from the adjusted trial balance without using a worksheet.

KEY TERMS

accruals (p. 125) Accruals are revenue and expense items that must be recorded during the adjustment process in order to achieve a proper matching of revenue and expense.

accrued expenses   (p. 125) An expense that has already been incurred, but is not yet due to be paid, such as unpaid wages at the end of an accounting period. This is an application of the matching concept.

accrued revenues   (p. 125) A revenue that has been earned, but has not yet been received, such as interest revenue on a note receivable. This is an application of the matching concept.

accumulated depreciation   (p. 118) The total amount of an asset's original cost that has been allocated to an expense since the asset was acquired. The account where these expenses are entered is called an asset *valuation account* or *contra-asset account.*

adjusted trial balance   (p. 131) A listing of accounts and their balances after the posting of adjusting entries to the accounts of the entity.

adjusting journal entry   (p. 115) An entry made in the accounts to reflect the correct balance sheet or income statement valuation of an item. This is an application of the matching concept.

book value   (p. 118) The balance sheet valuation of an item. The term is used often to describe the results of subtracting accumulated depreciation from the original cost of a long-term asset.

depreciation   (p. 118) The allocation of the cost of a long-term asset over its estimated useful life.

depreciation expense   (p. 118) That part of the original cost of a long-term asset allocated to a particular accounting period.

long-term asset   (p. 118) An asset that is long-lived (more than one year), used in the business, and not held for resale.

mixed accounts   (p. 115) Accounts containing both a balance sheet and an income statement portion at the time financial statements need to be prepared.

revenue recognition   (p. 101) Revenue is recognized as having been earned when the service is completed or the goods sold.

scrap value   (p. 119) The estimated amount for which an asset can be sold at the end of its useful life; also called *salvage value.*

straight-line method of depreciation   (p. 119) A simple method of calculating depreciation whereby it is assumed that equal benefit is received from the asset over its entire useful life. That is, as much benefit is gained from the asset in its first month of life as in its last month of useful life.

useful life   (p. 119) An estimate of the period of time an asset will be useful to an entity. This will vary depending on the amount of use the asset will have, rather than the type of asset. An automobile for a traveling salesperson will not last as long as one used exclusively to ferry executives visiting a corporate home office.

valuation account   (p. 118) An account that is subtracted from the original cost of the asset to arrive at the book value of the asset for balance sheet purposes; often called a *contra-asset account.*

SELF-TEST QUESTIONS FOR REVIEW   (Answers are at the end of this chapter.)

Q1, Q2

1. The operating cycle of an entity is
    (a) the same as the accounting period.
    (b) equal to 12 months.
    (c) usually much longer than one year.
    (d) usually much shorter than one year.

Q1, Q2

2. An example of an entity with an operating cycle longer than one year is
    (a) a fresh-fish market.
    (b) a ski resort.
    (c) a high-rise construction firm.
    (d) a restaurant.

Q3

3. Sometimes revenue is earned at the time cash is received. Which of the following is an example of this situation?
    (a)   Cash is received 9 days after a credit sale.
    (b)   Cash is received by an insurance company for a 12-month policy.
    (c)   Cash is received 30 days after a credit sale.
    (d)   Cash is received immediately on providing a service.

Q3

4. When cash is received from a customer, the amount might be recorded as
    (a)   a liability.
    (b)   an item of equity.
    (c)   an expense.
    (d)   None of the above

Q4

5. When a cost outlay results from a transaction, the amount might be recorded as
    (a)   an expense.
    (b)   an asset.
    (c)   Either (a) or (b)
    (d)   Neither (a) nor (b)

Q14

6. An adjusted trial balance proves that
    (a)   all transactions and adjustments have been recorded correctly.
    (b)   the adjustments made to the accounts are in balance.
    (c)   accounts receivable are stated correctly.
    (d)   accounts payable are stated correctly.
    (e)   All of the above

Q9

7. Depreciation Expense is most comparable to
    (a)   Equipment.
    (b)   Salaries Expense.
    (c)   Accumulated Depreciation.
    (d)   Long-term liabilities.

Q7, Q10

8. A mixed income statement account results in an adjustment to
    (a)   a balance sheet account.
    (b)   an income statement account.
    (c)   Neither (a) nor (b)
    (d)   Either (a) or (b)
    (e)   Both (a) and (b)

Q11

9. Which of the following is an example of an accrued revenue?
    (a)   Rent received in advance
    (b)   Cash received on the completion of a service
    (c)   Interest on a note receivable
    (d)   All of the above

Q3, Q4, Q9, Q12, Q13

10. The matching principle gives rise to which of the following?
    (a)   Depreciation expense
    (b)   Accrued revenue and expenses
    (c)   Prepaid expenses
    (d)   Revenue received in advance
    (e)   All of the above

DEMONSTRATION PROBLEM

The trial balance of White Corporation, before and after the posting of adjusting entries, follows.

	Trial Balance		Adjustments		Adjusted Trial Balance	
	Dr.	Cr.	Dr.	Cr.	Dr.	Cr.
Cash	$ 4,000				$ 4,000	
Accounts Receivable	5,000				5,000	
Prepaid Insurance	3,600				3,300	
Prepaid Rent	1,000				500	
Truck	6,000				6,000	
Accumulated Depreciation						$ 1,500
Accounts Payable		$ 7,000				7,400
Salaries Payable						1,000
Unearned Rent		1,200				600
Common Stock		2,700				2,700
Revenue		25,000				25,000
Rent Earned						600
Advertising Expense	700				700	
Commissions Expense	2,000				2,000	
Depreciation Expense					1,500	
Interest Expense	100				500	
Insurance Expense					300	
Rent Expense	5,500				6,000	
Salaries Expense	8,000				9,000	
Totals	$35,900	$35,900			$38,800	$38,800

Required

1. Determine the differences between the unadjusted and adjusted trial balance, and insert the amounts in the proper Adjustments column.

2. Prepare the adjusting entries that must have been recorded in the general journal.

3. Cross-reference these entries, using the alphabet, with the amounts in the Adjustments column, applying the matching concept.

SOLUTION TO DEMONSTRATION PROBLEM

1., 3.   **White Corporation**

	Trial Balance		Adjustments		Adjusted Trial Balance	
	Dr.	Cr.	Dr.	Cr.	Dr.	Cr.
Cash	$ 4,000				$ 4,000	
Accounts Receivable	5,000				5,000	
Prepaid Insurance	3,600			(a) $ 300	3,300	
Prepaid Rent	1,000			(b) 500	500	
Truck	6,000				6,000	
Accumulated Depreciation				(c) 1,500		$ 1,500
Accounts Payable		$ 7,000		(d) 400		7,400
Salaries Payable				(e) 1,000		1,000
Unearned Rent		1,200	(f) $ 600			600
Common Stock		2,700				2,700
Revenue		25,000				25,000
Rent Earned				(f) 600		600
Advertising Expense	700				700	
Commissions Expense	2,000				2,000	
Depreciation Expense			(c) 1,500		1,500	

(continued)

	Trial Balance		Adjustments		Adjusted Trial Balance	
	Dr.	Cr.	Dr.	Cr.	Dr.	Cr.
Interest Expense	100		(d) 400		500	
Insurance Expense			(a) 300		300	
Rent Expense	5,500		(b) 500		6,000	
Salaries Expense	8,000		(e) 1,000		9,000	
Totals	$35,900	$35,900	$4,300	$4,300	$38,800	$38,800

2. (a)   Insurance Expense   300
              Prepaid Insurance   300
              To record insurance expense for the period.

  (b)   Rent Expense   500
              Prepaid Rent   500
              To record rent expense for the period.

  (c)   Depreciation Expense   1,500
              Accumulated Depreciation   1,500
              To record depreciation of the truck for the period.

  (d)   Interest Expense   400
              Accounts Payable   400
              To record interest expense that accrued for the period.

  (e)   Salaries Expense   1,000
              Salaries Payable   1,000
              To record salaries earned for the period.

  (f)   Unearned Rent   600
              Rent Earned   600
              To record the portion of prepaid rent earned for the period.

DISCUSSION QUESTIONS

Q3-1   What is an operating cycle? How does it function?

Q3-2   In what manner do operating cycles overlap in practice? Use an example to explain.

Q3-3   The recording of some transactions causes more problems than the recording of others. Identify and explain two categories of such transactions.

Q3-4   Why is it important to identify the point at which the revenue of a business is actually earned?

Q3-5   When a deposit or advance payment is received, what is the accepted accounting practice to record its receipt? Identify and explain the practice.

Q3-6   Define cost outlay.

Q3-7   Identify and explain the accepted accounting practice to record cost outlays.

Q3-8   Is consistency an accounting principle or practice? What is its importance?

Q3-9   What are adjusting entries and why are they required? Why are some accounts described as being "mixed"?

Q3-10 What is the general method for unmixing asset accounts? Identify and describe the steps involved.

Q3-11 What is the general method for unmixing liability accounts? Identify and describe the steps involved.

Q3-12 Accountants do not unmix long-term-asset accounts. Why?

Q3-13 Depreciation Expense and Accumulated Depreciation are two accounts used in relation to long-term accounts. Why are they used?

Q3-14 Under what circumstances are cash receipts recorded as revenues?

Q3-15 Under what circumstances are cost outlays recorded as expenses?

Q3-16 What is the general method used in unmixing income statement accounts?

Q3-17 What is meant by the term *to accrue?* Give examples of items that accrue.

Q3-18 List the steps in the accounting cycle.

Q3-19 Which steps in the accounting cycle occur continuously throughout the accounting period?

Q3-20 Which steps in the accounting cycle occur at the end of the accounting period?

Q3-21 Refer to Real World Example 3-1. Accountants sometimes use the term *unearned revenue;* is this term a contradiction? Where would it fit in to the FASB definitions?

DISCUSSION CASE

The Bottom Line

Q11

"Everybody is talking GAAP, GAAP, GAAP," said Martin Ives, vice-chairman and director of research for the Governmental Accounting Standards Board, a private non-profit group that sets the GAAP guidelines. "I remember when."

"When" was before 1982. That was the last year New York state reported its financial operations on a cash basis accounting system. Revenues were recorded at the time they came in and expenditures at the time they went out.

That system allowed politicians to distort the financial condition of the state government honestly by moving receipts and disbursements from one fiscal year to another, by delaying payments or by speeding up collections.

For example, the state's fiscal year ends March 31. If the state ordered and received $100 million-worth of widgets in February, it could wait to pay for them until April 1, thereby pushing the $100 million disbursement into the next fiscal year.

When the books for the year ended March 31 were reviewed, the $100 million would not show up, even though the widgets had been ordered and put into use that year. In other words, the cash system made it possible to run today's operation by pushing some costs into tomorrow's budget.

LOOKING FOR A BETTER WAY

Nowhere was this technique more artfully employed than in aid to local school districts. By the late 1970s, it had become impossible to assess accurately the state's fiscal health. More and more officials began to look for an accurate way to determine it.

Under GAAP, expenditures are recorded when they are incurred rather than when the check is written. Revenues are recorded when they are due, rather than when the money is actually received.

So, if the state receives $100 million in widgets in February, they are charged against that fiscal year, even if the state doesn't get around to paying the bill until the next year.

When in the late 1970s state auditors began to analyze the accounts under GAAP, they realized how big New York's deficits had become. GAAP accounting did not help to eradicate the accumulated deficit (which now amounts to $4 billion), but it did define the size of it.

For Discussion

1. Identify the previous method of accounting used by New York and explain how it worked. What is the method used since 1982?

Source Jeffrey Schmalz, "Sometimes There's Just No Settling on the Bottom Line," *The New York Times,* March 17, 1985, p. 6-E. Copyright © 1985 by the New York Times Company. Reprinted by permission.

EXERCISES

Note: When answering these exercises, assume that no monthly accruals are made during the fiscal year.

Mixed income statement expense accounts (Q4, Q8, Q10)

E3-1 The following journal entry was made to record the purchase of a 12-month insurance policy dated April 1, 19X1:

Insurance Expense	1,800	
Cash		1,800

Required

What adjusting journal entry is necessary, assuming the entity has a fiscal year that ends on

1. September 30, 19X1?
2. December 31, 19X1?
3. February 28, 19X2?
4. March 31, 19X2?

Mixed balance sheet asset accounts (Q4, Q8, Q10)

E3-2 The following journal entry was made to record the purchase of a 12-month insurance policy dated April 1, 19X1:

Prepaid Insurance	1,800	
Cash		1,800

Required

What adjusting journal entry is necessary, assuming the entity has a fiscal year that ends on

1. September 30, 19X1?
2. December 31, 19X1?
3. February 28, 19X2?
4. March 31, 19X2?

Mixed balance sheet liability accounts (Q3, Q8, Q10)

E3-3 The following journal entry was made on April 1, 19X1, to record the receipt of $2,400 for an ad to be run in the entity's monthly magazine for a 2-year period:

Cash	2,400	
Prepaid Advertising		2,400

Required
What adjusting journal entry is necessary, assuming the entity has a fiscal year that ends on

1. September 30, 19X1?
2. December 31, 19X1?
3. February 28, 19X2?
4. March 31, 19X2?

**Mixed income state-
ment revenue accounts
(Q3, Q8, Q10)**

E3-4   The following journal entry was made on April 1, 19X1, to record the receipt of $2,400 for an ad run in the entity's monthly magazine for a 2-year period:

Cash	2,400	
Advertising revenue		2,400

Required
What adjusting journal entry is necessary, assuming the entity has a fiscal year that ends on

1. September 30, 19X1?
2. December 31, 19X1?
3. February 28, 19X2?
4. March 31, 19X2?

**Mixed balance sheet
fixed-asset accounts
(Q4, Q8–Q10)**

E3-5   The following journal entry was made to record the purchase of a truck on April 1, 19X1, that has an estimated useful life of 5 years with no salvage value:

Truck	24,000	
Cash		24,000

Required
What adjusting journal entry is necessary, assuming the entity has a fiscal year that ends on

1. September 30, 19X1?
2. December 31, 19X1?
3. February 28, 19X2?
4. March 31, 19X2?

**Accrual of expenses
(Q11)**

E3-6   A company obtained a note payable in the amount of $120,000, dated October 1, 19X1, due (payable) September 30, 19X2, and with a stated rate of interest on the note of 10%.

Required
What entry is necessary to record the accrual of interest expense on the note when the entity has a fiscal year that ends on

1. September 30, 19X1?
2. December 31, 19X1?
3. February 28, 19X2?
4. March 31, 19X2?

Accrual of revenue
(Q11)

E3-7   A company has a note receivable in the amount of $72,000, dated October 1, 19X1, due (payable) March 31, 19X2, and with a stated rate of interest on the note of 10%.

Required

What entry is necessary to record the accrual of interest revenue on a note receivable when the entity has a fiscal year that ends on

1. September 30, 19X1?
2. December 31, 19X1?
3. February 28, 19X2?
4. March 31, 19X2?

Accrual of income
taxes (Q11)

E3-8   An entity has a net income of $45,000 and pays a tax rate of 30%.

Required

What entry is necessary to record the accrual of income taxes if the fiscal year ends on December 31, 19X1, and if taxes are not payable until March 15, 19X2?

PROBLEMS

Journal entries, posting,
trial balances, financial
statements (Q3–Q14)

P3-1   Multi-Publishers Corp. was incorporated on June 1, 19X1, and had the following transactions during its first month of operation.

PART A

June	1	Issued common stock for $10,000
	1	Purchased equipment for $6,500 on account
	2	Purchased on account supplies costing $750. These supplies are expected to last three months.
	3	Paid for an ad in the local paper to run for two months at $250 per month
	5	Collected $12,000 representing three-month subscriptions to its *PC REVIEW* magazine, effective June 1
	14	Paid the following expenses: telephone, $350; rent for June, $500; salaries, $3,000
	16	Collected $5,000 from advertisers for the June edition of *PC REVIEW* magazine
	18	Paid for half of the equipment purchased June 1
	20	Paid $2,000 for supplies used for production during the first half of June. These supplies were in addition to the supplies purchased June 2.
	28	Paid the following expenses: telephone, $250; salaries, $3,000
	30	Received an invoice from the power company for $200 for electricity used during June

Required

1. Open ledger accounts for the following: Cash, Prepaid Advertising, Supplies, Equipment, Accounts Payable, Unearned Subscriptions, Common Stock, Advertising Revenue, Advertising Expense, Rent Expense, Revenue, Salaries Expense, Telephone Expense, Utilities Expense, Supplies Expense.

2. Prepare journal entries to record the June transactions. Post the entries to the ledger accounts.

PART B

At June 30 the following information is available to assist you in the preparation of the month-end adjusting entries.

a. The ad has run in the local newspaper during June, according to the agreement.

b. One month of the subscriptions collected June 5 has been earned.

c. A physical count of the supplies indicates that supplies costing $100 are on hand at the end of June.

d. The company pays a 5-percent commission to the firm that handles the paperwork on all subscriptions. This commission is due at the end of each month on subscriptions that have been earned.

e. Two days of salary for June 29 and 30 are unpaid; the unpaid amount will be included in the first Friday salary payment in July. The salary for each day during the week amounts to $300.

f. The equipment purchased on June 1 has an estimated useful life of 5 years and is estimated to have a salvage value of $500.

Required

3. Open additional ledger accounts for the following: Accumulated Depreciation, Salaries Payable, Commissions Expense, Depreciation Expense, Subscription Revenue.

4. Prepare all necessary adjusting entries. Post the entries to the ledger accounts.

5. Prepare an adjusted trial balance as of June 30.

6. Prepare a complete set of financial statements; an income statement, a balance sheet, and a statement of cash flows.

Note: P3-1 is designed for instructors who plan to skip Chapter 4.

Journal entries, posting, trial balances (Q3–14)

P3-2 Busy Contractors Corp. was incorporated on December 1, 19X1, and had the following transactions during December.

PART A

Dec. 1 Issued common stock for $5,000
      1 Paid $1,200 for three months' rent: December, January, and February
      1 Purchased a used truck for $10,000 on account
      1 Purchased on account supplies costing $1,000 that will be used during December
      3 Paid $1,800 for a years' insurance coverage on the truck. The policy was dated December 1.
      5 Sent invoices to customers totaling $4,500 for services performed to date
      6 Received $800 for services performed today
     14 Received $2,000 from customers to whom invoices were sent December 5
     14 Paid the following expenses: advertising, $350; interest, $100; telephone, $75; truck, $425; wages, $2,500
     20 Sent invoices to customers totaling $6,500 for services performed to date
     23 Signed a $9,000 contract for services to be performed in January
     28 Paid the following expenses: advertising, $200; interest, $150; truck, $375; wages, $2,500

29 Received $2,000 from customers for services to be performed in January. It is the policy of the company to record such advances as revenue at the time it is received.

31 Received an invoice from the power company in the amount of $100 for electricity used during December

Required

1. Open ledger accounts for the following: Cash, Accounts Receivable, Prepaid Insurance, Prepaid Rent, Truck, Accounts Payable, Common Stock, Service Revenue, Advertising Expense, Interest Expense, Supplies Expense, Telephone Expense, Truck Expense, Utilities Expense, Wages Expense.

2. Prepare journal entries to record the December transactions. Post the entries to the ledger accounts.

PART B

As of December 31, the following information is made available for the preparation of any required adjusting entries.

a. One month of the Prepaid Insurance has expired.

b. The December portion of the December 1 rent payment has expired.

c. A physical count indicates that supplies costing $350 are still on hand.

d. The amount collected on December 29 is unearned at December 31.

e. Busy determined that $1,500 in wages were earned by the employees during the last three days of December. This amount will be paid on the first regular payday in January.

f. The truck has an estimated useful life of 4 years with an estimated salvage value of $880.

Required

3. Open additional ledger accounts for the following: Supplies, Accumulated Depreciation, Wages Payable, Unearned Revenue, Depreciation Expense, Insurance Expense, Rent Expense.

4. Prepare all necessary adjusting entries. Post the entries to the ledger accounts.

5. Prepare an adjusted trial balance as of December 31.

Adjusting entries from adjusted and unadjusted data (Q3, Q4, Q6, Q8–Q11)

P3-3 The following accounts are extracted from the records of Stanley, Inc., as of December 31, its fiscal year-end.

		Unadjusted	Adjusted
		Balance	
a.	Prepaid Rent	$ 300	$ 600
b.	Wages Payable	500	700
c.	Income Tax Payable	-0-	1,000
d.	Unearned Commissions	2,000	3,000
e.	Unearned Revenue	25,000	20,000
f.	Advertising Expense	5,000	3,500
g.	Depreciation Expense—Equipment	-0-	500
h.	Supplies Expense	850	625
i.	Truck Expense	4,000	4,500

Required

For each of the listed accounts, prepare the adjusting entry that was evidently made.

Various adjusting
entries (Q3, Q4, Q6,
Q8–Q11)

P3-4 The trial balance of Hitchcock Films Corp. includes the following account balances as of December 31, 19X1, its fiscal year-end. No adjustments have yet been recorded.

	Debit	Credit
Prepaid Rent	$ 1,500	
Equipment	2,500	
Unearned Advertising		1,000
Insurance Expense	900	
Supplies Expense	600	
Telephone Expense	825	
Wages Expense	15,000	

The following information is available:

a. A physical count of supplies indicates that supplies costing $300 are still unused at the end of the year.

b. Although no invoice from the phone company has been received, it is estimated that these charges will be $75 for the month of December.

c. Hitchcock Films has determined that $125 in wages was earned by the employees during the last working day in December. This amount will be paid on the first regular payday in January.

d. The equipment was purchased December 1; it is expected to last 2 years and its estimated salvage value is $100. No depreciation has been recorded to date.

e. The prepaid rent is for December 19X1 and for January and February 19X2.

f. Half of the advertising has been earned as of December 31.

g. The $900 amount in Insurance Expense is for a one-year policy, effective July 1, 19X1.

Required

Prepare all necessary adjusting entries.

Various adjusting
entries (Q3, Q4, Q6,
Q8–Q11)

P3-5 The trial balance of Stratus Services, Inc., includes the following account balances as of December 31, its fiscal year-end. No adjustments have been recorded.

Temporary Investments	$10,000
Prepaid Insurance	600
Supplies	500
Bank Loan	5,000
Subscription Revenue	9,000
Salaries Payable	500
Rent Expense	3,900
Truck Expense	4,000

The following information is available:

a. The Temporary Investment balance represents an investment in interest-bearing investments; an accrued interest amounting to $250 has not been recorded.

b. The $600 for prepaid insurance is for a one-year policy, effective September 1.

c. A physical count indicates that supplies costing $300 are still on hand.

d. Interest on the bank loan is paid on the 15th day of each month; the unrecorded interest for the last 15 days of December is $25.

e. The Subscription Revenue is for six-month subscriptions to the corporation's *Investment Trends* report; the subscriptions began December 1.

f. Three days of salary amounting to $300 remain unrecorded as of December 31.

g. The monthly rent is $300.

h. The monthly invoice for maintenance on the truck has not been received. The estimated amount is $400.

Required
Prepare all necessary adjusting entries.

P3-6 The following accounts are taken from the record of Harrison Forbes, Inc., at the end of its first 12 months of operations, December 31, 19X1.

Besides the balances in each set of accounts, additional data are provided for adjustment purposes if applicable. Treat each set of accounts independently of the others.

Adjusting entries from T-account data (Q3, Q4, Q6–Q13)

a.

Truck	Depreciation Expense—Truck	Accumulated Depreciation—Truck
7,000		600			600

Additional information: The truck was purchased July 1 and has a useful life of 4 years and an estimated salvage value of $1,000.

b.

Unearned Rent	Rent Earned
	-0-		6,000

Additional information: The monthly rental revenue is $500. A part of Harrison's office was sublet during the entire 12 months at $500 per month.

c.

Supplies	Supplies Expense
		1,250	

Additional information: A physical inventory indicated supplies costing $300 were still on hand.

d.

Prepaid Rent	Rent Expense
1,200		4,400	

Additional information: The monthly rent is $400.

e.

Wages Expense		Wages Payable	
6,000			500

Additional information: Unrecorded wages as of December 31 were $750.

f.

Bank Loan		Interest Expense		Interest Payable	
	8,000	600			100

Additional information: The bank loan bears interest at 10%. The money was borrowed on January 1, 19X1.

g.

Utilities Expense		Utilities Payable	
1,200			200

Additional information: The December statement from the power company had not been received. The estimated amount is $150.

h.

Prepaid Insurance		Insurance Expense	
600		600	

Additional information: A $1,200 one-year insurance policy had been purchased effective April 1, 19X1; no other insurance policy is in effect.

i.

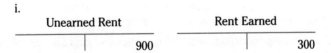

Unearned Rent		Rent Earned	
	900		300

Additional information: The Unearned Rent balance is applicable to November and December 19X1 and January 19X2.

j.

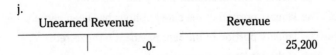

Unearned Revenue		Revenue	
	-0-		25,200

Additional information: $2,000 of the revenue has not been earned as of December 31.

Required

Prepare all necessary adjusting entries.

ALTERNATE PROBLEMS

Journal entries, posting, trial balances, financial statements (Q3–Q14)

AP3-1   Breen Productions, Inc., began operations on January 1, 19X1, with the issuance of common stock in exchange for $50,000.

PART A

The following are from the transactions of Breen Productions, Inc., during January 19X1.

a. Paid salaries of $15,000 during the month

b. Purchased on account supplies costing $750

c. Paid $8,000 for equipment

d. Invested $10,000 in a term deposit

e. Paid $1,200 for a one-year insurance policy, effective January 1

f. Collected $6,000 representing one-year subscriptions, beginning January 1

g. Paid $1,500 for three months of rent

h. Collected $600 for a two-month sublet of part of the company's warehouse, effective January 1

i. Paid $7,000 for a used truck

Required

1. Open ledger accounts for the following: Cash, Temporary Investments, Prepaid Insurance, Prepaid Rent, Supplies, Equipment, Truck, Accounts Payable, Unearned Rent, Unearned Subscriptions, Salaries Expense, Common Stock.

2. Prepare journal entries to record the January transactions. Post the entries to the ledger accounts.

PART B

As of January 31 the following information is made available for the preparation of the month-end adjusting entries.

j. Two days of salary amounting to $1,000 remain unpaid; the amount will be included in the first Friday salary payment in February.

k. A physical count indicates that supplies costing $250 are still on hand.

l. The equipment, purchased in transaction c on January 1, has a useful life of 3 years and an estimated salvage value of $800.

m. A report from the bank indicates that $100 has been earned on the money-market account during the past month. The interest will be paid by the bank at the end of February.

n. One month of the insurance policy has expired.

o. The January portion of the subscriptions has been earned.

p. The January portion of the rent payment has expired.

q. Half of the sublet has been earned.

r. The truck, purchased in transaction i on January 1, has a useful life of 4 years and an estimated salvage value of $1,000.

Required

3. Open additional ledger accounts for the following: Interest Receivable, Salaries Payable, Accumulated Depreciation—Equipment, Accumulated Depreciation—Truck, Interest

Earned, Rent Earned, Subscription Revenue, Depreciation Expense—Equipment, Depreciation Expense—Truck, Insurance Expense, Rent Expense, Supplies Expense.

4. Prepare all necessary adjusting entries. Post the entries to the ledger accounts.

5. Prepare an adjusted trial balance as of January 31.

6. Prepare a complete set of financial statements; an income statement, a balance sheet, and a statement of cash flows.

Note: AP3-1 is designed for instructors who plan to skip Chapter 4.

Journal entries, posting, trial balances (Q3–Q14)

AP3-2   The following transactions are from Storelli Services Corp. during January 19X1. The company started operations in late December with $15,000 invested in exchange for common stock.

PART A

a. Purchased a truck for $15,000

b. Received $12,000 in advance for advertising to be run during the next three months

c. Paid $600 for a one-year insurance policy, effective January 1

d. Received $150 as interest paid in advance on a loan made to a customer

e. Purchased on account supplies costing $500

f. Received $900 in advance for commissions to be earned in the future

g. Invested $5,000 in a money-market account. This is cash the company does not need immediately, but will need in the near future.

h. Paid $5,000 for equipment

i. Received $900 for a three-month sublet of some office space

j. Paid wages in the amount of $3,000 for January

Required

1. Open ledger accounts for the following: Cash, Temporary Investments, Prepaid Insurance, Equipment, Truck, Accounts Payable, Unearned Advertising Revenue, Commissions Earned, Rent Earned, Supplies Expense, Wages Expense, Common Stock, Advertising Revenue, Interest Earned.

2. Prepare journal entries to record the January transactions. Post the entries to the ledger accounts.

PART B

At the end of the month, the following information is made available for the preparation of any required adjusting entries.

k. The truck purchased in transaction *a* on January 1 has a useful life of 5 years and an estimated salvage value of $1,500.

l. One-third of the advertising revenue received in advance has been earned by the end of January.

m. The January portion of the insurance policy has expired.

n. One-half of the interest received in advance has now been earned.

o. A physical count indicates that supplies costing $200 are still on hand.

p. Approximately one-third of the commissions have been earned by the end of January.

q. A report from the bank indicates that $50 has been earned on the money-market account during the past month. The interest will be paid by the bank at the end of February.

r. The equipment, purchased in transaction *h* on January 1, is expected to have a useful life of 4 years and an estimated salvage value of $200.

s. One-third of the three-month sublet has been earned.

t. Three days of wages amounting to $150 remain unpaid; the amount will be included in the first Friday payment in February.

Required

3. Open additional ledger accounts for the following: Supplies, Accumulated Depreciation—Equipment, Accumulated Depreciation—Truck, Wages Payable, Depreciation Expense—Equipment, Depreciation Expense—Truck, Insurance Expense, Interest Receivable, Unearned Interest, Unearned Rent, Unearned Commissions, Unearned Revenue.

4. Prepare all necessary adjusting entries. Post the entries to the ledger accounts.

5. Prepare an adjusted trial balance as of January 31.

Adjusting entries from adjusted and unadjusted data (Q3, Q4, Q6, Q8–Q11)

AP3-3 The following accounts are from the records of Bedford, Inc., as of December 31, its fiscal year-end.

		Balance	
		Unadjusted	Adjusted
a.	Prepaid Insurance	$ 500	$ 300
b.	Supplies	850	400
c.	Accumulated Depreciation—Truck	-0-	1,200
d.	Salaries Payable	2,500	2,600
e.	Unearned Fees	5,000	1,000
f.	Income Tax Payable	-0-	3,500
g.	Revenue	50,000	45,000
h.	Commissions Expense	4,000	5,500
i.	Interest Expense	800	850

Required

For each of these accounts, prepare the adjusting entry that was probably recorded.

Various adjusting entries (Q3, Q4, Q6, Q8–Q11)

AP3-4 The trial balance of Eastwood Productions Corp. includes the following account balances at December 31, 19X1, its fiscal year-end. No adjustments have been recorded.

	Debit	Credit
Prepaid Insurance	$ 1,800	
Truck	19,000	
Unearned Commissions		$ 9,000
Rent Earned		-0-
Advertising Expense	5,000	
Salaries Expense	25,000	
Supplies Expense	900	

The following information is available:

a. A physical count indicates that supplies costing $200 have not been used as of December 31.

b. The prepaid insurance consists of a one-year policy, effective October 1.

c. The truck was purchased on July 1; it is expected to have a useful life of 6 years and its estimated salvage value is $1,000. No depreciation has been recorded during the year.

d. The unearned commissions as of December 31 actually amount to $7,500.

e. Eastwood determined that $200 in wages were earned by employees during the last working day in December. This amount will be paid on the first regular payday in January.

f. A rent payment has not yet been received for a sublet of part of a warehouse for two weeks during December. Payment of the $300 has been promised for the first week in January.

g. December advertising amounted to $300. The invoice has not been received as of the end of December.

Required

Prepare all necessary adjusting entries.

Various adjusting entries (Q3, Q4, Q6, Q8–Q11)

AP3-5 The trial balance of Bishop Court, Inc., includes the following account balances as of December 31, 19X1, its fiscal year-end. No adjustments have been recorded.

Temporary Investments	$15,000
Prepaid Rent	1,200
Bank Loan	7,500
Unearned Subscriptions	9,000
Insurance Expense	2,400
Salaries Expense	75,000
Supplies Expense	600
Utilities Expense	-0-
Supplies	-0-

The following information is available:

a. Accrued interest on the temporary investment amounts to $40 at December 31.

b. The prepaid rent is for November and December 19X1, and January 19X2.

c. Accrued interest on the bank loan amounts to $40 as of December 31.

d. One-third of the subscriptions remain unearned as of December 31.

e. Insurance expense includes the cost of a one-year insurance policy, effective January 1, 19X1, and the cost of a one-year renewal, effective January 1, 19X2. The premium cost for each year is $1,200.

f. Two days of salary have not yet been accrued at December 31; the usual salary for a five-day week is $2,500.

g. A physical count indicates that supplies costing $100 are still on hand.

h. The monthly invoice from the power company has not been received. The estimated amount is $200.

Required

Prepare all necessary adjusting entries.

Adjusting entries from
T-account data (Q3, Q4,
Q6–Q13)

AP3-6   The following accounts are taken from the records of Erma Brooks, Inc., at the end of its first 12 months of operations, December 31, 19X1. In addition to the balances in each set of accounts, additional data are provided for adjustment purposes, if applicable. Treat each set of accounts independently.

a.

Prepaid Rent	Rent Expense
-0-	5,200

Additional information: The monthly rent is $400.

b.

Bank Loan	Interest Expense	Interest Payable
10,000	850	-0-

Additional information: Unpaid interest on the bank loan amounts to $150.

c.

Supplies	Supplies Expense
-0-	800

Additional information: Supplies still on hand amount to $300.

d.

Salaries Expense	Salaries Payable
5,000	-0-

Additional information: Salaries earned by the employees but unpaid as of December 31 amount to $1,000.

e.

Prepaid Advertising	Advertising Expense
800	3,000

Additional information: Prepaid Advertising as of December 31 amounts to $1,200.

f.

Equipment	Depreciation Expense— Equipment	Accumulated Depreciation— Equipment
7,000	500	500

Additional information: The equipment was purchased on July 1 and has a useful life of 5 years with an estimated salvage value of $1,000.

g.

Unearned Rent		Rent Earned	
	-0-		10,000

Additional information: Unearned Revenue at December 31 amounts to $2,500.

h.

Prepaid Insurance		Insurance Expense	
100		500	

Additional information: The monthly insurance amounts to $50; $600 was paid for a one-year policy effective January 1, 19X1.

i.

Utilities Expense		Utilities Payable	
875			-0-

Additional information: The December statement from the power company had not been received by the end of the month. The estimated amount is $225.

Required
Prepare all necessary adjusting entries.

DECISION PROBLEM

Joe Campbell, a friend of your father, is considering investing in one of two construction corporations. Both began operations on January 1, 1989, and have been in operation for two years. Campbell shows you the following information on each corporation and asks you for your opinion on the financial health of each.

Fair Oaks Construction Corp.

Sales Payment Received 1989	$1,622,500
Expenses 1989	2,427,400
Accounts Receivable (Dec. 31, 1989)	1,947,600
Sales Payment Received 1990	947,400
Expenses 1990	1,747,400
Accounts Receivable (Dec. 31, 1990)	3,427,400

Orangevale Builders, Inc.

Sales Payment Received 1989	$1,240,000
Expenses 1989	977,200
Accounts Receivable (Dec. 31, 1989)	142,500
Sales Payment Received 1990	1,625,500
Expenses 1990	1,222,000
Accounts Receivable (Dec. 31, 1990)	247,000

Campbell also tells you that all of Fair Oaks' accounts receivable are for the construction of a post office in Folsom due for completion on June 1, 1991. The contract calls for a 5% penalty on the full $6 million contract price if the June 1 date is missed by more than 10 days. All construction is ahead of schedule, however, and no problems are anticipated.

Orangevale Builders builds for the residential market and does renovations to existing homes. Currently it has six projects in process.

Before leaving, Campbell also noted that Fair Oaks expects expenses for the first six months of 1991 to be $750,000 and is currently bidding on another post office project it is likely to get. Campbell added that the manager of Orangevale is complaining about the slow turnover of accounts receivable.

Required

1. From the information provided, what can you tell Joe Campbell?

2. What can you deduce about the credit practices of each company?

3. Should Campbell be worried about the large amount of accounts receivable for Fair Oaks?

4. Discuss the matching principle as it relates to these two entities.

5. What other information should Campbell consider before investing?

ANSWERS TO SELF-TEST QUESTIONS

1. **(d)** The true operating cycle is usually much shorter than one year. It amounts to the time it takes to convert cash into inventory, inventory into accounts receivable, and finally accounts receivable into cash. This process usually takes place several times within the accounting period.

2. **(c)** Of the entities listed, only a construction firm might have an operating cycle longer than one year. The fresh-fish market would have a cycle as short as one day, as might a restaurant. A ski resort would have an operating cycle equal to the snow season, and then would have a number of cycles within that ski season.

3. **(d)** Cash received immediately on providing a service will be recorded as revenue at that time. For the examples given in a and c, revenue would be recorded at the time of the sale, while the insurance company would recognize the revenue over the 12 months that the policy is in effect.

4. **(a)** The only answer that makes sense is a. When cash is received from a customer, it would not be recorded as an expense (outflow of an asset) or as an item of equity (claim against an asset). It would be recorded as a liability if the revenue would not be earned within the fiscal year in which it was received. Otherwise it is revenue.

5. **(c)** When a cost outlay is made, it either has a future benefit or no future benefit. If no future benefit is to be derived from the outlay, then it should be recorded as an expense. Otherwise, it should be recorded as an asset.

6. **(b)** The only thing a trial balance proves is that the debits equal the credits. Assuming that the *unadjusted* trial balance is in balance, an adjusted trial balance will balance if the adjustments made to the accounts are in balance.

7. **(b)** Depreciation Expense is an expense, just as salaries are an expense. The only difference is that salaries have an effect on cash flow while depreciation does not.

8. **(a)** A true mixed income statement account has an asset or a liability as part of its balance. The balance sheet portion must be identified and transferred to an asset or liability account.

9. **(c)** Accrued revenue is revenue that has been earned but not received. Both *a* and *b* represent revenue that has been received but not earned.

10. **(e)** All items listed are the result of the application of the matching principle. Each results from the process of matching expenses incurred against revenue earned in order to arrive at net income.

4 GAAP AND THE OPERATING CYCLE: PART TWO

As noted in Chapter 3, this chapter presents the worksheet approach to financial statement preparation. In a course mainly directed toward decision making, Chapter 4 could be eliminated without affecting required background information. The chapter describes the content and purpose of the worksheet, demonstrating how financial statements can be prepared directly from it. The concept of closing entries is introduced and their need demonstrated. After reversing entries are examined, the steps in the accounting process are again summarized.

After studying Chapter 4, you should be able to answer the following questions:

1 How does a worksheet assist in the preparation of financial statements? (pp.160–61)

2 Why are closing entries prepared, and what exactly is the closing procedure? (pp.166–70)

3 What is the purpose of a post-closing trial balance? (p.170)

4 What are reversing entries, and why are they prepared? (pp.172–73)

5 What steps occur continuously during the accounting period? (p.173)

6 What steps occur whenever interim or year-end financial statements are prepared? (p.173)

7 Which steps occur only at the fiscal year-end? (p.173)

8 How does preparation of reversing entries minimize the possibility of errors? (pp.173–74)

9 What simple rule is useful in the preparation of reversing entries for accruals? (pp.175–76)

THE WORKSHEET

Accountants usually use a columnar schedule to aid in preparing financial statements. This columnar schedule is called a **worksheet.** In Chapter 3, a trial balance for Saguaro Computers, Inc., was prepared as a separate schedule, following the recording and posting of the corporation's December transactions. As an alternate practice, the trial balance could be recorded directly on the worksheet. The arrangement of a typical worksheet consists of a series of debit and credit columns, as shown in Exhibit 4-1.

Q1: How worksheet helps

The worksheet is not a formal accounting record, as are the journal and ledger. Rather, it is an intermediate step that bridges the gap between the accounting records and the financial statements, serving as a tool for the accountant to prepare the formal financial statements. (See Exhibit 4-2.)

The worksheet organizes the many details brought together when statements are being prepared. It also provides an opportunity to check financial data; since its debit and credit column totals prove the equality of the account balances. An error is indicated whenever total debits do not equal total credits in any pair of columns. The worksheet is also a convenient place to calculate the net income or

EXHIBIT 4-1											

THE WORKSHEET

Account Number	Account Title	Trial Balance		Adjustments		Adjusted Trial Balance		Income Statement		Balance Sheet	
		Dr.	Cr.	Dr.	Cr.	Dr.	Cr.	Dr.	Cr.	Dr.	Cr.
		1		2		3		4		5	

The worksheet columns are explained below.

1. The debit and credit account balances are entered in these columns directly from the general ledger.
2. The adjusting entries for the period are recorded on the worksheet in the second pair of debit and credit columns.
3. The amounts in the preliminary trial balance and adjustment columns are combined, and the new balances are recorded in this third pair of debit and credit columns; these totals are referred to as an adjusted trial balance.
4. The revenue and expense account balances listed in the adjusted trial balance columns are transferred to the income statement debit and credit columns. The income statement will later be prepared from the amounts listed in these columns.
5. The asset, liability, and equity account balances listed in the adjusted trial balance columns are transferred to the balance sheet debit and credit columns. The statement of retained earnings and the balance sheet will later be prepared from the amounts listed in these columns.

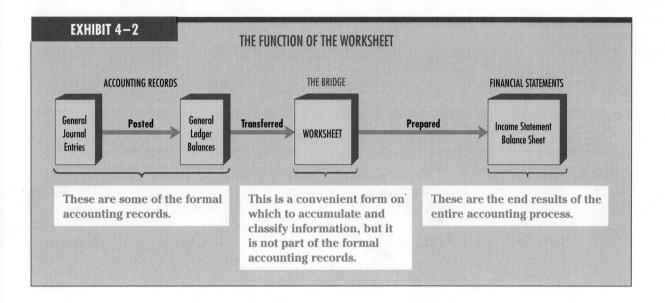

EXHIBIT 4-2

THE FUNCTION OF THE WORKSHEET

ACCOUNTING RECORDS   THE BRIDGE   FINANCIAL STATEMENTS

General Journal Entries → **Posted** → General Ledger Balances → **Transferred** → WORKSHEET → **Prepared** → Income Statement Balance Sheet

These are some of the formal accounting records.

This is a convenient form on which to accumulate and classify information, but it is not part of the formal accounting records.

These are the end results of the entire accounting process.

net loss for the period. It gives the accountant a preview of the final financial statements before their preparation.

A worksheet is unnecessary in practice if only a few accounts are in the trial balance and if only a few adjusting entries are required. The worksheet is very useful, however, when numerous accounts and adjustments must be organized before financial statements are prepared. In the case of Saguaro Computers, Inc., the December 31 worksheet might not be used by an experienced accountant, although its use may be convenient. In recent years, computers have lessened the need for worksheets in automated systems.

In the next few pages, a worksheet for SCI at December 31 is prepared to demonstrate the methodology. The use of the worksheet in the preparation of the corporation's year-end financial statements is also examined.

Recording a Trial Balance in the Worksheet

When all December transactions are journalized and posted, a trial balance is prepared on the worksheet to prove the equality of debit and credit balances in the ledger. The trial balance is recorded directly on the worksheet to prevent the duplication that would result from preparing the trial balance elsewhere and then transferring the identical information to the worksheet. Exhibit 4-3 illustrates the four steps required in worksheet preparation, discussed next.

STEP 1: THE TRIAL BALANCE IS RECORDED DIRECTLY IN THE WORKSHEET.

Accountants often refer to this trial balance as the *unadjusted trial balance,* because the adjusting entries required to match revenues with expenses are not yet included in the account balances. The preparation of financial statements from an unadjusted trial balance would cause misleading information to be communicated.

Following the recording of the unadjusted trial balance in the worksheet, the adjusting entries are entered in the second pair of columns.

EXHIBIT 4–3

THE WORKSHEET
Saguaro Computers, Inc.
For the Period Ended December 31, 19X1

| | | (Step 1) | | (Step 2) | | (Step 3) | | (Step 4) | | | |
| | | Trial Balance | | Adjustments | | Adjusted Trial Balance | | Income Statement | | Balance Sheet | |
Account Number	Account Title	Dr.	Cr.	Dr.	Cr.	Dr.	Cr.	Dr.	Cr.	Dr.	Cr.
101	Cash	11,695				11,695				11,695	
110	Accounts Receivable	3,500				3,500				3,500	
120	Notes Receivable	5,000				5,000				5,000	
161	Prepaid Insurance	1,200			(a) 100	1,100				1,100	
183	Equipment	2,000				2,000				2,000	
184	Truck	8,000				8,000				8,000	
201	Bank Loan		5,000				5,000				5,000
210	Accounts Payable		1,900				1,900				1,900
248	Unearned Rent		600	(b) 200			400				400
320	Common Stock		10,000				10,000				10,000
340	Retained Earnings		0								
450	Repair Revenue		23,895	(e) 2,000			21,895		21,895		
654	Rent Expense	1,200				1,200		1,200			
656	Salaries Expense	5,000		(h) 150		5,150		5,150			
668	Supplies Expense	2,100			(f) 495	1,605		1,605			
670	Truck Expense	1,400				1,400		1,400			
676	Utilities Expense	300				300		300			
	Totals	41,395	41,395								
631	Insurance Expense			(a) 100		100		100			
440	Rent Earned				(b) 200		200		200		
623	Deprec. Exp.-Eqpmt.			(c) 30		30		30			
193	Accum. Deprec.-Eqpmt.				(c) 30		30				30
624	Deprec. Exp.-Truck			(d) 240		240		240			
194	Accum. Deprec.-Truck				(d) 240		240				240
247	Unearned Repair Rev.				(e) 2,000		2,000				2,000
173	Supplies			(f) 495		495				495	
116	Interest Receivable			(g) 25		25				25	
430	Interest Earned				(g) 25		25		25		
226	Salaries Payable				(h) 150		150				150
632	Interest Expense			(i) 95		95		95			
222	Interest Payable				(i) 95		95				95
830	Income Tax Expense			(j) 6,000		6,000		6,000			
260	Income Tax Payable				(j) 6,000		6,000				6,000
	Totals			9,335	9,335	47,935	47,935	16,120	22,120	31,815	25,815
	Net Income							6,000			6,000
	Totals							22,120	22,120	31,815	31,815

The equality of these columns is proved to help ensure that no errors have been made.

Total Debit Balances = Total Credit Balances

STEP 2: THE ADJUSTMENTS ARE RECORDED IN THE APPROPRIATE COLUMNS OF THE WORKSHEET.

The adjustments prepared in Chapter 3 are recorded on the worksheet and identified by the following key letters:

(a)   The December expense portion of prepaid insurance

(b)   The December revenue portion of unearned rent

(c)   Depreciation on the equipment during December

(d)   Depreciation on the truck during December

(e)   The amount of unearned revenue in December

(f)   Repair supplies on hand at the end of December

(g)   Interest earned on note during December

(h)   Salaries accrued as of December 31

(i)   Interest expense on bank loans

(j)   Estimated income taxes as of December 31.

STEP 3: THE AMOUNTS IN THE TRIAL BALANCE COLUMNS ARE COMBINED WITH THOSE IN THE ADJUSTMENTS COLUMNS.

The accountant uses the worksheet to organize the many details that have to be brought together from the ledger and the schedule of adjustments before the financial statements can be prepared. After the recording of adjusting entries on the worksheet, an adjusted trial balance is calculated in the third pair of columns.

STEP 4: THE AMOUNTS IN THE ADJUSTMENTS COLUMNS ARE TRANSFERRED TO THE INCOME STATEMENT AND BALANCE SHEET COLUMNS.

The adjusted trial balance columns are transferred either to the income statement columns or to the balance sheet columns in this way:

$$\left.\begin{array}{l}\text{Expense Accounts}\\\text{Revenue Accounts}\end{array}\right\} \rightarrow \text{Income Statement Columns}$$

$$\left.\begin{array}{l}\text{Asset Accounts}\\\text{Liability Accounts}\\\text{Equity Accounts}\end{array}\right\} \rightarrow \text{Balance Sheet Columns}$$

Balancing the Worksheet

The income statement and balance sheet debit and credit columns are now totaled. The difference between the totals of the income statement columns is the net income of $6,000 at December 31; a net income exists because the total of the credit column exceeds the total of the debit expenses column. The $6,000 difference is entered in the income statement debit column and in the balance sheet credit column, as shown next.

Entering Net Income on this line brings the columns into balance. This is the self-balancing feature of the accounting equation.

Account Title	Adjusted Trial Balance		Income Statement		Balance Sheet	
	Dr.	Cr.	Dr.	Cr.	Dr.	Cr.
Totals	47,935	47,935	16,120	22,120	31,815	25,815
Net Income			6,000			6,000
Totals						

The next step in the completion of the worksheet is the addition of the income statement and balance sheet columns.

Account Title	Adjusted Trial Balance		Income Statement		Balance Sheet	
	Dr.	Cr.	Dr.	Cr.	Dr.	Cr.
Totals	47,935	47,935	16,120	22,120	31,815	25,815
Net Income			6,000			6,000
Totals			22,120	22,120	31,815	31,815

Note that the totals in the two income statement columns are equal, and that the totals in the two balance sheet columns are also equal. These balances indicate the equality of debits and credits maintained in recording the trial balance and adjustments in the worksheet. The fact that debits equal credits indicates that all calculations in the worksheet are mathematically correct.

If the worksheet reveals that expenses exceed revenues during a period (that is, when there is a net loss), the procedure is as follows:

Account Title	Adjusted Trial Balance		Income Statement		Balance Sheet	
	Dr.	Cr.	Dr.	Cr.	Dr.	Cr.
Totals	50,000	50,000	8,000	5,000	42,000	45,000
Net Loss				3,000 ←→ 3,000		
Totals			8,000	8,000	45,000	45,000

In this case, a $3,000 net loss exists, since the total of the income statement debit column exceeds that of the income statement credit column. The $3,000 difference is recorded in the income statement credit column and in the balance sheet debit column, and the columns are totaled.

PREPARATION OF FINANCIAL STATEMENTS FROM THE WORKSHEET

The data listed in the income statement and balance sheet columns of the worksheet are used to prepare the financial statements of Saguaro Computers, Inc., at the end of December. In the following pages, extracts from the worksheet demonstrate the tie-in between the worksheet and end-of-period financial statement preparation.

Income Statement Preparation

The income statement is prepared from the amounts in the income statement columns of the worksheet. Notice in Exhibit 4-4 that all the amounts contained in the income statement columns are rearranged and repeated in the formal statement.

A sole proprietor pays personal income tax on business income; a partner pays personal income tax on his/her share of a partnership's income. Accordingly, the income statement of a proprietorship or partnership does not include an income tax calculation. A corporation, however, pays income tax as a percentage of income from operations; for illustrative purposes, this rate is assumed to be 50%. The 50%

EXHIBIT 4-4

INCOME STATEMENT PREPARATION

Partial Worksheet

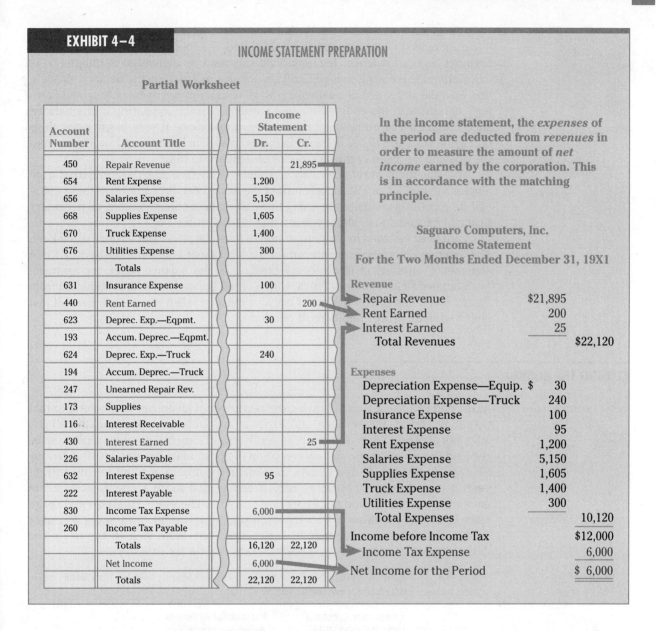

Account Number	Account Title	Income Statement Dr.	Income Statement Cr.
450	Repair Revenue		21,895
654	Rent Expense	1,200	
656	Salaries Expense	5,150	
668	Supplies Expense	1,605	
670	Truck Expense	1,400	
676	Utilities Expense	300	
	Totals		
631	Insurance Expense	100	
440	Rent Earned		200
623	Deprec. Exp.—Eqpmt.	30	
193	Accum. Deprec.—Eqpmt.		
624	Deprec. Exp.—Truck	240	
194	Accum. Deprec.—Truck		
247	Unearned Repair Rev.		
173	Supplies		
116	Interest Receivable		
430	Interest Earned		25
226	Salaries Payable		
632	Interest Expense	95	
222	Interest Payable		
830	Income Tax Expense	6,000	
260	Income Tax Payable		
	Totals	16,120	22,120
	Net Income	6,000	
	Totals	22,120	22,120

In the income statement, the *expenses* of the period are deducted from *revenues* in order to measure the amount of *net income* earned by the corporation. This is in accordance with the matching principle.

Saguaro Computers, Inc.
Income Statement
For the Two Months Ended December 31, 19X1

Revenue
Repair Revenue	$21,895	
Rent Earned	200	
Interest Earned	25	
Total Revenues		$22,120

Expenses
Depreciation Expense—Equip.	$ 30	
Depreciation Expense—Truck	240	
Insurance Expense	100	
Interest Expense	95	
Rent Expense	1,200	
Salaries Expense	5,150	
Supplies Expense	1,605	
Truck Expense	1,400	
Utilities Expense	300	
Total Expenses		10,120
Income before Income Tax		$12,000
Income Tax Expense		6,000
Net Income for the Period		$ 6,000

may seem high at this point, but in all situations a corporation will have to pay federal income tax as high as 34%. In many situations, the entity will have to pay a state income tax that could be as high as 15%, and in some cases, a city income tax. Therefore, assuming a 50% rate on income is not excessive. In a sense, it can be said that government is a silent partner in every business. Stockholders do not pay income tax on the corporation's income; rather, they are subject to tax only on the amount of cash dividends received by them.

Statement of Retained Earnings and Balance Sheet Preparation

Retained earnings represent the net income of a corporation that has been retained in the business; this amounts to $6,000 for Saguaro Computers, Inc., as of December 31, 19X1. The statement of retained earnings is the financial statement that, in effect, links the income statement with the balance sheet. Net income (or net loss) reported in the income statement is added (or deducted, if a loss) to any opening Retained Earnings account balance (less any dividends paid, as illustrated in Chapter 5) in calculating the ending Retained Earnings amount reported on the balance sheet. In this way, the statement of retained earnings reconciles the opening Retained Earnings amount with the ending Retained Earnings amount appearing in the balance sheet. Saguaro has no opening retained earnings, since it only began operations during the year. The $6,000 Retained Earnings balance at December 31, 19X1, becomes the opening Retained Earnings amount on January 1, 19X2.

The statement of retained earnings and the balance sheet are prepared from amounts in the balance sheet columns of the worksheet. Preparation of these financial statements is facilitated by using these worksheet columns, since all necessary financial information is already listed there (see Exhibit 4-5).

Care must be taken in the preparation of financial statements from a worksheet. The debit/credit relationship shown on the worksheet is not emphasized by these statements, although it is obviously present. In the balance sheet, for example, Accumulated Depreciation—Truck, with a credit balance of $240, is deducted from Truck, which has a debit balance. Care also must be taken to use each amount just once and in its proper debit/credit relation.

CLOSING THE BOOKS

Q2: Closing entries and procedure

At the end of a fiscal year, following the recording of all entries that belong to that operating period, the revenue and expense accounts have accumulated all the amounts affecting the business; these *revenue* and *expense accounts* must now be reduced to zero balances, so they can begin to accumulate the amounts that belong to a new fiscal year, and to update the Retained Earnings account for the current year. It is customary in business recordkeeping that these accounts accumulate amounts for a time period not exceeding one year. Therefore, **closing entries** are made to transfer the balances from these **temporary accounts. Permanent accounts** are those that have a continuing balance from one fiscal year to the next. The different types of temporary and permanent accounts are listed below.

At the end of the fiscal year, these accounts must be closed; that is, they must have a zero balance when the new fiscal year begins.

Temporary Accounts	Permanent Accounts
Revenue Accounts	Asset Accounts
Expense Accounts	Liability Accounts
	Stockholders' Equity Accounts

The periodic closing of revenue and expense accounts was not always a bookkeeping practice. Real World Example 4-1 (p. 168) describes a point in the evolution of accounting when accounts were closed less often.

The Closing Procedure

An intermediate summary account, called **Income Summary,** is used to close the revenue and expense accounts. The balances in these accounts are transferred to the Income Summary account. Since December 31 is the year-end of Saguaro Computers, Inc., closing journal entries are prepared at this date. The closing procedure for these accounts is illustrated in Exhibit 4-6 (p. 169) and explained next.

EXHIBIT 4–5

STATEMENT OF RETAINED EARNINGS AND BALANCE SHEET PREPARATION

Partial Worksheet

Account Number	Account Title	Balance Sheet Dr.	Balance Sheet Cr.
101	Cash	11,695	
110	Accounts Receivable	3,500	
120	Notes Receivable	5,000	
161	Prepaid Insurance	1,100	
183	Equipment	2,000	
184	Truck	8,000	
201	Bank Loan		5,000
210	Accounts Payable		1,900
248	Unearned Rent		400
320	Common Stock		10,000
340	Retained Earnings		
450	Repair Revenue		
654	Rent Expense		
656	Salaries Expense		
668	Supplies Expense		
670	Truck Expense		
676	Utilities Expense		
	Totals		
631	Insurance Expense		
440	Rent Earned		
623	Deprec. Exp.—Eqpmt.		
193	Accum. Deprec.—Eqpmt.		30
624	Deprec. Exp.—Truck		
194	Accum. Deprec.—Truck		240
247	Unearned Repair Rev.		2,000
173	Supplies	495	
116	Interest Receivable	25	
430	Interest Earned		
226	Salaries Payable		150
632	Interest Expense		
222	Interest Payable		95
830	Income Tax Expense		
260	Icome Tax Payable		6,000
	Totals	31,815	25,815
	Net Income		6,000
	Totals	31,815	31,815

> This is the date at which the assets, liabilities, and equity of the corporation are taken.

Saguaro Computers, Inc.
Balance Sheet
December 31, 19X1

Assets

Cash		$11,695
Accounts Receivable		3,500
Interest Receivable		25
Notes Receivable		5,000
Prepaid Insurance		1,100
Supplies		495
		$21,815
Equipment	$ 2,000	
Less: Accumulated Depreciation	30	1,970
Truck	$ 8,000	
Less: Accumulated Depreciation	240	7,760
		$31,545

Liabilities

Bank Loan	$ 5,000
Accounts Payable	1,900
Interest Payable	95
Salaries Payable	150
Income Tax Payable	6,000
Unearned Repair Revenue	2,000
Unearned Rent	400
	$15,545

Stockholders' Equity

Common Stock	$10,000	
Retained Earnings	6,000	16,000
		$31,545

> The statement of retained earnings shows the changes that occurred from November 1 to December 31, the end of the time period.

Saguaro Computers, Inc.
Statement of Retained Earnings
For the Two Months Ended December 31, 19X1

Balance, Nov. 1	$ -0-
Add: Net Income	6,000
Balance, Dec. 31	$ 6,000

REAL WORLD EXAMPLE 4-1
Closing Entries in Early Forms of Bookkeeping

In the Europe of around A.D. *1300, many of the elements of modern double-entry accounting were in place—but they were employed more for the keeping of records than for creating financial information. Accounts were sometimes kept open until a trading ship returned to port, for example.*

Early trading firms typically operated in separate ventures. Records of venture costs and receipts had been kept together well before the introduction of double entry. It was natural to continue with the venture as the focus of nominal [income statement] accounts in a double-entry system, particularly since ship captains or other parties were frequently entitled to share in the profits of individual ventures. In contrast, the need for periodic reckonings of profit of the business as a whole was much smaller for many businesses. Typically, a ledger was not closed and balanced except when a new one was to be opened or on special occasions such as the death of a partner. Owners were able to keep on top of their businesses by dint of personal contact, following the results of ventures, and reading the ledgers themselves.

There were some exceptions. Surviving records of banking and manufacturing companies of Florence provide evidence of a more advanced technique. The Medici bank, for example, required annual balance sheets (essentially listings of account balances) from its nine branches in Italy and abroad and used these as a means of control, especially watching for doubtful accounts receivable and excessive loans.* Examples can also be found of financial statements displaying such accrual techniques as prepayments, depreciation accounting, and allowances for taxes and contingencies. . . .

From the fifteenth century on, the advantage in trading and commerce moved from the Mediterranean to the Atlantic as discoveries widened the horizons of western civilization. Spain and Portugal led in the sixteenth century, to be succeeded by England and the Low Countries as maritime power shifted northward. The method of Venice followed the spread of commerce. Although, inevitably, adaptations and improvements were made over the course of time, the recordkeeping uses of accounts remained primary.

---

*See R. de Roover, "The Development of Accounting Prior to Luca Pacioli According to the Account-books of Medieval Merchants," in *Studies in the History of Accounting,* ed. Littleton and Yamey (London: Sweet & Maxwell, 1956), pp. 151–52.

Source Ross M. Skinner, *Accounting Standards in Evolution* (Toronto: Holt, Rinehart and Winston of Canada, Limited, 1987), pp. 8–9. By permission of author.

ENTRY 1: CLOSING THE REVENUE ACCOUNTS

The revenue accounts are closed in one compound closing journal entry to the Income Summary account. (All revenue accounts with credit balances are debited to bring them to zero. Their balances are transferred to the credit side of the Income Summary account.)

ENTRY 2: CLOSING THE EXPENSE ACCOUNTS

The expense accounts are closed in one compound closing journal entry to the Income Summary account. (All expense accounts with debit balances are credited to bring them to zero. Their balances are transferred to the debit side of the Income Summary account.)

EXHIBIT 4–6 CLOSING JOURNAL ENTRIES

Partial Worksheet

Account Number	Account Title	Income Statement Dr.	Cr.
450	Repair Revenue		21,895
654	Rent Expense	1,200	
656	Salaries Expense	5,150	
668	Supplies Expense	1,605	
670	Truck Expense	1,400	
676	Utilities Expense	300	
	Totals		
631	Insurance Expense	100	
440	Rent Earned		200
623	Deprec. Exp.—Eqpmt.	30	
193	Accum. Deprec.—Eqpmt.		
624	Deprec. Exp.—Truck	240	
194	Accum. Deprec.—Truck		
247	Unearned Repair Rev.		
173	Supplies		
116	Interest Receivable		25
430	Interest Earned		
226	Salaries Payable		
632	Interest Expense	95	
222	Interest Payable		
830	Income Tax Expense	6,000	
260	Income Tax Payable		
	Totals	16,120	22,120
	Net Income	6,000	
	Totals	22,120	22,120

General Journal

Date 19X1	Description	F	Debit	Credit
	Closing Entries			
Dec. 31	Repair Revenue		21,895	
	Rent Earned		200	
	Interest Earned		25	
	Income Summary			22,120
	To close revenue account balances			
	Income Summary		16,120	
	Depreciation Expense—Equipment			30
	Depreciation Expense—Truck			240
	Insurance Expense			100
	Interest Expense			95
	Rent Expense			1,200
	Salaries Expense			5,150
	Supplies Expense			1,605
	Truck Expense			1,400
	Utilities Expense			300
	Income Tax Expense			6,000
	To close expense account balances			
	Income Summary		6,000	
	Retained Earnings			6,000
	To close Income Summary account balance			

ENTRY 3: CLOSING THE INCOME SUMMARY ACCOUNT

The Income Summary account is next closed to the Retained Earnings account. The balance in the Income Summary account is transferred to Retained Earnings because the net income (or net loss) belongs to the stockholders.

The caption *Closing Entries* is inserted in the general journal on the line following the last adjusting entry. Unlike regular transaction entries, which require analysis and judgment, the closing process is purely mechanical and involves only the shifting and summarizing of amounts already recorded in the worksheet.

Posting the Closing Entries to the Ledger

As Entries 1 and 2 are posted to the ledger, the balances in all revenue and expense accounts are transferred to the Income Summary account. The posting and transfer of these balances is shown in Exhibit 4-7. Notice that a zero balance remains in each revenue and expense account after the closing entries are posted.

CLOSING REVENUE AND EXPENSE ACCOUNTS

After the closing of the revenue and expense accounts to the Income Summary account, the balance in the Income Summary account is equal to the net income of $6,000.

CLOSING THE INCOME SUMMARY ACCOUNT

The Income Summary account is now closed to Retained Earnings.

The Post-Closing Trial Balance

Q3: Purpose of post-closing trial balance

A **post-closing trial balance** is prepared immediately following the posting of closing entries and before the posting of transactions for the next accounting period. The purpose of its preparation is to ensure that the debits and credits in the general ledger are equal and that all revenue and expense accounts have in fact been closed. Exhibit 4-8 is the post-closing trial balance of Saguaro Computers, Inc. Note that only balance sheet accounts still have balances carried forward to the next accounting period. All revenue and expense accounts begin the new time period with a zero balance, so they can be used to accumulate amounts belonging to that new period. Accordingly, the accounting model, Assets = Liabilities + Equity, is not only the model for the balance sheet, but also the model for the post-closing trial balance.

THE SEQUENCE OF STEPS IN THE ACCOUNTING PROCESS

The periodicity, or time period, concept was introduced and its application explained in the preceding chapters; it assumes that an entity's business activities can be broken into meaningful accounting periods, for which financial statements are prepared. Certain accounting measurement problems result from the periodicity concept; accrual accounting and application of the matching of revenues with expenses are illustrated in Chapter 3.

The accounting process is the way in which the dollar amount of transactions during the accounting period is transformed into financial statement information. A sequence of steps is followed by the accountant during the time period; as noted

EXHIBIT 4-7

POSTING OF CLOSING REVENUE AND EXPENSE ACCOUNTS AND CLOSING OF INCOME SUMMARY ACCOUNT

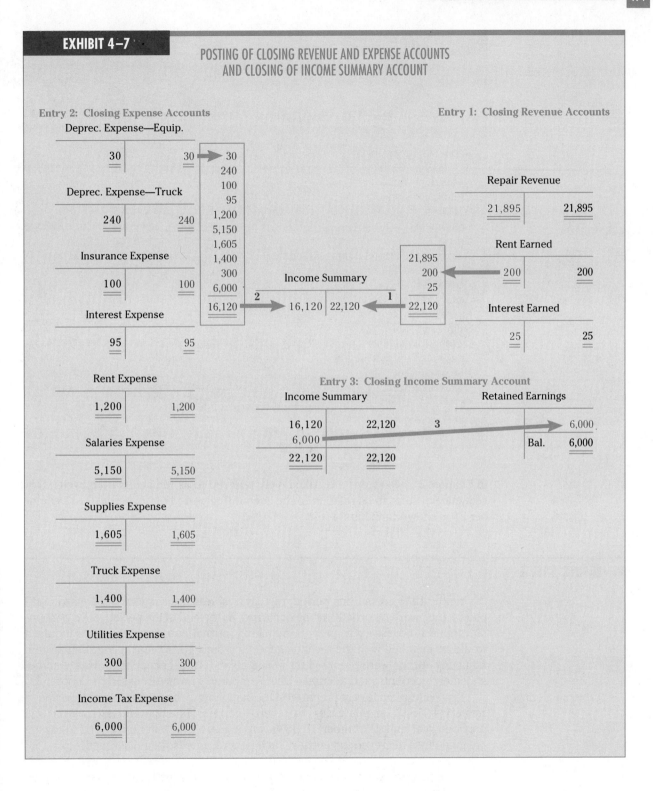

EXHIBIT 4-8			

Saguaro Computers, Inc.
Post-Closing Trial Balance
December 31, 19X1

	Account Balances	
	Debit	Credit
Cash	$11,695	
Accounts Receivable	3,500	
Interest Receivable	25	
Notes Receivable	5,000	
Prepaid Insurance	1,100	
Supplies	495	
Equipment	2,000	
Truck	8,000	
Accumulated Depreciation—Equipment		$ 30
Accumulated Depreciation—Truck		240
Bank Loan		5,000
Accounts Payable		1,900
Interest Payable		95
Salaries Payable		150
Income Tax Payable		6,000
Unearned Repair Revenue		2,000
Unearned Rent		400
Common Stock		10,000
Retained Earnings		6,000
Totals	$31,815	$31,815

in Chapter 2, these steps are collectively referred to as the accounting cycle. This sequence of steps in its relation to the accounting period of November 1 to December 31 is shown in Exhibit 4-9.

REVERSING ENTRIES

During the 19X1 accounting period, regular business transactions of Saguaro Computers, Inc., were recorded as they occurred. At the end of the period, SCI's accountant found it necessary to prepare adjusting journal entries so expenses incurred would be matched with the revenue generated during the same accounting period. Adjusting entries were prepared for mixed balance-sheet accounts, mixed income-statement accounts, and accruals. Their preparation was discussed in Chapter 3.

Q4: Reversing entries

Reversing entries are prepared at the beginning of the next accounting period—January 1, 19X2, in this case—to reverse certain adjusting entries made at the previous year-end, December 31, 19X1, for Saguaro Computers, Inc. The following are guidelines for reversing entries; each general rule is then discussed.

1. The preparation of reversing entries for *accrual* adjustments is recommended for problem solving in this text.

2. Reversing entries should be prepared for mixed income-statement account adjustments.

3. Reversing entries should not be prepared for mixed asset account adjustments.

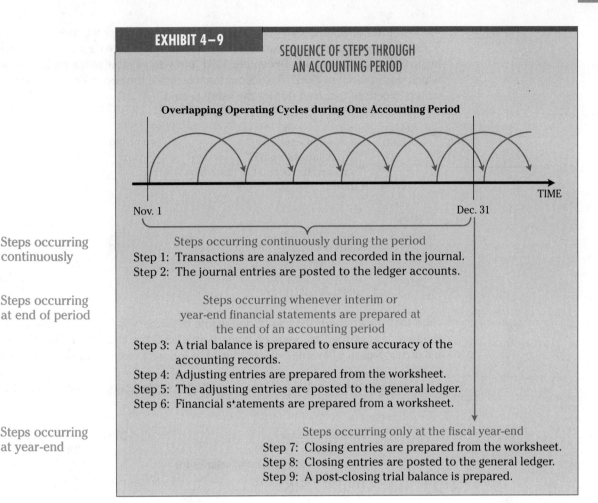

EXHIBIT 4-9

SEQUENCE OF STEPS THROUGH
AN ACCOUNTING PERIOD

Overlapping Operating Cycles during One Accounting Period

TIME

Nov. 1   Dec. 31

Steps occurring continuously during the period
Step 1: Transactions are analyzed and recorded in the journal.
Step 2: The journal entries are posted to the ledger accounts.

Steps occurring whenever interim or
year-end financial statements are prepared at
the end of an accounting period
Step 3: A trial balance is prepared to ensure accuracy of the
accounting records.
Step 4: Adjusting entries are prepared from the worksheet.
Step 5: The adjusting entries are posted to the general ledger.
Step 6: Financial statements are prepared from a worksheet.

Steps occurring only at the fiscal year-end
Step 7: Closing entries are prepared from the worksheet.
Step 8: Closing entries are posted to the general ledger.
Step 9: A post-closing trial balance is prepared.

Q5: Steps occurring
continuously

Q6: Steps occurring
at end of period

Q7: Steps occurring
at year-end

The use of reversing entries promotes the efficient operation of the accounting process, particularly in large corporations where numerous routine transactions are recorded. However, the use of computers in accounting has lessened the need for reversing entries.

Accrual Adjustments

Q8: Reversing entries
to minimize
errors

One category of adjusting entries illustrated in Chapter 3 is accruals. At the end of the accounting period, the accountant of Saguaro Computers, Inc., had found that some ledger accounts were incomplete because some revenues and expenses accrue. No accounting problem is caused by the absence of these items during the accounting period; the matching concept requires, however, that they be recorded when financial statements are prepared. The following SCI accounts required an accrual adjustment at December 31:

Income Statement Accounts	Balance Sheet Accounts
Interest Earned	Interest Receivable
Salaries Expense	Salaries Payable
Interest Expense	Interest Payable
Income Tax Expense	Income Tax Payable

These are the entries that should be reversed.

When no reversing entry is prepared, the following procedure, using one of SCI's adjusting entries as an example, can be followed. Three days of salary amounting to $150 was incurred in December 19X1, but was payable at the end of the week, which was in January 19X2. The accountant recorded the accrual so revenues would match expenses incurred during the same period.

19X1			
Dec. 31	Salaries Expense	150	
	Salaries Payable		150
	To record the accrual of three days' salaries.		

19X2			
Jan. 2	Salaries Expense	100	
	Salaries Payable	150	
	Cash		250
	To record the payroll for the week ended Jan. 2, 19X2.		

Note that the amount of expense applicable to January is only $100, the salary for the two days of the first week of January. In effect, the December 31, 19X1, credit balance in Salaries Payable is now reduced to zero as a result of the entry on January 2, 19X2.

Normally, when salaries are recorded after a year-end, the entry would be as follows:

	Salaries Expense	250	
	Cash		250
	To record the payment of salaries for one week.		

Without reversing entries, the entry necessary to record the first payment of salaries in January is not the normal entry used to record payroll, because the payment of $250 really represents the payment of the liability *salaries payable* as of December 31, 19X1, as well as the payment of salaries for the first two days of January.

PREPARATION OF REVERSING ENTRIES FOR ACCRUALS

Reversing entries are merely the reversal of an adjusting entry recorded at the end of an accounting period. They are dated as of the *first* day of the new period, after the closing entries have been posted, so the balance in all the revenue and expense accounts have been reduced to zero. The reversing entry for the accrual of salaries in the preceding example would be as follows:

19X2			
Jan. 1	Salaries Payable	150	
	Salaries Expense		150
	To reverse the adjusting entry for accrued salaries as of December 31, 19X1.		

The ledger accounts affected would now appear as follows:

Salaries Expense		Salaries Payable		
	150		150	Bal. 150
				-0-

Note that the Salaries Payable account has been reduced to zero as it was in the previous example when no reversing entry was made, but the Salaries Expense account now has a *credit* balance. The entry to pay the salaries on January 2, 19X2, now can be recorded in the normal manner as follows:

19X2
Jan. 2   Salaries Expense   250
              Cash   250

When the above entry is posted to the Salaries Expense account, the balance is $100, representing the salaries for the first two days of January. The ledger account appears as follows:

Salaries Expense	
250	150
Bal. 100	

The use of reversing entries resulted in the same salary expense for the first two days of January as without using reversing entries. However, the entry for the payment of salaries was recorded in the usual manner, thus minimizing errors. This is why it is said that reversing entries promote the operational efficiency of the accounting process.

The reversing entries of the other accruals for SCI follow:

19X1 Adjusting Entry			**19X2 Reversing Entry**		
Interest Receivable	25		Interest Earned	25	
Interest Earned		25	Interest Receivable		25
Interest Expense	95		Interest Payable	95	
Interest Payable		95	Interest Expense		95
Income Tax Expense	6,000		Income Tax Payable	6,000	
Income Tax Payable		6,000	Income Tax Expense		6,000

**19X2 Cash Payment
or Cash Receipt**

Cash	100	
Interest Earned		100
Interest Expense	100	
Cash		100
Income Tax Expense	6,000	
Cash		6,000

Q9: Rule for accruals   This simple rule may be useful in the preparation of reversing entries for accruals: *reverse any previous year's adjusting entry* (19X1 for Saguaro) *that follows with a cash payment or cash receipt the next year* (19X2 for Saguaro). Notice that all the reversing entries in the examples here resulted in a debit or a credit to Cash in the subsequent accounting period.

Mixed Income Statement Account Adjustments

As discussed in Chapter 3, mixed income statement accounts require adjustments. A mixed revenue account includes an unearned amount, such as unearned rent, for example. The unearned amount is therefore recognized as a liability and is transferred to a liability account at the end of the period. Similarly, a mixed expense account includes an unexpired amount; the unexpired amount is recognized as an asset and is transferred to an asset account at the end of the period. Adjusting entries are prepared for mixed accounts so revenues generated during the period are matched with expenses incurred to earn that revenue. Reversing entries should be prepared at the beginning of the next accounting period in order to return balances in mixed asset and liability accounts to their proper, before adjustment, location. The unexpired portion of one year's expense will usually expire in the subsequent year. The unearned portion of one year's revenue will usually be earned in the next year. Therefore, reversing entries transfer these amounts to their original location to remove any confusion that might otherwise result in further recordkeeping.

In effect, preparing reversing entries for mixed income-statement account adjustments allows the records to reflect management policies regarding certain types of transactions. If the policy is to record all payments for insurance as Insurance Expense, and if Prepaid Insurance is debited during the adjustment process, then the entry will have to be reversed in order to transfer the unexpired portion back to the expense account. If the policy is to record all revenue received as revenue, and if some of that revenue is unearned at the end of the year, then that amount is transferred to an Unearned Revenue (liability) account. In order to adhere to that policy, the unearned amount will have to be transferred back to the revenue account at the beginning of the new year.

Illustrative Problem:	**REVERSING ENTRIES FOR MIXED INCOME STATEMENT ACCOUNTS**

Reversing entries should be used to reverse adjustments previously made to mixed income statement accounts. SCI's adjusting entry for repair revenue can provide an example: $2,000 was received in December for repairs that were not done by December 31, 19X1; the repairs are currently scheduled to be made in January or February 19X2. An adjusting entry was prepared at December 31, so revenues earned would match expenses incurred during the same period.

The following reversing entry is made on January 1, 19X2, to return the repair revenue amount to its original location.

19X1 Adjusting Entry				19X2 Reversing Entry		
Dec. 31 Repair Revenue	2,000		Jan. 1	Unearned Repair Revenue	2,000	
Unearned Repair Revenue		2,000		Repair Revenue		2,000

This reversing entry returns to its proper location the amount expected to be earned as revenue in 19X2. In this way, all revenue earned in 19X2 will be recorded in the same account, Repair Revenue.

The other SCI mixed income statement amount recorded in December that required an adjustment was for supplies. A physical inventory of repair parts showed that supplies costing $600 were still on hand, thereby indicating that all supplies had not been used during the month. The original purchase of these parts had been recorded as an expense. The following reversing entry is made:

19X1 Adjusting Entry			19X2 Reversing Entry		
Dec. 31 Supplies	600		Jan. 1 Supplies Expense	600	
Supplies Expense		600	Supplies		600

This reversing entry returns to its proper location the amount expected to be used in January 19X2. In this way, all supplies used in 19X2 will be recorded in the same account, Supplies Expense.

Mixed Balance Sheet Account Adjustments

A mixed asset account includes an amount that has expired during the accounting period. Accordingly, its expired portion is transferred to expenses through an adjusting entry. A mixed liability account includes an amount that has been earned during the period. Therefore, the earned portion is transferred to revenue by an adjusting entry. No reversing entry is required at the beginning of the next accounting period because the balances remaining in the balance sheet accounts are already in their proper location. Regular business transactions can continue to be recorded in these accounts, and, as required, subsequent adjusting entries will remove the expired portion of asset accounts and the earned portion of liability accounts before preparation of the next year's financial statements. By not preparing reversing entries for mixed balance-sheet account adjustments, accountants automatically follow management policy. If the policy is to record a cash payment as an asset, or a cash receipt as a liability, after adjustment the unexpired or unearned amount is recorded in the proper balance sheet account.

Review of the Accounting Cycle

The accounting cycle consists of steps occurring continuously during its time period, steps occurring whenever financial statements are prepared, and steps occurring only at the fiscal year-end. These steps follow.

Steps occurring continuously during the accounting period:

STEP 1: TRANSACTIONS ARE ANALYZED AND RECORDED IN THE JOURNAL.
Journalizing consists of analyzing transactions as they occur, to see how they affect the accounting equation, and then recording the transactions chronologically in the general journal.

STEP 2: THE JOURNAL ENTRIES ARE POSTED TO LEDGER ACCOUNTS.
Posting consists of transferring debits and credits from the general journal to the appropriate ledger accounts. A balance is calculated after the recording of each debit and credit entry.

Steps occurring whenever financial statements are prepared:

STEP 3: THE EQUALITY OF DEBITS WITH CREDITS IS ESTABLISHED TO ENSURE ACCURACY.
Preparing a trial balance consists of listing account names and balances to prove the equality of total debit balances with total credit balances. These balances are listed directly onto the worksheet. The worksheet is then completed.

STEP 4: ADJUSTING JOURNAL ENTRIES ARE PREPARED FROM THE ADJUSTMENT COLUMNS OF THE WORKSHEET.

Preparing adjusting journal entries entails recording in the journal the necessary adjustments to match revenues with expenses.

STEP 5: THE ADJUSTING ENTRIES ARE POSTED TO THE LEDGER.

Posting adjusting entries involves transferring debits and credits from the general journal to the appropriate ledger accounts. A balance is calculated after the posting of each debit and credit entry.

STEP 6: THE SUMMARIZED TRANSACTIONS ARE COMMUNICATED TO INTERESTED PARTIES.

Preparing financial statements consists of using the data listed in the adjusted trial balance columns of the worksheet to prepare the income statement, the statement of retained earnings, and the balance sheet.

Steps occurring only at the fiscal year-end:

STEP 7: CLOSING JOURNAL ENTRIES ARE PREPARED FROM THE WORKSHEET.

Closing journal entries involves closing all revenue and expense accounts and transferring net income (loss) to retained earnings.

STEP 8: THE CLOSING ENTRIES ARE POSTED TO THE LEDGER.

Posting of closing entries consists of transferring debits and credits from the general journal to the appropriate ledger accounts. A balance is calculated after the posting of each debit and credit cntry.

STEP 9: THE EQUALITY OF DEBITS WITH CREDITS IS ESTABLISHED TO ENSURE ACCURACY.

Preparing a post-closing trial balance entails listing account names and balances to prove the equality of total debit and credit balances.

STEP 10: REVERSING ENTRIES ARE PREPARED AND POSTED TO THE LEDGER.

Reversing entries may be prepared after the closing process and, therefore, are dated the first day of the new accounting period, becoming the first transactions of the new period.

CHAPTER REVIEW

1 How does a worksheet assist in the preparation of financial statements? (pp. 160–61)
Financial statements can be prepared from the worksheet without formally posting the adjusting, closing, and reversing entries to the general ledger. Thus the worksheet facilitates the generation of timely financial reports.

2 Why are closing entries prepared, and what exactly is the closing procedure? (pp. 166–70)
Closing entries are necessary to update the balance sheet (retained earnings) and to reduce the balance in each income statement account to zero to get ready for the new fiscal year. The closing procedure includes closing the Revenue, Expense and Income Summary accounts.

3 What is the purpose of a post-closing trial balance? (p. 170)
The post-closing trial balance determines whether the accounts are still in balance

after all the transactions, year-end adjustments, and closing entries have been recorded and posted.

4   What are reversing entries, and why are they prepared? (pp. 172–73)

Reversing entries are simply that, the reversal of an adjusting entry. They are dated the first day of the new fiscal period, after the closing entries have been posted, and help to maintain management accounting policies regarding the recording of certain transactions, and help to facilitate the recording of everyday transactions in the new year.

5   What steps occur continuously during the accounting period? (p. 173)

The recording of economic events in the general journal and the posting of these transactions to the general ledger accounts occur continuously throughout an accounting period.

6   What steps occur whenever interim or year-end financial statements are prepared? (p. 173)

When interim financial statements are needed, a trial balance should be taken, adjusting entries made, an adjusted trial balance taken, and the financial statements then prepared from that adjusted trial balance. Reversing entries also may be necessary after the financial statements are prepared. At year-end, in addition to the above, closing entries will be required.

7   Which steps occur only at the fiscal year-end? (p. 173)

The closing entries are prepared and posted, and a post-closing trial balance is taken. Reversing entries may also be prepared and posted.

8   How does preparation of reversing entries minimize the possibility of errors? (pp. 173–74)

Everyday transactions can be recorded in the normal way without the need to go back to examine the adjusting entry made the previous year.

9   What simple rule is useful in the preparation of reversing entries for accruals? (pp. 175–76)

If an adjusting entry is followed by a cash receipt or disbursement during the next year, the adjusting entry should be reversed.

KEY TERMS

closing entries   (p. 166) The entries that reduce revenue and expense balances to zero in preparation for the next fiscal year, and update the Retained Earnings account for the current year.

income summary   (p. 166) A temporary account used to accumulate all revenue and expense balances at the end of the fiscal year. This account summarizes the net income (or loss) for the period and is closed to the Retained Earnings account.

permanent accounts   (p. 166) Accounts that have a continuing balance from one fiscal year to another; also called *real accounts*. All balance sheet accounts are permanent accounts.

post-closing trial balance   (p. 170) A listing of accounts and their balances after all temporary accounts have been closed; all temporary accounts should have a zero balance.

retained earnings   (p. 165) Net income that is not paid out as dividends; net income that is reinvested in the entity for expansion and growth of the entity.

reversing entries (p. 172) Entries made at the beginning of a new accounting period to reverse an adjusting entry made in the immediately preceding accounting period. The use of reversing entries facilitates the subsequent recording of transactions in the new accounting period.

temporary accounts (p. 166) Accounts that accumulate data for a fiscal year and are closed at the end of the fiscal year; also called *nominal accounts*. All revenue and expense accounts are temporary accounts.

worksheet (p. 160) A multi-column schedule used to organize the many details brought together to facilitate the preparation of financial statements.

SELF-TEST QUESTIONS FOR REVIEW   (Answers are at the end of this chapter.)

Q1
1. The use of a worksheet facilitates the preparation of
    (a) just a balance sheet.
    (b) just an income statement.
    (c) both an income statement and a balance sheet.
    (d) all the financial statements, including a statement of cash flows.

Q1
2. Worksheets are necessary
    (a) to properly prepare the financial statements at the end of an accounting period.
    (b) because someone reviewing the financial statements can trace the amounts back to the worksheet.
    (c) because it is a required part of the financial information package presented to the owners of the entity.
    (d) None of the above, because a worksheet is not necessary to prepare financial statements

Q2
3. Closing entries are prepared
    (a) before adjusting entries are posted.
    (b) before reversing entries are posted.
    (c) after both adjusting and reversing entries.
    (d) before the worksheet is prepared.

Q3
4. A trial balance should be prepared
    (a) before the worksheet is prepared.
    (b) after the worksheet is prepared.
    (c) before the closing entries are posted.
    (d) None of the above is a true statement

Q1
5. When statements are prepared from a worksheet
    (a) the balance sheet must be prepared before the income statement.
    (b) the income statement must be prepared before the balance sheet.
    (c) a statement of retained earnings cannot be prepared since needed information is not contained in the worksheet.
    (d) The statements can be prepared in any order.

Q2
6. The Income Summary account
    (a) appears on the balance sheet.
    (b) appears on the income statement.
    (c) appears on the statement of retained earnings.
    (d) does not appear on any of the statements.

Q7
7. Reversing entries are reflected on the
    (a) trial balance.
    (b) adjusted trial balance.
    (c) post-closing trial balance.
    (d) None of the above

Q7, Q8, Q9

8. Which of the following adjusting entries should not be reversed?
    (a) Entries affecting mixed balance sheet accounts
    (b) Entries affecting mixed income statement accounts
    (c) Entries affecting accrued revenue
    (d) Entries affecting accrued expenses

DEMONSTRATION PROBLEM

The following account balances are taken from the ledger of Andersen Services Corp. at the end of its fiscal year, June 30, 19X5. The corporation began operation on May 1, 19X5.

	Account Balances	
	Debit	Credit
Cash	$ 6,600	
Accounts Receivable	3,400	
Notes Receivable	2,000	
Prepaid Rent	2,400	
Office Supplies	750	
Service Supplies	1,000	
Equipment	12,000	
Accounts Payable		$ 3,600
Notes Payable		2,200
Common Stock		16,000
Revenue		8,335
Maintenance Expense	260	
Telephone Expense	45	
Utilities Expense	80	
Wages Expense	1,600	
Totals	$30,135	$30,135

At the end of June, the following additional information is made available:

a. The Notes Receivable account represents a 60-day, 20%, interest-bearing note signed by a customer on June 30.

b. The monthly rent is $600.

c. A physical count indicates that unused office supplies costing $375 and service supplies costing $600 remain on hand at the end of the fiscal year.

d. Equipment acquired on May 1 has an estimated useful life of 5 years and a salvage value of $1,200.

e. The note payable is to a local bank that charges 20% interest on its unsecured loans. The interest is due at the time the note matures. Interest in the amount of $75 (rounded) has accrued on the note as of June 30.

f. Employee wages that are earned but not paid are $300.

Required

1. Record the trial balance on the worksheet. Enter the following account titles on the worksheet: Service Supplies Expense, Rent Expense, Office Supplies Expense, Depreciation Expense—Equipment, Accumulated Depreciation—Equipment, Interest Expense, Interest Payable, and Wages Payable.

2. Complete the worksheet, using the additional information.

3. From the worksheet, prepare an income statement, a statement of retained earnings, and a balance sheet. (A statement of cash flows cannot be prepared from the information you have available.)

4. From the worksheet, prepare and post the adjusting and closing journal entries.

5. From the ledger, prepare a post-closing trial balance.

6. Prepare all necessary reversing entries if used.

SOLUTION TO DEMONSTRATION PROBLEM

1., 2.

Andersen Services Corp.
Worksheet
For the Year Ended June 30, 19X5

Account Title	Trial Balance Dr.	Trial Balance Cr.	Adjustments Dr.	Adjustments Cr.	Adjusted Trial Balance Dr.	Adjusted Trial Balance Cr.	Income Statement Dr.	Income Statement Cr.	Balance Sheet Dr.	Balance Sheet Cr.
Cash	6,600				6,600				6,600	
Accounts Receivable	3,400				3,400				3,400	
Notes Receivable	2,000				2,000				2,000	
Prepaid Rent	2,400			(b) 1,200	1,200				1,200	
Office Supplies	750			(c) 375	375				375	
Service Supplies	1,000			(c) 400	600				600	
Equipment	12,000				12,000				12,000	
Accounts Payable		3,600				3,600				3,600
Notes Payable		2,200				2,200				2,200
Common Stock		16,000				16,000				16,000
Revenue		8,335				8,335		8,335		
Maintenance Expense	260				260		260			
Telephone Expense	45				45		45			
Utilities Expense	80				80		80			
Wages Expense	1,600		(f) 300		1,900		1,900			
	30,135	30,135								
Rent Expense			(b) 1,200		1,200		1,200			
Service Supplies Expense			(c) 400		400		400			
Office Supplies Expense			(c) 375		375		375			
Deprec. Expense— Equipment			(d) 360		360		360			
Accum. Deprec.— Equipment				(d) 360		360				360
Interest Expense			(e) 75		75		75			
Interest Payable				(e) 75		75				75
Wages Payable				(f) 300		300				300
Totals			2,710	2,710	30,870	30,870	4,695	8,335	26,175	22,535
Net Income							3,640			3,640
Totals							8,335	8,335	26,175	26,175

3.

Andersen Services Corp.
Income Statement
For the Year Ended June 30, 19X5

Revenue		$8,335
Expenses		
Depreciation Expense	$ 360	
Interest Expense	75	
Maintenance Expense	260	
Office Supplies Expense	375	
Rent Expense	1,200	
Service Supplies Expense	400	
Telephone Expense	45	
Utilities Expense	80	
Wages Expense	1,900	
Total Expenses		4,695
Net Income		$3,640

Andersen Services Corp.
Statement of Retained Earnings
For the Year Ended June 30, 19X5

Balance, May 1	-0-
Add: Net Income	$3,640
Balance, June 30	$3,640

Andersen Services Corp.
Balance Sheet
June 30, 19X5

Assets			Liabilities		
Current Assets			*Current Liabilities*		
Cash	$6,600		Accounts Payable	$3,600	
Accounts Receivable	3,400		Notes Payable	2,200	
Notes Receivable	2,000		Interest Payable	75	
Prepaid Rent	1,200		Wages Payable	300	
Office Supplies	375		Total Current Liabilities		$6,175
Service Supplies	600				
Total Current Assets		$14,175			
Long-term Assets			**Stockholders' Equity**		
Equipment	$12,000		Common Stock	$16,000	
Less: Accum. Deprec.	360		Retained Earnings	3,640	
Total Long-term Assets		11,640	Total Stockholders' Equity		19,640
			Total Liabilities and		
Total Assets		$25,815	Stockholders' Equity		$25,815

4.

Andersen Services Corp.
General Journal
Page 2

Date 19X5		Description	F	Debit	Credit
		Adjusting Entries			
(a)		No Entry Required			
(b)	June 30	Rent Expense	654	1,200	
		Prepaid Rent	162		1,200
(c)	30	Office Supplies Expense	650	375	
		Office Supplies	170		375
(c)	30	Service Supplies Expense	667	400	
		Service Supplies	172		400
(d)	30	Depreciation Expense—Equipment	623	360	
		Accumulated Depreciation—Equipment	193		360
(e)	30	Interest Expense	632	75	
		Interest Payable	222		75
(f)	30	Wages Expense	677	300	
		Wages Payable	237		300

Andersen Services Corp.
General Journal
Page 3

Date 19X5	Description	F	Debit	Credit
	Closing Entries			
June 30	Revenue	460	8,335	
	Income Summary	360		8,335
30	Income Summary	360	4,695	
	Depreciation Expense—Equipment	623		360
	Interest Expense	632		75
	Maintenance Expense	641		260
	Office Supplies Expense	650		375
	Rent Expense	654		1,200
	Service Supplies Expense	667		400
	Telephone Expense	669		45
	Utilities Expense	676		80
	Wages Expense	677		1,900
30	Income Summary	360	3,640	
	Retained Earnings	340		3,640

Andersen Services Corp.
General Ledger

Cash	No. 101	Accounts Payable	No. 210	Common Stock	No. 320
6,600			3,600		16,000

Accounts Receivable	No. 110	Notes Payable	No. 220	Retained Earnings	No. 340
3,400			2,200	(30)	3,640

Notes Receivable			No. 120
2,000			

Prepaid Rent			No. 162
2,400	(b)	1,200	
Bal.	1,200		

Office Supplies			No. 170
750	(c)	375	
Bal.	375		

Service Supplies			No. 172
1,000	(c)	400	
Bal.	600		

Equipment		No. 183
12,000		

Accum. Deprec.— Equipment			No. 193
	(d)	360	

Interest Payable			No. 222
	(e)	75	

Wages Payable			No. 237
	(f)	300	

Income Summary			No. 360
(30)	4,695	(30)	8,335
(30)	3,640		
	8,335		

Revenue			No. 460
(30)	8,335		8,335

Deprec. Expense— Equipment			No. 623
(d)	360	(30)	360

Interest Expense			No. 632
(e)	75	(30)	75

Maintenance Expense			No. 641
	260	(30)	260

Office Supplies Expense			No. 650
(c)	375	(30)	375

Rent Expense			No. 654
(b)	1,200	(30)	1,200

Service Supplies Expense			No. 667
(c)	400	(30)	400

Telephone Expense			No. 669
	45	(30)	45

Utilities Expense			No. 676
	80	(30)	80

Wages Expense			No. 677
	1,600		
(f)	300		
	1,900	(30)	1,900

5.

Andersen Services Corp.
Post-Closing Trial Balance
June 30, 19X5

	Account Balances	
	Debit	Credit
Cash	$ 6,600	
Accounts Receivable	3,400	
Notes Receivable	2,000	
Prepaid Rent	1,200	
Office Supplies	375	
Service Supplies	600	
Equipment	12,000	
Accumulated Depreciation		$ 360
Accounts Payable		3,600
Notes Payable		2,200
Interest Payable		75
Wages Payable		300
Common Stock		16,000
Retained Earnings		3,640
Totals	$26,175	$26,175

$$\frac{\text{Total}}{\text{Debits}} = \frac{\text{Total}}{\text{Credits}}$$

6.

Andersen Services Corp.
General Journal   Page 4

Date 19X5	Description	F	Debit	Credit
	Reversing Entries			
July 1	Interest Payable	222	75	
	Interest Expense	632		75
1	Wages Payable	237	300	
	Wages Expense	677		300

DISCUSSION QUESTIONS

Q4-1   Accountants usually use a columnar schedule to aid in preparing financial statements. What is this columnar schedule called and how is it used?

Q4-2   Is the worksheet a formal accounting record, as are the journal and the ledger?

Q4-3   Under what circumstances is the use of a worksheet unnecessary?

Q4-4   Why is a trial balance recorded directly on a worksheet in practice? How do accountants refer to this trial balance?

Q4-5   Describe how the income statement and balance sheet columns of a worksheet are balanced.

Q4-6   The debit/credit relationship shown on the worksheet is not shown in the financial statements. Explain.

Q4-7   Customarily, in business recordkeeping, income statement accounts accumulate amounts for a time period not exceeding one year. Why is this custom necessary?

Q4-8   Identify which accounts are temporary and which are permanent.

Q4-9   What are the entries used to close the books at the fiscal year-end?

Q4-10 What is the Income Summary account, and why is one used?

Q4-11 Why is a post-closing trial balance prepared?

Q4-12 List the accounting steps when a worksheet is used.

DISCUSSION CASE
Enormous Successful Corporation

Consolidated Year-End Balance Sheet

Assets

Current Assets	19X6	19X5
Cash	$ 3,253,747,801	$1,157,353,991
Certificates of Deposit (note A)	3,000	41,664,812
Accounts Receivable (note B)	41,664,812	3,000
Other (note C)	24	24
Securities	806,459,528	317,655,290
	$ 4,101,875,165	$1,516,677,117
Less: Allowance for Doubtful Accounts (note D)	(41,664,812)	(39,969)
Inventories (note E)	821,000,002	721,000,002
Prepaid Expenses	89,997,765	1,630,599,554
Total Current Assets (note F)	$ 4,971,208,120	$3,868,236,704
Property, Plant, and Equipment (note G)	189,292,654	136,834,769
Intangibles	5	
Other Assets	4,896,977,562	4,996,997,562
Total Assets	$10,057,478,341	$9,002,069,035

Liabilities and Stockholders' Equity

Current Liabilities	19X6	19X5
Current Maturities of Long-Term Debt (note H)	$ 4,285,314	$ 4,385,414
Short-Term Notes Payable	624,833,824	624,833,826
Accounts Payable	432,198,765	198,765,432
Income Taxes Payable (note I)	321,987,654	87,654,321
Salaries, Wages, Commissions, etc.	160,998,827	160,998,837
Other	100,000,000	90,000,000
Total Current Liabilities	$ 1,644,304,384	$1,166,637,830
Deferred Income Taxes	$ 877,766,655	$ 988,877,766
Commitments and Contingent Liabilities (note J)	523,412	412,632,412
Stockholders' Equity		
Preferred Stock	305,816,903	245,355,077
Common Stock	436,258	436,278
Additional Paid-In Capital (note K)	7,242,630,729	6,288,129,672
Accumulated Deficit	(14,000,000)	(100,000,000)
Total Stockholders' Equity	$ 7,534,883,890	$6,433,921,027
Total Liabilities and Stockholders' Equity	$10,057,478,341	$9,002,069,035

To Our Stockholders:

We are pleased to announce that 19X6 was a very good year for your company, ENORMOUS SUCCESSFUL CORPORATION. In spite of uncertainties in Guatemala and a clouded outlook in Paterson, New Jersey, your company's assets increased by $1,055,409,306, easily keeping pace with liabilities. Our product groups improved their mix; our subsidiaries were written down; and our divisions were written *up*. Much of this success is a result of your company's decision in 19X1 to continue the operations of Bushey Dynamics, which had been operating at a sizable loss for as long as anyone could remember. Bushey is still presenting a debit profile, and its negative input produced this year a $480,000,000 tax-loss carry-over which justified the inclusion in "Other Assets" of a $748 extraordinary credit from the reserve taken the previous year for estimated write-down assets in 19X2. But why pat ourselves on the back? This balance sheet speaks for itself!

Covington Hornchurch
Chairman and President

Notes

A: CERTIFICATES OF DEPOSIT

Cycil Hornchurch, a director of your company, recommended that these certificates be withdrawn from the Second National Bank of Flat Bluff, Kentucky, because last May 24 a teller at the Second National Bank treated Mrs. Hornchurch with extreme disrespect.

B: ACCOUNTS RECEIVABLE

This is the amount outstanding on a loan made by your company to Tory Hornchurch, Jr., a promising young pork-belly trader. (To explain the amusing coincidence in surnames, Tory Hornchurch, Sr., is your Chairman's second-youngest brother.) The first repayment install-ment of $11,000,000, plus .002 percent interest, is expected any day now.

C: OTHER

This amount is a refund owed your company by the New York Telephone Company. Your company has written them eight letters about this item, since February, 19X5, and it is starting to get a little "hot under the collar."

D: DOUBTFUL ACCOUNTS

A precautionary listing, based on the fact that no one has heard from Tory Hornchurch, Jr., since he left for Peru's Urubamba Valley last August "to photograph a rare species of but-terfly" (his exact words).

E: INVENTORIES

Inventories are computed under the first-in, first-out method for the hard, fast-spinning, and breakable products group; under the last-in, last-out method for the slimy products group; and under the half-in, half-out method for the tall, skinny, pulverized products group. It should also be noted that, in 19X6, Porcumpansen-Bushey, one of our subsidiaries, changed its night for closing up shop and taking inventory from the first Monday of each month to the *second Tuesday*.

F: DISCONTINUED OPERATIONS

Every once in a while your company decides to discontinue an operation. Last March, for example, Bushey Dynamics stopped making wire rakes; in May, the Hornchurch Oilstone Factory floated away. In such cases, assets are usually diminished.

G: PROPERTY, PLANT, AND EQUIPMENT

Property, plant and equipment consists of land, buildings, machinery, furniture, and fixtures. Last March, Biff Klassfelder, the treasurer of ENORMOUS SUCCESSFUL CORPORATION, prepared a detailed list of your property, plant, and equipment, but it now appears that this list has somehow been obtained by Sheikh Abdul Hamanhi, of Qatar, who has promised to return it soon. Forehandedly, Biff had also written the totals on the inside of a matchbook. Property, plant, and equipment are carried at cost, naturally. Depreciation is on the straight-line method for financial statement purposes and on the bent-line method for tax purposes. Expenditures for repairs and minor betterments (such as the bells in our standby mainte-nance-inventory-exchange sub-office, which now go "ding" instead of "grr") are charged against operations.

H: LONG-TERM DEBT

The composition of long-term debt as of December 31, 19X6, is as follows:

IOUs held by Sheikh Hamanhi	$314,285,414,275
Mortgages on land and buildings (due 19X8)	975,314,453
Time payments on the Assistant Treasurer's Cadillac	4,010
Total	$315,260,732,738

I: INCOME TAXES

Your company and its subsidiaries file consolidated state and federal income tax returns, which are very, very complicated.

J: COMMITMENTS AND CONTINGENT LIABILITIES

As of December 31, 19X6, your company and its subsidiaries are obligated to pay $654,523,412 in fees to Claus F. Bushey and his brother, Bernie. Bernie Bushey, to be sure, owes $654,523,412 to Cyril Hornchurch, who has a tax-loss carry-forward from a 19X4 sale of wire rakes to the Greek & Italian Canned Salad & Spinach Corporation, of Harrisburg, Pennsylvania, which is owned by Claus F. Bushey's daughter-in-law. In addition, the Porcumpansen Corporation, which is a partly owned subsidiary of the Greek & Italian Canned Salad & Spinach Corporation and of K. C. Bushey and Sons, Inc.—a division of Bushey Dynamics—has contracted to have a two-car garage and sauna constructed at your company's executive Rest and Rehabilitation Center, at Gerber's Lake, at an estimated cost of $312,500. This facility will be leased to Dr. Cyril Hornchurch, Jr., Inc., a wholly owned subsidiary, at a rent yet to be determined. Meantime, Biff Klassfelder is listing our commitments and contingent liabilities in the $523,412 range.

As for the anti-trust suit that has been filed by the Justice Department against our Porcumpansen Low-Flying Avionics division, your company's lawyers cannot, of course, predict on which side the Supreme Court will come down, but your company does not believe in any case that the $2,500,000 judgment would have a lasting adverse effect on your company's operations, because Porcumpansen Low-Flying Avionics is carried on the books of its parent company, the Porcumpansen Corporation, at no value, and because Moleff-Dynamics (the parent company of the Porcumpansen Corporation) has not guaranteed the operations of Porcumpansen's subsidiaries, on the ground of "incomprehensibility."

K: ADDITIONAL PAID-IN CAPITAL

If Biff Klassfelder didn't put exactly the right amount on this line, liabilities would not equal assets.

Source Adapted from James Munves, "Annual Report," *The New Yorker,* March 7, 1977, pp. 32–33.

For Discussion

1. The transactions for an entity are first analyzed and then recorded; they are next summarized by account. From a review of the balance sheet and notes of the Enormous Successful Corporation, what observations can you make about the accounting process underlying the preparation of its balance sheet?

2. a. One concern of stockholders centers on the quality of management and the compensation it receives. From your reading of the preceding balance sheet and notes, what judgments can you make about these features at ESC? Provide specific details to support your answer.

   b. One concern of investors (which includes stockholders) is the way decisions about investments are made in a particular entity. How would you, as an investor in ESC, react to this balance sheet? Provide specific examples to support your answer.

3. For the reader of financial statements who is unfamiliar with accounting, how useful is any balance sheet and notes? Would an income statement be more useful?

4. Howard Ross has been quoted as saying about users of financial statements that: "Users get used to using what they are given. Investors who cannot get by with the information available are, I suppose, eliminated by a sort of Darwinian process—through losing the stuff to invest with." Comment on this observation.

EXERCISES

Preparing a worksheet from incomplete data (Q1)

E4-1   The following is an incomplete worksheet of Bernotas Corp. at its fiscal year-end, June 30, 19X2.

Bernotas Corp.
Worksheet
For the Year Ended June 30, 19X2

Account Title	Trial Balance Dr.	Trial Balance Cr.	Adjustments Dr.	Adjustments Cr.	Adjusted Trial Balance Dr.	Adjusted Trial Balance Cr.	Income Statement Dr.	Income Statement Cr.	Balance Sheet Dr.	Balance Sheet Cr.
Cash	600								?	
Accounts Receivable	?								1,500	
Prepaid Insurance	600			?					200	
Prepaid Rent	400			?					200	
Supplies	750			?					500	
Truck	5,000								?	
Accounts Payable		?								?
Common Stock		1,000								?
Revenue		9,000						?		
Advertising Expense	450						450			
Rent Expense	2,400		?				?			
Telephone Expense	300						300			
Totals	12,000	12,000								
Insurance Expense			?				400			
Supplies Expense			?				250			
Depreciation Expense			?				?			
Accumulated Deprec.				?						450
Totals			1,300	1,300			4,450	?	8,000	?
Net Income for Year							?			?
Totals							9,000	9,000	?	8,000

Required

Complete this worksheet.

Preparing and posting closing entries (Q2)

E4-2   Set up T accounts for the following: Revenue $10,000, Advertising Expense $200, Interest Expense $100, Rent Expense $2,400, Salaries Expense $5,000, and Income Summary -0-.

Required

1. Prepare all necessary closing entries.

2. Post the closing entries to the T accounts.

3. Balance and rule the T accounts.

Exercises 4-3, 4-4 and 4-5 are based upon the following ledger accounts and additional information taken from the records of Cristhop Corp. at the end of its fiscal year, December 31, 19X1.

Cash		Supplies		Advertising Expense	
Bal. 900		Bal. 700		Bal. 200	

Accounts Receivable		Common Stock		Salaries Expense	
Bal. 2,000			Bal. 3,800	Bal. 4,500	

Prepaid Insurance		Revenue		Telephone Expense	
Bal. 1,200			Bal. 7,750	Bal. 250	

Additional information:

a. The prepaid insurance is for a one-year policy, effective July 1, 19X1.

b. A physical count indicated that supplies costing $500 are still on hand.

c. The December statement from the phone company has not been received or recorded. The estimated amount is $50.

Recording and posting adjusting entries (Q1)

E4-3   Refer to ledger accounts and additional information for Cristhop Corp.

Required

Prepare and post all necessary adjusting entries.

Recording and posting closing entries (Q2)

E4-4   Refer to ledger accounts and additional information for Cristhop Corp.

Required

Prepare and post all necessary closing entries.

Recording and posting reversing entries (Q3)

E4-5   Refer to ledger accounts and additional information for Cristhop Corp.

Required

Prepare and post all necessary reversing entries.

Necessity of reversing entries (Q7–Q9)

E4-6   Prepaid Insurance had a balance of $800 before adjustment. The following adjusting entry was made:

Insurance Expense	350	
Prepaid Insurance		350

Required

Determine whether a reversing entry is necessary, and explain your reasoning.

Necessity of reversing
entries (Q7–Q9)

E4-7 Supplies Expense had a balance of $1,375 before adjustment. The following adjusting entry was made:

Supplies Inventory	475	
Supplies Expense		475

Required
Determine whether a reversing entry is necessary, and explain your reasoning.

Necessity of reversing
entries (Q7–Q9)

E4-8 Salaries Expense had a balance of $35,890 before adjustment. The following adjusting entry was made:

Salaries Expense	500	
Salaries Payable		500

Required
Determine whether a reversing entry is necessary, and explain your reasoning.

Necessity of reversing
entries (Q7–Q9)

E4-9 Accumulated Depreciation—Truck had a balance of $13,680 before adjustment. The following adjusting entry was made:

Depreciation Expense—Truck	1,000	
Accumulated Depreciation—Truck		1,000

Required
Determine whether a reversing entry is necessary, and explain your reasoning.

Necessity of reversing
entries (Q7–Q9)

E4-10 Unearned Advertising Revenue had a balance of $5,675 before adjustment. The following adjusting entry was made:

Unearned Advertising Revenue	3,500	
Advertising Revenue		3,500

Required
Determine whether a reversing entry is necessary, and explain your reasoning.

PROBLEMS

Worksheet, income
statement, and closing
entries (Q1, Q2)

P4-1 The following partial worksheet is taken from Umma Services, Inc., at the year ended December 31, 19X1.

Umma Services, Inc.
Partial Worksheet
For the Year Ended December 31, 19X1

Account Title	Adjusted Trial Balance Dr.	Cr.
Cash	500	
Accounts Receivable	10,000	
Truck	11,000	
Accumulated Deprec.		2,500
Bank Loan		10,000
Accounts Payable		6,000
Common Stock		1,000
Revenue		27,000

(continued)

Account Title	Adjusted Trial Balance	
	Dr.	Cr.
Advertising Expense	1,500	
Commissions Expense	5,000	
Depreciation Expense	2,500	
Insurance Expense	1,200	
Interest Expense	750	
Rent Expense	3,600	
Salaries Expense	10,000	
Supplies Expense	250	
Telephone Expense	200	
Totals		
Net Income for Year		
Totals		

Required

1. Calculate the totals of the adjusted trial balance debit and credit columns.

2. Complete the income statement and balance sheet columns of the worksheet.

3. Prepare the formal year-end income statement of the corporation.

4. Prepare all closing entries.

Worksheet, adjusting and reversing entries (Q1, Q7)

P4-2   The following partial worksheet and additional information are taken from the records of Davey Pencils, Inc., at the end of its first year of operations.

Davey Pencils Inc.
Partial Worksheet
For the Year Ended December 31, 19X1

Account Title	Trial Balance	
	Dr.	Cr.
Cash	3,300	
Accounts Receivable	4,000	
Prepaid Insurance	1,200	
Supplies	500	
Truck	8,500	
Accounts Payable		5,000
Unearned Rent		2,400
Common Stock		6,000
Revenue		16,600
Advertising Expense	200	
Commissions Expense	1,000	
Interest Expense	400	
Rent Expense	3,600	
Salaries Expense	7,000	
Telephone Expense	300	
Totals		
Insurance Expense		
Supplies Expense		
Depreciation Expense		
Accumulated Deprec.		
Salaries Payable		
Rent Earned		
Totals		
Net Income for Year		
Totals		

The following additional data are available:

a.   Prepaid insurance at December 31 amounts to $600.

b.   A physical count indicated that supplies costing $300 are still on hand.

c.   The truck was purchased on July 1 and has a useful life of 4 years with an estimated salvage value of $500.

d.   One day of salaries for December 31 is unpaid; the unpaid amount of $200 will be included in the first Friday payment in January.

e.   The unearned rent represents 6 months rental of warehouse space, effective October 1.

f.   The December statement from the phone company has not been received or recorded. The estimated amount is $100.

Required

1.   Prepare all necessary adjusting entries.

2.   Complete the worksheet.

3.   Prepare all necessary reversing entries.

Preparing closing entries, post-closing trial balance from a worksheet (Q1–Q3)

P4-3   The following columns are taken from the worksheet of Staedtler Service Corp.:

Staedtler Service Corp.
Partial Worksheet
For the Year Ended December 31, 19X1

Account Title	Income Statement Dr.	Income Statement Cr.	Balance Sheet Dr.	Balance Sheet Cr.
Cash			650	
Prepaid Insurance			1,100	
Supplies			700	
Equipment			3,000	
Accumulated Deprec.				250
Accounts Payable				2,000
Unearned Revenue				750
Income Tax Payable				725
Common Stock				1,000
Revenue		11,750		
Advertising Expense	400			
Commissions Expense	1,500			
Depreciation Expense	250			
Insurance Expense	100			
Rent Expense	2,400			
Salaries Expense	5,000			
Supplies Expense	300			
Telephone Expense	350			
Income Tax Expense	725			
Totals				
Net Income for Year				
Totals				

Required

1.   Complete the worksheet income statement and balance sheet columns.

2.   Prepare all closing entries.

3.   Prepare a post-closing trial balance.

Preparing an income statement and statement of retained earnings from closing entries (Q1)

P4-4 The following entries are extracted from the records of Village Cleaners, Inc.

General Journal   Page 1

Date 19X1	Description	F	Debit	Credit
	Closing Journal Entries			
Dec. 31	Revenue		30,000	
	Income Summary			30,000
	To close revenue account.			
31	Income Summary		25,000	
	Advertising Expense			500
	Commissions Expense			5,000
	Insurance Expense			1,200
	Rent Expense			3,600
	Truck Expense			4,700
	Wages Expense			10,000
	To close expense accounts.			
31	Income Summary		5,000	
	Retained Earnings			5,000
	To close the Income Summary account.			

Required

Using the data in the journal closing entries, prepare an income statement and a statement of retained earnings for the year-end, December 31, 19X1. (The balance in Retained Earnings was $10,000 on January 1, 19X1.)

Preparing balance sheet, income statement, and statement of retained earnings for closing (Q2, Q3)

P4-5 The following post-closing trial balance and closing entries are taken from the records of Folsom Services Corp.

Folsom Services Corp.
Post-closing Trial Balance
December 31, 19X1

	Account Balances	
	Debit	Credit
Cash	$ 3,500	
Accounts Receivable	7,500	
Supplies	1,000	
Truck	13,000	
Accumulated Depreciation		$ 3,000
Bank Loan		2,000
Accounts Payable		10,000
Common Stock		3,000
Retained Earnings		7,000
Totals	$25,000 =	$25,000

General Journal   Page 1

Date 19X1	Description	F	Debit	Credit
	Closing Journal Entries			
Dec. 31	Revenue		28,000	
	Income Summary			28,000
	To close revenue account.			
31	Income Summary		21,000	
	Advertising Expense			1,500
	Depreciation Expense			3,000
	Salaries Expense			10,000
	Supplies Expense			500
	Telephone Expense			2,000
	Truck Expense			4,000
	To close expense accounts.			
31	Income Summary		7,000	
	Retained Earnings			7,000
	To close the Income Summary account.			

Required

Using the data given, prepare an income statement, a statement of retained earnings, and a balance sheet as of December 31, 19X1, the end of the first year of operations for Folsom Services Corp.

ALTERNATE PROBLEMS

Worksheet, income statement, and closing entries (Q1, Q2)

AP4-1   The adjusted trial balance for Silva, Inc. appears below:

Silva Inc.
Partial Worksheet
For the Year Ended December 31, 19X1

Account Title	Adjusted Trial Balance	
	Dr.	Cr.
Cash	2,500	
Accounts Receivable	9,000	
Equipment	5,500	
Accumulated Deprec.		600
Bank Loan		5,000
Accounts Payable		6,000
Common Stock		3,000
Revenue		17,300

(continued)

		Adjusted Trial Balance	
Account Title		Dr.	Cr.
Advertising Expense		200	
Commissions Expense		3,000	
Depreciation Expense		600	
Interest Expense		500	
Rent Expense		2,400	
Salaries Expense		7,500	
Supplies Expense		400	
Telephone Expense		300	
Totals			
Net Income for the Year			
Totals			

Required

1. Calculate the totals of the adjusted trial balance debit and credit columns.

2. Complete the income statement and balance sheet columns of the worksheet.

3. Prepare the formal year-end income statement of the corporation.

4. Prepare all closing entries.

Worksheet, adjusting, and reversing entries (Q1, Q7)

AP4-2   The following partial worksheet is taken from Detroit Movers Corp. at the end of its first year of operations.

Detroit Movers Corp.
Partial Worksheet
For the Year Ended December 31, 19X1

		Trial Balance	
Account Title		Dr.	Cr.
Cash		1,500	
Accounts Receivable		7,000	
Prepaid Rent		1,200	
Supplies		100	
Equipment		3,500	
Accounts Payable			6,000
Unearned Commissions			3,000
Common Stock			1,000
Revenue			20,000
Advertising Expense		850	
Commissions Expense		3,600	
Interest Expense		550	
Rent Expense		4,400	
Supplies Expense		700	
Wages Expense		6,600	
Totals			
Depreciation Expense			
Accumulated Deprec.			
Wages Payable			
Unearned Revenue			
Interest Payable			
Totals			
Net Income for the Year			
Totals			

The following additional data are available:

a. Prepaid rent represents rent for the months of December 19X1 and January and February 19X2.

b. A physical count indicates that supplies costing $200 are still on hand as of December 31.

c. The equipment was purchased on July 1 and has a useful life of 3 years with an estimated salvage value of $500.

d. Wages for December 30 and 31 are unpaid; the unpaid amount of $300 will be included in the first Friday payment in January.

e. Revenue includes $2,500 received for work to be started in January 19X2.

f. Unrecorded interest expense amounts to $150.

Required

1. Prepare all necessary adjusting entries.

2. Complete the entire worksheet.

3. Prepare all reversing entries.

Preparing closing entries, post-closing trial balance from a worksheet (Q1–Q3)

AP4-3 The following columns are taken from the worksheet of Placerville Polish, Inc.

Placerville Polish, Inc.
Partial Worksheet
For the Year Ended December 31, 19X1

Account Title	Income Statement		Balance Sheet	
	Dr.	Cr.	Dr.	Cr.
Cash			2,700	
Prepaid Rent			900	
Supplies			600	
Equipment			5,000	
Accum. Depreciation				500
Accounts Payable				4,500
Unearned Revenue				1,500
Income Tax Payable				850
Common Stock				1,000
Revenue		14,500		
Advertising Expense	300			
Depreciation Expense	500			
Interest Expense	100			
Rent Expense	2,400			
Supplies Expense	400			
Truck Expense	2,500			
Utilities Expense	600			
Wages Expense	6,000			
Income Tax Expense	850			
Totals				
Net Income for Year				
Totals				

Required

1. Complete the worksheet income statement and balance sheet columns.

2. Prepare all closing entries.

3. Prepare a post-closing trial balance.

Preparing an income statement and statement of retained earnings from closing entries (Q1, Q2)

AP4-4   The following entries are extracted from the records of Aztec Repairs Corp.

General Journal

Page 1

Date 19X1	Description	F	Debit	Credit
	Closing Journal Entries			
Dec. 31	Revenue		14,400	
	Income Summary			14,400
	To close revenue account.			
31	Income Summary		12,400	
	Advertising Expense			300
	Interest Expense			1,000
	Maintenance Expense			700
	Salaries Expense			8,000
	Supplies Expense			2,000
	Telephone Expense			400
	To close expense accounts.			
31	Income Summary		2,000	
	Retained Earnings			2,000
	To close the Income Summary account.			

Required

Using the data from the above entries, prepare an income statement, and a statement of retained earnings for Aztec Repair Corp.'s year-end, December 31, 19X1. (The balance in Retained Earnings on January 1, 19X1, was $5,000.)

Preparing a balance sheet, income statement, and statement of retained earnings for closing (Q2, Q3)

AP4-5   The following post-closing trial balance and closing entries are taken from the records of Globe Services Corp.

	Account Balances	
	Debit	Credit
Cash	$ 2,500	
Accounts Receivable	10,000	
Prepaid Insurance	600	
Equipment	9,000	
Accumulated Depreciation		$ 1,000
Bank Loan		8,000
Accounts Payable		7,000
Common Stock		2,500
Retained Earnings		2,600
Totals	$22,100 =	$22,100

General Journal   Page 1

Date 19X1	Description	F	Debit	Credit
	Closing Journal Entries			
Dec. 31	Revenue		12,750	
	Income Summary			12,750
	To close revenue account.			
31	Income Summary		10,150	
	Advertising Expense			450
	Depreciation Expense			1,000
	Insurance Expense			600
	Rent Expense			2,400
	Supplies Expense			700
	Wages Expense			5,000
	To close expense accounts.			
31	Income Summary		2,600	
	Retained Earnings			2,600
	To close the Income Summary account.			

Required

Using the data above, prepare an income statement, a statement of retained earnings and a balance sheet as of December 31, 19X1, the first year of operations for Globe Services Corp.

DECISION PROBLEM

The first independent financial analysis of the 1980 Winter Olympics in Lake Placid showed an operating loss of $4,366,029.

The financial review, made at the insistence of government officials, also showed claims against the Lake Placid Olympic Organizing Committee of $21.5 million, arising mainly from construction disputes.

The unaudited financial statement was made by the accounting firm of Peat, Marwick and Mitchell. The indications are that the audited report of the Olympic Committee's books would not be more than $500,000 off the statement issued.

The statement said that it cost $60.8 million to administer and operate the games, with the major expenses in operations, $19.4 million, and marketing, $17 million.

The revenues—including television rights, $13 million; marketing and licensing contracts, $17.7 million; ticket sales, $12.2 million, and contributions, $7.4 million—totaled $56.4 million.

The report also showed construction costs of $72 million, most of which was paid by government. In addition, although the report did not mention it, an additional $40 million was contributed for improvement and renovation of government-owned facilities at Mount Van Hoevenberg, where the bobsled run was held, and at White Face Mountain, where the downhill speed skiing races and the slalom competitions were held.

The most expensive construction items were the $17.9 million housing complex for athletes at Ray Brook, which has just been converted into a prison; a new field-house in Lake Placid Village, $14.9 million, and the ski jumps, $5.9 million.

A footnote in the report also showed that the organizers had obligated themselves to pay $1.5 million as a fee and $2.3 million in costs to the Gilbane Construction Company, which supervised the construction.

Most of the claims against the committee are in $21.5 million in suits, filed or pending, by construction contractors. But, general counsel for the committee feels that these are exaggerated and it has included a reserve fund for potential damages within the $8.5 million it has requested from government.

Source Harold Faber, *The New York Times,* October 5, 1980, p. 51.

A Profit-Cost Statement
For the Winter Olympics

Revenues

Television Rights	$13,092,221
Marketing and Licensing	17,750,993
International Olympic Comm.	1,000,000
Contributions	7,368,835
Miscellaneous	590,177
Ticket Sales (net)	12,224,145
Accommodations	2,421,260
Proceeds on Disposal of Assets	751,605
Investment Income	625,710
Restricted Gifts	656,339
Total Revenues	$56,481,285

Administrative Costs

Executive	$ 8,897,343
Protocol	4,104,769
Marketing	17,014,290
Engineering and Construction	5,412,260
Operations	19,439,569
Press and Public Affairs	2,836,914
Sports	3,089,034
Other	53,135
Total Costs	$60,847,314
Deficit	$4,366,029

Required

1. Accountants usually assume that an entity is a going concern. Is the entity, the 1980 Winter Olympic Games, a going concern? Explain.

2. A cost outlay is usually recorded as an expense if it does not have the potential to produce future revenues. Why is the illustrated financial statement called a *profit-cost statement?* Explain.

3. The construction costs of $72 million have been excluded from the profit-cost statement. Is this acceptable from the point of view of matching of expenses with revenues? Why or why not?

4. An amount of $40 million-worth of improvements and renovations of government-owned facilities is excluded from the financial statements of the games. On the basis of what accounting principle could this be justified? Explain.

ANSWERS TO SELF-TEST QUESTIONS

1. **(c)** Both the balance sheet and an income statement, in addition to a statement of retained earnings, may be prepared from the type of worksheet illustrated in Chapter 4. A worksheet used to prepare a statement of cash flows is illustrated in Chapter 17.

2. **(d)** As was demonstrated in Chapter 3, a worksheet is not necessary to prepare the financial statements. It is merely a tool used by accountants to facilitate the preparation of the statements. Worksheets are not a published financial statement, but do aid in the review of financial statements prepared by a junior accountant.

3. **(b)** Since reversing entries are the first items recorded in the new accounting period, closing entries must come before reversing entries. Closing entries reduce the balances in all the revenue and expense accounts to zero to enable accountants to begin collecting financial information for the new period.

4. **(d)** A trial balance does not have to be prepared as a separate schedule, it can be recorded directly on the worksheet from the general ledger.

5. **(d)** Because the balance sheet columns on the worksheet have been updated by the amount of net income, the financial statements can be prepared in any order and before the adjusting and closing entries have been posted.

6. **(d)** The Income Summary account is an intermediate device that does not appear on any of the financial statements.

7. **(d)** Reversing entries are not reflected on any trial balance dated as of the last day in the entity's fiscal year.

8. **(a)** Entries affecting mixed balance sheet accounts are not reversed since the unexpired/unearned amounts are already reflected in asset/liability accounts. Mixed income statement account adjusting entries should be reversed to adhere to management policy, while accrual type adjustments should be reversed to facilitate efficient operations.

PART I
FINANCIAL STATEMENT ANALYSIS PROBLEM

Turn to the excerpts from the annual report of United Telecom at the back of the textbook, pp. 889–906, and refer to the data for the year ended December 31, 1989. Then answer the following questions:

1. What was the change in cash during the year 1989?

2. Was the change attributable to operating, investing, or financing activities?

3. Would you consider the outflow from investing activities as having a negative influence on United Telecom?

4. Was more long-term debt acquired or retired during 1989? What was the increase in cash during 1988? Can you identify a major source of that increase?

5. Has retained earnings increased or decreased during the last three years?

6. What amount of dividends did United Telecom pay during 1987?

7. What was United Telecom's net income for the year 1987?

8. What do you find unusual about your answers to the last two questions?

9. What type of services does United Telecom provide?

10. What does the accounting firm of Ernst and Young think of the performance and financial position of United Telecom?

PART II

OPERATING ACTIVITIES

PART II focuses on the operating activities of a merchandising entity. Chapter 5 introduces the student to the sales/collection and purchases/payment cycles of a merchandising operation. The concept of gross profit and its relationship to sales is explained, as well as cost of goods sold and its effect on year-end inventories.

Manual and computer-assisted accounting systems are introduced and examined in Chapter 6. The system utilized so far is not adequate to process the volume of transactions facing most entities. Recording payroll and all the related employee deductions is also investigated, as well as employer payroll taxes.

Internal controls and controls designed to protect cash are described in Chapter 7. Internal control systems are designed to maximize efficiency and to control an entity's assets, as well as ensure accuracy in recording and summarizing financial transactions.

Chapter 8 investigates the problems involved with the determination of inventory costs and introduces a number of methods used in the accounting profession to alleviate these problems. The effects of inventory valuation on the income statement are also discussed, in addition to methods of estimating inventory costs.

Chapter 9 closes the discussion of operating activities with a look into the problems in determining the cost of long-term assets, and the various methods used to allocate their costs over their estimated useful lives. Both tangible and intangible assets are discussed.

5 ACCOUNTING FOR MERCHANDISING OPERATIONS

In the first four chapters the focus was on service entities, where revenue was generated by performing services for a customer. In Chapter 5, the focus is on a merchandising concern, one that buys goods in the wholesale market, and sells the goods in the retail market at a profit. This profit, referred to as gross profit, is the difference between what an entity sells an item for and what the entity had to pay for that item. Gross profit is affected by a number of items, such as sales, sales returns and allowances, sales discounts, purchases, purchase returns and allowances, purchase discounts, transportation costs, and the increase or decrease in inventories. The first part of Chapter 5 discusses these issues and the related accounting problems. The worksheet and closing entries explained in Chapter 4 are adapted for a merchandising firm and classified financial statements are again discussed. The chapter concludes with a discussion of ratios that can be determined and evaluated from the classified financial statements. Both short-term liquidity ratios and efficiency ratios are introduced at this point. Other evaluation techniques are discussed in Chapter 16.

CHAPTER PREVIEW QUESTIONS

After studying Chapter 5, you should be able to answer the following questions:

1 In what way is the matching principle emphasized in the income statement prepared for a merchandising firm? (p.208)

2 What is the usefulness of the gross-profit calculation? (p.208)

3 What accounts are used to adjust sales revenue? (pp.209–12)

4 How is the cost of goods sold calculated? (pp.214–15)

5 What accounts are used to adjust purchase of merchandise for resale? (pp.215–17)

6 What is the periodic inventory system, and how does it differ from the perpetual inventory system? (p.218)

7 How is ending inventory recorded in the accounts under the periodic inventory system? (p.218)

8 What internal control feature is incorporated into the perpetual inventory system? (p.219)

9 How do closing entries for a merchandiser differ from those prepared for a service business? (pp.222–23)

10 What is the main advantage of classified financial statements? (pp.223–27)

11 How do extraordinary items differ from prior-period adjustments? (pp.227, 228–29)

12 What is the distinction between current items and noncurrent items disclosed in the balance sheet? (p.229)

13 What is short-term solvency analysis, and why is it important? (pp.231–34)

14 How can an entity measure whether or not the use of its assets is efficient? (pp.234–37)

THE CALCULATION OF GROSS PROFIT

Q1: Matching
principle

The income statement for a merchandising firm differs from that prepared for entities providing a service. The differences result from the fact that **merchandising** involves the purchase and subsequent resale of goods; matching the cost of the goods sold with the sales revenue generated from their sale is emphasized in the income statement. An income statement for a merchandising entity discloses this matching of cost with revenue in a manner different from a service business. It shows the calculation of a **gross profit,** the excess of sales revenue over the **cost of goods sold.** A simple gross profit analysis was made for the management of Saguaro Computers, Inc., when they were evaluating the start of their merchandising operations. The data involved the purchase for resale (rather than for internal use by SCI) of a portable computer for $2,000. They decided to sell the computer for $3,000. A gross-profit calculation was prepared as follows:

Partial Income Statement

Sales	(a)	$3,000
Cost of Goods Sold		2,000
Gross Profit	(b)	$1,000
Gross Profit (%)	(b) ÷ (a)	33⅓%

The $1,000 gross profit is essentially a subtotal calculation, which is usually shown separately in the income statement. The amount of gross profit is important to an entity's financial health in that it indicates the dollars the business has available to cover the cost of all other expenses that have been or will be incurred in selling the items, *and* to provide the owners a reasonable net income.

Q2: Usefulness of
gross profit

The relationship between total revenue and the gross profit is referred to as the gross-profit percentage. A gross-profit percentage can be calculated by dividing the gross profit by the sales amount. The sale of the portable computer that cost $2,000 results in a 33⅓% gross profit. Users of financial statements are interested in establishing this percentage in order to evaluate the performance of this entity with other entities in the same industry; they also want to know whether the percentage is increasing or decreasing from one accounting period to another. For decision-making purposes, it is important to identify the reasons causing a change in the gross-profit percentage. Of necessity, it must be attributable to a change in either the sales price or the cost, or possibly a combination of both. Real World Example 5-1 (pp. 210–11) is an illustration of the many facets that make up the cost of goods sold.

THE SALES AND COLLECTION CYCLE

A retail or wholesale merchandising entity accumulates revenue in a **Sales** account. Sales of merchandise on account result in an accounts receivable; the subsequent collection of cash completes the sales and collection cycle, which is sometimes identified as the revenue cycle. The distinct transactions making up this cycle are influenced by marketing techniques designed to increase sales. For example, a customer may be permitted to return merchandise if it is not satisfactory; an allowance may be given if the merchandise is damaged or differs cosmetically from that

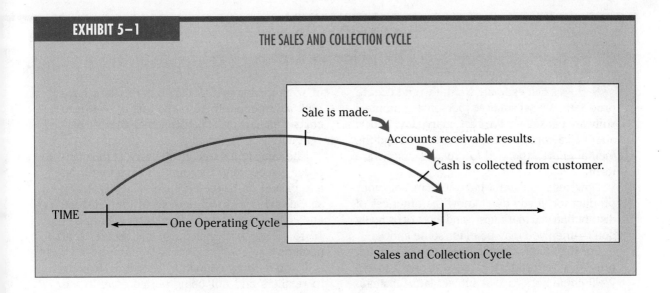

EXHIBIT 5-1

THE SALES AND COLLECTION CYCLE

Sale is made.

Accounts receivable results.

Cash is collected from customer.

TIME

One Operating Cycle

Sales and Collection Cycle

ordered. Collection techniques also affect the transactions in this cycle; discounts may be permitted for prompt payment. All these techniques are monitored by management through the creation of special general ledger accounts designed for sales returns and allowances or for sales discounts for a merchandising or a manufacturing business.

The sequence of events in the sales and collection cycle is illustrated in Exhibit 5-1.

Sales

Revenue resulting from the sale of merchandise is recorded in a Sales account. An accounts receivable results when the sale is made on account. The sale of Saguaro's portable computer for $3,000 on account is recorded as follows:

Accounts Receivable	3,000	
Sales		3,000

Q3: Adjusting sales revenue

The Sales account is a revenue account, similar to the Repair Revenue account used by SCI when recording the revenue earned in the repair process. Because Sales is a revenue account, it will normally have a credit balance. It is commonly referred to as *gross sales* if the merchandiser allows goods to be returned or allows discounts to be taken from the invoice price for early payment. The income statement would then present the information as follows:

Gross Sales		$XXXXXX
Less: Sales Returns	$XX	
Sales Discounts	XX	XXX
Net Sales		$ XXXXX

If sales returns and sales discounts are not allowed, then the revenue item would simply be referred to as *Sales*.

Only sales of merchandise purchased for resale are recorded in this account. The disposal of other corporate assets, such as equipment or a truck, are not

REAL WORLD EXAMPLE 5-1
The Price Is Right

W E can estimate what it would cost to produce a typical small PC [personal computer] software package in the customary vinyl folder: about $5 a copy, exclusive of overhead and the mental effort expended to create the software itself.

Now let's look at what you can sell your product for. If you don't know the practices of distribution and mark-ups—and most of us really don't—then you may be in for some shocks.

For the moment, we'll ignore the official list price of your product, or what it ought to be. We'll come back to that subject later. Instead, let's consider everything in terms of a percentage of the list price as is the custom in discussions of distribution and pricing.

Slicing Up the Pie

If we're lucky enough to sell our software to the end-user at 100 percent of the list price, that's all gravy for us. Unfortunately, we can't get it very much of the time. If we want to sell as many copies of our programs as possible and make as much money as possible, we have to get retailers, distributors, discounters, and others involved and give each a slice of the pie. As it turns out, they expect a bigger slice than most people imagine.

It's customary for a retail store to buy its goods at roughly 60 percent of the list price. It sounds as though they're getting 40 percent

of your customer's dollar, but retailers have rent, salespeople to pay, and lots of overhead costs. Retailers don't bank much of their 40 percent cut.

The same holds true, by the way, of the mail-order discounters. Discounters save overhead and pass it on to the end-user. They typically sell at about 70 to 75 percent of the list price and cover their costs and profit on a margin of 10 to 15 percent, instead of the retailer's 40 percent.

If you're lucky enough to be selling directly to retailers and not being buried alive in the process, then you're doing very nicely to be getting up to 60 percent of the list price of your programs. There is a good reason, though, why software distributors exist. Distributors act as buffers between software producers and computer retail stores. A retail store can turn to a distributor for one-stop shopping instead of ordering from dozens of suppliers and trying to keep track of who ships quickly and reliably and who takes frightfully long to send the goods. From the point of view of a retailer, the distributor smooths out the uneven response time from software producers. Budding software producers like us get a lot from distributors as well: one source of orders instead of a flood of phone calls from many stores, a sales force that knows all those computer stores, and an accounting department that knows how to pay its bills.

Distributors get their own slice of pie. Retail-

credited to the Sales account; rather, the cost of these assets is removed from the appropriate asset account, with a gain or loss being recognized.

SALES RETURNS AND ALLOWANCES

As noted earlier, it is not unusual for a merchandiser to allow the customer to return goods previously purchased. Retailers such as Macy's of California have very liberal return policies with no questions asked, while other merchandisers will allow a return only if the merchandise is defective or different from that ordered. Many times the customer will be offered a reduction in price if the item is not exactly what was ordered so the merchandiser can complete the sale and avoid the related problems of a return. Such a reduction is referred to as an *allowance,* and, therefore,

ers buy from the distributors at about 60 percent of list, and the distributors expect to buy from us at no more than 40 percent of list. Often they will require a price as low as 35 or even 30 percent.

The Publisher's Piece

If you end up selling your product for about 35 percent of the list price, you make a lot less profit than you might have expected. Let's suppose that you've created a game or some other piece of software that can't sell for a high ticket price. Typical game prices are $30, $35, $40 tops. Let's slice up the pie on a $30 product.

The customer pays 100 percent, $30. The retailer pockets 40 percent, $12, to cover costs and profit, passing on $18 to the distributor, who pockets 25 percent or $7.50. You get your 35 percent, some $10.50. But unlike everyone else, you've got the actual production cost, which we ball-park at $5, so your gross profit is a mere $5.50. For you, though, that's just a gross—out of it you have to cover your overhead, including any advertising you might be doing. Whatever is left is your profit as software author and software publisher—not sudden riches in anyone's book.

We've been assuming all along that you're both author and publisher of your own software. What if you don't plan on wearing both hats? Perhaps you've written something and you'd just as soon let someone else have the hassles of publishing it.

Although any kind of deal can be struck, the software publishing business has settled down to some stable standards that closely match the customs of the book publishing business. An often-quoted figure is a royalty to the author of 15 percent of the publisher's gross. That's not, as many people assume, 15 percent of the list price. In the case of software publishing, it's typically 15 percent of 35 percent of the list— or a net royalty of about 5 percent of list. For our hypothetical $30 software package, the royalty would be about $1.50 on each copy. That's far from a fat slice of the pie, but the author is relieved of all the business of making and selling and is responsible just for creating (which the business world never considered an important activity anyway).

It should be clear now why so much software is priced in the hundreds of dollars. It takes lots of investment in teams of programmers and in advertising to get big, serious software onto the streets. While a kitchen table software house might be able to thrive on a gross profit of $5 or $10, Ashton-Tate, MicroPro, and Peachtree can't. If a software publisher needs $100 gross profit to pay those hungry programmers, then his/her product is going to have a list price in the $300 to $400 range.

Source Peter Norton, "Make Sure the Price Is Right," *PC Magazine*, June 26, 1984. Reprinted by permission of the author.

the name of the account it is recorded in becomes **Sales Returns and Allowances.** Since this account is subtracted from the Sales account, it is called a *contra revenue* account and will normally have a debit balance. For example, a $100 allowance for damage to a SCI personal computer during shipment to a customer is recorded by the following entry:

Sales Returns and Allowances	100	
Accounts Receivable		100

Accounts Receivable was credited under the assumption the sale was made on account. If it were a cash sale, then the Cash account would be credited.

The Sales account could have been debited directly, but a separate account is used to accumulate the total amount of returns and allowances for the entire accounting period. A large balance in the account is a signal to management of a potential problem that requires study and resolution.

SALES DISCOUNTS

Another contra revenue account to Sales is **Sales Discounts.** These may apply to a sale made on account, if the customer pays within a time period specified on the sales invoice. For example, the sales terms may require payment within 30 days. However, a discount is often permitted if payment is made earlier. The exact terms are stated on the sales invoice of Saguaro Computers, Inc., as "2/10, n30." This short form means that the invoice must be paid within 30 days; however, if the customer chooses to pay within 10 days, a 2% discount can be deducted by the customer from the invoice amount.

Consider the sale on account of SCI's $3,000 personal computer (less the $100 allowance for damage), with the above terms. Payment within 10 days entitles the customer to a $58 discount, calculated as follows: $2,900 × 0.02 = $58. Note that the discount percentage is applied directly to the selling price involved. SCI receives $2,842 cash ($2,900 − $58) and prepares the following entry:

Cash	2,842	
Sales Discounts	58	
Accounts Receivable		2,900

The Sales Discounts account is deducted from Sales when an income statement is prepared. In this way, the reported sales revenue is reduced by the amount of the discount; in effect, sales discounts are considered a reduction of the selling price. If Saguaro had sold a computer and subsequently gave a $100 allowance and a $58 discount, these accounts would be deducted from sales in the calculation of net sales as follows:

Sales		$3,000
Less: Sales Returns and Allowances	$100	
Sales Discounts	58	158
Net Sales		$2,842

Because they are usually immaterial in amount, the balances of the Sales Returns and Allowances and Sales Discounts accounts are often omitted on income statements of merchandisers. If this were the case for SCI then the income statement would report only a net sales of $2,842. Sometimes too much information can be reported on the financial statements, making them less useful. The amounts of returns and allowances and discounts are more useful to management than to outside users of financial information.

THE PURCHASE AND PAYMENT CYCLE

A merchandising entity usually makes its purchases of items for resale on account; the subsequent payment of cash completes the purchase and payment cycle, which forms part of a broader revenue expenditure cycle that encompasses selling, general

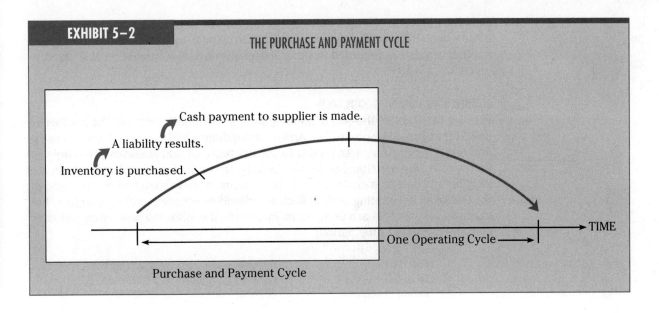

EXHIBIT 5–2

THE PURCHASE AND PAYMENT CYCLE

Cash payment to supplier is made.

A liability results.

Inventory is purchased.

TIME

One Operating Cycle

Purchase and Payment Cycle

and administrative, and other expenses. The distinct transactions of the purchase and payment cycle are the focus of this section. For example, purchasing activities include the occasional return of merchandise to a supplier; often an allowance is given by a supplier for damaged merchandise. These transactions result in the reduction of the amount due to the supplier. Purchasing activities involve the payment of transportation costs associated with the purchase. They also include discounts for prompt payment. These activities are monitored by management through the special general ledger accounts of Purchase Returns and Allowances, Purchase Discounts, and Transportation In. The sequences of events in the purchase and payment cycle is illustrated in Exhibit 5-2.

Combined, Exhibits 5-1 and 5-2 portray that goods are purchased on account, with the goods going into inventory; the supplier is paid for the goods; the goods are sold on account; and payment is received when the accounts receivable is collected and the cycle begins again. This might occur in practice, but more often than not these activities transpire in many combinations. Ideally, the goods would be sold and the accounts receivable collected before the supplier's invoice becomes due. Instead, the merchandiser must keep a careful outlook on his cash-flow situation. If credit terms for customers are more liberal than the terms offered by the supplier, the merchandiser can get into a cash-flow bind almost immediately. Businesses fail because of cash flow more than any other problem.

Purchases, the calculation of the cost of goods sold, and the accounting for inventory are discussed in the following sections.

Purchases

The cost of merchandise from suppliers is recorded in the **Purchases** account. An accounts payable results when the purchase is made on account. When SCI purchases a portable computer from its supplier on account, the transaction is recorded as follows:

Purchases	2,000	
Accounts Payable		2,000

Only the purchase of merchandise for resale is recorded in the Purchases account; it has a debit balance. Purchases of supplies to be used in the business or purchases of other assets are recorded in other more appropriate accounts, as discussed in preceding chapters.

ESTABLISHING COST OF GOODS SOLD

In order to establish the *cost of goods sold* in an accounting period, the number of items for sale must be controlled. An important difference between a merchandising firm and a service business relates to the existence of **merchandise inventory**— in this case, any merchandise for sale held by the entity between delivery from the supplier and sale to a customer. It is not unusual to have merchandise on hand at the end of an accounting period; such merchandise is called *ending inventory.* For example, assume Saguaro Computers, Inc., made the following purchases and sales during a particular time period:

Q4: Calculating cost of goods sold

Purchases	5	portable computers at $2,000 each
Less: Sales	-3	portable computers at $3,000 each
Ending Inventory	2	portable computers at $2,000 each

The gross-profit calculation for that period could be illustrated as follows:

Gross Profit Calculation

	Units		Dollars
Sales (net)	3		$9,000
Cost of Goods Sold			
Purchases	5	$10,000	
Less: Ending Inventory	-2	4,000	
Total Cost of Goods Sold	3		6,000
Gross Profit			$3,000

The format used for this calculation is patterned after the income statement. The *Units* column included in this calculation is not actually indicated on an income statement; it is shown here to demonstrate that sales of 3 units are matched with the purchase cost of 3 units in the calculation of gross profit. The remaining 2 units comprise ending inventory.

In this example, the cost of ending inventory is deducted from the cost of the 5 units purchased; thus, the cost of the 3 units sold is matched with the sales revenue generated from their sale. As stated earlier, this matching is required for the income statement of a merchandising firm. The deduction methodology for the calculation of cost of goods sold can be further understood by the following comparison:

Conventional Method		**Income Statement Method**	
Units Purchased	5	Units Purchased	5
Less: Units Sold	3	Less: Ending Inventory	2
Equals: Ending Inventory	2	Equals: Units Sold	3

The gross profit amount is a subtotal calculation on the income statement; its disclosure facilitates evaluation of an entity's operations during a particular time period. It is not required, but is often made. The gross profit may not be disclosed for any number of reasons; one often cited is marketing strategy—management often does not want competitors to have this information. Since the financial information used to calculate the gross profit (purchases and ending inventory, for example) must be revealed in the income statement in some manner, users of the statements can usually determine the gross profit even when it is not directly disclosed.

BEGINNING INVENTORY

The ending inventory of one accounting period becomes the beginning inventory of the next accounting period. Assume Saguaro Computers, Inc., had the following transactions in the next accounting period:

Beginning Inventory	2 portable computers at $2,000 each
Purchases	6 portable computers at $2,000 each
Sales	5 portable computers at $3,000 each

The following gross profit calculation is disclosed on the interim income statement of both accounting periods. Note that the ending inventory in Period 1 becomes the beginning inventory of Period 2.

	Period 1			Period 2	
	Units	Dollars		Units	Dollars
Sales (net)	3	$9,000		5	$15,000
Cost of Goods Sold					
Beginning Inventory	0			2	$ 4,000
Purchases	5	$10,000		6	12,000
Cost of Goods Available	5			8	$16,000
Less: Ending Inventory	−2	4,000		−3	6,000
Total Cost of Goods Sold	3	6,000		5	10,000
Gross Profit		$3,000			$ 5,000

Again, although units are not actually included in an income statement, they are shown here to emphasize the matching of costs with revenues. In Period 2, 8 portable computers are available for sale; 3 are not sold and are indicated as ending inventory. The cost of the 5 portable computers sold is matched with the revenue generated from their sale.

Students usually find it difficult to follow the income statement calculation of cost of goods sold. This calculation can be further illustrated as follows:

	Beginning Inventory
+	Purchases
=	Cost of Goods Available for Sale
−	Ending Inventory
=	Cost of Goods Sold

Q5: Adjusting purchases

This discussion has focused on purchases and ending inventory in the calculation of cost of goods sold. However, several other accounts are also used in merchandising operations. Two contra accounts deducted from purchases to arrive at net purchases are Purchase Returns and Allowances, and Purchase Discounts. Another account, Transportation In, is then added to net purchases to arrive at **cost of goods purchased.** These three accounts are necessary in merchandising operations to accumulate amounts for activities related to the purchase of merchandise for resale. They provide additional information for decision-making purposes.

PURCHASE RETURNS AND ALLOWANCES

Assume that one computer sent to Saguaro by a supplier is slightly damaged. When purchased merchandise is not satisfactory, it may be returned to the supplier, or the supplier may allow the purchaser to reduce the amount to be remitted. Such returns and allowances are accumulated in a separate account, **Purchase Returns and Allowances,** rather than recorded as a direct credit to the Purchases account. This financial information is important to management for evaluating suppliers. If the entity is constantly returning goods purchased from a particular supplier, then management has the opportunity to change suppliers. The cost of handling returned merchandise can run into millions of dollars per year for a large company. Assuming SCI received a $100 allowance for accepting a damaged computer, the entry would be as follows:

Accounts Payable	100	
Purchase Returns and		
Allowances		100

The Purchase Returns and Allowances account is a contra account and is deducted from Purchases when an income statement is prepared. In this way, the reported purchase cost is reduced by the returns and allowances.

PURCHASE DISCOUNTS

Another contra account, **Purchase Discounts,** accumulates purchase discounts. These apply to purchases made on account if payment is made within a time period specified in the supplier's invoice. For example, the terms on the $2,000 invoice for one portable computer received by Saguaro indicate "1/15, n45." This shorthand means that the $2,000 must be paid within 45 days; however, if payment is made within 15 days, a 1 percent discount can be taken.

Consider the slightly damaged computer received by SCI. If the 1/15, n45 terms apply to its purchase, and the accounting policy of the company is to take advantage of such discounts, Saguaro will make the payment within 15 days. The supplier's terms entitle Saguaro to deduct $19, calculated as follows: ($2,000 − $100) = $1,900 × 0.01 = $19. Therefore, an $1,881 cash payment is made to the supplier and is recorded as follows:

Accounts Payable	1,900	
Purchase Discounts		19
Cash		1,881

The Purchase Discounts account, a contra account, is deducted from Purchases in the income statement. In this way, the cost of purchases is reduced by the discounts taken.

Management must watch purchase discounts carefully. The terms of 1/15, n/45 allow the purchaser 30 days (45–15) beyond the free 15 days to pay the account. Since approximately twelve 30-day periods are in a year, the normal accounting period, this means management is paying 12% interest to "borrow" the money from the supplier. If the going rate of interest for short-term loans is less than 12%, then management is better off borrowing the money in order to take advantage of purchase discounts.

TRANSPORTATION IN

The purchase invoice for merchandise usually indicates who will pay the cost of transporting it. The term "fob" (meaning "free on board") is commonly used: **fob shipping point** means the purchaser pays, and **fob destination** means the supplier pays.

Assuming Saguaro's supplier sells on the basis of fob shipping point, the transportation cost is the responsibility of Saguaro, and its cash payment would be recorded as follows:

Transportation In	125	
Cash		125

The Transportation In account is added to the cost of Purchases in the income statement. In this way the reported cost of purchases is increased by the amount for transportation.

An alternate way of accounting for transportation could have been used in this case. Although Saguaro is responsible for the costs involved, the shipment could have been "freight prepaid" by the supplier. The supplier then would have paid the transportation and SCI would have to reimburse the supplier. Of course, no discount for prompt payment of the $125 would be allowed.

Alternatively, if Saguaro purchased from a supplier whose terms were *fob destination,* and the shipment had been sent "freight collect," then SCI would deduct the transportation charges from the invoice amount before remitting the balance to the supplier. The journal entries would appear as follows:

Purchases	4,000	
Accounts Payable		4,000
To record goods purchased fob destination.		
Accounts Payable	100	
Cash		100
To record the payment of an invoice for freight on goods shipped fob destination.		
Accounts Payable	3,900	
Cash		3,900
To record the amount due on goods shipped fob destination after deducting the amount paid for freight on arrival.		

The composition of the total cost of purchases made during the accounting period is therefore calculated as *purchases less purchase returns and allowances* and *purchase discounts plus transportation in.* The cost of purchases of SCI's computer is recorded as follows:

Purchases		$2,000
Less: Purchase Returns and Allowances	$100	
Purchase Discounts	19	119
Net Purchases		$1,881
Add: Transportation In		125
Total Cost of Goods Purchased		$2,006

The Cost of Goods Purchased also can be indicated as Cost of Purchases on the income statement.

Inventory

Q6: Periodic Inventory system

Q7: Recording ending inventory

THE PERIODIC INVENTORY SYSTEM

The method of accounting just described for purchases is called the **periodic inventory system.** Under this method, the total cost of goods available for sale is determined by adding the cost of beginning inventory to the cost of goods purchased during the accounting period. Then the goods on hand at the end of the year are counted and a cost for the inventory is determined. The theory is that if an entity subtracts the cost of the ending inventory from the cost of goods available for sale during the year, it will obtain the cost of the goods that must have been sold during the year. The major drawback to this method is that it inherently assumes that if the goods are not on hand at the end of the year, then they must have been sold during the year. Therefore, the cost of all goods *lost* (for various reasons, such as employee theft or spoilage) are reflected in the cost of goods *sold* for the year. The interrelationship between the disclosure of inventory in the income statement and Merchandise Inventory on the balance sheet can be illustrated as shown in Exhibit 5-3.

A physical count of inventory requires careful planning and accurate inventory-taking procedures. For instance, prenumbered inventory tags can be attached to all inventory items, with the quantity of items recorded on them; the numerical sequence and the quantities are subsequently checked to ensure that all counted items are accounted for.

The periodic inventory system is most useful where many different or low-value items are kept in stock and where maintaining detailed records would be expensive.

THE PERPETUAL INVENTORY SYSTEM

Under the **perpetual inventory system** a continuous balance of inventory on hand is calculated in terms of units and cost. As a purchase is received, the quantity

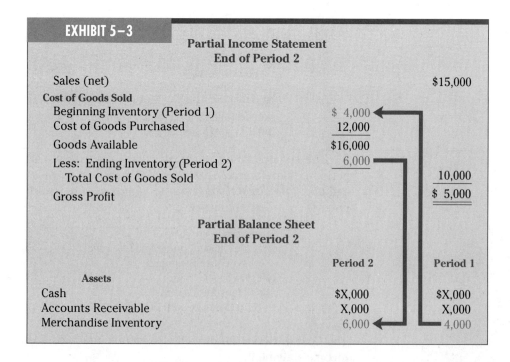

EXHIBIT 5-3

Partial Income Statement
End of Period 2

Sales (net)		$15,000
Cost of Goods Sold		
Beginning Inventory (Period 1)	$ 4,000	
Cost of Goods Purchased	12,000	
Goods Available	$16,000	
Less: Ending Inventory (Period 2)	6,000	
Total Cost of Goods Sold		10,000
Gross Profit		$ 5,000

Partial Balance Sheet
End of Period 2

	Period 2	Period 1
Assets		
Cash	$X,000	$X,000
Accounts Receivable	X,000	X,000
Merchandise Inventory	6,000	4,000

received is added to the quantity recorded as being on hand. When inventory is sold, the sold units are deducted and a new balance of inventory on hand is calculated. That balance at the end of the accounting period is checked against the quantities actually on hand. One cause of fluctuations in the gross-profit percentage can be inventory losses through theft and errors; if this is the case, management control over inventory needs to be strengthened.

Q8: Internal control feature

The perpetual inventory system, therefore, incorporates an important internal control feature. Losses resulting from theft and error can easily be determined when the actual quantity counted is compared with the quantities that ought to be on hand. This advantage is reduced, however, by the time and expense required for continuously updating the inventory records. Computerization makes this record-keeping easier and less expensive, particularly when the inventory system is tied into the sales system so that inventory is updated whenever a sale is recorded. Assuming SCI uses the perpetual method, the purchase of a computer for $2,000, and its subsequent sale for $3,000, would be recorded as follows:

Merchandise Inventory	2,000	
Accounts Payable		2,000
Accounts Receivable	3,000	
Sales		3,000
Cost of Goods Sold	2,000	
Merchandise Inventory		2,000

Note the balance in the Merchandise Inventory account in the general ledger reflects the cost of inventory that should be on hand (after purchasing the computer for resale, and before it is sold, one computer should be on hand). Therefore, a physical count of the goods should show whether any goods are "missing." Also note that Cost of Goods Sold is an account in the general ledger, and not an amount determined at the end of the year. The actual procedures involved in a perpetual inventory system and the impact of inventory errors on the income statement are further discussed in Chapter 8.

Purchase and Payment: Related Recording

DEBIT AND CREDIT MEMOS

The return of merchandise, the granting of an allowance, or the discovery of an invoicing error are among the reasons for the preparation of a source document referred to as a **debit** or **credit memo.**

Seller-Issued Memos

- A debit memo issued by a seller results in a debit to the customer's Accounts Receivable account. The increase in the amount due from the customer could be, for instance, the result of a calculation error in an original invoice that undercharged the customer.

- A credit memo issued by a seller results in a credit to the customer's Accounts Receivable account. This decrease in the receivable may be, for instance, the result of an allowance for damaged goods granted to the customer, or a return of the goods in question. A credit memo, from the seller's point of view, is a far more common document than a debit memo.

Purchaser-Issued Memos

■ A debit memo issued by a purchaser results in a debit to the supplier's Accounts Payable account. The decrease in the payable could be caused by a pricing error, an allowance granted for damaged or incorrect goods, or for the return of the goods.

■ A credit memo issued by a purchaser results in a credit to the supplier's Accounts Payable, thereby increasing it. This source document would be prepared based on the receipt of a debit memo from the seller and, as noted, is not a common document.

TRADE DISCOUNTS

The preceding discussion of sales and purchases involved the use of an established dollar amount for the invoice price. In practice, these amounts are often determined from a suggested list price in a catalogue indicating the merchandise offered. Trade discounts from the suggested list price are used to calculate prices for different categories of buyers and for different quantities. For example, a 30% discount may be offered to colleges and universities, and a different discount percentage to retailers. Trade discounts can be in terms of a percentage or dollar amount deducted from the suggested list price. When trade discounts are stated in terms of percentages for different classes of buyers, such as manufacturers, wholesalers, retailers, or the ultimate consumer, they are computed consecutively. For instance, assume an item has a list price of $1,000, the price the consumer would pay. But if the seller also sells to retailers, wholesalers, and manufacturers, trade discounts of 20-10-5 might be offered. If a retailer purchases the item, a 20% discount would be offered, resulting in a sales price of $800. If a wholesaler purchases the item, an *additional* 10% discount would be offered, resulting in a sales price of $720 ($800 − $80). If the buyer is a manufacturer, still an additional 5% discount would be offered, resulting in a sales price of $684 ($720 − $36). Trade discounts are used to determine the invoice price, and are not recorded in the accounts.

COMPLETION OF THE WORKSHEET

As with a service business, the completion of a worksheet for a merchandising firm organizes the many details that must be brought together when financial statements are being prepared. The worksheet also gives the accountant a preview of the final statements before they are actually prepared.

Exhibit 5-4 is a completed merchandising worksheet for 19X3 for Saguaro Computers, Inc., which is both merchandising and servicing computers. The worksheet for a merchandising firm differs in one respect from that of the service business: the treatment of inventory. Note the following:

1. Beginning inventory appears in the worksheet's trial balance debit column as $80,000. This amount has not changed during the year because Saguaro follows the periodic inventory system in recording the purchase of merchandise for resale in the Purchases Account. The Merchandise Inventory account remains unchanged until the closing entries are recorded.

2. The beginning inventory is transferred as a debit in the income statement columns of the worksheet. Remember that the beginning inventory is *added*

EXHIBIT 5–4

Saguaro Computers, Inc.
Worksheet
For the Year Ended December 31, 19X3

Account Number	Account Title	Trial Balance Dr.	Trial Balance Cr.	Adjustments Dr.	Adjustments Cr.	Adjusted Trial Balance Dr.	Adjusted Trial Balance Cr.	Income Statement Dr.	Income Statement Cr.	Balance Sheet Dr.	Balance Sheet Cr.
101	Cash	10,800								10,800	
110	Accounts Receivable	26,000								26,000	
150	Merchandise Inventory	80,000						80,000	120,000	120,000	
161	Prepaid Insurance	2,400			1,200					1,200	
183	Equipment	13,600								13,600	
193	Accum. Deprec.—Eqpmt.		-		1,600						1,600
201	Bank Loan—Current		39,000								39,000
210	Accounts Payable		25,000								25,000
260	Income Tax Payable		-		15,000						15,000
271	Bank Loan—Long-Term		48,500								48,500
320	Common Stock		10,000								10,000
340	Retained Earnings		21,750								21,750
350	Dividends	4,250								4,250	
500	Sales		308,500						308,500		
508	Sales Returns and Allowances	6,000						6,000			
509	Sales Discounts	2,500						2,500			
550	Purchases	240,000						240,000			
558	Purchase Returns and Allowances		12,600						12,600		
559	Purchase Discounts		2,400						2,400		
560	Transportation In	15,000						15,000			
610	Advertising Expense	10,000						10,000			
615	Commissions Expense	15,000						15,000			
620	Delivery Expense	6,000						6,000			
632	Interest Expense	10,000						10,000			
654	Rent Expense	3,600						3,600			
656	Salaries Expense	20,000						20,000			
669	Telephone Expense	1,080						1,080			
676	Utilities Expense	1,520						1,520			
	Totals	467,750	467,750								
623	Deprec. Expense—Eqpmt.			1,600				1,200			
631	Insurance Expense			1,200				1,600			
830	Income Tax Expense			15,000				15,000			
	Totals			17,800	17,800			428,500	443,500	175,850	160,850
	Net Income							15,000			15,000
	Totals							443,500	443,500	175,850	175,850

to the Purchases account in the cost-of-goods-sold computation on the income statement. Therefore, inserting the beginning inventory in the debit column guarantees that the amount will be added to the Purchases account during the closing process.

3. The ending inventory of $120,000 is recorded directly on the worksheet in two places:

   a. As a credit in the income statement columns. Remember, the ending inventory is *subtracted* from the summation of the beginning inventory and Purchases in the cost-of-goods-sold computation on the income statement. Therefore, the ending inventory is automatically subtracted from the total of beginning inventory and purchases by inserting the amount as a credit in the income statement columns of the worksheet.

   b. As a debit in the balance sheet columns. The amount of inventory on hand at year-end is an asset of the entity. Entering the amount as a debit in the balance sheet columns on the worksheet automatically includes ending inventory among the assets for presentation in the balance sheet.

Also, by inserting the $120,000 twice, once as a debit and once as a credit, the worksheet remains in balance. The recording of the ending inventory and the removal of the beginning inventory in the general ledger accounts is discussed later in this chapter.

After the recording of ending inventory in the worksheet, the columns are added and balanced, as explained in Chapter 4. Note that the adjusted trial balance columns are not filled out; this set of columns is simply an intermediate step between the recording of adjustments and the transfer of adjusted balances to the income statement and balance sheet columns. Leaving the adjusted trial balance columns blank reduces the time required to complete the worksheet without any corresponding loss of accuracy. Filling out the adjusted trial balance columns does, however, help locate errors. If the adjusted trial balance columns in the worksheet are used and they do not balance, an error has occurred between the trial balance and the adjusted trial balance. Otherwise, if the worksheet does not balance, an error could be anywhere on the worksheet after the trial balance.

Closing Entries

Q9: Closing entries for a merchandiser

The recording of adjusting entries from the worksheet and subsequent preparation of closing entries, as illustrated in Chapter 4, also applies to merchandisers. At the end of a fiscal year, the revenue and expense accounts are reduced to a zero balance, so they can begin to accumulate amounts of the new fiscal year. Closing entries are prepared to close these income statement accounts; dividend accounts are also closed at the end of the corporate year.

The closing process for merchandisers includes new Sales and Purchases accounts, as well as their contra accounts. The closing procedure remains the same as for service entities; all accounts listed in the worksheet's income statement columns are transferred to the Income Summary account. This includes the debit relating to beginning inventory and the credit relating to ending inventory.

Under the periodic inventory system, the opening inventory is removed, and ending inventory recorded, as part of the closing process. The following T account illustrates how this occurs.

		Merchandise Inventory	No. 150
Jan. 1	Beginning balance	80,000	
	Less: Beginning inventory		
	(closing entry posted)		80,000
	Balance	-0-	
	Add: Ending inventory	120,000	
Dec. 31	Ending balance	120,000	

The four closing entries prepared for Saguaro Computers, Inc., at December 31, 19X3, are shown in Exhibit 5-5. Note the inclusion of the Merchandise Inventory beginning and ending balances. The following explains the entries:

(1) All the amounts appearing in the *credit* column of the income statement are debited, and the Income Summary is credited for the total. Note that this entry accomplishes three tasks: the revenue accounts are closed, the contra-purchases accounts are closed, and the ending inventory is recorded in the asset account, Merchandise Inventory.

(2) All the amounts appearing in the *debit* column of the income statement are credited, and the Income Summary is debited for the total. Note that this entry accomplishes four tasks: the expense accounts are closed, the contra-revenue accounts are closed, the Merchandise Inventory account is relieved of the beginning inventory, and the balance in the Income Summary now represents the net income or loss for the accounting period.

(3) The Income Summary account is closed, either with a debit or credit, depending on whether the entity had a net income or a net loss, and Retained Earnings is either credited (net income) or debited (net loss). Because SCI had a net income of $15,000, the Income Summary has a $15,000 *credit* balance, as shown in Exhibit 5-5.

   If the entity had a net loss of $10,000, the Income Summary would have a *debit* balance and the closing entry would appear as follows:

Retained Earnings	10,000	
Income Summary		10,000

(4) The Dividends account is closed to Retained Earnings in a separate entry. Remember that dividends are distributions of income to the stockholders and, therefore, are not considered a determinant of net income.

CLASSIFIED FINANCIAL STATEMENTS

Q10: Advantage of classified financial statements

Accountants are concerned with the application of GAAP to the recording of financial transactions; the impact of GAAP on the accounting process has been the focus of preceding chapters. This section focuses on the disclosure in financial statements of financial information recorded in the company's books. The issues involved include financial statement preparation and **classification** (the way accounts are grouped).

EXHIBIT 5–5

CLOSING ENTRIES

General Journal

Date 19X1		Description	F	Debit	Credit
		Closing Entries			
(1)					
Dec.	31	Merchandise Inventory (ending)	150	120,000	
		Sales	500	308,500	
		Purchase Returns	558	12,600	
		Purchase Discounts	559	2,400	
		Income Summary	360		443,500
		To record ending inventory and to close income statement accounts with a credit balance.			
(2)					
	31	Income Summary	360	428,500	
		Merchandise Inventory (beginning)	150		80,000
		Sales Returns and Allowances	508		6,000
		Sales Discounts	509		2,500
		Purchases	550		240,000
		Transportation In	560		15,000
		Advertising Expense	610		10,000
		Commissions Expense	615		15,000
		Delivery Expense	620		6,000
		Depreciation Expense—Equipment	623		1,600
		Insurance Expense	631		1,200
		Interest Expense	632		10,000
		Rent Expense	654		3,600
		Salaries Expense	656		20,000
		Telephone Expense	669		1,080
		Utilities Expense	676		1,520
		Income Tax Expense	830		15,000
		To record the closing of beginning inventory and to close income statement accounts with a debit balance.			
(3)					
	31	Income Summary	360	15,000	
		Retained Earnings	340		15,000
		To close Income Summary account.			
(4)					
	31	Retained Earnings	340	4,250	
		Dividends	350		4,250
		To close Dividends account.			

The Classified Income Statement

In practice, the income statement of a merchandising firm is usually classified—that is, revenues and expenses are broken into categories with subtotals provided for each classification. This classification process highlights interrelationships of important amounts by making the information readily available.

The importance of the gross-profit subtotal was previously discussed; it represents the amount of sales revenue that remains to pay expenses necessary to operate the business (operating expenses) and to pay financing expenses, such as interest expense and the amount paid to the entity's silent partner, the government, as income tax expense. The balance is the bottom line—the net income. Net income represents the return on stockholders' investment and the amount available for dividends to stockholders. For bankers, it represents the ability of the entity to expand its operations through debt financing and to support increased interest charges resulting from increased debt. For labor unions, the entity's net income indicates a basis for increased salary demands in labor negotiations.

Exhibit 5-6 is a classified income statement of Saguaro Computers, Inc., for the year ended December 31, 19X3. It also includes the classification of **operating expenses** divided into two categories: selling expenses and general and administrative expenses.

Selling expenses are those incurred to sell the merchandise. General and administrative expenses are those incurred to administer the merchandising operations. While most operating expenses are easily distinguished as fitting one or the other category, some require allocation; for example, rent expense may include both the sales area and the office. Sometimes classification is made on the basis of expediency, particularly if the amounts involved are not material. For this reason Insurance Expense, which covers both the sales area and office space, has not been separately allocated by Saguaro.

Interest Expense is classified separately because of the impact financing the entity's activities through debt has on the calculation of net income.

The 19X3 year-end income statement illustrates all the major classifications required for Saguaro. Other entities may require further classifications indicating other subtotals to highlight important interrelationships relevant to specific aspects of their operations.

In practice, the financial statements would indicate not only the 19X3 data, but also the comparative data for the preceding year, 19X2 in this case. These are referred to as comparative financial statements; comparative amounts would be provided in each of the financial statements prepared.

Often a condensed income statement is reproduced in published annual reports. SCI's condensed statement could be designed as shown in Exhibit 5-7.

Note that for disclosure purposes, in accordance with GAAP, the depreciation has been shown separately from the amount of general and administrative expenses. The total amount still agrees with the selling and general and administrative expenses reported on the preceding classified income statement in Exhibit 5-6. One reason for disclosing the amount of depreciation is so readers of the financial information are able to partially assess the cash flow from operations. This subject is discussed in great detail in Chapter 17.

Other Income Statement Classifications

Three other classifications may appear on the income statement. All three would occur after the net income amount in Exhibit 5-6. Since they would be reported after the income is determined, the tax effect of these items would have to be listed with the items because, as shown in the income statement, income tax has already been deducted. The classifications are as follows:

1. **Discontinued operations.** If the entity had decided to stop producing or selling a major line of business, all revenues and expenses associated with

EXHIBIT 5-6

Saguaro Computers, Inc.
Income Statement
For the Year Ended December 31, 19X3

Revenue			
Sales			$308,500
Less: Sales Returns and Allowances		$ 6,000	
Sales Discounts		2,500	8,500
Net Sales			$300,000
Cost of Goods Sold			
Beginning Inventory (Jan. 1)		$ 80,000	
Purchases	$240,000		
Less: Purchase Returns and Allowances	$12,600		
Purchase Discounts	2,400	15,000	
Net Purchases	$225,000		
Add: Transportation In	15,000		
Cost of Goods Purchased		240,000	
Cost of Goods Available		$320,000	
Ending Inventory (Dec. 31)		120,000	
Total Cost of Goods Sold			200,000
Gross Profit			$100,000
Operating Expenses			
Selling Expenses			
Advertising Expense	$ 10,000		
Commissions Expense	15,000		
Delivery Expense	6,000		
Total Selling Expenses		$ 31,000	
General and Administrative Expenses			
Depreciation Expense—Equipment	$ 1,600		
Insurance Expense	1,200		
Rent Expense	3,600		
Salaries Expense	20,000		
Telephone Expense	1,080		
Utilities Expense	1,520		
Total General and Administrative Expenses		29,000	
Total Operating Expenses			60,000
Income from Operations			$ 40,000
Financing Expenses			
Interest Expense			10,000
Income (before income tax)			$ 30,000
Income Tax Expense			15,000
Net Income			$ 15,000

EXHIBIT 5–7

Saguaro Computers, Inc.
Income Statement
For the Year Ended December 31, 19X3

Net Sales		$300,000
Costs and Expenses		
Cost of Goods Sold	$200,000	
Selling, General and Administrative	58,400	
Depreciation Expense—Equipment	1,600	260,000
Income from Operations		$ 40,000
Financing Expenses		
Interest Expense		10,000
Income (before income tax)		$ 30,000
Income Tax Expense		15,000
Net Income		$ 15,000

that decision would be shown separately on the statement, below Net Income, along with the gain or loss determined from the sale of those assets used in the line of business.

Q11: Extraordinary items

2. **Extraordinary items.** If unusual and infrequent events occurred during the year that had a financial impact on the entity, the effect would be reported separately on the income statement, below Net Income. For example, businesses that suffered damage in the October 1989 earthquake in the Bay Area of California would separately report all expenses incurred in repairing that damage.

3. **Changes in accounting methods.** If an entity decided to change the method of accounting for a particular item, the financial effect of that change would be reported separately on the income statement, below Net Income.

Other calculations are also reported in the income statement to give additional information. One of these calculations is Earnings Per Share (EPS), which is discussed toward the end of this chapter.

The Statement of Retained Earnings

The net income (or loss) for the period, as well as dividends for the accounting period, are reported in the statement of retained earnings. This statement is a link between the income statement and balance sheet. The balance of the Retained Earnings account represents the earnings of the entity that have not been distributed to stockholders as dividends.

From its inception in 19X1 until the beginning of 19X3, Saguaro Computers, Inc., has retained $21,750. It earned $15,000 in 19X3 and paid a $4,250 cash dividend to stockholders during the year. A **dividend** results in the reduction of retained earnings, which consists of net income earned in the current or prior periods. The asset Cash is decreased by the payment, and Retained Earnings is also decreased.

EXHIBIT 5-8		
	Saguaro Computers, Inc. **Statement of Retained Earnings** **For the Year Ended December 31, 19X3**	
Balance, Jan. 1		$21,750
Add: Net Income		15,000
Total		$36,750
Less: Dividends		4,250
Balance, Dec. 31		$32,500

As noted, during 19X3, SCI declared and paid a $4,250 dividend authorized by its board of directors. This payment was recorded by the following entry:

Dividends	4,250	
Cash		4,250

The payment also could be recorded as follows;

Retained Earnings	4,250	
Cash		4,250

If the entity pays dividends only once during each year, the second entry would probably be the one recorded. Normally, however, corporations pay dividends more than once a year, generally four times per year. In that case the Dividends account used in the first example is debited, with the balance in dividends closed to Retained Earnings at the end of each accounting period. The pattern of recording dividend payments is similar to that used for assets and expenses. Debits record an increase in assets, expenses, and dividends.

SCI's 19X3 ending amount of earnings retained in the business is $32,500 ($21,750 + $15,000 − $4,250). This amount of retained earnings is represented by assets held by the corporation; these assets are available not only for use in the future expansion of the business but also to absorb any losses that may occur. If a net loss had occurred in 19X3, the amount of loss would have been deducted from the beginning Retained Earnings balance of $21,750.

Exhibit 5-8 is a statement of retained earnings for Saguaro Computers, Inc., for the year ended December 31, 19X3. Note that the Dividends balance is deducted on the statement. The net income for the year is taken from the income statement illustrated in Exhibit 5-6. This statement in Exhibit 5-8 discloses the changes during the year to the Retained Earnings account reported in the balance sheet at December 31, 19X3.

PRIOR-PERIOD ADJUSTMENTS

Q11: Prior Period
Adjustments

An additional category, referred to as **prior-period adjustments,** is also reported in the statement of retained earnings. This category relates to changes in the net income reported in the prior year. They are excluded from the current year's income statement; they are disclosed in the statement of retained earnings because the net income (or loss) of the prior year is included in the beginning Retained Earnings balance.

Prior-period adjustments are limited for the most part to the correction of accounting errors made in determining net income in past years. For instance, if SCI discovered during 19X4 that the ending inventory for 19X3 should have been $130,000, rather than $120,000, the following entry would be made:

Merchandise Inventory	10,000	
Retained Earnings		10,000

The credit to Retained Earnings is an adjustment to prior years' net income and therefore should be added to the beginning balance of Retained Earnings before Net Income for 19X4 is added.

The Classified Balance Sheet

Q12: Current versus noncurrent balance sheet items

The merchandiser's balance sheet, like that of a service entity, is prepared from amounts in the balance sheet columns of the worksheet. The classification of accounts into meaningful categories is designed to facilitate the analysis of balance sheet information. Assets and liabilities are customarily classified as either current or long-term. Current items are those that change or expire within a 12-month period. Refer to p. 66 of Chapter 2 for the discussion about the classified balance sheet.

BALANCE SHEET FORM

The balance sheet can be presented in either the *account form,* with the liabilities and equities presented to the right of the assets, or in the *report form,* with the liabilities and equities presented below the assets. Both formats are acceptable; the account form seems slightly more popular in published financial statements.

Some industries may begin the balance sheet with the Total Current Liabilities subtracted from the Total Current Assets, arriving at a difference known as **Working Capital.** After Working Capital, the Long-term Assets are added to arrive at a total. This total is now equal to the Total Long-term Liabilities plus Total Stockholders' Equity. The account-form balance sheet for SCI in Exhibit 5-9 illustrates the proper classifications.

After its financial statements, a corporation discloses what accounting policies it has followed in their preparation. These policies are summarized to facilitate the review and analysis of the financial statements. The matters covered could include revenue recognition, valuation of inventories, the accounting treatment of long-term-asset expenditures, the accounting for income taxes, and other issues significant to the business. Any changes in accounting policy from previous years must be noted.

In addition to a discussion of accounting policies, information that helps users of financial statements to understand individual items is disclosed in notes. These notes may explain extraordinary items or prior-period adjustments, details about income tax matters, transactions with related companies, commitments entered into by the company, and events subsequent to the data of the financial statements that are important and may affect the reader's interpretation.

The 19X3 financial statements of Saguaro Computers, Inc., include the following notes relating to the terms of its bank loan and a description of its common stock.

EXHIBIT 5–9

Saguaro Computers, Inc.
Balance Sheet
December 31, 19X3

Assets			Liabilities		
Current Assets			*Current Liabilities*		
Cash	$ 10,800		Bank Loan—Current	$39,000	
Accounts Receivable	26,000		Accounts Payable	25,000	
Inventory	120,000		Income Tax Payable	15,000	
Prepaid Insurance	1,200		Total Current Liabilities		$ 79,000
Total Current Assets		$158,000	*Long-term Liabilties*		
Long-term Assets			Bank Loan—Long term		
Equipment	$ 13,600		(note 1)		48,500
Less: Accum. Deprec.—			Total Liabilities		$127,500
Supplies	1,600				
Total Long-term Assets		12,000	**Stockholders' Equity**		
			Common Stock (note 2)	$10,000	
			Retained Earnings	32,500	
			Total Stockholders' Equity		42,500
			Total Liabilities and Stockholders'		
Total Assets		$170,000	Equity		$170,000

NOTE 1: BANK LOAN

The bank loan consists of a 12% demand bank loan. Under the terms of this bank loan, Saguaro has pledged its accounts receivable and inventory as collateral. In addition, certain personal guarantees have been made by one of the stockholders of Saguaro and certain insurance policies have been assigned to the bank.

NOTE 2: COMMON STOCK

The authorized capital of the company is comprised of 100,000 shares of common stock with a par value of $1, of which 10,000 shares are issued and outstanding. The rights of the stockholders include the right to vote at any meeting of stockholders, to receive any dividends declared by the company directors, and to receive the remaining property of the company on dissolution.

EVALUATION OF THE ENTITY

Accountants, analysts, and investors often talk about the solvency of a company. What does this mean? The term **solvency,** when applied to a company, refers to its ability to pay current liabilities as they become due. This is important to know because if a company is *insolvent,* then it is unable to pay its creditors who have provided goods and services on account. The implications of being insolvent are:

Current Liabilities

- Creditors can refuse to provide any further goods or services on account.
- Creditors can sue for payment.
- Creditors can put the company into bankruptcy.

Long-term Liabilities

■ Creditors can refuse to lend additional cash.

■ Creditors can demand repayment of their long-term debts under some circumstances.

Stockholders' Equity

■ Stockholders risk the loss of their investment if the corporation is placed into bankruptcy.

As of 19X3, Saguaro Computers, Inc., is a solvent corporation. What is the structure of SCI's creditor financing? An analysis of the company's balance sheet reveals the following liabilities:

	19X3
Current Liabilities	$79,000
Long-term Liabilities	48,500

This information indicates that the company's management relies on both short-term and long-term creditor financing. If the bank decides not to continue lending money to SCI, the company's ability to pay its other liabilities as they become due may be compromised. Management needs to be able to analyze SCI's short-term solvency.

SHORT-TERM SOLVENCY ANALYSIS

Q13: Short-term Solvency Analysis

Ratios are one way of evaluating any company's solvency. Two commonly used ratios are:

Short-term Solvency Analysis	Indicates
1. Current Ratio	How many current-asset dollars exist to pay current liabilities. This ratio is only a crude measure of solvency.
2. Acid-test Ratio	Whether the company is able to meet the immediate demands of creditors. This ratio is a more severe measure of solvency. Inventory and prepaid items are excluded from the calculation.

Current Ratio

An overall analysis of solvency is made by the **current ratio.** Is the firm able to repay short-term creditors? The current ratio answers this question by expressing a relationship between current assets and current liabilities—current assets are divided by current liabilities. These are the relevant SCI financial data required to calculate this ratio:

		19X3
Current Assets	(a)	$158,000
Current Liabilities	(b)	$ 79,000
Current Ratio	(a ÷ b)	2 : 1

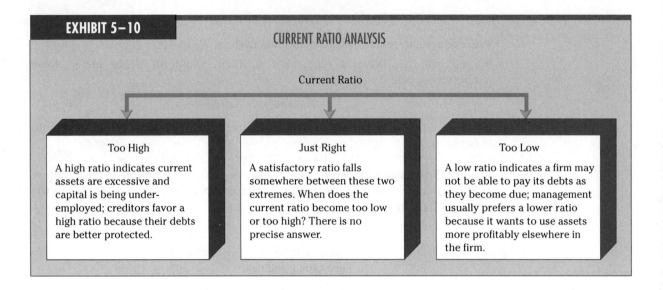

EXHIBIT 5-10

CURRENT RATIO ANALYSIS

Current Ratio

Too High

A high ratio indicates current assets are excessive and capital is being under-employed; creditors favor a high ratio because their debts are better protected.

Just Right

A satisfactory ratio falls somewhere between these two extremes. When does the current ratio become too low or too high? There is no precise answer.

Too Low

A low ratio indicates a firm may not be able to pay its debts as they become due; management usually prefers a lower ratio because it wants to use assets more profitably elsewhere in the firm.

The results of this calculation indicate how many current-asset dollars exist to pay current liabilities. In 19X3, $2 of current assets exist to pay each $1 of current liabilities. Is $2 adequate? Unfortunately, no one current ratio indicates whether an amount is adequate. Any given situation has three possibilities; these are described in Exhibit 5-10.

In the past, a current ratio of two-to-one (2 : 1) was considered necessary. For example, if an entity had $2 of current assets to pay each $1 of current liabilities, its management would have thought these current assets could shrink considerably and the firm would still be able to pay its debts. By this guide, the current ratio of Saguaro Computers, Inc., would be acceptable.

Today, however, analysts generally agree that no one ratio is sufficient for all businesses, and that other factors—such as the composition of current assets, the credit terms extended to customers, or the credit terms extended by suppliers—also must be considered to arrive at an acceptable ratio.

Dun and Bradstreet, as well as various trade publications, provides a range of current ratios that may be applicable to companies in a particular industry at one point in time. It is noteworthy that the adequacy of a current ratio depends on other developments within a company and, while a particular ratio may be satisfactory one year, it may not be adequate the next year.

COMPOSITION OF SPECIFIC ITEMS IN CURRENT ASSETS

In the following example, each company has a 2 : 1 current ratio. Is each company equally able to repay its short-term creditors?

	A	B
Current Assets		
Cash	$ 1	$10
Accounts Receivable	2	20
Inventory	37	10
Total Current Assets	$40	$40
Current Liabilities	$20	$20
Current Ratio	2 : 1	2 : 1

Each company has equal dollar amounts of current assets and current liabilities, but their debt-paying abilities are not equal. Company A must first sell some inventory and collect the resulting accounts receivable, or it can immediately sell its inventory as a single lot for cash, probably for less than its cost. This type of shrinkage is provided for in the 2 : 1 current ratio. The current ratio is, therefore, only a rough indicator of how able a firm is to pay its debts as they become due. The criticism of this ratio is that it doesn't consider the components of current assets in analyzing the solvency of a firm.

The Acid-Test Ratio

A more severe test of solvency is the so-called **acid-test ratio,** often called the *quick ratio.* It provides an indication of instant solvency—the ability to meet the immediate demands of creditors. To calculate this ratio, current assets have to be broken down into quick and nonquick current assets.

Quick Current Assets	Nonquick Current Assets
Cash	Inventory
Temporary investments	Prepaid items
Accounts receivable—trade	

These current assets are considered to be readily convertible into cash.

Cash could not be obtained immediately from these current assets.

Inventory and prepaid items are not usually convertible into cash in a short period of time. They are therefore excluded from **quick current assets** in the calculation of this ratio. The acid-test ratio is calculated by dividing the total of quick current assets by current liabilities. These are the relevant SCI financial data used to calculate the acid-test ratio:

		19X3
Quick Current Assets	(a)	$36,800
Current Liabilities	(b)	$79,000
Acid-Test Ratio	(a ÷ b)	0.47 (rounded): 1

This ratio indicates how many quick asset dollars (cash, temporary investments, and trade accounts receivable) exist to pay each $1 of current liabilities. As can be seen, Saguaro Computers, Inc., has $0.47 of quick assets to pay each $1 of current liabilities.

WHAT IS AN ADEQUATE ACID-TEST RATIO?

Analysts generally consider a one-to-one (1 : 1) acid-test ratio adequate to ensure that a firm is able to pay its current obligations. However, this is a fairly arbitrary guideline and is not necessarily reliable in all situations. A lower ratio than 1 : 1 can often be found in successful companies.

A company tries to keep in its current assets a reasonable balance among cash, receivables, and inventory. Unfortunately, there is no one indicator of what this balance really is. The balance is acceptable when debts are being paid. The "end of the rope" comes when current liabilities are not being paid.

WHAT IS THE RELATIONSHIP BETWEEN THE CURRENT RATIO AND THE ACID-TEST RATIO?

When taken together, these ratios give the financial statement reader a better understanding of the inventory implications for a company. While the current ratio may be favorable, the acid-test ratio may reveal that the current liabilities will not be met when they come due. This happens quite often when the credit terms offered by the entity's suppliers are not as generous as those offered to the entity's customers.

OPERATIONS EFFICIENCY ANALYSIS

Q14: Measuring efficiency

Each entity uses its assets as resources to earn net income. However, some entities do so more successfully than others. How can the efficiency with which a company is using its assets be established?

An evaluation of an entity's operations efficiency can be established through the calculation and study of relevant ratios. Of particular interest is the current status of the entity, the record of the entity over a number of years, and a comparison of the entity's financial performance with that of others in the same industry and in other industries.

Net income is the starting point for this **ratio analysis.** The efficient use of assets can be measured by expressing net income as a return on assets, on stockholders' equity, on sales, and on each share. An additional measurement used in the stock market to evaluate the selling price of shares relates the selling price to the share's earnings. This measure is referred to as the *price–earnings ratio.* These measurements indicate the following:

Operations Efficiency Analysis	Indicates
1. Return on Total Assets Ratio	How efficiently a company uses its assets as resources to earn net income.
2. Return on Stockholders' Equity Ratio	The adequacy of net income as a return on stockholders' equity.
3. Return on Sales Ratio	The percentage of sales revenue earned by the business after payment of creditor interest and income tax.
4. Return on Each Share/Earnings per Share	The amount of net income earned on each share of common stock.
5. Price–Earnings Ratio	The reasonableness of market price in relation to per-share earnings.

The relationship of the first three of these ratios to the balance sheet and income statement of an entity is shown in Exhibit 5-11.

Return on Total Assets Ratio

An efficient use of assets should result in a higher return on these assets; a less efficient use should result in a lower return. The return on total assets ratio is designed to measure this efficiency and is calculated as follows:

$$\frac{\text{Income from Operations}}{\text{Average Total Assets}}$$

Attention is focused on net income from operations, which is the amount earned by the entity from the use of its assets. Expenses not applicable to operations of the entity, such as interest (expenses to finance the entity) and income taxes (expenses on income due to the government) are excluded. The average of total assets is used in the calculation because the amount of assets used varies during the year.

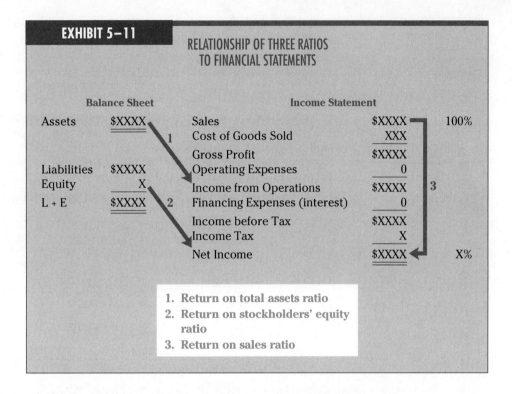

EXHIBIT 5-11

RELATIONSHIP OF THREE RATIOS
TO FINANCIAL STATEMENTS

	Balance Sheet		Income Statement		
Assets	$XXXX		Sales	$XXXX	100%
		1	Cost of Goods Sold	XXX	
			Gross Profit	$XXXX	
Liabilities	$XXXX		Operating Expenses	0	
Equity	X		Income from Operations	$XXXX	3
L + E	$XXXX	2	Financing Expenses (interest)	0	
			Income before Tax	$XXXX	
			Income Tax	X	
			Net Income	$XXXX	X%

1. Return on total assets ratio
2. Return on stockholders' equity ratio
3. Return on sales ratio

Since the ratio is based on average assets, the total assets of SCI at the end of 19X2 has to be included. Assuming SCI had total assets of $150,000 then, the average assets held during 19X3 would be $160,000, determined as follows:

Total Assets, Dec. 31, 19X2	$150,000
Total Assets, Dec. 31, 19X3	170,000
	$320,000

$$\frac{\$320,000}{2} = \$160,000 \text{ Average Assets during 19X3}$$

The return on total assets for SCI can now be calculated:

$$\frac{\text{Income from Operations}}{\text{Average Total Assets}} = \frac{\$40,000}{\$160,000} = 25\%$$

Is a 25% return good, bad, or just adequate? This question cannot be answered without knowing what the return was last year, and what the return is for other entities of the same size in the computer sales and repair field. Remember that the assets are provided by both creditors and stockholders. If the industry average for companies in the computer sales and repair field is 30% to 35%, then the management of SCI is not doing its job. If the industry average is 15% to 20%, then SCI is a good business in which to invest from either a creditor's or investor's point of view.

Return on Stockholders' Equity Ratio

The assets of an entity are financed by both creditors and stockholders. In return for their share of financing, creditors are paid interest. Stockholders have claim to whatever remains after interest and income taxes are paid. This return on stockholders' equity is measured through the following ratio:

$$\frac{\text{Net Income}}{\text{Average Stockholders' Equity}}$$

Net income after interest and income taxes is used in this calculation because only the balance remains to stockholders. Average equity is used because the amount of equity can vary during the year.

SCI's stockholders' equity at the end of 19X2 can be determined by adding the beginning balance in Retained Earnings ($21,750) to Common Stock ($10,000), or $31,750. Average Stockholders' Equity now can be determined:

Stockholders' Equity, Dec. 31, 19X2	$31,750
Stockholders' Equity, Dec. 31, 19X3	42,500
	$74,250

$$\frac{\$74,250}{2} = \$37,125 \text{ Average Stockholders' Equity}$$

The return on stockholders' equity can be calculated as follows:

$$\frac{\text{Net Income}}{\text{Average Stockholders' Equity}} = \frac{\$15,000}{\$37,125} = 40\%$$

Is a 40% return good, bad, or just adequate? This question cannot be answered without knowing what the return was last year, what the return is for other entities of the same size in the computer sales and repair field, and what the stockholders of SCI could earn if they had their money in an alternate investment. If the return on total assets were in the 5% to 6% range, the stockholders would be better off putting their money in a savings and loan to earn a very safe 7% to 8%. However, with a 40% return on total assets, the stockholders of SCI should be happy with their return.

Return on Sales Ratio

The efficiency, or *productivity*, of each sales dollar is established through the calculation of the return on sales. This percentage of sales revenue retained by the entity—after payment of creditor interest expenses and income taxes—is an index of performance that can be used to compare this entity with others in the same industry, or in other industries. The percentage of return on sales is calculated as follows:

$$\frac{\text{Net Income}}{\text{Net Sales}}$$

SCI's Return on Sales thus would be:

$$\frac{\text{Net Income}}{\text{Net Sales}} = \frac{\$15,000}{\$300,000} = 5\%$$

Again, nothing definitive can be said about a 5% return without knowing the return for SCI in the recent past and the return for others in the same industry. Some industries operate on a very low return on sales, such as below 1%, while others need 15% to 20% to survive.

Return on Each Share/Earnings per Share

The return to stockholders discussed earlier indicates the return on assets financed by stockholders. This return to stockholders also can be expressed on a per-share basis. That is, the amount of net income can be divided by the average number of common shares outstanding in order to establish how much net income has been earned for each share of stock:

$$\frac{\text{Net Income}}{\text{Average Number of Common Shares Outstanding}}$$

This expression of net income as a per-share amount is widely quoted in financial circles and, as noted, is called earnings per share (EPS). If preferred stockholders exist, their dividend claims on net income are deducted before net income is divided by the average number of shares of common stock outstanding:

$$\frac{\text{Net Income} - \text{Preferred Dividends}}{\text{Average Number of Common Shares Outstanding}}$$

Earnings per share is of particular interest to investors because of its importance in influencing stock market values. For this reason, in practice, EPS must be disclosed on the income statement.

Since SCI has no preferred stock outstanding, the EPS would be determined as follows:

$$\frac{\text{Net Income}}{\text{Average Number of Common Shares Outstanding}} = \frac{\$15,000}{10,000} = \$1.50$$

The average number of common shares outstanding was determined by reading note 2 for the balance sheet on p. 230. It was assumed that no changes occurred in the number of shares outstanding during the year. Therefore, the number outstanding at the end of the year would also be the average for the year. If the number of shares had changed during the year, a *weighted* average would be used to determine the number of shares outstanding. For instance, if shares were issued near the beginning of the year, they would be outstanding for more months than shares issued toward the end of the year.

Again, no real analysis can be made at this time without additional information. Of course an investor (stockholder) would want to compare the EPS with what had been paid for the stock, but that alone would not be indicative of a good or bad investment.

Price–Earnings Ratio

The price–earnings ratio is calculated by dividing the market value of a share by earnings per share:

$$\frac{\text{Market Price per Share}}{\text{Earnings per Share}}$$

This ratio indicates the reasonableness of market price in relation to per-share earnings. Assuming the market price of SCI's stock is $30, the price–earnings ratio would be calculated as follows:

$$\frac{\text{Market Price per Share}}{\text{Earnings per Share}} = \frac{\$30}{\$1.50} = 20$$

SCI's stock is selling for 20 times its earnings, indicating that investors currently feel that the company has future earning potential far beyond the $1.50 per share.

CHAPTER REVIEW

1 In what way is the matching principle emphasized in the income statement prepared for a merchandising firm? (p. 208)

In addition to matching operating expenses with revenue, in a merchandising operation, the cost of the goods being sold must be determined in order to match the costs against the revenue (sales) being generated. Determining the cost of the goods sold, while apparently an easily determined figure, can be much more of an estimate than expected. This dilemma will be addressed in Chapter 8.

2 What is the usefulness of the gross-profit calculation? (p. 208)

The gross profit for a merchandising firm is a very important figure. It tells management exactly how much remains to cover all operating and financing expenses and still yield a profit to the owners.

3 What accounts are used to adjust sales revenue? (pp. 209–12)

Gross sales may be adjusted by both Sale Returns and Allowances and Sales Discounts allowed for early payment.

4 How is the cost of goods sold calculated? (pp. 214–15)

Cost of goods sold is a residual calculation, that is, what can not be accounted for must have been sold. The ending inventory, determined by count, is subtracted from the summation of the beginning inventory and the purchases for the year. If the amount on hand at the end of the year is subtracted from what was available during the year the result should tell what was sold during the year.

5 What accounts are used to adjust purchase of merchandise for resale? (pp. 215–17)

The Purchases account is reduced by Purchase Returns and Allowances, and by Purchase Discounts to determine net purchases, while net purchases is increased by Transportation In to arrive at the cost of goods purchased.

6 What is the periodic inventory system, and how does it differ from the perpetual inventory system? (p. 218)

The periodic inventory system does not record changes in the inventory account during the year. When goods are purchased, a purchase account (not inventory) is debited. When goods are sold, only the sale and the related recognition of the revenue is recorded. It is not until the end of the accounting period that a physical inventory is taken, and the cost of goods sold then can be determined.

In a perpetual inventory system, as is noted on p. 219, the merchandise purchased is recorded in an inventory account, and when it is sold, the cost of the item is removed from the inventory and recorded in the Cost of Goods Sold account.

7 How is ending inventory recorded in the accounts under the periodic inventory system? (p. 218)

The easiest way to record ending inventory is to simply carry the beginning inventory from the trial balance debit column to the debit side of the income statement columns on the worksheet. This puts the worksheet out of balance, so the balancing amount, or ending inventory, is inserted in the credit side of the income statement columns and the debit side of the balance sheet columns. As described on p. 223, the ending inventory is posted to the accounts during the closing process.

8 What internal control feature is incorporated into the perpetual inventory system? (p. 219)

The major internal control feature incorporated into the perpetual inventory system is the fact that the entity can compare its ongoing inventory count of what is on hand at the end of the year with what is actually on hand, based on a physical count.

9   How do closing entries for a merchandiser differ from those prepared for a service business? (pp. 222–23)

> The closing entries are substantially the same. With a merchandiser, additional contra accounts both from sales (debits) and from purchases (credits) have to be closed out at the end of the accounting period. Also, the inventory must be adjusted. The beginning inventory must be taken off the records, and the ending inventory must be recorded. Inserting the respective amounts in the worksheet as described in the chapter guarantees that the beginning inventory will be taken off the record during the closing process, while the ending inventory will be recorded in the accounts.
>
> Other mechanical ways to record the change in inventory exist, but the one described here is the easiest.

10   What is the main advantage of classified financial statements? (pp. 223–27)

> Classified financial statements allow the user to more easily calculate financial ratios in order to evaluate the entity.

11   How do extraordinary items differ from prior-period adjustments? (pp. 227, 228–29)

> Extraordinary items are financial events that are both infrequent and unusual in nature; they are reported separately from net income, but on the face of the income statement. Prior-period adjustments, on the other hand, are corrections of accounting errors made in the past in determining net income. Prior-period adjustments are recorded directly in the Retained Earnings account and therefore bypass the income statement.

12   What is the distinction between current items and noncurrent items disclosed in the balance sheet? (p. 229)

> Current items are those that will occur within the next 12 months. Assets will be converted to cash, or be consumed, or will expire in some fashion, while current liabilities will come due and be paid.

13   What is short-term solvency analysis, and why is it important? (pp. 231–34)

> Short-term solvency analysis looks at the entity's ability to pay its debts as they mature or come due. If a business can not pay its debts as they come due, then supplies will be hard to come by, the telephone will be cut off, and similar repercussions will occur. Short-term solvency to any entity is of utmost importance.

14   How can an entity measure whether or not use of its assets is efficient? (pp. 234–37)

> Efficiency is measured in many ways, only a few of which have been mentioned in this chapter. Generally, net income is the central figure in the measurement of efficiency. It can be compared to total assets, stockholders' equity, sales, the number of shares outstanding, and to itself in past years. All of the ratios discussed in the text are important, but students must realize that any one ratio, taken by itself, is usually meaningless.

KEY TERMS

acid-test ratio   (p. 233) Quick current assets divided by current liabilities; also called the *quick ratio.*

classification   (p. 223) The grouping of accounts by category on financial statements.

cost of goods purchased   (p. 216) Purchases less purchase returns and allowances and purchase discounts, plus transportation in; also referred to as *cost of purchases.*

cost of goods sold   (p. 208) Accounting term used to describe the cost of merchandise sold during an accounting period.

current ratio   (p. 231) Current assets divided by current liabilities; also called the *working capital ratio.*

debit or **credit memo**   (p. 219) A source document that supports a journal entry recording a sale or purchase return or allowance, or other adjustments to an invoice.

dividend   (p. 227) A distribution to corporate stockholders; can consist of cash, property of the corporation, or shares of stock.

extraordinary items   (p. 227) Gains and losses that occur infrequently and that are unusual in nature; classified separately on the income statement.

fob destination   (p. 217) A term indicating that title to shipped goods passes when the goods reach their destination. The seller is responsible for transportation costs.

fob shipping point   (p. 217) A term indicating that title to shipped goods passes when the goods leave the shipping point. The buyer is responsible for transportation costs.

gross profit   (p. 208) The excess of the sales revenue over the net cost of the goods sold, also referred to as *gross margin.*

merchandise inventory   (p. 214) Goods held for resale by a retailer or a wholesaler.

merchandising   (p. 208) The activity of buying and selling items manufactured and assembled by other entities. The merchandiser does nothing to the goods other than to store them in inventory until they are sold.

operating expenses   (p. 225) Expenses incurred in the operation of the business, except items classified as *other expenses* or as *income tax expense.*

periodic inventory system   (p. 218) A system whereby a record of the beginning inventory and purchases during the period is kept. Ending inventory is determined by physically counting the goods on hand and assigning a cost to these goods; all goods not on hand at the end of the period are assumed to have been sold.

perpetual inventory system   (p. 218) A method of inventory valuation in which purchases and sales are recorded as they occur and a continuous balance of inventory on hand is calculated in terms of units and in terms of cost. The cost of goods sold is determined for each sale and is recorded. A physical count at the end of the period is used to verify the quantities that should be on hand.

prior-period adjustments   (p. 228) Gains and losses applicable to the net income reported in prior years; disclosed in the statement of retained earnings.

Purchases   (p. 213) An account used to accumulate the purchase cost of merchandise held for resale.

Purchase Discounts   (p. 216) A contra account to Purchases; cash discounts taken if payment is made within a certain discount period are recorded in this account.

Purchase Returns and Allowances   (p. 216) A contra account to Purchases; goods returned to suppliers or price adjustments allowed by suppliers are recorded in this account.

quick current assets   (p. 233) Assets that can be quickly converted into cash; usually includes cash, temporary investments, and accounts receivable.

ratio   (p. 231) The quotient resulting when one number is divided by another.

ratio analysis   (p. 234) Analysis of interrelationships of different financial statement items as a method of evaluating an entity's use of assets.

Sales   (p. 208) An account used to accumulate revenue transactions for merchandise sold to others.

Sales Discounts   (p. 212) A contra account to Sales; cash discounts taken by customers if payment is made within a certain discount period are recorded in this account.

Sales Returns and Allowances   (p. 211) A contra account to sales; goods returned by customers or price adjustments allowed to customers are recorded in this account.

solvency   (p. 230) The ability to pay current liabilities as they become due.

trade discount   (p. 220) A percentage or dollar amount used to calculate the actual sales or purchase price of merchandise.

Transportation In   (p. 217) An account used to accumulate freight charges on merchandise purchased for resale; these charges are added to the purchase cost of the merchandise.

working capital   (p. 229) The excess of current assets over current liabilities.

SELF-TEST QUESTIONS FOR REVIEW   (Answers are at the end of this chapter.)

Q4
1. Which of the following accounts are *not* used in the cost of goods sold computation?
   (a) Sales
   (b) Purchases
   (c) Ending Inventory
   (d) Beginning Inventory

Q3
2. When a customer is allowed to pay less than the invoice amount because of early payment, the difference between the amount paid and the invoice amount is recorded in which of the following accounts?
   (a) Purchase Discounts
   (b) Sales Returns and Allowances
   (c) Purchase Returns and Allowances
   (d) Sales Discounts

Q5
3. Trade discounts are recorded in which of the following accounts?
   (a) Purchase Discounts
   (b) Sales Discounts
   (c) It depends on whether the discount is allowed on a purchase or a sale.
   (d) Trade discounts are not recorded in the accounts.

Q4
4. Cost of Goods Purchased consists of which of the following?
   (a) Beginning Inventory plus Purchases less Transportation In
   (b) Beginning Inventory plus Net Purchases plus Transportation In
   (c) Beginning Inventory less Purchases plus Purchase Discounts plus Purchase Returns and Allowances plus Transportation In
   (d) Beginning Inventory plus Purchases plus Purchase Discounts plus Purchase Returns and Allowances less Transportation In

Q6
5. Taking a physical inventory is necessary when which of the following inventory systems is used?
   (a) Periodic
   (b) Perpetual
   (c) Both perpetual and periodic
   (d) A physical inventory is not necessary under either system.

Q11
6. Which of the following items are reported on the income statement?
   (a) Discontinued operations
   (b) Extraordinary items
   (c) Changes in accounting methods
   (d) All of the above

Q13
7. Which of the following ratios would be used to evaluate short-term solvency?
   (a) Price-earnings ratio
   (b) Acid-test ratio
   (c) Return on stockholders' equity ratio
   (d) Earnings per share ratio

Q14

8. Which of the following ratios would be used to evaluate the investment made by the owners of an entity?
   (a) Price-earnings ratio
   (b) Acid-test ratio
   (c) Return on stockholders' equity ratio
   (d) Earnings per share ratio

Q14

9. Which of the following ratios would indicate the reasonableness of the market value of an entity's stock?
   (a) Price-earnings ratio
   (b) Acid-test ratio
   (c) Return on stockholders' equity ratio
   (d) Earnings per share ratio

Q14

10. Which of the following ratios is applicable only in the chemical industry?
    (a) Price-earnings ratio
    (b) Acid-test ratio
    (c) Return on stockholders' equity ratio
    (d) Earnings-per-share ratio
    (e) None of the above

DEMONSTRATION PROBLEM

The following information is made available to you for John Stone, Inc. The year-end of the company is April 30.

John Stone, Inc.
Balance Sheet
April 30, 19X1

Assets			Liabilities	
Current Assets			Accounts Payable	$ 10
Cash		$ 20	Unearned Revenue	15
Accounts Receivable		30	Total Liabilities	$ 25
Merchandise Inventory		25		
Prepaid Insurance		16	**Stockholders' Equity**	
Total Current Assets		$ 91	Common Stock	10
			Retained Earnings	146
			Total Stockholders'	
			Equity	$156
Long-term Assets				
Equipment	$96			
Less: Accum. Deprec.—				
Equipment	6	90		
Total Assets		$181	Total Equities	$181

May Transactions:

May	2	Sales on Account	$100
	6	Purchases on Account	55
	8	Collection of Accounts Receivable	95
	12	Payment of Accounts Payable	40
	15	Dividends	20
	16	Sales Returns and Allowances	2
	23	Purchase Returns and Allowances	1
	27	Payment of Wages During May	10
	27	Payment of Other Expenses	8

Data for adjustment:

a. Accrued unpaid wages on May 31 amounted to $1.

b. A one-year insurance policy was purchased on January 1, 19X1.

c. Equipment has an estimated service life of 4 years.

d. The necessary deliveries were made to all customers who had paid in advance. All unearned revenue was earned in May.

e. A physical count of inventory was made on May 31, 19X1, and its cost was determined to be $20.

Required

1. Journalize the May transactions.

2. Post to appropriate general ledger accounts.

3. Prepare a trial balance on a worksheet.

4. Complete the worksheet.

5. Prepare an income statement, a statement of retained earnings, and a balance sheet as of May 31, 19X6.

6. Journalize the adjusting entries.

7. Post the adjusting entries.

8. Prepare a trial balance from the adjusted ledger accounts.

SOLUTION TO DEMONSTRATION PROBLEM

1.

John Stone, Inc.
General Journal
Page 1

Date 19X1	Description	F	Debit	Credit
May 2	Accounts Receivable	110	100	
	Sales	500		100
	To record sales for month.			
6	Purchases	550	55	
	Accounts Payable	210		55
	To record purchases for month.			
8	Cash	101	95	
	Accounts Receivable	110		95
	To record collections for month.			
12	Accounts Payable	210	40	
	Cash	101		40
	To record payments for month.			
15	Dividends	350	20	
	Cash	101		20
	To record dividends paid to stockholders.			
16	Sales Returns and Allowances	508	2	
	Accounts Receivable	110		2
	To record returns.			
23	Accounts Payable	210	1	
	Purchase Returns and Allowances	558		1
	To record allowance on purchase.			
27	Miscellaneous General Expense	652	8	
	Wages Expense	677	10	
	Cash	101		18
	To record payment of wages and other expenses.			

2.

Cash	No. 101		Accounts Payable	No. 210		Common Stock	No. 320		Sales	No. 500		Miscellaneous General Expenses	No. 652
20	40		40	10			10			100		8	
95	20		1	55									
	18			24		**Retained Earnings**	**No. 340**		**Sales Returns and Allowances**	**No. 508**		**Wages Expense**	**No. 677**
37							146		2			10	
Accounts Receivable	**No. 110**		**Unearned Revenue**	**No. 249**		**Dividends**	**No. 350**		**Purchases**	**No. 550**			
30	95			15		20			55				
100	2												
33									**Purchase Returns and Allowances**	**No. 558**			
Merchandise Inventory	**No. 150**									1			
25													
Prepaid Insurance	**No. 161**												
16													
Equipment	**No. 183**												
96													
Accum. Deprec.—Equipment	**No. 193**												
	6												

3., 4.

John Stone, Inc.
Worksheet
For the Month Ended May 31, 19X1

Account Title	Trial Balance Dr.	Trial Balance Cr.	Adjustments Dr.	Adjustments Cr.	Adjusted Trial Balance Dr.	Adjusted Trial Balance Cr.	Income Statement Dr.	Income Statement Cr.	Balance Sheet Dr.	Balance Sheet Cr.
Cash	37				37				37	
Accounts Receivable	33				33				33	
Merchandise Inventory	25				25		25	20	20	
Prepaid Insurance	16			(b) 2	14				14	
Equipment	96				96				96	
Accum. Deprec.—Equipment		6		(c) 2		8				8
Accounts Payable		24				24				24
Unearned Revenue		15	(d) 15							
Common Stock		10				10				10
Retained Earnings		146				146				146
Dividends	20				20				20	
Sales		100		(d) 15		115		115		
Sales Returns and Allowances	2				2		2			

(continued)

Account Title	Trial Balance		Adjustments		Adjusted Trial Balance		Income Statement		Balance Sheet	
	Dr.	Cr.	Dr.	Cr.	Dr.	Cr.	Dr.	Cr.	Dr.	Cr.
Purchases	55				55		55			
Purchase Returns and Allowances		1				1		1		
Miscellaneous Expense	8				8		8			
Wage Expense	10		(a) 1		11		11			
Wages Payable				(a) 1		1				1
Depreciation Expense—Equipment			(c) 2		2		2			
Insurance Expense			(b) 2		2		2			
Totals	302	302	20	20	305	305	105	136	220	189
Net Income for May							31			31
Totals							136	136	220	220

5.

John Stone, Inc.
Income Statement
For the Month Ended May 31, 19X1

Revenue

Sales		$115
Less: Sales Returns and Allowances		2
Net Sales		$113

Cost of Goods Sold

Beginning Inventory (May 1)		$25
Purchases	$55	
Less: Purchase Returns and Allowances	1	
Cost of Goods Purchased	54	
Cost of Goods Available	$79	
Ending Inventory (May 31)	20	
Total Cost of Goods Sold		59
Gross Profit		$ 54

Operating Expenses

Wages Expense	$11	
Insurance Expense	2	
Depreciation Expense	2	
Miscellaneous General Expense	8	23
Net Income		$ 31

John Stone, Inc.
Statement of Retained Earnings
For the Year Ended May 31, 19X1

Balance (April 30)	$146
Add: Net Income	31
Total	177
Less: Dividends	20
Balance (Dec. 31)	$157

John Stone, Inc.
Balance Sheet
May 31, 19X1

Assets

Current Assets		
Cash	$ 37	
Accounts Receivable	33	
Merchandise Inventory	20	
Prepaid Insurance	14	
Total Current Assets		$104
Long-term Assets		
Equipment	$ 96	
Less: Accum. Deprec.—Equipment	8	
Total Long-term Assets		88
Total Assets		$192

Liabilities

Accounts Payable	$ 24	
Wages Payable	1	
Total Liabilities		$ 25

Stockholders' Equity

Common Stock	$ 10	
Retained Earnings	157	
Total Stockholders' Equity		167
Total Liabilities and Stockholders' Equity		$192

6.

Date 19X1	Description	F	Debit	Credit
May 31	*Adjusting Entries*			
(a)	Wages Expense	667	1	
	Wages Payable	237		1
	To record Wages Payable.			
(b)	Insurance Expense	631	2	
	Prepaid Insurance	161		2
	To write off one month's insurance expense.			
(c)	Depreciation Expense—Equipment	623	2	
	Accumulated Depreciation—Equipment	193		2
	To record depreciation for one month.			
(d)	Unearned Revenue	249	15	
	Sales	500		15
	To transfer advances received to Revenue account.			

7.

Cash	No. 101
20	40
95	20
	18
37	

Accounts Receivable	No. 110
30	95
100	2
33	

Merchandise Inventory	No. 150
25	

Prepaid Insurance	No. 161
16	(b) 2
14	

Equipment	No. 183
96	

Accum. Deprec.— Equipment	No. 193
	6
(c)	2
	8

Accounts Payable	No. 210
40	10
1	55
	24

Wages Payable	No. 237
	(a) 1

Unearned Revenue	No. 249
(d) 15	15

Common Stock	No. 320
	10

Retained Earnings	No. 340
	146

Dividends	No. 350
20	

Purchases	No. 550
55	

Purchase Returns and Allowances	No. 558
	1

Sales	No. 500
	100
(d)	15
	115

Sales Returns and Allowances	No. 508
2	

Deprec. Expense— Equipment	No. 623
(c) 2	

Insurance Expense	No. 631
(b) 2	

Miscellaneous General Expenses	No. 652
8	

Wages Expense	No. 677
10	
(a) 1	
11	

8.

John Stone, Inc.
Adjusted Trial Balance
May 31, 19X1

	Account Balances	
	Debit	Credit
Cash	$ 37	
Accounts Receivable	33	
Merchandise Inventory	25	
Prepaid Insurance	14	
Equipment	96	
Accumulated Depreciation—Equipment		$ 8
Accounts Payable		24
Wages Payable		1
Common Stock		10
Retained Earnings		146

(continued)

	Account Balances	
	Debit	**Credit**
Dividends	20	
Sales		115
Sales Returns and Allowances	2	
Purchases	55	
Purchase Returns and Allowances		1
Depreciation Expense—Equipment	2	
Insurance Expense	2	
Miscellaneous General Expenses	8	
Wages Expense	11	
Totals	$305	$305

Note that Merchandise Inventory does not include the ending inventory amount at the adjusted trial balance stage. The ending inventory is recorded through the preparation and posting of closing journal entries (not required in this problem).

DISCUSSION QUESTIONS

Q5-1   How does the income statement prepared for a merchandising firm differ from that prepared for a service business?

Q5-2   What relationship does a gross-profit calculation express? Explain, using an example.

Q5-3   How does the gross profit appear on an income statement? Could it be omitted from the income statement?

Q5-4   Is the gross profit always disclosed on the income statement? Why or why not?

Q5-5   Contrast and explain the sales and collections cycle and the purchase and payment cycle.

Q5-6   What contra accounts are used for Sales and Purchases? What are their functions?

Q5-7   How is cost of purchases calculated?

Q5-8   List the components of the cost-of-goods-sold calculation.

Q5-9   Contrast the differences between the periodic inventory method and the perpetual inventory system.

Q5-10   How is ending inventory recorded on the worksheet of a merchandiser under the periodic inventory method? Illustrate your answer, using a $10,000 ending inventory as an example.

Q5-11   Explain how ending inventory is recorded in the accounts of a merchandiser.

Q5-12   Why is interest expense classified separately on the income statement?

Q5-13   What items are referred to as extraordinary? How are they disclosed?

Q5-14   What are prior-period adjustments? How do they differ from extraordinary items?

Q5-15   What categories of assets and liabilities are indicated on a classified balance sheet?

Q5-16   What are the implications for a firm to be insolvent?

Q5-17   What are financial ratios, and why are they calculated?

Q5-18   Distinguish between the current ratio and the acid-test ratio.

Q5-19   Is any one current ratio or acid-test ratio adequate for all businesses? Why or why not?

Q5-20   What ratios are relevant for an evaluation of an entity's operations efficiency?

Q5-21   Refer to Real World Example 5-1: what factors are disclosed regarding pricing by small and large organizations? How are these factors represented in the financial statements?

DISCUSSION CASE

Joe, the Restaurateur

Joe, the restaurateur, adds a rack of peanuts to the counter, hoping to pick up a little extra profit in the usual course of business. He is interviewed by his Accountant/Efficiency Expert.

EFF. EX.   Joe, you said you put in these peanuts because some people ask for them, but do you realize what this rack of peanuts is costing you?

JOE   It ain't gonna cost. 'Sgonna be a profit. Sure, I hadda pay $25 for a fancy rack to holda bags, but the peanuts cost 6¢ a bag and I sell 'em for 10¢. Figger I sell 50 bags a week to start. It'll take 12½ weeks to cover the cost of the rack. After that I gotta clear profit of 4¢ a bag. The more I sell, the more I make.

EFF. EX.   That is an antiquated and completely unrealistic approach, Joe. Fortunately, modern accounting procedures permit a more accurate picture which reveals the complexities involved.

JOE   Huh?

EFF. EX.   To be precise, those peanuts must be integrated into your entire operation and be allocated their appropriate share of business overhead. They must share a proportionate part of your expenditures for rent, heat, light, equipment depreciation, decorating, salaries for your waitresses, cook,— —

JOE   The cook? What'sa he gotta do wit'a peanuts? He don' even know I got 'em!

EFF. EX.   Look, Joe, the cook is in the kitchen, the kitchen prepares the food, the food is what brings people in here, and the people ask to buy peanuts. That's why you must charge a portion of the cook's wages, as well as part of your own salary to peanut sales. This sheet contains a carefully calculated costs analysis which indicates the peanut operation should pay exactly $1,278 per year toward these general overhead costs.

JOE   The peanuts? $1,278 a year for overhead? the nuts?

EFF. EX.   It's really a little more than that. You also spend money each week to have the windows washed, to have the place swept out in the mornings and keep soap in the washroom. That raises the total to $1,313 per year.

JOE (thoughtfully)   But the peanut salesman said I'd make money—put 'em on the end of the counter, he said—and get 4¢ a bag profit— —

EFF. EX. (with a sniff)   He's got an accountant. Do you actually know what the portion of the counter occupied by the peanut rack is worth to you?

JOE   Ain't worth nothing. No stool there—just a dead spot at the end.

EFF. EX.   The modern cost picture permits no dead spots. Your counter contains 60 square feet and your counter business grosses $15,000 a year. Consequently, the square foot of space occupied by the peanut rack is worth $250 per year. Since you have taken that area away from general counter use, you must charge the value of the space to the accountant.

JOE   You mean I gotta add $250 a year more to the peanuts?

EFF. EX.   Right. That raises their shares of the general operating costs to a grand total of $1,563 per year. Now, then, if you sell 50 bags of peanuts per week, these allocated costs will amount to 60¢ per bag.

JOE   WHAT?

EFF. EX.   Obviously, to that must be added your purchase price of 6¢ per bag, which brings the total to 66¢. So you see, by selling peanuts at 10¢ per bag you are losing 56¢ on every sale.

JOE   Somethin's crazy!

EFF. EX.   Not at all! Here are the figures. They prove your peanut operation cannot stand on its own feet.

JOE *(brightening)*   Suppose I sell lotsa peanuts—thousand bags a week 'stead a fifty?

EFF. EX. *(tolerantly)*   Joe, you don't understand the problem. If the volume of peanut sales increases, your operating costs will go up—you'll have to handle more bags, with more time, more depreciation, more everything. The basic principle of accounting is firm on that subject! "The Bigger the Operation the More General Overhead Costs that Must Be Allocated." No, increasing the volume of sales won't help.

JOE   Okay. You so smart, you tell me what I gotta do.

EFF. EX. *(condescendingly)*   Well—you could first reduce operating expenses.

JOE   How?

EFF. EX.   Move to a building with cheaper rent. Cut salaries. Wash the windows biweekly. Have the floor swept only on Thursday. Remove the soap from the washrooms. Decrease the area value of your counter. For example, if you can cut your expenses 50 percent that will reduce the amount allocated to peanuts from $1,563 down to $781.50 per year, reducing the cost to 36¢ per bag.

JOE *(slowly)*   That's better?

EFF. EX.   Much, much better. However, even then you would lose 26¢ per bag if you charge only 10¢. Therefore, you must also raise your selling price. If you want a net profit of 4¢ per bag you would have to charge 40¢.

JOE *(flabbergasted)*   You mean even after I cut operating costs 50 percent, I still gotta charge 40¢ for a 10¢ bag of peanuts? Nobody's that nuts about nuts! Who'd buy 'em?

EFF. EX.   That's a secondary consideration. The point is, at 40¢ you'd be selling at a price based upon a true and proper evaluation of your then-reduced costs.

JOE *(eagerly)*   Look! I gotta better idea. Why don't I just throw the nuts out—put 'em in a ash can?

EFF. EX.   Can you afford it?

JOE   Sure. All I got is about 50 bags of peanuts—cost about three bucks—so I lose $25 on the rack, but I'm outa this nasty business and no more grief.

EFF. EX. *(shaking head)*   Joe, it isn't quite that simple. You are in the peanut business! The minute you throw those peanuts out you are adding $1,563 of annual overhead to the rest of your operation. Joe—be realistic—can you afford to do that?

JOE *(completely crushed)*   It'sa unbelievable! Last week I was a make money. Now I'm in a trouble—justa because I think peanuts on a counter is a gonna bring me some extra profit—justa because I believe 50 bags of peanuts a week is a easy.

EFF. EX. *(with raised eyebrow)*   That is the object of modern cost studies, Joe—to dispel those false illusions.

Source "Peanuts—or The Higher Control of Business", *Cost and Management,* IV, 4 (July–August, 1970), p. 63. (Reprinted from the *New York Certified Public Accountant,* June, 1960.)

For Discussion

1. For financial statement purposes, some expenses have been shown in Chapter 5 to be common to both the selling and administrative functions; these expenses have to be apportioned between these functions on some equitable basis. In this case, the accountant/efficiency expert also believes that costs must further be apportioned among the types of items sold in the restaurant to enable Joe to make accurate business decisions. Is the accountant/efficiency expert correct? Why or why not?

2. If you prepared an income statement for Joe without any peanut sales and a second income statement showing the sale of 50 bags of peanuts a week, which income statement would show a larger net income? Why?

3. How accurate a picture has the accountant/efficiency expert given Joe? Does Joe make $0.04 a bag or doesn't he?

EXERCISES

Sales discounts, returns
and allowances (Q3)

E5-1   Sierra, Inc., uses the periodic inventory method. Its transactions during June 19X5 are as follows:

June 3 Sierra sold $1,500 of merchandise for credit to Pierre, Inc., for terms 2/10, net 30.
     8 Pierre returned $800 of defective merchandise purchased June 3.
   13 Sierra received payment from Pierre for the balance due.

Required

Prepare journal entries to record the above transactions.

Purchase discounts,
returns and allowances
(Q5)

E5-2   Center Corp. uses the periodic method of inventory. Its transactions during July 19X4 are as follows:

July 6 Purchased $600 of merchandise on account from St. Luke, Inc., for terms 1/10, net 30
    9 Returned $200 of defective merchandise
  15 Paid the amount due to St. Luke

Required

Prepare journal entries to record the above transactions.

Cost of goods sold
calculation (Q4)

E5-3   The following data pertain to Max Co.

Ending Inventory	$ 440
Beginning Inventory	375
Purchases	2,930
Purchase Discounts	5
Purchase Returns	20
Transportation In	105

Required

Calculate the cost of goods sold.

Cost of goods sold
computations (Q4)

E5-4   The following are computations for the cost of goods sold for Case A through Case F.

Amount	Case A	Case B	Case C
Beginning Inventory	$ 20	$ 50	$100
Purchases	300	500	600
Total	320	550	?
Ending Inventory	50	?	200
Cost of Goods Sold	?	390	500

	Case D	Case E	Case F
Beginning Inventory	$300	?	$300
Purchases	?	600	?
Total	850	?	950
Ending Inventory	?	450	?
Cost of Goods Sold	375	475	?

Required

Determine the missing amounts for the six cases given.

Correcting an income statement (Q1–Q5, Q10)

E5-5   The following income statement was prepared by the new accountant of Careless Company, Inc.

(1)	**Careless Company, Inc.**		
(2)	**Income Statement**		
(3)	**December 31, 19X5**		
	($000)		
(4)	Sales less: Returns and Allowances	$9,440	
(5)	Purchases: Discounts Earned	10	$9,450
(6)	Less: Cost of Goods Sold		
(7)	Ending Inventory	$ 880	
(8)	Add: Purchases	5,860	
(9)	Delivery Expense	360	
(10)	Goods Available for Sale	$7,100	
(11)	Beginning Inventory	750	6,350
(12)	Operating Profit		$3,100
(13)	Less: Expenses		
(14)	Salaries	$1,220	
(15)	Utilities	210	
(16)	Insurance	190	
(17)	Transportation In	205	
(18)	Property Tax	43	
(19)	Miscellaneous Expenses	260	2,428
(20)	Net Income (before income tax)		$ 672
(21)	Income Tax		312
(22)	Net Income		$ 360

Required

Identify the errors in the income statement by referring to the assigned line numbers and briefly explain why they are errors.

Preparing an income statement from closing entries (Q1–Q5, Q9, Q10)

E5-6   The following closing entry is taken from the journal of J.J. Jones, Inc., as of December 31, 19X4:

General Journal

Date 19X4	Description	F	Debit	Credit
Dec. 31	Sales		161,000	
	Purchase Returns and Allowances		1,500	
	Inventory (Dec. 31)		13,500	
	Purchases			84,000
	Rent Expense			18,000
	Advertising Expense			13,600
	Delivery Expense			4,800

Date 19X4	Description	F	Debit	Credit
	Office Supplies Expense			6,400
	Miscellaneous General Expense			11,650
	Inventory (Jan. 1)			11,250
	Income Summary			26,300
	To close revenue and expense accounts and to set up ending inventory.			

Required
Prepare an income statement in proper form.

Gross profit, gross profit rate, inventory systems (Q2, Q6, Q7)

E5-7 The following balances are taken from the records of D-Liver Corp. as of December 31, 19X2, its first year-end:

Transportation In	$ 500
Delivery Expense	1,200
Sales	25,000
Purchases	20,000
Sales Returns	2,000
Purchase Returns	1,000
Sales Discounts	400
Purchase Discounts	300
Interest Expense	4,000

The inventory as of December 31, 19X2, amounts to $7,900.

Required
1. Calculate the gross profit. (You are not required to prepare a partial income statement.)
2. What is the percentage of gross profit to net sales?
3. Is D-Liver using a periodic or perpetual inventory system? How can you tell?

Exercises 5-8 to 5-14 review various solvency and efficiency ratio analyses with decision making and are based on the following information taken from the records of B. J. Fuller Co.

Item	Dec. 31, 19X7	Dec. 31, 19X8
Current Assets	$100,000	$150,000
Quick Current Assets	50,000	60,000
Current Liabilities	80,000	90,000
Total Assets	750,000	950,000
Total Liabilities	300,000	400,000
Total Stockholders' Equity	450,000	550,000
Net Income	25,000	110,000
Net Income from Operations Before Tax	40,000	160,000
Sales	360,000	600,000
Dividends Paid	25,000	10,000
Number of Common Shares Outstanding	10,000	20,000
Market Price of the Common Shares	35	115

Assume that the information from the December 31, 19X7, balance sheet was unchanged from the December 31, 19X6, balance sheet.

Current ratio (Q13)   **E5-8**   Determine the current ratio for B. J. Fuller as of December 31, 19X7, and December 31, 19X8, and briefly comment on the change.

Acid-test ratio (Q13)   **E5-9**   Determine the acid-test ratio for B. J. Fuller as of December 31, 19X7, and December 31, 19X8, and briefly comment on the change.

Return on total assets (Q14)   **E5-10**   Determine the return on total assets for B. J. Fuller as of December 31, 19X7, and December 31, 19X8, and briefly comment on the change.

Return on stockholders' equity (Q14)   **E5-11**   Determine the return on stockholders' equity for B. J. Fuller as of December 31, 19X7, and December 31, 19X8, and briefly comment on the change.

Return on sales (Q14)   **E5-12**   Determine the return on sales for B. J. Fuller as of December 31, 19X7, and December 31, 19X8, and briefly comment on the change.

Earnings per share (Q14)   **E5-13**   Determine the earnings per share for B. J. Fuller as of December 31, 19X7, and December 31, 19X8, and briefly comment on the change.

Price-earnings ratio (Q14)   **E5-14**   Determine the price-earnings ratio for B. J. Fuller as of December 31, 19X7, and December 31, 19X8, and briefly comment on the change.

PROBLEMS

Preparation of an income statement (Q1–Q5, Q9, Q10)   **P5-1**   The following information is extracted from the income statement columns of the worksheet of the Nevada Co. as of December 31, 19X4.

Account Title	Income Statement Dr.	Cr.
Merchandise Inventory	184,000	200,000
Sales		781,600
Sales Returns and Allowances	16,400	
Sales Discounts	16,480	
Purchases	364,000	
Purchase Returns and Allowances		15,200
Purchase Discounts		4,800
Transportation In	6,560	
Salaries—Salespersons	88,000	
Advertising Expense	15,600	
Delivery Expense	69,200	
Miscellaneous Selling Expense	15,000	
Salaries—Office	80,000	
Property Taxes	13,500	
Miscellaneous Office Expense	32,440	
Supplies Expense	9,060	
Interest Income		840
Insurance Expense	11,160	
Depreciation Expense	22,080	
Interest Expense	2,112	
Income Tax Expense	18,530	
Totals	964,122	1,002,440
Net Income	38,318	
Totals	1,002,440	1,002,440

Required

1. Prepare an income statement in the correct format (record Depreciation Expense as General and Administrative Expense).

2. Prepare all necessary closing journal entries.

Journal entries for a merchandising entity (Q1, Q3, Q6)

P5-2 Beacon Hill Corp. was incorporated on July 2, 19X2, to operate a merchandising business. All its sales on account are made according to the following terms: 2/10, n/30. Its transactions during July 19X2 are as follows:

July 2 Issued common stock for $5,000 to George Hill, the incorporator and sole stockholder of the corporation

2 Purchased $3,500 of merchandise on account from Westmount Pencils, Inc., for terms 2/10, n/30

2 Sold $2,000 of merchandise on account to Meadow Tool Rentals, Inc.

3 Paid Concordia Rentals Corp. $500 for July rent

5 Paid Westwood Furniture, Inc. $1,000 for equipment

8 Collected $200 for a cash sale made today to Byron Peel

8 Purchased $2,000 of merchandise on account from MacDonald Distributors, Inc., for terms 2/15, n/30

9 Received the amount due from Meadow Tool Rentals Inc., for the July 2 sale (less discount)

10 Paid Westmount Pencils, Inc., for the July 2 purchase (less discount)

10 Purchased $200 of merchandise on account from Peel Products, Inc., for terms n/30

15 Sold $2,000 of merchandise on account to Condor Products Corp.

15 Purchased $1,500 of merchandise on account from Draper Door, Inc., for terms 2/10, n/30

15 Received a credit memo from MacDonald Distributors Inc., for $100 of defective merchandise included in the July 8 purchase

16 Condor Products Corp. returned $200 of merchandise: issued a credit memo

20 Sold $3,500 of merchandise on account to Pine Promotions Co.

20 Paid MacDonald Distributors Inc., for half the purchase made July 8 (less credit memo, less discount on payment)

24 Received half the amount due from Condor Products Corp. in partial payment for the July 15 sale (less discount on payment)

24 Paid Draper Door Inc., for the purchase made July 15 (less discount)

26 Sold $600 of merchandise on account to Daytona Sales Inc.

26 Purchased $800 of merchandise on account from Gold & Silver Co. for terms 2/10, n/30

31 Paid Real-Quick Transport Co. $350 for transportation to our warehouse during the month. (All purchases are fob shipping point.)

Required

Prepare journal entries to record the July transactions.

Journal entries for a merchandising entity (Q1, Q3, Q6)

P5-3 Lucerne Sales Corp. was incorporated on May 1, 19X1, to operate a merchandising business. All its sales on account are made according to the following terms; 2/10, net 30. Its transactions during May 19X1 are as follows:

May 1 Issued common stock for $2,000 to Harry Jones, the incorporator and sole stockholder of the corporation

1 Received $10,000 from Second National Bank as a demand bank loan

1 Paid Cadillac Corp. $1,500 for three months rent in advance

1 Paid Avanti Equipment Co. $5,000 for equipment

May 1 Purchased $2,000 of merchandise on account from St. Luke Wholesalers, Inc., for terms 2/10, n/30
     1 Sold $2,500 of merchandise on account to New York West Distributors
     2 Purchased $1,800 of merchandise on account from Rosedale Products Co. for terms n/30
     2 Sold $2,000 of merchandise on account to Terrebonne Sales, Inc.
     3 Collected $500 for a cash sale made today to Irwin Peabody
     5 Paid All State Insurance Inc. $1,200 for a one-year insurance policy, effective May 1
     5 Sold $1,000 of merchandise on account to Brock Stores Corporation
     6 Terrebonne Sales, Inc., returned $500 of merchandise: issued a credit memo
     8 Received a credit memo from St. Luke Wholesalers, Inc., for $300 of defective merchandise included in the May 1 purchase and returned subsequently to St. Luke
     8 Purchased $2,800 of merchandise on account from Elmhurst Novelties, Inc., for terms 2/15, n/30
     9 Received the amount due from New York West Distributors from the May 1 sale (less discount)
     9 Paid St. Luke Wholesalers, Inc., for the May 1 purchase (less discount and credit memo)
    10 Sold $400 of merchandise on account to Western Warehouse
    11 Received the amount due from Terrebonne Sales, Inc., (less the May 6 credit memo and discount)
    13 Paid Express Corporation $100 for transportation in
    15 Purchased $1,500 of merchandise on account from Hudson Distributors, Inc., for terms 2/10, n/30
    15 Sold $1,500 of merchandise on account to Roxboro Outlets, Inc.
    15 Paid $500 in commissions to Harry Jones
    19 Paid Rosedale Products Co. for the May 2 purchase
    19 Purchased $1,200 of merchandise on account from Mid-Island Stores Corp. for terms 1/10, n/30
    22 Purchased $600 of merchandise on account from Quick Sales Co. for terms n/30
    22 Paid Elmhurst Novelties, Inc., for the May 8 purchase (less discount)
    24 Paid Express Corporation $150 for transportation in
    25 Sold $900 of merchandise on account to Kirkland Center, Inc.
    26 Received the amount due from Brock Stores Corporation
    27 Paid $200 to Yale Deliveries, Inc., for deliveries made to customers
    28 Collected $300 for a cash sale made today to Joe Montclair
    28 Made a $200 cash purchase from Ballantyne Sales, Inc., today
    28 Sold $900 of merchandise on account to Lachine Wharf Corp.
    29 Purchased $100 of merchandise on account from Sidekicks, Inc.
    29 Paid Speedy, Inc., $300 for deliveries
    29 Paid Impetus Advertising Agency $400 for advertising materials used during May
    29 Paid the power company $100 for electricity
    29 Paid Harry Jones $350 commission
    30 Collected $1,000 on account from Roxboro Outlets, Inc.
    31 Paid Mid-Island Stores Corp. $700 on account
    31 Paid Harry Jones $100 for dividends declared today

Required

1. Prepare journal entries to record the May transactions.

2. Prepare any adjusting entries you believe are necessary as a result of the above transactions.

Preparation of a
balance sheet; ratio
analysis and decision
making (Q12, Q13)

P5-4 The following accounts and account balances are taken from the worksheet of Kapoor Enterprises, Inc., as of December 31, 19X6, its fiscal year-end.

| | Balance Sheet | |
Account Title	Dr.	Cr.
Cash	2,000	
Accounts Receivable	8,000	
Merchandise Inventory	19,000	
Prepaid Insurance	1,000	
Land	5,000	
Buildings	25,000	
Equipment	20,000	
Accum. Deprec.—Buildings		1,000
Accum. Deprec.—Equipment		4,000
Bank Loan (due 19X7)		5,000
Accounts Payable		7,000
Income Tax Payable		3,000
Mortgage Payable (due 19X9)		50,000
Common Stock		3,000
Retained Earnings		2,000
Dividends	1,000	
Totals	81,000	75,000
Net Income		6,000
Totals	81,000	81,000

Required

1. Using the above information, prepare a statement of retained earnings and a classified balance sheet.

2. Make the following calculations:
   a. The proportion of creditor to stockholders' claims on the assets of Kapoor
   b. The current ratio
   c. The acid-test ratio

3. Assume you are the loan officer of the bank where Kapoor has applied for a 120-day loan of $10,000. Would you grant the loan? Why or why not?

4. If the loan were granted, calculate the current ratio and acid-test ratio immediately following the receipt of the loan on January 2, 19X7.

Worksheet, adjusting,
closing, statements,
ratio analysis, decision
making (Q1–Q5, Q9,
Q10, Q12, Q13)

P5-5 The following trial balance has been extracted from the records of Diane Jewelry, Inc., as of December 31, 19X5, its fiscal year-end. The balances for Merchandise Inventory and Retained Earnings have not changed during the year.

| | Account Balances | |
	Debit	Credit
Cash	$ 750	
Accounts Receivable	12,000	
Merchandise Inventory	6,000	
Prepaid Rent	-0-	
Office Supplies	-0-	
Equipment—Office	4,400	
Accum. Depreciation		-0-
Bank Loan		$ 5,000

(continued)

	Account Balances	
	Debit	Credit
Accounts Payable		12,540
Income Tax Payable		2,400
Common Stock		2,000
Retained Earnings		1,500
Dividends	900	
Sales		50,000
Sales Returns	1,500	
Sales Discounts	500	
Purchases	35,000	
Purchase Returns		1,700
Purchase Discounts		300
Transportation In	1,000	
Advertising Expense	1,700	
Commissions Expense	4,800	
Delivery Expense	650	
Depreciation Expense	-0-	
Insurance Expense	350	
Interest Expense	600	
Office Supplies Expense	350	
Rent Expenses	1,950	
Telephone Expense	300	
Utilities Expense	290	
Income Tax Expense	2,400	
Totals	$75,440	$75,440

Required

1. Record the trial balance on a worksheet.

2. Prepare adjusting entries for the following and record them on the worksheet.
   a. A sale on account for $1,000 was made on December 31 but has not been recorded.
   b. A physical count indicates that $100 of supplies are still on hand.
   c. No depreciation has been recorded on the office equipment. $400 is estimated applicable to 19X5.
   d. The statement for use of the phone during December has not been received. The company estimates that the charge will be about $60.

3. Complete the worksheet. A physical count of inventory indicates that $8,000 of merchandise is still on hand at December 31, 19X5.

4. From the worksheet, prepare the following financial statements in good form:
   a. Classified income statement (The advertising, commissions, and delivery expenses are considered as selling expenses.)
   b. Statement of retained earnings
   c. Classified balance sheet

5. From the worksheet, prepare all necessary closing entries.

6. Answer the following questions:
   a. What is the proportion of creditor to stockholder claims on the assets of the corporation?
   b. What is the current ratio?
   c. What is the acid-test ratio?

7. Assume you are the loan officer of a bank to which the corporation has applied for an additional 3-month, $10,000 bank loan. Would you grant the loan? Why or why not?

8. If the loan were granted on January 2, 19X6, calculate the working capital, current ratio, and acid-test ratio immediately following receipt of the loan.

ALTERNATE PROBLEMS

Preparation of an
income statement
(Q1–Q5, Q9, Q10)

AP5-1 The following information is extracted from the income statement columns of the worksheet of the Arizona Co. as of December 31, 19X7.

Account Title	Income Statement Dr.	Cr.
Merchandise Inventory	365,000	418,000
Sales		948,000
Sales Returns and Allowances	27,800	
Sales Discounts	15,780	
Purchases	456,000	
Purchase Returns and Allowances		34,700
Purchase Discounts		17,450
Transportation In	9,700	
Salaries—Salespersons	112,000	
Advertising Expense	88,600	
Delivery Expense	98,000	
Miscellaneous Selling Expense	14,350	
Salaries—Office	56,800	
Property Taxes	23,500	
Miscellaneous Office Expense	17,500	
Supplies Expense	34,000	
Interest Income		34,000
Depreciation Expense	34,000	
Interest Expense	44,700	
Income Tax Expense	16,300	
Totals	1,414,030	1,452,150
Net Income	38,120	
Totals	1,452,150	1,452,150

Required

1. Prepare an income statement in the correct format (record Depreciation Expense as General and Administrative Expense).

2. Prepare all necessary closing entries.

Journal entries for a
merchandising entity
(Q1, Q3, Q6)

AP5-2 Simco Products, Inc., was incorporated on April 1, 19X1, to operate a merchandising business. All its sales on account are made according to the following terms: 2/10, n30. Its transactions during April 19X1 are as follows.

Apr. 1 Issued common stock for $3,000 to Rosco Simco, the incorporator and sole stockholder of the corporation

1 Purchased $4,000 of merchandise on account from Beaconsfield Wholesalers, Inc., for terms 2/10, n/30

1 Sold $3,000 of merchandise on account to Ahuntic Products Corp.

2 Collected $500 for a cash sale made today to George Kirkland

2 Purchased $750 of merchandise on account from Dorval Wholesalers, Inc., for terms n/30

2 Sold $1,200 of merchandise on account to Chambly Stores, Inc.

5 Received half the amount due from Ahuntic Products Corp. for the April 1purchase

8 Received the amount due from Chambly Stores, Inc., for the April 2 purchase

9 Paid Beaconsfield Wholesalers, Inc., for the April 1 purchase

Apr. 10   Purchased $2,000 of merchandise on account from Carlton Distributors, Inc. for terms 2/15, n/30
     11   Sold $500 of merchandise on account to Presidential Sales, Inc.
     12   Presidential Sales, Inc., returned $100 of merchandise: issued a credit memo
     15   Received a credit memo from Dorval Wholesalers, Inc., for $150 for defective merchandise included in the April 2 purchase and subsequently returned
     15   Purchased $1,500 of merchandise on account from Atwater Distributors, Inc., for terms 2/10, n/30
     19   Purchased $1,250 of merchandise on account from Kildare Sales, Inc., for terms n/30
     20   Sold $2,000 of merchandise on account to Salaberry Corp.
     20   Received the amount due from Presidential Sales, Inc., for the April 11 purchase
     22   Paid Carlton Distributors, Inc., for the April 10 purchase
     24   Paid Atwater Distributors, Inc., for the April 15 purchase
     27   Sold $800 of merchandise on account to Bishop Emporium Corp.
     30   Paid Rapid Delivery, Inc., $200 for deliveries made to customers during the month
     30   Paid Truck Forwarders, Inc., $500 for transportation to our warehouse during the month

Required
Prepare journal entries to record the April transactions.

Journal entries for a
merchandising entity
(Q1, Q3, Q6)

AP5-3   Rockland Wholesalers, Inc., was incorporated on March 1 to operate a merchandising business. All its sales on account are made according to the following terms: 2/10, n/30.

Mar. 1   Issued common stock for $410,000 to Michael Strong, the incorporator and sole stockholder of the corporation
      1   Paid Brunswick Fixtures, Inc., $4,000 for equipment
      1   Purchased $2,100 of merchandise on account from Mid-Island Stores Corp. for terms 2/10, n/30
      2   Sold $2,000 of merchandise on account to Kirkland Centers, Inc.
      2   Collected $300 for a cash sale made today to Irving Clayton
      3   Purchased $500 of merchandise on account from Quick Sales Co. for terms 1/10, n/30
      4   Sold $2,500 of merchandise on account to Western Warehouse
      4   Kirkland Centers, Inc., returned $200 of merchandise: issued a credit memo
      5   Purchased $1,400 of merchandise on account from St Luke Wholesalers, Inc., on account for terms n/30
      6   Received a credit memo from Mid-Island Stores Corp. for $100 of defective merchandise included in the March 1 purchase and subsequently returned to Mid-Island
      6   Sold $1,500 of merchandise on account to Lachine Wharf Corp.
      7   Purchased $600 of merchandise on account from Brock Stores Corporation for terms 2/15, n/30
      8   Received the amount due from Kirkland Centers, Inc.
     10   Paid Quick Sales Co. for the March 3 purchase
     11   Received $7,500 from Third National Bank as a demand bank loan
     12   Paid Fairview Realty Corp. $1,000 for two months rent, March and April
     12   Sold $700 of merchandise on account to Hudson Distributors, Inc.
     13   Received the amount due from Western Warehouse
     15   Paid Michael Strong $350 for commissions earned to date

Mar. 15 Paid Mid-Island Stores Corporation $1,000 on account

15 Purchased $1,000 of merchandise on account from Rosedale Products, Inc., for terms 2/15, n/30

18 Paid Brock Stores Corporation for half of the March 7 purchase

19 Collected $100 for a cash sale made today to Al Trudeau

20 Purchased $1,200 of merchandise on account from Sheraton Centers, Inc., for terms n/30

20 Paid $400 for a cash purchase from Roslyn Distributors, Inc.

20 Sold $600 of merchandise on account to Sidekicks, Inc.

21 Paid St. Luke Wholesalers, Inc., $700 on account

22 Received $500 on account from Lachine Wharf Corp.

23 Paid All-City Insurance Co. $2,400 for a one-year insurance policy, effective March 1

24 Paid $300 for a cash purchase from C.K.U. Emporium

25 Sold $1,400 of merchandise on account to Elmhurst Novelties, Inc.

26 Purchased $700 of merchandise on account from Grand Markets, Inc., for terms 2/10, n/30

30 Paid D-Liver Corp. $500 for deliveries

30 Paid Michael Strong $400 for commissions earned to date

30 Paid Bell-Bec $75 for the monthly telephone statement

30 Paid Johnson Visuals, Inc., $250 for advertising materials used during the month

31 Paid Michael Strong $200 for dividends declared today

Required

1. Prepare journal entries to record the March transactions.

2. Prepare any adjusting entries necessary as a result of the Rockland transactions.

Preparation of a balance sheet; ratio analysis and decision making (Q12, Q13)

AP5-4 The following information is taken from the balance sheet columns of the worksheet of Salem Enterprises for the year ended December 31, 19X5.

Account Title	Balance Sheet	
	Dr.	Cr.
Cash	23,500	
Accounts Receivable	32,000	
Merchandise Inventory	67,000	
Prepaid Insurance	6,000	
Land	10,000	
Buildings	88,000	
Equipment	45,000	
Accum. Depreciation—Buildings		37,000
Accum. Depreciation—Equipment		23,000
Bank Loan (due 19X5)		13,000
Accounts Payable		38,000
Income Tax Payable		22,000
Mortgage Payable (due 19X9)		38,500
Common Stock		15,000
Retained Earnings		23,000
Dividends	13,000	
Totals	284,500	209,500
Net Income		75,000
Totals	284,500	284,500

Required

1. Using the above information, prepare a statement of retained earnings and a classified balance sheet.

2. Determine the following ratios:
   a. Debit-to-equity
   b. Current
   c. Acid-test

3. Assume you are the loan officer of the bank where Salem has applied for a 120-day loan of $10,000. Would you grant the loan? Explain.

4. If the loan were granted, determine the current and acid-test ratios immediately after the receipt of the $10,000 on January 2, 19X6.

Worksheet, adjusting, closing, statements ratio analysis, decision making (Q1–Q5, Q9, Q10, Q12, Q13)

AP5-5   The following trial balance has been extracted from the records of Van der Aa Merchants, Inc., at December 31, 19X2, its fiscal year-end. The balances for Merchandise Inventory and Retained Earnings have not changed during the year.

	Account Balances	
	Debit	Credit
Cash	$ 1,500	
Accounts Receivable	5,000	
Merchandise Inventory	5,000	
Prepaid Insurance	1,300	
Prepaid Rent	600	
Equipment—Office	12,500	
Accumulated Depreciation		-0-
Bank Loan		$ 10,000
Accounts Payable		8,350
Income Tax Payable		3,600
Common Stock		3,000
Retained Earnings		2,000
Dividends	600	
Sales		75,000
Sales Returns	2,250	
Sales Discounts	750	
Purchases	60,000	
Purchase Returns		9,400
Purchase Discounts		600
Transportation In	2,000	
Advertising Expense	1,800	
Commissions Expense	7,200	
Delivery Expense	1,600	
Depreciation Expense	-0-	
Insurance Expense	1,100	
Interest Expense	1,200	
Rent Expense	3,300	
Telephone Expense	550	
Utilities Expenses	100	
Income Tax Expense	3,600	
Totals	$111,950	$111,950
	Total Debits	= Total Credits

Required

1. Record the above trial balance on a worksheet.

2. Prepare adjusting entries for the following and record them on the worksheet.
   a. The balance in Prepaid Rent consists of rent for the months of December 19X2 and January 19X3.
   b. Interest on the bank loan applicable to the month of December amounts to $100. This amount has not yet been recorded. Record as Interest Payable.
   c. No depreciation has yet been recorded on the office equipment; $500 is estimated applicable to 19X2.
   d. The statement for use of the phone during December has not been received. The company estimates that the charge will be about $50.
   e. The balance in Prepaid Insurance includes an amount applicable to December 19X2 and the 12 months of 19X3.

3. Complete the worksheet. A physical count of inventory indicates that $10,000 of merchandise is on hand at December 31, 19X2.

4. From the worksheet, prepare the following financial statements in proper form:
   a. Classified income statement (The advertising, commission and delivery expenses are considered as selling expenses.)
   b. Statement of retained earnings
   c. Classified balance sheet

5. From the worksheet, prepare all necessary closing entries.

6. Answer the following questions:
   a. What is the proportion of creditor to stockholder claims on the assets of the corporation?
   b. What is the current ratio?
   c. What is the acid-test ratio?

7. Assume that you are the loan officer of a bank to which the corporation has applied for an additional 6-month $5,000 bank loan. Would you grant the loan? Why or why not?

8. If the loan were granted on January 2, 19X3, calculate the working capital, current ratio, and acid-test ratio immediately following receipt of the loan.

DECISION PROBLEM

Nu-Vogue Hat Shop maintained incomplete records. After investigation, you uncovered the following assets and liabilities:

	19X6	
	January 1	**December 1**
Assets		
Cash	$ 2,680	$ 2,060
Accounts Receivable	13,400	13,660
Merchandise Inventory	6,200	7,600
Equipment (net of depreciation)	10,400	11,200
Prepaid Insurance	240	120
Total Assets	$32,920	$34,640

(continued)

	19X6	
Liabilities	January 1	December 1
Accounts Payable	$ 2,000	$ 4,400
Bank Loan		6,000
Accrued Liabilities	180	100
	$ 2,180	$10,500
Common Stock	1,600	4,000
Retained Earnings	29,140	20,140
Total Liabilities	$32,920	$34,640

An analysis of cash inflow and outflow showed:

Collections from Customers	$17,940
Proceeds of Bank Loan	6,000
Additional Common Stock Issued	2,400
Payment to Creditors	12,200
Payment of Expenses (selling)	9,000
Refunds on Sales	700
Dividends	3,000
Interest on Bank Loan	60
Purchase of Equipment	2,000

Required

1. Compute the net income (or loss) by analyzing the changes in retained earnings.

2. Prepare an income statement in the correct format.

3. Prepare a statement of cash flows.

ANSWERS TO SELF-TEST QUESTIONS

1. **(a)** Cost of goods sold is determined by adding purchases to beginning inventory, then subtracting the ending inventory from the resulting total. The sales account does not affect the cost of goods sold, but is used in conjunction with cost of goods sold to determine the gross profit.

2. **(d)** When a *customer* is allowed to pay less because of early payment, the amount is recorded in the Sales Discount account. When a *supplier* allows the entity to pay less for early payment, the amount is recorded in the Purchases Discount account. *Allowances* are allowed when the buyer decides to keep the items purchased even though they may be damaged, the wrong color, etc.

3. **(d)** Trade discounts are used to determine the selling price to a particular class of buyer (i.e. manufacturer, wholesaler, retailer, or the consumer). Once the selling price is determined, that is the amount recorded in the accounts. Therefore, the trade discount itself is not recorded.

4. **(b)** The Cost of Goods Purchased computation consists of the following: Beginning Inventory *plus* net purchases (Purchases *less* Purchase Returns and Allowances *and* Purchase Discounts = net purchases) *plus* Transportation In.

5. **(c)** A physical inventory must be taken at the end of an accounting period when a periodic inventory system is used. When a perpetual system is used, the physical inventory can be taken at any time. The items in inventory must be counted when a perpetual system is used to ensure the accuracy of the recordkeeping.

6. **(d)** All of the items mentioned are income statement categories. They are reported after net income from operations in the following order: discontinued operations, extraordinary items, and the effect of a change in accounting methods.

7. **(b)** The acid-test ratio measures the immediate debt-paying ability of an entity by comparing the most liquid assets (cash plus accounts receivable) with current liabilities. The other ratios listed are measures of the entity's efficiency.

8. **(c)** The owners of an entity (stockholders) would be interested in the return on stockholders' equity ratio, which evaluates the return they are earning on their investment.

9. **(a)** The price-earnings ratio compares the market value of one share of stock with the earnings-per-share ratio to determine how many times earnings that the stock is selling. If the market price of the stock is $50 and the earnings per share is $5, then the stock is selling for 10 times earnings.

10. **(e)** The acid-test ratio has nothing to do with the chemical industry and all the ratios listed would be applicable to any industry. The acid-test ratio is also known as the quick current ratio.

6 ACCOUNTING SYSTEMS

CHapter 6 introduces an accounting system designed to produce timely and accurate records. Special journals are investigated, along with control accounts and subsidiary ledgers. A system is presented to show how to gather and generate the information necessary to record the payroll and to satisfy the various taxing authorities. The use of computers to accomplish all of the above is also introduced.

CHAPTER PREVIEW QUESTIONS

After studying Chapter 6, you should be able to answer the following questions:

1 Does the volume of business transactions influence the design, number, and content of special journals? Explain. (p.268)

2 What are the common features used in the design of all special journals? (pp.268–69)

3 Can special journals be grouped into various cycles within the operating activity of an entity? (p.269)

4 What source documents are used by accountants in the sales and collection cycle? (pp.269–73)

5 What source documents are used in the purchase and payment cycle? (pp.273–78)

6 What is the interrelationship between the general ledger and subsidiary ledgers? (p.278)

7 How is equality maintained between the general ledger and the subsidiary ledgers? (p.278)

8 Is a one-write system of benefit to the accountant when designing an accounting system? (pp.282–83)

9 How are records designed to register the acquisition and subsequent payment of employee services? (pp.284–85, 287-89)

10 Are computers more of a help or a hindrance to the accountant when designing an accounting system? (pp.290–96)

SPECIAL JOURNALS

In Chapter 2, the general journal was introduced and used to record each financial transaction of Saguaro Computers, Inc. This procedure was useful for explaining the fundamentals of the accounting process, but it is practical only when a business has a small number of transactions.

The volume of transactions facing most entities makes it impractical to record each transaction in a general journal. It is not inconceivable for even a small business to have 200 to 300 customers and perhaps 50 to 100 suppliers of goods and services. Consider the number of journal entries that would be required to record sales and purchases on account, cash sales and cash purchases, cash receipts and cash disbursements, and payroll transactions. Recording these transactions in a general journal would be time consuming; the additional labor of posting entries to the general ledger would become overwhelming, increasing the possibility of posting errors so that the ledger does not balance.

In practice, transactions are grouped into a number of classifications common to most business entities and recorded in various **special journals,** as indicated here:

Transaction	Recorded in
Sales or services on account	Sales Journal
Collection of cash	Cash Receipts Journal
Purchases on account	Purchases Journal
Payment of cash	Cash Disbursements Journal
Payroll	Payroll Journal

Q1: Volume of trans-
    actions and
    special journals

Most entities maintain a separate journal in each of these categories, often collectively referred to as *books of original entry.* The frequency with which certain types of transactions occur determines how many and what types of journals an entity will use.

Q2: Features of
    special journals

The common feature in the actual design of all special journals is the use of multiple columns for debit and credit entries and for the recording of related information. In addition to reducing the time required for posting transactions, the use of multiple columns lessens the need to repeat information. Although the actual layout of the columns differs among entities and is also influenced by the availability of mechanical devices or electronic data processing, the following types of columns are always present:

Columns for Information	Columns for Recording Debits and Credits
Date of transaction	Accounts to be debited or
Name of other party involved	credited
Other details relevant to the	Amount debited or credited
transaction	for each transaction
Other details relevant to the	
posting information	

The column sequence used in this chapter is designed to emphasize the information to be recorded for each transaction and the equality of debits and credits. Once the methodology of special journals is understood, any variation in format can be easily accommodated by any accountant.

The use of special journals permits an efficient division of duties among employees. For example, while one employee is recording transactions in one journal, another can be recording other transactions in another journal. In this way, the recording process is expedited, and internal control is maintained.

The accounting system of each entity is organized to achieve certain objectives, which include the accurate recording of accounting information in the appropriate special journal. An additional objective is the accumulation of amounts in the appropriate general ledger and any **subsidiary ledgers** used by the entity. Internal control systems are designed to ensure this accuracy; they are also designed to maximize efficiency and to control the entity's assets. The control of cash is one area of particular concern for obvious reasons; internal controls are designed to protect it and also to ensure its accurate recording. These are more fully described in Chapter 7. Control of inventory was discussed briefly in Chapter 5. To help maintain bookkeeping accuracy, a **control account** that accumulates balances of particular accounts from a subsidiary ledger is maintained in the general ledger. In these ways, management can keep an eye on operating efficiency through its accounting system.

Q3: Special journals and operating cycles

Special journals can be grouped within a number of operating cycles continuously occurring within the entity. These cycles comprise major areas of the entity's activities; the preceding discussion has identified major categories of financial transactions and the applicable special journals.

The cycles focused on in this chapter, as in Chapter 5, are the sales and collection cycle and the purchase and payment cycle. The discussion in this chapter first begins with the inception of transactions in each of these cycles. It later focuses on the flow of data through the entity's accounts. Both are a part of the accounting process and lead to the reporting of information relevant to users of financial statements (the preparation of these statements was the emphasis of the preceding chapters). The payroll cycle is also introduced and examined in this chapter.

Accountants also are concerned with whether the information produced by each of these cycles is in accordance with generally accepted accounting principles.

The Sales and Collection Cycle

Q4: Documents for sales and collection cycle

The sales and collection cycle focuses on sales, accounts receivable, and the subsequent collection of cash. Transactions in this cycle begin with the preparation of a sales invoice, which is a source document. The collection of cash ends this cycle; the source document here is the deposit slip stamped by the bank as evidence of the deposit of cash and checks received. This information is recorded in the appropriate special journals, which are posted to the general ledger and a subsidiary customer ledger. (The interrelationship of the general and subsidiary ledgers is discussed in the next section.) The accounting process applicable to this cycle is illustrated in Exhibit 6-1.

SALES JOURNAL

All sales on account are recorded in the **sales journal.** (Cash sales are recorded in the cash receipts journal.) Exhibit 6-2 is an extract from the sales journal of Saguaro Computers, Inc., in which January sales have been recorded and the column totaled. The single amount column in this sales journal is designed for recording the debit to the Accounts Receivable account and the credit to the Sales account for each sale.

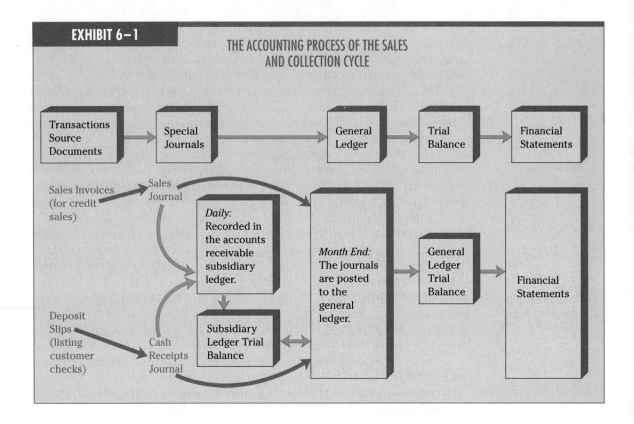

EXHIBIT 6-1

THE ACCOUNTING PROCESS OF THE SALES
AND COLLECTION CYCLE

Every entry in the sales journal includes a debit to Accounts Receivable and a credit to Sales. Recall that a sale would have been recorded in SCI's general journal as follows:

Jan. 5	Accounts Receivable	1,000	
	Sales		1,000
	To record a sale on account.		

Note that in the sales journal this transaction would be recorded on a single line, with a single entry recording debit and credit. Since such a sale can be recorded in a special journal, it need not be recorded in the general journal.

Other columns, if needed, could be added to the sales journal in Exhibit 6-2. For example, it could have a credit column for Sales Tax or columns for crediting sales by department or by product. In such cases, it would need a debit column for Accounts Receivable.

CASH RECEIPTS JOURNAL

All *receipts of cash* are recorded in the **cash receipts journal.** Exhibit 6-3 is a page from the cash receipts journal of Saguaro Computers, Inc., after January cash receipts have been recorded and the columns totaled. The columns used in this journal are designed to record the debits to the Cash and Sales Discounts accounts and the credits to Accounts Receivable, as well as to other accounts that might be affected.

Every entry in the cash receipts journal includes a debit to Cash; any other debit or credit entry depends on the transaction involved. For example, the receipt

EXHIBIT 6-2

SALES JOURNAL

Sales Journal

Date		Customer	Invoice Number	Terms	F	Accts. Rec.—Dr. Sales—Cr.
19X3						
Jan.	5	Devco Marketing, Inc.	301	net 30		1,000
	9	Perry Co.	302	2/10, net 30		200
	10	Horngren Corp.	303	2/10, net 30		650
	19	Bendix, Inc.	304	1/10, net 45		100
		Totals				1,950
1		2	3	4	5	6

Columns for Information

1. The date of the sales invoice is recorded in the Date column.
2. The name of the customer is recorded in the Customer column.
3. The sales invoice number is recorded in the Invoice Number column. Sales invoices are recorded in numerical sequence and all sales invoice numbers, including voided sales invoices, must be recorded.
4. The terms of the sale are listed in the Terms column. If the same terms are extended to all customers this column can be left out.
5. The use of this column is explained on p. 281.

Column for Recording of Sales on Account

6. The amount of the sale is recorded in this column as a debit to Accounts Receivable and a credit to Sales.

of the $5,000 loan from Heritage Fund would have been recorded in SCI's general journal as follows:

    Jan. 5   Cash   5,000
                    Notes Payable   5,000
              To record payment of mortgage.

Note that this transaction is recorded on a single line in the cash receipts journal, and that the equality of the debit and credit is still maintained through the use of the journal columns. The receipt of cash is recorded in the Debit Cash column; since the journal has no special column for Mortgage Payable, the account name and amount are entered in Other Accounts. Since the cash receipt is now recorded in a special journal, it is not recorded in the general journal.

The receipt of cash within the discount period would have been recorded in SCI's general journal as follows:

    Jan. 18   Cash   196
              Sales Discounts   4
                    Accounts Receivable   200
              To record receipt of cash.

EXHIBIT 6–3

CASH RECEIPTS JOURNAL

Cash Receipts Journal

		Debit		Credit					
Information					Accounts Receivable		Other Accounts		
Date	Cash Received From	Cash	Sales Disc.	✔	Amount	Account	F	Amount
19X3 Jan. 5	Heritage Fund	5,000				Notes Payable		5,000
18	Perry Co.	196	4		200			
22	Horngren Corp.	100			100			
	Totals	5,296	4		300			5,000
1	2	5	6	4	7	3	4	8

$5,300 $5,300

Columns for Information

1. The date of the receipt is recorded in the Date column.
2. The source of the cash receipt is written in the Cash Received From column. Cash receipts in payment of customers' accounts are shown individually, while cash sales are recorded as a daily total or weekly total amount, depending on the frequency and the dollar value of the transactions.
3. The Account column within the Other Accounts Credit column is used to record the name of general ledger accounts for which no special column has been provided. When applicable, cash sales are recorded here.
4. The use of these columns is explained on p. 280.

Columns for Recording Receipts of Cash/Columns for Debits

5. The amount of cash actually received is recorded in the Cash column.
6. Any cash discount granted a customer is recorded in the Sales Discount column.

Columns for Credits

7. The amount of accounts receivable paid by the customer is recorded in this column; the amount recorded is the total of cash received plus any sales discounts granted to the customer.
8. This column is for credits to general ledger accounts for which no special column has been provided in the cash receipts journal.

In this case, Perry Co. paid its account within 10 days and, accordingly, deducted 2% from the $200 amount of the sale ($200 $\times$ 0.02 = $4). Since this cash receipt is now recorded on a single line in a special journal, it is not recorded in SCI's general journal.

Other columns could be added to the cash receipts journal to meet the specific needs of another entity. For example, a Cash Sales column could be added for an entity that has frequent cash sales.

Since special journals are designed to facilitate not only the recording but also the posting process, the sequence of the debit and credit columns is often reversed in practice, as illustrated here.

Cash Receipts Journal — Page 1

Information			Credit					Debit	
Date			Accounts Receivable		Other Accounts				Sales
			F	Amount	Account	F	Amount	Cash	Disc.

The posting process and the subsidiary accounts receivable ledger are explained on pp. 278–279, 281.

The Purchase and Payment Cycle

Q5: Documents for purchase and payment cycle

This cycle focuses on purchases, accounts payable, and cash payments. (The acquisition of and payment for employee services are discussed later in this chapter.) Transactions in this cycle begin with the preparation of a purchase requisition and purchase order within the entity. The recording begins with an invoice from the supplier involved, which is the source document. The payment of cash completes this cycle; the source document here is the check prepared by the entity. These source documents are recorded in the appropriate special journals, the transaction then being posted to the general ledger and a subsidiary suppliers ledger. (The interrelationship of the general and subsidiary ledgers is discussed on p. 278.) The accounting process applicable to this cycle is illustrated in Exhibit 6-4.

During the month, purchases on account and payments on account are posted from the purchases journal and the cash disbursement journal to an accounts payable subsidiary ledger. The total debit and credit column balances in both the purchases and the cash disbursements journals are posted to the general ledger at the end of each month.

PURCHASES JOURNAL

All *purchases on account of merchandise for resale by the entity* are recorded in the **purchases journal.** (Cash purchases are recorded in the cash disbursements journal.) Exhibit 6-5 is a page from the purchases journal of Saguaro Computers, Inc., in which January purchases have been recorded and the column totaled.

Every entry in the purchases journal includes a debit to the Purchases account and a credit to Accounts Payable. The purchase from Peterson Co. would have been recorded in SCI's general journal as follows:

Jan. 3	Purchases	600	
	Accounts Payable		600
	To record purchase on account from Peterson Co.		

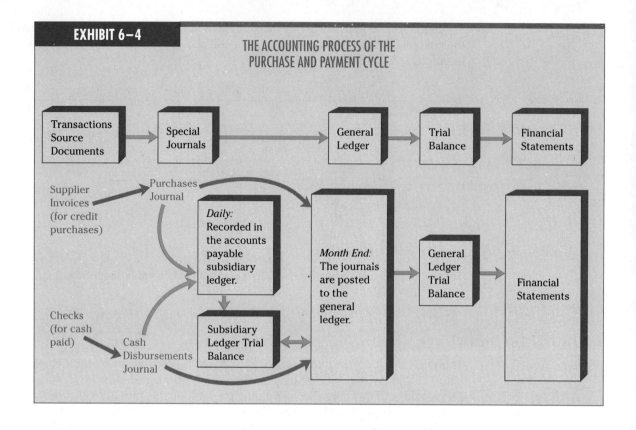

EXHIBIT 6-4

THE ACCOUNTING PROCESS OF THE
PURCHASE AND PAYMENT CYCLE

Note that this transaction is recorded on a single line in the purchases journal, with debit and credit recorded by a single entry.

Other columns could be added to meet specific needs. For example, a debit column for each department might be added, or for each class of products. Separate columns are frequently used for debits and credits. Since special journals are designed to facilitate not only the recording but also the posting process, the sequence of the debit and credit columns is often reversed in practice, as illustrated here.

Purchases Journal   Page 1

Information			Credit	Debit		
				Purchases		
Date		F	Accounts Payable	A	B	C

The posting procedure and the subsidiary accounts payable ledger are explained on pp. 279–82.

EXHIBIT 6–5

PURCHASES JOURNAL

Purchases Journal   Page 1

Date		Supplier	Terms	F	Purchase—Dr. Accts. Pay.—Cr.
19X3 Jan.	3	Peterson Co.	2/10, net 30		600
	4	Kensington, Inc.	net 30		350
	11	Canark Co.	net 30		500
	26	Jaycor, Inc.	2/10, net 30		250
					1,700

1   2   3   4   5

Columns for Information

1. The date of the supplier's invoice is recorded in the Date column.
2. The name of the supplier is recorded in the Supplier column.
3. The terms of purchase are listed in the Terms column.
4. The use of this column is explained on p. 283.

Columns for Recording Purchases on Account

5. The amount of the purchase is recorded in this column as a debit to Purchases and a credit to Accounts Payable.

CASH DISBURSEMENTS JOURNAL

All *payments of cash made by check* are recorded in the **cash disbursements journal.** Payments made in cash are usually handled as part of a petty cash fund (which is discussed in Chapter 7). Exhibit 6-6 is a page from the cash disbursements journal of Saguaro Computers, Inc., in which January cash disbursements have been recorded and the columns totaled. The columns in this cash disbursements journal are designed for recording debits to accounts applicable in a particular transaction and credits to Cash.

Every entry in the disbursements journal consists of a debit to some account and a credit to Cash. The payment to Peterson Co. on January 12 would have been recorded in SCI's general journal as follows:

Jan. 12	Accounts Payable	600	
	Purchase Discounts		12
	Cash		588
	To record payment, less discount of amount due Peterson Co.		

In this case, Saguaro paid Peterson Co. within 10 days and accordingly deducted $12 from the $600 amount of the purchase made on January 3 ($600 × 0.02 = $12).

EXHIBIT 6–6

CASH DISBURSEMENTS JOURNAL

Cash Disbursements Journal

| | Information | | Credit | | | | Debit | | | |
| | | | | | | Accounts Payable | | Other Accounts | | |
Date	Payee	Check Number	Cash	Purchase Discount	✔	Amount	Account	F	Amount
19X3									
Jan. 2	Kybo Properties	101	900				Rent Expense		900
8	Speedy Freight	102	50				Transportation In		50
12	Peterson Co.	103	588	12		600			
25	Glenco Co.	104	35				Supplies Expense		35
	Totals		1,573	12		600			985
			1						
			2						

| 1 | 2 | 3 | 6 | 7 | 4 | 8 | 5 | 4 | 9 |

$1,585 $1,585

Columns for Information

1. The date on the check is recorded in the Date column.
2. The name of the payee on the check is recorded in this column.
3. The check number, including any voided checks, is recorded here.
4. The use of these columns is explained on p. 282.
5. The Account column is used to record the titles of the general ledger accounts affected by the transaction, for which no special column has been provided.

Columns for Recording Payments of Cash/Columns for Credits

6. The actual amount of the check is recorded in the Cash column.
7. Any cash discounts allowed are recorded in the Purchase Discount column.

Columns for Debits

8. The original amount of the account payable is recorded here. The amount will be the total of the cash paid and any discounts taken.
9. The amount of any debit to a general ledger account for which no column has been provided is recorded in this column.

Since this cash receipt is now recorded on a single line in a special journal, it is not recorded in the general journal.

Other columns could be added to the cash disbursements journal to meet the specific needs of another entity, based on the frequency with which certain cash disbursements occur. Since special journals are designed to facilitate not only the recording but also the posting process, the sequence of the debit and credit columns could be reversed for the cash disbursements journal, as is shown next:

Cash Disbursements Journal   Page 1

| Information | | Debit | | | | | Credit | | |
| | | Accounts Payable | | Other Accounts | | | | | |
Date	Payee	✓	Amount	Account	F	Amount	Purchase Discounts	Cash	Check Number
19X2									
	Totals								

GENERAL JOURNAL

When special journals are used, the general journal is still used to record all other transactions that cannot be recorded in any of the special journals. For example, sales returns, purchase returns, and adjusting and closing entries continue to be recorded in the general journal.

Exhibit 6-7 shows three January entries in the general journal of Saguaro Computers, Inc., that are transactions that cannot be recorded in a special journal.

EXHIBIT 6–7

GENERAL JOURNAL

General Journal   Page 1

Date		Description	F	Debit	Credit
19X3 Jan.	12	Sales Returns and Allowances	508	100	
		Accounts Receivable	110✔		100
		To record return from Horngren Corp.			
	27	Accounts Payable	210✔	50	
		Purchase Returns and Allowances	558		50
		To record goods returned to Jaycor, Inc.			
	31	Depreciation Expense—Truck	624	200	
		Accumulated Depreciation—Truck	194		200
		To record depreciation for January.			

Note that a ✔ is entered into the Folio column (F) to indicate that the posting has also been made to the account of the customer and the supplier. This procedure is necessary whenever a control account is used.

Other Special Journals

Additional special journals also can be designed as required by an entity. In the sales and collection cycle, for example, a sales returns and allowances journal may be a labor-saving journal; in the purchase and payment cycle, a purchase returns and allowances journal may improve efficiency. The frequency with which these transactions occur determines the need for such additional special journals; the volume of other types of transactions would determine the need for other special journals.

THE GENERAL LEDGER AND SUBSIDIARY LEDGERS

Q6: Interrelationship between ledgers

Q7: Equality between ledgers

An entity often has a large number of customers; a department store, for example, may have in excess of 50,000 credit customers for whom detailed financial information has to be maintained. If each customer had an account in the general ledger, the general ledger would become unwieldy. For this reason, an accounts receivable subsidiary ledger is designed to include each customer's account. Only one Accounts Receivable account—in this case, the control account—is kept in the general ledger. After all transactions for the month have been recorded, the total of the accounts receivable subsidiary ledger should be equal to the balance in the control account:

General Ledger	Accounts Receivable Subsidiary Ledger		
Accounts Receivable	**Bendix, Inc.**	**Devco Marketing, Inc.**	**Horngren Corp.**
1,650	100	1,000	550

Control Total $1,650	=	Subsidiary Total $1,650

Other subsidiary ledgers, such as a long-term assets subsidiary ledger, also can be created to control volume.

A trial balance of the accounts receivable subsidiary ledger, also called a *schedule of accounts receivable,* is prepared at the end of the month to check that the subsidiary ledger total agrees with the Accounts Receivable control account in the general ledger.

Saguaro Computers, Inc.
Schedule of Accounts Receivable
January 31, 19X3

Bendix, Inc.	$ 100
Devco Marketing, Inc.	1,000
Horngren Corp.	550
Total	$1,650

Accounting information is initially recorded in special journals, as illustrated earlier. This information is next accumulated in both subsidiary and control accounts, a procedure referred to as the flow of accounting information through the accounts of an entity. This flow for each cycle can be illustrated by looking at the posting process for both control and subsidiary accounts.

Flow through the Sales and Collection Cycle Accounts

FLOW THROUGH THE ACCOUNTS RECEIVABLE CONTROL ACCOUNT

The total of the last column in the sales journal is posted to the general ledger at the end of each month to Accounts Receivable and Sales, as shown next. Note the reference *S1* in each account. This specifies that the amounts came from Page 1 of the sales journal. Such references make it easy to trace items as they flow through the account system.

Accounts Receivable	No. 110	Sales	No. 500
19X3		19X3	
Jan. 31 S1 1,950		Jan. 31 S1 1,950	

At the end of each month, the Cash and Sales Discount debit total and the Accounts Receivable credit total appearing in the cash receipts journal are posted to the appropriate general ledger account. The general ledger account number is then placed in parentheses below each total in the cash receipts journal to indicate that the amount has been posted to the proper account. The total of the Other Accounts column is not posted, but each amount listed in the column is posted to its respective general ledger account by name and number. (See Exhibit 6-8.)

FLOW THROUGH THE SUBSIDIARY ACCOUNTS

Each amount in the Accounts Receivable columns of the sales journal and the cash receipts journal is posted to the accounts receivable subsidiary ledger—usually daily. This posting updates the balance of each customer's account and makes the information readily available for trial balance preparation. Exhibit 6-9 illustrates the posting of the sales journal entries to the subsidiary ledger.

Note the posting to the Horngren account for $100 on January 22 from CR1 (cash receipts, Page 1) and the posting to the Perry account for $200 on January 19 from CR1. These are postings from the cash receipts journal in Exhibit 6-8.

Flow through the Purchase and Payment Cycle Accounts

FLOW THROUGH THE ACCOUNTS PAYABLE CONTROL ACCOUNT

At the end of each month, the Purchases debit and Accounts Payable credit total appearing in the purchases journal is posted to the appropriate general ledger accounts. The general ledger account number is placed in parentheses below the total in the purchases journal to indicate that the posting has been done. (The *P1* refers to Page 1 of the purchases journal.)

Purchases	No. 550	Accounts Payable	No. 210
19X3		19X3	
Jan. 31 P1 1,700		Jan. 31 P1 1,700	

At the end of each month, each debit and credit total appearing in the cash disbursements journal, except the Other Accounts debit total, is also posted to the appropriate general ledger account. The general ledger account number is placed

EXHIBIT 6-8

CASH RECEIPTS JOURNAL TRANSACTIONS POSTED TO THE GENERAL LEDGER

Cash Receipts Journal   Page 1

		Information		Debit		Credit				
							Accounts Receivable		Other Accounts		
Date		Cash Received From	Cash	Sales Disc.	✔	Amount	Account	F	Amount
19X3 Jan.	5	Heritage Fund	5,000				Notes Payable	280	5,000
	18	Perry Co.	196	4		200			
	22	Horngren Corp.	100			100			
		Totals	5,296	4		300			5,000
			(101)	(509)		(110)			(X)

> The posting reference *CR1* means that the amount came from Page 1 of the cash receipts journal. The *S1* refers to Page 1 of the sales journal.

> The *X* below the 5,000 indicates that the total is *not* posted to the general ledger. Rather, each entry in the column is posted individually. The general ledger account number is entered in the Folio column (F) to indicate that the posting has been made.

General Ledger

Cash	No. 101	Notes Payable	No. 280
19X3 Jan. 31 CR1 5,296		19X3 Jan. 31 CR1 5,000	

Accounts Receivable	No. 110	Sales Discounts	No. 509
19X3 Jan. 31 S1 1,950	19X3 Jan. 31 CR1 300	19X3 Jan. 31 CR1 4	

in parentheses below each total in the cash disbursements journal to indicate that the posting has been done. See Exhibit 6-10 (p. 282).

FLOW THROUGH THE SUBSIDIARY ACCOUNTS

Each amount in the Accounts Payable columns of the purchases journal and the cash disbursements journal is posted to the accounts payable subsidiary ledger—usually daily. This posting updates the balance of each creditor's account and makes the information readily available. The date of the entry in the subsidiary ledger account is the invoice date, which is needed if a discount is to be taken. See Exhibit 6-11 (p. 283).

EXHIBIT 6–9

POSTING OF SALES JOURNAL ENTRIES TO ACCOUNTS
RECEIVABLE SUBSIDIARY LEDGER

Note that the Folio column (F) is used to
indicate postings to the accounts receivable
subsidiary ledger. A check (✔) is entered
to indicate that the posting has been done.

Sales Journal   Page 1

Date		Customer	Invoice Number	Terms	F	Accts. Rec.—Dr. Sales—Cr.
19X3						
Jan.	5	Devco Marketing, Inc.	301	net 30	✔	1,000
	9	Perry Co.	302	2/10, net 30	✔	200
	10	Horngren Corp.	303	2/10, net 30	✔	650
	19	Bendix, Inc.	304	1/10, net 45	✔	100
		Totals				1,950

Note that the abbreviation *S* is used as a
posting reference from the sales journal;
CR stands for the cash receipts journal.

Accounts Receivable Subsidiary Ledger

Bendix, Inc.

Date		Invoice	F	Debit	Credit	Bal.
19X3						
Jan.	19	304	S1	100		100

Horngren Corp.

Date		Invoice	F	Debit	Credit	Bal.
19X3						
Jan.	10	303	S1	650		650
	22		CR1		100	550

Devco Marketing, Inc

Date		Invoice	F	Debit	Credit	Bal.
19X3						
Jan.	5	301	S1	1,000		1,000

Horngren Corp

Date		Invoice	F	Debit	Credit	Bal.
19X3						
Jan.	9	302	S1	200		200
	19		CR1		200	-0-

Note the posting of a debit to the Peterson account for $600 on January 12 from CD1 (cash disbursements, Page 1). This posting is from the cash disbursements journal in Exhibit 6-10.

A trial balance of the accounts payable subsidiary ledger, also called a *schedule of accounts payable,* is prepared at the end of the month to check that the subsidiary ledger total agrees with the Accounts Payable control account in the general ledger.

EXHIBIT 6-10

POSTING OF CASH DISBURSEMENT JOURNAL
ENTRIES TO GENERAL LEDGER

Cash Disbursements Journal   Page 1

Information			Credit			Debit			
					Accounts Payable		Other Accounts		
Date	Cash Paid To	Check Number	Cash	Purchase Discount	✔	Amount	Account	F	Amount
19X3									
Jan. 2	Kybo Properties	101	900				Rent Expense	654	900
8	Speedy Freight	102	50				Transportation In	560	50
12	Kensington, Inc.	103	588	12	✔	600			
25	Glenco Co.	104	35				Supplies Expense	668	35
	Totals		1,573	12		600			985
			(101)	(559)		(210)			(X)

The posting reference *CD1* means that the amount came from Page 1 of the cash disbursements journal. The *P1* refers to Page 1 of the purchases journal.

The *X* below the 985 total indicates that this total is *not* posted to the general ledger. Rather, each entry is posted individually. The general ledger account number is entered in the Folio column (F) to indicate that the posting has been made.

General Ledger

Cash		No. 101	Transportation In		No. 560	Accounts Payable			No. 210
19X3	19X3		19X3			19X3		19X3	
Jan. 31 CR1 5,296	Jan. 31 CD1 1,573		Jan. 31 CD1 50			Jan. 31 CD1 600		Jan. 31 P1 1,700	

Supplies Expense		No. 668	Rent Expense		No. 654	Purchase Discount		No. 559
19X3			19X3				19X3	
Jan. 31 CD1 35			Jan. 31 CD1 900				Jan. 31 CD1 12	

Saguaro Computers, Inc.
Schedule of Accounts Payable
January 31, 19X3

Canark Co.	$ 500
Jaycor, Inc.	250
Kensington, Inc.	350
Total	$1,100

The One-Write System

Q8: One-write system

Recording in the cash disbursements journal and posting to the subsidiary accounts payable journal can be simplified through the use of a **one-write system.** In fact, the check for the payment of an accounts payable can be prepared at the same

EXHIBIT 6–11

POSTING OF PURCHASES JOURNAL ENTRIES TO
ACCOUNTS PAYABLE SUBSIDIARY LEDGER

Purchases Journal   Page 1

Date		Supplier	Terms	F	Purchases—Dr. Accts. Pay.—Cr.
19X3					
Jan.	3	Peterson Co.	2/10, net 30	✔	600
	4	Kensington, Inc.	net 30	✔	350
	11	Canark Co.	net 30	✔	500
	26	Jaycor, Inc.	2/10, net 30	✔	250
		Totals			1,700

Note that the abbreviation *P* is used as a posting reference from the purchases journal; *CD* stands for the cash disbursements journal.

Note that the Folio column (F) is used to indicate postings to the accounts payable subsidiary ledger. A check (✔) is entered to indicate that the posting has been made.

Accounts Payable Subsidiary Ledger

Canark Co.

Date		Invoice	F	Debit	Credit	Bal.
19X3						
Jan.	11		P1		500	500

Kensington, Inc.

Date		Invoice	F	Debit	Credit	Bal.
19X3						
Jan.	4		P1		350	350

Jaycor, Inc.

Date		Invoice	F	Debit	Credit	Bal.
19X3						
Jan.	26		P1		250	250

Peterson Co.

Date		Invoice	F	Debit	Credit	Bal.
19X3						
Jan.	3		P1		600	600
	12		CD1	600		-0-

time. Using carbon-type paper, the blank check form is placed on top of the accounts payable subsidiary ledger card (A/P sub card) for the particular payee. Both the check and ledger card are then placed on the cash disbursements journal. When the check is prepared, the payee and the amount is "automatically" recorded in the accounts payable subsidiary ledger and in the cash disbursements journal. A one-write system is represented in Exhibit 6-12.

The one-write system is referred to as a pegboard system. As you can see in Exhibit 6-12, the carbon-type paper for each document is perforated and placed on a board with pegs along one edge. This aligns all the documents properly and allows for all three to be prepared at the same time. The computer is quickly replacing the pegboard system, but it is still used widely in noncomputerized accounting systems. Similar one-write systems are used for the sales and collection cycle and for the payroll cycle.

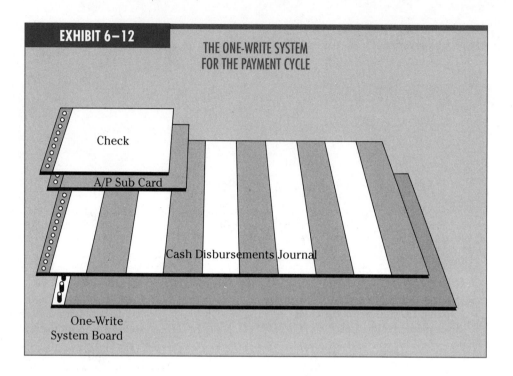

EXHIBIT 6-12

THE ONE-WRITE SYSTEM
FOR THE PAYMENT CYCLE

Check

A/P Sub Card

Cash Disbursements Journal

One-Write
System Board

THE PAYROLL CYCLE

The payment of salaries and wages can amount to well over one-half of total operating expenditures in service industries and a very material portion of total operating costs in the merchandising and manufacturing industries.

Before the accounting for salaries and wages is discussed, the two terms should be differentiated, and other aspects of payroll investigated.

Employees earning *salaries* generally receive a certain amount stated as so many dollars per month, or so much per year (that amount is divided by 12 to determine the monthly salary). Salaried employees are usually paid either bimonthly, such as on the 15th and on the 30th of each month, or once a month on the last day of each month. Overtime may or may not be paid, depending on the contract signed by the employee and employer. Overtime may be determined by the hours worked beyond the usual 8 per day or beyond 40 hours per week. Many times salaried employees are not paid overtime on a pay-period basis, but the time is taken as compensation time ("comp. time") with additional vacation days.

Q9: Records for
employee
services

Employees earning *wages* are generally paid weekly (52 times per year) or biweekly (26 times per year). They get paid for every hour worked, so time cards are used to measure the number of hours each employee works during a pay period. Overtime is generally paid at the rate of *time and one-half.* If an employee is earning $10 per hour regular time, any overtime hours worked would be paid at the rate of $15 per hour. The work year generally consists of 2,080 hours (40 per week × 52 weeks = 2,080 hours). Therefore the annual "salary" of a wage-earner can be quickly determined by multiplying the hourly rate by 2,080 hours. A wage of $10 per hour is equivalent to annual earnings of $20,800. On the other end of the continuum, someone paid a minimum wage of about $4 per hour earns $8,320 per year.

Conceptually, the payment of wages or salaries is quite simple, being no different than paying any other operating expense. The payment of rent, for example, would be recorded in the cash disbursements journal by the following general journal entry:

Rent Expense	XXX	
Cash (check number xxx)		XXX

It would then follow that the payment of salaries and wages would be recorded in the cash disbursements journal by the following general journal entry:

Salaries Expense	XXX	
Wages Expense	XXX	
Cash (check number xxx)		XXX

However, because of the number of required payroll deductions, and an even greater number of optional payroll deductions, the accounting for the payroll becomes quite complex. Before the accounting for payroll is explained, it will be helpful to investigate the required deductions and some of the optional deductions.

Required Payroll Deductions

FEDERAL INCOME TAX

Starting in the 1940s, the Internal Revenue Service (IRS) began the *withholding system* that is in effect today for all salaried and wage-earning employees. It is generally referred to as "pay as you go," but has been called the "let's-get-it-first-before-they-spend-it" approach.

Anyone who has had a job should know what withholding is and how it works. Tables published by the IRS show employers how much to withhold for federal income tax based on an employee's marital status, and based on how many exemptions the employee has claimed on the Employee Withholding Allowance Certificate (known as the W-4). Unless an employee signs a statement swearing he or she will have no tax liability for the current year, all employers must withhold federal income tax on employee earnings. What happens to the amounts withheld will be addressed later.

SOCIAL SECURITY TAX

Starting in the 1930s, Congress enacted legislation requiring most employees to contribute to a fund that would provide retirement benefits to employees and their families when the employee reached a certain age. The tax is formally known as the Federal Insurance Contributions Act and most often referred to as FICA. When the tax first went into effect, each worker's maximum contribution was less than $50 per year. That has increased over the years. By 1965 the maximum was almost $150; by 1990 the maximum was more than $3,800. Today, an employee earning more than $50,000 is paying the maximum amount as prescribed under the law.

STATE INCOME TAX

Very few states do not have a state income tax. All states that have an income tax also have a mandatory withholding program that is similar to that of the IRS. Employees are allowed to claim a certain number of exemptions and then an amount of state income tax is withheld based on marital status and the amount of earnings for a given time period.

Optional Payroll Deductions

Some of the "optional" deductions may not be optional at all in a given circumstance. Union dues, for instance, in many situations are required for employment. Health insurance is recommended and if the employer does not pay all of the premium, the employee may have to pay a portion—sometimes a substantial portion. Monthly premiums for health insurance in a group plan for a family range from $250 to $350. Most employers have some sort of pension plan for employees that may require the employee to contribute by way of payroll deduction. The accounting for pensions is quite complex and thus is covered in advanced accounting classes. An employee may request that the employer withhold part of his or her earnings and deposit it in a savings account, buy U.S. Savings Bonds or life insurance, or make contributions to United Way or other charities. The list is endless, and for the most part is beyond this discussion.

Combined, these deductions would be recorded by the following general journal entries, with estimated figures:

Salaries Expense	10,000	
Wages Expense	5,000	
Federal Withholding (W/H) Payable		2,500
State W/H Payable		1,000
FICA Payable		1,000
Health Insurance Payable		900
Union Dues Payable		750
U.S. Savings Bonds Payable		500
Pension Plan Payable		800
Payable to United Fund		300
Salaries Payable (net pay to		
employees)		7,250
Salaries Payable	7,250	
Cash (check numbers		
1389–1415)		7,250

First note that the employees are receiving less than one half of the amount earned, and that the journal entry is complex. The next section will examine the method the employer uses to pay all of the current liabilities created by such an entry.

WITHHOLDING PAYABLE

Both the various states and the federal government have set up guidelines for payment of withholding of income taxes. It depends on how much is withheld and in what period of time. If only minor amounts are withheld, such as less than $200 per calendar quarter, the IRS allows an employer to contribute the taxes on a quarterly basis. Larger amounts must be paid on a monthly basis, and if the amount is great enough, it might have to be paid within three banking days of the payroll. For federal tax purposes, most banks are registered depositories with the federal government and an employer only has to go to the bank to make the payments for withheld income taxes.

FICA PAYABLE

The social security tax is due quarterly and is paid in conjunction with the withholding taxes. The employer is not only responsible for the employee's contribution, but also must match the amount dollar for dollar. Currently the rates are 7.65% on all salaries and wages up to about $50,000. When the employer files the quarterly report, all FICA wages and salaries are multiplied by 14.3% to arrive at the amount that the employer must remit. How the entity records its share of the FICA contribution will be discussed later with other employer payroll costs.

OTHER DEDUCTIONS

Health insurance, union dues, and savings plans and contributions are generally paid monthly, while contributions to a pension plan might be monthly, quarterly, semiannually, or even annually.

The Payroll Journal

Q9: Records for employee services

Because listing all the deductions would be unwieldy for the general journal, a special **payroll journal** is used to facilitate the accounting for payroll. Exhibit 6-13 shows a page from the payroll journal of SCI in which a portion of the January payroll has been recorded. The columns have been totaled for display only, because the weekly payroll for all of January will be recorded in this journal.

Each entry in the payroll journal includes a debit to the expense accounts for each total of salaries and wages, credits to the appropriate liability accounts for the various required and optional deductions, and a credit to Salaries Payable.

Other columns are often found in payroll journals designed to meet the varying needs of entities.

Flow through the Control Account

At the end of the pay period, the totals for gross pay, deductions, and the net pay are posted from the payroll journal to the general ledger. The totals from the payroll journal in Exhibit 6-13 are reproduced in Exhibit 6-14 to illustrate the posting. Note that the account numbers are recorded below the column totals posted to the general ledger.

The amounts in the payroll journal may be posted directly to the general ledger, or may be recorded first in the general journal and then posted to the general ledger. If SCI followed the latter practice, the January 5, 19X3, payroll would be recorded in the general journal in the following manner:

19X3				
Jan. 5	Sales Salaries Expense	657	400	
	Delivery Wages Expense	658	250	
	Office Salaries Expense	659	300	
	Federal W/H Payable	253		86
	State W/H Payable	254		47
	FICA Payable	255		61
	Pensions Payable	256		16
	Health Insurance Payable	257		22
	Salaries Payable	226		491
	Wages Payable	237		227

RECORDING PAYROLL RELATED EXPENSES

As mentioned before, in addition to each employee contributing to social security, each employer must match that contribution up to the maximum income. The employer must also contribute to a federal unemployment fund, and in most states, to a state unemployment fund. The federal unemployment fund rate is now 6.2% on all wages up to $7,000 per year, but the federal government allows a credit

EXHIBIT 6-13

PAYROLL JOURNAL

Payroll Journal

	Information					Debit				Credit										
Week Ended				Hours		Rate	Salaries and Wages			Income Tax		Deductions								
Mo.	Day	Yr.	Employee Name	Reg.	OT	Reg.	OT	Sales	Delivery	Office	Fed.	State	FICA	Pension	Health	1	2	3	Total	Sal. or Wages Pay.	Chk. No.
1	5	X3	J. Abbott					400			42	20	26	7	9				104	296s	101
1	5	X3	N. Aitken							300	26	15	20	5	7				73	227w	102
1	5	X3	R. River	40		6.25			250		18	12	15	4	6				55	195s	103
								400	250	300	86	47	61	16	22				232	718	

| 1 | 2 | 3 | 4 | 5 | 6 | 7 | 8 | 9 | 10 | 11 | 12 | 13 |

Columns for Information

1. The date of the payroll check is recorded here.
2. The payee on the check is recorded in this column.
3. If the employee is a wage earner, the hours worked during the week, both regular and overtime, are recorded in these columns.
4. The hourly rate, if applicable, for each wage earner is recorded here.

Columns for Recording Payroll and Related Deductions

5. The amount of the salaries and wages before deductions (gross pay) is recorded in these columns as Sales Expense, Delivery Expense, or Office Expense, depending on the employee's position.
6. The amount of federal and state income taxes withheld from each employee is recorded in these columns.
7. The amount withheld for social security from each employee is recorded here. Later, some employees may not have a deduction for FICA if they have earned more than the maximum income for the year. Since this is January, each employee must contribute to the fund.
8. This column records the amount contributed by each employee to the pension fund of the employer.
9. The employee's share of the health insurance cost is recorded here.
10. Other optional deductions are recorded here in separate columns for such items as union dues, charitable contributions, or savings plans requested by the employee.
11. The total of all the deductions is recorded here as a control feature. The column is not necessary from a payroll point of view.
12. The net pay, the amount of the payroll check, is recorded in this column. This is the amount the employee actually receives for his or her efforts.
13. The check number of each payroll check is listed in this column.

against that rate of 5.4%, which in effect reduces the federal rate to .8%. The various state rates are tied to the number of former employees from that particular employer who are filing for unemployment benefits. The rate may go above the credit allowed by the federal government, but can go down to almost nothing if an employer has very few claims against the state for unemployment. No matter what rate is paid to the state, the employer still may take a credit of 5.4% for federal unemployment purposes.

EXHIBIT 6–14

POSTING FROM PAYROLL
JOURNAL TO GENERAL LEDGER

Column Totals from the Payroll Journal

400	250	300	86	47	61	16	22	232	718
(657)	(658)	(659)	(253)	(254)	(255)	(256)	(257)	(X)	(226 & 237)

The *X* below the total indicates that it is not posted to the general ledger. It is only a subtotal of deductions made from the gross pay.

General Ledger

Sales Salaries Expense		No. 657	Salaries Payable		No. 226
19X3 Jan. 5	Pa1	400		19X3 Jan. 5	Pa1	491

Delivery Wages Expense		No. 658	Wages Payable		No. 237
19X3 Jan. 5	Pa1	250		19X3 Jan. 5	Pa1	227

Office Salaries Expense		No. 659	Federal Withholding Payable		No. 253
19X3 Jan. 5	Pa1	300		19X3 Jan. 5	Pa1	86

State Withholding Payable   No. 254

19X3 Jan. 5   Pa1   47

FICA Payable   No. 255

19X3 Jan. 5   Pa1   61

The posting reference *Pa1* means that the amount came from Page 1 of the payroll journal.

Pension Payable   No. 256

19X3 Jan. 5   Pa1   16

Health Insurance Payable   No. 257

19X3 Jan. 5   Pa1   22

Assuming the state rate for SCI is 5% and the federal rate is .8%, and matching the earlier FICA deduction of $61, the taxes related to Saguaro's January 5 payroll would be recorded in the general ledger as follows:

Payroll Tax Expense	117	
FICA Payable		61
State Unemployment Payable		
(5% × $950)		48
Federal Unemployment Payable		
(.008 × $950)		8

The various state unemployment benefits are payable quarterly and the federal benefits annually. In both cases, as soon as the amounts due add up to a specified total, deposits such as those required for federal withholding of income taxes are required. The total amounts vary from state to state.

The employer may also contribute a portion to the health insurance premium of each employee (usually a major portion) and to the pension plan. Assuming SCI contributes $200 for health insurance and $175 to the pension plan for the January 5 payroll, the entry would be recorded in the general journal as follows:

Other Employee Benefits	375	
Health Insurance Payable		200
Pensions Payable		175

As mentioned before, the health insurance and pension contributions probably would be made on a monthly basis.

Flow through the Subsidiary Accounts: Individual Employee Records

Although the payroll journal maintains a record of all payroll transactions, it does not accumulate payroll data for each employee. Such cumulative individual employee data must be furnished to both the federal and state governments, and to each employee at the end of every calendar year. The W-2 form sent to employees at the end of the year shows their earnings for the year, deductions from their earnings for state and federal income taxes, and deductions paid into the Social Security fund. In order to aid in the accumulation of this information, **individual employee earnings records** are kept for each employee. The informational content is quite similar to that in the payroll journal, with the addition of a cumulative gross pay column for the purpose of calculating the employee's contribution to FICA and the employer's contribution to both state and federal unemployment. An example of the earnings records for three SCI employees is shown in Exhibit 6-15.

COMPUTERIZED ACCOUNTING SYSTEMS

Q10: Value of computers

A typical entity processes numerous routine accounting jobs, most of which involve some sort of recordkeeping. In small companies, all records may be kept manually, while a large corporation, such as General Motors or Seagram's, may have a totally computerized system. Bookkeepers may take care of the payroll, sales orders, inventory control, accounts receivable and payable, and the general ledger either manually or through automated processing. Computerized accounting may involve numerous systems with specific programs tailored to the entity's particular needs.

EXHIBIT 6–15

PAYROLL JOURNAL—INDIVIDUAL EMPLOYEE RECORDS

Individual Employee Earnings Record

Date Started:
Date Left:
Reason:

Social Security No.
Marital Status:
Dependents:

Employee No.:
Income Tax Exemption:
Rate:

	Week Ending			Hours	Earnings	Gross Pay			Income Tax			Deductions									
Mo.	Day	Yr.	Employee Name	Reg./OT	Reg./OT	Sales	Delivery	Office	Fed.	State	FICA	Pension	Health	1	2	3	Total	Net Pay	Chk. No.	Cumulative Gross Earnings
1	5	X3	J. Abbott			400			42	20	26	7	9				104	296	101	400

Individual Employee Earnings Record

Date Started:
Date Left:
Reason:

Social Security No.
Marital Status:
Dependents:

Employee No.:
Income Tax Exemption:
Rate:

	Week Ending			Hours	Earnings	Gross Pay			Income Tax			Deductions									
Mo.	Day	Yr.	Employee Name	Reg./OT	Reg./OT	Sales	Delivery	Office	Fed.	State	FICA	Pension	Health	1	2	3	Total	Net Pay	Chk. No.	Cumulative Gross Earnings
1	5	X3	N. Aitken					300	26	15	20	5	7				73	227	102	300

Individual Employee Earnings Record

Date Started:
Date Left:
Reason:

Social Security No.
Marital Status:
Dependents:

Employee No.:
Income Tax Exemption:
Rate:

	Week Ending			Hours	Earnings	Gross Pay			Income Tax			Deductions									
Mo.	Day	Yr.	Employee Name	Reg./OT	Reg./OT	Sales	Delivery	Office	Fed.	State	FICA	Pension	Health	1	2	3	Total	Net Pay	Chk. No.	Cumulative Gross Earnings
1	5	X3	R. River	40	250		250		18	12	15	4	6				55	195	103	250

EXHIBIT 6-16

A COMPUTERIZED STATEMENT OF
EARNINGS FOR INDIVIDUAL PAYCHECK

```
                    Saguaro Computers, Inc.
               STATEMENT OF EARNINGS AND DEDUCTIONS

   NAME: R. River          S.S.N.: 244-89-7153          EMPLOYEE NO.: 05225
```

EARNINGS	HRS/UNITS	AMOUNT	DEDUCTIONS	EARNINGS YEAR TO DATE
Regular	40	$250	Fed. Tax $18	$250
Overtime	0	.00	State Tax $12	
			FICA $15	
			Pension $4	
			Health $6	

```
   TOTAL EARNINGS: $250.00          TOTAL DEDUCTIONS: $55.00
   WEEK ENDING: X3/01/05          NET PAY: $195.00

   NOTE: Deposited at Golden One Credit Union
```

Payroll System

A computerized **payroll system** would accumulate data for individual employees in order to compute deductions for state and federal taxes, FICA, pensions, and health insurance. The system would, on the pay day, produce a paycheck for each employee, like the computer-printed statement of earnings and deductions illustrated in Exhibit 6-16. Notice that this statement notifies the employee that the paycheck has been automatically deposited in his or her bank account. Each employee's deductions are accumulated by the payroll system, so that reports for managerial purposes and for reporting taxes withheld for the IRS and the state government can be prepared through the system. In addition, the payroll system can communicate with the general ledger system to incorporate its payroll data for summarizing the financial status of the organization.

Sales Order Entry System

All merchandisers have some sort of organized procedure for processing customers' orders as they are received either in person, by telephone, or by mail. This procedure is called the **sales order entry system.** Large merchandisers have computerized their sales order entry system. Each order contains the customer's name, as well as a description of and the quantity of items to be sold. A good system can be designed to permit fast processing of orders, to update the inventory on hand, and to flag bad credit risks. Retail stores face special problems when dealing with sales order entry and inventory levels. A grocery store, for example, may sell one can of soup to a customer who may never shop at the same store again. Computerized systems have helped these retailers control these problems (see Real World Example 6-1).

REAL WORLD EXAMPLE 6-1
Computers in the Supermarket

ONE comprehensive use of computers by merchandisers is in the supermarket. Most items of merchandise are printed with the Universal Product Code (UPC), a series of bars and numbers that can be decoded by an optical scanner. A cashier passes each UPC over the optical scanner; the decoded information is displayed on the cash register. The computer records the sale, gives the customer an itemized receipt, and updates the inventory to preserve the perpetual inventory system. A further benefit is more efficiently produced information required for ordering and selecting products.

This decoding-inventory system is expensive: between $100,000 and $150,000 per store. It has been opposed by retail clerks who fear job losses and by consumer groups that want to prevent shopper exploitation by supermarkets that stop marking prices on individual items. Conversely, supermarket executives argue that this new system will cut retailer costs by millions and, thus, eventually benefit consumers through lower food costs. UPC symbols now appear on an estimated 92 percent of all packaged grocery goods, and the use of optical scanners is increasing.

```
               THANK YOU FOR SHOPPING
                  BEL AIR MARKETS
                    3510 PALMER DRIVE
                CAMERON PARK   CALIFORNIA

IRISH MIST                          18.99   T
JARLSBERG SWISS                      3.24   F
LONGHORN CHEESE                      2.10   F
PARMESAN WEDGES                      3.98   F
          2.29 LB @ 1LB / $0.49
GARNET YAMS                          1.12   F
FRISKIES BEEF STEW                   0.44   T
FRISKIES BEEF STEW                   0.44   T
FRISKIES BEEF STEW                   0.44   T
FRISKIES BEEF STEW                   0.44   T
FRISKIES BEEF STEW                   0.44   T
FRISKIES BEEF STEW                   0.44   T
FRISKIES BEEF STEW                   0.44   T
SIRLOIN TIP ROAST                   25.96   F
LOW-FAT MILK                         1.14   F
S/S CREAM                            0.93   F
S/S CREAM                            0.93   F
S/S CREAM                            0.93   F
EAGLE PRETZEL                        1.59   F
FL. YEAST                            0.96   F
SHELL PECANS                         3.89   F
SHEBA CAT FOOD                       0.67   T
SHEBA CAT FOOD                       0.67   T
SHEBA CAT FOOD                       0.67   T
          6 QTY       $0.36
ALPO LVR&CHX BANQ                    2.16   T
NLAND LOG                            1.99   T
LOGS                                 1.99   T
MAGAZINE                             1.95
HOME IMPROV                          2.75   T
PINE MT                              1.99   T

TAX                                  2.19
TOTAL                              $85.87


   ACCT # 1
CHECK                              $85.87

CHANGE                             $0.00
          34     ITEMS
   The employees at BEL AIR wish you
        a Happy Holiday Season !
   #                              2
0002 0015-0002  8432  SUN 12/24/90  3:51PM
```

Inventory Control System

As mentioned, a routine job that can be handled through computer procedures is inventory control. A computerized **inventory control system** can accumulate the number of units of each product purchased for inventory, deduct each item sold or used, and ensure that proper quantities of products are kept in stock. Automatic updates reduce the number of time-consuming manual counts needed to control inventory.

When a customer requests a product, a clerk enters the order into the sales order entry system; if the number is sufficient to fill the order, the goods are made available for shipment. The appropriate data are relayed to the accounts receivable system, which produces an invoice for the customer. If the goods are not in stock, the customer's order may be placed on back-order and the inventory control system will produce a notice to this effect indicating when the customer can expect the goods to be delivered.

A well designed inventory control system maintains an economical inventory level; it should have a warning procedure to notify managers when stock levels are too low. Most inventory control systems contain a variety of mathematical routines to help managers calculate an economical inventory level for each product.

Accounts Receivable System

The accounts receivable for a large merchandiser must be tracked efficiently. The high volume of transactions can be handled by a computerized **accounts receivable system** designed to calculate and print customers' purchases, payments, unpaid accounts, and account balances. The system also can calculate and print customers' invoices and management reports. Other output can include sales analyses that describe changing sales patterns and reports of current and past-due accounts. A more detailed presentation of accounts receivable is discussed in Chapter 7.

Accounts Payable System

The accounts payable a merchandiser owes to its suppliers also can be handled by a computerized system designed for the individual entity. An **accounts payable system** can control invoices received and generate checks to pay the invoices in much the same way the payroll system operates.

General Ledger System

The **general ledger system** in a computerized merchandising operation can determine whether the books balance, post to the general ledger, and produce financial statements.

Once a company has decided to computerize one or more of its routine activities, it must decide whether to develop its own software or buy a software package from a vendor. A computerized system developed by the company can have the advantage of being designed precisely for the company's particular needs. Vendor-supplied software, on the other hand, is quite inexpensive; for example, a general ledger package that operates on the IBM-PC is currently retailing for less than $100. Regardless of which way a company decides to go, it must be sure the general ledger system will be compatible with other systems the entity's computer already runs. Exhibit 6-17 illustrates the interrelationships of the various systems discussed in this section; the importance of the general ledger system is clear.

Management Uses of Computerized Accounting Systems

While the automation of routine data-processing tasks undoubtedly reduces accounting and other clerical expenses, the computer can do much more than

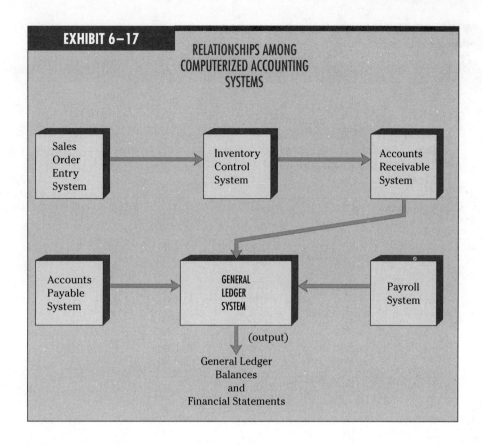

EXHIBIT 6–17

RELATIONSHIPS AMONG COMPUTERIZED ACCOUNTING SYSTEMS

Sales Order Entry System → Inventory Control System → Accounts Receivable System

Accounts Payable System → GENERAL LEDGER SYSTEM ← Payroll System

(output)

General Ledger Balances and Financial Statements

perform these programs. The computer's efficient organization of information can assist many levels of management in their decision-making roles. Again, programs can be designed to suit a particular entity's needs. For instance, based on trends in the historical sales results accumulated by the sales order entry system, forecasts for future sales can be calculated. A system that both reports routine data processing and generates information is called a **management information system** (MIS). Lately, **decision support systems** have also been introduced; unlike MIS, these systems permit the user to pose questions while the user is on-line. One of the most popular microcomputer applications of decision support systems is *spreadsheet analysis*.

SPREADSHEET

A **spreadsheet** is a table of columns and rows, as shown in Exhibit 6-18. Various commercial spreadsheets, such as Visicalc, Supercalc, and Lotus 1-2-3, perform many of the same functions, and operate using similar logic; however, some spreadsheet software packages may have additional features that others are lacking. A spreadsheet program prepares the computer to accept tables, values, or mathematical formulas into the preestablished spreadsheet cells.

The payroll information from Exhibit 6-13 of SCI's January 5 payroll journal has been entered into the spreadsheet program in Exhibit 6-18. The real advantage of a spreadsheet program is that, if a single datum changes, the entire spreadsheet is recalculated by the program. For instance, if the hourly wage of R. River is increased to $9 per hour, the user enters the new rate and the program automatically

EXHIBIT 6-18

A SPREADSHEET

```
1:: A :: B :: C :: D :: E  : :  G  ::  H  ::  I: :  K  ::  L   : :   N   :
                 Information  *      Debit    *    Credit    *           *
2:Employee      Hours   Rate *   Gross Pay    *   Total    Net*  Check    *
3:Name          Reg OT Reg OT *Sales  Deliv  Offic*Deductions  Pay*  Number   *
4:                           *                *               *           *
5:J. Abbott                  * 400            *     104     296*    101    *
6:N. Aitken                  *            300 *      73     227*    102    *
7:R. River      40           *       250      *      55     195*    103    *
8:                           *                *               *           *
9:                           *                *               *           *
10:                          *                *               *           *
11:                          *                *               *           *
12:                          *                *               *           *
13:                          *                *               *           *
14:                          *                *               *           *
15:                          *                *               *           *
16:                          *                *               *           *
17:                          *                *               *           *
18:Total                     * 400   250   300 *    232     718*           *
19:Total Gross Pay      950  *                *               *           *
20:                          *                *               *           *



>121
Widths    9 Memory:277 Last Col/Row:A1  ? for HELP
 1>
   Function keys: F1 = HELP : F2 = ERASE LINE/RETURN TO WORKSHEET
```

recalculates any amounts in the spreadsheet that are affected by the change. This is a simple example. A spreadsheet such as Lotus 1-2-3, with 2,043 rows and 254 columns, can perform calculations that would take hours with a calculator.

CHAPTER REVIEW

1 Does the volume of business transactions influence the design, number, and content of special journals? Explain. (p. 268)

Most definitely. If an entity operated with only a few transactions during an accounting period, the general journal would suffice. However, even small enterprises have hundreds or thousands of transactions during an accounting period, many of which are similar to each other in nature. These include inflows of cash, outflows of cash, sales on account, or purchases of merchandise for resale on account. The more similar transactions an entity has, the more the situation calls for special journals. The design, number, and content of the journals fit the exact situation of each entity.

2 What are the common features used in the design of all special journals? (pp. 268–69)
All special journals have two things in common; they provide columns of needed nonfinancial information, such as the date of the transaction, the name of the entity involved, the check number, and the terms, and they provide financial information, such as the amount of the check, the amount of the receipt, the total receivables, the total payables, and so on.

3 Can special journals be grouped into various cycles within the operating activity of an entity? (p. 269)
In part, special journals can be grouped. For instance, during the sales and collection cycle, the sales journal is used to record the sale on account, and the cash receipts journal is used to record the subsequent payment of that account. During the purchase and payment cycle, the purchases journal is used to record the purchase on account, while the cash disbursements journal is used to record the payment of the purchase.

4 What source documents are used by accountants in the sales and collection cycle? (pp. 269–73)
The sales invoice is the major document for the sale of an item, while the check received is the major external document for the collection portion of the cycle.

5 What source documents are used in the purchase and payment cycle? (pp. 273–78)
The purchase invoice is the major document for the purchase of merchandise for resale, while the check sent, along with its authorization, is the major document for the payment portion of the cycle.

6 What is the interrelationship between the general ledger and subsidiary ledgers? (p. 278)
Separate accounts are necessary for each customer an entity has and for each supplier if credit is granted. The general ledger would become too unwieldy if all these accounts were included, along with such accounts as Land, Buildings, Equipment, and Common Stock, to name a few. The control accounts for accounts receivable and accounts payable are part of the general ledger. Behind each control account exists a subsidiary ledger detailing the amount owed by each customer or the amount owed to each supplier. The total of the individual customer or supplier accounts must equal the balance in the control account in the general ledger. In an extremely small operation, subsidiary ledgers probably would not be needed, with general ledger accounts being maintained for each customer and each supplier granted credit. However, in situations where more than just a few customers and suppliers exist, subsidiary ledgers for accounts receivable and accounts payable are a must.

7 How is equality maintained between the general ledger and the subsidiary ledgers? (p. 278)
When an amount is entered in the columns for accounts receivable or accounts payable in any of the special journals, it is posted immediately to the subsidiary ledgers. At the end of the month, the total of those columns are posted to the general ledger control accounts. At this time, the two should be in balance, unless errors have been made.

8 Is a one-write system of benefit to the accountant when designing an accounting system? (pp. 282–83)

A one-write system is designed in such a manner that when an entry is made in one system, it is automatically (through carbon or carbonless paper) recorded in another. For instance, when a check is written, the date, payee, account number, and amount can be recorded simultaneously in the cash disbursements journal and in the subsidiary ledger of the supplier.

9 How are records designed to register the acquisition and subsequent payment of employee services? (pp. 284–85, 287–89)

Payroll journals and individual employee record cards, such as time cards, are used to gather the information necessary for the entity, the employee, and the various taxing authorities.

10 Are computers more of a help or a hindrance to the accountant when designing an accounting system? (pp. 290–96)

The answer to this question is open-ended. It strictly depends on the system and the programmer. The computer can take most of the drudgery out of the book-keeping process if it is designed properly. If it is not, it can add hours and hours to what should have been a minor task. The software available today is useful and generally adaptable to a variety of situations. The old adage still holds, however: "if you put garbage into the computer, you will get garbage out of the computer."

KEY TERMS

accounts receivable system   (p. 294) A computer system that generates monthly invoices to send to customers, maintains records of amounts due, and generates reports needed by management, such as overdue accounts and aging of receivables.

accounts payable system   (p. 294) A computer system that provides control over payment to suppliers, issues checks to suppliers and provides information necessary for effective cash management.

cash disbursements journal   (p. 275) A special journal used to record all payments made by check. Payments of cash, if made, should come from the petty cash fund.

cash receipts journal   (p. 270) A special journal used to record all receipts of cash.

control account   (p. 269) A general ledger account that has a subsidiary ledger containing the details to support the balance.

decision support system   (p. 295) An information system that managers can use to provide highly refined information to help make non-routine decisions.

general ledger system   (p. 294) An integrated computer system that records transactions, balances accounts, posts, and prepares the financial statements.

Individual Employee Earnings Record   (p. 290) A cumulative record of all gross earnings and related deductions from earnings for a particular employee.

inventory control system   (p. 292) A computer system used to monitor inventory quantity and to minimize inventory costs.

management information system (MIS)   (p. 295) An information and data processing system designed to aid in the performance of management functions. An MIS system includes all the computer systems introduced in Chapter 6.

one-write system (p. 282) A system that organizes information input, eliminates transposition errors, and establishes a clear audit trail.

payroll journal (p. 287) A special journal used to record the payroll information regarding gross and net pay, including the various deductions from an employee's pay.

payroll system (p. 291) A computer system that prepares payroll checks, maintains all payroll records, and prepares reports related to payroll activities.

purchases journal (p. 273) A special journal used to record all purchases for resale that are made on account.

sales journal (p. 269) A special journal used to record all sales on account.

sales order entry system (p. 292) A computer system that initiates shipping orders, keeps track of back-orders, and produces various reports needed by management and the accounting system.

special journals (p. 268) Multicolumn journals designed not only to record similar transactions chronologically but also to reduce the writing of repetitive information. They are often referred to collectively as the *books of original entry.* Any transaction that can not be recorded in a special journal is recorded in the general journal.

spreadsheet (p. 295) A program that allows the user to create a very large two-dimensional table and to change the data in many different ways.

subsidiary ledgers (p. 269) Separate ledgers that keep a group of homogeneous accounts that correspond to a related control account in the general ledger. Two examples include accounts receivable, accounts payable, and long-term assets ledgers.

SELF-TEST QUESTIONS FOR REVIEW   (Answers are at the end of this chapter.)

Q3

1. In which of the following journals would an entry for the sale of common stock be recorded?
    (a) General
    (b) Cash Receipts
    (c) Sales
    (d) Purchases
    (e) Cash Disbursements

Q3, Q4

2. In which of the following journals would an entry for the sale of merchandise for cash be recorded?
    (a) General
    (b) Cash Receipts
    (c) Sales
    (d) Purchases
    (e) Cash Disbursements

Q3, Q5

3. In which of the following journals would an entry for the purchase of merchandise for cash be recorded?
    (a) General
    (b) Cash Receipts
    (c) Sales
    (d) Purchases
    (e) Cash Disbursements

Q3, Q5

4. In which of the following journals would an entry for the return of merchandise previously purchased on account be recorded?
    (a) General
    (b) Cash Receipts

    (c) Sales
    (d) Purchases
    (e) Cash Disbursements

Q3, Q5

5. In which of the following journals would an entry for the purchase on account of merchandise for resale be recorded?
    (a) General
    (b) Cash Receipts
    (c) Sales
    (d) Purchases
    (e) Cash Disbursements

Q3, Q4

6. In which of the following journals would an entry for the sale of merchandise on account be recorded?
    (a) General
    (b) Cash Receipts
    (c) Sales
    (d) Purchases
    (e) Cash Disbursements

Q3

7. In which of the following journals would an entry for the purchase of fixed assets on account be recorded?
    (a) General
    (b) Cash Receipts
    (c) Sales
    (d) Purchases
    (e) Cash Disbursements

Q3, Q4

8. In which of the following journals would an entry for the collection of an account receivable be recorded?
    (a) General
    (b) Cash Receipts
    (c) Sales
    (d) Purchases
    (e) Cash Disbursements

Q6

9. Subsidiary ledgers must be in balance with their control accounts
    (a) at all times.
    (b) at the end of the month when the special journals are posted.
    (c) only at the end of the business year after all adjusting entries are posted.
    (d) only when a one-write system is used.
    (e) only if a general ledger computer system is in operation.

Q9

10. Which of the following taxes are deducted from employees' earnings to arrive at net pay?
    (a) The employees' share of the entity's income tax
    (b) Sales tax
    (c) FICA
    (d) Federal unemployment tax
    (e) All of the above

Q9

11. Which of the following is *not* considered a payroll tax expense?
    (a) Federal and state income taxes
    (b) State unemployment taxes
    (c) Federal unemployment taxes
    (d) Employers' share of employees' FICA
    (e) All of the above are considered payroll tax expense

DEMONSTRATION PROBLEM

Part A

Coda Sales, Inc., was incorporated on May 1, 19X1, to operate a merchandising business. Its sales journal, cash receipts journal, and general journal follow.

Sales Journal   Page 1

Date		Customer	Invoice Number	Terms	F	Accts. Rec.—Dr. Sales—Cr.
19X1						
May	1	Bloomfield Products Corp.	1	2/10, n/30		6,000
	2	Garland Stores, Inc.	2	2/10, n/30		2,400
	11	Summit Sales, Inc.	3	2/10, n/30		1,000
	20	Willowdale Corp.	4	2/10, n/30		4,000
	27	Cardinal Emporium Corp.	5	2/10, n/30		1,600
		Totals				15,000
						(110) (500)

Cash Receipts Journal   Page 1

Information			Debit			Credit			
					Accounts Receivable		Other Accounts		
Date		Cash Received From	Cash	Sales Disc.	✓ Amount	Account	F	Amount
19X1								
May	1	Common Stock	6,000			Common Stock	320	6,000
	2	Harvey Panda	1,000			Sales (cash)	500	1,000
	5	Bloomfield Products Corp.	2,940	60	3,000			
	8	Garland Stores, Inc.	2,352	48	2,400			
	20	Summit Sales, Inc.	784	16	800			
		Totals	13,076	124	6,200			7,000
			(101)	(509)	(110)			(X)

General Journal   Page 1

Date 19X1	Description	F	Debit	Credit
May 12	Sales Returns and Allowances	508	200	
	Accounts Receivable	110		200
	To record return from Summit Sales, Inc.			

Required

1. Open accounts receivable subsidiary accounts for each customer.

2. Post the appropriate information and amounts from each journal.

3. Calculate the balance in each accounts receivable subsidiary account.

Part B

Rapid Sales, Inc., was incorporated on June 2, 19X1, to operate a merchandising business. Its purchases journal, cash disbursements journal, and general journal follow.

Purchases Journal   Page 1

Date		Supplier	Terms	F	Purchases—Dr. Accts. Pay.—Cr.
19X1					
June	2	Atwater Pencils Co.	2/10, n/30		7,000
	8	Hymus Distributors, Inc.	2/15, n/30		4,000
	10	Park Products, Inc.	n/30		400
	15	MacKay Doors, Inc.	2/10, n/30		3,000
	26	Coolbrook Co.	2/10, n/30		1,600
		Totals			16,000
					(550) (210)

Cash Disbursements Journal   Page 1

	Information			Credit			Debit			
						Accounts Payable		Other Accounts		
Date		Cash Paid To	Check Number	Cash	Purchases Discounts	✓	Amount	Account	F	Amount
19X1										
June	3	Concordia Rentals Corp.	1	1,000				Rent Expense	654	1,000
	5	Westwood Furniture, Inc.	2	2,000				Equipment	183	2,000
	10	Atwater Pencils Co.	3	6,850	150		7,000			
	20	Hymus Distributors, Inc.	4	1,862	38		1,900			
	24	MacKay Doors, Inc.	5	2,940	60		3,000			
	31	Real Quick Transport Co.	6	700				Transportation In	560	700
		Totals		15,352	248		11,900			3,700
				(101)	(559)		(210)			(X)

General Journal   Page 1

Date		Description	F	Debit	Credit
19X1					
June	15	Accounts Payable	210	200	
		Purchase Returns and Allowances	558		200
		To record goods returned to Hymus Distributors, Inc.			

Required

1. Open accounts payable subsidiary accounts for each supplier.
2. Post the appropriate information and amounts from each journal.
3. Calculate the balance in each accounts payable subsidiary account.

SOLUTION TO DEMONSTRATION PROBLEM

Part A

Coda Sales, Inc.
Accounts Receivable Subsidiary Ledger

Bloomfield Products Corp.

Date 19X1	Description	F	Debit	Credit	Bal.
May 1		S1	6,000		6,000
5		CR1		3,000	3,000

Cardinal Emporium Corp.

Date 19X1	Description	F	Debit	Credit	Bal.
May 27		S1	1,600		1,600

Garland Stores, Inc.

Date 19X1	Description	F	Debit	Credit	Bal.
May 2		S1	2,400		2,400
		CR1		2,400	-0-

Summit Sales, Inc.

Date 19X1	Description	F	Debit	Credit	Bal.
May 11		S1	1,000		1,000
12		J1		200	800
20		CR1		800	-0-

Willowdale Corp.

Date 19X1	Description	F	Debit	Credit	Bal.
May 20		S1	4,000		4,000

Part B

Rapid Sales, Inc.
Accounts Payable Subsidiary Ledger

Atwater Pencils Co.

Date 19X1	Description	F	Debit	Credit	Bal.
June 2		P1		7,000	7,000
10		CD1	7,000		-0-

Coolbrook Co.

Date 19X1	Description	F	Debit	Credit	Bal.
June 26		P1		1,600	1,600

Hymus Distributors, Inc.

Date 19X1	Description	F	Debit	Credit	Bal.
June 8		P1		4,000	4,000
15		J1	200		3,800
20		CD1	1,900		1,900

Mackay Doors, Inc.

Date 19X1	Description	·F	Debit	Credit	Bal.
June 15		P1		3,000	3,000
24		CD1	3,000		-0-

Park Products, Inc.

Date 19X1	Description	F	Debit	Credit	Bal.
June 10		P1		400	400

DISCUSSION QUESTIONS

Q6-1   Special journals are often referred to as *books of original entry*. What are the advantages in using them?

Q6-2   What is the common feature in the actual design of all special journals? What types of columns are always present?

Q6-3   How does the use of special journals permit a better division of duties among employees?

Q6-4   In what special journal are cash sales recorded? cash purchases?

Q6-5   Special journals are designed to facilitate not only the recording but also the posting process. Explain how this improvement is achieved.

Q6-6   In order for special journals to facilitate the posting process, the sequence of the debit and credit columns is often reversed in practice. Explain how this column rearrangement facilitates the posting process.

Q6-7   What entries are recorded in the general journal when special journals are in use?

Q6-8   What is a control account? a subsidiary ledger?

Q6-9   Posting to subsidiary ledgers is often done on a daily basis, while posting to control accounts is done only at month-end. Why?

Q6-10   What is a source document?

Q6-11   How does a payroll journal differ from a cash disbursements journal?

Q6-12   How are employer-related payroll taxes recorded?

Q6-13   What is an employee earnings record, and why is it used?

Q6-14   For the sales order entry system, identify the inputs, what occurs to the data "in" the computer, and the output.

Q6-15   Some people argue that computers are intelligent and capable of decision making. Others argue that computers are simply dumb machines that execute what they are programmed to do. Take one side of this argument and support your position.

Q6-16   What are the limitations, if any, of spreadsheet programs?

DISCUSSION CASE
Making Dough with a PC

The Deerfield Bakery is managed by Karl Schmitt, whose family has been in the baking business since his great-grandfather began the tradition in Germany. From there the family moved to Chicago where it operated the bakery until moving to the present location 11 years ago.

Schmitt became part owner of the store in 1979 when he gave up his career as an actuary and brought with him the programming skills he gained in the business world.

Like many small business owners, Schmitt hoped that computers would bring greater efficiency to his operation, while preserving a craft that had been handed down through the family. But computerization didn't happen overnight; Schmitt experimented with both hardware and software to build the right system.

"We started with a Texas Instruments computer, but by 1980 we had outgrown it," he recalled. As more and more of the bakery's operations were automated, the business needed a machine with greater capabilities, so he turned to the Apple III. However, he had problems with the hardware so he bought a Commodore PET, but found it didn't meet his needs, either. When IBM announced its PC, Schmitt decided to wait for it. He bought one of the first PCs available in his area. Since the initial purchase, he has bought three more. Two of the PCs are used in the store in place of cash registers. The sales personnel punch in a code, which corresponds to the type of item and the price. The computer calculates the applicable tax, the total bill, and the change due. The printer produces a receipt. The computers also keep track of the various products and remind employees of their duties in other parts of the shop. The two other PCs are located in the company office upstairs from the shop. Both machines have combination clock calendars, printer interface and memory expansion cards, 320K disk drives, light pens, and color/graphics boards.

Schmitt has added a VOX board to upgrade one of the PCs to 14 megabytes. "I've written the programs so they can be run on floppies," he said. "I don't use the hard disk for original copy—it is more of a backup. If one machine goes down, I can run the program on the other machine on a floppy disk. This way, all of the programs can run on any of the PCs."

PROGRAMMING FOR BAKING

Finding the right software wasn't easy, either. When Schmitt began to computerize his business, he used off-the-shelf programs to handle accounts receivable and payable and other accounting procedures. However, he discovered that many of them did not adequately meet the needs of a small business.

"It's natural for commercial programmers to take the applications from large businesses—that's what they've done," he said. Unfortunately, a small business can't really use them, or it isn't economical to do so.

As an experienced computer programmer, Schmitt was not deterred by the lack of available commercial programs geared to his industry. He decided to write his own software, which could be tailored to the bakery's specific needs. He has written more than 60 programs in BASIC, which do anything from printing out recipes for each day's baking to making lists of how to decorate specialty cakes. According to Schmitt, he chose BASIC over COBOL or FORTRAN because it can be written quickly, and it can be compiled. Compiled programs execute quickly. While it is true that some of these functions would be performed by commercial programs, Schmitt believes that writing his own saved time and money.

There are also other advantages to customized programming. "Some commercial programs are designed to be so flexible that they are neither easy nor fast to operate," said Schmitt. "Part of what I expect from computers is speed. If a program doesn't run quickly, you've saved labor but thrown away the savings on the time spent operating it. Some programs are so user-friendly that they are cumbersome to use."

One problem that Schmitt remedied with his own software was slow printing speed. A commercial program he had used took 45 minutes to print checks because of pauses built into the software; his program, however, can produce checks as quickly as his Anadex dot-matrix printer can generate them. His accounting software consists of three programs chained together, and it handles tasks that once required 12 commercial programs.

The advantages of writing your own software are many, but most small-business owners probably don't have programming experience as extensive as Schmitt's. However, he believes that even a short, simple customized program can be helpful and he recommends at least giving it a try.

Schmitt has considered marketing his software, but decided against it because each operation's needs are so specific. "Someone else using our programs would run into the same problems I had with the commercial programs," he explained.

With the right hardware and software in place, the store can get down to the business of baking. Schmitt's programs include those for accounts receivable, bread recipes, cake recipes, and billing for wholesale accounts. He also uses programs for listing each type of decorative cake, determining price codes, and one for tallying cake orders to determine quantities of ingredients.

GETTING DOWN TO BAKING

Not every program is used every day, but most of them are central to the bakery's operations. When a customer calls in an order, the information is jotted down and later entered on the computer, where it is sorted by field (name, address, telephone number, type of order, price, and so forth). For example, this system allows you to examine all chocolate sheet cake orders at one time. At the end of the day, the telephone orders are combined with those from the wholesale customers (the bakery also sells some of its goods to supermarkets), and with the order of goods to stock the store. The computer will develop a recipe from this information, using another program.

Using this information the computer or an operator can decide to make, for example, 110 lb. of white bread loaves. The computer then creates a recipe and determines quantities for the necessary ingredients. In this case the recipe calls for 1.72 lb. of yeast, 5.43 lb. sweetened and condensed milk, 34.02 lb. of water, 64.25 lb. of flour, 0.9 lb. of diamalt, 1.26

lb. of salt, and 0.72 lb. of shortening. If prepared sweetened and condensed milk is unavailable, the computer automatically includes a recipe for it. It also provides other helpful hints for preparation. For instance, the program knows that flour comes in 100-pound sacks, so, in addition to calling for the required 64.25 pounds, it will note that you can simply remove 35.75 pounds of flour from the 100-pound sack. The recipe includes more than one set of mixing directions, each geared to a different machine in the bakery. The program specifies how long the mixing procedure will take, according to the machine used. A printout of the recipe is given to each baker when he begins work. For cakes or specialty items, the program will provide a decorations list along with a cake recipe.

"One of the biggest problems we had in the past," said Schmitt, "was misfiling of orders. A customer who had ordered a cake would come into the store, and we wouldn't have the cake ready—a sure way to damage your reputation. With the computer we print a list for the decorators each day, and all of the cakes are decorated to order.

"This is a prime example of the computer's value," he continued. "Management becomes easy when you have an alphabetical list of the cakes that have been ordered for a particular day. Without a computer, preparing a list like this one is such a time-consuming, tedious activity that many small businesses don't take the time to do it."

The Deerfield Bakery uses its PCs to keep track of more than 700 different confections and about 1,000 designs for cakes, which can cost up to $300 or $400. It also offers 18 different types of bread ranging from plain white to zucchini. In addition, each type of bread is available in a number of forms, such as muffins, loaves, and rolls. Each form requires a different proportion of ingredients. On a typical day the bakery will make from 30 to 40 different doughs. "When you include cake fillings, icings, and garnishes, you use more than 50 ingredients," said Schmitt. "It used to take up to 2 hours to total manually the next day's needs and then calculate the quantities. With the computer the process moves as quickly as punching the keyboard."

Source Michael Muskal, "Making Dough with the P.C.," *P.C. Magazine,* February 7, 1984.

For Discussion

1. What are some advantages and disadvantages of Karl Schmitt writing his own accounting computer programs?

2. Would you incorporate controls into Schmitt's system? If so, what sort of controls?

3. Can you pinpoint potential limitations in Schmitt's system?

EXERCISES

Note: In your answers to Exercises E-1 to E-6, the order of the column headings may vary from what is shown in the text. It is more important to understand the content than the form at this point.

Sales journal (Q2–Q4)

E6-1   Sketch a format for a sales journal and label the columns you have constructed without referring to the text.

Purchases journal (Q2, Q3, Q5)

E6-2   Sketch a format for a purchases journal and label the columns you have constructed without referring to the text.

Cash receipts journal (Q2–Q4)

E6-3   Sketch a format for a cash receipts journal and label the columns you have constructed without referring to the text.

Cash disbursements journal (Q2, Q3, Q5)

E6-4   Sketch a format for a cash disbursements journal and label the columns you have constructed without referring to the text.

Sales return and allowances journal (Q2–Q4)

E6-5 Sketch a format for a sales return and allowances journal and label the columns you have constructed without referring to the text.

Purchase returns and allowances journal (Q2, Q3, Q5)

E6-6 Sketch a format for a purchase returns and allowances journal and label the columns you have constructed without referring to the text.

GAAP and special journals (Q1)

E6-7 List the special journals required by GAAP and explain why they are required.

Employee payroll deductions (Q9)

E6-8 Name at least seven possible deductions your employer might take from your earnings before you receive the net check.

Balancing the control accounts with the subsidiary ledgers (Q6)

E6-9 Using an example, show how balance is achieved between the Accounts Receivable control account and the accounts receivable subsidiary ledger.

PROBLEMS

Purchases and cash disbursements journals, accounts payable subsidiary ledger, schedule (Q2, Q3, Q5)

P6-1 The following accounts payable subsidiary ledger accounts have been posted during March 19X2 from two books of original entry.

Accounts Payable Subsidiary Ledger

Avon Stores, Inc.

Date		Description	F	Debit	Credit	Bal.
19X2						
Bal.		(purchase made Feb. 2, 19X2, terms n/30)				1,000
Mar.	15	n/30	P3		500	
	17	n/30	P3		750	
	20		CD7	1,000		

Reynold Novelties

Date		Description	F	Debit	Credit	Bal.
19X2						
Mar.	3	2/10, n/30	P3		1,500	
	12		CD7	1,500		
	26	2/10, n/30	P3		1,250	

Fulton Place Products Inc.

Date		Description	F	Debit	Credit	Bal.
19X2						
Mar.	25	2/10, n/30	P3		3,000	
	31		CD7	1,500		

Otterburn College, Inc.

Date		Description	F	Debit	Credit	Bal.
19X2 Bal. Mar.	20 31	(purchase made Feb. 10, 19X2, terms n/30) n/30	P3 CD7	1,600	400	2,000

Richmond Renovators Corp.

Date		Description	F	Debit	Credit	Bal.
19X2 Mar.	10 24	2/15, n/30	P3 CD7	900	900	

Required

1. Calculate and record the balance in each of the above accounts.

2. Using the information in these accounts, prepare a purchases journal and calculate the column total.

3. Using the information in the subsidiary ledger accounts, prepare a cash disbursements journal and calculate all column totals. Assume that all cash disbursements in March were for the payment of accounts payable.

4. Open general ledger accounts for Cash, Accounts Payable, Purchases, and Purchase Discounts. Post the column totals of the purchases journal and cash disbursements journal.

5. Prepare a schedule of accounts payable as of March 31, 19X2. The total should agree with the balance in the general ledger Accounts Payable account. The February 28, 19X2, balance in this control account amounted to $3,000.

Sales and cash receipts journals, accounts receivable subsidiary ledger, schedule (Q2–Q4)

P6-2   The following accounts receivable subsidiary ledger accounts have been posted during January 19X3 from two books of original entry.

Accounts Receivable Subsidiary Ledger

Atwater Marketers Corp.

Date		Description	F	Debit	Credit	Bal.
19X3 Bal. Jan.	15		S6	1,000		5,250

Coolbrook Distributors

Date		Description	F	Debit	Credit	Bal.
19X3 Jan.	6 9 15		S6 S6 CR9	500 250	500	

Hymus Sales Corp.

Date		Description	F	Debit	Credit	Bal.
19X3 Bal.						1,500
Jan.	2		S6	1,200		
	11		CR6		2,700	

Mackay Products, Inc.

Date		Description	F	Debit	Credit	Bal.
19X3 Bal.						200
Jan.	7		S6	800		
	10		CR9		200	

Park Extension Co.

Date		Description	F	Debit	Credit	Bal.
19X3 Bal.						900
Jan.	18		CR9		900	
	25		S6	600		

TransCalifornia Sales, Inc.

Date			F	Debit	Credit	Bal.
19X3						
Jan.	10		S6	400		
	14		S6	300		
	19		CR9		400	

Required

1. Calculate and record the balance in each of the accounts.

2. Using the information in the subsidiary ledger accounts, prepare a sales journal complete with column totals. You may assume that all sales on account have terms of 2/10, net 30, and the first sale of the month was made on invoice number 31.

3. Using the information in the subsidiary ledger accounts, prepare a cash receipts journal and calculate all column totals. Assume that all cash receipts in January were from the collection of accounts receivable. Note that all eligible customers took discounts.

4. Open general ledger accounts for Cash, Accounts Receivable, Sales, and Sales Discounts. Post the column totals of the sales journal and cash receipts journal.

5. Prepare a schedule of accounts receivable as of January 31, 19X3; the total should agree with the balance in the general ledger Accounts Receivable account. The January 1, 19X3, balance in this control account amounted to $7,850.

Cash receipts and cash disbursements journals, posting to subsidiary ledgers, schedules (Q2–Q7)

P6-3 Beacon Hill Corp. was incorporated on July 2, 19X1, to operate a merchandising business. Its sales and purchases during July are recorded in the following journals.

Sales Journal Page 1

Date		Customer	Invoice Number	Terms	F	Accts. Rec.—Dr. Sales—Cr.
19X1						
July	2	Meadow Tool Rentals, Inc.	1	2/10, n/30		2,000
	15	Condor Products Corp.	2	2/10, n/30		2,000
	20	Pine Promotions Corp.	3	2/10, n/30		3,500
	26	Daytona Sales, Inc.	4	2/10, n/30		600
	31	Argyle, Inc.	5	2/10, n/30		1,900
						10,000
						(110) (500)

Purchases Journal Page 1

Date		Supplier	Terms	F	Purchases—Dr. Accts. Pay—Cr.
19X1					
July	2	Westmount Pencils Co.	2/10, n/30		3,500
	8	MacDonald Distributors, Inc.	2/15, n/30		2,000
	10	Peel Products, Inc.	n/30		200
	15	Draper Door, Inc.	2/10, n/30		1,500
	26	Gold & Silver Co.	2/10, n/30		800
					8,000
					(550) (210)

Other transactions during the month were as follows:

July 2 Issued common shares for $5,000 to George Hill, the incorporator and sole stockholder of the corporation

3 Issued check no. 1 to Concordia Rentals Corp. for $500 in payment of July rent

5 Issued check no. 2 to Westwood Furniture, Inc., for $1,000 in payment for equipment

8 Collected $200 for a cash sale made today to Byron Peel

9 Received the amount due from Meadow Tool Rentals, Inc., for the July 2 sale (less discount)

10 Issued check no. 3 to Westmount Pencils Co. in payment for the July 2 purchase (less discount)

15 Received a credit memo from MacDonald Distributors, Inc., for $100 because of defective merchandise included in the July 9 purchase.

16 Condor Products Corp. returned $200 of merchandise (issued a credit memo)

20 Issued check no. 4 to MacDonald Distributors, Inc., in payment of half the purchase made July 8 (less credit memo, less discount on payment)

24 Received half the amount due from Condor Products Corp. in partial payment for the July 15 sale (less discount on payment)

July 24   Issued check no. 5 to Draper Door, Inc., in payment of the purchase made July 15 (less discount)

    31   Issued check no. 6 to Real Quick Transport Co. for $350 in payment for transportation to our warehouse during the month (All purchases are fob shipping point.)

Required

1. Record the July transactions in the following journals:
   (a) cash receipts journal
   (b) cash disbursements journal
   (c) general journal

2. Calculate the total of each column in the cash receipts and cash disbursements journals. For each journal, ascertain whether total debits equal total credits.

3. Open subsidiary ledger accounts for each of the customers listed in the sales journal and post the sales transactions and appropriate cash receipts transactions to these accounts.

4. Open subsidiary ledger accounts for each of the suppliers recorded in the purchases journal and post the purchase transactions to these accounts.

5. Post the appropriate entries from the general journal to the subsidiary accounts receivable and subsidiary accounts payable accounts.

6. Open the following general ledger control accounts:
   (a) accounts receivable
   (b) accounts payable
   Post all appropriate balances from the cash receipts and cash disbursements journals and the appropriate amounts from the general journal.

7. Prepare a schedule of accounts receivable; the total should agree with the Accounts Receivable control account.

8. Prepare a schedule of accounts payable; the total should agree with the Accounts Payable control account.

Payroll, net pay, journal entries, payroll tax expense (Q2, Q3, Q5, Q9)

P6-4   The following payroll information for the week of March 7, 19X2, is taken from the records of Sandstone Services, Inc.

Gross Pay	$4,500
Less Deductions:	
Federal Income Tax	900
State Income Tax	300
FICA	300
Pension Plan	150
Health Insurance	30

Required

1. Determine the net pay.

2. Prepare the entry necessary to record the payroll in the general journal.

3. Prepare the entry necessary to record the payment of the payroll in the cash disbursements journal. (You may prepare this entry in general journal form.)

4. Assume the employer pays 5% for state unemployment and .8% for federal unemployment taxes. Prepare the entry necessary in the general journal to record the employer's payroll tax expense for the March 7 payroll.

ALTERNATE PROBLEMS

Purchases and cash disbursements journals, accounts payable subsidiary ledger, schedule (Q2, Q3, Q5)

AP6-1 The following accounts payable subsidiary ledger accounts have been posted for July 19X5 from two books of original entry.

Accounts Payable Subsidiary Ledger

Busy Warehouse, Inc.

Date		Description	F	Debit	Credit	Bal.
19X5						
July	15	2/10, n/30	P10		2,000	
	24		CD15	1,000		
	29		CD15	1,000		
	31	2/10, n/30	P10		500	

Crescent Shops, Inc.

Date		Description	F	Debit	Credit	Bal.
19X5						
Bal.		(purchase made June 3, 19X5, terms n/30)				3,000
July	10	n/30	P10		250	
	30		CD15	1,500		

Stadium Corp.

Date		Description	F	Debit	Credit	Bal.
19X5						
Bal.		(purchase made June 15, 19X5, terms n/30)				850
July	20	n/30	P10		250	
	25		CD15	550		

St. Lawrence Downtown, Inc.

Date		Description	F	Debit	Credit	Bal.
19X5						
July	9	2/15, n/30	P10		1,500	
	23		CD15	750		
	25	2/15, n/30	P10		500	
	30		CD15	750		

Walkley Cabinets Corp.

Date		Description	F	Debit	Credit	Bal.
19X5						
July	2	2/10, n/30	P10		600	
	11		CD15	600		

Required

1. Calculate and record the balance in each of the accounts.

2. Using the information in the accounts, prepare a purchases journal and calculate the column total.

3. Using the information in the subsidiary ledger accounts, prepare a cash disbursements journal and calculate all column totals. Assume that all cash disbursements in July were for the payment of accounts payable.

4. Open general ledger accounts for Cash, Accounts Payable, Purchases, and Purchase Discounts. Post the column totals of the purchases journal and cash disbursements journal.

5. Prepare a schedule of accounts payable as of July 31, 19X5; the total should agree with the balance in the general ledger Accounts Payable account. (The July 1, 19X5, balance of the control account amounted to $3,850.)

Sales and cash receipts journals, accounts receivable subsidiary ledgers, schedule (Q2–Q4)

AP6-2   The following accounts receivable subsidiary ledger accounts have been posted during June 19X4 from two books of original entry.

Accounts Receivable Subsidiary Ledger

Bloomfield Centers Corp.

Date		Description	F	Debit	Credit	Bal.
19X4						
Bal.						500
June	1		S8	400		
	6		S8	600		
	14		CR5		500	

Cardinal Cards Corp.

Date		Description	F	Debit	Credit	Bal.
June	5		S8	100		
	10		S8	300		
	22		CR5		400	

Cliff Distributors

Date		Description	F	Debit	Credit	Bal.
19X4 Bal.						2,000
June	1		CR5		1,000	
	10		S8	200		

Garland Products, Inc.

Date		Description	F	Debit	Credit	Bal.
19X4						
June	7		S8	800		
	21		CR5		800	

Summit Sales, Inc.

Date		Description	F	Debit	Credit	Bal.
19X4						
June	14		S8	200		
	20		S8	750		
	30		CR5		200	

Willowdale Sales, Inc.

Date		Description	F	Debit	Credit	Bal.
19X4 Bal.						2,500
June	15		S8	1,500		
	30		CR5		1,000	

Required

1. Calculate and record the balance in each of the accounts.

2. Using the information in the accounts, prepare a sales journal and calculate the column total. Note that all June sales journal entries are posted to the accounts and that terms for all sales are 2/15, net 30. The last sales invoice in May was number 78.

3. Using the information in the subsidiary ledger accounts, prepare a cash receipts journal and calculate all column totals. Assume that all cash receipts in June were from the collection of accounts receivable. Note that all eligible customers took discounts.

4. Open general ledger accounts for Cash, Accounts Receivable, Sales, and Sales Discounts. Post the column totals of the sales journal and cash receipts journal.

5. Prepare a schedule of accounts receivable as of June 30, 19X4; the total should agree with the balance in the general ledger accounts receivable account. The June 1, 19X4, balance in this control account amounted to $5,000.

Cash receipts and cash disbursements journals, posting to subsidiary ledgers, schedules (Q2–Q7)

AP6-3   Sim Products, Inc., was incorporated on April 1, 19X1, to operate a merchandising business. Its sales and purchases during April are recorded in the following journals.

Sales Journal   Page 1

Date		Customer	Invoice Number	Terms	F	Accts. Rec.—Dr. Sales—Cr.
19X1						
Apr.	1	Ahuntic Products Corp.	1	2/10, n/30		3,000
	2	Chambler Stores, Inc.	2	2/10, n/30		1,200
	11	Presidential Sales, Inc.	3	2/10, n/30		500
	20	Salaberry Corp.	4	2/10, n/30		2,000
	27	Bishop Emporium Corp.	5	2/10, n/30		800
						7,500
						(110) (500)

Purchases Journal   Page 1

Date		Supplier	Terms	F	Purchases—Dr. Accts. Pay.—Cr.
19X1					
Apr.	1	Beacon Sales, Inc.	2/10, n/30		4,000
	2	Drake Wholesalers	2/15, n/30		750
	10	Carlton Markers Corp.	n/30		2,000
	15	Atwater Distributors, Inc.	2/10, n/30		1,500
	19	Kildare Sales, Inc.	n/30		1,250
					9,500
					(550) (210)

Other transactions during April were as follows:

Apr. 1   Issued common shares for $3,000 to Rosco Simcoe, the incorporator and sole stockholder of the corporation

2   Collected $500 for a cash sale made today to George Kirkland

5   Received half the amount due from Ahuntic Products Corp. for the April 1 purchase (less discount)

8   Received the amount due from Chambler Stores, Inc., for the April 2 purchase (less discount)

9   Issued check no. 1 to Beacon Sales, Inc., in payment for the April 1 purchase (less discount on payment)

12   Presidential Sales, Inc., returned $100 of merchandise (issued a credit memo)

15   Received a credit memo from Drake Wholesalers for $50 because of defective merchandise included in the April 2 purchase and subsequently returned

20   Received the amount due from Presidential Sales, Inc., for the April 11 purchase (less return, less discount)

22   Issued check no. 2 to Carlton Markers Corp. in payment for the April 10 purchase (less discount on payment)

Apr. 24   Issued check no. 3 to Atwater Distributors, Inc., on account in partial payment of the April 15 purchase (less discount on payment)

30   Issued check no. 4 to Rapid Delivery, Inc., for $200 in payment for deliveries made to customers during the month

30   Issued check no. 5 to Truck Forwarders, Inc., for $500 in payment for transportation to our warehouse during the month (All purchases are fob shipping point.)   *free on board*

Required

1.   Record the April transactions in the following journals:
(a) cash receipts journal
(b) cash disbursements journal
(c) general journal

2.   Calculate the total of each column in the cash receipts and cash disbursements journals. For each journal, ascertain whether total debits equal total credits.

3.   Open subsidiary ledger accounts for each of the customers recorded in the sales journal, and post the sales transactions and appropriate cash receipts transactions to these accounts.

4.   Open subsidiary ledger accounts for each of the suppliers recorded in the purchases journal and post the purchase transactions to these accounts.

5.   Post all appropriate entries from the general journal to the subsidiary accounts receivable and subsidiary accounts payable accounts.

6.   Open the following general ledger control accounts:
a. Accounts Receivable
b. Accounts Payable
Post all appropriate balances from the cash receipts and disbursements journals, and appropriate amounts from the general journal.

7.   Prepare a schedule of accounts receivable; the total should agree with the Accounts Receivable control account.

8.   Prepare a schedule of accounts payable; the total should agree with the Accounts Payable control account.

Payroll, net pay, journal entries, payroll tax expense (Q2, Q3, Q5, Q9)

AP6-4   The following payroll information for the week of June 7, 19X2, is taken from the records of Sam and Sons Personnel Services, Inc.

Gross Pay	$3,000
Less Deductions:	
Federal Income Tax	600
State Income Tax	200
FICA	195
Pension Plan	100
Health Insurance	25

Required

1.   Determine the net pay.

2.   Prepare the entry necessary in the general journal to record the payroll.

3.   Prepare the entry necessary in the cash disbursements journal to record the payment of the payroll. (You may prepare this entry in general journal form.)

4.   Assume the employer pays 5% for state unemployment and .8% for federal unemployment. Prepare the entry necessary in the general journal to record the employer's payroll tax expense for the June 7 payroll.

DECISION PROBLEM

The North Star Corporation is a long-established family business, selling a limited line of highly priced, profitable merchandise to a few customers. The books of account consist of a general journal and a general ledger. The bookkeeper, who was somewhat set in his ways, has been with the company since it started and has provided accurate and timely statements every month.

In February of this year, the granddaughter of the original owner, having obtained her Bachelor of Business Administration (marketing major) degree, entered the business. She was aggressive and wanted to see the business expanded. Within six months, she had taken on several new lines that added numerous new customers. The volume of transactions increased from 200 to 2,000 per month. By the end of August, with the accounting statements for May 31 still not available, the bookkeeper had a nervous breakdown.

Required

1. What do you think might be the impact on the company of not having interim financial statements prepared?

2. Discuss in detail the recommendations you would have made with respect to the accounting system, if you had been the accountant and had observed the change in the company's expansion policy over this period.

ANSWERS TO SELF-TEST QUESTIONS

1. **(b)** Assuming that the sale of the common stock is in exchange for cash, the entry would be recorded in the cash receipts journal. In *any* transaction that involves an inflow of cash, the entry must be recorded in the cash receipts journal, no matter what the source. If the stock had been exchanged for a noncash asset such as land, the entry would be recorded in the general journal.

2. **(b)** Since this involved an inflow of cash, the entry would be recorded in the cash receipts journal.

3. **(e)** Since this involved an outflow of cash, the entry must be recorded in the cash disbursements journal. Purchases of merchandise on *account* would be recorded in the purchases journal.

4. **(a)** Unless a special journal was created to record purchase returns and allowances, all returns for credit would be recorded in the general journal. If cash had been *received* from the return, the entry would be recorded in the cash receipts journal.

5. **(d)** As mentioned in answer 3, the purchases journal is created to record the purchase on account of merchandise for resale.

6. **(c)** Like the purchases journal, the sales journal is created to record the sale of merchandise on account, assuming that the merchandise sold was purchased for resale.

7. **(a)** The general journal would be used. The purchases journal is only used to record the purchase of merchandise for resale; no other purchase of assets would be recorded in the purchases journal.

8. **(b)** If the receipt of cash is involved in a transaction, it must be recorded in the cash receipts journal.

9. **(b)** Entries to accounts receivable and accounts payable should be posted to the subsidiary ledgers immediately. The control accounts are usually only updated at the end of each month when the special journals are posted. In an on-line computer system,

the posting might be done simultaneously. If so, the ledgers would be in balance at all times, assuming no errors were made.

10. **(c)** Social security taxes are deducted from the earnings of all employees. The federal unemployment tax is an employer payroll-tax expense item. The sales tax has nothing to do with payroll, and the entity would be very happy if it could share its tax burden with all employees.

11. **(a)** The federal and state income taxes deducted from employees' earnings are passed on to the respective government agencies. It is not considered an expense of the entity. Answers *b, c,* and *d* are all considered payroll tax expenses.

7 CASH AND RECEIVABLES

THE collection of cash continues the operating cycle of an entity. It is important for management to design and implement a system of internal control over all assets of an entity, especially an asset as liquid as cash. This chapter examines the dual recording of cash transactions between the entity and the bank as one means of safeguarding cash. Small cost outlays for postage due and other minor expenditures can be paid in cash without losing control over cash outflows. Imprest systems for petty cash also will be examined. Since sales on account involve the granting of credit, by its very nature credit will result in accounts that cannot be collected. The amounts of uncollectible accounts must be estimated to achieve a proper matching of revenue and expenses.

After studying Chapter 7, you should be able to answer the following questions:

1   It has been said that an internal control system is used to ensure accurate accounting information. What are the objectives of such a system? (pp.322–23)

2   How does the preparation of a bank reconciliation facilitate control over cash? (p.323)

3   Give some examples of reconciling items regarding the amount of cash reported in the general ledger account that would require adjusting journal entries in the books of an entity. (pp.323–24)

4   Give some examples of reconciling items regarding the amount of cash reported by the bank that would require adjusting journal entries in the books of an entity. (pp.325–26)

5   Although a good system of internal control encompasses many facets, what is the one feature at the center of control over cash? (p.326)

6   What is the imprest petty cash system and how is it used to control this fund? (pp.332–33)

7   What problems regarding the matching principle arise when an entity allows goods to be sold on credit? (pp.333–34)

8   What are the two different methods used to determine and record estimated uncollectible accounts? (p.334)

9   Should emphasis be placed on the income statement or the balance sheet when estimating bad debts? (pp.334–37)

10   Why do credit balances in some customers' accounts present problems in measurement? (pp.339–40)

THE CONCEPT OF INTERNAL CONTROL

The accounting process transforms the dollar amounts of transactions into financial statement information for communication purposes. The steps involved and the generally accepted accounting principles applied to this accounting process have been discussed. The way transactions are processed in an accounting system was illustrated in the preceding chapter. **Internal controls** must be applied to the accounting system to ensure that transaction processing results in reliable records and that assets of the entity are protected. Internal controls comprise a plan of organization that attempts to accomplish the following four objectives.

Q1: Internal control objectives

1. Protect the entity's assets so as to receive the maximum benefit from them without waste or theft.
2. Provide accurate and reliable financial statements and other accounting reports.
3. Adhere to the policies prescribed by the entity's management.
4. Promote efficient operations by providing a system of checks and balances for all personnel involved in the operation.

Although not exactly a formal part of financial accounting, internal controls are useful in understanding the accounting process. When internal controls break down, disastrous results can take place. Over the years, in thousands of cases employees have embezzled millions of dollars from their respective employers. Recently in California, an accountant for one of the state agencies was caught in a cover-up that put more than $5 million in his pocket.

One part of a good system of internal controls is the accounting system itself, which must be designed to produce timely, accurate records. The chart of accounts is an important control; it describes what type of transaction should be recorded in each account. For example, assets are classified and recorded in asset accounts, and expenses are classified and recorded in expense accounts. In addition, financial statements, prepared according to generally accepted accounting principles, are useful not only to external users in evaluating the progress of the entity, but also to management for making decisions. The design of accounting records and documents is an important control. Financial information is entered and summarized in records and transmitted by documents. A good internal control measure requires that these records and documents be prepared at the time a transaction takes place or as soon as possible afterward, since they become less credible and the possibility of error increases with the passage of time. The documents also should be consecutively prenumbered to provide a control for missing documents.

Another internal control measure is the use of a procedures manual that sets out the procedures necessary for proper recordkeeping. Employees must be trained in the application of control procedures; they also must be competent to carry out their responsibilities. Incompetent or dishonest employees can make even the best control procedures ineffective.

Management is responsible for the installation and operation of the system of internal controls. Before auditing a company, a CPA will study the system of internal controls to determine how dependable the financial information generated by the system is, and to what extent the system must be tested.

The concept of internal controls serves as a prelude to the problems of accounting for cash. Although internal controls exist for all of the types of assets an entity may have, the controls become more important when the assets become more liquid. Cash, of course, is the most liquid of all the assets and probably most susceptible to theft. See Real World Example 7-1.

CASH COLLECTIONS AND PAYMENTS

The widespread use of banks for the deposit of **cash,** collection of negotiable instruments such as notes receivable, and the payment of checks not only facilitates cash transactions between entities, but also provides a safeguard for each entity's cash.

This involvement of banks as intermediaries between entities has accounting implications. Usually, the cash balance in the accounting records of a particular entity differs from the bank balance of that entity at any time period. The differences are usually attributable to the fact that, at the given time period, cash transactions recorded in the accounting records have not yet been recorded by the bank and, conversely, cash transactions recorded by the bank have not yet been recorded in the entity's accounting records.

Q2: Bank reconciliation of cash

Control over cash requires an accounting for the different book and bank cash balances; this accounting is accomplished through the preparation of a schedule frequently referred to as a **bank reconciliation.** The cash balances reported in the accounting records and the bank are established at a particular time, usually month-end. The balance of cash according to the entity's books appears in the general ledger Cash account; the cash according to the bank is reported in a bank statement. The bank reconciliation process calculates an adjusted book cash balance and adjusted bank cash balance. These adjusted amounts must agree.

The following are reconciling items usually appearing in the bank reconciliation; they are discussed in detail in later sections of this chapter.

Book Reconciling Items	Bank Reconciling Items
Collection of Negotiable Instruments	Deposits-in-Transit
NSF Checks	Outstanding Checks
Bank Charges	Bank Errors
Book Errors	

Book Reconciling Items

Q3: General ledger reconciling items

Collections are often made by a bank on behalf of its customers; these collections are frequently recorded in the entity's books only after receipt of the bank statement. Any differences require bank reconciliation and updating of the general ledger Cash account with adjusting journal entries.

Bank service charges for checks paid and other services provided are deducted from the customer's bank account; these reductions of cash are also customarily recorded in the entity's books following receipt of the bank statement. Checks returned to the bank because there were not sufficient funds (NSF) to cover them are charged to the entity's account. When these checks are first deposited, the bank accepts them at their face value. However, after the bank sends the checks for collection and discovers funds are insufficient in the maker's (check writer's) account, the bank reduces the entity's account. The entity may take the check and redeposit

REAL WORLD EXAMPLE 7-1
To Catch a Thief

FEW things are more discouraging to a company owner than discovering that somebody you've trusted has had his hand in the till. There are limitless opportunities in most small companies for people to steal. Often there are few procedures and controls in place—and for a reason. If you wanted to work in a big-corporation bureaucracy, you probably wouldn't have started your own company in the first place. Still, having no controls can be very costly. The fact is, embezzlers are drawn to a few weak spots that many small companies share. By concentrating on these, you can go a long way toward finding and preventing embezzlement in your company.

When managers are tempted to steal, there's often a shadowy accomplice: a messy set of books. I know of a controller in a manufacturing company, for example, who actually had the accounting records randomly stacked in two-foot-high piles around his office. He was the only person who could even hope to find anything there. One day when the president of the company was looking for something in one of the stacks, he came upon some suspicious-looking records quite by accident. When the dust settled, it turned out that the controller had given himself $40,000 worth of raises and bonuses over the course of the year.

Not infrequently—and often appropriately—"clean books" as a business goal become subordinate to more urgent concerns. But your books document the financial transactions of the business, and that includes criminal transactions. And, as with any criminal, the embezzler minimizes the chances of being caught if he or she destroys or hides the evidence, which is exactly what sloppy bookkeeping can accomplish.

Most embezzlers want to, and do, work alone. Someone, for example, who is completely responsible for every step of the weekly payroll can easily add imaginary employees to the payroll, increase wages, and tinker with payroll deductions for employee benefits and taxes. Payroll, accounts payable, accounts receivable, inventory, and investment portfolios are all wonderful targets for embezzlers. It follows, then, that if you segregate duties in some key areas so that what one employee is doing, another is checking, you'll probably keep temptation at bay—it's unlikely that a potential thief could successfully enlist another employee as an accomplice. So, as a general rule, try to separate the bookkeeping for an asset or event from the physical custody of the asset or management of the event.

You'll reduce your chances of hiring an

it, or it might have to return the check to the maker and have a new one issued. The check may be worthless if the account is closed and the maker is no where to be found.

In addition, checks deposited by the entity may be returned by the bank because they are outdated (checks over 6 months old are sometimes returned), postdated (checks that carry a future date), unsigned, illegible, or are rejected for some other reason. If the check is simply postdated, the entity can wait until that date passes, or request that the maker send a replacement check. No matter what the reason for the bank returning the check, the amount will have to be subtracted from the cash balance on the monthly bank reconciliation.

Errors made in recording deposits or disbursements also may be discovered during the reconciliation process. These errors may result in an increase or a decrease in the cash balance.

embezzler if you closely check the backgrounds of candidates for accounting and managerial positions. In my experience, someone who has embezzled once is likely to be a repeat offender. And why not? Embezzlers are rarely prosecuted—company owners are usually too embarrassed to press charges. Some say you'll never turn up something as dirty as embezzlement with reference and background checks, but I don't buy that. Usually a lot of people know about the problem when it's being investigated—and when the embezzler is forced to leave a company. I'm thinking of the owner of a closely held research-and-development company who, in the process of dealing with an embezzler, discussed the problem with his law and accounting firms, corporate officers and directors, the bank, the investment bankers, and the investors. Plus everyone in the embezzler's department knew why she had been fired.

If you follow these suggestions, it won't be easy for someone to pull a simple scam in your company. But to keep a check on exceptionally clever thieves, there's one more step you should take. Require your employees to take long enough vacations so that somebody else has to take over their responsibilities. Many of the embezzlement schemes are so fragile they require a lot of day-to-day maintenance, and they'll fall apart without it. A common example is "lapping"—whoever handles accounts receivables skims cash off the incoming collections, and uses other collections to cover for it, in essence robbing Peter to pay for Paul.

There's another reason to require employees to take vacations. You may well notice some changes occurring in your cash flow, say, or maybe a cost line item will suddenly drop. The most extreme story I've heard along these lines was about the assistant manager of a barely profitable concessions business who had worked for years without a vacation or break. Then, sadly, he had a heart attack and was out for months. Profits quadrupled. Predictably, the owner took a more than casual interest in the change. He discovered that the assistant manager had several tricks for increasing his own income at the expense of the business: taking a little money out of the cash register, selling some of his own inventory instead of the owner's, and buying supplies from vendors who understood that his palms needed a little grease. The plan was simple, and it was successful for years: a little here, a little there, and never so much from any one place that somebody would notice. Until he was forced to take time off.

Source Stephen Nelson, "To Catch a Thief," *Inc. Magazine,* January 1988, pp. 89–90. Reprinted with permission. Copyright © 1988 by Goldhirsh Group, Inc., 38 Commercial Wharf, Boston, MA 02110.

Bank Reconciling Items

Q4: Bank reconciling items

Checks are recorded in an entity's books as a reduction in cash at the time they are prepared and mailed or delivered. However, the actual outflow of cash does not occur until the check is presented to the bank for payment (anywhere from one day to a week or more, depending how long the payee holds the check before depositing it). Checks that are recorded in the entity's records as cash disbursements but are not yet paid by the bank are referred to as **outstanding checks.** The account-holder may ask the bank to certify a particular check. The **certified check** is then deducted immediately from the bank balance. In other words, a certified check does not have to clear the bank before the amount is deducted from the entity's account with the bank. A certified check is never considered an outstanding check. Cash receipts are recorded in an entity's books as an increase in cash at the time they are received. However, the bank will only record the increase when a deposit has been made. For instance, checks received on Friday may not be deposited until Monday, or if deposited after a certain time on Friday may not be recorded as deposited until Monday. Even if a weekend is not involved, a day or two may pass between the recording of a cash receipt by an entity and the recording of that receipt by the bank. When there is a time difference, these receipts are referred to as **deposits-in-transit.**

Bank errors sometimes occur. Possibly a check drawn on an account with a similar name or similar account number is charged to the wrong entity. Keypunching errors may occur when checks are entered. However, the number of bank errors has decreased over the years with the increase in sophistication of the computer systems.

Reconciling items per bank thus do not require adjusting journal entries in an entity's books because either they are bank errors or they have already been recorded.

Saguaro Computers, Inc., banks at the Second National Bank. The entity's bank account is carried as a liability in the records of the bank, since the amount is owed to SCI. Accordingly, credit memos included with the bank statement are for items that have increased the bank balance. Debit memos included with the bank statement are for items that have decreased the bank balance. These credit and debit memos must be taken into consideration when SCI prepares its bank reconciliations.

Illustrative Problem

BANK RECONCILIATION

Assume a bank reconciliation is prepared by Saguaro Computers, Inc., as of April 30. At this date, the general ledger Cash account shows a balance of $21,929 and includes the cash receipts and disbursements shown.

Cash   Acct. No.

Date 19X1	Description	F	Debit	Credit	Dr. or Cr.	Balance
Mar. 31	Balance				Dr.	20673
Apr. 30	April cash receipts	CR	9482		Dr.	30155
30	April cash payments	CP		8226	Dr.	21929

Extracts from SCI's accounting records are reproduced with the bank statement for April in Exhibit 7-1. Note the existence of outstanding checks from the preceding month's bank reconciliation (March).

Q5: Central control feature

The bank reconciliation underscores the reciprocal relationship between the bank's records and the depositor's. For each entry in the depositor's books, there should be a counterpart in the bank's books. This relationship is a must in any system of internal control: an independent *external* record that may be used to verify the *internal* record of the entity.

In the Books
1. All cash receipts are recorded by a debit to Cash.
2. All cash disbursements are recorded by a credit to Cash.

In the Bank
1. When the bank receives the cash, it credits the depositor's account.
2. When the bank pays the check, it debits the depositor's account.

The five steps in reconciling the cash per books with cash per bank are as follows. Refer to Exhibit 7-1.

EXHIBIT 7-1

THE RELATIONSHIP OF SCI'S COMPANY AND BANK RECORDS

Per Company Books

Outstanding Checks
as of March 31:

Check No.	Amount
580	$4,051✔
599	196✔
600	7✔

March 31 outstanding checks compared with checks cashed to see if still outstanding as of April 30.

Cash Disbursements
for April:

Check No.	Amount
601	$ 24✔
602	1,720✔
603	230✔
604	200✔
605	2,220✔
606	287
607	1,364
608	100
609	40
610	1,520
611	124✔
612	397✔

Cash disbursements compared with checks cashed to locate outstanding checks.

Cash Receipts for April:

Date	Amount
April 5	$1,570✔
10	390✔
23	5,000✔
28	1,522✔
30	1,000

Cash receipts compared with deposits to locate outstanding deposits.

Per Bank Records

The Bank Statement
It is customary for banks to send depositors a monthly statement together with the cancelled checks and notices of bank charges and credits. The statement shows the activities for the month; it should list:
1. Beginning balance
2. Deposits received and credits to the account
3. Checks paid and other charges to the account
4. Ending balance

The bank statement for April was as follows:

**Second National Bank
Statement of Account
with Saguaro Computers, Inc.**

Checks			Deposits	Date	Balance
				April 1	24,927
4,051✔				2	20,876
196✔	24✔	230✔	1,570✔	6	21,996
200✔			390✔	11	22,186
124✔	397✔	7✔		16	21,658
2,220✔←180	NSF			21	19,258
1,720✔	31		5,000✔	26	22,507
6 SC			1,522✔	29	24,023

CC — Certified Check	DM — Debit Memo
NSF — Not Sufficient Funds	CM — Credit Memo
SC — Service Charge	OD — Overdraft

STEP 1

The checks paid by the bank in April are matched. Any cancelled checks returned with the bank statement are compared with checks recorded as cash disbursements.

The bank reconciliation from the preceding month is inspected for the existence of any outstanding checks as of March 30.

In the Books
These checks were recorded in March; therefore, the Cash balance per books is correctly stated.

In the Bank
These outstanding March checks may or may not have been paid by the bank in April. If some of the checks have not yet been paid by the bank in April, the bank balance is overstated at April 30 by the amount of these checks.

In fact, SCI's March outstanding checks were paid by the bank in April; no corresponding adjustment is therefore required in the April 30 bank reconciliation—the cash balance per books and per bank are correctly stated in relation to these March outstanding checks.

The returned cancelled checks are compared with the checks recorded in the April cash disbursements journal. This comparison indicates that the following checks are outstanding because they have not yet been paid by the bank.

Check No.	Amount
606	$ 287
607	1,364
608	100
609	40
610	1,520

In the Books

These checks were recorded in April; therefore, the Cash balance per books is correctly stated.

In the Bank

These outstanding checks were not paid by the bank in April; therefore, the bank balance is overstated at April 30.

In reconciling the cash balance per books and per bank, the outstanding checks must be deducted from the bank's cash balance.

In some banks today the entity has a choice of receiving or not receiving the cancelled checks. The bank generally charges an additional service amount for returning the actual cancelled checks. If the customer chooses not to receive the check itself, the bank will provide copies of any checks the entity might need as physical evidence of a transaction. Other financial institutions, such as credit unions, offer no choice; the cancelled checks are not returned with the monthly statement.

STEP 2

Debit memos received with the statement must be examined.

In the Books

If these debit memos have not yet been recorded in April, then the Cash balance per books is overstated at April 30.

In the Bank

The bank has already made deductions from the cash balance per bank when these debit memos are recorded.

In reconciling the cash balances per books and per bank, these debit memos must be deducted from the Cash balance per books, if they were not recorded.

An examination of the April 30 bank statement shows that the bank had deducted the NSF check of John Donne for $180.

In the Books

The check of John Donne had originally been recorded as a cash receipt (a payment on account). During April, no entry was made regarding this returned check; therefore, the Cash balance per book is overstated at April 30.

In the Bank

The check of John Donne was originally deposited in the bank. However, John Donne's bank did not pay this check because of insufficient funds in Donne's account. The check was returned to SCI's bank and was then deducted from the company's cash balance.

In reconciling the cash balance per books and bank, this returned check must be deducted from the Cash balance per books. (A notice must be sent to Donne to request payment again, preferably by certified check.)

An examination of the April 30 bank statement also shows that the bank had deducted a service charge of $6 during April.

In the Books

This service charge was not deducted from the Cash balance per books during April; therefore, the Cash balance per books is overstated at April 30.

In the Bank

This service charge has already been deducted from the cash balance per bank.

In reconciling the cash balance per books and bank, this service charge must be deducted from the Cash balance per books.

STEP 3

The deposits shown on the bank Statement of Account are compared with the Cash Receipts for April recorded in the cash receipts journal. Both records are shown in Exhibit 7-1. This comparison indicates that the April 30 cash receipt amounting to $1,000 is not included as a deposit in the bank statement. This amount is an outstanding deposit, or a *deposit-in-transit.*

In the Books

The April cash receipts have been recorded in the books during April.

In the Bank

The April cash receipts have been deposited in the bank during April; however, the April 30 deposit was not recorded by the bank in April. Therefore, the cash balance per bank is understated at April 30.

In reconciling the cash balance per books and per bank, the outstanding deposit must be added to the cash balance per bank.

STEP 4

The March bank reconciliation is inspected for outstanding deposits at March 31.

In the Books

The cash receipts of March had been recorded in the books during March.

In the Bank

Any outstanding deposits at March 31 should have been recorded by the bank in April. If any March deposit is outstanding at April 30, an investigation should be made.

In reconciling the cash balance per books and per bank, any March outstanding deposit should be investigated. In fact, no deposits were in transit at March 31.

STEP 5

Any errors in the books or in the bank account that become apparent during the reconciliation process must be taken into consideration.

In the Books

Any error recorded in the books requires a correction in the Cash balance per books.

In the Bank

Any error recorded in the bank statement requires a correction in the cash balance per bank.

In reconciling the cash balance per books and per bank, any book error must be added or subtracted from the Cash balance per books; any bank error must be added or subtracted from the cash balance per bank.

An examination of the April 30 bank statement shows that the bank had deducted, in error, a check from Lou Board for $31. The bank indicated it would make a correction in May's bank statement.

In the Books

This check of Lou Board does not belong to Saguaro and does not require any change on the books.

In the Bank

This check of Lou Board should not have been deducted from the account of Saguaro; therefore, the cash balance per bank is understated at April 30.

In reconciling the cash balance per books and per bank, this bank error must be added to the cash balance per bank.

A bank reconciliation is prepared after the five steps have been completed; as shown in Exhibit 7-2, it accounts for the difference between the cash per books ($21,929) and the cash per bank ($24,023), and calculates adjusted cash balances as of April 30. The

EXHIBIT 7–2

Saguaro Computers, Inc.
Bank Reconciliation
April 30, 19XX

Cash per Books, Apr. 30		$21,929	Cash per Bank Statement, Apr. 30	$24,023
			Add: Outstanding Deposits	1,000
			Check Deducted in Error	31
				$25,054
Less: Bank Charges	$ 6		Less: Outstanding Checks	
NSF Checks	180	(186)	Check No. Amount	
			606 $ 287	
			607 1,364	
			608 100	
			609 40	
			610 1,520	(3,311)
Adjusted Cash Balance, Apr. 30		$21,743	Adjusted Cash Balance, Apr. 30	$21,743

——————— These balances must agree. ———————

Errors and adjustments in the "per books" section require journal entries in the general journal to correct the books, so the cash is shown at $21,743.

Outstanding deposits and checks should pass through the bank in May, thereby adjusting the cash balance in the bank. Other errors and adjustments must be reported to the bank so it can make the necessary corrections to Saguaro's account.

adjusted Cash balance in the books of SCI is the reported amount of cash in its interim balance sheet. The adjusted balance represents the actual cash that belongs to SCI, the amount that can still be withdrawn from the bank.

Updating the Accounting Records

The preparation of the bank reconciliation must be followed by an updating of the accounting records. As a general rule, every reconciling item used in the calculation of an adjusted cash balance *per books* requires the preparation of an adjusting journal entry to update the accounting records. A reconciling item added to the book Cash balance requires a debit to Cash, and a deduction from the bank cash balance requires a credit to Cash. The following adjusting journal entries are prepared as of April 30.

Apr. 30	Bank Charges Expense		6	
	Cash			6
	To record bank service charge for April.			
30	Accounts Receivable—NSF check		180	
	Cash			180
	To record amount due from John Donne.			

Note that these adjusting entries include all book reconciling items. The general ledger Cash account is then brought up to date, as illustrated in Exhibit 7-3.

Note that the balance in the general ledger Cash account is the same as the adjusted cash balance calculated on the bank reconciliation. Saguaro doesn't make any adjusting entries for bank reconciling items. The outstanding deposit and outstanding checks will probably be recorded by the bank in May. Adjustments for bank errors are made by the bank.

EXHIBIT 7-3   UPDATED CASH ACCOUNT IN SCI'S GENERAL LEDGER

Cash   Acct. No. 101

Date 19X1		Description	F	Debit	Credit	Dr. or Cr.	Balance
Mar.	31	Balance				Dr	20,673
Apr.	30	April cash receipts	CR	9,482		Dr	30,155
	30	April cash payments	CP		8,226	Dr	21,929
	30	Bank charge expense	J1		6	Dr	21,923
	30	NSF check	J1		180	Dr	21,743

This is the adjusted cash balance shown in the bank reconciliation.

Petty Cash Transactions

Q6: Imprest system

The payment of small amounts by check is not only inconvenient but also costly. The payment of postage due on some incoming mail, for example, might be less than the bank charge to process payment of a check. It is therefore useful to have a relatively small amount of cash on hand to pay small disbursements; this cash is usually referred to as a **petty cash fund.** There are different ways of handling such petty cash transactions; the imprest system is discussed in the following sections. Under this **imprest petty cash system,** a fixed petty cash fund is maintained, being increased or decreased in amount according to needs.

ESTABLISHING THE PETTY CASH FUND

Under the imprest system, a regular check is prepared in the amount of the petty cash fund; this check can be payable either to the Petty Cash account or to the custodian of the fund. If the fund is found subsequently to be too small, it can be increased; it can be decreased if changing circumstances result in its being too large. It is only in these cases that the Petty Cash general ledger account is affected.

Establishing the Fund			Increasing the Fund			Decreasing the Fund		
Petty Cash	200		Petty Cash	100		Petty Cash	50	
Cash		200	Cash		100	Cash		50

The amount of the fund is established by this entry.

The additional debit increases the fund to $300.

The credit of $50 decreases the fund to $250.

These transactions affect the size of the petty cash fund; they do not involve the record of disbursements paid out of the fund.

REIMBURSING THE PETTY CASH FUND

Payments are made out of the fund as required; payments should be supported by a petty cash voucher signed by the recipient of the payments, in addition to any supporting documents, such as a taxi receipt. When the amount of cash has been reduced to a predetermined level, then the petty cash fund is reimbursed for the total amount of payments made. A regular check is prepared in the total amount of all these payments and is made payable to Petty Cash or to the custodian, as the practice may be.

The check is recorded in the cash disbursements journal with the appropriate expense accounts debited. For example, the following compound journal entry would record the following payments: delivery charges, $35; light bulbs and other building maintenance items, $14; miscellaneous general expenses, $31 (including $30 for postage and a $1 shortage in the petty cash fund); and miscellaneous office supplies, $45. Because SCI has no specific postage account in its ledger (as noted on its chart of accounts), the $30 postage payment is recorded as Miscellaneous General Expense.

Delivery Expense	35	
Maintenance Expense	14	
Miscellaneous General Expense	31	
Office Supplies Expense	45	
Cash		125

To replenish the petty cash fund.

The shortage in a fund is usually recorded in a miscellaneous account. The petty cash vouchers and supporting documents should be marked paid at the time of reimbursement in order to prevent their reuse for duplicate reimbursements. The vouchers and shortage (or excess, as sometimes occurs) should be approved by a responsible employee.

Responsibility for the fund should be delegated to only one person, who should be held accountable for its contents. At any given time, the petty cash amount should consist of cash and supporting vouchers, all amounting to the Petty Cash fund balance.

COMPLETION OF THE SALES AND COLLECTIONS CYCLE—ACCOUNTS RECEIVABLE

Transactions in the sales and collections cycle were introduced in Chapter 5. In this cycle, sales are made, sales on account result in the creation of an **accounts receivable,** and the collection of cash completes the cycle. This section discusses the accounting treatment required when cash is not collected to complete the cycle; uncollected accounts receivable result in a cycle being completed without the collection of cash.

The extension of credit to an entity's customers produces this uncollectibility. The expectation of increased profits resulting from increased sales is a strong motivation to extend credit to customers. Also, competition may make the extension of credit a necessary business practice. Unfortunately, some accounts receivable are never collected; these are often referred to as bad debts.

A risk inherent in the sales and collections cycle, therefore, includes the possibility that some accounts receivable never will be collected. The existence of a good internal control system is designed to minimize bad debt losses. One such control is to permit sales on account only to credit-worthy customers; however, at some point, the decision of who is credit-worthy involves a trade-off between increasing this entity's sales, and its profit, or risking an increase in competitors' sales and potential profit. Even so, each entity realizes that a certain percentage of all credit sales will never be collected and some may be collected long after the sale is made.

Q7: Matching and credit

When applying the matching principle to the sales and collection cycle, accountants must estimate the dollar amount of uncollectible accounts in order to match this expense with the revenue resulting from the sale. Since the matching must take place before a particular account becomes uncollectible, the Accounts Receivable account cannot be directly reduced. The **Allowance for Doubtful Accounts** account is used to accumulate the estimates until such accounts are written off. This account is a contra account to Accounts Receivable and is disclosed on the balance sheet as follows.

Partial Balance Sheet
December 31, 19X4

Current Assets		
Cash		$ 5,000
Temporary Investments		10,000
Accounts Receivable	$25,000	
Less: Allowance for Doubtful Accounts	1,400	23,600
Inventory		50,000
Prepaid Expenses		3,450
Total Current Assets		$92,050

As can be seen, the contra account, Allowance for Doubtful Accounts, reduces the balance sheet valuation of Accounts Receivable to its **net realizable value**, the amount expected to be collected in cash. Note that it does not reduce the Accounts Receivable directly, because at this time it is merely an estimate. The entity does not know which customers' accounts will prove worthless or when, only that an estimate of $1,400 will eventually prove uncollectible. Unless the amount of estimated doubtful accounts is *immaterial* in relation to the balance of Accounts Receivable, the amount of the allowance should be disclosed on the face of the balance sheet. If the amount is deemed immaterial, then the information could be reported as follows:

> Accounts Receivable (net of an
> Allowance for Doubtful Accounts) $23,600

The Allowance account is eventually used to write off actual bad debts as they occur, directly reducing Accounts Receivable. In this manner, the actual accounts are not written off immediately, but an amount of estimated bad debts on the balance sheet is matched against revenue on the income statement, resulting in a more appropriate measure of net income.

Bad Debts Expense is usually classified in the income statement as a general and administrative expense since—for internal control purposes—the sales department should not authorize credit. This arrangement avoids a possible conflict between the approval of credit and the primary objective of a sales department, increasing the sales, particularly when sales bonuses are calculated on sales volume or remuneration includes a commission component. At year-end, the Bad Debts Expense account is closed to the Income Summary account.

Estimating Uncollectible Accounts Receivable

Q8: Uncollectible accounts methods

The use of an allowance account matches expenses and revenues and helps management to estimate sales and uncollectibles realistically. Once the estimate of uncollectible accounts is made, a journal entry is prepared with a debit to Bad Debts Expense and a credit to Allowance for Doubtful Accounts. Two different methods can be used to calculate the estimated amount; both follow the matching concept. One method focuses on the income statement, while the other focuses on the balance sheet.

Q9: Estimating bad debts

Income Statement Method

This method assumes that a certain percentage of sales on account made during the accounting period will result in bad debts. In order to match all expenses with sales revenue, an estimate of bad debts is made at the end of the accounting period on the basis of bad debts experienced in prior years (or expected this year) in relation to credit sales.

This estimated bad debts expense is calculated independent of any current balance in the Allowance for Doubtful Accounts account.

Balance Sheet Method

This method assumes that a certain amount of the accounts receivable as of the balance sheet date will not be collected in the next accounting period. In order to establish the amount expected to be collected (often called the realizable value of the receivables), an estimated uncollectible amount is calculated using an aging schedule. In this way, the net collectible amount can be reported on the balance sheet.

The estimated bad debts expense is the difference between the current allowance balance and the amount required at the end of the accounting period.

THE INCOME STATEMENT METHOD

Under this method, bad debts expense is calculated by applying an estimated loss percentage to net sales for the accounting period involved. The percentage can be calculated using actual losses experienced in prior years.

Year	Net Sales	Accounts Written Off	Loss Percentage
19X1	$150,000	500	
19X2	200,000	1,200	
19X3	250,000	1,300	
	$600,000	$3,000	0.005 = 0.5%

The average loss over three years is ½ of 1%. If management anticipates that similar losses may be applicable to 19X4, the estimated bad debts expense is calculated as follows: (19X4 sales) $300,000 × .005 = $1,500 estimated uncollectible accounts receivable. Under the income statement method, this $1,500 is recorded as the estimated uncollectible accounts receivable by the following entry:

Dec. 31	Bad Debts Expense	1,500	
	Allowance for Doubtful Accounts		1,500

When posted to the allowance account, the new account balance becomes $1,750.

The balance remaining in the account is $250.

The estimate of $1,500 is added to the existing balance.

Allowance for Doubtful Accounts	
	Bal. 250

Allowance for Doubtful Accounts	
	Bal. 250
	1,500
	1,750

The debit account also has been referred to as Doubtful Accounts Expense, Uncollectible Accounts Expense, or quite simply Bad Debts Expense. Bad Debts Expense is used throughout this text where applicable.

Note that the percentage loss is not .005 on a per-year basis. For instance, for year 19X1 the rate was .0033; for year 19X2, .006; and for year 19X3, .0052. The .005 rate is a weighted average for past years. Estimates also play a part in the above determination. The $1,300 for 19X3 accounts should include an estimate for the 19X3 sales that may become worthless in 19X4. Even some of the 19X2 sales may have not yet been collected.

Note also, that this method calculates the estimated uncollectible amount for the current year; it matches revenues for the year. In this way, the emphasis of the income statement method is on matching expenses with revenues; the remaining balance in the allowance account does not influence the true amount of bad debts expense for the accounting period. For instance, the resulting balance of $1,750 may be either too small or too large in relation to the balance in the Accounts Receivable.

THE BALANCE SHEET METHOD

The estimated bad debts expense also can be calculated by first determining how long the accounts receivable have remained unpaid. Obviously, the longer an account remains unpaid, the higher the probability that the account will prove worthless. An **aging of accounts receivable** is illustrated in the following schedule. Each account is classified as either not yet due or past due by the number of days indicated at the top of each column.

Analysis of Accounts Receivable by Age
December 31, 19X4

Customer	Total	Not Yet Due	1–30	31–60	61–90	Over 90
			Number of Days Past Due			
Bendix, Inc.	$ 1,000					$1,000
Devco Marketing, Inc.	6,000	$ 1,000	$3,000	$2,000		
Horngren Corp.	4,000	2,000	1,000		$1,000	
Perry Co.	5,000	3,000	1,000		1,000	
Others	9,000	4,000			5,000	
Totals	$25,000	$10,000	$5,000	$2,000	$7,000	$1,000

Each account balance is listed and extended to the appropriate not-yet-due or past-due columns. An estimated loss percentage is then applied to each total, thereby determining the estimated uncollectible amount, as shown.

Calculation of Estimated Uncollectible Amount
December 31, 19X4

	Accounts Receivable	Estimated Loss Percentage	Uncollectible Amount
Not yet due	$10,000	1%	100
Past due:			
1–30 days	5,000	3%	150
31–60 days	2,000	5%	100
61–90 days	7,000	10%	700
Over 90 days	1,000	40%	400
Totals	$25,000		$1,450

The estimated loss percentage can be calculated on the basis of prior experience with past due accounts—they usually become less collectible the longer they remain unpaid. The calculation here indicates that $1,450 is estimated as uncollectible at December 31, 19X4.

Under the balance sheet method, as noted, the estimated bad debts expense consists of the difference between the current balance remaining in Allowance for Doubtful Accounts and the estimated uncollectible amount required at year-end.

The balance remaining in the account is $250.

The estimated uncollectible amount is $1,450.

An amount of $1,200 must be recorded to bring the account to $1,450.

Allowance for Doubtful Accounts		
	Bal.	250

Allowance for Doubtful Accounts		
	Bal.	250
		1,450

Allowance for Doubtful Accounts		
	Bal.	250
		1,200
		1,450

Under the balance sheet method, therefore, the calculation of the bad debts expense of $1,200 is dependent on whatever balance remains at the end of the accounting period.

The amount is recorded by the following journal entry:

Dec. 31	Bad Debts Expense	1.200	
	Allowance for Doubtful Accounts		1,200

This entry records the amount necessary to bring the year-end balance in the allowance account to the estimate of $1,450. Of course, the allowance account could have a debit balance before adjustment if estimates made in the past were materially below the actual experience with uncollectible accounts. The amount of the estimate would be determined in the same manner as a credit balance before adjustment. Assuming the account had a debit balance of $400, the estimate is made as follows:

The balance remaining in the account is a debit of $400.	The estimated uncollectible amount is $1,450.	An amount of $1,850 must be recorded to bring the account to $1,450.

Allowance for Doubtful Accounts		Allowance for Doubtful Accounts		Allowance for Doubtful Accounts	
Bal. 400		Bal. 400		Bal. 400	
					1,850
			1,450		1,450

A credit to the allowance account of $1,850 was necessary to result in a $1,450 credit balance for balance sheet purposes. The entry to record this adjustment appears as follows:

Bad Debts Expense	1,850	
Allowance for Doubtful Accounts		1,850

Both the income statement and the balance sheet methods result in a matching on the income statement. But the two approaches are different and will result in different amounts appearing in the Bad Debts Expense account and in the Allowance for Doubtful Accounts account.

Writing Off Bad Debts

Once the estimated uncollectibles are in place, accounts receivable that are not collected in the subsequent year are written off to the allowance account. The example provided here is based on the uncollectible amount calculated by the balance sheet method. Assume that the account of Bendix, Inc., becomes uncollectible by Saguaro as a result of the bankruptcy of Bendix. The uncollectible account receivable is removed by this entry:

Apr. 1	Allowance for Doubtful Accounts	1,000	
	Accounts Receivable		1,000
	To write off the uncollectible account from Bendix, Inc.		

Note that the write-off of $1,000 is made to the contra allowance account, which is debited. In this way, both the Allowance for Doubtful Accounts account and Accounts Receivable are reduced.

Accounts Receivable		Allowance for Doubtful Accounts	
Bal. 25,000			Bal. 1,450
	1,000	1,000	

The balance remaining in the allowance account represents the estimated amount of other accounts receivable that also may become uncollectible. Note that the use of an allowance account for the write-off of an uncollectible account does not affect the net Accounts Receivable amount.

	Before Write-Off	After Write-Off
Accounts Receivable	$25,000	$24,000
Less: Allowance for Doubtful Accounts	1,450	450
Net Accounts Receivable	$23,550	$23,550

Note also that the balance in Bad Debts Expense is not affected by the Bendix account receivable write-off. The Bad Debts Expense account was debited to record the estimated bad debt expense and was closed to Income Summary at year-end.

The amount estimated as an allowance for doubtful accounts seldom agrees with the actual amount that proves uncollectible. A credit balance remains in the allowance account if fewer bad debts occur during the year than are estimated. A debit balance remains in the allowance account if more bad debts occur during the year than are estimated. Subsequently, an adjusting entry is prepared to set up the uncollectible balance that remains.

COLLECTION OF AMOUNTS PREVIOUSLY WRITTEN OFF

When Bendix, Inc., went bankrupt, its debt to Saguaro Computers, Inc., was written off in anticipation of no recovery of the amount owed. Later, an announcement was made that 25% of amounts owed by Bendix would in fact be paid by the trustee handling the bankruptcy. This new information required the reinstatement of the amount *expected* to be collected by SCI—$250 in this case. This transaction is recorded by the following journal entry:

Accounts Receivable	250	
Allowance for Doubtful Accounts		250

This entry reverses part of the amount previously written off and sets up the amount collected as a receivable. As a result, both accounts are increased.

Accounts Receivable		Allowance for Doubtful Accounts	
Bal. 25,000			Bal. 1,450
	1,000	1,000	
250			250

Since Bendix, Inc., is a bankrupt entity (a gone concern), its credit-worthiness is no longer an issue. It may occur, however, that the previously written off amount of an entity is reinstated and further sales contemplated. The reinstatement of the accounts receivable when full payment is anticipated has an effect on that customer's future credit worthiness. Therefore, Saguaro records recoveries on each customer's subsidiary ledger account as a credit reference.

The actual collection of the reinstated amount is recorded by a second journal entry.

Cash	250	
Accounts Receivable		250

The collection is thereby recorded in the normal manner.

The income statement and the balance sheet methods are applied when receivables are a material item in the entity's balance sheet. If credit sales amount to a very small percentage of total sales, the resulting receivables will probably not be material in relation to other current assets. When this is the case, the **direct write-off method** may be used. No estimate is made of accounts that may prove uncollectible in the future, so no matching of revenue and expense results. When an account proves to be uncollectible, the following journal entry is made:

Bad Debts Expense	500	
Accounts Receivable		500

Unless the account proves uncollectible in the year the sale was made, no matching results. The revenue will be recorded in one year and the expense related to that revenue recorded in the next year.

Credit Balances in Accounts Receivable

Q10: Credit balances and measurement

Accounts receivable subsidiary account balances usually have a debit balance because amounts are receivable from customers. Occasionally a credit balance occurs in some accounts as a result of double payment, merchandise being returned, or an allowance granted. Theoretically, the total amount of the credit balance accounts should be classified as a current liability, since these amounts are actually owed to the customer. In practice, these amounts are often netted against all other receivables with a debit balance and reported as Accounts Receivable on the balance sheet. However, if the credit balance amounts are *material* in relation to the debit balance amounts, then they should be reported as a current liability. For example, if the debit balances amount to $50,000 and the credit balances amount to $15,000, the net amount is $35,000. To report Accounts Receivable as $35,000 could materially understate current assets and current liabilities. It would be more accurate to report the $15,000 as current liabilities.

INSTALLMENT ACCOUNTS RECEIVABLE

The sale of merchandise on account was discussed under the assumption that single payments would be made. In practice, payments often consist of periodic payments, usually on a monthly basis; these are referred to as *installment accounts receivable*. Department stores, such as Macys and Weinstocks, often have installment accounts receivable. Because payment is made over a period of time under the installment method, it requires special rules in order to be recognized as revenue from sales. Often a portion of revenue is recorded as earned only as the payments are received; however, many possible variations exist. The accounting for installment sales is usually dealt with in more advanced accounting courses.

CHAPTER REVIEW

1 It has been said that an internal control system is used to ensure accurate accounting information. What are the objectives of such a system? (pp. 322–23)

Internal controls comprise a plan of organization that attempts to accomplish four objectives.

- Protect the entity's assets so as to receive the maximum benefit from them without waste or theft.
- Provide accurate and reliable financial statements and other accounting reports.
- Adhere to the policies prescribed by the entity's management.
- Promote efficient operations by providing a system of checks and balances for all personnel involved in the operation.

Although the safeguarding of an entity's assets is of utmost importance, the other objectives follow close behind.

2 How does the preparation of a bank reconciliation facilitate control over cash? (p. 323)

When a checkbook is used, two independent records of transactions exist, the bank's and the entity's. The results of these transactions (the cash balances) can then be compared and the differences accounted for. These may be simply timing differences, the result of an error, or an employee theft.

3 Give some examples of reconciling items regarding the amount of cash reported in the general ledger account that would require adjusting journal entries in the books of an entity. (pp. 323–24)

Debit and credit memos issued by the bank require adjusting entries in the entity's books if they have not been previously recorded. Examples of debit memos are memos that result from service charges, NSF checks, and the correction of errors that decreased the entity's Cash account. Debit memos are reductions in the account at the bank and have to be credited to the entity's Cash account. Examples of credit memos are memos that result from the collection of a note by the bank as an accommodation to the entity, and the correction of errors that increased the entity's account at the bank. Credit memos are increases in the account at the bank and have to be credited to the entity's Cash account. Errors in recording transactions in the books also might be discovered during the reconciliation process, which results in adjusting entries to either increase or decrease cash.

4 Give some examples of reconciling items regarding the amount of cash reported by the bank that would require adjusting journal entries in the books of an entity. (pp. 325–26)

Reconciling items per bank, such as outstanding checks or deposits in transit, either have already been recorded in an entity's books or are the correction of a *bank* error; therefore, no adjusting entries are required.

5 Although a good system of internal control encompasses many facets, what is the one feature at the center of control over cash? (p. 326)

The central feature is the dual nature of recording transactions when a checkbook is used. An *external* source (the bank) is used to verify the recording of all transactions of the entity *(internal)*. Errors and other discrepancies will be discovered when the reconciliation between the two takes place.

6 What is the imprest petty cash system and how is it used to control this fund? (pp. 332–33)

Imprest is the setting aside of a particular amount for a particular purpose. When the term is used with petty cash, it is a system where a small amount of cash (small depends on the situation, $50–$1,000) is kept on hand to pay for charges that are too small to support the cost of writing a check. First, a check is made payable to petty cash, or to the petty cash custodian by name. The check is cashed and the currency and coin placed in an appropriated place. Small expenditures taken from the fund will be replenished when the sum gets down to a predetermined amount. Each expenditure is supported by a voucher (an authorization). At the time the fund is replenished, these vouchers are summarized and classified and a check is again prepared in an amount equal to the amount spent for the various items. An entry is then made debiting the individual expense accounts and crediting Cash for the amount of the check. This, of course, will be recorded in the cash disbursements journal, but in general journal form it would appear as follows:

Miscellaneous Expense	XXX	
Cash		XXX

7 What problems regarding the matching principle arise when an entity allows goods to be sold on credit? (pp. 333–34)

When goods are sold on credit, invariably some sales are not going to be collected. How great of a problem this is depends on the industry and the state of the economy. When accounts receivable are not collected, and must be written off, a matching problem is created. The sale is generally made in one accounting period, with the resulting bad debt arising in a subsequent period. The revenue is thus recorded in one year and the expense in a subsequent year, preventing matching.

8 What are the two different methods used to determine and record estimated uncollectible accounts? (p. 334)

The two methods have been referred to as the income statement and the balance sheet methods. Although they both result in a matching of revenue and expense on the income statement, they take different avenues. The percentage-of-sales method focuses on the income statement by matching to sales revenue an estimated bad debts expense amount based on sales. The balance sheet method ignores the income statement and concentrates on the proper valuation of accounts receivable on the balance sheet. Many times an entity will use the percentage-of-sales method to prepare their monthly statements, then apply the percentage-of-accounts-receivable method to the balance sheet to determine if the percentage of sales method is sufficient.

9 Should emphasis be placed on the income statement or the balance sheet when estimating bad debts? (pp. 334–37)

This question has no definitive answer. In practice, a combination of the two approaches is used. During the year, a percentage of sales (income statement emphasis) is used to estimate bad debts expense, while at year-end an aging of the accounts receivable (balance sheet emphasis) is made to determine the adequacy of the balance in the Allowance for Doubtful Accounts account. Emphasis can not be placed on only one method.

10 Why do credit balances in some customers' accounts present problems in measurement? (pp. 339–40)

If a single customer overpays a bill for whatever reason, that particular account becomes a liability to the firm, rather than an asset, and should be reported as such. What usually happens is that the credit balance is just commingled with all the other receivables and the receivables are reported as one lump sum. If the amount of the overpayment is material in relationship to accounts receivable, or to current assets, or assets taken as a whole, then the amount should be transferred to an account in the current liability section of the balance sheet.

KEY TERMS

Accounts Receivable   (p. 333) An asset account arising from the sale of goods or services to customers on account. Receivables arising from other transactions, such as loans to officers or other employees, are *not* included in this account, but in separate accounts on the balance sheet.

aging of accounts receivable   (p. 336) The detailed analysis of trade accounts receivable by time elapsed since the creation of the receivable.

Allowance for Doubtful Accounts   (p. 333) A contra account to Accounts Receivable, showing the estimated amount of receivables that may never be realized in cash.

bank reconciliation   (p. 323) A reconciliation of the amount of cash in an entity's account reported by the bank and the amount of cash showing in the general ledger Cash account.

cash   (p. 323) Anything that will be accepted by a bank for deposit. This includes coin and currency from any recognized country, checks drawn on most banks, money orders, credit card charges such as VISA and Master Charge, and so on.

certified checks   (p. 325) Checks that are deducted from the maker's account when the check is issued, rather than when the check is returned to the bank after being cashed by the payee.

deposits-in-transit   (p. 326) Deposits that have been recorded on the books of the entity, but made too late to appear on the current bank statement.

direct write-off method   (p. 339) A method of accounting for uncollectible accounts when credit sales are a minor part of an entity's business. No estimates are made before an account proves uncollectible. The receivable is simply debited to bad debt expense at the time it is written off. There is no proper matching under the direct write-off method.

imprest petty cash system   (p. 332) A system whereby a fixed amount of currency and coin is set aside to be used to pay for minor expenditures. Entries are not made in the accounts for each expenditure, but only made when the fund is reimbursed.

internal control   (p. 322) The system used to ensure accurate record keeping and the timely preparation of financial statements, in order to safeguard the assets of the entity and to promote efficiency.

net realizable value   (p. 334) The amount an entity expects to receive from the "sale" of an asset. As the term is used in Chapter 7, it refers to the result from subtracting the Allowance for Doubtful Accounts account from Accounts Receivable. This is a measure of the amount of cash expected to flow into the entity as a result of collecting its receivables.

outstanding checks   (p. 325) Checks that have been recorded by the entity and sent to the payee, but because of time delays with the mail and whatever, have not cleared the bank at the time the statement is prepared.

petty cash fund   (p. 332) Cash that has been set aside for the payment of minor expenses.

SELF-TEST QUESTIONS FOR REVIEW   (Answers are at the end of this chapter.)

Q2–Q5

1. The major purpose of preparing a bank reconciliation is to
   (a) verify the accuracy of recording transactions.
   (b) determine if the bank made any errors.
   (c) gather information necessary to prepare month-end adjusting entries.
   (d) determine if the outstanding checks from last month cleared the bank at the recorded amount in the current month.
   (e) All of the above

Q4

2. Outstanding checks are
   (a) added to the balance per bank in a reconciliation.
   (b) deducted from the balance per books.
   (c) added to the balance per books.
   (d) deducted from the balance per bank.
   (e) None of the above

Q4

3. Deposits in transit are
   (a) added to the balance per bank in a reconciliation.
   (b) deducted from the balance per books.
   (c) added to the balance per books.
   (d) deducted from the balance per bank.
   (e) None of the above

Q4

4. Bank errors are
   (a) added to the balance per bank in a reconciliation.
   (b) deducted from the balance per books.
   (c) added to the balance per books.
   (d) deducted from the balance per bank.
   (e) None of the above

Q3

5. Errors made in the books are
   (a) added to the balance per bank in a reconciliation.
   (b) deducted from the balance per books.
   (c) added to the balance per books.
   (d) deducted from the balance per bank.
   (e) None of the above

Q3

6. Credit memos received from the bank are
   (a) added to the balance per bank in a reconciliation.
   (b) deducted from the balance per books.
   (c) added to the balance per books.
   (d) deducted from the balance per bank.
   (e) None of the above

Q3

7. Debit memos received from the bank are
   (a) added to the balance per bank in a reconciliation.
   (b) deducted from the balance per books.
   (c) added to the balance per books.
   (d) deducted from the balance per bank.

Q6

8. The Petty Cash account is
   (a) increased when the account is replenished.
   (b) increased when the amount in the account is formally reduced.
   (c) decreased when small expenditures are made from the fund.
   (d) debited when small expenditures are made from the fund.
   (e) None of the above

Q7–Q9

9. When an uncollectible account is written off using the income statement method,
   (a) net income is increased.
   (b) net income is decreased.
   (c) net income may increase or decrease, depending on the circumstances.
   (d) net income remains unchanged.

Q7–Q9

10. When an uncollectible account is written off using the balance sheet method,
   (a) net income is increased.
   (b) net income is decreased.
   (c) net income may increase or decrease, depending on the circumstances.
   (d) net income remains unchanged.

Q7

11. When an account is written off using the direct write-off method,
   (a) net income is increased.
   (b) net income is decreased.
   (c) net income may increase or decrease, depending on the circumstances.
   (d) net income remains unchanged.

DEMONSTRATION PROBLEM

Part A

The Paper Book Shop effectively controls its cash by depositing receipts on a daily basis and making all disbursements by check. After all the posting for the month of November was completed, the cash balance in the general ledger was $4,209. The statement received from the Guaranteed Bank showed the balance to be $4,440. The following data are available for the purpose of reconciling these balances:

(a) Cash receipts for November 30 amounting to $611 have been placed in the night depository and do not appear on the bank statement.

(b) Bank memos previously not available to Paper Book are included with the bank statement. A debit memo for an NSF check, originally received as payment for an account receivable of $130, is included. A debit memo for bank charges of $6 is also included. A credit memo advises Paper Book Shop that $494 has been deposited to the account ($500, less a bank charge of $6). This represents the net proceeds of a collection the bank had made on behalf of Paper Book Shop on a $500 note.

(c) Checks written during November but not included with the statement are no. 1154, $32; no. 1192, $54; no. 1193, $83; no. 1194, $109.

(d) Check no. 1042 is returned with the bank statement. The check was made for $494, the correct amount owed for office expense. The check was recorded in the books as $548.

(e) Checks outstanding at the end of October included no. 1014 for $152 and no. 1016 for $179. No 1016 was paid in the bank statement; no. 1014 was not.

Required
1. Prepare a bank reconciliation at November 30.
2. Prepare the necessary adjusting journal entries required to make the Cash account agree with the bank reconciliation adjusted cash balance as of November 30.

Part B

Lisa, Inc., had the following unadjusted account balances as of December 31, 19X5:

Accounts Receivable	$150,000
Allowance for Doubtful Accounts	3,000 credit
Sales	750,000

Required

1. Assume that Lisa, Inc., estimated its uncollectible accounts as of December 31, 19X5, to be 2% of Sales.
   (a) Prepare the appropriate adjusting entry to record the estimated uncollectible accounts as of December 31, 19X5.
   (b) Calculate the balance in the Allowance for Doubtful Accounts account after posting the adjusting entry.

2. Assume that Lisa, Inc., estimated its uncollectible accounts as of December 31, 19X5, to be 10% of the Accounts Receivable balance.
   (a) Prepare the appropriate adjusting entry to record the estimated uncollectible accounts as of December 31, 19X5.
   (b) Calculate the balance in the Allowance for Doubtful Accounts account after posting the adjusting entry.

3. Why do the calculated estimates of doubtful accounts differ in questions 1 and 2?

SOLUTION TO DEMONSTRATION PROBLEM

Part A

1.

Cash per Books, Nov. 30			$4,209
Add: Collection of Note	$500		
Less: Bank Fee	6	$494	
Error in Check No. 1042		54	548
Less: NSF Check		$130	
Service Charges		6	(136)
Adjusted Cash Balance per Books			$4,621

Cash per Bank Statement			$4,440
Add: Deposits in Transit			611
Less: Outstanding Checks			
Check No. 1014	$152		
1154	32		
1192	54		
1193	83		
1194	109		(430)
Adjusted Cash Balance per Bank			$4,621

2.

Cash	494	
Miscellaneous Expense	6	
Notes Receivable		500
To record the collection by the bank of a $500 note receivable, less a collection fee of $6.		

Cash	54	
Office Expense		54

To correct the recording of check no. 1042: recorded as $548, written in the amount of $494.

Accounts Receivable	130	
Cash		130

To record an NSF check received in payment of an account receivable.

Miscellaneous Expense	6	
Cash		6

To record bank service charges.

Resulting cash balance as of November 30, 19XX:

Cash

4,209	
494	130
54	6
4,621	

Part B

1. (a)

Bad Debts Expense	15,000	
Allowance for Doubtful Accounts		15,000

To record estimated bad debts based on 2% of Sales (.02 × $750,000 = $15,000).

(b) The allowance account will have a balance of $18,000: $15,000 (bad debts) + $3,000 (credit balance before adjustment).

2. (a)

Bad Debts Expense	12,000	
Allowance for Doubtful Accounts		12,000

To record estimated bad debts based on 10% of Accounts Receivable (.10 × $150,000 = $15,000 − $3,000, credit balance before adjustment).

(b) The allowance account will have a balance of $15,000: $12,000 (bad debts) + $3,000 (credit balance before adjustment).

3.   The percentage of sales approach (income statement method) focuses on the matching of revenue and expense, while the percentage of accounts receivable focuses on the balance sheet method or asset valuation.

DISCUSSION QUESTIONS

Q7-1   Describe an entity's system of internal control.

Q7-2   What does the term "cash" mean? What does it include?

Q7-3 What form does cash usually take? What form can it take?

Q7-4 How does the preparation of a bank reconciliation strengthen the internal control over cash?

Q7-5 What different reconciling items appear in a bank reconciliation?

Q7-6 What are the steps in preparing a bank reconciliation?

Q7-7 What is an NSF check?

Q7-8 What is a deposit in transit?

Q7-9 What is an imprest petty cash system?

Q7-10 What is the difference between establishing and replenishing the petty cash fund?

Q7-11 How does use of an Allowance for Doubtful Accounts account match expense with revenue?

Q7-12 How is bad debts expense classified in the income statement?

Q7-13 How does the income statement method calculate the estimated amount of uncollectible accounts?

Q7-14 What is an aging schedule for bad debts, and how is it used in calculating the estimated amount of uncollectible accounts?

Q7-15 How are credit balances in accounts receivable reported on the financial statements?

Q7-16 What is the role of the accountant in establishing and maintaining controls in organizations? Refer to Real World Example 7-1 when discussing your answer.

DISCUSSION CASE

Cash on the Balance Sheet

This chapter suggests that the proper balance sheet valuation for cash should be an adjusted amount determined by a bank reconciliation. If no debit or credit memos were received from the bank requiring journal entries on the books of a company and no errors were detected during the reconciling process, then the correct balance to be reported on the balance sheet would be the balance in the ledger account for cash. It has been suggested that in order to show "a true and fair view," cash on the balance sheet should be stated at an amount equal to the balance shown on the bank statement. The argument states that while checks are outstanding, they may be stopped by the company writing them, they may be held by the payee for a period of time, or they may become lost and never cashed. Deposits in transit may include checks returned by the bank for a variety of reasons, not the least of which is non-sufficient funds.

"It would seem, therefore, that the only accurate balance is that shown in the bank statement."

Source Adapted from a letter to the editor, *The Accountant,* August 28, 1965, p. 280.

For Discussion

Use the bank reconciliation in this chapter to discuss this case.

1. Usually there is a difference between the balance of cash shown in the books of an entity and the balance of cash shown by the bank statement. Accountants reconcile these different amounts when they prepare a bank reconciliation. Which is the correct balance of cash at the end of a time period—the balance per books or the balance per bank? Why?

2. If the cash balance per bank were used as the amount reported in the balance sheet, how would the following items be handled?
   (a) Outstanding checks   (b) Deposits in transit

3. Using the bank reconciliation in this chapter, prepare a bank reconciliation in accordance with the view that the cash balance shown in the bank statement is the proper cash balance to be reported in the balance sheet. (Note that the cash balance per books and the cash balance per bank would still be reconciled. Only the reconciling items used would change.)

EXERCISES

Bank reconciliation with deposits in transit, outstanding checks (Q2, Q4, Q5)

E7-1 First National Bank of Nevada sent its monthly statement for October 19X4 to Empire, Inc. The statement showed a cash balance of $13,569. Empire's general ledger showed a cash balance of $18,530. An analysis of the returned checks showed that checks totaling $2,592 were outstanding at the end of October, and the last deposit made by Empire on November 30, 19X4, in the amount of $7,553 was not reported on the bank statement.

Required
1. Prepare a bank reconciliation as of October 30, 19X4.
2. Prepare any journal entries necessary as a result of the reconciliation.

Bank reconciliation with deposits in transit, outstanding checks, service charges (Q2–Q5)

E7-2 The First National Bank of Nevada sent its monthly statement for October 19X4 to Empire, Inc. The statement showed a cash balance of $13,569. Empire's general ledger showed a cash balance of $18,530. An analysis of the returned checks showed that checks totaling $2,592 were outstanding at the end of October, and the last deposit made by Empire on November 30, 19X4, in the amount of $7,538 was not reported on the bank statement. Included with the bank statement was a debit memo for $15, representing service charges during October.

Required
1. Prepare a bank reconciliation as of October 30, 19X4.
2. Prepare any journal entries necessary as a result of the reconciliation.

Bank reconciliation with deposits in transit, outstanding checks, service charges, NSF check. (Q2–Q5)

E7-3 The First National Bank of Nevada sent its monthly statement for October 19X4 to Empire, Inc. The statement showed a cash balance of $13,569. Empire's general ledger showed a cash balance of $18,530. An analysis of the returned checks showed that checks totaling $2,592 were outstanding at the end of October, and the last deposit made by Empire on November 30, 19X4, in the amount of $7,188 was not reported on the bank statement. Included with the bank statement was a debit memo for $15, representing service charges during October, and a debit memo stating that one customer's check in the amount of $350 was returned because of nonsufficient funds.

Required
1. Prepare a bank reconciliation as of October 30, 19X4.
2. Prepare any journal entries necessary as a result of the reconciliation.

Bank reconciliation with deposits in transit, outstanding checks, service charges, NSF check, credit memo (Q2–Q5)

E7-4 The First National Bank of Nevada sent its monthly statement for October 19X4 to Empire, Inc. The statement showed a cash balance of $13,569. Empire's general ledger showed a cash balance of $18,530. An analysis of the returned checks showed that checks totaling $2,592 were outstanding at the end of October, and the last deposit made by Empire on November 30, 19X4, in the amount of $9,688 was not reported on the bank statement. Included with the bank statement was a debit memo for $15, representing service charges during October, and a debit memo stating that one customer's check in the amount of $350 was returned because of nonsufficient funds. There also was a credit memo stating that the bank had collected a note receivable in the amount of $2,500 that Empire had left with the bank.

Required

1. Prepare a bank reconciliation as of October 30, 19X4.

2. Prepare any journal entries necessary as a result of the reconciliation.

Bank reconciliation with deposits in transit, outstanding checks, service charges, NSF check, credit memo, bank error (Q2–Q5)

E7-5 The First National Bank of Nevada sent its monthly statement for October 19X4 to Empire, Inc. The statement showed a cash balance of $8,569. Empire's general ledger showed a cash balance of $18,530. An analysis of the returned checks showed that checks totaling $2,592 were outstanding at the end of October, and the last deposit made by Empire on November 30, 19X4, in the amount of $9,688 was not reported on the bank statement. Included with the bank statement was a debit memo for $15, representing service charges during October, and a debit memo stating that one customer's check in the amount of $350 was returned because of nonsufficient funds. There also was a credit memo stating that the bank had collected a note receivable in the amount of $2,500 that Empire had left with the bank. The statement also included a check in the amount of $5,000 that was charged to Empire's account in error.

Required

1. Prepare a bank reconciliation as of October 30, 19X4.

2. Prepare any journal entries necessary as a result of the reconciliation.

Petty cash imprest fund, creation and reimbursement (Q6)

E7-6 On July 1, 19X5, the management of Empire decided to fund a petty cash account to handle expenditures under $25. They estimated that a fund of $300 should be sufficient. During July, several payments were made from the fund, supported by notes explaining what the outflows were for, and the amount of each outflow. At the end of July was substantiation for expenditures of $275, and a count of the cash showed currency and coin in the amount of $20.

Required

Prepare the adjusting entry necessary to establish and replenish the fund. You may assume all the substantiated expenditures were for office expenses.

Income statement method of estimating bad debts, credit balance (Q7–Q9)

E7-7 The following balances appear in the unadjusted trial balance of Gabbs, Inc., at its year end, December 31, 19X5:

	Account Balances	
	Debit	Credit
Accounts Receivable	$100,000	
Allowance for Doubtful Accounts		$ 5,000
Sales (all on account)		600,000

Required

Assuming that Gabbs records estimated bad debts based on 3% of credit sales, prepare the entry necessary to record the estimated bad debts for the year 19X5.

Income statement
method of estimating
bad debts, debit
balance (Q7–Q9)

E7-8   The following balances appear in the unadjusted trial balance of Gabbs, Inc., at its year end, December 31, 19X5:

	Account Balances	
	Debit	Credit
Accounts Receivable	$100,000	
Allowance for Doubtful Accounts	5,000	
Sales (all on account)		$600,000

Required

Assuming that Gabbs records estimated bad debts based on 3% of credit sales, prepare the entry necessary to record the estimated bad debts for the year 19X5.

Balance sheet method
of estimating bad debts,
credit balance (Q7–Q9)

E7-9   The following balances appear in the unadjusted trial balance of Gabbs, Inc., at its year end, December 31, 19X5:

	Account Balances	
	Debit	Credit
Accounts Receivable	$100,000	
Allowance for Doubtful Accounts		$ 5,000
Sales (all on account)		600,000

Required

Assuming that Gabbs records estimated bad debts based on 12% of accounts receivable at year end, prepare the entry necessary to record the estimated bad debts for the year 19X5.

Balance sheet method
of estimating bad debts,
debit balance (Q7–Q9)

E7-10   The following balances appear in the unadjusted trial balance of Gabbs, Inc., at its year end, December 31, 19X5:

	Account Balances	
	Debit	Credit
Accounts Receivable	$100,000	
Allowance for Doubtful Accounts	5,000	
Sales (all on account)		$600,000

Required

Assuming that Gabbs records estimated bad debts based on 12% of accounts receivable at year end, prepare the entry necessary to record the estimated bad debts for the year 19X5.

Balance sheet method
of estimating bad debts
using aging, credit
balance (Q7–Q9)

E7-11   The following balances appear in the unadjusted trial balance of Gabbs, Inc., at its year end, December 31, 19X5:

	Account Balances	
	Debit	Credit
Accounts Receivable	$100,000	
Allowance for Doubtful Accounts		$ 5,000
Sales (all on account)		600,000

Required

Assuming that Gabbs records estimated bad debts based on the following aging process, prepare the adjusting journal entry necessary to record the estimated bad debts for the year 19X5.

Not yet due	$46,000 × 2%
Past due:	
1–30 days	18,000 × 4%
30–60 days	10,000 × 5%
61–90 days	5,000 × 25%
Over 90 days	21,000 × 50%

Balance sheet method of estimating bad debts using aging, debit balance (Q7–Q9)

E7-12 The following balances appear in the unadjusted trial balance of Gabbs, Inc., at its year end, December 31, 19X5:

	Account Balances	
	Debit	Credit
Accounts Receivable	$100,000	
Allowance for Doubtful Accounts	5,000	
Sales (all on account)		$600,000

Required

Assuming that Gabbs records estimated bad debts based on the following aging process, prepare the adjusting journal entry necessary to record the estimated bad debts for the year 19X5.

Not yet due	$46,000 × 2%
Past due:	
1–30 days	18,000 × 4%
30–60 days	10,000 × 5%
61–90 days	5,000 × 25%
Over 90 days	21,000 × 50%

PROBLEMS

Bank reconciliation with journal entries (Q2–Q5)

P7-1 The reconciliation of the cash balance per bank statement with the cash balance per general ledger usually results in one of five types of adjustments. These are as follows:

a. Additions to the reported general ledger cash balance

b. Deductions from the reported general ledger cash balance

c. Additions to the reported cash balance per the bank statement

d. Deductions from the reported cash balance per the bank statement

e. Providing information that has no effect on the current reconciliation

Required

1. Using the letters *a* to *e* from the list, indicate the appropriate adjustments for each of the following items that apply to XYZ Co. for December.

- The company has received a $3,000 loan from the bank, which was not recorded in the company books.
- A $250 check, certified on December 27, was not returned with the bank statement.
- Checks amounting to $4,290, shown as outstanding on the November reconciliation, still have not been returned by the bank.
- A $1,000 collection made by the bank has not been previously reported to XYZ.
- The bank has erroneously charged XYZ with a $1,100 check, which should have been charged to XXZ, Inc.
- A $350 check made out by ABC Company and deposited by XYZ has been returned by the bank marked NSF; this is the first knowledge XYZ has of this action.
- A check for $840 by KLM, Inc., a customer, which has been deposited in the bank, was erroneously recorded by the bookkeeper as $730.
- A $600 bank deposit of December 31 does not appear on the statement.
- Bank service charges amounting to $75 are reported to XYZ.
- The company declared a $1,500 cash dividend to shareholders on December 15.

2. Prepare a bank reconciliation using the data given. On December 31, the Cash account of XYZ Co. showed a balance of $84,293. The bank statement showed a balance of $90,568.

3. Prepare the journal entries required to adjust the Cash account of XYZ Co. to the reconciled balance.

Bank reconciliation with journal entries (Q2–Q5)

P7-2   The following is information for the Dallas Company.

a. Balance per the bank statement dated December 31 is $25,430.

b. Balance of the cash account on the company books as of December 31 is $11,040.

c. A check for $840 that had been deposited in the bank was erroneously recorded by the bookkeeper as $930.

d. A check for $2,100 deposited on December 21 is returned by the bank marked NSF; no entry has been made on the company records to reflect the returned check.

e. Among the cancelled checks is one for $345 given in payment of an account payable; the bookkeeper had recorded the check at $480 in the company records.

f. Bank service charges for December amount to $50.

g. The bank erroneously charged the Dallas Company account for a $10,000 check of the Houston Company; the check was found among the cancelled checks returned with the bank statement.

h. The bank had collected a $15,000 note plus accrued interest amounting to $75; $15,075 was credited to Dallas's account; a collection fee of $10 was debited to Dallas's account.

i. Bank deposit of December 31 for $1,570 does not appear on the bank statement.

j. Outstanding checks as of December 31: no. 197, $4,000; no. 199, $9,000.

Required

1. Prepare a bank reconciliation statement as of December 31.

2. Prepare the necessary adjusting journal entries to make the Cash account agree with the bank reconciliation adjusted cash balance as of December 31.

Allowance for Doubtful
Accounts, % sales,
% accounts receivable,
aging (Q7–Q9)

P7-3   Norkis, Inc., made $1,000,000 in sales during 19X2. Thirty percent of these were cash sales. During the year, $25,000 of accounts receivable were written off as being uncollectible. In addition, $15,000 of the accounts that were written off in 19X1 were unexpectedly collected. At its year-end, December 31, 19X2, Norkis had $250,000 of accounts receivable. The balance in the Allowance for Doubtful Accounts account was $15,000 credit as of December 31, 19X1.

	Accounts Receivable
Not yet due	$100,000
Past due:	
1–30 days	50,000
31–60 days	25,000
61–90 days	60,000
Over 90 days	15,000
Totals	$250,000

Required

1. Prepare journal entries to record the following 19X2 transactions:
   (a) The write-off of $25,000
   (b) The recovery of $15,000

2. Next, recalculate the balance in the Allowance for Doubtful Accounts account as of December 31, 19X2.

3. Prepare an adjusting entry required as of December 31, 19X2, for each of the following scenarios:
   (a) On the basis of experience, the estimated uncollectible accounts as of December 31, 19X2, is 3% of credit sales.
   (b) On the basis of experience, the estimated uncollectible accounts as of December 31, 19X2, is estimated at 5% of accounts receivable.
   (c) On the basis of experience, the estimated uncollectible accounts as of December 31, 19X2 is calculated as follows:

	Estimated Loss Percentage
Not yet due	2%
Past due:	
1–30 days	4%
31–60 days	5%
61–90 days	10%
Over 90 days	50%

Allowance for Doubtful
Accounts, aging
(Q7–Q9)

P7-4   The following balances are taken from the unadjusted trial balances of Pagnudo, Inc., at its year end, December 31, 19X4.

	Account Balances	
	Debit	Credit
Accounts Receivable	$150,000	
Allowance for Doubtful Accounts		$ 1,500
Sales	500,000	
Sales Returns and Allowances		50,000

An aging of accounts receivable as of December 31, 19X4, reveals the following information:

	Accounts Receivable	Estimated Loss Percentage
Not yet due	$ 50,000	2%
Past due:		
1–30 days	27,000	4%
31–60 days	40,000	5%
61–90 days	30,000	10%
Over 90 days	3,000	50%
Totals	$150,000	

The account for R. Wills of $1,000 is over 90 days past due. It is included in the aging of accounts receivable chart and has not yet been written off.

PART A: 19X4

Required

1. Prepare journal entries to record the write-off of R. Wills' account of $1,000 on December 31, 19X4.

2. Prepare the appropriate adjusting entry to set up the required balance in the Allowance for Doubtful Accounts account as of December 31, 19X4. (Hint: Remember that R. Wills' account has been written off.)

PART B: 19X5

The following transactions were made in 19X5:

(a) Sales on account were $700,000.

(b) Collections of accounts receivable amounted to $599,000.

(c) Pagnudo wrote off $10,000 of accounts receivables.

(d) An aging of accounts receivable as of December 31, 19X5, revealed the following information:

	Accounts Receivable	Estimated Loss Percentage
Not yet due	$170,000	2%
Past due:		
1–30 days	35,000	3%
31–60 days	-0-	4%
61–90 days	27,000	25%
Over 90 days	8,000	50%
Totals	$240,000	

Required

Prepare the appropriate adjusting entry to set up the required Allowance for Doubtful Accounts account balance as of December 31, 19X5.

Petty cash fund with increases, decreases (Q6)

P7-5   The following transactions were made by Hedges Corp. in March 19X3:

Mar. 1 Established a petty cash fund of $200
     12 Reimbursed the fund for the following:

Postage	$ 10
Office Supplies	50
Taxi Charges (Misc. Selling)	35
Meals (Misc. Selling)	25
	$120

Mar. 18 Increased the fund by an additional $200
     25 Reimbursed the fund for the following:

Office Supplies	$ 75
Taxi Charges (Misc. Selling)	30
	$105

     28 Reduced the amount of the fund to $350

Required

Prepare journal entries to record these transactions.

ALTERNATE PROBLEMS

Bank reconciliation
with journal entries
(Q2–Q5)

AP7-1   The preparation of the bank reconciliation is an important function of the accountant at Long Life, Inc. Normally, five types of adjustments are used:

(a) Additions to the reported general ledger cash balance

(b) Deductions from the reported general ledger cash balance

(c) Additions to the reported cash balance per the bank statement

(d) Deductions from the reported cash balance per the bank statement

(e) Providing information that has no effect on the current bank reconciliation

Required

1. Using the letters *a* to *e* from the list, indicate the appropriate adjustments for each of the following items derived from Long Life, Inc.'s, January bank statement.

- A bank collection of $2,000 was not previously reported to Long Life.
- A certified check amounting to $500 and dated January 15 was not returned with the January bank statement.
- The January 31 $1,000 deposit arrived too late at the bank to be included in the January statement.
- The $225 check of Phantom Truckers has been returned with the statement, marked NSF; the Long Life people are surprised.
- A check received for $540 was deposited by the accounts receivable clerk as $450.
- A debit memo for $13 for service charges is received with the bank statement.
- A $10,000 loan received from the bank is included in the bank statement only.
- A $150 December check has still not been paid by the bank.
- The bank has credited Long Life with a $2,000 deposit that should have been credited to Long Life Insurance.

2. Prepare a bank reconciliation using the data given. On January 31, the Cash account of Long Life, Inc., showed a balance of $24,848. The bank statement showed a balance of $37,850.

3. Prepare the journal entries required to adjust the Cash account of Long Life, Inc., to the reconciled balance.

Bank reconciliation
with journal entries
(Q2–Q5)

AP7-2   The following items relate to the activities of Eastern Company.

(a) At June 30, the Cash account shows a balance of $1,200.

(b) The June bank statement shows a balance of $64.

(c) Of four checks not returned by the bank in May, one still has not been returned in June: check no. 208 in the amount of $80.

(d) Eastern deposited cash received on June 29 (in the amount of $1,000) and June 30 (in the amount of $200) in the night depository as June 29 and 30, a Saturday and Sunday, respectively; these deposits do not appear on the bank statement.

(e) On checking the checks returned with the bank statement, Eastern found the following: check no. 214 properly made out for $45 was coded as a debit to office expense and a credit to cash for $54; a check of Western Company in the amount of $200 was incorrectly processed through Eastern's bank account by the bank.

(f) Bank service charge for the month totaled $5.

(g) Check no. 261 for $180 written in June was not returned with the cancelled checks.

Required

1. Prepare a bank reconciliation as of June 30.

2. Prepare the necessary adjusting journal entries to make the Cash account agree with the bank reconciliation adjusted cash balance as of June 30.

Allowance for Doubtful
Accounts, % sales,
% accounts receivable,
aging (Q7–Q9)

AP7-3   Baltas Corp. had $2,000,000 in sales during 19X3. Thirty percent of these were cash sales. During the year, $50,000 of accounts receivable were written off as being uncollectible. In addition, $30,000 of the accounts that were written off in 19X2 were unexpectedly collected. Accounts receivable at the year-end of Baltas, December 31, 19X3, amounted to $500,000. The balance in the Allowance for Doubtful Accounts account was $10,000 credit as of December 31, 19X2.

	Accounts Receivable
Not yet due	$200,000
Past due:	
1–30 days	100,000
31–60 days	50,000
61–90 days	120,000
Over 90 days	30,000
Totals	$500,000

Required

1. Prepare journal entries to record the following 19X3 transactions:
    (a) The write-off of $50,000
    (b) The recovery of $30,000

2. Next, recalculate the balance in the Allowance for Doubtful Accounts account as of December 31, 19X3.

3. Prepare an adjusting entry required as of December 31, 19X3, for each of the following scenarios:
    (a) On the basis of experience, the estimated uncollectible accounts as of December 31, 19X3, is 4% of credit sales.
    (b) On the basis of experience, the estimated uncollectible accounts as of December 31, 19X3, is 6% of accounts receivable.

(c) On the basis of experience, the estimated uncollectible accounts as of December 31, 19X3, is calculated as follows:

	Estimated Loss Percentage
Not yet due	1%
Past due:	
1–30 days	3%
31–60 days	4%
61–90 days	5%
Over 90 days	30%

Allowance for Doubtful Accounts, aging (Q7–Q9)

AP7-4 The following balances are taken from the unadjusted trial balance of McKenzie Corp. at its year-end, December 31, 19X5:

	Account Balances	
	Debit	Credit
Accounts Receivable	$ 300,000	
Allowance for Doubtful Accounts		$ 3,000
Sales	1,000,000	
Sales Returns and Allowances		100,000

An aging of accounts receivable as of December 31, 19X5, reveals the following information:

	Accounts Receivable	Estimated Loss Percentage
Not yet due	$100,000	2%
Past due:		
1–30 days	54,000	3%
31–60 days	80,000	4%
61–90 days	60,000	25%
Over 90 days	6,000	50%
Totals	$300,000	

The account for V. Barbieri of $2,000 is over 90 days past due. It is included in the aging of accounts receivable chart and has not yet been written off.

PART A: 19X5
Required

1. Prepare journal entries to record the write-off of V. Barbieri's account on December 31, 19X5.

2. Prepare the appropriate adjusting entry to set up the required balance in the Allowance for Doubtful Accounts account as of December 31, 19X5. (Hint: Remember that V. Barbieri's account has been written off.)

PART B: 19X6
The following 19X6 transactions were made in 19X6:

(a) Sales on account were $1,400,000.

(b) Collections of accounts receivable amounted to $1,198,000.

(c) McKenzie wrote off $20,000 of accounts receivables.

(d) An aging of accounts receivable as of December 31, 19X6, revealed the following information:

	Accounts Receivable	Estimated Loss Percentage
Not yet due	$340,000	2%
Past due:		
1–30 days	70,000	3%
31–60 days	-0-	4%
61–90 days	54,000	25%
Over 90 days	16,000	50%
Totals	$480,000	

Required

Prepare the appropriate adjusting entry to set up the required Allowance for Doubtful Accounts account balance as of December 31, 19X6.

Petty cash fund with increases, decreases (Q6)

AP7-5   The following transactions were completed by Harolds Corp. in July 19X9:

July 1   Established a petty cash fund of $1,000
     12   Reimbursed the fund for the following:

Postage	$120
Office Supplies	500
Taxi Charges (Misc. Selling)	130
Meals (Misc. Selling)	230
Totals	$980

     18   Increased the fund by an additional $200
     25   Reimbursed the fund for the following:

Office Supplies	$230
Taxi Charges (Misc. Selling)	75
Totals	$305

     28   Reduced the amount of the fund to $800

Required

Prepare journal entries to record these transactions.

DECISION PROBLEMS

Problem 1

Q2, Q5

You have been given the following bank reconciliation of AB, Inc., as of November 30 and asked to review the value of outstanding checks as of November 30 and of checks written from December 1 to December 15.

You obtained a bank statement and cancelled checks from the bank on December 15. Checks issued from December 1–15 per the books totaled $11,241. Checks returned by the bank on December 15 amounted to $29,219. Of the checks outstanding as of November 30,

$4,800 were not returned by the bank with the December 15 statement, and, of those issued per the books in December, $3,600 were not returned.

Required
1. Using the information relating to the checks, compare the checks returned by the bank on December 15 with the checks outstanding on November 30 and issued in December.
2. Suggest at least three possible explanations for any discrepancy that exists.

Bank Reconciliation
November 30

Cash per Books, Nov. 30	$12,817	Cash per Bank Statement, Nov. 30	$15,267
		Add: Outstanding Deposits	18,928
			$34,195
		Less: Outstanding Checks	(21,378)
		Adjusted Cash Balance, Nov. 30	$12,817

Problem 2

Q2, Q5

The internal control procedures for cash transactions in the Algonquin Corporation were not adequate. James Shifty, the cashier-bookkeeper, handled cash receipts, made small disbursements from the cash receipts, maintained accounting records, and prepared the monthly reconciliations of the bank account. As of November 30, the bank statement showed a balance of $17,500. The outstanding checks were as follows:

Check No.	Amount
7062	$268.55
7183	170.00
7284	261.45
8621	175.19
8623	341.00
8632	172.80

There was also an outstanding deposit of $3,347.20 as of November 30.

The Cash balance as shown on the company records was $20,258.31, which included some cash on hand. The bank statement for November included $200, arising from the collection of a note left with the bank; the company's books did not include an entry to record this collection.

Recognizing the weakness existing in internal control over cash transactions, Shifty removed the cash on hand and then prepared the following reconciliation in an attempt to conceal his theft.

Balance per Books	$20,258.31	Balance per Bank	$17,500.00
		Add: Outstanding Deposit	3,347.30
			$20,847.30
		Less: Outstanding Checks	

Check No.	Amount		
8621	$175.19		
8623	341.00		
8632	172.80	(588.99)
	Adjusted Cash Balance	$20,258.31

Required

1. Calculate the amount of cash taken by Shifty.
2. Explain how Shifty attempted to conceal his theft of cash.

Problem 3

Q8, Q9

Kingsman Miniatures Corporation had charge sales of $610,000 for the year, accounts receivable of $60,500, and a credit balance of $250 in the Allowance for Doubtful Accounts account at the end of the year.

Required

1. Record the bad debts expense for the year, using each of the following methods for the estimate:
   (a) The allowance for doubtful accounts is to be increased to 4% of accounts receivable.
   (b) Bad debts expense is estimated to be 0.45% of charge sales.
   (c) The allowance for doubtful accounts is to be increased to $3,700, as indicated by an aging schedule.
2. Which method would you choose and why?

ANSWERS TO SELF-TEST QUESTIONS

1. **(e)** No one major purpose to preparing the bank reconciliation exists. All of the answers fulfill the major objectives of a reconciliation.
2. **(d)** Since outstanding checks have been recorded and delivered, but have not yet been recorded by the bank as disbursements, they must be deducted from the balance per bank in order to reconcile.
3. **(a)** Since deposits in transit have already been received and recorded, the balance per books is correct. Therefore, they must be added to the balance per bank in order to reconcile.
4. **(e)** Bank errors may be either added *or* deducted from the balance per bank.
5. **(e)** Book errors may be either added *or* deducted from the balance per books.
6. **(c)** Credit memos received from the bank were credited to the entity's account at the bank. That account is a liability of the bank, so a credit to that account would increase the balance. Therefore, the credit memo must be added (debited) to the balance per books.
7. **(b)** Debit memos received from the bank were debited to the entity's account at the bank. That account is a liability of the bank, so a debit to that account would decrease the balance. Therefore, the debit memo must be deducted (credited) from the balance per books.
8. **(e)** The Petty Cash account is only affected when the fund is established, formally increased in amount, or formally decreased in amount.
9. **(d)** The objective of the income statement method is to match estimated bad debts with revenue in the year of the sale. Since the matching takes place when the estimate is made, net income is not affected. The entry to write off an account under this method is as follows:

Allowance for Doubtful Accounts	XXX	
Accounts Receivable		XXX

Note that no income statement account is affected. Also, since the Allowance account is subtracted from the Accounts Receivable on the balance sheet, the written-off account has no effect on the balance sheet.

10. **(d)** The objective of the balance sheet method is to match estimated bad debts with revenue in the year of the sale. Since the matching takes place when the estimate is made, net income is not affected. The entry to write off an account under this method is the same as for the income statement method, described in question number 9.

11. **(b)** Under the direct write-off method, no estimate of bad debts is made, and the entry to write off an account is as follows:

Bad Debt Expense	XXX	
Accounts Receivable		XXX

Therefore, net income is decreased when an account is written off.

8 INVENTORY

INVENTORY usually represents a material portion of current assets and definitely has a material effect on the determination of net income, because of its close tie with cost of goods sold. Chapter 8 examines the problems involved with assigning a cost to the inventory units on hand at the end of the year. Different cost flow assumptions will be investigated and compared, and different inventory systems will be presented, in addition to methods of estimating inventory costs.

After studying Chapter 8, you should be able to answer the following questions:

1 What are some of the flow-of-goods assumptions accountants make? (pp.365–66)

2 Is it neccessary that the flow of costs match the flow of goods when valuing the ending inventory? (pp.365–69)

3 Once the cost of inventory has been determined, is it possible another value may be used instead of cost? Why? (pp.369–70)

4 What impact does the use of the various cost flow assumptions have on the financial statements? (pp.371–74)

5 Once an inventory valuation method is decided on, can any changes be made in the future? (p.372)

6 Do the generally accepted methods of inventory valuation result in the proper measurement of net income? of asset values? (pp.373–74)

7 Between the perpetual and the periodic inventory systems, which one yields the most useful information? Why? (p.375)

8 What effect do inventory errors have on net income in the year the errors are made, and in the following year? (pp.380–81)

9 What methods, as opposed to taking a physical count, are available to determine the estimated cost of inventory? (pp.381–85)

DETERMINING THE COST OF INVENTORY

Determining inventory has two problems. The first, usually not difficult, involves determining the quantity of inventory at the end of an accounting period. The other problem involves assigning the most appropriate cost to this quantity, which *can* be difficult.

The cost of inventory can be determined in several different ways. Consider the following: five gadgets are purchased for resale on different dates during a period of rising prices.

1st purchase:	1 gadget at $1
2nd purchase:	1 gadget at $2
3rd purchase:	1 gadget at $3
4th purchase:	1 gadget at $4
5th purchase:	1 gadget at $5

At the end of the accounting period, four of these gadgets have already been sold and only one gadget remains in ending inventory. What is the cost of the one remaining gadget in ending inventory? Is it $1, $2, $3, $4, or $5?

Accountants are interested in achieving the best matching of revenue and expense on the income statement to achieve the most accurate determination of net income. Is the most accurate amount determined by assigning the gadget left at the end of the year its actual cost? In a small operation, or in the example, where only five items are purchased during the year, the actual cost of the item left at the end of the year probably could be determined. Logically, the item on hand at the end of the year would be the last one purchased, costing $5. However, if the gadget on hand at the end of the year is not perishable, then it could be the one that cost $4, $3, $2, or even $1, the cost of the first one purchased. If the stock is not rotated, it is possible that the one on hand at the end of the year is actually the first one purchased.

Assume the item on hand is the one purchased for $3 and that it was sold for $10 during the next accounting period. This would result in a recorded profit of $7 ($10 − $3). Remember that the gross profit amount discussed in Chapter 5 measures the dollars the owners have available to cover all other operating expenses and to provide themselves with a net income. Assuming in this example that all other operating expenses were covered by the gross profit from other sales, the sale in the next year of the $3 gadget would provide a net income of $7 to the owners. However, in order to maintain inventory levels, the owners must buy another gadget to replace the one just sold. How much will the owners have to pay to replace the gadget sold for $10? If prices increased from $1 to $5 during the last accounting period, it is reasonable to assume the prices will continue to climb in the next accounting period. Maybe the replacement item will cost $8. Yet the accounting system showed that the profit on the sale was $7 for an item that cost $3. In reality, the owner would have to use $5 ($8 − $3) of the $7 net income just to have enough cash to purchase the replacement gadget for $8. Therefore, did the matching of the $3 cost with the $10 sales price result in the most accurate measure of net income?

Accountants may use a number of methods to determine the cost of the ending inventory. The first part of this chapter discusses these methods, while later analyzing the differences between the periodic and perpetual inventory systems. The last section covers the estimation of inventory costs when a physical inventory count is impossible or impractical.

Specific Identification

In the example given, it was assumed that the owners determined that the item on hand was the one purchased for $3. If the inventory items are few in number, the **specific identification** method may be used. Obviously, its usefulness is limited to situations where the actual cost of the item on hand can be determined. However, as in the example, even though the $3 cost could be determined, if the owners had to replace that item for an identical one that costs $8, the specific identification method would not result in a realistic measure of profit on the transaction.

Another feature of the specific identification method that users might find objectionable is that management could manipulate net income by "choosing" the item to sell in a particular transaction. For example, instead of selling the $3 item for $10, management could look over the stock on hand and choose one costing $2 for an $8 profit, or one costing $7 for a $3 profit, depending on whether they wanted to increase net income for the stockholders, or decrease net income for the IRS.

The usefulness of this method is limited when the inventory consists of a large number of inexpensive items purchased at various times and at various prices during an accounting period. Consequently, accountants usually assign costs to inventory items based on an *assumed* **flow of goods.** The three choices are FIFO, LIFO, and average flow of goods, all described next. Once chosen, the assumed flow of goods should be used consistently in order to obtain comparable results.

The Actual Flow of Goods

THE FIFO ASSUMPTION

Q1: Flow-of-goods assumptions

Items in inventory flow through the entity depending on the nature of the item. For instance, assume a company sells eggs, a perishable good. This perishable nature requires a flow of goods that ensures that the first eggs on hand are sold first; the eggs acquired next are sold next, and so on. This is referred to in accounting as a **FIFO (first in, first out)** flow of goods, which can be thought of as a "conveyor belt" flow of goods. As each lot of eggs is purchased, it is placed on the conveyor belt. The eggs that are sold are the ones first in line. See Exhibit 8-1.

Q2: Flow of costs vs. flow of goods

Companies that choose the FIFO method of inventory valuation for accounting may have a flow of goods that is in fact a conveyor belt flow, or they may have just the opposite, such as is described next. The actual flow of goods can be in any

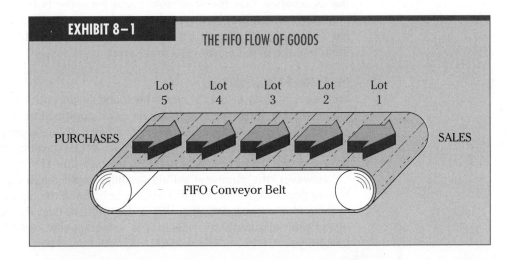

EXHIBIT 8–1   THE FIFO FLOW OF GOODS

Lot 5   Lot 4   Lot 3   Lot 2   Lot 1

PURCHASES   SALES

FIFO Conveyor Belt

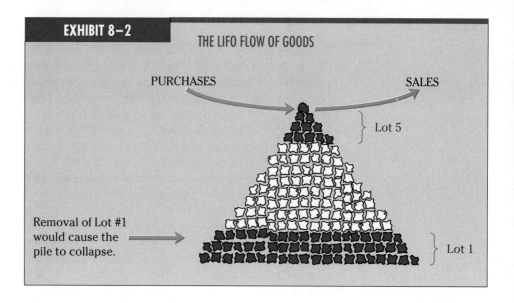

EXHIBIT 8–2

THE LIFO FLOW OF GOODS

PURCHASES

SALES

Lot 5

Removal of Lot #1
would cause the
pile to collapse.

Lot 1

order, but the firm can *assume* FIFO for determining cost flow for accounting purposes. For instance, assume the eggs in Lot 1 cost $10 per 100, while the eggs in Lot 2 cost $20 per 100, and so on. When 100 eggs are sold, under FIFO costing the eggs would be recorded at a cost of $10, since that was the cost of the first eggs purchased. The actual eggs sold could have been from Lot 1 or from Lot 2 or Lot 3, depending on the length of time between purchases.

THE LIFO ASSUMPTION

Rather than eggs, an entity may sell landscaping material, such as sand, gravel, or other such material. As the material is purchased, but before any is sold, each purchase is piled or dumped on the previous purchase, covering up most of it. The result is a pyramid of landscaping material, as illustrated in Exhibit 8-2.

As can be seen, the material at the top is the last to be purchased, but the first to be sold—hence, *last in, first out* or **LIFO.** Obviously, this is the actual flow of goods in entities that sell such material, but the LIFO inventory method can be the *assumed* flow of goods for any merchandiser. In other words, the landscaping business may sell sand off the top of the pile that may have cost $5 per ton, but make the assumption that the sand sold came from the bottom of the pile (the first purchase), which may have cost only $1 per ton. The company selling fresh eggs has an actual FIFO flow of goods, but may assume that the eggs sold came from the top of the pile, the last eggs purchased.

THE AVERAGE ASSUMPTION

The *average flow of goods* might be found in an entity that sells like items of nonperishable goods, such as gasoline or oil pumped into a tank when purchased and commingled with the existing liquid. When gasoline is pumped from the storage tank into the tank of a purchaser's car, the actual gasoline may have come from three or more different purchases. This average flow is shown in Exhibit 8-3.

However, the company selling gasoline could make either the average cost assumption, or the LIFO or FIFO assumption. Once the quantity of goods on hand at the end of an accounting period is determined, then the entity must make one of the three assumptions, unless it is using specific identification for valuating inventory.

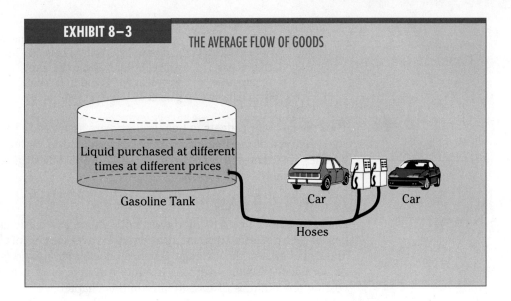

EXHIBIT 8–3   THE AVERAGE FLOW OF GOODS

Liquid purchased at different times at different prices

Gasoline Tank

Car   Car

Hoses

The Flow of Costs

Once the flow of goods has been assumed, the **flow of costs** can be assigned. In the previous FIFO example the eggs could have been assigned a cost of $1 to $5 per 100 count, while the tons of landscaping material (LIFO example) could have been assigned a cost of $1 to $5 per ton. The sequence of costs can be assigned to inventory items using any assumed flow of goods. The calculation of inventory cost under each of the three methods follows. The purchasing of the five gadgets at the beginning of the chapter will be used to illustrate the three inventory methods.

FIFO COST ASSUMPTION

Since the FIFO flow of goods assumes that the first unit on hand is the first to be sold, the unit acquired next is the next to be sold, and so on, the calculation of inventory cost corresponds to this assumed flow of goods. For example, the FIFO cost of one gadget remaining in ending inventory (four gadgets have been sold) would be $5, calculated as follows.

1st purchase:	1 gadget at $1	(1st to be sold)
2nd purchase:	1 gadget at $2	(2nd to be sold)
3rd purchase:	1 gadget at $3	(3rd to be sold)
4th purchase:	1 gadget at $4	(4th to be sold)
5th purchase:	1 gadget at $5	(assumed to be the cost of the item in ending inventory)

Thus the first four gadgets purchased are assumed to be the first four gadgets sold (first in, first out); the cost of the one item remaining is assumed to be the cost of the last item purchased.

LIFO COST ASSUMPTION

Since the LIFO flow of goods assumes that the last unit purchased is the first to be sold, the calculation of inventory cost has to correspond to this flow of goods. The LIFO cost of one gadget remaining in ending inventory (four gadgets have been sold) would be $1, calculated as follows.

```
1st purchase:     1 gadget at $1   (assumed to be the cost of
                                    the item in ending inventory)
2nd purchase:     1 gadget at $2   (4th to be sold)
3rd purchase:     1 gadget at $3   (3rd to be sold)
4th purchase:     1 gadget at $4   (2nd to be sold)
5th purchase:     1 gadget at $5   (1st to be sold).
```

Thus the last four gadgets to be purchased are assumed to be the first four gadgets sold; the cost of the item in inventory is assumed to be the cost of the first item purchased. Although this does not follow the actual flow of goods in many instances, it is still a valid assumption.

AVERAGE COST ASSUMPTION

Since the average cost method does not assume any particular flow of goods, the cost of each gadget sold is simply a computed average cost of all gadgets purchased. The calculation of this average depends on whether a *periodic* (weighted average) or *perpetual* (moving average) inventory system is in use. The moving-average costing procedure is discussed later in this chapter.

The calculation of inventory cost under the *weighted average* cost assumption follows:

```
1st purchase:     1 gadget at $ 1
2nd purchase:     1 gadget at $ 2
3rd purchase:     1 gadget at $ 3
4th purchase:     1 gadget at $ 4
5th purchase:     1 gadget at $ 5
                  ─                ──────
                  5                $15  ÷ 5 units = $3
```

Thus the four gadgets sold would be assumed to cost $3, and the item in ending inventory also would be assumed to have cost $3.

This is an example of a simple average since only one item was purchased at each price. If more than one item was purchased at different prices, the average would become weighted. Assume that in the previous example the quantity purchased doubled each time goods were purchased. Based on that assumption, the weighted average would be calculated as follows:

```
 1 unit  at  $1  =  $  1
 2 units at  $2  =     4
 4 units at  $3  =    12
 8 units at  $4  =    32
16 units at  $5  =    80
──                  ────
31       Totals     $129  ÷ 31 units = $4.16
```

Note that goods were purchased during the year at costs ranging from $1 to $5, yet the weighted average cost is more than $4. The **weighted average** takes into consideration the number of units purchased at each time rather than just the purchase price.

The three cost assumptions may be used with any flow of goods or costs. Therefore, a gasoline station that mixes all of its purchases together in one tank may still assume a FIFO or LIFO assumption, and the fresh-egg merchandiser may assume an average flow of goods.

The average method usually results in an inventory valuation that falls somewhere in-between the valuations under LIFO and FIFO.

The calculation of inventory cost under each of the three methods is summarized as follows.

1st purchase:	1 gadget at $ 1	← Under LIFO, inventory is given the cost of $1.
2nd purchase:	1 gadget at $ 2	
3rd purchase:	1 gadget at $ 3	
4th purchase:	1 gadget at $ 4	← Under FIFO, inventory is given the cost of $5.
5th purchase:	1 gadget at $ 5	

$15 ÷ 5 units = $3 ←

Under the average cost assumption, all unit costs are added together and the total divided by the number of units available for sale to calculate a $3 average cost per unit purchased.

LOWER OF COST OR MARKET

As discussed earlier, using historical cost under FIFO, LIFO, and weighted average assumptions is a generally accepted method of determining the cost of the ending inventory. However, in Chapter 2 the concept of conservatism was also discussed. It concerns the existence of two equally acceptable approaches, where the accountant takes the one that would have the least favorable effect on the financial condition of the entity.

Q3: Another value

Therefore, the **replacement cost** of an inventory item should be taken into consideration when determining the final valuation for inventory items. After the cost has been determined under LIFO, FIFO, or weighted average, the cost should be compared to the current market value (the actual cost to replace the item), and the *lower* of the two used as the inventory valuation. This method is known as the **lower of cost or market (LCM)** method. LCM, as applied on a unit-by-unit basis and on a group basis, is illustrated as follows.

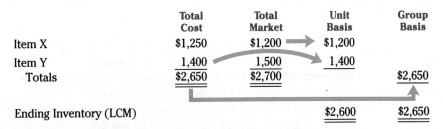

	Total Cost	Total Market	Unit Basis	Group Basis
Item X	$1,250	$1,200	$1,200	
Item Y	1,400	1,500	1,400	
Totals	$2,650	$2,700		$2,650
Ending Inventory (LCM)			$2,600	$2,650

These calculations (any of the inventory cost assumptions—FIFO, LIFO, average—can be used as "cost") result in the valuation of ending inventory as either $2,600 or $2,650. Under the unit basis, the lower of cost or market is selected for each item, resulting in a LCM cost of $2,600. Under the group basis, an increase in Item Y is offset by a decrease in Item X, resulting in a total LCM cost of $2,650. However, both methods, as well as subtotals of different product categories, are acceptable in the calculation of LCM.

The use of LCM is usually supported with an assumption that retail selling prices are expected to decline as inventory purchase cost declines. This assumption, however, is not always correct; and if declines in sales price do occur, they are not always proportional to the decline in inventory purchase cost, that is, "**market.**" The accountant's practice of conservatism is therefore invoked to justify use of LCM, although balance sheet valuation of inventory and measurement of net

REAL WORLD EXAMPLE 8-1
Surprise!

DURING the first year of running my own company, I thought we were doing really great. Then, at year end, I was shocked by a write-down of $66,000 in inventory that offset about a quarter of our pretax profits. I felt like I'd been kicked in the stomach. My illusion of having established control was shattered. Was it theft? Were our systems that screwed up? What was going on?

That was when I learned about accounting systems. In order to balance perfectly, they drive all sorts of errors into a misstatement of inventory throughout the year. Then, when you do your annual physical inventory and compare it with the books, you discover a discrepancy, usually a short-fall. For example, if you understate your costs when computing gross margins, it will show up on the books as more dollars of inventory than you actually have. If you understate product adjustment costs or scrap, that's another contribution to the shortfall. If a product is shipped and somehow not invoiced, same result. If a product is short-shipped by the vendor and not caught, more shortages. The list

goes on and on. And until all the accounting and procedural causes for inventory shrinkage are cleared up, your month-to-month operating statements will be misleading.

I'd like to say it was easy, but at Battery & Tire Warehouse Inc., it took us four years before we straightened out our system completely. And it's a grungy job. There are dozens of places to look for slipups, and only a methodical plugging away at the possibilities will bring you any answers. In the end, we resorted to doing a physical inventory every month, and then comparing the physical counts with the books to see what progress we'd make in our internal controls. By comparing each stockkeeping unit, we also were able to reassure ourselves that our problem was not any major organized theft—the unit count differences were pluses and minuses in a fairly random pattern typical of minor paperwork errors.

Our monthly operating statements now are reasonably clean and show what is actually happening. And personally, I have a much stronger feeling of control. That's why I've been

income is initially adversely affected. The business community seems to demand conservatism on the part of accountants.

This approach was first adopted in the days when conservatism was a dominant consideration for asset valuation. What it means is that, when the goods in inventory can be replaced for an amount that is less than their assumed cost, the inventory valuation should be reduced to this lower amount. A more accurate matching of costs and revenues in the next accounting period also results from this recognition of the lower cost of ending inventory, if sales prices are falling. See Real World Example 8-1.

LCM is most useful when inventory costs are decreased because of obsolescence or damage.

IMPACT OF DIFFERENT INVENTORY COST FLOWS

The application of different cost flow assumptions was just illustrated. If the cost of purchases did not increase during the period, then each method would allocate similar amounts to cost of goods sold and ending inventory. A problem arises,

surprised to learn over the past few years that many small and midsize companies experience year-end book-to-physical inventory shrinkage, but do little to attack it directly.

Some companies mask the year-end shrinkage problem by offsetting the loss with year-end windfalls, such as vendor rebates or FIFO (first in, first out) inflationary gains. We could have done that last year, for example, when our vendors raised their prices, which made our inventory worth $56,000 more. But what's the point of playing with numbers on the books? Such actions are useless if you're interested in getting the information you need to run your company. So we set up windfall gains as separate accounts and formally recognize shrinkage on its own.

A similarly useless game played by some managers is to build into their system automatic gains under the guise of conservatism. Back when I was in *Fortune 500* world, I was admonishing a division general manager for less than sterling profit results as the year was drawing to a close. His comment was, "Don't worry; we'll hit plan since we'll have a major year-end inventory pickup." I asked how he could

be so sure. "Oh, we always have a major gain since we are conservative in our manufacturing costs and scrap rates." After being pulled down from the ceiling I asked, dumbfounded, "How the hell do we know what our inventory shortfall should be? Maybe we're experiencing major problems and we'll have no way to tell. What have we done to scrap controls?"

Don't get me wrong—I think a certain amount of inventory shrinkage is inevitable. In our business as a $12-million distributor, we reserve $2,000 per month for shrinkage. This 0.2% covers miscellaneous breakage, some minor pilferage, mispulled product, and so on. The key point, though, is that we set up the reserve as a bona fide item on our books, so it can be compared with the actual shrinkage. To my mind, there are enough nasty surprises in running a business without adding inventory shrinkage to the list.

Source Charles J. Bodenstab, "Surprise! Surprise," *Inc. Magazine,* September 1988, p. 136. Reprinted with permission. Copyright © 1988 by Goldhirsh Group, Inc., 38 Commercial Wharf, Boston, MA 02110.

however, when purchase cost fluctuates during the accounting period. Typically, in a period of rapid inflation, cost increases can be significant. The resulting impact on the income statement, as well as on the balance sheet, is described next.

Impact on the Income Statement

Q4: Assumptions and statements

When costs are increasing, each cost flow method results in a different amount of ending inventory, cost of goods sold, and net income.

An example can be drawn from an analysis made for management of Saguaro Computers, Inc. Three different cost flows are being considered: FIFO, LIFO, and weighted average (average cost). Use is made of the data from the example concerning the cost increase from $1 to $5 during the period; the result was a total cost of $15 ($1 + $2 + $3 + $4 + $5). These increases reflected a period of rapidly rising prices. It is further assumed in this analysis that sales prices are also rising, and that the first four gadgets were sold for a total of $20 ($2 + $4 + $6 + $8). Operating expenses are assumed to remain constant at $6.

Note that the differences in net income are not caused by differences in the physical flow of goods; rather, they result from assumptions made about the flow of costs.

	FIFO Cost Flow		LIFO Cost Flow		Weighted Average Cost Flow	
Sales		$20		$20		$20
Cost of Goods Sold						
Purchases	$15		$15		$15	
Less: Ending Inventory	5		1		3	
Total Cost of Goods Sold		10		14		12
Gross Profit		$10		$ 6		$ 8
Less: Operating Expenses		6		6		6
Net Income		$ 4		$-0-		$ 2

As can be seen, the impact of different cost flow assumptions is dramatic. FIFO maximizes income when costs are rising and may result in a distorted net income amount. LIFO minimizes net income when costs are rising and results in a more accurate matching of current revenue with current costs; it also tends to approximate inflation-adjusted net income. Unfortunately, it also results in an unrealistic inventory valuation reported on the balance sheet. Weighted average results in a net income figure between those for FIFO and LIFO.

The choice of a particular inventory costing assumption can result in substantially different amounts of net income when costs are fluctuating (and inventory turns over quickly).

In view of the impact different cost flow assumptions can have on the financial statements, GAAP requires that the cost flow assumption used by an entity be disclosed in its financial statements.

A relationship between the cost of an ending inventory and the resulting net income is also apparent from the analysis. The FIFO method, with a larger ending inventory value ($5), also has the largest net income ($4). The LIFO method, with a smaller ending inventory value ($1), also has the lowest net income ($0). Therefore, one can conclude that, if ending inventory is higher or increases, net income also is higher or increases; if ending inventory is lower or decreases, net income also is lower or decreases.

This discussion results in the following axioms:

The higher the inventory valuation, the higher the net income, and the higher the income taxes

The lower the inventory valuation, the lower the net income, and the lower the income taxes

Q5: Changing valuation

Management obviously can manipulate the amount of net income simply by changing the assumptions made about the flow of goods. However, Chapter 2 also discusses the importance of consistency. For financial statement users to have applicable information, the accountant must be consistent in the adoption of different accounting methods. For these reasons, accountants must have an excellent and defendable reason to change the way inventories are valued. The IRS also requires excellent reasons for changing from one generally accepted method to another, and that a firm choosing LIFO valuation for accounting purposes use LIFO for tax purposes. However, an entity that chooses FIFO or weighted average for accounting purposes may use FIFO, LIFO, or weighted average for tax purposes.

PHANTOM PROFITS

Q6: Valuation and net income

The comparison of the effects of FIFO and LIFO costing methods on net income shows that a larger net income results when FIFO costing is used during a period of increasing prices. In the example, the net income on sales was $4 using FIFO and actually nil using LIFO. That is, FIFO showed profits of $4 more than LIFO. Such profits are sometimes referred to as **phantom profits.** The word "phantom" implies that these profits are an illusion. Why? Under FIFO, earlier costs are included in cost of goods sold. In the income statement these *earlier* costs are matched with *current* sales prices, with the result of a phantom profit of $4. Under LIFO, the most recent costs are included in cost of goods sold. In the income statement these *more recent* costs are matched with *current* sales prices, and a closer matching of costs with revenue is achieved. Therefore, LIFO costing, it is claimed, is more realistic with respect to the measurement of income.

In practice, a good matching occurs under LIFO only when purchases and sales occur frequently and in approximately the same quantity. Although LIFO usually results in a better matching on the income statement, the results may sometimes be disastrous. If an entity using LIFO is suddenly required to reduce inventory levels dramatically—such as happened to U.S. Oil inventories of firms using LIFO during the 1990 Persian Gulf crisis—the old, lower prices, would be moved to Cost of Goods Sold, and more material phantom profits would be produced than under FIFO. When inventory levels remain constant, LIFO results in a better income measurement, but a poorer asset valuation on the balance sheet.

Impact on the Balance Sheet

Despite its advantages in matching inventory costs with revenue in the income statement, a major disadvantage of LIFO costing is its understatement of the inventory on the balance sheet. This disadvantage in turn limits the significance and usefulness of this financial statement.

The gadget data used in the preceding discussions are repeated here to compare the inventory that would appear on the balance sheet under each of the three cost assumptions.

	FIFO	LIFO	Weighted Average
Ending Inventory	$5	$1	$3

As is obvious, LIFO provides an unrealistic ending inventory value. If this comparison of ending inventory under the three cost assumptions is representative of what occurs in practice—which it tends to be when prices are rising—care has to be exercised by the reader of financial statements in interpreting the amounts reported in them.

Q6: Valuation and assets

Full disclosure of the inventory costing assumption used in the financial statements is essential, because inventory is often the largest single item in the current assets section of the balance sheet.

Exhibit 8-4 compares the differences between the cost flow assumptions and specific identification and their impact on the income statement and balance sheet.

EXHIBIT 8–4

COMPARISON OF COST FLOW ASSUMPTIONS

	FIFO	LIFO	Weighted Average	Specific Identification
Physical Flow vs. Cost Flow	The flow of goods approximates the flow of costs in most cases.	The flow of goods does not approximate the flow of costs in most cases	No flow of costs occurs when using the weighted average since all units are assigned the same cost.	The flow of goods is the same as the flow of costs since costs are identified with specific goods.

INCOME STATEMENT

	FIFO	LIFO	Weighted Average	Specific Identification
Matching of Costs with Revenues	The earlier costs in beginning inventory and earlier purchases are matched with current revenues.	The most current costs are matched with current revenues.	An average cost for the period is matched with revenues.	The actual cost of each item sold is matched with the revenue resulting from the sale.
Net Income Determination	Maximizes income when prices are rising because the earlier (and lower) costs are included in cost of goods sold.	Minimizes net income when prices are rising because more current, and therefore higher, costs are included in cost of goods sold.	When prices are rising, results in a net income figure less than the FIFO calculation but more than the LIFO calculation.	When prices are rising (or falling), the user can arrange to sell identical higher-cost or lower-cost items.
	Therefore FIFO can result in a distorted net income figure.	Therefore LIFO results in a more accurate net income figure.	Therefore weighted average results in a net income figure between FIFO and LIFO.	Therefore specific identification can be more susceptible to net income manipulation.

BALANCE SHEET

	FIFO	LIFO	Weighted Average	Specific Identification
Inventory Valuation	Approximates replacement cost (particularly when inventory turnover is rapid), since ending inventory consists of most current costs.	May not approximate current replacement cost, since ending inventory consists of the earliest costs.	Does not approximate replacement cost as well as under FIFO, but ending inventory consists of average cost more current than under LIFO.	The actual cost of each item in inventory is included in ending inventory.
	Therefore FIFO results in a more current balance sheet inventory valuation.	Therefore LIFO can result in a distorted balance sheet inventory valuation.		

INVENTORY SYSTEMS

Q7: Most useful system

As mentioned in Chapter 5, two basic inventory systems exist: the periodic and the perpetual. The difference lies in the amount of recordkeeping used to account for the inventory. The periodic system is easy and inexpensi; however, the perpetual system can give management more useful and current information.

Periodic Inventory System

Under the periodic inventory system, as discussed in Chapter 5, the inventory is determined by a physical count. Therefore, the change in inventory is recorded only periodically, usually at the end of each year. A physical count requires careful planning and inventory-taking procedures: numbered inventory tags are attached to all inventory items; quantities counted are recorded on these tags; and the numerical sequence of the completed tags is subsequently checked to ensure that quantities are accounted for. The inventory descriptions and quantities are next transferred to inventory summary sheets, which also have blank columns for the entry of costs and the calculation of total costs.

Certified public accountants and other independent auditors will make test counts while they are observing the taking of the physical inventory to satisfy themselves that the inventory quantities used in determining the valuation of the inventory are reasonable.

After the physical count is completed, cost will be assigned using one of the flow assumptions discussed earlier in this chapter.

Perpetual Inventory System

The perpetual inventory system, as discussed in Chapter 5, requires a continuous balance of inventory on hand calculated in terms of units and often also in terms of cost. The use of this system requires maintaining a subsidiary inventory ledger; an example of a subsidiary accounts receivable ledger was illustrated in Chapter 6. An example of a subsidiary inventory ledger with recorded purchases and sales in terms of units is given in Exhibit 8-5.

As each purchase is received, the quantity received and the balance on hand are recorded in the appropriate columns. When inventory is sold, the units are recorded in the quantity sold column; a new balance on hand is also calculated and recorded. Thus, a change in inventory quantity is recorded each time a purchase or sale is made. The inventory at the end of an accounting period is one unit in Exhibit 8-5.

A physical count is made periodically to verify that the quantities are actually on hand.

Note the availability of columns for cost calculations. As purchases and sales are made, costs are assigned to the goods using whatever cost flow assumption designated.

Illustrative Problem   **FIFO COSTING UNDER THE PERPETUAL SYSTEM**

The purchases and sales from Exhibit 8-5 are repeated in Exhibit 8-6, incorporating unit costs under the FIFO assumption.

Under FIFO, the earliest purchase costs are assigned to sales. Note that the cost of ending inventory under the perpetual system is the same as it was for FIFO under the

EXHIBIT 8–5

INVENTORY RECORD CARD

	Purchased		Sold		Balance		
	Quantity	Unit Cost	Quantity	Unit Cost	Quantity	Unit Cost	Total Cost
Purchase 1	1				1		
Sale 1			1		0		
Purchase 2	1				1		
Purchase 3	1				2		
Sale 2			1		1		
Purchase 4	1				2		
Sale 3			1		1		
Purchase 5	1				2		
Sale 4			1		1		

periodic inventory system. When FIFO is used as the cost flow assumption, the calculation of ending inventory under both the perpetual and periodic systems will always be the same. (This correlation is not the case for LIFO or weighted average costing.)

Illustrative Problem

LIFO COSTING UNDER THE PERPETUAL SYSTEM

The example in Exhibit 8-5 is repeated in Exhibit 8-7, using the LIFO cost flow assumption.

Under LIFO, the cost of ending inventory is assumed to consist of the first unit purchased and not sold. In the case of Purchase 1, only one unit was on hand at the time of

EXHIBIT 8–6

INVENTORY RECORD CARD USING FIFO COSTING

	Purchased		Sold		Balance		
	Quantity	Unit Cost	Quantity	Unit Cost	Quantity	Unit Cost	Total Cost
Purchase 1	1	1			1	× 1	= 1
Sale 1			1	1	0	× 0	0
Purchase 2	1	2			1	× 2	2
Purchase 3	1	3			2	$\left.\begin{array}{l}1 \times 2\\1 \times 3\end{array}\right\}$	5
Sale 2			1	2	1	× 3	3
Purchase 4	1	4			2	$\left.\begin{array}{l}1 \times 3\\1 \times 4\end{array}\right\}$	7
Sale 3			1	3	1	× 4	4
Purchase 5	1	5			2	$\left.\begin{array}{l}1 \times 4\\1 \times 5\end{array}\right\}$	9
Sale 4			1	4	1	× 5	5

EXHIBIT 8–7

INVENTORY RECORD CARD USING LIFO COSTING

	Purchased		Sold		Balance		
	Quantity	Unit Cost	Quantity	Unit Cost	Quantity	Unit Cost	Total Cost
Purchase 1	1	1			1	× 1	= 1
Sale 1			1	1	0	× 0	0
Purchase 2	1	2			1	× 2	2
Purchase 3	1	3			2	$\left.\begin{array}{l}1 \times 2\\1 \times 3\end{array}\right\}$	5
Sale 2			1	3	1	× 2	2
Purchase 4	1	4			2	$\left.\begin{array}{l}1 \times 2\\1 \times 4\end{array}\right\}$	6
Sale 3			1	4	1	× 2	2
Purchase 5	1	5			2	$\left.\begin{array}{l}1 \times 2\\1 \times 5\end{array}\right\}$	7
Sale 4			1	5	1	× 2	2

the sale. Therefore, the cost of $1 left the system when Sale 1 was made. The first unit purchased and still on hand is Purchase 2 for $2.

The ending inventory cost under LIFO with the perpetual inventory system differs from that calculated under LIFO with the periodic system as follows:

	LIFO Periodic	LIFO Perpetual
Ending Inventory	$1	$2

The difference in amounts calculated is attributable to the fact that, under LIFO/perpetual, the most recent cost immediately prior to a sale leaves the system when the sale is actually made. Under LIFO/periodic, the calculation is made at year-end; therefore, the most recent cost at that date leaves the system. In periods of rising prices, LIFO/perpetual usually produces a higher ending inventory amount than LIFO/periodic.

Illustrative Problem

MOVING AVERAGE COSTING UNDER THE PERPETUAL SYSTEM

As mentioned earlier, weighted average costing is used for periodic inventory and moving average costing is used for perpetual inventory. The calculation of ending inventory under moving average costing is illustrated in Exhibit 8-8, using the same data as before. Under **moving average,** a weighted average is calculated each time a purchase is made. Accordingly, a weighted average is calculated after Purchases 3, 4, and 5 in Exhibit 8-8. No units were on hand to average with Purchase 2. The first average is added to the next purchase cost to calculate the next average. The ending inventory cost is $4.125 under moving average costing; under weighted average costing, ending inventory amounts to $3. In periods of rising prices, moving average usually produces a higher ending inventory than weighted average.

Inventory Systems Compared

The results produced by each of the cost flow assumptions under both periodic and perpetual systems are compared in the following diagram; these results also assume that prices are rising.

EXHIBIT 8–8　　INVENTORY RECORD CARD USING MOVING AVERAGE COSTING

	Purchased		Sold		Balance		
	Quantity	Unit Cost	Quantity	Unit Cost	Quantity	Unit Cost	Total Cost
Purchase 1	1	1			1	× 1	= 1
Sale 1			1	1	0	× 0	0
Purchase 2	1	2			1	× 2	2
Purchase 3	1	3			2	× 2.50	5
Sale 2			1	2.50	1	× 2.50	2.50
Purchase 4	1	4			2	× 3.25	6.50
Sale 3			1	3.25	1	× 3.25	3.25
Purchase 5	1	5			2	× 4.125	8.25
Sale 4			1	4.125	1	× 4.125	4.125

The moving average is calculated as follows:

$1 \times \$2.00 = \$2.00$	$1 \times \$2.50 = \$2.50$	$1 \times \$3.25 = \$3.25$
$1 \times \$3.00 = \$3.00$	$1 \times \$4.00 = \$4.00$	$1 \times \$5.00 = \$5.00$
2　　　　5.00	2　　　　6.50	2　　　　8.25
Average = $\$2.50$	Average = $\$3.25$	Average = $\$4.125$

	FIFO		LIFO		Average	
	Periodic	Perpetual	Periodic	Perpetual	Periodic	Perpetual
Ending Inventory	$5	$5	$1	$2	$3	$4.125

Ending inventory is always the same under both systems. FIFO always produces the highest ending inventory amount (and therefore income) when prices are rising because ending inventory consists of the most recent costs.

Ending inventory usually differs under both systems. LIFO/periodic usually produces a lower amount because ending inventory is calculated at the end of the period; under perpetual, the inventory balance is calculated after each sale. LIFO always produces the lowest ending inventory amount when prices are rising.

Ending inventory usually differs under both systems. Periodic/weighted average usually produces a lower amount than perpetual/moving average. Under periodic, one average cost is calculated for the whole period; under perpetual, an average is calculated following each purchase. An average method produces an ending inventory amount between those for FIFO and LIFO.

The differences between LIFO or FIFO costs calculated on either the periodic or the perpetual system will correspond to the magnitude of the change in prices during the period and to the rapidity of inventory turnover.

When prices are falling, the results produced under the different cost flow assumptions are reversed. LIFO produces the highest ending inventory, and FIFO the lowest. The average method produces an amount between those under LIFO and FIFO.

Under periodic inventory, the quantity of the ending inventory is determined by a complete physical count; the quantity in inventory is not readily available during the accounting period. When perpetual inventory is used, a continuous book inventory is kept for each type of item in inventory. The quantity in inventory is readily available at any time under this method.

Perpetual inventory incorporates an internal control feature that is lost under periodic inventory. Losses resulting from theft and error can easily be determined when the actual quantity of goods on hand is compared with the quantities shown in the inventory records as being on hand. This advantage is offset, however, by the time and expense required to update the inventory records continuously, particularly where thousands of different items of various sizes are in stock. Computerization makes this recordkeeping easier and less expensive, particularly when the inventory accounting system is tied in to the sales system in such a way that inventory is updated whenever a sale is recorded.

The perpetual inventory system also requires that the cost of inventory sold—which is an expense—be recorded periodically, so that a dollar amount of inventory is accurately shown in the general ledger.

The journal entries required under the FIFO/perpetual and FIFO/periodic systems differ for Purchase 1 and Sale 1, as illustrated next. Under the perpetual system, purchases are debited to the asset account Merchandise Inventory and when a sale is made, the cost of inventory is recorded as an expense.

Periodic Inventory			Perpetual Inventory		
Purchases	1		Merchandise Inventory	1	
Accounts Payable		1	Accounts Payable		1
To record Purchase 1.			To record Purchase 1.		
Accounts Receivable	2		Accounts Receivable	2	
Sales		2	Sales		2
To record Sale 1.			To record Sale 1.		
(No Entry Required)			Cost of Goods Sold	1	
			Merchandise Inventory		1
			To record the cost of Sale 1.		

Inventory Errors

A physical inventory count usually results in the discovery of shortages and excesses (overages). A perpetual inventory system provides better inventory control, since these differences are isolated when the counted quantity is compared with the quantity that should be on hand according to the perpetual inventory record.

The following comparative income statements illustrate the impact of an error in ending inventory one year and in the following year. A constant amount for sales, purchases, and inventory is assumed to highlight the impact of a $1,000 ending inventory understatement in 19X6 and the resulting $1,000 beginning inventory understatement in 19X7.

	19X6 Ending Inventory		19X7 Beginning Inventory	
	Correct	Understated	Understated	Correct
Sales	$30,000	$30,000	$30,000	$30,000
Cost of Goods Sold				
Beginning Inventory	$ 2,000	$ 2,000	$ 1,000	$ 2,000
Purchases	20,000	20,000	20,000	20,000
Goods Available for Sale	$22,000	$22,000	$21,000	$22,000
Less: Ending Inventory	2,000	1,000	2,000	2,000
Total Cost of Goods Sold	$20,000	$21,000	$19,000	$20,000
Gross Profit	$10,000	$ 9,000	$11,000	$10,000

Q8: Inventory errors

As can be seen, gross profit (and therefore net income) is understated in 19X6 as a result of the *ending* inventory being understated. The following year, 19X7, gross profit (and net income) is overstated as a result of the *beginning* inventory being understated. Therefore, the following conclusions can be made:

> Errors in ending inventory cause a like effect on net income; errors in beginning inventory cause an opposite effect on net income.

> When ending inventory is understated, net income will be understated; when beginning inventory is understated, net income will be overstated.

> Since ending inventory becomes beginning inventory at the beginning of the new accounting period, the *amount* of the error for the two years will be the same. Therefore inventory errors **counter-balance** themselves in the accounting process.

Note that in the comparison given, the correct incomes for 19X6 and for 19X7 total $20,000 ($10,000 + $10,000), and the total of the 19X6 and 19X7 misstated incomes is also $20,000 ($9,000 + $11,000).

Since inventory errors counter-balance, if the error is not found in the year it was made or during the next year, no entry is necessary to correct the records. If the error was discovered during 19X6, or at the end of 19X6 before the books were closed, the following journal entry would be made under a perpetual inventory system:

Merchandise Inventory	1,000	
Cost of Goods Sold		1,000

If the error was discovered at the beginning of 19X7 before the goods in question were sold, the following entry would be made:

Merchandise Inventory	1,000	
Retained Earnings		1,000

Remember that corrections of accounting errors are considered prior-period adjustments and as such are recorded in Retained Earnings.

If the error was discovered during 19X7 after the goods were sold, the following entry would be made:

Cost of Goods Sold	1,000	
Retained Earnings		1,000

If the error instead overstated the ending inventory, the opposite effect would occur, and the debit and credit entries would be reversed.

ESTIMATING INVENTORY COSTS

The two inventory systems and the various cost flow assumption methods discussed so far all rely on knowing the inventory quantities and then applying some unit cost to those quantities to determine a valuation for the ending inventory. In the remainder of this chapter, two additional methods will be discussed that determine the *estimated dollar amount for ending inventory,* rather than work from inventory quantities. Estimating inventories is useful for two reasons:

1. Useful for Inventory Control   Under the periodic inventory system, a physical inventory count determines the quantity of items on hand. When costs are assigned to these items and these individual costs are added, a total inventory amount is determined. Is this dollar amount correct? Should it be larger? How can one tell if an inventory shortage exists for comparison with the physical amount calculated? An estimate of what the amount should be is one answer.

2. Useful for the Preparation of Interim Financial Statements   Where a perpetual inventory system is not used, estimating the inventory amount offers a means of determining a company's inventory at frequent intervals, thereby avoiding the cost and inconvenience of taking a physical count each time monthly statements are being prepared.

Calculating Gross Profit

Q9: Other inventory cost methods

Two methods used to estimate the inventory dollar amount are the *gross profit method* and the *retail inventory method.*

Both the gross profit and the retail inventory method are based on the determination of the gross profit rate. The following partial income statement shows how to calculate the gross profit percentage rate.

Sales		$1,000	100%
Cost of Goods Sold			
Beginning Inventory	$100		
Net Purchases	700		
Cost of Goods Available	$800		
Less: Ending Inventory	200		
Total Cost of Goods Sold		600	60%
Gross Profit		$400	40%

The gross profit in this case is 40% ($400 ÷ $1,000)

Here, the gross profit is $400. This is the profit left over after the cost of the goods sold ($600) is deducted from net sales ($1,000). As calculated, the gross profit rate is 40% of net sales. The word *gross* is used by accountants in this case to indicate that the operating expenses necessary to run the business must still be deducted before net income can be calculated.

The calculation of the gross profit rate is the first step in making an estimate of the ending inventory.

Ending inventory estimation also requires an understanding of the relationship of ending inventory to cost of goods sold. As can be seen in the following comparative examples, some data from the preceding partial income statement has been removed.

<table>
<tr><td colspan="2">Cost of Goods Sold</td><td colspan="2">Cost of Goods Sold</td></tr>
<tr><td>Beginning Inventory</td><td>$100</td><td>Beginning Inventory</td><td>$100</td></tr>
<tr><td>Net Purchases</td><td>700</td><td>Net Purchases</td><td>700</td></tr>
<tr><td>Cost of Goods Available</td><td>$800</td><td>Cost of Goods Available</td><td>$800</td></tr>
<tr><td>Less: Cost of Goods Sold</td><td>600</td><td>Less: Ending Inventory</td><td>200</td></tr>
<tr><td>Estimated Ending Inventory</td><td>?</td><td>Estimated Cost of Goods Sold</td><td>?</td></tr>
</table>

If the entity had $800 of goods available for sale and it sold $600 of those goods, then $200 of goods should still be on hand.

This is the approach that will be taken to estimate ending inventories: If cost of goods sold can be estimated, then the estimated ending inventory can be determined.

If the entity had $800 of goods available for sale and has $200 of those goods on hand at the end of the year, then the cost of goods sold must be $600.

This is the approach taken thus far in Chapter 8: If the ending inventory can be determined, then the estimated cost of goods sold can be determined.

In these two examples, two questions are posed: What is the estimated ending inventory as of December 31, and what is the estimated cost of goods sold? Notice that once one of these two questions is answered, the answer to the other question can be easily determined. The cost of goods sold and ending inventory are two sides of the same coin. Knowing this relationship will make it easier to understand how estimating inventory works in the gross profit and retail inventory methods.

GROSS PROFIT METHOD

The **gross profit method** assumes that the *rate* (percentage) of gross profit on sales remains approximately the same from year to year. Therefore, if this rate can be determined, the dollar amount of inventory can be easily estimated. Assume that, during the previous two years, Saguaro Computers, Inc., has an average gross profit rate of 40%, as shown.

<table>
<tr><td></td><td colspan="3">Prior Years</td><td>This Year</td><td></td></tr>
<tr><td></td><td>1</td><td>2</td><td>Totals</td><td></td><td></td></tr>
<tr><td>Sales</td><td>$400</td><td>$600</td><td>$1,000</td><td>$2,000</td><td></td></tr>
<tr><td>Cost of Goods Sold</td><td>200</td><td>400</td><td>600</td><td>?</td><td></td></tr>
<tr><td>Gross Profit</td><td>$200</td><td>$200</td><td>$ 400</td><td>?</td><td>← Calculated as $800</td></tr>
<tr><td>Gross Profit Rate (%)</td><td>50%</td><td>33⅓%</td><td>40%</td><td>40%
assumed</td><td></td></tr>
</table>

In this case, the assumed gross profit rate for Year 3 is 40%, and the gross profit is calculated as $800 ($2,000 sales × 40% gross profit). Therefore, cost of goods sold must be the difference between $2,000 and $800, that is, $1,200. The income statement for Year 3 now can be completed.

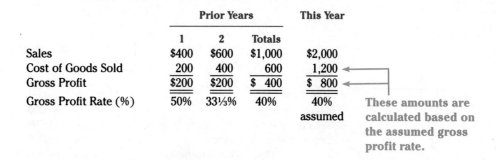

	Prior Years			This Year
	1	2	Totals	
Sales	$400	$600	$1,000	$2,000
Cost of Goods Sold	200	400	600	1,200
Gross Profit	$200	$200	$ 400	$ 800
Gross Profit Rate (%)	50%	33⅓%	40%	40% assumed

These amounts are calculated based on the assumed gross profit rate.

Using these figures, the partial income statement for Year 3 appears as follows, after the inclusion of the beginning inventory and purchases amounts:

Sales		$2,000
Cost of Goods Sold		
Beginning Inventory	$ 200	
Net Purchases	1,100	
Cost of Goods Available	$1,300	
Less: Estimated Ending Inventory	?	
Total Cost of Goods Sold		1,200
Gross Profit		$ 800

This information is always given to students for problem solving. In practice, if necessary, these amounts can be reconstructed from company and other records.

How much is the ending inventory as of December 31? It must be $100, the difference between the goods the company had available to sell ($1,300) and the amount it actually sold ($1,200).

The gross profit method of estimating inventory is particularly useful in situations where goods have been stolen or destroyed by fire; in these cases it is obviously impossible to make a physical inventory count. As noted before, it is also useful in preparing interim statements at almost any point in time management wants to do so.

RETAIL INVENTORY METHOD

The retail inventory method uses a calculation similar to what is used in determining estimated ending inventory under the gross profit method. It is based on redefining sales as cost of goods sold at retail. If sales is defined as cost of goods sold at retail, and ending inventory is the difference between cost of goods available for sale and cost of goods sold, then the ending inventory at retail can be estimated by subtracting sales from cost of goods available at retail.

In a retail establishment, inventory records are usually kept in terms of the retail price. If this is the case, the cost of goods available at retail is easily determined, as shown:

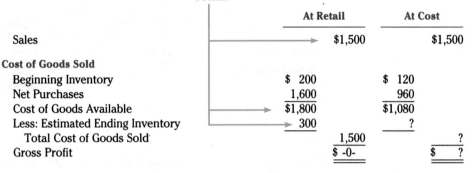

Retail prices of goods available for sale less sales equals inventory at retail.

	At Retail	At Cost
Sales	$1,500	$1,500
Cost of Goods Sold		
Beginning Inventory	$ 200	$ 120
Net Purchases	1,600	960
Cost of Goods Available	$1,800	$1,080
Less: Estimated Ending Inventory	300	?
Total Cost of Goods Sold	1,500	?
Gross Profit	$ -0-	$?

Note: When sales is defined as total cost of goods sold at retail, the gross profit is zero.

As can be seen, the ending inventory at retail is easily calculated by deducting sales during the period ($1,500) from the cost of goods available at retail ($1,800). How much is the ending inventory at retail for this company?

It sold	$1,500	(using retail sales prices)
It had available	1,800	(using retail cost of goods available prices)
It must still have	$ 300	(this is the ending inventory at retail prices)

How much is the ending inventory at cost? Ending inventory at retail is converted to cost by applying the cost percentage to the $300 ending inventory at retail prices. First, the cost percentage is calculated.

	Cost	Retail
Beginning Inventory	$ 120	$ 200
Net Purchases	960	1,600
Cost of Goods Available	$1,080	$1,800

The cost percentage is the ratio of cost of goods available to the retail price of those goods.

Cost Percentage
$$= \frac{\$1,080}{\$1,800} = 60\%$$

Note: The cost percentage is really the complement of the gross profit percentage. That is, if the gross profit percentage is 40%, then the cost percentage is 60% (100%–40%). Usually the cost percentage is calculated directly, as shown.

Then the cost percentage is used to convert to cost the $300 ending inventory at retail prices.

The retail inventory of $300 is converted to cost inventory of $180 using the cost percentage.

Ending Inventory at Retail = $300
Estimated Ending Inventory at Cost (60% of $300) = $180

The retail inventory method of estimating ending inventory is commonly used by department stores where inventory is taken at the selling price. It is easy to calculate and produces a relatively accurate cost of ending inventory, provided that no change in the cost percentage has occurred during the current period. This method results in an *average* cost of ending inventory, because the cost percentage is an average and therefore makes no assumption that goods are sold in any particular order.

Certain terms like *mark-ups* and *mark-downs* have become associated with the retail inventory method but are more appropriately dealt with in calculating cost percentage in a more advanced accounting course.

OTHER INVENTORY VALUATION METHODS

This chapter discusses generally accepted approaches to determining inventory costs. Other methods that have *not* gained acceptance may result in more usable information. One of these methods has been referred to as **NIFO** or *next in, first out*. This is a true replacement cost approach to inventory valuation. To demonstrate the application of NIFO, consider the example of the 5 gadgets that were purchased for $1, $2, $3, $4, and $5. Remember that 4 units were sold and one remained on hand at the end of the year. If the prices are assumed to remain constant during the first part of the next year, then to replace the 4 units sold, $20 ($5 × 4) would have to be spent. Under NIFO, cost of goods sold would be valued at $20. A comparison to the results obtained from FIFO and LIFO follows:

	Measurement of Income		
	FIFO Cost Flow	LIFO Cost Flow	NIFO Cost Flow
Sales	$20	$ 20	$ 20
Cost of Goods Sold			
Purchases	$15	$15	
Less: Ending Inventory	5	1	
Total Cost of Goods Sold	10	14	20
Gross Profit	$10	$ 6	$-0-
Less: Operating Expenses	6	6	6
Net Income (Loss)	$ 4	$-0-	$(6)

FIFO tells the user of financial information that the entity earned a net income of $4, and LIFO arrived at a break-even (zero profit), while NIFO shows a net loss of $6.

The reason for the differences is rising prices or inflation. The subject of inflation will be discussed in Chapter 18, rather than on a piecemeal basis throughout the text.

CHAPTER REVIEW

1 What are some of the flow-of-goods assumptions accountants make? (pp. 365–66)
FIFO, LIFO, Average, and NIFO are the assumptions. Costs may be assigned to items in inventory on a first in, first out basis, following the normal flow of goods, or on

a last in, first out basis. In between those two flow assumptions, costs may be based on an average flow. It is important to note that the actual flow of goods has no bearing on the choice made by the accountant. An approach that has been considered the most accurate would be to assign costs to inventory and to cost of goods sold based on replacement costs, that is, next in, first out.

2   Is it necessary that the flow of costs match the flow of goods when valuing the ending inventory? (pp. 365–69)

No. In most instances, where possible, stock (goods) is rotated so that the items purchased first are sold first (FIFO). For the items in ending inventory, however, any flow of goods may be assumed when assigning costs.

3   Once the cost of inventory has been determined, is it possible another value may be used instead of cost? Why? (pp. 369–70)

Once the cost of inventory has been determined using one of the flow assumptions, the accountant will sometimes compare that cost with the current replacement cost of the item. If the replacement cost (market) is below the determined cost, the lower valuation would be used. This is known as the *lower of cost or market,* or LCM method of inventory valuation.

4   What impact does the use of the various cost flow assumptions have on the financial statements? (pp. 371–74)

If prices remain relatively constant (no inflation), then the various flow assumptions will produce the same inventory valuation. If prices are rising, then the choice definitely has an impact on the financial statements. In periods of rising prices, FIFO will result in the highest measurement of net income and the highest inventory valuation, while LIFO will result in the lowest net income and the lowest inventory valuation. The average approach will fall somewhere in-between.

5   Once an inventory valuation method is decided on, can any changes be made in the future? (p. 372)

In order to be able to compare operating results of the current year with that of the past years, the accountant must strive for consistency in the application of alternative valuation methods. However, when it appears that a different method of measurement will produce more useful information, changes may be made.

6   Do the generally accepted methods of inventory valuation result in the proper measurement of net income? of asset values? (pp. 373–74)

Again, if prices are not changing, all the methods will arrive at approximately the same results. If prices are rising, the LIFO method gives a better matching of expenses and revenues on the income statement, but an unrealistic valuation on the balance sheet. FIFO, on the other hand, results in a realistic valuation on the balance sheet, but an inflated income figure on the income statement. Some current cost models have been suggested to better measure net income and asset values.

7   Between the perpetual and the periodic inventory systems, which one yields the most useful information? Why? (p. 375)

The perpetual system yields more useful information because it involves a running inventory in terms of quantities recorded in the books. Therefore, when a physical count is made, it can be compared to the book count and any differences can be investigated. Under the periodic system, the physical count must be accepted as valid.

8   What effect do inventory errors have on net income in the year the errors are made, and in the following year? (pp. 380–81)

When ending inventory is understated, the cost of goods sold is overstated and net income is understated. However, since ending inventory becomes the beginning inventory of the next accounting period, an understatement of the beginning inventory will understate cost of goods sold and overstate net income for the following year. This is why inventory errors are referred to as counter-balancing.

9 What methods, as opposed to taking a physical count, are available to determine the estimated cost of inventory? (pp. 381–85)

When inventory has been destroyed, stolen, or damaged in some way, the taking of a physical count may be impossible. Two methods may be used to estimate the value of the inventory without a physical count: the gross profit method and the retail inventory method. Both methods rely on the relationship of cost and profit to sales.

KEY TERMS

counter-balance (p. 380) The attribute inventory errors have on net income, caused by the fact that ending inventory becomes beginning inventory in the next accounting period.

FIFO (first in, first out) (p. 365) An inventory valuation method that assumes the first unit purchased is the first unit sold. An actual FIFO flow would be used with perishable goods.

flow of costs (p. 367) The sequence in which costs are assigned to merchandise sold and remaining in inventory.

flow of goods (p. 365) The sequence in which purchased goods are sold. Accountants can assume that the first unit purchased is always the first unit sold (FIFO), as should happen with perishable goods, that the last unit purchased is always the first unit sold (LIFO), or that the cost of goods sold, and therefore the ending inventory, is equal to the average cost incurred during the year.

gross profit method (p. 382) An inventory valuation method that estimates the amount of inventory without taking a physical count. Cost of goods sold is estimated using a historic gross profit rate, leaving the estimated inventory as a residual.

LIFO (last in, first out) (p. 366) An inventory valuation method that assumes the last unit purchased is the first unit sold. An actual LIFO flow would occur in the landscaping material business.

LCM (lower of cost or market) (p. 369) An inventory valuation method that compares the cost of inventory with the current replacement cost. If the current replacement cost is below the original cost of the item, then the replacement cost becomes the assumed cost of that item. It is an application of *conservatism.*

market (p. 369) The replacement cost of an item of inventory as of the balance sheet date.

moving average (p. 377) A weighted average approach to inventory valuation used in conjunction with a perpetual inventory system.

NIFO (next in, first out) (p. 385) A true replacement cost approach to inventory valuation. Cost of goods sold is determined by the amount spent to replace the item sold.

phantom profits (p. 373) A term used to describe the extra profits reported under FIFO as compared with LIFO. These profits are also referred to as *inventory profits* and *holding gains.*

replacement cost (p. 369) The amount of cash that would have to be spent to replace an asset, be it inventory, land, machinery, or buildings, at a particular point in time, usually as of the balance sheet date.

retail inventory method   (p. 383) An inventory valuation method that estimates the amount of inventory without taking a physical count. The retail value of the inventory is estimated, then converted to cost using a historic cost ratio.

specific identification   (p. 365) An inventory valuation method in which goods are identified with their actual cost. An assumption on the flow of costs or goods is not necessary.

weighted average   (p. 368) An inventory valuation method that assumes the units in inventory and the units sold came from a mixture of all units purchased at various costs during the year. It is called a *weighted* average since the number of units purchased at each of the various prices is part of the averaging.

SELF-TEST QUESTIONS FOR REVIEW   (Answers are at the end of this chapter.)

The following transactions took place in BM Corp. in 19X4:

Beginning Inventory	2000 units at $0.50
Purchases	1000 units at 2.00
	500 units at 1.00
	1000 units at 2.50
Sales	2000 units

Q1–Q3, Q9   Choose the best answer for each of the following, based on the given information:

1. Ending inventory under LIFO/periodic would be:
    (a) $3,000   (c) $2,660
    (b) $5,000   (d) $2,000

2. Ending inventory under FIFO/periodic would be:
    (a) $3,333   (c) $5,000
    (b) $2,660   (d) None of the above

3. Ending inventory under weighted average would be:
    (a) $5,000   (c) $3,000
    (b) $3,333   (d) None of the above

4. Cost of goods sold under LIFO/periodic would be:
    (a) $2,660   (c) $3,000
    (b) $4,000   (d) None of the above

5. Cost of goods sold under FIFO/periodic would be:
    (a) $4,000   (c) $2,660
    (b) $1,000   (d) None of the above

6. Cost of goods sold under weighted average would be:
    (a) $2,667   (c) $3,100
    (b) $1,000   (d) None of the above

The records of Qonqa, Inc., show the following information for 19X4. Sales during the period were $276,000. Beginning inventory amounted to $26,000 at cost and $80,000 at retail. Purchases were $200,000 at retail and $90,000 at cost. The company paid $4,000 for transportation in.

Choose the best answer for each of the following, based on the information given.

7. Gross profit at retail was:
    (a) $157,720   (c) -0-
    (b) $153,720   (d) None of the above

8. The ending inventory at retail was:
   (a) -0-   (c) $1,720
   (b) $4,000   (d) $9,333

9. The cost percentage would be calculated as follows:

   (a) $\dfrac{280,000}{120,000}$ (b) $\dfrac{120,000}{280,000}$ (c) $\dfrac{116,000}{280,000}$ (d) $\dfrac{280,000}{116,000}$

10. The ending inventory at cost was:
    (a) $1,720   (c) $4,000
    (b) $9,333   (d) -0-

11. The gross profit at cost was:
    (a) $157,720   (c) $153,770
    (b) -0-   (d) None of the above

12. The following are all characteristics of the retail method except:
    (a) Results in an average cost of ending inventory
    (b) Assumes goods are sold in a particular order
    (c) Is commonly used by department stores
    (d) Can be used to estimate the cost of ending inventory

DEMONSTRATION PROBLEM

Part A

The following transactions took place during January 19X9 at Kendriff, Inc. The beginning inventory consisted of 100 units of Brand X at $10 per unit. The following purchases were made during the month:

	Units	Unit Cost
Jan. 3	200	$10
11	400	9
19	500	8
24	600	7
30	200	6

During January, 1700 units were sold for $12 each.

Required

1. Calculate the cost of ending inventory and cost of goods sold under FIFO/periodic, LIFO/periodic, and weighted average.

2. Calculate the gross profit rate under each of these methods.

3. Under what circumstances will the cost of inventory under the LIFO assumption result in a lower net income than the FIFO assumption? in a higher net income than the FIFO assumption?

Part B

The accountant for Loyola, Inc., is concerned about the bookstore inventory. A physical count at May 31, 19X8, showed that $10,000 inventory (at cost) was on hand. The following information for the year then ended is available.

	At Retail	At Cost
Sales for the Year	$62,500	
Sales Returns	2,500	
Beginning Inventory	14,000	$10,000
Purchases for the Year	55,000	39,000
Purchase Returns	3,000	2,000
Transportation In		1,000

Required

1. Calculate the estimated ending inventory at retail.
2. Calculate the cost percentage (ratio of cost to retail).
3. Calculate the May 31, 19X8, estimated ending inventory at cost.
4. Why is the inventory calculated at cost different from the physical count at May 31?

Part C

The controller of Sir George Corp. is calculating the amount of inventory lost during the year ended May 31, 19X8. A physical count was not made at May 31 due to circumstances beyond his control. The following information for the year then ended is available from the general ledger.

Sales for the Year	$50,000
Sales Returns	5,000
Beginning Inventory	6,000
Purchases for the Year	35,000
Purchase Returns	3,000
Purchase Discounts	2,000
Transportation In	1,500
Delivery Expense	1,000
Depreciation Expense—Truck	400
Insurance Expense	100

The following are partial income statements of Sir George Corp. for years 19X5 to 19X7 (amounts are in thousands of dollars).

	19X5	19X6	19X7	Totals
Sales	$20	$30	$40	$
Cost of Goods Sold	10	20	30	
Gross Profit	$10	$10	$10	$

Required

Using the gross profit method, calculate the May 31, 19X8, estimated ending inventory at cost.

SOLUTIONS TO DEMONSTRATION PROBLEM

Part A

1. Use the following information to compare answers.

Date	Units	Unit Cost	Total Cost
Beginning Inventory	100	$10	$ 1,000
Jan. 3	200	10	2,000
11	400	9	3,600
19	500	8	4,000
24	600	7	4,200
30	200	6	1,200
	2,000		$16,000

	Units	FIFO/ Periodic	LIFO/ Periodic	Weighted Average
Beginning Inventory	100	$ 1,000	$ 1,000	$ 1,000
Purchases	1900	15,000	15,000	15,000
Cost of Goods Available	2000	$16,000	$16,000	$16,000
Less: Ending Inventory	300	1,900	3,000	2,400
Cost of Goods Sold	1700	$14,100	$13,000	$13,600

FIFO:

200 Units at $6	=	$1,200
100 Units at $7	=	700
FIFO Inventory	=	$1,900

LIFO:

100 Units at $10	=	$1,000
200 Units at $10	=	2,000
LIFO Inventory	=	$3,000

Weighted Average:

$$\frac{\text{Total Cost } \$16,000}{\text{Total Units } 2,000} = \$8 \text{ Average Cost}$$

Weighted Average Inventory = 300 Units at $8 = $2,400

2.

	FIFO/ Periodic	LIFO/ Periodic	Weighted Average
Sales (1700 × $12)	$20,400	$20,400	$20,400
Cost of Goods Sold	14,100	13,000	13,600
Gross Profit	$ 6,300	$ 7,400	$ 6,800
Gross Profit %	30.9%	36.3%	33⅓%

3. In a period of rising prices, the cost of inventory under the LIFO assumption will result in a lower net income than under the FIFO assumption. When prices are falling, LIFO will generate a higher net income than the FIFO assumption.

Part B

1. Use the following information to compare answers.

	At Retail		At Cost	
Sales		$62,500		$62,500
Less: Sales Returns		2,500		2,500
Net Sales		$60,000		$60,000
Cost of Goods Sold				
Beginning Inventory	$14,000		$10,000	
Purchases	55,000		39,000	
Less: Purchase Returns	(3,000)		(2,000)	
Transportation In			1,000	
Cost of Goods Available for Sale	$66,000		$48,000	
Less: Ending Inventory	(b) 6,000		?	
Total Cost of Goods Sold		(a) 60,000		?
Gross Profit		$ -0-		$?

(a) Cost of Goods Sold = Net Sales

(b) Ending Inventory = Cost of Goods Available − Cost of Goods Sold
    $66,000 − $60,000 = $6,000

2. Cost Percentage = Cost of Goods Available at Cost ÷ at Retail

$$\frac{\$48,000}{\$66,000} = 72.7\% \text{ (rounded)}$$

3. Estimated Ending Inventory at Cost = Cost Percentage × Retail Ending Inventory 72.7% × $6,000 = $4,362

4. The retail inventory method provides an accurate cost of ending inventory provided that no change in the cost percentage has occurred during the current period. The actual may differ from this estimate if a change in cost percentage has occurred.

Part C

	19X5	19X6	19X7	Totals
Sales	$20	$30	$40	$90
Cost of Goods Sold	10	20	30	60
Gross Profit	$10	$10	$10	$30
Gross Profit %	50%	33⅓%	25%	33⅓%

Gross profit percentage to be used is 33⅓%.

Note: Given the wide fluctuations in gross profit percentages, the method may not be very useful.

Sales			$50,000
Less: Sales Returns			5,000
Net Sales			$45,000
Cost of Goods Sold			
Beginning Inventory		$ 6,000	
Purchases		35,000	
Less: Purchase Returns	$3,000		
Purchase Discounts	2,000		
	$5,000	(5,000)	
Transportation In		1,500	
Cost of Goods Available		$37,500	
Less: Ending Inventory		?	
Total Cost of Goods Sold			30,000
Gross Profit			$15,000

Gross Profit = 33⅓% × $45,000 (Net Sales) = $15,000

Net Sales − Gross Profit = Cost of Goods Sold
$45,000 − $15,000 = $30,000

Cost of Goods Available − Cost of Goods Sold = Ending Inventory
$37,500 − $30,000 = $7,500

DISCUSSION QUESTIONS

Q8-1 Explain the importance of maintaining inventory levels for (a) management, (b) accountants, (c) investors and creditors.

Q8-2 How does a flow of goods differ from a flow of costs? Do generally accepted accounting principles require that the flow of costs be similar to the movement of goods? Explain.

Q8-3 What factors are considered in costing inventory? Which of these factors is most difficult to determine? Why?

Q8-4   Under the LIFO cost flow assumption, do ending inventories consist of the earliest or most recent costs? Do cost of goods sold include the earliest or most recent costs?

Q8-5   In recent years, the cost of goods acquired has been increasing because of inflation. What problems for financial reporting have resulted?

Q8-6   In a period of rising prices, which method of inventory valuation will result in the highest net income figure? the highest ending inventory amount?

Q8-7   Assume you are paid a year-end bonus according to the amount of net income earned during the year. When prices are rising, would you prefer to value inventories on a FIFO or a LIFO basis? Explain, using an example to support your answer. Would your choice be the same if prices were falling?

Q8-8   Why is consistency in inventory valuation necessary? Does the application of the consistency principle preclude a change from LIFO to FIFO? Explain.

Q8-9   The ending inventory of CBCA, Inc., is overstated by $5,000 at December 31, 19X4. What is the effect on 19X4 net income? What is the effect on 19X5 net income assuming that no other inventory errors have occurred during 19X5?

Q8-10   What are phantom profits? Where do they come from?

Q8-11   What is the primary reason for the use of LCM method of inventory valuation? What does the term *market* mean? What does *cost* refer to?

Q8-12   When should ending inventory be shown at cost, even though cost is higher than replacement cost?

Q8-13   What are the objections against LCM? Evaluate these objections.

Q8-14   A book inventory is required under the perpetual inventory system. What is the difference between a book inventory and a physical inventory?

Q8-15   What internal control feature of the perpetual inventory method is lost under the periodic inventory method? Would you recommend that a hardware store use the perpetual inventory method? Why or why not?

Q8-16   What procedure do the periodic and perpetual inventory systems both have in common?

Q8-17   Discuss the methods available to cost inventory under each of the periodic and perpetual inventory systems.

Q8-18   Contrast the journal entries required under the periodic and perpetual inventory systems.

Q8-19   Why is estimating inventory useful?

Q8-20   Do the gross profit and retail inventory methods use inventory quantities to calculate the dollar amount of inventory?

Q8-21   How does the calculation of ending inventory differ between the gross profit method and the retail inventory method? Use an example to illustrate.

Q8-22   When is the use of the gross profit method particularly useful?

Q8-23   Does the retail inventory method assume any particular movement of inventory? What cost flow is calculated under this method?

DISCUSSION CASES

Case 1: Control Data's Fall from Grace

It appeared to be quite a scoop. About three weeks ago, WTCN-TV, the NBC affiliate in Minneapolis, broadcast an interview with a man identified as "a former high-level Control

Data Corporation executive." He said the big data-processing company was suffering from low morale and technical problems and would soon lay off 5000 employees.

The broadcast was laced with intrigue. The man's voice was disguised and his face hidden from view—undermining the credibility, Control Data says, of the whole report. Nonetheless, the broadcast caused an uproar in Minneapolis, where Control Data employs nearly 18,000 people.

The company's switchboard was inundated with anxious calls. Control Data issued a memo to its employees, assuring them no lay-off was in the offing. And Richard C. Reid, Control Data's spokesman, still insists that there are "no plans for that at all."

But not even Reid could deny the broadcast's main point: Control Data, one of the giants of the computer industry, is in trouble.

Once a leading maker of mainframe computers, disk drives, and other data-processing gear, it has failed to keep up with sweeping changes in just about every market in which it competes. Analysts say its products have been late to market, costly, or out of touch with customer demand. The result has been a drop in profits and market share that is so steep that, some say, Control Data may never catch up.

Control Data's problems with 5¼-inch disk drives have been unnerving. The company's competitors rushed to market with the little units in 1977, when they became the storage device of choice for personal computer makers. Control Data did not produce its first 5¼-inch drive until 1980.

Early in 1981, many domestic manufacturers began producing 5¼-inch drives overseas in anticipation of an onslaught of lower-cost drives from Japan. That onslaught has now occurred. In the last six months alone, wholesale prices have fallen to about $75 a drive from $150. Control Data, however, did not move its production offshore until last year. Moreover, the rest of the industry began producing smaller units known as half-height drives in early 1983. Control Data's half-height versions did not appear until late that year.

The result, experts say, is that Control Data is stuck with a huge inventory of overpriced 5¼-inch drives that it must sell at a loss.

Source Eric N. Berg, "Control Data's Fall from Grace," *The New York Times,* February 17, 1985, p. 4-F. Copyright © 1985 by The New York Times Company. Reprinted by permission.

For Discussion

1. In light of this article, how would you, as potential investor, view the stated inventory on Control Data's published financial statements?

2. Should Control Data sell its inventory at a loss or hold it to wait for prices to rise? Explain.

Case 2: Surprise!

Read Real World Example 8-1 on pp. 370–71 and discuss the following questions:

For Discussion

1. Is Battery & Tire Warehouse using a periodic or perpetual inventory system? How can you tell?

2. Comment on the comparison of a physical inventory with a book inventory.

3. How can understating costs "show up on the books as more dollars of inventory than you actually have"?

4. Explain how ending inventory errors in 19X1 affect 19X1 and 19X2 incomes. What is the effect if other errors are also in the ending inventory of 19X2?

5. How could an increase in vendors' prices make the inventory of Battery & Tire Warehouse worth $56,000 more? Which inventory cost method is the entity using? Explain, using an example.

6. What is the meaning of the following comment: "So we set up windfall gains as separate accounts and formally recognize shrinkage on its own"?

7. Bodenstab writes, "A similarly useless game played by some managers is to build into their system automatic gains under the guise of conservatism"? What does he mean?

8. Could the situation described in Real World Example 8-1 lead management in other entities to make bad decisions? Explain.

EXERCISES

Exercises 8-1 through 8-12 draw on the following information taken from the records of King, Inc., for January 19X7. During the month 200 units of inventory were sold, 100 units during the period between the first and second purchases, and another 100 units between the fourth and fifth purchases.

	Units	Unit Cost
Beginning Inventory	100	$1
Purchase 1	10	1
Purchase 2	20	2
Purchase 3	30	3
Purchase 4	40	4
Purchase 5	50	5

Ending inventory—LIFO/periodic (Q1, Q7)

E8-1 Compute the cost of the ending inventory assuming a LIFO flow of costs and the use of a periodic inventory system.

Cost of goods sold—LIFO/periodic (Q1, Q7)

E8-2 Compute the cost of goods sold for January assuming a LIFO flow of costs and the use of a periodic inventory system.

Ending inventory—FIFO/periodic (Q1, Q7)

E8-3 Compute the cost of the ending inventory assuming a FIFO flow of costs and the use of a periodic inventory system.

Cost of goods sold—FIFO/periodic (Q1, Q7)

E8-4 Compute the cost of goods sold for January assuming a FIFO flow of costs and the use of a periodic inventory system.

Ending inventory—average/periodic (Q1, Q7)

E8-5 Compute the cost of the ending inventory assuming an average flow of costs and the use of a periodic inventory system.

Cost of goods sold—average/periodic (Q1, Q7)

E8-6 Compute the cost of goods sold for January assuming an average flow of costs and the use of a periodic inventory system.

Ending inventory—LIFO/perpetual (Q1, Q7)

E8-7 Compute the cost of the ending inventory assuming a LIFO flow of costs and the use of a perpetual inventory system.

Cost of goods sold—LIFO/perpetual (Q1, Q7)

E8-8 Compute the cost of goods sold for January assuming a LIFO flow of costs and the use of a perpetual inventory system.

Ending inventory—
FIFO/perpetual (Q1, Q7)

E8-9   Compute the cost of the ending inventory assuming a FIFO flow of costs and the use of a perpetual inventory system.

Cost of goods sold—
FIFO/perpetual (Q1, Q7)

E8-10   Compute the cost of goods sold for January assuming a FIFO flow of costs and the use of a perpetual inventory system.

Ending inventory—
average/perpetual
(Q1, Q7)

E8-11   Compute the cost of the ending inventory assuming an average flow of costs and the use of a perpetual inventory system.

Cost of goods sold—
average/perpetual
(Q1, Q7)

E8-12   Compute the cost of goods sold for January assuming an average flow of costs and the use of a perpetual inventory system.

Comparison of various
inventory methods
(Q1–Q4, Q6)

E8-13   Choose the method of inventory valuation that corresponds to each of the statements that follow.

1. FIFO   2. LIFO   3. Weighted average

- Matches actual flows of goods with actual flow of costs in most cases
- Matches new costs with new prices
- Matches old costs with new prices
- Results in phantom profits in a period of rising prices
- Results in the lowest net income in periods of falling prices
- Best matches current costs with current revenues
- Does not assume any particular flow of goods
- Results in the same inventory valuation, regardless of whether a periodic or perpetual inventory system is used
- Emphasizes income determination
- Emphasizes balance sheet valuation
- Values inventory at approximate replacement cost
- Results in lower income in a period of deflation
- Results in higher income in a period of deflation

Exercises E8-14 and E8-15 are based on the following data taken from the records of Turner Promotions Co.:

Beginning Inventory		Transportation In	$ 500
At retail	$ 7,000		
At cost	5,000	Purchase Returns	
		At retail	2,000
Purchases		At cost	1,500
At retail	25,000	Sales	22,000
At cost	16,000	Sales Returns	1,000

Retail method of esti-
mating inventory (Q9)

E8-14

Required

1.   Calculate the estimated ending inventory at cost, using the retail inventory method.

2.   Calculate the ending inventory at retail.

3. Calculate the cost percentage (ratio of cost to retail).

4. Calculate the ending inventory at cost.

Gross profit method of estimating inventory (Q9)

E8-15

Required

1. Calculate the ending inventory at cost, using the gross profit method. A gross profit rate of 35% is considered reasonable in the circumstances.

2. Explain why the ending inventory would be different under the two methods.

PROBLEMS

FIFO, LIFO, weighted average: Rising prices (Q1, Q2, Q4)

P8-1 The following purchases were made during 19X8 at Hooper Corporation. The beginning inventory consisted of 50 units at $1 each.

		Units	Unit Cost
Apr.	15	200	$2
May	25	200	$3
June	7	200	$4
Oct.	15	200	$5

Required

1. Calculate the number of units for beginning inventory, purchases, and goods available for sale. Also calculate cost of goods available as of December 31, 19X8, under FIFO/periodic, LIFO/periodic, and weighted average flows of goods.

2. If 200 units are on hand at December 31, 19X8, calculate the cost of this inventory under FIFO/periodic, LIFO/periodic, and weighted average flows of goods.

3. Calculate the number of units for goods available for sale, ending inventory, and goods sold. Calculate also the cost of goods sold under FIFO/periodic, LIFO/periodic, and weighted average flows of goods.

4. The president of Hooper Corporation has asked you to consider the implications of using the weighted average method over the LIFO or FIFO method. He is concerned that the reported income does not reflect the real income of the firm. Prepare some calculations showing the effect on net income of using the three inventory methods.

FIFO and LIFO: Falling prices, income taxes (Q1, Q2, Q4)

P8-2 The following data are taken from the records of Bethune, Inc., for the month of January 19X8.

	Purchases			Sales		
	Units	Unit Cost			Units	Unit Price
Beginning Inventory	25	$5				
Purchase 1	15	4		Sale 1	30	$6
Purchase 2	10	3		Sale 2	20	4
Purchase 3	35	2		Sale 3	50	2
Purchase 4	40	1				

Required

1. Calculate the amount of inventory at the end of January assuming that inventory is determined using FIFO/periodic.

2. How would the ending inventory differ if it was determined using LIFO/periodic?

3. Calculate the amount of gross profit under each of the above costing methods. Which method matches inventory costs more closely with revenues? Why?

4. Assume that the LIFO costing method was used and that the income tax was calculated at 50% of net income. Would more income tax be payable under the FIFO, or the LIFO method? Explain why.

LIFO and FIFO: rising prices (Q1, Q4, Q6)

P8-3   The Southern Co. made the following purchases during the year.

Jan.	7	8,000 units at $12.00 = $ 96,000
Mar.	30	9,000 units at $12.40 = $111,600
May	10	12,000 units at $12.00 = $144,000
July	6	16,000 units at $12.60 = $201,600
Sept.	2	6,000 units at $12.80 = $ 76,800
Dec.	14	7,000 units at $12.70 = $ 88,900

Ending inventory at December 31 amounted to 15,000 units. Selling price during the year was stable at $16 per unit. Beginning inventory at January 1 amounted to 4,000 units at $11.90 per unit.

Required

1. Prepare a schedule of inventory as of December 31 under both a FIFO/periodic and a LIFO/periodic system.

2. Prepare an income statement showing sales, cost of goods sold, and gross profit on both a FIFO and LIFO basis, using the above data.

3. Which method of inventory valuation matches revenues more closely with costs in this company under current conditions? Why?

4. The company is concerned about the continually increasing cost of its purchases. In January of the next year the cost price of each unit was $13. You are asked to explain the concept of phantom profits to the president. What will you say?

Inventory systems and journal entries (Q7)

P8-4   MacDonald Products Corp. sells gadgets. During the month of January 19X3, the number of gadgets purchased and sold are shown:

			Purchased			Sold			Balance		
			Quantity	Unit Cost	Total Cost	Quantity	Unit Cost	Total Cost	Quantity	Unit Cost	Total Cost
Jan.	1	Balance	100	$1							
	3	Purchase	100	1							
	8	Purchase	200	2							
	10	Sale				200	$3				
	15	Purchase	300	3							
	20	Sale				500	5				
	27	Purchase	400	1							

Required

1. Calculate the cost of the month-end inventory under each of the following costing assumptions:
   (a) FIFO/perpetual   (b) LIFO/perpetual   (c) Moving average

2. Prepare the journal entries required under the perpetual inventory system for the LIFO costing method.

3. Prepare the journal entries required under the periodic inventory system for the LIFO costing method.

4. Why are different journal entries prepared under each method?

Gross profit method of estimating inventory (Q9)

P8-5 Kamloops Retail Co. has consistently averaged 39% gross profit. The company's inventories, which are on a periodic basis, were recently destroyed by fire. The following data are available:

Sales	$305
Purchases	175
Beginning Inventory	25
Sales Returns	5
Purchase Returns	5
Delivery Expense	8
Transportation In	3
Repairs to Delivery Truck	3
Selling Commissions	6
Administrative Expenses	3

Required

1. Calculate the estimated ending inventory.

2. Prepare journal entries (with explanation) to record
   (a) The destruction of the inventory by fire
   (b) The recovery of $30 from the insurance company

3. Why did the insurance recovery exceed the inventory cost?

Retail method of estimating inventories (Q9)

P8-6 The president of Segovia Corp. is concerned that the year-end inventory amounting to $5,000 at cost is less than expected. Although a physical count was made and the costing was accurately calculated using FIFO, the president asks you to estimate the year-end inventory using the following data:

	At Retail	At Cost
Sales for the Year	$160,000	
Sales Returns	10,000	
Purchases for the Year	164,000	$80,000
Purchase Returns	4,000	2,000
Transportation In		1,000
Beginning Inventory	20,000	11,000

Required

1. Calculate the estimated ending inventory at retail.

2. Calculate the cost percentage (ratio of cost to retail).

3. Calculate the estimated ending inventory at cost.

4. Calculate the amount of inventory lost during the year.

5. Assuming that the current replacement cost of the inventory is covered by insurance, calculate the amount paid by the insurer if
   (a) The current replacement cost is 25% greater than the inventory FIFO cost
   (b) The insurer pays 80% of the current replacement cost

6. Prepare the journal entry to record the amount recovered from the insurer.

ALTERNATE PROBLEMS

FIFO, LIFO, weighted
average, specific identi-
fication; net income
(Q1, Q2, Q4, Q6)

AP8-1   The following transactions took place during January 19X6 at Kelly Corp. The beginning inventory consisted of 100 units at a total cost of $100.

		Units	Total Cost
Jan. 5	Purchase 1	100	$ 100
9	Purchase 2	200	400
16	Purchase 3	300	900
26	Purchase 4	400	1,600

Units sold during the month were as follows:

		Units	Total Cost
Jan. 10	Sale 1	200	$ 600
17	Sale 2	500	1,500

Required

1. Calculate the cost of ending inventory and the cost of goods sold under
   (a) FIFO/periodic
   (b) LIFO/periodic
   (c) Weighted average
   (d) Specific identification. Assume that the 700 units sold were identified as being made from the 100 units in beginning inventory, the 200 units purchased on January 9, and the 400 units purchased January 26.

2. The accountant for Kelly Corp. is concerned about the effect rising prices will have on income determination under the FIFO method they have been using. What is the difference in net income for 19X6 under FIFO and LIFO? If the income tax rate is 40%, how much more in taxes is Kelly Corp. paying under FIFO than under LIFO?

FIFO, LIFO, weighted
average, fluctuating
prices; income state-
ment and balance sheet
(Q1, Q2, Q4, Q6)

AP8-2   The Howell Co. is considering the use of different methods of calculating their ending inventory. The following data are applicable to its December operations:

Purchased		Sold	
Dec. 4	1000 units at $2.50	Dec. 5	600 units
11	800 units at $2.60	12	500 units
23	1600 units at $2.30	17	500 units
29	900 units at $2.40	27	400 units
		31	600 units

Required

1. Calculate the amount of ending inventory under
   (a) FIFO/periodic   (b) LIFO/periodic   (c) Weighted average/periodic

2. Which method presents the most appropriate balance sheet valuation of inventory? Explain, using appropriate amounts to support your answer.

3. Which method results in the most realistic income statement? Why?

FIFO, LIFO, weighted average, phantom profits (Q1, Q2, Q4, Q6)

AP8-3   The Single Product Co. had the following inventory transactions for the month of December:

Nov. 30	Inventory of	20 units at $4.60
Dec. 8	Purchased	80 units at $5.00
15	Purchased	40 units at $5.30
22	Purchased	60 units at $5.60
31	Purchased	40 units at $5.50

By December 31, 190 of the units had been sold by Single.

Required

1. Calculate the cost of the ending inventory using
   (a) FIFO/periodic   (b) LIFO/periodic   (c) Weighted average

2. The prices of the company's purchases have been increasing during the month and the controller is concerned about the possible existence of phantom profits under the FIFO method of costing inventory. If the sales price of each unit was $7 during December, prepare calculations necessary to isolate the existence of phantom profits.

FIFO, LIFO, moving average, perpetual, journal entries (Q1, Q7)

AP8-4   Janus Products, Inc., sells television sets. The following information relates to January 19X7 purchases and sales of Brand X 20-inch color television sets:

		Purchased			Sold			Balance		
		Quantity	Unit Cost	Total Cost	Quantity	Unit Cost	Total Cost	Quantity	Unit Cost	Total Cost
Jan. 1	Balance	6	$400							
2	Sale				1	$600				
3	Purchase	2	450							
7	Sale				2	700				
10	Sale				1	650				
15	Purchase	3	500							
20	Sale				4	750				
25	Purchase	1	500							
29	Sale				1	800				

Required

1. Calculate the cost of the month-end inventory under
   (a) FIFO/perpetual   (b) LIFO/perpetual   (c) Moving average

2. Prepare the journal entries required under the perpetual inventory method for
   (a) FIFO   (b) LIFO   (c) Moving average

Gross profit method of estimating inventory (Q9)

AP8-5   The Kenworth Mall housed the premises of the Handy Hardware Co. On the morning of November 1, fire gutted the hardware store and some of the other tenant shops. Handy Hardware had been at a popular location for homeowners and had, as a result, consistently earned a gross profit on net sales of 40% over the years. Appropriate data to date were as follows:

Sales	$1,220
Purchases	700
Purchase Returns	20
Sales Returns	16
Delivery Expense	30
Transportation In	12
Administrative Expense	8
Beginning Inventory (Jan. 1)	100
Advertising Expense	20
Salaries	85
Sales Discounts	4

Required

1. Calculate the estimated closing inventory.

2. Prepare the entries required to show the claim set up by Handy Hardware and the collection of a settlement in full of $60.

3. Did the insurance settlement exceed the inventory cost? Why?

Retail method of estimating inventories (Q9)

AP8-6   University Men's Shop, Inc., takes a year-end physical inventory at marked selling prices and reduces the total to a cost basis for year-end statement purposes. University also uses the retail method to estimate the amount of inventory that should be on hand at year-end. By comparison of the two totals, it is able to determine inventory shortages resulting from theft. The following information at the end of December is available.

	At Retail	At Cost
Sales	$234,680	
Sales Returns	3,740	
Beginning Inventory	36,200	$ 24,420
Purchases	239,800	166,770
Purchase Returns	3,900	2,830
Inventory Count (Dec. 31)	40,900	

Required

1. Use the retail method to estimate the year-end inventory at cost.

2. Use the retail method to reduce the shop's year-end physical inventory to a cost basis.

3. Prepare a schedule showing the inventory shortage at cost and at retail.

DECISION PROBLEMS

Problem 1

The president's assistant of Boswell, Inc., asks you to come to a board of directors meeting to explain some accounting problems to the members of the board. He indicates that the questions will be about the problems with inventories. As the controller of the firm, you are fully aware that the corporation has used the lower of FIFO cost or market value (LCM) in accounting for the inventory.

Required

At the board meeting the following questions are raised. How would you answer them?

1. What is the objective of determining the cost of the inventory and cost of goods sold in accordance with the principles of the LIFO method?

2. Are some accounting assumptions or conventions responsible for the development of this method?

3. What effect would the adoption of this method have on the financial statements?

Problem 2

Buck, Inc., reported net income (loss) for the years 19X7, 19X8, and 19X9 as follows:

19X7	$290.7 million
19X8	88.7 million
19X9	(7.6) million

In the company's annual report for 19X9, the following statement appeared in a footnote:

Inventories are stated at lower of cost or market for the period January 1, 19X7, through December 31, 19X8. Last in, first out (LIFO) method of inventory valuation had been used for approximately 60% of consolidated inventory. Cost of the remaining 40% of inventories was determined using first in, first out (FIFO) or average cost methods. Effective January 1, 19X9, the FIFO method of inventory valuation has been adopted for inventories previously valuated using LIFO method. This results in a more uniform valuation method throughout the corporation and makes financial statements with respect to inventory valuation comparable with those of the other manufacturers. As a result of adopting FIFO in 19X9, net loss reported is less than it would have been by approximately $20 million or $.40 a share. Inventory amounts at December 31, 19X9, are stated higher by $150 million than they would have been had LIFO been continued.

Required

1. Why do you think Buck made the change in its inventory costing method in 19X9 and not previously?

2. Do you believe the market regarded this change as cosmetic or that the price of Buck's shares was affected?

ANSWERS TO SELF-TEST QUESTIONS

1. **(d)** LIFO/periodic ending inventory:

2,000 units at $0.50 =	$1,000
500 units at $2.00 =	1,000
2,500	$2,000

2. **(c)** FIFO/periodic ending inventory:

   1,000 units at \$2.00 = \$2,000
     500 units at \$1.00 =   500
   1,000 units at \$2.50 = 2,500
   2,500   \$5,000

3. **(b)** Weighted average ending inventory:

   2,000 units at \$0.50 = \$1,000
   1,000 units at \$2.00 = 2,000
     500 units at \$1.00 =   500
   1,000 units at \$2.50 = 2,500
   4,500   \$6,000

   Weighted average cost:

$$\frac{\$6,000}{4,500} \times 2,500 \text{ units} = \$3,333 \text{ (rounded)}$$

4. **(b)** LIFO/periodic cost of goods sold:

     500 units at \$2.00 = \$1,000
     500 units at \$1.00 =   500
   1,000 units at \$2.50 = 2,500
   2,000   \$4,000

5. **(b)** FIFO/periodic cost of goods sold:

   2,000 units at \$0.50 = \$1,000

6. **(a)** Weighted average cost of goods sold:

   2,000 units at \$0.50 = \$1,000
   1,000 units at \$2.00 = 2,000
     500 units at \$1.00 =   500
   1,000 units at \$2.50 = 2,500
   4,500   \$6,000

   Weighted average cost:

$$\frac{\$6,000}{4,500} \times 2,000 \text{ units} = \$2,667 \text{ (rounded)}$$

7. **(c)** Use the following partial income statement to compare answers:

	At Retail	At Cost
Sales	\$276,000	\$276,000
Cost of Goods Sold		
Beginning Inventory	\$ 80,000	\$ 26,000
Purchases	200,000	90,000
Transportation In	—	4,000
Cost of Goods Available	\$280,000	\$120,000
Less: Ending Inventory	4,000	?
Total Cost of Goods Sold	276,000	
Gross Profit	\$ -0-	\$?

8. **(b)** Cost of Goods Sold = Net Sales

   Ending Inventory at Retail = Cost of Goods Available − Cost of Goods Sold
   \$4,000 = \$280,000 − \$276,000

9. **(b)**   Cost Percentage = Cost of Goods Available at Cost ÷ at Retail

$$43\% = \frac{\$120,000}{\$280,000}$$

10. **(a)**   Estimated Ending Inventory at Cost = Cost Percentage × Retail Ending Inventory
$1,720 = 43\% \times \$4,000$

11. **(a)**   The goods sold amount to $118,280 ($120,000 − $1,720). Therefore, the gross profit at cost is $157,720 ($276,000 − $118,280).

12. **(b)**

9 LONG-TERM ASSETS

Both tangible and intangible long-term assets are used in the normal operating activities of an entity. Since they are long-term, their historical cost must be allocated over the accounting periods that will benefit from their use. Chapter 9 will examine the determination of the historical cost of long-term assets, methods of allocating that cost over the useful life of the assets, disclosure requirements for financial statement purposes, subsequent disposal of long-term assets, and finally, the allocation of natural resources and intangible assets.

CHAPTER PREVIEW QUESTIONS

After studying Chapter 9, you should be able to answer the following questions:

1 What costs are included in the determination of the historical cost of a long-term asset? (pp.408–10)

2 If an entity constructs its own assets, should the historical cost be recorded as total cost incurred, or the cost of purchasing such an asset? (p.410)

3 After a long-term asset is placed in service, are any cash outflows ever added to the asset account, thereby increasing the historical cost? If so, what cash outflows are added, and which are expensed? (pp.410–11)

4 Differentiate between production-based and time-based depreciation methods. (pp.413–14)

5 What is the primary purpose of recording depreciation? (pp.413–14)

6 Are the methods of cost allocation used for financial reporting also accepted by the Internal Revenue Service? (pp.418–20)

7 Does one method of recording depreciation result in a better matching of revenue and expense on the income statement? (pp.420–21)

8 Does the book value of a long-term asset represent its estimated market value? Explain. (p.422)

9 What information regarding long-term assets should be disclosed in the financial statements? (pp.422–23)

10 Once a useful life has been estimated for a particular asset, is it possible to make revisions to that estimate in future years? (pp.424–25)

11 Why do accountants differentiate between exchanges involving similar and dissimilar assets? (p.426)

12 Is there a conceptual difference among the following terms: depreciation, depletion, and amortization? (pp.428–29)

13 Should intangible assets with indeterminable useful lives simply remain on the balance sheet with no allocation of revenue to the income statement? (pp.429–30)

14 If a patent has been issued to you, and later you spend $10,000 in court defending your right, should the payment be recorded as legal expense? (p.430)

ESTABLISHING THE COST OF LONG-TERM ASSETS

At the time of its acquisition, a long-term asset can be thought of as a bundle of services that will be consumed over a period of years, similar to an inventory of supplies being consumed over a period of months, or a one-year insurance policy expiring over a period of 12 months. The major difference is that supplies are visibly being consumed, and the allocation of a one-year insurance policy can be precisely measured.

Each year, as part of the above-mentioned bundle of services is consumed, a portion of its original cost must be transferred to the income statement as an expense. Eventually, this asset becomes no longer useful and must be replaced. The life cycle or **useful life** of a long-term asset is illustrated in Exhibit 9-1.

Capital Expenditures

Q1: Historical cost of long-term assets

Capital expenditures consist of the asset cost less any applicable cash discounts, plus any additional costs involved in preparing the asset for use. Assume that the asset equipment is purchased for a net price of $20,000, that transportation costs $500, installation requiring special wiring costs $1,000, construction of a cement foundation costs $2,500, and test runs to debug the equipment cost $2,000. The total historical cost of the asset, then, is $26,000. In addition to the purchase price or invoice cost of the asset acquired, the costs to prepare the asset for use are also **capitalized.** The various costs that may be incurred in the course of acquiring and preparing the asset for use are listed in Exhibit 9-2.

Well-established principles exist for determining what amounts should be included in the cost of the asset in most situations.

Generally accepted accounting principles require that all costs benefiting future accounting periods in which the asset will be used be included in the historical cost of the asset.

The preceding types of cost are clear examples of expenditures made in the course of acquiring the asset and preparing it for use. However, other expenditures are often more difficult to allocate. These are discussed next.

LAND

In addition to the costs listed in the preceding schedule, the land account will be charged with the cost of removing any useless structures found on the land. This

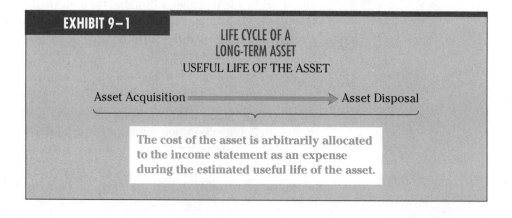

EXHIBIT 9-1

LIFE CYCLE OF A
LONG-TERM ASSET
USEFUL LIFE OF THE ASSET

Asset Acquisition ══════════⟶ Asset Disposal

The cost of the asset is arbitrarily allocated to the income statement as an expense during the estimated useful life of the asset.

EXHIBIT 9-2	CAPITAL EXPENDITURES		
	Land	**Building**	**Equipment**
Costs to Acquire the Asset	Purchase price Commission to real estate agent Legal fees	Purchase price Commission to real estate agent Legal fees	Invoice cost Transportation Insurance (during transportation)
Costs to Prepare Asset for Use	Costs of draining, clearing, and landscaping Assessments for streets and sewage system	Repair and remodelling costs before use Payments to tenants for premature termination of lease	Assembly Installation (including wages paid to company employees) Special floor foundations or supports Wiring Inspection Test run costs

cost is reduced by the proceeds, if any, obtained from the sale of the scrap. Assume that the total cost of a land parcel is $100,000 before an additional $15,000 is spent to raze an old building: $1,000 is expected to be received for salvaged materials. The historical cost of the land is $114,000.

Total Cost of Land		$100,000
Razing Costs for Building	$15,000	
Less: Salvage Proceeds	1,000	14,000
Total		$114,000

Frequently, land and useful buildings are purchased for a lump sum. If the buildings will be used for business purposes, the purchase price must be allocated to both the land and the buildings, because buildings are subject to depreciation. Land does not usually depreciate, since its utility for building or for other purposes does not diminish. The purchase price is usually allocated to the acquired assets on the basis of their market values. Assume that a lump sum of $150,000 is paid for land and buildings. After the market value of each is determined, this cost can be allocated as follows:

	Market Value	Percent of Total Market Value	Cost Allocation
Land	$ 50,000	25%	$ 37,500 ($150,000 × 25%)
Building	150,000	75%	112,500 ($150,000 × 75%)
Total	$200,000	100%	$150,000

The allocation also can be made on some other basis; it may be based on municipal assessed values or on estimates made by a professional appraiser.

As stated earlier, land does not normally depreciate. An exception to this rule occurs where nonrenewable mineral deposits or oil are to be removed from the land during future accounting periods. In such cases, the mineral deposit component of the land is subject to **depletion,** which is the term used to describe the allocation to the income statement of the portion of the land's cost assigned to nonrenewable resources. The topic of depletion is further discussed later in this chapter.

BUILDING AND EQUIPMENT

When an asset is purchased, its historical cost includes the net purchase price plus all costs to prepare the asset for use. In some cases, a business may construct its own building or equipment. In the case of a building, for example, cost includes all pertinent expenditures, including costs for excavation, building permits, insurance and property taxes during construction, engineering fees, the cost of labor incurred by having company employees supervise and work on the construction of the building, and the cost of any interest incurred to finance the construction during the construction period.

Q2: Constructing assets and cost

The cost of an asset constructed by the company is *never* recorded at the amount that it would have cost to have someone else construct the same building or piece of equipment. Accounting principles do not permit the recording of an unrealized profit—from construction of an asset at less than purchase cost, in this case.

In some cases, one asset is exchanged for another asset. Assume that a piece of land acquired several years ago at a cost of $25,000 is exchanged for a piece of equipment owned by another company. At the time of the exchange, the **fair market value (FMV)** of the land is $50,000 and the FMV of the equipment is $60,000. What is the cost of the equipment?

The rule followed by most accountants in this type of situation requires that the cost of the asset acquired (equipment) be the FMV of the asset given up (land, FMV $50,000); if the FMV of the land cannot be established or is not clear, then the FMV of the asset acquired (equipment, FMV $60,000) is used.

One exception to this rule occurs when one asset is traded in for a similar asset—an old piece of equipment for a new piece of equipment, for example. This topic is treated in another section of this chapter.

Betterments versus Extraordinary Repairs

As noted, all cash outlays made to purchase an asset and to prepare it for its particular use are considered capital expenditures.

Generally accepted accounting principles require expenditures to be capitalized when they will benefit more than one accounting period, when they are significant in amount, and when they can be measured with reasonably objective evidence.

Q3: Added cash outflows

In dealing with capital expenditures, a distinction should be made between a **betterment** and an **extraordinary repair.** A *betterment* results in a change to the asset that increases its efficiency; the estimated useful life of the asset does not change. For example, if a tape drive in a personal computer is replaced by a disk drive, the cost of the betterment is added to the existing asset cost and is depreciated over the existing asset's useful life. The cost of the replaced part and accumulated depreciation attributable to it are removed from the accounts.

An *extraordinary repair* results in a change of the estimated useful life of the asset. The cost of it is debited to accumulated depreciation rather than to asset cost, since it is viewed as reducing the previously recorded depreciation. The resulting net asset cost is then depreciated over the asset's remaining useful life. The accounting procedures in establishing the revised depreciation charges are discussed later in this chapter.

Not all asset-related expenditures incurred after the purchase of an asset are capitalized. Other expenditures, called **revenue expenditures,** are recorded directly as an expense. Examples of these expenditures include the cost of replacing parts of an asset (e.g., for a truck, new tires, new muffler, new battery), continuing expenditures for maintaining the asset in good working order (e.g., oil changes, antifreeze, transmission fluid changes), and costs of renewing structural parts of an asset (e.g., repairs of collision damage, repair or replacement of rusted parts).

An expenditure made to maintain an asset in satisfactory working order is a *revenue expenditure* of the accounting period in which the expenditure was made.

Although some revenue expenditures will benefit more than one accounting period, they do not increase the serviceability of the asset beyond its original useful life, and therefore are treated as normal maintenance costs.

Three criteria should be considered when establishing a policy to distinguish between capital and revenue expenditures incurred after the purchase and installation of an asset. They are explained in Exhibit 9-3.

The concept of *materiality* enters into the distinction between capital and revenue expenditures. As a matter of expediency, an expenditure of $200 that has all the characteristics of a capital expenditure would probably be expensed rather than capitalized in a large entity such as General Motors, because the effort to capitalize and depreciate the item is so much greater than the benefits to be derived. Policies are established by many companies to resolve the problem of distinguishing between capital and revenue expenditures. For example, all capital expenditures in excess of $1,000 would be capitalized; all capital expenditures under $1,000 would be expensed.

EXHIBIT 9-3

ASSET-RELATED EXPENDITURES FOLLOWING PURCHASE OF THE ASSET

Criterion	Capital Expenditure	Revenue Expenditure
1. Life of the Addition	Will benefit two or more accounting periods.	Will benefit the current accounting period.
2. Expenditure for Repairs	Will prolong the useful life of the asset beyond the original estimate.	Will not prolong the useful life of the asset beyond the original estimate.
3. Materiality of the Expenditure	Dollar amount of expenditure is large, is not made often, and will benefit two or more accounting periods.	Dollar amount of expenditure is small, is made relatively often, and does not materially affect net income.

THE NATURE OF DEPRECIATION

It is unfortunate but true that the sleek little sports car you want to own no matter what the cost will not last forever. How long it will last depends on a number of variables.

If it turns out to be a classic (1957 Chevy two-door hard-top), you take care of it (never drive it), you live where rust is not a factor (sunny California), and nobody ever hits you or you never hit anyone (in a vacuum), then it will not lose its value and will probably increase in value. If it is not a classic, no matter what you do, the car will eventually become worthless. Most **tangible long-term assets,** or physical assets, will wear out and come to the end of their usefulness. Henry Rand Hatfield, an eminent accountant and professor, wrote almost 80 years ago, "All machinery is on an irresistible march to the junk heap, and its progress, while it may be delayed, cannot be prevented by repairs."

The role of depreciation is to recognize this limited useful life and to allocate the cost of the asset over its useful life; that is, over the accounting periods expected to receive benefits from its use.

Assume that a machine acquired for $20,000 will have an estimated useful life of 5 years, after which time it will be scrapped for $2,000. The company has purchased for $20,000 a 5-year bundle of services, part of which will be used up each year, as shown in Exhibit 9-4.

Each year, part of the bundle of services of the asset is allocated to depreciation expense. The problem is: how do you measure the benefits that flow from an asset? Without this information (and it is difficult to obtain in practice), how do accountants rationally allocate the cost of an asset to a particular accounting period? The answer is that they can't! In practice, an estimate is made.

Assets included within the noncurrent asset category for long-term assets are as follows:

1. Depreciable tangible assets, such as buildings and equipment. **Depreciation** is the term used to describe the allocation of a tangible asset's cost to expense over its useful life.

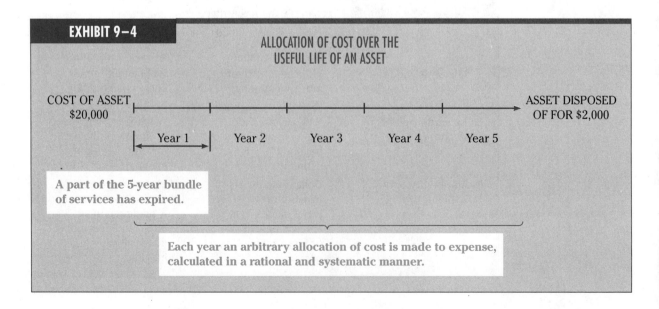

EXHIBIT 9–4

ALLOCATION OF COST OVER THE
USEFUL LIFE OF AN ASSET

COST OF ASSET
$20,000

ASSET DISPOSED
OF FOR $2,000

Year 1   Year 2   Year 3   Year 4   Year 5

A part of the 5-year bundle of services has expired.

Each year an arbitrary allocation of cost is made to expense, calculated in a rational and systematic manner.

2. Depreciable natural resource assets, such as oil and coal. *Depletion* is the term used to describe the allocation of a natural resource's cost to expense over its useful life.

3. Depreciable *intangible long-term assets,* such as patents and goodwill. **Amortization** is the term used to describe the allocation of an intangible asset's cost to expense over its useful life.

4. Other assets, such as investment assets and nonproduction assets.

Long-term Asset Cost Allocation Methods

Income determination is a primary objective of the depreciation process.

According to generally accepted accounting principles, a firm should adopt the method of allocating the cost of an asset to the depreciation expense that produces the most reasonable matching of depreciation costs with revenues earned.

The most frequently used methods to allocate the cost of long-term assets over their useful lives are

- Production methods
- Time-based methods
    Straight-line
    Sum-of-the-years'-digits
    Declining balance
    Internal Revenue Code

PRODUCTION METHODS

Q4: Production vs. time-based methods

Production methods of determining depreciation should be used in situations where wear and tear are the major factors in the decline of usefulness of the asset. The methods are also appropriate if the amount of use the asset receives varies from period to period. **Production depreciation** is determined on the basis of an equal amount for each unit produced. The unit may be an hour, a mile driven, a barrel of oil, a cubic foot of natural gas, a ton of ore, and so on. An estimate of the total number of units the asset will produce during its useful life must be made at the time the asset is put into service. An estimate also must be made of the amount to be realized on the disposal of the asset at the end of its useful life. For instance, assume that a machine costing $20,000 has a **salvage value** of $2,000 and is expected to have an estimated productive life of 10,000 units. If 1,500 units were processed during the current period, the depreciation expense for the period would be $2,700.

$$\frac{\text{Cost} - \text{Salvage Value}}{\substack{\text{Number of Units} \\ \text{of Estimated} \\ \text{Productive Life}}} = \frac{\text{Depreciation}}{\text{per Unit}} \times \frac{\text{Number of Units}}{\text{Produced}} = \frac{\text{Depreciation Expense}}{\text{for the Period}}$$

or, using the figures given:

$$\frac{\$20,000 - \$2,000}{10,000\,\text{Units}} = \$1.80 \times 1500\,\text{Units} = \$2,700\,\text{Depreciation Expense}$$

Q5: Objective of recording depreciation

Usage methods assume that the asset will contribute to the earning of revenues in relation to the amount of use during the accounting period. Therefore, the depreciation expense under this method records the decline in the capacity of the asset during the period. However, the purpose of depreciation is to allocate the cost of an asset over its useful life to match against revenue the costs incurred in producing that revenue. The purpose of depreciation does not include the determination of an estimated value of the asset for balance sheet purposes.

TIME-BASED METHODS

Time-based depreciation methods assign portions of an asset's cost to years rather than to units produced.

Straight-Line   The **straight-line depreciation** method—introduced briefly in Chapter 3—ignores asset usage and assumes that the asset will contribute to the earning of revenues equally during each period; that is, each period will receive services of equal value. Therefore, equal amounts of depreciation are recorded during each year of its useful life.

The straight-line method is appropriate for assets that make an equal contribution to operations during each year of their productive life. It is not appropriate when the asset does not contribute uniformly to operations during each year of its life.

Under the straight-line method, depreciation expense for each accounting period remains the same dollar amount during the useful life of the asset.

The straight-line method can be calculated as follows:

$$\frac{\text{Cost} - \text{Salvage Value}}{\text{Estimated Useful Life}} = \text{Depreciation Expense}$$

Assume that the same $20,000 machine used earlier, with an estimated service life of 5 years and an estimated net salvage value of $2,000, is depreciated on the straight-line method. The annual depreciation charge is:

$$\frac{\$20,000 - \$2,000}{5} = \$3,600$$

Exhibit 9-5 illustrates the arbitrary method of allocating costs in the straight-line method.

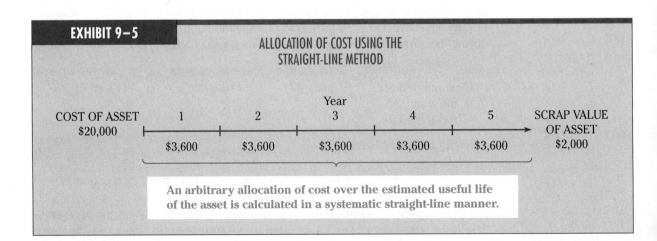

EXHIBIT 9-5

ALLOCATION OF COST USING THE STRAIGHT-LINE METHOD

COST OF ASSET $20,000	Year 1	2	3	4	5	SCRAP VALUE OF ASSET $2,000
	$3,600	$3,600	$3,600	$3,600	$3,600	

An arbitrary allocation of cost over the estimated useful life of the asset is calculated in a systematic straight-line manner.

The straight-line method considers depreciation as a function of time, and its main advantage is its simplicity of calculation. Since it is usually difficult to judge what the pattern of an asset's use will be, this method is least likely to be subject to bias.

ACCELERATED TIME-BASED METHODS

Both the production and the straight-line approach assign a constant amount for depreciation either to a unit produced or to a year's time. The methods do not take into consideration that as time passes, the asset will generally cost more to maintain through increased repair and maintenance expenses. In other words, as time passes, more costs are being matched against revenue, even though the amount of revenue being generated may remain the same. If straight-line depreciation and increasing repair and maintenance costs are assumed, a time period graph for total costs being charged to the income statement would appear as in Exhibit 9-6.

Notice that with equal amounts for depreciation each period, and increasing repair and maintenance costs, the total amount of expense charged to the income statement increases as time goes on.

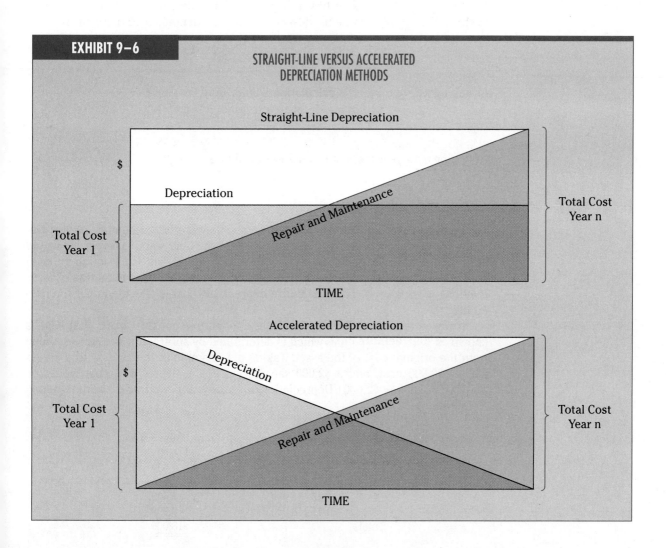

EXHIBIT 9-6

STRAIGHT-LINE VERSUS ACCELERATED
DEPRECIATION METHODS

If the amount of revenue produced from the asset remains relatively constant, then a mismatching occurs. Under an accelerated approach, a *decreasing* amount of depreciation is matched with an *increasing* amount of repair and maintenance expense, resulting in a more constant amount of total operating costs (depreciation plus repair and maintenance) charged against revenue. The time graph assuming an accelerated depreciation method is shown in Exhibit 9-6.

Accelerated depreciation methods also can be supported based on the assumption that the asset in many cases produces more revenue when it is new than in later years. Therefore, the earlier years should be charged with more depreciation than the later years to obtain a better matching of revenue and expense. Of the many accelerated methods used in practice today, this textbook will examine two major ones: sum-of-the-years'-digits method and declining-balance method.

Sum-of-the-Years'-Digits The **sum-of-the-years'-digits depreciation** method applies a decreasing rate to a constant balance to allocate more of an asset's cost in the earlier years of its useful life. The rate is expressed in the form of a fraction. The denominator is the sum of the number of years of the useful life of the asset. For instance, if an asset has a 5-year life, the denominator would be 15 ($1 + 2 + 3 + 4 + 5 = 15$). If the asset has a 10-year life, the denominator would be 55. A mathematic formula can be used to determine this denominator more easily.

$$\text{Denominator} = \frac{N(N + 1)}{2}$$

Assuming a 5-year life, the calculation would be

$$\frac{5(5 + 1)}{2} = 15$$

Assuming a 10-year life, the calculation would be

$$\frac{10(10 + 1)}{2} = 55$$

The numerator of the fraction for the decreasing rate is the number of years of useful life in *reverse order.* So, the numerator for the first year of a 5-year life would be 5, then 4 in the second year, 3 in the third year and so on. The fraction for each year of the 5-year life would be $\frac{5}{15}, \frac{4}{15}, \frac{3}{15}, \frac{2}{15}$, and $\frac{1}{15}$. Note that the summation of these fractions is equal to 1. Thus the entire depreciable cost is allocated over the useful life.

It was noted that a declining rate was applied to a constant base. That base is known as **depreciable cost,** which is determined by subtracting the salvage value from the original cost of the asset. Taking our example of the asset with a 5-year life, a $20,000 cost, and a $2,000 salvage value, the depreciable cost would be $18,000 ($20,000 − $2,000). Depreciation for the 5-year period would be determined as follows:

Year	Calculation		Depreciation Expense
1	5/15 ($18,000)	=	$ 6,000
2	4/15 (18,000)	=	4,800
3	3/15 (18,000)	=	3,600
4	2/15 (18,000)	=	2,400
5	1/15 (18,000)	=	1,200
Total			$18,000

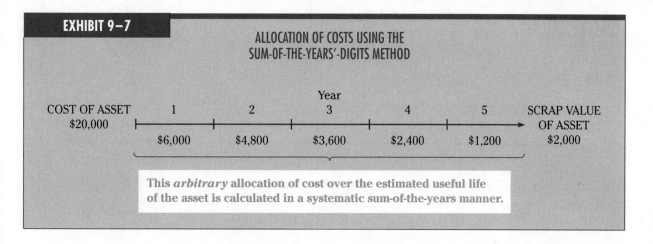

EXHIBIT 9–7

ALLOCATION OF COSTS USING THE
SUM-OF-THE-YEARS'-DIGITS METHOD

This *arbitrary* allocation of cost over the estimated useful life
of the asset is calculated in a systematic sum-of-the-years manner.

Exhibit 9-7 illustrates the arbitrary method of allocating costs in the sum-of-the-years'-digits method.

Declining Balance   Under the declining-balance method, a constant rate is applied to a declining balance. The rate can be determined by means of a mathematical formula, but in practice a multiple of the straight-line rate is used. For instance, if the useful life of an asset is 10 years, then 1/10 of the cost of the asset is written off each year, or 10%. If the useful life is 5 years, then 1/5 or 20% is written off; a 40-year asset, 1/40 or 2 1/2% per year, and so on. The most popular multiple is what is known as *double declining balance,* or 200% declining balance, which is twice the straight-line rate. Therefore, if **double declining-balance depreciation** is used on an asset with a 10-year life, the rate would be 20% (2 × 10%). The rate would be 40% for a 5-year asset (2 × 20%), and 5% for a 40-year asset (2 × 2 1/2%).

The rate selected should not change during the useful life, but the base to which it is applied does change. The rate is applied to the original cost of the asset, then *reduced* by the depreciation expense taken in each prior year and reapplied. Since the asset referred to here had a $20,000 cost and a 5-year life, double declining-balance depreciation for the 5-year period would be determined as follows:

Year	Carrying Value Calculation		Balance of Depreciating Cost		Constant Rate		Depreciation Expense
1	Total Cost	=	$20,000	×	40%	=	$8,000
2	$20,000 – 8,000	=	12,000	×	40%	=	4,800
3	12,000 – 4,800	=	7,200	×	40%	=	2,880
4	7,200 – 2,880	=	4,320	×	40%	=	1,728
5	4,320 – 1,728	=	2,592	×	40%	=	1,037 (rounded) 592

This method derives its name from the declining balance of depreciable cost.

Although $1,037 is the amount calculated, only $592 can be recorded as expense, so that scrap value of $2,000 remains.

Note that the constant rate is applied to the original cost in the first year, and then the original cost less depreciation expense taken in each prior year is added for

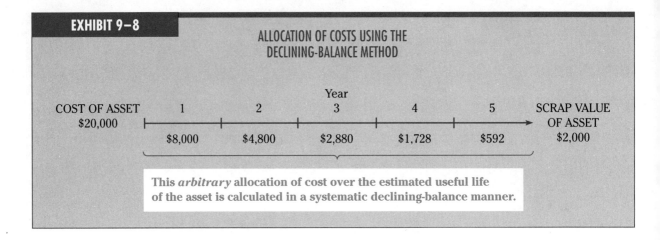

EXHIBIT 9–8

ALLOCATION OF COSTS USING THE
DECLINING-BALANCE METHOD

Year

COST OF ASSET $20,000	1	2	3	4	5	SCRAP VALUE OF ASSET $2,000
	$8,000	$4,800	$2,880	$1,728	$592	

This *arbitrary* allocation of cost over the estimated useful life
of the asset is calculated in a systematic declining-balance manner.

the next 4 years before the rate is reapplied. *Salvage value* was not subtracted from the original cost before applying the rate to determine depreciation. Note further, however, that the asset is not depreciated below its scrap value. In the fifth year, depreciation was determined to be $1,037. If that amount of depreciation were actually recorded, the **book value** (historical cost minus accumulated deprecia- tion) of the asset would be reduced to $1,555 ($2,592 − $1,037), which is below its salvage value. The amount of depreciation expense to be recorded in the last year is an amount that reduces the book value to reflect the salvage value. The book value at the end of the fourth year was $2,592; therefore, the depreciation in the fifth year amounts to $592.

Exhibit 9-8 illustrates the arbitrary method of allocating costs in the declining- balance method.

Q6: Cost allocation
and IRS

Internal Revenue Code   Prior to 1950, straight-line depreciation was the only accept- able method for computing depreciation for both the Internal Revenue Service and financial accounting. Starting in the early 1950s, Congress began building incentives into the tax code that were designed to promote investment. The tax code began to permit the use of accelerated methods of depreciation. Both sum-of-the-years'- digits and declining-balance depreciation methods were allowed. When investment in business assets was lacking, tax laws made it enticing for corporations to invest in those areas. Over the years, the IRS allowed 200% declining-balance depreciation for certain assets, 175% for others, and 150%, 125% and 100% (straight-line) for still others. The accelerated methods also were applied to GAAP for the reason discussed earlier in this chapter.

Companies attempted to use the same method for both tax and financial report- ing to avoid the hassle of accounting for the difference. Starting in 1981 and again in 1986, the IRS began allowing even more accelerated depreciation methods. Under the new methods, useful lives and salvage values were ignored, and the IRS set up various categories to include all assets. For instance, there were 3-year, 5-year, 10- year, and 15-year assets (3-5-10-15). Companies were allowed to depreciate assets over much shorter periods than they intended to use the assets. The new methods did not result in a proper matching of revenue and expense. Hence, for financial reporting, the methods discussed so far are used in practice, while the methods prescribed in the Internal Revenue Code are used to determine an entity's tax liability.

The depreciation method in effect for assets purchased between 1981 and 1986 was referred to as **Accelerated Cost Recovery Systems (ACRS)** and approximated a 150% declining-balance method for the early years, and a straight-line method in the later years of an asset. Only a half-year's depreciation was allowed in the year of purchase, no matter when the asset was purchased. This provision is known as the *half-year convention.* The percentages allowed each year were stated in the code. For instance, property classified as 5-year was given the percentages 15%, 22%, 21%, 21%, and 21%. For the $20,000 asset used in the previous examples, the depreciation would be

Year	Calculation		Depreciation Expense
1	$20,000 × 15%	=	$ 3,000
2	20,000 × 22%	=	4,400
3	20,000 × 21%	=	4,200
4	20,000 × 21%	=	4,200
5	20,000 × 21%	=	4,200
Total			$20,000

Congress changed the rules again in 1986 for assets purchased in 1987 and afterward. This version is called the **Modified Accelerated Cost Recovery System (MACRS).** Again assets were classified as 3-5-10-15, and so on, and various percentages were assigned to the year classifications. The write-off for some assets was accelerated, while the period for others was lengthened. The percentages stated, for instance, in the 1986 law for a 5-year asset were 20%, 32%, 19.2%, 11.52%, 11.52%, and 5.76%. The new percentages approximate the results under the 200% declining-balance method, with the half-year convention. Note that 6 percentages are listed for a 5-year asset. That is because Congress extended the half-year convention to include another half-year's depreciation during the sixth year. For the $20,000 asset, the depreciation would be

Year	Calculation		Depreciation Expense
1	$20,000 × 20%	=	$ 4,000
2	20,000 × 32%	=	6,400
3	20,000 × 19.2%	=	3,840
4	20,000 × 11.52%	=	2,304
5	20,000 × 11.52%	=	2,304
6	20,000 × 5.76%	=	1,152
Total			$20,000

Note the similar results if the 200% declining-balance method is used assuming the half-year convention.

$$\text{5-Year Life} = 20\% \times 2 = 40\%$$

Year	Calculation		Depreciation Expense
1	$20,000 × 40% × 1/2	=	$ 4,000
2	16,000 × 40%	=	6,400
3	9,600 × 40%	=	3,840
4	5,760 × 40%	=	2,304
5	3,456 × 40% = 1,382 →		1,456 (to retain $2,000
Total			$18,000 salvage value)

As shown, the percentages prescribed in the tax law result in the same depreciation expenses as the 200% method until the fifth year. Under MACRS, businesses may still choose straight-line depreciation for tax purposes or a declining-balance method, so long as the amount of depreciation in any year is not greater than it would have been under MACRS.

DEPRECIATION METHODS COMPARED

Which of the various methods of determining depreciation should be used? Obviously, for tax purposes, a firm will use the method prescribed under the law rather than one that allocates the cost over a longer period of time. In the examples in the earlier part of this chapter, the depreciation in the first year under straight-line was $3,600 per year, while under MACRS it was $4,000 the first year, $6,400 the second, and $3,840 the third. That is a total of $14,240 in depreciation expenses under MACRS, and $10,800 under straight-line, or a difference of $3,440. Assuming a combined federal and state income tax rate of 40%, $1,376 ($3,440 × 40%) less in taxes would be paid during the first three years under MACRS. Of course that changes in the later years, but entities using the faster method of write-off can defer income taxes.

Q7: Matching revenue and expense

But which method results in the best matching of revenue and expense on the income statement? Of the three categories examined in this chapter—production, time-based straight-line, and time-based accelerated, all can be defended in terms of matching, given certain assumptions.

Production

The production method assumes that the more a machine is used, the faster it will wear out. The more the machine is used, hopefully the more revenue is being earned, and the more depreciation is being charged (matched) against that revenue. This sounds like a perfect match. The production method, however, is based on the assumption that an accurate estimate can be made of the units the machine is capable of producing. How many miles will the delivery truck cover before it must be replaced? How many barrels of oil are in the ground? How many ounces of gold are in the gold field? How many gadgets can the gadget-making machine produce before it must be replaced? Such questions about the assumption are endless.

Time-based Straight-Line

The straight-line method is by far the easiest to apply, being based on the assumption that each year of an asset's useful life benefits in equal amounts. Assuming that a delivery truck will last 5 years because it is driven approximately 20,000 miles per year, then straight-line depreciation results in a proper matching of revenue and expense on the income statement. But, what is the useful life of a delivery truck? an oil well? a gold mine? a gadget-making machine?

Time-based Accelerated

Two accelerated methods used for financial reporting were examined: the sum-of-the-years'-digits and the declining balance. At this level, comparing the advantages and disadvantages of the two methods is unnecessary, but to analyze matching, it helps to examine the two assumptions on which the accelerated methods are based. One is that an asset produces more revenue in the earlier years of its useful life, and, therefore, those years should be charged with more depreciation than the later years. The other assumption is that revenue is earned equally over the life of the asset, but repair and maintenance expenses increase as the asset ages. Assigning more of the asset's cost to the earlier years results in a more even matching of total operating costs (depreciation plus repair and maintenance) to revenue.

On the surface, it appears that an accelerated method results in a better matching than straight-line, but the problem of properly estimating the useful life still exists. For instance, compare the results under the double declining-balance method (DDB) with the sum-of-the-years'-digits method (SYD):

Cost of Asset						Scrap Value of Asset
$20,000	1	2	3	4	5	$2,000
DDB	$8,000	$4,800	$2,880	$1,728	$ 592	
SYD	6,000	4,800	3,600	2,400	1,200	

During the first three years of the life of the asset, 87% ($15,680 ÷ $18,000), of the cost of the asset was allocated to the income statement under DDB, while 80% of the cost of the asset was allocated under SYD ($14,400 ÷ $18,000). Was 87% or 80% of the asset's revenue-producing ability actually used up during the first three years? Or was it closer to 75%? 70%? 65%? Under straight-line depreciation, 60% of the cost of the asset would have been allocated to the income statement during the first 60% or three years of the asset's life. Which method gives the proper matching? It is clear this question has no real answer.

Depreciation is nothing more than an estimate, a compromise between the other two extreme alternatives: expense the entire cost of the asset in the year it is purchased, or record it as an asset and expense in the year the asset is sold.

Phantom Profits

Another problem affecting depreciation that accountants have been unable to solve is the changing purchasing power of the dollar through inflation and the resulting effect on net income. In matching depreciation costs with revenues in the income statement, revenues are stated in dollars that have this year's purchasing power, while depreciation costs are stated in terms of old dollars, that is, dollars that had a different purchasing power.

Assume a machine was acquired 10 years ago at a cost of $100,000 and that the identical machine would cost $200,000 today. During this 10-year period, the firm's selling prices have also increased proportionately. In recording current sales revenue and matching these with 10-year-old costs, the firm shows a larger net income than it would if no inflation had occurred. The reported net income includes two different components: the normal income from operations and an income from comparing old costs with current revenues—a *holding gain*. As noted in Chapter 8, this holding gain is referred to as phantom profits. Recall that income taxes are calculated on the total net income, which includes these phantom profits; therefore, income tax, in real dollars, is paid on phantom profits.

The subject of inflation and what can be done with the *stable dollar assumption* when the dollar is unstable will be dealt with more fully in Chapter 18.

OTHER DEPRECIATION ISSUES

Long-term Assets on the Balance Sheet

The objective of the depreciation process is that the appropriate allocation of cost be matched with revenues for net income determination. The resulting balance sheet valuation of long-term assets is a secondary consideration. What are the implications of this emphasis?

- Depreciation allocation methods are all based on estimates, and estimates are subject to error. Accordingly, the undepreciated cost, or net book value, shown on the balance sheet will be the result of an estimate. Therefore, why should accountants be particularly concerned about the balance sheet value of long-term assets?

- Depreciation for a time period varies considerably, depending on the allocation method used. Accordingly, the undepreciated cost shown on the balance sheet of a firm can also vary considerably. Equipment, in amounts calculated earlier in this chapter, would appear on the balance sheet at the end of Year 1 as follows:

	Straight-Line Method	Double Declining- Balance Method
Long-term Assets		
Equipment	$20,000	$20,000
Less: Accumulated Depreciation	3,600	8,000
Net Book Value	$16,400	$12,000

- Historical cost is the commonly used basis for recording and depreciating long-term assets; its popularity is based on the fact that it is an objectively determined amount.

Q8: Book vs. market value

- Some readers misunderstand the significance of the undepreciated cost shown on the balance sheet. The net book value tends to be viewed as an estimate of the value of the asset. Referring to the figures given, is the value of the asset $16,400 or $12,000? Neither. Readers must be aware that the amounts shown for long-term assets are simply the remaining original cost of the asset that has not been transferred to the income statement and matched against revenue. A simple five-word definition for depreciation is found in accounting literature: *depreciation is allocation not valuation.*

FINANCIAL STATEMENT DISCLOSURE

Q9: Long-term asset disclosure

Besides a long-term asset's original cost, accumulated depreciation, and net book value on the balance sheet, and depreciation expense in the income statement, what other information would be useful to the readers of the financial statements?

- First of all, the amount of depreciation expense *must be reported* on the income statement. It must not be included in such classification totals as operating expenses, selling expenses, or general and administrative expenses. This information is necessary for assessing the effect of cash flows on operations, as is explained in Chapter 17.

- If summaries are reported on the balance sheet, such as totals for Land, Building, Equipment, and Accumulated Depreciation, a separate schedule should report the amount of accumulated depreciation related to the various depreciable long-term assets.

- Since so many methods for determining depreciation are acceptable, the method used to arrive at the amounts must be disclosed either on the face of the financial statements or, preferably, in the footnotes to them.

PARTIAL-YEAR DEPRECIATION

Assets may be both purchased and sold during the accounting year. Should depreciation be calculated for a whole year in such a case? The answer depends on individual circumstances and corporate accounting policy. A number of practices can be chosen. One is to record half a year's depreciation regardless of when an asset purchase or sale occurs during the year. Another alternative is to calculate partial depreciation from the month of asset purchase or sale. In the case of an asset purchased June 7, for example, depreciation for seven months would be recorded if the corporate fiscal year coincided with the calendar year. If the asset purchase had been made June 17, then only six months' depreciation would be recorded. The general rule to be followed in this case is the recording of depreciation from the month of acquisition (June) if the asset was purchased during the first half of the month (June 7); depreciation would be calculated from the next month (July) if the asset purchase was made during the second half of the month (June 17). For problem-solving in this text, it is recommended that this practice be used.

The annual calculation of straight-line depreciation for the $20,000 machine with an estimated useful life of 5 years and an estimated salvage value of $2,000 can be contrasted with partial-year depreciation for Year 1. The corresponding journal entries are included.

Purchase Jan. 1	Purchase June 7	Purchase June 17
The depreciation is allocated among 5 years as follows: ($20,000 − $2,000) ÷ 5 years = $3,600 per year	The depreciation is allocated as follows: $3,600 per year × 7/12 months = $2,100	The depreciation is allocated as follows: $3,600 per year × 6/12 months = $1,800

Deprec. Expense—			Deprec. Expense—			Deprec. Expense—		
Equip.	3,600		Equip.	2,100		Equip.	1,800	
Accum. Deprec.—			Accum. Deprec.—			Accum. Deprec.—		
Equip.		3,600	Equip.		2,100	Equip.		1,800

This example shows the recording of partial depreciation when an asset is purchased. Partial depreciation also must be recorded when asset disposal occurs.

Other partial-year depreciation policies are used in practice. For instance, no depreciation is taken the year an asset is purchased, and a full year's depreciation is taken when an asset is sold. Another is just the opposite: a full year's depreciation is taken the year an asset is purchased, and no depreciation is taken the year an asset is sold. The decision is up to management when policy is set. Remember that the IRS, under MACRS, requires the half-year convention, which in effect adds an extra year to the depreciation process.

GROUP DEPRECIATION

The preceding examples discussed the calculation of depreciation for individual assets. In practice, depreciation is usually calculated on a group basis, particularly when the assets are similar. In this situation, a **group rate** is used; an average useful life is calculated and applied to the total asset cost. A group rate also can be calculated for a mixture of dissimilar assets. In this case, the rate is referred to as a **composite rate.**

The calculation of group rates can be complex and is beyond the subject matter of this chapter. Advanced accounting courses examine not only the methodology used to establish group rates, but also the ramification of having assets replaced before the expiration of their estimated useful lives.

Revision of Depreciation Charges

Q10: Revisions to useful life estimates

The useful life of an asset is estimated at the time an asset is acquired and, as is the case with any estimate, it is subject to considerable error. The following ledger accounts show estimated accumulated depreciation after 2 years:

Equipment		Accumulated Depreciation	
20,000			3,600
			3,600

Total accumulated depreciation is $7,200.

The machine that cost $20,000 had been estimated to have a useful life of 5 years and a scrap value of $2,000. At the end of the first 2 years, it was determined that the asset would have a useful life of 10 years, but that scrap value would amount to only $1,000. At the end of 2 years, the remaining undepreciated cost of the asset was $12,800 (cost of $20,000 − $7,200 accumulated depreciation to date). In fact, the proper accumulated depreciation should be $3,800.

	Revised Estimates	Original Estimates
Equipment Cost	$20,000	$20,000
Less: Revised Scrap Value	1,000	2,000
Amount to Be Depreciated	$19,000	$18,000
Estimated Useful Life	10 years	5 years
Annual Depreciation	$ 1,900	$ 3,600
Accumulated Depreciation for Two Years	$ 3,800	$ 7,200

An excessive amount of depreciation has been recorded in Years 1 and 2.

What is the proper accounting procedure for this situation? The accepted procedure is to leave unchanged the depreciation recorded to date and to revise the annual depreciation to be recorded over the remaining estimated life of 8 years. This method is easy to apply. The amount of depreciation to be recorded in each of the remaining years is calculated as follows:

Actual Book Value ($20,000 − $7,200)	$12,800
Actual Scrap Value	1,000
Undepreciated Amount over Remaining 8 Years	$11,800
Depreciation for Each of the Next 8 Years Is $11,800 ÷ 8 Years =	$ 1,475

Accordingly, $1,475 would be recorded as the depreciation expense in the current year and in each of the next 7 years. Obviously the difference between $1,475 and $3,600 recorded in each of the 2 preceding years is substantial; however, the over-charge of depreciation in the first two years is offset by an undercharge of depreciation in the remaining 8 years. (If accurate information had been available at the outset, each year would have had a depreciation expense of $1,900.)

All revisions of accounting estimates are handled in this manner. That is, the prior years are left as recorded, and only the current and future years are affected by the change.

When changes are made from one depreciation method to another, other methods are employed to record the change. These procedures are quite complicated and are studied in more advanced accounting courses.

DISPOSAL OF LONG-TERM ASSETS

The disposal of a long-term asset requires the elimination of both its cost and accumulated depreciation from the balance sheet. As discussed, partial depreciation must be recorded when an asset disposal occurs. The sale, or abandonment and trade-in of assets are discussed next.

Sale or Abandonment of Long-term Assets

When an asset has reached the end of its useful life it can be either sold or abandoned. In either case, the asset cost and accumulated depreciation are removed from the records, following the recording of any partial depreciation that may be appropriate.

Recall the calculation of straight-line depreciation for the $20,000 machine with an estimated useful life of 5 years and an estimated salvage value of $2,000. Assume that the general ledger accounts of the equipment and its related accumulated depreciation amount contain the following entries:

Equipment		Accumulated Depreciation	
20,000			3,600
			3,600
			3,600
			3,600
			3,600

When a fully depreciated asset is abandoned, or simply thrown away, the asset is written off. Any proceeds from a sale of the asset may be recognized as a gain or loss.

Assume that the same machine is sold at the end of the fifth year, when accumulated depreciation amounted to $18,000. Book value at this date was $2,000 ($20,000 − $18,000). Three different situations are possible.

Sale at Book Value		Sale above Book Value	
The asset is sold for $2,000. The journal entry to record the sale is		The asset is sold for $3,000. The journal entry to record the sale is	
Cash	2,000	Cash	3,000
Accum. Deprec.—Equipment	18,000	Accum. Deprec.—Equipment	18,000
Equipment	20,000	Gain on Disposal	1,000
		Equipment	20,000

Sale below Book Value

The asset is sold for $1,000. The journal entry to record the sale is

Cash	1,000	
Accum. Deprec.—Equipment	18,000	
Loss on Disposal	1,000	
Equipment		20,000

In each of these cases, the cash proceeds must be recorded (by a debit) and the cost and accumulated depreciation must be removed from the accounts. At this point the debits of the journal entry must equal the credits. A credit difference represents a gain on disposal; a debit difference represents a loss. The gain actually represents an adjustment for too much depreciation recorded over the life of the asset. If the asset was sold for $3,000, then the salvage value when the asset was placed in service should have been $3,000, rather than $2,000. The loss actually represents an adjustment for too little depreciation recorded over the life of the asset. If the asset was sold for $1,000, then the original salvage value should have been $1,000, rather than $2,000. But remember, depreciation expense is an estimate, an estimate of the useful life, and an estimate of the salvage value at the end of its useful life.

Disposals Involving Trade-in

Many times an asset will be disposed of by exchanging it in a **trade-in** for a newer model, and in other situations a trade-in of one type of asset for one of a completely different nature occurs, such as a parcel of land in exchange for a machine or a vehicle. The term used to describe an exchange involving an old model for a new model, whether it be a car, truck, or gadget-producing machine, is **similar.** When the assets in question are quite different from one another (land for truck), the term used is **dissimilar.** Different ways of recording similar and dissimilar exchanges exist for accounting purposes.

Q11: Similar vs. dissimilar exchanges

Exchanges involving similar assets are believed to be continuations of previous decisions and, therefore, no gain or loss should be recorded, while exchanges involving dissimilar assets are thought to be the end of a previous decision and the beginning of a new decision. Therefore, a gain or loss should be recorded, based on the success or failure of the old decision.

SIMILAR ASSETS

If the assets in question are the same (they don't have to be identical), then the new asset is recorded at an amount equal to the book value of the asset given up, unless a loss is indicated. The book value of the asset given up would include both the asset itself (original cost, less any accumulated depreciation taken during the asset's lifetime) plus any cash paid in the transaction. When cash is received in the transaction, the accounting becomes more complex—another topic for more advanced accounting courses.

By recording the transaction in this manner, no gain is ever recorded when exchanging similar assets. For example, refer to the example used throughout this chapter. The asset cost $20,000 and had a 5-year life and a $2,000 salvage value. Assume the asset was used for 5 years and then traded in on a new model of the same asset costing $25,000. The book value of the old asset is $2,000 ($20,000 −

[5 × $3,600]). If a $3,000 price reduction or **trade-in allowance** is granted, then the cash required would be $22,000 ($25,000 − $3,000). If the $25,000 cost is the true cash price, then there is a $1,000 gain on the trade-in ($3,000 − $2,000 book value). The new asset is recorded at an amount equal to the book value of the asset given up—a cash payment of $22,000, plus the old asset's book value of $2,000, or a total of $24,000. The journal entry to record the transaction would appear as follows:

Equipment (new)	24,000	
Accum. Deprec.—Equipment	18,000	
Equipment (old)		20,000
Cash		22,000

A gain was indicated in the transaction because the trade-in allowance was greater than the book value. If the trade-in allowance had been only $1,000, then a loss of $1,000 would be indicated. Under the rule for recording similar assets, the new asset would include the cash payment of $24,000 ($25,000 − $1,000), plus the book value of the old asset, $2,000, or $26,000. The new asset thus would be recorded at an amount in excess of its fair market value, and the journal entry would appear as follows:

Equipment (new)	26,000	
Accum. Deprec.—Equipment	18,000	
Equipment (old)		20,000
Cash		24,000

However, under the historical cost assumption, assets should never be recorded at an amount in excess of their fair market value, so when a loss is indicated, the loss is recorded, and the new asset is recorded at its fair market value. The journal entry to record the transaction would appear as follows:

Equipment (new)	25,000	
Accumulated Depreciation	18,000	
Loss on Trade-in	1,000	
Equipment (old)		20,000
Cash		24,000

When the exchange involves similar assets, gains are not recognized, but losses are recorded under the rule of conservatism.

DISSIMILAR ASSETS

If the assets in question are not the same, then the new asset is recorded at its fair market value, and a gain or a loss is recorded. Assuming the $3,000 trade-in allowance results in a $1,000 gain, the journal entry to record the transaction would appear as follows:

Truck (new)	25,000	
Accum. Deprec.—Equipment	18,000	
Equipment (old)		20,000
Cash		22,000
Gain on Trade-in		1,000

Assuming the earlier $1,000 trade-in allowance that resulted in a $1,000 loss, the journal entry to record the transaction would appear as follows:

Truck (new)	25,000	
Accum. Deprec.—Equipment	18,000	
Loss on Trade-in	1,000	
Equipment (old)		20,000
Cash		24,000

EXCHANGES AND THE IRS

The IRS rules for exchanges are worded differently for "like-kind" (similar) exchanges and dissimilar exchanges, but the results are the same as for financial reporting except for "like-kind" exchanges that indicate a loss. For tax purposes, the loss would not be recorded, and the journal entry to record the transaction for *tax purposes* would appear as follows:

Equipment (new)	26,000	
Accum. Deprec.—Equipment	18,000	
Equipment (old)		20,000
Cash		24,000

Because exchanges involving the receipt of cash are quite complex, they are discussed in more advanced courses.

DEPLETION OF NATURAL RESOURCES

Q12: Depletion vs. depreciation, amortization

Natural resources include timberlands, mines, oil wells, and natural gas deposits, to name a few. They are recorded in asset accounts at cost. These natural resources are sometimes referred to as *wasting assets,* because the resource in most cases is not renewable and, once extracted, the asset value is reduced. This expiration of the asset is recorded in the books as *depletion.* (Natural resources deplete, while nonnatural assets depreciate.) The journal entry usually takes the following form:

Depletion Expense—Mine	xxx	
Accumulated Depletion—Mine		xxx

Theoretically, the depletion becomes a part of the inventory cost, which includes labor and other costs of extracting the ore (overhead). Therefore, depletion is a part of the cost of goods sold on the income statement. On the balance sheet, Accumulated Depletion—Mine is deducted from the cost of the mine resource:

Gold Mine	$xx,xxx	
Less: Accumulated Depletion—Mine	xxx	$xx,xxx

The periodic depletion charge is usually calculated on a usage basis called *units of production.* A depletion cost per unit is multiplied by the number of units extracted in order to calculate the periodic depletion expense. For example, a mine having an estimated 100,000 tons of nickel would have a cost of $3 per ton if its cost less salvage value amounted to $300,000 ($350,000 cost − $50,000 salvage value). If 20,000 tons are extracted during the year, the depletion would amount to $60,000.

$$\frac{\$350,000\,\text{Cost} \; - \; \$50,000\,\text{Salvage Value}}{100,000\,\text{Tons}} = \$3\,\text{per Ton} \times 20,000\,\text{Tons}$$

$$= \$60,000$$

The depletion for the year would be recorded in the general journal this way:

Depletion Expense—Mine	60,000	
Accumulated Depletion—Mine		60,000

In the example, the output of the mine was measured in tons. Usually the marketing unit is used as the unit of production in calculating depletion expense—*board feet* of lumber, *tons* of ore, *barrels* of oil, and *cubic feet* of natural gas.

The IRS allows depletion to be recorded as a percentage of revenue derived from the sale of the natural resource. The more revenue generated from the resource, the more depletion may be taken for tax purposes. Potentially, more depletion expense could be recorded under this method than was paid for the property. An example would be to allow depreciation of $1,000,000 to be recorded on an asset with a historical cost of $100,000. Of course, the IRS allows percentage depletion as an incentive to encourage exploration in certain areas. Different percentages are allowed for different types of natural resources.

INTANGIBLE ASSETS

The long-term assets discussed so far are physical substances; a parcel of land, a building, a truck, an auto, a gadget-maker, and so on. Another category is **intangible long-term assets,** those not made of a physical substance. Many of these assets give the owner certain rights, such as patents, trademarks, copyrights, franchises, secret processes and leaseholds. Other intangibles, such as goodwill and organization costs, do not carry a specific right with the cost outlay, but still have a future benefit requiring the amount to be recorded as an intangible asset.

Accountants have the same problems with intangible assets as they do with tangible assets. A historical cost must be determined and the amount must be capitalized, then allocated to the income statement so as to match the cost of generating the revenue (expense) with the revenue. If these rights are purchased from someone else, the measurement problem in determining the cost does not exist. The intangible asset will be recorded at historical cost. But, in many cases, these intangible rights are acquired through internal research and development, consuming hundreds of thousands of dollars. Many of these projects never result in an obtainable right. The measurement question becomes: how much research and development costs (R and D) should be capitalized when some efforts result in rights to future use and some efforts result in no rights? The generally accepted approach is to *expense* all R and D in the period in which it was incurred. Thus the capitalized costs of intangible assets obtained through internal research include only those costs directly related to obtaining the right, such as filing with the government for a patent, copyright, or trademark.

Q13: Intangible assets with no useful lives

Once the cost of the right has been determined, then the accountant must estimate the useful life of that right. Since many of these rights have indeterminable lives (a copyright is valid for the life of the author plus 50 years!), the accounting profession has placed an arbitrary maximum useful life of 40 years on such intangible assets. Once the useful life has been established, the cost of the intangible asset is *amortized* (allocated) over its useful life, generally on a straight-line basis. Some specific intangible assets are examined next.

Patents

Patents are granted by the United States government to give the holder the right to produce and sell a particular product. The legal life of a patent is 17 years, and the patent cannot be renewed. New patents, however, may be obtained as the product under the old patent has been refined or improved. As long as no one else has refined or improved the original idea before the creator, the right may be continuous. One of the most famous patent rights disagreements settled not too long ago was the right given to Edwin H. Land for his picture-in-a-minute camera, the Polaroid. Over the years the Polaroid Corporation refined and improved the camera and the process to include color and much shorter developing times, along with higher quality film and many other advancements. Kodak, on the other hand, had to wait until the original black-and-white Polaroid patent had expired before it could enter the market. The debate was not settled until Kodak was forced to stop selling not only its instant color camera, but also its film for the cameras that already had been sold. In fall 1990 Polaroid was awarded $909 million; it sought $12 billion.

Patents can be powerful tools, yet also can become totally worthless long before their 17-year legal lives are over. Because of changes in technology and the marketplace, patents are usually amortized over a much shorter period of time than their legal lives.

When recording amortization for an intangible asset such as a patent, the credit is usually recorded in the *asset* account rather than in an accumulated amortization account (similar to accumulated depreciation). Since tangible long-term assets are usually sold or traded at some point in time, it is important to maintain the original cost in the accounts. In most cases, however, it is not necessary to maintain the original cost of an intangible asset. An accumulated amortization account may or may not be used for an intangible asset when recording annual amortization. If an accumulated account is not used, the journal entry appears as follows:

Patent Amortization Expense	XXX	
Patents		XXX

Q14: Patents and court costs

If an entity is involved in a patent infringement suit on a patent it owns, all legal costs incurred in successfully defending the patent should be capitalized and amortized over the remaining life of the patent. If the suit is unsuccessful, all legal costs should be expensed, and any unamortized costs remaining on the balance sheet should be recorded as a loss.

Copyrights

A **copyright** is another intangible asset that confers on the holder an exclusive legal privilege: in this case, the federal government grants control over a published or artistic work for the life of the artist and 50 years afterward. This control extends to the reproduction, sale, or other use of the copyrighted material.

While the cost to obtain a copyright is minimal, the purchase of a copyrighted work can be substantial. Purchased copyrights are recorded at cost; this cost is amortized over the estimated useful life of the copyright, which is often less than its legal life. As with patents, the costs of any successful copyright infringement lawsuits or out-of-court settlements are added to the cost of the asset and amortized over its remaining useful life.

Trademarks

A **trademark** is a symbol or a word used by a company to identify itself or one of its products in the marketplace. Symbols are often logos printed on company stationery or displayed at company offices, on vehicles, or in advertising. Well-known word examples are Coke and Pepsi. The right to use a trademark can be protected by registering it with the government. Normally a trademark does not diminish in value through the passage of time or usage, but is affected by its success or lack of success. Trademarks are usually carried at cost and as intangible assets are amortized over 40 years or less.

Franchises

A **franchise** is a legal right granted by an entity or a government to sell particular products or to provide certain services using a specific trademark or trade name in a given territory. In return for the franchise, the franchisor often pays a fee that constitutes the franchise cost. McDonalds is one example of a franchised fast-food chain. The right to manufacture and sell Coke is another example.

Another example of a franchise is one granted by government for the provision of certain services within a given geographical location: for example, television stations authorized by the Federal Communications Commission, telephone services authorized in a particular state or county, or garbage collection authorized within a given community.

As with patents and copyrights, the cost of a franchise should be amortized over its useful life. In addition to the payment of a franchise fee that is capitalized, a franchise agreement usually requires annual payments. These payments, when incurred, are considered operating expenses.

Secret Processes

Secret processes or formulas or other such licenses also may have some costs that must be capitalized. Remember, however, costs associated with *developing* the process, unless incurred outside the company, are considered R and D and must be expensed. These costs should be amortized over a period not to exceed 40 years. Real World Example 9-1 illustrates how important a secret process can be to an entity.

Goodwill

What is goodwill? Good question. **Goodwill** is the most intangible of all intangible assets. It can mean that the entity has a good geographical location, a good employee–employer relationship, a good product, a secret process, and so on. Goodwill is seen as a composite of all of these and other factors that individually cannot be valued. Under GAAP, goodwill is not recorded unless it is purchased. About the only way goodwill can be purchased is if one going concern buys another going concern. Then, if the price paid exceeds the fair market value of all the assets less assumed liabilities (net assets), goodwill is measured by the difference.

REAL WORLD EXAMPLE 9-1
The Coca-Cola Secret

THE Coca-Cola Company says the secret formula for its cola flavoring ingredients is kept in a bank vault, which can be opened only by a vote of the board of directors. The formula for the soft drink long known by its trademark "Coke," the company adds, is known by only two senior chemists who are currently active at Coca-Cola (and apparently by one who has retired).

Early in 1985, in a brave marketing move, the company announced that it was discontinuing production of Coca-Cola and would replace it with a new Coke. This move followed several months of heatedly aggressive advertising campaigns by Coca-Cola and its competitors. One month after launching this new cola, the company changed once more in response to a massive consumer-testing effort; this time, it announced plans to bring back the former soft drink and market it under the name "Coca-Cola Classic," while retaining the new Coke as its flagship brand.

What's in that cola bottle? To start with, it apparently contains 99.8 percent water and sugar. After that, the mystery begins. The name "Coca-Cola" itself gives the best clue to the drink's principal flavoring ingredients, the coca leaf and the cola nut. In addition, the formula contains a complex blend of flavors and additives, with none standing out as a distinctive taste.

A modest amount of research turned up the following putative recipe for Coca-Cola Classic, which the company declines to confirm or dispute but which outside experts find reasonable:

Water, sugar, caramel (for coloring), caffeine, phosphoric acid, cinnamon, nutmeg, vanilla, glycerin, lavender, lime juice, other citrus oils, and fluid extract of guarana (which comes from the roasted, chestnut-like seed of a Brazilian tree, and contains caffeine and tannin).

Finally, there is the so-called secret ingredient, "merchandise No. 5": three parts coca leaves (with the cocaine removed) to one part cola nut.

In the late 1800s, Coke apparently contained a trace of cocaine, left over in the coca leaf after the "decocainizing" process. Shortly after 1900, however, the removal of cocaine from the leaf came under government supervision and, ever since, the drink has had to stand on its own as a pick-me-up.

Today, the coca flavoring for both colas is said to be extracted from coca leaves imported by the Stepan Chemical Company's Maywood, N.J., division. The cocaine, some 2000 to 3000 lb. a year, is reportedly sold for medicinal uses.

Whatever the ingredients, they remain Coca-Cola's secret—and the life blood of the corporation.

Editor's note: In 1988 a Coca-Cola Company spokesperson, Randy Donaldson, acknowledged that the coca leaf is used in the soft drink, but that it does not have cocaine in it and it is all strictly overseen by regulatory authorities.

If goodwill is recorded, then it must be amortized over the period of its expected benefit, not to exceed 40 years.

The subject of goodwill in business combinations (one firm buying a controlling interest in another) is further developed in Chapter 15.

Organization Costs

Organization costs are those incurred to incorporate or to establish another type of business organization. The period over which an entity will benefit from these costs is unlimited. Therefore, given the 40-year rule for intangibles, organization costs should be allocated over a period not to exceed 40 years. However, the IRS allows organization costs to be written off over a period not less than 60 months, so usually organization costs are amortized over 5 years.

Leases

The usual lease gives the lessee the right to occupy or use the property for the next month, or the next year, depending on the terms. In many cases, however, the lessee gains the same rights as the lessor in the transaction. When this happens, the lessee and the lessor treat the transaction as a purchase or a sale. This becomes quite complex, and is treated in more advanced accounting courses.

LEASEHOLDS
If a lessee makes an up-front payment to the lessor to secure a lease, a **leasehold,** this amount must be capitalized and amortized over the life of the lease.

LEASEHOLD IMPROVEMENTS
Even if the lessee does not gain the same rights as the lessor, if the lessee makes **leasehold improvements** to the property that will revert to the lessor at the end of the lease, that amount must be capitalized and amortized over the life of the lease, or the life of the improvement, if shorter.

Development of Software

As with a patent, the development of software for a computer application requires a material cost outlay. However, under GAAP, the cost of developing the software, an intangible asset, must be written off, and only the direct cost of licensing and marketing the software should be capitalized and written off over its estimated useful life.

CHAPTER REVIEW

1   What costs are included in the determination of the historical cost of a long-term asset? (pp. 408–10)

> All costs incurred in getting the asset to a point where it is operational are included in the historical cost. This would include the purchase price, less any discounts, plus freight, installation, and testing.

2   If an entity constructs its own assets, should the historical cost be recorded as total cost incurred, or the cost of purchasing such an asset? (p. 410)

> Only the actual cost of production should be included in the cost of self-constructed assets, unless this cost exceeds what would have been paid if the asset had been purchased from someone else. If the total production cost is less than the outside cost, then the asset should be recorded at actual cost.

3   After a long-term asset is placed in service, are any cash outflows ever added to the asset account, thereby increasing the historical cost? If so, what cash outflows are added, and which are expensed? (pp. 410–11)

> If a cash outflow is made that increases the operational efficiency (betterments) or the useful life of the asset (extraordinary repairs) after it is placed in service, these costs should be added to the asset. All other cash outflows should be expensed.

4 Differentiate between production-based and time-based depreciation methods. (pp. 413–14)

Production-based methods ignore the passage of time and instead determine the estimated number of units an asset is capable of producing, such as total miles on a truck. Time-based methods ignore production units such as number of miles and determine the estimated life of the asset in terms of years.

5 What is the primary purpose of recording depreciation? (pp. 413–14)

The primary purpose is simply to allocate the cost of a long-term asset over its useful life. No attempt is made to determine the decline in value of the asset. Depreciation is recorded *because* an item declines in value and will not last forever. If the asset will last forever (land), no depreciation is recorded. Depreciation is allocation, not valuation.

6 Are the methods of cost allocation used for financial reporting also accepted by the Internal Revenue Service? (pp. 418–20)

The IRS accepts methods only if they do not result in a faster write-off of the asset's cost. The IRS specifies that MACRS be used for assets purchased after 1986.

7 Does one method of recording depreciation result in a better matching of revenue and expense on the income statement? (pp. 420–21)

Depreciation is an estimate and by definition allows for errors. If more revenue is earned in the first years of an asset's life than in the last years, then an accelerated method will result in a better matching than straight-line. If the units produced by an asset fluctuate materially over its lifetime, then the production method will give a better matching. If revenue remains constant and repairs are minor during the life of the asset, then straight-line results in a good matching.

8 Does the book value of a long-term asset represent its estimated market value? Explain. (p. 422)

Depreciation is allocation, not valuation. The book value of a fixed asset is nothing more than the undepreciated portion of its historical cost. The market value of an asset is influenced by many factors, such as supply and demand, the condition of the asset, and the age of the asset, to name a few.

9 What information regarding long-term assets should be disclosed in the financial statements? (pp. 422–23)

Aside from the original cost and accumulated depreciation on the balance sheet, and depreciation expense on the income statement, the method used to determine depreciation must be disclosed, along with management's policy regarding partial-year depreciation.

10 Once a useful life has been estimated for a particular asset, is it possible to make revisions to that estimate in future years? (pp. 424–25)

Changes to the estimated useful life of an asset are made quite often. Accountants could go back and revise depreciation taken in the past but they have decided to simply allocate the remaining depreciable cost over the new estimate of the remaining useful life.

11 Why do accountants differentiate between exchanges involving similar and dissimilar assets? (p. 426)

Exchanges involving similar assets are believed to be continuations of previous decisions and, therefore, no gain or loss should be recorded, while exchanges involving dissimilar assets are thought to be the end of a previous decision and the beginning of a new decision. Therefore, a gain or loss should be recorded, based on the success or failure of the old decision.

12 Is there a conceptual difference among the following terms: depreciation, depletion, and amortization? (pp. 428–29)

No. All of the terms pertain to the allocation of a long-term asset over its useful life. Depreciation is used for tangible assets, while amortization is used for intangible assets, and depletion is used for natural resources.

13 Should intangible assets with indeterminable useful lives simply remain on the balance sheet with no allocation of revenue to the income statement? (pp. 429–30)

No. Although the useful life of intangible assets cannot be determined, revenue should still be charged with the portion of the cost. Therefore, an arbitrary period not to exceed 40 years is assumed for assets with indeterminable lives.

14 If a patent has been issued to you, and later you spend $10,000 in court defending your right, should the payment be recorded as legal expense? (p. 430)

It depends on whether you were successful or not. If you were successful, the fees should be capitalized and amortized over the remaining life of the patent. If you were unsuccessful, the patent should be written off as a loss and the legal fees included in the loss account.

KEY TERMS

Accelerated Cost Recovery Systems (ACRS) (p. 419)   The method of depreciation prescribed by the IRS starting in 1981. Depreciable assets are assigned to useful life groups based on their nature. Various percentages then were assigned to the years. The amount of depreciation approximated the results obtained under the 150% declining-balance method.

amortization (p. 413)   The process of allocating the cost of an intangible asset to each accounting period receiving benefit from that asset.

betterment (p. 410)   A capital expenditure that increases the operational efficiency of a long-term asset without extending its useful life.

book value (p. 418)   A term applied to the difference between the historical cost of a long-term asset and the total amount of accumulated depreciation.

capital expenditures (p. 408)   Cash outflows related to long-term assets that increase the operational efficiency of the asset, or extend its useful life. They include the asset cost, less applicable cash discounts.

capitalize (p. 408)   To record a cash outflow as an asset rather than as an expense. The term is used in this chapter in connection with capital expenditures applied to the asset cost.

composite rate (p. 424)   A depreciation rate applied to a group of related but different assets, rather than depreciation calculated on each asset.

copyright (p. 430)   The exclusive right granted by the federal government to publish a literary or artistic work. The right exists for the lifetime of the author plus 50 years.

depletion (p. 410)   The allocation of the cost of a natural resource to each accounting period receiving benefit from that resource.

depreciable cost (p. 416)   The portion of the cost of an asset to be allocated over its useful life; determined by subtracting the salvage value of the asset from its original cost.

depreciation (p. 412)   The allocation of the cost of a tangible long-term asset to each accounting period receiving benefit from that asset.

dissimilar (p. 426)   A term applied to transactions that involve the trade-in of one asset for another. If the assets are not related to one another, such as a parcel of land for a truck, the exchange involves *dissimilar assets*.

double declining-balance depreciation (p. 417)   A depreciation method that assigns a greater amount of asset cost to the earlier years of an asset's useful life and lesser amounts to the later years. The method uses a constant rate applied to a declining base. The rate is twice the straight-line rate, and the declining base is the book value of the asset at the beginning of the accounting period. Also referred to as *200% declining balance*. Extensions of the method include 175%, 150% and 125%.

extraordinary repair (p. 410)   A cost outlay that extends the useful life of a depreciable asset. The amount should be debited to the Accumulated Depreciation account, thereby reducing the book value of the asset allocated over its remaining useful life. The Accumulated Depreciation account, rather than the asset account, is debited, since the extraordinary repair is thought to be a reduction of estimated depreciation taken in past years.

fair market value (FMV) (p. 410)   The actual cash selling price of a new asset considered when trading in an old asset for a new one.

franchise (p. 431)   A legal right to render a service or to produce a good under a specific trademark or trade name.

goodwill (p. 431)   The value attached to the ability of an entity to make superior earnings as compared with other entities in the same industry. Goodwill is not recognized in the accounts unless it is purchased, generally arising when one corporations buys another at an amount in excess of the fair market value of the assets less the liabilities of the entity purchased. When goodwill is recorded, its cost is amortized over a period not to exceed 40 years.

group rate (p. 424)   A depreciation rate applied to a group of similar assets, rather than depreciation calculated on each asset.

intangible long-term assets (p. 429)   Long-term assets that are not physical substances, such as patents. Their cost is amortized over the accounting periods receiving benefits from the assets, but not over a period exceeding 40 years. *Straight-line amortization* is generally used.

leasehold improvements (p. 433)   Improvements made to leased property that will revert back to the lessor at the end of the lease. Classified as an intangible asset, the cost is amortized over the life of the lease or the life of the improvement if it is less than the life of the lease.

leaseholds (p. 433)   A payment made at the beginning of a lease in order to secure the lease. Classified as an intangible asset, the amount is amortized over the life of the lease.

Modified Accelerated Cost Recovery System (MACRS) (p. 419)   The method of depreciation prescribed by the IRS starting in 1987. Depreciable assets are assigned to useful-life groups based on their nature. Various percentages then are assigned to the year divisions. The amount of depreciation approximates the results obtained under the 200% declining-balance method.

natural resources (p. 428)   Also referred to as *wasting assets* and nonrenewable assets, they include such resources as oil, natural gas, timber, gold, and so on.

organization costs (p. 432)   Costs incurred during the process of incorporation. These costs are considered an intangible asset and should be amortized over a period not to exceed 40 years. Organization costs are generally amortized over a much shorter time such as the 5 years allowed by the IRS.

patent (p. 430)   A 17-year exclusive right granted by the federal government to an inventor to produce and sell a product.

production depreciation (p. 413)   A method of cost allocation related to number of units produced rather than to a period of time.

revenue expenditures (p. 411)   Cash outflows related to long-term assets that do not increase the operational efficiency of the asset or extend its useful life. Revenue expenditures are recorded as expenses in the year they are incurred.

salvage value (p. 413)   The estimated value of a long-term asset at the end of its useful life.

similar (p. 426)   A term applied to transactions that involve the trade-in of one asset for another. If the assets are related to one another, such as a truck for a truck, the exchange involves *similar assets*.

straight-line depreciation (p. 414)   A method of depreciation that allocates the cost of long-term assets to equal time periods rather than to units produced.

sum-of-the-years'-digits depreciation (p. 416)   An accelerated method of depreciation that allocates more of the asset's cost in the earlier years of its useful life than the later years. It is a declining rate expressed as a fraction applied to a constant base. The denominator of the fraction is the sum of the years in the useful life, and the numerator is the years of life in reverse order.

tangible long-term assets (p. 412)   Long-term assets that have physical substance, such as land, buildings, and equipment.

time-based depreciation (p. 414)   Depreciation methods that assign portions of an asset's cost to years rather than to units produced.

trade-in (p. 426)   A term used to describe an exchange of one asset for another, either similar or dissimilar.

trade-in allowance (p. 427)   A reduction in the cash price when an old asset is exchanged for a new one.

trademark (p. 431)   A legal right granted by the federal government to use a symbol or a word to identify a company or one of its products or services.

useful life (p. 408)   The estimated period during which an entity expects to benefit from the use of a long-term asset.

SELF-TEST QUESTIONS FOR REVIEW   (Answers are at the end of this chapter.)

Q5

1. The purpose of depreciation is to
   (a) determine an estimated remaining value of the asset for balance sheet purposes.
   (b) estimate the decline in usefulness of the asset during the current year.
   (c) allocate the cost of a long-term asset over its estimated useful life.
   (d) estimate the value of the asset in the used equipment market.

Note: Use the following information for questions 2–5: an asset is purchased for $18,000, with a 5-year life and a $3,000 salvage value.

Q4

2. Depreciation for the first year using straight-line depreciation would be
   (a) $5,000
   (b) $3,000
   (c) $7,200
   (d) $3,600

Q4

3. Depreciation for the first year using sum-of-the-years'-digits depreciation would be
   (a) $5,000
   (b) $3,000
   (c) $7,200
   (d) $3,600

Q4

4. Depreciation for the first year using double declining-balance depreciation would be
    (a) $5,000
    (b) $3,000
    (c) $7,200
    (d) $3,600

Q6

5. Depreciation for the first year using MACRS would be
    (a) $5,000
    (b) $3,000
    (c) $7,200
    (d) $3,600

Q11

6. When an asset is traded in on a new similar asset, the new asset is recorded at an amount equal to
    (a) the fair market value of the old asset.
    (b) the fair market value of the new asset.
    (c) the amount of cash paid in the transaction.
    (d) the book value of the old asset plus the amount of cash paid.

Q12

7. Which term is used to describe the allocation of the cost of a natural resource over its estimated useful life?
    (a) Depreciation
    (b) Amortization
    (c) Depletion
    (d) Assignment

DEMONSTRATION PROBLEM

A truck was purchased by Eric's Transportation, Inc., on January 1, 19X3. In addition to the purchase price of $20,000, Eric also had a two-way radio installed at a cost of $500, replaced the original bumpers in trade with heavy duty ones at a net cost of $700, and had pinstripes and his business logo painted on each side of the truck at a cost of $400. Eric estimates that the truck will last 4 years and have a salvage value of $3,600 at the end of the 4-year period.

Required

1. Prepare the journal entries necessary to record the purchase of the truck and the additional expenses paid for equipment and painting.

2. Determine depreciation under the following methods for the years 19X3 and 19X4, assuming Eric's business year-end is December 31:

    (a) Straight-line
    (b) Double declining-balance (DDB)
    (c) Sum-of-the-years'-digits (SYD)

3. Prepare journal entries to record the sale of the truck on June 30, 19X5, for $13,000, assuming straight-line depreciation was used.

4. Assume that the old truck was traded in January 1, 19X6, for a new truck, instead of being sold, and that straight-line depreciation was used. The new truck had a cash selling price of $28,000, and a $10,000 trade-in allowance was given for the old truck. Prepare the journal entries.

SOLUTION TO DEMONSTRATION PROBLEM

1. All of the additional costs are considered part of the cost of the truck, so the summary entry would appear as follows:

Truck	21,600	
Cash		21,600

Assuming that the radio, bumpers, and paint job involved three different businesses, four separate entries to the truck account and the cash account would be made to record the purchase.

2.

		19X3	19X4
(a)	Straight-line	$ 4,500	$4,500
(b)	DDB	10,800	5,400
(c)	SYD	7,200	5,400

(a) $21,600 - $3,600 = $18,000/4 = $4,500
(b) 4 years = 25% × 2 = 50%; $21,600 × 50% = $10,800
     $21,600 - $10,800 = $10,800; $10,800 × 50% = $5,400
(c) 1 + 2 + 3 + 4 = 10; $21,600 - $3,600 = $18,000 × 4/10 = $7,200
     $21,600 - $3,600 = $18,000 × 3/10 = $5,400

3.

Depreciation Expense	2,250	
Accumulated Depreciation		2,250
To record depreciation for 19X5 to June 30.		

Calculation

1/2 × $4,500 = $2,250

Cash	13,000	
Accum. Deprec.—Truck	11,250	
Truck		21,600
Gain on sale of truck		2,650
To record sale of truck on June 30, 19X5.		

Calculations

$4,500 + $4,500 + $2,250 = $11,250
$21,600 - $11,250 = $10,350 (book value); $13,000 - $10,350 = $2,650 (gain on the sale)

4.

Truck (new)	26,100	
Accum. Deprec.—Truck	13,500	
Truck (old)		21,600
Cash		18,000
To record January 19X6 trade-in of truck.		

Calculations

$4,500 × 3 = $13,500 (total depreciation)
$21,600 - $13,500 = $8,100 (book value)
$8,100 (book value) + $18,000 (cash) = $26,100

DISCUSSION QUESTIONS

Q9-1   The cost of an asset is said to be capitalized. What does this mean?

Q9-2   How does a capital expenditure differ from a revenue expenditure? Assume that you have purchased a minicomputer for business use; illustrate, using examples, capital and revenue expenditures associated with the computer.

Q9-3   CBCA, Inc., has purchased land and buildings for a lump sum. What does this mean? What is the acceptable manner of accounting for a lump sum purchase?

Q9-4   When one long-term asset is exchanged for another, how is the cost of the newly acquired asset determined?

Q9-5   Contrast the accounting for a betterment and an extraordinary repair. Give an example of each.

Q9-6   How does the concept of materiality affect the distinction between a capital and a revenue expenditure?

Q9-7   Long-term assets are often thought of as a bundle of services to be used over a period of years. The value of these services in the first year of the useful life of such assets, it is claimed, is not the same as in later years. Using a car as an example, indicate whether you agree or disagree.

Q9-8   Define tangible assets. How do they differ from intangible assets?

Q9-9   Distinguish among depreciation, depletion, and amortization. Give an example of each.

Q9-10   Assume that you have recently purchased a new sports car. Is a production or a time-based method preferable in recording depreciation? Why?

Q9-11   Why is salvage value ignored when depreciation is calculated according to the declining-balance method but not the straight-line method? Is this inconsistent? Why or why not?

Q9-12   What is the difference between the double declining-balance (DDB) method of depreciation and the sum-of-the-years'-digits (SYD) method?

Q9-13   How is the double declining-balance rate of depreciation calculated for an asset that is expected to have a 5-year useful life?

Q9-14   When referring to long-term-asset cost allocation, does GAAP stress balance sheet valuation or net income determination? Explain.

Q9-15   What are phantom profits in relation to long-term assets? Where do they come from?

Q9-16   The payment of income tax is often delayed through the use of MACRS, rather than a method that allocates the cost of the asset over a longer period, or more slowly over the same period. Is this delay equal to an interest-free loan? Will it be repaid?

Q9-17   Your friend is concerned that the calculation of depreciation relies too much on the use of estimates that are usually erroneous. Your friend believes that accountants should be precise. Do you agree that accountants are imprecise in the use of estimates for depreciation? Why or why not?

Q9-18   What is the proper accounting procedure to be followed when the previously estimated useful life of an asset is found to be erroneous? Why is more accurate information unavailable when long-term assets are initially acquired?

Q9-19   What is a trade-in? Explain whether one is or is not the same as the sale of an asset.

Q9-20   Why is the trade-in allowance, particularly in the case of a car, usually unrealistic? Why would a dealer give more trade-in allowance on a used car than it is worth?

Q9-21   What are wasting assets? Give some examples. Explain whether or not all assets are wasting.

Q9-22   Why is a declining-balance method unrealistic for natural resources? What method is permitted for income tax purposes?

Q9-23   What is a patent? Does a patent's useful life usually correspond to its true useful life? Why or why not? Support your answer with an example.

Q9-24   How does a copyright differ from a trademark? Give an example of each.

Q9-25   What is goodwill? Why is an entity's goodwill usually not recorded in its books?

DISCUSSION CASES

Case 1: J. R.'s Ranch

Q1

In the 1950s, Quaker Oats promoted its cereals with an unusual offer: the purchaser of a box of Quaker Oats was entitled to an inch-square piece of land in the Yukon. Now the same gimmick is being used to popularize not cereal but a serial. According to an advertisement in the *National Enquirer,* $25 will purchase a square foot of land in J. R.'s South Fork Ranch, the place where the television show *Dallas* was filmed.

"South Fork Ranch is mine," said J. R. Duncan, owner of 8,712,000 square feet of Texas soil, who was christened Joseph Rand Duncan, giving him the same initials as the popular *Dallas* character, J. R. Ewing. "By coincidence," said Duncan, "I have not been shot."

"We have actual deeds we send out with the documents to transfer the land to the new buyer," Duncan said, contrasting his land sale with the Quaker Oats giveaway, in which the individual deeds weren't formally registered.

Duncan said he was selling grazing land in the southeastern section of the ranch. Those who buy the land will have only limited rights to it. Although Duncan has built a separate entrance for the new ranch partners, there will be no picnic tables or kiddie rides. In fact, Duncan said he still intended to have his cattle graze the land. Duncan has also arranged to pay property taxes so the city clerk will not have to send thousands of assessment bills around the world.

As part of the deal for shooting on the ranch, Lorimar Productions, the makers of *Dallas,* have granted Duncan exclusive world-wide marketing rights for products carrying the South Fork name. Besides the obligatory T-shirts, belt buckles, and hatbands, Duncan has licensed the company to sell South Fork dirt and another gentleman to sell pieces of the fence.

"He's going to pay me to tear down my fence and cut it up in little pieces for wall plaques and desk weights," Duncan said. "And then he is going to build me a new fence. I'll tell you, I'm open to new ideas."

Source *The New York Times,* December 21, 1980, s. 3, p. 19. Copyright © 1980 by The New York Times Company. Reprinted by permission.

For Discussion

1. Would you pay $25 for a square foot of J. R.'s South Fork Ranch? Consider the following in your answer.
    (a) Your use of this land
    (b) Novelty value among your friends
    (c) Possible increase in value in the future as a collector's item
    (d) Other similar implications, including future land taxes applied to you if there were a default on tax payment

2. How much would Duncan receive for the land if all 8,712,000 square feet were sold? How would this compare to the probable current market value of this land?

3. If South Fork dirt is sold, would a part of the proceeds constitute a sale of land, depletion expense recovered, or something else? How would Duncan account for this? Prepare a few journal entries to illustrate your solution to this question.

4. (a) Is the original fence generally considered by accountants as part of the cost of the land, a land improvement, equipment, or something else? (b) If this land is sold as indicated in this article, what is the proper journal entry to record the sale? (c) If a new fence is going to be built on J. R.'s ranch by the purchaser of the old fence at no charge to Duncan, what is the proper journal entry, if any, to record the new fence? Discuss and illustrate with appropriate journal entries, if applicable. (d) Explain, using your knowledge of accounting theory, why the new fence would not be recorded, if you support this view.

5. What is your estimate of Duncan's probable success in
   (a) selling a square foot of J. R.'s ranch.
   (b) selling South Fork dirt.
   (c) Selling wall plaques and desk weights made from the fence on South Fork.

Case 2: Carpar

Q1, Q4, Q5, Q7, Q10

Carpar, a company producing auto parts, acquired a robot for its assembly line because it found its human workers could not perform at peak efficiency throughout the 8-hour day and produce uniform quality. At the same time that prices for its products were falling, costs were rising. The average worker cost Carpar $55,000 per year in salary and benefits. The company employs 12 people, 10 of whom are directly involved in production. Annual sales are worth about $1 million.

In February 1986, it bought the playback articulated robot to perform the coating operation, at a cost of $110,000. The robot is used on two 12-hour shifts and is operated by a worker with one year of experience. The robot's job is to take the work from the conveyor to the jig, attach it, and remove it when the coating is finished, a process that takes 25 seconds in all. Two other employees are in charge of robot teaching and maintenance. The maintenance cost of the robot is estimated to be $6,000 per year for the 10-year life of the robot. The robot can coat 3,200 pieces in 8 hours, as opposed to the 800 turned out by experienced workers. This result represents a 400% increase in productivity.

For Discussion

1. What would be the most appropriate method of depreciation to allocate the robot's cost over its full useful life?

2. Robots, which can be classified as long-term assets, can be depreciated over their useful life. Employees, who perform the same tasks, improve their work skills over time and receive remuneration according to their skill development, cost of living, and seniority. Compare the income statement bottom-line implications of using robots versus human employees.

3. Currently, major league baseball teams are allowed to depreciate their players' contracts over their expected playing careers for income tax purposes. Comment on this practice as it relates to GAAP.

EXERCISES

Straight-line vs. double declining-balance (Q7)

E9-1 Leopold, Inc., purchased a factory machine on January 1, 19X1, for $110,000. The machine is expected to have a useful life of 10 years with a scrap value of $10,000.

Required

Compute the depreciation for 19X1 and 19X2 using the

1. straight-line method.

2. double declining-balance method.

Lump sum allocation
(Q1)

E9-2   Vic Holdings, Inc., purchased a property including land and a building for $300,000. The market value of the land was $100,000 and the building, $300,000.

Required

Using these appraisals, prepare a journal entry to record the purchase.

Straight-line, declining-balance, sum-of-the-years'-digits (Q4)

E9-3   Tonka Corp. purchased a new car on January 1, 19X1, for $25,000. The estimated life of the car was 5 years, at which time the car would have a fair market value of $4,000.

Required

Calculate the depreciation for 19X1 and 19X2 using the

1. straight-line method.

2. sum-of-the-years'-digits method.

3. double declining-balance method.

Betterments and extraordinary repairs (Q3)

E9-4   Computer Pros, Inc., purchased an AT-compatible computer on January 1, 19X1. They estimated that it had a useful life of 3 years. In 19X2, Computer Pros made the following changes to the computer:

Mar. 1   Added a 150-meg hard disk at a cost of $1,000

Apr. 1   Added a new processing board for $2,000, which extended the life of the computer another 3 years

Required

1. Prepare a journal entry to record each of the above expenditures.

2. Discuss why the two transactions are treated differently in the accounting records.

Long-term asset cost
(Q1)

E9-5   Barbieri Corp. purchased a new laser printer to be used in its business. The printer, which was chosen from a number of alternatives, had a list price of $4,000, but Barbieri was able to purchase it for $3,250 The company expects it to have a useful life of approximately 5 years, after which time it will have a scrap value of $250. Barbieri is paying the delivery costs of $100, set-up and debugging costs of $300, and the costs of purchasing an appropriate table for $50. A sales tax of 10% was on the purchase price of the printer but not on the other costs.

Required

1. Calculate the total cost of the laser printer.

2. Barbieri asks you whether the straight-line or double declining-balance method of depreciation would be most appropriate for the printer. Make some calculations to support your answer, and compare the amounts you calculated.

3. Calculate the first year's depreciation, assuming the printer was purchased on January 2, 19X1, and the company's fiscal year ends December 31.

Revision of useful lives (Q4, Q10)

E9-6   Refer to the information in E9-1. At January 1, 19X3, Leopold revised its estimate of the machine's useful life from 10 to 6 years with no scrap value.

Required

Calculate the depreciation for 19X3 using the

1. straight-line method.
2. double declining-balance method.

Sale of long-term assets
(Q11)

E9-7   Refer to the information in E9-6. Leopold disposed of the machine at January 1, 19X4.

Required

Assuming that straight-line depreciation was used, prepare the necessary journal entries for the following cases:

1. The equipment was sold for $67,500.
2. The equipment was sold for $70,000.
3. The equipment was sold for $60,000.

Dissimilar exchange
(Q11)

E9-8   Simco, Inc., purchased a piece of land several years ago for $100,000. Now the company is going to exchange this land with a developer for equipment having a fair market value of $240,000. The land has a current fair market value of $200,000.

Required

Prepare the journal entry on the books of

1. Simco.
2. the developer.

Similar exchange (Q11)

E9-9   Refer to the information in E9-6. Leopold traded in the machine on a new model. The new model had a cash price of $150,000, but the company got a trade-in allowance of $100,000 on the old machine. The fair market value of the old machine was $95,000.

Required

Prepare the journal entry to record the trade-in on the equipment at January 1, 19X4 (include all depreciation to January 1, 19X4). Assume the straight-line method of depreciation is used.

Natural resources and
depletion (Q1, Q4, Q12)

E9-10   Eureka Corp. invested $1,000,000 in property and mineral rights, property estimated to contain 5,000,000 cubic feet of ore. Eureka spent $200,000 in developing the property to the point where mining could begin.

Required

Assuming that 200,000 cubic feet of ore was mined in the current year, and that 150,000 cubic feet of that ore was sold during the year, prepare the journal entries necessary to record the following:

1. The purchase of the property
2. The development costs
3. The production of the ore
4. The sale of the ore

Patents, cost,
amortization (Q14)

E9-11   A patent developed and registered to the Orange Corp. was sold to Fruit Exchange, Inc. Orange had spent $350,000 researching and developing the patent, and $10,000 in registration costs, including lawyer fees. Orange sold the patent rights to Fruit immediately on receiving notification that the patent was registered. The sales price agreed on was $975,000.

Required

1. Prepare entries for the books of Fruit Exchange to record the following:
   (a) The purchase
   (b) The amortization (Assume that a full year's amortization will be recorded in the year of acquisition.)
2. Prepare the entry for the books of Orange Corporation to record the sale of the patent.

Copyrights and amortization (Q13)

E9-12 Continental Corp. purchased the copyright from the author of a very successful text that they wanted to market on their own. The price was negotiated, and the rights were transferred to Continental on January 1, 19X7, for $50,000. The author was 43 years old when the copyright was registered to her.

Required
Prepare the journal entry to record the purchase of the copyright by Continental, and the entry to record amortization for the year 19X7.

PROBLEMS

Straight-line vs. sum-of-the-years'-digits (Q1, Q4, Q5, Q7)

P9-1 Mulberry Corp. purchased a business microcomputer on January 1, 19X3. The company year-end is December 31. The following information is available:

Cost	Useful Life	Salvage Value	Depreciation Method
$5,000	4 years	$1,000	(to be discussed)

Required

1. Calculate the depreciation expense for a 4-year period under each of these depreciation methods: straight-line and sum-of-the-years'-digits.
2. Since computers are subject to rapid changes in technology, the president asks you to explain what impact potential changes may have on the microcomputer's useful life. What factors should you cover in your explanation?
3. Which method of depreciation would you recommend in this case? Why?

Betterments and extraordinary repairs (Q1, Q3)

P9-2 On January 1, 19X2, Sanilac Construction Corp. purchased for $120,000 a new excavating machine for use in its business. The new machine was expected to have a useful life of 10 years with no salvage value. On January 2, 19X5, a device was added to the machine, increasing its output by 10%. The cost was $5,600. This addition brought no change to either life expectancy or salvage value. The machine was overhauled during the first week of January 19X9 for $36,000. The salvage value still remained the same, but the life expectancy was increased by 3 years.

Required
Prepare journal entries to record the

1. original purchase.
2. depreciation for 19X2 (straight-line; the year-end is December 31).

3. addition to the equipment.

4. depreciation for 19X5.

5. overhauling of the equipment.

6. depreciation for 19X9.

Various methods (Q4,
Q6, Q7)

P9-3   Liebman Trucks, Inc., purchased a delivery van on January 1, 19X3. The following
information is available:

Cost	Useful Life	Salvage Value	Depreciation Method
$11,000	4 years (consisting of 75,000 miles)	$2,000	(to be discussed)

Assume that this is a 3-year asset under MACRS and that the percentages are 33.33%, 44.45%,
14.81%, and 7.41%. The van was driven 20,000 miles in 19X3.

Required

1. Calculate the depreciation for 19X3 under each of the following methods:
    (a) Usage   (d) Double declining-balance
    (b) Straight-line   (e) MACRS
    (c) Sum-of-the-years'-digits

2. Compare the depreciation expense, accumulated depreciation, and net book value for
    19X3 for each of these methods:
    (a) Usage   (d) Double declining-balance
    (b) Straight-line   (e) MACRS
    (c) Sum-of-the-years'-digits

3. Which of these methods can be used for income tax purposes? Why?

4. Which method would result in the lowest income taxes paid in 19X3? Calculate the
    income tax saving in 19X3 if the income tax rate is 50%.

5. Which method results in the lowest income taxes paid in 19X6? Show details to support
    your answer. (Assume that the income tax rate is 50%.)

6. Is it fair to try to save on income taxes in 19X3?

Cost of the asset,
straight-line, revision of
useful life (Q1, Q10)

P9-4   The Oregon Co. purchased a machine on January 1, 19X6, for $23,000. Transpor-
tation charges paid by Oregon amounted to $600 and another $1,400 was incurred
for installation. The estimated salvage value of the machine is $1,000.

Required

1. Calculate the depreciable cost of the machine.

2. In journal entry form, record the depreciation each year of the expected life of the
    machine under the straight-line method (estimated life, 3 years).

3. On January 1, 19X7, Oregon changed the life estimate on the machine from a total of 3
    to a total of 5 years. Salvage value remains at an estimated $1,000. Calculate the depre-
    ciation that should be recorded in 19X7 and each year thereafter. The company used a
    straight-line method.

Nature of goodwill
(Q13)

P9-5   A bank manager, a friend of yours, discusses with you the matter of goodwill,
which appears so often in financial statements. She mentions that she does not
think that such an account should appear in the financial statements, particularly
since the rules for evaluation and presentation vary from one company to another.

Required

1. What is goodwill? Name some factors or situations that justify recording it.

2. Give the essential condition(s) that would justify showing goodwill in the financial statements.

P9-6

Part A

Trade of similar assets
(Q4, Q11)

Littleman Manufacturing, Inc., started business on May 1, 19X4. It commenced operations by signing a 20-year lease for a factory building. The year-end of the company is December 31. On May 5, 19X4, the company purchased equipment for $130,000. The equipment had an estimated useful life of 4 years, or a production of 100,000 units, with a salvage value of $10,000. The equipment over three years produced the following numbers of units: 19X4— 12,000; 19X5—30,000; and 19X6—20,000.

On January 4, 19X7, the company traded in all the original equipment on new equipment. The company traded in its old equipment and paid cash ($140,000) to receive delivery of the new equipment. The company had used the units-of-output (usage) method of calculating the depreciation on the manufacturing equipment. The fair market value of the original equipment was $60,000 at the date of the trade. The new equipment could have been purchased with no trade-in for $210,000.

Part B

Computing gain or loss
from fire (Q4, Q11)

On January 5, 19X5, Littleman Manufacturing, Inc., was able to buy a nearby warehouse for the storage of its finished product. The cost included land, $50,000; building, $300,000. The company signed a 10-year mortgage for $320,000 and paid the balance in cash. The building had a useful life of 50 years with no salvage value. On June 28, 19X9, the warehouse was totally destroyed by fire. Owing to a strike by the company employees at the time, the warehouse was empty and the company received $270,000 from the insurance company as settlement in full for the building. The building was depreciated on a straight-line basis.

Required

Prepare journal entries to record the transactions on the following dates:

1. May 5, 19X4 (Part A)   3. January 5, 19X5 (Part B)
2. January 4, 19X7 (Part A)   4. June 28, 19X9 (Part B)

ALTERNATE PROBLEMS

Straight-line vs. double
declining balance, pro-
duction (Q4, Q5, Q7)

AP9-1 Turner, Inc., a speculative mining organization, purchased a machine on April 1, 19X4. The following information is available:

Cost	Useful Life	Salvage Value	Depreciation Method
$40,000	3 years (consisting of 100,000 tons)	$4,000	(to be discussed)

The machine has an estimated life in production output of 100,000 tons. Actual output was Year 1—40,000 tons; Year 2—20,000 tons; Year 3—10,000 tons. The year-end of the company is March 31.

Required

1. Calculate the depreciation expense and the net book value at year-end for the 3-year period under each of these depreciation methods: straight-line, double declining-balance, and usage.

2. Assume that the machine is no longer useful at the end of 3 years and must be sold. Although depreciation has been recorded based on machine usage as calculated in number 1, the president believes that it could have been used to process an additional 30,000 tons. He fears that an excessive amount of depreciation has been charged against income during the 3 years, and that the company has issued incorrect financial statements. Do you agree? Why or why not?

Betterments, extraordinary repairs, fire loss (Q1, Q3, Q11)

AP9-2 On January 1, 19X1, Northern Construction, Inc., purchased new heavy-duty equipment and placed it in service. The cost to the company was $60,000. The equipment was expected to have no salvage value after a life expectancy of 10 years. On January 1, 19X4, a device was added to the equipment that increased its output by approximately 20%. The cost was $2,800. This addition brought no change to either life expectancy or salvage value.

The equipment was overhauled during the first week of January 19X8, for $18,000 cash. The salvage value still remained the same, but the life expectancy increased by 3 years. On July 1, 19X9, the equipment was a total loss following a fire. The insurance company arranged for settlement and paid the company $20,000.

Required

1. Prepare journal entries to record the
   (a) depreciation for 19X1 (straight-line; year-end is December 31).
   (b) addition to the equipment account after the January 2 addition.
   (c) depreciation for 19X3, 19X4, 19X5, 19X6, and 19X7.
   (d) overhauling of the equipment in January 19X8.
   (e) depreciation for 19X8.
   (f) fire loss and settlement on July 1, 19X9.

2. Post the appropriate part of these entries to the ledger accounts Equipment and Accumulated Depreciation—Equipment, and calculate the balance in each account.

Various methods (Q4, Q6, Q7)

AP9-3 Simon, Inc., purchased its first piece of equipment on January 1, 19X6. The following information pertains to this machine:

Cost	Useful Life	Salvage Value	Depreciation Method
$11,000	5 years	$1,000	(to be discussed)

As the chief accountant for the company, you are faced with making a choice of a depreciation method to be used.

Required

1. Calculate the straight-line and MACRS depreciation for 19X6, 19X7, and 19X8. Assume that the equipment is considered 5-year property; therefore, the rates for the first three years are 20%, 32%, and 19.2%.

2. Using the format provided, complete comparative partial income statements and balance sheets at December 31 for both the straight-line and MACRS depreciation.

Partial Income Statement	19X6	19X7	19X8
Net Income before Depreciation and Income Taxes	$30,000	$25,000	$35,000
Depreciation Expense	?	?	?
Income from Operations	$?	$?	$?
Income Taxes (50%)	?	?	?
Net Income	$?	$?	$?

Partial Balance Sheet			
Equipment	$?	$?	$?
Less: Accum. Deprec.—Equipment	?	?	?
Net Book Value	$?	$?	$?

3. Which depreciation method should be used for deferral of income taxes? Explain.

Cost of asset, straight-line, revision of useful life (Q1, Q10)

AP9-4 The Lamb Carpet Center purchased a cutting machine at the beginning of 19X4 for $46,000. Lamb paid additional charges of $1,200 and $2,800 for freight and installation, respectively. Salvage value was estimated at $2,000.

Required

1. Calculate the depreciable cost of the machine.

2. In journal form, record the depreciation for each year, using the straight-line method (estimated life, 3 years).

3. In January 19X5, Lamb revised the life estimate on the machine from 3 years to 5 years. Estimated salvage value remained at $2,000. Calculate the depreciation that should be recorded in 19X5 and each year thereafter. Use the straight-line method of depreciation.

Nature of goodwill and other intangibles (Q13, Q14)

AP9-5 In accounting, certain intangible assets are subject to the process of amortization, whereas others are not. Listed are three intangibles an accountant might encounter:

1. Trademarks

2. Patents

3. Goodwill

Required

Explain the accounting treatment you would suggest for each, incorporating in your answer reasons for the suggested treatment.

Revision of useful life of an asset (Q10)

AP9-6 On January 1, 19X1, Varas, Inc., purchased a machine for $30,000. The engineers had established a life duration for that machine of 20 years. The scrap value is estimated to be 10% of the original cost. On January 1, 19X8, experts were hired to review the expected life and scrap value of the machine. Here are the findings:

New Estimated Life	15 years
New Estimated Scrap Value	$6,000

Depreciation has not yet been recorded in 19X8. Assume that the straight-line method of depreciation is used.

Required

1. Calculate the book value of the machine at December 31, 19X7.

2. Calculate the undepreciated cost of the machine at January 1, 19X8, assuming that the straight-line method of depreciation is used.

3. Calculate the amount of depreciation expense to be recorded at December 31, 19X8, and prepare the necessary journal entry.

4. If the current replacement value of the machine is $51,000, comment on the existence of phantom profits in this company. Make some calculations to support your answer.

DECISION PROBLEMS

Problem 1

Newold, Inc., commenced construction of a new plant on July 1, 19X1. All construction activities were completed by March 31, 19X2, after which time the plant went into operation. The total cost incurred during the construction period included:

	(thousands)
Cost of Land (includes the cost of an old building on it)	$ 55
Engineering Fees	
Analysis of the subsoil	$ 8
Construction supervision	50
Analysis of the electrical system	30
Planning of a new production process (required in order to use new equipment that will be installed in the new building)	45
	$ 133
Subcontractor's Charges	
Demolition of the old building	$ 3
Wages and material (excluding landscaping)	531
Landscaping	4
	$ 538
Charges Included in the Company's Operating Accounts	
Wages of employees on construction site	$ 460
Construction materials	1,267
Taxes and interest (payable in advance, for the entire year commencing July 1, 19X1)	18
	$1,745

The company is to receive a government grant of $200,000 for having selected a recommended site as the actual location of the new plant.

Required

As controller of Newold, Inc., determine which of the above costs should be properly included in the cost of the new plant accounts. Briefly explain why you would include or exclude each cost item.

Problem 2

Jackson Mines Co., incorporated March 31, 19X1, had land bearing recoverable ore deposits, estimated by geologists to contain 800,000 tons. The cost of this land was $450,000, and it was estimated to be worth $50,000 after extraction of the ore. During this year, mine improvements totaled $17,500. Various buildings and sheds were constructed at a cost of $22,500. During the year, 35,000 tons were mined. Of this tonnage, 6,500 tons were on hand unsold on March 31, 19X2, the balance having been sold for $4.50 per ton. Expenses incurred and paid during the year, exclusive of depletion and depreciation, were as follows:

Mining	$84,000
Delivery	9,250
Administration	8,800

It is believed that buildings and sheds will be useful over the life of the mine only; therefore, depreciation should be recognized in terms of mine output.

Required
Prepare an income statement for the year ended March 31, 19X2.

Problem 3

Z Co. was incorporated on January 1, 19X3, and on that date purchased these assets:

Land	$100,000
Buildings	150,000
Equipment	75,000
Trucks and Automobiles	30,000

On December 14, 19X3, the president of Z Co. asks you for advice in selecting a realistic depreciation policy for the company. The president informs you that the subject has been discussed with the manager and the bookkeeper and that the following views have been expressed:

President   No depreciation should be provided for land and buildings, because the inherent increase in land values will more than compensate for any physical deterioration of the buildings. Equipment, trucks, and automobiles should be written off in the year of purchase in order to ensure that they will be purchased only in years when profits are sufficient to absorb the costs of such long-term assets.

Manager   No depreciation should be provided for land, because land is not used to earn profits. Buildings and equipment should be written off over the estimated useful lives of the assets—40 years for buildings and 10 years for equipment. Trucks and automobiles should be written off over a period of 3 years, since the company intends to trade them in for new ones every 3 years.

Bookkeeper   No depreciation should be provided for land, because few companies ever depreciate land and, therefore, any write-offs would not conform to GAAP. All other long-term asset costs should be written off by the declining-balance method, calculated on the following annual rates:

Buildings	8%
Equipment	25%
Trucks and Automobiles	35%

Required
What is your advice to the president of Z Co. as to the most acceptable depreciation policy for the company? Explain your comments on the validity of each of the views expressed by the president, the manager, and the bookkeeper.

ANSWERS TO SELF-TEST QUESTIONS

1. **(c)** Depreciation is allocation, not valuation.
2. **(b)** $18,000 − $3,000 = $15,000 ÷ 5 = $3,000
3. **(a)** $18,000 − $3,000 = $15,000 × 5/15 = $5,000
4. **(c)** 1/5 = 20% × 2 = 40%; $18,000 × 40% = $7,200
5. **(d)** $18,000 × 20% = $3,600
6. **(d)** When exchanges are made with similar assets, the asset received is recorded at the book value of the asset given up.
7. **(c)** *Depletion* is the term used to describe the allocation of the costs of natural resources over their useful lives.

PART II
FINANCIAL STATEMENT ANALYSIS PROBLEM

Turn to the excerpts (pp. 889–906) from the annual report of United Telecom (UT) for the year ended December 31, 1989, and answer the following questions:

1 According to the income statement, UT had discontinued some operations during 1987 and 1988.

    (a) What was the total gain (before tax) from the sale of the assets in 1988?
    (b) What was the total loss (before tax) from the sale of the assets in 1987?
    (c) Why would there be a tax effect when a loss occurs?
    (d) Why is information concerning discontinued operations reported net of tax?

2 The income statement for UT reports earnings per share (EPS) information.

    (a) What was the major cause for the decrease in EPS from 1988 to 1989?
    (b) Does this decrease represent a downturn in operating activities for UT? Explain.

3 Explain the comment found in note number 1 regarding cash: "At December 31, 1989 and 1988, outstanding checks in excess of cash balances of $155 and $161 million, respectively, are included in accounts payable."

4 Answer the following regarding Accounts Receivable:

    (a) Did the percentage of estimated uncollectible accounts increase or decrease from 1988 to 1989? Explain.
    (b) What reasons can you give for this seemingly material change?
    (c) Can you determine the method (income statement or balance sheet) that UT is using to determine its estimated uncollectible accounts?

5 What inventory method is UT using? Does your answer appear to contain a conflict? That is, can a company be using two different inventory methods at the same time?

6 Explain the comment in note number 1 regarding long-lived assets: "Generally, ordinary asset retirements and disposals are charged against accumulated depreciation with no gain or loss."

7 What depreciation method does UT use to record depreciation?

8 Does UT amortize intangible assets over their legal life? Explain. Do you think this is a reasonable policy?

PART III

FINANCING ACTIVITIES

The issuance of equity securities such as common stock, and the acquisition of long-term debt, comprise the financing activities of an entity. Equity financing is covered in Chapters 10, 11, and 12, while debt financing is covered in Chapter 13. Chapter 10 discusses how corporations use different types of equity instruments to obtain investment capital, and how these security transactions are recorded in the accounts.

Chapter 11 presents matters related to retained earnings and the distribution of retained earnings by means of dividends to the stockholders. Certain restrictions may be placed on retained earnings so dividends may not be paid. The restrictions are also investigated.

Chapter 12 examines equity financing from the point of view of noncorporate entities. Sole proprietors and partnerships also finance the entity through equity contributions, but the accounting is somewhat different from a corporate entity.

Chapter 13 discusses how entities obtain financing through long-term debt. As noted in Chapter 1, there must be a proper mix between debt and equity in order for an entity to operate most efficiently in regard to its owners. Bond issues are an important source of debt financing.

10 STOCKHOLDERS' EQUITY

CORPORATIONS may finance their operations through the issuance of shares of stock, or by borrowing on a long-term basis. Chapter 10 investigates the nature of a corporation, its structure, the nature of stock, and the various types of stock that may be issued. The components of stockholders' equity are identified and discussed, along with certain restrictions that may be placed on elements of stockholders' equity.

CHAPTER PREVIEW QUESTIONS

After studying Chapter 10, you should be able to answer the following questions:

1 What is meant by the limited liability characteristic of a corporation? Do any corporations have unlimited liability? Explain. (p. 459)

2 What are the rights of common stockholders? (p. 460)

3 Why do some common shares have a par value, while others have stated values and others have no value at all attached to them? (pp. 461–62)

4 What different classes of stock are available to investors in a corporation? Explain their differences. (pp. 462–63)

5 Are the rights of preferred stockholders the same as common? Explain. (pp. 462–63)

6 What are the various characteristics preferred stock might have? (pp. 462–63)

7 What is the difference between issued and outstanding stock? (p. 464)

8 What is meant by legal capital? Why is it important? (p. 466)

9 When shares of stock are issued for consideration other than cash, how is the transaction recorded? (pp. 466–67)

10 What is meant by a stock split? Why would a corporation elect to split the stock? (pp. 467–70)

11 When would the board of directors of a corporation want to put restrictions on the amount of retained earnings available for dividends? (pp. 470–72)

12 Are assets donated to a corporation recorded in the accounts? If so, how is the value of the asset determined? (pp. 472–73)

13 Is the market value of a share of stock the same as its book value? Explain. (pp. 473–74)

14 What accounting problems arise when shares of stock are sold on a subscription basis? (pp. 475–76)

THE CORPORATE STRUCTURE

The accounting equation expresses a relationship between assets owned by a corporation and the claims against those assets by creditors and stockholders. The accounting for assets and their financial statement disclosure was discussed in preceding chapters. The accounting for stockholders' equity is covered in this chapter. Corporate accounting for equity focuses on the distinction between the two main sources of stockholders' equity, illustrated in Exhibit 10-1.

These two basic components are discussed in detail in order to explain the main features of corporate accounting and the guidelines used by accountants for stockholders' equity disclosure.

Corporate Characteristics

The distinguishing characteristics of the corporation are that it is created by law, it has an unlimited life, it has limited liability, it can acquire capital easily, and it pays income tax on earnings.

CREATION BY LAW

In the United States, an entity can become a corporation under the laws of any of the fifty states. As noted in Real World Example 1-1 (Chapter 1) concerning incorporating in Delaware, some states have more favorable laws than others. In some countries, such as Canada, the federal government also may give life to a corporation. The laws of the fifty states differ in some respects, but most have the same basic underlying accounting rules and regulations. Although it is more difficult to form a corporation than other forms of the business unit (discussed in Chapter 12), the advantages far outweigh the disadvantages. Some of the more important advantages are discussed next.

UNLIMITED LIFE

A corporation has an existence separate from that of its owners. Individual stockholders may die, but the corporate entity continues. The life of a corporation comes

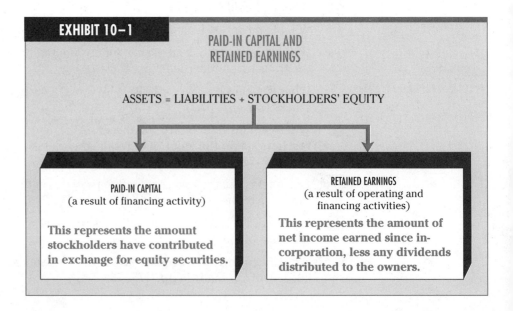

EXHIBIT 10-1

PAID-IN CAPITAL AND
RETAINED EARNINGS

ASSETS = LIABILITIES + STOCKHOLDERS' EQUITY

PAID-IN CAPITAL
(a result of financing activity)

This represents the amount stockholders have contributed in exchange for equity securities.

RETAINED EARNINGS
(a result of operating and financing activities)

This represents the amount of net income earned since incorporation, less any dividends distributed to the owners.

to an end only when it is dissolved, becomes bankrupt, or has its charter revoked. In general, it has many of the rights and responsibilities an individual citizen has. It can own property, for instance; it can sue and be sued.

LIMITED LIABILITY

Q1: Limited and
     unlimited liability

In the eyes of the law, a corporation is a separate, legal person. Since the corporation is viewed as such, the owners (stockholders) are not responsible for the debts of the corporation. Another way of stating this is that the owners are only liable for the amounts they have invested; they have *limited liability*. The corporate creditors cannot go after the individual assets of the owners. However, as will be shown in Chapter 12, it is possible for the creditors of a partnership or sole proprietorship to attach the personal assets of the owners, such as savings, homes, autos, and so on. Some businesses incorporated in countries that have been under British rule were required to have the word *limited* prominently displayed after the name of the corporation, signifying to creditors that the owners have limited liability.

In some corporations, stockholders have *unlimited* liability. These are collectively referred to as *professional corporations*. Up until about twenty years ago, professional people, such as accountants, lawyers, and doctors, could not incorporate, putting them at a disadvantage because of tax laws regarding pensions and other benefits granted corporations. Due to the nature of their work, professionals must be held responsible (liable) for their mistakes. Hence, the professional corporation was formed to allow professionals to take advantage of certain benefits granted to corporations without hiding behind the limited liability characteristic of corporations.

Some corporations exist solely for other benefits, such as the availability of pension plans and other tax benefits, rather than for the limited liability.

EASE OF ACQUIRING CAPITAL

A corporation is a multiple-ownership organization and *shares* are the ownership units. The issue of shares allows many individuals to participate in the financing of a corporation. Both small and large investors are able to participate because of the ease with which ownership can be transferred—shares are simply purchased or sold.

Of the many types of shares, differences exist with regard to voting rights, dividend rights, liquidation rights, and other preferential features. The rights of each stockholder depend on the class or type of shares held, and the amount of ownership by each stockholder depends on the number of shares he or she holds in relation to total shares outstanding. Through the issue and trading of shares on stock markets throughout the world, such as New York, American, Pacific Coast, Tokyo, London, and Toronto, large amounts of capital can be raised.

INCOME TAXES ON EARNINGS

Since corporations are considered persons in the eyes of the law, they are also persons in the eyes of the IRS. Corporate income tax rates in effect today range from 15% on incomes below $50,000 to 34% on incomes more than $335,000. In-between these two extremes, the rates are adjusted so that if a corporation earns more than $335,000, it pays federal income taxes of 34% on total earnings, even the first $50,000. With state income taxes, and in some situations even city income taxes, the combined tax burden for a corporation can easily amount to one-half of earnings. This tax effect plays an important part in most business decisions. Because corporate incomes are taxed, it has been said that there is *double taxation* of corporate profits. When dividend distributions are made from net income that has already been taxed, the dividends are taxable income to the stockholder receiving them. Therefore, if a corporation distributes 100% of its net income to its stockholders, the income is in effect taxed twice. If the stockholder is another corporation, parts of the tax code eliminate some, if not all, of this double taxation. At this level of accounting, it is enough to be aware that the tax burden of many corporations approaches 50%.

Aside from double taxation, the major disadvantage of the corporate form of ownership is government regulation. If the corporation is public, with shares traded on organized exchanges, it is regulated by the Securities and Exchange Commission (SEC) and another whole set of financial statements must be filed on forms provided by the SEC.

Rights of Stockholders

Ownership of a share of stock carries with it certain rights. Many times these rights are shown on the certificate issued by the corporation. Each share of stock must have the same rights as any other share within that class of stock. However, a corporation may have two, three, or even four classes of common stock, each with different rights attached to it. This chapter will discuss the general rights and privileges usually attached to a share of common stock. They are the following:

Q2: Stockholders' rights

1. *The right to vote each share.* Under the one share, one vote rule, stockholders receive the right to vote their shares in person at the annual stockholders' meeting. If they wish to do so, they may vote their shares by proxy: the company may solicit the votes of stockholders by mail, giving them the same privilege as if they were able to attend the annual meeting.

2. *The right to share in earnings of the entity through the distribution of dividends.* This is not an absolute right, as dividends must be declared by the board of directors before the dividends become a liability of the corporation.

3. *The right to a share by share distribution on liquidation of the corporation.* No stockholder will receive less than his or her fair share of the remaining corporate assets on liquidation.

4. *The right to maintain one's interest in a corporation.* Stockholders owning 10 shares out of 100 have a 10% interest in the corporation. If the corporation chooses to issue another 100 shares, and the stockholder does not purchase any, his or her interest falls from 10% to 5% ($10 \div 200$). Under the **preemptive right,** the corporation must offer existing stockholders the opportunity to maintain their interest in the corporation. Some states allow corporations to issue shares of stock that do not have the preemptive right attached to them. In those cases, a stockholder's interest falls involuntarily.

Stockholders' rights are attached to each share of common stock unless they are specifically addressed in the articles of incorporation, or on the stock certificate itself.

Board of Directors

The right to vote was mentioned as one of the basic rights with a share of common stock. Once a year, the stockholders at the annual meeting will vote to elect a board of directors. New board members might be elected, or old board members might be reelected. The board of directors then appoints or reappoints the officers of the corporation. The officers make up the basic management team that runs the daily operations of the corporation. The board of directors meets monthly or quarterly to review the operations of the corporation, and to set policy for future operations. The directors also decide whether the corporation was successful enough during the past accounting period to warrant the declaration of dividends to stockholders. Many times the board of directors will declare a dividend even if the past quarter was not as successful as planned, or even if the entity operated at a loss. Directors take pride in their dividend record and want to continue a distinctive record to any extent possible. However, unrestricted retained earnings from past successful years must be sufficient for the board to declare a dividend. Restrictions placed on retained earnings are discussed later in this chapter. The relationship between the board of directors and its corporation's management is discussed in Real World Example 10-1.

Corporate Terminology

Students sometimes have difficulty with the specialized meaning of terms required for corporate accounting. Three different classes of terms can be identified. These are shown in Exhibit 10-2 (p. 464) and are discussed later in this section.

STOCK CERTIFICATE VALUE

The various **State Corporation Acts** contain the rules and regulations that a registered corporation must abide by. These rules vary from state to state. Some states allow or require values to be placed on each share of stock issued by a corporation. It is important to note that the term *value* as used in this context has no relationship to the *market value* of a share of stock. The market value is the price each share of stock is selling for currently, today, on the various organized stock markets mentioned earlier. The **stock certificate** value, if it has one, is an arbitrary amount placed on the stock at incorporation either by implementation of the state law, or by an action of the board of directors. The three possibilities are *par value, no-par stated-value,* and true *no-par* shares.

PAR VALUE

Q3: Common shares and value

If the state in which the corporation is registered requires (or allows and the corporation chooses) a par value to be imprinted on each share, the stock is known as **par value stock.** The value is determined by the corporation and may be (but not necessarily) the amount the stock sells for on the day trading begins. The par value may be influenced by the investing market the corporation hopes to reach. If the corporation wants to obtain capital from individual investors, the par value will be low, in the $5 to $10 range. If the corporation wants to reach **institutional investors** with large sums to invest, the par value may be much higher, in the $100 range. It is important to remember that these are *arbitrary* values placed on shares of stock when the corporation comes into existence. Stock with a par value of $1 or even less may sell in the market for any amount, even hundreds of dollars per share. The par value becomes *legal capital,* a concept discussed later in this chapter.

NO-PAR AND NO-PAR STATED-VALUE

If the state in which the corporation is registered requires (or allows and the corporation chooses) no value to be placed on the stock, the stock is known as **no-par stock.** In this case, the legal capital is the total amount paid to the corporation

REAL WORLD EXAMPLE 10-1
Independence of the Board of Directors

THE board of directors must assure itself that the long-run interests of the corporation are being served and that management is acting in a responsible manner. To assess management's performance objectively, board members must be independent of those responsible for operating the corporation. Further, as key factors in an internal "credibility-added" function, board members must also appear to outsiders to be independent. When he was chairman of the United States Securities and Exchange Commission, Harold M. Williams suggested on several occasions that the following groups should not be allowed board membership: management, major customers and suppliers of goods and services, commercial bankers, outside counsel, investment brokers, and any other individuals whose positions might raise conflict of interest questions in the minds of reasonable third parties. Williams would, however, allow the corporation's chief executive officer (CEO) board membership as long as he/she did not chair the board. Although that suggested criterion for membership would improve the perception of the board's independence, the CEO's membership could have the effect of neutralizing the board's real independence.

Admission to the boardroom is a recognition of success. Good sense, effective judgment, initiative, and the right connections are universally regarded as desirable traits in new board members. Chief executive officers consider one other ingredient essential—loyalty. Loyalty develops rather naturally in novice board members; the initial board appointment understandably generates a sense of gratitude, a desire to be accepted quickly, and a recognition of an obligation to those who supported the selection. Any misplaced sense of self-importance quickly evaporates along with the mystique usually associated with the boardroom setting. A lesson soon learned after admission into the inner corporate circle is that the probability of success as a board member is significantly improved if operating management—particularly the CEO—is enthusiastically supported. Admission into the corridors of corporate power is, after all, a prestigious position worth holding onto.

To neutralize the support-of-management

---

for the shares. But the board of directors may choose to place an arbitrary value on the issued shares to establish a limit to legal capital or to establish an opening selling price. If the board of directors chooses to place an arbitrary value on the shares, the stock is known as **no-par stated-value stock.** The accounting for all three types of shares will be discussed with the concept of legal capital.

CLASSES OF STOCK

Q4: Classes of stock

Q5: Preferred stockholders

All corporations issue common stock, the basic unit of ownership having voting rights. Some corporations may issue more than one class of common stock, generally referred to as Class A common and Class B common. Corporations also may issue **preferred stock.** Preferred stock generally has no voting rights, or preemptive rights, but does carry with it the right to share in earnings through dividend payments, and the right to a partial sharing of the remaining assets in a liquidation. The share of dividends is usually fixed, either as a percentage of par value, or a

Q6: Characteristics of preferred stock

dollar amount per share. The stock is named *preferred* since the holders of these shares will receive dividend distributions *before* common stockholders, and upon

syndrome and replace it with effectiveness, the independence of the board vis-à-vis management must be established uncompromisingly. No member of management, particularly the CEO, should be allowed voting status on the board. Allowing the CEO membership would only perpetuate the status quo. Not permitting the CEO membership will neutralize his/her influence over board members and support the development of their real independence and ultimate effectiveness.

Membership restrictions, however, should not be allowed to erode the board's accessibility to management and vice versa. The CEO and other senior corporate operating managers should be present, by invitation, at most board meetings, and their opinions, comments, and views given significant consideration. The CEO should be able to request board meetings to consider topics of timely importance. Most senior operating executives will have little difficulty with the concept of reporting to a board over which they exert no formal control; convincing the board to approve major undertakings is no more than they would expect to have to accomplish, given their role within the corporation. Board scrutiny of their activity represents accountability commensurate with authority and position.

To some, however, the transition may not be palatable. What of the CEO who owns 51 percent of the voting stock in a public company? Is it reasonable to ask such a corporate head to remove himself as a voting member from the board? One response is that removal is the cost attached to using the securities markets to raise capital. Borrowing from or selling stock to the public necessitates increased accountability and, to discharge that accountability effectively, the CEO must report to, as opposed to direct the activity of, a board that has the requisite level of autonomy necessary to function in a responsible manner. When a company seeks or uses outside funds, shareholders should insist on the independence of the board of directors. The responsibility for establishing an effective internal monitoring system over operating management can then begin from a base of real as well as perceived objectivity.

Source "The Inside Story on Financial Statement Credibility," Donald S. Johnston and Morley Lemon, *CAMagazine,* June 1984. Reprinted with permission. Published by the Canadian Institute of Chartered Accountants, Toronto, Canada.

liquidation will receive the assigned share of assets *before* any assets are distributed to common stockholders. If the preferred stock is *cumulative,* it means that if **cumulative dividends** (preferred portion applied annually) are not paid in any one year, the *dividends in arrears* will be paid to preferred stockholders before any declared dividends are paid to the common stockholders. If the stock is *noncumulative,* only the preferred portion of the current year's declared dividend is paid to preferred stockholders. Although the dividend amount for the preferred stock is usually fixed in terms of a percentage of par value or a dollar amount per share, the stock can be *participating.* Participating stockholders may receive more than the stated portion of dividends if, after the initial distribution to all stockholders, funds remain in the declared dividend. If the preferred stock is *nonparticipating,* the holders will receive only the stated amount or percentage of par value. Although preferred stock has preference rights over common stock, the total rewards are generally limited, with common stockholders reaping more substantial rewards. Dividend distributions between common and preferred stock are further discussed in Chapter 11, while the concept of book value is discussed at the end of this chapter, showing the limited return preferred stockholders have in liquidation.

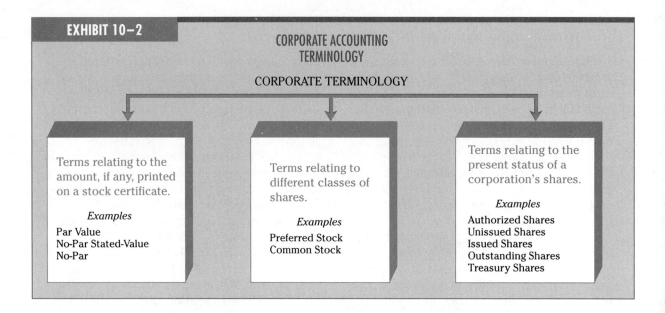

EXHIBIT 10-2

CORPORATE ACCOUNTING
TERMINOLOGY

CORPORATE TERMINOLOGY

Terms relating to the amount, if any, printed on a stock certificate.

Examples

Par Value
No-Par Stated-Value
No-Par

Terms relating to different classes of shares.

Examples

Preferred Stock
Common Stock

Terms relating to the present status of a corporation's shares.

Examples

Authorized Shares
Unissued Shares
Issued Shares
Outstanding Shares
Treasury Shares

STATUS OF SHARES

Q7: Issued vs. outstanding stock

When a corporation receives a charter to operate under the laws of a particular state, that charter will specify the number of shares of common (and possibly preferred) stock the corporation may issue. Once those shares have been issued, the corporation must apply for a further authorization from the state to issue more stock. The number of shares granted by the state of incorporation is known as authorized stock. This number is always disclosed in the *Stockholders' Equity* section of the balance sheet. At the date of incorporation, these shares are also referred to as unissued stock. As soon as some of the authorized shares are sold, they are referred to as issued stock. If none of the issued shares have subsequently been reacquired, they are also referred to as outstanding stock. If some of the issued shares have been reacquired but not formally retired, the reacquired shares are referred to as treasury stock. The difference between issued stock and outstanding stock is, therefore, the number of shares classified as treasury stock. The number of shares authorized, issued, and outstanding must be disclosed on the face of the balance sheet.

Graphically, these terms can be shown in Exhibit 10-3. To avoid confusion over these different classifications, take sufficient time to understand the distinctions among them before continuing to read this chapter.

PAID-IN CAPITAL TRANSACTIONS

Paid-in capital refers to all stockholders' equity contributed by investors rather than earned by the corporation. Stockholders' equity is composed of only two parts: investments (paid-in capital), and earnings (Retained Earnings). See Exhibit 10-4.

Recording Stock Transactions

The entry to record the sale of common stock depends on what, if any, value was placed on the shares at incorporation. Assume Saguaro Computers, Inc., has a

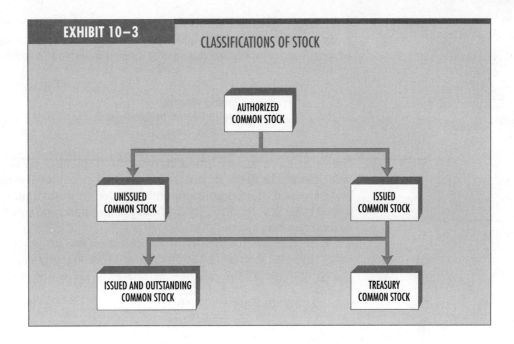

EXHIBIT 10–3

CLASSIFICATIONS OF STOCK

corporate charter authorizing it to issue 100,000 shares of $10 par value common stock. The entry to record the sale of 4,000 shares at $10 per share would be as follows:

Cash	40,000	
Common Stock		40,000

If SCI sold the 4,000 shares for $12, the entry would appear as follows:

Cash	48,000	
Common Stock		40,000
Paid-in Capital in Excess of Par		8,000

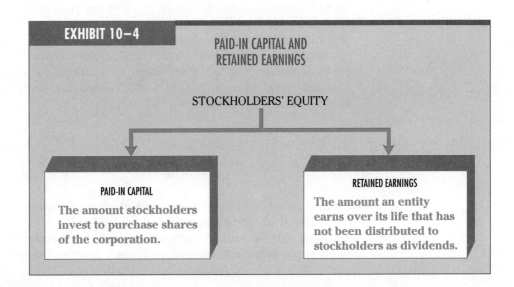

EXHIBIT 10–4

PAID-IN CAPITAL AND RETAINED EARNINGS

STOCKHOLDERS' EQUITY

PAID-IN CAPITAL

The amount stockholders invest to purchase shares of the corporation.

RETAINED EARNINGS

The amount an entity earns over its life that has not been distributed to stockholders as dividends.

If in the example the 100,000 shares were no-par but with a stated value of $10, the entry to record the sale of 4,000 shares at $10 would be the same as for par value, while the entry to record the sale of 4,000 shares at $12 would appear as follows:

Cash	48,000	
Common Stock		40,000
Paid-in Capital in Excess of		
Stated Value		8,000

Note that there is very little difference in accounting for par and no-par stated-value stock. The major difference between the two is legal in nature—the par value is determined at incorporation and included in the corporate charter, while the stated value is determined by the board of directors, and generally does not appear in the corporate charter.

If the Saguaro 100,000-share authorization was for no-par no-stated-value, the entry to record the sale of 4,000 shares at $10 would be same as for par value, while the entry to record the sale of 4,000 shares at $12 would appear as follows:

Cash	48,000	
Common Stock		48,000

Q8: Legal capital

The concept of legal capital can be introduced here briefly, but developed further later in the chapter. In the case of par or stated value stock, the legal capital is the par or stated value multiplied by the number of shares issued. In the examples so far, the legal capital for both the par and stated value would be $10,000, whether the 4,000 shares were sold for $10 or $12 each. In the case of no-par no-stated-value shares, the legal capital would be whatever was paid-in when the shares were issued, $10,000 or $12,000. **Legal capital** is the portion of stockholders' equity that *cannot* be distributed in the form of dividends. The discussion of legal capital will resume after more elements of paid-in capital are explored.

Q9: Exchanging stock for noncash assets

If shares of stock are issued in exchange for assets other than cash, such as land, a measurement problem is created. What amount should be recorded for the cost of the land—the market value of the land, or the market value of the stock? It depends on which value is more readily determinable. Since the land in question is external to the corporation, an appraised value (or several appraisals) of the land might be the best indication of the value to use in recording the transaction. If the stock is traded on a national exchange, the market value of the stock might be a better indication of the cost of the land.

Assume Saguaro acquires a parcel of land in exchange for 10,000 shares of $10 par value common stock actively traded on a national exchange and selling for $15. The land has an asking price of $175,000. The purchase of the land and the issuance of the shares would be recorded as follows:

Land	150,000	
Common Stock		100,000
Paid-in Capital in		
Excess of Par Value		50,000

In this instance, the market value of the stock is a more reliable determinant of cost of the land than the "asking price" of the land.

Many times shares of stock will be issued in exchange for professional time spent by attorneys, accountants, and others in accomplishing the incorporation. If

SCI issued 1000 shares of $10 par value stock in exchange for services valued at $13,000, the entry to record the issuance of the shares would be as follows:

Organization Costs	13,000	
Common Stock		10,000
Paid-in Capital in Excess of Par Value		3,000

Remember that organization costs are an intangible asset that must be amortized over a period not to exceed 40 years.

A corporation may repurchase its own shares through the stock exchange, just as anyone may purchase shares of stock. If the intent is to hold these shares temporarily, then to reissue them at a later date, these shares are known as *treasury stock.* Accounting for treasury stock is more fully discussed in Chapter 11. At this point it is enough to say that the shares would be purchased at their then market value. Assuming Saguaro repurchases 1,000 shares when the stock is selling for $15 per share, the entry to record the transaction would appear as follows:

| Treasury Stock | 15,000 | |
| Cash | | 15,000 |

Exhibit 10-5 demonstrates the effect several of these transactions have on the Stockholders' Equity section of SCI's balance sheet.

Note two factors affecting the balance sheet in Exhibit 10-5. The legal capital is $150,000, the total par value of the shares *issued,* not the shares outstanding, and treasury stock is treated as a reduction of total stockholders' equity, and *not* a reduction of paid-in capital.

ISSUING STOCK BELOW PAR OR STATED VALUE

Because the par or stated value of stock is a measure of legal capital, and legal capital is a portion of stockholders' equity that can not be paid out in the form of dividends, shares of common stock should not be issued in an amount less than par or stated value.

Stock Splits

Q10: Stock splits

The corporation may find its shares selling at a high price on the stock market, thereby putting them beyond the reach of many investors. To solve this problem, management may opt for a **stock split** to increase the marketability of a corporation's shares; the corporation issues, for example, three new shares to replace each old share. The old outstanding share certificates are *called in* and three new certificates are issued as replacements for each old share. The number of outstanding shares has now been tripled and the market price of each share tends to decrease to one-third of its former market price. This is illustrated by using some assumed data for Saguaro Computers, Inc.:

Number of Shares Issued	Total Par Value	Market Price per Share
10,000	$150,000 ($15 par)	$30
30,000	$150,000 ($5 par)	$10

EXHIBIT 10–5

PARTIAL BALANCE SHEET—STOCKHOLDERS' EQUITY

Assume the following for Saguaro Computers, Inc.:

1. The balance in retained earnings is $25,000.

2. The 100,000 authorized shares had a par value of $10.

3. Sold 4,000 shares for $12 per share

4. Issued 10,000 shares in exchange for land when the stock was selling at $15 per share

5. Issued 1,000 shares in exchange for professional services, valued at $13,000, incurred during incorporation

6. Reacquired 1,000 shares when the stock was selling at $15 per share

Stockholders' Equity

Paid-in Capital	
Common Stock, $10 Par Value, 100,000 shares authorized; 15,000 shares issued; 14,000 shares outstanding; 1,000 shares in the treasury	$150,000
Paid-in Capital in Excess of Par Value	61,000
Total Paid-in Capital	$211,000
Retained Earnings	25,000
Total	$236,000
Less: Treasury Stock at Cost	15,000
Total Stockholders' Equity	$221,000

As shown, the number of shares issued triples, while the market price per share decreases proportionately. Also note that the *issued* shares are split, not the *outstanding* shares. Since the par value of each share also decreases proportionately, the shares in the treasury would also have to be split.

The Stockholders' Equity section of Saguaro's balance sheet would appear as follows, assuming 100,000 shares were authorized before the split, and that SCI has $35,000 of retained earnings, no shares in the treasury, and paid-in capital in excess of par value of $45,000.

Before the split:

Stockholders' Equity

Paid-in Capital	
Common Stock, $15 Par Value, 100,000 shares authorized; 10,000 shares issued and outstanding	$150,000
Paid-in Capital in Excess of Par Value	45,000
Total Paid-in Capital	$195,000
Retained Earnings	35,000
Total Stockholders' Equity	$230,000

After the split:

Stockholders' Equity

Paid-in Capital

Common Stock, $5 Par Value, 300,000 shares authorized; 30,000 shares issued and outstanding	$150,000
Paid-in Capital in Excess of Par Value	45,000
Total Paid-in Capital	$195,000
Retained Earnings	35,000
Total Stockholders' Equity	$230,000

Note that only the number of shares authorized and issued change, along with the par value of each share. Total legal capital remains the same, as does total stockholders' equity. For this reason, no journal entry is needed to record a stock split. Only a memorandum in the Common Stock account is necessary, stating that the authorized number of shares has increased to 300,000 as the result of a "3-for-1" stock split, that the number of issued shares tripled to 30,000, and that the par value has decreased to $5 per share.

Stock splits can be in any ratio, with the most common being a 2-for-1 split. In that case, the number of shares doubles, and the par value and market value are reduced by 50%. A corporation could have a 10-for-1 split, or in the case of the Chicago Tribune, the split was 4,799 for 1 as discussed in Real World Example 10-2.

REAL WORLD EXAMPLE 10-2
This Stock Split Is 4799 for 1

TRIBUNE Co. yesterday announced a 4799-for-1 stock split as part of its move to become a publicly held company.

The company, owner of the *Chicago Tribune* and *New York Daily News* newspapers and the Chicago Cubs baseball team, will distribute 4799 shares of stock for each of the existing 7393 shares, said Stanton Cook, president and chief executive. The shares will be distributed October 3 to shareholders of record as of the close of business yesterday, he said. The company's current shares of stock are privately held and not publicly traded.

After the distribution, the stock will be listed on the New York Stock Exchange. A spokesman for the company said about 33.5 million shares would be outstanding and each is expected to be worth between $20 and $25.

The spokesman said Tribune Co. also is waiting for final government approval of its public statement of registration. The statement was filed about a month ago when the company announced that it would become a publicly held company.

Tribune also is planning to offer 5.5 million shares of additional common stock, which is expected to sell for between $22 and $26 a share, the spokesman said. That sale is contingent upon distribution of the common stock to current shareholders, he added.

In addition to the *Tribune,* the *Daily News,* and the Cubs, the company owns newspapers in Florida; WGN-TV in Chicago and several other broadcast properties; and operations in cable television, entertainment and newsprint, and forest products.

Source Associated Press, *The Gazette,* Montreal, February 27, 1983.

A **reverse stock split** is also possible. In a stock split, management wants to reduce the market price of the stock by increasing the number of shares in the hands of investors. In a reverse stock split, the opposite is true. Management wants to increase the market price of the stock by reducing the number of shares in the hands of the investors.

RETAINED EARNINGS RESTRICTIONS

Q11: Restrictions on retained earnings

The term retained earnings has been introduced throughout most of the chapters of this textbook. In this section of Chapter 10 and in Chapter 11, retained earnings is more fully developed. Examine Exhibit 10-6, the Saguaro balance sheet found in Exhibit 5-9 in Chapter 5.

In this balance sheet, the Retained Earnings amount is $32,500. If **retained earnings** represents net income retained in the business and not paid out in the form of dividends, then what portion of the $32,500 is available for the payment of dividends? Is the entire balance available for dividends? Theoretically, if no restrictions are placed on the Retained Earnings account by management, the balance is available for the payment of dividends. But when earnings are retained in the business, they are invested in income-producing assets, such as inventory and equipment. Also, some of the revenue reported on income statements in past years has not been collected in cash (Accounts Receivable). Therefore, what is the maximum amount of retained earnings SCI can declare and pay as dividends on December 31, 19X3? The answer is $10,800, the amount of cash on the balance sheet. But SCI has current liabilities that have to be addressed, and depending on how current

---

EXHIBIT 10-6

Saguaro Computers, Inc.
Balance Sheet
December 31, 19X3

Assets			Liabilities		
Current Assets			*Current Liabilities*		
Cash	$ 10,800		Bank Loan—Current	$39,000	
Accounts Receivable	26,000		Accounts Payable	25,000	
Inventory	120,000		Income Tax Payable	15,000	
Prepaid Insurance	1,200		Total Current Liabilities		$ 79,000
Total Current Assets		$158,000	*Long-term Liabilties*		
Long-term Assets			Bank Loan—Long Term		
Equipment	$ 13,600		(note 1)		48,500
Less: Accum. Deprec.—	1,600		Total Liabilities		$127,500
Supplies					
Total Long-term Assets		12,000	**Stockholders' Equity**		
			Common Stock (note 2)	$10,000	
			Retained Earnings	32,500	
			Total Stockholders' Equity		42,500
			Total Liabilities and Stockholders'		
Total Assets	$170,000		Equity		$170,000

they are, Saguaro could be in trouble. Having a balance in Retained Earnings and a balance in Cash does not mean a corporation is able to pay a dividend.

Aside from restrictions on retained earnings due to prudent cash management (like current liabilities), other restrictions may be placed on retained earnings for a variety of reasons. Maybe the company has plans to expand the plant in a few years and wants to restrict dividends to save the cash necessary to finance the plant expansion. A formal restriction may be placed on Retained Earnings by the following journal entry:

Retained Earnings	10,000	
Retained Earnings Appropriated		
for Plant Expansion		10,000

Now SCI's balance in (Unappropriated) Retained Earnings has been reduced to $22,500. Has cash been set aside for this expansion? No. Only dividends have been restricted. To set aside cash would require another entry, making a type of investment of that cash. This part of the transaction will be discussed in Chapter 14, "Short-term and Long-term Investment Portfolios." Assume SCI made the last journal entry for the next five years. Retained Earnings Appropriated for Plant Expansion now has a balance of $50,000. If the expansion occurs using exactly $50,000, the entry to record the new plant would be as follows:

Buildings	50,000	
Cash		50,000

Also, the following entry would have to be made, since the restriction on retained earnings is no longer necessary:

Retained Earnings Appropriated for		
Plant Expansion	50,000	
Retained Earnings		50,000

Does this entry mean that $50,000 more in Retained Earnings are now available for dividends? Yes. Does this mean that SCI has $50,000 more in cash with which to pay the dividends? No. In fact, it has $50,000 less in cash since it just spent $50,000 to expand the plant.

Graphically, the relationship between **restricted (appropriated)** and **unrestricted (unappropriated) retained earnings** appears as in Exhibit 10-7.

TERMINOLOGY

The term "appropriation of retained earnings" has been used in the form shown in the prior journal entries. The account could have been named Retained Earnings Restricted for Plant Expansion, or Retained Earnings Reserved for Plant Expansion. In fact, in practice an entry may not be made at all, and the restriction instead handled by a footnote to the financial statements. For SCI, the restriction could be disclosed as follows:

Retained Earnings (note 56)   32,500

Note 56
During the current year, the board of directors has established a policy of restricting retained earnings as to the payment of dividends. Accordingly, $10,000 of retained earnings are not available for dividends at the present time.

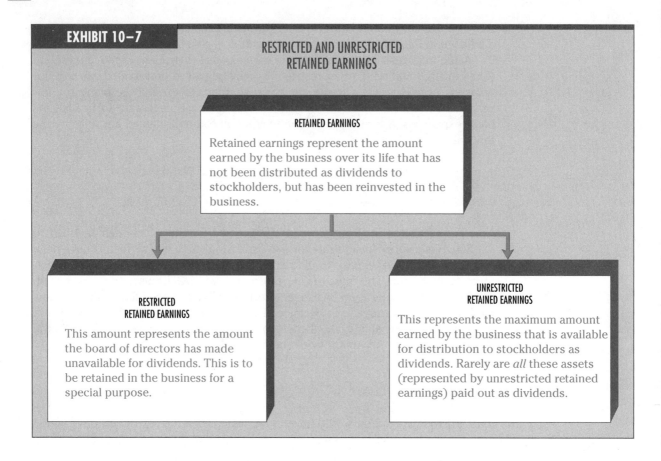

EXHIBIT 10–7

RESTRICTED AND UNRESTRICTED
RETAINED EARNINGS

RETAINED EARNINGS

Retained earnings represent the amount earned by the business over its life that has not been distributed as dividends to stockholders, but has been reinvested in the business.

RESTRICTED RETAINED EARNINGS

This amount represents the amount the board of directors has made unavailable for dividends. This is to be retained in the business for a special purpose.

UNRESTRICTED RETAINED EARNINGS

This represents the maximum amount earned by the business that is available for distribution to stockholders as dividends. Rarely are *all* these assets (represented by unrestricted retained earnings) paid out as dividends.

Footnotes to the financial statements have become an integral part of the financial package offered to investors. Examine the footnotes in United Telecom's annual report excerpts at the end of this textbook.

OTHER SOURCES OF STOCKHOLDERS' EQUITY

The emphasis in corporate accounting is on the distinctions among various sources of stockholders' equity. The accounting for legal capital has been discussed, along with accounting for amounts paid-in above legal capital (paid-in capital in excess of par value). The availability of retained earnings for the payment of dividends, and the use of retained earnings restrictions to indicate the unavailability of corporate assets for dividend payments was also discussed. These are all sources of stockholders' equity.

Most, if not all, of the many other sources of equity are reported as additional items under the Additional Paid-in Capital category under *Stockholders' Equity* on the balance sheet.

Q12: Donated assets

In many instances, assets may be donated to an entity by stockholders, or by entities outside the corporation. Known as **donated capital,** a common example would be a municipality donating a parcel of land to be used as a plant site as an inducement for a particular corporation to locate in that municipality. Nothing was paid for the land, but the property is still an asset of the corporation for business use, and, therefore, must be recorded at its fair market value. Assuming land with a fair market value of $50,000 is donated to Saguaro, the entry to record the acquisition is recorded as follows:

Land	50,000	
Donated Capital		50,000

The Donated Capital account is reported as part of Additional Paid-in Capital.

When *treasury stock* is purchased, and subsequently reissued at an amount above the cost of the stock, another paid-in account is created, as shown in the following entry where treasury stock costing $15,000 is sold for $18,000:

Cash	18,000	
Treasury Stock		15,000
Paid-in Capital from Treasury		
Stock Transactions		3,000

Treasury stock transactions are further developed in Chapter 11.

Many other sources of equity will be discussed later in this text and in more advanced accounting courses.

Components of Stockholders' Equity

The various components of stockholders' equity can now be shown graphically as in Exhibit 10-8.

BOOK VALUE PER SHARE

The **book value of common stock** must be handled with care. It is calculated as follows:

$$\frac{\text{Total Stockholders' Equity}}{\text{Number of Shares Outstanding}} = \text{Book Value per Share}$$

Since stockholders' equity can be viewed as a residual amount (Assets − Liabilities = Stockholders' Equity), the dollar amount of equity is determined by a host of accounting methods applied to a variety of assets and liabilities. Remember the many depreciation methods? the many inventory methods? the many ways of accounting for doubtful accounts? All of these decisions affect the dollar value of stockholders' equity. Therefore, it is important to treat book value per share carefully.

Q13: Book value vs. market value

A simple explanation of the measurement is that it determines the amount each stockholder would receive if all the assets were sold at exactly their book value (for example, long-term assets sold for an amount equal to their historical cost, less any depreciation taken since acquisition), and if all liabilities were satisfied (paid) at an amount equal to their book value. *Book value* does not measure the market value of the stock, or the liquidating value of the shares. It is simply another measurement used to make rational economic decisions.

The calculation of book value is fairly easy when only one class of stock is outstanding, as in the example. When more than one class of stock is outstanding, the determination becomes more complex. Since preferred stockholders have a preference right to assets on liquidation, the total book value of the *preferred stock*

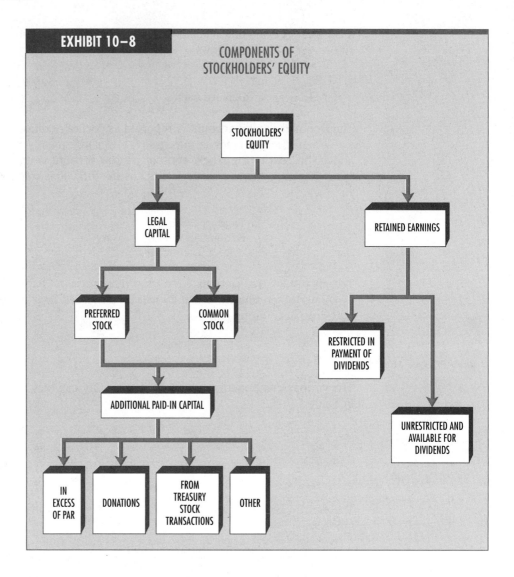

EXHIBIT 10–8

COMPONENTS OF
STOCKHOLDERS' EQUITY

must first be determined. This amount is then subtracted from total stockholders' equity in order to determine the total book value of the common stockholders. Then this is divided by the number of shares outstanding to obtain the book value per common share.

Book Value of Preferred Stock

The liquidating value of each preferred share is printed right on the certificate. It may be an amount equal to the par value, or an amount slightly higher. This is the amount of the **book value of preferred stock** on a per-share basis, unless the stock is cumulative. If the stock is cumulative, then any dividends that have not been paid in the past will be added to the liquidating value to arrive at the book value.

For example, assume the following facts: 10,000 shares of $100 par value, 6% cumulative preferred stock are outstanding with a liquidating value of $106 per share. No dividends have been paid for the last three years. The total of unpaid dividends is $180,000 ($18 per share × 10,000). A total of 350,000 shares of $10 par value common stock are outstanding, and total stockholders' equity amounts to $17,000,000. The following calculations determine the book value per share of common stock:

Cumulative Preferred Stockholders' Equity

Liquidation Value	$106 × 10,000 shares = $ 1,060,000
Unpaid Dividends	$ 18 × 10,000 shares = 180,000
Total Book Value ($124 per share)	$ 1,240,000
Total Stockholders' Equity	$17,000,000
Less: Preferred Stockholders' Equity	1,240,000
Common Stockholders' Equity	$15,760,000

$$\frac{\text{Common Stockholders' Equity}}{\text{Number of Shares Outstanding}} = \frac{\$15,760,000}{350,000} = \$45 \text{ (rounded)}$$

Note that the preferred stockholders' equity is determined *first*. In this manner, preferred stockholders are virtually assured of getting their investment back on liquidation, while the common stockholders hope for the best. As noted before, however, the common stockholders stand to reap the larger returns.

STOCK SUBSCRIPTIONS

Q14: Stock subscriptions

Up to this point, the discussion has assumed that shares issued in a new corporation are fully paid and their certificates are issued. In many cases, especially in new and relatively small corporations, stock is sold on a subscription basis. **Stock subscriptions** involve a contract with the corporation receiving a down payment along with a promise to make payments according to terms over a relatively short period of time, generally less than one year.

The rights of subscribing stockholders vary from state to state, so the presentation here for Saguaro is in general terms. At the time the agreement is signed, the following SCI journal entries would be made, based on the following assumptions: 1,000 shares of $10 par value common stock were subscribed to at $12 per share, with a 50% down payment, and the balance to be paid in two installments of $3,000 each.

Stock Subscriptions Receivable	12,000	
Common Stock Subscribed		10,000
Paid-in Capital in Excess of Par Value		2,000
To record the agreement to subscribe to 1,000 shares at $12 per share.		
Cash	6,000	
Stock Subscriptions Receivable		6,000
To record the down payment on stock subscriptions.		

Cash	3,000	
Stock Subscriptions Receivable		3,000
To record the receipt of the second payment on stock subscriptions.		
Cash	3,000	
Stock Subscriptions Receivable		3,000
To record the receipt of the third payment on stock subscriptions.		
Common Stock Subscribed	12,000	
Common Stock		12,000
To record the issuance of the certificates for common stock subscriptions.		

The Common Stock Subscribed account used in these entries would be disclosed in Saguaro's Stockholders' Equity section of the balance sheet as follows, using the information from Exhibit 10-5.

Stockholders' Equity

Paid-in Capital

Common Stock, $10 Par Value, 100,000 shares authorized; 15,000 shares issued; 14,000 shares outstanding; 1,000 shares in the treasury	$150,000
Common Stock Subscribed, 1,000 shares	10,000
Paid-in Capital in Excess of Par Value	63,000
Total Paid-in Capital	$223,000
Retained Earnings	25,000
Total	$248,000
Less: Treasury Stock at Cost	15,000
Total Stockholders' Equity	$233,000

Note that the number of shares included in the subscription are not included in the issued and outstanding amounts, but as a separate line item in stockholders' equity. Also note that the paid-in capital in excess of par value from the subscriptions is included with the rest of the amounts paid-in. After the stock certificates have been issued (after the final payment has been received), Saguaro's Stockholders' Equity section would appear as follows:

Stockholders' Equity

Paid-in Capital

Common Stock, $10 Par Value, 100,000 shares authorized; 16,000 shares issued; 15,000 shares outstanding; 1,000 shares in the treasury	$160,000
Paid-in Capital in Excess of Par Value	63,000
Total Paid-in Capital	$223,000
Retained Earnings	25,000
Total	$248,000
Less: Treasury Stock at Cost	15,000
Total Stockholders' Equity	$233,000

CHAPTER REVIEW

1 What is meant by the limited liability characteristic of a corporation? Do any corporations have unlimited liability? Explain. (p. 459)

Stockholders in a corporation generally risk only the "limited" amount that they choose to invest in the entity. The corporation is a legal "person;" therefore, creditors of the corporation cannot seek the personal assets of the stockholders to satisfy corporate liabilities. This has been referred to as the "corporate veil." Professional Corporations, on the other hand, do not have this feature. Doctors, lawyers, accountants, and the like may incorporate, but because of the nature of their work, are open to unlimited liability. Clients may sue and recover amounts from the individual assets of the professional person. This is why malpractice insurance is so necessary, and so expensive if available at all.

2 What are the rights of common stockholders? (p. 460)

Common stockholders generally have the following rights:
- The right to vote for the board of directors and other important matters.
- The right to share in the earnings of the corporation (dividends).
- The right to share in the remaining assets of a corporation in liquidation after creditors and preferred stockholders.
- The right to maintain their percentage ownership when new shares are being issued by the corporation.

3 Why do some common shares have a par value, while others have stated values and others have no value at all attached to them? (pp. 461–62)

It depends on the laws of the state in which the corporation receives its charter and on the choices of the corporation. Many states require that a value be placed on each share, known as par value. States that have no requirement allow the corporation to issue no-par stock. In some cases, the board of directors may elect, or be required, to place a stated value on the shares of stock.

4 What different classes of stock are available to investors in a corporation? Explain their differences. (pp. 462–63)

Corporations basically offer two classes of ownership; that represented by common stock, and that represented by preferred stock. The preferred stockholders have less at risk than do the common stockholders, but the rewards are far greater for the common stock investors. The preferred stock has almost a guaranteed, but limited, return, while common stock has no guarantee, but the returns are unlimited.

5 Are the rights of preferred stockholders the same as common? Explain. (pp. 462–63)

Depending on state law, the rights of the preferred stockholders can be the same as common stockholders, except for the right to maintain the same percentage of ownership. In most instances, however, preferred stockholders only have the right to dividends (share of earnings), and the right to their share of assets upon liquidation. They usually do not have voting or preemptive rights.

6 What are the various characteristics preferred stock might have? (pp. 462–63)

Preferred shares may have any of the following features, either alone or in combination:

- Cumulative
- Noncumulative
- Participating
- Nonparticipating

All preferred shares have a preference rate stated for dividends, either as a percentage of par value or as a dollar amount. If the board of directors fails to declare a dividend in any one year, the dividend will accumulate if the stock is *cumulative,* but it will be lost if the stock is *noncumulative.* If the stock is *participating,* the investor will have a chance to earn more than the preference rate.

7 What is the difference between issued and outstanding stock? (p. 464)

When stock is issued and then reacquired by the corporation (treasury stock), it is still considered issued, but not outstanding. Therefore, the difference between issued and outstanding is the number of shares of treasury stock a corporation owns.

8 What is meant by legal capital? Why is it important? (p. 466)

Legal capital is the portion of stockholders' equity that cannot be distributed to the stockholders in the form of dividends. It is generally measured by the total par value or stated value of the stock issued, or the total amount paid-in for no-par no-stated-value stock. It is important because it represents a creditor's cushion, an amount of corporate assets that a creditor knows will not be distributed to the owners of the corporation.

9 When shares of stock are issued for consideration other than cash, how is the transaction recorded? (pp. 466–67)

When shares are issued for consideration other than cash, the transaction is measured in terms of the fair market value of the assets given up, or the fair market value of the shares of stock, whichever is more easily obtainable. If the shares of stock are traded on an organized exchange, their value is readily obtainable; if not, the appraised value of the noncash item must be the amount recorded.

10 What is meant by a stock split? Why would a corporation elect to split the stock? (pp. 467–70)

A stock split is a corporation action to increase by a certain percentage the number of shares of stock outstanding. Splits are usually expressed in a ratio, such as 2-for-1, which means that the number of shares are being doubled, reducing the market value of each share by 50%. If the market value of the stock increases beyond a certain amount, the stock becomes out of reach for most investors. So, to promote activity in the stock market, the corporation may choose to reduce the market value by increasing the number of shares outstanding.

11 When would the board of directors of a corporation want to put restrictions on the amount of retained earnings available for dividends? (pp. 470–72)

The board of directors may want to restrict the amount of retained earnings available for dividends for a number of reasons. Some restrictions are due to prudent cash management, such as investing or paying off current liabilities. The corporation may be starting on a plant expansion program that will require a sizable amount of cash to finance the operation. Other reasons, not given in the textbook, might include restrictions for the eventual retirement of long-term debt, or unresolved contingencies such as a pending lawsuit.

12 Are assets donated to a corporation recorded in the accounts? If so, how is the value of the asset determined? (pp. 472–73)

Yes, assets donated to a corporation are recorded in the accounts. The value of the asset is determined at its fair market value on the date the donation is made.

13 Is the market value of a share of stock the same as its book value? Explain. (pp. 473–74)

No. The book value of a share of stock is determined by the following formula:

$$\frac{\text{Stockholders' Equity}}{\text{Number of Shares Outstanding}} = \text{Book Value per Share}$$

Therefore, book values are based on historical costs. The market value is determined by the stock market itself: how much are investors willing to pay for a share of a particular corporation's stock? The more investors that want the stock, the higher the price and vice versa.

14 What accounting problems arise when shares of stock are sold on a subscription basis? (pp. 475–76)

When shares are sold on a subscription basis, the stockholders are basically paying the amount due over a period of time. Problems arise because the shares are not issued until the contract is fully paid. Therefore, the corporation must carry a receivable from the subscribing stockholder and an equity item for the par value of the stock in question, along with additional paid-in capital for the amount of the subscription price in excess of par value.

KEY TERMS

appropriated retained earnings (p. 471) See restricted retained earnings.

authorized stock (p. 464) The number of shares a corporation may issue as stated in the corporate charter.

book value of common stock (p. 473) The amount of the net assets of a corporation represented by one share of common stock. It is determined by dividing the number of common shares outstanding into the stockholders' equity accruing to the common stockholders. Total stockholders' equity is first reduced by the portion accruing to the preferred stockholders.

book value of preferred stock (p. 474) The amount preferred stockholders would receive on a corporation's liquidation. It generally consists of the stock's par value, or a liquidating value if offered, plus the dividend in arrears on cumulative preferred stock.

cumulative dividend (p. 463) An undeclared dividend that accumulates and has to be paid in the future before any dividends can be paid to common stockholders. Once a dividend is declared, the fixed percentage of par value or dollar amount per share for preferred stock is awarded for each year dividends were not paid.

donated capital (p. 472) The portion of paid-in capital that represents assets contributed by stockholders and other interested parties.

institutional investors (p. 461) Investors, usually corporations such as banks, savings and loans, pension plans, and insurance companies, of large sums—billions of dollars every year.

issued stock (p. 464) Authorized stock that has been issued. Treasury shares that have been reacquired are still considered issued stock.

legal capital (p. 466) The portion of paid-in capital that cannot be distributed to the stockholders in the form of dividends.

no-par stated-value stock (p. 462) Common shares that the state of incorporation requires no par value to be attached, but that have an arbitrary stated value placed on each share by the board of directors.

no-par stock (p. 461) Common shares that the state of incorporation requires no value to be attached, and on which the board of directors places no arbitrary value.

outstanding stock (p. 464) Authorized shares that have been issued and are currently in the hands of stockholders, not in the treasury.

paid-in capital (p. 464) That portion of stockholders' equity contributed by stockholders and others, rather than earned by the corporation.

par value stock (p. 461) Common shares that have an arbitrary value imprinted on them when authorized. Par value does not in any way measure market value or book value.

States may or may not require stock to be issued with a par value. If the state does not require a par value, corporations still may elect to issue par value stock. The term applies to both common and preferred stock.

preemptive right (p. 460)   The right of each stockholder to maintain his or her percentage ownership in the corporation. When new shares are issued, under this right the existing stockholders must be offered the right to a proportional interest in the new shares.

preferred stock (p. 462)   A class of stock that has a preference over common stock. Holders of preferred stock are entitled to payment of dividends before common stockholders, and usually have a prior claim to corporate assets on liquidation.

restricted retained earnings (p. 471)   That portion of the assets earned by a corporation, but not currently available for dividends through an action of the board of directors.

retained earnings (p. 470)   That portion of stockholders' equity earned by a corporation, but not distributed to its owners in the form of dividends.

reverse stock split (p. 470)   An action taken by the board of directors to reduce the number of shares outstanding. It usually involves exchanging the original shares for a smaller number of new shares. The par value is increased, and the market price of the stock is usually increased proportionately.

State Corporation Acts (p. 461)   Each state in the Union has legislation that governs corporations incorporated in that state and corporations registered to do business in that state. These acts are many and varied. The material presented in this textbook is based on general applications, and in some cases, may not be applicable to a particular state.

stock certificate (p. 461)   A legal document signifying the number of shares of a particular class of stock an investor owns. The rights attached to the ownership are usually stated on the certificate.

stock split (p. 467)   An action taken by the board of directors that increases the number of shares outstanding. It usually involves exchanging the original shares for a larger number of new shares. The par value is reduced, and the market price of the stock is usually reduced proportionately.

stock subscriptions (p. 475)   A contract between the corporation and some stockholders to pay for their shares over a period of time. The stock certificate is not issued until the contract is fully paid, but subscribing stockholders do have some of the rights of fully paid holders. The number of rights depend on the various state corporation acts.

treasury stock (p. 464)   Shares of the issuing corporation that have been issued and reacquired, but not retired. Treasury stock will normally be reissued at a later time.

unappropriated retained earnings (p. 471)   See unrestricted retained earnings.

unissued stock (p. 464)   The shares of stock that have been authorized to be issued, but have not been at a point in time.

unrestricted retained earnings (p. 471)   That portion of the assets earned by a corporation currently available for dividends. The amount of available cash, however, would dictate cash dividends.

SELF-TEST QUESTIONS FOR REVIEW   (Answers are at the end of this chapter.)

Q2, Q4

1. Which of the following classes of stock normally has the right to vote in major corporate matters?
    (a) Preferred stock
    (b) Participating preferred stock
    (c) Cumulative preferred stock
    (d) Common stock

Q2   2. Who makes the day-to-day operating decisions under the corporate form of ownership?
    (a) Stockholders
    (b) Board of Directors
    (c) Officers of the corporation
    (d) Combined management team

Q7   3. No difference exists between the number of shares issued and the number of shares outstanding unless which one of the following is present?
    (a) Treasury shares
    (b) Par value shares
    (c) No-par value shares
    (d) Formally retired shares

Q9   4. When new shares are issued in exchange for noncash assets, the asset received will be recorded at an amount equal to the
    (a) par value of the stock.
    (b) book value of the stock.
    (c) fair market value of the stock.
    (d) fair market value of the noncash asset.
    (e) Either *c* or *d*, depending which is more determinable.

Q10   5. When par value common stock is split on a 2-for-1 basis, the
    (a) market value usually doubles.
    (b) par value doubles.
    (c) par value is reduced by 50%.
    (d) number of shares outstanding is reduced by 50%.

Q11   6. Restrictions placed on retained earnings
    (a) ensure that cash will be available for that restriction.
    (b) allow the board of directors more flexibility in determining the amount of the dividends.
    (c) restrict the amount of retained earnings available for dividends.
    (d) reduce the amount of cash available for dividends.

Q13   7. When assets such as land are donated to a corporation,
    (a) no entry is recorded, since assets are usually recorded at cost and the cost is zero.
    (b) land is recorded at the amount recorded on the books of the donor.
    (c) land is recorded at its current fair market value and a liability account is credited since the corporation will probably pay for it when it has the money.
    (d) land is recorded at its fair market value and an element of stockholders' equity is credited for an equal amount.

Q14   8. With stock subscriptions, stockholders receive a certain number of shares of stock each month, similar to a magazine subscription.
    (a) The above statement is true.
    (b) The above statement is false.
    (c) The above statement has some truth to it.
    (d) The above statement is true only if each stockholder receives the same number of shares each month.

DEMONSTRATION PROBLEM

Part A

Wade, Inc., received a charter that authorized it to issue 100 shares of $3 par value common stock. The following transactions were completed during 19X6:

Jan.   5   Sold and issued 30 shares of common stock for a total of $150

Jan. 12 Exchanged 50 shares of common stock for assets listed at their fair market values: Machinery, $100; Building, $100; Land, $50

30 Subscriptions were received on 10 shares of common stock at $6 each. Down payments amounting to 20% accompanied the subscription contracts.

Feb. 28 Received payment of the balance due on the subscriptions of Jan. 30; the stock was then issued

Dec. 31 Closed the net income of $41 to retained earnings
Paid a total dividend on common stock of $20

Required

1. Prepare the journal entries necessary to record these transactions.

2. Prepare a Stockholders' Equity section of the balance sheet as of the following dates:
   (a) January 31
   (b) February 28
   (c) December 31

Part B

The Stockholders' Equity section of the Dresden Manufacturing Co. balance sheet as of December 31, 19X6, follows:

Stockholders' Equity

Paid-in Capital
Preferred Stock, $10 Par Value, 6% Noncumulative
and nonparticipating, 1,000 shares authorized;
40 shares issued and outstanding $ 400
Common Stock, $1 Par Value, 4,000 shares
authorized; 2,000 shares issued and outstanding   2,000
Total Legal Capital $2,400
Paid-in Capital in Excess of Par Value
Common Stock $200
Preferred Stock   100   300
Total Paid-in Capital $2,700
Retained Earnings
Unrestricted   900
Total Stockholders' Equity $3,600

Required

1. Determine the book value of the preferred and common stock as of December 31, 19X6. The dividends have not been paid for two years on the preferred stock.

2. Assume that the common stock was split 2-for-1 on January 2, 19X7, and no other changes were made in any other accounts other than those affected by the stock split. Determine the book values.

SOLUTION TO DEMONSTRATION PROBLEM

Part A

1. Jan. 5   Cash   150
                Common Stock   90
                Paid-in Capital in Excess of Par
                  Value   60
             To record the issuance of 30 shares of
             $3 par value common stock for $150.

Jan. 12	Land	50	
	Building	100	
	Machinery	100	
	Common Stock		150
	Paid-in Capital In Excess of Par Value		100
	To record the issuance of 50 shares of $3 par value common stock in exchange for land, buildings, and equipment.		

(The market values of the individual noncash assets were used, since the total market value of the stock [50 shares × $5 = $250] was equal to the total market value of the noncash assets.)

Jan. 30	Cash	12	
	Subscriptions Receivable	48	
	Common Stock Subscribed		30
	Paid-in Capital in Excess of Par Value		30
	To record the subscriptions to 10 shares of common stock at an agreed on value of $6 per share. The contract required a 20% down payment.		
Feb. 28	Cash	48	
	Stock Subscriptions Receivable		48
	To record the payment of the balance due on the Jan. 30 stock subscriptions.		
Feb. 28	Common Stock Subscribed	30	
	Common Stock		30
	To record the issuance of the stock certificates on payment in full of the Jan. 30 stock subscriptions.		
Dec. 31	Income Summary	41	
	Retained Earnings		41
	To record the 19X6 net income.		
Dec. 31	Retained Earnings	20	
	Cash		20
	To record the declaration and payment of 19X6 dividends.		

2. (a) January 31

Stockholders' Equity

Paid-in Capital
Common Stock, $3 Par Value, 100 shares authorized; 80 shares issued and outstanding	$240
Common Stock Subscribed	30
Total Legal Capital	$270
Paid-in Capital in Excess of Par Value—Common	190
Total Paid-in Capital	$460
Retained Earnings	
Unrestricted	-0-
Total Stockholders' Equity	$460

Note that the balance in Common Stock to Be Issued is part of legal capital, but it is not considered issued and outstanding because the stock certificates will not be issued until the contract is fully paid.

(b) February 28

Stockholders' Equity

Paid-in Capital
    Common Stock, $3 Par Value, 100 shares
        authorized; 90 shares issued and outstanding $270
        Paid-in Capital in Excess of Par Value—Common   190
        Total Paid-in Capital $460
Retained Earnings
    Unrestricted   -0-
        Total Stockholders' Equity $460

Note that the only change is that the shares subscribed to have now been issued and are outstanding. No other amounts change between January 31 and February 28.

(c) December 31

Stockholders' Equity

Paid-in Capital
    Common Stock, $3 Par Value, 100 shares
        authorized; 90 shares issued and outstanding $270
        Paid-in Capital in Excess of Par Value—Common   190
        Total Paid-in Capital $460
Retained Earnings
    Unrestricted ($41–$20)   21
        Total Stockholders' Equity $481

Part B

1. The book value of the preferred stock is equal to its par value of $10. The calculation is as follows:

$$\frac{\text{Total Book Value of Preferred}}{\text{Number of Shares Outstanding}} = \frac{\$400}{40} = \$10$$

Note two areas of concern. The paid-in capital in excess of par value does not attach to the preferred stock in liquidation. The preferred holders are only entitled to the par value or in some cases a *stated* liquidating value. Also note that the dividends in arrears were not considered in the calculation. The reason is simple; the preferred shares were *noncumulative.* If the preferred stock had been *cumulative,* the dividends in arrears would have been $48 (6% × $400 total par × 2 years), and the calculation would have been as follows:

$$\frac{\text{Total Book Value of Preferred}}{\text{Number of Shares Outstanding}} = \frac{\$448}{40} = \$11.20$$

The $11.20 consists of the par value of $10, plus 2 unpaid $.60 dividends.
The book value of the common stock would be determined as follows:

$$\frac{\text{Total Stockholders' Equity} - \text{Preferred Equity} = \text{Common Equity}}{\text{Number of Shares Outstanding}} = \frac{\$3,600 - \$400}{2,000} = \$1.60$$

2. Remember that book value is a liquidation value based on the book value of the net assets. If all the assets were sold for an amount equal to their book value, and all liabilities were paid in an amount equal to their book value, each common stockholder would receive $1.60, while each preferred stockholder would receive $10.

After the stock split, the preferred stock book value would be the same, as follows:

$$\frac{\text{Total Book Value of Preferred}}{\text{Number of Shares Outstanding}} = \frac{\$400}{40} = \$10$$

The common stock book value would be reduced by 50%, as follows:

$$\frac{\text{Total Stockholders' Equity} - \text{Preferred Equity} = \text{Common Equity}}{\text{Number of Shares Outstanding}} = \frac{\$3,600 - \$400}{4,000} = \$.80$$

In a stock split, nothing changes other than the number of shares of common stock outstanding, and the par value.

DISCUSSION QUESTIONS

Q10-1 What are some advantages and disadvantages of the corporate form of organization?

Q10-2 What is meant by the limited liability feature of corporations? How does it influence creditors?

Q10-3 In what way is there double taxation for a corporation? Are there tax advantages with a corporate form of organization?

Q10-4 What rights are attached to common shares? Where are these rights indicated?

Q10-5 What is a board of directors and whom does it represent? Are the directors involved in the daily management of the entity?

Q10-6 Corporate accounting involves the use of specialized terminology. Explain:
(a) The different terms relating to the amount, if any, printed on a share certificate
(b) The different classes of shares
(c) The different terms relating to the current status of a corporation's shares

Q10-7 The word *value* has a specific meaning for accountants. What exactly does it mean? Give examples of different uses.

Q10-8 Distinguish between par value stock and no-par value stock.

Q10-9 In what way is stock "preferred"? In which way is it similar to common stock? Different from common stock?

Q10-10 Distinguish among authorized, unissued, issued, and outstanding shares.

Q10-11 What is legal capital? What significance does it have?

Q10-12 *Paid-in capital* is a generic term. What does it include? Must the assets represented by it be legally kept in the corporation for the protection of creditors?

Q10-13 Why do corporations sometimes opt for a stock split? What is a reverse stock split?

Q10-14 Assume a 2-for-1 stock split occurs. Explain:
(a) The effect on the par value of each share split
(b) The effect on the total amount of issued and outstanding shares

Q10-15 In what way have retained earnings been plowed back into an entity?

Q10-16 What is the difference between restricted and unrestricted retained earnings? Why would some retained earnings be restricted? Prepare the journal entry used to make a restriction.

Q10-17   Are restrictions of retained earnings the best method for indicating and explaining management's intentions? Explain.

Q10-18   Define *donated capital*. Where is donated capital classified in the balance sheet?

Q10-19   Identify the major components of the stockholders' equity section of a balance sheet. Why are these components distinguished?

Q10-20   What does book value of shares represent? How is it calculated?

Q10-21   A corporate entity has both preferred and common classes of shares. How is the book value of common shares calculated in this case? What is meant by the liquidating value of preferred shares?

Q10-22   Does the book value change from year to year? Of what value is its calculation to the reader of financial statements?

Q10-23   The market price of a share is less than its book value; is it a bargain? Why or why not?

Q10-24   Refer to Real World Example 10-1. What is the function of the board of directors? What are the similarities between the board of directors and the firm's auditors in their relationship with the firm's stockholders?

DISCUSSION CASE

A Reverse Stock Split

Q10

Askin Service Corp. and Motor Oil Refinery Holding Co. of Chicago have reached an agreement in principle for the combination of the two companies.

Askin, which has been reducing its retail operations and has announced a plan to enter the energy field, would issue 10,520,298 common shares and warrants to purchase another 450,000 in the transaction, which would result in a transfer of control to the Chicago firm.

Askin currently has 818,922 shares outstanding and warrants to buy 400,000 additional shares.

Askin said the companies are considering a possible reverse split to reduce the shares outstanding of the combined company. The transaction is subject to the approval of a definite contract by the boards of Askin and Motor Oil Refinery and the stockholders of Askin.

For Discussion

1.   The company is reported to be considering a reverse stock split. What are the implications of this decision for the market price of shares, the number of stockholders and the stockholder base, and the number of shares outstanding?

2.   A student friend, a major in hotel administration, is having difficulty understanding the idea of a stock split. Someone has suggested using, instead of shares, a banana to be split. How is it comparable and how is it not comparable?

3.   Prepare a short example of a reverse stock split, using a banana split to get the idea across.

EXERCISES

Issuance of par value, stated value, and no-par shares (Q3)

E10-1   A corporation received a charter authorizing it to issue 5,000 shares of common stock.

Required

Prepare the entries necessary to record the issuance of 1,000 shares for $20,000, assuming that the stock is as follows:

1. $1 par value

2. $10 par value

3. $25 par value

4. No-par with a $5 stated value

5. No-par stock

Donated assets (Q9)

E10-2 A tract of land has been given to a corporation by a major stockholder. The land has a fair market value of $50,000, and its owner has had offers recently as high as $50,000.

Required

What journal entry, if any, is necessary to record the above "transaction"?

Authorized, issued, and outstanding shares (Q7)

E10-3 A corporation has common shares with the following statuses:

Unissued	45,000
Issued	35,000
Outstanding	28,000

Required

Determine the following:

1. Number of shares authorized

2. Number of shares in the treasury

3. Maximum number of shares that could ever be outstanding

4. Number of shares used to determine the book value of the stock

Stock subscriptions (Q14)

E10-4 A corporation allowed stockholders to subscribe to shares of common stock under the following agreement:

■ The issue price is $23 per share.
■ 20% of the total price must be paid on signing the contract.
■ 40% is due after two months.
■ The balance is due after an additional 2 months.

Required

Prepare the journal entries necessary to record the subscription to 20,000 shares of the company's $10 par value common stock.

Net assets vs. stock-holders' equity (Q11)

E10-5 A corporation has 10,000 common shares outstanding only, with a total stock-holders' equity as follows:

Legal Capital	$ 43,000
Paid-in Capital	86,000
Retained Earnings—Restricted	100,000
Retained Earnings—Unrestricted	75,000
Total Stockholders' Equity	$304,000

Required

What is the amount of net assets currently available to the corporation for operations? Can you determine the amount of assets and liabilities making up the net assets?

Book value of common stock (Q12)

E10-6   A corporation has 10,000 common shares outstanding only, with a total stockholders' equity as follows:

Legal Capital	$ 43,000
Paid-in Capital	86,000
Retained Earnings—Restricted	100,000
Retained Earnings—Unrestricted	75,000
Total Stockholders' Equity	$304,000

Required

What is the book value of the common stock?

Exchanging common stock for cash and non-cash assets (Q9)

E10-7   Perry Corp. received a charter to issue 10,000 shares of $1 par value common stock. The following transactions took place shortly thereafter:

- Issued 1,000 shares for $1,000 to the founding president
- Issued 500 shares for $750 to an attorney who agreed to represent the corporation in legal matters
- Issued 2,000 shares to investors who thought the idea had potential. They invested a total of $3,000.
- Issued 2,000 shares in exchange for operating equipment with undeterminable market value, although the asking price was $3,500

Required

Prepare the journal entries necessary to record the Perry transactions.

Stockholders' Equity section of balance sheet (Q12)

E10-8   The following information for 19X9 was taken from the general ledger of the Carstairs Corp.:

Long-term Debt	$ 100,000
Retained Earnings—Restricted for Plant Expansion	50,000
Revenues (total for 19X9)	2,500,000
Retained Earnings (January 1, 19X9)	75,000
Donated Land	50,000
Dividends	300,000
Retained Earnings—Restricted for Lawsuits Pending	50,000
Common Stock, $8 Par Value, 12,500 authorized, issued, and outstanding	100,000
Expenses (total for 19X9)	2,000,000
Paid-in Capital in Excess of Par Value	60,000
Paid-in Capital from Donated Assets	50,000

Required

1. Prepare the Stockholders' Equity section of the balance sheet in the correct format.
2. Calculate the book value of the common stock.
3. Describe what the calculated book value means to an individual stockholder.

PROBLEMS

Issuance of preferred
and common stock,
stockholders' equity,
stock split. (Q3, Q4,
Q8–Q10)

P10-1   Price Co. was incorporated on June 1, 19X5, with an authorization to issue 20,000 shares of $50 par value, 5% cumulative preferred stock, and 100,000 shares of common stock.

Required

1. Prepare journal entries to record the following transactions;
   (a) Issued 3,000 shares of preferred for $65 per share
   (b) Issued 2,000 shares of preferred for $50 per share
   (c) Issued 5,000 shares of common for $7 per share, assuming it is
      (1) $5 par value.
      (2) no-par, with a stated value of $2.
      (3) no-par no-stated-value.
   (d) Issued 5,000 shares of common in exchange for land valued at $50,000 when the stock was selling daily for $8 per share. Assume the stock had a par value of $5 per share.
   (e) Issued 1,000 shares of common to promoters of the corporation whose services were mutually valued at $10,000, assuming the common is
      (1) $5 par value.
      (2) no-par with a stated value of $2.
      (3) no-par no-stated-value.

2. Prepare the Stockholders' Equity section of the balance sheet as of the end of the first year. Assume that no dividends were declared or paid, that net income was $36,000, and that the common stock had a par value of $5.

3. Early the next year, the common stock was split 2-for-1. Prepare a new Stockholders' Equity section, assuming that no other transactions occurred.

Book value of common
shares (Q3, Q12)

P10-2   The following is the Stockholders' Equity section of the balance sheet of Red River Foods, Inc.:

Stockholders' Equity

Paid-in Capital

Common Stock, $10 Par Value, 500 shares authorized; 300 shares issued and outstanding	$3,000
Paid-in Capital in Excess of Par Value—Common	70
Total Paid-in Capital	$3,070
Retained Earnings	
Unrestricted	500
Total Stockholders' Equity	$3,570

Required

1. What is the book value of the common stock?

2. On December 31, the Red River common stock was trading at a record high of $24 per share. Why would investors be willing to buy stock at amounts that materially exceed the book value of the shares?

3. If the common stock had been no-par no-stated-value, how would the $70 paid-in capital in excess of par value be recorded?

4. What is the maximum amount of dividends that could be declared at this time?

Exchanging common
stock for cash and non-
cash assets, subscrip-
tions, stockholders'
equity (Q3, Q9, Q14)

P10-3   Big City Carpet Co. was incorporated January 2, 19X5. Its charter authorized the company to issue 100,000 common shares with a $5 par value. The following transactions occurred during the first half of 19X5:

Jan.   2   Issued 20,000 shares for $7.50 per share
        3   Issued 15,000 shares to Brown Wholesalers in exchange for carpet-cutting equipment. Brown had paid $75,000 for the equipment, but could have sold it for $120,000 to another company for cash.
        9   Accepted subscriptions for 10,000 shares at $8 per share with a cash payment of $40,000, and the balance due June 29.
June 29   The subscription balance due of $40,000 was paid, and the stock certificates issued.
      30   Net income for the first 6 months totaled $16,500, of which $2,900 was earned in January.

Required

1. Prepare journal entries to record the Big City transactions. Closing entries are not necessary.

2. Prepare two Stockholders' Equity sections, one as of January 31 and another as of June 30, 19X5.

Treasury stock, stock
splits, restriction on
retained earnings (Q7,
Q10)

P10-4   The Stockholders' Equity section of the balance sheet of the Alexandria and Ivaninsky Works, Inc., as of December 31, 19X1, follows:

Stockholders' Equity

Paid-in Capital		
Preferred Stock, $15 Par Value, 8% cumulative and nonparticipating, 1,000 shares authorized; 1,000 shares issued and outstanding		$15,000
Common Stock, $5 Par Value, 10,000 shares authorized; 4,800 shares issued and outstanding		24,000
Total Legal Capital		$39,000
Paid-in Capital in Excess of Par Value		
Common Stock	$ 7,000	
Preferred Stock	1,000	8,000
Total Paid-in Capital		$47,000
Retained Earnings		
Restricted for Plant Expansion	$12,000	
Unrestricted	20,000	
Total Retained Earnings		32,000
Total Stockholders' Equity		$79,000

The following transactions took place during 19X2:

Jan. 24   Reacquired 400 shares of common stock for $10 per share
Feb. 16   Reissued the Jan. 24 shares for $12 each
Aug. 13   Split the common stock 2-for-1
Oct. 18   Board authorized an addition of $5,000 to Retained Earnings Restricted for Plant Expansion
Dec. 31   Net Income of $19,500 closed to retained earnings

Required
1. Prepare the journal entries necessary for the AIW transactions.
2. Prepare a Stockholders' Equity section of the balance sheet as of December 31, 19X2.

ALTERNATE PROBLEMS

Issuance of preferred and common stock, stockholders' equity, stock split (Q3, Q4, Q8–Q10)

AP10-1 Sable Co. was incorporated on July 1, 19X1, with an authorization to issue 50,000 shares of $100 par value, 5% cumulative preferred stock and 200,000 shares of common stock.

Required
1. Prepare journal entries to record the following transactions:
   (a) Issued 5,000 shares of preferred for $105 per share
   (b) Issued 7,000 shares of preferred for $100 per share
   (c) Issued 5,000 shares of common for $15 per share, assuming it is
       (1) $1 par value.
       (2) no-par, with a stated value of $10.
       (3) no-par no-stated-value.
   (d) Issued 10,000 shares of common in exchange for land valued at $180,000 when the stock was selling daily for $15 per share. Assume the stock had a par value of $1 per share.
   (e) Issued 1,000 shares of common to promoters of the corporation whose services were mutually valued at $20,000, assuming the common is
       (1) $1 par value.
       (2) no-par, with a stated value of $10.
       (3) no-par no-stated-value.

2. Prepare the Stockholders' Equity section of the balance sheet as of the end of the first year. Assume that no dividends were declared or paid, that net income was $106,000, and that the common stock had a par value of $1.

3. Early the next year, the common stock was split 1-for-2. Prepare a new Stockholders' Equity section, assuming that no other transactions occurred.

Book value of common shares (Q3, Q12)

AP10-2 The following is the Stockholders' Equity section of the balance sheet of Lone Pine Foods, Inc.:

Stockholders' Equity

Paid-in Capital
Common Stock, $15 Par Value, 5,000 shares authorized;

3,000 shares issued and outstanding	$ 45,000
Paid-in Capital in Excess of Par Value—Common	7,000
Total Paid-in Capital	$ 52,000
Retained Earnings	
Unrestricted	50,000
Total Stockholders' Equity	$102,000

Required
1. What is the book value of the common stock?
2. On December 31, the Lone Pine common stock was trading at a record high of $124 per share. Why would investors be willing to buy stock at amounts that materially exceed the book value of the shares?

3. If the common stock had been no-par no-stated-value, how would the $7,000 paid-in capital in excess of par value be recorded?

4. What is the maximum amount of dividends that could be declared at this time?

Exchanging common stock for cash and non-cash assets, subscriptions, stockholders' equity (Q3, Q9, Q14)

AP10-3 Littleton Carpet Co. was incorporated January 2, 19X1. Its charter authorized the company to issue 200,000 common shares with a $1 par value. The following transactions occurred during the first half of 19X1:

Jan.	2	Issued 40,000 shares for $9.50 per share
	3	Issued 15,000 shares to Brown Wholesalers in exchange for carpet-cutting equipment. Brown had paid $75,000 for the equipment, but could have sold it for $150,000 to another company for cash.
	9	Accepted subscriptions for 10,000 shares at $11 per share with a cash payment of $60,000, and the balance due June 29.
June	29	The subscription balance due of $50,000 was paid, and the stock certificates issued.
	30	Net income for the first 6 months totaled $36,500, of which $5,000 was earned in January.

Required

1. Prepare journal entries to record the Littleton transactions. Closing entries are not necessary.

2. Prepare two Stockholders' Equity sections, one as of January 31 and another as of June 30, 19X1.

Treasury stock, stock splits, restriction on retained earnings (Q7, Q10)

AP10-4 The Stockholders' Equity section of the balance sheet of the Annie Cox Works, Inc., as of December 31, 19X1, follows:

Stockholders' Equity

Paid-in Capital		
Preferred Stock, $100 Par Value, 12% cumulative and nonparticipating, 10,000 shares authorized; 5,000 shares issued and outstanding		$ 500,000
Common Stock, $10 Par Value, 30,000 shares authorized; 10,000 shares issued and outstanding		100,000
Total Legal Capital		$ 600,000
Paid-in Capital in Excess of Par Value		
Common Stock	$307,000	
Preferred Stock	100,000	407,000
Total Paid-in Capital		$1,007,000
Retained Earnings		
Restricted for Plant Expansion	$120,000	
Unrestricted	200,000	
Total Retained Earnings		320,000
Total Stockholders' Equity		$1,327,000

The following transactions took place during 19X2:

Jan.	24	Reacquired 600 shares of common stock for $55 per share
Feb.	16	Reissued the Jan. 24 shares for $63 per share
Aug.	13	Split the common stock 5-for-1
Oct.	18	Board authorized an addition of $95,000 to Retained Earnings Restricted for Plant Expansion
Dec.	31	Net Income of $78,000 closed to retained earnings

Required

1. Prepare the journal entries necessary for the ACW transactions.

2. Prepare a Stockholders' Equity section of the balance sheet as of December 31, 19X2.

DECISION PROBLEM

Two Stockholders' Equity sections for Parker Sisters, Inc., as of December 31, 19X3, and December 31, 19X4, follow.

Stockholders' Equity (December 31, 19X3)

Paid-in Capital		
Preferred Stock, $50 Par Value, 10% cumulative and nonparticipating, 10,000 shares authorized; 4,000 shares issued and outstanding		$ 200,000
Common Stock, $15 Par Value, 100,000 shares authorized; 50,000 shares issued; 40,000 shares outstanding		750,000
Common Stock to Be Distributed		75,000
Total Legal Capital		$1,025,000
Paid-in Capital in Excess of Par Value		
Common Stock	$300,000	
Preferred Stock	20,000	320,000
Total Paid-in Capital		$1,345,000
Retained Earnings		
Unrestricted	$345,000	
Restricted	350,000	
Total Retained Earnings		695,000
Total		$2,040,000
Less: Treasury Stock at Cost ($35 per share)		350,000
Total Stockholders' Equity		$1,690,000

Note: The preferred stock dividends have not been paid in 3 years, leaving dividends in arrears for a total of $60,000.

Stockholders' Equity (December 31, 19X4)

Paid-in Capital

Preferred Stock, $50 Par Value, 10% cumulative and nonparticipating, 10,000 shares authorized; 6,000 shares issued and outstanding		$ 300,000
Common Stock, $15 Par Value, 100,000 shares authorized; 70,000 shares issued and outstanding		1,050,000
Total Legal Capital		$1,350,000
Paid-in Capital in Excess of Par Value		
Common Stock	$675,000	
Preferred Stock	30,000	
Paid-in Capital from Treasury Stock	100,000	805,000
Total Paid-in Capital		$2,155,000
Retained Earnings		
Unrestricted	$795,000	
Restricted	-0-	
Total Retained Earnings		795,000
Total		$2,950,000
Less: Treasury Stock		-0-
Total Stockholders' Equity		$2,950,000

Note: The net income for 19X4 was $200,000. Dividends were declared and paid during 19X4 and preferred shares were issued on December 31, 19X4.

Required

Identify and explain all stockholders' equity transactions that took place during 19X4.

ANSWERS TO SELF-TEST QUESTIONS

1. **(d)** Generally common stock is the voting stock of a corporation. If preferred stock has a voting right, it will be so stated on the certificate and is not governed by whether the stock is participating or cumulative.

2. **(d)** The answer to this question might be debatable, given that the officers of the corporation usually make the major decisions concerning the operations, but the day-to-day operations are governed by actions of the entire management team, including the officers if necessary.

3. **(a)** By definition, the difference between issued and outstanding stock is the number of treasury shares the corporation has repurchased. All issued stock is outstanding if the corporation owns no shares of its own stock. Formally retired shares are no longer considered outstanding or issued.

4. **(e)** In noncash transactions, the fair market value of the shares given up in exchange for the new asset is usually used to valuate the new asset. In some cases, especially when *new* shares are issued, the fair market value of the asset received is more determinable.

5. **(c)** If par value common stock is split 2-for-1, the old shares are called in and twice as many new shares are issued at one-half the par value of the old shares. Answers *a*, *b*, and *d* would be true if this were a reverse stock split of 1-for-2.

6. **(c)** Restrictions placed on retained earnings reduce the amount of retained earnings available for dividend distribution. No cash is set aside, and restrictions allow the board of directors *less* flexibility in determining the amount of dividends to declare.

7. **(d)** Land *is* recorded under historical cost even if it was of no *cost* to the corporation. It is recorded at its fair market value with an offset (credit) to an additional paid-in capital account called Donated Capital.

8. **(b)** This question involves a little lightheartedness. Stock subscriptions are nothing more than a time-payment approach to stockholders who do not have the up-front cash. There is no truth to this statement.

11 DIVIDEND DISTRIBUTIONS

As earnings are retained in a corporation, the board of directors must decide if any of those earnings should be distributed to the stockholders as dividends. The amount of retained earnings represents the maximum amount the directors may declare for an income dividend, but the amount of available cash weighs more heavily in dividend decisions. Chapter 11 investigates dividends in general and examines different classes of stock on which dividends are paid. Dividend distributions made up of the corporation's own stock are discussed, as well as decisions made by the board of directors to repurchase the corporation's own stock after it has been issued.

After studying Chapter 11, you should be able to answer the following questions:

1 Are all the components of stockholders' equity available for distribution as dividends? (pp. 498–99)

2 Why would the board of directors choose not to declare a dividend? (p. 499)

3 Once a dividend is declared, can the board of directors vote to rescind it? (pp. 499–500)

4 Three dates have been identified in regard to dividends; what accounting events take place on each of the dates? (pp. 500–501)

5 What is a property dividend and how does its accounting differ from a cash dividend? (p. 502)

6 Do any shares of a corporation have preference over other shares in dividend distributions? If so, why would a corporation give preference to some shares and not to others? (pp. 502–6)

7 What effect does a stock dividend have on the net assets of the corporation? (pp. 506–7)

8 What effect does a stock dividend have on the stockholders' investment account? (pp. 507–8)

9 Why would a corporation choose to buy back shares that were previously issued? (p. 512)

10 Are dividends paid on stock the corporation has repurchased? (p. 512)

DIVIDENDS

Components of Stockholders' Equity

Stockholders' equity consists of the rights to assets contributed by stockholders and others, and the rights to assets earned and retained in the business. The distinction between the sources of these assets is important. It relates to the availability of assets for distribution to stockholders as **dividends.** Exhibit 11-1 is an adaptation of Exhibit 10-7 in Chapter 10.

Q1: Equity as dividends

The legal capital portion in Exhibit 11-1 outlined in *box 1* is *never* available for dividend distribution. *Box 2* is currently not available for dividends because of a restriction placed on the assets by an action of the board of directors. Paid-in capital, *box 3,* may be available for dividends by an action of the board of directors, but any distribution would be considered a **liquidating dividend,** since it would be a return *of* investment, rather than a return *on* investment. Unrestricted retained

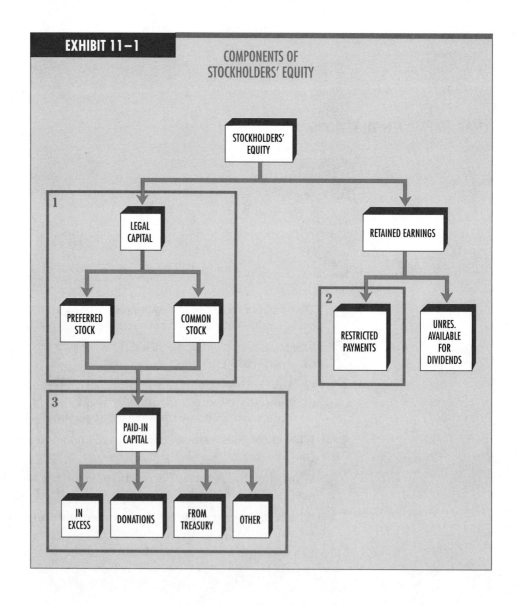

EXHIBIT 11–1

COMPONENTS OF STOCKHOLDERS' EQUITY

earnings are always available for dividend distribution if Cash is sufficient, and if the board of directors decides to declare a dividend.

Both creditors and stockholders are interested in the amount of assets that can be distributed as dividends. Legal capital and restricted retained earnings represent assets unavailable for distribution as dividends. These categories are intended to protect creditors because they prevent stockholders from withdrawing assets as dividends to the point where assets become insufficient to pay creditors; they are also intended to ensure the continued operation of the business.

Stockholders' equity is classified in Exhibit 11-1 to emphasize the distinction between assets available for dividends and assets unavailable for dividends. However, such a diagram is not published by corporations in their financial statements. Rather, the reader of financial statements must understand and be able to interpret the information on the balance sheet and in its notes.

A word of caution—the various state corporation acts have different provisions for dividend distribution, and this discussion does not refer to any particular state law. Most states, however, follow these general guidelines.

Dividend Policy

Q2: Not declaring dividends

Sometimes a board of directors may choose not to declare any dividend. Financial conditions in the corporation may make the payment impractical or even impossible, such as would occur if a deficit were in the Retained Earnings account. A **deficit** exists whenever Retained Earnings has a *debit* balance. The board of directors also may decide not to pay dividends even when the corporation has unrestricted retained earnings.

1. *Cash may not be adequate.* Corporations regularly reinvest their earnings in assets in order to make more profits. Growth occurs in this way and reliance on creditor financing can be minimized.

2. *The policy of the corporation may preclude dividend payments.* Some corporations pay no dividends. They reinvest their earnings in the business. Stockholders benefit through increased earnings, which are translated into increased market prices for the corporation's shares. The pressure from stockholders for the corporation to provide dividends is reduced in this way. This type of dividend policy is often found in growth-oriented corporations.

3. *No laws require dividends to be paid.* The board of directors may decide that no dividends should be paid. If stockholders are dissatisfied, they can elect a new board or, failing that, sell their shares.

4. *Dividends may be issued in shares of the corporation rather than in cash.* Stock dividends may be issued to conserve cash or to increase the number of shares to be traded on the stock market. Stock dividends are discussed later in this chapter.

The difficulty faced in deciding on the declaration of a dividend is discussed in Real World Example 11-1.

Dividend Declaration

Q3: Rescinding dividends

Dividends can be paid only if they have been officially declared by the board of directors. The board must pass a formal resolution authorizing the dividend payment. Notices of the dividend are then published. It is noteworthy that once a

REAL WORLD EXAMPLE 11-1
A Tough Call: The Dividend

Du Pont's board of directors will gather tomorrow in one of the ornate rooms at the chemical company's headquarters in Wilmington, Del., for what has become an annual fall ritual: the vote on whether to award an extra dividend on top of the $0.60 quarterly dividend.

Some analysts believe the vote will indicate just how difficult the board expects the next couple of quarters to be. With the economy in such straits, and Du Pont's chemical business having a difficult time, there are some questions as to whether the board will part with the traditional bonus, which has been as high as $0.75 and has been paid in eight out of the last 11 years. Last year shareholders received an extra $0.35.

"No one knows what will happen," said a spokesman for Du Pont. "The finance committee will consider it first because they have all the information on earnings and the economy, and then they will send the recommendation onto the full board, which meets right after the finance committee."

The decision might produce a lively debate between the board members who are large shareholders and need the dividends, like the three Seagram representatives, and the more frugal-minded executives of Du Pont, according to William Young, a vice-president at Dean Witter Reynolds.

Most analysts think the odds are high that the extra dividend will be awarded simply because it does not really cost Du Pont all that much—around $80 million if $0.35 is awarded, according to Young—and not awarding the special payment could alienate shareholders who have stuck by the company during a difficult year.

Source *The New York Times,* November 14, 1984, p. 27-f. Copyright © 1984 by The New York Times Company. Reprinted by permission.

dividend declaration has been made public, the dividend cannot be rescinded. At this point, the dividend becomes a liability and must be paid. An example of a dividend notice is shown in Exhibit 11-2.

Three different and important dates are associated with the dividend. Usually dividends are declared on one date, the **date of dividend declaration;** they are payable to stockholders on a second date, the **date of record;** and the dividend itself is actually paid on a third date, the **date of payment.**

DATE OF DIVIDEND DECLARATION

Q4: Dividend dates

The dividend declaration provides an official notice of the dividend. It specifies the amount of the dividend and which stockholders will receive the dividend. The liability for the dividend is recorded in the books of the corporation on its declaration date. Stockholders become creditors of the corporation until the dividend is paid.

DATE OF RECORD

Stockholders who own the shares on the date of record will receive the dividend even if they have sold the share before the dividend is actually paid. This date is usually a week or two after the date of declaration. This is important for corporations whose shares are actively traded on the stock market. Investors whose names appear in the stockholders' ledger on the date of record will receive the dividend.

EXHIBIT 11–2   A TYPICAL DIVIDEND NOTICE

Saguaro Computers, Inc.

Dividend Notice

On May 25, 19X1, the Board of Directors of Saguaro Computers, Inc., declared a semi-annual dividend of $0.50 per share on common shares. The dividend will be paid on June 26, 19X1, to stockholders of record on June 7, 19X1.

By Order of the Board
[signed]
Lee Cactus
Secretary

May 25, 19X1

Shares sold on the stock market after the date of record are sold *ex-dividend,* that is, without any right to the dividend.

DATE OF PAYMENT

The dividend is actually paid on this date to investors whose names appear in the stockholders' ledger on the date of record. This date is several weeks after the date of record, in order to allow share transfers to be recorded to the date of record and dividend checks to be prepared.

Accounting for Dividends

Dividends are usually paid as **cash dividends.** They also can be paid in other assets of the corporation, or in shares of the corporation itself. (The latter case is discussed in a later section.) When dividends are declared in assets other than cash, they are usually referred to as **property dividends.** Property dividends often create problems in dividing the property pro-rata (in proportion), because of the difficulty distributing to stockholders in proportion to the number of shares they own. Usually, inventory of the corporation and temporary investments are the first assets to be considered for property dividends. The journal entries for cash and property dividends take the following form:

Cash Dividends			Property Dividends		
Declaration date			*Declaration date*		
Dividends	xxx		Dividends	xxx	
Dividends Payable		xxx	Dividends Payable		xxx
Payment date			*Payment date*		
Dividends Payable	xxx		Dividends Payable	xxx	
Cash		xxx	Inventory		xxx
			Investments		xxx

Remember, the Dividends account is closed to Retained Earnings in a separate entry during the closing process. If a balance sheet is prepared between the date

Q5: Property
dividend

of declaration and the date of payment, the Dividends Payable account is reported in the current liability section of the balance sheet.

Before property dividends are distributed, the assets must first be adjusted to their fair market value. If the inventory in the prior example was valued using the LIFO method, its book value may be substantially below the inventory's fair market value. If the LIFO value of the inventory in question was $6,000, but the inventory could be sold for $15,000, then the following entry must be made:

Inventory	9,000	
Gain on Inventory Distributed As		
a Property Dividend		9,000

The same would be true with the investments distributed in the prior example. If the historical cost of the investments was $15,000 and their current market value was $48,000, then the following entry must be made:

Investments	33,000	
Gain on Investments Distributed		
As a Property Dividend		33,000

STOCKHOLDER PREFERENCE TO DIVIDENDS

Q6: Preferred shares

Preferred stockholders are usually entitled to dividends before any dividends are distributed to common stockholders. They may also receive other dividend preferences, depending what rights have been attached to preferred shares at the date of incorporation. Two additional preferences can be

- The accumulation of undeclared dividends from one year to the next—referred to as *cumulative dividends,* as compared with *noncumulative dividends,* which do not accumulate
- The participation of preferred stock with common stock in dividend distributions beyond the usual preferred dividends—referred to as a *participating* feature of preferred stock, as compared with a *nonparticipating* feature

The relationships among these dividend preferences are shown in Exhibit 11-3.

Cumulative Dividend Preferences

The *cumulative* preference on **cumulative preferred stock** means that an unpaid dividend based on a predesignated percentage or amount accumulates from year to year and is payable from future earnings after a dividend declaration is made by the entity. These accumulated dividends must be paid before any dividends are paid on common stock. The unpaid dividends are usually referred to as *dividends in arrears.* Dividends in arrears are not recorded as a liability on the balance sheet of the company unless and until they have been declared by the board of directors. Note disclosure of dividends in arrears, however, must be made in the financial statements.

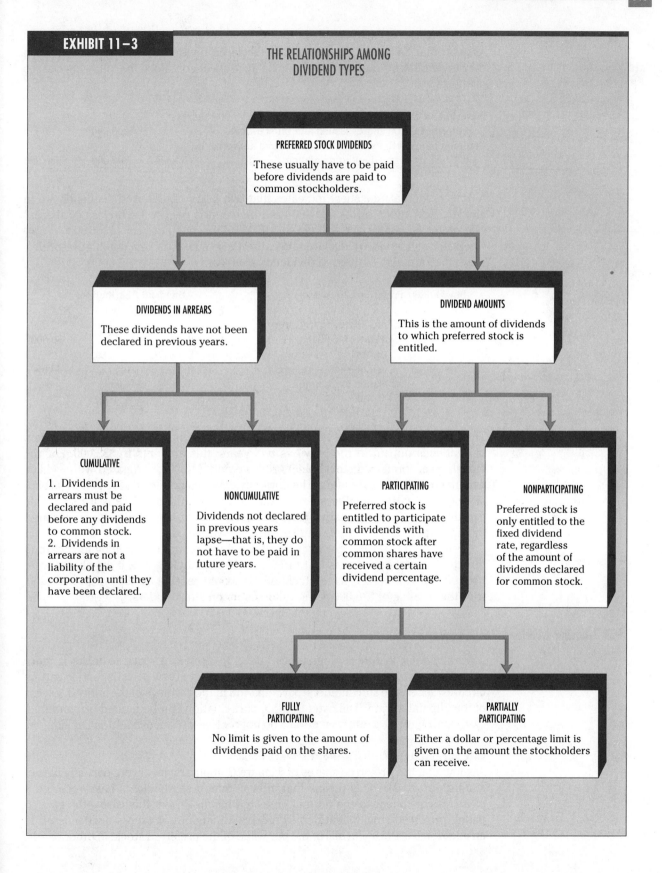

EXHIBIT 11–3

THE RELATIONSHIPS AMONG
DIVIDEND TYPES

PREFERRED STOCK DIVIDENDS

These usually have to be paid before dividends are paid to common stockholders.

DIVIDENDS IN ARREARS

These dividends have not been declared in previous years.

DIVIDEND AMOUNTS

This is the amount of dividends to which preferred stock is entitled.

CUMULATIVE

1. Dividends in arrears must be declared and paid before any dividends to common stock.
2. Dividends in arrears are not a liability of the corporation until they have been declared.

NONCUMULATIVE

Dividends not declared in previous years lapse—that is, they do not have to be paid in future years.

PARTICIPATING

Preferred stock is entitled to participate in dividends with common stock after common shares have received a certain dividend percentage.

NONPARTICIPATING

Preferred stock is only entitled to the fixed dividend rate, regardless of the amount of dividends declared for common stock.

FULLY PARTICIPATING

No limit is given to the amount of dividends paid on the shares.

PARTIALLY PARTICIPATING

Either a dollar or percentage limit is given on the amount the stockholders can receive.

CASE 1: CUMULATIVE PREFERRED STOCK

Assume that Saguaro Computers, Inc., declared dividends totaling $92,000 when the Stockholders' Equity section of its balance sheet contained the following classes of shares:

Preferred Stock, $100 Par Value, 8% cumulative; 3,000 shares authorized; 2,000 shares issued and outstanding	$200,000	
Common Stock, $10 Par Value, 35,000 shares authorized; 30,000 shares issued and outstanding	300,000	$500,000

A note to the balance sheet indicates that two years of preferred dividends are in arrears. How much of the $92,000 cash dividend is paid to each class of shares? The preferred shares are entitled to $16,000 dividends per year ($200,000 × 8%) whenever dividends are declared. Because these shares have a cumulative preference, they are also entitled to dividends in arrears.

Stockholder Preference to Dividends		Dividend Distribution		
		To Preferred	*To Common*	*Balance*
	Total Dividend Declared	—	—	$92,000
1st Preference:	Arrears ($16,000 × 2 years)	$32,000	—	60,000
2nd Preference:	Current Year—Preferred	16,000	—	44,000
	Balance to Common	—	$44,000	-0-
	Total	$48,000	$44,000	

The cumulative preference has resulted in the payment to preferred stockholders of dividends unpaid in the previous two years; this amounts to $32,000. For the current year, preferred stockholders receive only $16,000, compared with $44,000 paid to common stockholders. The normally cautious preferred stockholder is usually content with a smaller share of the profits as long as there is a reasonably certain return. The cumulative feature ensures that, if any dividends are declared by the corporation, the preferred stockholder will be paid.

For noncumulative preferred stock, a dividend not declared by the board of directors in any one year is lost forever. In the example given, if the shares were noncumulative, the preferred stockholders would receive $16,000 of the $92,000, with the balance of $76,000 going to the common stockholders.

Participating Dividend Preferences

A *participating* feature is sometimes added to preferred stock to make it more attractive to stockholders. Participating preferred stock permits, under certain circumstances, the stockholders' participation in the earnings of the entity in excess of the stipulated rate. The extent of this participation can be limited or unlimited. Nonparticipating preferred stocks do not receive a share of additional dividends.

CASE 2: PARTIALLY PARTICIPATING PREFERRED SHARES

Assume that the preferred shares of Saguaro Computers, Inc., were partially participating up to 10%. This means that after common stockholders have received a payment equivalent to the normal preferred claim—8% in this case—the participating preferred stock is entitled to receive an amount of excess dividends up to an additional 2% (10% in all) of the par value of the preferred stock. In other words, once common stockholders receive 8% of the par value of their shares in dividends, both common and preferred stockholders are entitled to a pro-rata share of excess dividends up to 10%. Then common stockholders are entitled to any dividend funds remaining.

Stockholder Preference to Dividends		Dividend Distribution		
		To Preferred	*To Common*	*Balance*
	Total Dividend Declared	—	—	$92,000
1st Preference:	Arrears ($16,000 × 2 years)	$32,000	—	60,000
2nd Preference:	Current Year—Preferred 8%	16,000	—	44,000
3rd Preference:	Current Year—Common 8% to Match Preferred 8%			
	($300,000 × 8%)	—	$24,000	20,000
4th Preference:	Current Year—1% to Each Class			
	($200,000 × 1%)	2,000	—	15,000
	($300,000 × 1%)	—	3,000	
5th Preference:	Current Year—Additional 1% to Each Class =			
	10% to Each Class	2,000	3,000	10,000
	Balance to Common	—	10,000	-0-
	Total	$52,000	$40,000	

In this case, preferred stockholders receive $52,000, compared with $40,000 for common stockholders. If the dividends declared had been insufficient to pay $24,000 ($300,000 × 8%) for the current year in the third preference, however, the participating feature would not have come into effect for preferred stockholders. Notice also that dividends were sufficient to pay more than 10% of par value to common stockholders, who receive the balance of $10,000 after the fifth preference.

CASE 3: FULLY PARTICIPATING PREFERRED SHARES

Case 2 presented the calculation of dividends when preferred stockholders were partially participating in dividends. Preferred stock also may be fully participating. What would the dividend distribution be if preferred stockholders were fully participating with common stockholders in Saguaro Computers, Inc., rather than being limited to 10% participation?

Stockholder Preference to Dividends		Dividend Distribution		
		To Preferred	*To Common*	*Balance*
	Total Dividend Declared	—	—	$92,000
1st Preference:	Arrears ($16,000 × 2 years)	$32,000	—	60,000
2nd Preference:	Current Year—Preferred 8%	16,000	—	44,000
3rd Preference:	Current Year—Common 8% to Match Preferred 8%	—	$24,000	20,000
4th Preference:	Current Year—the Balance Is Distributed in Proportion of Each Class of Shares to Total Stated Capital			
	Preferred = $\frac{\$200,000}{\$500,000} \times \$20,000 =$	8,000		
	Common = $\frac{\$300,000}{\$500,000} \times \$20,000 =$		12,000	-0-
	Total	$56,000	$36,000	

In this case, preferred stockholders receive $56,000, compared with $36,000 for common stockholders. Obviously, the fully participating preference here allows preferred stockholders to receive more dividends than common stockholders.

Investments in shares of a corporation carry with them an element of risk that the investment may be lost if the corporation is unsuccessful. Different classes of shares are therefore used to appeal to investors whose willingness to take risks differ. The Saguaro Computers, Inc., preferred stockholders have taken less risk than the common stockholders. The preference features attached to the stock have made it perform quite well in the three cases. Common stockholders have received less with the participating feature than preferred stockholders. These examples have been used to illustrate the different preferences that can be given to preferred stock. In practice, fully participating features are seldom provided for preferred shares. While cumulative features do occur, participating features are rarely found.

STOCK DIVIDEND DISTRIBUTIONS

Q7: Stock dividends and net assets

A **stock dividend** is a dividend payable to stockholders in shares of the declaring corporation, generally in place of a cash or property dividend. The stockholders are satisfied, and the corporation is able to conserve cash for reinvestment and expansion, reducing the need to finance these activities through long-term debt.

Assume that Saguaro Computers, Inc., declares a 10% stock dividend to common stockholders. Just before the declaration, the Stockholders' Equity section of the balance sheet appeared as follows:

Stockholders' Equity

Paid-in Capital	
Common Stock, $3 Par Value, 20,000 shares authorized;	
5,000 shares issued and outstanding	$ 15,000
Paid-in Capital in Excess of Par Value	10,000
Retained Earnings	
Unrestricted	100,000
Total Stockholders' Equity	$125,000

If at the date of declaration the stock is selling on one of the organized exchanges for $12, an amount equal to $6,000 (500 × $12) would be transferred from Retained Earnings to Paid-in Capital.

A stock dividend is usually expressed as a percentage of outstanding shares. In this case, if 5,000 shares are outstanding, and the dividend declared is 10%, then the board of directors chose to issue 500 shares (5,000 × 10%). If 500 shares with a par value of $3 each are issued, then the Common Stock account would be credited with $1,500 (500 × $3 par). If the shares are selling at $12 at the time of the declaration, the market value of shares distributed would be $6,000 (500 × $12). Therefore, $6,000 should be transferred out of Retained Earnings, with $1,500 being credited to the Common Stock account, and the difference of $4,500 to the Paid-in Capital in Excess of Par Value account. The entry would then appear as follows:

Retained Earnings	6,000	
Common Stock		1,500
Paid-in Capital in Excess of Par		
Value		4,500

The reasoning behind this entry will be discussed later in the chapter, but first it is important to examine the effect of a stock dividend on an individual investor.

If one investor in SCI owns 1,000 shares, then he or she would receive 100 shares as a result of this dividend (1,000 shares × 10%). Since no corporate assets were distributed in the stock dividend, theoretically the market price of the shares should fall proportionately to compensate for the increased number of shares. If the market price of one share of stock was $12, the investor with 1,000 shares would have an investment with a market value of $12,000. If that investor's shares increased to 1,100 shares, the market price per share *should* drop to $10.91 ($12,000 ÷ 1,100) under the assumption that the total market value of the investment should not change. This analysis can be shown as follows:

	Before Stock Dividend	After Stock Dividend
Market Price of One Share	$12	$10.91
Total Market Value of Shares:		
1,000 × $12	$12,000	
1,100 × $10.91		$12,000

Theoretically, the total market value should stay the same before and after the stock dividend. In reality, this is seldom the case. The market price of the stock may fall an immaterial amount or may even increase because of some other element in the market, such as news of slowing inflation, lower gasoline prices, or even news from other countries such as the changes that took place in Eastern Europe in the late 1980s and early 1990s.

Whatever happens, the stockholder seldom loses ground when a stock dividend is distributed, unless it is a very large percentage of the outstanding stock. Most stock dividends are in the neighborhood of 1% to 10% of the outstanding stock, and do not have a material affect on the actual market price. This is why the market price of the stock is used to measure the amount of retained earnings to be transferred to the Paid-in Capital section of the balance sheet. If a board of directors is considering a larger stock dividend, such as 50%, it usually treats the transaction as a stock split rather than a stock dividend. This situation is discussed later in this chapter.

If the market price of the stock is not materially affected, then the stockholder has received something of value in a stock dividend. Assuming the market price of each share does not change after Saguaro's stock dividend, the total value to the investor who owns 1,000 shares has increased by $1,200, as is shown:

Before:	1,000 shares × $12 =	$12,000
After:	1,100 shares × $12 =	$13,200
Increase:		$ 1,200

Since no assets were transferred, and increases in market values are not recognized under historical cost, no journal entry is made by the stockholder who receives a stock dividend. Only the number of shares that the stockholder owns changes. The cost basis of *each* share now owned decreases, as is shown next, assuming that the investor originally paid $8 per share.

Before:	$8,000 ÷ 1,000 = $8 per share
After:	$8,000 ÷ 1,100 = $7.30 (rounded) per share

Q8: Stock dividends and stockholders' account

The ownership interest in the corporation does not change as the result of a stock dividend. In the prior example, the investor who owned 1,000 shares out of 5,000 shares had a 20% interest in the corporation (1,000 ÷ 5,000 = 20%). If in a

10% stock dividend 500 shares are distributed, the corporation now has 5,500 shares outstanding, of which the investor now owns 1,100 shares or a 20% interest (1,100 ÷ 5,500 = 20%).

The stockholders' dollar interest in the corporation also does not change with the issuance of a stock dividend. Refer to Saguaro's partial balance sheet on p. 506. After the journal entry was posted, SCI's Stockholders' Equity section on the balance sheet changed to the following:

Stockholders' Equity

Paid-in Capital
    Common Stock, $3 Par Value, 20,000 shares authorized;

5,500 shares issued and outstanding	$ 16,500
Paid-in Capital in Excess of Par Value	14,500
Retained Earnings	
Unrestricted	94,000
Total Stockholders' Equity	$125,000

Notice that before and after the stock dividend, the stockholder owns a 20% interest in Saguaro, which has a stockholders' equity of $125,000. Or it could be said that the book value of the stockholder's interest in the corporation has not changed as a result of the stock dividend ($125,000 × 20% = $25,000).

Accounting for Stock Dividends

For small stock dividends, generally below 25% of the outstanding shares, an amount equal to the market value of the shares is used to determine the total market value of the dividend. As noted earlier, this requires a transfer, or **capitalization of Retained Earnings,** from Retained Earnings in the Stockholders' Equity section of the balance sheet to Paid-in Capital. This transfer is illustrated in Exhibit 11-4, using SCI's example.

Since the dividend is recorded at market value, $6,000 of retained earnings is *capitalized* as a result of the dividend, and is no longer available for cash dividend distributions. Of the $6,000 transferred to Paid-in Capital, the par value, or $1,500, is added to legal capital, making it *unavailable for dividends,* while the balance of $4,500 becomes the Paid-in Capital in Excess of Par Value, which may become available in the future for liquidating dividends.

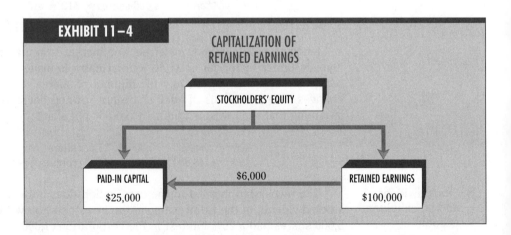

EXHIBIT 11-4

CAPITALIZATION OF RETAINED EARNINGS

STOCKHOLDERS' EQUITY

PAID-IN CAPITAL $25,000 $6,000   RETAINED EARNINGS $100,000

After the transfer has been recorded, stockholders' equity becomes the following:

Paid-in Capital: $ 25,000 + $6,000 = $ 31,000
Retained Earnings: $100,000 − $6,000 =   94,000
                                         $125,000

Note that only the composition of stockholders' equity changed, not the total. No assets were distributed or liabilities created.

Stock dividends, like cash dividends, usually encompass three dates; the date of declaration, the date of record, and the date of distribution. The entry for SCI's transfer, shown on p. 506, assumes that the declaration and distribution took place at the same time. If the dividend was declared at one time and distributable at another (the typical situation), the entry on the declaration date would appear as follows:

Retained Earnings	6,000	
Common Stock to be Distributed		1,500
Paid-in Capital in Excess of Par Value		4,500

Note that the only change is that a new account has been created that would appear in the Stockholders' Equity section of the balance sheet if one is prepared before distribution as follows:

Stockholders' Equity

Paid-in Capital
Common Stock, $3 Par Value, 20,000 shares authorized;
    5,000 shares issued and outstanding .... $ 15,000
Common Stock to Be Distributed (1,000 shares at par) 1,500
Paid-in Capital in Excess of Par Value 14,500
Retained Earnings
Unrestricted 94,000
    Total Stockholders' Equity $125,000

When the shares are actually distributed on the payment date, the following entry will be made:

Common Stock to be Distributed	1,500	
Common Stock		1,500

Stock Dividend versus Stock Split

If, instead of a 10% dividend, Saguaro Computers, Inc., had distributed a 50% stock dividend, the outcome might be quite different, depending whether the transaction is treated as a stock dividend or as a stock split. A 50% stock dividend would have the same economic effect as a 1-1/2-for-1 stock split. In a 50% stock dividend, 2,500 of SCI's authorized shares would be issued (50% × 5,000) and 7,500 shares would be outstanding (5,000 + 2,500), while in a 1-1/2-for-1 stock split, the old 5,000 shares would be called in and 7,500 (5,000 × 1-1/2) new shares would be issued. In both cases, 7,500 shares would be outstanding after the stock transaction. The effect of each on the balance sheet, however, would be quite different. Remember that for a stock dividend an amount must be transferred from Retained Earnings to

Common Stock. When Saguaro issued a 10% stock dividend, the entry appeared as follows:

Retained Earnings	6,000	
Common Stock		1,500
Paid-in Capital in Excess of Par Value		4,500

The transfer from Retained Earnings to Paid-in Capital was measured by the market value of the 500 shares of stock (500 × $12). Market value was used since a small stock dividend does not have a proportionate or sometimes not even a measurable effect on the market price, even though more shares are outstanding. A 50% stock dividend would have a measurable and maybe even a proportionate effect on the market price, so market value is not used. Many times only the par value is used to measure the value of the dividend. If par value were used in the 50% stock dividend, the entry would be as follows:

Retained Earnings	7,500	
Common Stock		7,500

The $7,500 is the total par value of the additional 2,500 shares issued ($3 × 2,500). Stockholders' Equity would appear on the balance sheet as follows after the 50% dividend:

Stockholders' Equity

Paid-in Capital
Common Stock, $3 Par Value, 20,000 shares authorized;
7,500 shares issued and outstanding	$ 22,500
Paid-in Capital in Excess of Par Value	10,000
Retained Earnings	
Unrestricted	92,500
Total Stockholders' Equity	$125,000

Note that the unrestricted retained earnings has been reduced by $7,500, leaving $92,500 available for future dividends. If the stock transaction had taken the form of a 1-1/2-for-1 stock split, Stockholders' Equity would appear as follows:

Stockholders' Equity

Paid-in Capital
Common Stock, $2 Par Value, 30,000 shares authorized;
7,500 shares issued and outstanding	$ 15,000
Paid-in Capital in Excess of Par Value	10,000
Retained Earnings	
Unrestricted	100,000
Total Stockholders' Equity	$125,000

Remember that in a stock split the number of shares authorized, issued, and outstanding changes, as well as the par value of each share, but the *total* par value does not change. Therefore no change occurs in paid-in capital or retained earnings, leaving $100,000 in unrestricted retained earnings available for future dividends, $7,500 more than for the 50% stock dividend.

Usually, large stock dividends are treated as stock splits so retained earnings do not have to be permanently *capitalized.*

TREASURY STOCK

Once again, the many and varied state incorporation acts influence the accounting for shares of a corporation's own stock that the corporation has reacquired. If these shares are not retired and placed back in the authorized but unissued category—a transaction discussed in a more advanced accounting course—then they are known as treasury stock, as introduced in Chapter 10. Of the several methods to account for treasury stock, most are taught in a more advanced course. The **cost method** of accounting for treasury stock will be discussed here because it is the one used most often in practice. Under the cost method, the Treasury Stock account is debited for the amount paid to reacquire the shares. Assuming that $15,000 was paid to purchase 1,000 shares, the entry would be as follows:

Treasury Stock	15,000	
Cash		15,000

Recall from Chapter 10 that the Treasury Stock account is a contra account to *total* stockholders' equity and therefore is subtracted at the very end of the equity section.

When the shares are subsequently sold again, the entry depends on whether the shares are sold for more or less than cost. If one-half of the reacquired 1,000 shares in the last example are sold for $17 per share, the entry would be as follows:

Cash (500 × $17)	8,500	
Treasury Stock (500 × $15)		7,500
Paid-in Capital from Treasury Transactions		1,000

Note that the par value of the shares had no bearing on these entries.

If the remaining 500 shares are subsequently sold for $14 per share, the entry would be as follows:

Cash (500 × $14)	7,000	
Paid-in Capital from Treasury Transactions	500	
Treasury Stock (500 × $15)		7,500

Note that when treasury shares are reissued for less than cost ($15), the difference is taken out of paid-in capital from previous treasury stock transactions, if the amount in the account is sufficient, as it is in this transaction. Instead assume that the remaining 500 shares were reissued for $11 per share. The entry would appear as follows *if* the paid-in capital were sufficient:

Cash (500 × $11)	5,500	
Paid-in Capital from Treasury Transactions	2,000	
Treasury Stock (500 × $15)		7,500

However, the Paid-in Capital from Treasury Transactions had only a $1,000 balance, the maximum that could be debited to the account, so the entry would be as follows:

Cash (500 × $11)	5,500	
Paid-in Capital from Treasury		
Transactions	1,000	
Treasury Stock (500 × $15)		7,500

But this entry does not balance. Where does the remaining $1,000 shortage come from? The answer depends on the various state laws, but a general answer applies at this level: from Retained Earnings. The *correct* entry appears as follows:

Cash (500 × $11)	5,500	
Retained Earnings	1,000	
Paid-in Capital from Treasury		
Transactions	1,000	
Treasury Stock (500 × $15)		7,500

Q9: Buying back shares

Why does a corporation buy its own shares? The answers are many and varied. The corporation may have no more authorized shares remaining unissued and sees a need in the future for such shares for stock dividends or stock options (to be discussed in Chapter 14). Sometimes, if the market is going down, the corporation may be able to slow the effect on its own shares by buying some. Other courses in the business curriculum explain other situations when it is advantageous for a corporation to purchase its own shares.

Dividends and Treasury Stock

Q10: Dividends and repurchased stock

When a corporation declares cash or property dividends, the distribution is based on the number of shares outstanding, not the number of shares issued. That is, cash and property dividends are not paid to shares in the treasury. The entry to record the declaration and payment of a cash dividend is as follows:

Retained Earnings	XXX	
Cash		XXX

If the corporation declared and paid cash dividends to shares in the treasury, the receipt of the dividend would have to be recorded as follows:

Cash	XXX	
Dividend Income		XXX

Since the Dividend Income account is closed to Retained Earnings, the previously reported income of the corporation would be reported again on a future income statement; that is, the same income would be reported twice.

When the corporation splits the common stock, the shares in the treasury also will be split, and if a stock dividend is declared, the corporation may or may not declare the dividend on the shares in the treasury. The accounting for these transactions, however, is covered in more advanced courses.

CHAPTER REVIEW

1 Are all the components of stockholders' equity available for distribution as dividends? (pp. 498–99)

No, the portion designated as legal capital cannot be distributed in the form of dividends. Legal capital consists of the *total* par or stated value of stock having such a value, or the total amount paid in for no-par no-stated-value shares. Also, the board of directors may have placed some restrictions on retained earnings for various reasons. If any of the restrictions are in place at dividend declaration time, that component of stockholders' equity is not available. If dividend declarations are made from paid-in capital, the distribution is referred to as a liquidating dividend.

2 Why would the board of directors choose not to declare a dividend? (p. 499)

A corporation's dividend payment record is important to investors. Therefore, the board of directors of companies with established dividend payment records will do everything possible to maintain that record. If, however, the company is in a very poor cash position, the board may decide to forego the declaration. Many new companies will have a policy of not declaring dividend payments until they have become established. All earnings are then plowed back into the company, lessening the need for outside long-term debt financing.

3 Once a dividend is declared, can the board of directors vote to rescind it? (pp. 499–500)

No. Once declared, a cash or property dividend becomes a liability of the corporation and must be paid. The declaration of a *stock dividend* may be rescinded.

4 Three dates have been identified in regard to dividends; what accounting events take place on each of the dates? (pp. 500–501)

- The date of declaration: the liability is established and an entry is made debiting Retained Earnings and crediting a liability account.
- The date of record: the liability to a specific stockholder is determined; no entry is recorded in the accounting records.
- The date of payment: the asset, either cash or property, is distributed to the stockholders and an entry is made debiting the liability account and crediting Cash or other assets.

5 What is a property dividend and how does its accounting differ from a cash dividend? (p. 502)

A property dividend is a distribution of assets other than cash to the stockholders. The property must first be increased or decreased in the accounting records to its fair market value before being distributed to the stockholders. A gain or loss would be recorded at the same time.

6 Do any shares of a corporation have preference over other shares in dividend distributions? If so, why would a corporation give preference to some shares and not to others? (pp. 502–6)

The board of directors is not required to declare a dividend on any shares. When dividends are declared, however, *preferred shares* will receive dividends before *common shares*. If the preferred shares have a cumulative feature, dividends not declared and paid in past years will accumulate and must be paid when a dividend is declared before common stockholders receive any distributions.

Corporations may give preference to some shares (preferred) over others (common) to promote investment into the entity. For a new corporation, preferred shares are easier to sell than common since they are perceived as a less risky investment. If the corporation fails, preferred stockholders will receive their share of remaining assets, if any, before common stockholders.

7 What effect does a stock dividend have on the net assets of the corporation? (pp. 506–7)

A stock dividend has no effect on net assets. The only movement is within the Stockholders' Equity section of a balance sheet, with no effect on assets or liabilities. The net assets are simply spread over a greater number of shares. The entry to record a stock dividend is as follows:

Retained Earnings	XXX	
Common Stock		XXX
Paid-in Capital in Excess of Par Value		XXX

8 What effect does a stock dividend have on the stockholders' investment account? (pp. 507–8)

A stock dividend has no dollar effect on such an account. Stock dividends are not considered income to the recipient, since no assets are distributed. The investor's total cost is now spread over a greater number of shares, reducing the cost basis per share. *If* the investor records investments at market value rather than cost, a small stock dividend probably would increase the total market value, because the market price per share does not fall proportionately to the increased number of shares.

9 Why would a corporation choose to buy back shares that were previously issued? (p. 512)

The corporation may choose to buy its own shares (treasury stock) for a number of reasons. All the authorized shares may have been issued, and, rather than getting a new authorization from the state of incorporation, the board of directors may choose to buy shares from the market place, just as any other investor. The shares may be needed for a planned stock dividend, or for a stock option plan to encourage employees to stay with the corporation. In some cases, the corporation can influence the market price of stock by buying and selling its own shares. A corporation may also repurchase its own shares and formally retire them when stockholder investment is no longer needed.

10 Are dividends paid on stock the corporation has repurchased? (p. 512)

No, cash and property dividends are not paid on shares in the treasury. Stock dividends *may* be distributed on treasury shares, and stock splits normally affect the number of shares in the treasury.

KEY TERMS

capitalization of Retained Earnings (p. 508)   The transfer on a balance sheet from Retained Earnings to Paid-in Capital as the result of a stock dividend.

cash dividend (p. 501)   A distribution to stockholders made in cash.

cost method (p. 511)   A term used to describe a method of accounting for treasury stock. When purchased, the stock is recorded at cost through an entry debiting Treasury Stock, and crediting Cash.

cumulative preferred stock (p. 502)   Stock on which an unpaid dividend will accumulate until paid. As long as dividends are in arrears, common stockholders may not receive any dividend distributions.

date of dividend declaration (p. 500)   The date the board of directors elects to declare a dividend. The act creates a liability of the corporation at this time.

date of payment (p. 500)   The date assets are distributed or the shares of the corporation's own stock are issued as dividends to stockholders on the ledger on the date of record.

date of record (p. 500)   The date the individual stockholder who will receive a dividend is identified, usually a week or two after the declaration.

deficit (p. 499)   A debit balance in the Retained Earnings account of a corporation.

dividends (p. 498)   Distributions of corporate assets to stockholders in the form of cash or other assets, *or* distributions of the corporation's own stock to owners.

liquidating dividend (p. 498)   A dividend that is charged against Paid-in Capital, rather than Retained Earnings.

noncumulative preferred stock (p. 504)   Stock on which unpaid dividends do not accumulate. Once an annual dividend is not distributed, the right to that distribution is lost forever to the stockholder.

nonparticipating preferred stock (p. 504)   Stock that is *only* entitled to the stated preference dividend. No further distributions are made above the stated rate.

participating preferred stock (p. 504)   Stock that *may* receive dividend distributions above the stated rate or amount.

property dividend (p. 501)   A distribution to stockholders made with assets other than cash, such as the entity's inventory or shares the entity owns in another corporation.

stock dividend (p. 506)   A dividend distribution consisting of shares of the corporation's own stock, usually accomplished by a capitalization (transfer) of retained earnings (to Paid-in Capital).

SELF-TEST QUESTIONS FOR REVIEW   (Answers are at the end of this chapter.)

Q3, Q4

1. On which of the following dates regarding dividends does the corporation become liable to pay the dividend?
    (a)   Ex-dividend date
    (b)   Payment date
    (c)   Record date
    (d)   Declaration date

Q5

2. Which of the following distributions would be considered a property dividend?
    (a)   Automobiles by an auto leasing company
    (b)   Cigarettes from a tobacco company
    (c)   Common shares held in another company
    (d)   Land
    (e)   All of the above

Q6

3. The participating factor in preferred shares refers to which of the following?
    (a)   The right to participate in the management of the company
    (b)   The right to vote
    (c)   The right to share in earnings above the preference amount
    (d)   The right to participate in board of directors meetings

Q7, Q8

4. Which of the following would be considered a stock dividend?
    (a)   Cattle distributed to owners of a cattle company
    (b)   Shares of ABC company's common stock distributed by XYZ company to its preferred stockholders
    (c)   Common shares of DDD company distributed to common stockholders of DDD company
    (d)   Common shares of DDD company distributed to preferred stockholders of DDD company

Q9

5. Which of the following transactions would result in treasury stock being recognized?
   (a) The purchase of Treasury notes issued by the United States government
   (b) The purchase of Treasury notes issued by the state of incorporation
   (c) The purchase of common shares of ERA company by ERA company to be reissued at a later time
   (d) The purchase of common shares of ERA company by ERA company to be immediately retired
   (e) All of the above

DEMONSTRATION PROBLEM

Part A

The following is a dividend announcement published in a financial newspaper on October 27, 19X2:

Cavendish, Inc.

At a meeting held on October 25, 19X2, the board of directors declared a cash dividend of $1.00 per share on the outstanding Common Shares, payable on January 2, 19X3, to stockholders of record at the close of business on November 30, 19X2.
W. S. Golden
Secretary

Required

1. What is the dividend declaration date?

2. What is the significance of the words "stockholders of record at the close of business on November 30, 19X2"?

3. If 5,000 common shares are outstanding, prepare the journal entries necessary for declaration and payment of dividends.

Part B

The Stockholders' Equity section of the Jaleh Co. balance sheet as of December 31, 19X1, follows.

Stockholders' Equity

Paid-in Capital
Preferred Stock, $50 Par Value, 6% cumulative and nonparticipating, 10,000 shares authorized; (?) shares issued and outstanding ... $32,000
Common Stock, $1 Par Value, 40,000 shares authorized; (?) shares issued and outstanding ... 20,000
Total Legal Capital ... $52,000
Paid-in Capital in Excess of Par Value
Common Stock ... $23,500
Preferred Stock ... 1,000 ... 24,500
Total Paid-in Capital ... $76,500
Retained Earnings
Unrestricted ... 3,800
Total Stockholders' Equity ... $80,300

Required

1. How many shares of preferred and common stock are outstanding?

2. Dividends have been paid on the preferred stock up to January 1, 19X1. No dividends, however, have been paid for the year 19X1. How will this be disclosed in the financial statements for the year ended December 31, 19X1?

3. The directors of the Jaleh Co. are anxious to commence dividend payments to all stockholders as soon as possible. What is the minimum amount of dividend that must be declared in 19X2 in order for common stockholders to receive a dividend?

Part C

The Stockholders' Equity section of the Prairie Machine Company balance sheet as of December 31, 19X3, follows.

Stockholders' Equity

Paid-in Capital

Preferred Stock, $100 Par Value, 6% cumulative and nonparticipating, 10,000 shares authorized; (?) shares issued and outstanding		$ 32,000
Common Stock, $10 Par Value, 40,000 shares authorized; (?) shares issued and outstanding		40,000
Total Legal Capital		$72,000
Paid-in Capital in Excess of Par Value		
Common Stock	$23,500	
Preferred Stock	1,000	24,500
Total Paid-in Capital		$96,500
Retained Earnings		
Unrestricted	39,000	
Restricted	20,000	
Total Retained Earnings		59,000
Total Stockholders' Equity		$155,500

Required

1. Prepare the journal entry to record the declaration of the semiannual preferred stock dividend on December 28, 19X3.

2. Assume the directors declared a common stock dividend of 10% on January 2, 19X4, distributable January 30 to stockholders of record on January 23; the fair market value of Prairie Machine common stock was $15 per share. No shares had been issued after the December 31, 19X3, figures were prepared. Prepare journal entries to record the declaration and issue of the stock dividend.

SOLUTION TO DEMONSTRATION PROBLEM

Part A

1. October 25, 19X2.

2. Stockholders who on November 30, 19X2, are registered will receive the dividend; at this date, all stock transactions are closed off and dividend checks are prepared.

3. 19X2

Oct. 25	Dividends (or Retained Earnings)	5,000	
	Dividends Payable		5,000

To record the declaration of a $1 per share cash dividend.

19X3

Jan. 2	Dividends Payable	5,000	
	Cash		5,000

To record the payment of a previous declared dividend.

Part B

1. At this time, 640 shares of preferred stock and 20,000 shares of the common stock are outstanding. This is determined by dividing the par value of each class of stock into the total par value.

$$\frac{\$32,000}{\$50} = 640; \quad \frac{\$20,000}{\$1} = 20,000$$

2. The disclosure would be by way of a note to the balance sheet:

> As of December 31, 19X1, dividends on the 6% cumulative preferred shares were in arrears to the extent of $3 per share [$50 × 6%] and amounted in total to $1,920.

3. More than $3,840 would have to be declared in order to pay the dividends in arrears and the current dividend for 19X2 (640 shares × $3 = $1,920 × 2 = $3,840).

Part C

1. 19X3

Dec. 28	Dividends (or Retained Earnings)	960	
	Dividends Payable		960

To record the declaration of a preferred stock dividend.

Calculation: 1/2 × 6% × $32,000 = $960

2. 19X4

Jan. 2	Retained Earnings	6,000	
	Common Stock to Be Distributed		4,000
	Paid-in Capital in Excess of Par Value		2,000

To record the declaration of a 10% stock dividend.

Prairie Machine has 4,000 shares of common stock outstanding. A 10% dividend would result in the issuance of 400 shares. The debit to Retained Earnings would be based on market value (400 × $15 = $6,000), while the Common Stock to Be Distributed account would be credited with the par value of the shares to be issued (400 × $10 = $4,000). The difference would be credited to Paid-in Capital in Excess of Par Value.

Jan. 30	Common Stock to Be Distributed	4,000	
	Common Stock		4,000

To record the issuance of the stock certificates.

DISCUSSION QUESTIONS

Q11-1 Stockholders' equity represents the net assets of a corporation. Distinguish between assets that are available for dividend purposes and those that are not. Legal capital represents which assets?

Q11-2 When a board of directors is making a decision involving the declaration of dividends, what are some of the main considerations used?

Q11-3 If a corporation is making a substantial net income each year, why might it not pay any dividends?

Q11-4 Distinguish among the date of dividend declaration, the date of record, and the date of payment.

Q11-5 Is a corporation legally required to declare a dividend? At what point do dividends become a liability of the corporation?

Q11-6 What is the difference in accounting between cash dividends and property dividends? Give a sample journal entry for each.

Q11-7 Explain the different dividend preferences that may be attached to preferred shares. Why would preferred shares have these preferences over common shares? Does it mean that purchasing preferred shares is better than purchasing common shares?

Q11-8 What are dividends in arrears? Are they a liability of the corporation?

Q11-9 Distinguish between a stock dividend and a cash dividend. Which is preferable from a stockholder's point of view? Why?

Q11-10 How does a stock dividend differ from a stock split?

Q11-11 Is there any dollar effect on an investor's portfolio when a stock dividend is declared and paid? Why or why not?

Q11-12 Does a stock dividend result in a change in an investor's percentage of corporate ownership? Explain, using an example.

Q11-13 What does a capitalization of retained earnings refer to when made in relation to the declaration and payment of a stock dividend?

Q11-14 How is a stock dividend recorded at the date of declaration? at the date of payment?

Q11-15 Can a corporation own shares in itself? under what circumstances?

Q11-16 Are all reacquired shares actually treasury shares? Explain.

Q11-17 How is the accounting for reacquired shares handled under the cost method?

Q11-18 Refer to Real World Example 11-1. What should the investor in an entity look for: dividends or stock price? Discuss.

DISCUSSION CASE
Dividend Choices

(Q2, Q3, Q5, Q8)

A regional banking corporation plans to provide stockholders with various options for enlarging their holdings. Under the plan, stockholders could receive dividends in three ways: as a cash dividend, which is the present plan; as a cash dividend that would be reinvested automatically in the bank's common stock at a discount of 5% from the average market price over a determined period; and as a stock dividend.

In addition, common stockholders would be entitled to purchase shares directly from the corporation at the average market price, subject to a limitation of $5,000 per stockholder per quarter. The plan is subject to the waiver of preemptive rights by stockholders.

For Discussion

1. What are the advantages and disadvantages of each of the choices offered to stock-holders under the new plan?

2. Which would you prefer and why?

3. The stockholders must waive their preemptive right. What is the preemptive right, and why would the stockholders be asked to waive it?

4. What effect would each of the three dividend forms have on stockholders' ownership percentage?

5. Would stockholders' equity increase, decrease, or remain the same, given the various choices?

EXERCISES

Liquidating dividends (Q1)

E11-1   A corporation has 10,000 common shares outstanding only, with a total stock-holders' equity as follows:

Legal Capital	$ 43,000
Paid-in Capital in Excess of Par Value	86,000
Retained Earnings—Restricted	100,000
Retained Earnings—Unrestricted	75,000
Total Stockholders' Equity	304,000

Required

What is the maximum amount of assets that could be distributed by the board of directors to the stockholders as liquidating dividends at this time?

Income dividends (Q1)

E11-2   A corporation has 10,000 common shares outstanding only with a total stock-holders' equity as follows:

Legal Capital	$ 43,000
Paid-in Capital in Excess of Par Value	86,000
Retained Earnings—Restricted	100,000
Retained Earnings—Unrestricted	75,000
Total Stockholders' Equity	304,000

Required

What is the total amount of cash that could be distributed by the board of directors to the stockholders as income dividends at this time?

Declaration and payment of cash dividends (Q3, Q4)

E11-3   Lonie Corp. has 100,000 shares of common stock outstanding on January 1, 19X1. On May 24, 19X1, the board of directors declare the semiannual cash dividend of $.50 per share. The dividend will be paid on July 13 to stockholders of record June 13, 19X1.

Required

Prepare the necessary journal entries for the following dates:

1. May 24

2. June 13

3. July 13

Cumulative preferred
dividends in arrears
(Q3, Q6)

E11-4   Maxwell, Inc., has 1,000 cumulative preferred shares outstanding on which the $500 dividend was not paid in 19X3. The corporation had 5,000 shares of common stock outstanding when the board of directors declared a $2,000 cash dividend at the end of 19X4. The number of preferred shares outstanding did not change during 19X4.

Required

Determine the dividends that will be paid on each share of preferred and common stock for the year 19X4.

Stock dividends on
common stock (Q7)

E11-5   The Stockholders' Equity section of the Royal Corporation balance sheet appears as follows on December 31, 19X7:

Paid-in Capital
Common Stock, $5 Par Value, 60,000 shares authorized;

35,000 shares issued and outstanding	$175,000
Paid-in Capital in Excess of Par Value	25,000
Total Paid-in Capital	$200,000
Retained Earnings	100,000
Total Stockholders' Equity	$300,000

On January 15, 19X8, the board of directors declared a 10% stock dividend to be distributed on March 7 to stockholders of record on February 7, 19X8. The stock was selling for $20 per share on January 15.

Required

Prepare the necessary entries for the following dates:

1. January 15
2. February 7
3. March 7

Noncumulative partici-
pating preferred stock
(Q6)

E11-6   The Kerry corporation has the following shares outstanding:

(a) 5,000 shares of $100 par value, 8% noncumulative participating preferred stock

(b) 50,000 shares of $10 par value common stock

Required

Determine how a total of $90,000 of dividends will be allocated between the preferred and common stockholders.

Preferred dividends in
arrears: balance sheet
(Q6)

E11-7   The following note appears on the balance sheet of Fidelity Data, Inc.:

As of December 31, 19X2, dividends on the cumulative preferred stock were in arrears for three years to the extent of $15 per share, amounting to $15,000.

Required

1. Does the amount of dividends in arrears appear as a liability on the December 31, 19X2, balance sheet? Explain your answer.

2. Does Fidelity have a deficit balance in retained earnings?

3. The controller for Fidelity projects a net income after taxes of $38,000 for the year 19X3. If dividends equal to 50% of net income are distributed at the end of 19X3, will common stockholders receive a dividend? Explain.

4. If the projected net income was $50,000 for 19X3, how much would the common stockholders receive?

Treasury stock
transactions (Q9)

E11-8 The following transactions took place during 19X6 in the Mailer Corp.:

Jan.   28 Purchased 2,000 shares of Mailer Corp. stock for $35 per share. This stock will
be reissued in a short period of time.

Feb.   14 Sold 500 of the shares repurchased on Jan. 28 for $40 per share

March 17 Sold 1,000 shares from the Jan. 28 transaction for $33 per share

April 15 Sold the remaining 500 shares from the Jan. 28 transaction for $30 per share

Required
Prepare the necessary journal entries to record these stock transactions.

PROBLEMS

Cash and stock divi-
dends: balance sheet
(Q4, Q6)

P11-1 Note the following transactions:

(a) Declaration of a stock dividend

(b) Declaration of a cash dividend

(c) Issue of new shares in place of old shares associated with a stock split

(d) Distribution of stock dividend in *a*

(e) Payment of cash dividend in *b*

Required
Using a column for each, indicate in terms of assets, liabilities, and stockholders' equity
the effects of the items given. For no change indicate *0*; for an increase, +; and for a
decrease, −.

Types of preferred
stock (Q6)

P11-2 The ABM Company had outstanding shares as follows: 1,000 shares 6% preferred
stock, $100 par value; and 5,000 shares common stock, $100 par value. For the
years 19X3 to 19X7, net income was $48,000; $32,000; $3,000; $10,000; and $40,000,
respectively. The company policy is to pay out all net income as dividends. No
dividends were in arrears on December 31, 19X2.

Required
Calculate for 19X3 to 19X7, using columns for *a* through *d*, the amount of dividends for both
preferred and common stock, assuming the

(a) preferred is cumulative and nonparticipating.

(b) preferred is cumulative and fully participating.

(c) preferred is noncumulative and fully participating.

(d) preferred is noncumulative and nonparticipating.

Cash dividends on
preferred and common
shares, stock dividends
on common shares,
stockholders' equity
(Q1, Q4, Q6, Q7)

P11-3 The Stockholders' Equity section of the balance sheet of Boyle Services, Inc., on
December 31, 19X7, appears as follows.

Stockholders' Equity

Paid-in Capital

Preferred Stock, $100 Par Value, 6% cumulative and nonparticipating, 5,000 shares authorized; 200 shares issued and outstanding	$20,000
Common Stock, $10 Par Value, 2,000 shares authorized; 100 shares issued and outstanding	1,000
Total Legal Capital	$21,000

(continued)

Paid-in Capital in Excess of Par Value		
Common Stock	$1,300	
Preferred Stock	1,000	2,300
Total Paid-in Capital		$23,300
Retained Earnings		
Unrestricted		3,300
Total Stockholders' Equity		$26,600

The following transactions occurred during 19X8:

Mar. 15 Declared the regular semiannual $3-per-share dividend on the preferred stock and $0.50-per-share dividend on the common stock to holders of record April 1, payable April 30

Apr. 30 Paid the dividends previously declared

June 1 Declared a 10% stock dividend to common stockholders of record July 1, to be distributed July 15. The closing price of the stock on June 1 was $16, which was designated by the board of directors as the fair market value of the dividend.

July 15 Distributed the stock dividend declared on June 1.

Sep. 15 Declared the regular semiannual $3-per-share dividend on the preferred stock and a $0.50-per-share dividend on the common stock

Oct. 30 Paid the dividends previously declared

Dec. 15 Declared a 10% stock dividend to common stockholders of record Jan. 10, 19X9, to be distributed Jan. 15. The closing price of the stock on Dec. 15 was $18, which was designated by the board of directors as the fair market value of the dividend.

     31 Net income for the year ended Dec. 31, 19X8, was $3,000

Required
1. Prepare all necessary journal entries, including any adjusting and closing entries necessary as of December 31, 19X8.

2. Prepare the Stockholders' Equity section of the balance sheet as of December 31, 19X8.

Treasury stock
transactions (Q9)

P11-4   The following transactions pertain to the activities of the New Mexico Corp., a company incorporated under the laws of a state that follows the general guidelines presented in this textbook. The company has 400,000 shares of $10 par value common stock authorized and 300,000 shares issued and outstanding. As of January 1, 19X4, New Mexico has unrestricted retained earnings of $75,000.

19X4

Feb. 7 Purchased 2,000 shares of its own stock on the open market for $35 per share

Apr. 14 Sold 1,500 of the treasury shares purchased on Feb. 7 for $38 per share

19X5

Sept. 12 Sold the remaining 500 shares in the treasury from the purchase of Feb. 7, 19X4, for $12 (19X5 has not been a good year in the stock market). No treasury stock transactions occurred prior to Feb. 7, 19X4.

Nov. 1 The board of directors of New Mexico Corp. declared a 1% stock dividend to stockholders of record Nov. 18, 19X5, to be distributed Dec. 26, 19X5. The stock had somewhat recovered, since New Mexico's common stock was selling for $16 per share on Nov. 1.

     18 Recorded the journal entry required on the date of record

Dec. 26 Recorded the distribution of the stock dividend declared on Nov. 1

Required
Prepare the necessary journal entries to record these stock transactions.

ALTERNATE PROBLEMS

Cash and stock dividends: balance sheet (Q4, Q6)

AP11-1   Note the following transactions:

(a)   Declaration of a cash dividend

(b)   Declaration of a stock dividend

(c)   Payment of the cash dividend in *a*

(d)   Distribution of stock dividend in *b*

(e)   Issue of new shares in place of old shares associated with a stock split

Required
Using a column for each, indicate in terms of assets, liabilities, and stockholders' equity the effects of the items given. For no change, indicate *0*; for increase, +; for decrease, −.

Types of preferred stock (Q6)

AP11-2   The Retained Earnings account of the ABC Co. was $400,000 on January 1, 19X5. During the following years, the company's dividend declarations were as follows:

19X5	$48,000	19X7	$ 2,000	19X9	$42,000
19X6	30,000	19X8	14,000		

ABC Co. had outstanding shares as follows: 1,000 shares 8% preferred stock, $100 par value; and 2,000 shares common stock, $100 par value.

Required
Calculate for 19X5 to 19X9, using columns for *a* through *d*, the amount of dividends for both preferred and common stock, assuming the

(a)   preferred is cumulative and nonparticipating.

(b)   preferred is cumulative and fully participating.

(c)   preferred is noncumulative and fully participating.

(d)   preferred is noncumulative and nonparticipating.

Cash dividends on preferred and common shares, stock dividends on common shares, Stockholders' Equity (Q1, Q4, Q6, Q7)

AP11-3   On December 31, 19X4, the Stockholders' Equity section of the Fingal Company balance sheet was as follows:

Stockholders' Equity

Paid-in Capital
Preferred Stock, $10 Par Value, 6% cumulative and
   nonparticipating, 1,000 shares authorized; 40 shares

issued and outstanding		$ 400
Common Stock, $1 Par Value, 4,000 shares authorized; 2,000		
shares issued and outstanding		2,000
Total Legal Capital		$2,400
Paid-in Capital in Excess of Par Value		
Common Stock	$200	
Preferred Stock	100	300
Total Paid-in Capital		$2,700
Retained Earnings		
Unrestricted		900
Total Stockholders' Equity		$3,600

The following transactions occurred during 19X5:

Feb. 15 Declared the regular semiannual dividend on its preferred stock and a $0.05-per-share dividend in the common stock to holders of record Mar. 5, payable Apr. 1

Apr.   1 Paid the dividends declared Feb. 15

May   1 Declared a 10% stock dividend to common stockholders of record May 15 to be issued June 15, 19X6 (The common stock closed at a price of $2 on this date on the stock exchange; this price was designated by the board as the fair market value.)

June 15 Paid the dividends declared May 1

Aug. 15 Declared the regular semiannual dividend on preferred stock and a dividend of $0.05 per share on the common stock to holders of record Aug. 31, payable Oct. 1

Oct.   1 Paid the dividends declared Aug. 15

Dec. 15 Declared a 10% stock dividend to common stockholders of record Dec. 20 to be issued on Jan. 15, 19X9 (The common stock closed at a price of $3 on this date on the stock exchange; this price was designated by the board as the fair market value.)

       31 Net income for the year ended Dec. 31, 19X5, was $1,400

Required

1. Prepare all necessary journal entries, including any adjusting and closing entries necessary as of December 31, 19X5.

2. Prepare the Stockholders' Equity section of the balance sheet as of December 31, 19X5.

Treasury stock transactions (Q9)

AP11-4 The following transactions pertain to the activities of the New Hampshire Corp., a company incorporated under the laws of a state that follows the general guidelines presented in this textbook. The company has 300,000 shares of $5 par value common stock authorized and 100,000 shares issued and outstanding. As of January 1, 19X7, New Hampshire has unrestricted retained earnings of $48,000.

19X7

Feb.   7 Purchased 2,000 shares of its own stock on the open market for $14 per share

Apr. 14 Sold 1,500 of the treasury shares purchased on Feb. 7 for $15 per share

19X8

Sept. 12 Sold the remaining 500 shares in the treasury from the purchase of Feb. 7, 19X7, for $12.

19X9

Nov.   1 The board of directors of New Hampshire Corp. declared a 5% stock dividend to stockholders of record Nov. 18, 19X9, to be distributed Dec. 26, 19X9. The stock was selling for $22 per share on Nov. 1, 19X9.

Dec. 18 Recorded the journal entry required on the date of record

       26 Recorded the distribution of the stock dividend declared on Nov. 1

Required

Prepare the necessary journal entries to record these stock transactions.

DECISION PROBLEMS

Problem 1

The Wayne-Kett Plastics Co. was incorporated in June 19X2. Preferred shares were issued in January, 19X4, for $100 per share and carried a $6-per-share cumulative dividend up to January 1, 19X7. The last audited balance sheet showed the following accounts (summarized):

Balance Sheet Items
June 30, 19X7

Cash	$ 22,000
Accounts Receivable	72,000
Merchandise Inventory	80,000
Temporary Investments	60,000
Net Long-term Assets	620,000
Intangible Assets	30,000
Other Assets	16,000
Totals	$900,000
Current Liabilities	$ 76,000
Long-term Debt	120,000
Preferred Stock, $100 Par Value	100,000
Common Stock, $10 Par Value	300,000
Paid-in Capital in Excess of Par Value	
Preferred	8,000
Common	46,000
Retained Earnings	250,000
Totals	$900,000

The board of directors had not declared a dividend since incorporation; instead, the profits were used to expand the company. The board is planning to declare a year-end dividend (December 19X7).

Required

1. If the required dividend on the preferred and $0.50 per share on the common stock were to be paid in December, what amount would be required? Prepare the necessary journal entries for the declaration of such dividends.

2. Should the board of directors go through with their decision to declare and pay the dividend determined in no. 1?

3. If the dividends in no. 1 are paid in 19X7 as proposed, the company expects to implement the following policy: retain 50% of net income for expansion and pay 50% in dividends. Determine the necessary 19X8 net income to implement the policy if a $1-per-share dividend is to be paid on the common stock.

Problem 2

Toward the end of the current year, the board of directors of the Denver Corp. is presented with the following Stockholders' Equity section of the balance sheet.

Stockholders' Equity

Paid-in Capital	
Common Stock, $20 Par Value, 5,000 shares authorized; 1,500	
shares issued and outstanding	$30,000
Paid-in Capital in Excess of Par Value—Common	18,000
Total Paid-in Capital	$48,000
Retained Earnings	
Unrestricted	24,000
Total Stockholders' Equity	$72,000

Denver Corp. has paid dividends of $3.60 per share in each of the last five years. After careful consideration of the company's cash needs, the board of directors declared a stock dividend of 300 shares of common stock (20%). Shortly after the stock dividend had been distributed and before the end of the year, the company declared a cash dividend of $3 per share.

James Brown owned 360 shares of Denver Corp. common stock, which he acquired several years ago. The market price of this stock when the stock dividend was declared was $60 per share.

Required

Answer the following questions, showing calculations.

1. What is Brown's share of the net assets of Denver Corp. before the stock dividend action? What is his share after the stock dividend action? Explain whether or not any changes occur as a result of the stock dividend.

2. What are the probable reasons why the market value of Brown's stock differs from the amount of net assets per share shown on the books?

3. Compare (with comment) the amount of cash dividends that Brown receives this year with dividends received in previous years.

4. On the day the common stock went ex-dividend (with respect to the stock dividend), its quoted market value fell from $60 to $50 per share. Did this represent a loss to Brown? Explain.

5. If the Denver Corp. had announced that it would continue its regular cash dividend of $3.60 per share on the increased number of shares outstanding after the stock dividend, would you expect the market value of the common stock to react in any way different from the change described in no. 4? Why?

ANSWERS TO SELF-TEST QUESTIONS

1. **(d)** The corporation becomes liable immediately on the declaration of a cash or property dividend. The liability is paid (assets distributed) on the date of payment to the person owning the share of stock as of a particular date (record date). The ex-dividend date is the date on which the dividend no longer is attached to a share in the marketplace.

2. **(e)** A property dividend is a distribution of *assets* other than cash. All of these are asset distributions, although it might be difficult to distribute land to thousands of stockholders.

3. **(c)** The participation factor allows the preferred stockholder to receive more than the stated preference amount if a large enough dividend is declared. Before such stockholders can begin to participate, the common stockholders must receive the same percent dividend as the preference rate given. Stockholders do not participate directly in the management of the corporation or the board of directors meetings. Common stockholders participate indirectly by voting for the members of the board of directors. Preferred stockholders may or may not have the right to vote.

4. **(c)** A stock dividend is a distribution of a company's common stock to the common stockholders. Cattle and shares of another company's stock are examples of property dividends. Common shares distributed to holders of preferred stock might be referred to as a dividend paid in common stock to preferred holders, but they would not be considered stock dividends.

5. **(c)** By definition, treasury stock is the company's own stock that has been issued, reacquired, and not retired. If the stock is retired, it reverts back to the status of *authorized* but unissued stock in some states, while in others it is permanently retired and cannot be reissued.

12 SOLE PROPRIETORSHIPS AND PARTNERSHIPS

Corporations are not the only type of business organization. Many more partnerships and sole proprietorships exist than corporations. From an accounting perspective, however, the only differences are found in the equity section of the balance sheets. Even those differences are mainly from a financing point of view. From an operating point of view, revenue and expense accounts are still closed to the income summary, but the Income Summary account is closed to the "capital" account of the owner (sole proprietor) or owners (partners).

From a financing activity perspective, the accounting for sole proprietorships and partnerships is far less complicated than for a corporation. For corporations, the sources of all capital paid-in must be accounted for, and in addition, the "capital" earned and retained in the business is accounted for separately from that paid-in. In a sole proprietorship or a partnership, no distinction is made between paid-in capital and retained earnings. Both amounts are recorded in the capital accounts of the owner(s).

Payments made to stockholders are referred to as *dividends,* while payments made to sole proprietors or partners are referred to as *drawings.* Chapter 12 will investigate the accounting problems with these two forms of business ownership only from the viewpoint of differences found in the equity section of the balance sheets. Chapter 12 also reminds students of the uses that can be made of accounting data even at the noncorporate level.

CHAPTER PREVIEW QUESTIONS

After studying Chapter 12, you should be able to answer the following questions:

1 How does the accounting differ between a corporation and a sole proprietorship or partnership? (pp. 530–32)

2 Does double taxation on sole proprietorship or partnership profits occur as on corporate profits? Explain. (pp. 530–33)

3 If you were going to start your own business, would you choose the corporate form or a sole proprietorship? Why? (p. 531)

4 Does a sole proprietorship or partnership have limited liability? Explain. (p. 532)

5 Do partners have an absolute right to any noncash assets that they individually contribute to the partnership? (pp. 532–33)

6 If you and a business associate were going to start your own business, would you choose the corporate form or a partnership? Why? (p. 533)

7 Describe some possible ways partners may decide to divide profits and losses. Should they have a different formula for profits than for losses? (pp. 538–40)

8 If a new partner is admitted to the partnership, is the old partnership liquidated? (pp. 541–42)

9 Is there more than one way to admit a new partner to the organization? (pp. 542–45)

10 Is there more than one way to record the withdrawal of a partner from the organization? (pp. 545–47)

11 What does the term liquidation refer to in regard to partnerships? (p. 547)

SOLE PROPRIETORSHIPS

Q1: Accounting
differences

A **sole proprietorship** is nothing more than an unincorporated entity owned by only one person. Imagine a corporation owned by only one stockholder; it would seem unnecessary to account for legal capital and paid-in capital separately, or to account for profits retained in the business. That is why the owners' (stockholders') equity section of the balance sheet usually contains only one account, referred to as **Capital—Owner,** or more specifically, "Capital—Brown" (naming the owner). All investments of assets made by the owner are recorded as credits to this account, while withdrawals of assets are recorded as debits. After the revenue and expense accounts have been closed to the Income Summary, the balance in the Income Summary account is closed to the Capital—Owner account. The balance always reflects the total amount invested and earned by the owner, less any withdrawals the owner made since the entity was formed. If Don Brown contributed (invested) $100,000 cash into his entity, the journal entry would be as follows:

Cash	100,000	
Capital—Brown		100,000

If noncash assets are invested, they are recorded at their fair market value on the date invested. If Brown instead contributed equipment with a fair market value of $50,000, the entry would be as follows:

Equipment	50,000	
Capital—Brown		50,000

Q2: Double taxation

Since a sole proprietorship is not considered a separate entity, the IRS taxes the earnings of the unincorporated entity only through its owner. Therefore, no double taxation occurs, as it does with a corporation. When the owner withdraws profits from the business, the dollars are not taxed to the owner as with corporate dividends. Any assets, cash or otherwise, are recorded by a debit to the owner's **Drawing account.** If owner Brown removed inventory with a fair market value of $10,000 from the store, the entry to record the transaction would be as follows:

Drawing—Brown	10,000	
Inventory		10,000

If the owner had withdrawn $10,000 in cash, the entry would be as follows:

Drawing—Brown	10,000	
Cash		10,000

If the owner withdrew assets other than cash, and those assets had a fair market value higher than the book value, then a gain would have to be recorded. Assuming Brown removed land that had a book value of $10,000 but an established fair market value of $14,000, the entry would be as follows:

Drawing—Brown	14,000	
Land		10,000
Gain on Disposal of Land		4,000

If the assets withdrawn by the owner had a market value *below* the book value, a loss should be recorded.

The only time income is recorded by a sole proprietor is at the end of the year when the Income Summary account is closed to the owner's Capital account. The amount of income is not affected by the amount of drawings the owner made during the year, just as the amount of dividends paid to the stockholders of a corporation do not affect the amount of earnings for that corporation. Remember, dividends were closed to retained earnings after the income for the year was added to retained earnings.

Once the net income for the year is determined (in the same manner as a corporation, according to GAAP), that income (or loss) is closed to the owner's Capital account as follows, assuming a net income of $37,500.

Income Summary	37,500	
Capital—Brown		37,500

Assuming that the drawings for the year were $14,000, the entry to close the Drawing account would be as follows:

Capital—Brown	14,000	
Drawing—Brown		14,000

In a sole proprietorship, the statement of retained earnings is referred to as a **statement of owner's capital,** and for Brown would appear as follows:

Statement of Owner's Capital

Balance, January 1, 19X4	$150,000
Add: Net Income	37,500
	$187,500
Less: Drawings	14,000
Balance, December 31, 19X4	$173,500

Q3: Sole proprietorships vs. corporations

Other than the differences already described, accounting for a corporation does not differ from accounting for a sole proprietorship. In summary, the sole proprietorship is not taxed as a separate entity. In fact, legally, the sole proprietorship is *not* an entity, but for accounting purposes, under the entity concept (Chapter 1), it is assumed to be a separate entity. Drawings (dividends) are not considered income to the owner since the sole proprietorship is not a legal entity.

Advantages of a sole proprietorship include ease of formation and the lack of double taxation. Disadvantages include the unlimited liability of the sole proprietor, which will be discussed further in relation to partnerships.

PARTNERSHIPS

In reality (from an accounting point of view), a partnership is nothing more than multiple sole proprietorships. A **partnership** combines the abilities and capital of any number of individuals who together own and operate a business. A partnership is an accounting entity, like the sole proprietorship, but it is not a legal entity, like a corporation. Therefore, a partnership has a limited life, along with a number of other unique characteristics.

Partnership Characteristics

The characteristics that influence equity accounting for a partnership include limited life, unlimited liability, mutual agency, co-ownership of assets, and the special need to share the profits or losses of the operation by some equitable means.

LIMITED LIFE

The life of a partnership may be limited by a clause in the **partnership agreement** stipulating that the partnership will terminate after a particular period of time or completion of the partnership objective. More often, however, an existing partnership is dissolved when a new partner is admitted, or an existing partner withdraws or dies. Partner dissolution does not necessarily mean that the business is also dissolved; usually the business continues under a new partnership agreement. Accounting for partnership capital therefore involves issues related to the formation and dissolution of partnerships and to the allocation of the profits and losses to the individual partners.

UNLIMITED LIABILITY

Q4: Limited liability

While a partnership business is an entity that exists separately from its owners, it does not have a separate legal life, as a corporation does. A partnership has **unlimited liability**—each partner is personally liable for debts that the partnership cannot pay. In the event that a partner is unable to pay his or her share of partnership debts, the other partners can be called on to pay personally for such debts. Accounting for partnerships includes issues related to the payment of partnership debts from personal assets of individual partners. The liability of some partners can be limited if the partnership agreement stipulates that certain partners are "limited." The remaining or "general" partners, however, still have unlimited liability. A sole proprietor, like a general partner, has unlimited liability.

MUTUAL AGENCY

Unless otherwise stated in the partnership agreement, each partner is able to make legally binding decisions, not only on the partnership, but also on the other partners known as **mutual agency.** The only exception involves activities that fall outside the normal activities of the partnership. For example, a partnership formed to sell used cars would not normally include the buying and selling of footwear; in this case, used-car partners would not be legally bound to footware contracts signed by only one of the partners. A clear understanding of mutual agency implications is important, since it focuses on one of the pitfalls of the partnership form of business organization. Real World Example 12-1 discusses this and other problem areas for unwary partners.

CO-OWNERSHIP OF ASSETS

Q5: Right to noncash assets

Unless the partnership agreement specifies otherwise, all assets, including noncash assets, contributed to the partnership by individual partners are jointly owned by all partners. Each partner, therefore, has a claim against all partnership assets up to the amount of his or her capital balance. Therefore, partnership assets are often sold on liquidation to facilitate their distribution to partners in the form of cash.

SHARING OF PROFITS AND LOSSES

The partnership agreement usually stipulates the manner in which profits and losses will be shared. If no such provision is specified, then partners share all profits and losses equally. Accounting issues related to the division of profits and losses are discussed later in this chapter.

Advantages of a Partnership

Q6: Partnerships vs. corporations

The major advantage of a partnership over the corporate form of business owner-ship is the ease with which it can be formed. No legal requirements exist, not even a written partnership agreement, although every partnership *should* have one. The major advantage of a partnership over a sole proprietorship is the amount of capital that can be raised; the more partners, the more capital may be available.

Since a partnership is not a legal entity, it is not taxed as such, and no double taxation occurs. The individual partners pay taxes on their share of the earnings, so earnings are only taxed once.

Disadvantages of a Partnership

The disadvantages far outweigh the advantages of a partnership. The disadvantages can be examined from the viewpoint of each of the partnership characteristics mentioned earlier.

LIMITED LIFE

The units of ownership in a partnership are not as easy to transfer as in a corpo-ration. If a partner dies or wants to retire or leave the partnership for whatever reason, a valuation problem is created. Every time the number of partners changes in either direction, the partnership is dissolved and a new entity is formed.

UNLIMITED LIABILITY

Each partner is individually responsible for the debts of the partnership. If the partnership is in trouble, the creditors can go after the assets of *any* partner they so choose to satisfy partnership debts. The corporate form of ownership, on the other hand, has the protection of limited liability.

MUTUAL AGENCY

Each partner can bind the other partners in a contract by his or her actions. Dis-satisfied partners have used this as a tactic to get back at other partners.

CO-OWNERSHIP OF ASSETS

Once assets have been contributed to a partnership, they become partnership assets and do not necessarily revert back to the investing partner at the end of the partnership.

SHARING OF PROFITS AND LOSSES

No matter how partners try to be equitable, something often goes awry and some partners become unhappy.

Also, more tax incentives generally exist for doing business in the corporate form rather than the partnership form. In recent years the individual and corpo-rate rates for income taxes have become somewhat equal. For many years, the corporate income-tax rates were lower than the individual rates at the upper-income levels, making the corporate form a more palatable choice.

REAL WORLD EXAMPLE 12-1
Why Partnerships Break Up

Two and a half years ago, four of us started out on a great adventure together—our own consulting partnership. For six months, we struggled along with no clients. Then we hit the big time: a $1.3-million contract. But somehow our success at attracting clients was greater than our ability to work together harmoniously. This April, our original partnership broke up. The experience was one of the toughest I've ever gone through—but it taught me some valuable lessons about what makes a partnership succeed.

When it became apparent, after several attempted salvage operations, that there were irreconcilable differences in our partnership, we called in our attorney. "Splitting up a partnership," he said, "is just like a divorce without the kids." He meant to reassure us with the comment about kids, but I found that the dissolution of a partnership can be just as emotional as a divorce. Like ours, many partnerships consist of friends and former colleagues, and many other partnerships include relatives. Couple these personal relationships with the intense involvement required to run a small business, and you can see why a failing partnership creates misunderstandings, bruised egos, bitterness, hurt feelings, and anger.

Of course, no one puts together a partnership thinking about the unpleasantness of breaking it up. The key is to recognize that a partnership arrangement is subject to some stresses that are not found in other corporate structures. After our partnership broke up, I began to analyze our experiences, and I found that there were three basic rules that were responsible for our successes when we heeded them, and for our problems when we didn't.

Rule 1: Share and Share Alike

Very simple, right? Most partners have every intention of doing just that. The problem is to make reality conform with the intent. Unfortunately, as George Orwell pointed out, some of us are more equal than others. Human nature being what it is, some people are more exploitative or manipulative, and some are more easily exploited and manipulated.

Because of various backgrounds and experiences, partners may have different opinions on what risk is justifiable, how money should be managed, and what the work ethic really means. Before you sign your name to a partnership agreement, assess just how everyone views such questions. This will provide a good indication of how equal everyone is likely to be three months or three years later.

Also ask if each partner can contribute enough money. Our experience confirmed that there are those months when the cash flow slows to a trickle or does not flow at all. When that happens, the partners may have to do without. Most partners may agree to such a sacrifice in the excitement of beginning a new venture, but when it comes time to actually go without pay, some partners simply may not be able to do so. The ledger sheet may eventually be brought back into balance, but the psychological effects of unequal sacrifice will probably remain.

Set aside at least one meeting to discuss nothing but the personal ability of each partner to persevere through periods of reduced income. This is not a time to be timid or to worry about being "impolite." Spell out what will be expected of each partner (and it had better be much the same for each) if the worst case occurs. If you have the time, continue to talk about personal financial positions on a regular basis.

The need for the partners to contribute *themselves* equally to the company is even more important than how much money they can contribute. In many cases, partnerships are formed because one partner can contribute something that the other partners cannot, and that's what a good partnership is all about. But a merger of disparate specialists, no matter how good they are in their particular areas, has a distinct disadvantage. In young, small businesses, every-

Source Stephen G. Thomas, "Why Partnerships Break Up," *Inc. Magazine*, 1984. Reprinted with permission. Copyright © 1984 by Goldhirsh Group, Inc., 38 Commercial Wharf, Boston, MA 02110.

one has to do a little bit of everything. In our case, the four partners were the entire company for the first six months. That meant that each of us had to raise money, keep the books, research and produce our services, type, make coffee, get the mail, and sweep the steps. If your partners will not share in such tasks—especially when everyone's personal hard work is the only thing that will earn money—friction and failure are inevitable. The only safeguard is to spell out from the start who is going to do what, making sure that the tasks and levels of effort are reasonably equitable.

There is no secret of success: it's hard work. If your partners don't see it that way, beware. If everyone is committed to lots of hard work, determine exactly how hard it is going to be. Is everyone going to do his share of overtime? If one of your partners loves golf, sailing, skiing, or even church or service organizations more than anything else, does that mean more than the company? Remember, your partners are not likely to change their characters or habits just because you are now a partnership.

But if recreation and outside interests are recognized by the partnership as desirable aspects of the partners' lives, spell it out so that time legitimately taken away from the company is available to everyone in equal portions. One week for a partner to serve as a counselor at scout camp should be matched with one week for the other partners, whether it be for running marathons, lying on a sunny beach, or working for the United Way.

Rule 2: Get It in Writing

In each of the cases mentioned above, your best bet is to get it in writing. Write down who is going to do what tasks. Write down how much everyone is going to work. Write down how much money each partner will invest and where that money will come from. Write down how much money in wages will be given up when there is limited income. Write down your goals and expectations for marketing, production, and routine management. Write down a plan to monitor progress. Write down who will go to

training sessions, seminars, and conferences. Write down who will get what perquisites.

All of this writing serves three related purposes: planning, recordkeeping, and protection. Writing everything out will allow you to encounter and solve many of your problems before they jeopardize your company or destroy your friendships. Once you get going, you should continue to plan on paper. A record of your agreements on goals, policies, and procedures protects the company in general and the partners in particular. If you have agreed to limit spending on a particular marketing target, and the marketing partner exceeds the limit with no results, a reprimand is in order. It's especially important to keep written records because, if worst comes to worst—if the partnership falters and the separation is contested—the record will protect the partners who are not at fault by showing exactly who did what.

Let's say you have three basic goals. You want to hold administrative costs to 20%, you want to produce three handmade bamboo fly rods and 150 flies per week, and you want to double the demand for your products within three months. Develop and write the plan in outline fashion, in as much detail as you can imagine. Start with the goal: three rods and 150 flies. Decide who will be responsible: Partner A. Decide who will do the work: Partner A (75%) and Partner B (25%). Allocate the time to accomplish the task: one week. Plan what will be done if the target of doubling your demand in three months is not met; record at least five options. When each goal is developed and addressed in this fashion, write the whole thing up formally, and have each partner sign it. If this is done for each main goal, no one aspect of the business should get so far off the track that it endangers the other aspects of the company itself.

These written plans are the basis for the overall operation of the company. They provide the focus for the management meeting you should hold at least once a week. To make these meetings worth anything, a recording secretary

(continued)

must keep complete and objective minutes. These minutes must then be reviewed at each subsequent meeting so that everyone is satisfied that interim operating procedures are mutually acceptable.

Like a report outline, company plans provide frameworks for action. Don't deviate from them capriciously. As circumstances dictate change, review your plans with all of the partners. Some seemingly simple change that you're sure is appropriate may be seen quite differently by another partner.

While this may all sound ominously formal, structured, and time-consuming, it is much more costly in both time and dollars to proceed on an ill-defined course or, worse, to operate at cross-purposes with your partners. If you fail to write everything down (and there are always plenty of good excuses for not doing it), and things start to go wrong, be assured that no one will agree on what was said six months ago.

Rule 3: Don't Lie

Generally, none of us tells big lies that lead to fraud or other criminal acts. But there are those little white lies—more pleasant ways of putting the truth, or simply lack of candor—that can occur, and they can be devastating to a partnership.

There is a great deal of pressure to dismiss, ignore, or avoid bad news. Bad news, however, is not necessarily a sign of personal failure, nor is it usually the result of some totally external factor inflicted on the company by unknown agents. Instead, it is information that must be addressed in the context of your company plans. Only if you get sound and adequate information can you overcome problems.

If one partner is responsible for raising money, and all of the partners have agreed that a certain action is dependent on raising $30,000 from normally acceptable sources, it is not really a favor to the company if the money-raiser gets $10,000 from selling his car, $10,000 from his kindly old aunt, and $10,000 from a loan shark, and neglects to tell you that it didn't come from the bank. The consequences of such efforts, even if they happen to have some short-term advantages, are detrimental to company planning because they are based on false premises. It is always possible that the banks are refusing your loan request for a good reason, a reason that the company should be aware of. If the company is going beyond conventional sources for

Partnership Accounting

Business transactions for a partnership are recorded in the same manner as those for a corporation or a sole proprietorship. As in a sole proprietorship, the only significant difference between a partnership and a corporation is the treatment of owners' equity. The accounting for equity is the same as a sole proprietorship, except that a Capital account and a Drawing account are kept for each partner. Investments made by the partners, along with their share of profit or loss and their drawings, are all recorded in the Capital account.

PARTNERSHIP CAPITAL ACCOUNTS
Each partner has an individual account credited with their capital contributions to the partnership. The following entry records a $5,000 cash investment by partner A.

Cash	5,000	
Capital—A		5,000
To record investment by A.		

loans, it had better be a partnership decision. In this example, there is the additional danger that personal concerns will adversely affect company performance. Your company should not be forced into making decisions based on a partner's having to walk to work, getting into disputes with relatives, or being threatened with bodily harm.

It's particularly easy to lie to yourself about employee relations. If the employees are not producing, you must find out why and face the consequences. Most people find it difficult to fire employees, and many managers have trouble urging, cajoling, or demanding the required work from employees. Use the style that best suits you when it comes to supervision, but don't lie to yourself. In most cases, you simply can't afford to "wait three more months" for an employee to get the hang of it. And, in fact, it does the employee little good to assume that his work is acceptable when it is not. Employees must understand clearly what is expected of them and then be given adequate opportunity and support to meet those goals. If the person is not suited for the position, send him on his way with suggestions for more appropriate employment. Delay only compounds the problem and your level of stress.

You may also notice a tendency to oversell yourself or the company. This is lying. Some people can work 112 hours a week, but most of us can't. You can't plan effectively if you don't assess your capabilities realistically. The same is true at the company level. You really don't gain anything by selling what you can't deliver, and there's no better method for shutting off the flow of contracts.

Lying or not confiding in your other partners is harmful mainly because it denies your business the chance to benefit from all your partners' experience. You are partners because each one of you is bright, talented, and full of useful contributions to the company. Don't fail to use your own resources by hiding unpleasant situations from your partners. They may not think the situation is as grave as you do.

Partnerships are a great way to combine resources, and much of their effectiveness comes from a merger of human and intangible qualities. Your accountant, attorney, or banker can be invaluable with corporate and financial concerns, but it is your partners who are your greatest assets. Choose them wisely, ask hard questions, and don't take them—or yourself—for granted. You have to work at your partnership as much as you do at your business.

If noncash assets are contributed, then the appropriate asset account is debited for an amount equal to the asset's fair market value.

Partner withdrawals of assets from the partnership are recorded in each partner's Drawing account. If partner A withdraws $1,000 cash, for example, the following entry is recorded:

Drawing—A	1,000	
Cash		1,000
To record drawings by A.		

At year-end, each partner's Drawing account is closed to his or her Capital account. The following closing entry would close partner A's Drawing account, assuming no further drawings have been made.

Capital—A	1,000	
Drawing—A		1,000
To close A's Drawing account.		

The Drawing account is closed directly to the Capital account of each partner.

DIVISION OF PARTNERSHIP PROFITS AND LOSSES

Q7: Division of profits, losses

Partnership profits and losses are divided equally among partners, if no profit-and-loss-sharing ratio is indicated in the partnership agreement. Otherwise, the ratio specified in the agreement is used; this ratio can be fixed, such as 3 : 2 or ⅔ to ⅓, for example. Profits and losses also may be shared according to a formula specified in the agreement. This formula usually considers three factors: a return to each partner for the amount of his or her capital invested in the partnership, an allocation to each partner for services rendered, and a further division of any remaining profit (or resulting loss) in the profit-and-loss-sharing ratio. Although a partnership agreement may not include separate calculations for each of these factors, the ratio should be determined after considering their impact on each partner's remuneration.

Division Using a Fixed Ratio

The division of profits and losses according to a fixed ratio is appropriate when each partner makes an equal contribution to the business. Ideally, each partner would have an equal amount of capital invested in the partnership and would devote an equal amount of time and effort in the business. However, usually the amount of capital differs, and time and effort devoted to the business is unequal. The initial calculation of a fixed ratio for inclusion in the partnership agreement would consider the weight of these factors.

Assuming that A and B share profits in the ratio of 3 : 2, a $15,000 profit would be divided and recorded by the following entry.

Income Summary	15,000	
Capital—A (3/5 × 15,000)		9,000
Capital—B (2/5 × 15,000)		6,000
To record division of partnership profits.		

Division Using Capital Balances

An alternate method of allocating partnership profits and losses uses partners' Capital balances. This method is most suitable where large amounts are invested by partners and where profits are mainly attributable to these invested amounts. Use of this method must be specified in the partnership agreement; otherwise, profits and losses are divided equally among partners.

Assuming that use of Capital balances are indicated in the A and B partnership agreement and that these balances are the same for each partner, the $15,000 profit would be divided equally in this case (by coincidence). It is recorded as follows:

Income Summary	15,000	
Capital—A		7,500
Capital—B		7,500
To record division of partnership profits.		

Note that the partnership agreement should indicate whether the beginning, ending, or average Capital balances are to be used in dividing profits and losses. Each balance would result in a different allocation unless the capital invested in the partnership by each partner did not change during the year. Thus the use of beginning or ending Capital balances may not be an equitable method in many circumstances.

The use of beginning or ending capital would be equitable if the partners made no additional investments or withdrawals during the year. If any investments or withdrawals were made, then a *weighted average balance* should be used to determine the allocation of profit or loss. An example of a weighted average calculation follows. The calculation is based on the following Capital account assumptions:

Beginning Balance, January 1, 19X4	$ 60,000
Investment, April 1, 19X4	20,000
Investment, August 1, 19X4	30,000
Withdrawal, October 1, 19X4	(10,000)
Ending Balance (before share of profit)	$100,000

$60,000 × 12/12 (full year) =	$60,000
20,000 × 9/12 (9 months) =	15,000
30,000 × 5/12 (5 months) =	12,500
(10,000) × 3/12 (3 months) =	(2,500)
Weighted Average Capital for 19X4 =	$85,000

Division Using Salary and Interest Allocations

Since the time and effort devoted by individual partners to the business is often unequal, and the amount of Capital balance varies among partners, another allocation method can be chosen. Profits and losses can be divided using an allocation through **partner salary** and **interest on Capital balances** to each partner, in accordance with individual contributions. Any remaining profits and losses can be divided through the profit-and-loss-sharing ratio. The salary and interest allocations are not deducted as expenses on the income statement; *salary* and *interest* used here refer only to individual factors used in dividing profits and losses among partners.

Before beginning their partnership, A and B recognized that A deserved more salary compensation because of his technical skills and the fact that he had been earning more than B. Accordingly, the following salary allocations were specified in their partnership agreement: $7,000 to A and $5,000 to B. The agreement also indicated that 12% interest should be allocated to their Capital balances and that any remaining profit and loss should be shared in the ratio of 3 : 2.

The following calculation shows how a $15,000 profit is divided according to these provisions of the A and B partnership agreement. Remember that these salary and interest amounts have not been paid to partners; rather they are a means of allocating partnership net income to partners. Both A and B have average Capital balances during the year of $10,000.

	A	B	Total
Amount of Profit to Be Allocated to Partners			$15,000
Interest Allocation			
A: $10,000 × 12%	$1,200		
B: $10,000 × 12%		$1,200	2,400
Balance			$12,600
Salary Allocation	7,000	5,000	12,000
Balance			$ 600

Balance Allocated in Profit-and-Loss-
  Sharing Ratio
    A: $600 × 3/5 360
    B: $600 × 2/5 .... 240 } 600
    Balance .... -0-
  Allocated to Partners $8,560 $6,440

The following entry records this profit allocation between A and B:

Income Summary	15,000	
Capital—A		8,560
Capital—B		6,440

If the $15,000 partnership income had been inadequate to cover the salary and interest allocated to A and B, the difference would have been allocated in the profit-and-loss-sharing ratio. Assuming that partnership net income had amounted to $9,000, the following calculation of amounts allocated to the partners would be made:

	A	B	Total
Amount of Profit to Be Allocated to Partners			$ 9,000
Interest Allocation			
A: $10,000 × 12%	$1,200		
B: $10,000 × 12%		$1,200	2,400
Balance			$ 6,600
Salary Allocation	7,000	5,000	12,000
Balance			($ 5,400)
Balance Allocated in Profit-and-Loss-Sharing Ratio			
A: $5,400 × 3/5	(3,240)		
B: $5,400 × 2/5		(2,160)	5,400
Balance			-0-
Allocated to Partners	$ 4,960	$ 4,040	

These calculations illustrate the allocation of partnership net income using a combination of interest and salary elements, with any remaining balance being allocated to partners according to their profit-and-loss-sharing ratio. Alternately, the partnership agreement may only provide for allocation of a salary, with the remaining balance being allocated according to the profit-and-loss-sharing ratio. In practice, the agreement may also provide periodic drawings to individual partners, equal to their salary allocation; as previously noted, the Drawing account is then closed to each partner's Capital account at year-end.

PARTNERSHIP FINANCIAL STATEMENTS

Partnership and proprietorship financial statements are similar. The income statement of a partnership might include this allocation of income to individual partners:

A and B
Income Statement
For the Year Ended December 31, 19X4

Revenue		
Sales		$150,000
Cost of Goods Sold		90,000
Net Income		$ 15,000
Net Income Allocation:		
A	$8,560	
B	6,440	$ 15,000

A **statement of partners' capital** replaces the statement of retained earnings. It shows partner contributions to the business, changes in capital resulting from net income (or loss) allocations, and drawings representing withdrawals during the period. The partners' capital statement for A and B would appear as follows:

A and B
Statement of Partners' Capital
For the Year Ended December 31, 19X4

	A	B	Total
Capital Balance, Jan. 1	$ 5,000	$ 5,000	$10,000
Add: Investments, Jan. 2	5,000	5,000	10,000
Net Income	8,560	6,440	15,000
	$18,560	$16,440	$35,000
Less: Drawing	7,000	5,000	12,000
Capital Balance, Dec. 31	$11,560	$11,440	$23,000

It is assumed in this statement of partners' capital that each partner made additional $5,000 investments during the year and that net income is divided using salary and interest allocations.

The balance sheet of a partnership shows the Capital balance of each partner if there are only a few partners. Otherwise, only a total Capital amount is indicated, with details appearing in the statement of partners' capital. Note that no separate accounts are opened to represent owner capital contributions and net income earned and retained in the business, as occurs in corporate financial statements. The partners' equity of A and B may appear as follows on the balance sheet:

Partners' Equity	
Capital—A	$11,560
Capital—B	11,440
Total Equity	$23,000

ADMISSION OF A NEW PARTNER

Q8: New partner and liquidation

The admission of a new partner results in the creation of a new partnership. Although the business of the former partnership need not discontinue, the former partnership ceases to exist with the admission of a new partner. Since the liability, agency, and profit-sharing arrangements will be altered, a new partnership agreement is required.

For illustrative purposes, the following balance sheet data are used for the A and B partnership:

Assets		Liabilities and Equity		
Cash	$ 5,000	Liabilities		$ 7,000
Other Assets	22,000	Capital—A	$10,000	
		Capital—B	10,000	20,000
		Total Liabilities		
Total Assets	$27,000	and Equity		$27,000

Q9: Admitting new partner

A new partner, C, wants to enter the A and B partnership. He or she can be admitted either by purchasing an existing partner's interest or by contributing assets to the partnership. In either case, the admission of a new partner must be approved by the existing partners.

Purchase of an Existing Partner's Interest

Assume C is going to purchase B's interest in the A and B partnership. The **purchase of a partnership interest** from an existing partner is a private transaction between the new partner and the existing partner who is selling his or her interest in the partnership. The new partner C makes a payment to the existing partner B, who in turn transfers his or her partnership interest. This type of purchase does not affect the assets of the partnership. Only an entry recording the change in ownership is made in the partnership books. The following entry illustrates the recording of C's purchase of B's interest:

Capital—B	10,000	
Capital—C		10,000
To record transfer of B's partnership		
interest to C.		

C could have paid less than $10,000 or substantially more than $10,000 for B's interest. Remember, that the balances in the Capital accounts are determined by the recorded values of the assets and liabilities (assets − liabilities = owners' equity) and do not purport to be estimates of fair market value. If C believes that the fair market value of B's interest is $15,000, then C may be willing to pay $15,000 to B. The amount paid is a private transaction between B and C; it is not reflected in the partnership records. C also could have purchased half of B's interest. In this case, only half of B's capital would be transferred to C by the following entry:

Capital—B	5,000	
Capital—C		5,000
To record transfer of half of B's		
partnership interest to C.		

INVESTMENT IN THE PARTNERSHIP

Rather than purchase an existing partner's interest, the new partner could contribute cash and other assets in return for a partnership interest. This **investment into a partnership** differs from the purchase of an existing partner's interest; in this case, both the assets and equity of the partnership are increased. Assume the same data exist in the A and B balance sheet. Assume in this case that C contributes assets at their fair market value of $10,000 (referred to as *Other Assets* for illustrative purposes) to the partnership for a one-third interest in the partnership capital after his investment. This investment is recorded as follows:

Other Assets	10,000	
Capital—C		10,000
To record C's investment in the partnership.		

The A, B, and C partnership balance sheet, following the investment, appears as follows:

Assets		Liabilities and Equity		
Cash	$ 5,000	Liabilities		$ 7,000
Other Assets ($22,000 + $10,000)	32,000	Capital—A	$10,000	
		Capital—B	10,000	
		Capital—C	10,000	30,000
		Total Liabilities		
Total Assets	$37,000	and Equity		$37,000

Note that C's $10,000 investment results in a $10,000 Capital balance; the total partnership capital amounts to $30,000, of which C has a one-third ownership interest.

C may receive more or less than a $10,000 Capital balance. Under some circumstances, a bonus may be given either to the new partner or to the existing partners. The admission of a new partner and the recognition of a bonus is shown in Exhibit 12-1.

BONUS TO THE NEW PARTNER

The partnership may want to add a new partner who can offer certain technical skills, management abilities, or some other desirable business strengths. To entice a desirable individual, a **bonus to the new partner** may be offered in excess of the amount invested by that person. In this case, the existing partners allocate a portion of their capital to C.

Assume that C invests assets at their fair market value of $4,000 into the partnership for a one-third ownership interest. The new total capital amounts to $24,000; of this amount, $8,000 (one-third) belongs to C. The determination of these amounts is illustrated as follows:

Capital—A	$10,000
Capital—B	10,000
Capital Balance	$20,000
Investment by C	4,000
Capital of New Partnership	$24,000
Capital—C ($24,000 × ⅓)	$ 8,000

The new partner's bonus of $4,000 is recorded as follows:

Other Assets	4,000	
Capital—A	2,000	
Capital—B	2,000	
Capital—C		8,000

The $4,000 of assets invested by C results in an $8,000 Capital balance by reducing the capital of both A and B. In this journal entry, it is assumed that A and B share profits and losses equally; accordingly, they both have an equal $2,000 capital reduction.

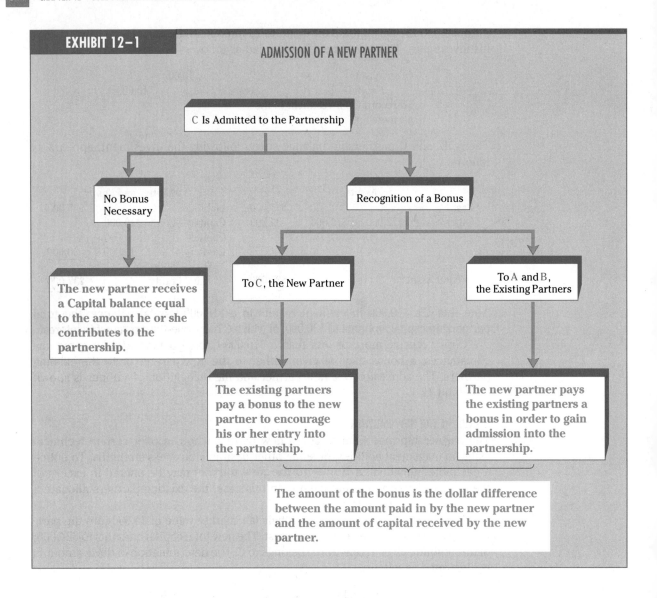

EXHIBIT 12–1

ADMISSION OF A NEW PARTNER

C Is Admitted to the Partnership

No Bonus Necessary

Recognition of a Bonus

The new partner receives a Capital balance equal to the amount he or she contributes to the partnership.

To C, the New Partner

To A and B, the Existing Partners

The existing partners pay a bonus to the new partner to encourage his or her entry into the partnership.

The new partner pays the existing partners a bonus in order to gain admission into the partnership.

The amount of the bonus is the dollar difference between the amount paid in by the new partner and the amount of capital received by the new partner.

The partnership balance sheet following the recording of C's investment would appear as follows:

Assets		Liabilities and Equity		
Cash	$ 5,000	Liabilities		$ 7,000
Other Assets ($22,000 + $4,000)	26,000	Capital—A	$8,000	
		Capital—B	8,000	
		Capital—C	8,000	24,000
		Total Liabilities		
Total Assets	$31,000	and Equity		$31,000

Note that ownership interests are reflected in the balances of the Capital accounts. In the example, C was admitted for a one-third ownership interest and therefore has a capital balance of $8,000 from the total capital of $24,000. The ownership interest has no bearing on the share of profits and losses C will have in the new partnership. That is a separate issue resolved among the partners. If the agreement is silent as to how profits and losses will be divided, then all partners will share equally.

BONUS TO EXISTING PARTNERS

If the partnership business is particularly successful and profitable, the new partner may pay **bonuses to the current partners** as an admission requirement. In this case, the new partner has less capital than his or her contribution of assets to the partnership; a portion of this contribution is allocated to existing partners. The determination of this allocation follows.

Assume that C invests assets at their fair market value of $13,000 in the partnership for a one-third ownership interest. The new total capital amounts to $33,000; of this amount, $11,000 (one-third) belongs to C.

Capital—A	$10,000
Capital—B	10,000
Capital Balance	$20,000
Investment by C	13,000
Capital of New Partnership	$33,000
Capital—C ($33,000 × ⅓)	$11,000

The bonus of $2,000 to existing partners is recorded as follows:

Other Assets	13,000	
Capital—A		1,000
Capital—B		1,000
Capital—C		11,000

The $13,000 invested by C results in an $11,000 Capital balance; the balance is allocated to A and B in their profit-sharing ratio, which they are assumed to share equally. Accordingly, both A and B receive a $1,000 increase in each of their Capital balances as a result of C's $13,000 investment in the partnership.

The partnership balance sheet, following the recording of C's investment, would appear as follows:

Assets		Liabilities and Equity		
Cash	$ 5,000	Liabilities		$ 7,000
Other Assets ($22,000 + $13,000)	35,000	Capital—A	$11,000	
		Capital—B	11,000	
		Capital—C	11,000	33,000
		Total Liabilities		
Total Assets	$40,000	and Equity		$40,000

Note again that ownership interests are reflected in the balances of the Capital accounts. In the example, C was admitted for a one-third ownership interest and has a capital balance of $11,000 from the total capital of $33,000.

WITHDRAWAL OF AN EXISTING PARTNER

Q10: Withdrawal of a partner

The withdrawal of a partner can be accounted for as a sale to a new partner, as a sale to one or more of the existing partners, or through a payment of partnership assets to the withdrawing partner. The following balance sheet shows the A, B, and C partnership:

Assets		Liabilities and Equity		
Cash	$ 5,000	Liabilities		$ 7,000
Other Assets	32,000	Capital—A	$10,000	
		Capital—B	10,000	
		Capital—C	10,000	30,000
		Total Liabilities and		
Total Assets	$37,000	Equity		$37,000

Sale to a New Partner

This method is similar to the one discussed earlier of the purchase of an existing partner's interest to admit a new partner. One partner sells his or her interest to another person. No change occurs in either the assets or the capital of the partnership as a result of this transaction. Payment for the ownership interest is a private transaction; of course, the existing partners must approve the new arrangement.

Sale to the Remaining Partners

An alternate method is for the withdrawing partner to sell his or her ownership interest to the remaining partner(s). This transaction is also private. The assets and the total equity of the partnership are not altered. An entry is made to record the change in the partnership books. If C wants to withdraw, and A and B both purchase C's interest, the following entry would be recorded:

Capital—C	10,000	
Capital—A		5,000
Capital—B		5,000
To record transfer of C's partnership interest to A and B.		

Although more or less than $10,000 may have been paid personally by A and B to C, the record to transfer C's ownership is based on the recorded balance.

Payment from Partnership Assets

A third method involves the withdrawing partner being paid the amount of his or her Capital balance. This causes no recording difficulties. If the payment is in cash, the following entry would be made:

Capital—C	10,000	
Cash		10,000
To record C's withdrawal from partnership.		

Usually, however, the withdrawing partner may receive either more or less than his or her recorded Capital balance. The difference can result from undervalued or overvalued partnership assets, anticipated future profitable operations in excess of normal return, or interpersonal difficulties. As a result, the partners determine an agreed amount that is due to C; the difference is treated as a bonus to either the withdrawing partner or the remaining partners. That is, the Capital balances of the remaining partners absorb the difference in the remaining partners' profit-and-loss-sharing ratio. In this case, the two remaining partners are assumed to share the difference equally.

If C is paid $2,000 more than his Capital balance, the Capital balances of both A and B would each be reduced by $1,000.

Capital—C	10,000	
Capital—A	1,000	
Capital—B	1,000	
Cash		12,000
To record C's withdrawal from the partnership.		

C, therefore, receives a total of $12,000, represented by the $10,000 Capital balance and a bonus of $2,000, which is paid equally by A and B.

If C is paid $3,000 less than his Capital balance, the Capital balances of both A and B would be increased by $1,500.

Capital—C	10,000	
Capital—A		1,500
Capital—B		1,500
Cash		7,000
To record C's withdrawal from the partnership.		

C receives $7,000 in cash; the $3,000 difference, shared equally by A and B, increases their Capital balances.

The bonus approach for both incoming and outgoing partners is the most prevalent method of recording these types of transactions. Since a new entity is created every time the makeup of the partnership changes, the assets could be revaluated in either direction before the new partner comes in or the old partner withdraws. This would eliminate the need for the bonus approach in many instances. Because of some of the complexities involved, more advanced accounting courses cover asset revaluation.

On the death of a partner, the partnership business may be continued under a new partnership agreement; settlement of the deceased partner's ownership interest is made in accordance with provisions in the partnership agreement.

LIQUIDATION OF A PARTNERSHIP

Q11: Partnership liquidation

The **liquidation of a partnership** results in a termination of the partnership business; its assets are sold, debts are paid, and any remaining cash (or unsold assets) is distributed to the partners in settlement of their Capital balances. The amount of cash available to partners is influenced by the sale of partnership assets at a gain or loss. The following partnership post-closing balance sheet as of January 1, 19X4, illustrates the accounting for the liquidation of the A, B, and C partnership.

Assets			Liabilities and Equity		
Cash	$ 5,000		Accounts Payable		$ 7,000
Other Assets	32,000		Capital—A	$10,000	
			Capital—B	10,000	
			Capital—C	10,000	30,000
			Total Liabilities		
Total Assets	$37,000		and Equity		$37,000

For purposes of this section, profits and losses are assumed to be shared in a ratio of 5 : 3 : 2, or 50%, 30% and 20%.

Gains on Sale of Assets

Each partner's share of gains realized on the sale of assets is recorded as an increase in his or her Capital account. If other assets are sold for $42,000, the following entry is prepared to record the gain.

Cash	42,000	
Gain on Realization of Assets		10,000
Other Assets		32,000
To record the gain on sale of other assets.		

The $10,000 gain is then divided among the partners in their 5 : 3 : 2 profit-and-loss-sharing ratio.

Gain on Realization of Assets	10,000	
Capital—A		5,000
Capital—B		3,000
Capital—C		2,000
To record the division of the gain from sale of other assets.		

The liabilities are then paid; the journal entry to record the payment follows.

Accounts Payable	7,000	
Cash		7,000
To record payment of liabilities.		

At this point, the partnership balances would appear as shown next.

Assets		Equity	
Cash	$40,000	Capital—A	$15,000
		Capital—B	13,000
		Capital—C	12,000
Total Assets	$40,000	Total Equity	$40,000

The following entry is made to record payment of the three Capital account balances:

Capital—A	15,000	
Capital—B	13,000	
Capital—C	12,000	
Cash		40,000
To record payment of Capital accounts.		

Note that all Capital account balances are zero, following the distribution of cash.

Loss on Sale of Assets

In this case, losses resulting from the **realization of assets**—their conversion to cash—are also allocated to partners in their profit-and-loss-sharing ratio. The discussion that follows deals with the situation in which each partner's Capital balance is sufficient to absorb his or her share of the loss. The subsequent discussion covers the situation in which one partner's Capital balance is insufficient to absorb his or her share of the loss.

ADEQUATE AMOUNT OF CAPITAL BALANCES

Assume that the sale of the $32,000 of other assets in the example given earlier realizes only $22,000. The following entry records the sale:

Cash	22,000	
Loss on Realization of Assets	10,000	
Other Assets		32,000
To record loss on sale of assets.		

The $10,000 loss is then allocated to each partner in accordance with the 5 : 3 : 2 profit-and-loss-sharing ratio.

Capital—A	5,000	
Capital—B	3,000	
Capital—C	2,000	
Loss on Realization of Assets		10,000
To record the division of loss from sale of assets.		

The payment of liabilities is then recorded.

Accounts Payable	7,000	
Cash		7,000
To record payment of accounts payable.		

The partnership balances are then determined. The assets include the $15,000 cash from the sale of the assets, plus the beginning Cash balance of $5,000. This equals the equities after the loss is subtracted from each partner's Capital account of $10,000.

Assets		Equity	
Cash	$20,000	Capital—A	$ 5,000
		Capital—B	7,000
		Capital—C	8,000
Total Assets	$20,000	Total Equity	$20,000

The following entry records the distribution of cash to the partners:

Capital—A	5,000	
Capital—B	7,000	
Capital—C	8,000	
Cash		20,000
To record payment of Capital accounts.		

Note that the balance in each Capital account is zero following the distribution of cash.

INADEQUATE AMOUNT OF CAPITAL BALANCES

Partnership assets may have to be sold at a considerable loss, resulting in a debit balance in one partner's account following allocation of the loss. Assume that the sale of the previous $32,000 of other assets realizes only $8,000. The following entry records the sale:

Cash	8,000	
Loss on Realization of Assets	24,000	
Other Assets		32,000
To record loss on sale of assets.		

This $24,000 loss is then allocated to each partner in accordance with the 5 : 3 : 2 profit-and-loss-sharing ratio.

Capital—A	12,000	
Capital—B	7,200	
Capital—C	4,800	
Loss on Realization of Assets		24,000
To record the division of loss from sale of assets.		

The payment of liabilities is then recorded.

Accounts Payable	7,000	
Cash		7,000
To record payment of accounts payable.		

The partnership balances now appear as follows:

Assets		Equity	
Cash	$6,000	Capital—A	$(2,000)
		Capital—B	2,800
		Capital—C	5,200
Total Assets	$6,000	Total Equity	$6,000

As can be seen, A has a debit balance in A's Capital account. A would be expected to contribute $2,000 cash to the partnership to make up this debit balance. If A does not contribute this amount, then this $2,000 debit balance is allocated to the remaining partners in their agreed profit-and-loss-sharing ratio, in this case 3 : 2. The following entry illustrates the allocation of A's debit balance to B and C.

Capital—B	1,200	
Capital—C	800	
Capital—A		2,000
To record allocation of A's debit balance.		

At this point, the partnership balances are:

Assets		Equity	
Cash	$6,000	Capital—B	$1,600
		Capital—C	4,400
Total Assets	$6,000	Total Equity	$6,000

EXHIBIT 12–2

A, B, and C
Statement of Partnership Liquidation
January 19X3

	Cash	Other Assets	Liabilities	A	B	C
Balance, Jan. 1	$ 5,000	$32,000	$7,000	$10,000	$10,000	$10,000
Sale of Other Assets	8,000	(32,000)				
Allocation of Loss ($24,000)				(12,000)	(7,200)	(4,800)
	$13,000	-0-	$7,000	($ 2,000)	$ 2,800	$ 5,200
Payment of Liabilities	(7,000)		(7,000)			
	$ 6,000		-0-			
Allocation of A's Debit Balance				2,000		
B: 3/5 × $2,000					(1,200)	
C: 2/5 × $2,000						(800)
				-0-	$ 1,600	$ 4,400
Distribution of Cash	(6,000)				(1,600)	(4,400)
	-0-				-0-	-0-

The distribution of cash to B and C would be recorded by the following entry.

Capital—B	1,600	
Capital—C	4,400	
Cash		6,000

To record payment of Capital accounts.

Liquidation Statement

A liquidation statement can be prepared to show the progress of the liquidation over a period of time. The data involving the sale of $32,000 of other assets for $8,000, allocation of loss to the partners, payment of liabilities, allocation of A's debit balance to B and C, and final distribution of cash are summarized in Exhibit 12-2.

CHAPTER REVIEW

1 How does the accounting differ between a corporation and a sole proprietorship or partnership? (pp. 530–32)

The only differences are found in the equity section of the balance sheet. Since a corporation is a legal "person," equity must be accounted for by source under the major headings of Paid-in Capital and Retained Earnings. Since both the sole proprietorship and the partnership are not legal entities, the need to account for equity by source is not present. Capital accounts are created for each partner or for the sole proprietor, and investments, share of income, and drawings are all recorded in the one account.

2 Does double taxation on sole proprietorship or partnership profits occur as on corporate profits? Explain. (pp. 530–33)

Once again, since the partnership and sole proprietorship forms of business organization are not separate legal entities, their profits are not taxed. The profits or losses pass directly through to the owners and are taxed on their individual returns. Therefore, the profit is only taxed once—not twice as in a corporation.

3 If you were going to start your own business, would you choose the corporate form or a sole proprietorship? Why? (p. 531)

A corporation would be better, even though it would have only one owner. This would allow protection of personal assets to the extent possible. (If the business chosen were in one of the professions, the limited liability protection of the corporation would be unavailable, but the corporate form would provide certain tax advantages.)

4 Does a sole proprietorship or partnership have limited liability? Explain. (p. 532)

No. The corporation had limited liability because it was considered to be a legal entity, separate from its owners. The sole proprietorship and the partnership form of organization are not separate legal entities, and therefore have *unlimited liability*. A partner's or sole proprietor's personal assets—house, car, savings—are all at risk. Only a limited partner would have stipulated liability limits; other partners (general partners) would continue to bear unlimited liability.

5 Do partners have an absolute right to any noncash assets that they individually contribute to the partnership? (pp. 532–33)

Individual partners have *no* right whatsoever to any assets contributed by them. Once an asset is invested into the partnership, it becomes partnership property. Depending on the type of asset, an automobile for instance, provisions might be included in the partnership agreement stating that *if* the asset is still in the partnership at the time the business is ending, the partner may choose the automobile as part of his or her share, but it would be valued at the current fair market value.

6 If you and a business associate were going to start your own business, would you choose the corporate form or a partnership? Why? (p. 533)

The corporate form would definitely be preferred over the partnership for all the reasons stated in the answer to question number 3.

7 Describe some possible ways partners may decide to divide profits and losses. Should they have a different formula for profits than for losses? (pp. 538–40)

Many factors should be taken into consideration when determining profit-and-loss-sharing agreements. At least *all* of the following should be considered;

- Time devoted
- Experience and abilities
- Amount invested

If all of these factors are about equal, then profits and losses should be divided equally. If any are not equal, the agreement should take the inequality into consideration by equitably allocating profits and losses. If the partnership agreement makes no mention of profit sharing, then profits and losses are divided equally. If the agreement only mentions profits, then losses will be divided in the same manner as profits.

Profit-sharing agreements are one of the most difficult problems to solve in forming a partnership. Because of changes that occur over time, the agreement must be constantly updated. Many times when the agreements are drawn up, the partners can only see good (profits), and not bad (losses). Sometimes the most equitable agreement for profits turns out to be the most unequitable if the business suffers a loss. The partners should determine if the agreement will be as equitable for profits as well as losses, and if not, develop a separate agreement for losses.

8 If a new partner is admitted to the partnership, is the old partnership liquidated? (pp. 541–42)

When a new partner is admitted to the partnership (or an old partner withdraws), the old partnership is *dissolved* and a new one *formed.* No liquidation occurs.

9 Is there more than one way to admit a new partner to the organization? (pp. 542–45)

An incoming partner may *purchase an interest* in the partnership from one of the existing partners or may *invest* directly into the business. If an interest is purchased, the transaction is external to the partnership, much the same as buying a share of stock from one of the existing stockholders of a corporation. The only entry made on the books of the partnership is to transfer equity from the old to the new partner as follows:

Capital—Old Partner	XXX	
Capital—New Partner		XXX

The dollar amount is the portion of equity purchased, and not the purchase price of the transaction. When an interest is purchased, it has no effect on the net assets of the partnership.

If a partner chooses to invest into the partnership, then the entry is as follows;

Assets (cash or noncash)	XXX	
Capital—New partner		XXX

The dollar amount recorded for assets would be the fair market value of the property invested.

10 Is there more than one way to record the withdrawal of a partner from the organization? (pp. 545–47)

The same options are available for a withdrawing partner as an incoming partner. The withdrawing partner may sell his or her interest to a new partner, as described in question number 8, *or* the withdrawing partner may sell his or her interest to *existing* partners, as is shown in the following entry:

Capital—Withdrawing Partner	XXX	
Capital—Old Partner A		XXX
Capital—Old Partner B		XXX

Again, the dollar amount is the portion of equity sold and not the sales price. In the two transactions, the net assets of the partnership were not affected.

The partners may agree to buying the interest of the withdrawing partner. If this is the case, partnership assets are paid to the withdrawing partner, as in the following entry:

Capital—Withdrawing Partner	XXX	
Assets (cash or non cash)		XXX

The dollar amount of assets going to the withdrawing partner would be an agreed upon amount.

11 What does the term liquidation refer to in regard to partnerships? (p. 547)
A liquidation occurs when the partners decide to end their relationship by selling all the noncash assets, satisfying all debts of the partnership, and distributing the remaining assets to the partners according to their interest in the business.

KEY TERMS

bonuses to current partners (p. 545)   A means of compensating the current members of a partnership for a job well done when admitting a new partner into the partnership.

bonuses to new partners (p. 543)   A means used to entice needed investors to join a partnership. The new partner will have a Capital balance in excess of the amount invested.

Capital—Owner (p. 530)   The account that takes the place of paid-in capital and retained earnings in a sole proprietorship or a partnership. Original and additional investments are recorded here, as well as withdrawals, profits, and losses.

Drawing account (p. 530)   The account that in a sole proprietorship or a partnership takes the place of the Dividends account in a corporation. Whenever a partner or a sole proprietor takes assets out of the business, cash or noncash, the Drawing account is charged with the fair market value of those assets.

interest on Capital balances (p. 539)   When unequal amounts of capital are invested into a partnership by the various partners, the profit-sharing agreement should allow interest on Capital balances as a means of more equitably allocating net income to the partners.

investment into a partnership (p. 542)   One way of admitting a new partner. Both cash and noncash assets are invested in exchange for an interest in the partnership.

liquidation of a partnership (p. 547)   When a partnership is liquidated, all the assets are sold for cash, the liabilities are paid, and cash is distributed to the partners according to their interest in the partnership.

mutual agency (p. 532)   A characteristic of a partnership that allows one partner to bind all the other partners in contracts related to the business.

partner salary (p. 539)   When unequal amounts of time or abilities are invested into a partnership by the various partners, the profit-sharing agreement should allow for salary allowances as a means of more equitably allocating net income to the partners. The salaries are not paid to the partners, but are used to allocate net income.

partnership (p. 531)   An unincorporated form of business organization in which the entity is owned by two or more persons.

partnership agreement (p. 532)   A written document that describes all important matters regarding a partnership. The most important parts of the agreement detail how profits and losses are to be divided, and how to value a withdrawing or deceased partner's share of the business.

purchase of a partnership interest (p. 542)   One way of admitting a new partner. The new partner purchases an interest directly from an existing partner in a transaction external to the partnership.

realization of assets (p. 548)   The realization of assets takes place during a liquidation of a partnership. As assets are sold for cash, they are said to be *realized*.

sole proprietorship (p. 530)   An unincorporated form of business organization in which the entity is owned by only one person.

statement of owner's capital (p. 531)   A statement that shows the changes in owner's equity of a sole proprietorship during an accounting period.

statement of partners' capital (p. 541)   A statement that shows the changes in owners' equity of a partnership during an accounting period.

unlimited liability (p. 532)   Since a sole proprietorship or a partnership is not considered to be a legal entity, the owners have unlimited liability in that creditors of the business may proceed against the personal assets of the owners.

SELF-TEST QUESTIONS FOR REVIEW   (Answers are at the end of this chapter.)

Q2, Q4, Q6

1. Which of the following is a major advantage of the partnership form of business organization?
    (a) Limited liability
    (b) Unlimited liability
    (c) Mutual agency
    (d) Double taxation
    (e) None of the above

Q2–Q4

2. Which of the following is a major advantage of the sole proprietorship for   f business organization?
    (a) Limited liability
    (b) Unlimited liability
    (c) Mutual agency
    (d) Double taxation
    (e) None of the above

Q7

3. If a partnership agreement is silent about how profits and losses should be allocated, these results from operations would be allocated
    (a) according to the ratio of capital balances.
    (b) according to the salary level each partner earned before coming to the partnership.
    (c) equally for losses, but according to the Capital balances for profits.
    (d) equally for both profits and losses.

Q9

4. If C is admitted to the partnership of A and B with an investment less than the amount credited to her Capital account, this would be an example of
    (a) a bonus to the old partners.
    (b) a bonus to the new partner.
    (c) a bonus to the partnership.
    (d) a bonus to no one.

Q1–Q4, Q6

5. What is the major difference between a partnership and a sole proprietorship?
    (a) Lack of double taxation for a partnership
    (b) Ease of formation for a sole proprietorship
    (c) Legal requirements for a partnership
    (d) The number of owners
    (e) No major differences exist between the two forms of ownership.

Q9

6. When a new partner is admitted to a partnership, the old entity is said to be
    (a) dissolved.
    (b) liquidated.
    (c) increased in size.
    (d) strengthened.

Q1

7. When a sole proprietor withdraws noncash assets from the business, the
    (a) fair market value of the asset is debited to his or her Drawing account.
    (b) fair market value of the asset is recorded as income for tax purposes.
    (c) book value of the asset is debited to his or her Drawing account.
    (d) book value of the asset is recorded as income for tax purposes.

Q11

8. After the noncash assets have been sold and the liabilities paid in the liquidation of a partnership, the cash is distributed to the partners
    (a) in terms of the income-sharing ratio.

(b)   in terms of the Capital balances immediately before the liquidation process began.
(c)   in terms of the Capital balances after all gains and losses from liquidation have
       been posted to the accounts and all debit balances in the partners' Capital accounts
       have been satisfied.
(d)   according to the needs of each of the partners.

DEMONSTRATION PROBLEM

Part A

X and Y have decided to establish a partnership in a local mall. They are evaluating two
plans for a profit-and-loss-sharing agreement:

Plan A   X to receive a salary of $15,000 per year, the balance to be divided in their
1 : 2 Capital balance ratios of $50,000 for X and $100,000 for Y.
Plan B   X to receive a salary of $1,000 per month; 8% per year interest each on their
investments; and the balance divided equally.

Required
Calculate the division under each plan, assuming: (a) a profit of $60,000, and (b) a loss of
$30,000.

Part B

F, G, and H, are partners, sharing profits equally. They decide to admit Q for an equal
partnership with one-quarter of the total capital. The balances of the partners' Capital accounts
follow:

Capital—F	$30,000
Capital—G	26,000
Capital—H	19,000
Total	$75,000

Required
Prepare journal entries to record admission of Q, using the bonus method:

1.   Assume Q invests $15,000.

2.   Assume Q invests $45,000.

Part C

The following balance sheet is for the partnership of Allan, Billie, and Carrie.

Allan, Billie, and Carrie
Balance Sheet
November 1, 19X2

Assets		Liabilities and Partners' Equity	
Cash	$ 20,000	Liabilities	$ 50,000
Other Assets	180,000	Capital—Allan (40%)	37,000
		Capital—Billie (40%)	65,000
		Capital—Carrie (20%)	48,000
		Total Liabilities and	
Total Assets	$200,000	Equity	$200,000

Figures shown parenthetically reflect the agreed profit-and-loss-sharing percentages. The partnership is dissolved and liquidated by selling the other assets for $100,000 and paying off the creditors.

Required

The partners are unclear as to how to divide the proceeds of liquidation. You have been handling the accounting for the partnership, so they ask you to prepare the schedule of partnership liquidation (use the format shown on p. 551).

SOLUTIONS TO DEMONSTRATION PROBLEM

Part A

X and Y Partnership

Profit and Loss Sharing Plan		(a) Profit $60,000		(b) Loss $30,000	
		X	Y	X	Y
Plan A	Salary	$15,000	-0-	$ 15,000	-0-
	Balance	15,000	$30,000	(15,000)	$(30,000)
		$30,000	$30,000	-0-	$(30,000)
Plan B	Salary	$12,000	-0-	$ 12,000	-0-
	Interest	4,000	$ 8,000	4,000	$ 8,000
	Balance	18,000	18,000	(27,000)	(27,000)
	Totals	$34,000	$26,000	$(11,000)	$(19,000)

Part B

1.

Capital—F	$ 30,000
Capital—G	26,000
Capital—H	19,000
Capital Balance	$ 75,000
Investment by Q	15,000
Capital of New Partnership	$ 90,000
Q's Capital ($90,000 × 1/4)	$ 22,500

The new partner's bonus is recorded as follows:

Cash	15,000	
Capital—F	2,500	
Capital–G	2,500	
Capital—H	2,500	
Capital—Q		22,500

2.

Capital—F	$ 30,000
Capital—G	26,000
Capital—H	19,000
Capital Balance	$ 75,000
Investment by Q	45,000
Capital of New Partnership	$120,000
Q's Capital ($120,000 × 1/4)	$ 30,000

The bonus to existing partners is recorded as follows:

Cash	45,000	
Capital—F		5,000
Capital—G		5,000
Capital—H		5,000
Capital—Q		30,000

Part C

Allan, Billie, and Carrie
Statement of Partnership Liquidation
November 19X2

	Cash	Other Assets	Liabilities	Allan	Billie	Carrie
Balance, Nov. 1, 19X2	$ 20,000	$180,000	$50,000	$37,000	$65,000	$48,000
Sale of Other Assets	100,000	(180,000)				
Allocation of Loss ($80,000)				(32,000)	(32,000)	(16,000)
	$120,000	-0-	$50,000	$ 5,000	$33,000	$32,000
Payment of Liabilities	(50,000)		(50,000)			
	$ 70,000		-0-			
Distribution of Cash	(70,000)			(5,000)	(33,000)	(32,000)
	-0-			-0-	-0-	-0-

DISCUSSION QUESTIONS

Q12-1   Is a sole proprietorship a separate entity? Explain.

Q12-2   What differentiates a sole proprietorship from a partnership?

Q12-3   What similarities exist between an accounting firm organized as a sole proprietorship and an accounting firm organized as a corporation?

Q12-4   Are profits from a sole proprietorship taxed twice as in a corporation?

Q12-5   Identify and briefly explain five unique characteristics of a partnership.

Q12-6   What are the advantages and disadvantages of a partnership?

Q12-7   How does accounting for a partnership differ from that for a corporation?

Q12-8   How are partnership profits and losses divided among partners?

Q12-9   Why are salary and interest allocations included in the division of profits and losses?

Q12-10   How are partners' Capital balances disclosed in the balance sheet?

Q12-11   What is a partnership bonus? How is it determined when a new partner is admitted?

Q12-12   Distinguish between the sale of a withdrawing partner's interest to a new partner and its sale to existing partner(s).

Q12-13   Explain how a debit balance in one partner's Capital account is handled if that partner is unable to contribute additional assets to cover the debit balance.

Q12-14   What is the difference, if any, between the dissolution of a partnership and the liquidation of a partnership?

Q12-15   Are partners personally liable for the personal debts of other partners?

Q12-16   Do all partners have to agree to the admission of a new partner, or would a simple majority suffice?

Q12-17   What are the similarities and differences between a statement of owners' equity and a statement of partners' equity?

DISCUSSION CASE

To Incorporate or Not?

(Q1, Q2, Q4–Q6)

Adam, Porter, and Ida Clark own and operate as partners a family business known as Clarks' Raiders. Along with ten employees and equipment valued at about $200,000, they travel the carnival and rural fair circuit each summer with a crowd-thrilling automobile stunt show. Business is seasonal, and each of the three owns a home in the Midwest, where the families are located permanently. The partners feel that they could double the amount of annual revenue with the addition of more equipment and the hiring and training of two or three more drivers. Ida and Porter are in favor of such action, but Adam is hesitant. He points out that twice during the past season, a car ran into a section of bleachers, causing damages amounting to thousands of dollars; it was fortunate that the costs did not run into the hundreds of thousands. He has heard something about limited liability of the corporate form of business, but really doesn't understand what it would mean to Clarks' Raiders. All three partners agree to seek your advice.

For Discussion

Using this partnership, what are some advantages and disadvantages of changing to the corporate form of business?

EXERCISES

Closing income summary account: corporation, sole proprietorship, partnership (Q1)

E12-1 All the revenue and expense accounts have been closed to the Income Summary account, which has a credit balance of $45,000.

Required

Prepare the necessary journal entry to close the Income Summary account, assuming the business is organized as a

1. sole proprietorship.
2. partnership with three partners.
3. corporation.

Allocation of profit, loss in partnership (Q7)

E12-2 All the revenue and expense accounts of a partnership have been closed to the Income Summary account, which has a *credit* balance of $45,000. The partnership agreement is silent between the two partners.

Required

1. Determine the proper allocation of the balance in the Income Summary account.
2. Prepare the entry necessary to close the Income Summary account.

Allocation of profit, loss in partnership (Q7)

E12-3 All the revenue and expense accounts of a partnership have been closed to the Income Summary account, which has a *debit* balance of $45,000. The partnership agreement is silent between the two partners.

Required

1. Determine the proper allocation of the balance in the Income Summary account.
2. Prepare the entry necessary to close the Income Summary account.

Allocation of profit, loss in partnership (Q7)

E12-4 All the revenue and expense accounts in a partnership of A and B have been closed to the Income Summary account, which has a credit balance of $42,000. The partnership agreement for division of income is as follows: Profit shall be divided between the two partners using weighted average Capital balances. The activity in their respective capital accounts follows:

	A	B
Beginning Balance	$36,000	$20,000
Investment, March 31	10,000	
Investment, July 31		30,000
Withdrawal, June 1	(6,000)	
Withdrawal, Sept. 30		(10,000)

Required

1. Determine the proper allocation of the ending balance in the Income Summary account.

2. Prepare the entry necessary to close the Income Summary account.

Allocation of partner-
ship loss (Q7)

E12-5   The partnership agreement in E12-4 referred to profits and income.

Required

How would a loss of $42,000 be allocated?

Allocation of profit, loss
in partnership (Q7)

E12-6   All the revenue and expense accounts in a partnership of A and B have been closed to the Income Summary account, which has a credit balance of $63,500. The partnership agreement has the following profit and loss allocations: interest allowances of 10% on weighted average Capital balances; salary allowances of $30,000 to A and $15,000 to B; and any remaining profits or losses shall be allocated in a 1 : 2 ratio. A's average capital for the year was $40,000, while B's was $25,000.

Required

1. Determine the proper allocation of the balance in the Income Summary account.

2. Prepare the entry necessary to close the Income Summary account.

Allocation of profit, loss
in partnership (Q7)

E12-7   Consider the partnership agreement in E12-6.

Required

How would a net income of $30,500 be allocated?

Admission of new
partner by purchasing
an interest (Q9)

E12-8   The partnership of A and B had the following Capital balances when they decided to admit C into the partnership: A, $40,000; B, $60,000. All profits and losses had been split evenly. C will purchase 1/5 of A's interest for $12,000 and 1/12 of B's interest for $8,000.

Required

Prepare the entry necessary to record C's purchase.

Admission of new part-
ner by investment (Q9)

E12-9   The partnership of A and B had the following Capital balances when they decided to admit C into the partnership: A, $40,000; B, $60,000. All profits and losses had been split evenly. C will invest $50,000 for a 1/3 interest in the partnership's net assets.

Required

Prepare the entry necessary to record C's investment.

Admission of new part-
ner by investment (Q9)

E12-10   The partnership of A and B had the following Capital balances when they decided to admit C into the partnership: A, $40,000; B, $60,000. All profits and losses had been split evenly. C will invest $50,000 for a 30% interest in the partnership's net assets.

Required

Prepare the entry necessary to record C's investment.

Admission of new partner by investment (Q9)

E12-11 The partnership of A and B had the following Capital balances when they decided to admit C into the partnership: A, $40,000; B, $60,000. All profits and losses had been split evenly. C will invest $50,000 for a 40% interest in the partnership's net assets.

Required

Prepare the entry necessary to record C's investment.

Distribution of cash in partnership liquidation (Q10)

E12-12 The partnership of A, B, and C has decided to liquidate. Profits and losses are allocated in a 5 : 3 : 2 ratio. All the assets have been sold and all the liabilities have been paid.

Required

How would the remaining cash of $16,000 be distributed, assuming the Capital balances show the following amounts?

A	$4,000
B	6,000
C	6,000

Distribution of cash in partnership liquidation (Q10)

E12-13 The partnership of A, B, and C has decided to liquidate. Profits and losses are allocated in a 5 : 3 : 2 ratio. All the assets have been sold and all the liabilities have been paid.

Required

How would the remaining cash of $16,000 be distributed, assuming the Capital balances show the following amounts?

A	$ (4,000)
B	10,000
C	10,000

Partnership liabilities, no cash (Q10)

E12-14 The partnership of A, B, and C is in the process of liquidating. After all noncash assets have been sold and all available cash paid to creditors, the balance sheet appears as follows:

Assets	Liabilities and Equity		
(None)	Accounts Payable		$20,000
	Capital—A	$ (6,000)	
	Capital—B	(9,000)	
	Capital—C	(5,000)	(20,000)
-0-			-0-

The profit-and-loss agreement calls for an allocation in a 4 : 4 : 2 ratio. The personal financial position of the three partners is as follows:

	Assets	Liabilities
A	$65,000	$50,000
B	22,000	35,000
C	67,000	15,000

Required

1. Assuming the creditors decide to go after the personal assets of C, how much can they recover from C?

2. What is the maximum amount A could be required to contribute to the partnership?

3. Will partner B be required to pay $9,000 of the $22,000 in assets to the partnership?

PROBLEMS

Journal entries, closing, statement of owner's capital for sole proprietorship (Q1, Q2)

P12-1 The following transactions took place during January 19X8 after Ray Brown decided to open Brown's Antiques:

Jan. 1 Invested antiques with a wholesale fair market value of $100,000 into the business

2 Invested cash of $20,000 into the business

9 Sold antiques with a wholesale value of $15,000 for $24,600. Brown uses the perpetual method of recording inventories.

15 Paid operating expenses of $13,000

24 Sold antiques with a wholesale value of $25,000 for $47,800

30 Paid operating expenses of $14,000

31 Took $5,000 cash as salary for January

Required

1. Prepare journal entries for Brown's transactions.

2. Determine the net income.

3. Assume all income statement accounts have been closed to the Income Summary account. Close the Income Summary and Drawing accounts.

4. Prepare a statement of owner's capital for Ray Brown as of January 31, 19X8.

5. How did Brown's Antiques do for the month of January?

Allocation of net income (Q7)

P12-2 On January 1, 19X3, XYZ partnership had Capital balances of $60,000, $100,000, and $20,000 for X, Y, and Z, respectively. In 19X3 the partnership reported net income of $40,000. None of the partners withdrew any assets in 19X3. The partnership agreed to share profits and losses as follows: a monthly salary allowance of $2,000, $2,500, and $4,000 to X, Y, and Z, respectively; an annual interest allowance of 10% to each partner based on his or her capital balance at the beginning of the year; and any remaining balance to be shared in a 5 : 3 : 2 ratio.

Required

1. Using the format shown in this chapter, prepare a schedule to allocate the 19X3 net income to the partners.

2. Assume all the income statement accounts for 19X3 have been closed to the Income Summary account. Prepare the entry to record the division of the 19X3 net income.

Admission of new partner by investment (Q9)

P12-3 Crane and Davis are partners sharing profits and losses 60% and 40%, respectively. On July 1, their interests in the firm are as follows: Crane, $23,000; Davis, $18,600. Hughes is admitted as a partner with an investment of $16,000.

Required

Record the investment by Hughes in general journal form, assuming Hughes receives the following:

1. Credit for the actual investment made

2. A ⅓ interest, with a bonus to Hughes

3. A ¼ interest, with a bonus to the existing partners

Partnership liquidation,
insolvent partner (Q11)

P12-4 The A, B, and C partnership has decided to liquidate. The general ledger shows the following balances on March 1, 19X3:

Cash	$ 10,000
Other Assets	125,000
Accounts Payable	10,000
Capital—A	25,000
Capital—B	37,500
Capital—C	62,500

Proceeds from the sale of noncash assets during March were $42,500.

Required

Prepare a statement of partnership liquidation. Net income and losses are shared equally; the partners have no other assets.

ALTERNATE PROBLEMS

Journal entries, closing, statement of owner's capital for sole proprietorship (Q1, Q2)

AP12-1 The following transactions took place during July 19X3 after Roy Thompson decided to open Roy's Antique Automobiles:

July 1 Invested automobiles with a wholesale fair market value of $1,000,000 into the business

2 Invested cash of $200,000 into the business

9 Sold an automobile with a wholesale value of $35,000 for $75,000. Thompson uses the perpetual method of recording inventories.

15 Paid operating expenses of $33,000

24 Sold an automobile with a wholesale value of $25,000 for $61,000

30 Paid operating expenses of $24,000

30 Took $15,000 cash as salary for January

Required

1. Prepare journal entries for RAA's transactions.

2. Determine the net income.

3. Assume all income statement accounts have been closed to the Income Summary account. Close the Income Summary and Drawing accounts.

4. Prepare a statement of owner's capital for Roy Thompson as of July 31, 19X3.

5. How did RAA do for the month of July?

Allocation of net income (Q7)

AP12-2 On January 1, 19X9, the partnership of Harry, Mary, and Beth had balances of $40,000, $30,000, and $60,000, respectively. During 19X9 the partnership earned $81,000. None of the partners withdrew any assets during the year, and no additional investments were made. The income-sharing plan found in the partnership agreement follows: a monthly salary allowance of $2,000, $3,000, and $4,000 for Harry, Mary, and Beth, respectively; an annual interest allowance of 10% on the partners' weighted average capital balance during the year; a bonus to Beth of 5% of net income after salary and interest allowances; and any remaining profit or loss to be shared in a 4 : 4 : 2 ratio.

Required

1. Using the format shown in this chapter, prepare a schedule to allocate the 19X9 net income to the partners.

2. Assume all the income statement accounts for 19X9 have been closed to the Income Summary account. Prepare the entry to record the division of the 19X9 net income.

Admission of new part-
ner by investment (Q9)

AP12-3   Jackson and Peterson are partners sharing in profits and losses in a 2 : 3 ratio, respectively. On August 1 their capital balances were $35,000 and $25,000, respectively. Mercer is admitted as a partner with an investment of $30,000.

Required

Record the investment by Mercer in journal form, assuming Mercer receives the following:

1. A 1/3 interest
2. A 1/4 interest
3. A 2/5 interest

Partnership liquidation,
insolvent partner

AP12-4   A, B, C, and D have a partnership sharing profits 40%, 30%, 20%, and 10% respectively. Assume all partners are unable to contribute any amount to the partnership. The audited balance sheet follows:

A, B, C, and D Partnership
Balance Sheet
January 1, 19X3

Assets		Liabilities and Equity	
Cash	$ 4,000	Liabilities	$20,000
Noncurrent assets	54,000	Capital—A	4,000
		Capital—B	9,600
		Capital—C	18,400
		Capital—D	6,000
		Total Liabilites	
Total Assets	$58,000	and Equity	$58,000

The partnership is liquidated during January 19X3, and the noncash assets realized were $26,000.

Required

Prepare a statement of partnership liquidation.

DECISION PROBLEMS

Problem 1

Q11

A partnership of R, S, and T has sold all of its assets and paid out all of its cash to its creditors. No cash or other assets remain in the partnership. The following liability and Capital balances remain. (Figures shown in parentheses reflect the partners' profit-and-loss-sharing percentage.)

Liabilities and Equity

Liabilities	$21,000 Cr.
Capital—R (40%)	66,000 Dr.
Capital—S (20%)	20,000 Cr.
Capital—T (40%)	25,000 Cr.

Required

1. Assuming all partners are personally bankrupt, briefly explain what the creditors of the partnership may do.
2. Assume instead the following information regarding the personal solvency of the partners:

	Assets	Liabilities
R	$ 6,000	$28,000
S	38,000	14,000
T	7,000	8,000

Indicate the course of action you expect the creditors to take, given these circumstances.

Problem 2

Q7

Partners A and B are subject to the following agreement for the sharing of profits and losses: annual salaries are allowed—$12,000 to A, $14,000 to B; interest at 10% is allowed on original capital contributions of $100,000 from A and $70,000 from B; any remainder is to be split in the ratio of 3 : 2.

Required

How much net income must be earned by the partnership for A to be allocated a total of $47,000?

ANSWERS TO SELF-TEST QUESTIONS

1. **(e)** All of the terms listed either do not apply to a partnership or represent disadvantages, not advantages. Limited liability is an advantage of the corporation; a partnership has unlimited liability, but it is not an advantage. A partnership does have mutual agency, but it is not usually viewed as an advantage. A partnership does not have double taxation as does a corporation.

2. **(e)** All of the terms listed either do not apply to a sole proprietorship or represent disadvantages, not advantages. Limited liability is an advantage of the corporation; a sole proprietorship has unlimited liability, but it is not an advantage. The concept of mutual agency does not apply to a sole proprietorship. A sole proprietorship does not have double taxation, as does a corporation.

3. **(d)** If the partnership agreement does not address profit and loss sharing, both should be allocated equally. Any profit-sharing agreement will be used to allocate losses as well. Answer *b* does not make much sense.

4. **(b)** If C is admitted with an investment less than the credit to her Capital account, then the transaction indicates a bonus to the new partner. This easily can be seen in a journal entry, as follows:

Cash	14,000	
Capital—A	2,000	
Capital—B	2,000	
Capital—C		18,000

5. **(d)** Like a partnership, a sole proprietorship does not have double taxation, and a partnership is almost as easy to form as a sole proprietorship. The only major difference is the number of owners: a partnership has more than one.

6. **(a)** Whenever the makeup of the partners changes in a partnership, the old entity is dissolved and a new one formed. Liquidation refers to the sale of all noncash assets and the payment of all liabilities, with the distribution of cash being the final transaction of the business.

7. **(a)** Any asset taken from the business, whether it be a sole proprietorship, partnership, or corporation, is recorded at its fair market value. The distribution of noncash assets in a sole proprietorship or a partnership is not considered a taxable activity.

8. **(c)** The final step in liquidation is to distribute the cash to the partners. Cash will be distributed according to the partners' ending Capital balances, which have been reduced by all losses, including any losses incurred as the result of an insolvent partner with a debit balance.

13 FINANCING ACTIVITIES: LONG-TERM DEBT

A corporation has two choices when deciding how to finance its operations: debt or equity. Chapters 10, 11, and 12 examined equity financing arrangements in corporations, sole proprietorships, and partnerships. This chapter discusses debt financing. Remember that a proper mix must occur between debt and equity to maximize the return to the common stockholders. Chapter 13 first explores the decision to issue bonds, including the advantages and disadvantages of having debt outstanding. The chapter continues with a section on bond terminology that students must master to have a firm understanding of accounting for bonds. Since bonds carry a fixed interest rate, and the market rate of interest fluctuates daily, bonds may be issued at an amount above or below their face value, creating an amount referred to as a *bond premium* or a *bond discount*. These amounts must be allocated (amortized) over the life of the bond as an adjustment to interest expense. Chapter 13 investigates two widely used methods to amortize the bond premium or discount. An appendix at the end of this chapter includes an introduction to both present-value and future-value analyses, which should help students understand why bonds sell at amounts other than their face value. Since present and future value analyses are used extensively in the business curriculum, the topic is timely. However, accounting for bonds can be taught without the appendix.

After studying Chapter 13, you should be able to answer the following questions:

1 Do stockholders and bondholders have similar rights? Explain. (p.568)

2 Will issuing bonds usually result in higher earnings-per-share (EPS) amounts for the common stockholders? (p.570)

3 Why is it said that the issuing corporation benefits when it has bonds outstanding during periods of inflation? (p.571)

4 What are the major disadvantages of issuing bonds over stock? (p.571)

5 Do all bonds have some sort of security behind them? (p.572)

6 Do bondholders usually have the right to convert their bonds into common stock? Would this feature be of any advantage to the issuing corporation? the investing corporation? (p.573)

7 Would a corporation usually use a sinking fund in connection with serial bonds outstanding? (p.574)

8 Bonds have a face value (par value); when would bonds sell above or below face value? Explain. (p.575)

9 Why are bond premiums and discounts treated as adjustments to interest expense over the life of the bond issue? (p.578)

10 What problem arises when a corporation decides to retire unmatured bonds? Explain. (pp.583–84)

11 What problem arises when bonds are issued after the date of original authorization and, therefore, between interest dates? (pp.584–85)

12 It is said that the effective interest method of bond amortization results in more accurate information than the straight-line method. Why? (pp.586–87)

13 What are some areas of financial accounting where present or future value analysis is used? (pp.593–97)

THE DECISION TO ISSUE BONDS

Corporations acquire long-term financing through the issue of stocks and bonds. In Chapter 11, the acquisition of capital from stocks is discussed. This chapter examines the acquisition of capital—that is, the financing of the corporation—through issues of bonds.

A **bond** is a debt security that requires a future payment of money, as well as periodic interest payments during its life. A contract called a **bond indenture** is prepared between the corporation and the future bondholders. It specifies the terms with which the corporation will comply. One of these terms may be a restriction on further borrowing by the corporation. A **trustee** is appointed to be an intermediary between the corporation and the bondholder.

Rights of Bondholders

Q1: Stockholder vs. bondholder rights

Ownership of a bond certificate carries with it certain rights. These rights are printed on the certificate and vary among bond issues. The various characteristics applicable to bond issues are the subject of more advanced courses in finance and are not treated here. It is appropriate to point out, however, that individual bondholders always acquire two rights.

1. It is the right of the bondholder to receive the face value of the bond at a specified date in the future, referred to as the **maturity date;** and

2. It is the right of the bondholder to receive periodic interest payments, usually semiannually, at a specified percent of the bond's face value.

Bond Authorization

Every corporation is legally required to follow a well-defined sequence in authorizing a bond issue. The bond issue is presented to the board of directors by management and may have to be approved by stockholders. Legal requirements must be complied with and disclosure is required in the financial statements of the corporation.

Stockholder approval is an important step because bondholders are creditors with a prior claim on the assets of the corporation if liquidation occurs. Further, dividend distributions may be restricted during the life of the bonds, for which stockholder acceptance is necessary. These restrictions are usually reported to the reader of financial statements through note disclosure.

Recording the Bond Authorization

Assuming that Saguaro Computers, Inc., decides to issue bonds amounting to $30 million to finance its expansion, the amount of authorized bonds, their interest rate, and their maturity date can be shown in the accounts as follows:

General Journal
Memorandum

19X1
Jan. 1   Authorized to issue $30,000,000 of 12%
3-year bonds due January 1, 19X4.

General Ledger
Bonds Payable
(Due January 1, 19X4)

19X1
Jan. 1   Authorized to issue $30,000,000 of 12%
3-year bonds, dated January 1, 19X1.

Different general ledger accounts are opened for each type of bond approved. The caption used for the bonds payable should generally indicate the type of bonds involved in the issue.

Bond Issues in the Financial Statements

Each bond issue is disclosed separately in the financial statements because each issue may have different characteristics. The descriptive information disclosed to readers of financial statements includes the interest rate and maturity date of the bond issue. Also disclosed in a note are any restrictions imposed on the corporation's activities and on assets pledged, if any.

The Bond Financing Decision

A corporation should evaluate many factors when considering issuing bonds as a means of financing. The more important of these are discussed here.

IS CASH REQUIRED NOW, THE IMMEDIATE FUTURE, OR IN THE DISTANT FUTURE?

Bonds, like common stock, are authorized in a given amount. They all can be issued at once or in a piecemeal fashion, depending on the corporation's cash needs. The danger is, however, that bond prices can fluctuate more widely than stock prices, since the bond prices are tied to the market rate of interest. It is possible to issue bonds at a discount if authorized but unissued bonds are held during a period when interest rates are rising. The problem must be considered because interest rates on authorized bonds are fixed and do not change with changes in the market interest rate.

IMPORTANT TERMS OF THE BONDS

The interest rate of the bonds, their maturity date, and other important provisions—such as being convertible into common shares and restrictions on future dividend distributions of the corporation—are also considered. The success of a bond issue often depends on the proper combination of these and other similar features.

ASSETS OF THE CORPORATION TO BE PLEDGED

The pledging of mortgageable assets is an important consideration for bondholders because it safeguards their investment. It is important to the corporation because the pledging of all these assets may restrict future borrowings. The total amount of authorized bonds is usually a fraction of the mortgageable assets—for example, 50%. The difference is the margin of safety to bondholders, since it permits the proceeds from the sale of these assets to shrink substantially yet still cover reimbursement of bondholders should the need arise.

OTHER METHODS OF RAISING CASH

Various alternate methods of raising cash, such as issues of common or preferred stock, are also reviewed by management in order to determine whether to issue bonds.

Many factors influence management in its choice between the issue of bonds and the issue of common stock. One of the most important considerations is the potential effect of each of these financing methods on the current owners of the corporation, that is, the common stockholders. How would their earnings per share be affected?

Consider the example of Saguaro Computers, Inc., which has 100,000 common shares outstanding, is a growth company, and is profitable. SCI requires $30 million in cash to finance its seventh new plant, complete with new equipment. Management is currently reviewing three financing options:

Plan 1   Issue 12% bonds, due in three years
Plan 2   Issue 8% preferred stock
Plan 3   Issue an additional 200,000 shares of common stock

Erecting a new plant and placing it in operation should result in a net income of $6 million before interest expense, if any, and income taxes (assumed to be 50% of net income and calculated after the deduction of interest expense from net income).

Management has prepared the following analysis to compare and evaluate each financing option. Study the details of this schedule and consider which plan is most attractive to the common stockholders.

Q2: Earnings per share

	Plan 1 Issue Bonds	Plan 2 Issue Preferred Stock	Plan 3 Issue Common Stock
Net Income before Interest and Income Taxes	$6,000,000	$6,000,000	$6,000,000
Less: Bond Interest Expense	3,600,000	-0-	-0-
Earnings before Taxes	$2,400,000	$6,000,000	$6,000,000
Less: Income Tax at 50%	1,200,000	3,000,000	3,000,000
Balance	$1,200,000	$3,000,000	$3,000,000
Less: Preferred Dividends at 8%	-0-	2,400,000	-0-
Net Available to Common Stockholders	$1,200,000	$ 600,000	$3,000,000
Common Shares Outstanding	100,000	100,000	300,000
Earnings per Common Share	$12	$6	$10

Based on the earnings per share, it becomes clear that Plan 1, the issue of bonds, has several advantages for existing common stockholders.

Advantage 1: Earnings per Share   If the additional long-term financing were acquired through the issue of bonds (Plan 1), the corporate **earnings per share (EPS)**, the amount of net income allocated to each common share, would be $12. (EPS was discussed at the end of Chapter 5.) This EPS is greater than the EPS earned through financing with either preferred or additional common shares. On this basis alone, the issue of bonds is more financially attractive to existing common stockholders. However, long-term financing with bonds has other notable advantages.

Advantage 2: Control of the Corporation   Bondholders have no vote in the corporation. If common shares were issued, existing stockholders might lose some management control because corporate ownership would be distributed over a larger number of stockholders. In the SCI case, outstanding common shares would increase from 100,000 to 300,000. Percent interest in the corporation would decrease for each stockholder unless the preemptive right is in place and all existing stockholders contributed the $30 million on a pro rata basis.

Advantage 3: Income Tax Expenses   Interest expense is deductible for income tax purposes. Dividend payments are distributions of retained earnings and are not deducted from net income and are not deductible for tax purposes. With a 50% income tax rate, the after-tax interest expense to the corporation is only 6% (12% × 50%). By contrast, dividends to preferred stockholders would be 8% and would not be tax deductible.

Q3: Bonds and inflation

Advantage 4: The Impact of Inflation   The corporation would receive $30 million with today's purchasing power. If the purchasing power of the dollar declines in three years, the $30 million borrowed would be repaid in dollars with a considerably lower purchasing power; an unrecognized gain thereby would accrue to the common stockholders.

BOND FINANCING DISADVANTAGES

Q4: Bond disadvantages

Some disadvantages to long-term financing with bonds also must be carefully reviewed by management and the board of directors. The most serious disadvantage is the possibility that the corporation might earn less than $6 million before interest expense and income taxes. The bond interest expense is a fixed amount. If net income were to fall below the $3,600,000 annual interest expense, one of the other plans might become more advantageous.

Another disadvantage is the fact that bonds have to be repaid at maturity, whether or not the corporation is financially able to do so, while shares do not have to be repaid.

Since the securities market and corporate net earnings remain uncertain, no mathematical formula can solve this financial problem. The financing decision requires sound judgment, based on past experiences and projected future needs. For more discussion on such corporate decisions, see Real World Example 13-1.

BOND CHARACTERISTICS AND TERMINOLOGY

Students sometimes encounter difficulty with the new terminology involved in accounting for bonds. Three main types of bond terminology can be identified. These are shown in Exhibit 13-1 and are discussed next.

Classification of Bonds

Each corporation issuing bonds has unique financing needs and attempts to satisfy various borrowing situations and investor preferences. Many types of bonds have been created to meet these varying needs. Some of the common types are described here.

REAL WORLD EXAMPLE 13-1
Assessing Corporate Capital Needs

THE first step in determining how much capital a company needs and how it should be raised begins with the business plan. . . . A business plan forces managers to examine questions of growth and capital requirements. Drawing up pro formas makes obvious how much money the company will need to meet its goals.

Management then needs to ask whether the company can generate the capital needed from internal sources. It is usually preferable to reinvest excess cash than give up owners' equity or saddle the firm with more debt.

If the company cannot internally generate enough funds, management should ask if it should reduce its goals and thus eliminate the need for external financing. Does management want the company to grow so quickly that it will need outside funding—and its burdens?

If the answer is yes, management must address these questions:

1) How much capital is needed?
2) When is it needed?

3) What will the company do if it cannot raise the funds? It is foolhardy to make the commitments required for growth and then find out the capital to fulfill them can't be raised. Plan ahead for contingencies.

4) Who in the company will manage the program? It is important to assign responsibilities early on and to establish a timetable.

5) Will the company require outside help to raise the funds? Typically, any major effort will involve auditors and counsel.

6) How much management time and corporate cash will a successful capital raising program require? Will the drain on either resource be excessive? Management tasks may have to be restructured to compensate for the new demands of the financing program.

7) Will the company's business plan be good enough to convince capital sources of the company's need and its ability to fulfill whatever commitments will be required?

BONDS CAN BE SECURED OR UNSECURED

Q5: Bond security   **Secured bonds** are backed by mortgageable assets of the corporation. These mortgageable assets are pledged as security for the bonds, and these secured bonds are consequently referred to as *mortgage bonds*.

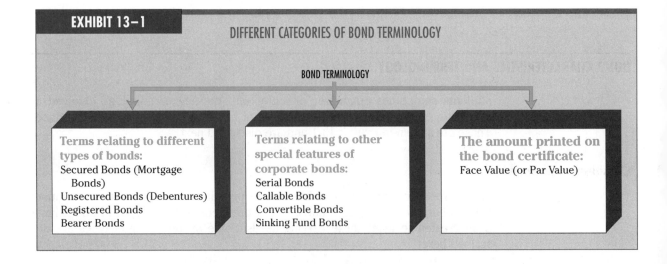

EXHIBIT 13–1   DIFFERENT CATEGORIES OF BOND TERMINOLOGY

BOND TERMINOLOGY

Terms relating to different types of bonds:
Secured Bonds (Mortgage Bonds)
Unsecured Bonds (Debentures)
Registered Bonds
Bearer Bonds

Terms relating to other special features of corporate bonds:
Serial Bonds
Callable Bonds
Convertible Bonds
Sinking Fund Bonds

The amount printed on the bond certificate:
Face Value (or Par Value)

Debt, Equity, or Other?

Every type of financing has its advantages and disadvantages. Debt means a drain on cash flow to meet interest payments. What's more, depending on the type of debt, assets may have to be pledged as security, the lender may impose other restrictive covenants on the firm, sinking funds may have to be established and paid into, and more.

Equity, on the other hand, generally will not drain cash flow. But equity can represent a permanent forfeiture of ownership of at least part of the company. Avoiding equity give-up is often an overriding concern of owner/managers. Some sales of equity, however, can contain buy-back provisions. Used primarily in venture capital financings, this structure gives managers the opportunity to buy back some of the equity sold to venture capitalists if the company meets or exceeds some predetermined performance criteria.

What about the other financing forms? These are the so-called off-balance-sheet techniques.

Off-balance-sheet capital is often preferable to any other form because its position—off the balance sheet—does not affect either the debt or equity ratios of the company. But off-balance-sheet financing typically applies to a limited number of special situations. Moreover, it requires extensive legal and accounting expertise that may make it expensive to structure.

After carefully analyzing the pluses and minuses of each financing alternative, management should be able to decide which type it prefers. Then, the question is: is it feasible?

Here, the advice of the firm's auditors, lawyers, and/or consultants is beneficial. Management, however, can do some of its own homework. To determine whether additional debt or equity is even a possibility, management can examine the financials of other, comparable firms.

Source *Inc. Magazine,* December 1984, pp. 193–94. Reprinted with permission. Copyright © 1984 by Goldhirsh Group, Inc., 38 Commercial Wharf, Boston, MA 02110.

Unsecured bondholders are ordinary creditors of the corporation and **unsecured bonds** are secured only by the future financial success of the corporation. Such bonds are commonly referred to as *debenture bonds.* These debenture bonds usually command a higher interest rate because of the added risk for investors.

BONDS CAN BE REGISTERED OR BEARER BONDS

Registered bonds require the name and address of the owner to be recorded by the corporation or its trustee, since interest is paid by check.

The title to *bearer bonds* passes on delivery of the bonds. Payment of interest is made when the bearer clips coupons attached to the bond and presents them to a bank.

Special Features of Bonds

Special features can be attached to bonds in order to make them more attractive to investors, as discussed next.

VARYING MATURITY DATES

When **serial bonds** are issued, the bonds *mature* on more than one date, as indicated on the bond contract. Investors are able to choose bonds with a term that agrees with their investment plans. For example, in a $30-million serial bond issue,

$10 million of the bonds may mature each year for three years. If all the bonds mature on one day in the future, they are referred to as **term bonds.**

The issue of bonds with a **call provision** permits the issuing corporation to redeem, or call, the bonds before their maturity date. The bond indenture usually indicates the **call price** at which bonds are redeemable. Borrowers are thereby protected in the event that market interest rates decline below the bond contract interest rate. In such an event, the higher interest rate bonds can be called to be replaced by bonds bearing a lower interest rate.

CONVERSION PRIVILEGE

Q6: Bonds to common stock

Bonds with a conversion feature are called **convertible bonds;** this feature allows the bondholder to convert the bonds or a portion of the bonds to a specific number of the corporation's voting common stock. This allows the bondholder to enjoy the security of being a creditor to begin with, while having the option of becoming an owner if the corporation is successful.

SINKING FUND REQUIREMENT

Q7: Sinking fund

The corporation is required to deposit funds at regular intervals, usually with a trustee, when **sinking fund** bonds are issued. This feature ensures the availability of adequate cash for the redemption of the bonds at maturity.

RESTRICTION OF DIVIDENDS

The corporation issuing bonds may be required to restrict its retained earnings, thereby limiting the amount of dividends that can be paid from assets represented by retained earnings. The creation of such a restriction is discussed in Chapter 10.

In the final analysis, a bond is only as good as the quality of the assets pledged, if any, as its security and its interest rate. The other provisions in a bond contract are of limited or no value if the issuing corporation is in financial difficulties. A corporation in such difficulties may not be able to sell its bonds, regardless of the attractive provisions attached to them.

Face Value

Each bond has an amount printed on the face of the bond certificate. This is called the **face value** of the bond; it is also commonly referred to as the *par value* of the bond. When the cash received is the same as a bond's face value, the bond is said to be issued *at par.* A common face value of bonds is $1,000, although bonds of other denominations exist. A sale of a $1,000 bond for $1,000 is referred to as a sale at its par value. A $1,000 bond is sold at a **bond premium** when it is sold for more than its face value. If the same bond is sold for less than $1,000, then it has been sold at a **bond discount.**

With a face value of $1,000, a $30-million bond issue can be divided into 30,000 bonds. This number permits a large number of individuals and institutions to participate in corporate financing. As pointed out earlier, the opportunity to raise large amounts of capital is one of the important advantages of the corporate form of organization.

Interest paid to bondholders is *always* calculated on the face value of the bond—the contract amount—regardless of whether the bonds are issued at par,

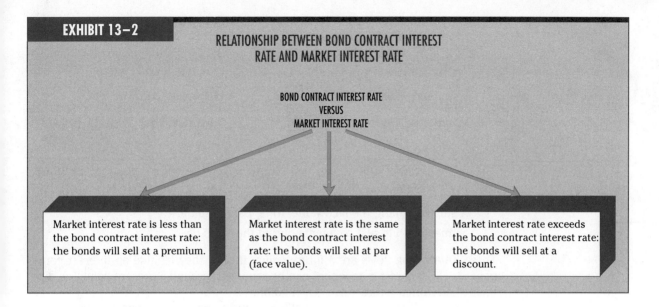

EXHIBIT 13-2

RELATIONSHIP BETWEEN BOND CONTRACT INTEREST
RATE AND MARKET INTEREST RATE

BOND CONTRACT INTEREST RATE
VERSUS
MARKET INTEREST RATE

Market interest rate is less than the bond contract interest rate: the bonds will sell at a premium.

Market interest rate is the same as the bond contract interest rate: the bonds will sell at par (face value).

Market interest rate exceeds the bond contract interest rate: the bonds will sell at a discount.

at a premium, or at a discount. For example, a $1,000 bond with a contract interest rate of 12% pays the following total annual interest:

$$\$1,000 \times 12\% = \$120 \text{ annual interest}$$

This interest is usually paid semiannually, that is, $60 every six months.

Q8: Above or below face value

Why would investors pay a premium for a corporate bond? Why would a corporation sell its bonds at a discount? The answer to these questions lies in the relationship between the bond contract interest rate and the prevailing **market interest rate.** Exhibit 13-2 illustrates the relationship between the bond contract interest rate and the prevailing market interest rate.

The amortization of a bond premium or discount can be made by the straight-line method or by the effective interest method. These are discussed later in this chapter.

Balance Sheet Presentation

Bonds payable are classified as long-term liabilities for disclosure on the balance sheet.

Long-term Liabilities
Bonds Payable
Authorized—$30,000,000, 12%, Due 19X4
Issued— $100,000

When the bonds become payable within one year from the balance sheet date, then they are classified on the balance sheet as a current liability, unless they will be retired with the proceeds of a new debt in the coming 12 months if contracts have already been signed for that new debt.

The bond discount or premium accounts are called *valuation accounts.* They are subtracted from (discounts) or added to (premiums) the Bond Payable account in the liability section of the balance sheet, as shown:

Long-term Liabilities		Long-term Liabilities	
Bonds Payable		Bonds Payable	
Authorized—		Authorized—	
$30,000,000,		$30,000,000,	
12%, Due 19X4		12%, Due 19X4	
Issued—	$100,000	Issued—	$100,000
Less: Discount on		Add: Premium on	
Bonds	(12,000)	Bonds	6,000
Total Liabilities	$ 88,000	Total Liabilities	$106,000

THE PRICE OF A BOND

The selling price of a bond can be determined by the *present value* of all future cash flows associated with the bond:

1. A single amount, the face value, to be paid at maturity
2. Semiannual interest payments during the bond life

These future cash flows are a future value; that is, they include an interest component. This interest component can be removed through a present value (as distinguished from a future value) calculation.

The time value of money, usually referred to as interest, and the method of calculating present value are further discussed in the appendix of this chapter. The next two sections focus on the accounting for bonds.

THE BOND ACCOUNTING PROCESS

Bond accounting often appears quite complex to students. They soon find themselves embroiled in a mass of confusing variables, such as bonds issued between interest dates, interest dates that do not coincide with the corporation's year-end, and the determination and recording of the amortization of bond premiums or discounts. These problems are discussed in the material that follows.

Since authorized bonds are issued by a corporation as cash is required, some bonds may be sold at par, while others are sold at a premium or discount. The issue price of a bond is usually quoted at a percentage of its face value. A bond issued at par is said to sell at 100 (100% of par value). If an issue is quoted as selling at 106, that would mean 106% of par (a $100,000 issue would sell for $106,000). If that same issue was quoted as selling at 88, that would mean 88% of par ($88,000 on a $100,000 issue). The amount of interest paid, however, is always based on a percentage of face value. The selling price of a bond is determined by a number of factors. The factor most identifiable is how the investor views the bond contract interest rate in relation to the prevailing market interest rate.

Assuming that Saguaro sells $100,000 of its 12%, 3-year bonds with interest paid every 6 months, the journal entries to record the issue at par (100), at a premium (106), and at a discount (88) follow:

Cash	100,000		Cash	106,000	
Bonds Payable		100,000	Premium on Bonds		6,000
			Bonds Payable		100,000

Cash	88,000	
Discount on Bonds	12,000	
Bonds Payable		100,000

Amortizing Premiums and Discounts Using the Straight-Line Method

When a premium or discount results from a bond issue, it must be allocated over the period the bond is outstanding as an adjustment to interest expense, a process called **amortization.** If a $100,000 bond issue is sold for $106,000, only $100,000 must be paid at maturity, resulting in a decrease of $6,000 in the cost of borrowing (interest expense). If the same bonds were sold for $88,000, however, $100,000 would have to be paid at maturity, resulting in an additional $12,000 to the cost of borrowing.

Two methods are used to determine the amount of amortization to record in any given interest period: the **straight-line method** and the **effective interest method.** The straight-line method of amortization results in a constant amount of interest expense recorded over the life of the bond issue, while the effective interest method results in a constant interest rate reflected in the amount of interest expense recorded over the life of the bond issue. The straight-line method will be demonstrated first, and the effective interest method will be investigated in the next section. The effective interest method is required by GAAP if it results in interest expense that is materially different from that under the straight-line method. The straight-line method more clearly shows students the effect of amortization on interest expense.

The effect of the straight-line amortization process on the carrying value of the bond liability (par value plus premium or minus discount) is diagrammed in Exhibit 13-3.

Interest on a Bond

Interest begins to accumulate from the previous interest payment date of the bond and is usually paid semiannually, regardless of when the bond is actually sold. As

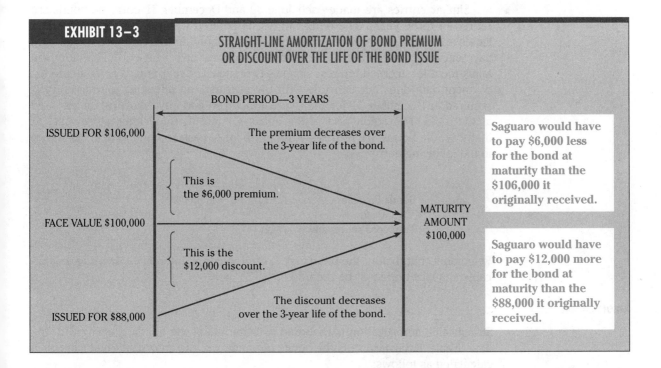

EXHIBIT 13-3

STRAIGHT-LINE AMORTIZATION OF BOND PREMIUM OR DISCOUNT OVER THE LIFE OF THE BOND ISSUE

BOND PERIOD—3 YEARS

ISSUED FOR $106,000

The premium decreases over the 3-year life of the bond.

This is the $6,000 premium.

FACE VALUE $100,000

MATURITY AMOUNT $100,000

This is the $12,000 discount.

The discount decreases over the 3-year life of the bond.

ISSUED FOR $88,000

Saguaro would have to pay $6,000 less for the bond at maturity than the $106,000 it originally received.

Saguaro would have to pay $12,000 more for the bond at maturity than the $88,000 it originally received.

noted earlier, interest paid to bondholders is *always* calculated on the face value of the bond, regardless of whether the bonds are issued at par, at a premium, or at a discount. For example, SCI's $100,000 bond issue with an interest rate of 12% pays the following total annual interest:

$$\$100,000 \times 12\% = \$12,000 \text{ annual interest}$$

Individual bondholders would receive $6,000 each semiannually.

Q9: Adjustments to interest expense

Under the straight-line method, it is recommended that bond premiums and discounts be amortized each time bond interest expense is recorded. The recording of amortization emphasizes that it is an adjustment of bond interest expense. The interest payments for the first year of SCI's $100,000 bond issue, together with the appropriate amortization entry, are recorded as follows:

Payment of Interest

June 30	Bond Interest Expense	6,000	
	Cash		6,000
Dec. 31	Bond Interest Expense	6,000	
	Cash		6,000
	To record semiannual bond interest.		

Amortization of Premium			**Amortization of Discount**		
Bond Premium	1,000		Bond Interest Expense	2,000	
Bond Interest Expense		1,000	Bond Discount		2,000
To record amortization of bond premium.			To record amortization of bond discount.		
Bond Premium	1,000		Bond Interest Expense	2,000	
Bond Interest Expense		1,000	Bond Discount		2,000
To record amortization of bond premium.			To record amortization of bond discount.		

The determination of these amounts is shown on p. 579.

Similar entries are made each June 30 and December 31 until the bonds are retired in three years. The bond interest is entered in a separate Bond Interest Expense account, because it is usually a large amount. In this example, the interest payment date, December 31, is also the corporation's year-end. Therefore, no adjustment for accrued interest expense is required at year-end. When the interest payment date does not coincide with the year-end, an adjusting journal entry is required at December 31 for the interest incurred and any amortization required at that date. The credit part of the entry is made to Bond Interest Payable. At maturity, the bonds are retired by the payment of cash to bondholders, as shown in the following entry:

19X4			
Jan. 1	Bonds Payable	100,000	
	Cash		100,000
	To record retirement of bonds.		

Remember that, before the bonds are retired, the final interest payment and applicable amortization must be recorded.

Amortization

Straight-line amortization is recorded over the life of the bonds, starting with the date of sale. If Saguaro sells the bonds on January 1, the amortization at June 30 is calculated as follows:

Amortization of Premium		Amortization of Discount	
Premium is	$6,000	Discount is	$12,000
Months left are	36	Months left are	36
Months amortized	6	Months amortized	6

Calculation
($6,000 ÷ 36) × 6 = $1,000

Calculation
($12,000 ÷ 36) × 6 = $ 2,000

Premium Amortization Adjusting Entry		*Discount Amortization Adjusting Entry*	
Bond Premium	1,000	Bond Interest Expense	2,000
Bond Interest Expense	1,000	Bond Discount	2,000

The amortization of a premium reduces bond interest expense.

The amortization of a discount increases bond interest expense.

Note that the amortization of the premium requires a debit to Bond Premium in order to decrease the $6,000 premium balance. The credit is made to Bond Interest Expense and thereby reduces the $6,000 interest expense recorded. The credit required to amortize Bond Discount results in a debit to Bond Interest Expense. The amortization represents, therefore, an additional interest expense over the $6,000 interest expense recorded.

These SCI ledger accounts illustrate the reduction in interest expense.

These SCI ledger accounts illustrate the increase in interest expense.

Premium on Bonds		Bond Interest Expense	
	6,000	6,000	
1,000			1,000
1,000		6,000	
2,000	6,000		1,000
	4,000	12,000	2,000
		10,000	

Discount on Bonds		Bond Interest Expense	
12,000		6,000	
	2,000	2,000	
	2,000	6,000	
12,000	4,000	2,000	
8,000		16,000	

The premium is reduced each interest period by amortization.

Amortization of a bond premium results in a decrease of bond interest expense.

The discount is reduced each interest period by amortization.

Amortization of a bond discount results in an increase of bond interest expense.

HOW IS THE AMORTIZATION OF THE PREMIUM RECORDED IN THE BOOKS?

It is sound accounting practice to allocate part of the premium to each semiannual interest payment period. The effect of amortizing the premium at each interest payment date during the three years is shown in Exhibit 13-4, which should be studied carefully.

The total interest expense over the life of the bonds consists of $36,000 of interest less the $6,000 amortization of the premium. The $6,000 premium received when the bond was sold represents a reduction of the corporation's bond interest expense during each year of the bond's life. The interest actually paid to bondholders is still $36,000. The interest expense to SCI is $30,000. This decrease of $6,000 results from the favorable bond interest rate in relation to the prevailing market interest rate. In other words, receiving $106,000 on January 1, 19X1, is to the corporation's benefit as it only has to repay $100,000 on January 1, 19X4. This benefit is reflected in a reduced net annual interest expense during the life of the bonds.

EXHIBIT 13–4

EFFECT OF STRAIGHT-LINE AMORTIZATION OF BOND PREMIUM AT EACH INTEREST PAYMENT DATE

19X1		Bonds Payable	Premium Amortization	Cash Interest Paid	Actual Annual Interest Expense
Jan. 1	Sale of Bonds	+$100,000	+$6,000	-0-	-0-
June 30	Premium Amortization		– 1,000	+$ 6,000	$10,000
Dec. 31	Premium Amortization		– 1,000	+ 6,000	
	Balance	+$100,000	+$4,000	$12,000	$10,000
19X2					
June 30	Premium Amortization		– 1,000	+$16,000	$10,000
Dec. 31	Premium Amortization		– 1,000	+ 6,000	
	Balance	+$100,000	+$2,000	$12,000	$10,000
19X3					
June 30	Premium Amortization		–$1,000	+$ 6,000	$10,000
Dec. 31	Premium Amortization		–$1,000	+ 6,000	
	Balance	+$100,000	-0-	$12,000	$10,000
19X4					
Jan. 1	Bonds Repaid	– 100,000			
		-0-			

Part of the premium has been written off each period.

The interest expense of the corporation has been reduced by the premium amortization.

Therefore, accountants record the decrease in bond interest expense as an amortization of the premium. The annual interest expense of $10,000 is lower than the 12% bond interest paid of $12,000. Accordingly, whenever a corporation sells a bond for more than its face value, the corporation's total cost of borrowing is decreased.

HOW IS THE BOND DISCOUNT AMORTIZED IN THE BOOKS?

The discount is amortized through the straight-line method by equal periodic debits to Bond Interest Expense over the three-year life of the bonds. This amortization is recorded every time Bond Interest Expense is entered in the books. The effect of amortizing the discount at each interest payment date during the three years is shown in Exhibit 13-5. Study it closely.

The total interest expense over the life of SCI's bonds sold at a discount consists of $36,000 interest plus the $12,000 amortization of the discount. The $12,000 discount on the bond issue represents an increase of the corporation's bond interest expense during each year of the bond's life. The interest actually paid to bondholders is still $36,000. However, the interest expense to the corporation is actually $48,000. The additional $12,000 compensates investors for the unfavorable bond interest rate in relation to the prevailing market interest rate. In other words, receiving only $88,000 on January 1, 19X1, is an additional cost to the corporation since

EXHIBIT 13–5

EFFECT OF STRAIGHT-LINE AMORTIZATION OF BOND DISCOUNT AT EACH INTEREST PAYMENT DATE

19X1		Bonds Payable	Discount Amortization	Cash Interest Paid	Actual Annual Interest Expense
Jan. 1	Sale of Bonds	+$100,000	–$12,000	-0-	-0-
June 30	Discount Amortization		+ 2,000	+$ 6,000	$16,000
Dec. 31	Discount Amortization		+ 2,000	+ 6,000	
	Balance	+$100,000	–$ 8,000	$12,000	$16,000
19X2					
June 30	Discount Amortization		+ 2,000	+$16,000	$16,000
Dec. 31	Discount Amortization		+ 2,000	+ 6,000	
	Balance	+$100,000	–$ 4,000	$12,000	$16,000
19X3					
June 30	Discount Amortization		+ 2,000	+$16,000	$16,000
Dec. 31	Discount Amortization		+ 2,000	+ 6,000	
	Balance	+$100,000	-0-	$12,000	$16,000
19X4					
Jan. 1	Bonds Repaid	– 100,000			
		-0-			

Part of the discount has been written off each period.

The interest expense of the corporation has been increased by the discount amortization.

it must repay $100,000 on January 1, 19X4. This additional cost is reflected in the increased net annual interest expense during the life of the bonds.

Therefore, in the case of bonds issued at a discount, the actual annual interest expense of $16,000 is higher than the 12% bond interest expense of $12,000. Accordingly, whenever a corporation sells a bond for less than its face value, the corporation's total cost of borrowing is increased because of discount amortization.

Operation of a Bond Sinking Fund

The fund set up to retire bonds is called a *sinking fund* because the assets in the fund are tied up or "sunk." The assets in the sinking fund cannot be used for any purpose other than the redemption of the bonds at maturity, or before maturity, if permitted in the bond indenture.

The operation of a bond sinking fund has three phases:

1. The contributions to the fund
2. The earnings of the assets in the fund
3. The use of assets in the funds to retire bonds payable

Each of these phases is discussed next, using the data of Saguaro Computers, Inc. Assume that its bonds contain a sinking fund feature. Bonds amounting to $100,000 are issued at par on the authorization date, January 1, 19X1, and are due in three years. The bond indenture requires an annual contribution at the end of each of the three years to provide for the retirement of the bonds at maturity. Assets in the sinking fund are guaranteed by the trustee to earn 10% annually.

The required annual contributions to the sinking fund, together with anticipated compound interest on the amount deposited, are assumed to equal the $100,000 needed to retire the bonds at the end of three years. If equal amounts, each called an **annuity,** are to be deposited with the trustee and the fund is to earn 10% compounded annually, the annual deposit required can be calculated using an annuity table.

The following schedule accumulates the annuities and the 10% annual revenue earned by the assets in the sinking fund.

	Annual Contributions	10% Annual Revenue	Annual Total	Fund Balance
Dec. 31				
19X1	$30,211	-0-	$30,211	$ 30,211
19X2	30,211	$3,021 (10% × $30,211)	33,232	63,443
19X3	30,211	$6,346* (10% × $63,443)	36,557	100,000

*Increased to adjust the fund balance to $100,000.

Note: The determination of the annual contribution of $30, 211 will be demonstrated in the appendix to this chapter.

The annual contributions to the fund and earnings of the assets in the fund are recorded as follows, using 19X2 amounts from this schedule.

Recording Annual Contribution			**Recording Fund Earnings**		
Bond Sinking Fund	30,211		Bond Sinking Fund	3,021	
Cash		30,211	Sinking Fund Revenue		3,021

The annual contribution is invested by the trustee.   The earnings remain in the fund but are recorded in the corporation's books.

The bond sinking fund is reported on the balance sheet as a long-term investment. The bond sinking fund revenue is reported on the income statement as "Other Income."

When Saguaro management receives notice from its trustee that the bonds have been retired on January 1, 19X4, the following entry is made to remove the bond liability from SCI's books.

	19X4		
	Jan. 1	Bonds Payable	100,000	
		Bond Sinking Fund		100,000
		To record the retirement of bonds by the trustee.		

This entry eliminates both the Bonds Payable and Bond Sinking Fund accounts.

In this example, the trustee guaranteed a 10% return on investments in the sinking fund and an assumption has been made that only 10% was earned by the fund. In practice, it is possible that a balance of cash may still remain in the fund.

The trustee returns such a balance to the corporation, which records the receipt of cash as follows:

```
19X4
Jan. 1    Cash                                    XXX
                Bond Sinking Fund                           XXX
          To record receipt of balance in sinking
          fund.
```

Bond Redemption

The *redemption*, or retirement, of bonds at their maturity date requires a cash payment to bondholders; the cash payment is the face value of the bonds. The accounting entry for the retirement of Saguaro Computers, Inc.'s bonds on January 2, 19X4, follows.

```
19X4
Jan. 1    Bonds Payable                        100,000
                Cash                                      100,000
```

A bond issue also can be retired in whole, or in part, before its maturity date. Here are several different possibilities:

1. The bonds can be repurchased on the open market if the sale is financially advantageous to the issuer.

2. A *call provision* is sometimes included in a bond indenture permitting early redemption at a specified price, usually higher than face value. The issuer may decide to exercise this call provision if it is financially advantageous.

3. The bondholder may be able to exercise a conversion feature if one was provided for in the bond indenture. In the next example, it is assumed that SCI's $100,000 bond issue can be converted into 2,000 shares of $10 par value common stock at the option of the bondholder.

Q10: Retiring unmatured bonds

Whenever bonds are retired before the maturity date, the amount payable to bondholders is the face amount of the bonds or the amount required by a call provision. Any unamortized premium or discount must also be removed from the accounts. The accounting required for SCI's January 1, 19X1, issue of $100,000 face value 12% bonds has been illustrated. Suppose that $50,000 face value bonds are redeemed at 102 on December 31, 19X1, when the account balances are as follows:

19X1	Bonds Payable		Premium on Bonds	
Jan. 1		100,000		6,000
June 30			1,000	
Dec. 31			1,000	
			2,000	
				Bal. 4,000

Since $50,000 of the bonds are redeemed, only half of the $4,000 premium balance ($2,000) is applicable to the redeemed bonds.

The retirement by repurchase or by conversion is shown next. Note that the $50,000 face value bonds are converted into 1,000 shares of $10 par value common stock, and that the carrying value of the bonds (face value plus the unamortized premium in this case) becomes the carrying value of the common stock issued (par value plus paid-in capital in excess of par value).

Retirement by Repurchase		
Bonds Payable	50,000	
Premium on Bonds	2,000	
Gain on Bond Retirement		1,000
Cash (102 × $50,000)		51,000

In this case, the retirement results in a gain; under different circumstances, a loss may result.

Retirement by Conversion		
Bonds Payable	50,000	
Premium on Bonds	2,000	
Common Stock		10,000
Paid-in Capital in Excess		
of Par Value		42,000

In this case, Paid-in Capital in Excess of Par Value is credited for the difference between the carrying value of the bond and the par value of the stock ($52,000–$10,000).

The SCI retirement occurred on an interest payment date, December 31, 19X1; interest and premium amortization was already recorded. If the retirement had occurred between interest payment dates, then accrued interest also would be paid to the bondholders and amortization would be recorded in the issuer's books.

In addition to retirement by repurchase or conversion of bonds, it is also possible for an existing bond issue to be replaced by a new issue, usually at a lower interest rate; this is referred to as **refunding a bond issue.** Outstanding bonds also can be repurchased with assets accumulated in a bond sinking fund, as previously shown.

Sale of Bonds between Interest Dates

Q11: Between interest dates

Not all bonds are issued on the date when interest begins to accumulate on the bond. In bond transactions, the investor pays the issue price of the bonds plus an amount for accrued interest. In turn, the first interest payment is for one full interest period—six months—thereby returning to the purchaser the accrued interest paid plus the interest earned from the date of purchase to the next interest payment date. For example, consider the sale of an additional $50,000 of SCI bonds on April 1, 19X1. Interest began to accumulate on January 1 and, regardless of the date on which the bond was issued, a six-month interest payment is made to the bondholder on June 30. This payment is to the bondholder even though the bond has been held for only three months, from April 1 to June 30. The $50,000 of bonds is said to be sold at *par plus accrued interest.* The bonds could also have been sold at a premium or a discount and accrued interest. See Exhibit 13-6.

ACCRUED INTEREST

As noted, interest begins to accumulate from the previous interest payment date of the bond and is usually paid semiannually, regardless of when the bond is actually sold. If the bond is sold between interest dates, the purchaser pays the accrued interest at the date of purchase.

In this case, $1,500 of interest has accrued on the bond from January 1 to April 1. When the bond is sold between interest dates specified in the bond indenture, it is accepted practice for the purchaser to pay accrued interest at the date of purchase, that is, April 1. This amount, $1,500, is returned to the investor by the corporation at the next interest date, which in this case is June 30.

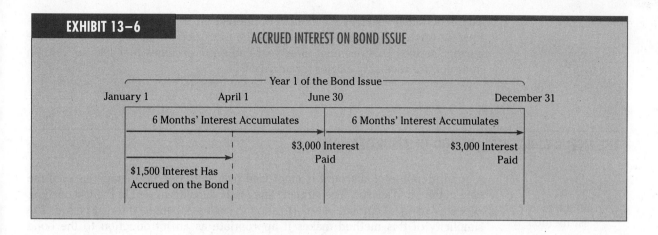

EXHIBIT 13-6

ACCRUED INTEREST ON BOND ISSUE

Assuming reversing entries are not used, Saguaro records the receipt of the accrued interest in a liability account, because this amount is due to the bondholders:

Recording the Bond Issue			Payment of Interest		
Cash	51,500		Bond Interest Expense	1,500	
Bond Interest Payable		1,500	Bond Interest Payable	1,500	
Bond Payable		50,000	Cash		3,000

The investor pays the issue price of the bonds plus accrued interest.

The next interest payment returns the accrued interest to the bondholder (previously recorded as a liability), plus the interest earned since he or she purchased the bond.

SCI makes the regular semiannual interest payment on June 30. For this example, the interest calculation applies only to the $50,000 bonds issued on April 1 and excludes interest on the bonds sold January 1.

AMORTIZING PREMIUMS AND DISCOUNTS

If the sale made on April 1 had been made at a premium (106) or at a discount (88), the amortization at June 30 would be as follows:

Amortization of Premium		Amortization of Discount	
Premium is $50,000 × 6% = $3,000		Discount is $50,000 × 12% = $6,000	
Months left are	33	Months left are	33
Months amortized	3	Months amortized	3
Calculation		*Calculation*	
($3,000 ÷ 33) × 3 = $272.73		($6,000 ÷ 33) × 3 = $545.45	

It is necessary to calculate the number of months remaining in the life of the bonds at the date bonds are sold.

If the bond has interest payment dates that do not coincide with the year-end of the issuing corporation, an adjusting journal entry is required at year-end to record interest incurred at that date:

Adjusting Entry			Payment of Interest after Year-End		
Bond Interest Expense	X		Bond Interest Expense	X	
Bond Interest Payable		X	Bond Interest Payable	X	
			Cash		XX

The bondholder receives six months of interest on the payment date. Part of the interest was recorded as an expense in the prior period; part is recorded in the current period. This payment after year-end entry assumes that the corporation does not use reversing entries for accruals.

THE EFFECTIVE INTEREST METHOD OF AMORTIZATION

Q12: Effective interest method

A bond premium or discount is amortized over the bond life remaining from the date of the bond's issue. The straight-line method, as discussed in the last section, allocates an equal amount of amortization to each semiannual interest period. The simplicity of this method makes it appropriate as an introduction to the bond accounting process. The major drawback to the straight-line method is that a different percentage of interest or rate is recorded in the accounts for each interest period, given the carrying value of the debt. For instance, consider the example of the SCI bonds sold at a premium for $106,000. During the first six months, $6,000 of interest was paid and $1,000 of the premium was amortized, reducing bond interest expense to $5,000. The bond liability at the beginning of the six-month period was $106,000. Therefore, the interest *rate* reflected in the financial statements is determined as follows:

$$\frac{\text{Interest Expense}}{\text{Carrying Value of the Liability}} = \text{Interest Rate for Six Months}$$

$$\frac{\$5,000}{\$106,000} = 4.72\%$$

The next six months the rate would be

$$\frac{\$5,000}{\$105,000} = 4.76\%$$

The last six months the rate would be

$$\frac{\$5,000}{\$101,000} = 4.95\%$$

The bonds paid interest at 6% semiannually, but SCI reported interest rates climbing from 4.72% to 4.95%. Since the bonds sold at a premium, the market rate of interest must have been below the 6%, but the straight-line method does not reflect the market rate or report interest expense that reflects the market rate.

When Saguaro's bonds were sold for $88,000, the amount of interest paid the first six months was the same $6,000, but interest expense was increased by $2,000, the amount of amortization of the discount. Therefore, the interest rate for the first 6 months would be

$$\frac{\$8,000}{\$88,000} = 9.09\%$$

The next six months the rate would be

$$\frac{\$8,000}{\$90,000} = 8.89\%$$

The last six months the rate would be

$$\frac{\$8,000}{\$98,000} = 8.16\%$$

The bonds paid interest at 6% semiannually, but Saguaro reported interest rates climbing from 8.19% to 9.09%. Since the bonds sold at a discount, the market rate of interest must have been above the 6%, but the straight-line method does not determine the market rate or report interest expense that reflects the market rate.

Calculating Interest Payments and Premium Amortization

The *effective interest method* applies the market rate of interest to the carrying value of the bond to determine interest expense. The amount of amortization is therefore the difference between that interest expense and the amount of cash paid for interest. It follows that the amount of interest expense and the amount of amortization will differ each period. If the bond is sold at a premium, the amount of interest expense decreases as the carrying value of the bond decreases, while if the bond is sold at a discount, the amount of interest expense increases as the carrying value of the bond increases. The determination of these amounts is facilitated by an amortization table.

A number of assumptions are reflected in the premium amortization table in Exhibit 13-7. SCI has issued 12% bonds in the amount of $100,000 that were sold for $110,485. Interest is payable semiannually and the bonds mature in three years.

EXHIBIT 13-7

Issue of $100,000, 12% Bonds Payable for $110,485
Amortization Table
Using Market Interest Rate of 8%

Year	Period	A Bond Carrying Value	B ($\frac{1}{2}$ × 8% × A) Using 8% Market Rate to Calculate 6-Month Interest Expense	C 6% Actual Cash Interest Paid	D (C − B) 6-Month Premium Amortization	E (A − D) Dec. 31 Bond Carrying Value
19X1	1	$110,485	$4,419 (4% × $110,485)	$6,000	$1,581	$108,904
	2	108,904	4,356 (4% × 108,904)	6,000	1,644	107,260
19X2	3	107,260	4,290 (4% × 107,260)	6,000	1,710	105,550
	4	105,550	4,222 (4% × 105,550)	6,000	1,778	103,772
19X3	5	103,772	4,151 (4% × 103,772)	6,000	1,849	101,923
	6	101,923	4,077 (4% × 101,923)	6,000	1,923	100,000

This amount is the interest expense for each 6-month period.

Note the use of a constant interest rate under this method.

This amount is the amortization for each 6-month period.

The bonds were sold the day they were authorized to yield an 8% return (the market rate of interest) to the investor. The present value of the principal and interest payments is determined to be $110,485 (see the chapter appendix), an amount that will yield the investor an 8% return on the investment even though the bonds pay interest at the rate of 12%. Note that 4% (1/2 × 8%) is applied to the carrying value of the bonds at the beginning of the period. The carrying value of the bonds decrease each six-month period by the amount of the amortization determined for the previous six-month period. As noted, the objective of amortization is to reduce the carrying value of the liability to its face or par value by the maturity date.

The calculation in column D provides the premium amortization amount for each period. In period 1, for example, the difference between the $4,419 market rate interest expense (column B) and the $6,000 actual bond contract interest paid (column C) determines the premium amortization at $1,581 (column C − column B).

Columns E and A show the decreasing carrying value of the bonds during their three-year life; these are the amounts actually used, it is claimed, in financing the entity. Accordingly, the effective interest method calculates interest expense at a constant 4% of the bond financing in effect each period. In this way, interest expense (column B) decreases each period as less bond financing is used. From a theoretical point of view, it is preferable to show a financing interest expense that decreases (column B), as the amount of financing decreases (column A).

Note that if the interest rate for each period were calculated using the interest expense amounts from Exhibit 13-7, the rate would be the same for each period, unlike the varying amounts resulting from the application of the straight-line method in the exhibit. The calculations are shown next for the first two and the last interest payment periods.

$$\frac{\$4,419}{\$110,485} = 4\%$$

The next six months the rate would be

$$\frac{\$4,356}{\$108,904} = 4\%$$

The last six months the rate would be

$$\frac{\$4,077}{\$101,923} = 4\%$$

RECORDING INTEREST PAYMENTS AND PREMIUM AMORTIZATION

Journal entries to record interest payments and amortization of a premium under the effective interest method are made every June 30 and December 31 in the same manner as for straight-line amortization. The actual interest paid to bondholders amounts to $6,000 each semiannual period; the amount of premium amortization for each period is taken from column D of the amortization table in Exhibit 13-7. These are the entries for period 1.

Payment of Interest			Amortization of Premium		
June 30	Bond Interest Expense	6,000		Bond Premium	1,581	
	Cash		6,000	Bond Interest Expense		1,581
	To record semiannual bond interest.			To record amortization of bond premium.		

The entries for each remaining period are similar; only the amounts used for premium amortization differ, as shown in column D of the amortization table. After the posting of the June 30 entries, the following balances result:

Balance Sheet Accounts			Income Statement Account
Bonds Payable	Premium on Bonds		Bond Interest Expense
100,000		10,485	6,000
	1,581		1,581
		8,904	4,419

The bond carrying value is $108,904 ($100,000 + $8,904) as of June 30; this is the amount that appears in column E of the amortization table.

This amount is the expense determined in column B of the amortization table.

Calculating Interest Expense and Discount Amortization

The following assumptions are reflected in the discount amortization table in Exhibit 13-8. SCI has issued 12% bonds in the amount of $100,000 that were sold for $90,754. Interest is payable semiannually and the bonds mature in three years. The bonds were sold the day that they were authorized to yield a 16% return (the market rate of interest) to the investor. The present value of the principal and interest payments is determined to be $90,754 (see the chapter appendix), an amount that will yield the investor a 16% return on the investment even though the bonds pay interest at

EXHIBIT 13-8

Issue of $100,000, 12% Bonds Payable for $90,754
Amortization Table
Using Market Interest Rate of 16%

Year	Period	A Bond Carrying Value	B ($\frac{1}{2}$ × 16% × A) Using 8% Market Rate to Calculate 6-Month Interest Expense	C 6% Actual Cash Interest Paid	D (B − C) 6-Month Discount Amortization	E (A − D) Dec. 31 Bond Carrying Value
19X1	1	$90,754	$7,260 (8% × $90,754)	$6,000	$1,260	$ 92,014
	2	92,014	7,361 (8% × 92,014)	6,000	1,361	93,375
19X2	3	93,375	7,470 (8% × 93,375)	6,000	1,470	94,845
	4	94,845	7,588 (8% × 94,845)	6,000	1,588	96,433
19X3	5	96,433	7,715 (8% × 96,433)	6,000	1,715	98,148
	6	98,148	7,852 (8% × 98,148)	6,000	1,852	100,000

This amount is the interest expense for each 6-month period.

Note the use of a constant interest rate under this method.

This amount is the amortization for each 6-month period.

the rate of 12%. Note that 8% ($1/2 \times 16\%$) is applied to the carrying value of the bonds at the beginning of the period. The carrying value of the bonds increase each six-month period by the amount of the amortization determined for the previous six-month period.

The calculation in column D provides the discount amortization amount. In period 1, for example, the difference between the $7,260 market rate interest expense (column B) and the $6,000 actual bond contract interest paid (column C) determines the discount amortization at $1,260 (column B − column C).

Columns E and A show the increasing carrying value of the bonds during their three-year life; these are the actual amounts used, it is claimed, in financing the entity. Accordingly, the effective interest method calculates interest expense at a constant 8% of each period's balance of bond financing. In this way, interest expense (column B) increases each period as financing increases. From a theoretical point of view, it is preferable to show a financing interest expense that increases (column B), as the amount of financing increases (column A).

Note that if the interest rate for each period were calculated using the interest expense amounts from Exhibit 13-8, the rate would be the same for each period, unlike the varying amounts resulting from the application of the straight-line method in the exhibit. The calculations are shown next for the first two and the last interest payment periods.

$$\frac{\$7,260}{\$90,754} = 8\%$$

The next six months the rate would be

$$\frac{\$7,361}{\$92,014} = 8\%$$

The last six months the rate would be

$$\frac{\$7,852}{\$98,148} = 8\%$$

RECORDING INTEREST PAYMENTS AND DISCOUNT AMORTIZATION

Journal entries to record interest payments and amortizations are made each June 30 and December 31 in the same manner as for the straight-line method (shown earlier). The actual interest paid to bondholders amounts to $6,000 each semi-annual period; the amount of discount amortization is taken directly from column D of the amortization table. These are the entries for period 1.

	Payment of Interest				Amortization of Discount		
June 30	Bond Interest Expense	6,000			Bond Interest Expense	1,260	
	Cash		6,000		Bond Discount		1,260
	To record semiannual bond interest.				To record amortization of bond discount.		

The entries for each remaining period are similar; only the amounts used for discount amortization differ, as shown in column D of the amortization table. After the posting of the June 30 entries, the following balances result:

Balance Sheet Accounts		Income Statement Account
Bonds Payable	Discount on Bonds	Bond Interest Expense

Bonds Payable	Discount on Bonds		Bond Interest Expense
100,000	9,246		6,000
		1,260	1,260
	7,986		7,260

The bond carrying value is $92,014 ($100,000 − $7,986) as of June 30; this is the amount in column *E* of the amortization table.

This amount is the expense determined in column *B* of the amortization table.

Comparison of the Effective Interest Method with the Straight-Line Method

A further comparison of the two amortization methods can be made using the data applicable to the issue of SCI's bonds at a discount; $100,000 face value bonds are issued for $90,754, resulting in a discount of $9,246 ($100,000 − $90,754). Under the straight-line method, this $9,246 discount is amortized in equal amounts over the 3-year life of the bonds. The discount is calculated for 6-month periods, because amortization is recorded at the time semiannual interest payments are made. The straight-line method amortization is calculated as follows:

Discount is	$9,246
Months left are	36
Months amortized	6

Calculation
($9,246 ÷ 36) × 6 = $1,541

As explained earlier, amortization of a discount increases interest expense. Therefore, the $1,541 is added to the $6,000 interest payment to calculate the $7,541 interest expense applicable to each 6-month period.

Under the effective interest method, the $9,246 discount amortization is calculated in column *D* of the amortization table in Exhibit 13-8. The relevant details are shown in Exhibit 13-9 to compare with the appropriate calculations under the straight-line method. For convenience, all percentage calculations are rounded.

As can be seen, a constant financing expense of 8% each 6-month period (16% per annum) occurs under the effective interest method. The financing rate varies from period to period under the straight-line method. Theoretically, accounting purists insist that a correct financing charge is calculated only under the effective interest method. However, others argue that, from a practical point of view, the difference in the amounts calculated is not material and the additional accuracy obtained using the market interest is not worth the effort involved. Note that the total interest expense of $45,246 for the 3-year period is the same under both methods. The straight-line method is widely used because of its simplicity. As noted before, GAAP requires the use of the effective interest method when its application would result in interest expense that is materially different from that under straight-line. If the difference is not material, straight-line amortization of bond premiums or discounts is acceptable.

This comparison involved the issue of bonds at a discount. A similar comparison for bonds issued at a premium would indicate a similar difference in the

EXHIBIT 13–9

COMPARISON OF CALCULATIONS UNDER TWO METHODS

		Effective Interest Method			Straight-Line Method		
Year	Period	Carrying Value (A)	Interest Expense (B)	(B ÷ A) %	Carrying Value	Interest Expense	%
19X1	1	$90,754	$ 7,260	8	$90,754	$ 7,541	8.3
	2	92,014	7,361	8	92,295	7,541	8.2
19X2	3	93,375	7,470	8	93,836	7,541	8
	4	94,845	7,588	8	95,377	7,541	7.9
19X3	5	96,433	7,715	8	96,918	7,541	7.8
	6	98,148	7,852	8	98,459	7,541	7.7
			$45,246			$45,246	

Under this method the financing percentage is constant.

Under this method the financing percentage varies.

calculation of a periodic financing charge. Under the straight-line method, however, the financing charge percentage would increase in the case of a premium, rather than decrease as here.

Accrual of Bond Interest at Year-End

In these examples, interest is paid at June 30 and December 31; here, the year-end coincided with the December 31 payment. When these two dates do not coincide, it is necessary to accrue interest at year-end and to record an appropriate amount of amortization. These adjustments are made to comply with the matching concept, which specifies that all expenses be matched with revenues for that same year. The adjusting entry accruing interest requires a credit to Bond Interest Payable.

Assume that the fiscal year-end is September 30, but that interest on bonds is still paid June 30 and December 31. In this case, three months of interest has to be accrued (July, August, and September); amortization must also be recorded for three months. The amount of interest would be $3,000 ($100,000 × 12% × ¼); the amount of amortization, assuming the effective interest method is used, would be half of the appropriate semiannual periodic amortization recorded in column D of whichever amortization table applies.

APPENDIX: TIME VALUE OF MONEY ANALYSIS—PRESENT AND FUTURE VALUES

A comparison of *present value analysis* to *future value analysis* easily shows that interest is the cause of present values shrinking and future values growing. **Present value analysis** examines amounts to be received in the future and takes out the interest factor, what would be earned on the amount over a period of time, leaving only the "present values." **Future value analysis,** on the other hand, examines present values and adds to them the interest to be earned over a period of time to arrive at the future values.

Taking the two concepts together, if $1 is invested today at 10%, that $1 will grow to $1.10 at the end of one year and to $1.21 ($1.10 × 10% = $.11; $1.10 + .11 = $1.21) the next year. From a future value perspective on this simple example, it would be said that the future value of $1 invested at 10% would be $1.10 after the first year and $1.21 by the end of the second year. Present value analysis would show that the present value of $1.21 to be received in one year would be $1.10, and the present value of the same $1.21 to be received at the end of two years is $1.

Present value Tables I and II and future value Tables III and IV are provided at the end of this appendix, pp. 598–601.

Present Value Calculations

Q13: Use of present/
future analyses

Any amount to be received in the future can be discounted in a similar manner to determine its present value, that is, the amount that excludes the interest on money. Consider Saguaro's issue of 12%, $100,000-face value, 3-year bonds discussed in this chapter. In this example, interest is payable semiannually each June 30 and December 31 for three years. With this information, the present value of the future cash flows can be determined.

1. The $100,000 single amount is to be paid at the end of three years.
2. The $6,000 semiannual interest payments are to be paid to bondholders for 6 periods during the 3-year bond life ($100,000 × 12% = $12,000 interest per year; the amount paid every semiannual period is $6,000). The individual payments are referred to as annuities.

PRESENT VALUE OF A SINGLE FUTURE AMOUNT

The illustration given earlier stated that the present value of $1.10 to be received at the end of one year if the interest rate is 10% is $1. That is clear since $1 × 10% = $.10 and $1 + .10 = $1.10. It follows that if the $1.10 was left to accumulate one more year's interest, it would grow to $1.21, and the present value of the $1.21 to be received in two years was still the $1. Using the factors given in Table I for the present value of 1, these results also could be determined. Under the 10% column for one year is the factor .909. If the $1.10 is multiplied by the factor .909, the result is $1 ($1.10 × .909). The present value of $1.10 to be received in one year is $1.

Under the 10% column for two years is the factor .826. If the $1.21 in the example is multiplied by the factor .826, the result is $1 ($1.21 × .826). The present value of $1.21 to be received in two years is $1.

The present value of *any amount* to be received at some point in the future can be determined using the present value factors in **Table I.** For instance, the present value of $65,873 to be received in 13 years, assuming an annual interest rate of 12%, is $15,085 ($65,873 × .229).

The present value of SCI's principle payment due after 6 six-month periods can now be determined under different market-rate-of-interest assumptions for its $100,000 bond issue.

Calculation 1: The market interest rate is 12% (per annum)   Since semiannual interest payments are made, the six-month rate is half the annual rate. Therefore, the compounding rate is 6% (12% × ½) in this case; this 3-year bond has 6 periods.

According to Table I, the present value of $1 compounded at 6% for 6 periods, is 0.705. The present value of the bonds is therefore calculated as follows: $100,000 × 0.705 = $70,500 (rounded).

Calculation 2: The market interest rate is 8% (per annum)   Again since semiannual interest payments are made, the six-month rate is half the annual rate. Therefore, the compounding rate this time is 4% (8% × ½); this 3-year bond has 6 periods.

According to Table I, the present value of $1 compounded at 4% for 6 periods is 0.790. The present value of the bonds is therefore calculated as follows: $100,000 × 0.790 = $79,000 (rounded).

Calculation 3: The market interest rate is 16% (per annum)   For these semiannual interest payments, the six-month rate is 8% (16% × ½); this 3-year bond has 6 periods.

According to Table I, the present value of $1 compounded at 8% for 6 periods is 0.63. The present value of the bonds is therefore calculated as follows: $100,000 × 0.63 = $63,000.

PRESENT VALUE OF MULTIPLE FUTURE AMOUNTS

Table I gives the present value of $1 to be received at the end of one year as .909 and the factor of $1 to be received at the end of two years as .826. It follows that the present value of $1 to be received at the end of *each* of the next two years would be $1.74 ($.91 [$1 × .909] + $.83 [$1 × .826]). An easier calculation is to multiply $1 with the *sum* of the two factors 1.735 (.909 + .826). An even easier alternative is to utilize the factors in Table II, the present values of an annuity of $1 to be received at the end of any number of periods. Note the factor of 1.736 under the 10% column for two years. (Because these factors have been rounded, the figures might differ slightly.) The present value of any annuity can be determined using **Table II.** For instance, the present value of $4,782 to be received at the end of each year for 19 years is $45,926 ($4,782 × 9.604), assuming an interest rate of 8%.

The present value of the interest annuities on SCI's bonds can now be determined under the same interest rate assumptions used for the principal.

Calculation 1: The market interest rate is 12% (per annum)   According to Table II, the present value of an annuity of $1 compounded at 6% (12% × ½) for 6 periods is 4.917. The present value of an annuity of $6,000 is therefore calculated as follows: $6,000 × 4.917 = $29,502.

Calculation 2: The market interest rate is 8% (per annum)   Again using Table II, the present value of an annuity of $1 compounded at 4% (8% × ½) for 6 periods is 5.242. The present value of an annuity of $6,000 is therefore calculated as follows: $6,000 × 5.242 = $31,452.

Calculation 3: The market interest rate is 16% (per annum)   The present value of an annuity of $1 compounded at 8% (16% × ½) for 6 periods is 4.6230 according to Table II. The present value of an annuity of $6,000 is therefore calculated as follows: $6,000 × 4.623 = $27,738.

Now the theoretical selling price of the Saguaro Computers, Inc., bonds can be determined under each of the market rate of interest assumptions. Simply add the principal and interest present values together for each assumption.

CALCULATING THE PRESENT VALUE OF A BOND

Scenario 1: The bond contract interest rate (12%) is the same as the market interest rate (12%)
In this case, the bonds are sold at face value. An investor is willing to pay face value because the present value of the future cash flow is $100,000.

1. The $100,000 bond face value is due at the end of six periods. The present value of this cash flow is calculated as

$$\$100{,}000 \times 0.705 \ (\text{Table I}) \qquad \$70{,}500$$

2. The semiannual $6,000 interest is to be received for six periods in total. The present value of this cash flow is calculated as

$$\$6{,}000 \times 4.917 \ (\text{Table II}) \qquad \underline{29{,}502}$$
Total present value of these bonds is $\qquad \underline{\$100{,}002} \approx \$100{,}000$

When the bond contract interest rate is the same as the market interest rate, the present value of all cash flows is the same as the bond's face value; other things—such as risk or inflation—being equal, the bond will sell for this amount.

In practice, however, the market interest rate is not the same as the bond contract interest rate, or some other factor (risk or inflation) creates an impact. Scenarios 2 and 3 deal with this situation.

Scenario 2: The bond contract interest rate (12%) is greater than the market interest rate (8%)
Here the bonds are sold at a premium. An investor is willing to pay more than face value because the present value of the future cash flow amounts to $110,452.

1. The $100,000 bond face value is due at the end of six periods. The present value of this cash flow is calculated as

$$\$100{,}000 \times 0.790 \ (\text{Table I}) \qquad \$79{,}000$$

2. The semiannual $6,000 interest is to be received for six periods in total. The present value of this cash flow is calculated as

$$\$6{,}000 \times 5.242 \ (\text{Table II}) \qquad \underline{31{,}452}$$
Total present value of these bonds is $\qquad \underline{\$110{,}452}$

Therefore, when the bond contract interest rate is greater than the market interest rate, the present value of all cash flows is greater than the face value of the bonds, other things being equal. This excess amount, calculated as $10,452 in this example, is considered to be a premium.

Scenario 3: The bond contract interest rate (12%) is less than the market interest rate (16%)
In this case, the bonds are sold at a discount. An investor will pay less than face value because the present value of future cash flow amounts to only $90,738.

1. The $100,000 bond face value is due at the end of six periods. The present value of this cash flow is calculated as

$$\$100{,}000 \times 0.630 \ (\text{Table I}) \qquad \$63{,}000$$

2. The semiannual $6,000 interest is to be received for six periods in total. The present value of this cash flow is calculated as

$6,000 × 4.623 (Table II)   27,738
Total present value of these bonds is $90,738

Therefore, when the bond contract interest rate is less than the market interest rate, the present value of all cash flows is less than the face value of the bonds, and other things being equal, the bond will sell for $90,738.

Note that the present value of the bonds under the 8% assumption ($110,452) is very close to the example used earlier for the effective interest method ($110,485). The only difference is that Tables I and II round the numbers for ease in calculating the values. For example, in Scenario 2, the actual factor for the present value of an annuity for 6 periods at 8% is 5.242137, and the present value of $1 for the same period is .790315. If the actual factors are used rather than the rounded ones, the present value of the two cash flows would be $110,485. The same is true for the bonds issued at a discount ($90,738 versus $90,754).

Future Value Calculations

This appendix contains two other tables: Table III, the future value of $1 at a point in time, and Table IV, the future value of an annuity of $1. The factors in **Table III** can be explained by the following example, utilizing the information from the present-value section of this appendix. The three calculations there determined that the present value of the $100,000 bond principle to be received at the end of 6 six-month periods at 6% was approximately $70,500; at 4%, the present value was $79,000; and at 8%, the present value was $63,000. In each of these cases, the future value was known and the present value was needed. In a given situation, the present value might be known and the future value needed.

If the present value at 6% of the $100,000 future cash flow is $70,500, then a factor of 1.4184397 ($100,000 ÷ $70,500) could be applied to the $70,500 to arrive at the future value of $100,000 as follows:

$70,500 × 1.4184397 = $100,000

If the present value at 4% of the $100,000 future cash flow is $79,000, then a factor of 1.2658227 ($100,000 ÷ $79,000) could be applied to the $79,000 to arrive at the $100,000 as follows:

$79,000 × 1.2658227 = $100,000

If the present value at 8% of the $100,000 future cash flow is $63,000, then a factor of 1.5873015 ($100,000 ÷ $63,000) could be applied to the $63,000 to arrive at the $100,000 as follows:

$63,000 × 1.5873015 = $100,000

Note that the factor from Table III for 6 periods and 6% is 1.419; for 4%, 1.265; and for 8%, 1.587. Table III factors are all rounded versions of the factors calculated from the present value information. Table III is a reciprocal of Table I.

If the present value of a number is known, for instance the current balance in a savings account, the future balance can be determined using Table III for any point in time, assuming a constant interest rate and no withdrawals occurred. If you have $5,000 in a savings account today, and you are 20 years old, how much will you have when you are 70 years old if you withdraw nothing and the account earns a constant rate of 10%? You would have more than one-half million dollars, $587,000 ($5,000 × 117.4).

Table IV shows you how a consistent savings plan will grow during a period of constant deposits and constant interest rates. Consider the bondholder of SCI's 12%, 3-year, $100,000 bonds that pay interest semiannually. If the investor (assuming one person purchased all the bonds) invests the $6,000 interest annuity into a savings account that pays 10%, how much will accumulate by the end of the three years?

Date	Deposit	Interest	Balance
June 30, 19X1	$6,000	—	$ 6,000
Dec. 31, 19X1	6,000	$ 300	12,300
June 30, 19X2	6,000	615	18,915
Dec. 31, 19X2	6,000	946	25,861
June 30, 19X3	6,000	1,293	33,154
Dec. 31, 19X3	6,000	1,658	40,812

This schedule indicates that the investor would have $40,812 at the end of the three-year period. That amount could have been determined directly from Table IV by multiplying the $6,000 annuity by the factor of 6.802 found under 5% for 6 periods ($6,000 × 6.802).

Reversing the situation, what amount would the investor have to put into a savings account at the end of each six-month period in order to have a $40,812 balance at the end of the three years? To calculate the answer, divide the needed amount by the same factor found in Table IV under the 5% column for 6 periods.

$$\frac{\$40,812}{6.802} = \$6,000$$

Remember the discussion about the bond sinking fund required by the bond indenture in an earlier section? The required payment was $30,211. How was this amount determined? Using Table IV, for 3 periods and 10%, the factor is 3.31. It can be shown that a payment of $30,211 for 3 years will accumulate $100,000 rounded (3.31 × $30,211). In reverse, the question would be as follows: If $100,000 were needed at the end of 3 years, and interest would remain constant at 10%, how much would have to be invested each year to accumulate the $100,000? Mathematically, all that is necessary is to divide the factor of 3.31 into the $100,000 to arrive at the required payment to the sinking fund, as is shown:

$$\frac{\$100,000}{3.31} = \$30,211$$

Both present and future value analyses are used extensively in accounting, finance, and other areas of business. Students will be exposed to their application in numerous other courses required to obtain a related degree. This appendix is meant to be a brief introduction to the topic as it relates to bond transactions. Present value analysis will be examined again in the chapters covering the investor's side of bond transactions.

PRESENT VALUE TABLES

TABLE I	PRESENT VALUE OF $1 RECEIVED IN THE FUTURE								

Periods Hence	Rate per Compounding Period									
	2%	3%	4%	5%	6%	8%	10%	12%	15%	20%
1	0.980	0.971	0.962	0.952	0.943	0.926	0.909	0.893	0.870	0.833
2	0.961	0.943	0.925	0.907	0.890	0.857	0.826	0.797	0.756	0.694
3	0.942	0.915	0.889	0.864	0.840	0.794	0.751	0.712	0.658	0.579
4	0.924	0.889	0.855	0.823	0.792	0.735	0.683	0.636	0.572	0.482
5	0.906	0.863	0.822	0.784	0.747	0.681	0.621	0.567	0.497	0.402
6	0.888	0.838	0.790	0.746	0.705	0.630	0.564	0.507	0.432	0.335
7	0.871	0.813	0.760	0.711	0.665	0.583	0.513	0.452	0.376	0.279
8	0.854	0.789	0.731	0.677	0.627	0.540	0.467	0.404	0.327	0.233
9	0.837	0.766	0.703	0.645	0.592	0.500	0.424	0.361	0.284	0.194
10	0.821	0.744	0.676	0.614	0.558	0.463	0.386	0.322	0.247	0.162
11	0.804	0.722	0.650	0.585	0.527	0.429	0.350	0.287	0.215	0.135
12	0.789	0.701	0.625	0.557	0.497	0.397	0.319	0.257	0.187	0.112
13	0.773	0.681	0.601	0.530	0.469	0.368	0.290	0.229	0.163	0.093
14	0.758	0.661	0.577	0.505	0.442	0.340	0.263	0.205	0.141	0.078
15	0.743	0.642	0.555	0.481	0.417	0.315	0.239	0.183	0.123	0.065
16	0.728	0.623	0.534	0.458	0.394	0.292	0.218	0.163	0.107	0.054
17	0.714	0.605	0.513	0.436	0.371	0.270	0.198	0.146	0.093	0.045
18	0.700	0.587	0.494	0.416	0.350	0.250	0.180	0.130	0.081	0.038
19	0.686	0.570	0.475	0.396	0.331	0.232	0.164	0.116	0.070	0.031
20	0.673	0.554	0.456	0.377	0.312	0.215	0.149	0.104	0.061	0.026
30	0.552	0.412	0.308	0.231	0.174	0.099	0.057	0.033	0.015	0.004
40	0.453	0.307	0.208	0.142	0.097	0.046	0.022	0.011	0.004	0.001
50	0.372	0.228	0.141	0.087	0.054	0.021	0.009	0.003	0.001	—

TABLE II

PRESENT VALUE OF $1 ANNUITY RECEIVED AT END OF EACH PERIOD

Periods Hence	Rate per Compounding Period									
	2%	3%	4%	5%	6%	8%	10%	12%	15%	20%
1	0.980	0.971	0.962	0.952	0.943	0.926	0.909	0.893	0.870	0.833
2	1.942	1.914	1.886	1.859	1.833	1.783	1.736	1.690	1.626	1.528
3	2.884	2.829	2.775	2.723	2.673	2.577	2.487	2.402	2.283	2.106
4	3.808	3.717	3.630	3.546	3.465	3.312	3.170	3.037	2.855	2.589
5	4.714	4.580	4.452	4.330	4.212	3.993	3.791	3.605	3.352	2.991
6	5.601	5.417	5.242	5.076	4.917	4.623	4.355	4.111	3.784	3.326
7	6.472	6.230	6.002	5.786	5.582	5.206	4.868	4.564	4.160	3.605
8	7.326	7.020	6.733	6.463	6.210	5.747	5.335	4.968	4.487	3.837
9	8.162	7.786	7.435	7.108	6.802	6.247	5.760	5.328	4.772	4.031
10	8.983	8.530	8.111	7.722	7.360	6.710	6.145	5.650	5.019	4.192
11	9.787	9.253	8.761	8.306	7.887	7.139	6.495	5.988	5.234	4.327
12	10.575	9.954	9.385	8.863	8.384	7.536	6.814	6.194	5.421	4.439
13	11.348	10.635	9.986	9.394	8.853	7.904	7.103	6.424	5.583	4.533
14	12.106	11.296	10.563	9.899	9.295	8.244	7.367	6.628	5.724	4.611
15	12.849	11.938	11.118	10.380	9.712	8.560	7.606	6.811	5.847	4.675
16	13.578	12.561	11.652	10.838	10.106	8.851	7.824	6.974	5.954	4.730
17	14.292	13.166	12.166	11.274	10.477	9.122	8.022	7.120	6.047	4.775
18	14.992	13.754	12.659	11.690	10.828	9.372	8.201	7.250	6.128	4.812
19	15.679	14.324	13.134	12.085	11.158	9.604	8.365	7.366	6.198	4.844
20	16.351	14.878	13.590	12.462	11.470	9.818	8.514	7.469	6.259	4.870
30	22.397	19.600	17.292	15.373	13.765	11.258	9.427	8.055	6.566	4.979
40	27.356	23.115	19.793	17.159	15.046	11.925	9.779	8.244	6.642	4.997
50	31.424	25.730	21.482	18.256	15.762	12.234	9.915	8.304	6.661	4.999

FUTURE VALUE TABLES

| TABLE III | | | | | FUTURE VALUE OF $1 AFTER A GIVEN NUMBER OF TIME PERIODS | | | | | |

Periods Hence	Rate per Compounding Period									
	2%	3%	4%	5%	6%	8%	10%	12%	15%	20%
1	1.020	1.030	1.040	1.050	1.060	1.080	1.100	1.120	1.150	1.200
2	1.040	1.061	1.082	1.103	1.124	1.166	1.210	1.254	1.323	1.440
3	1.061	1.093	1.125	1.158	1.191	1.260	1.331	1.405	1.521	1.728
4	1.082	1.126	1.170	1.216	1.262	1.360	1.464	1.574	1.749	2.074
5	1.104	1.159	1.217	1.276	1.338	1.469	1.611	1.762	2.011	2.488
6	1.126	1.194	1.265	1.340	1.419	1.587	1.772	1.974	2.313	2.986
7	1.149	1.230	1.316	1.407	1.504	1.714	1.949	2.211	2.660	3.583
8	1.172	1.267	1.369	1.477	1.594	1.851	2.144	2.476	3.059	4.300
9	1.195	1.305	1.423	1.551	1.689	1.999	2.358	2.773	3.518	5.160
10	1.219	1.344	1.480	1.629	1.791	2.159	2.594	3.106	4.046	6.192
11	1.243	1.384	1.539	1.710	1.898	2.332	2.853	3.479	4.652	7.430
12	1.268	1.426	1.601	1.796	2.012	2.518	3.138	3.896	5.350	8.916
13	1.294	1.469	1.665	1.886	2.133	2.720	3.452	4.363	6.153	10.699
14	1.319	1.513	1.732	1.980	2.261	2.937	3.798	4.887	7.076	12.839
15	1.346	1.558	1.801	2.079	2.397	3.172	4.177	5.474	8.137	15.407
16	1.373	1.605	1.873	2.183	2.540	3.426	4.595	6.130	9.358	18.488
17	1.400	1.653	1.948	2.292	2.693	3.700	5.054	6.866	10.761	22.186
18	1.428	1.702	2.026	2.407	2.854	3.996	5.560	7.690	12.375	26.623
19	1.457	1.754	2.107	2.527	3.026	4.316	6.116	8.613	14.232	31.948
20	1.486	1.806	2.191	2.653	3.207	4.661	6.728	9.646	16.367	38.338
30	1.811	2.427	3.243	4.322	5.743	10.060	17.450	29.960	66.212	237.376
40	2.208	3.262	4.801	7.040	10.290	21.720	45.260	93.050	267.864	1,469.772
50	2.692	4.384	7.107	11.470	18.420	46.900	117.400	289.000	1,083.657	9,100.438

| TABLE IV | | | FUTURE VALUE OF $1 ANNUITY
PAID EACH PERIOD FOR A NUMBER OF TIME PERIODS | | | | | | | |

Periods Hence	Rate per Compounding Period									
	2%	3%	4%	5%	6%	8%	10%	12%	15%	20%
1	1.000	1.000	1.000	1.000	1.000	1.000	1.000	1.000	1.000	1.000
2	2.020	2.030	2.040	2.050	2.060	2.080	2.100	2.120	2.150	2.200
3	3.060	3.091	3.122	3.153	3.184	3.246	3.310	3.374	3.473	3.640
4	4.122	4.184	4.246	4.310	4.375	4.506	4.641	4.779	4.993	5.368
5	5.204	5.309	5.416	5.526	5.637	5.867	6.105	6.353	6.742	7.442
6	6.308	6.468	6.633	6.802	6.975	7.336	7.716	8.115	8.754	9.930
7	7.434	7.662	7.898	8.142	8.394	8.923	9.487	10.090	11.070	12.920
8	8.583	8.892	9.214	9.549	9.897	10.640	11.440	12.300	13.730	16.500
9	9.755	10.160	10.580	11.030	11.490	12.490	13.580	14.780	16.790	20.800
10	10.950	11.460	12.010	12.580	13.180	14.490	15.940	17.550	20.300	25.960
11	12.170	12.810	13.490	14.210	14.970	16.650	18.530	20.650	24.350	32.150
12	13.410	14.190	15.030	15.920	16.870	18.980	21.380	24.130	29.000	39.580
13	14.680	15.620	16.630	17.710	18.880	21.500	24.520	28.030	34.350	48.500
14	15.970	17.090	18.290	19.600	21.020	24.210	27.980	32.390	40.500	59.200
15	17.290	18.600	20.020	21.580	23.280	27.150	31.770	37.280	47.580	72.040
16	18.640	20.160	21.820	23.660	25.670	30.320	35.950	42.750	55.720	87.440
17	20.010	21.760	23.700	25.840	28.210	33.750	40.540	48.880	65.080	105.900
18	21.410	23.410	25.650	28.130	30.910	37.450	45.600	55.750	75.840	128.100
19	22.840	25.120	27.670	30.540	33.760	41.450	51.160	63.440	88.210	154.700
20	24.300	26.870	29.780	33.070	36.790	45.760	57.280	72.050	102.400	186.700
30	40.570	47.580	56.080	66.440	79.060	113.300	164.500	241.300	434.700	1,181.200
40	60.400	75.400	95.030	120.800	154.800	259.100	442.600	767.100	1,779.000	7,343.000
50	84.580	112.800	152.700	209.300	290.300	573.800	1,164.000	2,400.000	7,218.000	45,497.000

CHAPTER REVIEW

1 Do stockholders and bondholders have similar rights? Explain. (p. 568)

Bondholders have absolute rights to share in earnings through the payment of interest and to the return of their investment (principal) when the bond matures. Stockholders have the right to share in earnings, but only if any exist and if the board of directors declares a dividend. Stockholders only have a right to the return of their investment when the corporation is liquidated and if the remaining assets are sufficient to return it. Bondholders do not have the right to vote, as do stockholders, and the preemptive right has no meaning to bondholders.

2 Will issuing bonds usually result in higher earnings-per-share amounts for the common stockholders? (p. 570)

The answer to this question extends far beyond what is taught in introductory courses, but was included to promote discussion. The discussion early in the chapter shows that the EPS would be $12 if bonds were issued, $6 if preferred stock were issued, and $10 if additional common stock were issued, assuming that the project provided $6,000,000 in profit before cost of borrowing and income taxes. If the same calculations are made assuming smaller and smaller assumed profit figures, students can readily see that the answer to this question depends on how much profit will be provided from the new investment. Generally, bonds are cheaper to issue than preferred stock, since the interest payments are deductible, but if interest payments are not covered, or barely covered, then issuing more common stock would be best to increase EPS.

3 Why is it said that the issuing corporation benefits when it has bonds outstanding during periods of inflation? (p. 571)

If a corporation borrows money (issues bonds) during a period of inflation, the dollars they pay back when the bond matures are not worth as much as the dollars they borrowed, thereby providing an unrecognized gain.

4 What are the major disadvantages of issuing bonds over stock? (p. 571)

Interest must be paid on bonds, or the bonds go into default, and control of the corporation could pass to the bondholders. The principal also must be repaid at a certain point in time, creating a need to make sure cash is available to retire the debt. Also, if the corporation's earnings fall below the annual interest requirement, having debt outstanding forces the corporation into a net loss position.

5 Do all bonds have some sort of security behind them? (p. 572)

All bonds have some security behind them, in that bondholders are creditors of the corporation and as such stand in front of the owners at liquidation. Many bonds are debenture bonds, which means that the main security is the creditworthiness of the corporation. Some bonds are fully secured, in that the bondholders have an absolute right to particular assets, usually real estate.

6 Do bondholders usually have the right to convert their bonds into common stock? Would this feature be of any advantage to the issuing corporation? the investing corporation? (p. 573)

A bond issue *may* be issued with a conversion feature. The main advantage to the issuing corporation is that the convertible bonds are easier to sell because the creditor can become an owner at his or her choosing. If the corporation is successful, the bondholders will likely convert, negating the corporation's need to repay the principal at maturity. The advantage to the investing corporation is that it can become an owner of a successful corporation while first enjoying the benefits of a creditor until the corporation reaches the successful years.

7 Would a corporation usually use a sinking fund in connection with serial bonds outstanding? (p. 574)

Serial bonds have various maturity dates, while term bonds have only one. If the serial bonds begin to mature one year after issue, and the same face value amounts mature each year, a sinking fund is scarcely needed. It is usually used in connection with term bonds.

8 Bonds have a face value (par value); when would bonds sell above or below face value? Explain. (p. 575)

Since bonds have an interest rate that does not fluctuate, they may be issued during a period of time that the market rate of interest is above or below that fixed rate. If so, the market price of the bond will reflect that difference. If the market rate is above the fixed rate, the bonds will sell below par (at a discount), adjusting the fixed rate to reflect the market rate. If the market rate is below the fixed rate, the bonds will sell above par (at a premium).

9 Why are bond premiums and discounts treated as adjustments to interest expense over the life of the bond issue? (p. 578)

When bonds are sold at a premium, say $106,000 for $100,000 par, the $6,000 does not have to be paid at maturity. For a 10-year, 5% bond, $50,000 in interest (5% × $100,000 × 10) must be paid. Because the $6,000 premium does not have to be returned, it reduces this $50,000 interest cost to $44,000, or $4,400 per year. Hence, $600 of the premium is amortized each year to offset the payments. The alternative would be to record the entire $6,000 as income in either the first year of the issue or in the year the bonds mature, which would not result in a proper matching of revenue and expenses.

The same can be said of a discount. If $100,000 par value bonds are sold for $94,000, an *additional* $6,000 must be paid at maturity, increasing the total cost of borrowing to $56,000 or $5,600 per year, with $600 of the discount being amortized to offset the cost. These two analyses assume straight-line amortization.

10 What problem arises when a corporation decides to retire unmatured bonds? Explain. (pp. 583–84)

The corporation must remove from the accounts all the related valuation and prepaid accounts. For bonds, this would entail the Bonds Payable account, along with valuation accounts such as Premium on Bonds, Discount on Bonds, and any unamortized bond-issue costs. Then a gain or loss would be recorded, based on the difference between the net carrying cost and the amount that had to be paid to retire the bonds.

11 What problem arises when bonds are issued after the date of original authorization and, therefore, between interest dates? (pp. 584–85)

A corporation pays a full six-month interest on each bond that is outstanding. Because of this, whenever a bond is sold between interest dates, the purchaser must pay to the corporation the interest that has accrued on the bond since the last interest date or the date of issue, whichever is later.

12 It is said that the effective interest method of bond amortization results in more accurate information than the straight-line method. Why? (pp. 586–87)

The effective interest method provides a *constant* interest *rate* for reporting in the financial statements. Under the straight-line method, the interest *rate increases* if the bonds were sold at a discount, or it *decreases* if the bonds were sold at a premium, because interest expense remains a constant amount.

13   What are some areas of financial accounting where present or future value analysis is used? (pp. 593–97)

Many of the uses of present and future value analyses are beyond the scope of this textbook, but as is demonstrated in the appendix, present value analysis is used to determine the price a bond should sell for, given the relationship between the fixed rate of interest and the market rate of interest. A bond should sell for an amount equal to the present value of the interest payments plus the present value of the principle to be paid at maturity. Future value analysis is used to determine bond sinking fund requirements.

The time value of money analyses will be used throughout the course work for business majors.

KEY TERMS

amortization (p. 577)   The allocation of the bond premium or bond discount to interest expense over the time the bond issue will be outstanding.

annuity (p. 582)   A series of payments or receipts made at equal time intervals. The payment of interest on a bond issue is an annuity, as well as payments into a bond sinking fund.

bond (p. 568)   A debt security that requires the periodic payment of interest at a stated rate, and the repayment of face or par value at some date in the future. The maturity date may be a single date in the future (term bonds) or multiple dates (serial bonds).

bond discount (p. 574)   An amount under the face value received when a bond is issued. The situation usually exists when the market rate of interest is higher than the stated rate of interest on the bond issue.

bond indenture (p. 568)   The printed agreement that specifies the terms that the issuing corporation has agreed to abide by.

bond premium (p. 574)   An amount in excess of the face value received when a bond is issued. The situation usually exists when the market rate of interest is below the stated interest rate on the bond issue.

call price (p. 573)   The amount a corporation must pay to redeem a bond in order to exercise the call provision of the issue.

call provision (p. 573)   A provision in the bond indenture that allows the issuing corporation to redeem the bonds before the maturity date. The call price is usually in excess of face value.

convertible bonds (p. 573)   A bond issue that may, at the option of the bondholder, be exchanged for shares of common stock of the issuing corporation.

debenture bonds   See *unsecured bonds*.

earnings per share (EPS) (p. 570)   The amount of net income allocated to each share of common stock outstanding. The amount is usually based on a weighted average of the number of shares outstanding.

effective interest method (p. 577)   A method of amortizing bond premiums or discounts that results in a constant *rate* being recorded as interest expense over the life of the bonds.

face value (p. 574)   The amount repaid when a bond issue matures. This amount, printed on the bond, is also referred to as the *par value*.

future value analysis (p. 593)   Determines the future value of a present value, either as a single amount or as an annuity. A single amount will grow only because of the time value of money; an annuity will grow because of the time value of money and the periodic deposits. This analysis can be used to determine sinking-fund deposit requirements for a *term bond* issue. See the chapter appendix.

market interest rate (p. 575)   The current rate of interest being paid on similar securities.

maturity date (p. 568)   The date specified in the bond indenture for the return of the face or par value of the bonds to the investors.

mortgage bonds   See *secured bonds.*

par value   See *face value.*

present value analysis (p. 592)   Determines the present value of an amount or series of amounts to be received in the future. The purchase price of a bond may be estimated by determining the present value of the principal to be received 5, 10, or 20 years from the issue, and then adding the results to the present value of the interest annuity. See the chapter appendix.

refunding a bond issue (p. 584)   The act of issuing a new bond issue and using the proceeds to retire an older bond issue, presumably at a dollar savings.

secured bonds (p. 572)   A bond issue secured by physical assets of the issuing corporation, usually referred to as *mortgage bonds.*

serial bonds (p. 573)   A bond issue that has more than one maturity date for the repayment of principal. In a very common serial bond situation, 1/10 of the principal is due each year for a 10-year period.

sinking fund (p. 574)   An investment fund usually used in connection with an issue of term bonds. With the principal payment coming at one time in the future, the corporation must provide for the retirement of the bonds. An amount determined by means of present and future value analyses is deposited in a fund each year and is invested in income-producing securities.

straight-line method (p. 577)   A method of amortizing bond premiums or discounts that results in a constant *amount* being recorded as interest expense over the life of the bonds.

term bonds (p. 573)   A bond issue that has only one maturity date for the repayment of the principal. No matter how long the bonds will be outstanding, all of them mature (become due) on the same date.

trustee (p. 568)   An intermediary between the corporation issuing the bonds and the bondholders. The trustee represents the bondholders and will often hold title to property securing the bonds, if any.

unsecured bonds (p. 572)   A bond issue secured only by the good name of the corporation. If the corporation is successful, the bondholders will be paid; if not, they may not receive the interest they are entitled to, or even the principal. These bonds are often referred to as *debenture bonds.*

SELF-TEST QUESTIONS FOR REVIEW   (Answers are at the end of this chapter.)

Q2

1. If the net cost of debt securities is less than the return on investment, the earnings per share would
   (a)   remain the same whether debt or equity securities were issued.
   (b)   increase if debt securities were issued instead of equity securities.
   (c)   decrease if debt securities were issued instead of equity securities.
   (d)   increase if equity securities were issued instead of debt securities.

Q3

2. The decision to issue bonds can be influenced by the degree of inflation or deflation in the economy. It is better to issue debt securities when the economy is in
   (a) an inflationary period.
   (b) a deflationary period.
   (c) either period, since the state of the economy does not influence the decision.
   (d) It is never better to issue debt securities over equity securities.

Q8

3. When the market rate of interest is equal to the stated rate of interest on a bond issue, the bonds
   (a) will probably not sell until the situation changes.
   (b) will sell at a premium.
   (c) will sell at a discount.
   (d) should sell at an amount equal to the face or par value.

Q8, Q9

4. When bonds sell at a premium, the total cost of borrowing the funds will
   (a) stay the same since the amount of interest paid remains the same.
   (b) increase because the bonds sold for more than their face value.
   (c) decrease because the bonds were sold at a premium.
   (d) be undeterminable until the bonds mature, and the actual cost is known.

Q12

5. Straight-line amortization of a bond premium is the best method, since the amount of interest expense
   (a) remains the same over the life of the bond issue.
   (b) increases over the life of the bond issue.
   (c) decreases over the life of the bond issue.
   (d) None of the above

Q12

6. The effective interest method of amortizing a bond premium or discount results in
   (a) an increasing amount of amortization.
   (b) a decreasing amount of amortization.
   (c) a constant amount of amortization because a constant rate is used.
   (d) The question cannot be answered since whether the bonds were sold at a premium or a discount has to be known.

Q9

7. The amortization of a bond discount will
   (a) increase interest expense.
   (b) decrease interest expense.
   (c) cause no change in interest expense since the rate of interest is stated in the indenture, and that amount must be paid regardless of whether the bond was sold at a premium or discount.
   (d) decrease the carrying value of the bond issued.

Q9

8. The amortization of a bond premium will
   (a) increase interest expense.
   (b) decrease interest expense.
   (c) cause no change in interest expense since the rate of interest is stated in the indenture, and that amount must be paid regardless of whether the bond was sold at a premium or discount.
   (d) increase the carrying value of the bond issued.

Q13

9. What is the future value of $7,000 if invested at 10% annual interest for the next 50 years?
   (a) $821,800
   (b) $350,000
   (c) $385,000
   (d) $1,567,900

Q13

10. What is the present value of $1,000,000 to be received 50 years from now at 10% interest?
    (a) $1,000,000
    (b) -0-
    (c) $9,000
    (d) $99,150

DEMONSTRATION PROBLEM

Part A

Bolovision Corp., a profitable growth company with 200,000 shares of common stock outstanding, is in need of approximately $40 million in new funds to finance required expansion. Currently, no other securities are outstanding. Management has three options open: sell $40 million of 12% bonds at face value; sell 10% preferred stock—400,000 shares at $100 per share; or sell another 200,000 shares of common stock at $200 per share. Operating income (before interest and income tax) on completion of the expansion is expected to average $12 million per annum; the income tax rate is 50%.

Required

1. Prepare a schedule calculating the following items to determine the earnings per common share. Use three columns to show the earnings per share for $12 million each of bonds, preferred stock, and common stock.

> Net Income before Interest and Income Taxes
> Less: Bond Interest Expense
> Earnings before Taxes
> Less: Income Tax at 50%
> Balance
> Less: Preferred Dividends
> Net Available to Common Stockholders
> Common Shares Outstanding
> Earnings per Common Share

2. Which financing option is most advantageous to the common stockholders?

3. What are the advantages of issuing shares rather than bonds? of issuing bonds rather than shares?

Part B

Watfor Corp. was authorized to issue $500,000 face value bonds. The corporation issued $100,000 of face value bonds on January 1, 19X1.

Date of Authorization	Term	Bond Contract Interest Rate	Interest Payment Dates
January 1, 19X1	3 years	12%	Semiannually on June 30 and December 31

Required

Answer the questions for each of the following cases:

> Case A: The bonds were issued at face value and purchased at par.
> Case B: The bonds were issued for $112,000 and purchased at a premium.
> Case C: The bonds were issued for $88,000 and purchased at a discount.

1. How much cash does Watfor receive for the bonds?

2. How much annual interest must the corporation pay? On what face value amount?

3. Prepare the journal entry to record the sale of the bonds.

4. Record the entries applicable to interest payment and straight-line amortization for June 30, 19X1, and for December 31, 19X1.

Part C

Maple Leaf Distributors was authorized to issue $500,000 of face value bonds. On January 1, 19X1, the corporation issued $200,000 of face value bonds for $210,152. On this date the market rate of interest was 10%.

Date of Authorization	Term	Bond Contract Interest Rate	Interest Payment Dates
January 1, 19X1	3 years	12%	Semiannually on June 30 and December 31

Required

1. Calculate the amount of interest paid every interest payment date.

2. Prepare an amortization table like the one in Exhibit 13-7. (The carrying value at January 1, 19X1 is $210,152 and periodic interest is $10,507 for the first 6 months.) For convenience, round all column B calculations to the nearest dollar. Use the effective interest method of amortization.

3. Calculate the financing percentage ($B \div A$) under the effective interest method of amortization for each 6-month period. For convenience, round all percentage calculations to the nearest percent.

4. Comment on the financing percentage that results in each period. Do you think this financing percentage should remain constant from period to period? Why or why not?

SOLUTION TO DEMONSTRATION PROBLEM

Part A

	Bonds	Preferred Shares	Common Shares
1.			
Net Income before Interest and Income Taxes	$12,000,000	$12,000,000	$12,000,000
Less: Bond Interest Expense	4,800,000(a)	-0-	-0-
Earnings before Taxes	$ 7,200,000	$12,000,000	$12,000,000
Less: Income Tax at 50%	3,600,000	6,000,000	6,000,000
Balance	$ 3,600,000	$ 6,000,000	$ 6,000,000
Less: Preferred Dividends	-0-	4,000,000(b)	
Net Available to Common Stockholders	$ 3,600,000	$ 2,000,000	$ 6,000,000
Common Shares Outstanding	200,000	200,000	400,000
Earnings per Common Share	$18	$10	$15

(a) $40 million × 12% = $4.8 million
(b) 400,000 × $100 × 10% = $4,000,000

2. Issuing bonds is the most advantageous financing option to the common stockholders, since it results in higher earnings per common share. A second advantage is that bond-

holders normally do not have any control over managerial decisions. Issuing shares will distribute control over a larger number of stockholders and the present stockholders' control would be diluted. A third advantage is that interest expense is deductible for tax purposes, while dividends are paid out of after-tax dollars. The last advantage is the impact of inflation. By borrowing today's dollars and repaying the same dollars later on, the investor in effect gains purchasing power, since today's dollars are worth more than tomorrow's dollars in a period of inflation. One disadvantage, which may make another option more advantageous, is that interest expense is fixed and the investor risks the possibility that the corporation will not earn enough income to cover the interest expense in any given year.

3. The advantage of issuing shares rather than bonds is that the corporation may not earn enough to cover the fixed interest expense for bonds in a given year. The advantages of issuing bonds rather than shares are the following: The earnings per common share would be higher and, therefore, more attractive to stockholders; stockholders retain management control, since bondholders cannot vote; interest expense is tax deductible, while dividends are paid out of after-tax dollars; and money borrowed today in a period of inflation will have less purchasing power by the time it is repaid.

Part B

	Case A		Case B		Case C	
1.	$100,000		$112,000		$88,000	
2.	$12,000 annual interest on $100,000 face value		$12,000 annual interest on $100,000 face value		$12,000 annual interest on $100,000 face value	
3.	Cash 100,000		Cash 112,000		Cash 88,000	
	Bonds Payable	100,000	Premium on Bonds	12,000	Discount on	
			Bonds Payable	100,000	Bonds	12,000
					Bonds Payable	100,000
4.	June 30, 19X1		June 30, 19X1		June 30, 19X1	
	Bond Interest		Bond Interest		Bond Interest	
	Expense 6,000		Expense 6,000		Expense 6,000	
	Cash	6,000	Cash	6,000	Cash	6,000
			Amortization:		Amortization:	
			Premium on		Bond Interest	
			Bonds 2,000		Expense 2,000	
			Bond Interest		Discount on Bonds	2,000
			Expense	2,000		
	December 31, 19X1		December 31, 19X1		December 31, 19X1	
	Bond Interest		Bond Interest		Bond Interest	
	Expense 6,000		Expense 6,000		Expense 6,000	
	Cash	6,000	Cash	6,000	Cash	6,000
			Amortization:		Amortization:	
			Premium on		Bond Interest	
			Bonds 2,000		Expense 2,000	
			Bond Interest		Discount on Bonds	2,000
			Expense	2,000		

Part C

1. Interest payment every 6 months: $200,000 × 12% × 1/2 = $12,000

2.

Amortization Table
Using Market Interest Rate of 10%

Year	Period	A Jan. 1 Bond Carrying Value	B ([½ of 10% = 5%] × A) Using 10% Market Rate to Calculate 6-Month Interest Expense	C 6% Actual Cash Interest Paid	D (C − B) 6-Month Premium Amortization	E (A − D) Dec. 31 Bond Carrying Value
1	1	$210,152	$10,507 (5% × $210,152)	$12,000	$1,493	$208,659
	2	208,659	10,433 (5% × 208,659)	12,000	1,567	207,092
2	3	207,092	10,355 (5% × 207,092)	12,000	1,645	205,447
	4	205,447	10,272 (5% × 205,447)	12,000	1,728	203,719
3	5	203,719	10,186 (5% × 203,719)	12,000	1,814	201,905
	6	201,905	10,095 (5% × 201,905)	12,000	1,905	200,000

3. The financing percentage for each 6-month period is 5%.

4. The financing charge remains constant from period to period under the effective interest method. It would vary slightly under the straight-line method. Purists will argue that the interest rate should remain constant in order to be correct. From a practical point of view, the difference from period to period is not material under the straight-line method, and the effective interest method is not worth the effort. The straight-line method is much simpler to use and is acceptable if the results are not materially different from those under the effective interest method.

DISCUSSION QUESTIONS

Q13-1 A corporation can be financed in a number of ways. Explain the different ways and give examples. What factors influence management in the choice of a financing method?

Q13-2 What is a bond? a bond indenture? Why is a trustee usually necessary?

Q13-3 A bondholder has certain rights. List and explain these rights.

Q13-4 What is the significance of stockholder approval before an issue of bonds?

Q13-5 How are different bond issues reported in the financial statements of a corporation?

Q13-6 Management is considering three different financing options: the issue of preferred shares, of common shares, and of bonds. The directors of the corporation have concluded that attention should be devoted to observing the expected effect on earnings per common share in the selection of a financing method. What are the advantages of issuing bonds? preferred shares? common shares?

Q13-7 Three different categories of bond terminology are identified in this chapter. Identify these categories and list the major types falling within each category.

Q13-8 Why would investors pay a premium for a corporate bond? Why would a corporation issue its bonds at a discount? Explain, using the relationship between the bond contract interest rate and the prevailing market interest rate.

Q13-9 How is the bond premium or bond discount reported in the balance sheet?

Q13-10 How is the price of a bond determined? Give an example.

Q13-11   If the bond contract interest rate is greater than that required in the market, what is the effect on the selling price of the bond? Why?

Q13-12   What are the different methods used in amortizing premiums and discounts? Explain.

Q13-13   How is the interest paid to bondholders calculated? How does this practice affect the sale of bonds between interest dates?

Q13-14   How is the amortization of a bond premium recorded in the books? bond discount?

Q13-15   Explain a bond sinking fund. What are the three phases in its operation?

Q13-16   What are the different possibilities in the redemption of bonds before their maturity?

Q13-17   If a bond is sold between interest dates, what is the accepted practice for handling accrued interest? Why has the practice evolved in this form?

Q13-18   From a theoretical point of view, why is the effective interest method of amortization more acceptable than the straight-line method? Evaluate the usefulness of the effective interest method from a practical point of view.

Q13-19   Explain how the amortization under the effective interest method is calculated. Use an example.

Q13-20   How does the calculation of a periodic financing charge differ from the effective interest method and the straight-line method?

Q13-21   Distinguish between future value and present value. What is the time value of money? Why is it important?

Q13-22   Explain compound interest. What is its relationship to both future value and present value?

Q13-23   Why is it necessary to discount future cash flows when calculating the present value of a bond? Explain, using the different cash flows associated with bonds.

Q13-24   How does the use of mathematical tables facilitate the calculation of present values?

Q13-25   Contrast the calculation of present value when (a) the market interest rate is greater than the bond contract interest rate, and (b) the market interest rate is less than the bond contract interest rate.

DISCUSSION CASE

Jasmine Technologies, Inc.

Like many an entrepreneur before him, Dennis Chang was long on chutzpah and short on cash. After bouncing around the computer industry for eight years, he had a business plan modeled after IBM's and Apple Computer's. But he had no savings, no investors, and no willing lenders.

He still doesn't. Yet for the fiscal year ended last September, his San Francisco company, Jasmine Technologies, Inc., logged sales of more than $35 million on its disk drives and other Macintosh-compatible components. Chang, 40, financed this astonishing growth with some of the most reluctant lenders around: his suppliers.

Supplier financing is often messy and precarious. It had one serious advantage for Chang, however; it was his only option.

Source Ellyn E. Spragins, "Supply-Side Financing," *Inc. Magazine,* February 1989. Reprinted with permission. Copyright © 1989 by Goldhirsh Group, Inc., 38 Commercial Wharf, Boston, MA 02110.

Everyone knows the official textbook rule on such backdoor finance. It says: Put off paying your suppliers as long as possible—period. That's fine if you already have suppliers. But if like Chang you barely have a product, much less a track record, it simply doesn't apply. The trick was to get not only his raw materials, but his office equipment, advertising—his entire business—on credit.

Fortunately, Chang didn't know the first thing about official finance. "Everything I was doing was intuitive, seat of the pants," he recalls—thus the birth of Finesse Finance . . .

Chang's first lesson was about the power of the personal guarantee. With no other means of selling or distributing its Macintosh-clone peripherals, Jasmine was relying on an advertisement in *Macworld* magazine to educate Macintosh users, to promote its product, and to produce prepaid orders. Trouble was, *Macworld* insisted that Chang pay for his ads. But he couldn't; he had to get them on credit.

All it took was conversation—a couple of months of it. Chang was on the phone almost every day with San Francisco account executive Penny Rigby and the magazine's credit department. They discussed Chang's education, previous jobs, personal finances, business plan, marketing strategy. In the end, he consented to personally guarantee a credit line of about $30,000, an obligation he could meet only by selling his house.

By the end of those months of talking, Rigby and the credit people were emotionally committed to him. Chang's guarantee gave the magazine's bean counters a security blanket—so they could do what they already wanted to do, which was to back Chang. Lesson one: The power of the personal guarantee lies mostly in what you do before you give it.

Now, Chang was really rolling. Or so he thought, until he tried to find a leasing company that would agree to rent him some telephones, typewriters, copiers, and computers. It didn't take long before the solution hit him: he'd simply "recycle" his personal guarantee. All the money he had was $40,000 of equity in his house. Guaranteeing $12,000 to $15,000 in payments to a leasing company couldn't make him any more vulnerable. What's more, he soon discovered, few ever asked how many other credit lines he had personally guaranteed. And therein lay the second lesson: The first guarantee devalues all subsequent guarantees, but your suppliers don't know that.

For some people, Chang learned, getting paid wasn't nearly as important as growth, or, say, bucking the status quo. These were the suppliers who were motivated by the same thing that drove him, his soul mates in ambition. He spent hours with such small companies describing his vision of Jasmine's future. "I sold them on the value of our growth," Chang says.

Chang got two of his most important vendor relationships by being a Good Samaritan to one that stumbled. Chang offered to buy a huge batch of excess inventory of platters from a grateful disk supplier. The disk maker also introduced Chang to Arrow Electronics, Inc., where Chang bumped into the invisible credit limit.

"Arrow initially gave us a $50,000 credit line," remembers Chang. "We were growing 30% a month, so we exceeded it." Nothing happened. Jasmine paid Arrow's bills, then it again exceeded the credit limit. Again nothing happened. Eureka! "I finally realized that we didn't really have a credit limit. I started ordering products like crazy."

It wasn't long before Chang faced a new problem with his vendors. It was no longer a matter of persuading them to be his suppliers—it was that little matter of how to pay them. In the beginning, he had made certain all bills were paid on time. But now Jasmine's growth was chewing up cash. Chang looked at his suppliers and saw a few dozen small, relatively unimportant ones and a handful of crucial ones. Rather than spend all his money on the important suppliers, he devised a kind of reverse triage: he'd pay the small bills right away and drag out the big ones. He figured that if they shut him off, the small vendors could hurt him just about as much as the big ones. And besides, he could afford to pay the little bills. And the big vendors? Well, they would get plenty of Dennis Chang's private currency—personal attention.

He talked to them every day. He returned their phone calls immediately. He took their families out to breakfast or lunch. If he managed to scrape together part of the money Jasmine owed, he personally hand delivered the check. In short, he paid them with evidence of his intense commitment. When the cash crisis was over, he found, those suppliers felt like partners in his success.

Despite that success, it's clear that supplier financing is no substitute for more conventional forms of capital. With no outside equity in the company, Jasmine's heavy reliance on suppliers' credit makes it look terribly overleveraged. That, in turn, makes the company unappealing to banks and other lenders. Lack of both equity and borrowing capacity means it has no cushion against a temporary drop in sales, such as it suffered early last year.

There is an up side, though. It worked. It worked well enough that Jasmine is no longer a seed company or a start-up—it's up and running hard. And that makes a world of difference to potential investors. Chang says he's constantly being approached by venture capitalists, investment bankers, and other investors, but he's not letting them turn his head. As usual, he has a plan: "The longer we hold them off, the less we have to give away of our company," he explains.

This could be the start of chapter two of Finesse Finance—but that's another story.

For Discussion

1. What exactly is supplier financing? Explain how it works. Why is supplier financing messy and precarious?

2. How could Chang finance $35 million in sales without savings, investors, or willing lenders? Are any ethical issues involved in this situation?

3. Chang's personal guarantee "gave the magazine's bean counters a security blanket." Who are the bean counters?

4. How many times did Chang recycle his personal guarantee? Could any entrepreneur have used this technique? How? Exactly how does "Finesse Finance" work?

5. Explain Chang's invisible credit line with Arrow.

6. Discuss Chang's "private currency."

7. Explain in what way Jasmine is overleveraged.

EXERCISES

E13-1 to E13-13 are based on the following data:

Agave Corp. issues $100,000 of 8% bonds dated January 1, 19X0. Interest is payable on June 30 and December 31 for the next 10 years. The entire $100,000 matures on December 31, 19X9.

Entries for bonds at par (Q8)

E13-1 Assume the bonds are sold on January 1, 19X0, at their face value.

Required

Prepare the journal entries necessary on the following dates:

1. January 1, 19X0

2. June 30, 19X0

3. December 31, 19X0

Entries for bonds above par (Q8)

E13-2 Assume the bonds are sold on January 1, 19X0, at 115, and straight-line amortization is used.

Required

Prepare the journal entries necessary on the following dates:

1. January 1, 19X0
2. June 30, 19X0
3. December 31, 19X0

Entries for bonds below par (Q8)

E13-3   Assume the bonds are sold on January 1, 19X0, at 87, and straight-line amortization is used.

Required

Prepare the journal entries necessary on the following dates:

1. January 1, 19X0
2. June 30, 19X0
3. December 31, 19X0

Entries for bonds at par between interest dates (Q8, Q11)

E13-4   Assume the bonds are sold on April 1, 19X0, at their face value.

Required

Prepare the journal entries necessary on the following dates:

1. April 1, 19X0
2. June 30, 19X0
3. December 31, 19X0

Entries for bonds above par between interest dates (Q8, Q11)

E13-5   Assume the bonds are sold on April 1, 19X0, at 115, and straight-line amortization is used.

Required

Prepare the journal entries necessary on the following dates:

1. April 1, 19X0
2. June 30, 19X0
3. December 31, 19X0

Entries for bonds below par between interest dates (Q8, Q11)

E13-6   Assume the bonds are sold on April 1, 19X0, at 87, and straight-line amortization is used.

Required

Prepare the journal entries necessary on the following dates:

1. April 1, 19X0
2. June 30, 19X0
3. December 31, 19X0

Bonds at par retired early (Q10)

E13-7   Assume all the Agave bonds are repurchased through the market on December 31, 19X4, at par.

Required

Prepare all the journal entries necessary on Dec. 31, 19X4, assuming the bonds were sold at face value on January 1, 19X0.

Bonds above par retired early (Q10)

E13-8   Assume all the Agave bonds are repurchased through the market on December 31, 19X4, at 106.

Required

Prepare all the journal entries necessary on Dec. 31, 19X4, assuming the bonds were sold at 115 on January 1, 19X0.

Bonds below par retired early (Q10)

E13-9   Assume all the Agave bonds are repurchased through the market on December 31, 19X4, at 95.

Required

Prepare all the journal entries necessary on Dec. 31, 19X4, assuming the bonds were sold at 87 on January 1, 19X0.

Entries for bonds at par, effective interest method (Q13)

E13-10   Assume the bonds were sold to yield 8% to the investor.

Required

1. Determine the selling price of the bond issue.

2. Prepare the journal entries necessary on the following dates:
   (a) January 1, 19X0
   (b) June 30, 19X0
   (c) December 31, 19X0

Entries for bonds below par, effective interest method (Q9, Q12, Q13)

E13-11   Assume the bonds were sold to yield 10% to the investor.

Required

1. Determine the selling price of the bond issue.

2. Prepare the journal entries necessary on the following dates:
   (a) January 1, 19X0
   (b) June 30, 19X0
   (c) December 31, 19X0

Entries for bonds above par, effective interest method (Q9, Q12, Q13)

E13-12   Assume the bonds were sold to yield 6% to the investor.

Required

1. Determine the selling price of the bond issue.

2. Prepare the journal entries necessary on the following dates:
   (a) January 1, 19X0
   (b) June 30, 19X0
   (c) December 31, 19X0

Calculation of sinking fund deposit (Q7, Q13)

E13-13   Assume the bond issue in E13-12 required a sinking fund.

Required

What is the annual contribution to this fund if the following assumptions are made?

1. The contribution is made at the end of the year.

2. The fund will earn an annual interest rate of 12%.

PROBLEMS

Financing decisions: bonds, preferred stock, common stock (Q2)

P13-1   The board of directors of Oligopoly, Inc., has approved management's recommendation to expand the production facilities. The firm currently manufactures only heavy machinery, but plans are being developed for diversifying the corporation's activities through the production of smaller and more versatile equipment. The directors have decided to emphasize the expected effect on earnings per common share in selection of a financing method. They are considering the following financing methods: sell $2 million of 12% bonds at face value; sell 8% preferred stock—20,000 shares at $100 a share (no other preferred shares are outstanding); or sell another 50,000 shares of common stock at $400 a share (currently 40,000 common shares are outstanding). Operating income (before interest and income tax) is expected to average $1,000,000 per annum following the expansion; the income tax rate is expected to be 50%.

Required
1. Calculate the earnings per common share for each alternative: 12% bonds, preferred stock, and common stock.
2. Which financing method best meets the board of directors' criteria?
3. What factors should the board of directors consider, in addition to earnings per share?

Straight-line amortization, entries, balance sheet (Q8, Q9)

P13-2   Computer Stores Corp. was authorized to issue $300,000 of face value bonds. On January 1, 19X1, the corporation issued $150,000 of face value bonds for $147,000.

Date of Authorization	Term	Bond Contract Interest Rate	Interest Payment Dates
January 1, 19X1	3 years	12%	Semiannually on June 30 and December 31

Part A

Required
1. Calculate the amount of
   (a) interest paid every interest payment date.
   (b) amortization to be recorded at each interest payment date. Use the straight-line method.
2. Prepare a schedule, like the one in Exhibit 13-5, to show the effect of discount amortization at each interest payment date. Note that amortization is recorded each time interest expense is recorded.
3. Prepare the journal entries to record the interest and amortization as of June 30, 19X1.
4. Prepare a partial balance sheet showing the bond liability on the following dates:
   (a) December 31, 19X1 (Note that the bonds are a long-term liability on this date, since they will not be redeemed in 19X2.)
   (b) December 31, 19X2 (Note that the bonds are a current liability on this date, since they will be redeemed on January 1, 19X4.)

Part B

Bond sinking fund (Q7)

The bond indenture contained a sinking fund provision requiring equal annual contributions that are transferred to a trustee who guarantees a 10% annual return. Annual contributions are to be made on December 31, 19X1, 19X2, and 19X3. The amount of the contributions and the 10% revenue in the sinking fund are calculated as follows:

December 31	Annual Contribution	10% Annual Revenue	Annual Total	Fund Balance
19X1	$45,317	-0-	$45,317	$ 45,317
19X2	45,317	$4,532 (10% × $45,317)	49,849	95,166
19X3	45,317	9,517 (10% × $95,166)	54,834	150,000

Required

5. Prepare journal entries to record the
    (a) annual contribution in each of the three years.
    (b) 10% annual revenue in each of the three years.
    (c) redemption of the bonds at maturity.

6. Show how the annual contribution was determined.

Bonds at par, below par, above par, with entries (Q8, Q9)

P13-3   On the date of bond authorization, Axel Corp. issued $100,000 of face value bonds.

Date of Authorization	Term	Bond Contract Interest Rate	Interest Payment Dates
January 1, 19X1	3 years	12%	Semiannually on June 30 and December 31

Required

Consider these cases.

Case A: The bonds are issued at face value.
Case B: The bonds are issued for $103,000.
Case C: The bonds are issued for $94,000.

For each case, do the following:

1. Calculate the amount of
    (a) interest paid every interest payment date.
    (b) amortization to be recorded at each interest payment date, if applicable. Use the straight-line method.

2. Prepare journal entries to record the
    (a) issue of bonds on January 1, 19X1.
    (b) payment of interest on June 30, 19X1.
    (c) amortization on June 30, 19X1.
    (d) payment of interest on December 31, 19X1.
    (e) amortization on December 31, 19X1.
    (f) payment of interest on December 31, 19X3.
    (g) amortization on December 31, 19X3.
    (h) redemption of the bonds at maturity, January 1, 19X4.

3. Calculate the amount of interest expense shown in the income statement as of December 31, 19X1. Is this amount the same as cash interest paid by Axel? Why or why not?

Amortization table, straight-line, rates (Q8, Q9, Q12)

P13-4   Beaver Products, Inc., which uses straight-line amortization, was authorized to issue $1,000,000 face value bonds. On January 1, 19X1, Beaver issued $300,000 of face value bonds for $272,263.

Date of Authorization	Term	Bond Contract Interest Rate	Interest Payment Dates
January 1, 19X1	3 years	12%	Semiannually on June 30 and December 31

Required

1. Calculate the amount of
   (a) interest paid every interest payment date.
   (b) amortization to be recorded at each interest payment date. Use the straight-line method.

2. Prepare an amortization table like the one in Exhibit 13-8, but use the straight-line method. Note that amortization is recorded each time interest expense is recorded.

3. Calculate the financing percentage under the straight-line method of amortization for each 6-month period. For convenience, round all percentage calculations to one decimal place.

4. Comment on the financing percentage that results in each period. Do you think this financing percentage should vary from period to period? Why or why not?

Straight-line vs. effective interest, entries (Q8, Q9, Q12, Q13)

P13-5 Peripherals Corp. was authorized to issue $1,000,000 of face value bonds. The corporation issued $100,000 of face value bonds on the date of bond authorization for $107,721. The market rate of interest on the issue date was 10%.

Date of Authorization	Term	Bond Contract Interest Rate	Interest Payment Dates
January 1, 19X4	5 years	12%	Semiannually on June 30 and December 31

Required
Consider these cases.

Case A: Peripherals uses the straight-line method of amortization.
Case B: The company uses the effective interest method of amortization.

Prepare an amortization table to calculate the amount of amortization applicable to the first three 6-month periods. For each case, do the following:

1. Calculate the amount of
   (a) interest paid on $100,000 of face value bonds every interest payment date.
   (b) amortization to be recorded at each interest payment date. For convenience, round all calculations to the nearest dollar.

2. (a) Prepare a schedule comparing the financing charge for the first year. For convenience, round all percent calculations to one decimal place.
   (b) Comment on the financing percentage. Which method is most appropriate? Why?

3. Prepare journal entries to record the
   (a) issue of the bonds.
   (b) payment of interest and amortization applicable as of June 30, 19X4.
   (c) payment of interest and amortization applicable as of December 31, 19X4.
   (d) redemption of the bonds at maturity, January 1, 19X6.

Determining issue prices (Q8, Q9, Q12, Q13)

P13-6 Dana's Toy Patch, Inc., was authorized to issue $500,000 of face value bonds.

Date of Authorization	Term	Bond Contract Interest Rate	Interest Payment Dates
January 1, 19X3	5 years	12%	Semiannually on June 30 and December 31

The following transactions occurred during 19X3:

Jan. 31   Issued $500,000 of face value bonds
June 30   Paid the semiannual interest on the issued bonds and made an entry to record straight-line amortization
Dec. 31   Paid the semiannual interest on the issued bonds and made an entry to record amortization

Required

Consider these cases.

Case A: The bonds were issued at a price to yield 12%.
Case B: The bonds were issued at a price to yield the 16% market rate of interest.
Case C: The bonds were issued at a price to yield the 8% market rate of interest.

For each case, do the following:

1. Calculate the
   (a) amount of each semiannual interest payment on the issued bonds.
   (b) issue price of the bonds, consisting of the present value of the bond face value and the present value of the 10 semiannual interest payments to be made during the 5-year period. For convenience, round all calculations to the nearest dollar.
   (c) amount of amortization applicable to each interest payment date. Use the straight-line method; round all calculations to the nearest dollar.

2. Prepare journal entries to record the 19X3 transactions.

ALTERNATE PROBLEMS

Financing decisions: bonds, preferred stock, common stock (Q2)

AP13-1   The financing structure of Dome Sands Corp. is currently as follows:

Current Liabilities	$200,000
Bonds Payable	-0-
Preferred Stock—8%	100,000
Common Stock—50,000 shares	500,000
Retained Earnings	300,000

Management is considering a plant expansion costing $1,000,000. Several different factors have been considered in the selection of a financing method; the effect of alternative financing methods on earnings per common share remains to be analyzed. The following financing methods are being considered: sell $1 million of 12% bonds at face value; or sell another 10,000 common shares at $100 per share. Dome is a profitable growth company and operating income (before interest and tax) is expected to average $200,000 per annum; the income tax rate is 50%.

Required

1. Prepare a schedule to compare the effect on earnings per common share of each of the financing options.

2. Based on earnings per common share, which method is financially advantageous to common stockholders?

3. What other factors should be considered before a final decision is made?

Part A

Straight-line amortization, entries, balance sheet (Q8, Q9)

AP13-2 Mercury Software, Inc., was authorized to issue $500,000 of face value bonds. On January 1, 19X1, the corporation issued $200,000 of face value bonds for $212,000.

Date of Authorization	Term	Bond Contract Interest Rate	Interest Payment Dates
January 1, 19X1	3 years	12%	Semiannually on June 30 and December 31

Required

1. Calculate the amount of
   (a) interest paid every interest payment date.
   (b) amortization to be recorded at each interest payment date. Use the straight-line method.

2. Prepare a schedule, like the one in Exhibit 13-4, to show the effect of premium amortization at each interest payment date. Note that amortization is recorded each time interest expense is recorded.

3. Prepare the journal entries to record the interest and amortization as of June 30, 19X1.

4. Prepare a partial balance sheet showing the bond liability on the following dates:
   (a) December 31, 19X1 (Note that the bonds are a long-term liability on this date, since they will not be redeemed in 19X2.)
   (b) December 31, 19X2 (Note that the bonds are a current liability on this date, since they will be redeemed on January 1, 19X4.)

Part B

Bond sinking fund (Q7)

The bond indenture contained a sinking fund provision requiring equal annual contributions that are transferred to a trustee who guarantees a 10% annual return. Annual contributions are made on December 31, 19X1, 19X2, and 19X3. The amount of the contributions and the 10% revenue in the sinking fund are calculated as follows:

December 31	Annual Contribution	10% Annual Revenue	Annual Total	Fund Balance
19X1	$60,423	-0-	$60,423	$ 60,423
19X2	60,423	$ 6,042 (10% × $ 60,423)	66,465	126,888
19X3	60,423	12,689 (10% × 126,888)	73,112	200,000

Required

5. Prepare journal entries to record the
   (a) annual contribution in each of the three years.
   (b) 10% annual revenue in each of the three years.
   (c) redemption of the bonds at maturity.

6. Show how the annual contribution was determined.

Bonds at par, below par, above par, with entries (Q8, Q9)

AP13-3 Andrew's Computer Corner Corp. was authorized to issue $500,000 of face value bonds. The corporation issued $250,000 of face value bonds on January 1, 19X4.

Date of Authorization	Term	Bond Contract Interest Rate	Interest Payment Dates
January 1, 19X4	3 years	12%	Semiannually on June 30 and December 31

Required

Consider these cases.

Case A: The bonds are issued at face value.
Case B: The bonds are issued for $256,000.
Case C: The bonds are issued for $242,800.

For each case, do the following:

1. Calculate the amount of
   (a) interest paid on the issued bonds every interest payment date.
   (b) amortization, if any, applicable to each interest payment date. Use the straight-line method.

2. Prepare journal entries to record the
   (a) issue of the bonds.
   (b) payment of interest and recording of amortization, if any, on June 30, 19X4.
   (c) payment of interest and recording of amortization, if any, on December 31, 19X4.

3. Calculate the amount of interest expense shown in the income statement as of December 31, 19X4. Is this amount the same as cash paid by Andrew's in 19X4? Why or why not?

4. On December 31, 19X4, the corporation exercised a call feature included in the bond indenture and retired the $250,000 of face value bonds issued January 1, 19X4. The bonds were called at 103. Prepare the December 31 journal entry to record the exercise of the call option.

Amortization table, straight-line, rates (Q8, Q9, Q12)

AP13-4 Maple Leaf Distributors was authorized to issue $500,000 of face value bonds. On January 1, 19X1, the corporation issued $200,000 of face value bonds for $210,152.

Date of Authorization	Term	Bond Contract Interest Rate	Interest Payment Dates
January 1, 19X1	3 years	12%	Semiannually on June 30 and December 31

Required

1. Calculate the amount of
   (a) interest paid every interest payment date.
   (b) amortization to be recorded at each interest payment date. Use the straight-line method.

2. Prepare an amortization table. Note that amortization is recorded each time interest expense is recorded.

3. Calculate the financing percentage under the straight-line method of amortization for each 6-month period. For convenience, round all percentage calculations to one decimal place.

4. Comment on the financing percentage that results in each period. Do you think this financing percentage should vary from period to period? Why or why not?

Straight-line vs. effective interest, entries (Q8, Q9, Q12, Q13)

AP13-5 Jasper, Inc., was authorized to issue $250,000 of face value bonds. These bonds were issued on the authorization date for $216,449. The market rate of interest on the issue date was 16%.

Date of Authorization	Term	Bond Contract Interest Rate	Interest Payment Dates
January 1, 19X1	5 years	12%	Semiannually on June 30 and December 31

Required
Consider these cases.

> Case A: Jasper, Inc., uses the straight-line method of amortization.
> Case B: The company uses the effective interest method of amortization.

Prepare an amortization table to calculate the amount of amortization applicable to the first two 6-month periods. For each case, do the following:

1. Calculate the amount of
   (a) interest paid on the $250,000 of face value bonds every interest payment date.
   (b) amortization to be recorded at each interest payment date. For convenience, round all calculations to the nearest dollar.

2. (a) Prepare a schedule comparing the financing charge for the first year. For convenience, round all percent calculations to one decimal place.
   (b) Comment on the financing percentage. Which method is most appropriate? Why?

3. Prepare journal entries to record the
   (a) issue of the bonds.
   (b) payment of interest and amortization applicable as of June 30, 19X1.
   (c) payment of interest and amortization applicable as of December 31, 19X4.
   (d) redemption of the bonds at maturity, January 1, 19X6.

Determining issue
prices (Q8, Q9, Q12,
Q13)

AP13-6   James's Aluminum Products, Inc., was authorized to issue $1,000,000 of face value bonds.

Date of Authorization	Term	Bond Contract Interest Rate	Interest Payment Dates
January 1, 19X7	3 years	12%	Semiannually on June 30 and December 31

The following transactions occurred during 19X7:

Jan.   1   Issued $100,000 of face value bonds
June 30   Paid the semiannual interest on the issued bonds and made an entry to record straight-line amortization
Dec. 31   Paid the semiannual interest on the issued bonds and made an entry to record amortization

Required
Consider these cases.

> Case A: The bonds were issued at a price to yield 12%.
> Case B: The bonds were issued at a price to yield the 16% market rate of interest.
> Case C: The bonds were issued to yield the 10% market rate of interest.

For each case, do the following:

1. Calculate the
   (a) amount of each semiannual interest payment on the issued bonds.
   (b) issue price of the bonds, consisting of the present value of the bond face value and the present value of the 6 semiannual interest payments to be made during the 3-year period. For convenience, round all calculations to the nearest dollar.

(c) amount of amortization applicable to each interest payment date. Use the straight-line method; round all calculations to the nearest dollar.

2. Prepare journal entries to record the 19X7 transactions.

DECISION PROBLEM

Q8, Q9, Q12

Beaver Products, Inc., which uses effective interest amortization, was authorized to issue $1,000,000 of face value bonds. On January 1, 19X1, Beaver issued $300,000 of face value bonds for $272,263.

Date of Authorization	Term	Bond Contract Interest Rate	Interest Payment Dates
January 1, 19X1	3 years	12%	Semiannually on June 30 and December 31

Required

1. Were the bonds issued at a premium or a discount?
2. Was the market rate of interest above or below the 12% contract rate of interest? Explain.
3. Determine what the market rate of interest must have been for the bonds to sell for $272,263.
4. What is the amount of interest under the straight-line method?
5. What is the amount of interest under the effective interest method for the first interest payment period?
6. Is the difference material?
7. Which method of amortization would you recommend? Why?

ANSWERS TO SELF-TEST QUESTIONS

1. **(b)** As demonstrated in the text, EPS normally increases when debt securities are issued instead of equity securities if the return on investment is greater than the net cost of debt. In this situation, earnings per share would *decrease* if equity securities were issued instead of debt securities.
2. **(a)** It is always better to borrow during a period of inflation. The borrowed dollars will be worth more than the repaid dollars, thereby giving the borrower an unrecognized gain. There must be a proper mix between debt and equity in order to maximize the return to the common stockholders.
3. **(d)** All other things considered equal, when the market rate of interest is the same as the contract or stated rate of interest, the bonds should sell at face value. However, other totally unrelated factors can affect the market price of a bond.
4. **(c)** When bonds are sold at a premium, the issuing corporation receives dollars that do not have to be paid back. These dollars are considered a decrease in the cost of borrowing, rather than a source of income.
5. **(d)** Answer *a* is a true statement regarding straight-line amortization, but straight-line amortization is *not* the best method. The effective interest method is required unless the difference between the two is immaterial.

6. **(a)** The effective interest method results in an increasing amount of amortization whether the bonds were issued at a premium or a discount. If bonds are issued at a discount, the amount of interest *expense* increases, while the amount of cash paid for interest remains constant and below the amount of interest expense, thereby resulting in an increase in amortization. When the bonds are issued at a premium, interest *expense* decreases while the amount of cash paid for interest remains constant and above the amount of interest expense, thereby resulting in an increase in amortization.

7. **(a)** Bonds issued at a discount increase the cost of borrowing. More must be paid back to bondholders than was received. This amount is added to interest paid to arrive at interest expense. The amount of cash paid as interest remains the same, but interest expense increases.

8. **(b)** Bonds issued at a premium decrease the cost of borrowing. Fewer dollars must be paid back than were received. This amount is deducted from interest paid to arrive at interest expense. The amount of cash paid remains the same, but interest expense decreases.

9. **(a)** Table III in the appendix shows the factor for the future value of $1 to be received in 50 years at a constant interest rate of 10% is 117.4. Therefore, the future value of $7,000 would be $7,000 × 117.4 = $821,800.

10. **(c)** Table I in the appendix shows the factor for the present value of $1 to be received in 50 years at an interest rate of 10% is .009. Therefore, the present value of that $1,000,000 your uncle promised to give you when you turned 72 years old is only $9,000.

PART III
FINANCIAL STATEMENT ANALYSIS PROBLEM

Turn to the excerpts (pp. 889–906) from the annual report of United Telecom (UT) for the year ended December 31, 1989, and answer the following questions:

1 What is the par value of UT's common stock? How many shares were outstanding at the end of 1989? 1988?

2 What was the book value per common share at December 31, 1989? 1988? Can you determine the cause of this material change?

3 What entry was made to record the stock dividend? Do you find a conflict between the entry and what was described in Chapter 10?

4 How much of UT's retained earnings is available for dividends? What are the various restrictions on retained earnings?

5 If all the convertible bonds that are outstanding as of December 31, 1989, were converted, what would be the increase in paid-in capital?

6 Did dividends per share change as a result of the stock dividend? Explain.

7 Has UT's issuance of long-term debt increased or decreased over the last three years?

8 Has the retirement of long-term debt increased or decreased over the last three years?

9 What is the lowest interest rate on long-term debt that UT currently has outstanding? What is the highest? Would UT be better off paying the old debt rather than waiting for the bonds to mature?

10 What qualities does the preferred stock have? What advantage do the holders of redeemable preferred shares have over those with nonredeemable shares?

11 Does UT have more debt or more equity financing outstanding? Is this a healthy situation?

PART IV

INVESTING ACTIVITIES

P_{ART} IV investigates the investing activities of an entity. In many cases the major part of these activities consists of the acquisition of long-term assets used in the operation of the business. Because of its close tie with operating activities, accounting for the acquisition and use of long-term assets was discussed in Part II, along with the other operating activities of an entity. The accounting for other investing activities in Part IV includes recording the investment of cash not currently needed for operating or financing activities, and the acquisition of a long-term position in another corporation, either through debt or equity. In Chapters 10, 11, and 13 the issuance of stock and debt instruments was investigated from the point of view of the issuing entity. Chapters 14 and 15 cover accounting issues from the point of view of the investing entity.

In Chapter 14, the relative risk of investing in stocks or bonds will be reviewed, along with accounting issues involved with both short-term and long-term investments in stocks and bonds.

Chapter 15 investigates the accounting issues involved when one corporation invests in enough common shares to exercise control over another corporation. This condition usually exists when more than 50% of the stock is acquired. When this occurs, the two entities are considered one from an economic and accounting point of view. The individual financial statements are combined to reflect one economic entity, rather than two different legal entities.

14 SHORT-TERM AND LONG-TERM INVESTMENT PORTFOLIOS

CORPORATIONS will often invest in securities of another corporation. The reasons are many and varied. On a short-term basis, the main reason may be to utilize idle cash, cash not currently needed but that will be needed in the foreseeable future. Short-term investments are usually made in securities that are readily converted into cash as financing needs or operating needs arise. Common and preferred shares are generally purchased for long-term investments, as are bonds of other corporations. If enough common shares are purchased (more than 50% of the outstanding shares), the investing corporation has effective control over the board of directors and the management of that company. In some cases, significant influence can be exercised over a corporation with substantially less than 50% of the outstanding shares. Chapter 14 investigates problems that arise in accounting for short-term investments in stocks and bonds, as well as long-term investments in bonds and common stock when the degree of control is less than 50%. Chapter 15 investigates situations where control over another corporation exists, and the ensuing necessity of preparing consolidated statements.

After studying Chapter 14, you should be able to answer the following questions:

1 Are debt instruments (bonds) a more secure form of investment than equity instruments (common stock)? Explain. (pp.630–31)

2 What four possible valuation methods may be used to record investments? Give examples of when each may be used. (p.631)

3 What factors determine the classification of investments into short- or long-term portfolios? (pp.631–32)

4 Is it possible an investment in the short-term portfolio could be moved to the long-term portfolio? How about from the long- to short-term portfolio? (p.632)

5 Why are the premiums and discounts on bond investments in the short-term portfolio not amortized? (pp.632–33)

6 Does the application of LCM to stock investments in the short-term portfolio affect net income? Explain. (pp.636–37)

7 Why are stock dividends not considered income to the investor? (p.637)

8 Does the application of LCM to stock investments in the long-term portfolio affect net income? Explain. (pp.640–41)

9 What is the equity method of accounting for investments? Why is it required? (pp.641–42)

10 Why are the premiums and discounts on bond investments in the long-term portfolio amortized? (pp.643–44)

11 Why is the effective interest method of amortization required by GAAP over the straight-line method? (p.651)

THE INVESTMENT DECISION

Every corporate entity is financed by capital transferred to it by stockholders, bondholders, and other creditors. The preceding chapters have viewed stocks and bonds from the point of view of the issuing corporations. This chapter views stocks and bonds from the viewpoint of the *purchasing entity*—the investor who transfers capital into a corporation. Investments in a corporation can take various forms, as shown in Exhibit 14-1.

Q1: Security of investments

No investor is guaranteed against a loss of invested capital if the business entity is unsuccessful. In fact, both share and debt investments can be lost if a corporation becomes bankrupt and assets remain insufficient to be distributed to investors. Alternatively, cash may be insufficient to pay interest to debt investors even when a corporation is not bankrupt. This, in fact, has occurred—for instance, at Chrysler Corporation.

In normal circumstances, bondholders are more secure than stockholders and are able to institute legal action to obtain at least partial repayment of their investment and the interest owed them, even if this would result in the liquidation of the corporation.

Stockholders are unable to force the repayment of their investment, unless the privileges and rights attached to the shares include a redeemable or conversion feature; usually stockholders are also unable to force a corporation to pay dividends. Why, then, would someone wish to invest in shares of a corporation? Several reasons follow.

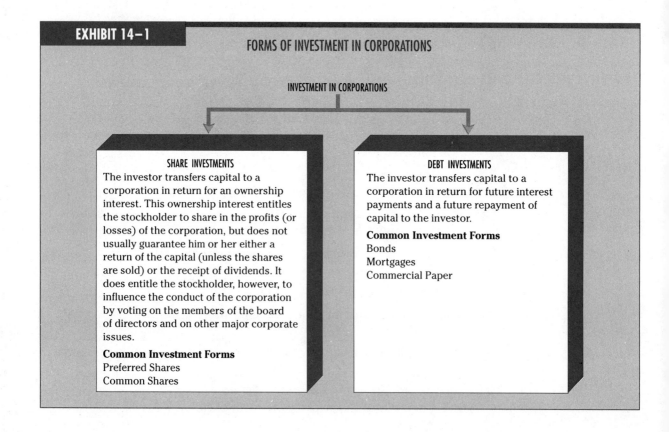

EXHIBIT 14–1

FORMS OF INVESTMENT IN CORPORATIONS

INVESTMENT IN CORPORATIONS

SHARE INVESTMENTS
The investor transfers capital to a corporation in return for an ownership interest. This ownership interest entitles the stockholder to share in the profits (or losses) of the corporation, but does not usually guarantee him or her either a return of the capital (unless the shares are sold) or the receipt of dividends. It does entitle the stockholder, however, to influence the conduct of the corporation by voting on the members of the board of directors and on other major corporate issues.

Common Investment Forms
Preferred Shares
Common Shares

DEBT INVESTMENTS
The investor transfers capital to a corporation in return for future interest payments and a future repayment of capital to the investor.

Common Investment Forms
Bonds
Mortgages
Commercial Paper

1. While it is true that an investor does risk capital, he or she also expects rewards in return. If the corporation is successful, the investor in common stock will increase the value of the investment substantially. This is *capital appreciation.*

2. The investor in common stock has a vote in the running of the corporation. The investor has an opportunity to participate in setting the goals of the corporation.

3. Dividends may be declared by the corporation and may become substantial in relation to the amount of the investor's original investment. If dividends are not declared but are reinvested within the corporation, the value of the investment in common stock should increase.

Valuation of Investments

Four alternate methods are acceptable for the valuation of investments on the balance sheet.

ALTERNATIVE 1: ORIGINAL COST

Q2: Four valuation methods

Investments are reported at their acquisition cost, or **original cost,** which includes the original amount paid, brokerage fees, and any other such costs. Under this method, the market value is disclosed on the balance sheet in parentheses, even if market value declines below cost, provided that the decline is not expected to be permanent. In this method the temporary decline does not appear on the income statement.

ALTERNATIVE 2: LOWER OF COST OR MARKET (LCM)

Under the **lower of cost or market** method, cost is compared with market value of the securities at each balance sheet date, and the lower of the two is used on the balance sheet. The actual asset account is not reduced if market is less than cost. A contra asset account (called a valuation account) is used to recognize a reduction from cost to market. The account is named **Allowance to Reduce Securities to Market.** In this method, the decline may be reported on the income statement as a separate item, or in the Stockholders' Equity section of the balance sheet. The distinction between a short-term and a long-term investment determines where unrealized losses should be reported.

ALTERNATIVE 3: CURRENT MARKET VALUE

The **current market value** as of the balance sheet date is taken as the value of investments, regardless of what cost is. This is not a generally accepted method of valuing these securities and is seldom used in practice, except by some financial institutions, where a majority of the assets are securities in other entities.

ALTERNATIVE 4: EQUITY METHOD

Under the **equity method,** the original investment is recorded at cost, but the investment is increased by the share of *earnings* reported by the issuing corporation, the **investee,** and decreased by any portion of that income distributed in the form of dividends. In this manner, a percentage relationship is maintained between the balance in the investment account and the stockholders' equity of the corporation that had issued the shares. Market value may or may not be disclosed, but the investment is not written down to the market value if market is below the balance in the account.

Q3: Classifying
     investments

Q4: Changing
     portfolios

The various alternatives just reviewed are all used in certain circumstances, depending on the classification of the investment and the intent of management. Investments in securities are generally divided into two categories: the **short-term portfolio** and the **long-term portfolio.** No set number of months, or years for that matter, determines the classification. The reason for making the investment and management's plan of disposal (near future, or sometime in the distant future) are the factors taken into consideration when investments in securities are classified. If management is making the investment in common stock for control purposes or to exercise significant influence over the corporation, the investments will be recorded in the long-term portfolio. Since the intent of management controls the classification, then if the original investment plan changes, the classification of the investment also changes. Securities may be moved from the short-term to the long-term portfolio and vice versa.

Alternative 1, original cost, is used to account for most investments, other than equity securities (common and preferred shares issued by a corporation). These would include investments such as certificates of deposits (similar to savings accounts), money market funds, and like investments. Investments in corporate bonds included in the short-term portfolio are usually valued at cost, while bonds included in the long-term portfolio are valued at cost plus or minus discount or premium amortization.

Alternative 2, LCM, is used to valuate marketable equity securities in both the short- and long-term portfolios when the percentage of shares owned does not allow the investor the ability to exercise significant influence over the operation of that entity.

Alternative 3, current market value, is normally not used. In some particular entities, such as financial institutions whose assets are almost exclusively made up of securities, market value is more appropriate.

Alternative 4, the equity method, is used when one corporation owns enough shares of common stock in another corporation to exercise significant influence over the operation of that corporation.

The next section investigates the problems involved in accounting for securities included in the short-term portfolio, while the third section discusses stock investments included in the long-term portfolio, and the last section examines bonds included in the long-term portfolio.

SHORT-TERM PORTFOLIO INVESTMENTS

Investments included in the short-term portfolio are generally referred to as **marketable securities,** in that they are highly marketable, that is, they can be converted to cash in a relatively short period of time. Most of these investments are made in order to utilize idle cash and are traded on the organized exchanges. As mentioned before, this category can include any number of different types of securities, such as treasury bills, certificates of deposit, money market funds, government funds, private funds, and corporate stocks and bonds. This discussion will be limited to the accounting for stocks and bonds in the short-term portfolio, because no real accounting problems occur with other short-term investments.

Short-term Investments in Bonds

Q5: Short-term bonds
     and amortization

Bonds purchased for short-term purposes do not need amortization of the premium or discount. Remember that from the issuing corporation's point of view, the premium or discount on a bond issue is amortized *over the life* of the issue. The amortization served to increase interest expense in the case of a discount and decrease interest expense in the case of a premium. The amortization period cannot be determined for bonds purchased as a short-term investment, so no amortization is recorded. When bonds are purchased as a long-term investment, the assumption is made that the bonds will be held to maturity. Therefore, amortization is recorded by the investor in the same manner as the issuing corporation. (This accounting is discussed later.)

The purchase price of a bond includes all costs the investor incurred in making the investment. Assume Saguaro Computers, Inc., purchased ten $1,000 bonds at 98, plus brokerage commissions and other fees of $400. The entry to record the investment would be as follows:

| Marketable Securities | 10,200 | |
| Cash | | 10,200 |

Since bonds are quoted in terms of a percentage of face value, 10 bonds selling at 98 would cost $9,800. The total cost should include the costs incurred in the investment; therefore, $9,800 + $400 = $10,200.

Chapter 13 stated that when bonds are issued between interest dates, the *purchaser* must pay the interest accrued since the last payment date. If the bonds in this example were 10% bonds that pay interest semiannually and were sold 3 months after an interest date, $250 ($10,000 × 10% × 3/12) of accrued interest would be paid at the time of purchase. Just as the **payment of accrued interest** to the corporation is not considered part of the proceeds from the sale of the bonds, it is also not considered part of the cost of the investment. An Interest Receivable account is created at the time of purchase. The entry for SCI would be as follows:

Marketable Securities	10,200	
Interest Receivable	250	
Cash		10,450

When the first interest check is received by the investor, it will reflect interest for an entire six-month period, returning to the investor the accrued interest paid at date of purchase. Saguaro's entry to record the receipt of the first interest check of $500 ($10,000 × 5%) would appear as follows:

Cash	500	
Interest Receivable		250
Bond Interest Earned		250

If an accounting year-end occurs between interest payment dates, interest must be accrued for proper matching of revenue and expenses. Assuming the accounting year-end falls two months after an interest payment date, $167 ($10,000 × 10% × 2/12) of interest must be accrued as follows:

| Interest Receivable | 167 | |
| Bond Interest Earned | | 167 |

The entry made when the full six months' interest is received four months into the new year would depend on whether reversing entries were made.

No reversing entries

Cash	500	
Interest Receivable		167
Bond Interest Earned		333

Reversing entries

Cash	500	
Bond Interest Earned		500

When short-term bond investments are sold on an interest date, the interest income is recorded as noted and, in addition, an entry must be made to record the receipt of cash and a gain or loss in the investment. Assuming Saguaro sold the bonds on an interest date for $12,800, less brokerage commissions and other fees of $500, the entry would be as follows:

Cash	12,300	
Marketable Securities		10,200
Gain on Sale of Securities		2,100

If the bonds were sold between interest dates, the purchaser would have to pay the accrued interest. Assuming SCI sold the bonds instead one month after an interest payment date, the accrued interest would be $83 ($10,000 × 10% × 1/12) and the entry would be as follows:

Cash	12,383	
Marketable Securities		10,200
Gain on Sale of Securities		2,100
Bond Interest Earned		83

SHORT-TERM INVESTMENTS IN BONDS AND LCM

Although normally recorded at cost, short-term bond investments may be subjected to lower of cost or market rules. Because current assets are supposed to be the most liquid of a corporation's assets, many financial ratios (Chapter 16) are based on total current assets. If the market price of bonds included in the Current Assets section of a balance sheet (marketable securities) is below cost, and the bonds may be sold in a short period of time, they should be valued at their net realizable value for balance sheet purposes. To value them at their net realizable value has the same affect as valuing them on a LCM basis. If Saguaro's $10,200 bond investment in the last example had a market value of $8,000 on December 31, and the intention was to sell those bonds shortly after the start of the new year, the following entry would be made:

Unrealized Loss on Securities	2,200	
Allowance to Reduce Securities to Market		2,200

Note that the Marketable Securities account is not reduced directly, but a contra-asset account is created to measure the decline. The following would appear on the balance sheet:

Current Assets

Marketable Securities	$10,200	
Less: Allowance to Reduce Securities to Market	(2,200)	$8,000

The Unrealized Loss on Securities account would appear in the income statement for the year ended December 31. When the bonds are sold in the future, the accounting is the same as for the sale of shares of stock under LCM, which is shown next.

Short-term Investments in Stock: No Significant Influence

If an investing corporation owns only 100 shares or 1,000 shares or even 100,000 shares of a very large corporation, it does not have the ability to influence decisions made by the board of directors or management. As the investing corporation owns more and more of the outstanding shares, the likelihood increases that significant influence can be exercised. In that case, the equity method must be used as explained in the third section of this chapter. If significant influence cannot be exercised, the LCM method must be used for accounting.

LOWER OF COST OR MARKET METHOD

Assume SCI purchased 1,000 shares of another corporation's common stock for $7.75 per share, with brokerage commissions and other fees amounting to $250. The total purchase price therefore would be $8,000 ([1,000 × $7.75] + $250), and the entry to record the investment would be as follows:

Marketable Securities	8,000	
Cash		8,000

When cash dividends are received after the investment, the entry is as follows:

Cash	XXX	
Dividend Income		XXX

Since dividends do not accrue, an investor does not have to pay for dividends that theoretically accrue during the period of time between dividend declarations. However, if the investor buys shares of stock after a dividend has been declared, but before the date of record, the market price will reflect the amount of the declared dividend, and that portion of the purchase price should not be included in the cost of the investment. In the last example, if a $.50-per-share dividend had been declared but the date of record had not passed before SCI purchased the 1,000 shares, the entry would be as follows:

Investment in Stock	7,500	
Dividends Receivable	500	
Cash		8,000

When the dividend is received, the entry would be as follows:

Cash	500	
Dividends Receivable		500

The $500 would not be considered as income, but as a return of a portion of the purchase price.

At the end of the accounting period, a comparison must be made between the cost of the stock, $8,000, and the market value of the 1,000 shares. Assuming that their market value is $12,000, the only accounting information that need be disclosed is that fact. If the market value of the shares is only $7,000, then the unrealized loss must be reflected in Saguaro's financial statements. The entry would be as follows:*

Unrealized Loss on Securities	1,000	
Allowance to Reduce Securities		
to Market		1,000

Q6: Stock, LCM, short-term, net income

The entry assumes that the Allowance account had a zero balance before adjustment.

The **Unrealized Loss** account would appear on the income statement in the *other expenses* category. As with bonds, the Allowance account is a contra-asset account subtracted from the asset account Marketable Securities on the balance sheet, and would appear as follows:

Current Assets		
Marketable Securities	$8,000	
Less: Allowance to Reduce Securities to Market	(1,000)	$7,000

Note that historical cost is maintained in the asset account through the use of the Allowance account, and that the loss is *unrealized*. The loss is considered unrealized since no sale has taken place. In order for an actual (realized) loss to be recorded, the securities would have to be sold at the lower price.

When SCI sells the stock in the next accounting period, the entry would be the same as if the account was recorded at cost, rather than LCM. Assuming the shares were sold for $7,000, less brokerage and other fees of $200, the entry would be as follows:

Cash	6,800	
Realized Loss on Sale of Securities	1,200	
Marketable Securities		8,000

Note that the balance in the Allowance account was not taken into consideration when Saguaro recorded the sale of the securities. The Allowance account is adjusted only at the end of the year. In the previous example, the balance in the Allowance account was increased to $1,000; it was assumed that the balance prior to adjustment was zero. Continuing with the example where the shares were subsequently sold for $6,800, if SCI purchases no other securities during the remainder of the year, then the balance in Marketable Securities is zero, and the *desired* balance in the Allowance account is zero. But the balance in the Allowance account is still $1,000 from the entry made at the end of the previous accounting period. To obtain the desired balance of zero, the following entry must be made:

Allowance to Reduce Securities to		
Market	1,000	
Recovery of Unrealized Losses		1,000

The balance in the Allowance account is now zero, and the **Recovery of Unrealized Losses** would be reported on SCI's income statement netted against the Realized Loss account as follows:

---

*If securities of more than one entity were owned, the LCM rule would be applied in the aggregate. This is fully explained in more advanced accounting courses.

Other Expenses

Realized Loss on Sale of Securities	$1,200
Less: Recovery of Unrealized Losses	(1,000)
Net Loss on Securities	$ 200

The end result on the income statements for the two years would be:

Year 1

Unrealized Loss on Securities	$1,000

Year 2

Net Loss on Securities	$ 200

Over the two-year period, Saguaro purchased securities for $8,000 and sold them later for $6,800, leaving a total loss of $1,200, which is exactly what the accounting records show.

EFFECT OF STOCK DIVIDENDS

Q7: Stock dividends and income

Returning to Saguaro's purchase of 1,000 shares for a total of $8,000, assume that SCI receives 100 shares from a stock dividend when the market price of the stock was $12 per share. Theoretically, the total market price of Saguaro's investment should remain the same when a stock dividend is distributed, since no corporate assets have been distributed. If the market value just before the stock dividend is $12,000 (1,000 shares × $12), the market price per share after the distribution should be $10.91 ($12,000 ÷ 1,100 shares). In reality, the market price does not drop proportionately. In fact, as demonstrated in Chapter 11, in many cases the market price does not drop at all. If it does not drop, the market value of the investment would increase to $13,200 (1,100 shares × $12).

No journal entry is made by SCI, however, since no corporate assets were distributed. Saguaro would simply compute a new cost basis for each of the 1,100 shares now held; the new cost basis per share would be $7.27 ($8,000 ÷ 1,100 shares). When the shares are sold in the future, the gain or loss would be measured from the $7.27 per share, rather than the original cost of $8 per share.

The same is true for the investor when a corporation splits the outstanding stock; the investor will have more shares (split) or less shares (reverse split) with the same total cost basis. For instance, if the investor had purchased 1,000 shares for $8 per share, and the stock split 2-for-1, the cost basis per share would be reduced to $4 per share ($8,000 ÷ 2,000 shares). Conversely, if the stock were split on a 1-for-2 basis (reverse split), the investor's cost basis would be increased to $16 per share ($8,000 ÷ 500 shares). For an interesting extension of stock splits, see Real World Example 14-1.

For the effect a stock dividend has on the issuing corporation, review the material on pp. 506–9 in Chapter 11. For the effect a stock split has on the issuing corporation, review the material on pp. 467–69 in Chapter 10.

Short-term Investments in Stock: Significant Influence

Significant influence is usually assumed when a corporation owns more than 20% of the outstanding stock of another corporation. Under normal circumstances, if 20% of the outstanding stock of a corporation is owned by another corporation, the intent of the investing management is to hold that stock on a long-term basis. Therefore, this situation is investigated in the next section.

REAL WORLD EXAMPLE 14-1
A Different Approach to Stock Splits

Splitting a stock into pieces is in the headlines today, with the announcement that Shearson Lehman Hutton Inc. has agreed to try it for several corporations, including American Express Co. and Dow Chemical Co.

But, like sawing the lady in half, it's an old trick.

Americus trusts have been doing it on a small scale since 1983, and on a large scale since 1987. In the Americus arrangement, the type of security called the Score carries the potential for big capital gains or losses. The other part called the Prime contains the right to the stock's stream of dividends, plus certain other benefits. Some $6 billion of Americus trust units are currently outstanding.

Investors in these split-apart securities have discovered that some of them can be as volatile as firecrackers. Americus Scores, which resemble Shearson's new price appreciation certificates, plunged an average of 69% between August 1987 and last week. Over the same period, however, the Primes outperformed the stock market as a whole.

"What we did was separate the most volatile part of a stock from its more conservative attributes," said Joseph Debe, chairman of Americus Shareowner Service Corp. "An investor can buy the part that's most suitable to his requirements. You can blend it any way that you want."

A series of Americus trusts have been sponsored by the company. Currently 26 of them are operating. Ths trusts, which last for five years, work like this:

A shareholder owns 1,000 shares of Dow Chemical. The holder gives those shares to the trust in exchange for 1,000 Dow Chemical Primes and 1,000 Dow Chemical Scores. The underlying stock trades on the New York Stock Exchange.

The Primes and Scores trade on the American Stock Exchange.

Scores, in theory, should be highly volatile, providing chances for big gains or losses. And so far, at least, that's the way it has worked in practice—although the result has been mainly losses because most of the Americus trusts were launched in August 1987, just as the stock market hit its all-time peak.

As a result, holders of Scores have been knocked to the canvas. the worst loss in the period from August 1987 to last week was on Xerox Corp. Scores, which were down 87%. The mildest loss for the period was 29% on Exxon Corp. Scores.

Holders of Primes, on the other hand, have done nicely. On average, Primes have risen 2% since August 1987. The best gain in the Prime category since August 1987 is 22% on the Ford Motor Co. Prime. The biggest loss is 12% on the Prime for Sears, Roebuck & Co.

Over the same period, the 26 common stocks that form the basis for the trusts have declined an average of 20%.

While Primes are a pillow, Scores are a firecracker. Based on one common Wall Street measure of volatility, Primes are about half as volatile as ordinary stock. Scores are about twice as volatile as ordinary stock and four times as volatile as Primes. However, Exxon Score holders have been luckier than most: If they acquired their Scores early enough, they've made more money than Exxon Prime holders have.

There are several differences between the Americus trusts and the new split securities devised by Shearson.

For starters, Shearson's new securities carve up common stock into three pieces, rather than two. Americus Scores are fairly similar to

Shearson's equity appreciation certificates. But the attributes of the Americus Prime will be divided between a bond and a preferred stock.

Another big difference is that the Shearson-designed split securities can't be exchanged for ordinary common stock until some 30 years from now. The Americus trusts are designed to dissolve in five years. And in the meantime, Americus units can be recombined any time and redeemed for shares of common stock.

That means the Shearson-designed securities may sometimes trade at a discount from the value of the underlying common stock, said Peter A. Broms, a senior vice president with Kidder, Peabody & Co. there's precedent for that, he said, in the history of a small group of so-called dual-purpose mutual funds that separate a portfolio's capital appreciation from its dividend flow and allow investors to choose one or the other.

The tax treatment is also different. When investors traded in shares for Americus units, it didn't trigger a tax on any appreciation in the stock up to that point. But Congress has since changed the rules. So individual investors buying the new securities may trigger a capital gain or loss for tax purposes.

All of these differences, along with the relatively short history of the Americus trusts, make it hard to predict exactly how Shearson's new stock fragments will behave in the market. But the investors' experience with Americus trusts suggests that they will lend themselves to various trading strategies.

For example, Patrick J. James, a senior associate with the San Diego money management partnership Rice Hall James & Associates, converted 10,000 shares of Merck & Co. into Americus units on behalf of a Midwest university endowment fund. Mr James sold off all the Scores, and used the proceeds to buy extra Primes. That increased the income from the holding about 40%, while insulating the account, as it turned out, from an 18% drop in the value of the common stock. Primes, however, will decline if the underlying common drops far enough.

Mr. James did similar maneuvers with several other Americus trusts for other clients, though in most cases he sold off only 30% or 40% of the Scores. Now he's considering repurchasing some Scores at lower prices. Indeed, as he noted, many Scores are still selling below the prices at which they traded right after the October 1987 stock market crash.

Another strategy, which Kidder's Mr. Broms likes, is to buy Scores along with a zero-coupon bond. Zero-coupon bonds pay no interest. Instead, they're issued at a deep discount to their face value, and investors' gains come from the difference between that discounted price and the face value they receive at maturity.

The combination of Scores and zero-coupon bonds can assure the investor of at least breaking even over a period of 3½ years. For example, an investor could buy a zero-coupon bond for $700 and Scores for $300. At maturity, the bond would pay $1,000, assuring the investor of coming out even. And if the stock soars, the Score will do even better. The tandem, however, underperforms the common stock if the stock price rises but doesn't really soar.

Many other fancy maneuvers have also been tried with Americus units, and more will doubtless be invented for Shearson's new units. Said Mr. Debe, "Imitation is the sincerest form of flattery."

Source From "Splitting Up Stocks Offers One Way to Score Volatility," John R. Dorfman, *Wall Street Journal,* December 6, 1988. Reprinted by permission of *Wall Street Journal,* © 1988 Dow Jones & Company, Inc. All Rights Reserved Worldwide.

LONG-TERM PORTFOLIO INVESTMENTS: STOCK

No Significant Influence

It is not uncommon for one corporation to own shares in another corporation on a long-term basis, even where no significant influence exists. If a corporation cannot exercise significant influence but management intends to hold the stock as a long-term investment (as opposed to utilizing idle cash), then the investment will be carried in the long-term portfolio, and accounted for under the LCM method used for the short-term portfolio.

The major difference between the LCM rules for long- and short-term portfolios is the reporting of the Unrealized Loss account created at the end of the year when the market value of the stock holdings is below cost. In the previous section, when the total cost was compared with the total market value of Saguaro's short-term portfolio, the following entry was made:

Unrealized Loss on Securities	1,000	
Allowance to Reduce Securities		
to Market		1,000

If that investment were considered long-term, the entry would be as follows:

Unrealized Loss on Securities		
(long-term)	1,000	
Allowance to Reduce Securities		
to Market (long-term)		1,000

Q8: Stock, LCM, long-term, net income

The most important difference is *not* the addition of "long-term" to the account titles, but the reporting of the Unrealized Loss account. When LCM is applied to the long-term portfolio, the unrealized loss is reported as an element of *stockholders' equity* on the balance sheet and does not affect net income. The main reason for this is that if the investment is held for long-term purposes, it is unlikely the investment will be sold in the near future at the depressed market price. In fact, when the securities are eventually sold, they could be sold at a substantial *gain or loss.* Therefore, net income should not be affected by decreases in the market value during the term of the long-term investments.

The Allowance account is adjusted annually, and assuming SCI sold the shares during the next year for $6,800, the desired balance in the Allowance account would be zero, and the following entry would be made at the end of the second year:

Allowance to Reduce Securities to		
Market (long-term)	1,000	
Unrealized Loss on Securities		
(long-term)		1,000

Note that the entry is merely a reversal of the entry creating the loss and allowance accounts. The income statement is unaffected.

The entry to record the sale of the shares would be exactly like the short-term assumption, except for the name of the credit account, as follows:

Cash	6,800	
Realized Loss on Sale of Securities	1,200	
Long-term Investments		8,000

The credit account here is Long-term Investments; the account could have been named Investment in Stock, or simply Investments. In this text, the title of the account will be Long-term Investments to differentiate it from short-term investments, which were recorded in the Marketable Securities account. Those investments could have been recorded in a Short-term Investments account.

Note that the income statement was not affected the year the securities were purchased, but a $1,200 realized loss was reported on the income statement the year the securities were sold, for a total loss of $1,200, as was the case for the short-term investment. The difference lies in the fact that with the short-term assumption, $1,000 of the loss was reported in the year of purchase, and a net loss of $200 was reported in the year of sale.

Significant Influence

Q9: Equity method

If the investing corporation can exercise significant influence, then the *equity method* must be used. Depending on the size of the issuing corporation, and how closely (very few stockholders) the stock is held, owning as little as 5% could allow the stockholder to exercise significant influence over the entity. On the other hand, owning as much as 49% in a very closely held corporation could prevent the stockholder from exercising any influence. As noted, it is generally assumed that holding 20% or more of the outstanding stock of a corporation allows the stockholder to exercise influence and thereby requires the use of the equity method of accounting. If it can be shown that the 20% holdings do not allow the ability to exercise influence, then the investment would be accounted for under LCM.

Under the equity method, a percentage relationship is maintained between the balance in the investment account and the stockholders' equity of the firm issuing the securities. In order to do so, the investment is first recorded at its original cost, but then the investment account is increased by the stockholders' share of the reported net income. Assume Saguaro Computers, Inc., owns 30% of the outstanding stock of a company that reports $100,000 of net income. The entry under the equity method would be as follows:

Long-term Investments	30,000	
Equity in Earnings of Investee		30,000

This entry increases the balance in the Long-Term Investments account by the same amount that the owners' share of the retained earnings increases as the result of earnings for the current year. The entry also records on the income statement, in the **Equity in Earnings of Investee** account, the investor's share of earnings for the year.

The investment account must be decreased by any dividends paid during the current year, since dividends are considered distributions of current net income. If the dividends paid during the year by the same corporation amounted to $60,000, SCI would make the following entry to record the dividends received as the 30% stockholder:

Cash	18,000	
Long-term Investments		18,000

Note that the dividends are not considered income since they are deemed to be paid out of current earnings, and current earnings were recorded as the stockholders' share of net income, as shown earlier. If Saguaro were to record the dividend distribution as income, that amount of income then would be recorded as a credit twice, once as a share of earnings, and again as a distribution of those earnings.

When investments carried under the equity method are sold, the entry is identical to those for other stock and bond investments. Assuming the balance in the same investment account is $378,000 at the time SCI sells the shares for $589,000, the entry would be as follows:

Cash	589,000	
Long-term Investments		378,000
Gain on Sale of Securities		211,000

If the degree of ownership in the issuing corporation should decrease through the sale of partial interests, and the stockholder can no longer exercise significant influence, the investment should be accounted for using LCM again.

Actual Control

When one corporation owns more than 50% of another's outstanding stock, control is said to exist. Under normal circumstances, the stockholder who owns more than 50% of the voting stock can control the membership on the board of directors, thereby controlling the entity. When this takes place, it is assumed that only one *economic entity* exists, even though two *legal entities* actually exist. This is more obvious when it is assumed one corporation owns 100% of the outstanding stock of another corporation. In reality, only the stockholders of the corporation owning the 100% interest exist, leaving only one entity in an economic sense.

When actual control exists, the financial statements are mechanically combined into one set of statements referred to as **consolidated financial statements.** This topic is discussed in Chapter 15.

LONG-TERM PORTFOLIO INVESTMENTS: BONDS

The accounting for long-term investments in bonds is essentially the reverse of the accounting required by the bond issuer described in Chapter 13. The accounting for the long-term investments in bonds is similar to the accounting for short-term investments in bonds and the receipt of interest; the only exception is the accounting for the amortization of premiums and discounts.

Purchase Cost of Bonds

Investments in bonds are always recorded at cost; *cost* includes brokerage charges and any other applicable acquisition costs. The purchase price is affected by such factors as risk and the rate of inflation, but is largely determined by how investors view the bond contract interest rate in relation to the prevailing market interest rate.

1. If the bond contract interest rate is the same as that required in the market, then the bonds are usually purchased at par.

2. If the bond contract interest rate is greater than that required in the market, then the bonds are usually purchased at a premium (more than face value) to yield the investor the lower market rate.

3. If the bond contract interest rate is less than that required in the market, then the bonds are usually purchased at discount (less than face value) to yield the investor the higher market rate.

The sale of bonds by Saguaro Computers, Inc., is illustrated in Chapter 13. The same data are used here as an example of an investor's purchase of these 12%, 3-year, $100,000 bonds paying interest semiannually on June 30 and December 31 of each year. Their purchase at a premium and a discount is shown:

Purchased at a Premium			Purchased at a Discount		
Investment in Bonds	106,000		Investment in Bonds	88,000	
Cash		106,000	Cash		88,000

Note that the cost of the purchase is recorded at cost; no separate discount or premium account is required. (Other applicable costs were not included in this example.) The account title Investment in Bonds will be used in this section of the chapter to identify the type of investment. In practice, all long-term investments would be recorded in one account, either titled Investments or Long-term Investments, with a subsidiary ledger identifying each type of investment.

Amortizing Premiums and Discounts

Q10: Amortizing bond premiums, discounts

In practice, the amount of premium or discount is amortized over the life remaining from the purchase date of the bond. It is also accepted practice to record amortization each time a journal entry is made to record interest earned. Therefore, where bond interest earned is recorded, an appropriate amount of amortization is also recorded. The periodically recorded amortization will change the carrying value of the investment (see Exhibit 14-2).

When the bond is redeemed at maturity, the following journal entry is recorded:

19X4			
Jan. 4	Cash	100,000	
	Investment in Bonds		100,000
	To record retirement of Saguaro Computers, Inc., bond.		

The balance in the Investment in Bonds account is reduced (or increased) to face value at maturity; this entry reduces the balance in that account to zero.

The straight-line method of amortization is used in the following examples to demonstrate the application of GAAP. Remember from Chapter 13 that the **effective interest method** of amortization is required if the results are materially different from the results under straight-line. The effective interest method will be demonstrated again at the end of this section. Under the straight-line method, an equal amount of amortization is allocated to each semiannual period. The simplicity of calculation is this method's main advantage. The amortization is calculated as follows:

Amortization of a Premium			**Amortization of a Discount**	
Premium is	$6,000		Discount is	$12,000
Months left are	36		Months left are	36
Months amortized	6		Months amortized	6

Calculation   *Calculation*

($6,000 ÷ 36) × 6 = $1,000   ($12,000 ÷ 36) × 6 = $2,000

AMORTIZING PREMIUMS IN INVESTOR'S BOOKS

In practice, the bond premium is commonly amortized using the straight-line method over the life of the bonds, until no premium remains at maturity. As noted, it is accepted practice to record an appropriate amount of premium amortization each time a journal entry is made to record interest. The amount of amortization applicable to each interest receipt period is calculated as follows:

$6,000 Premium ÷ 3 Years ÷ 2 Interest Payments per Year
= $1,000 Amortization per Interest Period

The journal entries to record the receipt of interest and the appropriate amortization are as follows:

Receipt of Interest			**Amortization of Premium**	
Cash	6,000		Bond Interest Earned	1,000
Bond Interest Earned		6,000	Investment in Bonds	1,000

This entry decreases the investment account and also the bond interest earned. The interest rate is therefore lower than the 12% bond interest rate.

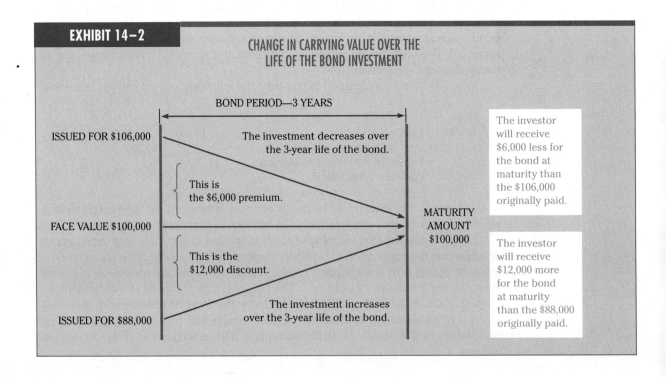

EXHIBIT 14–2

CHANGE IN CARRYING VALUE OVER THE LIFE OF THE BOND INVESTMENT

BOND PERIOD—3 YEARS

ISSUED FOR $106,000

The investment decreases over the 3-year life of the bond.

This is the $6,000 premium.

FACE VALUE $100,000

MATURITY AMOUNT $100,000

This is the $12,000 discount.

The investment increases over the 3-year life of the bond.

ISSUED FOR $88,000

The investor will receive $6,000 less for the bond at maturity than the $106,000 originally paid.

The investor will receive $12,000 more for the bond at maturity than the $88,000 originally paid.

Similar entries are made each June 30 and December 31 until the SCI bonds mature in three years. Bond interest earned is usually recorded in a separate general ledger account. Note that premium amortization *reduces* the bond interest earned; the yield to the investor is less than the bond contract interest rate, in this case. In contrast, the discount amortization *increases* the bond interest earned, thereby increasing, in excess of the bond contract interest rate, the yield to the investor.

In these examples, the December 31 interest date coincides with the investor corporation's year-end. Therefore, no adjustment for bond interest earned is required at year-end. When the interest payment date does not coincide with the fiscal year-end, an adjusting journal entry is required at December 31 for the interest earned until that date and for the appropriate amount of amortization. The adjusting entry accruing interest to December 31 requires a debit to Bond Interest Receivable and a credit to Bond Interest earned.

The recording of amortization during the three-year life of the bond issue is shown in Exhibit 14-3. Study the effect of premium amortization on both the Investment in Bonds and the Bond Interest Earned accounts. Note that the amortization reduces the balance in the investment account to its face value of $100,000.

The amount of premium has been amortized from the date of purchase to the date of maturity. If no amortization had been recorded, the amount of premium

---

EXHIBIT 14–3

EFFECT OF PREMIUM AMORTIZATION ON INVESTOR'S ACCOUNTS

19X1		Investment in Bonds	Cash Interest Received	Actual Annual Interest Earned
Jan. 1	Purchase of Bonds	+$106,000		
June 30	Interest Received		+$6,000	
	Premium Amortization	− 1,000		$10,000
Dec. 31	Interest Received		+ 6,000	
	Premium Amortization	− 1,000		
	Balance	$104,000	$12,000	$10,000
19X2				
June 30	Interest Received		+$6,000	
	Premium Amortization	− 1,000		$10,000
Dec. 31	Interest Received		+ 6,000	
	Premium Amortization	− 1,000		
	Balance	$102,000	$12,000	$10,000
19X3				
June 30	Interest Received		+$6,000	
	Premium Amortization	− 1,000		$10,000
Dec. 31	Interest Received		+ 6,000	
	Premium Amortization	− 1,000		
	Balance	$100,000	$12,000	$10,000
19X4				
Jan. 1		− 100,000		
		-0-		

would be recognized as a loss in the accounting period during which the bonds mature. Such a loss would reflect only the failure to adjust the Bond Interest Earned account in earlier accounting periods.

AMORTIZING BOND DISCOUNTS IN INVESTOR'S BOOKS

The discount is amortized by periodic *debits* to the Investment in Bonds account and *credits* to Bond Interest Earned. Since interest is paid every six months, the periodic amortization is recorded as follows:

$$\$12,000 \text{ Discount} \div 3 \text{ Years} \div 2 \text{ Interest Payments per Year}$$
$$= \$2,000 \text{ Amortization per Interest Period}$$

Amortization is recorded every time bond interest expense is entered in the books:

Receipt of Interest			Amortization of Discount		
Cash	6,000		Investment in Bonds	2,000	
Bond Interest Earned		6,000	Bond Interest Earned		2,000

The debit to the investment account increases the amount of the investment recorded in the books; the credit to Bond Interest Earned represents additional interest earned over the 12% bond interest rate.

The recording of amortization during the three-year life of the bond is shown in Exhibit 14-4. Study the effect of the discount amortization on both the Investment in Bonds and the Bond Interest Earned accounts.

Interest received by the terms of the bond contract amounted to $12,000 per year; however, the interest earned was actually $16,000 per year. This additional interest usually compensates for the unfavorable bond interest rate in relation to the rate required in the securities market for this type of bond.

Study the following ledger accounts, which illustrate this increase over the first year of the bonds' term:

	Investment in Bonds		Bond Interest Earned	
The investment	88,000			6,000
account is increased	2,000			2,000
each interest period				6,000
by amortization.	2,000			2,000
	92,000			16,000

In the case of bonds purchased at a discount, bond interest earned consists of the 12% bond rate plus the amortized discount. Whenever an investor purchases bonds for less than face value, the investor's total interest earned is increased because of the discount amortization.

COMPARISON OF RECORDING BY THE BOND INVESTOR AND THE ISSUER

The following comparison of entries on the books of the investor and the issuer (pp. 647–48) illustrates the accounting for bonds. The comparison stresses the fact that the accounting for the investor is virtually the **mirror image** of the accounting for the issuer.

EXHIBIT 14–4

EFFECT OF DISCOUNT AMORTIZATION ON INVESTOR'S ACCOUNTS

19X1		Investment in Bonds	Cash Interest Received	Actual Annual Interest Earned
Jan. 1	Purchase of Bonds	+$ 88,000		
June 30	Interest Received		+$6,000	
	Discount Amortization	+ 2,000		$16,000
Dec. 31	Interest Received		+ 6,000	
	Discount Amortization	+ 2,000		
	Balance	$ 92,000	$12,000	$16,000
19X2				
June 30	Interest Received		+$6,000	
	Discount Amortization	+ 2,000		$16,000
Dec. 31	Interest Received		+ 6,000	
	Discount Amortization	+ 2,000		
	Balance	$ 96,000	$12,000	$16,000
19X3				
June 30	Interest Received		+$6,000	
	Discount Amortization	+ 2,000		$16,000
Dec. 31	Interest Received		+ 6,000	
	Discount Amortization	+ 2,000		
	Balance	$100,000	$12,000	$16,000
19X4				
Jan. 1		– 100,000		
		-0-		

	Transaction	Recorded by the Investor		
19X1				
Jan. 1	Investor purchases SCI's $100,000 of bonds at 106.	Investment in Bonds Cash	106,000	106,000

June 30	SCI pays semiannual interest on bond. The bond premium is amortized for 6 months.	Cash
		  Bond Interest Earned
		Bond Interest Earned
		  Investment in Bonds
			6,000
			
			1,000
				
				6,000
				
				1,000

Dec. 31	SCI pays semiannual interest on bond. The bond premium is amortized for 6 months.	Cash
		  Bond Interest Earned
		Bond Interest Earned
		  Investment in Bonds
			6,000
			
			1,000
				
				6,000
				
				1,000

Recorded by the Issuer (SCI)

19X1

Jan. 1	Cash	106,000	
	Bonds Payable		100,000
	Premium on Bonds		6,000
June 30	Bond Interest Expense	6,000	
	Cash		6,000
	Premium on Bonds	1,000	
	Bond Interest Expense		1,000
Dec. 31	Bond Interest Expense	6,000	
	Cash		6,000
	Premium on Bonds	1,000	
	Bond Interest Expense		1,000

Note the mirror image is true throughout the analysis, aside from the fact that the issuing corporation normally uses a separate premium or discount account, while the investing corporation simply debits the cost of the investment to the asset account without setting up separate accounts. The investor could use separate accounts just as well as the issuing corporation could not use separate accounts.

Effective Interest Method: Long-term Bond Investments

It might help students to review this section and the Chapter 13 appendix before studying this application of the effective interest method. Remember that the price of bonds is influenced by the market interest rate and how it compares with the stated interest rate on the bond itself. The stated rate does not change over the life of the bond, but the market rate can change daily.

BONDS ISSUED AT A DISCOUNT

Since bond investors are purchasing the right to receive two future cash flows, an annual or semiannual interest payment and a one-time return of principal when the bond matures, the purchase price approximates the present value of each of these flows. Taking the example of SCI's 12%, semiannual 3-year bond issue of $100,000 that sold at a discount for $88,000, what market interest rate approximates the $88,000 selling price? The calculations follow. The present value of the following two flows must be determined: $6,000 received each of the next six 6-month periods and $100,000 received at the end of the six 6-month periods.

Assuming a 16% market interest rate

$$1/2 \times 16\% = 8\% \text{ semiannually}$$

$$\$6,000 \times 4.623 \text{ (present value of 6 payments at 8\%)} = \$27,738$$

$$\$100,000 \times .630 \text{ (present value of one payment at 8\%)} = \$63,000$$

$$\$27,738 + \$63,000 = \$90,738$$

If the bonds sold for $88,000, and the present value of the two flows totals $90,738, then the market interest rate must be higher than 16%.

EXHIBIT 14-5

Investment of $100,000, 12% Bonds for $86,516
Amortization Table
Using Market Interest Rate of 18%

Period 19X1	A Bond Carrying Value	B (1/2 × 18% × A) Effective Interest at 9%	C 6% Interest Received	D (B − C) Discount Amortization	E (A − D) Bond Carrying Value
Jan. 1	$86,516				
June 30	86,516	$7,786	$6,000	$1,786	$ 88,302
Dec. 31	88,302	7,947	6,000	1,947	90,249
19X2					
June 30	90,249	8,122	6,000	2,122	92,371
Dec. 31	90,371	8,313	6,000	2,313	94,684
19X3					
June 30	94,684	8,521	6,000	2,521	97,205
Dec. 31	97,213	8,795*	6,000	2,795	100,000

*Increased by $47 for rounding errors.

Assuming an 18% market interest rate

$1/2 \times 18\% = 9\%$ semiannually

$6,000 \times 4.486$ (present value of 6 payments at 9%) = $26,916

$100,000 \times .596$ (present value of one payment at 9%) = $59,600

$26,916 + $59,600 = $86,516

If the bonds sold for $88,000 and the present value of the future flows totals $86,516, then the market interest rate must be less than 18%. Therefore, the market interest rate is somewhere between 16% and 18%. Rather than use a fractional interest rate, assume the bonds sold at a discount for $86,516 (rather than for $88,000) with a market rate of 18% for the purpose of discussing amortization under the effective interest method.

First of all, an amortization table must be constructed. See Exhibit 14-5. The journal entries to record the receipt of the semiannual interest can easily be made from the amortization table. The entry to record the receipt of the June 30, 19X1, interest would appear as follows:

Cash	6,000	
Investment in Bonds	1,786	
Bond Interest Earned		7,786

Note that the transaction is recorded in a compound entry. This is usually the case when applying the effective interest method because the amount of amortization is dependent on and derived from the amount of interest income recorded and the amount of cash received. Under the straight-line method, the amount of amortization is calculated directly and then added to interest income. The compound entry could have been made into separate entries, as follows:

Cash	6,000	
Bond Interest Earned		6,000
Investment in Bonds	1,786	
Bond Interest Earned		1,786

The entries for each interest payment would be recorded either way, taking the information from the amortization table. For instance, the final interest payment would be recorded as follows:

Cash	6,000	
Investment in Bonds	2,795	
Bond Interest Earned		8,795

After the last entry is posted to the Investment in Bonds account, the account should have a balance of $100,000, and the following entry is made on maturity date:

Cash	100,000	
Investment in Bonds		100,000

BONDS ISSUED AT A PREMIUM

In the example used for straight-line amortization, SCI's $100,000 bonds were also assumed to sell at a premium for $106,000. For the effective interest method, a market interest rate that approximates $106,000 must be determined. Start by assuming a rate *below* the contract interest rate of 12%.

Assuming a 10% market interest rate

$1/2 \times 10\% = 5\%$ semiannually

$6,000 \times 5.076$ (present value of 6 payments at 5%) = $30,456

$100,000 \times .746$ (present value of one payment at 5%) = $74,600

$30,456 + $74,600 = $105,056

These calculations prove that the actual market rate of interest is a little above the 10% rate, but rather than use fractional interest rates, assume the bonds sold for $105,056 (rather than for $106,000).

First an amortization table must be constructed. See Exhibit 14-6. The journal entries to record the receipt of the semiannual interest can easily be made from the amortization table. The entry to record the receipt of the June 30, 19X1, interest would appear as follows:

Cash	6,000	
Investment in Bonds		747
Bond Interest Earned		5,253

Note that the transaction is recorded in a compound entry, as was shown for the discount amortization. The compound entry could have been made into separate entries, as follows:

Cash	6,000	
Bond Interest Earned		6,000
Bond Interest Earned	747	
Investment in Bonds		747

EXHIBIT 14–6

Investment of $100,000, 12% Bonds for $105,056
Amortization Table
Using Market Interest Rate of 10%

Period 19X1	A Bond Carrying Value	B $(1/2 \times 10\% \times A)$ Effective Interest at 5%	C 6% Interest Received	D $(C - B)$ Premium Amortization	E $(A - D)$ Bond Carrying Value
Jan. 1	$105,056				
June 30	105,056	$5,253	$6,000	$747	$104,309
Dec. 31	104,309	5,215	6,000	785	103,524
19X2					
June 30	103,524	5,176	6,000	824	102,700
Dec. 31	102,700	5,135	6,000	865	101,835
19X3					
June 30	101,835	5,092	6,000	908	100,927
Dec. 31	100,927	5,073*	6,000	927	100,000

*Increased by $27 for rounding errors.

The entries for the rest of the interest payments would be recorded either way, using the amortization schedule. The final interest payment would be recorded as follows:

Cash	6,000	
Investment in Bonds		927
Bond Interest Earned		5,073

After the last entry is posted to the Investment in Bonds account, the account should have a balance of $100,000, and the following entry is made on maturity date:

Cash	100,000	
Investment in Bonds		100,000

Q11: Effective interest and GAAP

The effective interest method is required under GAAP because it reflects the actual interest rate being earned by the investor on the investment, given the purchase price and the bonds' stated rate of interest. The straight-line method may still be used, however, as long as the results under the straight-line method are not materially different from the results under the effective interest method.

CHAPTER REVIEW

1 Are debt instruments (bonds) a more secure form of investment than equity instruments (common stock)? Explain. (pp. 630–31)

Since the principal portion of debt instruments has a due date, and the interest on debt instruments must be paid, it is said that bonds are a more secure form of investments. Dividends do not have to be distributed as with shares, and when everything is said and done, no assets may be available for distribution to equity security holders, especially common stockholders. However, no laws guarantee that a company in trouble will be able to pay the interest on bonds, or to retire the debt when it comes due.

2 What four possible valuation methods may be used to record investments? Give examples of when each may be used. (p. 631)

Original cost, lower of cost or market (LCM), current market value, and the equity method all have been used to valuate investments in securities.

Cost is generally used with most investments classified in the short-term portfolio. The major exception to the rule is investments in common stock where significant influence cannot be exercised on the investee. In this case LCM is applied to the investment.

Investments in stock, both short- and long-term, are carried under the lower of cost or market method if significant influence cannot be exercised. LCM also can be applied to an investment carried in the short-term portfolio if the net realizable value is below cost.

Current market value is used in some specialized industries where a major part of a company's assets consists of investments in securities traded on the various markets.

The equity method is used to record investments in common stock where the percentage owned is sufficient to exercise significant influence over the operation of the issuing corporation.

3 What factors determine the classification of investments into short- or long-term portfolios? (pp. 631–32)

The intent of management is the overriding factor in the classification of investments. If idle cash is invested, the securities are normally carried in the short-term portfolio. Other investments made to control or to exert influence over the operations of another corporation are carried in the long-term portfolio.

4 Is it possible an investment in the short-term portfolio could be moved to the long-term portfolio? How about from the long- to short-term portfolio? (p. 632)

Yes, investments can be moved both ways. Since management's intent is the major deciding factor, when the intent changes, the classification can change.

5 Why are the premiums and discounts on bond investments in the short-term portfolio not amortized? (pp. 632–33)

Premiums and discounts are amortized by the *issuing* corporation over the time the bonds will be outstanding, which generally means from date of issue to the maturity date, a determinable period of time. If the bonds are being held as a short-term investment, no time over which to amortize the premium or discount can be determined.

6 Does the application of LCM to stock investments in the short-term portfolio affect net income? Explain. (pp. 636–37)

Yes. When LCM is applied to the short-term portfolio, unrealized losses and their recovery are considered income statement accounts and directly affect the measurement of net income.

7 Why are stock dividends not considered income to the investor? (p. 637)

Since no corporate assets have been distributed to the investor, income cannot be measured. The investor simply calculates a new cost basis by spreading the total original investment over a greater number of shares.

8 Does the application of LCM to stock investments in the long-term portfolio affect net income? Explain. (pp. 640–41)

> No, temporary changes in the market should not affect net income if the investments are considered long-term—that is, not to be sold in the foreseeable future. Unrealized losses are treated as an element of stockholders' equity rather than as an income statement item.

9 What is the equity method of accounting for investments? Why is it required? (pp. 641–42)

> The equity method of accounting for investments is used when the investor can exercise significant influence over the operation of the issuing corporation. It records as an increase in the investment account the investor's share of the net income reported by the issuing corporation, and records as a decrease in the investment account any of that net income distributed in the form of dividends. In doing so, a percentage relationship is maintained between the balance in the investment account and the total stockholders' equity. The intention is that if the investor can exercise significant influence, this relationship should be maintained since the investment account does in fact represent an interest in the stockholders' equity of the issuing corporation.

10 Why are the premiums and discounts on bond investments in the long-term portfolio amortized? (pp. 643–44)

> They are amortized for the same reason they are amortized by the issuing company—to adjust the interest being earned to reflect a more realistic amount. If the bonds are considered a long-term investment, the assumption is that management will hold the bonds until maturity. If this is the case, then the premiums and discounts are really an adjustment to the amount of interest earned over the life of the bond.

11 Why is the effective interest method of amortization required by GAAP over the straight-line method? (p. 651)

> The effective interest method determines the exact interest rate being earned on the investment and then uses this rate to record interest earned. As explained in Chapter 13, under the straight-line method, the amount of interest recorded as earned is constant, but when compared to the balance in the investment account, the rate is actually either increasing or decreasing, depending on whether the investment was made at a premium or a discount.

KEY TERMS

Allowance to Reduce Securities to Market (p. 631)   A valuation account under the lower of cost or market method of valuing securities used to indirectly reduce the valuation of securities when the market price is below cost. The asset account is not reduced directly.

consolidated financial statements (p. 642)   Two or more sets of financial statements combined when one corporation owns from 51% to 100% of another corporation and is presumed to have control over that corporation. Such control from an economic viewpoint results in only one company.

current market value (p. 631)   A valuation method used for investments in securities. The investment is adjusted annually to its current value, whether that value is above *or* below the investment cost. It is used in some industries where a majority of the assets are securities in other entities.

effective interest method (p. 643)   A method of amortizing the premium or discount on a long-term investment in bonds that results in a constant rate of interest reported as earned over the life of the investment.

Equity in Earnings of Investee (p. 641)   The name of the account on the income statement that results from the application of the equity method. The balance in the account represents the owners' share of the reported earnings of the investee.

equity method (p. 631)   A method of accounting for investments applied when the investor has sufficient ownership interest to exercise significant influence over the corporation. Under the method, a relationship is maintained between the balance in the investment account and the investor's share of the stockholders' equity of the corporation.

investee (p. 631)   The term applied to the corporation over which an investor has the ability to exercise significant influence.

long-term portfolio (p. 632)   Investment securities that management does not intend to liquidate in the near future.

lower of cost or market (LCM) (p. 631)   A method of valuating equity securities held in either short-term or long-term portfolios when significant influence cannot be exercised on the issuing corporation.

marketable securities (p. 632)   The term usually applied to securities convertible to cash in a short time period and traded on the organized exchanges across the nation and around the world.

mirror image (p. 646)   A term applied to the accounting for bonds by the investor and the issuing corporation. One is a mirror image of the other.

original cost (p. 631)   A valuation method for investments in securities. The investments are reported at their acquisition cost, and current market values may be disclosed. No entry is made to write the investment up or down to current market value.

payment of accrued interest (p. 633)   A phrase used to describe the fact that bond investors must pay at the time the bond is purchased the interest that has accrued on a bond since the last interest payment date. The amount is returned to the investor on the next interest date, when the investor is paid for a full six months' interest.

Recovery of Unrealized Losses (p. 636)   The account title used when the Allowance to Reduce Securities to Market account must be decreased when applying LCM to equity securities in the short-term portfolio.

short-term portfolio (p. 631)   Investment securities that management intends to liquidate in the near future.

Unrealized Loss (p. 636)   The account title used when the Allowance to Reduce Securities to Market account must be increased when applying LCM to equity securities in the short-term portfolio. The loss is considered unrealized since no sale has taken place. In order for an actual (realized) loss to be recorded, the securities would have to be sold at the lower price.

SELF-TEST QUESTIONS FOR REVIEW   (Answers are at the end of this chapter.)

Q7

1. The declaration and distribution of a stock dividend that does not affect the market price of the stock will
    (a) increase the balance in the stock investment account.
    (b) decrease the balance in the stock investment account.
    (c) increase the cost allocated to each share.
    (d) decrease the cost allocated to each share.
    (e) None of the above

Q5, Q10

2. If an issuing corporation's bonds are selling in the market at an amount in excess of 100, it indicates that
   (a) the bonds are selling for more than $100.
   (b) good news has influenced the market price.
   (c) the bonds carry an interest rate above the rate being paid on similar bonds.
   (d) the market rate of interest is higher than the rate paid on the bonds.
   (e) None of the above

Q6

3. The lower of cost or market approach when applied to the short-term portfolio will
   (a) increase net income.
   (b) decrease net income.
   (c) increase or decrease net income, depending on the situation.
   (d) have no affect on net income.

Q8

4. The lower of cost or market approach when applied to the long-term portfolio will
   (a) increase net income.
   (b) decrease net income.
   (c) increase or decrease net income, depending on the situation.
   (d) have no affect on net income.

Q3, Q4, Q9

5. Control of a corporation is indicated when one corporation
   (a) owns 20% or more of the outstanding stock.
   (b) can exercise influence over another.
   (c) owns more than 50% of the outstanding stock.
   (d) is appointed by the courts to manage another corporation.

Q2

6. The equity method of accounting should be used if
   (a) 20% or more of the outstanding stock is owned.
   (b) 50% or more of the outstanding stock is owned.
   (c) between 20% and 50% of the outstanding stock is owned.
   (d) the degree of ownership allows the stockholder to exercise significant influence over the corporation.

Q10

7. Amortization of a discount on a bond investment will
   (a) increase interest earned.
   (b) decrease interest earned.
   (c) have no effect on the income statement.
   (d) decrease the balance in the investment account.

DEMONSTRATION PROBLEM

Part A

Mountain Wagons, Inc., had the following short-term investment transactions in marketable securities during 19X8.

Jan.   1   Purchased $50,000 face-value, 12% bonds of Crescent Restaurants, Inc., at 102, plus $1,000 brokerage fees (semiannual interest is payable on June 30 and December 31)

Apr. 15   Purchased 1,000 shares of Bishop Court, Inc., for $14.75 per share, plus $250 brokerage fees

May 25   Received a 10% stock dividend from Bishop Court, Inc. (recorded a memo entry in the Investment account noting the new number of shares held)

June   7   Received a $0.10-per-share cash dividend for the shares in Bishop

30   Received the semiannual interest on the Crescent bonds

Oct.   4   Sold the bonds of Crescent Restaurants, Inc., at 99, less brokerage fees of $1,000 (recorded accrued interest at this date amounting to $1,578)

Dec. 31   The market value of a Bishop share was $10 on this date.

Required
1. Prepare journal entries to record the 19X8 transactions.
2. How should the market value of Bishop shares be disclosed in the December 31, 19X8, balance sheet of Mountain Wagons, Inc.? Prepare any journal entries necessary.

Part B

Brandon Corp. purchased 20,000 shares representing a 20% interest in Curtis Corp. for $10 per share on January 1, 19X8. The following transactions occurred during the year.

Apr.   15   Curtis paid a $0.25-per-share dividend.
June   7   Curtis distributed a 10% stock dividend.
Oct.   4   Curtis paid a $0.15-per-share dividend.
Dec.   31   Curtis reported net income of $50,000; Brandon exercises a significant control over Curtis.

Required
1. Prepare journal entries to record
   (a)   the purchase of the 20,000 shares as a long-term investment.
   (b)   receipt of Brandon's share of dividends paid by Curtis.
   (c)   Brandon's share of net income reported by Curtis.
2. Prepare a T account that shows the changes in the investment account during the year and the amount that would appear on the year-end balance sheet.
3. What amount would appear on the year-end income statement?

Part C

Cord City, Inc., paid $147,000 for $150,000 face-value bonds of Computer Stores Corp. The bonds, which were acquired on January 1, 19X1, as a long-term investment, had the following features.

Date of Authorization	Term	Bond Contract Interest Rate	Interest Payment Dates
January 1, 19X1	3 years	12%	Semiannually on June 30 and December 31

Required
1. Calculate the amount of
   (a)   interest received every interest payment date.
   (b)   amortization to be recorded at each interest payment date. Use the straight-line method of amortization.
2. Prepare the ledger for the Investment in Bonds account of Cord City, Inc., to show the purchase of the bonds and the semiannual amortization amounts until redemption. (Note that amortization is recorded each time bond interest income is recorded.)
3. Prepare the journal entries to record the interest and amortization as of June 30, 19X1.

Part D

Desert Tile Corp. sold a 10%, 3-year bond issue of $100,000 to yield the investor, Thunder Co., a 12% return on investment. The bonds pay interest *annually*.

Required

1. Did the bond sell at a premium or a discount?

2. How much did the investor pay for the bond?

3. Prepare an amortization table for the investor for the three-year period.

4. Prepare the journal entry required to record the *receipt* of the first interest payment.

SOLUTION TO DEMONSTRATION PROBLEM

Part A

1. Jan. 1	Marketable Securities		52,000	
	Cash			52,000
	To record the purchase of $50,000 bonds of Crescent Restaurants, Inc., at 102, plus brokerage charges.			
	Apr. 15	Marketable Securities	15,000	
		Cash		15,000
	To record the purchase of 1,000 shares of Bishop Court, Inc., at $14.75, including $250 brokerage fees (cost per share, $15).			
	May 25	Memorandum		
	Received a 10% stock dividend bringing the number of shares of Bishop Court, Inc., held to 1100. The cost per share is $13.64 ($15,000 ÷ 1100).			
	June 7	Cash	110	
		Dividend Income		110
	To record the receipt of a $0.10 per share dividend on 1,100 shares of Bishop Court Inc.			
	30	Cash	3,000	
		Bond Interest Earned		3,000
	To record the receipt of semiannual interest on bonds of Crescent Restaurants, Inc.			
	Oct. 4	Cash	(a) 50,078	
		Loss on Sale of Securities	(b) 3,500	
		Bond Interest Earned		1,578
		Marketable Securities		52,000
	To record sale of Crescent Restaurants, Inc., bonds at 99, less brokerage fees of $1,000 plus accrual interest.			

(a) $50,000 × 99% = $49,500; ($49,500 − 1,000) + $1,578 = $50,078

(b) $48,500 − $52,000 = $3,500

2. GAAP requires that equity investments in the short-term portfolio be recorded under the LCM rules, which recognize an unrealized loss on the income statement through the use of a valuation account contra to the asset account. The journal entry would be as follows:

Unrealized Loss on Securities	4,000	
Allowance to Reduce Securities to Market		4,000

$$\$15,000 - (1,100 \times \$10) = \$4,000$$

Part B

1. (a)

Jan. 1	Long-term Investments	200,000	
	Cash		200,000
	To record purchase of 20,000 shares of Curtis Corp.		

(b)

Apr. 15	Cash	5,000	
	Long-term Investments		5,000
	To record receipt of $0.25-per-share dividend from Curtis (20,000 × $.25).		
June 7	Memorandum		
	Curtis distributed a 10% stock dividend, bringing the number of shares held to 22,000.		
Oct. 4	Cash	3,300	
	Long-term Investments		3,300
	To record receipt of a $0.15-per-share dividend from Curtis (22,000 × $.15).		

(c)

Long-term Investments	10,000	
Equity in Earnings of Investee		10,000
To record share of Curtis Corp. reported net income.		

2.

Long-Term Investments

(purchase) 200,000	5,000 (dividends)
(Share of income) 10,000	3,300 (dividends)
Bal. 201,700	

3. The Equity in Earnings of Investee, $10,000, would appear on the income statement.

Part C

1. (a) Amount of interest received every 6 months: $150,000 × 12% × 1/2 = $9,000
   (b) Amortization every 6 months:

Face Value	$150,000
Investment	147,000
Discount	$ 3,000
Amortization ($3,000 ÷ 6)	$500

2.   **Investment in Bonds**

Date 19X1	Description	Debit	Credit	Dr. or Cr.	Balance
Jan. 1	Purchase of Computer Stores Corp. Bonds	147,000		Dr.	147,000
June 30	Discount Amortization	500		Dr.	147,500
Dec. 31	Discount Amortization	500		Dr.	148,000
19X2					
June 30	Discount Amortization	500		Dr.	148,500
Dec. 31	Discount Amortization	500		Dr.	149,000
19X3					
June 30	Discount Amortization	500		Dr.	149,500
Dec. 31	Discount Amortization	500		Dr.	150,000
19X4					
Jan. 1	Bonds Redeemed		150,000		-0-

3.

Receipt of Interest		Discount Amortization	
Cash	9,000	Investment in Bonds	500
Bond Interest Earned	9,000	Bond Interest Earned	500

Part D

1. The bond was sold below face value or at a discount since the market rate of interest is above the stated rate of interest.

2. The investor would pay an amount equal to the present value of the two cash flows, interest and principal. The calculations follow.

   $100,000 × .712 (present value of one payment at 12%) = $71,200

   $10,000 × 2.402 (present value of three payments at 12%) = $24,020

   Purchase price of the bond: $71,200 + $24,020 = $95,220

3.   **Amortization Table**

	A	B	C	D	E
Period 19X1	Bond Carrying Value	Effective Interest at 12%	10% Interest Received	$(B - C)$ Discount Amortization	$(A - D)$ Bond Carrying Value
Jan. 1	$95,220				
19X2					
Jan. 1	95,220	$11,426	$10,000	$1,426	$ 96,646
19X3					
Jan. 1	96,646	11,598	10,000	1,598	98,244
19X4					
Jan. 1	98,244	11,756*	10,000	1,756	100,000

*Reduced by $33 for rounding error.

4.

Cash	10,000	
Investment in Bonds	1,426	
Bond Interest Earned		11,426

DISCUSSION QUESTIONS

Q14-1 Is an investor guaranteed against the loss of an investment? Explain.

Q14-2 How can bondholders obtain repayment of their investment? Are stockholders more secure than bondholders? Explain.

Q14-3 Why would someone prefer to invest in the shares of a corporation rather than in bonds?

Q14-4 What are four alternative methods for investment disclosure on the balance sheet?

Q14-5 What are marketable securities? How are they classified on the balance sheet?

Q14-6 What are long-term investments? How are they classified on the balance sheet?

Q14-7 Is amortization of any bond premium or discount recorded for short-term investments in bonds? Why or why not?

Q14-8 If the purchase price of shares includes dividends that have been declared but not yet paid at the time of share purchase, how is the subsequent receipt of the dividend recorded? Do dividends accrue?

Q14-9 Does the price of bonds include accrued interest? How is accrued interest recorded by the investor?

Q14-10 How is the gain or loss on sale of marketable securities classified on the income statement?

Q14-11 How are equity securities accounted for when the investor cannot exercise significant influence on the issuing corporation?

Q14-12 How are equity securities accounted for when the investor can exercise significant influence on the issuing corporation?

Q14-13 What is the major difference, as far as asset valuation and income determination, between the LCM and equity methods of accounting for long-term equity securities?

Q14-14 How do investments in common stock differ from investments in preferred stock as far as investor control of a corporation is concerned?

Q14-15 Identify and discuss three levels of voting influence by an investor corporation over the investee corporation.

Q14-16 Explain how the price of a bond is influenced by the bond contract interest rate and the prevailing market interest rate.

Q14-17 Compare the straight-line method of amortization with the effective interest method for long-term investments.

DISCUSSION CASE

Compound Interest

WHY IS GROWTH ESSENTIAL?

Unless your investments beat inflation, they have no "real" growth. High growth enables the magic of compounding to work best—to generate large sums of money over time. Every additional percentage point makes a big difference.

ANNUAL INVESTMENT	% RETURN	GROWS TO AMOUNT INDICATED WITHIN:				
		10 YEARS	15 YEARS	20 YEARS	25 YEARS	30 YEARS
$1,000	8	$ 15,645	$ 29,324	$ 49,423	$ 78,954	$ 122,346
	10	17,531	34,950	63,002	108,182	180,943
	12	19,655	41,753	80,699	149,334	270,293
	14	22,045	49,980	103,768	207,333	406,737
	16	24,733	59,925	133,841	289,088	615,162
	18	27,755	71,939	173,021	404,272	933,319
	20	31,150	86,442	224,026	566,377	1,418,258
TOTAL INVESTED		$ 10,000	$ 15,000	$ 20,000	$ 25,000	$ 30,000
$3,500	8	$ 54,759	$102,635	$ 172,980	$ 276,340	$ 428,211
	10	61,359	122,324	220,509	378,636	633,302
	12	68,791	146,136	282,446	522,669	946,024
	14	77,156	174,931	363,189	725,665	1,423,580
	16	86,565	209,738	468,442	1,011,809	2,153,066
	18	97,143	251,787	605,574	1,414,952	3,266,615
	20	109,026	302,547	784,090	1,982,321	4,963,903
TOTAL INVESTED		$ 35,000	$ 52,500	$ 70,000	$ 87,500	$ 105,000
$5,500	8	$ 86,050	$161,284	$ 271,826	$ 434,249	$ 672,902
	10	96,421	192,224	346,514	595,000	995,189
	12	108,100	229,643	443,843	821,337	1,486,609
	14	121,245	274,892	570,726	1,140,330	2,237,054
	16	136,031	329,558	736,123	1,589,985	3,383,389
	18	152,653	395,665	951,616	2,223,497	5,133,252
	20	171,327	475,432	1,232,141	3,115,075	7,800,418
TOTAL INVESTED		$ 55,000	$ 82,500	$ 110,000	$ 137,500	$ 165,000

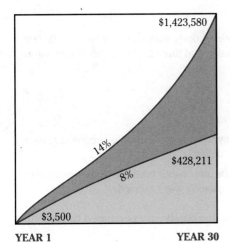

$1,423,580

14%

$428,211

8%

$3,500

YEAR 1   YEAR 30

Extra growth does pay off in a big way through the effects of compounding. For example, $3,500 invested at 14% grows to $1,423,580 over 30 years compared to just $428,211 for an investment yielding 8% over the same period (see graph). The trick, clearly, is to achieve high rates of growth without sacrificing security.

For Discussion
1. Comment on the usefulness of this type of analysis.
2. Refer to Exhibit 6-18. How might a spreadsheet analysis be used in this instance?

EXERCISES

E14-1 through E14-6 are based on the following information: Murphy Corp. purchased some securities in order to utilize cash on hand that was not needed immediately for financing or operating activities. The cost of the securities amounted to $107,500, including brokerage commissions and other fees of $1,500.

Short-term portfolio; no significant influence (Q2, Q7)

E14-1 Assume the securities purchased were 4,300 shares of Alta Corp. common stock, which amounted to 3% of the outstanding stock of Alta.

Required
1. Prepare the journal entry to record the investment.
2. Prepare the entry to record the receipt of a dividend amounting to $1.25 per share.
3. Prepare the entry to record the receipt of a 10% stock dividend. The market price of the stock on the day the shares were received was $32.

Sale of shares after
stock dividend (Q2, Q7)

E14-2 Assume the same facts as for E14-1. Shortly after the receipt of the stock dividend, 1,000 of the shares owned were sold for $38 per share, less commissions and fees of $700.

Required

1. Prepare the journal entry to record the sale of the 1,000 shares.

2. Prepare the entry necessary on the last day of the fiscal year, assuming the market value of the remaining shares is $24 per share.

Short-term portfolio:
bond premium (Q2, Q5)

E14-3 Assume that the securities purchased were bonds with a face value of $100,000, an interest rate of 12% payable semiannually, and three full years remaining before the bond matures.

Required

1. Prepare the journal entry to record the investment.

2. Prepare the entry to record the first interest payment. Amortization is recorded at each interest payment date under the straight-line method.

3. Prepare the entry to record the sale of the bonds after two interest payments have been received. Cash of $104,000 net of $1,000 commissions was received.

Short-term portfolio:
accrued interest on
bonds (Q2, Q5)

E14-4 Assume the same facts as for 14-3, but that the bonds were purchased two months after an interest payment date.

Required

1. Determine the amount of accrued interest included in the purchase price.

2. Prepare the journal entry necessary to record the investment.

3. Determine how much amortization would be recorded at the first interest payment date.

Short-term portfolio:
LCM valuation on bonds
(Q2, Q5, Q6)

E14-5 Assume that the market value of the bonds referred to in E14-3 was $110,000 as of the end of the current fiscal year.

Required
What journal entry is necessary to record the increase in value?

Short-term portfolio:
LCM valuation on bonds
(Q2, Q5, Q6)

E14-6 Assume that the market value of the bonds referred to in E14-3 was $99,000 as of the end of the current fiscal year.

Required

1. What journal entry is necessary to record the decrease in value?

2. Do you agree with your answer to number 1? Explain.

E14-7 through E14-11 are based on the following change in assumptions from E14-1 to E14-6:

Assume that management changed its mind and immediately decided to hold the securities purchased for $107,500 as a long-term investment.

20% acquisition, no
significant influence
(Q4, Q6, Q8)

E14-7 Assume that the purchase resulted in the acquisition of 20% of the outstanding stock of the issuing corporation, and that no significant influence could be exercised with the 20% interest.

Required

1. Prepare the journal entry to record the investment.

2. Prepare the entry to record the receipt of a dividend amounting to $1.25 per share.

3. Prepare the entry necessary to record Murphy's share of the corporation's reported earnings of $50,000.

4. Prepare the entry necessary to record the fact that the stock had fallen by $2 per share at the end of the year.

5. Determine the balance in the Investment account at the end of the year. What amount will be reported on the balance sheet?

20% acquisition, signifi-
cant influence (Q4, Q9)

E14-8 Assume that the purchase resulted in the acquisition of 20% of the outstanding stock of the issuing corporation, and that Murphy was able to exercise significant influence with the 20% interest.

Required

1. Prepare the journal entry to record the investment.

2. Prepare the entry to record the receipt of a dividend amounting to $1.25 per share.

3. Prepare the entry necessary to record Murphy's share of the corporation's reported earnings of $50,000.

4. Prepare the entry necessary to record the fact that the stock had fallen by $2 per share at the end of the year.

5. Determine the balance in the Investment account at the end of the year. What amount will be reported on the balance sheet?

Long-term portfolio:
bond premium (Q4–Q6,
Q8)

E14-9 Assume that the securities purchased were bonds with a face value of $100,000, an interest rate of 12% payable semiannually, and three full years remaining before the bond matures.

Required

1. Prepare the journal entry to record the investment.

2. Prepare the entry to record the first interest payment. Amortization is recorded at each interest payment date under the straight-line method.

Long-term portfolio:
subsequent sale of
bonds with premium
(Q4–Q6, Q8)

E14-10 Assume that the securities purchased were bonds with a face value of $100,000, an interest rate of 12% payable semiannually, and three full years remaining before the bond matures.

Required

1. Determine the carrying value of the investment after the second interest payment.

2. Prepare the journal entry to record the sale of the bonds for $106,000, including brokerage commissions and other fees of $1,000.

Long-term portfolio:
effective interest
method, bond premium
(Q4–Q6, Q8, Q10)

E14-11 Assume that the securities purchased were bonds with a face value of $100,000, an interest rate of 12% payable semiannually, and three full years remaining before the bond matures. Assume that the bonds were purchased to yield an annual market rate of interest of 10%.

Required

1. Determine the amount of brokerage commissions and other fees included in the $107,500 purchase price.

2. Determine the amount of interest and amortization for the first interest payment, using the effective interest method.

3. Prepare the journal entry to record the receipt of the first interest payment.

PROBLEMS

Short-term portfolio: stocks and bonds (Q2, Q5, Q6)

P14-1   Morton Services, Inc., had the following transactions affecting their short-term portfolio during 19X7.

Jan. 1   Purchased $25,000 of 12% bonds of St. Luke Farms, Inc., at 95, plus $250 in brokerage commissions and fees

Feb. 28   Purchased 200 shares of Cody Canyon Winery common stock for $20 per share, plus $60 in brokerage commissions and fees

June 30   Received the semiannual interest payment on the St. Luke bonds

Oct. 4   Received a $.50-per-share dividend from Cody

Dec. 31   Received the semiannual interest payment on the St. Luke bonds

      31   The market value of the bonds was 90 and the shares were selling at $15.

Required

1. Prepare the necessary journal entries to record the 19X7 transactions.

2. Prepare any adjusting entries you believe are necessary for the short-term investments. It is the policy of Morton to carry all short-term investments in bonds at cost, with no adjustment to LCM.

3. Show how these investments would be reported on the balance sheet as of December 31, 19X7.

4. The Cody stock was sold for $25 per share, less brokerage commissions and fees of $70 on Apr. 11, 19X8. Prepare the entry to record the sale.

5. Prepare any adjusting entry necessary on December 31, 19X8, as a result of the investments.

6. Show how the income statement would be affected for the year 19X8, assuming that the St. Luke bonds were still held as a short-term investment.

Equity method vs. LCM (Q2, Q3, Q6, Q8, Q9)

P14-2   Peter Corporation (PC) purchased 20,000 shares as a long term investment, representing a 20% interest in Sol O. Sun, Inc., for $100,000 on January 1, 19X7. The following transactions occurred subsequently.

19X7

June 30   Sol paid $5,000 in dividends to its stockholders.

Dec. 31   Sol reported net income of $10,000 for 19X7.

19X8

June 30   Sol paid $50,000 in dividends to its stockholders.

Dec. 31   Sol reported net income of $75,000 for 19X8.

Required

Consider these cases.

Case A: PC has a significant influence over Sol.
Case B: PC does not have a significant influence over Sol.

For each case do the following:

1. Prepare journal entries to record
   (a) the purchase of the 20,000 shares by PC.
   (b) receipt of PC's share of dividends paid by Sol.
   (c) PC's share of Sol's net income, if applicable.

2. If the market value of the 20,000 shares declined by $1 per share at December 31, 19X7, prepare the journal entry required under the LCM method to record an unrealized loss. Explain how this decline would be reported in the financial statements.

3. Prepare a schedule to compare the amounts reported on the balance sheet and on the income statement of PC for 19X7.

Long-term investments: effective interest method (Q2, Q3, Q8, Q10, Q11)

P14-3 Cedarville, Inc., purchased bonds of Alturas Mfg. on January 1, 19X2. The bonds had a face value of $100,000, carried an interest rate of 12%, and were purchased at an amount that would yield a 10% market rate. The bonds were dated January 1, 19X2, and mature on January 1, 19X4. Interest is payable semiannually on June 30 and December 31. Cedarville intends to hold the bonds until maturity.

Required

1. Did the bonds sell at a premium or a discount? Why?

2. How much did Cedarville pay for the bonds?

3. Prepare an amortization table for the two-year period for Cedarville, using the effective interest method.

4. Prepare the journal entry required to record the receipt of the first interest payment.

5. Prepare the entry necessary on the day the bonds mature.

Mirror image effect of bond issues (Q2, Q10)

P14-4 Muller Marketing Marauders, Inc., the year-end for which is December 31, acquired $75,000 of face value bonds of Guelph Collegiate, Inc., at 98. The bonds, which were acquired on January 1, 19X3, as a long-term investment, had the following features:

Date of Authorization	Term	Bond Contract Interest Rate	Interest Payment Dates
January 1, 19X3	3 years	12%	Semiannually on June 30 and December 31

Required

1. Calculate the amount of
   (a) interest applicable to each six-month period.
   (b) amortization to be recorded at each interest date. Use the straight-line method.

2. Prepare a T account for the Investment in Bonds account of Muller, recording the purchase and the amortization of the discount until redemption of the bonds.

3. Using a comparative format similar to the one on pp. 647–48, prepare all journal entries required on the books of both Muller and Guelph in 19X3. The year-end for Guelph is also December 31.

ALTERNATE PROBLEMS

Short-term portfolio: stocks and bonds (Q2, Q5, Q6)

AP14-1   Abbot Services, Inc., had the following transactions affecting their short-term portfolio during 19X3.

Jan.   1   Purchased $75,000 of 14% bonds of St. Luke Farms, Inc., at 95, plus $750 in brokerage commissions and fees.
Feb. 28   Purchased 400 shares of Big Canyon Brewery common stock for $15 per share, plus $100 in brokerage commissions and fees.
June 30   Received the semiannual interest payment on the St. Luke bonds.
Oct.   4   Received a $.75-per-share dividend from Big Canyon.
Dec. 31   Received the semiannual interest payment on the St. Luke bonds.
        31   The market value of the bonds was 90 and the shares were selling at $8.

Required

1. Prepare the necessary journal entries to record the 19X3 transactions.

2. Prepare any adjusting entries you believe are necessary for the short-term investments. It is the policy of Abbot to carry all short-term investments in bonds at cost, with no adjustment to LCM.

3. Show how the investments would be reported on the balance sheet as of December 31, 19X3.

4. The Big Canyon stock was sold for $25 per share, less brokerage commissions and fees of $100 on Apr. 11, 19X4. Prepare the entry to record the sale.

5. Prepare any adjusting entry necessary on December 31, 19X4, as a result of the investments.

6. Show how the income statement would be affected for the year 19X4, assuming that the St. Luke bonds were still held as a short-term investment.

Equity method vs. LCM (Q2, Q3, Q6, Q8, Q9)

AP14-2   The Sulphur Corp. purchased as a long-term investment 50,000 shares of Jungo, Inc., common stock for $500,000. This represented a 15% interest in the company. The purchase was made on July 1, 19X3. The following transactions occurred during 19X3 and 19X4.

19X3
Oct.   1   Jungo paid a cash dividend of $50,000.
Dec. 31   Jungo reported a net income of $300,000, which was earned evenly over the year.

19X4
Oct.   1   Jungo paid a cash dividend of $90,000.
Dec. 31   Jungo reported a net income of $500,000, which was earned evenly over the year.

Required
Consider these cases.

Case A: Sulphur can exercise significant influence over Jungo as a result of the investment.
Case B: Sulphur cannot exercise significance influence over Jungo as a result of the investment.

For each case, do the following:

1. Record all journal entries indicated by the information.

2. The market value had declined by $3 per share as of December 31, 19X3. Explain how the decline in value would be reported in the financial statements.

3. Prepare a schedule to compare the amounts reported on the balance sheet and the income statement of Sulphur for 19X3.

Long-term investments: effective interest method, (Q2, Q3, Q8, Q10, Q11)

AP14-3   Denio, Inc., purchased bonds of Sheldon Mfg. on January 1, 19X7. The bonds had a face value of $100,000, carried an interest rate of 8%, and were purchased at an amount that would yield a 10% market rate. The bonds were dated January 1, 19X7, and mature on January 1, 19X9. Interest is payable semiannually on June 30 and December 31. Denio intends to hold the bonds until maturity.

Required

1. Did the bonds sell at a premium or a discount? Why?

2. How much did Denio pay for the bonds?

3. Prepare an amortization table for the two-year period for Denio, using the effective interest method.

4. Prepare the journal entry required to record the receipt of the first interest payment.

5. Prepare the entry necessary on the day the bonds mature.

Mirror image effect of bond issues (Q2, Q10)

AP14-4   Mags, Inc., paid $110,000 for $100,000 of face-value bonds of Ski Corp. Both corporations have December 31 as their year-end. The bonds, which were acquired as a long-term investment on January 1, 19X1, had the following features.

Date of Authorization	Term	Bond Contract Interest Rate	Interest Payment Dates
January 1, 19X1	2 years	12%	Semiannually on July 1 and January 1

Required

1. Calculate the amount of
   (a) interest applicable to each six-month period.
   (b) amortization to be recorded at each interest date. Use the straight-line method.

2. Prepare a T account for the Investment in Bonds account for Mags, Inc., recording the purchase and the amortization of the premium until redemption of the bonds.

3. Using a comparative format similar to the one on pp. 647–48, prepare all journal entries required on the books of both Mags, Inc., and Ski Corp. for the year ended December 31, 19X1.

DECISION PROBLEM

Q2, Q3, Q9

Honest Ned's Corp. has 100,000 shares outstanding. The following data are applicable to 19X6 and 19X7.

	Dividends Paid	Net Income (Loss)
19X6	$100,000	$(300,000)
19X7	200,000	400,000

Part A

E. Tonne, Inc., purchased 55,000 shares of Honest Ned's for $220,000 on January 1, 19X6.

Required

1. Identify the relationship between these two corporations.

2. Indicate what method of accounting can be used in the records of E. Tonne, Inc., for this long-term investment.

3. Assuming the equity method is used, prepare journal entries for 19X6 to record
   (a) the purchase of the 55,000 shares.
   (b) the receipt of E. Tonne's share of 19X6 dividends paid by Honest Ned's.
   (c) E. Tonne's share of Honest Ned's 19X6 income.
   (d) a decline of $40,000 in the market value of Honest Ned's shares held by E. Tonne.

4. Assuming the equity method is used, prepare journal entries for 19X7 to record
   (a) the receipt of E. Tonne's share of 19X7 dividends paid by Honest Ned's.
   (b) E. Tonne's share of Honest Ned's 19X7 income.
   (c) an unrealized recovery of $10,000 of the decline in market value of Honest Ned's shares held by E. Tonne. The market value of the shares had improved during the year.

Part B

Sim and Sons, Inc., purchased 35,000 shares, representing a 35% interest in Honest Ned's Corp., for $160,000 on January 1, 19X7. Sim and Sons is a fierce competitor of E. Tonne, Inc. The purchase of these shares was viewed with concern by E. Tonne, Inc.

Required

5. Identify the relationship between Honest Ned's Corp. and Sim and Sons.

6. Indicate what method of accounting would be used in the records of Sim and Sons for this long-term investment.

7. Assuming Sim and Sons uses the equity method, prepare journal entries to record
   (a) the purchase of 35,000 shares.
   (b) the receipt of Sim and Sons' share of 19X7 dividends paid by Honest Ned's.
   (c) Sim and Sons' share of Honest Ned's income.
   (d) The sale of the 35,000 shares on January 1, 19X8, to E. Tonne, Inc., at $6 per share, a price considerably above the stock market price of these shares. Why would E. Tonne, Inc., pay more than market value for these shares?

ANSWERS TO SELF-TEST QUESTIONS

1. **(d)** Even if the declaration did affect the market price, no corporate assets are distributed to the stockholders. Therefore, it would not affect the balance in the investment account. The cost basis *per share* does decrease, however, since the same total cost is now spread over more shares.

2. **(c)** Bonds are quoted in terms of a percentage of face value, face value being equal to 100. If bonds are selling above face value, it means that they are paying an interest rate above the market, or above the rate being paid on similar bonds.

3. **(c)** Lower of cost or market when applied to the short-term portfolio affects net income. If the Allowance account is increased, a loss will be recorded and net income will decrease. If the Allowance account is decreased, recovery of unrealized losses will be recorded, which will increase net income.

4. **(d)** When LCM is applied to the long-term portfolio, net income is not affected. Since temporary changes in the market may well reverse themselves in future years, the Unrealized Loss account created when long-term securities are written down is reported as a contra account in stockholders' equity.

5. **(c)** Control is generally assumed when one stockholder owns more than 50% of the outstanding stock. Such a stockholder should be able to appoint a majority of the members of the board of directors, thereby gaining control.

6. **(d)** If "all of the above" were a choice, it probably would be a safe bet. The equity method must be used when a stockholder has sufficient shares to be able to have an influence on the corporation. The ability to exercise significant influence is usually presumed when a stockholder owns 20% or more of the outstanding stock, making *a, b,* and *c* all correct, but in certain circumstances even a 49.9% interest would not allow one to exercise influence, and in other circumstances a 10% share would allow that stockholder to exercise significant influence.

7. **(a)** When an investor amortizes a bond discount, the entry increases both the Investment account and interest earned.

15 BUSINESS COMBINATIONS

W<small>HENEVER</small> the percentage of ownership of a corporation reaches 50%, the element of control comes into play. From an economic standpoint, whenever one corporation can exercise control over another, only one entity exists. This is more clearly seen when one corporation owns *all* of the outstanding voting stock of another corporation. In that case only one stockholder has ownership in the second corporation, and that stockholder is the investing corporation. Since that investing corporation is owned by its stockholders, only one set of stockholders exists, and therefore only one entity. But the two corporations are two *legal* entities. Chapter 15 investigates business combinations from a conceptual viewpoint first, and then examines the mechanics needed to mathematically combine the two legal entities to form one economic entity.

After studying Chapter 15, you should be able to answer the following questions:

1 Does owning more than 50% of the voting stock of another corporation signify that the investing corporation has control over the corporation? (p.672)

2 What is the distinction in a business combination between a purchase and a pooling of interests? (p.672)

3 When consolidated financial statements are prepared, does each corporation continue to maintain its own legal existence as a separate entity? (p.675)

4 What is the meaning of the term "reciprocal accounts"? Why are they eliminated in the consolidating process? (pp.675–76)

5 When does goodwill arise in the consolidating process? (pp.676–78)

6 What are the mechanics involved in the preparation of consolidated financial statements? (p.679)

7 When eliminating entries are made, are they posted to the books of the parent corporation? the subsidiary? Explain. (pp.679–80)

8 When does minority interest exist? (p.681)

9 Why is a pooling of interest recorded at the book value of the net assets of a subsidiary rather than fair market value, as is the practice in a purchase situation? (pp.686–87)

10 Should lower of cost or market be used in valuing securities when the element of control exists? (pp.688–89)

BUSINESS COMBINATIONS

Q1: Stock ownership
and control

Often a corporation acquires a **controlling interest** in another corporation; usually this control is accomplished through the purchase of voting shares. As mentioned earlier, when the number of shares purchased amounts to more than 50%, the investor controls the voting shares of the other corporation, which is then referred to as a **subsidiary** of the investing **parent company.** When control exists, the individual financial statements of the parent and its subsidiary are combined for the parent company's reporting purposes, as if the two legal companies were one economic entity. If the parent company acquired *all* the outstanding stock of the subsidiary, the parent could elect to take the subsidiary out of legal existence, thereby leaving only one corporation (with no need to combine financial statements). This chapter focuses on business combinations where the two corporations remain in legal existence, creating the need for **consolidated financial statements.**

Q2: Purchase vs.
pooling

Business combinations are identified either as a purchase or a pooling of interests. In a **purchase,** between 51% and 100% of the outstanding shares of a corporation are acquired with a combination of assets (cash or other assets), liabilities (usually a long-term debt such as bonds), or equity securities (such as preferred or common stock). The transaction could consist of entirely cash, entirely long-term debt, or entirely common stock. Most purchase acquisitions consist of a combination of cash and debt, which means that a portion of the stockholders of the subsidiary have been bought out. They no longer exist as owners of either company. In a **pooling of interests,** only common stock of the parent is exchanged for common stock of the subsidiary, thereby making the stockholders of the subsidiary now stockholders of the parent company. Since the owners (stockholders) are the same after the transaction as before, it is said that the interests of the owners have been pooled—hence the term *pooling of interests.* The two types of business combinations, purchase and pooling of interests, are contrasted in Exhibit 15-1.

The combining accounting process for a purchase and a pooling are different. The two main sections after this discuss the combination of financial statements when a purchase occurs, while the last section introduces the methodology of combining financial statements when a pooling of interests occurs.

The Accounting Equation Reviewed

Since net assets are the focus of both a purchase and a pooling of interests, it is useful to review the accounting equation at this point. Simply stated, the accounting equation indicates that total assets belonging to an entity must always equal the total claims against those assets. Both creditors and owners contribute these assets and the accounting equation recognizes these contributions.

ASSETS	=	LIABILITIES	+	EQUITY
(Resources owned by the entity)		(Creditors' claims to assets)		(Owners' claims to assets)

The equation also expresses the equality between assets and total claims by both creditors and owners to these assets.

Business combinations focus on the owners' claim to the net assets of a subsidiary; that is, the amount of net assets left for the owners after all other claims

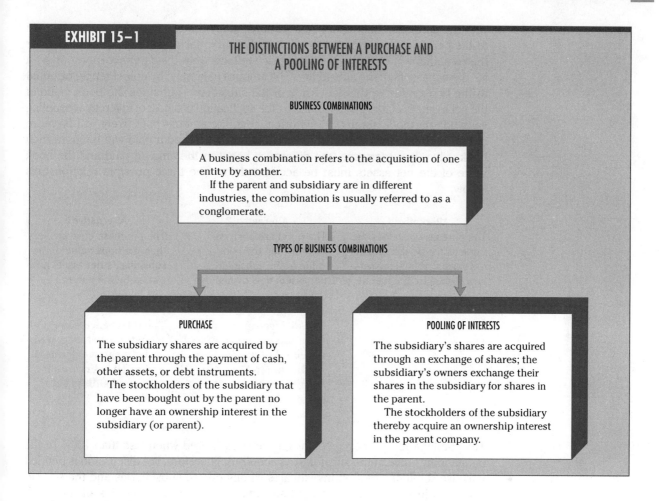

EXHIBIT 15-1

THE DISTINCTIONS BETWEEN A PURCHASE AND
A POOLING OF INTERESTS

BUSINESS COMBINATIONS

A business combination refers to the acquisition of one
entity by another.
   If the parent and subsidiary are in different
industries, the combination is usually referred to as a
conglomerate.

TYPES OF BUSINESS COMBINATIONS

PURCHASE

The subsidiary shares are acquired by
the parent through the payment of cash,
other assets, or debt instruments.
   The stockholders of the subsidiary that
have been bought out by the parent no
longer have an ownership interest in the
subsidiary (or parent).

POOLING OF INTERESTS

The subsidiary's shares are acquired
through an exchange of shares; the
subsidiary's owners exchange their
shares in the subsidiary for shares in
the parent.
   The stockholders of the subsidiary
thereby acquire an ownership interest
in the parent company.

have been addressed. The accounting equation can therefore be restated in the
following manner to emphasize owners' claims to net assets:

ASSETS	–	LIABILITIES	=	EQUITY
(Resources owned by the entity)		(Creditors' claims to assets)		(Owners' claims to remaining assets)

Since assets less liabilities is also referred to as net assets, the term *net assets*
can be said to be synonymous with owners' equity, that is, the owners' claims to
the assets of the entity. The discussion of business combinations focuses on the
net assets of a subsidiary. In other words, *the balance in the investment account
represents the investor's share of the stockholders' equity (or net assets) of the
subsidiary.*

Recording the Acquisition

Recording the purchase of a controlling interest is no different from the acquisitions
discussed in Chapter 14. The acquisition cost includes not only the amount paid
for the common shares, but also brokerage fees and any other costs associated

with the purchase. In business acquisitions, many times a *finder's fee* must be paid to the person or corporation who found the potential subsidiary and arranged for the combination. The total purchase price reflects what the parent corporation paid for the net assets of the subsidiary. The amount paid may, by coincidence, be equal to the book value of the net assets of the subsidiary, but since the book value of the net assets is actually determined by the application of a host of different accounting valuation methods applied to historical cost, the amount paid likely will be more or less than the book value. In most situations, the amount paid will be more than book value. In either case, the difference between the amount paid and the book value of the net assets must be accounted for. The three possible relationships follow:

Alternative 1	**Alternative 2**	**Alternative 3**
The purchase cost was the same as the book value of the subsidiary's net assets now owned by the parent.	The purchase cost was greater than the book value of the subsidiary's net assets now owned by the parent.	The purchase cost was less than the book value of the subsidiary's net assets now owned by the parent.
	The difference can result from the existence of unrecorded goodwill applicable to the subsidiary and to an undervaluation of the subsidiary's assets.	The difference can result from the existence of so-called negative goodwill and to an overvaluation of the subsidiary's assets.

The combination process becomes more complicated when less than 100% of the outstanding stock of the subsidiary is acquired. Therefore, the discussion is divided into two sections: the first investigates wholly owned subsidiaries and the second discusses less than wholly owned subsidiaries, where the interests of the other stockholders (the minority interest) must be considered.

WHOLLY OWNED SUBSIDIARIES

The following discussion is based on the assumption that the parent company (P) has acquired *all* of the outstanding stock of the subsidiary (S) in a cash transaction that took place on December 31, 19X8.

Recording the Acquisition

The acquisition cost for each of the three alternatives is recorded in the combined journal entries shown next. In each case, the parent has acquired a 100% ownership interest in the subsidiary. Note that the amount paid differs in each case.

	Acquisition of 100% Ownership Interest		
	Alternative 1	Alternative 2	Alternative 3
Investment in Subsidiary	20,000	25,000	16,000
Cash	20,000	25,000	16,000

Although this purchase is with cash, the acquisition also can be made through a payment of other assets. Regardless, the parent purchases a 100% ownership interest in the subsidiary's net assets; none of the subsidiary's previous owners then has an ownership interest in the subsidiary. In this example, the parent and the subsidiary remain as separate legal entities.

Preparation of Consolidated Financial Statements

Q3: Separate entities

Although some exceptions occur, the individual financial statements of the parent and its subsidiary are combined for reporting purposes, as if the two were one economic entity and not two separate corporations; this reporting process is in accordance with GAAP. Although accountants prepare this single composite financial report, both parent and subsidiary are, and continue to be, two separate legal entities.

The combination of statements consists of two steps. First, the changes that occurred as a result of the acquisition are indicated in the parent's balance sheet; the balances immediately before and immediately after the purchase are shown. Next the balances of both parent and subsidiary are combined and disclosed. Note that liabilities are not listed in the subsidiary's trial balance in the analysis example to follow. This exclusion emphasizes both that the parent is actually purchasing the net assets of the subsidiary and that the assets are the focus of the consolidation. An example that incorporates liabilities is in the illustrative problem.

ALTERNATIVE 1

In this alternative it is assumed that the purchase price representing the fair market value of the net assets is equal to the book value of the net assets of the subsidiary. Since the purchase is made on December 31, 19X8 (after closing entries have been posted), it is easy to indicate and compare the changes to the parent's financial position immediately after the purchase. See Exhibit 15-2. Next, the balances of both parent and subsidiary are combined. Note that the combination process involves the elimination of *reciprocal accounts* (indicated with arrows).

Q4: Reciprocal accounts

Note that the consolidated column is identical to the parent's column before its investment in the subsidiary. This correlation results because the combined group has the same resources before and after the acquisition in this example.

The important point to note is that the combination process combines only certain amounts. Other amounts, usually referred to as **reciprocal accounts,** are not combined; reciprocal accounts are eliminated in the combination process. The parent Investment in Subsidiary account and the subsidiary equity accounts comprise one example of reciprocal accounts that are eliminated for the following reasons:

- The combined entity cannot have an investment in itself, from a consolidation point of view

- The inclusion of the parent's Investment account and the subsidiary's equity accounts would show more assets and equity than actually exist in the combined financial entity. In other words, the inclusion of these reciprocal accounts would result in a double counting of assets and equity in the combined financial statements.

The combination, therefore, eliminates the parent's Investment account and the subsidiary's reciprocal equity accounts. Intercompany transactions, such as a loan from the parent to the subsidiary or a payment of interest by the subsidiary to the

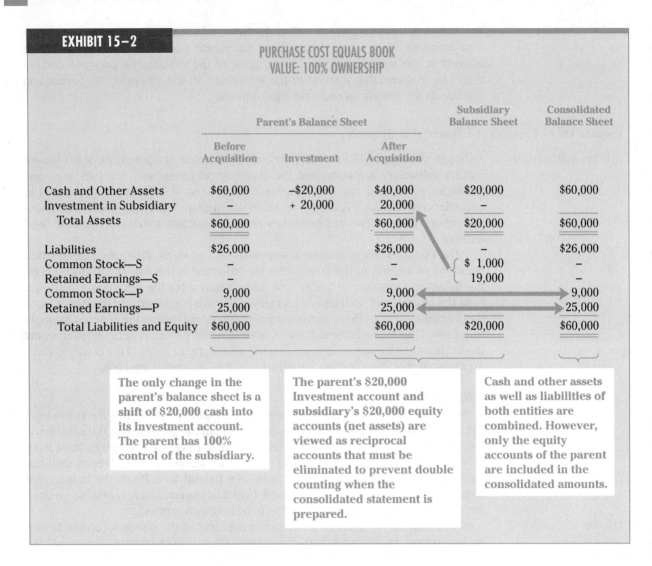

EXHIBIT 15-2

PURCHASE COST EQUALS BOOK
VALUE: 100% OWNERSHIP

	Parent's Balance Sheet			Subsidiary Balance Sheet	Consolidated Balance Sheet
	Before Acquisition	Investment	After Acquisition		
Cash and Other Assets	$60,000	–$20,000	$40,000	$20,000	$60,000
Investment in Subsidiary	–	+ 20,000	20,000	–	
Total Assets	$60,000		$60,000	$20,000	$60,000
Liabilities	$26,000		$26,000	–	$26,000
Common Stock—S	–		–	$ 1,000	–
Retained Earnings—S	–		–	19,000	–
Common Stock—P	9,000		9,000		9,000
Retained Earnings—P	25,000		25,000		25,000
Total Liabilities and Equity	$60,000		$60,000	$20,000	$60,000

The only change in the parent's balance sheet is a shift of $20,000 cash into its Investment account. The parent has 100% control of the subsidiary.

The parent's $20,000 Investment account and subsidiary's $20,000 equity accounts (net assets) are viewed as reciprocal accounts that must be eliminated to prevent double counting when the consolidated statement is prepared.

Cash and other assets as well as liabilities of both entities are combined. However, only the equity accounts of the parent are included in the consolidated amounts.

parent, also would be eliminated. This is necessary because if these transactions were not eliminated, the loan, for example, would be reported both as an asset and a liability representing the same item on the balance sheet. The income statement would report both an interest revenue and an interest expense representing the same item. In this example, since no intercompany transactions occurred, no other eliminations are required.

Although reciprocal accounts are eliminated in the combination process, it is important to note that no journal entries are actually recorded in the books of either parent or subsidiary. Worksheet entries are prepared and used only toward preparation of consolidated financial statements. (See the illustrative problem in this section.)

ALTERNATIVE 2

Q5: Goodwill from consolidation

In this alternative, the purchase cost is $25,000; the subsidiary's net assets recorded in its books remain at $20,000, as in Alternative 1. A balance sheet (shown in Exhibit 15-3) is prepared to show the changes occurring in the parent's balance sheet immediately after the purchase; the balances of both parent and subsidiary are then

EXHIBIT 15–3

PURCHASE COST IS MORE THAN BOOK
VALUE: 100% OWNERSHIP

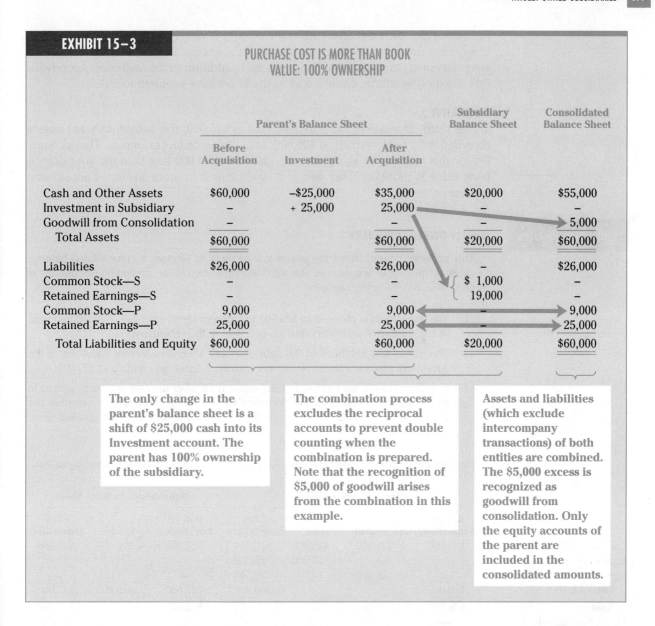

	Parent's Balance Sheet			Subsidiary Balance Sheet	Consolidated Balance Sheet
	Before Acquisition	Investment	After Acquisition		
Cash and Other Assets	$60,000	–$25,000	$35,000	$20,000	$55,000
Investment in Subsidiary	–	+ 25,000	25,000	–	–
Goodwill from Consolidation	–		–	–	5,000
Total Assets	$60,000		$60,000	$20,000	$60,000
Liabilities	$26,000		$26,000	–	$26,000
Common Stock—S	–		–	$ 1,000	–
Retained Earnings—S	–		–	19,000	–
Common Stock—P	9,000		9,000	–	9,000
Retained Earnings—P	25,000		25,000	–	25,000
Total Liabilities and Equity	$60,000		$60,000	$20,000	$60,000

The only change in the parent's balance sheet is a shift of $25,000 cash into its Investment account. The parent has 100% ownership of the subsidiary.

The combination process excludes the reciprocal accounts to prevent double counting when the combination is prepared. Note that the recognition of $5,000 of goodwill arises from the combination in this example.

Assets and liabilities (which exclude intercompany transactions) of both entities are combined. The $5,000 excess is recognized as goodwill from consolidation. Only the equity accounts of the parent are included in the consolidated amounts.

combined. Note that, this time, the combination process involves not only the elimination of reciprocal accounts, but also the creation of **goodwill from consolidation** (discussed briefly in Chapter 9); this goodwill arises because the parent has paid $5,000 in excess of the subsidiary's $20,000 net assets. (It is assumed for this example that the $5,000 payment is for goodwill in the subsidiary. In other examples, the $5,000 excess could represent an undervaluation of assets in addition to the existence of goodwill.)

Note that the total of the consolidated column ($60,000) is identical to the parent's column total ($60,000) before its investment in the subsidiary. The combined group has the same resources before and after the acquisition, in this alternative. However, the individual components within the asset amounts differ because of the existence of goodwill.

In this alternative, the parent paid $25,000 to purchase ownership claims to $20,000 of net assets in the subsidiary. The $5,000 excess was paid for goodwill in the subsidiary. Although goodwill is an asset, it is never recorded in the accounts of an entity unless it has been purchased. If the excess amount was attributable to an undervaluation of the subsidiary's assets, in addition to the existence of goodwill, this situation would be disclosed as in the illustrative problem to follow.

ALTERNATIVE 3

In this third alternative, the purchase cost is $16,000; the subsidiary's net assets recorded in its books remain at $20,000, as in the preceding examples. The accounting for this acquisition at a purchase cost that is $4,000 less than the subsidiary's book value is more complex, and is fully explained in more advanced accounting courses.

Illustrative Problem

WHOLLY OWNED SUBSIDIARY

This problem demonstrates the use of a worksheet to prepare a consolidated balance sheet at the date of acquisition. The same example used in the preceding discussions is used, with the following changes:

1. The investment is changed to $26,500 to incorporate an example of an amount paid in recognition of an undervaluation of assets in the subsidiary.

2. The assets and liabilities of the subsidiary are altered to include liabilities in the subsidiary's balance sheet. Net assets (assets − liabilities) remain at $20,000.

3. P made a $15,000 loan to S at December 31, 19X8, after the acquisition, as agreed in the acquisition negotiations. P recorded the loan as a receivable; S recorded the amount as a payable. These are reciprocal accounts that must be eliminated on consolidation.

Here are the individual balance sheets of P and S immediately before and after acquisition.

	Parent's Balance Sheet				**Subsidiary's Balance Sheet**		
	Before Acquisition	Investment	Loan	After Acquisition	Before Acquisition	Loan	After Acquisition
Cash and Other Assets	$60,000	− $26,500	− $15,000	$18,500	$22,000	+ $15,000	$37,000
Loans Receivable—S	—	—	+ 15,000	15,000	—		—
Investment in Subsidiary	—	+ 26,500		26,500	—		—
Total Assets	$60,000			$60,000	$22,000	$15,000	$37,000
Liabilities	$26,000			$26,000	$ 2,000		$ 2,000
Loans Payable—P	—			—		+ 15,000	15,000
Common Stock—S	—			—	1,000		1,000
Retained Earnings—S	—			—	19,000		19,000
Common Stock—P	9,000			9,000	—		—
Retained Earnings—P	25,000			25,000	—		—
Total Liabilities and Equity	$60,000			$60,000	$22,000	$15,000	$37,000

The parent's balance sheet has two changes: $26,500 of cash is used for the investment, and $15,000 of cash is used for the loan. Note that the total assets have not changed.

The only change in the subsidiary's balance sheet is the receipt of $15,000 cash and the creation of loans payable of the same amount. Note that the total assets and total equity have changed, although net assets have not.

These comparisons are included to show the changes resulting from the investment and the loan. The preparation of consolidated financial statements requires the elimination of reciprocal accounts; the elimination of the Investment in Subsidiary account and the subsidiary's equity accounts was considered already. The Loan Receivable and Loan Payable accounts are also reciprocal accounts, since total assets and total liabilities of the combined economic entity did not increase.

Again assume that, on December 31, 19X8, P corporation purchased a 100% ownership interest in S by paying $26,500 to the stockholders of S for their shares. Included in the purchase price was an amount in recognition of unrecorded goodwill in S and an undervaluation of an asset of S of $1,500.

Q6: Preparation of statements

On this date, as agreed in the acquisition, P also lent $15,000 to S. Here are the balance sheets prepared immediately after the purchase and recording of the loan.

	P	S	
	Book Value	Book Value	Market Value
Cash and Other Assets	$18,500	$37,000	$38,500
Loans Receivable—S	15,000	—	
Investment in Subsidiary	26,500	—	
Total Assets	$60,000	$37,000	
Liabilities	$26,000	$ 2,000	2,000
Loans Payable—P	—	15,000	15,000
Common Stock—S	—	1,000	
Retained Earnings—S	—	19,000	
Common Stock—P	9,000	—	
Retained Earnings—P	25,000	—	
Total Liabilities and Equity	$60,000	$37,000	

How much was included in the purchase price in recognition of undervalued assets in S?

Market Value of S Assets	$38,500
Book Value of S Assets	37,000
S Assets Undervalued	$ 1,500

How much was included in the purchase price in recognition of unrecorded goodwill in S?

Purchase Payment	$26,500
P Purchased 100% of S	20,000
Excess	$ 6,500
Excess from Asset Undervaluation	1,500
Balance Is Goodwill	$ 5,000

Q7: Eliminating entries

Note that in Exhibit 15-3, the reciprocal accounts disappeared when the parent's and subsidiary's balance sheets were added together. This approach is fine for illustrative purposes, but in practice a worksheet would be used to combine the two financial statements. The worksheet for this example appears in Exhibit 15-4. The eliminating entries, labeled *a* and *b* on the worksheet, appear here in journal form, but they are not posted to any records. These are worksheet entries only. Note that it would be difficult to post either of these entries since the various accounts affected appear on two different corporations' records.

Worksheet Entry

Loans Payable—P	(a) 15,000	
Loans Receivable—S		(a) 15,000

To eliminate intercompany loan.

Worksheet Entry

Common Stock—S	(b) 1,000	
Retained Earnings—S	(b) 19,000	
Assets—S	(b) 1,500	
Goodwill from Consolidation	(b) 5,000	
Investment in Subsidiary		(b) 26,500

To eliminate the Investment in
Subsidiary and subsidiary
equity accounts and set up
undervaluation of S's assets and
unrecorded goodwill.

A formal consolidated balance sheet is then prepared from the worksheet and also appears in Exhibit 15-4.

PARTIALLY OWNED SUBSIDIARIES

Q8: Minority interest

Since control of a corporation is usually achieved with an investment in stock of slightly more than 50%, there is no conceptual reason why a parent corporation would have to (or want to) own 100% of the stock, unless the parent wanted to take the subsidiary out of legal existence. In many, perhaps most business combinations, the parent owns less than 100%, creating the need to account for the **minority interest** in the subsidiary. In the discussion that follows, a 75% acquisition is assumed, creating a minority interest in the net assets of the subsidiary of 25%. The three alternatives investigated in the first part of the chapter are again addressed. They are referred to as Alternative 4, where the purchase price equals the book value of the net assets; Alternative 5, where the purchase price is more than the book value of the net assets; and Alternative 6, where the purchase price is less than the book value of the net assets.

Recording the Purchase

The acquisition cost for the alternatives already discussed is recorded here. This time the parent has acquired a 75% ownership interest in the subsidiary. Note that the amount paid differs in each case.

Acquisition of 75% Ownership Interest

	Alternative 4	Alternative 5	Alternative 6
Investment in Subsidiary	15,000	18,000	13,000
Cash	15,000	18,000	13,000

Although the purchase involves the payment of cash, the acquisition also can be made through a payment of other assets. Regardless, the parent in effect purchases a 75% ownership interest in the subsidiary's net assets; 75% of the subsidiary's previous owners no longer have any ownership interest in the subsidiary.

EXHIBIT 15-4

Consolidated Worksheet

| | Book Balances | | Eliminations | | |
	P	S	Debit	Credit	Consolidated
Debits					
Cash and Other Assets	$18,500	$37,000	(b) $1,500		$57,000
Loans Receivable—S	15,000	–		(a) $15,000	–
Investment in Subsidiary	26,500	–		(b) 26,500	–
Goodwill from Consolidation	–	–	(b) 5,000		5,000
Total Debits	$60,000	$37,000			$62,000
Credits					
Liabilities	$26,000	$ 2,000			$28,000
Loans Payable—P	–	15,000	(a) 15,000		–
Common Stock—S	–	1,000	(b) 1,000		–
Retained Earnings—S	–	19,000	(b) 19,000		–
Common Stock—P	9,000	–			9,000
Retained Earnings—P	25,000	–			25,000
Total Credits	$60,000	$37,000	$41,500	$41,500	$62,000

P & S Corporation
Consolidated Balance Sheet
December 31, 19X8

Assets		Liabilities and Equity		
Cash and Other Assets	$57,000	Liabilities		$28,000
Goodwill from Consolidation	5,000	Common Stock	$ 9,000	
		Retained Earnings	25,000	34,000
		Total Liabilities and		
Total Assets	$62,000	Equity		$62,000

Preparation of Consolidated Financial Statements

The combination of individual parent and subsidiary financial statements is then prepared for the partially owned subsidiary. As before, accountants prepare consolidated financial statements to show a financial picture of the whole operation, as if they were one economic entity.

ALTERNATIVE 4

In this alternative, the purchase cost is $15,000 ($20,000 × 75%); this is the amount of the subsidiary's net assets recorded in the books. The December 31, 19X8, purchase changes the parent's balances immediately after the purchase, as shown in Exhibit 15-5. Then the amounts of both parent and subsidiary are combined. Note that the combination process results in the recognition of the 25% minority interest.

Note that the consolidated column total ($65,000) is $5,000 larger than the parent's column total ($60,000) before its investment in the subsidiary. The consolidated statements include both the parent and minority interests; therefore, the

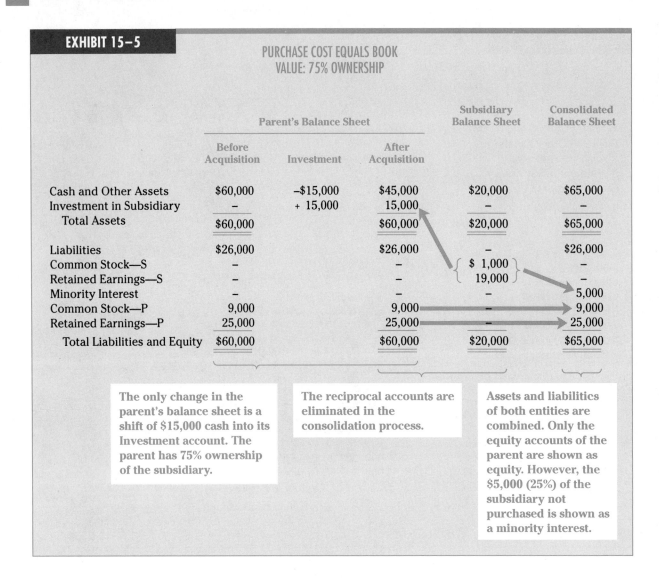

EXHIBIT 15–5

PURCHASE COST EQUALS BOOK
VALUE: 75% OWNERSHIP

	Parent's Balance Sheet			Subsidiary Balance Sheet	Consolidated Balance Sheet
	Before Acquisition	Investment	After Acquisition		
Cash and Other Assets	$60,000	–$15,000	$45,000	$20,000	$65,000
Investment in Subsidiary	–	+ 15,000	15,000	–	–
Total Assets	$60,000		$60,000	$20,000	$65,000
Liabilities	$26,000		$26,000	–	$26,000
Common Stock—S	–		–	$ 1,000	–
Retained Earnings—S	–		–	19,000	–
Minority Interest	–		–	–	5,000
Common Stock—P	9,000		9,000	–	9,000
Retained Earnings—P	25,000		25,000	–	25,000
Total Liabilities and Equity	$60,000		$60,000	$20,000	$65,000

The only change in the parent's balance sheet is a shift of $15,000 cash into its Investment account. The parent has 75% ownership of the subsidiary.

The reciprocal accounts are eliminated in the consolidation process.

Assets and liabilities of both entities are combined. Only the equity accounts of the parent are shown as equity. However, the $5,000 (25%) of the subsidiary not purchased is shown as a minority interest.

consolidated statements are increased when minority interests exist in a controlled subsidiary.

In this case, the combination of both entities eliminates the parent's Investment account and 75% of the subsidiary's equity accounts; the ownership interest of the subsidiary's remaining stockholders (25%) is recognized as a minority interest. The consolidated column, therefore, indicates that both the parent and the minority stockholders of the subsidiary have an ownership interest in the consolidated net assets of the combined group. An important difference between the parent and the minority interest, however, is that the parent is in the position of control of the subsidiary's operations.

ALTERNATIVE 5

In this alternative, the purchase cost is $18,000; this amount is $3,000 greater than the 75% ownership interest in the subsidiary's net assets ($20,000 × 75% = $15,000). The changes occurring in the parent's balances immediately before and after the purchase are prepared; then, the balances of both parent and subsidiary are com-

EXHIBIT 15–6

PURCHASE COST IS MORE THAN BOOK VALUE: 75% OWNERSHIP

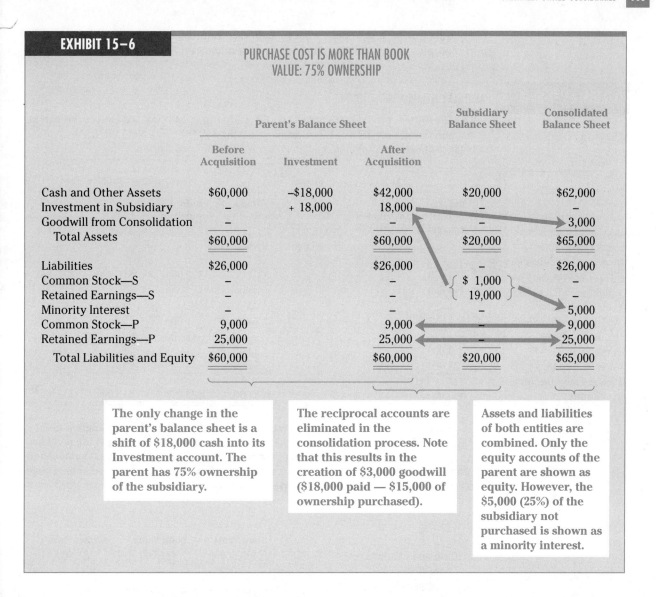

	Parent's Balance Sheet			Subsidiary Balance Sheet	Consolidated Balance Sheet
	Before Acquisition	Investment	After Acquisition		
Cash and Other Assets	$60,000	–$18,000	$42,000	$20,000	$62,000
Investment in Subsidiary	–	+ 18,000	18,000	–	–
Goodwill from Consolidation	–		–	–	3,000
Total Assets	$60,000		$60,000	$20,000	$65,000
Liabilities	$26,000		$26,000	–	$26,000
Common Stock—S	–		–	$ 1,000	–
Retained Earnings—S	–		–	19,000	–
Minority Interest	–		–	–	5,000
Common Stock—P	9,000		9,000	–	9,000
Retained Earnings—P	25,000		25,000	–	25,000
Total Liabilities and Equity	$60,000		$60,000	$20,000	$65,000

The only change in the parent's balance sheet is a shift of $18,000 cash into its Investment account. The parent has 75% ownership of the subsidiary.

The reciprocal accounts are eliminated in the consolidation process. Note that this results in the creation of $3,000 goodwill ($18,000 paid — $15,000 of ownership purchased).

Assets and liabilities of both entities are combined. Only the equity accounts of the parent are shown as equity. However, the $5,000 (25%) of the subsidiary not purchased is shown as a minority interest.

bined. See Exhibit 15-6. Note that the combination process results in the recognition of goodwill from consolidation, as well as the recognition of the 25% minority interest. The goodwill refers to the parent's payment of $3,000 in excess of its 75% ownership of the subsidiary's $20,000 net assets. In other situations, this $3,000 excess could result from an undervaluation of assets in addition to the existence of goodwill. An example incorporating an asset undervaluation appears in the illustrative problem to follow.

Note that, as with Alternative 4, the consolidated column ($65,000) is also $5,000 greater than the parent's column ($60,000) before its investment in the subsidiary. The consolidated statements include both the parent and minority interests and are increased when minority interests exist in a controlled subsidiary.

ALTERNATIVE 6

In this alternative, the purchase cost is $13,000; the subsidiary's net assets recorded in its books remain at $20,000, as in the preceding examples. The accounting for this acquisition at a purchase cost $7,000 less than the subsidiary's book value is more complex and is fully explained in more advanced accounting courses.

Illustrative Problem

PARTIALLY OWNED SUBSIDIARY

This illustrative problem is identical to the earlier one, with one exception: the parent has purchased only 75% of the subsidiary, paying $19,500 cash. Here are the individual balance sheets of P and S immediately before and after acquisition.

	Parent's Balance Sheet				Subsidiary's Balance Sheet		
	Before Acquisition	Investment	Loan	After Acquisition	Before Acquisition	Loan	After Acquisition
Cash and Other Assets	$60,000	− $19,500	− $15,000	$25,500	$22,000	+ $15,000	$37,000
Loans Receivable—S	—		+ 15,000	15,000	—		—
Investment in Subsidiary	—	+ 19,500		19,500	—		—
Total Assets	$60,000			$60,000	$22,000	$15,000	$37,000
Liabilities	$26,000			$26,000	$ 2,000		$ 2,000
Loans Payable—P	—			—		+ 15,000	15,000
Common Stock—S	—			—	1,000		1,000
Retained Earnings—S	—			—	19,000		19,000
Common Stock—P	9,000			9,000	—		—
Retained Earnings—P	25,000			25,000	—		—
Total Liabilities and Equity	$60,000			$60,000	$22,000	$15,000	$37,000

On December 31, 19X8, P corporation purchased a 75% ownership interest in S by paying $19,500 to 75% of the stockholders of S for their shares. Included in the purchase price was an amount in recognition of unrecorded goodwill in S and an undervaluation of an asset. On this date, P also lent $15,000 to S. The balance sheets prepared immediately after the purchase and recording of the loan appeared as follows:

	P	S	
	Book Value	Book Value	Market Value
Cash and Other Assets	$25,500	$37,000	$38,500
Loans Receivable—S	15,000	—	
Investment in Subsidiary	19,500	—	
Total Assets	$60,000	$37,000	
Liabilities	$26,000	$ 2,000	$ 2,000
Loans Payable—P	—	15,000	$15,000
Common Stock—S	—	1,000	
Retained Earnings—S	—	19,000	
Common Stock—P	9,000	—	
Retained Earnings—P	25,000	—	
Total Liabilities and Equity	$60,000	$37,000	

How much was included in the purchase price in recognition of undervalued assets in S?

	100%	75%
Market Value of S Assets	$38,500 × 75% purchased =	$28,875
Book Value of S Assets	37,000 × 75% purchased =	27,750
S Assets Undervalued	$ 1,500	$ 1,125

How much was included in the purchase price in recognition of unrecorded goodwill in S?

Purchase Payment	$19,500
P Purchased 75% of S	15,000
Excess	$ 4,500
Excess from Asset Undervaluation	1,125
Balance Is Goodwill	$ 3,375

The amount of minority interest is calculated.

Net Assets of S	$20,000
P purchased 75% of S	15,000
Minority Interest	$ 5,000

The worksheet elimination entries, labeled *a* and *b*, needed to consolidate the individual balance sheets are prepared.

Worksheet Entry

Loans Payable—P	(a) 15,000	
Loans Receivable—S		(a) 15,000

To eliminate intercompany loan.

Worksheet Entry

Common Stock—S	(b) 1,000	
Retained Earnings—S	(b) 19,000	
Assets—S	(b) 1,125	
Goodwill from Consolidation	(b) 3,375	
Minority Interest		(b) 5,000
Investment in Subsidiary		(b) 19,500

To eliminate the Investment in
Subsidiary and subsidiary
equity accounts and set up the
undervaluation of S's assets, the
unrecorded goodwill, and the
minority interest.

A consolidated worksheet is prepared for December 31, 19X8, immediately following the purchase of S's shares and the loan of $15,000.

Consolidated Worksheet

	Book Balances		Eliminations		
	P	S	Debit	Credit	Consolidated
Debits					
Cash and Other Assets	$25,500	$37,000	(b) $ 1,125		$63,625
Loans Receivable—S	15,000	—		(a) $15,000	—
Investment in Subsidiary	19,500	—		(b) 19,500	—
Goodwill from Consolidation	—	—	(b) 3,375		3,375
Total Debits	$60,000	$37,000			$67,000

(continued)

Consolidated Worksheet

Credits	Book Balances P	Book Balances S	Eliminations Debit		Eliminations Credit		Consolidated
Liabilities	$26,000	$ 2,000					$28,000
Loans Payable—P	—	15,000	(a)	15,000			—
Minority Interest					(b)	5,000	5,000
Common Stock—S	—	1,000	(b)	1,000			—
Retained Earnings—S	—	19,000	(b)	19,000			—
Common Stock—P	9,000	—					9,000
Retained Earnings—P	25,000	—					25,000
Total Credits	$60,000	$37,000		$39,500		$39,500	$67,000

A consolidated balance sheet is prepared for December 31, 19X8, immediately following the acquisition of S.

P & S Corporation
Consolidated Balance Sheet
December 31, 19X8

Assets		Liabilities and Equity		
Cash and Other Assets	$63,625	Liabilities		$28,000
Goodwill from Consolidation	3,375	Minority Interest		5,000
		Common Stock	$ 9,000	
		Retained Earnings	25,000	34,000
		Total Liabilities and		
Total Assets	$67,000	Equity		$67,000

POOLING OF INTERESTS

Q9: Pooling and book value

Remember that in a purchase the stockholders of the subsidiary are usually "bought out," that is, they accept cash or debt instruments in exchange for their shares in the subsidiary. Therefore, the parent stockholders become the new "owners" of the subsidiary. In a *pooling of interest,* the old owners of the subsidiary become new owners of the parent company, thereby leaving the owners as a group unchanged. If the owners remain the same, then under the historical cost assumption no change in ownership has occurred, and the net assets of the subsidiary should not be revalued to fair market value. Therefore, any investment recorded as a pooling of interest should be recorded at the book value of the acquired firm.

As noted earlier, a pooling of interest can only involve an exchange of common stock for common stock. In the examples throughout this chapter, the equity of the subsidiary consisted of common stock of $1,000 and retained earnings of $19,000. Assuming an agreement whereby the stockholders of the subsidiary accept 3,000 shares of $1 par value common stock of the parent in exchange for all their shares in the subsidiary, then the combination should be recorded as a pooling of interest. If book values are to be maintained, the parent's Investment account must be recorded at $20,000, as was the case for Alternative 1. If 3,000 shares of $1 common stock are issued in the transaction, then Common Stock must be credited for $3,000. The journal entry at this point would appear as follows:

Investment in Subsidiary	20,000
Common Stock	3,000
?	17,000

Since the group of subsidiary stockholders is pooling its interests with the group of parent stockholders, the subsidiary stockholders still want to keep their interest in the undistributed profits (retained earnings) of the subsidiary. Therefore, in any pooling of interest, retained earnings of the subsidiary are recorded on the parent's books to the extent possible. The entry to record the exchange of stock would appear as follows:

Investment in Subsidiary	20,000
Common Stock	3,000
Retained Earnings	17,000

After the exchange entry, the combining process can take place. It is quite similar to the accounting for Alternatives 1 and 4, when the fair market value (purchase cost) of the net assets of the subsidiary was equal to the book value of those net assets. Compare Exhibit 15-7 with the other examples in this chapter.

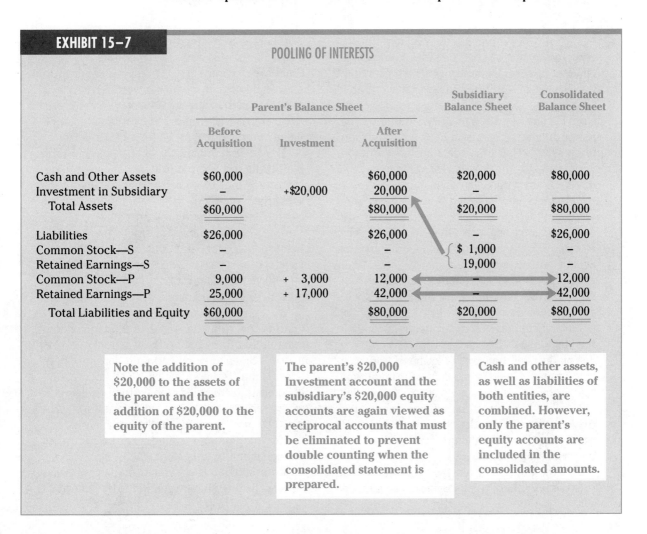

EXHIBIT 15-7 POOLING OF INTERESTS

	Parent's Balance Sheet			Subsidiary Balance Sheet	Consolidated Balance Sheet
	Before Acquisition	Investment	After Acquisition		
Cash and Other Assets	$60,000		$60,000	$20,000	$80,000
Investment in Subsidiary	–	+$20,000	20,000	–	
Total Assets	$60,000		$80,000	$20,000	$80,000
Liabilities	$26,000		$26,000	–	$26,000
Common Stock—S	–		–	$ 1,000	–
Retained Earnings—S	–		–	19,000	–
Common Stock—P	9,000	+ 3,000	12,000	–	12,000
Retained Earnings—P	25,000	+ 17,000	42,000	–	42,000
Total Liabilities and Equity	$60,000		$80,000	$20,000	$80,000

Note the addition of $20,000 to the assets of the parent and the addition of $20,000 to the equity of the parent.

The parent's $20,000 Investment account and the subsidiary's $20,000 equity accounts are again viewed as reciprocal accounts that must be eliminated to prevent double counting when the consolidated statement is prepared.

Cash and other assets, as well as liabilities of both entities, are combined. However, only the parent's equity accounts are included in the consolidated amounts.

APPLICATION OF LCM WHERE CONTROL EXISTS

Q10: LCM and control

As noted in Chapter 13, when securities are purchased with the intent to hold them for long-term purposes, the lower of cost or market (LCM) should be applied and the unrealized loss reported as a contra element in stockholders' equity. In situations where significant influence exists, the equity method should be used with on write-down for LCM. In situations where control exists, LCM should not be recorded in the accounts, since temporary declines in the market price of the stock are of no importance to users of financial information.

For an interesting discussion on the application of GAAP, see Real World Example 15-1. Should LCM have been applied to any investments in common stock right after the October 19, 1987, trading date when the world markets dropped 33% in

REAL WORLD EXAMPLE 15-1
LCM and the October 19, 1987, Decline

STRANGE that so many academics still cling to the illusion that the stock market is an efficient pricing mechanism. If the stock market were truly efficient, it would never have reached 2700 on the Dow in the summer of 1987, nor would it have crashed to 1750 little more than a month later. To argue that this was efficient pricing would be to argue that the corporate world lost one-third of its real value in a single month. Clearly this is an unsustainable view.

Despite piles of research from academics and government regulatory agencies, there is still no clear consensus on what triggered Black Monday. But it happened and could happen again, without reasonable cause, says Avner Arbel, 52, professor of finance at Cornell University. Arbel isn't lulled by the market's subsequent recovery. He is convinced that the crash is but a symptom of dangerous inefficiency in the stock market.

For decades the textbooks have told business students that the stock market is rational, that stock prices accurately reflect all publicly available information. This efficient market theory is the basis of hundreds of investment strategies aimed at identifying both "undervalued and overvalued" securities.

But the theory certainly does not hold true today, says Arbel. No single kernel of information can account for the market's precipitous crash 21 months ago. To Arbel, this indicates that the stock market was riding a wave of speculative buying. In academic terms, the stock market had become inefficient. What's more, Arbel warns that unless the causes of this inefficiency are corrected, another crash is likely.

Arbel thinks he knows what lies behind the inefficient and volatile pricing: insider trading. He argues that today's stock market gyrations are largely fueled by information not available to the general public—especially takeover rumors. The big moves in stocks have mostly been in takeover situations and the like, and here, Arbel says, the mass of investors are at an enormous disadvantage vis-à-vis the deal-makers, big traders, and institutions.

With investing increasingly dominated by institutions, Arbel has reached the radical conclusion that there are really two stock markets in the U.S., each running on a different pool of information. The first market we all know about. It consists of the traditional stock exchanges, where prices are based on information provided by news accounts, brokerage analysts, and disclosure documents filed with the Securities & Exchange Commission.

More sinister is a second market, or what Arbel calls the "shadow market." Here the stock

one day? Although the discussion in the *Forbes* article centers around the efficient market theory (beyond the scope of this textbook), it does point out some problems that may exist when applying GAAP.

FINANCIAL STATEMENTS AFTER DATE OF ACQUISITION

The accounting problems become quite complex at this point, whether the business combination has been accounted for as a purchase or as a pooling of interest. This material is discussed in more advanced accounting courses. Students who are considering a major in accounting will want to take Advanced Accounting, which in most universities in the United States covers consolidated theory. Consolidated

prices of companies involved in mergers and restructuring are determined away from the market, be it in a company's boardroom or in the offices of its investment banker. Generally, this information isn't available to the public on a timely basis. Instead, it remains the preserve of a few big institutions and professional traders. In time, prices on the traditional stock markets rise or fall to meet the shadow market, leaving savvy shadow players clutching fat profits.

"How can a pricing be efficient if stocks double overnight because of discussions that go on in boardrooms?" Arbel gripes.

Soured on the game, he says, individual investors have turned away from the market. "In an odd way the small investor knows the market is inefficient, and he doesn't trust it."

The implications of this could mean trouble for new companies seeking equity financing. Individual investors have provided crucial financing for small companies such as Apple Computer, which had virtually no institutional investors back in 1981. Or take a well-known stock like Disney; only 8% of its shares were owned by institutions as recently as 1970. *Forbes'* database shows that initial public stock offerings—a sector of the market especially reliant on individual investors—dropped from $18.8 billion in 1986 to some $5.2 billion last year.

In his recent book, *Crash* (Longman, $22.95),

Arbel reaches conclusions on his own, but he admits that much of his research comes straight from official studies of the 1987 crash. Up to now, unfortunately, many of those studies have been all but ignored.

To make the stock market more efficient, Arbel would eliminate the specialist system, which failed to hold up stock prices in the face of massive selling. He would also create one centralized market and one government agency to oversee it. During heavy downward market moves, Arbel supports a halt in trading to give the market a chance to catch its breath. To help alleviate small investors' fears, Arbel recommends more effective policing of institutional activity and more timely public disclosure of merger negotiations.

In short, Arbel wants to see more federal policing. But is that really the answer? A market that prices stocks so cheaply that they are susceptible to substantial premiums in takeover situations may not be efficient in the first place. Could it be that the takeover game, far from being a cause of inefficiency, is itself a product of pricing inefficiency?

Source Matthew Schifrin, "Dangerously inefficient," *Forbes,* July 10, 1989. Reprinted by permission of *Forbes* magazine. © Forbes Inc., 1989.

income statements must be prepared, and many intercompany transactions accounted for. The topic was introduced in Chapter 15 for the majority of students who must have an introduction to consolidated statements in order to be prepared for introductory courses in finance.

CHAPTER REVIEW

1   Does owning more than 50% of the voting stock of another corporation signify that the investing corporation has control over the corporation? (p. 672)

Yes, when one corporation owns more than 50% of another corporation, control is presumed. In some situations, the ownership position may only be temporary, or control might be in the hands of the courts in bankruptcy cases, but normally control is assumed at the 51% level.

2   What is the distinction in a business combination between a purchase and a pooling of interests? (p. 672)

In a purchase, the stockholders of the subsidiary accept cash, other assets, or debt instruments in exchange for their ownership interests in the subsidiary, thereby having no interest in the parent or subsidiary after the transaction. In a pooling of interests, the stockholders of the subsidiary accept ownership interests (common stock) of the parent corporation in exchange for their ownership interests in the subsidiary, thereby becoming stockholders of the parent company, which now owns the subsidiary.

3   When consolidated financial statements are prepared, does each corporation continue to maintain its own legal existence as a separate entity? (p. 675)

Yes, otherwise consolidated financial statements would not be needed. If the parent company takes the subsidiary out of legal existence, only one company would exist, the parent, and only one set of financial statements. The need for consolidated financial statements arises when two separate legal entities have common ownership.

4   What is the meaning of the term "reciprocal accounts"? Why are they eliminated in the consolidating process? (pp. 675–76)

Reciprocal accounts are the accounts referred to in the answer to question number 6 that represent the same thing. They must be eliminated to avoid double counting.

5   When does goodwill arise in the consolidating process? (pp. 676–78)

Goodwill arises in a business combination recorded as a purchase when the price paid for the net assets of the subsidiary exceeds the fair market value of the individual net assets. It appears only on the consolidated balance sheet, and not on the individual statements of the parent or the subsidiary.

6   What are the mechanics involved in the preparation of consolidated financial statements? (p. 679)

The balance in the Investment account represents the parent's interest in the net assets (stockholders' equity) of the subsidiary. Therefore, the Investment account on the books of the parent and the Stockholders' Equity section of the subsidiary's balance sheet both represent the same assets. Two accounts that represent the same thing must be eliminated against one another in order to avoid double counting. Intercompany receivables and payables (for example, S owes P $50,000) also must be eliminated, since otherwise the balance sheet would carry an asset (Accounts Receivable) and a liability (Accounts Payable) that represent the same claim. Many more intercompany accounts must be eliminated during consolidation.

7 When eliminating entries are made, are they posted to the books of the parent corporation? the subsidiary? Explain. (pp. 679–80)

Eliminating entries are not posted to any general ledger because accounts of two different entities are affected, and posting them to the general ledgers of the parent and the subsidiary would cause both sets of books to be out of balance.

8 When does minority interest exist? (p. 681)

Minority interest exists in any business combination where the parent owns less than 100% of the outstanding voting stock. The account Minority Interest represents the remaining stockholders' interest in the net assets of the subsidiary.

9 Why is a pooling of interest recorded at the book value of the net assets of a subsidiary rather than fair market value, as is the practice in a purchase situation? (pp. 686–87)

Since the owners of the two corporations do not change in a pooling, historical cost must be maintained in the books of the parent and of the subsidiary. If the ownership does not change, then a continuity exists that is not subject to revaluation.

10 Should lower of cost or market be used in valuing securities when the element of control exists? (pp. 688–89)

No, when control exists, the investment is deemed to be permanent (long-term) and temporary decreases in the market price of the securities are of no importance to the users of financial information.

KEY TERMS

business combination (p. 672) The acquisition of one corporation by another corporation, usually through acquiring a controlling interest represented by purchasing more than 50% of the outstanding voting stock.

consolidated financial statements (p. 672) The result of combining the financial statements of the parent and its subsidiary(ies); these must be prepared when one corporation (parent) owns a controlling interest in another corporation (subsidiary).

controlling interest (p. 672) Where one corporation owns more than 50% of the outstanding voting stock of another corporation.

goodwill from consolidation (p. 677) The excess of the purchase price of a business combination accounted for as a purchase over the fair market value of the net assets of the subsidiary. It appears as an asset only on the consolidated balance sheet, not on the individual balance sheet of the parent or its subsidiary.

minority interest (p. 681) The remaining stockholders' interest in a subsidiary in which a parent corporation has a controlling interest, but does not own 100% of the outstanding voting stock. Appears only on the consolidated financial statements, and not on the individual balance sheets of the parent or its subsidiary.

parent company (p. 672) A corporation that owns a controlling interest in another corporation, referred to as the subsidiary.

pooling of interests (p. 672) The method of accounting for a business combination in which the stockholders of the subsidiary give up their ownership interest in the subsidiary in exchange for ownership interests (common stock) in the parent corporation, thereby becoming owners of the parent corporation, which in turn owns the subsidiary.

purchase (p. 672) A business combination in which the stockholders of the subsidiary give up their ownership interest in the subsidiary in exchange for cash, other assets, or debt instruments of the parent. The stockholders no longer have an ownership interest in the subsidiary or the parent.

reciprocal accounts (p. 675)   Accounts that represent the same claim as other accounts when combining financial statements of a parent and its subsidiary(ies). The major reciprocal accounts are the Investment account on the books of the parent, and the stockholders' equity accounts on the books of the subsidiary. They both represent the owners' claim to the net assets of the subsidiary.

subsidiary (p. 672)   The corporation in which another corporation, the parent, has a controlling interest.

SELF-TEST QUESTIONS FOR REVIEW   (Answers are at the end of this chapter.)

Q5

1. Consolidated goodwill arises from
    (a) business combinations accounted for as a purchase.
    (b) business combinations accounted for as a pooling of interest.
    (c) either a purchase or a pooling.
    (d) neither a purchase or a pooling.

Q4

2. When the purchase price of a business combination is equal to the book value of the net assets of the subsidiary,
    (a) no reciprocal accounts have to be eliminated.
    (b) all reciprocal accounts must be eliminated, as in any combination.
    (c) no reciprocal accounts exist.
    (d) only reciprocal receivables and payables need to be eliminated.

Q1

3. A controlling interest only is presumed when one corporation owns
    (a) more than 20% of the voting stock and can exercise significant influence over the corporation.
    (b) 100% of the outstanding voting stock of another corporation.
    (c) more than 50% of the voting stock of another corporation.
    (d) all of the preferred stock and can exercise significant influence over the corporation.

Q6

4. Stockholders' Equity on the consolidated balance sheet will be
    (a) equal to the sum of the stockholders' equities of the parent and the subsidiary.
    (b) greater than the sum of the stockholders' equities of the parent and the subsidiary.
    (c) equal to the stockholders' equity of the parent corporation if the parent owns 100% of the subsidiary.
    (d) equal to the stockholders' equity of the subsidiary.

Q8

5. The Minority Interest account
    (a) appears as an asset on the consolidated balance sheet.
    (b) appears between Liabilities and Stockholders' Equity on the consolidated balance sheet.
    (c) appears only on the financial statements of the subsidiary.
    (d) appears only on the balance sheet of the parent.
    (e) is not a balance sheet account.

Q5

6. Goodwill from consolidation arises when the purchase price is
    (a) greater than the book value of the net assets of the subsidiary.
    (b) greater than the fair market value of the net assets of the subsidiary.
    (c) equal to the book value of the net assets of the subsidiary.
    (d) equal to the fair market value of the net assets of the subsidiary.

Q2

7. The consideration given by the parent in a business combination accounted for as a purchase can include the following:
    (a) Cash
    (b) Noncash assets
    (c) Debt securities

(d) Equity securities
(e) All of the above

Q2, Q9

8. The consideration given by the parent in a business combination accounted for as a pooling of interest can include the following:
(a) Cash
(b) Noncash assets
(c) Debt securities
(d) Equity securities
(e) All of the above

DEMONSTRATION PROBLEM

Part A

On January 1, 19X2, P corporation purchased 100% of S's shares by paying $300,000 cash to the stockholders of S for their shares. The purchase price included an amount in recognition of an undervaluation in the asset land and also an amount in recognition of goodwill in S. The balance sheet balances of both corporations immediately after the purchase are recorded in this partial consolidation worksheet.

	Book Balances	
	P	S
Cash and Other Assets	$350,000	$150,000
Investment in Subsidiary	300,000	—
Land—S	—	200,000
Goodwill from Consolidation	—	—
Total Assets	$650,000	$350,000
Liabilities	$225,000	$100,000
Common Stock—P	250,000	—
Retained Earnings—P	175,000	—
Common Stock—S	—	200,000
Retained Earnings—S	—	50,000
Total Liabilities and Equity	$650,000	$350,000

Required

1. Calculate the amount by which land is undervaluated. Assume that the current market value of land is $225,000.

2. Calculate the amount of goodwill included in the purchase price.

3. Prepare the worksheet elimination entry needed to consolidate the individual balance sheets.

4. Complete the consolidated worksheet, using the form in the illustrative problems in the chapter.

Part B

The following consolidated worksheet was prepared on December 31, 19X2, following the purchase of a controlling interest in S by P corporation. On that date, P also had other transactions with S.

Consolidated Worksheet

Debits	Book Balances P	Book Balances S	Eliminations Debit	Eliminations Credit	Consolidated
Cash	$ 6,000	$ 2,000			$ 8,000
Accounts Receivable	14,000	11,000		$ 1,000	24,000
Notes Receivable	5,000	—		5,000	—
Investment in Subsidiary	40,000	—		40,000	—
Long-term Assets (net)	110,000	43,000			153,000
Goodwill from Consolidation	—	—	$ 5,000		5,000
Total Debits	$175,000	$56,000			$190,000
Credits					
Accounts Payable	$ 20,000	$ 1,000	1,000		$ 20,000
Notes Payable	—	5,000	5,000		—
Minority Interest	—	—		15,000	15,000
Common Stock—P	100,000	—			100,000
Retained Earnings—P	55,000	—			55,000
Common Stock—S	—	40,000	40,000		—
Retained Earnings—S	—	10,000	10,000		—
Total Credits	$175,000	$56,000	$61,000	$61,000	$190,000

Required

1. What percentage of S's shares was purchased by P? (*Hint:* Start by calculating the percentage of S owned by minority stockholders.)

2. Was the purchase of S's shares made at book value? Explain.

3. Record the worksheet elimination entries needed to consolidate the individual balance sheets. Explain why each entry is required.

4. Prepare a consolidated balance sheet as of December 31, 19X2.

SOLUTION TO DEMONSTRATION PROBLEM

Part A

1.

	S Book Value	Market Value	Undervaluation
Land	$200,000	$225,000	$25,000

2.

Purchase Payment	$300,000
P Purchased 100% of S	250,000
Excess	$ 50,000
Undervaluation of Land	25,000
Goodwill from Consolidation	$ 25,000

3.

Common Stock—S	200,000	
Retained Earnings—S	50,000	
Land	25,000	
Goodwill from Consolidation	25,000	
Investment in Subsidiary		300,000

To eliminate the Investment account and set up revaluation of land and goodwill from consolidation.

4.

Consolidated Worksheet

| | Book Balances | | Eliminations | | |
	P	S	Debit	Credit	Consolidated
Debits					
Cash and Other Assets	$350,000	$150,000			$500,000
Investment in Subsidiary	300,000	—		$300,000	—
Land	—	200,000	$ 25,000		225,000
Goodwill from Consolidation	—	—	25,000		25,000
Total Debits	$650,000	$350,000			$750,000
Credits					
Liabilities	$225,000	$100,000			$325,000
Common Stock—P	250,000	—			250,000
Retained Earnings—P	175,000	—			175,000
Common Stock—S	—	200,000	$200,000		—
Retained Earnings—S	—	50,000	50,000		—
Total Credits	$650,000	$350,000	$300,000	$300,000	$750,000

Part B

1. Total Assets S − Total Liabilities = $56,000 − 6,000 = $50,000

   Minority Interest = $15,000 ÷ $50,000 = 30%; if minority interest holds 30%, then P owns 70%.

2. If the purchase had been made at book value, then 70% of S's common stock and retained earnings would equal the investment cost.

$$70\% (\$40,000 + \$10,000) = \$35,000$$

   Investment = $40,000; therefore, purchase was not made at book value. Also, goodwill appears on the consolidated worksheet.

3.

Accounts Payable	1,000	
Accounts Receivable		1,000
To eliminate intercompany amounts owed.		
Notes Payable	5,000	
Notes Receivable		5,000
To eliminate intercompany amounts owed.		
Common Stock—S	40,000	
Retained Earnings—S	10,000	
Goodwill from Consolidation	5,000	
Investment in Subsidiary		40,000
Minority Interest		15,000
To eliminate the Investment account and set up minority interest and goodwill.		

4.

P & S Corporation
Consolidated Balance Sheet
December 31, 19X2

Assets

Current Assets		
Cash	$ 8,000	
Accounts Receivable	24,000	
Total Current Assets		$ 32,000
Long-term Assets (net)		153,000
Goodwill from Consolidation		5,000
Total Assets		$190,000

Liabilities and Equity

Current Liabilities		
Accounts Payable		$ 20,000
Minority Interest		15,000
Stockholders' Equity		
Common Stock	$100,000	
Retained Earnings	55,000	
Total Stockholders' Equity		155,000
Total Liabilities and Equity		$190,000

Note: In current practice the Minority Interest account is normally reported between the Liability section of the balance sheet and Stockholders' Equity. In theory the account is neither a liability of the consolidated entity, nor an element of stockholders' equity of the consolidated entity.

DISCUSSION QUESTIONS

Q15-1 What is a business combination?

Q15-2 What is the distinction between a parent and a subsidiary?

Q15-3 Distinguish between a purchase and a pooling of interests.

Q15-4 Does a parent corporation acquire the net assets or the equity of a subsidiary? Explain.

Q15-5 Why does a subsidiary maintain its own accounting records?

Q15-6 Why would the purchase cost of a subsidiary exceed the subsidiary's net assets?

Q15-7 Why are reciprocal accounts eliminated in the preparation of consolidated financial statements?

Q15-8 How are intercompany transactions handled in a combination? Why?

Q15-9 Describe the procedure used in the preparation of consolidated financial statements.

Q15-10 How does goodwill arise on consolidation?

Q15-11 How does partial ownership of a subsidiary result in a minority interest?

Q15-12 How does the preparation of consolidated financial statements differ for a pooling of interests and a purchase?

DISCUSSION CASE

Which Solution?

Q8

Turn to p. 698 and read the data for E15-1 through E15-7. Then read E15-5 and examine the following two solutions to the three requirements for the exercise.

Solution 1

1.	Purchase Payment (8,000 × $70)		$560,000
	Book Value of Net Assets (80% × $400,000)		320,000
	Excess		$240,000
	Land (80% × $50,000)	$ 40,000	
	Buildings (80% × $95,000)	76,000	
	Equipment (80% × $55,000)	44,000	160,000
	Goodwill		$ 80,000

2.	Investment in Subsidiary	560,000	
	Cash		560,000

3.	Common Stock	200,000	
	Retained Earnings	200,000	
	Land	40,000	
	Buildings	76,000	
	Equipment	44,000	
	Goodwill	80,000	
	Investment in Subsidiary		560,000
	Minority Interest (20% ×		
	$400,000)		80,000

Solution 2

1.	Purchase Price (8,000 × $70) ÷ .80		$700,000
	Book Value of Net Assets		400,000
	Excess		$300,000
	Land	$ 50,000	
	Buildings	95,000	
	Equipment	55,000	200,000
	Goodwill		$100,000

2.	Investment in Subsidiary	560,000	
	Cash		560,000

3.	Common Stock	200,000	
	Retained Earnings	200,000	
	Land	50,000	
	Buildings	95,000	
	Equipment	55,000	
	Goodwill	100,000	
	Investment in Subsidiary		560,000
	Minority Interest (20% ×		
	$700,000)		140,000

Required

Compare the two solutions to E15-5 and comment on your investigation.

EXERCISES

E15-1 through E15-7 are based on the following data: P corporation acquires control of S corporation by purchasing the outstanding shares from the stockholders of S corporation. The agreed on price is $75 per share for all 10,000 shares outstanding, or $70 per share if less than 100% of the stockholders want to take part in the transaction. At the time of the acquisition, the stockholders' equity of S corporation consisted only of common stock and retained earnings.

Acquisition and elimi-
nation entries, goodwill
(Q4–Q7)

E15-1 Assume P corporation acquired 100% of the outstanding stock of S corporation, and S's stockholders' equity at the date of acquisition appeared as follows:

Common Stock	$200,000
Retained Earnings	550,000

Required
1. Determine the amount of goodwill evident in the combination.
2. Prepare the journal entry necessary to record the acquisition of the shares.
3. Prepare the elimination entry necessary to remove the reciprocal accounts prior to combining the financial statements of the two companies.

Acquisition and elimi-
nation entries, revalua-
tion of land, goodwill
(Q4–Q7)

E15-2 Assume P corporation acquired 100% of the outstanding stock of S corporation, and S's stockholders' equity at the date of acquisition appeared as follows:

Common Stock	$200,000
Retained Earnings	350,000

Some land the subsidiary owns has a market value of $200,000 in excess of its historical cost.

Required
1. Determine the amount of goodwill evident in the combination.
2. Prepare the journal entry necessary to record the acquisition of the shares.
3. Prepare the elimination entry necessary to remove the reciprocal accounts prior to combining the financial statements of the two companies.

Acquisition and elimi-
nation entries, revalua-
tion of noncash assets,
goodwill (Q4–Q7)

E15-3 Assume P corporation acquired 100% of the outstanding stock of S corporation, and S's stockholders' equity at the date of acquisition appeared as follows:

Common Stock	$200,000
Retained Earnings	350,000

Some land the subsidiary owns has a market value of $50,000, while some buildings were appraised at $95,000 and equipment at $55,000, all in excess of historical cost.

Required
1. Determine the amount of goodwill evident in the combination.
2. Prepare the journal entry necessary to record the acquisition of the shares.
3. Prepare the elimination entry necessary to remove the reciprocal accounts prior to combining the financial statements of the two companies.

Acquisition and elimination entries, revaluation of noncash assets, goodwill (Q4–Q7)

E15-4   Assume P corporation acquired 100% of the outstanding stock of S corporation, and S's stockholders' equity at the date of acquisition appeared as follows:

Common Stock	$200,000
Retained Earnings	250,000

Some land the subsidiary owns has a market value of $50,000, while some buildings were appraised at $95,000 and equipment at $55,000, all in excess of historical cost.

Required

1. Determine the amount of goodwill evident in the combination.
2. Prepare the journal entry necessary to record the acquisition of the shares.
3. Prepare the elimination entry necessary to remove the reciprocal accounts prior to combining the financial statements of the two companies.

Acquisition and elimination entries, revaluation of noncash assets, goodwill, minority interest (Q4–Q8)

E15-5   Assume P corporation acquired 80% of the outstanding stock of S corporation, and S's stockholders' equity at the date of acquisition appeared as follows:

Common Stock	$200,000
Retained Earnings	200,000

Some land the subsidiary owns has a market value of $50,000, while some buildings were appraised at $95,000 and equipment at $55,000, all in excess of historical cost.

Required

1. Determine the amount of goodwill evident in the combination.
2. Prepare the journal entry necessary to record the acquisition of the shares.
3. Prepare the elimination entry necessary to remove the reciprocal accounts prior to combining the financial statements of the two companies.

Acquisition and elimination entries, goodwill, minority interest (Q4–Q8)

E15-6   Assume P corporation acquired 80% of the outstanding stock of S corporation, and S's stockholders' equity at the date of acquisition appeared as follows:

Common Stock	$200,000
Retained Earnings	500,000

Required

1. Determine the amount of goodwill evident in the combination.
2. Prepare the journal entry necessary to record the acquisition of the shares.
3. Prepare the elimination entry necessary to remove the reciprocal accounts prior to combining the financial statements of the two companies.

Acquisition and elimination entries, revaluation of noncash assets, goodwill, minority interest (Q4–Q8)

E15-7   Assume P corporation acquired 80% of the outstanding stock of S corporation, and S's stockholders' equity at the date of acquisition appeared as follows:

Common Stock	$200,000
Retained Earnings	200,000

Some land the subsidiary owns has a market value of $50,000 above historical cost, while some buildings were appraised at $95,000 above historical cost and equipment at $55,000 *below* historical cost.

Required

1. Determine the amount of goodwill evident in the combination.

2. Prepare the journal entry necessary to record the acquisition of the shares.

3. Prepare the elimination entry necessary to remove the reciprocal accounts prior to combining the financial statements of the two companies.

PROBLEMS

100%, 60% acquisitions, goodwill (Q4–Q8)

P15-1 On December 31, 19X1, P corporation purchased an interest in S by paying cash to the stockholders of S for their shares. S is a newly formed developer of computer microchips that was about to begin manufacturing operations. Included in the purchase price was an amount in recognition of goodwill in S. Immediately before this purchase, the balance sheets of the corporations appeared as follows:

	P	S	
	Book Value	Book Value	Market Value
Cash and Other Assets	$450,000	$150,000	$150,000
Liabilities	$ 75,000	—	
Common Stock	175,000	$150,000	
Retained Earnings	200,000	—	
Total Liabilities and Equity	$450,000	$150,000	

Required

Consider these cases.

Case A: P purchased 100% of S's shares by paying $175,000 cash.
Case B: P purchased 60% of S's shares by paying $100,000 cash.

For each case, do the following:

1. Calculate the amount of goodwill included in the purchase.

2. Calculate the amount of the minority interest, if applicable.

3. Prepare the entry to record in P's books the purchase of S's shares.

4. Prepare the worksheet elimination entry needed to consolidate the balance sheets.

5. Prepare a consolidated balance sheet as of December 31, 19X1, immediately following the purchase of S's shares.

70% acquisition, long-term assets, goodwill (Q4–Q8)

P15-2 On June 30, 19X3, P corporation purchased 70% interest in S by paying $225,000 cash to the stockholders of S for their shares. Included in this purchase price were amounts in recognition of an undervaluation in S's long-term assets and of goodwill in S. On this date S owed $50,000 to P; this amount is included in the accounts receivable of P and the accounts payable of S. The financial statements of both corporations immediately preceding the purchase are reproduced here.

	P	S	
	Book Value	Book Value	Market Value
Cash	$275,000	$ 30,000	$ 30,000
Accounts Receivable	150,000	20,000	20,000
Inventory	200,000	110,000	110,000
Long-term Assets (net)	335,000	225,000	330,000
Total Assets	$960,000	$385,000	

(continued)

	P	S	
	Book Value	Book Value	Market Value
Accounts Payable	$ 50,000	$160,000	$160,000
Common Stock	115,000	100,000	
Retained Earnings	795,000	125,000	
Total Liabilities and Equity	$960,000	$385,000	

Required

1. Prepare the entry to record in P's books the purchase of S's shares.

2. Calculate the amount of the undervaluation in S's long-term assets.

3. Calculate the amount of goodwill included in the purchase price.

4. Prepare the worksheet elimination entries needed to consolidate the individual balance sheets.

5. Prepare a consolidated worksheet.

6. Prepare a consolidated balance sheet as of June 30, 19X3, immediately after the purchase of S's shares.

100%, 60% acquisitions, goodwill (Q4–Q8)

P15-3 On January 2, 19X3, P purchased an interest in S. The following condensed financial statements of S and P were prepared immediately before the purchase:

	P	S	
	Book Value	Book Value	Market Value
Assets	$150,000	$190,000	
Liabilities	$ 10,000	$ 10,000	
Equity	140,000	?	
Total Liabilities and Equity	$150,000		

Required
Consider these cases.

Case A: P purchased 100% of S's shares January 2, 19X3, by paying $210,000 to stockholders of S. Included in the purchase price was an amount in recognition of unrecorded goodwill in S.

Case B: P purchased 60% of S's shares January 2, 19X3, by paying $125,000 to stockholders of S. Included in the purchase was an amount in recognition of unrecorded goodwill in S.

For each case, do the following:

1. Prepare the entry to record on P's books the purchase of S's shares.

2. Calculate the amount of minority interest to be shown on the consolidated balance sheet immediately after the purchase of S's shares.

3. Calculate the amount of goodwill to be shown on the consolidated balance sheet immediately after the purchase of S's shares.

4. Prepare the worksheet elimination entry needed to remove the Investment in Subsidiary account on P's books and S's equity immediately after the purchase of S's shares.

70% acquisition, noncash assets, goodwill (Q4–Q8)

P15-4 P is an investment company that has assets consisting of cash and investments. On December 31, 19X7, P purchased 70% of S's shares by paying $185,000 to stockholders of S. The balance sheet and other financial information of S immediately before the purchase are as follows:

	S				**S**	
	Book Value	Market Value			Book Value	Market Value
Cash	$ 75,000	$ 75,000	Accounts Payable		$ 55,000	$ 55,000
Land	40,000	85,000	Bonds Payable		80,000	80,000
Building (net)	110,000	190,000	Common Stock		120,000	
Equipment (net)	60,000	20,000	Retained Earnings (Jan. 2, 19X7)		140,000	
Goodwill	50,000	—	Net loss for the year		(60,000)	
Total Assets	$335,000		Total Liabilities and Equity		$335,000	

Required

1. Included in the purchase price was an amount in recognition of the undervaluation and overvaluation of various balance sheet items. Calculate this net amount.

2. Was any amount included in the purchase price in recognition of unrecorded goodwill for S? Explain.

3. What amount of assets and liabilities of S would appear on the consolidated balance sheet immediately after the purchase of S's shares by P?

4. Calculate the amount of minority interest that would appear on the consolidated balance sheet immediately after purchase of S's shares by P.

100%, 70%, and 60% acquisitions, assets, no goodwill (Q4–Q8)

P15-5 On December 31, 19X8, P corporation purchased an interest in S by paying $120,000 cash to the stockholders of S for their shares. Included in this purchase price was an amount in recognition of an undervaluation of the net assets of S. Assume no goodwill exists. Here are some summarized financial data from the balance sheets of both corporations immediately after the purchase.

	P	**S**
	Book Value	Book Value
Net Assets	$400,000	$90,000
Common Stock	$100,000	$30,000
Retained Earnings	300,000	60,000

Required

Consider these cases.

Case A: P purchased 100% of S.
Case B: P purchased 70% of S.
Case C: P purchased 60% of S.

For each case, do the following:

1. Calculate the amount of the undervaluation of S's net assets.

2. Prepare the worksheet elimination entry needed to consolidate the individual balance sheets.

3. What amounts would be reported on the consolidated balance sheet for
   (a) Net Assets?
   (b) Common Stock? Retained Earnings?

ALTERNATE PROBLEMS

100%, 60% acquisitions, inventory, long-term assets, goodwill (Q4–Q8)

AP15-1 On January 2, 19X2, P corporation purchased an interest in S by paying cash to the stockholders of S for their shares. The financial statements and other financial information of both corporations immediately before the purchase are as follows:

	P	S	
	Book Value	Book Value	Market Value
Cash and Other Assets	$205,000	$ 90,000	$90,000
Inventory	95,000	60,000	70,000
Long-term Assets	165,000	50,000	65,000
Total Assets	$465,000	$200,000	
Liabilities	$ 55,000	$ 45,000	$45,000
Common Stock	260,000	95,000	
Retained Earnings	150,000	60,000	
Total Liabilities and Equity	$465,000	$200,000	

Required

Consider these cases.

Case A: P purchased 100% of S's shares for $180,000 cash.
Case B: P purchased 60% of S's shares for $120,000 cash.

For each case, do the following:

1. Prepare the entry to record in P's books the purchase of S's shares.

2. Calculate the amount of the minority interest, if any.

3. Was any amount included in the purchase price in recognition of unrecorded goodwill in S? If so, calculate the amount of such goodwill.

4. Calculate the consolidated balances for inventory and goodwill as of January 2, 19X2, immediately after the purchase.

5. Prepare the worksheet elimination entry needed to consolidate the individual balance sheets.

6. Prepare a consolidated balance sheet as of January 2, 19X2, immediately after the purchase of S's shares.

70% acquisition, long-term assets, bonds payable, goodwill (Q4–Q8)

AP15-2 On December 31, 19X2, P corporation purchased a 70% interest in S by paying $200,000 cash to the stockholders of S for their shares. The purchase price included an amount of an undervaluation of long-term assets and bonds payable and also an amount in recognition of goodwill in S. Here are the balance sheets of both corporations immediately after the purchase.

	P	S	
	Book Value	Book Value	Market Value
Assets			
Current Assets	$ 65,000	$160,000	$160,000
Investment in Subsidiary	200,000	—	
Long-term Assets (net)	585,000	225,000	270,000
Goodwill from Consolidation	110,000	—	
Total Assets	$960,000	$385,000	
Liabilities and Equities			
Current Liabilities	$ 50,000	$ 60,000	$ 60,000
Bonds Payable (5-year life)	200,000	100,000	115,000
Common Stock	250,000	75,000	
Retained Earnings	460,000	150,000	
Total Liabilities and Equity	$960,000	$385,000	

Required
Do the following for the date of acquisition:

1. Calculate the undervaluation of long-term assets and bonds payable.
2. Calculate the amount of goodwill included in the purchase price.
3. Calculate the amount of minority interest.
4. Prepare the worksheet elimination entry needed to consolidate the individual balance sheets.
5. Prepare a consolidation worksheet as of December 31, 19X2.

60% acquisition, accounts receivable, goodwill (Q4–Q8)

AP15-3   On December 31, 19X6, P corporation purchased a 60% interest in S by paying $150,000 cash to stockholders of S for their shares. Included in this purchase price was an excess of cost over book value. At that date, P owed $15,000 to S; the amount is included as an accounts payable in P's books and as an accounts receivable in S's books. Immediately after the purchase, the balance sheets of both corporations appeared as follows:

	P	S	
	Book Value	Book Value	Market Value
Cash and Other Assets	$ 90,000	$105,000	$109,000
Accounts Receivable	160,000	95,000	95,000
Investment in Subsidiary	150,000	—	
Total Assets	$400,000	$200,000	
Accounts Payable	$ 60,000	$ 25,000	$ 25,000
Common Stock	225,000	100,000	
Retained Earnings	115,000	75,000	
Total Liabilities and Equity	$400,000	$200,000	

Required
1. Calculate the excess of cost over book value of the investment in S.
2. Prepare the worksheet elimination entries needed to consolidate the individual balance sheets.
3. Prepare a consolidation worksheet.
4. Prepare a consolidated balance sheet as of December 31, 19X6, immediately after the purchase of S's share.

100%, 75% acquisitions, patent, goodwill (Q4–Q8)

AP15-4   The following are financial statements and other financial information of P corporation and S as of December 31, 19X6:

	P	S	
	Book Value	Book Value	Market Value
Cash and Other Assets	$160,000	$ 30,000	$ 30,000
Patent	—	75,000	150,000
Total Assets	$160,000	$105,000	
Liabilities	$ 50,000	$ 45,000	$ 45,000
Common Stock	10,000	15,000	
Retained Earnings	100,000	45,000	
Total Liabilities and Equity	$160,000	$105,000	

Required

Consider these cases.

Case A: P purchased 100% of S's shares December 31, 19X6, by paying $150,000 to stock-holders of S.

Case B: P purchased 75% of S's shares December 31, 19X6, by paying $135,000 to stock-holders of S.

Case C: P purchased 75% of S's shares December 31, 19X6, by paying $30,000 to stockholders of S. Assume that the market value of a patent owned by S was $55,000 on this date.

For each case, do the following:

1. Prepare the journal entry to record in P's books the purchase of S's shares.

2. Included in the purchase price was an amount in recognition of an undervaluation (overvaluation) in the asset patent. Calculate this amount.

3. Was any amount included in the purchase price in recognition of unrecorded goodwill in S? If so, calculate the amount.

4. Prepare the worksheet elimination entry needed to consolidate the individual balance sheets.

5. Prepare a consolidated balance sheet as of December 31, 19X6, immediately after the purchase of S's shares.

90% acquisition, good-will (Q4–Q8)

AP15-5 On January 2, 19X6, P corporation purchased a 90% interest in S by paying $120,000 cash to the stockholders of S for their shares. Included in this purchase price was an amount in recognition of goodwill in S. Here is selected financial information from the balance sheets of both corporations immediately before the purchase.

	P	S
Common Stock	$120,000	$75,000
Retained Earnings	70,000	25,000

Required

Do the following as of January 2, 19X6:

1. Prepare the entry to record in P's books the purchase of S's shares.

2. Prepare the worksheet elimination entry needed to consolidate the individual balance sheets immediately after the purchase. (Assume that no other reciprocal accounts exist.)

3. Calculate the amount of equity (common stock and retained earnings) that would appear on the consolidated balance sheet.

DECISION PROBLEM

Q4–Q8

On December 31, 19X5, P corporation purchased an interest in S by paying cash to the stockholders of S for their shares. The following financial statements and other financial information are for that date, immediately before the purchase.

	P	S	
	Book Value	Book Value	Market Value
Cash and Other Assets	$500,000	$200,000	$60,000
Liabilities	$125,000	$ 60,000	
Common Stock	150,000	80,000	
Retained Earnings	225,000	60,000	
Total Liabilities and Equity	$500,000	$200,000	

Required

Consider these cases.

> Case A: P purchased 100% of S's shares by paying $140,000 cash.
> Case B: P purchased 100% of S's shares by paying $180,000 cash.
> Case C: P purchased 70% of S's shares by paying $98,000 cash.
> Case D: P purchased 70% of S's shares by paying $110,000 cash.

For each case, answer the following:

1. Prepare the entry to record in P's book the purchase of S's shares.

2. Was any amount included in the purchase price in recognition of overvalued or under-valued assets in S? How can you tell? If applicable, calculate the amount.

3. Was any amount included in the purchase price in recognition of unrecorded goodwill in S? If so, calculate the amount.

4. Prepare the worksheet elimination entry needed to consolidate the individual balance sheets.

5. If the assets of the subsidiary have a market value of $60,000 and a book value of $200,000, should the assets be written down permanently on the books of S?

6. Determine the amount of consolidated retained earnings available for dividends.

7. Prepare the consolidated balance sheet immediately after the purchase of S's shares.

ANSWERS TO SELF-TEST QUESTIONS

1. **(a)** Since a pooling is recorded at an amount equal to the book value of the net assets of the subsidiary, goodwill can only arise in a purchase acquisition.

2. **(b)** The equality or inequality of the purchase price to the book value of the net assets of the subsidiary has nothing to do with reciprocal accounts. When the financial statements of two related companies are consolidated, certain accounts in the general ledger of both companies represent the same thing—hence, the term *reciprocal*. These accounts must be eliminated against one another during the process of combining the two companies.

3. **(c)** A controlling interest is usually presumed when one corporation owns more than 50% of the voting stock of another corporation. Significant influence over the corporation may be exercised by owning substantially less than 50%, however. Generally it is presumed that a corporation can exercise significant influence when 20% or more of the outstanding stock is owned, although in any given case, the ability to exercise significant influence could occur with ownership as low as 5% or no less than 49%.

4. **(c)** At this level of understanding, it can be said that the amount reported as stock-holders' equity for the parent after acquisition also will be the amount reported as stockholders' equity on the consolidated balance sheet.

5. **(b)** Much discussion surrounds this point, but the Minority Interest account is *usually* reported between Liabilities and Stockholders' Equity.

6. **(b)** Goodwill from consolidation can arise when the purchase price is above book value (*a*), but that excess may be allocated to other noncash assets that appear to be undervaluated. If the purchase price exceeds the fair market value of the net assets, then consolidated goodwill exists.

7. **(e)** The consideration in a purchase can be a combination of all of the items listed or 100% of any one of the items listed. Although when the consideration is made up of 100% of common stock, it will probably be recorded as a pooling of interest.

8. **(d)** In order for a business combination to be recorded as a pooling of interest, the consideration must take the form of common stock of the parent. This subject is fully explored in advanced accounting courses.

PART IV
FINANCIAL STATEMENT ANALYSIS PROBLEM

Turn to the excerpts (pp. 889–906) from the annual report of United Telecom (UT) for the year ended December 31, 1989, and answer the following questions:

1 Does UT have any investments in companies where it does not have control, but is able to exercise significant influence? Explain.

2 From the balance sheet and related notes, can you determine how much UT has in temporary investments (marketable securities)?

3 Did UT have any investments in bonds of other companies during the time period covered? Explain.

4 Explain in your own words what the account *Minority Interests* on the balance sheet represents.

5 What was the reason for the seemingly material decrease in the Minority Interest account on the balance sheet from 1988 to 1989?

6 A Minority Interest account also appears on the income statement. Can you explain the difference between the two accounts? (*Note:* This was not explained in the text).

7 Did UT have any wholly owned subsidiaries during the period covered by the financial statements? Explain.

8 Does UT have investments in any unconsolidated subsidiaries during the period covered by these financial statements? Explain.

9 In Chapter 15, it is mentioned that intercompany items such as assets and liabilities that are related to each other should be eliminated. Explain the appearance of intercompany revenues and intercompany expenses in the income statement prepared for United Telecom.

PART V

DISCLOSURE AND FINANCIAL REPORTING

FINANCIAL statements report information for analysis to stockholders and other interested parties at regular intervals. Although stockholders actually own the entity, they alone do not finance it; creditors finance some of its activities and, together with stockholders, form the entity's financial structure. This financial structure is carefully evaluated by readers of financial statements to ascertain whether stockholders' equity is inadequate or excessive. Management must decide the proportion of debt to equity financing. Then by analyzing financial statements, owners and creditors evaluate such decisions. In order for the financial information to be useful, it must be timely, and users should be able to depend on it for making investment decisions. Financial ratios constitute one way to evaluate an entity's financial position. Various ratios are illustrated in Chapter 16; these allow users to evaluate solvency and operational efficiency.

While the income statement, statement of retained earnings, and balance sheet have been the focus of preceding chapters, the statement of cash flows is discussed in detail in Chapter 17. It is designed to inform users of the cash inflows and outflows from an entity's three main activities: operating, financing, and investing.

16 ANALYSIS OF FINANCIAL STATEMENTS

Reading financial statements provides some users all the information they need to make decisions. However, most users of financial information must go beyond mere reading of the information. Chapter 16 introduces some ratios that will provide users information about the relative position the company is in regarding debt and equity financing, its solvency position in both the short term and long term, and the efficiency of its operations from a number of different viewpoints.

After studying Chapter 16, you should be able to answer the following questions:

1 Why is the ratio between debt and equity important to users of financial information? (pp.712–13)

2 What are the relative advantages of short-term and long-term debt? (p.713)

3 Can an entity be considered insolvent when its assets exceed its liabilities? Explain. (p.714)

4 Are any weaknesses inherent with some of the ratios used to evaluate solvency? Explain. (p.719)

5 How can a corporation determine the length of its operating cycle? (p.724)

6 What are some of the ratios available to an entity to evaluate the efficiency of its operations? (p.725)

7 What is meant by *trading on the equity*? (pp.726–27)

8 Since entities have a considerable amount of their resources invested in long-term assets, what ratios are available to evaluate this material investment? (pp.729–30)

9 What is required to make an accurate comparison of financial information from one year to the next? between entities in the same industry? between entities in different industries? (p.732)

10 What is horizontal analysis? Differentiate between it and vertical analysis. (pp.732–34)

FINANCIAL STRUCTURE: SAGUARO COMPUTERS, INC.

The accounting equation expresses a relationship between assets owned by an entity and the claims against those assets. Although stockholders own a corporation, they alone do not finance the corporation; creditors also finance some of its activities. Together, creditor and stockholder equity are said to form the **financial structure** of a corporation.

Saguaro Computers, Inc.'s Financial Structure (19X5)
(thousands)

ASSETS = LIABILITIES + STOCKHOLDERS' EQUITY
$2,486 $1,255 $1,231

Financial analysts and would-be investors look very carefully at the financial structure of a corporation, that is, at the amount of stockholder claims against the assets of a corporation compared to the creditor claims. SCI has a high reliance on debt in its financial structure; creditors have a substantial claim against its assets.

The long-term financial strength of a corporation depends on its financial structure. In any given situation, a company is said to be *underfinanced* if stockholders' equity is inadequate; it is considered to be *overfinanced* if stockholders' equity is excessive. The proportion of creditor-to-stockholder claims is calculated by dividing total liabilities by total stockholders' equity. Saguaro's situation for a three-year period is presented here:

	(thousands)		
	19X5	**19X4**	**19X3**
Total Liabilities (a)	$1,255	$ 917	$ 269
Stockholders' Equity (b)	1,231	1,195	1,148
Debt-to-Equity Ratio (a) ÷ (b)	1.02	.77	.235

The ratios show that SCI has a little more than $1 of debt for each $1 contributed by the stockholders either through direct investment or reinvestment through retained earnings. Over the past three years, SCI has been relying more and more on debt to finance its operations. The **debt-to-equity ratio** should be cause for concern for Saguaro's board of directors.

Q1: Importance of ratio

On the one hand, management's reliance on debt financing is good. Additional issues of shares would require existing stockholders to contribute additional capital under the preemptive right or to share some of their control with new stockholders, thereby reducing some stockholders' percentage of ownership. Debt financing may be more financially attractive to existing stockholders if the return to the stockholders is greater than the cost of the debt.

On the other hand, management's reliance on debt financing is troublesome. If too much debt exists, creditors may not be willing to extend additional financing, should it be necessary. This potential is one risk of excessive debt financing. Another risk derives from the fact that interest has to be paid on this debt and repayment of the debt is required. The terms and timing of these payments are agreed to when the debt is issued. Total earnings of SCI could be reduced if heavy interest payments have to be paid. Each of these risks could threaten the survival of the company.

The proportion of debt-to-equity financing is decided by management. A reasonable balance has to be maintained. Although no specific figures can be stated as the most appropriate debt-to-equity ratio, techniques are available for discovering the optimum balance. They involve the weighing of leverage (the proportion of debt) against the risk involved; this is the subject matter of finance studies and cannot be covered in an accounting course. What can be attempted, however, is an evaluation of an existing financial structure.

Short-term versus Long-term Debt

Q2: Short-term vs. long-term debt

Both short-term and long-term financing strategies have their advantages. The advantage of some short-term debt is that it does not require interest payments to creditors; for example, accounts payable do not usually require payment of interest if they are paid within credit terms. A further advantage of short-term debt is that income is not reduced by the debt. Short-term debt also has its disadvantages: payment is required in a short period of time, and an increase in the proportion of short-term debt is more risky because each debt has to be paid off and new ones obtained more frequently.

Long-term debt's advantages are that payment may be made over an extended period of time, and that risk is reduced by this longer repayment period governed by a contractual agreement. The disadvantages of long-term debt are that interest payments are required for specified times, and that these interest payments reduce income. As a general rule, long-term financing should be used to finance long-term assets.

SAGUARO'S CREDITOR FINANCING STRUCTURE

An analysis of the company's balance sheet reveals the following liabilities:

	(thousands)		
	19X5	19X4	19X3
Current Liabilities	$1,255	$917	$269
Long-term Liabilities	—	—	—

This information indicates that SCI management relies solely on short-term debt financing, part of which is $300,000 of accounts payable that bears no interest. The risk they have assumed is the need to replace existing liabilities, as they come due and are paid, with new liabilities. If creditors become unwilling to offer new short-term financing, Saguaro's ability to pay its other liabilities may be compromised. In fact, this is happening. Existing creditors have become less willing to extend new credit, and the bank is asking for the repayment of SCI's loan. At this point, the company may have reached the end of its short-term financing rope.

IS SAGUARO INSOLVENT?

Accountants, analysts, and investors often talk about the **solvency** of a company. The term, when applied to a company, refers to its ability to pay its **current liabilities** as they become due. If a company is insolvent, then it is unable to pay the creditors who have provided it with goods and services on account. These are the implications of being insolvent, as first presented in Chapter 5:

Current Liabilities

- Creditors can refuse to provide any further goods or services on account.
- Creditors can sue for payment.
- Creditors can put the company into receivership or bankruptcy.

Long-term Liabilities

- Creditors can refuse to lend additional cash.
- Creditors can demand repayment of their long-term debts under some circumstances.

Stockholders' Equity

- Stockholders may be unwilling to invest in additional shares of common stock of the company.
- Stockholders risk the loss of their investment if the corporation is placed in bankruptcy.

Q3: Insolvency

Currently, SCI is unable to pay its creditors. Although sales are rapidly increasing and an acceptable gross profit is being earned, the company is technically insolvent.

A company normally keeps a reasonable balance in its current assets among cash, receivables, and inventory. Unfortunately, no one indicator tells what a "reasonable" balance really is. The balance is acceptable when debts are being paid. And when current liabilities are not being paid, as is the case for Saguaro Computers, Inc., a reasonable balance does not exist.

Study the following components of Saguaro's 19X5 current assets:

Current Assets (19X5)	(thousands)	% Composition
Cash	$ 19	1.33
Marketable Securities	37	2.58
Accounts Receivable—Trade	544	37.96
Inventory	833	58.13
Total Current Assets	$1,433	100.00

Given this financial balance, SCI appears to have an overinvestment both in receivables and in inventory—together they amount to approximately 96% of its current assets—although a final evaluation must relate investment to sales and cost of goods sold. Consider the current debts of the company in 19X5.

Current Liabilities (19X5)	(thousands)	
Bank Loan	$ 825	These are the short-term
Accounts Payable—Trade	300	creditors of SCI. Short-
Accrued Liabilities	82	term solvency analysis
Income Tax Payable	48	emphasizes factors im-
Total Current Liabilities	$1,255	portant to these creditors.

The short-term creditors would be particularly concerned about these factors:

1. Trade accounts payable are due within the next 60 days. Will SCI be able to pay them?
2. Saguaro has asked its bankers for additional loans. The bankers are unwilling to provide new loans and are asking for repayment of existing bank loans.
3. How will SCI cope with accrued liabilities and income taxes payable?

Obviously, Saguaro is in trouble!

SCI has $19,000 cash on hand and $37,000 in marketable securities (which can be converted immediately into cash) to pay current liabilities. One alternative at this time appears to be to collect receivables as quickly as it can and sell inventory at whatever price it can get. This desperate action would undoubtedly result in losses that would jeopardize the company's existence. Another alternative might be to renegotiate its short-term bank loan into a long-term bank loan.

SHORT-TERM SOLVENCY ANALYSIS

Ratios are one way of evaluating any company's solvency. Commonly used ratios, first introduced in Chapter 5, are summarized next in a table that describes what they can be expected to indicate. Information from the comparative Saguaro financial statements for 19X5, 19X4, and 19X3 in Exhibit 16-1 are used for detailed analysis of SCI's financial position.

Short-term Solvency Analysis	Indicates
1. Current Ratio	How many current asset dollars exist to pay current liabilities. (This ratio is only a crude measure of solvency.)
2. Acid-Test Ratio	Whether the company is able to meet the immediate demands of creditors. (This ratio is a more severe measure of solvency. Inventory and prepaid items are excluded from the calculation.)
3. Management Decisions Related to Receivables	
(a) Accounts Receivable Collection Period	The average time needed to collect receivables.
(b) Accounts Receivable Turnover	How often during the year accounts receivable have been converted into cash.
4. Management Decisions Related to Inventory	
(a) Number of Days of Sales in Inventory	How many days of sales can be made with existing inventory.
(b) Inventory Turnover	How many times during the year inventory has been sold and replaced.
5. Revenue Operating Cycle	How much time passes between the purchase of inventory and the subsequent collection of cash.

The following financial information (see also p. 717) from Exhibit 16-1 is used in the analysis of SCI's short-term solvency.

	(thousands)		
	19X5	**19X4**	**19X3**
Current Assets			
Cash	$ 19	$ 24	$ 50
Marketable Securities	37	37	37
Accounts Receivable—Trade	544	420	257
Merchandise Inventory	833	503	361
Total Current Assets	$1,433	$984	$705

EXHIBIT 16–1

Saguaro Computers, Inc.
Balance Sheets
December 31

Assets		(thousands)	
Current Assets	19X5	19X4	19X3
Cash	$ 19	$ 24	$ 50
Marketable Securities	37	37	37
Accounts Receivable—Trade	544	420	257
Merchandise Inventory	833	503	361
Total Current Assets	$1,433	$ 984	$ 705
Long-term Assets			
Land	$ 200	$ 200	$ 100
Buildings	350	350	200
Equipment	950	950	700
	$1,500	$1,500	$1,000
Less: Accumulated Depreciation— Buildings and Equipment	(447)	(372)	(288)
Total Long-term Assets	$1,053	$1,128	$ 712
Total Assets	$2,486	$2,112	$1,417

Liabilities			
Current Liabilities	19X5	19X4	19X3
Bank Loan	$ 825	$ 570	–
Accounts Payable—Trade	300	215	144
Other Liabilities	82	80	75
Income Tax Payable	48	52	50
Total Current Liabilities	$1,255	$ 917	$ 269

Stockholders' Equity			
Paid-in Capital	$1,000	$1,000	$1,000
Retained Earnings	231	195	148
Total Stockholders' Equity	$1,231	$1,195	$1,148
Total Liabilities and Stockholders' Equity	$2,486	$2,112	$1,417

Saguaro Computers, Inc.
Combined Statements of Income and Retained Earnings
For the Years Ended December 31

		(thousands)	
	19X5	19X4	19X3
Sales	$3,200	$2,800	$2,340
Cost of Goods Sold	2,500	2,150	1,800
Gross Profit	$ 700	$ 650	$ 540
Expenses	584	533	428
Net Income	$ 116	$ 117	$ 112
Beginning Retained Earnings	195	148	96
	$ 311	$ 265	$ 208
Less: Dividends	80	70	60
Ending Retained Earnings	$ 231	$ 195	$ 148

Other related information included in total expenses:

Interest Expense	$ 89	$ 61	–
Income Tax Expense	95	120	$ 97

	(thousands)		
	19X5	19X4	19X3
Current Liabilities			
Bank Loan	$ 825	$570	—
Accounts Payable—Trade	300	215	$144
Other Liabilities	82	80	75
Income Tax Payable	48	52	50
Total Current Liabilities	$1,255	$917	$269
Net Working Capital	$ 178	$ 67	$436

Working Capital

The calculation of working capital is a starting point in short-term solvency analysis. For accountants, **working capital** refers to the mathematical difference between current assets and current liabilities at a particular point in time. The calculation is most useful to the reader when it is compared with the working capital of previous years. For example, an increase in working capital informs the reader about the entity's increased ability to pay its debts.

In the SCI schedule, working capital amounts to $178,000 in 19X5 and represents current assets in excess of current liabilities. This working capital indicates short-term solvency in a dollar amount; notice the dollar difference in working capital between 19X5 and 19X3.

The current ratio discussed next determines this same short-term solvency in terms of a ratio; a ratio is usually easier to interpret than an absolute dollar amount.

THE CURRENT RATIO

Is the firm able to repay short-term creditors? The **current ratio** answers this question by expressing the working capital as a ratio of current assets to current liabilities—current assets are divided by current liabilities. The relevant SCI financial data required to calculate this ratio follows:

	(thousands)		
	19X5	19X4	19X3
Current Assets (a)	$1,433	$984	$705
Current Liabilities (b)	$1,255	$917	$269
Current Ratio (a ÷ b)	1.14	1.07	2.62

The results of this calculation are an indication of how many current asset dollars exist to pay current liabilities. In 19X5, $1.14 of current assets exists to pay each $1 of current liabilities. Is $1.14 adequate? Unfortunately, no one current ratio can be defined as adequate in all situations. Exhibit 16-2 diagrams the possibilities, first illustrated in Exhibit 5-4.

Saguaro is suffering from cash shortages and is unable to pay its debts as they become due. Therefore, its current ratio of 1.14 is clearly inadequate and should be regarded unfavorably; the 19X4 ratio of 1.07 is also inadequate. Without other information, one cannot conclude whether 2.62, the 19X3 ratio, is just right or too high. Some analysts, as noted in Chapter 5, believe a corporation should maintain a 2 : 1 current ratio, depending on the industry in which the firm operates. For example, if a firm has $2 of current assets to pay each $1 of current liabilities, these current assets could shrink considerably in worth and the firm likely would still be able to pay its debts. However, it is recognized that no one current ratio is applicable to all entities; other factors—such as the composition of current assets, the credit

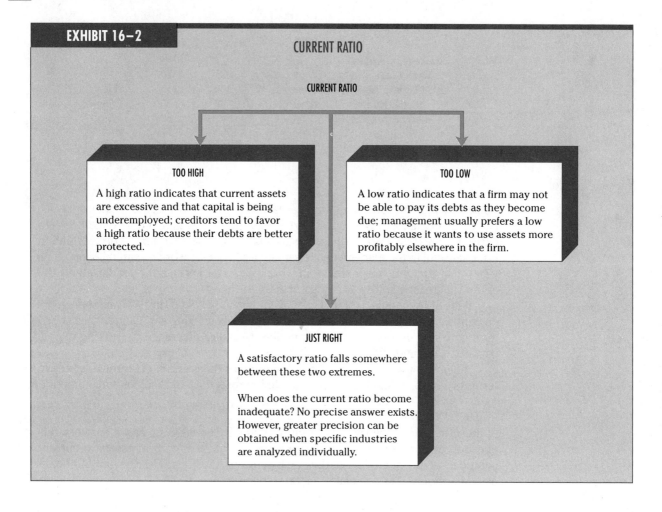

EXHIBIT 16-2

CURRENT RATIO

CURRENT RATIO

TOO HIGH

A high ratio indicates that current assets are excessive and that capital is being underemployed; creditors tend to favor a high ratio because their debts are better protected.

TOO LOW

A low ratio indicates that a firm may not be able to pay its debts as they become due; management usually prefers a low ratio because it wants to use assets more profitably elsewhere in the firm.

JUST RIGHT

A satisfactory ratio falls somewhere between these two extremes.

When does the current ratio become inadequate? No precise answer exists. However, greater precision can be obtained when specific industries are analyzed individually.

terms extended by suppliers—also must be considered to arrive at an acceptable ratio.

Dun and Bradstreet, as well as trade publications, provides a range of current ratios that may be applicable to companies in a particular industry at a given time. Note that the adequacy of a current ratio depends on other developments within a company and that, while a given ratio may be satisfactory one year, it may not be the next year.

COMPOSITION OF SPECIFIC ITEMS IN CURRENT ASSETS

In the following example, each company has a 2 : 1 current ratio. Are the companies equally able to repay their short-term creditors?

	A Corp.	B Corp.
Current Assets		
Cash	$ 1,000	$10,000
Accounts Receivable	2,000	20,000
Merchandise Inventory	37,000	10,000
Total Current Assets	$40,000	$40,000
Current Liabilities	$20,000	$20,000
Current Ratio	2 : 1	2 : 1

The companies have equal dollar amounts of current assets and current liabilities, but they have different debt paying abilities. A Corp. could first sell some inventory and collect the resulting receivables, or it can immediately sell its inventory as a single lot for cash, probably for less than it cost. (This type of shrinkage is provided for in the 2 : 1 current ratio discussed previously.) Clearly, B Corp. is in a better position to repay short-term creditors.

Q4: Ratio weaknesses

Since the current ratio doesn't consider the components of current assets, it is only a rough indicator of how able a firm is to pay its debts as they become due. This weakness is partly remedied by another ratio, the acid-test ratio.

The Acid-Test Ratio

As discussed in Chapter 5, a more severe test of solvency is provided by the so called **acid-test ratio;** often called the *quick ratio,* it provides an indication of instant solvency—the ability to meet the immediate demands of creditors. To calculate this ratio, current assets have to be broken down into **quick current assets** and nonquick current assets.

Quick Current Assets	Nonquick Current Assets
Cash	Inventory
Marketable Securities	Prepaid Items
Accounts Receivable—Trade	
These current assets are considered to be readily convertible into cash.	Cash could not be obtained immediately from these current assets.

Inventory and prepaid items cannot usually be converted into cash in a short period of time. They are, therefore, excluded from quick assets in the calculation of this ratio. The acid-test ratio is derived by dividing the total of quick current assets by current liabilities. The relevant SCI financial data required to calculate this ratio follows:

	(thousands)		
	19X5	19X4	19X3
Quick Current Assets (a)	$ 600	$481	$344
Current Liabilities (b)	$1,255	$917	$269
Acid-Test Ratio (a ÷ b)	0.478	0.525	1.28

This ratio indicates how many quick asset dollars (cash, marketable securities, and trade accounts receivable) exist to pay each dollar of current liabilities. As can be seen, only 47.8 cents of quick assets are available to pay each $1 of current liabilities in 19X5. This amount is clearly inadequate; 52.5 cents in 19X4 is also inadequate. The 19X3 ratio may be a reasonable guide for the adequacy of quick current assets. Of particular concern to financial analysts would be the trend of the acid-test ratio over the three years.

What is an adequate acid-test ratio? It is generally considered that a 1 : 1 acid-test ratio is adequate to ensure that a firm will be able to pay its current obligations. However, this is a fairly arbitrary guideline and is not reliable in all situations. A lower ratio than 1 : 1 often can be found in successful companies.

When taken together, the current and acid-test ratios give the financial statement reader a better understanding of a company's financial health. While the current ratio may be favorable, the acid-test ratio may alert the reader to a preponderance of nonquick assets in the company.

Management Decisions Related to Receivables

Short-term solvency is affected by management decisions related to trade accounts receivable. Lax collection of receivables can result in a shortage of cash to pay current obligations. The effectiveness of management decisions relating to receivables is analyzed by calculating the accounts receivable collection period and the accounts receivable turnover.

ACCOUNTS RECEIVABLE COLLECTION PERIOD

The acid-test ratio is a more severe test of solvency than the current ratio, but it also can be misleading if accounts receivable are high because of slow receivables collection. The calculation of the **accounts receivable collection period** establishes the average time needed to collect an amount. This figure indicates the efficiency of collection procedures when the collection period is compared with the firm's sales terms (in SCI's case, net 30). To calculate this ratio, the *average* annual accounts receivable is divided by the net credit sales and the result is multiplied by 365 days. The relevant Saguaro financial data required to make the calculation appear next.

	(thousands)	
	19X5	**19X4**
Net Credit Sales (a)	$3,200	$2,800
Average Accounts Receivable (b)		
[(Beginning Balance + Ending Balance) ÷ 2]	$ 482	$ 338
Average Collection Period		
[(b ÷ a) × 365]	55 days	44 days

When Saguaro's 30-day sales terms are compared to the average 55-day collection period for 19X5, it is obvious that an average of 25 days of sales (55 days − 30 days) have gone uncollected beyond the regular credit period. Moreover, the trend is toward an increase in this collection period over that of the previous year. Therefore, some overextension of credit and possibly ineffective collection procedures are indicated by this ratio. Quicker collection would improve SCI's cash position.

Whether the increase in collection period is good, bad, or just right depends on other factors, such as increasing sales or increasing profits. Therefore, the average collection period is subject to further interpretation before a conclusion can be made. The ratio does provide, however, an indication of the effectiveness of credit and collection procedures in 19X5.

ACCOUNTS RECEIVABLE TURNOVER

A further insight into the quality of trade accounts receivable is provided through the calculation of the **accounts receivable turnover.** This ratio indicates how often accounts receivable have been converted into cash during the year. The higher the turnover, the less investment exists in accounts receivable.

Higher Turnover Indicates:	Lower Turnover Indicates:
1. Accounts receivable are more liquid.	1. Accounts receivable are less liquid.
2. Accounts receivable have decreased in relation to sales.	2. Accounts receivable have increased in relation to sales.
3. Investment in accounts receivable has decreased in relation to sales.	3. Investment in accounts receivable has increased in relation to sales.

The accounts receivable turnover is calculated by dividing net credit sales during the year by average accounts receivable. The relevant SCI financial data required to calculate this ratio follow.

	(thousands)	
	19X5	19X4
Net Credit Sales (a)	$3,200	$2,800
Average Accounts Receivable (b)		
[(Beginning Balance + Ending Balance) ÷ 2]	$ 482	$ 338
Accounts Receivable Turnover (a ÷ b)	6.64 times	8.28 times

As can be seen, the accounts receivable turnover has decreased during 19X5, that is, accounts receivable were converted into cash fewer times during the year than in the previous year. This simply means that trade receivables were less liquid in 19X5. The danger exists that they were less collectible in 19X5, because older receivables may be buried in the total amount of receivables.

Management Decisions Related to Inventory

The acid-test ratio showed how short-term solvency is affected by management decisions involving inventory, since an overinvestment in inventory can reduce the amount of cash available to pay current liabilities. The effectiveness of management decisions relating to inventory can be further analyzed by calculating the number of days of sales in inventory and the inventory turnover.

NUMBER OF DAYS OF SALES IN INVENTORY

If current assets are tied up in inventory, then accounts payable cannot be paid within the discount period, a situation that would not be beneficial for the company. One method of analyzing whether an overinvestment in inventory occurred is to calculate how many days of sales can be made with the existing inventory. The **number of days of sales in inventory** is calculated by dividing average inventory by the cost of goods sold and multiplying the result by 365 days. The relevant SCI financial data required to calculate this ratio follow.

	(thousands)	
	19X5	19X4
Cost of Goods Sold (a)	$2,500	$2,150
Average Inventory (b)		
[(Beginning Balance + Ending Balance) ÷ 2]	$ 668	$ 432
Number of Days of Sales in Inventory [(b ÷ a) × 365]	97.5 days	73.3 days

More days of sales remain in 19X5 inventory, which means Saguaro is increasing its investment in inventory. The 97.5 days of sales in inventory for 19X5 indicates that SCI can handle approximately 3 months of sales with its existing inventory.

INVENTORY TURNOVER

An **inventory turnover ratio** also can be calculated for Saguaro to measure how many times inventory has been sold and replaced during the year. This analysis is important because a gross profit is earned each time inventory is turned over. The ratio is calculated by dividing cost of goods sold by average inventory. The relevant SCI financial data required to calculate this ratio follow:

	(thousands)	
	19X5	**19X4**
Cost of Goods Sold (a)	$2,500	$2,150
Average Inventory (b)		
[(Beginning Balance + Ending Balance) ÷ 2]	$ 668	$ 432
Inventory Turnover (a ÷ b)	3.74 times	4.98 times

Inventory has turned over fewer times in 19X5 than in 19X4. In other words, inventory was sold and replaced less often in 19X5. Usually a high turnover is considered favorable and a low turnover is considered troublesome. However, the situation is more complex.

A high turnover is usually a sign of good inventory management, because the amount of assets tied up in inventory is lower, and an optimum amount of inventory is being purchased. A high turnover is also important for controlling inventory losses owing to obsolescence or deterioration. It tends to indicate that these problems will be avoided. Also, inventory-related expenses such as insurance and taxes are lower because less storage space is being used for inventory. It should be noted, however, that a high turnover can have negative consequences if turnover becomes so rapid that, at any point in time, items customers want to purchase are out of stock.

A low turnover is usually a sign of poor inventory management, because an excessive investment in inventory ties up assets that could be used for other purposes, and an excessive amount of inventory is being purchased. Further, a low turnover tends to indicate that problems will be encountered in obsolescence (such as styling in women's shoes) or deterioration (groceries). Such inventories may become unsaleable. However, the positive aspect of low turnover is that delivery time to customers can be shorter, and customers can always count on items being in stock. Customers remain satisfied and loyal.

Whether Saguaro's reduced turnover is positive or negative depends on management's objectives. Is management increasing inventory to provide for increased sales in 19X6, or is inventory being poorly managed?

Inadequate information precludes a precise answer. Consider, however, the following factors about SCI:

Analyst's Questions	Facts
1. Is inventory turnover decreasing because of inadequate sales volume?	Sales volume is rapidly increasing.
2. Is an excessive inventory being purchased?	Sales are expected to increase in 19X6. Therefore, the 19X5 inventory should be considered in relation to anticipated 19X6 sales.
3. Are slow-moving items responsible for the decreasing turnover?	Saguaro sells computer hardware and software, which are much in demand.

Based on this analysis, it appears that the increased days of sales in inventory and the decreased inventory turnover can be explained in relation to Saguaro's anticipated 19X6 sales. The problem appears to be not so much an overinvestment in inventory in relation to sales, but an overinvestment in inventory in relation to the financial strength of the corporation. In the final analysis, a reasonable balance between inventory, sales, and the company's financial strength has to be maintained. Management must decide how to strike this balance. The calculation of inventory ratios can only give an insight into the quality of these management decisions.

WHAT IS AN ADEQUATE INVENTORY TURNOVER?

Since no management aims to tie up assets in inventory, it is important for managers to uncover the underlying circumstances when turnover is low. Is the company "stuck" with its inventory (as automobile manufacturers were at one time with their big cars)? Or has the company stockpiled inventory (such as oil) because of anticipated shortages or price increases, which occurred during the Persian Gulf Crisis in 1990?

Turnovers vary from industry to industry and a firm's performance should be compared with industry averages. However, a problem with industry averages occurs when information in published financial statements is incomplete—for example, cost of goods sold is often not shown separately. Accordingly, sales, rather than cost of goods sold, is often used in practice to make calculations and comparisons. The resulting ratio, however, does not give the actual inventory; it gives the sales dollars from average inventory. Such a figure may not be entirely useful for judging performance.

The Revenue Operating Cycle

Every business repeats a **revenue operating cycle** over and over again. Inventory is purchased, an accounts receivable occurs when a sale is made, and cash is generated when the receivable is collected. This cycle is illustrated in Exhibit 16-3.

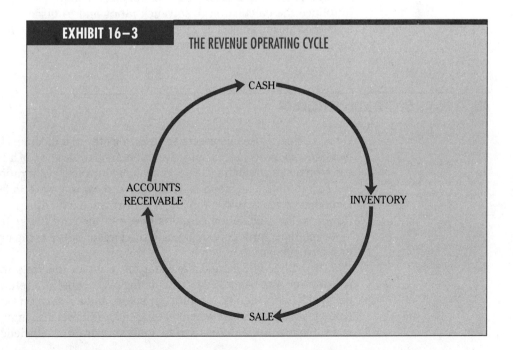

EXHIBIT 16–3   THE REVENUE OPERATING CYCLE

CASH

INVENTORY

SALE

ACCOUNTS RECEIVABLE

Q5: Length of
    operating cycle

How much time elapses at Saguaro between the purchase of inventory and the subsequent collection of cash? That is, how long does it take SCI to complete one revenue operating cycle? The amount of time required to complete a single cycle can be calculated by adding the number of days it takes to turn over inventory to the number of days it takes to collect receivables that result from sales. The relevant SCI financial data required to calculate this ratio follows. The data is taken from prior calculations.

	19X5	19X4
Average Number of Days to Turn Over Inventory	97 days	73 days
Average Number of Days to Collect Receivables	55 days	44 days
Number of Days to Complete Cycle	152 days	117 days

In 19X5, 152 days were required to complete this cycle, compared to 117 days in 19X4. If accounts payable are due within 60 days, it is obvious that SCI will not be able to pay these liabilities with cash from the revenue operating cycle. Moreover, the situation in 19X5 is worse than it was in 19X4.

What Is Causing Saguaro's Financial Problems?

The company is faced with financing its sales to customers and maintaining an adequate inventory in relation to sales, without having the financial strength to do so. Although inventory turnover could be improved, it is doubtful that accounts receivable could be collected much more rapidly. SCI is experiencing rapid growth and is not able to cope with its solvency requirements.

The company has relied too much on short-term financing for its expansion and increased receivable and inventory requirements. SCI is no longer able to rely on this short-term financing and must reconsider its short-term and long-term financing objectives and requirements.

The preceding analysis used the financial data of Saguaro Computers, Inc., to introduce the calculation of solvency ratios and to discuss the merits and weaknesses of these ratios. The ratios that can be used to analyze the operations efficiency of a company are discussed next.

ANALYSIS OF OPERATIONS EFFICIENCY

Every company uses its assets as resources to earn income. However, some companies do so more successfully than others. An evaluation of a company's efficiency can be made through the calculation and study of relevant ratios. Ratios can reveal the current financial status of a company, show the trend in its performance over a number of years, and compare its performance with others in the same industry. However, the calculation of ratios does not indicate the state of such factors as labor relations, product quality, and the impact of the company's operations in its own environment.

The net income earned is the starting point for this ratio analysis. The efficient use of assets can be judged by calculating net income as a return on assets, a return on stockholders' equity, a return per share, and a return on sales. The reasonableness of a company's investment in long-term assets is also important. The following is a summary of the ratios used to analyze operations efficiency:

Q6: Efficiency ratios

Analysis of Operating Efficiency	**Indicates:**
1. Return on Total Assets	How efficiently a company uses its assets as resources to earn a profit.
2. Return on Stockholders' Equity	The adequacy of net income as a return on stockholders' equity.
(a) Trading on the Equity	The use of borrowed money to generate a higher return in the business than the rate being paid on the borrowed money.
(b) Bondholder Protection: Times-Interest-Earned Ratio	The ability of a company to pay interest to long-term creditors.
3. Earnings per Share	The amount of income earned on each share of common stock.
(a) Price-to-Earnings Ratio	The reasonableness of market price in relation to per-share earnings.
(b) Dividend-Yield Ratio	The cash return expected from an investment in a company's shares.
4. Return-on-Sales Ratio	The percentage of sales revenue left in the business after payment of expenses, creditor interest, and income taxes.
5. Management Decisions Relating to Long-term Assets	
(a) Ratio of Sales to Long-term Assets	The adequacy of sales in relation to the investment in long-term assets.
(b) Ratio of Long-term Assets to Stockholders' Equity	The amount of stockholders' equity tied up in long-term assets.

Return on Total Assets

An efficient use of assets should result in a higher return on these assets; a less efficient use results in a lower return. The **return on total assets** ratio is designed to measure the efficiency with which assets are used. The ratio is calculated by the following formula:

$$\frac{\text{Income from Operations}}{\text{Average Total Assets}}$$

This ratio focuses attention on income from operations, which is the amount earned by the corporation from the use of its assets. Expenses not applicable to operations of the company are excluded, such as expenses to finance the company (interest) and income taxes. Average total assets are used in the calculation because the amount of assets used varies during the year.

Return on Stockholders' Equity

The assets of a company are financed by both creditors and stockholders. In return for their share of financing, creditors are paid interest. Stockholders receive credit for whatever remains after interest is paid to creditors and income taxes are paid to the government. This **return on stockholders' equity** is calculated as a ratio by using the following formula:

$$\frac{\text{Net Income for the Year}}{\text{Average Stockholders' Equity}}$$

Net income after interest and income taxes is used in this calculation because only the balance remains to stockholders. Average equity is used because the amount of equity can vary during the year.

TRADING ON THE EQUITY

Q7: Trading on equity

Trading on the equity is not, strictly speaking, a ratio, but it is closely related to the return on stockholders' equity, which in turn is influenced by the use of long-term credit or financing. This use of borrowed funds can generate a higher return than the rate used to borrow the funds. Consider the following example, involving Companies H and D:

	Company H	Company D
Total Assets	$400,000	$400,000
Long-term Liabilities (12%)	—	200,000
Equity	400,000	200,000

Although both H and D have the same amount of assets, H has no long-term liabilities, while D has $200,000 of 12% long-term liabilities. If both companies have $100,000 net income from operations, do they have a similar return on stockholders' equity?

	Company H	Company D
Income from Operations	$100,000	$100,000
Interest Expense ($200,000 × 12%)	—	24,000
	$100,000	$ 76,000
Income Tax (50% assumed)	50,000	38,000
Net Income	$ 50,000	$ 38,000

Notice that the use of long-term creditor financing resulted in a lower income figure for Company D, because of the interest expense. Now consider the implications of this lower income as a return on stockholders' equity:

	Company H	Company D
Income from Operations (a)	$100,000	$100,000
Net Income (b)	50,000	38,000
Total Assets (c)	400,000	400,000
Stockholders' Equity (d)	400,000	200,000
Return on Total Assets (a ÷ c)	25%	25%
Return on Stockholders' Equity (b ÷ d)	12.5%	19%

The return on total assets is 25% for both companies; however, the return on stockholders' equity is considerably greater (19%) for Company D. This means that Company D borrowed funds at 12% to earn 25% in its business and this resulted in a 6.5% gain to stockholders. That is, trading on the equity magnified the return on stockholders' equity by 6.5%.

However, risk is involved in trading on the equity. While it magnifies the return on equity when the return on borrowed funds exceeds the cost of borrowing those funds, the opposite occurs when the cost of the borrowed funds exceeds the return on those borrowed funds. In general, companies with stable earnings can carry more debt in their financial structure than companies with fluctuating earnings.

BONDHOLDER PROTECTION: TIMES-INTEREST-EARNED RATIO

Bondholders and other long-term creditors are aware that their funds are used for leverage and that the risk is that the cost of borrowed funds may exceed the borrowing company's return on those borrowed funds. Therefore, they are interested in the **times-interest-earned ratio,** which is designed to measure the ability of a company to pay interest. It indicates the amount by which income from operations could decline before a default on interest would result. The ratio is calculated by the following formula:

$$\frac{\text{Income from Operations}}{\text{Interest Expense}}$$

Income tax is excluded in the calculation of this ratio because taxes are paid after interest. Income from operations is presumed to be income *before* the deduction of interest on debts. For 19X5, then, Saguaro's income from operations is $300,000, composed of net income of $116,000, interest expense of $89,000, and income tax expense of $95,000. The calculation of the ratio would be as follows:

$$\$300,000 \div \$89,000 = 3.4 \text{ (approximately)}$$

When this ratio approaches 1.0, the entity is in danger of defaulting on the interest payments, with the possibility of control passing to the creditors.

Earnings Per Share

The return to stockholders calculated earlier indicates the overall return on assets financed by stockholders. This return to stockholders also can be expressed on a per-share basis. That is, the amount of net income can be divided by the average number of common shares outstanding to establish how much net income has been earned for each share of stock. This ratio is calculated by the following formula:

$$\frac{\text{Net Income for the Year}}{\text{Average Number of Common Shares Outstanding}}$$

The expression of net income as a per-share amount is a widely quoted statistic in financial circles, and as noted in Chapter 5, is commonly referred to as earnings per share (EPS). The EPS calculation is required as an integral part of the income statement. In some complex situations, more than one earnings-per-share figure might be required. This problem is resolved in more advanced accounting courses. Note that the term refers to earnings per *common* share. Therefore, if some preferred shares are outstanding, the numerator should be reduced by any preferred dividends that have been paid or must be paid in the future (cumulative). The ratio formula then would be as follows:

$$\frac{\text{Net Income for the Year} - \text{Preferred Dividends}}{\text{Average Number of Common Shares Outstanding}}$$

PRICE-TO-EARNINGS RATIO

Earnings per share is of particular interest to investors because of its importance in influencing share market values. Additional measurements used in the stock market to evaluate the selling price of shares are the price-to-earnings ratio and the dividend yield. The **price-to-earnings ratio** is calculated by dividing the market value of a share by earnings per share:

$$\frac{\text{Market Price per Share}}{\text{Earnings per Share}}$$

This ratio indicates the market price in relation to per-share earnings. In fact, it only indicates investors' beliefs as to whether a particular share is overvalued or undervalued.

DIVIDEND-YIELD RATIO

The **dividend-yield ratio** is calculated by dividing annual dividends per share by a share's current market price.

$$\frac{\text{Dividends per Share}}{\text{Market Price per Share}}$$

This ratio indicates how large a return can be expected from an investment in the company's shares.

Return-on-Sales Ratio

The efficiency, or productivity, of each sales dollar is established through the calculation of the **return-on-sales ratio.** This percentage of sales revenue retained by the company—after payment of operating expenses, creditor interest expenses, and income taxes—is an index of performance that can be used to compare the company to others in the same industry. This ratio is calculated by the following formula:

$$\frac{\text{Net Income for the Year}}{\text{Net Sales}}$$

Note that each industry has different acceptable returns on sales. Consider the following:

Food		Steel	
Company	Return on Sales	Company	Return on Sales
Oshawa Group	1.02	Stelco, Inc.	7.5
Steinberg, Inc.	1.24	Algoma Steel Corp.	10.3
Loblaw Companies	0.48	Dofasco, Inc.	9.54

The comparison of return on sales between different industries is meaningless if other characteristics of each industry are not considered. Sales volume, accounts receivable turnover, and inventory turnover vary from industry to industry.

		Ratios	
Industry	Sales Volume	Receivables Turnover	Inventory Turnover
Food	high	not applicable	high
Steel	high	low	low

Any comparison of companies in different industries has to take distinctive industry characteristics into consideration for an accurate analysis. It is particularly difficult to evaluate the financial performance of so-called conglomerates. In the financial statements of conglomerates, products in different industries are combined and one return on sales is calculated. This ratio is virtually meaningless and an informative comparison with other companies cannot easily be made.

Publicly owned corporations falling within the jurisdiction of the Securities and Exchange Commission (SEC) are required to report separately the financial status of each different type of business. From this information, a more useful analysis can be made through the calculation of an individual return on sales for each component of the conglomerate.

Management Decisions Related to Long-term Assets

Q8: Ratios and long-term assets

Corporations usually have a considerable amount of their resources tied up in long-term assets used to produce products to be sold. The financial strength and success of these corporations depends on the reasonableness of their investment in these assets.

An analysis of these investment decisions can be made by calculating the ratio of sales to long-term assets and the ratio of long-term assets to stockholders' equity.

RATIO OF SALES TO LONG-TERM ASSETS

Are sales adequate in relation to the investment in long-term assets? The calculation of the **ratio of sales to long-term assets** provides one answer to this question by establishing the number of sales dollars earned for each dollar invested in long-term assets. The ratio is calculated by the following formula:

$$\frac{\text{Net Sales}}{\text{Average Net Long-term Assets}}$$

From the comparative balance sheet of Saguaro Computers, Inc., the average net long-term assets for 19X4 would be calculated as ($712,000 + $1,128,000) ÷ 2 = $920,000. The ratio of sales to long-term assets would be the 19X4 sales, $2,800,000, divided by $920,000, or $3.04.

A low ratio in relation to other companies in the same industry may indicate their overinvestment in these assets or inefficiency in their use. The financial position of the company can be jeopardized by such errors in judgment; they are difficult to correct in the short run. It is important to recognize that results obtained by this ratio may be affected by one or both of the following factors:

1. Long-term assets are recorded at historic cost, while sales are made at current (inflation increased) prices.

2. The age of the long-term assets can distort a comparison of companies. Two companies with the same investment can show entirely different results because the different ages of their assets results in differing net amounts for long-term assets in their financial statements.

RATIO OF LONG-TERM ASSETS TO STOCKHOLDERS' EQUITY

How much of stockholders' equity is tied up in long-term assets? The **ratio of long-term assets to stockholders' equity** calculates the amount of equity tied up in these assets and thus indicates what amount of equity is left over for working capital purposes. The ratio is calculated by the following formula:

$$\frac{\text{Average Net Long-term Assets}}{\text{Average Stockholders' Equity}}$$

No magic formula exists to indicate the proper amount of working capital to be provided by stockholders' equity. It is expected, however, that some part of the working capital should be provided by stockholders' equity.

SAGUARO COMPUTERS, INC.'S PERFORMANCE

The following financial information from Saguaro Computers, Inc., is used in the calculation of ratios in this section. The ratios help to establish how efficiently the company uses its assets as resources to earn net income.

		(thousands)	
	19X5	19X4	19X3
Income from Operations (a)	$300	$280	$209
Financing Charges—Interest	(89)	(61)	—
Income Tax	(95)	(102)	(97)
Net Income (b)	$116	$117	$112
Average Net Long-term Assets (c)			
[(Beginning and Ending Balances) ÷ 2]	$1,091	$ 920	—*
Average Total Assets (d)			
[(Beginning and Ending Balances) ÷ 2]	2,299	1,765	—*
Average Stockholders' Equity (e)			
[(Beginning and Ending Balances) ÷ 2]	1,213	1,172	—*
Net Sales (f)	3,200	2,800	$2,340
Common Shares Outstanding (g)	100	100	100
Calculation of Selected Ratios			
1. Return on Total Assets (a ÷ d)	13%	15.9%	—*
2. Return on Stockholders' Equity (b ÷ e)	9.6%	9.98%	—*
3. Earnings per Share (b ÷ g)	$1.16	$1.17	$1.12
4. Return on Sales (b ÷ f)	3.6%	4.2%	4.8%
5. Sales to Long-term Assets (f ÷ c)	$2.93	$3.04	—*
6. Long-term Assets to Stockholders' Equity (c ÷ e)	$0.90	$0.78	—*

*The figure for 19X2 is not available for calculation of an average for 19X3.

Analysis of Operating Efficiencies

RETURN ON TOTAL ASSETS
Saguaro's net income was 13% of average total assets in 19X5, a decrease from 15.9% in 19X4. This decrease is disappointing not only because it seems to indicate

a less efficient use of company assets, but also because the decrease has occurred during a period of rapidly expanding sales. Although average total assets have increased almost 30% (from $1,765,000 to $2,299,000 in 19X5), its net income has remained virtually unchanged. It may be that the investment in long-term assets during this period has not yet begun to pay off. In all probability, however, other efficiency factors are affecting this disappointingly decreased return on total assets.

RETURN ON STOCKHOLDERS' EQUITY

In 19X5, Saguaro earned a 9.6% return on stockholders' equity (represented by common stock and retained earnings), compared to 9.98% in 19X4. Is a 9% to 10% return adequate? It is consistent with previous years. A comparison with other companies in the same industries and the industry average would give an indication of Saguaro's relative performance. Such averages are published by Dun and Bradstreet and in other trade publications.

EARNINGS PER SHARE

Saguaro's EPS has remained relatively constant over the three-year period because its expansion was financed by debt.

RETURN ON SALES

Saguaro has a lower return on sales in 19X5 than in 19X4; this decline should be viewed with some concern. Comparison has to be made with other firms in the same industry to evaluate SCI's performance. The return on total assets and on equity should also be examined when appraising the efficiency of asset use.

A low return on sales is not necessarily unfavorable, if it is accompanied by a high return on stockholders' equity. What is unsettling in SCI's case is that both return on sales and return on stockholders' equity are declining. It is important to isolate the reasons for this decline in Saguaro's performance. A **gross profit percentage** is widely used to establish whether additional sales are being made as a result of lower sales prices. A study of SCI's gross profit shows the following:

	(thousands)		
	19X5	19X4	19X3
Net Sales (a)	$3,200	$2,800	$2,340
Cost of Goods Sold	2,500	2,150	1,800
Gross Profit (b)	$ 700	$ 650	$ 540
Gross Profit Percentage (b ÷ a)	21.9%	23.2%	23.1%

Saguaro's gross profit percentage has remained fairly constant over the three-year period. Therefore, the decrease in the return on sales must be occurring within the operating expense category rather than from lack of sales.

Saguaro's Management Decisions Related to Long-term Assets

It is important to analyze the reasonableness of Saguaro's increased investment in long-term assets in the current circumstances.

SALES TO LONG-TERM ASSETS

In 19X5, SCI made $2.93 of sales for each dollar invested in long-term assets, a little less than the $3.04 it earned in 19X4. Much will depend on the results of 19X6. Sales have been rapidly expanding and market acceptance of any computer related innovation is assured; this growth is more important than the ratios. The long-term asset expansion does not appear unwise in the circumstances.

LONG-TERM ASSETS TO STOCKHOLDERS' EQUITY

What does appear unwise is Saguaro's method of financing its expansion. Consider the amount of stockholders' equity tied up in this expansion, calculated as follows:

	(thousands)	
	19X5	19X4
Average Net Long-term Assets (a)	$1,091	$ 920
Average Stockholders' Equity (b)	1,213	1,172
Long-term Assets to Stockholder's Equity (a ÷ b)	0.90	0.78

A significant change has occurred between 19X4 and 19X5. The amount of stockholders' equity tied up in long-term assets has increased from $0.78 for each dollar invested in plant and equipment to $0.90; therefore, less working capital is being provided by stockholders' equity. The proportion of $0.90 to each dollar in long-term assets is not necessarily troublesome in itself. What is dangerous is the shortage of working capital provided from operations.

TREND ANALYSIS

When evaluating the various ratios used in this chapter, management frequently focuses attention on *trends* that have become apparent. Most public companies provide comparative ratios with their financial statements. The period of comparison usually is not less than 5 years and often covers 10 years or more. This **trend analysis** permits a better evaluation of a company's financial strength and profitability. In order for this trend analysis to be useful, however, GAAP must be applied consistently over the period of time covered in the trend analysis. If the method of valuing inventory, for instance, is changed from year to year, the many ratios based on inventory, current assets, and total assets could fluctuate to the point of making them useless. It also facilitates comparisons with other companies in the same industry, with the industry average, and with companies in other industries. Each July, Dun and Bradstreet publishes *Key Business Ratios* for various corporations. Moody's and Standard and Poor's reporting services also provide financial information covering extended periods of time.

Q9: Accurate comparisons

Q10: Horizontal vs. vertical analysis

Percentages can be used to analyze amounts appearing in financial statements. They can be calculated horizontally and vertically.

Horizontal Analysis   In **horizontal analysis** the balance for one year is compared with the balance for one or more other years. The difference, or change, is shown

EXHIBIT 16-4

BALANCE SHEETS

Horizontal Analysis

	19X5	19X4	Change Amount	Percentage
Current Assets	$1,433	$ 984	+$449	+45.63
Long-term Assets	1,053	1,128	-$ 75	- 6.65
Totals	$2,486	$2,112	+$374	+17.71
Current Liabilities	$1,255	$ 917	+$338	+36.86
Stockholders' Equity	1,231	1,195	+ 36	+ 3.01
Totals	$2,486	$2,112	+$374	+17.71

Notice the special columns introduced here. Analysis of the changes indicates a large increase in current assets, together with a large increase in current liabilities. A small decline in long-term assets and a small increase in stockholders' equity occurred. The percentage change must always be interpreted together with the dollar amount of change to avoid incorrect conclusions; percentages can sometimes be misleading.

Vertical Analysis

	Common Size Percentages	
	19X5	19X4
Current Assets	57.64	46.59
Long-term Assets	42.36	53.41
Totals	100.00	100.00
Current Liabilities	50.48	43.42
Stockholders' Equity	49.52	56.58
Totals	100.00	100.00

In the common size balance sheets, it is clear that the composition of the assets has changed with an overall shift to current assets in 19X5. It also shows that an increase in current liabilities has occurred. Vertical analysis places the balance sheet components in comparable terms through the conversion of all dollar amounts into percentages.

as a dollar amount and also as a percentage. The percentage is calculated by dividing the dollar amount of change by the older of the two amounts being compared.

Vertical Analysis In **vertical analysis**, each amount on a financial statement is expressed as a percentage of a base. Net sales is the base in the income statement, total assets is the base for assets, and total equities is the base for equities in the balance sheet. Statements prepared in this manner are referred to as **common size financial statements.**

Horizontal and vertical analyses of the balance sheets and income statements of Saguaro Computers, Inc., are shown in Exhibits 16-4 and 16-5. The percentages calculated in these analyses become more informative when compared to earlier years.

EXHIBIT 16–5

INCOME STATEMENTS

Horizontal Analysis   **Vertical Analysis**

				Change			Common Size Percentages	
	19X5	19X4	Amount	Percentage		19X5	19X4
Sales	$3,200	$2,800	+400	+14.29	Sales	100.00	100.00
Cost of Goods Sold	2,500	2,150	+350	+16.28	Cost of Goods Sold	78.12	76.79
Gross Profit	$ 700	$ 650	+ 50	+ 7.69	Gross Profit	21.88	23.21
Expenses	584	533	+ 51	+ 9.57	Expenses	18.25	19.04
Net Income	$ 116	$ 117	– 1	– 0.85	Net Income	3.63	4.17

Note that although sales and gross profit increased, net income decreased. This decrease in net income resulted from an increase in cost of goods sold and expenses. The increased sales were insufficient to offset the increased cost of merchandise and increased expenses.

Notice the relative change in the components of the statement. For example, cost of goods sold increased in 19X5 relative to sales, while expenses in 19X5 relative to sales decreased. The decrease in expenses, however, was insufficient to offset an increase in Cost of Goods Sold.

Further analysis is usually undertaken in order to establish answers to the following questions:

Horizontal Analysis

1. What caused this change?

2. Is the change favorable or negative?

These and other similar questions call attention to weak areas and help to spot trends in financial strength and profitability.

Vertical Analysis

1. How do the percentages of this company compare with other companies in the same industry? in other industries?

2. Why is such a large portion of assets tied up in current assets?

These and other similar questions call attention to areas that may require further study.

In fact, the published financial statements of actual companies tend to reduce the amount of information that can be used for analysis so that competitors will be left in the dark as much as possible. Accordingly, gross profits are often not shown separately and cost of goods sold is combined with operating expenses to prevent its calculation by the reader. The lack of individual breakdowns of salaries, audit fees, promotion expenses, and so on also prevent the statement reader from obtaining a detailed picture of a corporation's activities. Therefore, stockholders, analysts, and others are left in the dark. The calculation of all of the percentages and ratios possible from the figures provided will shed at least some light on the situation.

SUMMARY OF RATIOS

The ratios covered in this chapter are summarized in Exhibit 16-6. A commentary on ratio analyses appears in Real World Example 16-1.

EXHIBIT 16–6	SUMMARY OF RATIOS	
Reliance on Debt	**Calculation of Ratio**	**Indicates**
Debt-to-Equity Ratio	$$\dfrac{\text{Total Liabilities}}{\text{Total Stockholders' Equity}}$$	What is the proportion of debt financing to owners' equity.
Short-term Solvency Analysis 1. Current Ratio	$$\dfrac{\text{Current Assets}}{\text{Current Liabilities}}$$	How many current asset dollars exist to pay current liabilities. (This is only a crude measure of solvency.)
2. Acid-Test Ratio	$$\dfrac{\text{Quick Current Assets}}{\text{Current Liabilities}}$$	Whether the company is able to meet the immediate demands of creditors. (This is a more severe measure of solvency. Inventory and prepaid items are excluded from the calculation.)
3. Management Decisions Related to Receivables (a) Accounts Receivable Collection Period	$$\dfrac{\text{Average Accounts Receivable}}{\text{Net Credit Sales}} \times 365$$	What is the average time needed to collect receivables.
(b) Accounts Receivable Turnover	$$\dfrac{\text{Net Credit Sales}}{\text{Average Accounts Receivable}}$$	How often during the year accounts receivable have been converted into cash.
4. Management Decisions Related to Inventory: (a) Number of Days of Sales in Inventory	$$\dfrac{\text{Average Inventory}}{\text{Cost of Goods Sold}} \times 365$$	How many days of sales can be made with existing inventory.
(b) Inventory Turnover	$$\dfrac{\text{Cost of Goods Sold}}{\text{Average Inventory}}$$	How many times during the year inventory has been sold and replaced.
5. Revenue Operating Cycle	Average Number of Days to Turn Over Inventory + Average Number of Days To Collect Receivables	How much time between the purchase of inventory and the subsequent collection of cash.

(continued)

EXHIBIT 16–6 (cont.)

Analysis of Operating Efficiency	Calculation of Ratio	Indicates
1. Return on Total Assets	$$\frac{\text{Income from Operations}}{\text{Average Total Assets}}$$	How efficiently a company uses its assets as resources to earn a profit.
2. Return on Stockholders' Equity	$$\frac{\text{Net Income for the Year}}{\text{Average Stockholders' Equity}}$$	The adequacy of net income as a return on stockholders' equity.
(a) Trading on the Equity (This is not a ratio, but is related to the return on stockholders' equity, which in turn is influenced by the use of long-term financing.)	[See example on p. 000.]	The use of borrowed money to generate a higher return in the business than the rate being paid on the borrowed money.
(b) Bondholder Protection: Times-Interest-Earned Ratio	$$\frac{\text{Income from Operations}}{\text{Interest Expense}}$$	The ability of a company to pay interest to long-term creditors.
3. Earnings per Share	$$\frac{\text{Net Income for the Year} - \text{Preferred Dividends}}{\text{Average Number of Common Shares Outstanding}}$$	The amount of income earned on each share of common stock.
(a) Price-to-Earnings Ratio	$$\frac{\text{Market Price per Share}}{\text{Earnings per Share}}$$	The reasonableness of market price in relation to per-share earnings.
(b) Dividend-Yield Ratio	$$\frac{\text{Dividends per Share}}{\text{Market Price per Share}}$$	The cash return expected from an investment in a company's shares.
4. Return-on-Sales Ratio		
(a) Net Income	$$\frac{\text{Net Income for the Year}}{\text{Net Sales}}$$	The percentage of sales revenue left in the business after payment of expenses, creditor interest, and income taxes.
(b) Gross Income	$$\frac{\text{Gross Profit}}{\text{Net Sales}}$$	
5. Management Decisions Related to Long-term Assets		
(a) Ratio of Sales to Long-term Assets	$$\frac{\text{Net Sales}}{\text{Average Net Long-term Assets}}$$	The adequacy of sales in relation to the investment in long-term assets.
(b) Ratio of Long-term Assets to Stockholders' Equity	$$\frac{\text{Average Net Long-term Assets}}{\text{Average Stockholders' Equity}}$$	The amount of stockholders' equity tied up in long-term assets.

REAL WORLD EXAMPLE 16-1
Calculating the Z Score

S OMEONE once said that if you have one clock, you always know what time it is, but if you have several clocks, you are never quite sure. I often get that feeling when I calculate financial ratios. This is because the dozens of financial ratios I use seem to provide different answers to the same simple question. "How'd we do?"

So I've been on the lookout recently for financial models that summarize one general aspect of overall company performance. One example is the Z score, which, though developed to measure the likelihood of bankruptcy, can be used as a handy measure of overall financial performance.

The original Z score was created by Edward I. Altman in the mid-1960s. It is the most widely used of the many bankruptcy classifications that exist, and it has stood the test of time.

To get the Z score, you simply take the figures for the four ratios, which Altman calls X1, X2, etc., from your financial statements. Multiply their values by coefficients Altman has derived, and add up the results. The formula, explained in detail below, looks like this:

$$6.56(X1) + 3.26(X2) + 6.72(X3) + 1.05(X4)$$

If a company's total score is greater than 2.60, things are looking good. If it is less than 1.10, bankruptcy may well be in sight. Figure 2 shows the financial statements and Z-score calculations for a hypothetical company, The BC Corp., which at 5.206 has scored well above the danger point.

The interesting thing about the Z score is that it is a good analytic tool no matter what shape your company is in. To find your company's Z score, first calculate the four ratios.

$$X1 = \frac{\text{Working Capital}}{\text{Total Assets}}$$

This measure of liquidity compares net liquid assets to total assets. The net liquid assets, or working capital, are defined as current total assets minus current total liabilities. Generally,

Figure 1
The Z Score Bankruptcy Classification Model

Ratio Names		Description	Coefficient	Mean Ratio Values Altman's Sample Cos.	
				Bankrupt	Nonbankrupt
X1	=	$\frac{\text{Working Capital}}{\text{Total Assets}}$	6.56	(0.061)	0.414
X2	=	$\frac{\text{Retained Earnings}}{\text{Total Assets}}$	3.26	(0.626)	0.355
X3	=	$\frac{\text{EBIT}}{\text{Total Assets}}$	6.72	(0.318)	0.154
X4	=	$\frac{\text{Net Worth}}{\text{Total Liabilities}}$	1.05	0.494	2.684

Cutoff Values		Mean Scores	
Safe if greater than	2.60	Nonbankrupt	7.70
Bankrupt if less than	1.10	Bankrupt	(4.06)

Source *Corporate Financial Distress,* Edward I. Altman, John Wiley & Sons, 1983.

(continued)

Figure 2

BC Corp.
Balance Sheet
December 1986
(All values in $1,000)

Assets	
Current Assets	
Cash	13
Receivables	109
Inventory	272
Prepaid Expenses	9
Total Current Assets	403
Net Fixed Assets	169
Total Assets	572

Liabilities	
Current Liabilities	
Accounts Payable	82
Notes Payable	50
Other Current Liabilities	35
Total Current Liabilities	167
Long-term Debt	130
Total Liabilities	297

Shareholders' Equity	
Common Stock	110
Retained Earnings	165
Net Worth	275
Total Liabilities and Equity	572

BC Corp.
Income Statement
1986
(All values in $1,000)

Income Statement	
Sales	845
Cost of Goods Sold	
Materials	250
Direct Labor	245
Utilities	32
Indirect Labor	28
Depreciation	31
Total Cost of Goods Sold	586
Gross Profit	259
Operating Expense	
Selling Expense	99
General and Administrative Expenses	110
Total Operating Expense	209
Earnings before Interest and Taxes	50
Interest Expense	14
Earnings before Taxes	36
Taxes	8
Net Income	28

Stock Data
December 31, 1986

Stock Data	
Stock Price (in dollars)	3
Shares Outstanding	100
Market Value of Equity	300

Z Score Calculations

Ratio	Description	Formula	Result		Coefficient		Z Score
X1	$\dfrac{\text{Working Capital}}{\text{Total Assets}}$	$\dfrac{403 - 167}{572}$	= 0.413	×	6.560	=	2.707
X2	$\dfrac{\text{Retained Earnings}}{\text{Total Assets}}$	$\dfrac{165}{572}$	= 0.288	×	3.260	=	0.940
X3	$\dfrac{\text{EBIT}}{\text{Total Assets}}$	$\dfrac{50}{572}$	= 0.087	×	6.720	=	0.587
X4	$\dfrac{\text{Net Worth}}{\text{Total Liabilities}}$	$\dfrac{275}{297}$	= 0.926	×	1.050	=	0.972

Z Score: 5.206

when a company experiences financial difficulties, working capital will fall more quickly than total assets, causing this ratio to fall.

$$X2 = \frac{\text{Retained Earnings}}{\text{Total Assets}}$$

This ratio is a measure of the cumulative profitability of your company. To some degree, the ratio also reflects the age of your company, because the younger it is, the less time it has had to build up cumulative profits. This bias in favor of older firms is not surprising, given the high failure rate of young companies.

When a company begins to lose money, of course, the value of total retained earnings begins to fall. For many companies, this value—and the X2 ratio—will become negative.

$$X3 = \frac{\text{EBIT}}{\text{Total Assets}}$$

This is a measure of profitability, or return on assets, calculated by dividing your firm's EBIT (earnings before interest and taxes) for one year by its total assets balance at the end of the year.

You can also use it as a measure of how productively you are using borrowed funds. If the ratio exceeds the average interest rate you're paying on loans, you are making more money on your loans than you are paying in interest.

To calculate this ratio in the middle of a fiscal year, use your month-end balance sheet and the EBIT from an income statement showing the most recent 12 months of activity.

$$X4 = \frac{\text{Net Worth}}{\text{Total Liabilities}}$$

This ratio is the inverse of the more familiar debt-to-equity ratio. It is found by dividing your firm's net worth (also known as stockholders' equity) by its total liabilities.

After you've calculated these four ratios, simply multiply the X1 ratio by its coefficient, shown in Figure 1, the X2 by its coefficient, and so on; add the results; and then compare the total with Altman's cutoff values, also shown in Figure 1.

The purpose of calculating your own Z score is to warn you of financial problems that may need serious attention and to provide a guide for action. If your Z score is lower than you would like, you should examine your financial statements to determine the reason why.

Start by calculating the scores from previous periods, comparing them with your current score. (Graph them if possible.) If the trend is down, try to understand what has changed to create ratios that are dragging your scores down. Monitoring the trend in your Z scores can also help you evaluate your turnaround efforts.

Another way to analyze your score is to compare your results with those of other companies. You could refer to Robert Morris Associates (RMA) *Annual Statement Studies,* which provide detailed financial ratios by Standard Industrial Classification code. (Ratio X2 cannot be calculated from RMA data, however, because retained earnings aren't included.) Compare your own calculations with industry ratios, and find the ones that are out of line.

When you use bankruptcy classification models, including the Z score, keep this reservation in mind: they are by no means infallible. They can complement the other reports and analyses that you use within your company. Seldom, however, should you use any of the models as your only means of financial analysis.

Source Charles W. Kyd, "How are you doing," *Inc. Magazine,* February 1987, p. 122–25. Reprinted with permission. Copyright © 1987 by Goldhirsh Group, Inc., 38 Commercial Wharf, Boston MA 02110.

CHAPTER REVIEW

1 Why is the ratio between debt and equity important to users of financial information? (pp. 712–13)

Volumes have been written over time in answer to this question. At the introductory level, it is important to realize that a firm does not have to utilize any debt whatsoever, financing instead entirely by owner investment and retained earnings. In many cases, the cost to borrow is below what an entity is earning on the resources; therefore, the return to the owners is greater if debt financing can be utilized. Debt financing can go too far, however, and in bad times could backfire. If an entity is placed in a position where it cannot pay the interest on a debt, control could pass from the owners to the creditors.

For these reasons, the relationship between debt and equity is a closely watched ratio. Owners would like to see it as high as possible, while creditors would like to see it as low as possible. The mix must be beneficial to all.

2 What are the relative advantages of short-term and long-term debt? (p. 713)

Short-term debt usually has no costs, while long-term debt always has costs. The main disadvantages to short-term debt are the limited amount that can be borrowed and the due date of the repayment. Short-term debt, accounts payable and the like, usually is due within 30 to 60 days and usually will have a very low ceiling. Long-term debt, on the other hand, can have maturities as long as 20 years (the railroads used to issue 100-year bonds) and an almost unlimited upper limit.

3 Can an entity be considered insolvent when its assets exceed its liabilities? Explain. (p. 714)

Yes, anytime an entity is not meeting currently due debt, it is said to be insolvent and creditors may force a judgment in bankruptcy. A firm may have assets significantly above the amount of debt it owes, but because of a lack of cash, may not be able to pay its current liabilities.

4 Are any weaknesses inherent with some of the ratios used to evaluate solvency? Explain. (p. 719)

Numbers are an inherent weakness; they can be made to say what management chooses. One of the most used ratios regarding short-term solvency is the current ratio, also called the working capital ratio. It is simply a ratio of current assets to current liabilities. If a firm has twice as many dollars of current assets than current liabilities, the ratio is 2:1, meaning $2 in current assets are available to satisfy every $1 in current debt. Although this sounds healthy, the *makeup* of the current assets is important. If a majority of the company's current assets are represented by inventory, and it has an operating cycle longer than the average due dates of the current liabilities, then it is going to have trouble meeting current debt.

5 How can a corporation determine the length of its operating cycle? (p. 724)

It is possible to determine the average collection period for accounts receivable and the average number of days of sales to turn over inventory during a particular accounting period. The sum of these two statistics measures the average number of days in the operating cycle. For example, if the inventory has an average of 45 days' supply, and the average collection period is 45 days, the operating cycle, the time it takes cash to be turned into cash again, would be 90 days.

6 What are some of the ratios available to an entity to evaluate the efficiency of its operations? (p. 725)

A number of ratios compare net income to another base to measure efficiency. Net income can be used to calculate the following:

Return on Total Assets = Income from Operations ÷ Average Total Assets

Return on Stockholders' Equity = Net Income for the Year ÷ Average Stockholders' Equity

Earnings per Share = Net Income for the Year ÷ Average Number of Common Shares Outstanding

Return on Sales = Net Income for the Year ÷ Net Sales

This is not an exhaustive list, but it does include some of the more common relationships.

7 What is meant by *trading on the equity?* (pp. 726–27)

Trading on the equity is a phrase used to describe the situation whereby the cost of borrowed funds is less than the rate earned on the funds. If debt is costing 12% and the return on stockholders' equity is 15%, the firm is said to be trading on the equity.

8 Since entities have a considerable amount of their resources invested in long-term assets, what ratios are available to evaluate this material investment? (pp. 729–30)

Investment in long-term assets can be compared to sales and to stockholders' equity. When comparing assets to sales, an amount is calculated representing the number of sales dollars for each dollar of long-term assets. The number then can be compared to industry averages, and with the same number the previous year. For instance, if long-term assets generated $3.10 in sales for each dollar invested, and the industry average was $2.50, it could be said that the utilization of long-term assets was above average. If the same figure the year before was $2.80, it could be said that the entity is improving its return on long-term assets. The comparison of investment in long-term assets to stockholders' equity determines the percentage of owner financing of long-term assets. The higher that percentage is, the lesser the amount available for working capital.

9 What is required to make an accurate comparison of financial information from one year to the next? between entities in the same industry? between entities in different industries? (p. 732)

In order to make comparisons from one year to the next, the application of GAAP must be consistent. If material changes are made annually, the ratio comparisons become meaningless. Accountants strive for uniformity of the application of GAAP in firms within the same industry so financial information such as ratios can be compared from firm to firm. Firms in different industries can be compared by means of trend analysis and both horizontal and vertical analyses.

10 What is horizontal analysis? Differentiate between it and vertical analysis. (pp. 732–34)

Horizontal analysis is the comparison of the same information for two or more years to determine the amount of the change and percentage increase or decrease. For instance, if accounts receivable were $100,000 last year and $125,000 this year, the change represents a $25,000 increase or 25%. Vertical analysis is the comparison of one item to others in the same group for a given year. For instance, the $100,000 of accounts receivable might have represented 35% of current assets last year, while the $125,000 represents 45% of current assets this year.

KEY TERMS

accounts receivable collection period (p. 720)   The average time needed to collect an account; the average annual accounts receivable is divided by net credit sales and the result is multiplied by 365 days.

accounts receivable turnover (p. 720)   Indicates how often during the year accounts receivable have been converted to cash; net credit sales is divided by average accounts receivable.

acid-test ratio (p. 719)   Quick current assets divided by current liabilities; this indicates the ability of the entity to meet the immediate demands of the creditors. A more severe measure of solvency than the current ratio, it is also known as the *quick current ratio.*

common size financial statements (p. 733)   Statements that have been restated in percentage form, such as an income statement that expresses all components as a percentage of sales.

current liabilities (p. 713)   Obligations of an entity that come due during the next accounting period or during the next operating cycle if it's longer.

current ratio (p. 717)   Current assets divided by current liabilities; this indicates the number of current asset dollars available to pay current liabilities. A crude measure of solvency, it is also known as the *working capital ratio.*

debt-to-equity ratio (p. 712)   A comparison of total debt with total stockholders' equity. It indicates what percentage of the assets are financed with debt and what percentage financed with owner contribution, either by investment or by earnings.

dividend-yield ratio (p. 728)   Indicates the cash return that can be expected from a particular investment; dividends per share is divided by the market price per share.

financial structure (p. 712)   Sometimes referred to as the *capital structure,* it is the right-hand side of the balance sheet, the liabilities and stockholders' equity of an entity. It answers the question, how were the assets financed? debt? equity? internally (retained earnings)?

gross profit percentage (p. 731)   Indicates the percentage of each sales dollar available to cover all operating expenses, interest, taxes, and ultimately, profit to the owners; gross profit is divided by sales.

horizontal analysis (p. 732)   The analysis of financial statements through the calculation of percentage *changes* in statement components over two or more years.

inventory turnover ratio (p. 722)   Indicates how many times the inventory has been sold and replaced during the year; cost of goods sold is divided by average inventory.

number of days of sales in inventory (p. 721)   Indicates how many days' supply of inventory is on hand; the average inventory is divided by cost of goods sold and the result is multiplied by 365 days.

price-to-earnings ratio (p. 728)   Indicates the reasonableness of the market price in relation to how much is being earned in return for the investment; the market price per share is divided by the earnings per share.

quick current assets (p. 719)   Assets that can be converted into cash in a short period of time. These include cash, accounts receivable, and marketable securities.

ratio of long-term assets to stockholders' equity (p. 729)   Indicates the percentage of equity being used to acquire long-term assets; average net long-term assets is divided by average stockholders' equity.

ratio of sales to long-term assets (p. 729)   Indicates the adequacy of sales in relation to the investment in long-term assets; net sales is divided by average long-term assets. To be meaningful, the number must be compared with that of last year's, or with others in the industry.

return-on-sales ratio (p. 728)   Indicates the percentage of each sales dollar that ends up in retained earnings and is available for distribution as dividends; net income for the year is divided by net sales.

return on stockholders' equity (p. 725)   Indicates the adequacy of earnings as a return on the investment by the owners of the entity; net income for the year is divided by average stockholders' equity.

return on total assets (p. 725)   This indicates how efficiently a company uses its assets in the earnings process; income from operations is divided by average total assets.

revenue operating cycle (p. 723)   The time it takes to buy inventory, sell it, and to collect the cash from the sale. A shorter definition has been offered as "cash to cash." It can be determined by adding the accounts receivable collection period to the number of days' supply of inventory.

solvency (p. 713)   The ability of an entity to pay its debts (current liabilities) as they become due.

times-interest-earned ratio (p. 727)   Indicates the ability of the entity to pay the interest on long-term debt, such as bonds; income from operations is divided by interest expense.

trading on the equity (p. 726)   Utilizing debt as a means of financing when the return on the amount borrowed exceeds the cost of borrowing the funds.

trend analysis (p. 732)   The comparison of data for several years when analyzing financial statements for evaluation of a company's financial strength and profitability.

vertical analysis (p. 733)   The analysis of the composition of a financial statement through the restating of all items in the statement as percentages; comparison of the percentages between two or more years shows the change in composition of the statement components. Once restated in percentages, the statements are referred to as *common size financial statements.*

working capital (p. 717)   The excess of current assets over current liabilities; also referred to as *net working capital.*

SELF-TEST QUESTIONS FOR REVIEW   (Answers are at the end of this chapter.)

Here are the simplified balance sheet and income statement for Kong, Inc.

Balance Sheet
December 31, 19X2

Assets		Liabilities and Stockholders' Equity	
Cash	$ 72	Accounts Payable	$ 60
Accounts Receivable (net)	88	Bonds Payable	80
Merchandise Inventory	100	Mortgage Payable	70
Prepaid Expenses	40	Preferred Stock (10%)	60
Land	220	Common Stock	250
Building (net)	100	Retained Earnings	100
Total Assets	$620	Total Liabilities and Stockholders' Equity	$620

Income Statement
For the Year Ended December 31, 19X2

Sales	$240
Cost of Goods Sold	144
Gross Profit	$ 96

(continued)

Operating Expenses		
Salaries	$44	
Depreciation	6	
Interest	8	58
Income (before income tax)		38
Income Tax Expense		18
Net Income		$ 20

Assume the average of all balance sheet items is equal to the year-end figure, and that all preferred dividends have been paid currently. The number of common shares outstanding is 10.

Q4

1. The current ratio is approximately
   (a) 4.33   (d) 2.14
   (b) 2.66   (e) None of the above
   (c) 5

Q6

2. The return on total assets is approximately
   (a) 6.1%   (d) 15.4%
   (b) 7.4%   (e) None of the above
   (c) 4.8%

Q6

3. The inventory turnover is approximately
   (a) 0.96   (d) 1.50
   (b) 1.44   (e) None of the above
   (c) 2.40

Q4

4. The acid-test ratio is approximately
   (a) 4.2   (d) 2.66
   (b) 5   (e) None of the above
   (c) 3.33

Q6

5. The times-interest-earned ratio is approximately
   (a) 5.75   (d) 7.25
   (b) 4.75   (e) None of the above
   (c) 2.5

Q6

6. The earnings per share of common stock is
   (a) $1.40   (d) $4.60
   (b) $2.00   (e) None of the above
   (c) $3.80

Q6

7. Eighty percent of sales are on account. The accounts receivable collection period is
   (a) under 108 days.
   (b) over 170 days.
   (c) between 150 and 165 days.
   (d) between 109 and 148 days.
   (e) None of the above

Q6

8. The return on stockholders' equity is approximately
   (a) 8%   (d) 4.9%
   (b) 9.3%   (e) None of the above
   (c) 6.4%

DEMONSTRATION PROBLEM

Consider the following financial statement data.

Balance Sheet Data

Cash	$ 20	Current Liabilities	$ 20
Accounts Receivable (net)	20	Bonds Payable (10%)	60
Merchandise Inventory	40	Common Stock (8 shares)	80
Plant (net)	140	Retained Earnings	60
Total Assets	$220	Total liabilities and equity	$220

Income Statement Data

Sales	$100
Cost of Goods Sold	50
Gross Profit	$ 50
Operating Expenses (incl. interest)	20
Income (before income tax)	$ 30
Income Tax Expense	10
Net Income	$ 20

Assume that the average of all balance sheet items is equal to the year-end figure and that all sales were on credit.

Required
1. Calculate the following ratios:
   - (a) Return on total assets (assume interest has been paid)
   - (b) Return on stockholders' equity
   - (c) Times-interest-earned ratio
   - (d) Earnings per share
   - (e) Inventory turnover
   - (f) Accounts receivable collection period
   - (g) Ratio of sales to long-term assets
   - (h) Current ratio
   - (i) Acid-test ratio
   - (j) Debt-to-equity ratio
2. Which of these ratios measure short-term solvency?

SOLUTION TO DEMONSTRATION PROBLEM

1. (a) $\dfrac{\text{Income from Operations}}{\text{Average Total Assets}} = \dfrac{30 + (10\% \times 60)}{220} = 16.36\%$

   (b) $\dfrac{\text{Net Income for the Year}}{\text{Average Stockholders' Equity}} = \dfrac{20}{140} = 14.3\%$

   (c) $\dfrac{\text{Income from Operations}}{\text{Interest Expense}} = \dfrac{30 + (10\% \times 60)}{(10\% \times 60)} = 6\text{ times}$

   (d) $\dfrac{\text{Net Income for the Year}}{\text{Number of Common Shares Outstanding}} = \dfrac{20}{8} = \$2.50$

   (e) $\dfrac{\text{Cost of Goods Sold}}{\text{Average Inventory}} = \dfrac{50}{40} = 1.25$

(f) $\dfrac{\text{Average Accounts Receivable}}{\text{Net Credit Sales}} \times 365 = \dfrac{20}{100} \times 365 = 73\,\text{days}$

(g) $\dfrac{\text{Net Sales}}{\text{Average Net Long-term Assets}} = \dfrac{100}{140} = 71\%$

(h) $\dfrac{\text{Current Assets}}{\text{Current Liabilities}} = \dfrac{80}{20} = 4$

(i) $\dfrac{\text{Cash and Accounts Receivable}}{\text{Current Liabilities}} = \dfrac{40}{20} = 2$

(j) $\dfrac{\text{Stockholders' Equity}}{\text{Total Liabilities}} = \dfrac{140}{80} = 1.75$

2. (e) Inventory turnover; (f) Accounts receivable collection period; (h) Current ratio; (i) Acid-test ratio

DISCUSSION QUESTIONS

Q16-1 Why are analysts and investors concerned with the financial structure of a particular corporation? How is it possible that the corporation is overfinanced or underfinanced?

Q16-2 Is the reliance on creditor financing advisable or inadvisable? Explain its impact on net income.

Q16-3 Discuss the advantages and disadvantages of short-term debt financing compared to long-term debt financing.

Q16-4 Explain what *solvency* means. When a corporation is insolvent, what are the implications to stockholders? to creditors?

Q16-5 How is it possible that a corporation making an acceptable gross profit on operations can actually be insolvent?

Q16-6 What ratios can be calculated to evaluate solvency? Explain what each one indicates.

Q16-7 (a) Define *working capital*. Distinguish between the current ratio and the acid-test ratio.
　　　　(b) "The current ratio is, by itself, inadequate to measure short-term solvency." Discuss this statement.

Q16-8 Two firms have the same working capital. Explain how it is possible that one is able to provide its short-term creditors with a guarantee from its current assets, while the other firm is not.

Q16-9 Management decisions relating to accounts receivable and inventory can affect solvency. Explain. What is an acceptable accounts receivable turnover? an acceptable inventory turnover?

Q16-10 Discuss the advantages and disadvantages of increasing inventory turnover.

Q16-11 Financial analysts compute inventory turnover by dividing cost of goods sold by average inventory. Why is it not theoretically correct to estimate the turnover of inventories by dividing net sales by the average inventory?

Q16-12 What is the revenue operating cycle? How is its calculation useful in evaluating solvency?

Q16-13 Identify and explain four ratios (and any associated calculations) that evaluate a corporation's efficiency. What does each ratio specify?

Q16-14 How is trading on the equity related to the overfinancing or underfinancing of a corporation? Provide an example.

Q16-15 "Leverage is useful but only if you can pay the interest." Discuss this statement.

Q16-16 The ratio of sales to long-term assets is used to determine adequacy of sales revenue in relation to investment in long-term assets. Discuss what factors may affect the usefulness of this ratio.

Q16-17 Comparisons need to be made to determine what is an acceptable or unacceptable ratio. On what basis can comparison be made?

Q16-18 Distinguish between a horizontal and a vertical analysis of financial statements.

DISCUSSION CASES

Case 1: Murphy, Inc.

Q1, Q4, Q6–Q8

The following are condensed comparative financial statements of Murphy, Inc., for the three years ended December 31, 19X5, 19X4, and 19X3.

Balance Sheets
December 31

	19X5	19X4	19X3
Current Assets			
Cash	$ 21	$ 8	$ 17
Accounts Receivable—Trade	38	30	20
Merchandise Inventory	60	40	30
Prepaid Expenses	1	2	3
Total Current Assets	$120	$ 80	$ 70
Total Long-term Assets	260	150	76
Total Assets	$380	$230	$146
Current Liabilities			
Accounts Payable	$ 98	$ 78	$ 48
Income Tax Payable	2	2	2
Total Current Liabilities	$100	$ 80	$ 50
Bonds Payable	50	50	—
Common Stock	200	80	80
Retained Earnings	30	20	16
Total Liabilities and Equity	$380	$230	$146

Income Statements
For the Years Ended December 31

	19X5	19X4	19X3
Sales	$210	$120	$100
Cost of Goods Sold	158	80	55
Gross Profit	$ 52	$ 40	$ 45
Operating Expenses	42	36	37
Net Income	$ 10	$ 4	$ 8

Additional information:

The company's accounts receivable as of December 31, 19X2, totaled $20. Its merchandise inventory as of December 31, 19X2, was $20. Credit terms are net 60 days from date of invoice.

For Discussion

1. What is your evaluation of
    (a) the financial structure of the corporation?
    (b) the proportion of stockholder and creditor claims to its assets?
    (c) the structure of its short-term and long-term credit financing?

2. Evaluate the short-term solvency of the corporation.
    (a) Calculate appropriate ratios for the three years.
    (b) Comment on the significant features in the corporation's balance sheet and income statement, including those apparent from the ratios calculated.

Case 2: Fitz, Inc., and Roy Corp.

Q1, Q4, Q6–Q8

The following are condensed comparative financial statements of Fitz, Inc., and Roy Corp. for the last four years.

Balance Sheets
December 31
(0, 000s)

	Fitz, Inc.				Roy Corp.			
	19X5	19X4	19X3	19X2	19X5	19X4	19X3	19X2
Current Assets	$185	$165	$155	$140	$480	$450	$410	$381
Current Liabilities	160	135	130	110	272	251	170	180
	$ 25	$ 30	$ 25	$ 30	$208	$199	$240	$201
Long-term Assets (net)	535	397	392	378	599	603	572	601
	$560	$427	$417	$408	$807	$802	$812	$802
Bonds Outstanding								
12% Due in 10 Years	$120	—	—	—				
15% Due in 7 Years					$400	$400	$400	$400
Paid-in Capital								
Cumulative Preferred, 5%								
(200 shares)	200	$200	$200	$200	200	200	200	200
Common (100 shares)	100	100	100	100	50	50	50	50
Retained Earnings	140	127	117	108	157	152	162	152
	$560	$427	$417	$408	$807	$802	$812	$802

Income Statements
For the Years Ended December 31
(0, 000s)

	Fitz, Inc.				Roy Corp.			
	19X5	19X4	19X3	19X2	19X5	19X4	19X3	19X2
Sales	$600	$540	$528	$516	$330	$220	$320	$270
Cost of Goods Sold	460	430	420	410	105	75	100	90
Gross Profit	$140	$110	$108	$106	$225	$145	$220	$180
Operating Expenses	70	50	50	50	155	155	160	156
Income (loss) from Operations	$ 70	$ 60	$ 58	$ 56	$ 70	$(10)	$ 60	$ 24
Income Tax Expense	35	30	29	28	30	—	30	12
Net Income (loss)	$ 35	$ 30	$ 29	$ 28	$ 40	$(10)	$ 30	$ 12
Dividends Paid								
Preferred	$ 10	$ 10	$ 10	$ 10	$ 20	—	$ 10	$ 10
Common	12	10	10	10	15	—	10	—

The current stock market quotations for common shares of these corporations are as follows: Fitz, Inc., $2.60; Roy Corp., $5.

For Discussion

1. What is your evaluation of
   (a) the financial structure of each corporation?
   (b) the proportion of stockholder and creditor claims to their assets?
   (c) the structure of their short-term and long-term creditor financing?

2. Evaluate the success with which each corporation is using its assets to earn net income.
   (a) Calculate appropriate ratios for each corporation.
   (b) Comment on the significant features in each corporation's balance sheet and income statement, including those apparent from the ratios calculated.

3. Which corporation would be a better investment if you were planning to purchase common shares? Support your decision with the necessary calculations.

Case 3: Achilles Corp.

Q1, Q4, Q6–Q8

The following are condensed comparative financial statements of Achilles Corp. for the three years ended December 31, 19X2, 19X1, and 19X0.

Balance Sheets
December 31

	19X2		19X1		19X0	
Current Assets						
Cash		$ 24		$ 9		$ 20
Accounts Receivable	$ 46		$ 37		$ 24	
Less: Allowance for Doubtful Accounts	1	45	1	36	—	24
Merchandise Inventory		72		48		36
Prepaid Expenses		3		3		4
Total Current Assets		$144		$ 96		$ 84
Long-term Assets	$405		$234		$118	
Less: Accumulated Depreciation	93	312	54	180	27	91
Total Assets		$456		$276		$175
Current Liabilities						
Accounts Payable		$ 90		$ 72		$ 40
Accrued Liabilities		30		24		20
Total Current Liabilities		$120		$ 96		$ 60
Bonds Payable		60		60		—
Total Liabilities		$180		$156		$ 60
Stockholders' Equity						
Common Stock (no-par value)		240		96		96
Retained Earnings		36		24		19
Total Liabilities and Stockholders' Equity		$456		$276		$175

Income Statements
For the Years Ended December 31

	19X2		19X1		19X0	
Sales		$252		$144		$120
Cost of Goods Sold						
Beginning Inventory	$ 48		$ 36		$ 24	
Purchases	213		108		78	
Cost of Goods Purchased	$261		$144		$102	
Ending Inventory	72		48		36	
Total Cost of Goods Sold		189		96		66
Gross Profit		$ 63		$ 48		$ 54
Selling and Administrative Expenses		37		34		30
Income from Operations		$ 26		$ 14		$ 24
Interest Expense		6		6		—
Income (before income tax)		$ 20		$ 8		$ 24
Income Tax Expense		8		3		9
Net Income		$ 12		$ 5		$ 15

Statements of Retained Earnings
For the Years Ended December 31

	19X2	19X1	19X0
Balance, Jan. 1	$ 24	$ 19	$ 12
Add: Net Income	12	5	15
Total	$ 36	$ 24	$ 27
Less: Dividends	—	—	8
Balance, Dec. 31	$ 36	$ 24	$ 19

Additional information:

All sales are on credit; credit terms are net 60 days after invoice date. Twenty shares of common stock were outstanding in years 19X0 and 19X1. On January 1, 19X2, an additional 30 shares of common stock were sold for $144. Beginning balance of accounts receivable on January 2, 19X0, was $19. Net long-term assets on January 1, 19X0, were $91. Total assets on January 1, 19X0, were $165. Total stockholders' equity on January 1, 19X0, was $101.

Required

1. From this information, calculate the following for each of the three years:
   (a) *Short-term solvency*
   Current ratio
   Acid-test ratio
   Accounts receivable collection period
   Number of days of sales in inventory
   Revenue operating cycle
   (b) *Long-term solvency*
   Return on total assets
   Return on stockholders' equity
   Times interest earned
   Earnings per share
   Return on sales
   Debt-to-equity ratio
   Ratio of sales to long-term assets

2. Do a short-term solvency analysis of Achilles Corp. What conclusion can be drawn from each of the financial ratios calculated in number 1 (a)?

3. Do a long-term solvency analysis of Achilles Corp. What conclusion can be drawn from each of the financial ratios calculated in number 1(b)? Was Achilles Corp. wise to expand operations?

EXERCISES

E16-1 through E16-6 are based on the following data taken from the records of Pleasant Products, Inc.

	(thousands)	
	19X2	19X1
Current Assets		
Cash	$ 10	$ 15
Temporary Investments	35	50
Accounts Receivable	200	150
Inventory	600	400
Current Liabilities	$400	$300

Short-term solvency ratios (Q4)

E16-1

Required
1. Determine the following ratios:
   (a) Current
   (b) Acid-test
2. What observations can you make about the short-term solvency of the corporation?

Management decisions related to receivables (Q6)

E16-2 Assume net credit sales for the year 19X2 amounted to $1,065.

Required
1. Determine the following:
   (a) Average accounts receivable collection period
   (b) Accounts receivable turnover
2. What observations can you make about the collection policies of the corporation?

Management decisions related to inventories (Q6)

E16-3 Assume cost of goods sold amounted to $852.

Required
1. Determine the following:
   (a) Number of days of sales in inventory
   (b) Inventory turnover
2. What observations can you make about management's inventory policies?

Gross profit rate (Q6)

E16-4 Use the information in E16-1, E16-2, and E16-3.

Required
1. Determine the following:
   (a) Gross profit rate of Pleasant Products, Inc.
   (b) Revenue operating cycle
2. What observations can you make about the gross profit rate and the operating cycle?

Vertical analysis (Q10)   **E16-5**

Required

From the information given, use vertical analysis to comment on the makeup of the current assets.

Horizontal analysis   **E16-6**
(Q10)

Required

From the information given, use horizontal analysis to comment on the trend in current assets.

E16-7 through E16-14 are based on the following balance sheet and income statement data for Peters Co.:

Balance Sheet *(thousands)*

Current Assets		*Current Liabilities*	
Cash	$ 55	Accounts Payable	$ 75
Accounts Receivable	48	Bonds Payable	60
Merchandise Inventory	70	Common Stock (15 shares)	150
Plant (net)	170	Retained Earnings	58
Total Current Assets	$343	Total Current Liabilities	$343

Income Statement	*(thousands)*
Sales	$145
Cost of Goods Sold	87
Operating Expenses	35
Interest Expense	8
Income Tax Expense	7
Net Income	$ 8

Assume that the average of all balance sheet items is equal to the ending balances and all sales were on credit.

Return on total assets   **E16-7**
(Q6)

Required

Determine the return on total assets and comment on your answer.

Return on stockholders'   **E16-8**
equity (Q6)

Required

Determine the return on stockholders' equity and comment on your answer.

Times-interest-earned   **E16-9**
ratio (Q6)

Required

Determine the times-interest-earned ratio and comment on your answer.

Earnings per share (Q6)   **E16-10**

Required

Determine the earnings per share and comment on your answer.

Return on sales (Q6)	**E16-11**

Required

Determine the return on sales and comment on your answer.

Ratio of sales to long-term assets (Q6, Q8)	**E16-12**

Required

Determine the ratio of sales to long-term assets and comment on your answer.

Ratio of long-term assets to stockholders' equity (Q6, Q8)	**E16-13**
	Required

Determine the ratio of long-term assets to stockholders' equity and comment on your answer.

Reliance on debt (Q1)	**E16-14**

Required

Determine the debt-to-equity ratio and comment on your answer.

PROBLEMS

Short-term and long-term solvency ratios (Q2, Q4)

P16-1   The following is the balance sheet of Cosmos Corp.

Balance Sheet
December 31, 19X0

Assets		Liabilities and Stockholders' Equity	
Current Assets		*Current Liabilities*	
Cash	$ 100	Accounts Payable	$ 300
Accounts Receivable	200	Wages Payable	50
Merchandise Inventory	500	Dividends Payable	50
Prepaid Expenses	50	Total Current Liabilities	$ 400
Total Current Assets	$ 850	Bonds Payable	800
Long-term Assets	1,000	Total Liabilities	$1,200
		Common Stock	500
		Retained Earnings	150
		Total Liabilities and	
Total Assets	$1,850	Stockholders' Equity	$1,850

Required

1. Based on this information, calculate the following:
    (a) Current ratio
    (b) Acid-test ratio
    (c) Debt-to-equity ratio

2. What do these ratios tell you about Cosmos Corp.?

3. What other financial statements are necessary to complete the analysis of Cosmos Corp.?

Solvency and efficiency
(Q4, Q6)

P16-2 The following information for 19X2 was gathered from the December 31, 19X2, financial statements of Unicorn Corp.

Balance Sheet		Income Statement	
Cash	$ 60	Net Credit Sales	$800
Accounts Receivable (net)	140	Cost of Goods Sold	600
Merchandise Inventory	250	Gross Profit	$200
Prepaid Expenses	10	Selling and Administrative Expenses	100
Long-term Assets (net)	330	Income from Operations	$100
Total Assets	$790	Interest Expense	20
Accounts Payable	$100	Income (before income tax)	$ 80
Notes Payable (6 months)	20	Income Tax Expense	30
Current Portion of Bonds		Net Income	$ 50
Payable	60		
Bonds Payable	140		
Preferred Stock, 10% (8 shares)	120		
Common Stock (50 shares)	250		
Retained Earnings	100		
Total Liabilities and			
Stockholders' Equity	$790		

Information from the December 31, 19X1, statements follows.

Accounts Receivable	$180
Merchandise Inventory	200
Long-term Assets (net)	250
Retained Earnings	80

Required

1. Compute the following for 19X2:
   (a) Debt-to-equity ratio
   (b) Current ratio
   (c) Acid-test ratio
   (d) Accounts receivable collection period
   (e) Inventory turnover
   (f) Return on stockholders' equity
   (g) Earnings per share

2. Compute dividends per share (common stock) for 19X2.

Preparing balance
sheet, incomplete data
(Q4, Q6)

P16-3 Ajax Corp.'s books were destroyed in a fire. The controller of the corporation can only remember the following few odd pieces of information to reconstruct the financial statements:

- The current ratio was 3.75 to 1.
- Sales for the year were $73,000.
- Inventories were $20,000 and were equal to long-term assets and to bonds payable.
- The accounts receivable collection period was 40 days.
- The bonds payable was 10 times cash.
- Total current assets were twice common stock.

Required

Using this information, prepare Ajax Corp.'s balance sheet as of April 30, 19X1.

Vertical analysis of
income statement (Q10)

P16-4 You are an accountant analyzing Zeus Corp.'s income statements. Zeus Corp. has
expanded its production facilities by 200% since 19X0. The condensed comparative income statements follow.

Income Statements
For the Years Ending December 31

	19X2	19X1	19X0
Sales	$250	$150	$120
Cost of Goods Sold	190	100	60
Gross Profit	$ 60	$ 50	$ 60
Selling and Administrative Expenses	35	34	35
Net Income	$ 25	$ 16	$ 25

Required

1. Prepare a vertical analysis of Zeus Corp.'s income statement for the three years.

2. What important inferences can be drawn from this analysis?

ALTERNATE PROBLEMS

Short-term and long-
term solvency ratios
(Q2, Q4)

AP16-1 The following is the balance sheet of Shingle Springs Corp.

Balance Sheet
December 31, 19X4

Assets		Liabilities and Stockholders' Equity	
Current Assets		*Current Liabilities*	
Cash	$ 250	Accounts Payable	$ 350
Accounts Receivable	150	Wages Payable	100
Merchandise Inventory	600	Dividends Payable	50
Prepaid Expenses	80	Total Current Liabilities	$ 500
Total Current Assets	$1,080	Bonds Payable	1,200
Long-term Assets	1,820	Total Liabilities	$1,700
		Common Stock	1,000
		Retained Earnings	200
		Total Liabilities and	
Total Assets	$2,900	Stockholders' Equity	$2,900

Required

1. Based on this information, determine the following:
   (a) Current ratio
   (b) Acid-test ratio
   (c) Debt-to-equity ratio

2. What do these ratios tell you about Shingle Springs?

3. What other financial statements are necessary to complete the analysis of Shingle
   Springs Corp.?

Solvency and efficiency
ratios (Q4, Q6)

AP16-2   The following financial statements belong to Banzai Corp.

Balance Sheet
December 31, 19X0

Assets		Liabilities and Stockholders' Equity	
Current Assets		*Current Liabilities*	
Cash	$ 20	Accounts Payable	$ 30
Accounts Receivable	60	Wages Payable	10
Merchandise Inventory	90	Total Current Liabilities	$ 40
Total Current Assets	$170	Bonds Payable (8%)	100
Long-term Assets (net)	110	Total Liabilities	$140
		Common Stock	100
		Retained Earnings	40
		Total Liabilities and	
Total Assets	$280	Stockholders' Equity	$280

Income Statement
For the Year ended December 31, 19X0

Sales	$300
Cost of Goods Sold	180
Gross Profit	$120
Selling and Administrative Expenses	80
Net Income	$ 40

Additional information:

Income tax was 50% of net income; it is included in selling and administrative expenses. Beginning balances of balance sheet accounts were the same as ending balances. All sales were on credit.

Required

The significance of certain ratios or tests follows. Give the name of the corresponding ratio or test, and calculate the ratios for Banzai Corp.

1. Primary test for solvency

2. A more severe test of immediate solvency

3. Test of efficiency of collection

4. Indication of liquidity of inventory

5. Reflection of financial strength and cushion for creditors

6. Indication of the net productivity of each sales dollar

7. Indication of management's ability to use efficiently the resources provided

Preparing balance
sheet, incomplete data
(Q4, Q6)

AP16-3   The incomplete balance sheet of Alpha Co. follows.

Balance Sheet
December 31, 19X1

Assets

Current Assets		
Cash	$ 30,000	
Accounts Receivable	?	
Merchandise Inventory	?	
Total Current Assets		$?

(continued)

Assets

Long-term Assets	$?	
Less: Accumulated Depreciation	100,000	?
Total Assets		$?

Liabilities and Stockholders' Equity

Current Liabilities		
Accounts Payable	$ 50,000	
Accrued Liabilities	?	
Total Current Liabilities		$120,000
Bonds Payable, 8%		?
Common Stock		?
Retained Earnings		?
Total Liabilities and Stockholders' Equity		$?

Required

Use the following information as of December 31, 19X1, to complete Alpha Co.'s balance sheet.

- The amount of working capital is $150,000.
- The par value of the stock is $10 per share.
- Market price per share is $15.
- Price-to-earnings ratio is 3.
- Income before payment of interest and income tax is $80,000.
- The ratio of stockholder equity to total assets is 0.60 to 1.
- Income tax equals $30,000.
- The acid-test ratio is 1.5 to 1.
- Times interest earned is 8.

Vertical analysis of income statement data (Q10)

AP16-4 The following information is taken from the records of P. Jones Corp.:

	19X3	19X2
Sales	$1,397	$1,122
Cost of Goods Sold	935	814
Selling Expenses	154	121
General Expenses	88	77
Other Revenue	4	7
Other Expenses	2	9
Income Tax	134	66

Required

1. Prepare a vertical analysis of the income statement.
2. Indicate the favorable and unfavorable changes.

DECISION PROBLEMS
Problem 1

Q4, Q6

You are the bank manager of North Bank. Two companies, A and B, are seeking bank loans. You are given the following financial statements. Assume that a fair comparison between companies A and B can be made with these data. *Ignore income tax.*

Balance Sheets
December 31, 19X1

Assets	Company A	Company B	Liabilities and Stockholders' Equity	Company A	Company B
Cash	$ 80	$ 165	Current Liabilities	$ 240	$ 300
Accounts Receivable (net)	125	235	Long-term Liabilities	600	500
Merchandise Inventory	480	660	Common Stock	250	640
Total Current Assets	$ 685	$1,060	Retained Earnings	100	160
Long-term Assets (net)	505	540			
			Total Liabilities and		
Total Assets	$1,190	$1,600	Stockholders' Equity	$1,190	$1,600

Note: Receivables and inventories are not significantly different from the balances as of December 31, 19X0.

Income Statements
For the Year Ended December 31, 19X1

	Company A	Company B
Sales (credit)	$1,500	$900
Cost of Goods Sold	1,050	540
Gross Profit	$ 450	$360
Selling and Administrative Expenses	150	200
Income from Operations	$ 300	$160
Interest Expense	60	50
Net Income	$ 240	$110

Required

1. From this information, calculate the following for each company:
   (a) *Short-term solvency ratios*

Current ratio	Accounts receivable turnover
Acid-test ratio	Number of days of sales in inventory
Accounts receivable collection period	Inventory turnover

   (b) *Long-term solvency ratios*
   Return on total assets
   Times interest earned
   Debt-to-equity ratio

2. From these ratios, determine the company to which you would grant a 6-month, 12% loan of $150 without security, and give reasons for your choice.

Problem 2

Q4, Q6

As controller of Athena Corp., you have calculated the following ratios, turnovers, and percentages to enable you to answer questions the directors are likely to ask at their next meeting.

	19X2	19X1	19X0
Current Ratio	3.1	2.6	2.0
Acid-Test Ratio	0.8	1.2	1.5
Inventory Turnover	9.5 times	10.0 times	11.2 times
Accounts Receivable Turnover	7.1 times	7.5 times	7.6 times
Return on Stockholders' Equity	12.0%	13.3%	14.1%
Return on Total Assets	12.6%	12.8%	13.3%
Sales Percentage Trend	123.0	118.0	100.0
Selling Expenses to Net Sales Ratio	13.9%	13.9%	14.2%

Required

Using these statistics, answer each question with a brief explanation to support each answer.

1. Is it becoming easier for the company to take advantage of cash discounts?
2. Is the company collecting its accounts receivable more rapidly than before?
3. Is the company's investment in accounts receivable decreasing?
4. Is the company's investment in inventory increasing?
5. Is the stockholders' investment becoming more profitable?
6. Did the dollar amount of selling expenses decrease during the three-year period?

ANSWERS TO SELF-TEST QUESTIONS

1. **(c)** Current Ratio $= \dfrac{\text{Current Assets}}{\text{Current Liabilities}}$;

$$\dfrac{\text{Cash + Accounts Receivable + Merchandise Inventory + Prepaid Expenses}}{\text{Accounts Payable}}$$

$$= \dfrac{300}{60} = 5$$

2. **(b)** Return on Total Assets $= \dfrac{\text{Income from Operations}}{\text{Average Total Assets}}$;

$$\dfrac{\text{Income before Taxes + Interest Expense}}{\text{Total Assets}} = \dfrac{38 + 8}{620} = 7.4\%$$

3. **(b)** Inventory Turnover $= \dfrac{\text{Cost of Goods Sold}}{\text{Average Inventory}} = \dfrac{144}{100} = 1.44$

4. **(d)** Acid-Test Ratio $= \dfrac{\text{Quick Current Assets}}{\text{Current Liabilities}}$;

$$\dfrac{\text{Cash + Accounts Receivable}}{\text{Accounts Payable}} = \dfrac{72 + 88}{60} = 2.66$$

5. **(a)** Times-Interest-Earned Ratio $=$

$$\dfrac{\text{Income from Operations + Interest Expense}}{\text{Interest Expense}} = \dfrac{38 + 8}{8} = 5.75$$

6. **(a)** Earnings per Share $= \dfrac{\text{Net Income } - \text{ Preferred Dividends}}{\text{Number of Common Shares Outstanding}}$

$$= \dfrac{20 - (\$60 \times 10\%)}{10} = \dfrac{20 - 6}{10} = \$1.40$$

7. **(e)** Accounts Receivable Collection Period $= \dfrac{\text{Average Accounts Receivable}}{\text{Net Credit Sales}}$

$$\times 365 = \dfrac{88}{(80\% \times 240)} \times 365 = \dfrac{88}{192} \times 365 = 167 \text{ days}$$

8. **(d)** Return on Stockholders' Equity $= \dfrac{\text{Net Income for the Year}}{\text{Average Stockholders' Equity}}$;

$$\dfrac{\text{Net Income for the Year}}{\text{Preferred Stock + Common Stock + Retained Earnings}} = \dfrac{20}{60 + 250 + 100} = 4.9\%$$

17

STATEMENT OF CASH FLOWS

CHAPTER 17 investigates the statement of cash flows, which was introduced in Chapter 1 and discussed on a rudimentary basis in Chapters 1 through 5. This chapter fully explains the statement and demonstrates practical approaches to preparing it. The statement is approached from the direct method of presentation, which is recommended. The indirect method is then discussed and students are shown a worksheet that may be used to assemble the necessary data to construct the statement under both the direct and the indirect methods. The chapter concludes with an appendix that offers a classroom approach to preparing the statement (the T-account approach), which may save more time in solving problems than the worksheet.

The statement of cash flows completes the financial picture of any entity. This statement tells the story that the income statement does not tell of what happens between two balance sheets. Since the income statement is based on the accrual method of accounting, where revenues are recorded when earned and expenses recorded when incurred, the profit so measured does not reflect cash flows. The income statement also includes items that do not represent an inflow or outflow of cash, but are properly reported as increases in revenues or expenses. It does not contain information about the financing or investing activities of an entity.

The statement of cash flows converts the information from the income statement to reflect cash inflow or outflow from operating activities, and then proceeds to report all financing and investing activities that had an effect on cash.

CHAPTER PREVIEW QUESTIONS

After studying Chapter 17, you should be able to answer the following questions:

1 What information is disclosed on the statement of cash flows that is not determinable from the other financial statements? (p.762)

2 What are some of the more important questions answered by the information provided on the statement of cash flows? (p.762)

3 Does net income represent the increase (or net loss the decrease) in cash from operating activities? Explain. (p.767)

4 What is the difference between the direct and the indirect method of reporting cash flows from operating activities? Is one preferred over the other? (pp.768–70)

5 How is it possible to report a net loss on the income statement yet report a sizable increase in cash from operating activities? (pp.770–71)

6 Is it possible to report a sizable net income yet an outflow of cash from operating activities? (p.771)

7 What other information is required if the direct method is used to report cash flows from operating activities? (p.773)

8 What approaches are available to help accountants prepare the statement of cash flows? (p.775)

FINANCIAL STATEMENT REPORTING

No single financial statement is more important than another. The income statement is important in that it details the revenues earned and the expenses incurred by an entity over a period of time. The revenues are recorded under the accrual basis and the expenses are matched against that revenue to determine the net income for the period. Obviously, an entity must operate at a profit or it will soon be a gone, rather than a going, concern. The amount of net income is then reported on the statement of retained earnings as an addition to the beginning balance, and any dividends declared during the period are subtracted from this total to arrive at the ending balance of retained earnings.

A balance sheet that reports the financial position of the entity at a point in time, the last day of the accounting period, is then prepared. The balance sheet reports the financial resources (assets) available to the entity, the liabilities (claims against the assets by outsider creditors) the entity has, and the equity that the owners have in the assets.

All three of these statements, discussed in the first 16 chapters of the text, are needed to properly communicate financial information to the users of that information. The three statements, however, do not disclose any cash flow information.

Q1: Cash flow information

The **statement of cash flows** discloses the amount of cash available as a result of an entity's operating activities, either directly as inflows and outflows or indirectly through a series of adjustments to the amount of net income for the year, and as a result of the entity's investing and financing decisions. The definition of *cash* may be expanded to include cash equivalents such as marketable securities and other short-term highly liquid assets. The cash flow statement provides users with the answer to questions such as the following:

Q2: Questions answered by cash flow statements

- How much cash was generated from operations?
- Was any cash generated from operations?
- How can a net income occur at the same time as a net outflow of cash from operations?
- What was done with the cash provided from operations?
- If so much cash was generated from operations, why did the Cash account decrease so much during the year?
- Is most of the cash coming from borrowing and other financing decisions?
- Are operations being funded by selling off excess assets? (If so, the owners will not be in business very long.)

The list could multiply. All financial statements contain important information. But the statement of cash flows provides urgently needed information. An entity cannot operate very long without cash.

THE STATEMENT OF CASH FLOWS

The statement of cash flows is divided into three main sections, which are then summarized in a fourth section where the increase or decrease in cash is reconciled with the beginning and ending balance of cash. The first section of the statement reports net cash flow from **operating activities.** Inflows of cash from operating activities usually come from the sale of goods or services, while outflows of cash go to the entities supplying the necessary assets consumed during operations, such as cost of goods sold, employee services, general and administrative expenses, interest expense, and of course, payments to the government. The direct method shows the source of the inflows and outflows, while the indirect method shows adjustments to net income that convert net income to cash provided from operating activities.

The next section reports cash flows from **investing activities,** those resulting from management decisions regarding the purchase or sale of noncurrent assets. Outflows in this section represent the purchase of assets such as land, buildings, and equipment for operations; the purchase of intangible assets such as patent rights and copyrights; or the purchase of long-term investments. For example, shares of stock of another corporation might be purchased for control purposes, or in order to exercise significant influence over the operations of that corporation. Inflows from investing activities would result from the eventual sale of the just-mentioned assets. Dividends and interest received from the long-term investments would be reflected in the operating activities section, because of its close tie with the income statement and the determination of income tax liabilities.

The third section of the statement reports cash flows from **financing activities,** those resulting from management decisions regarding the debt and equity mix. Inflows might come from the issuance of common or preferred stock, the sale of treasury stock, or the issuance of bonds or other long-term debt securities. Outflows might reflect management decisions to retire common or preferred stock, to purchase treasury stock, or to retire bonds or other long-term debt securities. The payment of dividends would be reported as an outflow from financing activities, while the payment of interest on long-term debt securities is usually reflected in the operating activities section because of its close tie with the income statement and the determination of income tax liabilities. For a more complete list of the types of cash flows found under the three major activity categories, see Real World Example 17-1.

Any transaction that has an effect on cash should be reported in some manner on the statement of cash flows. Transactions that do not affect cash but are the results of financing or investing decisions should be disclosed in the financial statements, but not as a part of the actual cash flow statement. For example, if an entity issues common stock in exchange for a parcel of land, the transaction is both an investing decision (the purchase of land) and a financing decision (the issuance of common stock). This transaction should not be reported on the statement of cash flows as an inflow from financing and an outflow from investing because no actual flow of cash occurs. It must be disclosed, but in such a manner that it does not lead financial statement readers to conclude that it had an effect on cash.

The Saguaro Computers, Inc., comparative balance sheet and income statement in Exhibits 17-1 and 17-2 (pp. 766–67) are used in this chapter to illustrate the preparation of a statement of cash flows.

In Chapters 1 and 2, the statement of cash flows was prepared directly from the Cash account. Dealing with very few transactions made this approach possible. Chapter 17 will investigate more feasible methods to prepare this statement.

ANALYSIS OF CASH FLOWS

The following five steps are used in the preparation of a statement of cash flows:

Step 1 Calculate the increase or decrease in the Cash account.
Step 2 Calculate cash flows from operating activities.

REAL WORLD EXAMPLE 17-1
How Cash Flows Are Classified

Statement no. 95 [FASB] has sounded the death knell of the "sources and uses" format. Instead, it provides explicit criteria for classification of cash flows as investing or financing activities. All other cash flows are considered operating activities.

Investing activities

Cash paid to:
Acquire property, plant, and equipment and other productive assets (including capitalized interest), provided the cash is paid close to the time of purchase.

Acquire a business.

Purchase debt (other than cash equivalents) or equity securities (including investments accounted for by the equity method) of other entities.

Make loans to another entity.

Purchase loans from another entity.

Cash received from:
Sales of property, plant, and equipment and other productive assets.

Sales of a business unit, such as a subsidiary or division.

Sale of debt (other than cash equivalents) or equity securities of other entities.

Collection of principal on loans made to another entity.

Sale of loans made by the entity.

Financing activities

Cash paid to:
Owners in the form of dividends or other distributions.

Repay amounts borrowed, including amounts related to short-term debt, long-term debt, capitalized lease obligations and seller-financed debt.

Reacquire treasury stock and other equity securities.

Cash received from:
Issuing equity securities, such as common stock.

Issuing bonds, mortgages, notes and other short- or long-term borrowings.

Operating Activities

Cash received from:
Sales of goods or services, including receipts from the collection or sale of trade accounts and short- and long-term notes receivable (including sales-type leases).

Returns on loans (interest) and on equity securities (dividends), including dividends from equity-method investees.

All others for transactions not defined as investing or financing activities. This includes amounts received to settle lawsuits, proceeds of insurance settlements not pertaining directly to investing or financing activities, and cash refunds from suppliers.

Cash paid to:
Acquire materials for manufacture or goods for

Step 3   Analyze the changes in Noncurrent Asset, Liability, and Equity accounts, and identify transactions that resulted in cash inflows and outflows.
Step 4   Analyze any current accounts not used in the measurement of income.
Step 5   Prepare a classified statement of cash flows in the correct format. The net increase or decrease in cash shown in the statement of cash flows must equal the amount calculated in Step 1.

Step 1   Calculation of the Increase or Decrease in Cash

The change in the Cash account for Saguaro Computers, Inc., is calculated by comparing the end-of-year balance with the beginning-of-year balance.

resale, including principal payments on trade accounts and both short- and long-term notes payable to suppliers.

Employees for compensation.

Creditors for interest.

Governments for taxes, duties, fines, and other fees or penalties.

Other suppliers for other goods and services.

All others for transactions not defined as investing or financing activities. This includes payments to settle lawsuits, cash contributions to charities, and cash refunds to customers.

Reconciling Net Income and Net Cash From Operations

In reconciling net income and net cash from operating activities, Statement no. 95 requires companies to present *all major classes of adjustments.* Typical reconciling items are

Accruals of expected future operating cash receipts and payments

Accounts receivable.

Notes receivable from customers arising from sale of goods or services.

Interest receivable.

Accounts payable.

Notes payable to suppliers to acquire materials for manufacture or goods for resale.

Interest payable.

Income taxes payable.

Excess of income of equity-method investees over dividends received.

Other accrued expenses.

Deferrals of past operating cash receipts and payments

Inventory.

Deferred income.

Deferred expenses.

Prepaid expenses.

Noncash expenses/income

Depreciation.

Depletion.

Deferred income taxes.

Amortization of intangible assets.

Amortization of debt issuance costs.

Amortization of discounts on securities.

Provision for bad debts.

Provision for losses on long-lived assets.

Gains or losses from transactions where cash flows are investing or financing activities

Sale of property, plant, and equipment and other productive assets.

Sales of debt (other than cash equivalents) or equity securities of other entities.

Sale of loans.

Sale of business operations.

Return of an investment, such as a liquidating dividend.

Retirement of debt.

Source John J. Mahoney, CPA, Mark V. Sever, CPA, and John A. Theis, CPA, "How Statement No. 95 Classifies Cash Flows" table in "Cash Flow: FASB Opens the Floodgates," May 1988. Reprinted with permission from the *Journal of Accountancy.* Copyright © 1988 by AICPA.

			Change in Cash (*thousands*)	
	19X8	19X7	Debit Change	Credit Change
Cash	$27	$150	—	$123

Cash has decreased by $123,000 during the year. Rather than cash having been generated during the year, it has been deployed in this case, because it has decreased.

The amount of available cash is important to financial statement readers. An increase in cash is usually required for growth, since additional sales result in more receivables being financed and in a larger amount of liabilities incurred as a result

EXHIBIT 17–1

Saguaro Computers, Inc.
Balance Sheets
December 19X8 and 19X7

(thousands)

Assets	19X8	19X7	Debit Changes	Credit Changes
Current Assets				
Cash	$ 27	$ 150		$123
Marketable Securities	25	50		25
Accounts Receivable	350	400		50
Merchandise Inventory	900	450	$ 450	
Prepaid Expenses	20	10	10	
Total Current Assets	$1,322	$1,060		
Investments	$ 140	$ 220		80
Long-term Assets				
Land	$ 70	$ 70		
Building	1,200	400	800	
Machinery (note 1)	1,000	700	300	
Less: Accumulated Depreciation (note 2)	(550)	(300)		250
Total Long-term Assets	$1,720	$ 870		
Total Assets	$3,182	$2,150		
Liabilities				
Current Liabilities				
Accounts Payable	$ 235	$ 145		90
Accrued Liabilities	25	30	5	
Income Tax Payable	40	25		15
Total Current Liabilities	$ 300	$ 200		
Long-term Liabilities				
Mortgage Payable	1,000	500		500
Total Liabilities	$1,300	$ 700		
Stockholders' Equity				
Common Stock	$1,210	$ 800		410
Retained Earnings (note 3)	672	650		22
Total Stockholders' Equity	$1,882	$1,450		
Total Liabilities and Stockholders' Equity	$3,182	$2,150		
Total Changes			$1,565	$1,565

Notes to the Balance Sheet:

1. Machinery costing $50,000 with accumulated depreciation of $10,000 was sold for $30,000 cash.

2. This item represents an increase in an asset contra account, which in turn represents a decrease in an asset account.

3. Dividends of $58,000 were declared and paid during 19X8.

EXHIBIT 17-2

Saguaro Computers, Inc.
Income Statement
For the Year Ended December 31, 19X8

(thousands)

Sales		$1,200
Cost of Goods Sold		674
Gross Profit		$ 526
Operating Expenses		
Depreciation Expense—Buildings and Machinery	$260	
Other Expenses	120	380
		$ 146
Income from Operations		
Gain on Sale of Long-term Investments	$ 24	
Loss on Sale of Machinery	(10)	14
Income (before income tax)		$ 160
Income Tax Expense		80
Net Income		$ 80

of increased purchases. Excess cash is unproductive; however, inadequate cash can affect the entity's liquidity, that is, its ability to pay its debts as they become due. Cash management deals with the optimal amount of cash to be kept on hand.

In the case of SCI, the statement reader is faced with the following question. Is the decrease in cash a result of good cash management? Or does it signal a liquidity problem? Also, what are the cash inflows and outflows that resulted in the $123,000 cash decrease?

Step 2 Calculation of Cash Flows from Operating Activities

Q3: Net income and operating activities

Determining cash flow from operating activities is the next step in preparing a statement of cash flows. The net income of $80,000 reported on the income statement has been determined on the basis of accrual accounting and other requirements of GAAP. Net income on the accrual basis does not purport to be a measure of the increases or decreases in cash as a result of operating activities. Many items on the accrual-basis income statement do not impact cash flows, items such as depreciation and other cost allocations, gains and losses, and selected accounts affected by changes in certain current balance sheet accounts (for example, changes in Accounts Receivable determine the amount of cash received from sales).

Because of the many income statement items that do not affect cash, two approaches can be taken to convert the income statement information to a measure of cash flows from operating activities. The items on the income statement that affect cash can be addressed (the direct approach), or the items that do not affect cash can be eliminated (the indirect approach). The direct method will be demonstrated first.

THE DIRECT METHOD

Q4: Direct method

The *direct method* is recommended by the accounting profession, and was the basis for the statement of cash flows introduced in Chapters 1 and 2. From a learning point of view, the direct method is also easier to understand. The indirect method is presented because it has been the traditional approach used in practice.

The **direct method** focuses on the income statement items that do have an impact on cash flows. The first step, therefore, is to identify these items. From Exhibit 17-2, the following items would have an effect on cash; Sales, Cost of Goods Sold, Other Expenses, and Income Tax Expense. Certain accounts on the balance sheet, however, affect these items on the income statement. The amount of cash received from sales is influenced by the amount of accounts receivable at the beginning and end of the year. The cash paid out to suppliers for cost of goods sold is controlled by the amount of inventory and of accounts payable at the beginning and end of the year. Cash paid for other expenses is affected by the accrued expenses and prepaid expenses at the beginning and end of each year, while the cash paid for income taxes is affected by the amount of income taxes payable at the beginning and end of each year. Actually, the significance is not in the amounts of the items at the beginning and end of the year but in the *change* in the accounts during that time. Each of these interrelated SCI income statement items and balance sheet accounts will be examined next as they apply to the statement of cash flows.

Sales The amount of Saguaro sales was reported as $1,200. However, during the year, accounts receivable decreased by $50. If accounts receivable decreased, it indicates that more cash was collected during the year than is reflected in the Sales account. Stated another way, the amount reported as sales is *understated from a cash-flow point of view*. The amount of cash actually received from customers was $1,250;

Sales	$1,200*
Add: Decrease in Accounts Receivable	50
Cash Received from Customers	$1,250

An increase in Accounts Receivable must be subtracted from Sales, since an increase indicates that less cash was collected during the year, resulting in an overstatement in Sales from a cash-flow perspective.

Cost of Goods Sold Cost of Goods Sold must be adjusted by the change in two balance sheet accounts, Merchandise Inventory and Accounts Payable. Accounts payable are usually limited to trade accounts payable, which refer to liabilities a merchandiser has incurred as a result of buying items for resale from its suppliers. Adjusting cost of goods sold by the change in both accounts can determine the amount of cash paid to suppliers. If the merchandise inventory increased during the year by $450, it indicates that more inventory was purchased during the year than was sold, resulting in a further outflow of cash not reflected in the income statement as Cost of Goods Sold. This increase in inventory must be added to Cost of Goods Sold. If the inventory had decreased during the year, it shows that more goods were sold during the year than were purchased, that is, goods sold during the current year

---

*Throughout the remainder of this chapter, the zeroes representing thousands have been omitted in order to avoid such large numbers. For example, $1,200,000 will appear as $1,200.

were purchased in a previous year. If the goods were purchased in a previous year, chances are that the cash was paid out in the previous year, not in the current year. A decrease in inventory would be subtracted from Cost of Goods Sold.

On the other hand, if accounts payable increased during the year, it indicates that more goods were purchased than were paid for, and cost of goods sold is overstated from a cash-flow perspective. The increase in Accounts Payable must be subtracted from Cost of Goods Sold. If accounts payable had decreased, it shows that more inventory was paid for during the year than was purchased, and the decrease would be added to Cost of Goods Sold. The cash paid to suppliers during the year amounted to $1,034, determined as follows:

Cost of Goods Sold	$ 674
Add: Increase in Merchandise Inventory	450
Less: Increase in Accounts Payable	(90)
Cash Paid to Suppliers	$1,034

Other Expenses Other Expenses must be adjusted by the change in Prepaid Expenses and the change in Accrued Liabilities, much like the adjustment to Cost of Goods Sold. If prepaid expenses increased during the year, it indicates that more expenses were paid in cash than were matched against revenue during the year, resulting in an understatement in other expenses from a cash-flow perspective. The increase in Prepaid Expenses must be added to Other Expenses. Had prepaid expenses decreased during the year, the decrease would be subtracted from Other Expenses, indicating an overstatement from a cash-flow viewpoint. A decrease in accrued liabilities during the year shows that more cash was paid for other expenses than is reflected on the income statement, and therefore the decrease must be added to Other Expenses. If accrued liabilities had increased, the change would have been subtracted from Other Expenses. The amount of cash paid for other expenses therefore would be $135, determined as follows:

Other Expenses	$120
Add: Increase in Prepaid Expenses	10
	$130
Add: Decrease in Accrued Liabilities	5
Cash Paid for Other Expenses	$135

Income Taxes Income Tax Expense must be adjusted by the change in Income Tax Payable during the year. If taxes payable increased by $15, it indicates that more income tax expense appears on the income statement than was paid during the year, from a cash-flow perspective. The increase in Income Tax Payable must be subtracted from Income Tax Expense. If the Income Tax Payable account had decreased during the year, the change would have been added to Income Tax Expense. The cash paid to the government amounted to $65, determined as follows:

Income Tax Expense	$80
Less: Increase in Income Tax Payable	(15)
Cash Paid to the Government	$65

The Cash Flows from Operating Activities section of the statement of cash flows for Saguaro now would appear as follows:

Cash Flows from Operating Activities

Inflows:

Cash Received from Customers		$1,250
(Outflows):		
Cash Paid to Suppliers	$(1,034)	
Cash Paid for Other Expenses	(135)	
Cash Paid to the Government	(65)	
Total Cash Outflows		(1,234)
Net Cash Inflow from Operating Activities		$16

THE INDIRECT METHOD

Q4: Indirect method

As mentioned before, under the **indirect method** the statement of cash flows eliminates income statement items that do not impact cash flows, while adjusting certain income statement accounts for balance sheet items that affect the amount of cash flows. The latter adjustments are the same as those made under the direct approach to sales, cost of goods sold, other expenses, and income tax expense, but under the indirect method, the adjustments are made to net income, rather than to the individual income statement items. The Cash Flows from Operating Activities section of the statement of cash flows is instead divided into three sections, all of which are considered adjustments to net income; expenses and revenues not involving cash, losses and gains not due to normal operations, and net debit and credit changes in current asset and liability accounts used in the measurement of income.

Expenses and Revenues Not Involving Cash   Income statement items not involving cash consist of noncash accounts used in the determination of net income. A partial list of the more common accounts follows:

Debits	Credits
Depreciation Expense	Amortization of Bond Premium
Depletion Expense	Equity in Earnings of Investee
Amortization Expense	
Amortization of Bond Discount	

The debit items must be added back to net income since no outflow of cash occurred, while the credit items must be subtracted from net income because no inflow of cash occurred as a result of the transaction. For instance, remember that under the *equity method* of recording investments, used when the entity can exercise significant influence, the investor's share of the investee's net income is recorded with the following journal entry:

Long-term Investments	XXX (% share of net income)
Equity in Earnings of Investee	XXX (% share of net income)

The credit account, Equity in Earnings of Investee, appears on the income statement as an increase in net income. However, because no corresponding inflow of cash occurred, it must be subtracted from net income on the statement of cash flows to determine the cash provided from operating activities.

Q5: Net loss and cash increase

Losses and Gains Not Due to Normal Operations   Losses and gains appearing on the income statement do not directly impact cash flows, but they are related to transactions affecting investment and financing decisions that generate cash flows. Examples include the decision to retire bonds before the maturity date or the sale of previ-

Q6: Net income and
cash outflow

ously purchased real estate. The resulting cash flows from these transactions are reported in other sections of the statement of cash flows and, therefore, must be removed from the Cash Flows from Operating Activities section. Since losses are deducted when determining net income, they must be added back, and conversely, gains added to net income must be subtracted out when determining cash flows from operating activities. Take, for example, the following entry:

Cash	100	
Land		40
Gain on Sale of Land		60

As will be shown in the next section, the $100 is an inflow from investing activities. Under accrual accounting, the $60 is reported on the income statement and net income is increased by $60. Since the amount of the inflow was $100 and not $60, in order to avoid double counting and to arrive at a proper determination of cash flows from operating activities, the gain would have to be subtracted from net income. Conversely, a loss would be added back to net income.

Net Changes in Current Accounts   A third category of adjustments to net income involves the following balance sheet accounts used in accrual accounting:

Current Assets	Current Liabilities
Accounts Receivable (net)	Accounts Payable
Merchandise Inventory	Accrued Liabilities
Prepaid Expenses	Income Tax Payable
Supplies Expense	

These current asset and current liability accounts have offsetting expense and revenue items in the income statement that affect net income. Examples of offsetting items are sales on account and purchases on account. If cash has not yet been received or paid, the offsetting amount must be omitted when calculating cash flow from operations. This is done by calculating the net debit or net credit change in the income-statement-related current asset and current liability accounts, as follows for SCI:

	19X8	19X7	(thousands) Debit	Credit
Current Assets				
Accounts Receivable	$350	$400		$50
Merchandise Inventory	900	450	$450	
Prepaid Expenses	20	10	10	
Current Liabilities				
Accounts Payable	235	145		90
Accrued Liabilities	25	30	5	
Income Tax Payable	40	25		15
			Debits are deducted from net income.	Credits are added to net income.

The reason that debits are deducted from net income and credits are added back is not readily apparent. It becomes clearer when each item is analyzed individually.

The analysis of this category is much the same as that used for discussing the direct method. Under that method, if accounts receivable decreased, it indicated that more cash was collected than is reflected in the Sales account. The decrease amount was therefore added back to Sales to arrive at Cash Received from Customers. Since the indirect method starts with reported net income, the adjustments are made to Net Income rather than to Sales. If an adjustment is added to Sales under the direct method, it would be added to Net Income under the indirect method. Note, however, that under the direct method, the increase in inventory was *added* to Cost of Goods Sold, while under the indirect method, it is *subtracted* from Net Income. Adding the increase to Cost of Goods Sold increased the actual cost of goods sold, which therefore decreases net income.

Mistakes can be easily made when switching back and forth between the direct and the indirect method. While the increase in Prepaid Expenses was added to Other Expenses under the direct method, it is subtracted from Net Income under the indirect method for the same reason given for the increase in inventory. While the increase in Accounts Payable was *subtracted* from Cost of Goods Sold because the cash was not paid out, it is *added* to Net Income for the same reason. The direction of the change will be the same under both the direct and indirect methods when adjusting current revenue accounts, but the two methods will oppose each other when adjusting expense and cost-of-goods-sold accounts.

The Cash Flows from Operating Activities section of the cash flow statement for Saguaro under the indirect method appears as follows:

Cash Flows from Operating Activities

Net Income		$ 80
Add: Expenses Not Requiring Cash:		
Depreciation Expense	$260	
Losses Not Due to Normal Operations:		
Loss on Sale of Machinery	10	
Net Credit Changes in Current Accounts:		
Decrease in Accounts Receivable	50	
Increase in Accounts Payable	90	
Increase in Income Tax Payable	15	425
Less: Gains Not Providing Cash:		
Gain on Sale of Long-term Investments	(24)	
Net Debit Changes in Current Accounts:		
Increase in Merchandise Inventory	(450)	
Increase in Prepaid Expenses	(10)	
Decrease in Accrued Liabilities	(5)	(489)
Net Cash Inflow from Operating Activities		$16

Compare Saguaro's Cash Flows from Operating Activities section under the indirect method with the same section under the direct method, repeated as follows:

Cash Flows from Operating Activities

Inflows:		
Cash Received from Customers		$1,250
(Outflows):		
Cash Paid to Suppliers	$(1,034)	
Cash Paid for Other Expenses	(135)	
Cash Paid to the Government	(65)	
Total Cash Outflows		(1,234)
Net Cash Inflow from Operating		
Activities		$16

Note that in both cases, a seemingly healthy $80,000 net income for Saguaro has shrunk to an apparently unhealthy $16,000 when net income was converted from the accrual basis to the cash basis.

The results in terms of the net increase or decrease in cash as a result of operating activities are the same under both the direct and the indirect methods, but the statement's informational content is quite different. Some people in the profession believe that the direct approach is more understandable to statement users than the indirect method. The major drawback to using the direct method is that a *reconciliation schedule* of net income and cash provided from operating activities must be included as part of the statement of cash flows. This requirement means that an entity choosing the recommended direct method must include the same information provided in the operating activities section under the indirect method. The indirect method has been used for many years in the past and appears to be the method used in practice today. Note the United Telecom annual report at the end of the text; the statement of cash flows is reported under the indirect method. As shown, the only difference between the two methods is the Cash Flows from Operating Activities section. The discussion of the other two sections, Cash Flows from Investing Activities and Cash Flows from Financing Activities, continues with Steps 3 and 4. These steps complete the analysis of the accounts that provide information for the completion of the statement of cash flows.

Q7: Additional information, direct method

Step 3   Analysis of Changes in Noncurrent Accounts

Step 3 is to analyze the cash inflows and outflows included in noncurrent account transactions. The transactions involving these accounts follow.

(*thousands*)

1. Long-term investments costing $80 were sold for $104.
2. A building was purchased for $800.
3. Machinery costing $50 was sold for $30. Depreciation of $10 had been recorded on this machine.
4. Machinery was purchased for $350.
5. Depreciation expenses of $260 were recorded during the year.
6. A mortgage of cash in the amount of $500 was taken out on one of SCI's buildings.
7. A sum of $410 was received from the sale of no-par common stock.
8. Dividends totaling $58 were declared and paid during the year.
9. Net income for the year amounted to $80.

The impact of these transactions on Cash is determined by reconstructing the journal entry for each transaction, a *journal entry extension* approach.

Transaction 1   Long-term investments costing $80 were sold for $104.

Cash	104	
Investments		80
Gain on Sale of Long-term Investments		24

Analysis This is a cash inflow from investing activities of $104,000.
Note: The gain affects the determination of Cash Flows from Operating Activities under the indirect method.

Transaction 2 A building was purchased for $800.

Building	800	
Cash		800

Analysis This is a cash outflow from investing activities of $800.

Transaction 3 Machinery costing $50 was sold for $30. Depreciation of $10 had been recorded on this machine.

Cash	30	
Accumulated Depreciation—Machinery	10	
Loss on Sale of Machinery	10	
Machinery		50

Analysis This is a cash inflow from investing activities of $30,000.
Note: The loss affects Cash Flows from Operating Activities under the indirect method.

Transaction 4 Machinery was purchased for $350.

Machinery	350	
Cash		350

Analysis This is a cash outflow from investing activities of $350.

Transaction 5 Depreciation expenses of $260 were recorded during the year.

Depreciation Expense—Buildings and		
Machinery	260	
Accumulated Depreciation		260

Analysis This has no impact on cash flow.
Note: Depreciation Expense affects Cash Flows from Operating Activities under the indirect method.

Transaction 6 A mortgage of cash in the amount of $500 was taken out on one of SCI's buildings.

Cash	500	
Mortgage Payable		500

Analysis This is a cash inflow from financing activities of $500 since cash was received by assuming the long-term debt.

Transaction 7 A sum of $410 was received from the sale of no-par value common stock.

Cash	410	
Common Stock		410

Analysis This is a cash inflow from financing activities of $410.

Transaction 8 Dividends totaling $58 were declared and paid during the year.

Retained Earnings	58	
Cash		58

Analysis This is a cash outflow from financing activities of $58.

Note: Dividends Payable would have been credited when the dividends were declared, and Cash credited later when the dividends were paid, but since they were declared and paid during the same year, the credit was made to Cash.

Transaction 9 Net income for the year amounted to $80.

Income Summary	80	
Retained Earnings		80

Analysis This has no impact on cash flow.

Note: Net income is used as a basis for determining Cash Flows from Operating Activities under the indirect method.

Q8: Available approaches

The transactions analysis used here is a derivation of the *journal entry extension model,* one approach to gather the information to complete the investing and financing sections of the statement of cash flows. A different, formal worksheet approach is presented later in this chapter, while another approach, often referred to as the T-account approach, is presented in the appendix to this chapter. The transactions approach is satisfactory in limited situations when the number of transactions is small and to the point. This approach should be enough for those students who are not majoring in accounting. The more formal worksheet is used to assemble the information in practice in order to leave an easily followed audit trail.

One more step still must be performed before the final step, the actual preparation of the statement. The current accounts related to operations were examined in Step 2, and the noncurrent accounts were examined in Step 3. Step 4 examines the changes in current accounts not related to operations.

Step 4 Analysis of Current Accounts Not Used in the Measurement of Income

The current accounts analyzed in Step 2 were related to items on the income statement. Other accounts, such as for short-term investments in marketable securities, dividends payable, and the current portion of long-term debt, might be present and have an effect on cash flow. In this example, only short-term investments (Marketable Securities) need to be addressed. As mentioned before, the short-term investments in marketable securities may be considered equivalent to cash. Here, Cash is limited to just that, cash, so any change in marketable securities must be examined. Saguaro's account has decreased by $25, indicating that some securities have been sold. Since the income statement shows no gain or loss for Marketable Securities (it has a gain on the sale of long-term investments), it must be assumed that these securities were sold at book value. The journal entry is as follows:

Cash	25	
Marketable Securities		25

Analysis This is a cash inflow from investing activities of $25.

Step 5 Preparation of the Formal Statement of Cash Flows

On the basis of the foregoing analysis, the statement of cash flows for SCI can now be prepared. See Exhibits 17-3, 17-4, and 17-5. Exhibit 17-3 was prepared under the direct method. As noted, this method requires the inclusion of a reconciliation between net income and net cash flows from operating activities. The schedule in Exhibit 17-4 is an integral part of the statement of cash flows prepared under the direct method.

The more traditional cash flow statement under the indirect method would appear as shown in Exhibit 17-5.

EXHIBIT 17–3

Saguaro Computers, Inc.
Statement of Cash Flows (Direct Method)
For the Year Ended December 31, 19X8

Cash Flows from Operating Activities

Inflows:

Cash Received from Customers			$1,250
(Outflows):			
Cash Paid to Suppliers	$(1,034)		
Cash Paid for Other Expenses	(135)		
Cash Paid to the Government	(65)		
Total Cash Outflows		(1,234)	
Net Cash Inflow from Operating Activities			$ 16

Cash Flows from Investing Activities

Inflows:

Sale of Marketable Securities	25		
Sale of Long-term Investments	104		
Sale of Machinery	30		
Total Cash Inflows		159	
(Outflows):			
Purchase of Building	(800)		
Purchase of Machinery	(350)		
Total Cash Outflows:		(1,150)	
Net Cash Outflow from Investing Activities			(991)

Cash Flows from Financing Activities

Inflows:

Issuance of Common Stock	410		
Increase in Long-term Debt	500		
Total Cash Inflows		910	
(Outflows):			
Payment of Dividends		(58)	
Net Cash Inflow from Financing Activities			852
Net Outflow of Cash			$(123)
Cash Balance, Jan. 1, 19X8			150
Cash Balance, Dec. 31, 19X8			$ 27

EXHIBIT 17-4

**Reconciliation of Net Income
to Net Cash Flows from
Operating Activities**

Net Income		$ 80
Add: Expenses Not Requiring Cash:		
Depreciation Expense—Buildings and Machinery	$260	
Losses Not Due to Normal Operations:		
Loss on Sale of Machinery	10	
Net Credit Changes in Current Accounts:		
Decrease in Accounts Receivable	50	
Increase in Accounts Payable	90	
Increase in Income Tax Payable	15	425
Less: Gains Not Providing Cash:		
Gain on Sale of Long-term Investments	(24)	
Net Debit Changes in Current Accounts:		
Increase in Merchandise Inventory	(450)	
Increase in Prepaid Expenses	(10)	
Decrease in Accrued Liabilities	(5)	(489)
Net Cash Inflow from Operating Activities		$ 16

Noncash Financing and Investing Activities

Many times an important financing or investing activity will not involve cash. An example is a transaction whereby a parcel of land is acquired through a direct issue of common stock, the journal entry being as follows:

Land	40	
Common Stock		40

Since transactions of this type do not affect cash, the transaction should not be reported on the statement of cash flows. Instead, such a transaction should appear as a footnote to the financial statements so users are aware it has taken place.

The more complex statements of cash flows require a more organized system to analyze the changes in all the noncash accounts. The next section presents a formal worksheet approach to solving the more complex problems, while the chapter appendix presents a much quicker method than the worksheet, which may be used to solve most textbook problems. The T-account method in the appendix is generally not used in practice because it lacks an organized audit trail.

THE WORKSHEET APPROACH TO SOLVING CASH-FLOW PROBLEMS

The **worksheet approach** provides the accountant a clean, organized tool to gather all the information necessary to prepare a complex statement of cash flows. Since it is necessary to account for all the changes in all the general ledger accounts other than Cash, the worksheet format has two columns for the balance sheet accounts—one on the left and one on the right. The left-hand column presents the

EXHIBIT 17–5

Saguaro Computers, Inc.
Statement of Cash Flows (Indirect Method)
For the Year Ended December 31, 19X8

Cash Flows from Operating Activities

Net Income			$ 80
Add: Expenses Not Requiring Cash:			
Depreciation Expense—Building and Machinery	$260		
Losses Not Due to Normal Operations:			
Loss on Sale of Machinery	10		
Net Credit Changes in Current Accounts:			
Decrease in Accounts Receivable	50		
Increase in Accounts Payable	90		
Increase in Income Tax Payable	15	425	
Less: Gains Not Providing Cash:			
Gain on Sale of Long-term Investments	(24)		
Net Debit Changes in Current Accounts:			
Increase in Merchandise Inventory	(450)		
Increase in Prepaid Expenses	(10)		
Decrease in Accrued Liabilities	(5)	(489)	
Net Cash Inflow from Operating Activities			$ 16

Cash Flows from Investing Activities

Inflows:			
Sale of Marketable Securities	25		
Sale of Long-term Investments	104		
Sale of Machinery	30		
Total Cash Inflows		159	
(Outflows):			
Purchase of Building	(800)		
Purchase of Machinery	(350)		
Total Cash Outflows:		(1,150)	
Net Cash Outflow from Investing Activities			(991)

Cash Flows from Financing Activities

Inflows:			
Issuance of Common Stock	410		
Increase in Long-term Debt	500		
Total Cash Inflows		910	
(Outflows):			
Payment of Dividends		(58)	
Net Cash Inflow from Financing Activities			852
Net Outflow of Cash			(123)
Cash Balance, Jan. 1, 19X8			150
Cash Balance, Dec. 31, 19X8			$ 27

balance sheet accounts at the beginning of the year, while the right-hand one shows the account balances at the end of the year. The columns in-between, therefore, are used to account for the differences. Before proceeding further, examine the completed worksheet in Exhibit 17-6 on pp. 787–88. Notice how the worksheet entries flow from the balance sheet accounts through the income statement accounts and into the amounts appearing on the statement of cash flows. The same income statement amounts and transactions used in the earlier part of this chapter are used in describing the worksheet approach.

The basic format of the worksheet is as follows:

Balance Sheet Accounts	Balances	Changes		Balances
	Dec. 31, 19X7	Debit	Credit	Dec. 31, 19X8
Income Statement Accounts				
Statement of Cash Flows		Inflow	Outflow	

As discussed earlier, the basic concept for preparing the statement of cash flows is to account for all the changes in all the noncash accounts. In doing so, all the changes to the Cash account during the year also will be identified, and the accountant is able to then classify the changes as results of operating, investing, or financing activities. For example, if the current asset and liability accounts were examined, Accounts Receivable would be the first account analyzed. Since the change in accounts receivable affects the amount of cash received from customers during the year, that amount could be determined and recorded on the worksheet by the following entry:

Cash Received from Customers	1,250	
Accounts Receivable		50
Sales		1,200

This entry is labeled *a* on the worksheet (Exhibit 17-6); it would be posted to the various sections as follows:

Balance Sheet Accounts	Balances	Changes		Balances
	Dec. 31, 19X7	Debit	Credit	Dec. 31, 19X8
Accounts Receivable	400		(a) 50	350
Income Statement Accounts				
Sales			(a) 1,200	1,200
Statement of Cash Flows		Inflow	Outflow	
Cash Flows from Operating Activities				
Cash Received from Customers		(a) 1,250		

Note that the change in Accounts Receivable has been accounted for, sales for the year have been recorded, and Cash Received from Customers has been posted to the proper worksheet section for the statement of cash flows. When each noncash account has been analyzed, all the changes will be accounted for, all the cash flows will be identified, and all the information necessary to prepare the statement of cash flows will be assembled on the worksheet.

The next current account affecting operations is Merchandise Inventory. In an earlier section of this chapter, discussing the direct approach, the change in inventory, the change in accounts payable, and cost of goods sold were used to determine the amount of cash paid to suppliers during the year. This information could be recorded by the following worksheet entry:

Merchandise Inventory	450	
Cost of Goods Sold	674	
Accounts Payable		90
Cash Paid to Suppliers		1,034

This entry is labeled *b* on the worksheet; it would be posted to the various sections as follows:

Balance Sheet Accounts	Balances	Changes		Balances
	Dec. 31, 19X7	Debit	Credit	Dec. 31, 19X8
Merchandise Inventory	450	(b) 450		900
Accounts Payable	145		(b) 90	235
Income Statement Accounts				
Cost of Goods Sold		(b) 674		674
Statement of Cash Flows		Inflow	Outflow	
Cash Paid to Suppliers			(b) 1,034	

Note that the changes in two balance sheet accounts, Merchandise Inventory and Accounts Payable, are accounted for, Cost of Goods Sold is recorded in the income statement section, and Cash Paid to Suppliers has been determined and posted to the Statement of Cash Flows section of the worksheet.

The next current account on the balance sheet affecting operations is Prepaid Expenses. Earlier, the change in Prepaid Expenses, the change in Accrued Liabilities, and Other Expenses on the income statement were used to determine the amount of cash paid for other expenses. This information could be recorded by the following worksheet entry:

Prepaid Expenses	10	
Accrued Liabilities	5	
Other Expenses	120	
Cash Paid for Other Expenses		135

This entry is labeled *c* on the worksheet; it would be posted to the various sections as follows:

Balance Sheet Accounts	Balances	Changes		Balances
	Dec. 31, 19X7	Debit	Credit	Dec. 31, 19X8
Prepaid Expenses	10	(c) 10		20
Accrued Liabilities	30	(c) 5		25
Income Statement Accounts				
Other Expenses		(c) 120		120
Statement of Cash Flows		Inflow	Outflow	
Cash Paid for Other Expenses			(c) 135	

Note that the changes in two more balance sheet accounts, Prepaid Expenses and Accrued Liabilities, are accounted for, while Other Expenses is recorded in the income statement section, and Cash Paid for Other Expenses has been determined and is posted to the Statement of Cash Flows section of the worksheet.

The next current account on the balance sheet affecting operations still to be analyzed is Income Tax Payable. As shown earlier, the changes in income tax payable and income tax expense were used to determine the amount of cash paid to the government. This information could be recorded by the following worksheet entry:

Income Tax Expense	80	
Income Tax Payable		15
Cash Paid to the Government		65

This entry is labeled *d* on the worksheet; it would be posted to the various sections as follows:

Balance Sheet Accounts	Balances	Changes		Balances
	Dec. 31, 19X7	Debit	Credit	Dec. 31, 19X8
Income Tax Payable	25		(d) 15	40
Income Statement Accounts				
Income Tax Expense		(d) 80		80
Statement of Cash Flows		Inflow	Outflow	
Cash Paid to the Government			(d) 65	

Note that the change in Income Taxes Payable has been accounted for, Income Tax Expense is recorded on the income statement section, and Cash Paid to the Government has been determined and is correctly recorded in the Statement of Cash Flows section of the worksheet.

Now that the current accounts affecting operations have all been examined and the changes accounted for, the next step in preparing the worksheet would be to examine the changes in the current nonoperating accounts, if any. It was noted earlier that some marketable securities were sold during the year at cost. The entry given was as follows:

Cash	25	
Marketable Securities		25

That entry could be changed slightly to fit the worksheet approach in this part of the chapter as follows:

Sale of Marketable Securities	25	
Marketable Securities		25

This entry is labeled *e* on the worksheet; it would be posted to the various sections as follows:

Balance Sheet Accounts	Balances	Changes		Balances
	Dec. 31, 19X7	Debit	Credit	Dec. 31, 19X8
Marketable Securities	50		(e) 25	25
Income Statement Accounts				
(no gain or loss)				
Statement of Cash Flows		Inflow	Outflow	
Cash Flows from Investing Activities				
Sale of Marketable Securities		(e) 25		

Note that the change in Marketable Securities has now been accounted for, and the cash received from the sale is reported in the Statement of Cash Flows section of the worksheet.

All the noncurrent accounts also must be examined to account for all the changes and to identify further inflows and outflows from investing and financing activities.

It was noted that long-term investments costing $80,000 were sold for $104,000, resulting in a gain of $24,000. The entry could be adapted to fit the worksheet as follows:

Sale of Long-term Investments	104	
Gain on Sale of Long-term Investments		24
Investments		80

This entry is labeled *f* on the worksheet; it would be posted to the various sections as follows:

Balance Sheet Accounts	Balances	Changes		Balances
	Dec. 31, 19X7	Debit	Credit	Dec. 31, 19X8
Investments	220		(f) 80	140
Income Statement Accounts				
Gain on Sale of Long-term Investments			(f) 24	24
Statement of Cash Flows		Inflow	Outflow	
Sale of Long-term Investments		(f) 104		

Note that the change in the Investments account has been identified, and the cash flow from the transaction is recorded in the correct section of the worksheet.

The Land account is next. However no apparent changes occurred in the account during the year. Since Cash is affected by changes in noncash accounts, given the information available, cash was not affected by the Land account. The account could have increased and decreased by the same amount during the year, but no information to that effect is available.

In another transaction, a building was purchased in the amount of $800. The entry given at that point could be adapted to fit the worksheet solution as follows:

Building	800	
Purchase of Building		800

This entry is labeled *g* on the worksheet; it would be posted to the various sections as follows:

Balance Sheet Accounts	Balances	Changes		Balances
	Dec. 31, 19X7	Debit	Credit	Dec. 31, 19X8
Building	400	(g) 800		1,200
Income Statement Accounts				
(no effect)				
Statement of Cash Flows		Inflow	Outflow	
Purchase of Building			(g) 800	

Note that the change in the Building account has been identified and the cash flow from the transaction is recorded in the correct section of the worksheet.

Machinery costing $50 was sold in another SCI transaction for $30 after $10 in depreciation was taken. The entry given at that point could be adapted to fit the worksheet as follows:

Sale of Machinery	30	
Accumulated Depreciation—Machinery	10	
Loss on Sale of Machinery	10	
Machinery		50

This entry is labeled *h* on the worksheet; it would be posted to the various sections as follows:

Balance Sheet Accounts	Balances	Changes		Balances
	Dec. 31, 19X7	Debit	Credit	Dec. 31, 19X8
Machinery	700	?	(h) 50	1,000
Accumulated Depreciation	300	(h) 10	?	550
Income Statement Accounts				
Loss on Sale of Machinery		(h) 10		10
Statement of Cash Flows		Inflow	Outflow	
Sale of Machinery		(h) 30		

Note that more changes occur in the Machinery and Accumulated Depreciation accounts, designated by question marks. It was noted in a different Saguaro transaction that machinery was purchased in the amount of $350. The entry could be adapted to fit the worksheet as follows:

Machinery	350	
Purchase of Machinery		350

Labeled *i* on the worksheet, this entry would be posted to the various sections as follows:

Balance Sheet Accounts	Balances	Changes		Balances
	Dec. 31, 19X7	Debit	Credit	Dec. 31, 19X8
Machinery	700	(i) 350	(h) 50	1,000
Income Statement Accounts				
(no effect)				
Statement of Cash Flows		Inflow	Outflow	
Sale of Machinery		(h) 30		
Purchase of Machinery			(i) 350	

Now the rest of the changes in the Machinery account have been identified. The cash flow from the transaction also has been recorded on the worksheet.

As for the change in the Accumulated Depreciation account still to be identified, it was noted earlier that depreciation expenses of $260,000 were recorded on the income statement. The journal entry for this does not have to be adapted to fit the worksheet, since cash flows were not affected. The entry given earlier could be posted as follows:

Depreciation Expense—Buildings and		
Machinery	260	
Accumulated Depreciation		260

Labeled *j* on the worksheet, this entry would be posted to the various sections as follows:

Balance Sheet Accounts	Balances	Changes		Balances
	Dec. 31, 19X7	Debit	Credit	Dec. 31, 19X8
Accumulated Depreciation	300	(h) 10	(j) 260	550
Income Statement Accounts				
Depreciation Expense— Buildings and Machinery		(j) 260		260
Statement of Cash Flows		Inflow	Outflow	
(no effect)				

Note that the change in the Accumulated Depreciation account is now fully explained and any cash flows have been posted to the correct section.

The next account to be analyzed is Mortgage Payable. A mortgage was taken out on one of Saguaro's buildings for $500,000 and could be recorded by the following worksheet entry:

| Increase in Long-term Debt | 500 | |
| Mortgage Payable | | 500 |

This entry is labeled *k* on the worksheet; it would be posted to the various sections as follows:

Balance Sheet Accounts	Balances	Changes		Balances
	Dec. 31, 19X7	Debit	Credit	Dec. 31, 19X8
Mortgage Payable	500		(k) 500	1,000
Income Statement Accounts				
(no effect)				
Statement of Cash Flows		Inflow	Outflow	
Cash Flows from Financing Activities				
Increase in Long-term Debt		(k) 500		

The next account to be analyzed is the Common Stock account. As was noted, $410,000 of common stock was issued on a no-par basis. The entry given earlier could be modified as shown:

| Issuance of Common Stock | 410 | |
| Common Stock | | 410 |

This entry is labeled *l*; it would be posted to the various sections as follows:

Balance Sheet Accounts	Balances	Changes		Balances
	Dec. 31, 19X7	Debit	Credit	Dec. 31, 19X8
Common Stock	800		(l) 410	1,210
Income Statement Accounts				
(no effect)				
Statement of Cash Flows		Inflow	Outflow	
Issuance of Common Stock		(l) 410		

Note that the change in Common Stock is now fully explained, and its effect on cash flow is posted to the cash-flow section of the worksheet.

The last account to analyze is Retained Earnings. Dividends were paid in the amount of $58,000 which could be recorded in the following worksheet entry:

| Retained Earnings | 58 | |
| Payment of Dividends | | 58 |

Net income for the year amounted to $80,000 and could be recorded by the following worksheet entry:

Net Income	80	
Retained Earnings		80

Labeled *m* and *n* respectively, these entries could be posted to the various sections of the worksheet as follows:

Balance Sheet Accounts	**Balances**	**Changes**		**Balances**
	Dec. 31, 19X7	**Debit**	**Credit**	**Dec. 31, 19X8**
Retained Earnings	650	(m) 58	(n) 80	762
Income Statement Accounts				
Net Income		(n) 80		80
Statement of Cash Flows		**Inflow**	**Outflow**	
Payment of Dividends			(m) 58	

Note that the change in Retained Earnings is now fully explained, Net Income is recorded on the income statement section, and the effect on cash flow is correctly posted to the cash-flow section of the worksheet.

At this point, the only account that has not been analyzed is Cash. However, because all the other accounts have been analyzed, Cash in effect has been analyzed. If all the inflows and outflows of cash in the operating section of the worksheet were netted together, the net inflow of cash from operating activities would be $16,000. That information could be recorded by the following worksheet entry:

Cash	16	
Net Cash Inflow from Operating Activities		16

If all of the inflows and outflows of cash in the investing section of the worksheet were netted together, the net outflow of cash from investing activities would be $991,000. That information could be recorded by the following worksheet entry:

Net Cash Outflow from Investing Activities	991	
Cash		991

If all of the inflows and outflows of cash in the financing section of the worksheet were netted together, the net inflow of cash from financing activities would be $852,000. That information could be recorded by the following worksheet entry:

Cash	852	
Net Cash Inflow from Financing Activities		852

The three net entries are labeled *o*, *p*, and *q* respectively; they would be posted to the worksheet as follows:

Balance Sheet Accounts	Balances	Changes		Balances
	Dec. 31, 19X7	Debit	Credit	Dec. 31, 19X8
Cash	150	(o) 16 (q) 852	(p) 991	27

Income Statement Accounts				
(no effect)				

Statement of Cash Flows		Inflow	Outflow	
Net Cash Inflow from Operating Activities			(o) 16	
Net Cash Outflow from Investing Activities		(p) 991		
Net Cash Inflow from Financing Activities			(q) 852	

Since all of the noncash accounts have been examined, all the information has been gathered to construct the formal statement of cash flows. The entire worksheet as it would appear after these entries is illustrated in Exhibit 17-6.

Notice that the Statement of Cash Flows section of the worksheet provides all the information necessary to prepare a statement of cash flows under the direct method. A worksheet also could be derived that results in the information necessary

EXHIBIT 17–6

WORKSHEET FOR STATEMENT OF CASH FLOWS, DIRECT METHOD

Balance Sheet Accounts	Balances Dec. 31, 19X7	Changes Debit	Changes Credit	Balances Dec. 31, 19X8
Cash	150	(o) 16 (q) 852	(p) 991	27
Marketable Securities	50		(e) 25	25
Accounts Receivable	400		(a) 50	350
Merchandise Inventory	450	(b) 450		900
Prepaid Expenses	10	(c) 10		20
Investments	220		(f) 80	140
Land	70			70
Building	400	(g) 800		1,200
Machinery	700	(i) 350	(h) 50	1,000
Accumulated Depreciation	(300)	(h) 10	(j) 260	(550)
Accounts Payable	(145)		(b) 90	(235)
Accrued Liabilities	(30)	(c) 5		(25)
Income Tax Payable	(25)		(d) 15	(40)
Mortgage Payable	(500)		(k) 500	(1,000)
Common Stock	(800)		(l) 410	(1,210)
Retained Earnings	(650)	(m) 58	(n) 80	(672)
Check Totals	–0–	2,551	2,551	–0–

(continued)

EXHIBIT 17–6 (cont.)

Income Statement Accounts		Changes		Balances
		Debit	Credit	Dec. 31, 19X8
Sales			(a)1,200	1,200
Cost of Goods Sold		(b) 674		674
Other Expenses		(c) 120		120
Depreciation Expense—Building and Machinery		(d) 260		260
Income Tax Expense		(j) 80		80
Gain on Sale of Long-term Investments			(f) 24	24
Loss on Sale of Machinery		(h) 10		10
Net Income		(n) 80		80
Check Totals		1,224	1,224	–0–
Statement of Cash Flows		Inflow	Outflow	
Cash Flows from Operating Activities				
Cash Received From Customers		(a)1,250		
Cash Paid to Suppliers			(b)1,034	
Cash Paid for Other Expenses			(c) 135	
Cash Paid to the Government			(d) 65	
Net Cash Inflow from Operating Activities			(o) 16	
Check Totals		1,250	1,250	
Cash Flows from Investing Activities				
Sale of Marketable Securities		(e) 25		
Sale of Long-term Investments		(f) 104		
Sale of Machinery		(h) 30		
Purchase of Building			(g) 800	
Purchase of Machinery			(i) 350	
Net Cash Outflow from Investing Activities		(p) 991		
Check Totals		1,150	1,150	
Cash Flows from Financing Activities				
Increase in Long-term Debt		(k) 500		
Issuance of Common Stock		(l) 410		
Payment of Dividends			(m) 58	
Net Cash Inflow from Financing Activities			(q) 852	
Check Totals		910	910	

to prepare the statement of cash flows under the indirect method. Worksheet entries would be constructed to account for all the changes in the noncash accounts in the general ledger, but the income statement accounts would not have to be examined since the indirect approach begins with Net Income in the Cash Flows from Operating Activities section of the statement of cash flows. The worksheet for the indirect method appears in Exhibit 17-7, while the corresponding worksheet journal entries are cross-referenced in Exhibit 17-8. No explanations are given, since the items have been analyzed already in this chapter.

Refer back to Exhibits 17-3 through 17-5, pp. 776–78, and examine the statements of cash flows prepared from the worksheets using the direct and indirect

EXHIBIT 17–7

WORKSHEET FOR STATEMENT OF CASH FLOWS, INDIRECT METHOD

Balance Sheet Accounts	Balances Dec. 31, 19X7	Changes Debit	Changes Credit	Balances Dec. 31, 19X8
Cash	150	(o) 16	(p) 991	
		(q) 852		27
Marketable Securities	50		(e) 25	25
Accounts Receivable	400		(a) 50	350
Merchandise Inventory	450	(b) 450		900
Prepaid Expenses	10	(c) 10		20
Investments	220		(f) 80	140
Land	70			70
Building	400	(g) 800		1,200
Machinery	700	(i) 350	(h) 50	1,000
Accumulated Depreciation	(300)	(h) 10	(j) 260	(550)
Accounts Payable	(145)		(b) 90	(235)
Accrued Liabilities	(30)	(c) 5		(25)
Income Tax Payable	(25)		(d) 15	(40)
Mortgage Payable	(500)		(k) 500	(1,000)
Common Stock	(800)		(l) 410	(1,210)
Retained Earnings	(650)	(m) 58	(n) 80	(672)
Check Totals	–0–	2,551	2,551	–0–

Statement of Cash Flows		Increase	Decrease	
Cash Flows from Operating Activities				
Decrease in Accounts Receivable		(a) 50		
Increase in Merchandise Inventory			(b) 450	
Increase in Prepaid Expenses			(c) 10	
Increase in Accounts Payable		(b) 90		
Decrease in Accrued Liabilities			(c) 5	
Increase in Income Tax Payable		(d) 15		
Gain on Sale of Long-term Investments			(f) 24	
Loss on Sale of Machinery		(h) 10		
Depreciation Expense—Building and Machinery		(j) 260		
Net Income		(n) 80		
Net Cash Inflow from Operating Activities			(o) 16	
Check Totals		505	505	
Cash Flows from Investing Activities				
Sale of Marketable Securities		(e) 25		
Sale of Long-term Investments		(f) 104		
Purchase of Building			(g) 800	
Sale of Machinery		(h) 30		
Purchase of Machinery			(i) 350	
Net Cash Outflow from Investing Activities		(p) 991		
Check Totals		1,150	1,150	
Cash Flows from Financing Activities				
Increase in Long-term Debt		(k) 500		
Issuance of Common Stock		(l) 410		
Payment of Dividends			(m) 58	
Net Cash Inflow from Financing Activities			(q) 852	
Check Totals		910	910	

EXHIBIT 17-8   WORKSHEET JOURNAL ENTRIES, INDIRECT METHOD

(a) Decrease in Accounts Receivable	50	
Accounts Receivable		50
(b) Merchandise Inventory	450	
Increase in Accounts Payable	90	
Accounts Payable		90
Increase in Merchandise Inventory		450
(c) Accrued Liabilities	5	
Prepaid Expenses	10	
Increase in Prepaid Expenses		10
Decrease in Accrued Liabilities		5
(d) Increase in Income Tax Payable	15	
Income Tax Payable		15
(e) Sale of Marketable Securities	25	
Marketable Securities		25
(f) Sale of Long-term Investments	104	
Investments		80
Gain on Sale of Long-term Investments		24
(g) Buildings	800	
Purchase of Building		800
(h) Sale of Machinery	30	
Loss on Sale of Machinery	10	
Accumulated Depreciation	10	
Machinery		50
(i) Machinery	350	
Purchase of Machinery		350
(j) Depreciation Expense—Buildings and Machinery	260	
Accumulated Depreciation		260
(k) Increase in Long-term Debt	500	
Mortgage Payable		500
(l) Issuance of Common Stock	410	
Common Stock		410
(m) Retained Earnings	58	
Payment of Dividends		58
(n) Net Income	80	
Retained Earnings		80
(o) Cash	16	
Net Cash Inflow from Operating Activities		16
(p) Net Cash Outflow from Investing Activities	991	
Cash		991
(q) Cash	852	
Net Inflow of Cash from Financing Activities		852

methods, and the reconciliation of net income with net cash flows from operating activities. The worksheet is a very useful tool to use in complex situations. For instructors who prefer to use the T-account approach, it is presented in the chapter appendix with the same balances and transactions used throughout this chapter.

No matter which approach is used, the end results will be the same. The journal entry extension model (with transactions analysis) can be used in very simple textbook situations, while the T-account method is more adaptable to more complex textbook problems. The worksheet approach is used extensively in practice, with many software programs now available to cut down on the preparation time immensely.

Cash-flow information is extremely important to the major users of financial statements. Owners must have information about future cash flows to plan on future financing at the most advantageous interest rates. Both short-term and long-term cash needs must be met for an entity to survive. Creditors must have cash flow information in order to evaluate potential borrowers. Positive future cash flows are a must if the lender is going to be paid on time. Investors want cash flow information to evaluate comparable investments in terms of the generation of cash and the payment of cash dividends.

The accrual method of accounting used to determine net income is still by far the most informative measure of net income. The cash basis of determining net income does not address the matching of revenue and expenses, and therefore does not provide a very useful earnings figure. However, accurate cash flow information is essential if a business expects to continue to survive.

The statement of cash flows is a required financial statement that must be included in the basic package of financial information. Although the statement has been referred to by different names over the years, its content has remained basically the same.

APPENDIX: THE T-ACCOUNT APPROACH TO SOLVING CASH-FLOW PROBLEMS

Since any approach to the preparation of a statement of cash flows requires an examination of the changes in all the noncash accounts, T accounts could be set up for each of the accounts. The journal entries used to prepare the worksheet could then be posted to them. The time involved in setting up the T accounts is minimal compared to the time to set up a formal worksheet, and the necessary information is still generated. The **T-account approach** is recommended for textbook problems and in exam situations where time is limited.

The Direct Method

The entries used to prepare the worksheet under the direct method are reproduced here for demonstrating the mechanics of the T-account approach.

(a)	Cash Received from Customers	1,250	
	Accounts Receivable		50
	Sales		1,200
(b)	Merchandise Inventory	450	
	Cost of Goods Sold	674	
	Accounts Payable		90
	Cash Paid to Suppliers		1,034
(c)	Prepaid Expenses	10	
	Accrued Liabilities	5	
	Other Expenses	120	
	Cash Paid for Other Expenses		135

(d)	Income Tax Expense	80	
	Income Tax Payable		15
	Cash Paid to the Government		65
(e)	Sale of Marketable Securities	25	
	Marketable Securities		25
(f)	Sale of Long-term Investments	104	
	Gain on Sale of Long-term		
	Investments		24
	Investments		80
(g)	Buildings	800	
	Purchase of Building		800
(h)	Sale of Machinery	30	
	Accumulated Depreciation—Machinery	10	
	Loss on Sale of Machinery	10	
	Machinery		50
(i)	Machinery	350	
	Purchase of Machinery		350
(j)	Depreciation Expense—Buildings and		
	Machinery	260	
	Accumulated Depreciation		260
(k)	Increase in Long-term Debt	500	
	Mortgage Payable		500
(l)	Issuance of Common Stock	410	
	Common Stock		410
(m)	Retained Earnings	58	
	Payment of Dividends		58
(n)	Net Income	80	
	Retained Earnings		80

T accounts first must be created for each of the noncash accounts in the general ledger. Under the direct approach, this includes the income statement accounts as well as the balance sheet accounts. Under the indirect method, only the balance sheet accounts need be included.

The T accounts do not have to be very involved, but must show at a minimum the change in the account from the beginning to the end of the year. When the various journal entries are posted to the T accounts, the changes are thus accounted for and their effects on cash flows are determined and posted to the proper T account—operating, investing, or financing. Note that each T account begins with its change during the year given on the worksheet and is then underlined.

In posting entry *a*, for instance, the following T accounts would be created:

Accounts Receivable		Sales		Cash Flows—Operating	
50			1,200	-0-	-0-
(a) 50			(a) 1,200	(a) 1,250	

Entry *b* would be posted as follows:

Merchandise Inventory	Cost of Goods Sold	Accounts Payable
450	674	90
(b) 450	(b) 674	(b) 90

Cash Flows—Operating
(b) 1,034

Entry *c* would be posted as follows:

Prepaid Expenses	Accrued Liabilities	Other Expenses
10	5	120
(c) 10	(c) 5	(c) 120

Cash Flows—Operating	
-0-	-0-
	(c) 135

Entry *d* would be posted as follows:

Income Tax Expense	Income Tax Payable	Cash Flows—Operating	
80	15	-0-	-0-
(d) 80	(d) 15		(d) 65

Entry *e* would be posted as follows:

Marketable Securities	Cash Flows—Investing	
25	-0-	-0-
(e) 25	(e) 25	

Entry *f* would be posted as follows:

Investments	Gain on Sale of Long-term Investments	Cash Flows—Investing	
80	24	-0-	-0-
(f) 80	(f) 24	(f) 104	

Entry *g* would be posted as follows:

Buildings	Cash Flows—Investing	
800	-0-	-0-
(g) 800		(g) 800

Entry *h* would be posted as follows:

Accumulated Depreciation		Machinery		Loss on Sale of Machinery	
	250	300		10	
(h) 10			(h) 50	(h) 10	

Cash Flows—Investing	
-0-	-0-
(h) 30	

Note that the changes in the Machinery and the Accumulated Depreciation accounts have not been accounted for in full. Therefore, the accounts must be further analyzed.
Entry *i* would be posted as follows:

Accumulated Depreciation		Machinery		Loss on Sale of Machinery	
	250	300		10	
(h) 10		(i) 350	(h) 50	(h) 10	

Cash Flows—Investing	
-0-	-0-
(h) 30	(i) 350

The change in the Accumulated Depreciation account still has not been fully accounted for.
Note: Other accounts not affected by this entry are presented here because the accounts are so interrelated.
Entry *j* would be posted as follows:

Depreciation Expense		Accumulated Depreciation		Machinery	
260			250	300	
(j) 260		(h) 10	(j) 260	(i) 350	(h) 50

Loss on Sale of Machinery		Cash Flows—Investing	
10		-0-	-0-
(h) 10		(h) 30	(i) 350

Note that now all the general ledger account changes so far have been fully accounted for.
Entry *k* would be posted as follows:

Cash Flows—Financing		Mortgage Payable	
-0-	-0-		500
(k) 500			(k) 500

Entry *l* would be posted as follows:

Common Stock		Cash Flows—Financing	
	410	-0-	-0-
	(l) $\overline{410}$	(l) 410	

Entry *m* would be posted as follows:

Cash Flows—Financing		Retained Earnings	
-0-	-0-		22
	(m) 58	(m) 58	

Entry *n* would be posted as follows:

Income Summary		Retained Earnings	
80			22
(n) $\overline{80}$		(m) 58	(n) $\overline{80}$

A summary of the three cash-flow T accounts now can be made:

	Cash Flows from Operating Activities	
	Inflow	Outflow
(a) Cash received from Customers	1,250	
(b) Cash Paid to Suppliers		1,034
(c) Cash Paid for Other Expenses		135
(d) Cash Paid to the Government		65
Net Cash Inflow from Operating Activities (to balance)		16
Check Totals	1,250	1,250

	Cash Flows from Investing Activities	
	Inflow	Outflow
(e) Sale of Marketable Securities	25	
(f) Sale of Long-term Investments	104	
(g) Purchase of Building		800
(h) Sale of Machinery	30	
(i) Purchase of Machinery		350
Net Cash Outflow from Investing Activities (to balance)	991	
Check Totals	1,150	1,150

	Cash Flows from Financing Activities	
	Inflow	Outflow
(k) Increase in Long-term Debt	500	
(l) Issuance of Common Stock	410	
(m) Payment of Dividends		58
Net Cash Inflow from Financing Activities (to balance)		852
Check Totals	910	910

As shown, the T-account approach is far less time-consuming when working a problem from the text or in a test situation. Its use, however, is limited by the size of the undertaking, and the necessary underlying audit trail.

The Indirect Method

Turn to Exhibit 17-8 for the worksheet entries prepared when the indirect approach was used in the chapter.

Entry *a* would be posted to T accounts as follows:

Accounts Receivable		Cash Flows—Operating	
	50	-0-	-0-
	(a) 50	(a) 50	

Entry *b* would be posted as follows:

Merchandise Inventory		Cash Flows—Operating		Accounts Payable	
	450	-0-	-0-		90
	(b) 450	(b) 90	(b) 450		(b) 90

Entry *c* would be posted as follows:

Accrued Liabilities		Prepaid Expenses		Cash Flows—Operating	
	5	10		-0-	-0-
	(c) 5	(c) 10			(c) 10
					(c) 5

Entry *d* would be posted as follows:

Income Tax Payable		Cash Flows—Operating	
	15	-0-	-0-
	(d) 15	(d) 15	

Entry *e* would be posted as follows:

Marketable Securities		Cash Flows—Investing	
	25	-0-	-0-
	(e) 25	(e) 25	

Entry *f* would be posted as follows:

Investments		Cash Flows—Investing		Cash Flows—Operating	
80		-0-	-0-	-0-	-0-
(f) 80		(f) 104			(f) 24

Entry *g* would be posted as follows:

Buildings		Cash Flows—Investing	
800		-0-	-0-
(g) 800			(g) 800

Entry *h* would be posted as follows:

Machinery		Accumulated Depreciation		Cash Flows—Investing	
300			250	-0-	-0-
	(h) 50	(h) 10		(h) 30	

Cash Flows—Operating	
-0-	-0-
(h) 10	

Entry *i* would be posted as follows:

Machinery		Accumulated Depreciation		Cash Flows—Investing	
300			250	-0-	-0-
(i) 350	(h) 50	(h) 10		(h) 30	(i) 350

Cash Flows—Operating	
-0-	-0-
(h) 10	

Entry *j* would be posted as follows:

Machinery		Accumulated Depreciation		Cash Flows—Investing	
300			250	-0-	-0-
(i) 350	(h) 50	(h) 10	(j) 260	(h) 30	(i) 350

Cash Flows—Operating	
-0-	-0-
(h) 10	
(j) 260	

Note: Certain T accounts for entries *h*, *i*, and *j* were repeated because the entries affect many of the same accounts.

Entry *k* would be posted as follows:

Mortgage Payable		Cash Flows—Financing	
	500	-0-	-0-
	(k) 500	(k) 500	

Entry *l* would be posted as follows:

Common Stock		Cash Flows—Financing	
	410	-0-	-0-
	(l) 410	(l) 410	

Entry *m* would be posted as follows:

Retained Earnings		Cash Flows—Financing	
	22	-0-	-0-
(m) 58			(m) 58

Entry *n* would be posted as follows:

Retained Earnings		Cash Flows—Financing		Cash Flows—Operating	
	22	-0-	-0-	-0-	-0-
(m) 58	(n) 80		(m) 58	(n) 80	

A summary of the three cash-flow T accounts now can be made:

	Cash Flows from Operating Activities	
	Increase	Decrease
(a) Decrease in Accounts Receivable	50	
(b) Increase in Accounts Payable	90	
(b) Increase in Merchandise Inventory		450
(c) Increase in Prepaid Expenses		10
(c) Decrease in Accrued Liabilities		5
(d) Increase in Income Tax Payable	15	
(f) Gain on Sale of Long-term Investments		24
(h) Loss on Sale of Machinery	10	
(j) Depreciation Expense—Buildings and Equipment	260	
(n) Net Income	80	
Net Cash Inflow from Operating Activities (to balance)		16
Check Totals	505	505

Cash Flows from Investing Activities

	Inflow	Outflow
(e) Sale of Marketable Securities	25	
(f) Sale of Long-term Investments	104	
(g) Purchase of Building		800
(h) Sale of Machinery	30	
(i) Purchase of Machinery		350
Net Cash Outflow from Investing Activities (to balance)	991	
Check totals	1,150	1,150

Cash Flows from Financing Activities

	Inflow	Outflow
(k) Increase in Long-term Debt	500	
(l) Issuance of Common Stock	410	
(m) Payment of Dividends		58
Net Cash Inflow from Financing Activities (to balance)		852
Check Totals	910	910

Notice that the summary T accounts for investing and financing activities are the same for both the direct and indirect methods, but, while the summary T accounts for operating activities differ, both methods result in the same net cash inflow from operating activities.

CHAPTER REVIEW

1 What information is disclosed on the statement of cash flows that is not determinable from the other financial statements? (p. 762)

The income statement explains part of the change in the Retained Earnings account. Outside of that, a void exists in the information about what happened between the beginning and ending balance sheets in terms of the asset, liability, and equity accounts. The statement of cash flows fills this void by presenting the cash flows from each of the entity's three main activities; operating, investing, and financing.

2 What are some of the more important questions answered by the information provided on the statement of cash flows? (p. 762)

The list included here is from the chapter material, and is by no means all-inclusive. You should be able to double or even triple this list.

- How much cash was generated from operations?
- Was any cash generated from operations?
- How can a net income occur at the same time as a net outflow of cash from operations?
- What was done with the cash provided from operations?
- If so much cash was generated from operations, why did the Cash account decrease so much during the year?

- Is most of the cash coming from borrowing and other financing decisions?
- Are operations being funded by selling off excess assets?

3 Does net income represent the increase (or net loss the decrease) in cash from operating activities? Explain. (p. 767)

No, net income is determined on the basis of accrual accounting and other requirements of GAAP. Net income on the accrual basis does not purport to be a measure of the increases or decreases in cash from operating activities. Many items on the accrual-basis income statement do not have an effect on cash flows. Depreciation, for example, is an expense, but does not represent an outflow of cash. Other changes in some balance sheet accounts do affect items on the income statement in terms of cash flows. For example, the change in accounts receivable determines the amount of cash received from sales.

4 What is the difference between the direct and the indirect method of reporting cash flows from operating activities? Is one preferred over the other? (pp. 768–70)

The *direct method* determines what items on the income statement do have an effect on cash and adjusts them to reflect cash flows. For instance, if Accounts Receivable increases, the amount reported on the income statement for Sales is overstated in terms of cash inflows, so the increase in Accounts Receivable will be subtracted from Sales to arrive at Cash Received from Customers. All other accounts on the income statement that have an effect on cash are adjusted in the same manner.

The *indirect method* involves the income statement items that do not have an effect on cash flows. In the example given, the increase in Accounts Receivable would be subtracted from Net Income, because the increase in receivables did not provide a cash inflow. Depreciation and other like items are added back to net income because cash was not affected when the item was recorded.

5 How is it possible to report a net loss on the income statement yet report a sizable increase in cash from operating activities? (pp. 770–71)

Certain items that may be material to net income are added back to net income to arrive at the net cash inflow from operating activities. Depreciation alone may change a net loss into a positive cash flow from operating activities, as is shown;

Net Loss	$(456,000)
Add: Depreciation Expense	900,000
Cash Flow from Operating Activities	$ 444,000

6 Is it possible to report a sizable net income yet report an outflow of cash from operating activities? (p. 771)

Yes, a net income can be reported with a cash outflow from operating activities. Certain items that may be material to net income are subtracted from net income to arrive at the Net Cash Flow from Operating Activities. A gain on the sale of land alone may change net income into a negative Cash Flows from Operating Activities, as is shown:

Net Income	$ 35,000
Gain on Sale of Land	60,000
Cash Flows from Operating Activities	$(25,000)

7 What other information is required if the direct method is used to report cash flows from operating activities? (p. 773)

If the direct method is used, then a *reconciliation* of net income with cash flows from operating activities must be included in the financial package. This in effect requires the use of the indirect method along with the direct method if the direct method is chosen for the statement. Although the direct method is recommended, it will probably not be used because adding information costs money—an unfortunate situation.

8 What approaches are available to help accountants prepare the statement of cash flows? (p. 775)

For a very simple textbook-type problem, the T account for Cash may be examined to determine all of the information necessary to prepare a statement of cash flows. This was observed in Chapter 1. As the problems become slightly more complex, the *journal entry extension* approach may be used. Each journal entry affecting noncurrent accounts is extended to examine its effect on cash. For more complex textbook problems, the student has the choice between the T-account approach or the worksheet approach. From an audit trail point of view, the worksheet is superior, but time-consuming. The T account approach suffices for most classroom situations.

KEY TERMS

direct method (p. 768) One of two formats for the Cash Flows from Operating Activities section of the statement of cash flows. The method takes a positive approach, in that it reflects the income statement items that *do* have an effect on Cash.

financing activities (p. 763) The activities of an entity that result from financing decisions made by management. Inflows come from the issuance of common or preferred stock, or from long-term borrowing through mortgages or bonds payable. The outflows include the retirement of the just-mentioned securities, in addition to the payment of dividends. Because of a close tie to the income statement and the determination of income tax liability, interest expense on long-term borrowing is currently being reported as an outflow from *operating* activities.

indirect method (p. 770) One of two formats for the Cash Flows from Operating Activities section of the statement of cash flows. The method takes a negative approach, in that it reflects the income statement items that *do not* have an effect on cash.

investing activities (p. 763) The activities of an entity that result from investment decisions by management. Inflows result from the sale of assets previously purchased, while outflows result from the purchase of long-term assets. The assets would include land, buildings, and equipment that a company needs for operating, as well as intangible assets, such as patents and copyrights, and long-term investments.

operating activities (p. 762) The activities of an entity that result from operating decisions made by management. Inflows result from the sale of goods or services, while outflows result from efforts to generate the inflows. The Net Cash Inflow from Operating Activities can be determined using either the direct or the indirect method.

statement of cash flows (p. 762) A financial statement that reports the cash flows from the three major activities of an entity: operating, investing, and financing.

T-account approach (p. 791) A textbook approach used to gather the information necessary to prepare a statement of cash flows. Since the statement involves accounting for differences in an entity's accounts from the beginning of the year to the end, a T account is set up for each account, showing the change in that account.

worksheet approach (p. 777) A practical approach used to gather the information necessary to prepare a statement of cash flows. Since the statement involves accounting for differences in an entity's accounts from the beginning of the year to the end, the worksheet consists of balance sheets at the beginning and the end of the year. The changes in the various accounts from the beginning to the end of the year are then analyzed and summarized by activity.

SELF-TEST QUESTIONS FOR REVIEW   (Answers are at the end of this chapter.)

Q3, Q4

1. An increase in Accounts Receivable would be reported in a statement of cash flows prepared using the indirect method as a(n)
   (a) addition to net income.
   (b) deduction from net income.
   (c) inflow from investing activities.
   (d) outflow from investing activities.
   (e) inflow from financing activities.
   (f) outflow from financing activities.

Q1, Q2

2. The issuance of bonds payable due in ten years would be reported in a statement of cash flows as a(n)
   (a) addition to net income.
   (b) deduction from net income.
   (c) inflow from investing activities.
   (d) outflow from investing activities.
   (e) inflow from financing activities.
   (f) outflow from financing activities.

Q1, Q2

3. The purchase of treasury stock would be reported in a statement of cash flows as a(n)
   (a) addition to net income.
   (b) deduction from net income.
   (c) inflow from investing activities.
   (d) outflow from investing activities.
   (e) inflow from financing activities.
   (f) outflow from financing activities.

Q3, Q4

4. A decrease in Wages Payable would be reported in a statement of cash flows prepared using the indirect method as a(n)
   (a) addition to net income.
   (b) deduction from net income.
   (c) inflow from investing activities.
   (d) outflow from investing activities.
   (e) inflow from financing activities.
   (f) outflow from financing activities.

Q1, Q2

5. The purchase of a bus to move the employees from the parking lot to the factory would be recorded in a statement of cash flows as a(n)
   (a) addition to net income.
   (b) deduction from net income.
   (c) inflow from investing activities.
   (d) outflow from investing activities.
   (e) inflow from financing activities.
   (f) outflow from financing activities.

Q1, Q2

6. The payment of preferred stock dividends would be reported in a statement of cash flows as a(n)
   (a) addition to net income.
   (b) deduction from net income.
   (c) inflow from investing activities.
   (d) outflow from investing activities.
   (e) inflow from financing activities.
   (f) outflow from financing activities.

Q1, Q2

7. The payment of common stock dividends would be reported in a statement of cash flows as a(n)
   (a) addition to net income.

    (b) deduction from net income.
    (c) inflow from investing activities.
    (d) outflow from investing activities.
    (e) inflow from financing activities.
    (f) outflow from financing activities.

Q1, Q2

8. The sale of stock purchased in past years in another corporation would be reported in a statement of cash flows as a(n)
    (a) addition to net income.
    (b) deduction from net income.
    (c) inflow from investing activities.
    (d) outflow from investing activities.
    (e) inflow from financing activities.
    (f) outflow from financing activities.

Q1, Q2

9. The purchase of stock in another corporation would be reported in a statement of cash flows as a(n)
    (a) addition to net income.
    (b) deduction from net income.
    (c) inflow from investing activities.
    (d) outflow from investing activities.
    (e) inflow from financing activities.
    (f) outflow from financing activities.

Q1, Q2

10. The sale of land donated to the entity would be reported in a statement of cash flows as a(n)
    (a) addition to net income.
    (b) deduction from net income.
    (c) inflow from investing activities.
    (d) outflow from investing activities.
    (e) inflow from financing activities.
    (f) outflow from financing activities.

DEMONSTRATION PROBLEM

Part A

From the following information regarding Brennan Co. as of December 31, 19X8, prepare a statement of cash flows under the direct method, including any required schedules.

Sales	$4,000
Cost of Goods Sold	2,000
Depreciation Expense	120
Other Expenses	280
Income Tax Expense	280
Increase in Wages Payable	20
Increase in Accounts Receivable	40
Decrease in Merchandise Inventory	50
Amortization of Patents	5
Retirement of Long-term Liabilities	250
Issuance of Common Stock	500
Amortization of Bond Premium	6
Declaration of Dividend	30
Cash Balance, Jan. 1, 19X5	3,000

Part B

Using the above information, prepare a statement of cash flows under the indirect method, including any required schedules.

SOLUTION TO DEMONSTRATION PROBLEM

Part A

Brennan Co.
Statement of Cash Flows (Direct Method)
For the Year Ended December 31, 19X8

Cash Flows from Operating Activities

Inflows:

Cash Received from Customers		$3,960	
(Outflows):			
Cash Paid to Suppliers	$(1,950)		
Cash Paid for Other Expenses	(261)		
Cash Paid to the Government	(280)		
Total Cash Outflows		(2,491)	
Net Cash Inflow from Operating Activities			$1,469

Cash Flows from Investing Activities

(none)

Cash Flows from Financing Activities

Inflows:

Issuance of Common Stock		500	
(Outflows):			
Decrease in Long-term Debt		(250)	
Net Cash Inflow from Financing Activities			250
Net Inflow of Cash			$1,719
Cash Balance, Jan. 1, 19X8			3,000
Cash Balance, Dec. 31, 19X8			$4,719

Calculations

Cash Received from Customers:

Sales	$ 4,000
Less: Increase in Accounts Receivable	(40)
	$ 3,960

Cash Paid to Suppliers:

Cost of Goods Sold	$ 2,000
Less: Decrease in Merchandise Inventory	(50)
	$ 1,950

Cash Paid for Other Expenses:

Other Expenses	$ 280
Less: Increase in Wages Payable	(20)
Less: Amortization of Patents	(5)
	255
Add: Amortization of Bond Premium	6
	$ 261

Reconciliation of Net Income to Net Cash Flow from Operating Activities

Net Income		$1,320
Add: Expenses Not Requiring Cash:		
Depreciation Expense	$ 120	
Patent Amortization	5	
Net Credit Changes in Current Accounts:		
Decrease in Merchandise Inventory	50	
Increase in Wages Payable	20	195
Less: Expense Reductions Not Providing Cash:		
Amortization of Bond Premium	(6)	
Net Debit Changes in Current Accounts:		
Increase in Accounts Receivable	(40)	(46)
Net Cash Inflow from Operating Activities		$1,469

Determination of Net Income

Sales	$ 4,000
Less: Cost of Goods Sold	(2,000)
Depreciation Expense	(120)
Other Expenses	(280)
Income Tax Expense	(280)
Net Income	$ 1,320

Part B

Brennan Co.
Statement of Cash Flows (Indirect Method)
For the Year Ended December 31, 19X8

Cash Flows from Operating Activities

Net Income		$1,320	
Add: Expenses Not Requiring Cash:			
Depreciation Expense	$120		
Patent Amortization	5		
Net Credit Changes in Current Accounts:			
Decrease in Merchandise Inventory	50		
Increase in Wages Payable	20	195	
Less: Expense Reductions Not Providing Cash:			
Amortization of Bond Premium	(6)		
Net Debit Changes in Current Accounts:			
Increase in Accounts Receivable	(40)	(46)	
Net Cash Inflow from Operating Activities			$1,469

Cash Flows from Investing Activities
(none)

(continued)

Cash Flows from Financing Activities
Inflows:

Issuance of Common Stock	500	
(Outflows):		
Retirement of Long-term Debt	(250)	
Net Cash Inflow from Financing Activities		250
Net Inflow of Cash		$1,719
Cash Balance, Jan. 1, 19X8		3,000
Cash Balance, Dec. 31, 19X8		$4,719

DISCUSSION QUESTIONS

Q17-1   Using an example, explain in your own words the function of a statement of cash flows. Why is it prepared? What does it communicate to the reader of financial statements? What is its advantage over a balance sheet?

Q17-2   Why are financing and investing activities of a corporation important to financial statement readers?

Q17-3   Explain in your own words how an increase in accounts receivable during the year affects the cash flow from operations. How does a decrease in accounts receivable affect it?

Q17-4   Is a statement of cash flows really only a summary of cash receipts and disbursements recorded in the corporation's Cash account?

Q17-5   What effect does the declaration of a cash dividend have on cash flow? the payment of a dividend declared and paid during the current year? the payment of a dividend declared in the preceding year?

Q17-6   Why does an increase or a decrease in the Marketable Securities account not affect the amount of cash provided by operations?

Q17-7   Why is it possible that cash may have decreased during the year, even though the net income during the same period has been substantial?

Q17-8   Why does the net income for the year usually differ from the increase (decrease) in cash flow from operating activities for the same year? What causes the difference?

Q17-9   What causes cash to be depleted? Give examples of items that cause an outflow of cash.

Q17-10   Explain how balance sheet items are analyzed to identify the inflow and outflow of cash that occurred during the year.

Q17-11   The T-account method is often used for instructional purposes in illustrating the preparation of a statement of cash flows. How does the T-account method work?

Q17-12   What is the basic format of a statement of cash flows? Prepare a model format under both the direct and indirect methods.

DISCUSSION CASE

Ben & Jerry's

Q1, Q2   Presented here are Ben & Jerry's statements of cash flows for 1985 to 1987.

Ben & Jerry's Homemade, Inc.
Statement of Cash Flows
Years Ended December 31, 1987

	1987	1986	1985
Cash provided by operations:			
Net income	$1,444,538	$1,016,375	$ 550,625
Add charges not affecting working capital:			
Depreciation	751,248	566,227	251,006
Deferred income taxes	108,000	97,000	48,000
Amortization and reduction of unearned compensation	62,020	58,118	
Loss on disposition of assets	23,341		72,442
	2,389,147	1,737,720	922,073
Cash provided (used) by working capital:			
Accounts receivable	(1,271,447)	(817,039)	(430,684)
Income taxes	(730,091)	744,746	(154,749)
Inventories	(403,701)	(628,890)	(372,653)
Prepaid expenses	14,484	(5,824)	(16,958)
Accrued royalties		(33,820)	(18,180)
Accounts payable	25,586	(462,574)	1,010,393
Accrued payroll and related costs	42,947	159,546	18,336
Accrued expenses	25,940	196,360	23,264
Deferred revenue	120,000		
Franchise deposits	298,750	156,850	31,100
	(1,877,532)	(690,645)	89,869
Cash provided by operations	511,615	1,047,075	1,011,942
Cash provided (used) by investing activities:			
Additions to property, plant and equipment	(2,917,442)	(2,876,768)	(3,504,865)
(Increase) decrease in other assets	(703,422)	2,324	(3,548)
Proceeds from sale of assets	11,000		19,417
Construction funds	(4,600,000)		1,322,759
	(8,209,864)	(2,874,444)	(2,166,237)
Cash provided (used) by financing activities:			
Repayment of long-term debt	(138,994)	(134,113)	(74,212)
Increase in long-term debt	6,036,525		613,475
Proceeds from issuance of preferred stock			9,000
Proceeds from issuance of common stock		161,438	5,850,000
Issuance costs of common stock including underwriter discounts			(794,393)
Purchase of treasury stock	(24,342)		
Unearned compensation		(161,438)	
Purchase of fractional shares	(8,779)		
	5,864,410	(134,113)	5,603,870
Increase (decrease) in cash and cash equivalents and certificates of deposit	(1,833,839)	(1,961,482)	4,449,575
Cash and cash equivalents and certificates of deposit at beginning of period	3,399,921	5,361,403	911,828
Cash and cash equivalents and certificates of deposit at end of period	$1,566,082	$3,399,921	$5,361,403

Source From the Ben & Jerry's Homemade, Inc., Annual Report for the Year Ended December 31, 1987. Reprinted with permission.

For Discussion

1. In 1986 and 1987, cash and cash equivalents and certificates of deposit decreased. Does Ben & Jerry's have a problem with cash flow?

2. How is Ben & Jerry's using most of its cash?

EXERCISES

Classifying activities: operating, investing, financing (Q1)

E17-1   The choices when determining how a particular item might be disclosed on a statement of cash flows are as follows: Operating (O), Investing (I), Financing (F), Noncash (NC), or Not Disclosed (ND).

Required
In what section would the following be disclosed?

1. Net Income
2. Purchase of Land
3. Sale of Bonds
4. Purchase of a Truck
5. Sale of Treasury Stock

6. Depreciation Expense
7. Sale of Machinery
8. Purchase of Treasury Stock
9. Sale of a Patent
10. Issuance of Common Stock

The following data are used to answer E17-2 and E17-3. Assume that this is all the information needed to answer the exercises.

The income statement of Swipe Company included the following for the year ended December 31, 19X5:

Sales	$3,500
Cost of Goods Sold	2,400
Operating Expenses	1,000
Net Income	100

Depreciation amounted to $400.
Income taxes amounted to $30 and are included in operating expenses.
Accounts receivable increased $800 during the year.
Inventory decreased $200 during the year.
Accounts payable decreased $500 during the year.
Taxes payable remained constant during the year.

Cash flows from operating activities: indirect method (Q3, Q4)

E17-2

Required
Compute the cash flows from operating activities during the year under the indirect method.

Cash flows from operating activities: direct method (Q3, Q4, Q6)

E17-3

Required
Compute the cash flows from operating activities during the year under the direct method.

E17-4 through E17-6 are based on the following information:

Net Income	$6,000
Depreciation Expense	2,000
Sale of Common Stock	3,000

Issuance of Bonds	$7,000
Sale of Land	9,000
Purchase of Inventory	1,000
Purchase of Equipment	4,000
Payment of a Dividend	5,000
Payment of Salaries	9,000

Cash flows from invest-
ing activities (Q1)

E17-4

Required
Determine the cash flows from investing activities.

Cash flows from financ-
ing activities (Q1)

E17-5

Required
Determine the cash flows from financing activities.

Cash flows from operat-
ing activities (Q3)

E17-6

Required
Determine the cash flows from operating activities.

E17-7 through E17-10 are based on the following information:

Sales	$9,000
Cost of Goods Sold	5,000
Expenses (including income taxes, but	
not depreciation)	2,000
Depreciation	500
Income Tax Expense	800
Accounts Receivable Increased	2,000
Inventory Decreased	3,000
Accounts Payable Increased	1,000
Income Tax Payable Decreased	7,000
Amortization of Patents	300

Cash received from
customers (Q4)

E17-7

Required
Determine the amount of cash received from customers.

Cash paid to suppliers
(Q4)

E17-8

Required
Determine the amount of cash paid to suppliers.

Cash paid for expenses
(Q4)

E17-9

Required
Determine the amount of cash paid for expenses other than income taxes.

Cash paid to
government (Q4)

E17-10

Required
Determine the amount of cash paid to the government for income taxes.

PROBLEMS

Statement of cash flows: direct method (Q4, Q8)

P17-1   During the year ended December 31, 19X3, Poor Company reported $95,000 in sales; $50,000 in cost of goods sold; $20,000 in other expenses; and $5,000 in income taxes. The following transactions occurred during the year:

Depreciation Expense	$3,000
Increase in Wages Payable	500
Increase in Accounts Receivable	900
Decrease in Merchandise Inventory	1,200
Amortization of Patent	100
Maturity of Long-term Liabilities	5,000
Issuance of Common Stock	12,500
Amortization of Bond Discount	150

■ Long-term assets costing $10,000 were acquired through the issuance of common stock with a par value of $10,000.

■ On December 15, 19X3, the board of directors declared a cash dividend of $5,000, payable to stockholders of record on January 15, 19X4. The payment date is January 31.

■ At the same time the cash dividend was declared, the company also declared a stock dividend of 1,000 shares when the market price was $10 per share. The shares will be distributed on January 16, 19X4.

■ Old machinery was sold for $6,000 cash. The original cost was $15,000 and it is one-half depreciated. This was reported as an ordinary item on the income statement and was included in Other Expenses.

■ Accounts payable decreased by $1,000.

■ The cash balance on January 1, 19X3, was $10,000.

Required
Without using a worksheet, prepare a statement of cash flows under the direct method and explain what this statement tells you about Poor Company.

Statement of cash flows: indirect method (Q4, Q8)

P17-2

Required
Using the data in P17-1, prepare a statement of cash flows under the indirect method. Which method yields the better information for the user of financial data?

Statement of cash flows: direct method, worksheet (Q4, Q8)

P17-3   Kwick-Change Corp. reported the following information regarding its financial position during 19X2:

Comparative Balance Sheets
December 31, 19X1, and 19X2

Assets	19X2	19X1	Increase or Decrease
Cash	$ 7,875	$6,225	$1,650
Accounts Receivable (net)	1,350	1,200	150
Merchandise Inventory	8,895	6,000	2,895
Prepaid Insurance	90	75	15
Land	1,500	-0-	1,500
Machinery	6,750	6,000	750
Accumulated Depreciation	(450)	(300)	(150)
Totals	$26,010	$19,200	$6,810

(continued)

Liabilities and Stockholders' Equity	19X2	19X1	Increase or Decrease
Accounts Payable	$ 375	$ 300	75
Dividends Payable	750	150	600
Bonds Payable, 9%	4,500	-0-	4,500
Premium on 9% Bonds	135	-0-	135
Convertible Preferred Stock	-0-	2,250	(2,250)
Common Stock, $10 Par Value	13,500	12,000	1,500
Paid-in Capital in Excess of Par Value	750	-0-	750
Retained Earnings	6,000	4,500	1,500
Totals	$26,010	$19,200	$6,810

The income statement for Kwick-Change contained the following information:

Sales	$10,000
Cost of Goods Sold	4,000
Depreciation Expense	300
Interest Expense	255
Other Expenses	795
Loss on Trade-in of Machinery	150
Income Tax Expense	2,250
Net Income	2,250

Additional information:

- Dividends of $150 were paid during the year, and a dividend of $750 was declared at the end of the year, payable in 19X3.
- During the year, the company traded an old machine for a new one. The new machine had a cash selling price of $2,250. The old one had an original cost of $1,500, and $150 of depreciation had been taken. A cash difference of $1,050 also was paid.
- On January 1, 19X2, $3,000 of 9% bonds were issued at 105. The bonds are due in 10 years, and interest is due on December 31 of each year.
- On December 31, 19X2, 9% bonds with a face value of $1,500 were exchanged for a parcel of land having a fair market value of $1,500.
- The convertible preferred stock was converted during the year into 150 shares of $10 par value common stock.
- The premium on the bonds is amortized using the straight-line method.

Required

1. Prepare the worksheet necessary to prepare a statement of cash flows under the direct method.

2. Prepare a formal statement of cash flows with any necessary reconciliations.

3. What does the statement of cash flows tell you about the company?

Statement of cash flows: indirect method, worksheet (Q4, Q8)

P17-4

Required

Using the information from P17-3, answer the following:

1. Prepare the worksheet necessary to prepare a statement of cash flows under the indirect method.

2. Prepare a formal statement of cash flows with any necessary reconciliations.

3. What does the statement of cash flows tell you about the company?

Statement of cash flows: direct method, T accounts (Q4, Q8)

P17-5 Comparative balance sheet information for Medicine Hat Corp. for December 31, 19X1, and 19X2 follow.

(thousands)

Debits	19X2	19X1
Cash	$ 10	$ 8
Accounts Receivable (net)	18	10
Merchandise Inventory	24	20
Long-term Investments	10	24
Long-term Assets	94	60
Totals	$156	$122

Credits	19X2	19X1
Accumulated Depreciation	$ 14	$ 10
Accounts Payable	16	12
Notes Payable—Long-term	40	32
Common Stock	60	50
Retained Earnings	26	18
Totals	$156	$122

The Income Statement for 19X2 is shown next.

Income Statement
For the Year Ended December 31, 19X2

Sales		$300
Cost of Goods Sold		(200)
Gross Profit		$100
Operating Expenses		
Expenses, including Income Tax	$ (78)	
Depreciation	(6)	(84)
Income from Operations		$ 16
Other Gains (Losses)		
Gain on Disposal of Long-term Assets		2
Loss on Disposal of Investments		(4)
Net Income		$ 14

Additional data concerning changes in the noncurrent accounts during 19X2 follow:

- Cash dividends paid, $6
- Issue of shares for cash, $10
- Long-term assets disposed during the year cost $6.
- Ignore income taxes.

Required
1. Prepared a statement of cash flows under the direct method using the T-account approach.
2. Explain what this statement of cash flows tells you about Medicine Hat Corp.

Statement of cash flows: indirect method, T accounts (Q4, Q8)

P17-6

Required
Using the data from P17-5, answer the following:
1. Prepare a statement of cash flows under the indirect method using the T-account approach.
2. Explain what this statement of cash flows tells you about Medicine Hat Corp.
3. Do you prefer one form of the statement of cash flows over the other? Explain.

ALTERNATE PROBLEMS

Statement of cash flows: direct method (Q4, Q8)

AP17-1 During the year ended December 31, 19X3, Rich Company reported $125,000 in sales; $70,000 in cost of goods sold; $35,000 in other expenses; and $7,000 in income taxes. The following transactions occurred during the year:

Depreciation Expense	$5,000
Decrease in Wages Payable	900
Decrease in Accounts Receivable	1,300
Increase in Merchandise Inventory	1,700
Amortization of Patent	895
Maturity of Long-term Liabilities	11,000
Issuance of Common Stock	17,000
Amortization of Bond Discount	450

■ Long-term assets costing $10,000 were acquired through the issuance of common stock with a par value of $10,000.

■ On December 15, 19X3, the board of directors declared a cash dividend of $15,000, payable to stockholders of record on January 7. The payment date has been set for January 31.

■ At the same time the cash dividend was declared, the company also declared a stock dividend of 1,000 shares when the market price was $10 per share. The shares will be distributed on January 16, 19X4.

■ Old machinery was sold for $15,000 cash. The original cost was $25,000 and it is one-half depreciated. This was reported as an ordinary item on the income statement.

■ Accounts payable decreased by $10,000.

Required

Without using a worksheet, prepare a statement of cash flows under the direct method and explain what this statement tells you about Rich Company.

Statement of cash flows: direct method (Q4, Q8)

AP17-2

Required

Using the data in AP17-1, prepare a statement of cash flows under the indirect method. Which method yields the better information for the user of financial data?

Statement of cash flows: direct method, worksheet (Q4, Q8)

AP17-3 Opry, Inc., reported the following data on its financial position in 19X2:

Comparative Balance Sheets
December 31, 19X1, and 19X2

Assets	19X2	19X1	Increase or Decrease
Cash	$ 918,750	$ 726,250	$192,500
Accounts Receivable (net)	157,500	140,000	17,500
Merchandise Inventory	1,037,750	700,000	337,750
Prepaid Insurance	10,500	8,750	1,750
Land	175,000	-0-	175,000
Machinery	787,500	700,000	87,500
Accumulated Depreciation	(52,500)	(35,000)	(17,500)
Totals	$3,034,500	$2,240,000	$794,500

(continued)

Liabilities and Stockholders' Equity	19X2	19X1	Increase or Decrease
Accounts Payable	$ 43,750	$ 35,000	
Dividends Payable	87,500	17,500	70,000
Bonds Payable, 9%	525,000	-0-	525,000
Premium on 9% Bonds	15,750	-0-	15,750
Convertible Preferred Stock	-0-	262,500	(262,500)
Common Stock, $10 Par Value	1,575,000	1,400,000	175,000
Paid-in Capital in Excess of Par Value	87,500	-0-	87,500
Retained Earnings	700,000	525,000	175,000
Totals	$3,034,500	$2,240,000	$794,500

The income statement for Opry contained the following information:

Sales	$3,000,000
Cost of Goods Sold	2,000,000
Depreciation Expense	35,000
Interest Expense	29,750
Other Expenses	392,750
Loss on Trade-in of Machinery	17,500
Income Tax Expense	262,500
Net Income	262,500

Additional information:

■ Dividends of $17,500 were paid during the year, and a dividend of $87,500 was declared at the end of the year, payable in 19X3.

■ During the year, the company traded an old machine for a new one. The new machine had a cash selling price of $262,500. The old one had an original cost of $175,000, and $17,500 of depreciation had been taken. A cash difference of $122,500 also was paid.

■ On January 1, 19X2, $350,000 of 9% bonds were issued at 105. The bonds are due in 10 years, and interest is due on December 31 of each year.

■ On December 31, 19X2, 9% bonds with a face value of $175,000 were exchanged for a parcel of land having a fair market value of $175,000.

■ The convertible preferred stock was converted during the year into 17,500 shares of $10 par value common stock.

■ The premium on the bonds is amortized using the straight-line method.

Required

1. Prepare the worksheet necessary to prepare a statement of cash flows under the direct method.

2. Prepare a formal statement of cash flows with any necessary reconciliations.

3. What does the statement of cash flows tell you about the company?

Statement of cash flows: indirect method, worksheet (Q4, Q8)

AP17-4

Required

Using the information from AP17-3, answer the following:

1. Prepare the worksheet needed to do a statement of cash flows under the indirect method.

2. Prepare a formal statement of cash flows with any necessary reconciliations.

3. What does the statement of cash flows tell you about the company?

Statement of cash flows, direct method, T accounts (Q4, Q8)

AP17-5 The president of Costa Company is concerned about the company's cash position at the end of December 19X2. The following data summarizes the financial position of the company for 19X1 and 19X2:

	(thousands)	
Debits	**19X2**	**19X1**
Accounts Receivable	$ 170	$ 208
Building	610	500
Cash (overdraft)	(50)	50
Merchandise Inventory	110	125
Land	175	90
Long-term Investments	40	100
Machinery	300	170
Prepaid Expenses	5	4
Bond Discount	4	5
Totals	$1,364	$1,252
Credits		
Accounts Payable	$ 70	$ 50
Accumulated Depreciation	241	218
Bonds Payable	100	50
Common Stock	500	450
Notes Payable—Trade	25	-0-
Retained Earnings	423	480
Wages Payable	5	4
Totals	$1,364	$1,252

Additional information:

- A dividend of $.15 per share was declared and paid on the 500,000 outstanding shares.
- Shares issued during the year were sold at par value.
- Some shares held as a long-term investment were sold during the year to finance a portion of the new building. These shares had a cost of $60,000 and were sold for $40,000.
- Machinery was sold during the year for $2,000. The original cost was $10,000 and depreciation of $6,000 had been recorded.

Additional data from the income statement follows:

	(thousands)
Sales	$1,350
Cost of Goods Sold	720
Depreciation Expense	29
Other Expenses	546
Loss on Sale of Machinery	2
Loss on Sale of Investments	20
Income Tax Expense	15
Net Income	18

Required

1. Using the T-account approach, prepare a statement of cash flows.

2. Evaluate the cash position of Costa Company.

Statement of cash flows: **AP17-6**
indirect method,
T accounts (Q4, Q8)

Required

1. Using the data from AP17-5 and the T-account approach, prepare a statement of cash flows under the indirect method.

2. Evaluate the cash position of Costa Company.

DECISION PROBLEM

Sal Vage is a successful realtor who owns and operates three hotels. In September 19X8, she told her auditor, "Claude Hopper bought the White Sands Hotel five years ago. It hasn't yet shown a profit, and he's approached me with an offer to sell the assets at net book value of $1.5 million, even though the property has been appraised at $2 million.

"Claude had no previous experience in the hotel business. I believe that with proper management the White Sands would be a very good investment. From mid-May to mid-September, customers are being turned away. During December and January, the hotel is closed. In my judgment, the room rates are too low at White Sands compared with similar hotels.

"As you know, my primary interest is in cash flow. Because it is not a cash flow item, I consider depreciation to be an irrelevant expense. In order to raise the $1.5 million purchase price, I would have to sell some relatively secure bonds, which are now earning 10% interest. I am interested in investing in the White Sands only if I can obtain a cash flow of at least double the interest I would be losing.

"Mr. Hopper has agreed to let you review his hotel's books."

An income statement for the year ended September 30, 19X8, prepared by Claude Hopper and his staff is presented here. After reviewing this statement, Sal Vage asked her auditor to prepare a statement for 19X9 indicating the projected cash flow based on the following assumptions:

- Room rates from June 1 to September 30 would be raised $15, but the occupancy rate would drop 10%.

- Neither room rates nor occupancy rates would change from February 1 to May 31 or from October 1 to November 30.

- The hotel would remain open during December and January, with 50 daily rentals at a reduced daily rate of $40.

- Variable expenses per room rented would continue as at present.

- Advertising expenses would be increased by $20,000.

- Fixed salaries would be reduced by $10,000.

- Sal Vage would not assume the existing loan from the Bank of America; she would sell bonds if she decided to purchase the hotel.

- The income tax rate is 40%.

White Sands Hotel
Income Statement
For the Year Ended September 30, 19X8

Revenues (total room rentals—15,000) (Note 1)		$1,050,000
Less: Variable Expenses		510,000
Contribution Margin		$ 540,000
Less: Fixed Expenses		
Depreciation—Hotel		$ 60,000
Depreciation—Equipment, Furniture, and Fixtures		60,000
Depreciation—Outdoor Facilities		30,000
Fixed Portion of Utility Expenses		20,000
Property Taxes		40,000
Tennis and Pool Attendants		30,000
Building Maintenance and Security		40,000
Bookkeeping and Front Desk		50,000
Advertising		60,000
Hotel and Room Management		60,000
Legal and Auditing		25,000
Payroll Taxes		10,000
Interest on Loans from Bank of America		90,000
Miscellaneous		25,000
Total		$ 600,000
Net Loss		$ (60,000)

1. Includes 7,500 room rentals from June 1 to September 30, and 7,500 room rentals from February 1 to May 31 and October 1 to November 30. Room rates are fixed throughout the year at $70.

Required

1. Prepare a statement of projected cash flows based on these assumptions, and determine whether Sal Vage's investment criterion would be met.

2. Evaluate Sal Vage's investment criterion.

ANSWERS TO SELF-TEST QUESTIONS

1. **(b)** If Accounts Receivable increased, the amount reported as Sales on the income statement is overstated from a cash inflow perspective. Under the indirect method, this increase is subtracted from net income to correct the overstatement. Under the direct method, the increase is subtracted directly from the Sales amount to arrive at cash inflow from customers.

2. **(e)** Since the decision to issue debt instead of equity is a financing decision, the cash inflow from a bond issue would be reported as an inflow from financing activities.

3. **(f)** Since the decision to issue common stock is a financing decision, and the issuance is reported as an inflow from financing activities, then the repurchase of those shares would be reported as an outflow from financing activities.

4. **(b)** If Wages Payable decreased during the year, more cash was paid during the year than is reflected in the Wages Expense amount on the income statement. From a cash flow perspective, Wages Expense is understated. Under the indirect method, this decrease would be subtracted from net income to correct the understatement of Wages Expense. Under the direct approach, the decrease would be added to the amount for Wages Expense to correct the understatement, and to report the amount of cash outflow paid to employees.

5. **(d)** The purchase of any long-term asset would be reported as an outflow from investing activities.

6. **(f)** Since the decision to issue preferred stock is a financing decision, the payment of dividends on those shares would be considered an outflow from financing activities.

7. **(f)** Since the decision to issue common stock is a financing decision, the payment of dividends on those shares would be considered an outflow from financing activities.

8. **(c)** Since the decision to purchase the shares was the result of an investing decision, the resulting inflow of cash from the subsequent sale of the shares would be reported as an investing activity.

9. **(d)** The decision to invest in the stock of another company is the result of an investment decision, and therefore would be reported as an outflow from investing activities.

10. **(c)** It does not matter whether the land was donated to the entity or purchased by the entity; the proceeds from the sale of long-term assets would be reported as an inflow from investing activities. If the land had not been donated, chances are that a similar parcel would have been purchased and reported as an outflow from investing activities.

PART V
FINANCIAL STATEMENT ANALYSIS PROBLEM

Turn to the excerpts (pp. 889–906) from the annual report of United Telecom (UT) for the year ended December 31, 1989, and answer the following questions:

1
- Determine the financial ratios identified as *a* through *p* for the years 1988 and 1989.
- For each ratio state whether the trend is favorable or unfavorable. Explain your position.
- After all the ratios have been calculated, make some general comments regarding the overall financial position of UT.

(a) **Debt-to-equity ratio** Assume that minority interest is considered a part of equity.

(b) **Current ratio**

(c) **Acid-test ratio** Assume that the quick assets include cash, temporary investments, and all receivables.

(d) **Accounts receivable collection period** Assume that all revenue is from credit transactions.

(e) **Accounts receivable turnover.** Assume that all revenue is from credit transactions.

(f) **Number of days sales in inventory** Since UT is mainly a service organization, use only the expenses reported from complementary businesses to determine this relationship.

(g) **Inventory turnover** Use only the revenue from complementary businesses to determine this ratio.

(h) **Length of the operating cycle**

(i) **Return on total assets**

(j) **Return on stockholders' equity**

(k) **Number of times interest earned**

(l) **Price-earnings ratio**

(m) **Dividend yield ratio**

For items *l* and *m,* you may assume that the market price of UT's common stock was as follows: 1985, $12; 1986, $13; 1987, $12; 1988, $23; 1989, $38.

(n) **Return on sales**

(o) **Sales to long-term assets ratio**

(p) **Long-term assets to stockholders' equity ratio**

2 In reference to the statement of cash flows for UT for the years ending 1987, 1988, and 1989, answer the following questions:

(a) Is the statement presented under the direct or indirect method? Explain.

(b) With the information given, is it possible to express the information by both the direct *and* indirect methods? Explain.

(c) Cash provided from operating activities remained relatively constant from 1988 to 1989, while net income decreased from $509 million in 1988 to $363 million in 1989, a decrease of more than 29%! Explain how this could happen.

(d) Cash decreased from $617 million in 1988 to $115 million in 1989. What is the major source of this decrease? Would it be a wise assumption that cash may continue to decrease at this alarming rate? Explain.

(e) In a statement of cash flows prepared under the direct method, the amount of taxes and interest paid is disclosed on the face of the statement. How can these amounts be determined from a statement prepared under the indirect method?

(f) In 1987, dividends of $195 million were paid during a year when UT suffered a net loss of $52 million. Is this possible, or was the declaration of the dividend by the board of directors an illegal or unwise decision? Explain.

PART VI

SPECIAL TOPICS

P_{ART} VI examines the two remaining issues of importance to students of introductory financial accounting courses. However, if course time is short, the elimination of this material will not significantly limit students' understanding of financial accounting. Although the two issues seem unrelated, they are related mathematically and are therefore explored here in one chapter, separately. The first issue, international accounting, is easier to grasp than the second issue, inflation accounting. For instance, suppose the exchange rate for the Canadian dollar were .84. That means a Canadian dollar could be purchased for 84 cents of U.S. currency. A Canadian, however, would have to pay $1.19 in Canadian currency to purchase each U.S. dollar ($1.00 ÷ 84 = $1.19.) Similarly, if the inflation rate were 19% during a one-year period, a U.S. dollar at the end of the year would only be worth 84 cents ($1.00 ÷ 119%) in terms of the same dollar at the beginning of the year. The U.S. dollar would still buy $1 in goods or services at the end of the year, but the same goods now would cost $1.19 instead of $1. Therefore, mathematically at least, these two issues have the same implications. Although the United States has not had a yearly inflation rate above 13% in recent times, many countries have inflation rates far in excess of 19%. Chapter 18 explores these two issues in two sections, beginning with a discussion of international accounting.

18 INTERNATIONAL AND INFLATION ACCOUNTING

CHAPTER 18 explores two issues regarding financial accounting yet to be addressed: accounting issues outside the United States, and measurement issues concerning accounting valuation and inflation. Chapter 15 explored the problems involved when one corporation owns more than 50% of another corporation, resulting in control over that entity. Because of this common ownership, the financial statements are consolidated to reflect the fact that it is only one economic entity. The first part of Chapter 18 addresses the problems involved when the company owned by another is located in a foreign country and the accounting records are kept in terms of a currency other than the U.S. dollar. It would be difficult to add 1,000,000 U.S. dollars to 1,000,000 Japanese yen when a yen has a U.S. dollar equivalent of less than a penny. Next the inflation issue is addressed. The balance sheet consists of a number of assets and liabilities, especially long-term assets and liabilities, that are acquired in different years when the rate of inflation may have fluctuated. Yet the dollar costs of those items are added together to arrive at total assets or total liabilities. Can useable information be generated by an accounting system that adds the cost of a truck purchase in 1977 to the cost of one purchased in 1990, when the 1990 truck costs more than twice as much? An inflation rate must be applied to a beginning-of-year U.S. dollar to obtain an equivalent end-of-year dollar valuation just as to express a foreign currency unit in terms of the U.S. dollar, an exchange rate must be applied to convert the unit.

After studying Chapter 18, you should be able to answer the following questions:

1 What is the difference between a foreign translation and foreign transactions? (pp.824, 827)

2 Is GAAP universal? Explain. (pp.824–25)

3 Should the records of foreign subsidiaries be converted to reflect GAAP before or after being translated into U.S. dollars? (p.825)

4 How is a balance sheet that is prepared using a different monetary unit converted to the U.S. dollar? (pp.825–26)

5 For a purchased subsidiary, should goodwill be determined in terms of the foreign currency unit and then converted to the U.S. dollar? (p.826)

6 What measurement problems are encountered when foreign transactions are denominated in terms of the U.S. dollar? (pp.827–28)

7 Are foreign exchange rates static? Do they ever change? (pp.828–29)

8 Should exchange gains and losses arising from foreign transactions affect net income? (pp.829–31)

9 Should adjustments be made at the balance sheet date to receivables and payables arising from foreign transactions? (pp.829–31)

10 How can it be said that international and inflation accounting are related? Explain. (p.831)

11 What is the difference between general price indexes and specific price indexes? (p.831)

12 What are the current requirements for inflation-adjusted data? (p.831)

13 Purchasing power gains will result during periods of inflation. Is this statement true or false? Explain. (pp.836–38)

14 Is it correct to say that accounting for inflation may be accomplished through either current cost or constant dollar accounting, since the end result is the same? (p.838)

15 Current cost is an extension of historical cost, while constant dollar is a departure from GAAP. Is this statement true or false? Explain. (p.840)

16 Does LIFO inventory costing result in an income statement that approximates current cost accounting? Explain. (pp.840–41)

17 If current costs are used in the accounts for long-term assets, will depreciation provide enough cash for the replacement of the assets? (p.841)

18 How does realized net income under current cost accounting relate to net income determined under GAAP? (pp.841–43)

INTERNATIONAL ISSUES

This introduction to international issues will begin with a brief review of Chapter 15, "Business Combinations," where the problems involved with common ownership between companies were examined. When one company owns another, consolidated financial statements are prepared. At this textbook level, only the preparation of a balance sheet at the date of the acquisition of the controlling interest was shown. The balance sheets of the two corporations were added together, and the reciprocal accounts (the double-counted items such as the investment account and the stockholders' equity of the subsidiary) were eliminated against one another. The intercompany receivables and payables also were eliminated, and the consolidated balance sheet formed the economic (although not legal) entity of parent plus subsidiary (P and S).

What happens when the subsidiary or parent company is located in a foreign country, such as Canada? The general ledger and all the other accounting records will be in terms of the Canadian dollar, while the general ledger of the affiliate in the United States will be in terms of the U.S. dollar. If the two units of monetary measure have a different equivalent value, some adjustments must be made before the amounts can be added together to arrive at any meaningful sum.

Foreign Translations

Q1: Foreign translation

Foreign translations become necessary when a parent company has a subsidiary located in a foreign country and consolidated financial statements must be prepared. Normally, the accounting records of the subsidiary are kept according to the accounting rules and regulations of the subsidiary's country, and the transactions are measured in terms of that country's currency.

DIFFERENCES CAUSED BY GAAP

Q2: GAAP and world

When a subsidiary of a U.S. parent has accounting records kept in terms of the accounting rules and regulations of another country, material differences might exist between values on the balance sheet under U.S. GAAP and the values determined under the other country's rules.

For example, in Canada the research and development costs associated with a patent are capitalized when the patent rights are granted, while in the United States, research and development costs are expensed when incurred. Only costs directly associated with the granting of the patent rights, such as legal and registration fees, are capitalized. As a result, the difference in the balance sheet valuation of a patent could be material. Suppose the research and development costs amounted to $1,000,000, while the legal and registration costs were $100,000. In Canada, the patent would be carried on the balance sheet and amortized based on $1,100,000, while in the United States, the balance sheet valuation would be only $100,000, a 91% difference from the Canadian value. In other words, the Canadian value is 10 times higher or 1,000% greater, a material difference.

Also, in Canada the consensus tends to be that FIFO should be used for inventory valuation if the flow of goods is FIFO, while the LIFO method should be used if the flow of goods is LIFO. In most cases the flow of costs tends to follow the flow of goods in inventory valuation. In the United States, the determination of inventory valuation is not tied to the flow of goods; an assumed flow of costs allows any acceptable method of costing. Since inventory valuation under FIFO and LIFO can differ substantially, adding a LIFO inventory value to a FIFO value, even after converting for the difference between the Canadian and the U.S. dollar, can be significant.

Since this textbook does not focus on **international accounting** the comparison of United States and Canadian GAAP will stop here. This was a comparison between two industrialized countries in North America. Similar comparisons could be made between the United States and the United Kingdom, Europe, Japan, and other countries in industrialized Asia. Even greater differences would become apparent when the United States is compared with Russia, China, or countries in Africa.

Q3: Conversion to GAAP

As international trade expands, more international agreements are made, but the many differences still require adjustments before the accounts of a foreign parent or subsidiary can be translated into U.S. dollar equivalents. The accounting records should first be adjusted for differences in GAAP before they are translated into U.S. dollars. Although in many cases the results would be the same, material differences can exist. This topic is discussed in more advanced accounting courses.

DIFFERENCES CAUSED BY THE MEASUREMENT UNIT

The foreign translation differences caused by the measurement unit were introduced in this chapter's preface. If the **exchange rate** (conversion factor) on the balance sheet date for the U.S. and Canadian dollar, for example, is other than one for one, then the Canadian dollar balance sheet must be converted into U.S. dollars (or vice versa) before the two balance sheets can be added. The question is, what exchange rate should be used to convert one measurement unit into another?

The accountant has many choices. The exchange rate in effect on the date of the balance sheet is one. It is published in a variety of sources on a daily basis, such as the *Wall Street Journal, New York Times, San Francisco Chronicle, Los Angeles Times,* and *Chicago Tribune.* This rate is referred to as the *current rate.* The *average exchange rate* for the current year could be used, or the exchange rate in effect when the item was recorded. This rate is referred to as the **historic rate.**

GAAP suggests that if the currency in which the books are kept is the currency in which the entity operates (functional currency), then the current rate should be used for all asset and liability accounts, and the average rate for all the income statement accounts. The paid-in capital accounts should be translated at the rate in effect when the stock was issued, and the retained earnings figure becomes the balancing amount after the translation of all the other accounts at the suggested rates. After the start-up retained earnings is determined, the next year's retained earnings can be determined by taking the beginning-of-the-year translated amount, adding translated net income, and subtracting translated dividends.

Q4: Balance sheet conversion

Since the preparation of consolidated income statements and retained earnings statements is beyond the scope of this textbook, the following example taken from P15-2 on p. 700 consists of only a balance sheet conversion on the date the acquisition of S by P for $225,000 took place:

	S		S
Account Title	**Canadian Dollars**	**Exchange Rate**	**U.S. Dollars**
Cash	30,000	.84	25,200
Accounts Receivable	20,000	.84	16,800
Inventory	110,000	.84	92,400
Long-term Assets (net)	225,000	.84	189,000
Total Assets	385,000		323,400
Accounts Payable	160,000	.84	134,400
Common Stock	100,000	.84	84,000
Retained Earnings	125,000	.84	105,000
Total Equities	385,000		323,400

Q5: Determining
goodwill

Note that all the balance sheet items were converted at the current rate of $.84 U.S. (assumed to be the balance sheet rate). All the assets and liabilities should be converted using the exchange rate in effect at the balance sheet date, while the equity accounts should use the historic rate, in this case the same as the current rate. In this example, the book value of the net assets is $189,000 ($323,400 − $134,400). If the parent corporation purchased 70% of the subsidiary's outstanding stock, including amounts in recognition of an undervaluation of long-term assets and goodwill, then the book value of what was purchased must be $132,300 (70% × $189,000), with an excess of $92,700, as shown:

Purchase Price	$225,000
Book Value of Net Assets Purchased (70%)	132,300
Excess (undervaluation and goodwill)	$ 92,700

As stated in the problem, long-term assets have a market value of $330,000. Assuming that this is measured in U.S. dollars, then this is an increase of $141,000 over the U.S. dollar book value equivalent of $189,000 for the long-term assets. Since only 70% was acquired, only 70% of the increase or $98,700 (70% × $141,000) would be recorded as long-term assets. However, the maximum allocable excess is $92,700, so the entire excess would be allocated to long-term assets, and nothing to goodwill. The results follow the same concepts as P15-2; only the numbers differ. As explained in Chapter 15, preparation of a consolidated worksheet, and eventually a balance sheet, requires worksheet elimination entries.

The worksheet elimination entry for the $50,000 S owed P on the purchase date would be as follows:

Accounts Payable	42,000	
Accounts Receivable		42,000
To eliminate $50,000 Canadian owed to the parent corporation when the exchange rate was $.84 U.S.		

(This entry assumes that proper adjusting entries were made on the books of the parent for the foreign transactions addressed later in this chapter.)

The major worksheet elimination entry to prevent double counting would appear as follows:

Common Stock	84,000	
Retained Earnings	105,000	
Long-term Assets	92,700	
Investment in Subsidiary		225,000
Minority Interest		56,700

The minority interest is determined by multiplying 30% by the book value of the net assets of the Canadian subsidiary converted to U.S. dollars ($84,000 + $105,000 = $189,000 × 30% = $56,700). The consolidated worksheet, with P's amounts from P15-2, would appear as shown in Exhibit 18-1.

The consolidated balance sheet for the entity would be prepared from the right-hand column, just as was done in Chapter 15.

The main purpose of the discussion on P15-2 was to show how financial statements from two different countries could be consolidated by applying exchange rates to the balance sheet of one of the companies. These procedures could have

EXHIBIT 18-1

CONSOLIDATED WORKSHEET FROM BALANCE SHEET CONVERSION

Accounts	Book Balances		Eliminations		Consolidated
	P	S	Debit	Credit	
Debits					
Cash	$ 50,000	$ 25,200			$ 75,200
Accounts Receivable	150,000	16,800		$ 42,000	124,800
Inventory	200,000	92,400			292,400
Long-term Assets	335,000	189,000	$ 92,700		616,700
Investment in Subsidiary	225,000	–		225,000	–
Totals	$960,000	$323,400			$1,109,100
Credits					
Accounts Payable	50,000	134,400	42,000		142,400
Minority Interest	–	–	–	56,700	56,700
Common Stock—P	115,000	–	–	–	115,000
Retained Earnings—P	795,000	–	–	–	795,000
Common Stock—S	–	84,000	84,000	–	–
Retained Earnings—S	–	105,000	105,000	–	–
Totals	$960,000	$323,400	$323,700	$323,700	$1,109,100

been accomplished in reverse by multiplying all the amounts on the parent company books by $1.19, the U.S. equivalent of the Canadian dollar (1.00 ÷ .84). Also, keep in mind that the amounts on the Canadian company's books would have to be adjusted to reflect U.S. GAAP first before being converted to U.S. dollar equivalents. If the U.S. company's balance sheet items were to be converted into Canadian dollars, the amounts first would have to be adjusted to reflect Canadian GAAP.

FOREIGN TRANSACTIONS

Q1: Foreign transactions

Q6: Denominated in dollars

Another major accounting issue of concern for U.S. companies operating in international markets is the recording of **foreign transactions,** those **denominated in** (measured in) a currency other than the U.S. dollar. What happens when the supplier of a U.S. company is located in Canada? If goods are ordered, chances are that the U.S. company will receive an invoice that requires payment in Canadian dollars.

This problem is illustrated in the following example. Saguaro Computers, Inc., (a United States company) and CC (Canadian Company) are in a customer/supplier relationship. Note that the two entities do not have common ownership. CC's sales price for goods sold to SCI is $100,000 Canadian. The entry made on CC's books would be as follows:

Accounts Receivable	100,000	
Sales		100,000

To record the sale of goods to SCI with terms of n90.

No mention of what denomination is necessary, since it would be understood that CC's unit of measure is the Canadian dollar. Note also that SCI can take advantage of liberal credit terms offered by CC. Basically, CC is offering three months of free credit, which, like individuals, most corporations would maximize. An entry is also required on Saguaro's books. The transaction recorded on SCI's books would have to be recorded at the U.S. dollar equivalent on the date of the transaction. Assume that the transaction took place February 26, 1990, when the Canadian dollar was trading at $.84 U.S. Therefore, $100,000 Canadian would have a value of $84,000 on this date. The journal entry would be as follows:

Purchases (or Merchandise Inventory)	84,000	
Accounts Payable		84,000
To record the purchase of merchandise for resale from CC for $100,000 Canadian when the exchange rate was $.84 U.S. The terms of the sale required payment within 90 days.		

Note that if the transaction had no credit terms (cash on delivery), the entry would be recorded as follows:

Purchases (or Merchandise Inventory)	84,000	
Cash		84,000
To record the purchase of merchandise for resale from CC for $100,000 Canadian when the exchange rate was .84 U.S.		

To buy the goods, Saguaro would have to purchase a draft for $100,000 Canadian from a bank, paying it $84,000. If CC would accept a check drawn for $84,000 U.S., and a U.S. dollar had an exchange rate of $1.19 Canadian, then the receipt of the cash would be recorded on CC's books as follows:

Cash ($84,000 U.S. × $1.19 Canadian)	100,000	
Sales		100,000
To record a cash sale to SCI receiving a check for $84,000 U.S. when the exchange rate was $1.19.		

Note that each exchange rate can be expressed in terms of the respective currency.

Q7: Exchange rates

Since the arrangement is not a cash transaction, but a credit purchase for SCI, a problem arises. During the 90-day period, the exchange rate between the Canadian and U.S. dollars would fluctuate daily, depending on world markets and the strength or weakness of the U.S. dollar in those markets. (Students who plan on majoring in international business will take a course in international finance, where world money markets will be studied in depth.) The account payable to CC is due May 26, 1990, in the amount of $100,000 Canadian. Assume that on that day the exchange rate for a Canadian dollar is $.80 U.S. This exchange rate also may be expressed as 1.25 Canadian per U.S. dollar (1.00 ÷ .80). If SCI sends Canadian dollars in payment, the charge for a Canadian draft in the amount of $100,000 would be $80,000. When this check is recorded in Saguaro's books, the entry would be as follows:

Accounts Payable	84,000	
Cash		80,000

However, the entry obviously does not balance. Because of the fluctuation of the world money markets, SCI has ended up with a *foreign exchange gain* of $4,000 that must be recorded. The gain is the result of satisfying an $84,000 account payable with a cash payment of $80,000. If the exchange rate had been $.90 U.S., a foreign exchange loss of $6,000 would have resulted ($90,000–$84,000). **Foreign exchange gains and losses** result when the U.S. dollar equivalent is different on the date of receipt or payment than it was on the date the transaction was recorded.

One approach would be to report that the goods purchased 90 days before really only cost $80,000, and the entry could be completed as follows:

Accounts Payable	84,000	
Cash		80,000
Purchases (or Merchandise		
Inventory)		4,000

This entry shows that the goods were purchased at the net cost of $80,000, due to the credit terms of n90, instead of $84,000. But the credit terms should *not* affect the cost of the merchandise. This approach also creates other problems if the goods have already been sold, or if a year-end closing has already taken place.

Since the cost of the goods should not be affected by the credit terms, then for a better approach begin with the unbalanced entry as follows:

Accounts Payable	84,000	
Cash		80,000

Q8: Exchange gains, losses

The difference should be recorded as a foreign exchange gain on the income statement when the bill is paid, as follows:

Accounts Payable	84,000	
Cash		80,000
Foreign Exchange Gain		4,000

To record the payment of the amount
of $100,000 Canadian due to CC when
the exchange rate was $.80 U.S.

When CC receives the draft for $100,000 Canadian, the entry would appear as follows:

Cash	100,000	
Accounts Receivable		100,000

To record the receipt of a draft for
$100,000 Canadian from SCI.

If CC had agreed to accept the equivalent amount of U.S. dollars, then the receipt of the $80,000 check would be recorded as follows:

Cash ($80,000 U.S. × 1.25)	100,000	
Accounts Receivable		100,000

To record the receipt of $80,000 U.S.
from SCI when the exchange rate was
$1.25.

Q9: Adjustments and foreign transactions

If a year-end closing occurred during the 90-day credit period, adjustments of Saguaro's accounts payable and possibly CC's accounts receivable would have to be made. Assume that March 31, 1990, had been the year-end for both SCI and CC, and that the exchange rate was $.83 U.S. for a Canadian dollar and $1.21 Canadian for a U.S. dollar (rounded: 1:00 ÷ .83 = 1.20482). An adjusting entry would be required on SCI's books as follows:

Accounts Payable	1,000	
Foreign Exchange Gain		1,000
To adjust accounts payable to the		
actual amount owed CC on March 31,		
1990 ($100,000 Canadian × $.83 U.S.		
= $83,000). Original amount was		
$84,000.		

Since the transaction is denominated in terms of the Canadian dollar, the accounts receivable on CC's books would not have to be adjusted; payment of $100,000 Canadian or its equivalent will eventually be received.

If the sale made by CC on February 26, 1990, had been denominated in U.S. dollars rather than in Canadian dollars, then if the year-end came before payment, CC would have to adjust its receivable instead of SCI adjusting its payable. If the original transaction had been measured as $84,000 U.S., then CC would have recorded the sales transaction as follows:

Accounts Receivable ($84,000 U.S. ×		
$1.19 C)	100,000	
Sales		100,000
To record the sale of goods to SCI in		
the amount of $84,000 U.S. with terms		
of net 90 days.		

Assuming no year-end closing occurred during the 90 days, the following entry would be made when CC received the check for $84,000 U.S.:

Cash ($84,000 U.S. × $1.25)	105,000	
Accounts Receivable		100,000
Foreign Exchange Gain		5,000
To record the receipt of $84,000 U.S.		
from SCI when the exchange rate was		
$1.25 U.S.		

If the fiscal year-end of CC was on March 31, 1990, an adjustment of the account receivable from SCI would be made as follows:

Accounts Receivable	1,640	
Foreign Exchange Gain		1,640
To adjust accounts receivable to the		
actual amount due from SCI on March		
31, 1990 ($84,000 U.S. × $1.21		
Canadian = $101,640 − $100,000).		

As an example of an exchange fluctuation that resulted in a loss, consider the elimination entry made in the last section for a $50,000 loan to a subsidiary.

Accounts Payable	42,000	
Accounts Receivable		42,000
To eliminate $50,000 Canadian owed to		
the parent corporation when the		
exchange rate was $.84 U.S.		

When the accounts of the Canadian subsidiary were converted into U.S. dollars, the account payable for $50,000 Canadian became $42,000 U.S., requiring a debit to the payable account for $42,000. What was the exchange rate when the account receivable for $50,000 Canadian was first recorded? If it had been $.84 U.S., no adjustment would have been necessary, since the balance in the receivable account still would be $42,000. However, it is unlikely that the exchange rate would remain the same after the passage of some time. If the exchange rate was $.88 U.S. at the time the receivable was recorded by the U.S. parent corporation, the Accounts Receivable would have a balance of $44,000 ($50,000 Canadian × $.88 U.S.). If at the balance sheet date, the rate had fallen to $.84 U.S., a *foreign exchange loss* would have to be recognized before the two reciprocal accounts could be eliminated against one another, as follows:

Foreign Exchange Loss	2,000	
Accounts Receivable		2,000

At this point, the balance in both the receivable and the payable would be the same and the elimination entry would be the one given earlier.

Foreign translations and transactions are only two areas of concern in international business and were examined on a very elementary level here. Because international business has become relevant to even small companies, its problems must be introduced in less advanced courses in business and in the language of business—accounting.

Q10: International and inflation accounting

This chapter will now address the problem of accounting for inflation in an entity's accounts. As mentioned in the Part VI introduction, mathematically speaking, accounting for inflation is related to international accounting problems since it deals with monetary units of different values. Inflation, however, involves the value of the U.S. dollar measured at different points in time.

ACCOUNTING FOR INFLATION

Accounting for inflation involves two basic approaches: accounting for general inflation and accounting for inflation within a specific industry. Over the last 20 years, the price of energy has increased substantially, while the price of computers has not only dropped substantially, but also the operational efficiency of computers has increased almost beyond belief from the knowledge available 20 years ago. The two approaches to accounting for inflation are known as price level accounting, or more currently as *constant dollar accounting* and as *current cost accounting*. Constant dollar accounting uses general price indexes to determine valuations. When specific price indexes are used to convert historical cost amounts, the results are the approximate current cost of the item being valued.

Q11: General vs. specific price indexes

This section of the chapter also will be divided into two parts. The first part will consider the problems with constant dollar accounting, while the second part will discuss current cost accounting. It should be noted that, at the present time, corporations are not required to present any inflation-adjusted data with the basic package of financial information. Requirements in the past were when inflation rates in the United States were very high, but they were relaxed when inflation rates fell to much more acceptable levels. Who is to say what will happen to inflation in the future? The theory of accounting for inflation is presented here for two reasons:

Q12: Inflation-adjusted data

material inflation will return, and historical cost should be questioned as to whether it is the most viable measure of the value of the assets and liabilities of an entity.

Constant Dollar Accounting

Constant dollar accounting consists of extending the historical cost values on the financial statements to reflect **general inflation.** An entire set of price-level adjusted statements could be prepared, or more simply, key statement amounts, such as Net Income, Inventory, and Property, Plant, and Equipment, might be adjusted to reflect general levels of price increases. These three amounts seem to be most affected by inflation when comparing historical costs to current costs. Current assets and liabilities are just that, *current,* and therefore result in historical cost values that usually approximate current cost values. Inventory, one of the three key amounts, may be an exception, especially if the inventory is carried under the LIFO costing method. Long-term liabilities tend to remain fixed in the amount to be repaid, so the balance sheet values tend to reflect that amount, assuming the debt is held until maturity. Using general price indexes to adjust historical cost values makes the application of constant dollar accounting quite easy on the surface.

A number of general price-level indexes are available, but the one most often quoted when referring to constant dollar accounting is the **Consumer Price Index** for all Urban Users (CPI-U). The index is computed on a continual basis by the federal government and is quite readily available. Actual CPI information will not be presented in this text in order to use more rounded figures that are easier to work with. However, the numbers used will approximate the actual index. Until recently, the CPI has used 1967 as a base year. Had the U.S. Department of Labor continued to use 1967 as a base year, the index would have exceeded 400 by 1990 or 1991. The following are some approximate CPI indexes since 1960 (all these index numbers are computed in relation to the base year 1967):

1960	89	1969	110	1974	148	1980	247	1986	335
1964	93	1970	116	1976	171	1982	289	1989	379
1967	100	1972	125	1979	217	1984	311	1991	407

The index numbers from 1984 on are estimates, because the Department of Labor changed the base year to 1982 when the index became too high. The higher numbers are presented here to demonstrate the dramatic decrease in the purchasing power of the dollar in the last 30 years.

First of all, what do these numbers mean? The Department of Labor takes a *market basket* approach to determine the index at any point in time. The "basket" includes such categories as food, clothes, shelter, transportation, utilities, and other daily necessities. The total average cost of these items is then determined. After a period of time, the cost for the same items is calculated again, and an index number defining the change is determined. After a period of time, the cost for the same items is calculated again and an index number determined. See Real World Example 18-1 for a presentation of inflation rates for the last 12 years and for the first quarter of 1990. The article also tells the makeup of the market basket currently used and the recent changes in the cost of the items in that basket. The rate of inflation is determined by comparing the CPI-U at two different times. For example, assuming that the index for the year 1968 was 104, this conveys a 4% increase in the average cost of the basket items. What was the total inflation rate from 1976 to 1982, using the index numbers given in the textbook?

1982	289
1976	171
6-Year Change	118

118 ÷ 171 = 69% Increase

Think about a 69% increase in the level of prices in a 6-year period! That means a textbook that cost $20 in 1976 would cost $34 ($20 × 169%) in 1982 if costs in the publishing industry increased at the same rate as general inflation. In 1991 that same textbook would cost $48 (407 − 171 = 236; 236 ÷ 171 = 138%; $20 × 238%). No wonder parents who went to college survived on a much smaller book budget. Not all items fit the assumption that their inflation followed the general inflation rate. If the hand-held calculator industry followed general inflation, consumers would be paying more than $650 for a 6-function machine that constantly needs batteries or a nearby source of electricity.

How do inflation indexes relate to financial accounting? In the examples that follow, assumed index numbers are used, rather than those presented earlier, to obtain more rounded numbers so their significance can be seen more easily. The discussion will be limited to the effects of general inflation on the balance sheet and the income statement.

BALANCE SHEET CONVERSION

A very simple balance sheet will be used to show the effect of price-level adjustments on various items. In the first example, assume Saguaro Computers, Inc., was incorporated on January 1, 19X1, when the CPI was 100. On the same date, $100,000 cash was received in exchange for common stock (no-par). SCI immediately invested $80,000 of the cash in land and buildings that cost $30,000 and $50,000, respectively. A balance sheet prepared on January 1, 19X1, would appear as follows:

Balance Sheet
January 1, 19X1

Assets		Liabilities and Equity	
Cash	$ 20,000	Common Stock	$100,000
Land	30,000		
Building	50,000		
Total Assets	$100,000	Total Liabilities and Equity	$100,000

Assume Saguaro was not involved in any transactions during the year, and that the cash was not invested in any income-producing account. The year-end balance sheet would therefore appear the same as for January 1. If the CPI had increased to 120 by the end of the year, the constant-dollar balance sheet for SCI would be prepared from the worksheet shown in Exhibit 18-2 (p. 836).

Saguaro suffered a loss during the year when no transactions took place. This can be explained by examining the Cash account. Cash of $20,000 was held during a year when inflation was 20%. In order to have the same purchasing power at the end of the year as was enjoyed at the beginning of the year, SCI would have to have $24,000 [$20,000 (120 ÷ 100)] at the end of the year. But SCI only had $20,000 in cash, representing a loss of $4,000, the $4,000 needed to balance the worksheet. This loss is referred to as a **purchasing power loss.** To have the same purchasing power as $20,000 at the beginning of the year, $24,000 in cash is needed.

If Saguaro had purchased inventory in the amount of $20,000, the beginning and ending balance sheets would have appeared as shown on p. 836.

REAL WORLD EXAMPLE 18-1
Inflation Hits 8-Year High

WASHINGTON — Consumer prices shot up during the first three months of the year at an annual rate of 8.5 percent, the most rapid quarterly rise in nearly eight years, the Labor Department reported Tuesday.

Higher prices for housing and apparel accounted for more than two-thirds of March's 0.5 percent increase, which was considerably more than most analysts expected and which sent bond prices tumbling.

The widespread assumption was that the Federal Reserve has lost, at least for the foreseeable future, any leeway it might have had to reduce interest rates and might eventually have to raise them.

"It couldn't have been worse if you'd designed it that way," said Donald Straszheim, chief economist at Merrill Lynch in New York. "This is not the kind of numbers the Fed likes to see. Any hopes they will push interest rates down in the short run are not realistic."

Another government report issued Tuesday suggested that inflation would not be cooled by a slowing economy any time soon.

The Federal Reserve, introducing an updated index to measure industrial production, said that factory output increased a strong 0.7 percent in March. The Fed revised February's industrial output up to 0.8 percent from the originally reported 0.6 percent.

"We are in a split situation," said Irwin L. Kellner, chief economist at Manufacturers Hanover in New York. "Some industries are hurting and corporate profits fell last year.

Yet there's enough inflationary pressure that the Fed has no choice but to keep a tight grip on money and credit. There's a real danger of a collision down the road. The economy as a whole has escaped so far, but statistics like these could bring us down before the year is out."

In Tuesday's inflation report, some analysts were particularly disconcerted by the fact that the so-called core rate of inflation—the Consumer Price Index excluding food and energy—rose even faster than the index as a whole, by seven-tenths of 1 percent.

This meant that the increase could not be easily dismissed, as frequently occurs, by pointing to aberrations such as harsh weather pushing up the price of fuel oil or fresh vegetables.

"You take away the special stuff and you still have a reading on inflation that is not very favorable," said Edward F. McKelvey, a senior vice president at Goldman, Sachs & Co.

"Inflation is worse than we thought."

But while economists generally agreed that there was little consolation to be found in Tuesday's figures, several suggested that future reports would reflect considerably diminished price pressures.

Patrick C. Jackman, senior economist in the Labor Department branch that prepares the price index, called the first quarter "very bad" but observed that prices of much food and energy had now moderated or turned lower and that the price of apparel would almost certainly fall in April after soaring at a 21.4 annual clip during the first quarter.

Jackman also said a 1 percent rise in homeowners' costs last month, which contributed to a rise of five-tenths of 1 percent in the housing category, did not reflect any indentifiable factor that would continue to push prices higher.

Housing accounts for 42 percent of the price index, with food and transportation almost equally splitting another 35 percent.

The other four categories are medical, clothing, entertainment and "other" goods and services.

Consumer prices are nonetheless climbing faster than those at the producer level.

The Labor Department last week reported a decline of two-tenths of 1 percent in the

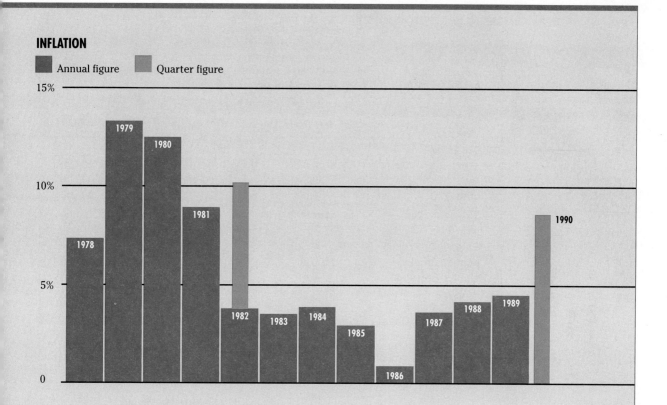

INFLATION

■ Annual figure   ■ Quarter figure

Producer Price Index for Finished Goods in March.

A major part of the difference, according to some economists, is that 55 percent of the consumer index consists of services, which rose seven-tenths of 1 percent last month.

That is a 6.3 percent rate of increase for the six months through March.

The producer index, a tabulation of prices received by domestic producers for their goods, contains no directly measured services.

Service jobs have been expanding smartly and, with the nation's unemployment rate of 5.2 percent hovering just above 16-year lows, it appears that a tight labor market is generating cost pressures.

Some of the tightest labor markets are in metropolitan areas where bidding for certain kinds of workers has raised rates of pay substantially and put pressure on prices.

These wage pressures are likely to be given additional impetus by the April 1 rise in the minimum wage to $3.80, from $3.35 an hour.

One of those stressing the impact of wage pressure on inflation is Kathryn L. Kobe, a vice president of Joel Popkin & Co.

Kobe predicts that the core inflation rate will rise to 5 percent this year, from 4.4 percent in 1989.

All seven of the major Consumer Price Index categories showed price acceleration during the first quarter, making the total the fastest quarterly inflation since the 10.1 percent posted in the second quarter of 1982.

For 1989, the rate was 4.6 percent.

Source The Sacramento Bee News Service, "Inflation hits 8-year high," April 18, 1990. Reprinted with permission.

EXHIBIT 18-2

PURCHASING POWER LOSS

Saguaro Computers, Inc.
Constant Dollar Worksheet
December 31, 19X1

	Historical Cost	Conversion Factor	Constant Dollars
Assets			
Cash	$ 20,000	(see discussion)	$ 20,000
Land	30,000	120/100	36,000
Building	50,000	120/100	60,000
Totals	$100,000		$116,000
Liabilities and Equity			
Common Stock	$100,000	120/100	$120,000
Retained Earnings	–0–	(to balance)	(4,000)
Totals	$100,000		$116,000

Balance Sheet
January 1, 19X1

Assets		Liabilities and Equity	
Inventory	$ 20,000	Common Stock	$100,000
Land	30,000		
Building	50,000		
Total Assets	$100,000	Total Liabilities and Equity	$100,000

EXHIBIT 18-3

NO PURCHASING POWER LOSS

Saguaro Computers, Inc.
Constant Dollar Worksheet
December 31, 19X1

	Historical Cost	Conversion Factor	Constant Dollars
Assets			
Inventory	$ 20,000	120/100	$ 24,000
Land	30,000	120/100	36,000
Building	50,000	120/100	60,000
Totals	$100,000		$120,000
Liabilities and Equity			
Common Stock	$100,000	120/100	$120,000
Retained Earnings	–0–	(to balance)	–0–
Totals	$100,000		$120,000

The worksheet to convert this balance sheet would appear as shown in Exhibit 18-3. Notice that the amount of retained earnings needed to balance amounted to zero. SCI had no purchasing power loss during the year because it held no cash during a period of inflation.

If Saguaro Computers had acquired the building in the last example for $100,000, paying $50,000 down and assuming a mortgage for the balance, the beginning and ending balance sheets would appear as follows:

Balance Sheet
January 1, 19X1

Assets		Liabilities and Equity	
Inventory	$ 20,000	Mortgage Payable	$ 50,000
Land	30,000	Common Stock	100,000
Building	100,000		
Total Assets	$150,000	Total Liabilities and Equity	$150,000

Q13: Purchasing power gains

The worksheet to convert to constant dollars would appear as shown in Exhibit 18-4. Notice that the amount of retained earnings needed to balance amounted to an increase of $10,000. SCI had a **purchasing power gain** during the year because debt was held during a period of inflation.

In the first example cash was held during an inflationary period and Saguaro suffered a purchasing power loss. In the second example, no cash was held, and no purchasing power loss occurred. In the third example, no cash was held, but some long-term debt was outstanding and SCI enjoyed a purchasing power gain. This can be explained by studying the difference between monetary and nonmonetary assets and liabilities.

Monetary Items A **monetary item** is an asset or liability that is fixed in terms of a monetary unit. That **monetary unit** may be the U.S. dollar, the Canadian dollar,

EXHIBIT 18–4	PURCHASING POWER GAIN

Saguaro Computers, Inc.
Constant Dollar Worksheet
December 31, 19X1

	Historical Cost	Conversion Factor	Constant Dollars
Assets			
Inventory	$ 20,000	120/100	$ 24,000
Land	30,000	120/100	36,000
Building	100,000	120/100	120,000
Totals	$150,000		$180,000
Liabilities and Equity			
Mortgage Payable	$ 50,000	(see discussion)	$ 50,000
Common Stock	100,000	120/100	120,000
Retained Earnings	–0–	(to balance)	10,000
Totals	$150,000		$180,000

the Australian dollar, the British pound sterling, the French franc, the Russian ruble, and so on. At any point in time a monetary item can be measured by the balance in its account. For instance, in the first example earlier, the amount of cash was fixed at $20,000. The monetary unit may have been worth more or less then that at another point in time, but the item still was 20,000 of the monetary unit.

Monetary items can be assets or liabilities, while nonmonetary items can be assets, liabilities, or equities. An entity has very few monetary assets, while most of its liabilities are monetary in nature. If an entity has an account payable of $100,000, the entity owes 100,000 of the monetary unit being used by the entity and not some other amount. If an entity had a mortgage of $50,000, it owes $50,000 and not some other amount. On the other hand, the building in the examples was recorded as either $50,000 or $100,000. Does that mean that when the building is sold the entity will receive either $50,000 or $100,000? No, when the building is sold, the building's monetary value will be measured by the net cash received. Cash and Accounts Receivable are the most common monetary assets that an entity will have on its balance sheet.

Because monetary items are fixed in terms of the number of monetary units, they are not converted when preparing constant dollar financial statements. Note that in the examples Cash and Mortgage Payable were not converted. This historical cost valuation is also the constant dollar valuation, since the balances consist of a fixed number of monetary units.

Note again that in the example where cash was held during a year of inflation, the result was a purchasing power loss, while when the mortgage payable was held during the year, the result was a purchasing power gain. If monetary assets are held during a period of inflation, a purchasing power loss will occur because the dollars held during the year will not be worth as much as at the beginning of the year. If monetary liabilities are held during a period of inflation, a purchasing power gain will result, since the dollars borrowed will have a greater purchasing power than the dollars paid back in the future.

Nonmonetary Items Nonmonetary items must be converted on the balance sheet when converting historical cost to constant dollars in order to measure them in common units of measurement. Note in the second example that Saguaro had no monetary assets or liabilities and therefore no purchasing power gain or loss. As long as an entity holds a neutral position in monetary items, no purchasing power gain or loss occurs.

INCOME STATEMENT CONVERSION

The income statement also can be converted into constant dollars. If it can be assumed that sales are made and expenses are incurred evenly over the year, they can be converted into constant dollars using the average index for the year.

Exhibit 18-5 is an income statement for Saguaro Computers, Inc., a few years after the balance sheet examples. The building that SCI had purchased for $100,000 with the mortgage of $50,000 had a useful life of 10 years. The income statement is for 19X5, when the CPI was 160 on January 1 and 180 on December 31 and had an average during the year of 170. The average CPI for 19X4 was 150.

As can be seen from the worksheet, the GAAP (historical cost) net income of $2,000 has become a loss of $6,700 when applying the effect of inflation based on the CPI. In converting cost of goods sold to constant dollars it was assumed that the beginning inventory was purchased at mid-year 19X4, and therefore the average CPI for 19X4 was used. The ending inventory was assumed to be purchased at the

EXHIBIT 18–5

CONVERSION OF HISTORICAL COST TO CONSTANT DOLLARS

Saguaro Computers, Inc.
Income Statement
For the Year Ended December 31, 19X5

Revenue		
Sales		$42,000
Cost of Goods Sold		
Beginning Inventory	$ 6,000	
Purchases	28,000	
Goods Available for Sale	$34,000	
Ending Inventory	9,000	
Total Cost of Goods Sold		25,000
Gross Profit		$17,000
Operating and Financing Expenses		
Selling and Administrative Expenses	$ 3,000	
Depreciation Expense	10,000	
Interest Expense	1,000	
Income Tax Expense	1,000	
Total Expenses		15,000
Net Income		$ 2,000

The following worksheet was prepared to convert the historical-cost income statement into constant dollars:

Constant Dollar Worksheet
December 31, 19X4

	Historical Cost	Conversion Factor	Constant Dollars
Sales	$42,000	180/170	$44,500*
Cost of Goods Sold			
Beginning Inventory	$ 6,000	180/150	7,200
Purchases	28,000	180/170	29,600
Ending Inventory	9,000	180/180	9,000
Total Cost of Goods Sold	25,000		27,900
Selling and Administrative Expenses	3,000	180/170	3,200
Depreciation Expense	10,000	180/100	18,000
Interest Expense	1,000	180/170	1,100
Income Tax Expense	1,000	180/170	1,100
Net Income	$ 2,000		$(6,700)

*Rounded to the nearest $100.

end of the year, 19X5. Note that the depreciation is converted using the CPI when the building was purchased at incorporation (100).

In addition to the apparent net loss when constant dollars are taken into consideration, SCI could have suffered a price-level loss during the year, which would make matters worse.

Q14: Current cost vs. constant dollar

Constant dollar information can be helpful if used correctly. Its function is the subject of more advanced courses. The major drawback to constant dollar accounting is that readers of financial statements tend to view the resulting balance sheet values as estimates of current values, which is not the case. Remember the example of the hand-held calculator? The numbers were close to actual amounts. A 6-function hand calculator sold for $200 in 1972. Using constant dollar analysis, the current balance sheet valuation of the calculator would be almost $650 [$200 (407 ÷ 125)]! How much does a 6-function calculator cost today? At the time of this writing, they cost less than $7, do not require batteries, and have a lot more than 6 functions. If constant dollar financial information attempts to measure current *values,* then a 1991 6-function calculator would be valued at about $650, as just determined. Obviously this is not a measure of the current *cost* of the calculator. The $650 simply tells how many of today's dollars would be necessary to purchase the calculator in 1972.

Another method to measure the effect of inflation on financial information uses current cost data. This is discussed next.

Current Cost Accounting

Q15: Valuation and GAAP

Constant dollar information is useful to an extent, but only if it is not viewed as measuring current value. Current cost information is far more relevant and useful, if the information can be obtained. While constant dollar accounting is an extension of historical cost accounting, **current cost accounting** is an abrupt change from the "protection" of historical cost (GAAP). The major problem is determining current cost, which is not as easy as it may seem. Some items on the balance sheet can simply be looked up, such as inventory purchased on a daily, weekly, or monthly basis, but what about long-term assets? How is increased operational efficiency considered? What is the current cost of the calculator that sold for $200 in 1972? Is it relevant? What is the current cost of a building when the area around the plant has just been rezoned from agricultural to commercial? or rezoned from commercial to residential? What is the current cost of the special machinery custom built just for a particular operation when no other similar equipment exists on the face of the earth?

In reality, most current cost information is difficult and costly to obtain and, therefore, accountants have stayed with historical cost. There have been attempts to adopt current cost accounting in the past and there will be attempts in the future. The material is presented here so students will have a basic understanding of the issues involved.

Q16: LIFO and current cost

In Chapter 8 inventory valuation was discussed at length, including the application of various methods of costing the inventory in order to more accurately match the cost of goods sold with the sales revenue from the sale of the goods. Comparisons showed how LIFO inventory valuation resulted in a better matching of revenue and expenses when prices were rising. Wouldn't the application of the true replacement cost (current cost) be even a better matching? For example, assume an item is sold for $100. It was purchased several months before at a cost of $40. Similar items have been purchased in recent months for $60. Today, the item could be purchased in the market for $80. What is the gross profit on the sale of the item for $100 under FIFO, LIFO, and current cost?

	FIFO	LIFO	Current Cost
Sales	$100	$100	$100
Cost of Goods Sold	40	60	80
Gross Profit	$ 60	$ 40	$ 20

What is the correct gross profit from the transaction? FIFO and LIFO are acceptable for GAAP, but current cost is not. If the entity did not have operating expenses, and gross profit equalled net income, how much in dividends could be declared at the end of the year with the information available?

If $60 are paid in dividends from the sale of the item for $100, under the FIFO assumption $40 would be left to replace the item sold, which now costs $80. An additional $40 would have to come from somewhere to keep the operation going. The same could be said under the LIFO assumption. If $40 are paid in dividends from the $100, $60 would be left to replace the item now costing $80. Although LIFO puts the entity in a better position than FIFO, an additional $20 would still have to come from somewhere. It must be taken from past profits, or from equity or debt borrowing. However, if current cost data had been used in the accounts, the net income under the assumptions would be $20. If $20 are declared as a dividend, then the entity would have sufficient cash to replace the item sold.

Another area where current cost can have an impact is depreciation and other cost allocations, such as depletion of natural resources and the amortization of intangibles. In all of these situations, the current value of the item could be substantially more than the historical cost of the asset that is the basis for the cost allocation, and therefore more than the amount charged against revenue on the income statement.

Q17: Depreciation and current costs

For instance, assume a machine costing $100,000 is being depreciated over a 10-year period. It is anticipated that the asset will be replaced at the end of 10 years with a new one with equal capabilities. When $10,000 of depreciation is recorded in the first year, does it provide any cash for the eventual replacement of the machine? No, management must provide for cash to be set aside if a fund is to be available. Supposedly, depreciation does allow management to have the opportunity to set aside cash. If depreciation were the only expense of an entity (Sales − Depreciation Expense = Net Income), then net income is the residual amount remaining after providing funds for the replacement of the machine. This calculation shows that taking depreciation does provide the opportunity to set aside cash, but management must first choose to do so. It also points to one of the fallacies of historical cost: depreciation is based on historical cost and not on replacement values. Even if management does set aside cash for the replacement of the machine, it is doubtful that it will be enough cash since depreciation is based on the purchase price of the asset and not its replacement cost. Assuming that the replacement cost of the machine at the end of 10 years is $150,000, and management has accumulated $100,000, where will the additional $50,000 come from? Once again, it must be taken from past profits, equity issues, or new debt.

CURRENT COSTS AND THE INCOME STATEMENT

To demonstrate the application of current costs on the income statement, assume the following; Saguaro Computers, Inc., buys 10 units of inventory at $6 per unit. Between the purchase and the end of the year, SCI sells 4 of the units at $15 each.

EXHIBIT 18–6

HISTORICAL VERSUS CURRENT COST

Historical Cost	
Sales (4 × $15)	$60
Cost of Goods Sold (4 × $6)	24
Net Income	$36
Current Cost	
Sales (4 × $15)	$60
Cost of Goods Sold (4 × $11)	44
Operating Income	$16
Realized Holding Gain on Items Sold ($11 – $6 = $5; $5 × 4)	20
Realized Net Income	$36
Unrealized Holding Gain on Items in Inventory ($11 – $6 = $5; $5 × 6)	30
Current Cost Net Income	$66

At the end of the year, the replacement cost of the units has increased from $6 to $11. Also, the cost of the item sold is the only expense Saguaro has, and therefore net income is the same as gross profit. Two shortened income statements, one based on historical cost accounting (GAAP) and the other on current cost accounting, are shown in Exhibit 18-6.

Under current cost accounting, **holding gains** are identified. In Exhibit 18-6, Cost of Goods Sold, is measured using the current cost of the item ($11), while the items actually cost $6. This results in a holding gain of $5 per unit. By purchasing the items for $6, and selling them above the current cost of $11, Saguaro has realized the holding gain on the 4 items that have been sold. When the realized holding gains is added to operating net income, realized net income results in the amount of $36.

Q18: Realized net income

Note that net income under historical cost is also $36. Is this a coincidence? No. Historical cost net income also reflects realized holding gains, but buries the gain in net income without disclosing the amount. By burying the gain, historical cost net income is overstated from a current cost point of view. Since cost of goods sold under historical cost is only $24, and it will cost $44 to replace the items sold, $20 of the $36 net income is needed to maintain inventory levels. Therefore, available net income is really only $16, the amount reported as operating income under the current cost approach. The current cost model discloses how much is available for dividends (operating income), along with the **realized holding gains** to reach realized income (GAAP). One further adjustment is made to the income statement for the **unrealized holding gains** on the items remaining in inventory. Of the 10 items purchased, only 4 were sold, leaving 6 items in inventory at a cost of $6 each. But, as of the balance sheet date, each of those items have a replacement cost of $11, resulting in a $5 holding gain for each item. Since these items have not been sold, the gain is *unrealized,* and it is reported as an adjustment of realized net income to arrive at the current cost net income.

The question regarding understated depreciation also could be demonstrated on the income statement, but this is more complex and is taught in more advanced courses. However, the concept of separating realized and unrealized holding gains is the same.

CURRENT COSTS AND THE BALANCE SHEET

The major impacts current cost accounting has on the balance sheet are in inventory and long-term asset valuations. The remainder of the items on the balance sheet are relatively close to current costs. Of course, retained earnings is also affected, because of the historical cost overstatement of net income caused by the understatement of cost of goods sold, depreciation, and other cost allocation amounts.

The understatement of inventory on the balance sheet causes misstatements of the various ratios (Chapter 16) based on current assets and on inventory itself. The current ratio, inventory turnover, and number of days of sales in inventory all could be affected, although the major problem is in the current ratio. The other two ratios are based on cost of goods sold, which would be adjusted if current cost is used.

All of the operating efficiency ratios discussed in Chapter 16 would be affected by current cost, since many of them are based on the relationship of net income to other balance sheet items.

Current cost accounting has been discussed seriously in the accounting literature for at least 30 years. The accounting profession has resisted most movements toward the current cost method because of the difficulty in gathering accurate information, instead opting to stay within the safe confines of the historical cost method. Historical costs are known quantities and are quite verifiable; current costs are estimates and in most cases cannot be verified. Although current cost information is more *relevant*, historical cost data is more *reliable*.

As was mentioned in the beginning of this chapter, inflation-adjusted information was required of U.S. companies in the past. Disclosure of what an entity's net income would have been under both current cost and constant dollar accounting was required, along with the current value of property, plant, and equipment and inventory. Purchasing power gains and losses needed to be disclosed, as well as holding gains net of inflation.

Of the information required then, only **holding gains net of inflation** have not been discussed. A simple example can be applied to the information in the first part of this section. It was assumed CPI indexes were used to convert a balance sheet to constant dollar accounting, and that the index increased from 100 to 120 during the year. On that balance sheet was a parcel of land purchased for $30,000. On the year-end constant dollar balance sheet, the land was recorded as $36,000 [$30,000 (120 ÷ 100)]. If that land had a current selling price of $50,000, a holding gain of $20,000 ($50,000 − $30,000) would result, but inflation would have consumed $6,000 of that gain. Therefore, the holding gain net of inflation for the parcel of land would be $14,000 ($20,000 − $6,000).

Currently, GAAP does not require the disclosure of any inflation-adjusted information, although GAAP recommends that information on a current cost basis adjusted for inflation be disclosed in the financial statement of large corporations. The material was introduced here at the introductory level to make students aware that problems occur with historical cost, and that such information will be required again when inflation rises to unacceptable levels.

CHAPTER REVIEW

1 What is the difference between a foreign translation and foreign transactions? (pp. 824, 827–28)

Foreign translations involve determining the proper exchange rates to apply to various items in the financial statements of a foreign subsidiary before the statements can be consolidated with its U.S. parent. Foreign transactions involve economic events between two entities denominated (measured) in currency other than the U.S. dollar. The invoice amount must first be converted into the U.S. dollar equivalent before the transaction can be recorded. Extended credit terms are usually offered in foreign trade, and with the daily fluctuations of world currencies, the amount recorded is often different from the amount received or paid, resulting in a foreign exchange gain or loss.

2 Is GAAP universal? Explain. (pp. 824–25)

GAAP is hardly universal within the confines of the United States, let alone worldwide. Many differences exist between U.S. GAAP and the other industrialized countries of the world. Even more material differences may exist between the U.S. and nonindustrialized countries.

3 Should the records of foreign subsidiaries be converted to reflect GAAP before or after being translated into U.S. dollars? (p. 825)

This point has been much discussed, and the general consensus is that the foreign amounts should be first converted to U.S. GAAP, and then converted to U.S. dollars. In most cases the results will be the same, but in some areas the difference could be material. This area of discussion is covered in more advanced courses.

4 How is a balance sheet that is prepared using a different monetary unit converted to the U.S. dollar? (pp. 825–26)

If an entity's books are kept in the currency that the entity is operating in, then the assets and liabilities are translated at the current rate (the rate in effect on balance sheet date) and the paid-in capital amounts at their historic rate. Retained Earnings then becomes the balancing amount.

5 For a purchased subsidiary, should goodwill be determined in terms of the foreign currency unit and then converted to the U.S. dollar? (p. 826)

No. This question is similar to number 3. In a consolidation, the foreign subsidiary records should be first converted to U.S. dollars before any goodwill from consolidation is determined. The accounting records of the foreign subsidiary must be first converted to reflect U.S. GAAP before being converted to U.S. dollars.

6 What measurement problems are encountered when foreign transactions are denominated in terms of the U.S. dollar? (pp. 827–28)

No problems occur as long as the entity in question is a U.S. company. If the transaction is denominated in the U.S. dollar, it can be recorded just as any other transaction. The problems arise when transactions are denominated in other currencies that must be first converted into U.S. dollars. Then the company must account for the difference between the amount eventually paid and the amount that could have been paid on the transaction date.

7 Are foreign exchange rates static? Do they ever change? (pp. 828–29)

This is a very naive question. The exchange rates change hourly or more frequently, just as stock prices change. A study of international finance explores this very complex subject area.

8 Should exchange gains and losses arising from foreign transactions affect net income? (pp. 829–31)

Yes, transaction gains and losses have a direct effect on cash flow. If a payable is on the books at $50,000, and $42,000 is received in full satisfaction of the account, then a cash flow adjustment of $8,000 must be reflected in the income statement.

9 Should adjustments be made at the balance sheet date to receivables and payables arising from foreign transactions? (pp. 829–31)

Yes, even if the adjustment is not made because of an offsetting item on the books of a subsidiary, an adjustment should be made on the parent's balance sheet. The receivable or payable is first reported on the books at its U.S. dollar equivalent, and since that amount fluctuates, the balance sheet valuation should project the dollar equivalent on that date.

10 How can it be said that international and inflation accounting are related? Explain. (p. 831)

Since both types of accounting require the translation of one monetary unit to another, they are related. With international accounting, when a company controlled by a U.S. parent corporation keeps its general ledger in terms of another currency, the ledger must be first translated into U.S. dollars before consolidated financial statements can be prepared. Similarly, if the accounts of a U.S. company are to reflect the effects of general inflation, the balance sheet valuation for various items must be translated into current U.S. dollars before being added to one another.

11 What is the difference between general price indexes and specific price indexes? (p. 831)

The answer to this question is the same as if the question were posed, what is the difference between constant dollar and current cost accounting? Constant dollar accounting uses general price indexes to determine accounting valuations, while current cost uses specific price indexes to determine the values. The example of the hand-held calculator in the text fully explains this difference.

12 What are the current requirements for inflation-adjusted data? (p. 831)

No requirements exist today. When inflation was reaching two digits (above 9%) during the late 1970s and the early 1980s, the profession became concerned about the situation and began to require that certain information be included in the basic accounting information package. However, when the inflation rate quieted down during the mid-1980s, the requirements were dropped, although it was strongly suggested that the information be provided. When inflation again becomes a two-digit affair, the information will be again required.

13 Purchasing power gains will result during periods of inflation. Is this statement true or false? Explain. (pp. 836–38)

Purchasing power gains will result during periods of inflation when more monetary liabilities are carried during the year than monetary assets. The dollars paid back will not be worth as much as the dollars borrowed. The situation reverses itself when monetary assets are involved. The dollars that the entity receives will not be worth as much as the dollars involved in the original transaction.

14 Is it correct to say that accounting for inflation may be accomplished through either current cost or constant dollar accounting, since the end result is the same? (p. 838)

No! The two accounting methods are diametrically opposed. Current cost measures just that—how much the item would cost today if purchased today—while constant dollar accounting restates historical cost valuations into the number of today dollars that would have been required to purchase the item when it was acquired. The end results are not the same.

15 Current cost is an extension of historical cost, while constant dollar is a departure from GAAP. Is this statement true or false? Explain. (p. 840)

The reverse is true. Constant dollar accounting applies general price indexes to historical cost amounts (GAAP) to determine the dollar equivalent in constant dollars. Current cost accounting, however, is just that—the determination of the current cost of the item. Specific price indexes might be used, but the result is the same as the current cost of the item at hand. The constant dollar valuation is *not* a measure of the current value of the asset.

16 Does LIFO inventory costing result in an income statement that approximates current cost accounting? Explain. (pp. 840–41)

The answer depends on the rate at which prices are rising. If prices rose rapidly during the past year, but leveled off at year-end and into the next year, then LIFO inventory costing results in an income statement close to one completed under current cost. If prices continued to rise after the last purchase, then LIFO doesn't match current cost with revenue. LIFO comes much closer to current cost than FIFO does regarding the income statement, but as noted in Chapter 7, LIFO results in a poor balance sheet valuation for inventory.

17 If current costs are used in the accounts for long-term assets, will depreciation provide enough cash for the replacement of the assets? (p. 841)

Depreciation does not provide *any* cash flow. If management sets aside cash equal to the amount of depreciation on the income statement, then depreciation provides some cash for replacement. If management can estimate the amount necessary to replace the current operating asset, and sets that amount aside, instead of an amount based on historical cost, then depreciation could be said to provide cash for replacement.

18 How does realized net income under current cost accounting relate to net income determined under GAAP? (pp. 841–43)

As shown in the text, realized net income under current cost accounting is the same as net income determined under GAAP. The reason is that under current cost accounting, the realized holding gains are disclosed, while under historical cost these same gains are hidden in the GAAP income amount.

KEY TERMS

constant dollar accounting (p. 832)   An application of general price-level indexes to historical cost amounts in the financial statements. The result is the determination of a purchasing power gain or loss, and the expression of statement amounts in common dollars.

Consumer Price Index (CPI) (p. 832)   A U.S. Department of Labor index that prices a *market basket* of goods at various times during the year in order to determine the general inflation rate for the year.

current cost accounting (p. 840)   A departure from historical cost, where assets and liabilities are valued at their current value as determined by reference to market prices.

denominated in (p. 827)   A phrase used to describe the measurement or monetary unit in which a transaction takes place. Most transactions that take place are denominated in U.S. currency, but some are denominated in a foreign currency unit.

exchange rate (p. 825)   Refers to the factor used to convert a different monetary unit to the U.S. dollar. The monetary unit may be a foreign currency unit or a U.S. dollar unadjusted for inflation.

foreign exchange gains and losses (p. 829)   The results of foreign transactions when the amount eventually paid on the transaction differs from the original dollar amount of the transaction.

foreign transactions (p. 827)   Economic events denominated in a currency other than the U.S. dollar. If the transaction is other than cash, a measurement problem arises because of the daily fluctuation in the exchange rate of other currencies in relation to the U.S. dollar.

foreign translation (p. 824)   The area of accounting that revolves around a subsidiary or parent company operating in a foreign country and using a monetary unit other than the U.S. dollar.

general inflation (p. 832)   Measured by some general price index, such as the Consumer Price Index. Balance sheet valuations are converted, and the purchasing power gain or loss is determined by the difference between the converted and the unconverted amounts.

historic rate (p. 825)   The exchange rate that should be used to convert nonmonetary items on the balance sheet to their constant dollar equivalents. The rate in effect when a balance sheet item is recorded.

holding gains (p. 841)   The difference between the historical cost of an item and its current cost. If an item cost $5 and the current cost is $7, then the holding gain is $2.

holding gains net of inflation (p. 843)   The difference between the historical cost of an item and its current cost, adjusted for inflation. If an item cost $100 at the beginning of the year and $130 at the end, during which inflation was 10%, the holding gain would be $30, and the holding gain net of inflation would be $20 ($100 $\times$ 0.1 = $10; $100 + $10 = $110; $130 − $110 = $20).

international accounting (p. 825)   A subject area that encompasses the entire world. The many GAAP vary from country to country.

monetary items (p. 837)   Balance sheet asset or liability accounts that are fixed in terms of the number of monetary units to be received as a result of the account. For example, if the balance sheet amount for Cash is $50,000, that means the entity has $50,000.

monetary unit (p. 837)   A unit of measurement, not tied to any norm. The unit could be the French franc or the Russian ruble. The unit also could be the U.S. dollar at the beginning of the year compared to the end of the year.

nonmonetary items (p. 838)   All balance sheet assets and liabilities that are not monetary in nature. They are not fixed in terms of a number of monetary units to be received or paid and must be converted.

purchasing power gain (p. 836)   The increase in purchasing power due to holding more monetary liabilities than monetary assets during a period of inflation.

purchasing power loss (p. 833)   The decline in purchasing power due to holding more monetary assets than monetary liabilities during a period of inflation.

realized holding gains (p. 842)   Holding gains on items in inventory that have been sold during the year, or on depreciable assets used during the year and reflected in Depreciation Expense on a current cost basis.

unrealized holding gains (p. 842)   Holding gains on items in inventory that have not been sold during the year, or on depreciable assets held at year-end when current costs are recorded in the accounts.

SELF-TEST QUESTIONS FOR REVIEW   (Answers are at the end of this chapter.)

Q3, Q4

1. If a patent is recorded in the general ledger of a Canadian subsidiary of a U.S. parent at $1,500,000 Canadian, what is the U.S. dollar equivalent, if the amount includes capitalized research and development costs of $1,200,000 Canadian and the exchange rate is $1.30 Canadian or $.77 U.S.?
    (a) $1,950,000
    (b) $390,000
    (c) $1,155,000
    (d) $231,000

Q7, Q8

2. If the exchange rates between Canada and the United States are quoted as $1.25 Canadian or $.80 U.S., and you present a U.S. dollar to an Canadian bank, disregarding any service charges, you will receive Canadian currency with what face value?
    (a) This cannot be answered since the two rates cannot be determined one from the other.
    (b) $1.00 Canadian
    (c) $1.25 Canadian
    (d) $.80 Canadian

Q7, Q8

3. If the exchange rates between Canada and the United States are quoted as $1.25 Canadian or $.80 U.S., and you present a Canadian dollar to a U.S. bank, disregarding any service charges, you will receive U.S. currency with what face value?
    (a) This cannot be answered since one rate cannot be determined from the other.
    (b) $1.00 U.S.
    (c) $1.25 U.S.
    (d) $.80 U.S.

Q7, Q8

4. If the exchange rates between Canada and the United States are quoted as $1.25 Canadian or $.80 U.S., and you hold a receivable measured in Canadian currency, for each Canadian dollar, you will receive U.S. currency with what face value?
    (a) This cannot be answered since it is unknown when the receivable is due.
    (b) $1.00 U.S.
    (c) $1.25 U.S.
    (d) $.80 U.S.

Q7, Q8

5. If the exchange rates between Canada and the United States are quoted as $1.25 Canadian or $.80 U.S., and you have a payable measured in U.S. dollars, you will have to pay for each dollar owed the equivalent of what?
    (a) This cannot be answered since it is unknown when the receivable is due.
    (b) $1.00 U.S.
    (c) $1.25 U.S.
    (d) $.80 U.S.

For self-test question numbers 6 through 10, assume the following:

Historical CPI	100 (when all assets were acquired)
Beginning of Current Year CPI	120
Average CPI for Current Year	130
End of Current Year CPI	140

Q12, Q12, Q15

6. What fraction would be used to convert the amount of Cash on the year-end balance sheet to reflect constant dollars?
    (a) 140/120
    (b) 140/140
    (c) 140/100
    (d) 140/130
    (e) None of the above

Q11, Q12, Q15   7. What fraction would be used to convert the amount of bonds payable at the beginning of the year to reflect constant dollars?
    (a) 140/120
    (b) 140/140
    (c) 140/100
    (d) 140/130
    (e) None of the above

Q11, Q12, Q15   8. What fraction would be used to convert the amount of Land on the year-end balance sheet to reflect constant dollars?
    (a) 140/120
    (b) 140/140
    (c) 140/100
    (d) 140/130
    (e) None of the above

Q11, Q12, Q15   9. What fraction would be used to convert the amount of Depreciation Expense on the income statement to reflect constant dollars?
    (a) 140/120
    (b) 140/140
    (c) 140/100
    (d) 140/130
    (e) None of the above

Q11, Q12, Q15   10. What fraction would be used to convert the amount of Beginning Inventory on the income statement to constant dollars, assuming the inventory was purchased at the end of the year before?
    (a) 140/120
    (b) 140/140
    (c) 140/100
    (d) 140/130
    (e) None of the above

Q11, Q15   11. Which of the following measurement approaches yields the most useful information?
    (a) Constant dollar
    (b) Current cost
    (c) Current cost adjusted for inflation
    (d) Historical cost

DEMONSTRATION PROBLEM

Part A

Donaldson Co., which is a wholly owned subsidiary of USA Co., operates in Britain and keeps its records in terms of the pound sterling. The exchange rate at the end of the current year is P.S. .592 per $1 U.S. and $1.69 U.S. per pound sterling. The exchange rates when the controlling interest was acquired were P.S. .374 per $1 U.S. and $2.67 U.S. per pound sterling.

Required
Convert the following trial balance information in pound sterling to U.S. dollars:

Current Assets	P.S. 190,000	
Long-term Assets	234,000	
Current Liabilities		P.S. 135,000
Long-term Debt		100,000
Common Stock		89,000
Retained Earnings		100,000
Totals	P.S. 424,000	P.S. 424,000

Part B

USA Co. purchased some goods from its Japanese supplier on March 4, 19X1, for Y 3,456,703. The goods arrived today FOB destination with credit terms of net 180 days. The yen is trading today for $.00673 and Y 148.6. The exchange rates when payment is due are $.00543 and Y 184.2.

Required

Prepare the journal entry to record the purchase of the goods and the entry to record the subsequent payment for those goods.

Part C

Assume the following CPI rates:

December 31, 19X8	345
Average for 19X8	317
January 1, 19X5	289

Required

What is the constant dollar valuation for the following historical cost values found on the December 31, 19X8, balance sheet?

Sales during 19X8	$2,500,000
Cash	600,000
Accounts Receivable	150,000
Bonds Payable (issued Jan. 1, 19X5)	300,000
Common Stock (issued Jan. 1, 19X5)	400,000
Interest Expense	50,000

Part D

Assume the following:

- Land was purchased on January 1, 19X9, for $100,000.
- Inflation was 10% during 19X9.
- The current value of the land at December 31, 19X9, is $140,000.

Required

Determine the following:

1. The constant dollar value of the land as of December 31, 19X9

2. The holding gain based on current values

3. The holding gain after inflation

4. The gain that would be recorded under historical cost if the land were sold for $148,000 on February 1, 19X0

SOLUTION TO DEMONSTRATION PROBLEM

Part A

Donaldson Company
Worksheet to Convert Pound Sterling to U.S. Dollars

Account	Pound Sterling	Conversion Rate	U.S. Dollars
Current Assets	190,000	.592	112,480
Long-term Assets	234,000	.592	138,528
Total Assets			251,008
Current Liabilities	135,000	.592	79,920
Long-term Debt	100,000	.592	59,200
Common Stock	89,000	.374	33,286
Retained Earnings	100,000	(to balance)	78,602
Total Liabilities and Equity			251,008

Part B

Purchases	23,264	
Accounts Payable		23,264

To record the purchase of
merchandise invoiced at Y 3,456,703
when the exchange rate was $.00673.

Accounts Payable	23,264	
Cash		18,770
Foreign Exchange Gain (or loss)		4,494

To record the payment of Y 3,456,703
when the exchange rate was $.00543.

Part C

Constant Dollar Valuations

Account	Historical Cost	Conversion Factor	Constant Dollar
Sales	$2,500,000	345/317	$2,720,820
Cash	600,000	Monetary	600,000
Accounts Receivable	150,000	Monetary	150,000
Bonds Payable	300,000	Monetary	300,000
Common Stock	400,000	345/289	477,509
Interest Expense	50,000	345/317	54,416

Part D

1. $110,000 [($100,000 × 10%) + $100,000]

2. $40,000 ($140,000 − $100,000)

3. $30,000 ($140,000 − $110,000)

4. $48,000 ($148,000 − $100,000)

DISCUSSION QUESTIONS

Q18-1   Why are international and inflation accounting discussed in the same chapter?

Q18-2   What is the method currently used to convert currencies of different values into a common value?

Q18-3   What other possible methods could be used to convert currencies of differing monetary values?

Q18-4   What needs to be done if the currencies are from countries with different generally accepted accounting principles?

Q18-5   Must all foreign subsidiaries be consolidated with their U.S. parent?

Q18-6   What measurement problem exists when foreign transactions are measured in monetary units other than the recording company?

Q18-7   Should exchange gains and losses from foreign transactions be recorded on the income statement? Why?

Q18-8   Should foreign exchange losses be reported separately from exchange gains?

Q18-9   What adjusting entries are necessary at the end of a fiscal year if any receivables or payables are denominated in foreign currencies?

Q18-10   Should the records of a foreign subsidiary be kept in terms of the U.S. dollar to eliminate the need for a foreign translation, and in some cases, to eliminate the problems caused by foreign transactions?

Q18-11   Accountants make the assumption that the U.S. monetary unit, the dollar, has a stable value. Is this a valid assumption? Has it ever been a valid assumption?

Q18-12   Would you rather have a dollar now or a dollar a year from now? Answer in terms of inflation and not the time value of money.

Q18-13   Are the results from applying constant dollar accounting comparable to the results obtained under current cost?

Q18-14   Define a monetary item. Are monetary items assets or liabilities?

Q18-15   Purchasing power losses occur during a period of inflation. Is this a true statement? Why?

Q18-16   What is the major drawback with constant dollar accounting?

Q18-17   Why has current cost accounting not been accepted as GAAP?

Q18-18   What is wrong with historical cost accounting?

Q18-19   Is there a measure of current cost net income that results in the same information as historical cost? Explain.

Q18-20   Should income taxes be based on accounting for net income as defined under GAAP? Why?

DISCUSSION CASE

Saguaro Computers, Inc.

Q11, Q14, Q15

The following income statement and worksheet information for Saguaro Computers, Inc., is taken from the chapter material.

Saguaro Computers, Inc.
Income Statement
For The Year Ended December 31, 19X5

Revenue		
Sales		$42,000
Cost of Goods Sold		
Beginning Inventory	$ 6,000	
Purchases	28,000	
Goods Available for Sale	$34,000	
Ending Inventory	9,000	
Total Cost of Goods Sold		25,000
Gross profit		$17,000
Operating and Financing Expenses		
Selling and Administrative Expenses	$ 3,000	
Depreciation Expense	10,000	
Interest Expense	1,000	
Income Tax Expense	1,000	
Total Expenses		15,000
Net Income		$ 2,000

Saguaro Computers, Inc.
Worksheet to Convert Historical Dollars to Constant Dollars

Account	Historical Cost	Conversion Factor	Constant Dollars
Sales	$42,000	180/170	$44,500*
Cost of Goods Sold			
Beginning Inventory	$ 6,000	180/150	$ 7,200
Purchases	28,000	180/170	29,700
Ending Inventory	9,000	180/180	9,000
Total Cost of Goods Sold	25,000		27,900
Selling and Administrative Expenses	3,000	180/170	3,200
Depreciation Expense	10,000	180/100	18,000
Interest Expense	1,000	180/170	1,700
Income Tax Expense	1,000	180/170	1,700
Net Income	$ 2,000		$ (8,000)

*Rounded to the nearest $100.

Required

Discuss the significance of the constant dollar amounts versus the historical amounts on the income statement.

EXERCISES

E18-1 through E18-4 are based on the following data:

Cash	$100,000
Land	200,000
Depreciation Expense	50,000

Salaries Expense	$ 30,000
Common Stock	300,000
Retained Earnings	150,000

These accounts are measured in Canadian dollars. Assume the following exchange rates:

	Canadian	U.S.
Balance Sheet Date	1.45	.69
Average for Current Year	1.30	.77
Land Purchased	1.25	.80
Depreciable Assets Purchased	1.20	.83
Common Stock Issued	1.05	.95
Retained Earnings Recorded	Fluctuated	Fluctuated

Converting foreign to U.S. dollars (Q4)

E18-1

Required

What is the U.S. dollar equivalent for the following accounts?

1. Cash
2. Land
3. Depreciation Expense
4. Salary Expense
5. Common Stock
6. Retained Earnings

Converting U.S. dollars to foreign (Q4)

E18-2   Assume that the amounts in the accounts listed are measured in terms of U.S. dollars rather than Canadian dollars.

Required

What is the Canadian dollar equivalent for the following accounts?

1. Cash
2. Land
3. Depreciation Expense
4. Salary Expense
5. Common Stock
6. Retained Earnings

Converting historical cost values to constant dollars (Q4)

E18-3   Assume that the amounts given as Canadian exchange rates (1.45, 1.30, 1.25, 1.20, and 1.05) are instead general price indexes at the various dates.

Required

What is the constant dollar valuation for the following accounts?

1. Cash
2. Land
3. Depreciation Expense
4. Salary Expense

5. Common Stock

6. Retained Earnings

Converting historical cost values to current costs (Q4)

E18-4 Assume that the amounts given as Canadian exchange rates (1.45, 1.30, 1.25, 1.20, and 1.05) are instead specific price indexes at the various dates.

Required

What is the current cost valuation for the following accounts?

1. Cash

2. Land

3. Depreciation Expense

4. Salary Expense

5. Common Stock

6. Retained Earnings

Consolidated goodwill, foreign subsidiary (Q5)

E18-5 The following information is available:

	Canadian	U.S.
Book Value of Assets	$400,000	
Book Value of Liabilities	150,000	
Acquisition of 100% of Canadian Company		$300,000
Current Exchange Rate	1.25	.80
Fair Market Value of Assets		350,000
Fair Market Value of Liabilities		120,000

Required

Determine the amount of goodwill that will be recorded on the consolidated balance sheet of the combined companies at the date of acquisition.

E18-6 through E18-9 are based on the following assumptions: A Canadian company sold some merchandise to a U.S. company in the amount of $100,000 U.S. with credit terms of net 60. On that date, the exchange rates were $1.70 Canadian or $.59 U.S., and 60 days later the exchange rates were $1.50 Canadian and $.67 U.S.

Foreign transactions, U.S. dollars, U.S. company (Q1, Q6, Q8)

E18-6

Required

What journal entries would the U.S. company make to record the purchase and payment for this transaction?

Foreign transactions, U.S. dollars, foreign company (Q1, Q6, Q8)

E18-7

Required

What journal entries would the Canadian company make to record the sale and payment for this transaction?

For E18-8 and E18-9 assume the same facts except that the transaction was denominated in Canadian dollars.

Foreign transactions, foreign currency, U.S. company (Q1, Q6, Q8)

E18-8

Required

What journal entries would the U.S. company make to record the purchase and payment for this transaction?

Foreign transactions, currency, company (Q1, Q6, Q8)

E18-9

Required

What entries would the Canadian company make to record the sale and payment for this transaction?

Purchasing power gain or loss, monetary assets same as liabilities (Q13)

E18-10 The following entry records the only transaction that takes place during the year:

Building	500,000	
Common Stock		500,000

Required

If the inflation rate for the current year was 8%, what is the purchasing power gain or loss to the entity?

Purchasing power gain or loss, monetary assets in excess of liabilities (Q13)

E18-11 The following entry records the only transaction that takes place during the year:

Cash	500,000	
Common Stock		500,000

Required

If the inflation rate for the current year was 8%, what is the purchasing power gain or loss to the entity if the cash was not invested?

Purchasing power gain or loss, monetary assets less than liabilities (Q13)

E18-12 The following entry records the only transaction that takes place during the year:

Land	500,000	
Bonds Payable		500,000

Required

If the inflation rate for the current year was 8%, what is the purchasing power gain or loss to the entity?

Holding gains and holding gains net of inflation (Q18)

E18-13 Assume the following:

A parcel of land is acquired on January 1, 19X1, at a cost of $50,000. The inflation rate for the next 12 months is 7%, and the land has a current value at the end of the 12 months of $78,000.

Required

Determine the following:

1. Constant dollar valuation at the end of 12 months
2. The holding gain for the 12 months
3. The holding gain net of inflation for the 12 months
4. The gain measured by historical cost if the land is sold at the end of the 12 months for market price.

PROBLEMS

Foreign translation, yen to dollars (Q4)

P18-1 USA Co. owns a controlling interest in Japan Co. and must therefore prepare consolidated financial statements. Japan Co. is located in Tokyo and the general ledger reflects the Japanese yen (Y). The following exchange rates were in effect on the various dates listed:

	Yen per Dollar	Dollars per Yen
Balance Sheet Date	148.60	.00673
Average for Past Year	125.7	.00796
Beginning of Current Year	107.5	.00930
Inventory Purchased	112.6	.00888
Buildings Purchased	214.5	.00466
Land Purchased	262.0	.00382
Common Stock Issued	278.2	.00359

Japan Co. showed the following trial balance information on the date USA Co. bought the controlling interest:

Cash	Y 1,000,000	
Accounts Receivable	500,000	
Inventory	300,000	
Land	700,000	
Buildings	1,500,000	
Accounts Payable		Y 350,000
Bonds Payable		1,700,000
Common Stock		900,000
Retained Earnings		1,050,000
Totals	Y 4,000,000	Y 4,000,000

Required
Prepare a trial balance for Japan Co. in terms of U.S. dollars so the consolidated financial statements may be prepared.

Foreign transactions (Q1, Q6, Q8)

P18-2 USA Co. buys its goods directly from its French supplier, and sells most of its goods to companies in the U.S., but sometimes to customers in Japan. The transactions between USA and its French supplier are all denominated in the French franc, while invoices to customers in Japan are denominated in the yen as an accommodation.

The following exchange rates were in effect on the various dates listed:

Date	Francs/Dollar	Dollars/Franc	Yen/Dollar	Dollars/Yen
Jan. 1, 19X5	F 5.71	$.17512	Y 148.6	$.00673
June 1, 19X5	6.00	.16667	160	.00625
Sept 1, 19X5	6.25	.16000	175	.00571
Dec 31, 19X5	6.68	.14970	200	.00500

During 19X5 the following transactions took place:

Jan. 1 USA purchased merchandise from its French supplier invoiced at F 100,000 with credit terms of net 150 days.

June 1 USA paid F 100,000 to its French supplier.
USA sold merchandise to a customer in Japan for Y 1,000,000, with credit terms of net 90 days.

Sept. 1   USA received a draft for Y 1,000,000 from its Japanese customer.
USA purchased merchandise from its French supplier invoiced at F 200,000 with credit terms of net 180 days.

Required

Prepare all journal entries required to record these transactions, including any necessary adjusting entries at December 31, 19X5.

Constant dollar accounting (Q11, Q14)

P18-3   The income statement and balance sheet are presented here for Colfax Corp. for the year ended December 31, 19X7.

Income Statement
For the Year Ended December 31, 19X7

Revenue		
Sales		$200,000
Cost of Goods Sold		
Beginning Inventory	$ 20,000	
Purchases	150,000	
Cost of Goods Available	$170,000	
Ending Inventory	40,000	
Total Cost of Goods Sold		130,000
Gross Profit		$ 70,000
Operating Expenses		
Salaries Expense	15,000	
Rent Expense	8,000	
Utilities Expense	2,000	
Depreciation Expense—Building	15,000	
Depreciation Expense—Equipment	10,000	
Total Operating Expenses		50,000
Income (before income tax)		$ 20,000
Income Tax Expense		8,000
Net Income		$ 12,000

Balance Sheet
December 31, 19X7

Assets

Current Assets			
Cash		$20,000	
Accounts Receivable		15,000	
Merchandise Inventory		40,000	
Total Current Assets			$ 75,000
Long-term Assets			
Land		10,000	
Buildings	$100,000		
Less: Accumulated Depreciation	60,000	40,000	
Equipment	$ 78,000		
Less: Accumulated Depreciation	34,000	44,000	
Total Long-term Assets			94,000
Total Assets			$169,000

(continued)

Liabilities

Current Liabilities

Accounts Payable	$37,000	
Income Tax Payable	8,000	
Total Current Liabilities		$ 45,000

Long-term Liabilities

Bonds Payable		50,000
Total Liabilities		$ 95,000

Stockholders' Equity

Common Stock	6,000	
Retained Earnings	68,000	
Total Stockholders' Equity		74,000
Total Liabilities and Stockholders' Equity		$169,000

The following is a listing of the CPI on various dates:

December 31, 19X7	234
Average for Year	208
January 1, 19X7	182
Common Stock Issued	100
Beginning Inventory Purchased	175
Land Purchased	105
Buildings Purchased	110
Equipment Purchased	135
Bonds Issued	142

Required

1. Prepare a worksheet to convert the income statement to constant dollars, assuming a purchasing power gain of $5,000, and that the Ending Inventory came from average purchases during the year.

2. Prepare a worksheet to convert the balance sheet to constant dollars as of December 31, 19X7.

3. What information does the problem contain that would support a purchasing power gain?

Current cost income statement (Q18)

P18-4   The following transactions took place during 19X4 at Floor Bros. Printing Co.:

■ Purchased 1,000 desk units at $750 each

■ Sold 675 of the desk units for $1,200 each, including installation

■ At December 31, 19X4, the current replacement cost of the desk units in FBP's market area is $900.

■ Operating expenses of $282,000 were paid during the year.

Required

1. Prepare a current cost income statement for the year 19X4 for Floor Bros.

2. Prepare a historical cost income statement for the year 19X4 for FBP.

3. Comment on the results.

ALTERNATE PROBLEMS

Foreign translation,
dollars to yen (Q4)

AP18-1   Japan Co. owns a controlling interest in USA Co. and must therefore prepare consolidated financial statements. USA Co. is located in Seattle and the general ledger reflects the U.S. dollar. The following exchange rates were in effect on the various dates listed:

	Yen per Dollar	Dollars per Yen
Balance Sheet Date	148.60	.00673
Average for Past Year	125.7	.00796
Beginning of Current Year	107.5	.00930
Inventory Purchased	112.6	.00888
Buildings Purchased	214.5	.00466
Land Purchased	262.0	.00382
Common Stock Issued	278.2	.00359

USA Co. showed the following trial balance information on the date Japan Co. bought the controlling interest:

Cash	$1,000	
Accounts Receivable	500	
Inventory	300	
Land	700	
Buildings	1,500	
Accounts Payable		$ 350
Bonds Payable		1,700
Common Stock		900
Retained Earnings		1,050
Totals	$4,000	$4,000

Required
Prepare a trial balance for USA Co. in terms of the Japanese yen so the consolidated financial statements may be prepared.

Foreign transactions
(Q1, Q6, Q8)

AP18-2   French Co. buys its goods directly from its Japanese supplier, and sells most its goods to companies in France, but sometimes to customers in the United States. The transactions between French Co. and its Japanese supplier are all denominated in the Japanese yen, while invoices to customers in the United States are denominated in the U.S. dollar as an accommodation.

The following exchange rates were in effect on the various dates listed:

Date	Francs/Dollar	Dollars/Franc	Yen/Franc	Francs/Yen
Jan. 1, 19X5	F 5.71	$.17512	Y 26.002	F .03843
June 1, 19X5	6.00	.16667	24.567	.04071
Sept. 1, 19X5	6.25	.16000	28.816	.03070
Dec. 31, 19X5	6.68	.14970	23.119	.04325

During 19X5 the following transactions took place:

Jan. 1   French Co. purchased merchandise from its Japanese supplier invoiced at Y 1,000,000 with credit terms of net 150 days.

June 1   French Co. paid Y 1,000,000 to its Japanese supplier.
French Co. sold merchandise to a customer in the United States for $100,000, with credit terms of net 90 days.

Sept. 1   French Co. received a draft for $100,000 from its U.S. customer.
French Co. purchased merchandise from its Japanese supplier invoiced at
Y 1,800,000 with credit terms of net 180 days.

Required

Prepare all journal entries required to record these transactions on the books of French Co.,
including any necessary adjusting entries at December 31, 19X5.

Constant dollar
accounting (Q11, Q14)

AP18-3   The income statement and balance sheet are presented here for Auburn Corp. for
the year ended December 31, 19X7.

Income Statement
For the Year Ended December 31, 19X7

Revenue		
Sales		$200,000
Cost of Goods Sold		
Beginning Inventory	$ 20,000	
Purchases	150,000	
Cost of Goods Available	$170,000	
Ending Inventory	40,000	
Total Cost of Goods Sold		130,000
Gross Profit		$ 70,000
Operating Expenses		
Salaries Expense	15,000	
Rent Expense	8,000	
Utilities Expense	2,000	
Depreciation Expense—Building	15,000	
Depreciation Expense—Equipment	10,000	
Total Operating Expenses		50,000
Income (before income tax)		$ 20,000
Income Tax Expense		8,000
Net Income		$ 12,000

Balance Sheet
December 31, 19X7

Assets

Current Assets			
Cash		$20,000	
Accounts Receivable		15,000	
Merchandise Inventory		40,000	
Total Current Assets			$ 75,000
Long-term Assets			
Land		10,000	
Buildings	$100,000		
Less: Accumulated Depreciation	60,000	40,000	
Equipment	$ 78,000		
Less: Accumulated Depreciation	34,000	44,000	
Total Long-term Assets			94,000
Total Assets			$169,000

(*continued*)

Liabilities

Current Liabilities

Accounts Payable	$37,000	
Income Tax Payable	8,000	
Total Current Liabilities		$ 45,000

Long-term Liabilities

Bonds Payable		50,000
Total Liabilities		$ 95,000

Stockholders' Equity

Common Stock	6,000	
Retained Earnings	68,000	
Total Stockholders' Equity		74,000
Total Liabilities and Stockholders' Equity		$169,000

The following is a listing of the CPI on various dates:

December 31, 19X7	162
Average for Year	186
January 1, 19X7	210
Common Stock Issued	125
Beginning Inventory Purchased	200
Land Purchased	120
Buildings Purchased	115
Equipment Purchased	110
Bonds Issued	167

Required

1. Prepare a worksheet to convert the income statement to constant dollars, assuming a purchasing power loss of $5,000, and that the Ending Inventory came from average purchases during the year.

2. Prepare a worksheet to convert the balance sheet to constant dollars as of December 31, 19X7.

3. What information does the problem contain that would support a purchasing power loss?

Current cost income statement (Q18)

AP18-4   The following transactions took place during 19X4 at Ceiling Tile Co.:

- Purchased 500 wall units at $1,750 each

- Sold 234 of the wall units for $2,350 each, including installation

- At December 31, 19X4, the current replacement cost of the wall units in CT's market area is $1,400.

- Operating expenses of $382,000 were paid during the year.

Required

1. Prepare a current cost income statement for the year 19X4 for Ceiling Tile.

2. Prepare a historical cost income statement for the year 19X4 for CT.

3. Comment on the results.

DECISION PROBLEM

Refer to E18-13. Determine the required amounts and comment on the various items and how they relate or do not relate to each other. The data and the requirements are reprinted here as a convenience.

A parcel of land is acquired on January 1, 19X1, at a cost of $50,000. The inflation rate for the next 12 months is 7%, and the land has a current value at the end of the 12 months of $78,000.

Required
Determine the following:

1. Constant dollar valuation at the end of 12 months
2. The holding gain for the 12 months
3. The holding gain net of inflation for the 12 months
4. The gain measured by historical cost if the land is sold at the end of the 12 months for market price.

ANSWERS TO SELF-TEST QUESTIONS

1. **(d)** Before foreign general ledgers can be converted to U.S. dollars, the values must be first converted to U.S. GAAP. Therefore, the patent would have to be reduced by the following journal entry:

Retained Earnings	1,200,000	
Patent		1,200,000

To write off the cost of research and development capitalized under Canadian GAAP.

This entry would be recorded on a worksheet prepared to convert Canadian GAAP to U.S. GAAP and not posted to the Canadian general ledger. The remaining $300,000 Canadian would then be converted to U.S. dollars using the $.77 exchange rate: $300,000 C × $.77 = $231,000.

2. **(c)** The exchange rates as stated show that a U.S. dollar is worth $1.25 Canadian, so you would receive $1.25. Canadians would have to pay $1.25 C to receive one U.S. dollar ($1.25 C × $.80 = $1.00 U.S.).

3. **(d)** A Canadian dollar would be worth $.80 U.S., given the exchange rates. A U.S. citizen would have to pay $.80 U.S. for one Canadian dollar ($.88 × $1.25 C = $1.00 C).

4. **(a)** Since when the receivable is due or what the exchange rate will be on the date it is due are unknown, the U.S. dollar equivalent cannot be determined. The receivable would be valued at 80% of book value if this were a balance sheet date.

5. **(b)** Since the payable is measured in U.S. dollars, the recorded value is the amount to be paid.

6. **(b)** Since cash is a monetary asset, it already reflects constant dollars.

7. **(b)** Since bonds payable are a monetary liability, the recorded amount already reflects constant dollars.

8. **(c)** The land was purchased when the index was 100, and the year-end index is 140.

9. **(c)**   The depreciable assets were purchased when the index was 100; therefore, the depreciation of those assets would be based on an index of 100, and the current index is 140.

10. **(a)**   The beginning inventory was purchased when the index was 120, and the year-end index is 140.

11.   This question really has no answer. If "useful" is defined as *relevant,* then the answer would be *b* or *c*, depending on the level of inflation. If "useful" is defined as *reliable,* then the answer would have to be *d.*

PART VI
FINANCIAL STATEMENT ANALYSIS PROBLEM

Turn to the excerpts (pp. 889–906) from the annual report of United Telecom (UT) for the year ended December 31, 1989, and answer the following questions:

1 Assume the following:

- Monetary assets include cash, all receivables, and the refund from the Internal Revenue Service.
- Monetary liabilities include all liabilities.
- Inflation increased 10 points on the index each year, starting in 1985 (index for 1985 = 100).
- The change in the net monetary position during any year took place at the average inflation rate for the year. *Note to instructor:* You may explain this calculation based on the next example.

Determine the purchasing power gain or loss for 1987, 1988, and 1989. The calculation for 1985–1986 follows as an example.

	1985	1986
Monetary Assets	$ 624	$ 642
Monetary Liabilities	(4,031)	(4,609)
Net Monetary Position	(3,407)	(3,967)
Net Monetary Position, Jan. 1, 1986	(3,407)	110/100 = (3,748)
Change during the Year	(560)	110/105 = (587)
Total		(4,335)
Net Monetary Position, Dec. 31, 1986	(3,967)	(3,967)
Purchasing Power Gain		368

Note that once the net monetary position is known for the beginning and end of each year, and an assumption is made regarding when the change took place during the year, then the purchasing power gain or loss can be determined. Can you explain why a purchasing power gain occurred, rather than a loss?

2 Assume that the net income under GAAP was equal to the constant-dollar net income before the purchasing power gain or loss for each year. Was the purchasing power gain or loss determined in question 1 material in relation to the GAAP net income for the years 1987 through 1989?

3 Assume that UT is a Canadian subsidiary of a U.S. corporation that was to be consolidated with the U.S. parent for the year ending December 31, 1989. The Canadian dollar was trading at $.84 U.S. while the U.S. dollar was trading at $1.19 Canadian.

(a) If the U.S. parent used the LIFO inventory and wanted to convert UT's inventory reflecting LIFO to U.S. dollars, what adjustments to inventory must be made before conversion to the U.S. dollar? The LIFO valuation of the inventory for 1989 was $109.6 million Canadian.

(b) Once the adjustment in *a* was made, how would the Canadian dollar amount for inventory be converted into U.S. dollars?

(c) If the total current liabilities are all payable in U.S. dollars, but are shown on the UT balance sheet at their Canadian dollar equivalent, at what amount will

UT's current liabilities be reported on the consolidated balance sheet of UT's U.S. parent, assuming that none of the liabilities are intercompany?

(d) If UT's accounts payable at December 31, 1989, are all payable in U.S. dollars, at what amount will the accounts payable appear on the consolidated balance sheet for UT's parent as of December 31, 1989, assuming that all of the accounts are due to the U.S. parent? What amount of foreign exchange gain or loss will appear on UT's separate income statement, assuming the liabilities were incurred when the Canadian dollar was trading for $1.25 U.S.?

(e) Assume UT's long-term debt is all payable in Canadian dollars, and 50% is payable to the U.S. parent. How will the long-term debt appear in the consolidated balance sheet of the U.S. parent?

APPENDIX A

ETHICS

Appendix A contains the American Institute of Certified Public Accountants (AICPA) Code of Professional Conduct. This code is the primary statement of ethical responsibility for Certified Public Accountants. (From 1973—when AICPA rules were collected and codified—to 1988, the AICPA called the earlier version of this selection simply the Code of Ethics.) The Code sets out the accounting profession's responsibilities to clients, colleagues, and the public.

Note that the AICPA Code contains two sections; Principles and Rules. Principles are general and aspirational. Rules are specific, and the Code requires adherence by all members.

The two parts of the Code suggest two aspects of ethical decision making. First, sometimes ethical issues are readily apparent. Some situations involve a clear decision between right and wrong, for example. Should an accountant conspire to misstate earnings, for example, to benefit a client? The answer is clearly no. Specific rules help accountants navigate known ethical dilemmas—when they are recognized as such.

But sometimes accountants cannot find a rule specific to the situation at hand. Or in some complex situations accountants may need to analyze transactions in depth to determine whether or not an ethical issue exists. If accountants cannot find a rule governing questionable behavior, they are responsible for making a vigorous effort to try. General principles can provide some guidance when the ethics of a situation are unclear.

The Code itself moves from the general (Principles) to the specific (Rules), as shown.

AICPA CODE OF PROFESSIONAL CONDUCT

As adopted January 12, 1988

Introduction

COMPOSITION, APPLICABILITY, AND COMPLIANCE

The Code of Professional Conduct of the American Institute of Certified Public Accountants consists of two sections—(1) the Principles and (2) the Rules. The Principles provide the framework for the Rules, which govern the performance of professional services by members. The Council of the American Institute of Certified Public Accountants is authorized to designate bodies to promulgate technical standards under the Rules, and the bylaws require adherence to those Rules and standards.

The Code of Professional Conduct was adopted by the membership to provide guidance and rules to all members—those in public practice, in industry, in government, and in education—in the performance of their professional responsibilities.

Compliance with the Code of Professional Conduct, as with all standards in an open society, depends primarily on members' understanding and voluntary actions, secondarily on reinforcement by peers and public opinion, and ultimately on disciplinary proceedings, when necessary, against members who fail to comply with the Rules.

Section 1—Principles

PREAMBLE

Membership in the American Institute of Certified Public Accountants is voluntary. By accepting membership, a certified public accountant assumes an obligation of self-discipline above and beyond the requirements of laws and regulations.

These Principles of the Code of Professional Conduct of the American Institute of Certified Public Accountants express the profession's recognition of its responsibilities to the public, to clients, and to colleagues. They guide members in the performance of their professional responsibilities and express the basic tenets of ethical and professional conduct. The Principles call for an unswerving commitment to honorable behavior, even at the sacrifice of personal advantage.

ARTICLE I
Responsibilities

In carrying out their responsibilities as professionals, members should exercise sensitive professional and moral judgments in all their activities.

As professionals, certified public accountants perform an essential role in society. Consistent with that role, members of the American Institute of Certified Public Accountants have responsibilities to all those who use their professional services. Members also have a continuing responsibility to cooperate with each other to improve the art of accounting, maintain the public's confidence, and carry out the profession's special responsibilities for self-governance. The collective efforts of all members are required to maintain and enhance the traditions of the profession.

ARTICLE II
The Public Interest

> Members should accept the obligation to act in a way that will serve the public interest, honor the public trust, and demonstrate commitment to professionalism.

A distinguishing mark of a profession is acceptance of its responsibility to the public. The accounting profession's public consists of clients, credit grantors, governments, employers, investors, the business and financial community, and others who rely on the objectivity and integrity of certified public accountants to maintain the orderly functioning of commerce. This reliance imposes a public interest responsibility on certified public accountants. The public interest is defined as the collective well-being of the community of people and institutions the profession serves.

In discharging their professional responsibilities, members may encounter conflicting pressures from among each of those groups. In resolving those conflicts, members should act with integrity, guided by the precept that when members fulfill their responsibility to the public, clients' and employers' interests are best served.

Those who rely on certified public accountants expect them to discharge their responsibilities with integrity, objectivity, due professional care, and a genuine interest in serving the public. They are expected to provide quality services, enter into fee arrangements, and offer a range of services—all in a manner that demonstrates a level of professionalism consistent with these Principles of the Code of Professional Conduct.

All who accept membership in the American Institute of Certified Public Accountants commit themselves to honor the public trust. In return for the faith that the public reposes in them, members should seek continually to demonstrate their dedication to professional excellence.

ARTICLE III
Integrity

> To maintain and broaden public confidence, members should perform all professional responsibilities with the highest sense of integrity.

Integrity is an element of character fundamental to professional recognition. It is the quality from which the public trust derives and the benchmark against which a member must ultimately test all decisions.

Integrity requires a member to be, among other things, honest and candid within the constraints of client confidentiality. Service and the public trust should not be subordinated to personal gain and advantage. Integrity can accommodate the inadvertent error and the honest difference of opinion; it cannot accommodate deceit or subordination of principle.

Integrity is measured in terms of what is right and just. In the absence of specific rules, standards, or guidance, or in the face of conflicting opinions, a member should test decisions and deeds by asking: "Am I doing what a person of integrity would do? Have I retained my integrity?" Integrity requires a member to observe both the form and the spirit of technical and ethical standards; circumvention of those standards constitutes subordination of judgment.

Integrity also requires a member to observe the principles of objectivity and independence and of due care.

ARTICLE IV
Objectivity and Independence

A member should maintain objectivity and be free of conflicts of interest in discharging professional responsibilities. A member in public practice should be independent in fact and appearance when providing auditing and other attestation services.

Objectivity is a state of mind, a quality that lends value to a member's services. It is a distinguishing feature of the profession. The principle of objectivity imposes the obligation to be impartial, intellectually honest, and free of conflicts of interest. Independence precludes relationships that may appear to impair a member's objectivity in rendering attestation services.

Members often serve multiple interests in many different capacities and must demonstrate their objectivity in varying circumstances. Members in public practice render attest, tax, and management advisory services. Other members prepare financial statements in the employment of others, perform internal auditing services, and serve in financial and management capacities in industry, education, and government. They also educate and train those who aspire to admission into the profession. Regardless of service or capacity, members should protect the integrity of their work, maintain objectivity, and avoid any subordination of their judgment.

For a member in public practice, the maintenance of objectivity and independence requires a continuing assessment of client relationships and public responsibility. Such a member who provides auditing and other attestation services should be independent in fact and appearance. In providing all other services, a member should maintain objectivity and avoid conflicts of interest.

Although members not in public practice cannot maintain the appearance of independence, they nevertheless have the responsibility to maintain objectivity in rendering professional services. Members employed by others to prepare financial statements or to perform auditing, tax, or consulting services are charged with the same responsibility for objectivity as members in public practice and must be scrupulous in their application of generally accepted accounting principles and candid in all their dealings with members in public practice.

ARTICLE V
Due Care

A member should observe the profession's technical and ethical standards, strive continually to improve competence and the quality of services, and discharge professional responsibility to the best of the member's ability.

The quest for excellence is the essence of due care. Due care requires a member to discharge professional responsibilities with competence and diligence. It imposes the obligation to perform professional services to the best of a member's ability with concern for the best interest of those for whom the services are performed and consistent with the profession's responsibility to the public.

Competence is derived from a synthesis of education and experience. It begins with a mastery of the common body of knowledge required for designation as a certified public accountant. The maintenance of competence requires a commitment to learning and professional improvement that must continue throughout a member's professional life. It is a member's individual responsibility. In all engagements and in all responsibilities, each member should undertake to achieve a level of competence that will assure that the quality of the member's services meets the high level of professionalism required by these Principles.

Competence represents the attainment and maintenance of a level of understanding and knowledge that enables a member to render services with facility and acumen. It also establishes the limitations of a member's capabilities by dictating that consultation or referral may be required when a professional engagement exceeds the personal competence of a member or a member's firm. Each member is responsible for assessing his or her own competence—of evaluating whether education, experience, and judgment are adequate for the responsibility to be assumed.

Members should be diligent in discharging responsibilities to clients, employers, and the public. Diligence imposes the responsibility to render services promptly and carefully, to be thorough, and to observe applicable technical and ethical standards.

Due care requires a member to plan and supervise adequately any professional activity for which he or she is responsible.

ARTICLE VI
Scope and Nature of Services

A member in public practice should observe the Principles of the Code of Professional Conduct in determining the scope and nature of services to be provided.

The public interest aspect of certified public accountants' services requires that such services be consistent with acceptable professional behavior for certified public accountants. Integrity requires that service and the public trust not be subordinated to personal gain and advantage. Objectivity and independence require that members be free from conflicts of interest in discharging professional responsibilities. Due care requires that services be provided with competence and diligence.

Each of these Principles should be considered by members in determining whether or not to provide specific services in individual circumstances. In some instances, they may represent an overall constraint on the nonaudit services that might be offered to a specific client. No hard-and-fast rules can be developed to help members reach these judgments, but they must be satisfied that they are meeting the spirit of the Principles in this regard.

In order to accomplish this, members should

- Practice in firms that have in place internal quality-control procedures to ensure that services are competently delivered and adequately supervised.

- Determine, in their individual judgments, whether the scope and nature of other services provided to an audit client would create a conflict of interest in the performance of the audit function for that client.

- Assess, in their individual judgments, whether an activity is consistent with their role as professionals (for example, Is such activity a reasonable extension or variation of existing services offered by the member or others in the profession?).

Section II—Rules

APPLICABILITY
The bylaws of the American Institute of Certified Public Accountants require that members adhere to the Rules of the Code of Professional Conduct. Members must be prepared to justify departures from these Rules.

Interpretation Addressing the Applicability of the AICPA Code of Professional Conduct   For purposes of the Applicability Section of the Code, a "member" is a member or international associate of the American Institute of CPAs.

1. The Rules of Conduct that follow apply to all professional services performed except (a) where the wording of the rule indicates otherwise and (b) that a member who is practicing outside the United States will not be subject to discipline for departing from any of the rules stated herein as long as the member's conduct is in accord with the rules of the organized accounting profession in the country in which he or she is practicing. However, where a member's name is associated with financial statements under circumstances that would entitle the reader to assume that United States practices were followed, the member must comply with the requirements of Rules 202 and 203.

2. A member may be held responsible for compliance with the rules by all persons associated with him or her in the practice of public accounting who are either under the member's supervision or are the member's partners or shareholders in the practice.

3. A member shall not permit others to carry out on his or her behalf, either with or without compensation, acts, which if carried out by the member, would place the member in violation of the rules.

DEFINITIONS

[Pursuant to its authority under the bylaws ... to interpret the Code of Professional Conduct, the Professional Ethics Executive Committee has issued the following definitions of terms appearing in the code effective November 30, 1989.]

Client   A client is any person or entity, other than the member's employer, that engages a member or a member's firm to perform professional services or a person or entity with respect to which professional services are performed. The term "employer" for these purposes does not include those entities engaged in the practice of public accounting.

Council   The Council of the American Institute of Certified Public Accountants.

Enterprise   For purposes of the Code, the term "enterprise" is synonymous with the term "client."

Financial Statements   Statements and footnotes related thereto that purport to show financial position which relates to a point in time or changes in financial position which relate to a period of time, and statements which use a cash or other incomplete basis of accounting. Balance sheets, statements of income, statements of retained earnings, statements of changes in financial position, and statements of changes in owners' equity are financial statements.

Incidental financial data included in management advisory services reports to support recommendations to a client and tax returns and supporting schedules do not, for this purpose, constitute financial statements; and the statement, affidavit, or signature of preparers required on tax returns neither constitutes an opinion on financial statements nor requires a disclaimer of such opinion.

Firm   A proprietorship, partnership, or professional corporation or association engaged in the practice of public accounting, including individual partners or shareholders thereof.

Institute   The American Institute of Certified Public Accountants.

Interpretations of Rules of Conduct   Pronouncements issued by the division of professional ethics to provide guidelines concerning the scope and application of the rules of conduct.

Member   A member, associate member, or international associate of the American Institute of Certified Public Accountants.

Practice of Public Accounting   The practice of public accounting consists of the performance for a client, by a member or a member's firm, while holding out as CPA(s), of the professional services of accounting, tax, personal financial planning, litigation support services, and those professional services for which standards are promulgated by bodies designated by Council, such as Statements of Financial Accounting Standards, Statements on Auditing Standards, Statements on Standards for Accounting and Review Services, Statements on Standards for Management Advisory Services, Statements of Governmental Accounting Standards, Statement on Standards for Attestation Engagements, and Statement on Standards for Accountants' Services on Prospective Financial Information.

However, a member or a member's firm, while holding out as CPA(s), is not considered to be in the practice of public accounting if the member or the member's firm does not perform, for any client, any of the professional services described in the preceding paragraph.

Professional Services   Professional services include all services performed by a member while holding out as a CPA.

Holding Out   In general, any action initiated by a member that informs others of his or her status as a CPA or AICPA-accredited specialist constitutes holding out as a CPA. This would include, for example, any oral or written representation to another regarding CPA status, use of the CPA designation on business cards or letterhead, the display of a certificate evidencing a member's CPA designation, or listing as a CPA in local telephone directories.

RULES

Rule 101   Independence
A member in public practice shall be independent in the performance of professional services as required by standards promulgated by bodies designated by Council.

Rule 102   Integrity and Objectivity
In the performance of any professional service, a member shall maintain objectivity and integrity, shall be free of conflicts of interest, and shall not knowingly misrepresent facts or subordinate his or her judgment to others.

Rule 201   General Standards

A member shall comply with the following standards and with any interpretations thereof by bodies designated by Council.

A. *Professional Competence.* Undertake only those professional services that the member or the member's firm can reasonably expect to be completed with professional competence.

B. *Due Professional Care.* Exercise due professional care in the performance of professional services.

C. *Planning and Supervision.* Adequately plan and supervise the performance of professional services.

D. *Sufficient Relevant Data.* Obtain sufficient relevant data to afford a reasonable basis for conclusions or recommendations in relation to any professional services performed.

Rule 202   Compliance With Standards

A member who performs auditing, review, compilation, management advisory, tax, or other professional services shall comply with standards promulgated by bodies designated by Council.

Rule 203   Accounting Principles

A member shall not (1) express an opinion or state affirmatively that the financial statements or other financial data of any entity are presented in conformity with generally accepted accounting principles or (2) state that he or she is not aware of any material modifications that should be made to such statements or data in order for them to be in conformity with generally accepted accounting principles, if such statements or data contain any departure from an accounting principle promulgated by bodies designated by Council to establish such principles that has a material effect on the statements or data taken as a whole. If, however, the statements or data contain such a departure and the member can demonstrate that due to unusual circumstances the financial statements or data would otherwise have been misleading, the member can comply with the rule by describing the departure, its approximate effects, if practicable, and the reasons why compliance with the principle would result in a misleading statement.

Rule 301   Confidential Client Information

A member in public practice shall not disclose any confidential client information without the specific consent of the client.

This rule shall not be construed (1) to relieve a member of his or her professional obligations under rules 202 and 203, (2) to affect in any way the member's obligation to comply with a validly issued and enforceable subpoena or summons, (3) to prohibit review of a member's professional practice under AICPA or state CPA society authorization, or (4) to preclude a member from initiating a complaint with or responding to any inquiry made by a recognized investigative or disciplinary body.

Members of a recognized investigative or disciplinary body and professional practice reviewers shall not use to their own advantage or disclose any member's confidential client information that comes to their attention in carrying out their official responsibilities. However, this prohibition shall not restrict the exchange of information with a recognized investigative or disciplinary body or affect, in any way, compliance with a validly issued and enforceable subpoena or summons.

Rule 302   Contingent Fees
Professional services shall not be offered or rendered under an arrangement whereby no fee will be charged unless a specified finding or result is attained, or where the fee is otherwise contingent upon the findings or results of such services. However, a member's fees may vary depending, for example, on the complexity of services rendered.

Fees are not regarded as being contingent if fixed by courts or other public authorities, or, in tax matters, if determined based on the results of judicial proceedings or the findings of governmental agencies.

Rule 501   Acts Discreditable
A member shall not commit an act discreditable to the profession.

Rule 502   Advertising and Other Forms of Solicitation
A member in public practice shall not seek to obtain clients by advertising or other forms of solicitation in a manner that is false, misleading, or deceptive. Solicitation by the use of coercion, over-reaching, or harassing conduct is prohibited.

Rule 503   Commissions
The acceptance by a member in public practice of a payment for the referral of products or services of others to a client is prohibited. Such action is considered to create a conflict of interest that results in a loss of objectivity and independence.

A member shall not make a payment to obtain a client. This rule shall not prohibit payments for the purchase of an accounting practice or retirement payments to individuals formerly engaged in the practice of public accounting or payments to their heirs or estates.

Rule 505   Form of Practice and Name
A member may practice public accounting only in the form of a proprietorship, a partnership, or a professional corporation whose characteristics conform to resolutions of Council.

A member shall not practice public accounting under a firm name that is misleading. Names of one or more past partners or shareholders may be included in the firm name of a successor partnership or corporation. Also, a partner or shareholder surviving the death or withdrawal of all other partners or shareholders may continue to practice under such name which includes the name of past partners or shareholders for up to two years after becoming a sole practitioner.

A firm may not designate itself as "Members of the American Institute of Certified Public Accountants" unless all of its partners or shareholders are members of the Institute.

Source American Institute of Certified Public Accountants, *AICPA Professional Standards Code of Conduct Bylaws* (New York: AICPA, 1989).

GOVERNMENTAL AND NONPROFIT ACCOUNTING

"The chief business of the American people is business," President Calvin Coolidge declared in 1925. But it was not the only business. Even in 1925 much of the **gross national product (GNP)** was created by the governmental and nonprofit sectors of the economy. Today almost half of the GNP represents nonbusiness activity. Because governmental units and nonprofit organizations share many characteristics, they both will sometimes be discussed under the single term *nonbusiness entities*.

Just how do accountants track the financial performance of entities that are not concerned with making a profit? Answering that question is the job of this brief introduction.

NONBUSINESS VERSUS BUSINESS ACCOUNTING

One way to understand governmental and nonprofit accounting is to reconsider accounting for business. A single business may be involved in various business activities, each of which could be associated with its own assets, liabilities, and equities. But financial accountants report only the overall effect of those activities.

Why does it make sense for a company that sells both apples and oranges to produce financial reports combining those economic activities? (Actually, company managers may want to see reports segregating sales of apples and oranges—but that is the domain of managerial accounting.) For the purposes of financial accounting, the unifying goal of the business entity is to produce net income.

FUNDS AND FUND ACCOUNTING

One could say that all the activities of the business are reported in a single *fund* because of the unifying goal of making a profit. But for governments and most nonprofit groups, performance is measured by how well the entity meets stated objectives and by changes in its resources. Nonbusiness objectives cannot be measured by an improvement in net income. Because overall net income is not the primary issue, the activities concerning the main objectives of the entity are accounted for in separate funds.

A **fund** can be defined as a bundle of assets, liabilities, and equity related to a specific goal or subgoal of a nonbusiness entity. Each fund is a self-contained unit and merits its own set of accounts. The separation of such funds allows full accountability. Nonbusiness entities typically receive financial resources that can only be used for set purposes. Taxpayers or donors have a vested interest in knowing that these monies are spent for their intended purpose. Therefore, nonbusiness accounting systems help provide control over the entity's resources.

Nonbusiness financial statements will often use the term *increase in fund balance* in place of *net income,* and *fund balance* or *entity capital* in place of *owners' equity.* For example, note the use of *entity capital* in Exhibit B-1, the balance sheet for the nonprofit Saguaro Chamber Orchestra.

Note also in Exhibit B-1 the listing of several types of funds making up entity capital. The existence of such funds are at the root of nonbusiness accounting, also called **fund accounting.** In the absence of the profit motive, nonbusiness entities organize multiple funds in support of multiple goals.

In fund accounting, the names of the funds and even the types of the funds can vary greatly from one nonbusiness entity to another. The formats of financial statements also vary greatly. A full discussion of the types of funds and financial statements is beyond the limits of this appendix.

BASES OF ACCOUNTING FOR NONBUSINESS ENTITIES

Accrual Basis of Accounting

Recall from Chapter 2 that businesses use the **accrual method of accounting.** Under the accrual basis, revenues are recorded when earned and expenses are recorded when they are incurred. Thus a business accountant measures income by recording revenue when it is earned and matching that against expenses incurred to earn that revenue. For a business, it is useful to tie income measurement to selling for evaluating business performance.

In contrast, nonbusiness entities may use several bases of accounting—including the accrual basis. The accrual basis is appropriate for nonbusiness organizations or programs that still produce revenue. Examples include many hospitals, universities, and municipal utilities. These entities are very much like profit-making institutions in their needs to evaluate performance by measuring net income. Soon most governmental entities will be adopting the accrual basis.

Cash Basis of Accounting

Opposite to the accrual basis is the **cash basis of accounting.** Under the cash basis, the timing of entries is much different. Revenues are recorded when received

EXHIBIT B–1

Saguaro Chamber Orchestra
Balance Sheet
June 30, 19X1 and 19X2

Assets	19X1	19X2
Current Assets		
Cash	$211,304	$171,223
Marketable Securities	275,444	60,721
Accounts Receivable (net of Allowance for Doubtful Accounts)	68,022	27,561
Grants Receivable	–0–	7,200
Other	41,958	16,753
Total Current Assets	$596,728	$283,458
Noncurrent Assets		
Investments and Endowment Funds Cash	276,997	265,150
Property and Equipment at Cost (net of Accumulated Depreciation)	56,138	42,104
Rent and Other Deposits	3,876	9,210
Total Assets	$933,739	$599,922
Liabilities and Entity Capital		
Current Liabilities		
Accounts Payable and Accrued Expenses	$112,891	$166,962
Deferred Revenues—Subscriptions	288,430	189,712
Deferred Revenues—Grants	41,526	–0–
Current Portion of Long-term Debt	55,000	55,000
Total Current Liabilities	$497,847	$411,674
Long-term Debt Contingencies	39,000	59,720
Entity Capital		
Plant Fund	32,360	67,504
Endowment Funds	285,847	261,740
Unrestricted Funds	78,685	(200,716)
Total Liabilities and Entity Capital	$933,739	$599,922

and expenses are recorded when they are paid.

Keeping books on a cash basis is much like keeping a checkbook. You can see why a business might have real problems with this approach; its important economic events are not always tied to a cash inflow or outflow. The cash basis ignores events that give assurance of future receipts or that obligate the entity to make future payments. Concepts like depreciation have no place under the cash basis, for example.

Very few entities use the cash basis. However, it may be surprising to some that the federal government still keeps its books on a cash basis. Critics argue that under the cash basis, the federal government reports deficits far lower than would be reported under the accrual accounting that companies use. Long-term planning, especially for the replacement of aging assets, they argue, would be better served by a move toward an accrual basis of accounting. Ironically, the federal government has made the same recommendations to financially troubled cities in the wake of the federal bailout of New York City in the early 1980s.

Modified Accrual Basis of Accounting

Currently, most nonbusiness entities use a **modified accrual basis of accounting.** This approach shares elements of both the cash and accrual bases. Under the modified accrual basis of accounting, revenues are recorded when they are *measurable* and *available*. This approach often results in the recording of revenues on a cash basis, especially for a nonprofit organization. Expenses are generally recorded when the *liability* is incurred (if measurable).

As an example of how revenues are recorded under the modified accrual basis, consider a governmental unit, the County of Saguaro. The county sends out property-tax bills in the total amount of $750,000. Saguaro estimates from previous experience that 6 percent of the taxes will prove uncollectible. Under the modified accrual basis, the following journal entry is recorded when the bills are sent out:

Taxes Receivable	750,000	
Allowance for Uncollectible Taxes		45,000
Tax Revenue		705,000

Note that the authoritative standards treat property taxes as unique. The funds are measurable and available since the tax lien is enforceable. Other kinds of taxes, such as sales taxes, are recorded as though under the cash basis, because the amounts to be received are not measurable beforehand, or because the revenues are not immediately available.

It may be useful to compare briefly the differences between recording of expenditures under the accrual basis and under the modified accrual basis. In the first journal entry, assume that the County of Saguaro recorded the transaction under the accrual basis.

Accrual Basis Expenditure

(expense)	Insurance Expenditure	3,500	
(liability)	Accounts Payable		3,500

The *expense* of the insurance is the event that triggers the recording of this entry. Now assume the County of Saguaro recorded the transaction under the modified accrual basis.

Modified Accrual Basis Expenditure

(expense)	Insurance Expenditure	3,500	
(liability)	Accounts Payable		3,500

In the second journal entry, the triggering event is incurring the *liability* for the insurance premium. Although the two journal entries look the same, they are initiated by different economic events—and might well be recorded on different dates.

Some prepaid expense transactions may be treated differently under the modified accrual basis. For example, supplies are recorded under the accrual basis as an asset when purchased, then transferred to an expense account when used. This is shown in the following entry, which records the use of $1,200 in supplies.

Supplies Expense	1,200	
Supplies Inventory		1,200

Under the modified accrual basis, the supplies could have been recorded as an expense when purchased, rather than starting in the asset account, Supplies Inventory. This modified approach is usually taken when the budget is based on spending the money, rather than on using the assets purchased with the money.

ACCOUNTING STANDARDS FOR GOVERNMENTAL UNITS AND NONPROFIT ENTITIES

As with the accounting standards for business entities, those for governmental units and nonprofit entities continue to develop and evolve over time. For governmental units, the authority for accounting standards varies according to the level of government. The U.S. Congress oversees accounting for the federal government through the **Office of Management and Budget (OMB)** and the **General Accounting Office (GAO).**

In 1984 the Financial Accounting Foundation, which directs the Financial Accounting Standards Board (FASB), established a parallel organization, the Governmental Accounting Standards Board (GASB). The GASB sets standards for state and local governments. Other organizations established standards before GASB; most notable among them was the **National Council on Governmental Accounting (NCGA).** NCGA standards that were in effect in 1984 were adopted by the GASB. For some governmental units that operate like businesses (municipal utilities and city hospitals), the FASB and GASB issue joint standards.

Many organizations have contributed to the accounting standards for nonprofit organizations, the FASB chief among them. Some nongovernmental entities, like universities, hospitals, and utilities, are required to follow FASB rules and regulations.

Recently the GASB passed a five-year structure review and continues to fulfill short-term and long-term goals to regularize reporting procedures. The FASB is increasingly active in establishing accounting standards for nonprofits in its jurisdiction. And the AICPA has issued additional audit standards related to governmental and nonprofit organizations. GAAP for nonprofit entities develops apace.

To learn more about accounting for nonprofit entities, see Patricia P. Douglas, *Governmental and Nonprofit Accounting: Theory and Practice* (San Diego: Harcourt Brace Jovanovich, 1991). For more information on the control aspects of nonprofit accounting, see Mary T. Ziebell and Don T. DeCoster, *Management Control Systems in Nonprofit Accounting* (San Diego: Harcourt Brace Jovanovich, 1991).

MICROSTUDY+®
OPERATING
INSTRUCTIONS

INTRODUCTION

These brief operating instructions will help you start using MicroStudy +, the software study aid. After you study a chapter in the textbook, use MicroStudy + to reinforce your understanding. The program is as flexible and comprehensive as possible to speed the learning process. More complete operating instructions are available within the program itself.

HARDWARE AND SOFTWARE REQUIREMENTS

MicroStudy + is available on both 5¼-inch and 3½-inch disks for use with most DOS-based microcomputers, such as the IBM PC® or PS/2®. Use the PC DOS or MS DOS version 2.1 or higher.

Your instructor will tell you how to get or make a copy of the MicroStudy + software. Typically the publisher gives each school a master disk for these purposes. You may run the software from an individual floppy disk or you can copy it onto a hard disk drive.

GETTING STARTED

These instructions assume that you know how to start your computer and obtain a DOS prompt, such as

A>

The instructions also assume you will be running the software from the A drive.

1. At the **A**> prompt, type

STUDY

(in either upper or lower case), and then press the <**Return**> key.

2. Next, you will see one or more introductory screens. Typically a screen will display for several seconds and then the next screen will replace it automatically, until the Main Menu appears.

3. At the Main Menu, take a minute to review your menu choices.

1. Select Chapter in Textbook for Review
2. Study Chapter Preview Questions
3. List Key Terms in the Chapter
4. Vocabulary Building with Matching Exercises
5. True/False Statement Drill
6. Multiple Choice Question Drill
7. Review Instructions for Using MICROSTUDY+
8. Set or Change the Operating Environment
<**Esc**> to Exit

For more detailed operating instructions, choose menu option 7 by obtaining the Main Menu and then pressing the <**7**> key.

Good luck with your studies.

STUDENT INSTRUCTIONS FOR *WHAT IF? ELECTRONIC SPREADSHEET TEMPLATES FOR DECISION MAKING*

by Kent Finkle

INTRODUCTION

What If? Electronic Spreadsheet Templates for Decision Making introduces the spreadsheet as a decision-making tool. Spreadsheets allow you to concentrate on the important accounting concepts without the burden of calculations. You can solve different versions of a problem in a short time. The use of the spreadsheet facilitates this kind of "what if" analysis.

This particular collection of spreadsheets is build around the Demonstration Problems that occur in each chapter of the textbook.

BEFORE YOU BEGIN

To use this free software ancillary, you will need the following:

1. *These instructions.* Here you will find general information on the design and intent of the *What If?* software.

2. *A copy of the template disk.* The publisher will provide each campus with a master copy of the software. Your instructor will tell you how and where the disk is available for copying onto your own diskette.

3. *Access to Lotus 1-2-3, Release 2.0 or above (and preferably the Lotus tutorial).* Some campuses will be able to provide this spreadsheet software for your use. (You may use another spreadsheet program, such as *VP Planner* or *Quattro*, in place of Lotus 1-2-3. Keep in mind that some of the HBJ templates run as long as 525 rows, however. Be sure that the spreadsheet software will accommodate templates of this size.)

4. *Access to a DOS-based microcomputer, such as the IBM PC or PS/2.* Again, some campuses may have microcomputers available for your use.

WHAT YOU NEED TO KNOW

Microcomputers

These instructions assume you know how to operate a DOS-based microcomputer. If you do not, instruction is available from a variety of sources.

Lotus 1-2-3

These instructions are no substitute for a complete Lotus tutorial. Lotus 1-2-3 typically comes with a full tutorial, and instructions on using Lotus are available from a variety of sources. You should have a rough familiarity with the basics of Lotus before you begin.

File Name Conventions

Each demonstration problem spreadsheet resides in its own file, one for each demonstration problem in the textbook. File names begin with PROB01.WK1, the solution to the demonstration problem at the end of the first chapter, and continue in order (PROB02.WK1, PROB03.WK1, and so on).

GETTING STARTED

See the Lotus manual or tutorial for full operating instructions. The following brief instructions are here as a reminder only. For simplicity, we assume that you will run the Lotus software from the C drive of a microcomputer, and that the HBJ templates will be read from the A drive.

1. Obtain the C> prompt, as

C>

2. Insert the *What If?* disk in disk drive A and then close the disk drive door.
3. Type

LOTUS

(using either uppercase or lowercase), and then press the <**Return**> key.
4. At the Lotus main menu, use the arrow keys to highlight

1-2-3

then press the <**Return**> key.
5. After Lotus 1-2-3 loads, the worksheet grid appears on-screen.

6. Press the / (slash) key to bring up the 1-2-3 menu along the top of the screen.

7. Then press the **F** key (or highlight the word *File* and press <**Return**>).

8. Next press the **D** key (or highlight the word *Directory* and press <**Return**>).

9. Now type **A:** to designate the drive/directory where files are located, and press <**Return**>.

10. Next press the **R** key (or highlight the word *Retrieve* and press <**Return**>). The file names of available templates will appear on a line near the top of the screen.

11. Assuming you want to load the template from Chapter 1, use the arrow keys to highlight

PROB01.WK1

and press <**Return**>.

12. The template will load onto the screen. Use the <**PgUp**> and <**PgDn**> keys to move through the template and read the instructions.

Note: Additional "What if?" instructions appear on each template in the screen just to the right of the first screen. See the next section, "Spreadsheet Layout," for more information.

SPREADSHEET LAYOUT

The data entry area, the requirements of the problem, and the solution to the problem appear in a series of screens. The templates are programmed so that when they are first loaded you will see the initial screen, and the upper-left-hand corner of the worksheet area will correspond to cell A1. The first series of screens will repeat the instructions from the Demonstration Problems in the textbook for easy reference.

You can move from an earlier screen to a later screen by pressing the <**PgDn**> key. To return to an earlier screen, press the <**PgUp**> key. You can return to the first screen as well by pressing the <**Home**> key.

Typically, additional instructions appear on the screen to the right of the initial screen. To locate these additional instructions, first press the <**Home**> key. (This places your cursor in the upper-left corner of the spreadsheet, in the cell A1.) Now press the <**Tab**> key, and the "what if?" instruction screen will appear. To remove the instructions from your screen (that is, to return to the original screen), press the <**Home**> key again. These instructions provide additional "what if?" analysis to expand on the textbook instructions. The additional instructions will help you utilize the unique capabilities of the spreadsheet.

SPREADSHEET STYLE

The templates offer you an introduction to, and an example of, organized, structured spreadsheet programming. In business, management uses the complex web of data and formulas called a spreadsheet to choose between alternatives involving large sums of money. Accountants must therefore take steps to ensure the accuracy and integrity of their templates. Errors can quickly creep into such a complicated design. Any template can contain an error, but these templates illustrate good spreadsheet programming practices, minimizing the risk of costly mistakes.

First, good spreadsheet design separates the input data in the template from the formulas using the data. In all the templates provided, the user enters data in a clearly marked area well separated from the formulas. Second, spreadsheet formulas using cell addresses can be difficult to read and understand, even by the maker of the template. Instead of cell addresses, the templates give names to cells, indicating the accounting principle behind the calculation. Lotus calls descriptive names of cells or groups of cells "range names." Use of range names instead of cell addresses improves readability. For example, consider the following typical spreadsheet formula:

$$(1) \ B15 * C18 - E45$$

This formula provides no clue to the accounting concept behind the calculation. What does *B15* mean? Why multiply it by the *C18* cell address, whatever it may be? Further, why subtract the mysterious *E45* cell from the product of the first two terms? By contrast, the use of range names creates a formula numerically equivalent, but much easier to understand:

$$(2) \ PRICE * QUANTITY.SOLD - EXPENSES$$

Now the relationship is clear. Where possible, the template expresses all formulas with range names like those in formula *(2)*, rather than cell addresses.

THE LIMITATIONS OF TEMPLATES

First-time users of electronic spreadsheets should note that all preprogrammed templates have their limitations. Each template in the *What If?* package is programmed under assumptions basic to the corresponding Demonstration Problem. Each template will yield useful results, as long as the inputs stay within reasonable bounds and no major changes occur in the underlying assumptions. To change major assumptions and accounting relationships, reprogramming or redesigning the template (beyond the scope of this introduction) is required.

We hope these templates will help you understand the accounting principles involved and gain an appreciation for careful spreadsheet design.

1989 UNITED TELECOM ANNUAL REPORT

THE FOLLOWING PAGES ARE AN EXTRACT FROM THE 1989 ANNUAL REPORT FOR UNITED TELECOMMUNICATIONS, INC.

SELECTED FINANCIAL DATA

	December 31,				
	1989	1988	1987	1986	1985
	(Millions of Dollars Except per Share Data)				
Net operating revenues	$7,549.0	$6,493.0	$2,935.1	$3,012.7	$3,083.8
Income (loss) from continuing operations	362.9	141.8	(33.5)	198.0	36.0
Income (loss) per common share from continuing operations*	1.72	0.68	(0.19)	1.00	0.17
Earnings (loss) per common share*	1.72	2.48	(0.28)	0.91	0.09
Dividends per common share*	0.97	0.96	0.96	0.96	0.96
Total assets	9,821.3	9,816.9	6,558.4	6,379.1	5,767.4
Long-term debt	3,747.0	3,674.8	3,047.6	2,683.3	1,947.7
Redeemable preferred stock	36.9	38.9	40.9	42.7	44.3

*Common share data reflects the 1989 two-for-one stock split.

BUSINESS SEGMENT INFORMATION

	1989	1988	1987
	(Millions of Dollars)		
Long-Distance Communications Services			
Net operating revenues	$4,323.6	$3,405.4	
Operating expenses			
Local interconnection	1,890.3	1,738.0	
Other operations expenses	737.1	637.8	
Selling, general and administrative	1,045.5	876.1	
Depreciation and amortization	424.1	344.6	
Business restructuring charge		195.0	
Total operating expenses	4,097.0	3,791.5	
Operating income (loss)	$ 226.6	$ (386.1)	
Property additions	$ 705.0	$ 734.7	
Identifiable assets at December 31[1]	$4,285.2	$3,583.1	
Local Communications Services			
Net operating revenues			
Local service	$ 903.6	$ 847.9	$ 810.2
Network access	1,016.9	979.1	914.2
Long-distance service	411.5	391.7	349.1
Miscellaneous	305.0	291.0	315.4
Total net operating revenues	2,637.0	2,509.7	2,388.9
Operating expenses			
Plant operations	811.7	737.5	661.8
Depreciation and amortization	517.9	533.3	531.9
Other	671.7	642.1	558.6
Total operating expenses	2,001.3	1,912.9	1,752.3
Operating income	$ 635.7	$ 596.8	$ 636.6
Property additions	$ 658.6	$ 676.4	$ 653.4
Identifiable assets at December 31[1]	$5,032.0	$4,873.5	$4,711.2
Complementary and Other			
Net operating revenues	$ 762.1	$ 698.6	$ 628.0
Operating income	$ 47.7	$ 42.1	$ 42.7
Depreciation and amortization	$ 19.9	$ 28.7	$ 31.8
Property additions	$ 25.4	$ 27.7	$ 42.1
Identifiable assets at December 31[1]	$2,018.0	$2,048.2	$2,049.7

[1]Includes assets eliminated in consolidation of $1,513.9, $687.9 and $202.5 million for December 31, 1989, 1988 and 1987, respectively.

See accompanying notes to consolidated financial statements.

CONSOLIDATED STATEMENTS OF INCOME

	Years Ended December 31,		
	1989	1988	1987
	(In Millions Except per Share Data)		
Net operating revenues			
Long-distance communications services	$4,323.6	$3,405.4	
Local communications services	2,637.0	2,509.7	$2,388.9
Complementary businesses	762.1	698.6	628.0
Intercompany revenues	(173.7)	(120.7)	(81.8)
Total net operating revenues	7,549.0	6,493.0	2,935.1
Operating expenses			
Long-distance communications services (including business restructuring charge of $195.0 in 1988 — NOTE 2)	4,097.0	3,791.5	
Local communications services	2,001.3	1,912.9	1,752.3
Complementary businesses	714.4	656.5	585.3
Intercompany expenses	(173.7)	(120.7)	(81.8)
Total operating expenses	6,639.0	6,240.2	2,255.8
Operating income	910.0	252.8	679.3
Other (income) expense, net	(11.5)	7.1	(31.2)
Interest charges, net of capitalization	359.8	320.4	265.9
Equity in loss of US Sprint — NOTE 2			580.4
Minority interest — NOTE 2	33.4	(223.4)	
Income (loss) from continuing operations before income taxes	528.3	148.7	(135.8)
Income tax provision (benefit) — NOTE 8	165.4	6.9	(102.3)
Income (loss) from continuing operations	362.9	141.8	(33.5)
Discontinued operations (net of income tax expense of $260.0 in 1988 and benefit of $10.3 in 1987) — NOTE 4		367.1	(18.0)
Net income (loss)	362.9	508.9	(51.5)
Preferred stock dividends	3.0	3.3	3.5
Earnings (loss) applicable to common stock	$ 359.9	$ 505.6	$ (55.0)
Earnings (loss) per share — NOTE 5			
From continuing operations	$ 1.72	$ 0.68	$ (0.19)
From discontinued operations		1.80	(0.09)
Total	$ 1.72	$ 2.48	$ (0.28)
Weighted average number of common shares outstanding	209.1	204.4	199.6

See accompanying notes to consolidated financial statements.

CONSOLIDATED BALANCE SHEETS

	As of December 31,	
	1989	1988
	(Millions of Dollars)	

Assets

	1989	1988
Current assets		
Cash and temporary cash investments	$ 114.8	$ 617.1
Accounts receivable, net of allowance for doubtful accounts of $168.8 ($202.5 in 1988)	998.7	850.3
Notes receivable	84.4	330.6
Inventories held for resale	124.7	131.3
Deferred income taxes—NOTE 8	33.5	44.7
Prepayments and other assets	153.1	151.0
Total current assets	1,509.2	2,125.0
Property, plant and equipment—NOTES 2 and 7		
Long-distance communications services	4,281.4	3,493.0
Local communications services	7,213.9	6,900.8
Complementary and other	259.6	275.4
	11,754.9	10,669.2
Less accumulated depreciation	3,870.0	3,339.4
	7,884.9	7,329.8
Intangible assets, net of accumulated amortization of $130.7 ($92.0 in 1988)	122.4	124.3
Other assets	304.8	237.8
	$ 9,821.3	$ 9,816.9

Liabilities and Shareholders' Equity

	1989	1988
Current liabilities		
Current maturities of long-term debt—NOTE 7	$ 384.3	$ 148.5
Accounts payable	738.7	716.9
Accrued local interconnection and leased facilities costs	318.5	292.1
Advance billings	67.5	63.3
Accrued taxes	237.9	313.2
Accrued interest	107.0	100.8
Other	424.9	514.1
Total current liabilities	2,278.8	2,148.9
Long-term debt—NOTE 7	3,747.0	3,674.8
Deferred credits and other liabilities		
Deferred income taxes—NOTE 8	934.2	792.1
Deferred investment tax credits—NOTE 8	156.7	188.8
Other	126.0	137.3
	1,216.9	1,118.2
Minority interest—NOTE 2	464.8	958.9
Redeemable preferred stock—NOTE 6	36.9	38.9
Commitments and contingencies—NOTE 11		
Common stock and other shareholders' equity		
Common stock, authorized 250,000,000 shares, par value $2.50—NOTE 5	517.8	256.6
Employees stock purchase installments—NOTE 5	22.3	7.3
Non-redeemable convertible preferred stock	4.0	2.4
Capital in excess of par or stated value	650.0	882.5
Retained earnings—NOTE 7	882.8	728.4
	2,076.9	1,877.2
	$ 9,821.3	$ 9,816.9

See accompanying notes to consolidated financial statements.

CONSOLIDATED STATEMENTS OF CASH FLOWS

	Years Ended December 31,		
	1989	1988	1987
	(Millions of Dollars)		
Operating Activities			
Net income (loss)	$ 362.9	$ 508.9	$ (51.5)
Adjustments to reconcile net income (loss) to net cash provided by operating activities:			
Depreciation and amortization	961.9	906.6	563.7
Deferred income tax provision (benefit) and investment tax credits	108.2	94.4	(63.3)
Minority interest	33.4	(223.4)	
Net gain on sale of discontinued operations		(371.2)	
Business restructuring charge		195.0	
Changes in operating assets and liabilities:*			
(Increase) decrease in accounts receivable, net	(136.3)	125.2	(11.4)
Decrease in other current assets	7.4	24.8	1.2
Net increase (decrease) in accounts payable, accrued expenses and other current liabilities	(172.3)	3.1	73.1
Other, net	7.0	(83.3)	(22.9)
Net cash provided by operating activities	1,172.2	1,180.1	488.9
Investing Activities			
Additions to property, plant and equipment	(1,389.0)	(1,438.8)	(695.5)
Acquisitions, net of cash acquired	(604.9)		
Collection of notes receivable	300.0		
Issuance of notes receivable	(53.8)	(317.1)	
Investment in and advances to US Sprint, net of equity in pre-tax loss			(132.1)
Net proceeds from sales of plant and equipment	80.0	57.0	31.3
Net proceeds from sale of discontinued operations		775.3	
Other, net	(21.5)	7.2	(4.6)
Net cash used for investing activities	(1,689.2)	(916.4)	(800.9)
Financing Activities			
Proceeds from long-term borrowings	470.3	578.4	630.2
Principal payments on long-term debt	(353.3)	(303.7)	(190.7)
Minority interest contributions and advances	64.0	202.3	
Decrease in short-term notes payable and commercial paper		(31.3)	(5.6)
Proceeds from common stock issued	35.1	28.8	30.1
Dividends paid	(203.1)	(198.3)	(194.5)
Other, net	1.7	2.8	8.7
Net cash provided by financing activities	14.7	279.0	278.2
Increase (Decrease) in Cash and Temporary Cash Investments	(502.3)	542.7	(33.8)
Cash and Temporary Cash Investments at Beginning of Year	617.1	74.4	108.2
Cash and Temporary Cash Investments at End of Year	$ 114.8	$ 617.1	$ 74.4

*Net of the effects of acquisitions in 1989 and the consolidation of US Sprint accounts in 1988.
See accompanying notes to consolidated financial statements.

CONSOLIDATED STATEMENTS OF COMMON STOCK AND OTHER SHAREHOLDERS' EQUITY

Years Ended December 31, 1989, 1988 and 1987

	Common Stock	Employees Stock Purchase Installments	Non-Redeemable Convertible Preferred Stock	Capital in Excess of Par or Stated Value	Retained Earnings	Total
			(Millions of Dollars)			
Balance at January 1, 1987 (98,536,141 shares issued and outstanding)	$246.4	$ 6.0	$2.9	$810.5	$662.0	$1,727.8
Net loss					(51.5)	(51.5)
Common stock dividends, $.96 per share—NOTE 5					(191.0)	(191.0)
Preferred stock dividends					(3.5)	(3.5)
Installments received		10.9				10.9
Conversion of preferred stock and debentures	0.5		(0.3)	1.7		1.9
Additional common stock issued	2.8	(0.9)		28.2		30.1
Other, net	1.7			(1.5)	1.2	1.4
Balance at December 31, 1987 (100,546,896 shares issued and outstanding)	251.4	16.0	2.6	838.9	417.2	1,526.1
Net income					508.9	508.9
Common stock dividends, $.96 per share—NOTE 5					(195.0)	(195.0)
Preferred stock dividends					(3.3)	(3.3)
Installments received		12.3				12.3
Conversion of preferred stock and debentures	0.9		(0.2)	6.1		6.8
Additional common stock issued	4.3	(21.0)		45.5		28.8
Other, net				(8.0)	0.6	(7.4)
Balance at December 31, 1988 (102,621,257 shares issued and outstanding)	256.6	7.3	2.4	882.5	728.4	1,877.2
Net income					362.9	362.9
Common stock dividends, $.97 per share—NOTE 5					(200.1)	(200.1)
Preferred stock dividends					(3.0)	(3.0)
Installments received		15.0				15.0
Two-for-one stock split	258.7		2.0	(260.7)		
Conversion of preferred stock and debentures	0.5		(0.4)	0.9		1.0
Additional common stock issued	2.0			33.1		35.1
Other, net				(5.8)	(5.4)	(11.2)
Balance at December 31, 1989 (207,100,810 shares issued and outstanding)	$517.8	$22.3	$4.0	$650.0	$882.8	$2,076.9

See accompanying notes to consolidated financial statements.

NOTES TO CONSOLIDATED FINANCIAL STATEMENTS

1. Accounting Policies

Basis of Consolidation

The accompanying consolidated financial statements include the accounts of United Telecommunications, Inc. (United) and its wholly-owned subsidiaries. The 1989 and 1988 consolidated financial statements also include the accounts of US Sprint Communications Company Limited Partnership (US Sprint), a partnership which was owned equally by subsidiaries of United and GTE Corporation (GTE) at December 31, 1988. Consolidation of US Sprint commenced in 1988 as a result of United's assumption of management control of US Sprint and continued for 1989 as United increased its percentage ownership in US Sprint in 1989 to 80.1 percent. GTE's 19.9 percent and 50 percent ownership interests in US Sprint during 1989 and 1988, respectively, are reflected in the consolidated financial statements as Minority Interest. United's investment in US Sprint is accounted for using the equity method in the 1987 consolidated financial statements. See Note 2 for additional information concerning United's investment in US Sprint.

In accordance with industry practice, revenues and related net income of non-regulated operations attributable to transactions with United's regulated telephone operations have not been eliminated in the accompanying financial statements. Intercompany revenues of such entities amounted to $173, $183 and $165 million in 1989, 1988 and 1987, respectively. All other significant intercompany transactions have been eliminated.

Classification of Operations

United's long-distance communications services segment includes the operations of US Sprint, an 80.1 percent-owned limited partnership at December 31, 1989, and Sprint Services, a wholly-owned business unit of United. US Sprint provides domestic voice and data communications services across certain specified geographical boundaries, as well as international long-distance communications services. Sprint Services, established in the fourth quarter of 1988, began providing operator services (principally to US Sprint) and "900" services in 1989. Revenues for long-distance communications services are recorded based on communication services rendered after deducting an estimate of the services which will not be collected. Activities of the long-distance communications services segment are not rate-regulated.

Local communications services consist principally of the revenues and operating expenses of United's rate-regulated telephone operations. These operations provide local exchange services,

access by telephone customers and other carriers to United's local exchange facilities and long-distance services within specified geographical areas.

Complementary businesses consist of all other operations of United. The primary business activities within this classification include wholesale distribution of telecommunications products and the publishing and marketing of white and yellow page telephone directories.

Certain amounts in the accompanying consolidated financial statements for 1988 and 1987 have been reclassified to conform to the presentation of amounts in the 1989 consolidated financial statements. These reclassifications had no effect on net income in either year.

Cash and Temporary Cash Investments

Temporary cash investments generally include highly liquid investments with original maturities of three months or less and are stated at cost, which approximates market value.

At December 31, 1989 and 1988, outstanding checks in excess of cash balances of $155 and $161 million, respectively, are included in accounts payable.

Inventories Held for Resale

Inventories held for resale are stated at the lower of cost (principally first-in, first-out method) or market.

Property, Plant and Equipment

Property, plant and equipment are recorded at cost. Maintenance and repair costs are expensed as incurred. Generally, ordinary asset retirements and disposals are charged against accumulated depreciation with no gain or loss.

Income Taxes

United and its eligible subsidiaries file a consolidated federal income tax return. United's share of the US Sprint partnership tax attributes is also included in the consolidated tax return.

United claims the full investment tax credit (ITC) and reduces the tax basis of depreciable assets by the full credit claimed. ITC related to non-regulated property is included in income on a current basis. ITC related to regulated telephone property is deferred and amortized over the property's useful life. Deferred income taxes applicable to the tax effect of the basis reduction are provided at the time the related investment tax credit is reflected in income.

In accordance with Accounting Principles Board Opinion No. 11, deferred income taxes are provided for all differences in timing of reporting income and expenses for book and tax purposes, except for items that are not allowable by various regulatory commissions as an expense for rate-making purposes. The cumulative net amount of such timing differences for which deferred income taxes have not been provided approximated $85 million as of December 31, 1989.

Depreciation

The cost of property, plant and equipment is generally depreciated over their estimated useful lives on a straight-line basis. The weighted average annual composite depreciation rates for the local communications services rate-regulated segment, excluding special amortizations and non-recurring charges described below, were 6.9, 7.3 and 8 percent in 1989, 1988 and 1987, respectively.

Depreciation rate increases granted by regulatory commissions to the regulated telephone operating companies during 1989, 1988 and 1987 resulted in additional depreciation of $4, $18 and $19 million, respectively. In addition, depreciation expense for 1989, 1988 and 1987 includes special short-term amortizations and non-recurring charges approved by regulatory commissions totaling approximately $37, $51 and $38 million, respectively. After considering the effects of the related long-distance and network access revenue increases and income taxes, these items collectively reduced net income during 1989, 1988 and 1987 by $22, $29 and $27 million, respectively.

Interest Charged to Construction

Regulatory commissions allow the local communications services companies to capitalize an allowance for funds expended during construction which includes both interest and equity return components. Amounts capitalized will be recovered over the service lives of the respective assets constructed as the resulting higher depreciation is recovered through increased revenues. Interest costs associated with the construction of capital assets for United's other operations are capitalized in accordance with Statement of Financial Accounting Standards No. 34, "Capitalization of Interest Cost." Total interest amounts capitalized during 1989, 1988 and 1987, including an allowance for funds expended during construction capitalized by the local communications services companies, totaled $21, $25 and $3 million, respectively. The 1987 total does not include US Sprint amounts.

Intangible Assets

Intangible assets include costs assigned to individual customers, trade names and other intangible assets of the long-distance communications services segment. These assets are being amortized over their estimated lives of generally five years using the straight-line method.

Earnings per Share

Earnings (loss) per common share is based on the weighted average number of shares both outstanding and issuable assuming exercise of all dilutive options. As more fully described in Note 5, a two-for-one stock split was effected in 1989 in the form of a stock dividend. As a result, prior years' earnings per share amounts have been retroactively adjusted in the accompanying consolidated financial statements to give effect to the stock split.

2. Investment in US Sprint

Formation of the Partnership

On July 1, 1986, United combined its US Telecom voice and data communications operations with those of GTE Sprint and GTE Telenet to form US Sprint, a partnership then owned equally by US Telecom, Inc. and GTE Communications Services, Inc., wholly-owned subsidiaries of United and GTE, respectively. The partnership was formed to provide both domestic and international long-distance voice and data communications services.

Changes in the Partners' Ownership Percentages and the Partnership Agreement

In July 1988, UCOM, Inc. (UCOM), a wholly-owned subsidiary of United, agreed to acquire from GTE an additional 30.1 percent interest in US Sprint effective January 3, 1989. United assumed day-to-day management control of US Sprint operations in July 1988 and received final regulatory approval of the transaction in December 1988. On January 3, 1989, UCOM completed the acquisition and paid GTE $585 million in cash. The final purchase price, which has not yet been determined, will be adjusted and finalized in accordance with provisions of the acquisition agreement.

As a result of the acquisition:

- US Sprint became a limited partnership, with US Telecom owning a 50 percent general partnership interest and UCOM and GTE owning 30.1 percent and 19.9 percent limited partnership interests, respectively.
- US Sprint will repay to GTE its advances outstanding at December 31, 1988, with interest, in installments over a three-year period to commence on a date yet to be determined.
- United may, at its option, purchase all or a portion of GTE's remaining limited partnership interest in US Sprint through December 31, 1995. Such interest may be purchased until December 30, 1990, at the

corresponding net book value of such interest on the last day of the month of exercise, excluding the effect of cumulative losses, if any, incurred by US Sprint after December 31, 1988. During the remaining option period, United may purchase the additional interest in US Sprint at the greater of net book value at December 31, 1988, or net book value as of the last day of the month of exercise of the option.

- GTE may, at its option, require United to purchase all or a portion of its remaining partnership interest at any time during the period December 31, 1991, through December 31, 1995, at a price equal to the net book value of the partnership interest being purchased as of the last day of the month in which the option is exercised.
- US Telecom, as general partner, now determines whether and to what extent additional capital contributions from the partners are needed by US Sprint. GTE is required to contribute its proportionate share of US Sprint's capital requirements, subject to a cumulative upper limit of $225 million, and is required to make additional advances to US Sprint in an amount equal to one-third of the additional capital contributions, subject to a cumulative upper limit of $75 million. At December 31, 1989, GTE had made capital contributions and advances to US Sprint of $49 and $16 million, respectively, that were subject to these limits.

If United had owned 80.1 percent of US Sprint during 1988, United's unaudited pro forma net income and earnings per common share for that period would have been reduced to $405 million and $1.97, respectively, reflecting United's greater pro forma share of US Sprint's 1988 loss. Consolidated revenue and expense levels in the 1989 and 1988 financial statements are not affected by the different ownership interests in US Sprint since US Sprint results have been consolidated in both 1989 and 1988.

Business Restructuring Charges

In 1987, US Sprint recorded a $350 million pre-tax charge to operations which included a $260 million write-down of its interim analog-microwave network made redundant by the earlier than expected transition of traffic to its new fiber-optic network and a $76 million increase in its provision for uncollectible accounts. Efforts to dispose of the interim analog-microwave network did not meet

management's expectations and more costs were incurred to keep the interim network in operation than originally anticipated. Operating expenses of long-distance communications services reflected in the 1988 consolidated financial statements include a $195 million pre-tax charge recorded in December 1988 principally to reflect the final disposition of these assets. The effect of these charges, after related minority interest and income tax effects, was to reduce income from continuing operations by $64 and $109 million for 1988 and 1987, respectively.

Related Party Transactions

United's 1989 and 1988 consolidated financial statements include local interconnection charges from GTE of $236 and $177 million, respectively, for long-distance calls made from or to GTE's local telephone service territories. Amounts charged to US Sprint were generally established under tariffs approved by federal and state regulatory commissions. Interest costs on funds advanced to US Sprint by GTE totaled $16 million for each of the years ended December 31, 1989 and 1988, and have been included in United's consolidated financial statements.

1987 Summarized Financial Information

Summarized income statement data for US Sprint for the year ended December 31, 1987, follows (millions of dollars):

Net operating revenues	$ 2,672.4
Operating expenses, excluding business restructuring charge	3,486.5
Business restructuring charge	274.0
Other expenses, net	32.1
Interest charges, net of capitalization	34.7
Loss before income taxes	$(1,154.9)

Interest on funds advanced to US Sprint by United during 1987 aggregated $20 million. The 1989 and 1988 amounts have been eliminated in the consolidated financial statements. Generally, interest is computed based on United's actual cost of borrowings.

3. Acquisitions and Property Exchange

On August 15, 1989, US Sprint acquired 100 percent of the outstanding stock of Private Transatlantic Telecommunications Systems, Inc. (PSI), which owns a 50 percent interest in the PTAT transatlantic fiber-optic cable system. Cable and Wireless, based in London, owns the other 50 percent interest in the PTAT transatlantic cable system. In addition, US Sprint acquired all the assets and assumed all the liabilities of Long Distance/USA in October 1989. Based in Hawaii, Long Distance/USA provides long-distance communications services, with an emphasis in the hospitality industry.

These acquisitions have been accounted for as purchases, with the fair values of assets acquired and liabilities assumed equal to approximately $295 and $271 million, respectively. The 1989 consolidated statement of income includes the results of operations of PSI and Long Distance/USA from their respective dates of acquisition. Had PSI and Long Distance/USA been acquired as of January 1, 1988, the effects of the acquisitions on United's 1989 and 1988 consolidated results of operations would not have been material.

Effective July 1, 1989, United's local communications services segment exchanged all of its telephone properties located in Iowa and Arkansas and certain of its properties located in Missouri for similar assets owned by Contel of Kansas, Inc. and The Kansas State Telephone Company, both Contel Corporation subsidiaries. The net recorded value of assets relinquished in the exchange totaled approximately $65 million. No gain or loss was recognized as a result of these nonmonetary transactions, as the properties received in the exchange were recorded at the net recorded value of the assets relinquished.

4. Discontinued Operations

In October 1988, United sold United TeleSpectrum, Inc., a wholly-owned subsidiary providing cellular telephone and paging services, for approximately $775 million. United recorded a net gain from discontinued operations of $367.1 million in 1988 (net of related income taxes of $260 million) due to the sale of United TeleSpectrum.

Operating revenues and expenses for discontinued operations were not material.

The amount of income taxes allocated to discontinued operations is the incremental tax effects resulting from such operations. In 1988, such incremental effects included an increase in income tax expense of $26 million realized upon the utilization of ITC carryforwards in amounts less than those previously recognized for financial reporting purposes (see Note 8).

5. Common Stock

On October 10, 1989, the board of directors of United declared a two-for-one stock split, effected in the form of a stock dividend on United's outstanding common shares, payable on December 28, 1989. As a result of the common stock split, United transferred $258.7 million from capital in excess of par or stated value to common stock to reflect the par value of the additional shares issued, which remained at $2.50 per share. All shares and per share amounts have been retroactively adjusted to reflect the increased number of shares as a result of the stock split.

The stock option plans of United reserve common stock for issuance to officers, key employees and outside directors. Both incentive and nonqualified options are granted at 100 percent of the market price at date of grant.

Options outstanding as of December 31, 1989, include 892,000 options that provide for the granting of stock appreciation rights as an alternate method of settlement upon exercise. The stock appreciation rights feature allows the optionee to elect to receive any gain in the stock price on the underlying option directly from United, either in stock or in cash or a combination of the two, in lieu of exercising the option by payment of the purchase price. Of the 263,950 options bearing the stock appreciation rights feature that were exercised in 1989, 149,208 were settled by the election of cash payments aggregating $790,000.

A summary of stock option activity under the plans is as follows:

	Number of Shares	Per Share Exercise Price		Aggregate Exercise Amount
		Low	High	(Millions of Dollars)
Shares under option as of January 1, 1989 (1,134,712 shares exercisable)	3,006,402	$ 8.56	$22.56	$39.7
Granted	945,250	21.69	39.31	23.0
Exercised				
Options without stock appreciation rights	403,570	8.69	21.69	4.9
Options with stock appreciation rights	263,950	8.69	14.34	3.3
Terminated and expired	401,198	9.25	24.38	6.2
Shares under option as of December 31, 1989 (1,003,556 shares exercisable)	2,882,934	$ 8.56	$39.31	$48.3

Approximately 2.9 million common shares were available for future grants under the plans at December 31, 1989.

At December 31, 1989, elections to purchase 2,308,256 and 582,752 United common shares were outstanding under the 1988 Employees Stock Purchase Plan and the 1989 US Sprint Employee Stock Purchase Plan. The purchase prices under the plans cannot exceed $13.12 and $34.34 per share, respectively, such prices representing 85 percent of the average market price on the respective offering dates. Both plans terminate on June 30, 1990.

In September 1989, United redeemed the Rights issued to holders of United common stock pursuant to the Shareholder Rights Plan adopted August 12, 1986, and adopted a new Shareholder Rights Plan. The redemption price for the Rights was five cents per Right. The cost of the redemption has been recorded as a direct charge to retained earnings.

Under the new Plan, shareholders of record as of September 8, 1989, were granted Preferred Stock Purchase Rights at the rate of one Right for each common share held. Each Right, which is exercisable and detachable upon the occurrence of certain takeover events, will entitle shareholders to buy units consisting of one one-hundredth of a newly-issued share of Preferred Stock-Fourth Series, Junior Participating at a price of $235 per unit, or, in certain circumstances, common stock. Under certain circumstances, Rights beneficially owned by an acquiring person become null and void. United's Preferred Stock-Fourth Series is without par value. It is voting, cumulative and accrues dividends equal generally to the greater of $10 or one hundred times the aggregate per share amount of all common stock dividends. No shares of Preferred Stock-Fourth Series were issued or outstanding at December 31, 1989. Following the 1989 two-for-one common stock split, the number of Rights associated with each share of common stock was adjusted so that each share has one-half of a Right attached. The Rights may be redeemed by United at a price of one cent per Right, and expire on September 8, 1999.

Information regarding United common stock is as follows:

	Number of Shares	
	Issued in 1989	Reserved at December 31, 1989
Conversion of preferred stock	161,991	1,607,126
Conversion of debentures	36,354	162,854
Officers' and key employees' stock options	246,650	3,000,142
US Sprint Employee Stock Option Plan	13,890	356,750
Directors Option Plan		300,000
Automatic Dividend Reinvestment Plan	321,634	1,795,017
1988 Employees Stock Purchase Plan	39,294	8,917,464
1989 US Sprint Employee Stock Purchase Plan	282	582,752
Savings plans	132,585	6,535,799
Business combinations	50,000	
Two-for-one stock split	103,476,873	
	104,479,553	23,257,904

6. Redeemable Preferred Stock

United has 20,000,000 and subsidiaries have 4,068,548 authorized shares of preferred stock, including non-redeemable preferred stock. The redeemable preferred stock outstanding as of December 31 is summarized below:

	1989		1988	
	Shares	Amount (Millions of Dollars)	Shares	Amount (Millions of Dollars)
United, third series — stated value $100, non-participating, non-voting, cumulative 7¾% annual dividend rate	256,000	$25.6	268,000	$26.8
Subsidiaries — stated values ranging from $1 to $100, annual dividend rates ranging from 5.0% to 12.0%	339,220	11.3	356,980	12.1
	595,220	$36.9	624,980	$38.9

United's third series is redeemed from a sinking fund at the rate of 12,000 shares, or $1.2 million per year, until 2008, at which time all remaining shares are to be redeemed. United may redeem additional shares at $103.59 per share during 1990, and at declining amounts in succeeding years.

The redeemable preferred stocks of subsidiaries are presented at par value or carrying value, whichever more closely corresponds to the involuntary liquidation preference. The annual redemption requirements are $.7 million for 1990, 1991 and 1992, $.8 million for 1993, and $.7 million for 1994.

In the event of default, the holders of United's redeemable preferred stock are entitled to elect a certain number of directors until all arrears in dividend and sinking fund payments have been paid.

7. Debt and Related Dividend Restrictions

Long-term debt, as of December 31, is presented below:

	Maturing	1989	1988
		(Millions of Dollars)	
Corporate			
Senior notes			
7.52%	1989		$ 50.0
7.50%	1990	$ 200.0	200.0
8.42% to 9.50%	1991	225.0	225.0
8.10% to 8.25%	1992	215.0	215.0
9.75%	1993	100.0	100.0
8.60% to 9.71%	1994	225.0	175.0
9.40% to 10.45%	1995 to 1997	410.0	410.0
Debentures			
9.40% to 11.00%	1999 to 2000	52.3	58.2
Subordinated debentures			
5.00% (1)	1993	2.3	3.3
9.75% (2)	2010	104.9	141.8
Subordinated notes			
8.90%	1993	200.0	200.0
Commercial paper and bank notes, classified as long-term debt,			
8.33% to 9.13%	1993	193.5	51.6
Other			
6.13% to 14.63%	1990 to 2007	17.0	17.4
Long-Distance Communications Services			
Vendor financing agreements			
8.00% to 10.18% (3)	1990 to 2001	405.2	321.3
Minority interest advances (4)	(4)	186.8	170.5
Other			
6.41% to 15.00%	1990 to 1993	15.9	13.1
Local Communications Services			
First mortgage bonds			
4.50% to 7.25%	1990 to 1994	58.6	75.0
2.00% to 11.00%	1995 to 1999	192.0	195.1
5.63% to 12.75%	2000 to 2004	303.0	307.1
4.00% to 10.38%	2005 to 2009	244.0	246.1
7.50% to 13.75%	2010 to 2014	48.7	49.1
8.00% to 14.45%	2015 to 2019	297.6	132.7
Debentures			
4.35% to 12.00%	1990 to 2016	232.4	234.6
Commercial paper and bank notes, classified as long-term debt,			
9.01% to 10.00%	1993	11.3	30.5
Other			
2.00% to 13.88%	1990 to 2016	17.2	16.2
Complementary Businesses			
Senior note			
11.70%	2000	40.0	40.0
Vendor financing agreements			
10.18%	2001	116.9	122.0
Other			
6.20% to 10.70%	1991 to 1993	16.7	22.7
Total		4,131.3	3,823.3
Less current maturities		384.3	148.5
Total Long-term Debt, Excluding Current Maturities		$3,747.0	$3,674.8

(1) Convertible into 162,854 shares and 235,692 shares at December 31, 1989 and 1988, respectively, of United common stock at $14 per share.
(2) Exchangeable for 2,124,165 shares of The Southern New England Telephone Company (SNET) common stock owned by United and included in other assets at cost of $63 million (market value of $191 million) at December 31, 1989. United may, at its option, pay cash in an amount equal to the market value of the SNET common stock otherwise payable under the exchange provisions in lieu of exchanging the SNET common stock.
(3) GTE has guaranteed $144 million of US Sprint's borrowings at December 31, 1989.
(4) The average interest rates on advances from GTE were 9.1 and 8.9 percent for 1989 and 1988, respectively. See Note 2 concerning repayment terms of the portion of these advances outstanding at December 31, 1988. The remaining portion of these advances is due in 1999.

Long-term debt maturities during each of the next five years are as follows:

Year	Amount
	(Millions of Dollars)
1990	$384.3
1991	478.3
1992	445.9
1993	537.2
1994	373.3

Property, plant and equipment totaling approximately $6.9 billion is either pledged as security for first mortgage bonds and certain notes or is restricted for use as mortgaged property.

Balances of notes payable and commercial paper of United and its subsidiaries as of December 31, 1989, and the weighted average interest rates for such borrowings for the year then ended, are as follows:

	Amount Outstanding	Weighted Average Interest Rate
	(Millions of Dollars)	
Bank notes	$ 10.9	9.62%
Master trust notes	42.1	9.32%
Commercial paper	151.8	9.34%
Total	$204.8	

Bank notes, Master Trust notes and commercial paper that United ultimately intends to replace by new long-term debt borrowings are classified as long-term debt. Such amounts were $205 and $83 million as of December 31, 1989 and 1988, respectively.

United and its subsidiaries' one-year bank notes are renewable at various dates throughout the year. United and its subsidiaries pay a fee to certain commercial banks to support current and future credit requirements based upon loan commitments. Lines of credit may be withdrawn by the banks if there is a material adverse change in the financial condition of United or its subsidiaries.

United has a Master Trust Note Agreement with the trust division of a bank to borrow funds on demand. Interest on such borrowings is at a rate that yields interest equivalent to the most favorable discount rate paid on 180-day commercial paper.

United and several of its subsidiaries issue commercial paper on a discount basis. Also, certain of United's subsidiaries participate in a financing agreement whereby two banks provide an $80 million letter of credit and long-term revolving credit agreement to support commercial paper issued for these subsidiaries. A fee is paid to the banks for this commitment, which expires July 31, 1992, and contains a provision to annually extend the term of the financing agreement for one year.

As of December 31, 1989, United and its subsidiaries had a total of $984 million of credit available made up of various bank commitments, a $700 million revolving credit agreement with a syndicate of domestic and international banks and the subsidiaries' letter of credit and long-term revolving credit agreement. Unused lines of credit available to United as of December 31, 1989, were $823 million, of which $631 million is available on a long-term basis under the $700 million revolving credit agreement and the subsidiaries' letter of credit and revolving credit agreement.

The most restrictive covenant applicable to dividends results from the $700 million revolving credit agreement. Among other restrictions, the agreement requires United to maintain a consolidated tangible net worth of $1.55 billion. At December 31, 1989, $610 of United's $883 million consolidated retained earnings is restricted from payment of dividends. The indentures and the $80 million financing agreement of United's subsidiaries contain various provisions restricting the payment to United of cash dividends on common stock. As of December 31, 1989, $709 million of the related subsidiaries' $1.4 billion total retained earnings is restricted. The flow of cash in the form of advances between United and its subsidiaries is generally not restricted.

8. Income Taxes

Income tax provision (benefit) for the years 1989, 1988 and 1987 includes the following components:

	1989	1988	1987
	(Millions of Dollars)		
Federal income tax provision (benefit)			
Current	$ 41.9	$122.2	$ (59.3)
Deferred	120.6	126.5	(27.7)
Deferred investment tax credit, net	(31.8)	(35.1)	(38.7)
	130.7	213.6	(125.7)
State income tax provision			
Current	15.3	50.3	10.0
Deferred	19.4	3.0	3.1
	34.7	53.3	13.1
Total income tax provision (benefit)	$165.4	$266.9	$(112.6)

Following are the differences which cause the effective income tax rate to vary from the statutory federal income tax rate of 34 percent in 1989 and 1988 and 40 percent in 1987:

	1989	1988	1987
	(Millions of Dollars)		
Net income (loss)	$362.9	$508.9	$ (51.5)
Preferred stock dividends of subsidiaries	1.1	1.2	1.2
	364.0	510.1	(50.3)
Income tax provision (benefit)	165.4	266.9	(112.6)
Income (loss) before income taxes	$529.4	$777.0	$(162.9)
Income tax provision (benefit) at the applicable statutory income tax rate	$180.0	$264.2	$ (65.2)
Less:			
Investment tax credit included in income	32.3	47.7	70.6
Statutory reduction of investment tax credit carryover		(26.3)	
Expected federal income tax provision (benefit) after investment tax credit	147.7	242.8	(135.8)
Effect of:			
Timing differences required to be flowed through by regulatory commissions	6.8	8.3	9.5
Deferred taxes reversing at prior year rates	(14.7)	(17.7)	(13.8)
Investment tax credit basis reduction	3.0	6.9	15.4
Equity in earnings of unconsolidated partnership subsidiary			(4.1)
State and local taxes, net of federal income tax effect	22.9	35.2	7.9
Other, net	(0.3)	(8.6)	8.3
Income tax provision (benefit), including investment tax credit	$165.4	$266.9	$(112.6)
Effective income tax rate	31%	34%	69%

Deferred income tax results from the differences in the timing of recognizing certain revenues and expenses for income tax and financial statement purposes. The sources of the differences for 1989, 1988 and 1987, along with the income tax effect of each, are as follows:

	1989	1988	1987
	(Millions of Dollars)		
Excess of tax depreciation and cost of removal over book depreciation	$124.5	$104.7	$93.5
Writedowns for partnership valuation and business restructuring charges	20.4	(1.3)	(36.7)
Revenues billed but not recognized for accounting purposes	2.3	(5.9)	(6.1)
Tax leasing arrangements	(3.3)	(3.0)	(3.5)
Capitalized cost differences between book and tax methods	36.3	9.4	3.2
Bad debts	4.0	(12.2)	9.6
Investment tax credit carryovers	(25.7)	79.8	(96.0)
Exchangeable debentures	9.5		
Deferred revenue	6.7	(10.7)	
Reserves deferred for tax purposes	7.0	(16.1)	0.7
Alternative minimum tax credit carryovers	(49.6)		
Other	7.9	(15.2)	10.7
	$140.0	$129.5	$(24.6)

United generated no regulated telephone deferred ITC in 1989. In both 1988 and 1987, regulated telephone ITC recapture exceeded ITC deferred by $1 million. ITC of $1, $13 and $33 million in 1989, 1988 and 1987, respectively, applicable primarily to construction of the long-distance communications network, is included in income on a current basis. Under special transition rules included in the Tax Reform Act of 1986 (Act), United has retained the benefit of ITC for its share of 1986 and subsequent construction expenditures for the long-distance communications network. Under the Act, reductions in ITC carryovers equal to $30 million were also required, of which $26 million was recognized in 1988.

For financial reporting purposes, unused ITC of $26, $13 and $96 million in 1989, 1988 and 1987, respectively, was applied as a reduction of deferred income taxes. Deferred income taxes of $93 million were restored in 1988 to reflect ITC carryovers utilized to reduce income taxes paid.

For income tax purposes, United has available at December 31, 1989, ITC carryovers of $42 million. The carryovers expire in the years 2002 through 2004 if not previously utilized. Additionally, $50 million of alternative minimum tax credit carryovers are available to offset regular income tax in future years.

Two United subsidiaries have available pre-acquisition tax loss carryforwards of approximately $47 million and ITC carryforwards of approximately $3 million. The utilization of these carryforwards is subject to the ability of the subsidiaries to generate taxable income on a separate company basis. These carryforwards expire in varying amounts annually from 1994 through 1998.

9. Pension Plan and Other Post Employment Benefits

Substantially all employees of United and its subsidiaries, including US Sprint, are covered by noncontributory defined benefit pension plans (the United Plan and the US Sprint Plan). For participants of the United Plan represented by collective bargaining agreements, benefits are based on schedules of defined amounts as negotiated by the respective parties. For remaining United Plan participants, benefits through December 31, 1989, are based on years of service and each participant's compensation for the highest five consecutive years during the last 10 years of employment. For participants of the US Sprint Plan, benefits are based on years of service and adjusted career average compensation, with credit for prior years of service with United or GTE for those employees who transferred to US Sprint from these companies during the six months ended December 31, 1986.

Effective January 1, 1990, the United Plan was amended for non-bargaining participants to also provide retirement benefits based upon years of service and adjusted career average compensation. For such participants employed at December 31, 1989, benefits for service rendered prior to January 1, 1990, will be based upon participants' compensation for the five-year period ending on December 31, 1989. Participants of this group who become eligible to retire prior to January 1, 2000, will receive the larger of the benefit amounts calculated under the two benefit formulas. The January 1, 1990, benefit formula change had no effect on 1989 net pension cost or the funded status of the Plans at December 31, 1989, and is not expected to increase future pension costs and funding requirements.

The funding policy of each plan is to contribute each year an actuarially determined amount consistent with applicable federal income tax regulations. The funding objective for each plan is to accumulate funds at a relatively stable rate over participants' working lives so that benefits are fully funded at retirement. At December 31, 1989, United Plan assets consist principally of investments in corporate equity securities and U.S. government and corporate debt securities. US Sprint Plan assets consist of investments in corporate equity securities, U.S. government and corporate debt securities, and receivables from the United and GTE pension plans. These receivables represent amounts necessary to fund the prior service cost granted to former United and GTE employees.

United calculates and records pension cost in accordance with Statement of Financial Accounting Standards No. 87, "Employers' Accounting for Pensions," which prescribes the use of the projected unit credit actuarial cost method. In accordance with generally accepted accounting principles for rate-regulated enterprises, United recognized pension costs for its rate-regulated operations in 1987 consistent with those methods used in setting rates. United adopted the revised Uniform System of Accounts (USOA) effective January 1, 1988. In adopting the revised USOA, many of the accounting differences between United's local communications services operations and its non-regulated operations were eliminated, including those differences pertaining to pension cost recognition. Accordingly, United's method of recognizing pension costs for its rate-regulated subsidiaries in 1989 and 1988 is generally consistent with that of its non-regulated operations.

A summary of the components and assumptions used in the calculation of 1989, 1988 and 1987 net pension cost follows. The 1987 amounts do not include the US Sprint Plan.

	1989	1988	1987
	(Millions of Dollars)		
Service cost — benefits earned during the period	$ 35.2	$ 32.5	$27.2
Interest cost on projected benefit obligation	63.9	58.5	49.7
Actual return on plan assets	(230.2)	(113.6)	(27.1)
Net, other	129.1	20.7	(31.7)
Net pension cost (credit)	$ (2.0)	$ (1.9)	$18.1
Discount rate	9.00%	8.75%	8.00%
Expected long-term rate of return on plan assets	8.00%	8.00%	8.25%
Anticipated composite rate of future increases in compensation	7.41%	7.29%	6.50%

The following table sets forth the funded status and amounts recognized in the consolidated balance sheets for the United and US Sprint Plans at December 31, 1989 and 1988:

	1989	1988
	(Millions of Dollars)	
Actuarial present value of benefit obligations		
Vested benefit obligation	$ (503.0)	$ (473.9)
Accumulated benefit obligation	$ (567.7)	$ (532.2)
Projected benefit obligation	$ (783.3)	$ (740.2)
Plan assets at fair value	1,296.9	1,085.7
Plan assets in excess of the projected benefit obligation	513.6	345.5
Unrecognized net gains	(239.8)	(59.7)
Unrecognized prior service cost	10.0	6.7
Unamortized portion of transitional asset at December 31	(267.1)	(290.0)
Prepaid pension cost	$ 16.7	$ 2.5

In addition to providing pension benefits, United provides certain health care and life insurance benefits for retired employees. Substantially all employees who retired on or before December 31, 1989, became eligible for these post-employment benefits. Effective January 1, 1990, retiring employees are eligible for health care and life insurance benefits on a shared cost basis with the employer company based upon years of service at retirement.

These health care and life insurance benefits for retirees and active employees were provided through an insurance company whose premiums were based principally on the benefits paid during the year. United recognizes the cost of providing these benefits for its retirees and active employees in its consolidated financial statements by expensing the insurance premiums, which were $109, $85 and $36 million in 1989, 1988 and 1987, respectively. The 1987 amount does not include US Sprint. The cost of providing 1989 benefits for the 4,535 retirees is not separable from the cost of providing benefits for the 39,581 active employees.

10. Operating Leases

Gross rental expense, reflected in continuing operations, aggregated $238, $222 and $55 million for 1989, 1988 and 1987, respectively. Gross rental expense in 1987 does not include amounts applicable to US Sprint.

Minimum rental commitments as of December 31, 1989, for all non-cancelable operating leases are as follows:

Year	Amount
	(Millions of Dollars)
1990	$213.3
1991	164.9
1992	111.4
1993	52.7
1994	38.9
Thereafter	114.4

The amount of rental commitments applicable to subleases, contingent rentals and executory costs is not significant.

11. Commitments and Contingencies

On July 10, 1989, the Equal Employment Opportunity Commission dismissed a class action suit filed in 1976 against United and certain of its subsidiaries alleging sex discrimination. In addition, various other suits arising in the ordinary course of business are pending against United and its subsidiaries, including US Sprint. Management cannot predict the ultimate outcome of these actions, but believes they will not result in a material effect on United's consolidated financial position.

United's consolidated capital expenditures for the year ending December 31, 1990, will approximate $1.6 billion. Normal purchase commitments have been made for these planned expenditures.

Under an agreement expiring in 1992, US Sprint may sell, on a continuing basis, up to $300 million of its accounts receivable. Subsequent collections of accounts receivable sold are typically reinvested in the pool of eligible receivables to maintain an aggregate outstanding balance of such receivables at a constant amount. Receivables sold that remained uncollected at December 31, 1989 and 1988, aggregated $300 million. Average monthly proceeds from the sale of accounts receivable were $250 and $231 million in 1989 and 1988, respectively. United and GTE are obligated to repurchase any defaulted receivables in proportion to their respective ownership interest upon the occurrence of certain events.

12. Supplemental Cash Flows Information

	For the Years Ended December 31,		
	1989	1988	1987
	(Millions of Dollars)		
Cash paid (refunded) for:			
Interest (net of amounts capitalized)	$374.3	$301.4	$250.1
Income taxes	$180.7	$ (16.6)	$ (80.1)

In connection with 1989 acquisitions referred to in Note 3, liabilities assumed were as follows (in millions):

Fair value of assets acquired	$295.0
Cash paid	24.4
Liabilities assumed	$270.6

Net recorded value of properties relinquished in the exchange of assets with Contel, as described in Note 3, totaled $65 million.

During 1988, $383 million of advances received by US Sprint from GTE were converted to capital contributions.

See the consolidated statements of common stock and other shareholders' equity for amounts of common stock issued as the result of conversions of preferred stock and debentures.

Management Report

The management of United Telecommunications, Inc. has the responsibility for the integrity and objectivity of the information contained in the annual report. Management is responsible for the consistency of reporting such information and for ensuring that generally accepted accounting principles are used.

In discharging this responsibility, management maintains a comprehensive system of internal controls and supports an extensive program of internal audits, and has made organizational arrangements providing appropriate divisions of responsibility and established communication programs aimed at assuring that its policies, procedures and codes of conduct are understood and practiced by its employees.

The consolidated financial statements included in the annual report have been examined by Ernst & Young, independent auditors. They believe that the consolidated financial statements presented are neither misleading nor contain material errors.

The responsibility of the Board of Directors for these financial statements is pursued primarily through its Audit Committee. The Audit Committee, composed entirely of directors who are not officers or employees of United, meets periodically with the independent auditors both with and without management to assure that their respective responsibilities are being fulfilled. The independent auditors have full access to the Audit Committee to discuss auditing and financial reporting matters.

William T. Esrey, President

Report of Independent Auditors

The Board of Directors and Shareholders
United Telecommunications, Inc.

We have audited the accompanying consolidated balance sheets of United Telecommunications, Inc. (United) at December 31, 1989 and 1988, and the related consolidated statements of income, common stock and other shareholders' equity, and cash flows for each of the three years in the period ended December 31, 1989. These financial statements are the responsibility of United's management. Our responsibility is to express an opinion on these financial statements based on our audits. The financial information of US Sprint Communications Company (US Sprint), an 80.1 percent owned limited partnership effective January 3, 1989, and a 50 percent owned general partnership before that date, is presented on a consolidated basis in 1989 and 1988 and using the equity method in 1987 (see Note 1). The 1987 financial statements of US Sprint were examined by other auditors whose report has been furnished to us, and our opinion on United's 1987 consolidated financial statements, insofar as it relates to the amounts included for US Sprint, is based solely on the report of the other auditors.

We conducted our audits in accordance with generally accepted auditing standards. Those standards require that we plan and perform the audit to obtain reasonable assurance about whether the financial statements are free of material misstatement. An audit includes examining, on a test basis, evidence supporting the amounts and disclosures in the financial statements. An audit also includes assessing the accounting principles used and significant estimates made by management, as well as evaluating the overall financial statement presentation. We believe that our audits and the 1987 report of the other auditors provide a reasonable basis for our opinion.

In our opinion, based on our audits and, in 1987, on the report of the other auditors, the financial statements referred to above present fairly, in all material respects, the consolidated financial position of United Telecommunications, Inc. at December 31, 1989 and 1988, and the consolidated results of its operations and its cash flows for each of the three years in the period ended December 31, 1989, in conformity with generally accepted accounting principles.

Ernst & Young
Kansas City, Missouri
February 6, 1990

CONSOLIDATED STATEMENTS OF INCOME
FOR THE YEARS ENDED DECEMBER 31,

	1989	1988	1987	1986	1985
	(Millions of Dollars Except per Share Data)				
Net operating revenues					
Long-distance communications services	$4,323.6	$3,405.4		$ 212.4	$ 342.6
Local communications services	2,637.0	2,509.7	$2,388.9	2,311.4	2,302.3
Complementary businesses	762.1	698.6	628.0	555.6	456.9
Intercompany revenues	(173.7)	(120.7)	(81.8)	(66.7)	(18.0)
Total net operating revenues	7,549.0	6,493.0	2,935.1	3,012.7	3,083.8
Operating expenses					
Long-distance communications services	4,097.0	3,791.5		322.2	837.5
Local communications services	2,001.3	1,912.9	1,752.3	1,643.6	1,659.9
Complementary businesses	714.4	656.5	585.3	525.2	446.9
Intercompany expenses	(173.7)	(120.7)	(81.8)	(66.7)	(18.0)
Total operating expenses	6,639.0	6,240.2	2,255.8	2,424.3	2,926.3
Operating income	910.0	252.8	679.3	588.4	157.5
Other (income) expense, net	(11.5)	7.1	(31.2)	(42.5)	(19.9)
Interest charges, net of capitalization	359.8	320.4	265.9	211.3	187.9
Equity in loss of US Sprint			580.4	153.3	
Minority interest	33.4	(223.4)			
Income (loss) from continuing operations					
before income taxes	528.3	148.7	(135.8)	266.3	(10.5)
Income tax provision (benefit)	165.4	6.9	(102.3)	68.3	(46.5)
Income (loss) from continuing operations	362.9	141.8	(33.5)	198.0	36.0
Discontinued operations		367.1	(18.0)	(17.5)	(15.2)
Net income (loss)	362.9	508.9	(51.5)	180.5	20.8
Preferred stock dividends	3.0	3.3	3.5	3.7	4.0
Earnings (loss) applicable to common stock	$ 359.9	$ 505.6	$ (55.0)	$ 176.8	$ 16.8
Earnings (loss) per share*					
From continuing operations	$ 1.72	$ 0.68	$ (0.19)	$ 1.00	$ 0.17
From discontinued operations		1.80	(0.09)	(0.09)	(0.08)
Total	$ 1.72	$ 2.48	$ (0.28)	$ 0.91	$ 0.09
Cash dividends per common share*	$ 0.97	$ 0.96	$ 0.96	$ 0.96	$ 0.96

*Common share data reflects the 1989 two-for-one stock split.

CONSOLIDATED BALANCE SHEETS AT DECEMBER 31,

	1989	1988	1987	1986	1985
Assets			(Millions of Dollars)		
Current assets					
Cash and temporary cash investments	$ 114.8	$ 617.1	$ 74.4	$ 108.2	$ 110.2
Accounts receivable, net	998.7	850.3	450.4	439.0	513.5
Notes receivable	84.4	330.6			
Inventories held for resale	124.7	131.3	86.7	82.2	113.6
Income tax refund			74.0	94.7	
Deferred income taxes	33.5	44.7	21.7	20.5	52.0
Prepayments and other assets	153.1	151.0	101.1	86.2	98.0
Total current assets	1,509.2	2,125.0	808.3	830.8	887.3
Investment in and advances to US Sprint			1,187.9	1,065.9	
Property, plant and equipment					
Long-distance communications services	4,281.4	3,493.0			541.6
Local communications services	7,213.9	6,900.8	6,555.3	6,303.6	6,104.4
Complementary and other	259.6	275.4	414.3	406.1	372.6
	11,754.9	10,669.2	6,969.6	6,709.7	7,018.6
Less accumulated depreciation	3,870.0	3,339.4	2,625.5	2,429.0	2,300.2
	7,884.9	7,329.8	4,344.1	4,280.7	4,718.4
Intangible assets, net	122.4	124.3			
Other assets	304.8	237.8	218.1	201.7	161.7
	$ 9,821.3	$ 9,816.9	$6,558.4	$6,379.1	$5,767.4
Liabilities and Shareholders' Equity					
Current liabilities					
Current maturities of long-term debt	$ 384.3	$ 148.5	$ 123.2	$ 49.9	$ 42.8
Accounts payable	738.7	716.9	390.3	381.9	586.1
Accrued local interconnection and leased facilities costs	318.5	292.1			
Advance billings	67.5	63.3	59.4	44.9	41.6
Accrued taxes	237.9	313.2	80.5	85.7	19.9
Accrued interest	107.0	100.8	72.6	56.8	45.2
Other	424.9	514.1	199.1	165.2	324.2
Total current liabilities	2,278.8	2,148.9	925.1	784.4	1,059.8
Long-term debt	3,747.0	3,674.8	3,047.6	2,683.3	1,947.7
Deferred credits and other liabilities					
Deferred income taxes	934.2	792.1	623.3	648.7	554.4
Deferred investment tax credits	156.7	188.8	223.9	262.6	282.1
Other	126.0	137.3	171.5	229.6	186.7
	1,216.9	1,118.2	1,018.7	1,140.9	1,023.2
Minority interest	464.8	958.9			
Redeemable preferred stock	36.9	38.9	40.9	42.7	44.3
Common stock and other shareholders' equity					
Common stock	517.8	256.6	251.4	246.4	239.8
Employees stock purchase installments	22.3	7.3	16.0	6.0	13.6
Non-redeemable convertible preferred stock	4.0	2.4	2.6	2.9	3.3
Capital in excess of par or stated value	650.0	882.5	838.9	810.5	763.9
Retained earnings	882.8	728.4	417.2	662.0	671.8
	2,076.9	1,877.2	1,526.1	1,727.8	1,692.4
	$ 9,821.3	$ 9,816.9	$6,558.4	$6,379.1	$5,767.4

Accelerated Cost Recovery Systems (ACRS) The method of depreciation prescribed by the IRS starting in 1981. Depreciable assets are assigned to useful life groups based on their nature. Various percentages then were assigned to the years. The amount of depreciation approximated the results obtained under the 150% declining-balance method.

account A record designed to classify and summarize the effect of economic events on a particular element in an entity (such as cash, equipment, or accounts payable).

account form balance sheet A balance sheet in which liabilities and equities are listed to the right of assets.

accounting The process of identifying, measuring, and communicating economic information to permit informed judgments and decisions by the users of the information.

accounting cycle The individual steps required to process accounting information during an accounting period.

accounting equation The foundation on which accounting is developed and the basic formula for the balance sheet. It expresses the dollar amounts of assets, liabilities, and equities and can be stated as ASSETS = LIABILITIES + EQUITY.

accounts payable Amounts due (payables) to suppliers of goods or services for which no cash has been paid.

accounts payable system A computer system that provides control over payment to suppliers, issues checks to suppliers and provides information necessary for effective cash management.

Accounts Receivable An asset account arising from the sale of goods or services to customers on account. Receivables arising from other transactions, such as loans to officers or other employees, are *not* included in this account, but in separate accounts on the balance sheet.

accounts receivable collection period The average time needed to collect an account; the average annual accounts receivable is divided by net credit sales and the result is multiplied by 365 days.

accounts receivable system A computer system that generates monthly invoices to send to customers, maintains records of amounts due, and generates reports needed by management, such as overdue accounts and aging of receivables.

accounts receivable turnover Indicates how often during the year accounts receivable have been converted to cash; net credit sales is divided by average accounts receivable.

accrual method of accounting Method of accounting that recognizes revenues when they are earned and expenses when they are incurred; ignores when cash is received or paid in recognizing revenues or expenses; also referred to as the accrual basis of accounting.

accruals Accruals are revenue and expense items that must be recorded during the adjustment process in order to achieve a proper matching of revenue and expense.

accrued expenses An expense that has already been incurred, but is not yet due to be paid, such as unpaid wages at the end of an accounting period. This is an application of the matching concept.

accrued revenues A revenue that has been earned, but has not yet been received, such as interest revenue on a note receivable. This is an application of the matching concept.

accumulated depreciation The total amount of an asset's original cost that has been allocated to an expense since the asset was acquired. The account where these expenses are entered is called an asset *valuation account* or *contra-asset account.*

acid-test ratio Quick current assets divided by current liabilities; this indicates the ability of the entity to meet the immediate demands of the creditors. A more severe measure of solvency than the current ratio, it is also known as the *quick current ratio.*

"adding apples and oranges" An old cliché in accounting. It is believed or accepted that monetary units (dollars) from different time periods can be added together to get meaningful amounts. Because those dollars have different values caused by inflation, the sum is not meaningful. Just as adding apples and oranges gives us mixed fruit, adding dollars of different values gives us mixed dollars.

adjusted trial balance A listing of accounts and their balances after the posting of adjusting entries to the accounts of the entity.

adjusting journal entry An entry made in the accounts to reflect the correct balance sheet or income statement valuation of an item. This is an application of the matching concept.

aging of accounts receivable The detailed analysis of trade accounts receivable by time elapsed since the creation of the receivable.

Allowance for Doubtful Accounts A contra account to Accounts Receivable, showing the estimated amount of receivables that may never be realized in cash.

Allowance to Reduce Securities to Market A valuation account under the lower of cost or market method of valuing securities used to indirectly reduce the valuation of securities when the market price is below cost. The asset account is not reduced directly.

American Accounting Association (AAA) The membership of this group consists mainly of accounting educators, who promote most of the research conducted today in accounting. The group has contributed much of the base for accounting theory.

American Institute of Certified Public Accountants (AICPA) A national professional accounting association that has been very active in the development of GAAP in this century. This group also develops and grades the national Certified Public Accountants (CPA) Examination.

amortization The process of allocating the cost of an intangible asset to each accounting period receiving benefit from that asset. An example is the allocation of the bond premium or bond discount to interest expense over the time the bond issue will be outstanding.

annuity A series of payments or receipts made at equal time intervals. The payment of interest on a bond issue is an annuity, as well as payments into a bond sinking fund.

appropriated retained earnings See restricted retained earnings.

"arm's length" transaction A business transaction assumed to take place at market value. No secret agreements are included, and the monetary value decided on would be the same for anyone involved in similar transactions. An objectively determined transaction.

assets Probable future economic benefits obtained or controlled by a particular entity as a result of past transactions or events.

auditor's report An opinion of a professional accountant on the financial statements of an entity; states whether the financial statements fairly present the financial position and operating results of the entity and whether these statements have been prepared according to GAAP.

authorized stock The number of shares a corporation may issue as stated in the corporate charter.

balance sheet A financial report showing the assets, liabilities, and equities of an entity on a specific date; also referred to as a statement of financial position or a statement of financial condition.

bank reconciliation A reconciliation of the amount of cash in an entity's account reported by the bank and the amount of cash showing in the general ledger Cash account.

betterment A capital expenditure that increases the operational efficiency of a long-term asset without extending its useful life.

board of directors Elected representatives of a corporation's stockholders.

bond A debt security that requires the periodic payment of interest at a stated rate, and the repayment of face or par value at some date in the future. The maturity date may be a single date in the future (term bonds) or multiple dates (serial bonds).

bond discount An amount under the face value received when a bond is issued. The situation usually exists when the market rate of interest is higher than the stated rate of interest on the bond issue.

bond indenture The printed agreement that specifies the terms that the issuing corporation has agreed to abide by.

bond premium An amount in excess of the face value received when a bond is issued. The situation usually exists when the market rate of interest is below the stated interest rate on the bond issue.

bonuses to current partners A means of compensating the current members of a partnership for a job well done when admitting a new partner into the partnership.

bonuses to new partners A means used to entice needed investors to join a partnership. The new partner will have a Capital balance in excess of the amount invested.

book value The balance sheet valuation of an item. The term is used often to describe the results of subtracting accumulated depreciation from the original cost of a long-term asset.

book value of common stock The amount of the net assets of a corporation represented by one share of common stock. It is determined by dividing the number of common shares outstanding into the stockholders' equity accruing to the common stockholders. Total stockholders' equity is first reduced by the portion accruing to the preferred stockholders.

book value of preferred stock The amount preferred stockholders would receive on a corporation's liquidation. It generally consists of the stock's par value, or a liquidating value if offered, plus the dividend in arrears on cumulative preferred stock.

business combination The acquisition of one corporation by another corporation, usually through acquiring a controlling interest represented by purchasing more than 50% of the outstanding voting stock.

call price The amount a corporation must pay to redeem a bond in order to exercise the call provision of the issue.

call provision A provision in the bond indenture that allows the issuing corporation to redeem the bonds before the maturity date. The call price is usually in excess of face value.

capital expenditures Cash outflows related to long-term assets that increase the operational efficiency of the asset, or extend its useful life. They include the asset cost, less applicable cash discounts.

Capital—Owner The account that takes the place of paid-in capital and retained earnings in a sole proprietorship or a partnership. Original and additional investments are recorded here, as well as withdrawals, profits, and losses.

capitalization of Retained Earnings The transfer on a balance sheet from Retained Earnings to Paid-in Capital as the result of a stock dividend.

capitalize To record a cash outflow as an asset rather than as an expense. The term is used in this chapter in connection with capital expenditures applied to the asset cost.

cash Anything that will be accepted by a bank for deposit; serves as a unit of account, a medium of exchange, and a store of purchasing power. Includes coin and currency from any recognized country, checks drawn on most banks, money orders, credit card charges such as VISA and Master Charge, and so on.

cash disbursements journal A special journal used to record all payments made by check. Payments of cash, if made, should come from the petty cash fund.

cash dividend A distribution to stockholders made in cash.

cash receipts journal A special journal used to record all receipts of cash.

certified checks Checks that are deducted from the maker's account when the check is issued, rather than when the check is returned to the bank after being cashed by the payee.

certified management accountant (CMA) A professional accountant, generally in industry, who has passed the CMA Examination and has satisfied all other professional requirements.

certified public accountant (CPA) A professional accountant who has passed the CPA Examination and has satisfied all other professional requirements for admittance.

chart of accounts A list of account names and numbers used in the general ledger; usually found in financial statement presentation order.

classification The grouping of accounts by category on financial statements.

closing entries The entries that reduce revenue and expense balances to zero in preparation for the next fiscal year, and update the Retained Earnings account for the current year.

common size financial statements Statements that have been restated in percentage form, such as an income statement that expresses all components as a percentage of sales.

common stock The class of stock that is a basic ownership unit in a corporation. Ownership carries the right to vote and to share in dividends.

composite rate A depreciation rate applied to a group of related but different assets, rather than depreciation calculated on each asset.

compound journal entry A journal entry that includes more than one account that is debited, or more than one account that is credited.

conservatism When making a choice between equally defensible alternatives, the accountant will choose the one that will produce the least favorable results for the entity. This presents the most conservative estimate of financial position or net income.

consistency The consistent application of accounting principles from one accounting period to the next. This makes it possible to compare one year's financial statements with another year, when changes are made in the application of accounting principles.

consolidated financial statements Two or more sets of financial statements combined when one corporation (parent) owns from 51% to 100% of another corporation (subsidiary) and is presumed to have control over that corporation. Such control from an economic viewpoint results in only one company.

constant dollar accounting An application of general price-level indexes to historical cost amounts in the financial statements. The result is the determination of a purchasing power gain or loss, and the expression of statement amounts in common dollars.

Consumer Price Index (CPI) A U.S. Department of Labor index that prices a *market basket* of goods at various times during the year in order to determine the general inflation rate for the year.

control account A general ledger account that has a subsidiary ledger containing the details to support the balance.

controlling interest Where one corporation owns more than 50% of the outstanding voting stock of another corporation.

convertible bonds A bond issue that may, at the option of the bondholder, be exchanged for shares of common stock of the issuing corporation.

copyright The exclusive right granted by the federal government to publish a literary or artistic work. The right exists for the lifetime of the author plus 50 years.

cost–benefit judgment The measuring of the cost of providing information with the benefit the users will receive from having access to the information. If the cost exceeds the benefit, the information will not be provided.

cost of goods purchased Purchases less purchase returns and allowances and purchase discounts, plus transportation in; also referred to as *cost of purchases.*

cost of goods sold Accounting term used to describe the cost of merchandise sold during an accounting period.

cost method A term used to describe a method of accounting for treasury stock. When purchased, the stock is recorded at cost through an entry debiting Treasury Stock, and crediting Cash.

counter-balance The attribute inventory errors have on net income, caused by the fact that ending inventory becomes beginning inventory in the next accounting period.

credit The right side of an account.

creditors Individuals to whom money is owed by an entity; often referred to as *primary claims.*

cumulative dividend An undeclared dividend that accumulates and has to be paid in the future before any dividends can be paid to common stockholders. Once a dividend is declared, the fixed percentage of par value or dollar amount per share for preferred stock is awarded for each year dividends were not paid.

cumulative preferred stock Stock on which an unpaid dividend will accumulate until paid. As long as dividends are in arrears, common stockholders may not receive any dividend distributions.

current assets Economic resources to be converted to cash or consumed during the next year.

current cost accounting A departure from historical cost, where assets and liabilities are valued at their current value as determined by reference to market prices.

current liabilities Obligations of an entity that come due during the next accounting period or during the next operating cycle if it's longer.

current market value A valuation method used for investments in securities. The investment is adjusted annually to its current value, whether that value is above *or* below the investment cost. It is used in some industries where a majority of the assets are securities in other entities.

current ratio Current assets divided by current liabilities; this indicates the number of current asset dollars available to pay current liabilities. A crude measure of solvency, it is also known as the *working capital ratio*.

date of dividend declaration The date the board of directors elects to declare a dividend. The act creates a liability of the corporation at this time.

date of payment The date assets are distributed or the shares of the corporation's own stock are issued as dividends to stockholders on the ledger on the date of record.

date of record The date the individual stockholder who will receive a dividend is identified, usually a week or two after the declaration.

debenture bonds See *unsecured bonds*.

debit The left side of an account.

debit or **credit memo** A source document that supports a journal entry recording a sale or purchase return or allowance, or other adjustments to an invoice.

debt-to-equity ratio A comparison of total debt with total stockholders' equity. It indicates what percentage of the assets are financed with debt and what percentage financed with owner contribution, either by investment or by earnings.

decision support system An information system that managers can use to provide highly refined information to help make non-routine decisions.

deficit A debit balance in the Retained Earnings account of a corporation.

denominated in A phrase used to describe the measurement or monetary unit in which a transaction takes place. Most transactions that take place are denominated in U.S. currency, but some are denominated in a foreign currency unit.

depletion The allocation of the cost of a natural resource to each accounting period receiving ben-

efit from that resource.

deposits-in-transit Deposits that have been recorded on the books of the entity, but made too late to appear on the current bank statement.

depreciable cost The portion of the cost of an asset to be allocated over its useful life; determined by subtracting the salvage value of the asset from its original cost.

depreciation The allocation of the cost of a tangible long-term asset to each accounting period receiving benefit from that asset.

depreciation expense That part of the original cost of a long-term asset allocated to a particular accounting period.

direct method One of two formats for the Cash Flows from Operating Activities section of the statement of cash flows. The method takes a positive approach, in that it reflects the income statement items that *do* have an effect on Cash.

direct write-off method A method of accounting for uncollectible accounts when credit sales are a minor part of an entity's business. No estimates are made before an account proves uncollectible. The receivable is simply debited to bad debt expense at the time it is written off. There is no proper matching under the direct write-off method.

dissimilar A term applied to transactions that involve the trade-in of one asset for another. If the assets are not related to one another, such as a parcel of land for a truck, the exchange involves *dissimilar assets*.

dividends Distributions of corporate assets to stockholders in the form of cash or other assets, *or* distributions of the corporation's own stock to owners. Since they are distributions of net income, they are not determinants of net income; therefore, they are not subtracted from revenue as are expenses.

dividend-yield ratio Indicates the cash return that can be expected from a particular investment; dividends per share is divided by the market price per share.

donated capital The portion of paid-in capital that represents assets contributed by stockholders and other interested parties.

double declining-balance depreciation A depreciation method that assigns a greater amount of asset cost to the earlier years of an asset's useful life and lesser amounts to the later years. The method uses a constant rate applied to a declining base. The rate is twice the straight-line rate, and the declining base is the book value of the asset at the beginning of the accounting period. Also referred to as *200% declining balance*. Extensions of the method include 175%, 150% and 125%.

double-entry bookkeeping system The method of accounting that recognizes the dual nature of each transaction—that is, both the property is accounted for (assets) and who has the right to that property (equity).

Drawing account The account that in a sole proprietorship or a partnership takes the place of the Dividends account in a corporation. Whenever a partner or a sole proprietor takes assets out of the business, cash or noncash, the Drawing account is charged with the fair market value of those assets.

earnings per share The amount of net income allocated to each share of common stock outstanding. The amount is usually based on a weighted average of the number of shares outstanding.

effective interest method A method of amortizing the premium or discount on a long-term investment in bonds that results in a constant *rate* of interest reported as earned over the life of the investment.

entity A unit of accountability that exists separately from its owners; the term *legal entity* is used when referring to a corporation, which has a legal existence separate from its owners.

entity assumption The business enterprise is always assumed to be separate from its owners.

equity Claims against assets of the entity; consists of creditor claims and owner claims.

Equity in Earnings of Investee The name of the account on the income statement that results from the application of the equity method. The balance in the account represents the owners' share of the reported earnings of the investee.

equity method A method of accounting for investments applied when the investor has sufficient ownership interest to exercise significant influence over the corporation. Under the method, a relationship is maintained between the balance in the investment account and the investor's share of the stockholders' equity of the corporation.

exchange rate Refers to the factor used to convert a different monetary unit to the U.S. dollar. The monetary unit may be a foreign currency unit or a U.S. dollar unadjusted for inflation.

expenses An outflow of assets or the resources of an entity used up, or obligations incurred during a time period, in the course of performing revenue-producing services.

extraordinary items Gains and losses that occur infrequently and that are unusual in nature; classified separately on the income statement.

extraordinary repair A cost outlay that extends the useful life of a depreciable asset. The amount should be debited to the Accumulated Depreciation account, thereby reducing the book value of the asset allocated over its remaining useful life. The Accumulated Depreciation account, rather than the asset account, is debited, since the extraordinary repair is thought to be a reduction of estimated depreciation taken in past years.

face value The amount repaid when a bond issue matures. This amount, printed on the bond, is also referred to as the *par value.*

fair market value (FMV) The actual cash selling price of a new asset considered when trading in an old asset for a new one.

Federal Reserve Board A federal board that oversees much of the banking activity in the United States.

fiduciary relationship A relationship based on mutual trust between two or more individuals.

FIFO (first in, first out) An inventory valuation method that assumes the first unit purchased is the first unit sold. An actual FIFO flow would

be used with perishable goods.

financial accounting The area of accounting that focuses on users outside the entity, such as owners (stockholders), creditors, and the government.

Financial Accounting Standards Board (FASB) A board funded by the Financial Accounting Foundation to establish accounting rules and regulations. Unlike its predecessors, this is an independent, full-time, paid group of individuals.

Financial Executives Institute (FEI) A group of accountants who hold higher management positions in the financial hierarchy in large corporations.

financial structure Sometimes referred to as the *capital structure,* it is the right-hand side of the balance sheet, the liabilities and stockholders' equity of an entity. It answers the question, how were the assets financed? debt? equity? internally (retained earnings)?

financial transaction The financial aspect of a transaction, expressed in terms of dollars.

financing activities The activities of an entity that result from financing decisions made by management. Inflows come from the issuance of common or preferred stock, or from long-term borrowing through mortgages or bonds payable. The outflows include the retirement of the just-mentioned securities, in addition to the payment of dividends. Because of a close tie to the income statement and the determination of income tax liability, interest expense on long-term borrowing is currently being reported as an outflow from *operating* activities.

fiscal year An arbitrary twelve-month period beginning on the first day of any month. Fiscal years are used many times instead of calendar years, so the year ends when the business activity is at its lowest point.

flow of costs The sequence in which costs are assigned to merchandise sold and remaining in inventory.

flow of goods The sequence in which purchased goods are sold. Accountants can assume that the first unit purchased is always the

first unit sold (FIFO), as should happen with perishable goods, that the last unit purchased is always the first unit sold (LIFO), or that the cost of goods sold, and therefore the ending inventory, is equal to the average cost incurred during the year.

fob destination A term indicating that title to shipped goods passes when the goods reach their destination. The seller is responsible for transportation costs.

fob shipping point A term indicating that title to shipped goods passes when the goods leave the shipping point. The buyer is responsible for transportation costs.

footing A total of a column of figures; the difference between the debit and credit balances is then calculated.

foreign exchange gains and losses The results of foreign transactions when the amount eventually paid on the transaction differs from the original dollar amount of the transaction.

foreign transactions Economic events denominated in a currency other than the U.S. dollar. If the transaction is other than cash, a measurement problem arises because of the daily fluctuation in the exchange rate of other currencies in relation to the U.S. dollar.

foreign translation The area of accounting that revolves around a subsidiary or parent company operating in a foreign country and using a monetary unit other than the U.S. dollar.

franchise A legal right to render a service or to produce a good under a specific trademark or trade name.

future value analysis Determines the future value of a present value, either as a single amount or as an annuity. A single amount will grow only because of the time value of money; an annuity will grow because of the time value of money and the periodic deposits. This analysis can be used to determine sinking-fund deposit requirements for a *term bond* issue. See the chapter appendix.

general inflation Measured by some general price index, such as the Consumer Price Index. Balance sheet valuations are converted, and the purchasing power gain or loss is determined by the difference between the converted and the unconverted amounts.

general journal A chronological record of an entity's financial transactions; often referred to as a book of original entry.

general ledger A book that contains the asset, liability, equity, revenue, and expense accounts of an entity.

general ledger system An integrated computer system that records transactions, balances accounts, posts, and prepares the financial statements.

generally accepted accounting principles (GAAP) A set of constantly changing accounting principles and practices that have become generally accepted and are used by accountants in the preparation of financial statements.

going-concern assumption The entity will remain in existence indefinitely.

goodwill The value attached to the ability of an entity to make superior earnings as compared with other entities in the same industry. Goodwill is not recognized in the accounts unless it is purchased, generally arising when one corporations buys another at an amount in excess of the fair market value of the assets less the liabilities of the entity purchased. When goodwill is recorded, its cost is amortized over a period not to exceed 40 years.

goodwill from consolidation The excess of the purchase price of a business combination accounted for as a purchase over the fair market value of the net assets of the subsidiary. It appears as an asset only on the consolidated balance sheet, not on the individual balance sheet of the parent or its subsidiary.

Governmental Accounting Standards Board (GASB) Another board funded by the Financial Accounting Foundation to establish accounting rules and regulations for governmental units.

gross profit The excess of the sales revenue over the net cost of the goods sold, also referred to as *gross margin*.

gross profit method An inventory valuation method that estimates the amount of inventory without taking a physical count. Cost of goods sold is estimated using a historic gross profit rate, leaving the estimated inventory as a residual.

gross profit percentage Indicates the percentage of each sales dollar available to cover all operating expenses, interest, taxes, and ultimately, profit to the owners; gross profit is divided by sales.

group rate A depreciation rate applied to a group of similar assets, rather than depreciation calculated on each asset.

historical-cost assumption The belief that the most objective measure of an asset's worth is the amount paid for the asset. Subsequent changes in the value of the asset are not recorded.

historic rate The exchange rate that should be used to convert non-monetary items on the balance sheet to their constant dollar equivalents. The rate in effect when a balance sheet item is recorded.

holding gains net of inflation The difference between the historical cost of an item and its current cost, adjusted for inflation. If an item cost $100 at the beginning of the year and $130 at the end, during which inflation was 10%, the holding gain would be $30, and the holding gain net of inflation would be $20 ($100 × 0.1 = $10; $100 + $10 = $110; $130 − $110 = $20).

horizontal analysis The analysis of financial statements through the calculation of percentage *changes* in statement components over two or more years.

imprest petty cash system A system whereby a fixed amount of currency and coin is set aside to be used to pay for minor expenditures. Entries are not made in the accounts for each expenditure, but only made when the fund is reimbursed.

income determination and matching assumption The determination of income by the accrual basis of accounting, where revenue is recognized when earned and expenses are recognized when incurred. The expenses are then matched against the revenue generated to determine net income.

income statement A financial report summarizing the entity's progress during a time period; summarizes revenue earned and expenses incurred, and calculates net income for the period.

income summary A temporary account used to accumulate all revenue and expense balances at the end of the fiscal year. This account summarizes the net income (or loss) for the period and is closed to the Retained Earnings account.

indirect method One of two formats for the Cash Flows from Operating Activities section of the statement of cash flows. The method takes a negative approach, in that it reflects the income statement items that *do not* have an effect on cash.

Individual Employee Earnings Record A cumulative record of all gross earnings and related deductions from earnings for a particular employee.

institutional investors Investors, usually corporations such as banks, savings and loans, pension plans, and insurance companies, of large sums—billions of dollars every year.

intangible long-term assets Long-term assets that are not physical substances, such as patents. Their cost is amortized over the accounting periods receiving benefits from the assets, but not over a period exceeding 40 years. *Straight-line amortization* is generally used.

interest on Capital balances When unequal amounts of capital are invested into a partnership by the various partners, the profit-sharing agreement should allow interest on Capital balances as a means of more equitably allocating net income to the partners.

interim financial statement A financial statement that does *not* report the activities and financial position for an entire business year. An interim statement could be for *any* period of time, from one day to 11 months. Financial statements for a 12-month period are not referred to as interim statements.

internal control The system used to ensure accurate record keeping and the timely preparation of financial statements, in order to safeguard the assets of the entity and to promote efficiency.

Internal Revenue Service (IRS) The agency of the federal government that collects various taxes for the U.S. Treasury. The IRS has different rules for determining income for tax purposes than those used to determine income for financial accounting purposes. In many cases, an entity will maintain two sets of records, one for the IRS and one using GAAP for financial reporting.

international accounting A subject area that encompasses the entire world. The many GAAP vary from country to country.

International Accounting Standards Committee (IASC) A group that has issued many international accounting standards that have been translated into a number of languages.

International Federation of Accountants (IFAC) A group made up of professional accounting bodies from more than 50 countries in the world. It was founded primarily to nurture international discussion on accounting issues.

inventory control system A computer system used to monitor inventory quantity and to minimize inventory costs.

inventory turnover ratio Indicates how many times the inventory has been sold and replaced during the year; cost of goods sold is divided by average inventory.

investee The term applied to the corporation over which an investor has the ability to exercise significant influence.

investing activities The activities of an entity that result from investment decisions by management. Inflows result from the sale of assets previously purchased, while outflows result from the purchase of long-term assets. The assets would include land, buildings, and equipment that a company needs for operating, as well as intangible assets, such as patents and copyrights, and long-term investments.

investment into a partnership One way of admitting a new partner. Both cash and noncash assets are invested in exchange for an interest in the partnership.

issued stock Authorized stock that has been issued. Treasury shares that have been reacquired are still considered issued stock.

journal entry An entry recorded in the general journal with at least one debit and one credit.

journalizing The process of recording a transaction in a journal.

LCM (lower of cost or market) An inventory valuation method that compares the cost of inventory with the current replacement cost. If the current replacement cost is below the original cost of the item, then the replacement cost becomes the assumed cost of that item. It is an application of *conservatism*.

leasehold improvements Improvements made to leased property that will revert back to the lessor at the end of the lease. Classified as an intangible asset, the cost is amortized over the life of the lease or the life of the improvement if it is less than the life of the lease.

leaseholds A payment made at the beginning of a lease in order to secure the lease. Classified as an intangible asset, the amount is amortized over the life of the lease.

ledger account An account kept in a book called a ledger.

legal capital The portion of paid-in capital that cannot be distributed to the stockholders in the form of dividends.

leverage The use of borrowed capital in an attempt to earn more in the business than the rate of interest paid on the borrowed capital.

liabilities Probable future economic sacrifices of economic benefits arising from the present obligations of an entity to transfer assets or provide services to other entities in the future as a result of past transactions or events.

LIFO (last in, first out) An inventory valuation method that assumes the last unit purchased is the first unit sold. An actual LIFO flow would occur in the landscaping material business.

liquidating dividend A dividend that is charged against Paid-in Capital, rather than Retained Earnings.

liquidation of a partnership When a partnership is liquidated, all the assets are sold for

cash, the liabilities are paid, and cash is distributed to the partners according to their interest in the partnership.

liquidation value The valuation of assets at their net realizable value; based on the assumption that the entity will go out of business and will sell its assets.

long-term asset An asset that is long-lived (more than one year), used in the business, and not held for resale; sometimes referred to as *fixed assets*.

long-term liabilities Obligations that do not require repayment for one or more years.

long-term portfolio Investment securities that management does not intend to liquidate in the near future.

lower of cost or market (LCM) A method of valuating equity securities held in either short-term or long-term portfolios when significant influence cannot be exercised on the issuing corporation.

management information system (MIS) An information and data processing system designed to aid in the performance of management functions. An MIS system includes all the computer systems introduced in Chapter 6.

managerial accounting The area of accounting that focuses on users inside the entity, such as management and owners (such as sole proprietors or partners) who are closer to the day-to-day operations of the business.

market The replacement cost of an item of inventory as of the balance sheet date.

market interest rate The current rate of interest being paid on similar securities.

marketable securities The term usually applied to securities convertible to cash in a short time period and traded on the organized exchanges across the nation and around the world.

materiality The judgment call an accountant must make when deciding to disclose a given piece of information. The more immaterial the item is, the lesser the chance that it will be disclosed, since too much information can cloud the issue.

maturity date The date specified

in the bond indenture for the return of the face or par value of the bonds to the investors.

merchandise inventory Goods held for resale by a retailer or a wholesaler.

merchandising The activity of buying and selling items manufactured and assembled by other entities. The merchandiser does nothing to the goods other than to store them in inventory until they are sold.

minority interest The remaining stockholders' interest in a subsidiary in which a parent corporation has a controlling interest, but does not own 100% of the outstanding voting stock. Appears only on the consolidated financial statements, and not on the individual balance sheets of the parent or its subsidiary.

mirror image A term applied to the accounting for bonds by the investor and the issuing corporation. One is a mirror image of the other.

mixed accounts Accounts containing both a balance sheet and an income statement portion at the time financial statements need to be prepared.

Modified Accelerated Cost Recovery System (MACRS) The method of depreciation prescribed by the IRS starting in 1987. Depreciable assets are assigned to useful-life groups based on their nature. Various percentages then are assigned to the year divisions. The amount of depreciation approximates the results obtained under the 200% declining-balance method.

monetary items Balance sheet asset or liability accounts that are fixed in terms of the number of monetary units to be received as a result of the account. For example, if the balance sheet amount for Cash is $50,000, that means the entity has $50,000.

monetary unit A unit of measurement, not tied to any norm. The unit could be the French franc or the Russian ruble. The unit also could be the U.S. dollar at the beginning of the year compared to the end of the year.

mortgage bonds See *secured bonds.*

moving average A weighted average approach to inventory valuation used in conjunction with a perpetual inventory system.

mutual agency A characteristic of a partnership that allows one partner to bind all the other partners in contracts related to the business.

National Association of Accountants (NAA) A group made up mostly of accountants in industry. This group develops and grades the **Certified Management Accountants (CMA)** Examination.

natural resources Also referred to as *wasting assets* and nonrenewable assets, they include such resources as oil, natural gas, timber, gold, and so on.

net assets The excess of assets over liabilities; often referred to as *equity.*

net income The excess of revenue over expenses for a period of time.

net loss The excess of expenses over revenue for a period of time.

net realizable value The amount an entity expects to receive from the "sale" of an asset. As the term is used in Chapter 7, it refers to the result from subtracting the Allowance for Doubtful Accounts account from Accounts Receivable. This is a measure of the amount of cash expected to flow into the entity as a result of collecting its receivables.

NIFO (next in, first out) A true replacement cost approach to inventory valuation. Cost of goods sold is determined by the amount spent to replace the item sold.

noncumulative preferred stock Stock on which unpaid dividends do not accumulate. Once an annual dividend is not distributed, the right to that distribution is lost forever to the stockholder.

nonmonetary items All balance sheet assets and liabilities that are not monetary in nature. They are not fixed in terms of a number of monetary units to be received or paid and must be converted.

nonparticipating preferred stock Stock that is *only* entitled to the stated preference dividend. No further distributions are made above the stated rate.

no-par stated-value stock Common shares that the state of incorporation requires no par value to

be attached, but that have an arbitrary stated value placed on each share by the board of directors.

no-par stock Common shares that the state of incorporation requires no value to be attached, and on which the board of directors places no arbitrary value.

note A written promise by a borrower to repay a specified amount.

number of days of sales in inventory Indicates how many days' supply of inventory is on hand; the average inventory is divided by cost of goods sold and the result is multiplied by 365 days.

one-write system A system that organizes information input, eliminates transposition errors, and establishes a clear audit trail.

operating activities The activities of an entity that result from operating decisions made by management. Inflows result from the sale of goods or services, while outflows result from efforts to generate the inflows. The Net Cash Inflow from Operating Activities can be determined using either the direct or the indirect method.

operating cycle The cash-to-cash sequence of events for the revenue-producing operations of an entity.

operating expenses Expenses incurred in the operation of the business, except items classified as *other expenses* or as *income tax expense.*

organization costs Costs incurred during the process of incorporation. These costs are considered an intangible asset and should be amortized over a period not to exceed 40 years. Organization costs are generally amortized over a much shorter time such as the 5 years allowed by the IRS.

original cost A valuation method for investments in securities. The investments are reported at their acquisition cost, and current market values may be disclosed. No entry is made to write the investment up or down to current market value.

outstanding checks Checks that have been recorded by the entity and sent to the payee, but because of time delays with the mail and whatever, have not cleared the bank at the time the statement is prepared.

outstanding stock Authorized shares that have been issued and are currently in the hands of stockholders, not in the treasury.

Luca Pacioli The first person to publish a description of double-entry record-keeping, designed to ensure the accuracy of transactions being recorded. His book *Arithmetic, Geometry and Proportion* was published in 1494 in Italy.

paid-in capital That portion of stockholders' equity contributed by stockholders and others, rather than earned by the corporation.

parent company A corporation that owns a controlling interest in another corporation, referred to as the subsidiary.

participating preferred stock Stock that *may* receive dividend distributions above the stated rate or amount.

partner salary When unequal amounts of time or abilities are invested into a partnership by the various partners, the profit-sharing agreement should allow for salary allowances as a means of more equitably allocating net income to the partners. The salaries are not paid to the partners, but are used to allocate net income.

partnership An unincorporated form of business organization in which the entity is owned by two or more persons, each of whom has unlimited liability for the obligations of the entity.

partnership agreement A written document that describes all important matters regarding a partnership. The most important parts of the agreement detail how profits and losses are to be divided, and how to value a withdrawing or deceased partner's share of the business.

par value See *face value*.

par value stock Common shares that have an arbitrary value imprinted on them when authorized. Par value does not in any way measure market value or book value. States may or may not require stock to be issued with a par value. If the state does not require a par value, corporations still may elect to issue par value stock. The term

applies to both common and preferred stock.

patent A 17-year exclusive right granted by the federal government to an inventor to produce and sell a product.

payment of accrued interest A phrase used to describe the fact that bond investors must pay at the time the bond is purchased the interest that has accrued on a bond since the last interest payment date. The amount is returned to the investor on the next interest date, when the investor is paid for a full six months' interest.

payroll journal A special journal used to record the payroll information regarding gross and net pay, including the various deductions from an employee's pay.

payroll system A computer system that prepares payroll checks, maintains all payroll records, and prepares reports related to payroll activities.

periodic inventory system A system whereby a record of the beginning inventory and purchases during the period is kept. Ending inventory is determined by physically counting the goods on hand and assigning a cost to these goods; all goods not on hand at the end of the period are assumed to have been sold.

periodicity assumption The belief that the life of a business enterprise can be divided into arbitrary units of time, ususally one year, for the purpose of measuring net income and financial position.

periodicity concept The assumption that the entire life of a business can be divided into arbitrary periods of 12 months or less. This assumption allows for the issuance of timely financial statements so users can measure the performance and accomplishments of the enterprise. This also has been known as the time-period assumption.

permanent accounts Accounts that have a continuing balance from one fiscal year to another; also called *real accounts*. All balance sheet accounts are permanent accounts.

perpetual inventory system A method of inventory valuation in

which purchases and sales are recorded as they occur and a continuous balance of inventory on hand is calculated in terms of units and in terms of cost. The cost of goods sold is determined for each sale and is recorded. A physical count at the end of the period is used to verify the quantities that should be on hand.

petty cash fund Cash that has been set aside for the payment of minor expenses.

phantom profits A term used to describe the extra profits reported under FIFO as compared with LIFO. These profits are also referred to as *inventory profits* and *holding gains.*

pooling of interests The method of accounting for a business combination in which the stockholders of the subsidiary give up their ownership interest in the subsidiary in exchange for ownership interests (common stock) in the parent corporation, thereby becoming owners of the parent corporation, which in turn owns the subsidiary.

post-closing trial balance A listing of accounts and their balances after all temporary accounts have been closed; all temporary accounts should have a zero balance.

posting The process of transferring amounts from the journal to a ledger account.

preemptive right The right of each stockholder to maintain his or her percentage ownership in the corporation. When new shares are issued, under this right the existing stockholders must be offered the right to a proportional interest in the new shares.

preferred stock A class of stock that has a preference over common stock. Holders of preferred stock are entitled to payment of dividends before common stockholders, and usually have a prior claim to corporate assets on liquidation.

present value analysis Determines the present value of an amount or series of amounts to be received in the future. The purchase price of a bond may be estimated by determining the present value of the principal to be received 5, 10, or 20 years from the issue, and then adding the results to the present value of the interest annuity. See the chapter appendix.

price-to-earnings ratio Indicates the reasonableness of the market price in relation to how much is being earned in return for the investment; the market price per share is divided by the earnings per share.

prior-period adjustments Gains and losses applicable to the net income reported in prior years; disclosed in the statement of retained earnings.

production depreciation A method of cost allocation related to number of units produced rather than to a period of time.

property dividend A distribution to stockholders made with assets other than cash, such as the entity's inventory or shares the entity owns in another corporation.

proprietorship An entity owned by one person who has unlimited liability for the obligations of the entity; often referred to as a *sole proprietorship*.

purchase A business combination in which the stockholders of the subsidiary give up their ownership interest in the subsidiary in exchange for cash, other assets, or debt instruments of the parent. The stockholders no longer have an ownership interest in the subsidiary or the parent.

Purchase Discounts A contra account to Purchases; cash discounts taken if payment is made within a certain discount period are recorded in this account.

purchase of a partnership interest One way of admitting a new partner. The new partner purchases an interest directly from an existing partner in a transaction external to the partnership.

Purchase Returns and Allowances A contra account to Purchases; goods returned to suppliers or price adjustments allowed by suppliers are recorded in this account.

Purchases An account used to accumulate the purchase cost of merchandise held for resale.

purchases journal A special journal used to record all purchases for resale that are made on account.

purchasing power gain The increase in purchasing power due to holding more monetary liabilities than monetary assets during a period of inflation.

purchasing power loss The decline in purchasing power due to holding more monetary assets than monetary liabilities during a period of inflation.

quick current assets Assets that can be converted into cash in a short period of time. These include cash, accounts receivable, and marketable securities.

ratio The quotient resulting when one number is divided by another.

ratio analysis Analysis of interrelationships of different financial statement items as a method of evaluating an entity's use of assets.

ratio of long-term assets to stockholders' equity Indicates the percentage of equity being used to acquire long-term assets; average net long-term assets is divided by average stockholders' equity.

ratio of sales to long-term assets Indicates the adequacy of sales in relation to the investment in long-term assets; net sales is divided by average long-term assets. To be meaningful, the number must be compared with that of last year's, or with others in the industry.

realization of assets The realization of assets takes place during a liquidation of a partnership. As assets are sold for cash, they are said to be *realized*.

realized holding gains Holding gains on items in inventory that have been sold during the year, or on depreciable assets used during the year and reflected in Depreciation Expense on a current cost basis.

reciprocal accounts Accounts that represent the same claim as other accounts when combining financial statements of a parent and its subsidiary(ies). The major reciprocal accounts are the Investment account on the books of the parent, and the stockholders' equity accounts on the books of the subsidiary. They both represent the owners' claim to the net assets of the subsidiary.

Recovery of Unrealized Losses The account title used when the

Allowance to Reduce Securities to Market account must be decreased when applying LCM to equity securities in the short-term portfolio.

refunding a bond issue The act of issuing a new bond issue and using the proceeds to retire an older bond issue, presumably at a dollar savings.

relevance The usefulness and timeliness of accounting information. Can it be used to reduce the uncertainty associated with decision making?

reliability The dependability of accounting information. Can the user employ the information to evaluate alternative possibilities?

replacement cost The amount of cash that would have to be spent to replace an asset, be it inventory, land, machinery, or buildings, at a particular point in time, usually as of the balance sheet date.

report form balance sheet A balance sheet in which liabilities and equities are listed below the assets.

restricted retained earnings That portion of the assets earned by a corporation, but not currently available for dividends through an action of the board of directors.

retail inventory method An inventory valuation method that estimates the amount of inventory without taking a physical count. The retail value of the inventory is estimated, then converted to cost using a historic cost ratio.

retained earnings That portion of stockholders' equity (net income) earned by a corporation, but not distributed to its owners in the form of dividends.

return-on-sales ratio Indicates the percentage of each sales dollar that ends up in retained earnings and is available for distribution as dividends; net income for the year is divided by net sales.

return on stockholders' equity Indicates the adequacy of earnings as a return on the investment by the owners of the entity; net income for the year is divided by average stockholders' equity.

return on total assets This indicates how efficiently a company uses its assets in the earnings process; income from operations is divided by average total assets.

revenue An inflow of assets to an entity in return for services performed or goods sold during that period.

revenue expenditures Cash outflows related to long-term assets that do not increase the operational efficiency of the asset or extend its useful life. Revenue expenditures are recorded as expenses in the year they are incurred.

revenue operating cycle The time it takes to buy inventory, sell it, and to collect the cash from the sale. A shorter definition has been offered as "cash to cash." It can be determined by adding the accounts receivable collection period to the number of days' supply of inventory.

revenue recognition Revenue is recognized when earned. This is usually at the time the good or service is provided, although in some cases revenue may be recognized before all the goods or services have been provided, or in some other cases, the revenue may not be recorded until the cash has been received.

reverse stock split An action taken by the board of directors to reduce the number of shares outstanding. It usually involves exchanging the original shares for a smaller number of new shares. The par value is increased, and the market price of the stock is usually increased proportionately.

reversing entries Entries made at the beginning of a new accounting period to reverse an adjusting entry made in the immediately preceding accounting period. The use of reversing entries facilitates the subsequent recording of transactions in the new accounting period.

Sales An account used to accumulate revenue transactions for merchandise sold to others.

Sales Discounts A contra account to Sales; cash discounts taken by customers if payment is made within a certain discount period are recorded in this account.

sales journal A special journal used to record all sales on account.

sales order entry system A computer system that initiates shipping orders, keeps track of back-

orders, and produces various reports needed by management and the accounting system.

Sales Returns and Allowances A contra account to sales; goods returned by customers or price adjustments allowed to customers are recorded in this account.

salvage value The estimated value of a long-term asset at the end of its useful life.

scrap value The estimated amount for which an asset can be sold at the end of its useful life; also called *salvage value*.

secured bonds A bond issue secured by physical assets of the issuing corporation, usually referred to as *mortgage bonds*.

Securities and Exchange Commission (SEC) An agency of the U.S. government that has the legal power to develop accounting principles and reporting practices for companies whose stock is traded on domestic markets. The commission has asked the accounting profession to regulate its own practices, but it monitors the situation very closely.

serial bonds A bond issue that has more than one maturity date for the repayment of principal. In a very common serial bond situation, 1/10 of the principal is due each year for a 10-year period.

short-term portfolio Investment securities that management intends to liquidate in the near future.

similar A term applied to transactions that involve the trade-in of one asset for another. If the assets are related to one another, such as a truck for a truck, the exchange involves *similar assets*.

sinking fund An investment fund usually used in connection with an issue of term bonds. With the principal payment coming at one time in the future, the corporation must provide for the retirement of the bonds. An amount determined by means of present and future value analyses is deposited in a fund each year and is invested in income-producing securities.

sole proprietorship An unincorporated form of business organization in which the entity is owned by only one person.

solvency The ability of an entity to

pay its debts (current liabilities) as they become due.

source documents The raw data from which the financial transactions of a business are recorded. They include such items as bank deposit slips, cancelled checks, sales invoices, purchase invoices, insurance policies, and invoices from various service suppliers such as phone, electricity, and natural gas companies.

special journals Multicolumn journals designed not only to record similar transactions chronologically but also to reduce the writing of repetitive information. They are often referred to collectively as the *books of original entry*. Any transaction that can not be recorded in a special journal is recorded in the general journal.

specific identification An inventory valuation method in which goods are identified with their actual cost. An assumption on the flow of costs or goods is not necessary.

spreadsheet A program that allows the user to create a very large two-dimensional table and to change the data in many different ways.

stable-unit-of-measure assumption The monetary unit used to measure the value of an economic event has the same value from year to year. In the United States, the monetary unit is the U.S. dollar.

State Corporation Acts Each state in the Union has legislation that governs corporations incorporated in that state and corporations registered to do business in that state. These acts are many and varied. The material presented in this textbook is based on general applications, and in some cases, may not be applicable to a particular state.

statement of cash flows A financial statement that shows the inflows and outflows of cash as a result of the entity's three main activities—operating, investing, and financing—for a period.

statement of owner's capital A statement that shows the changes in owner's equity of a sole proprietorship during an accounting period.

statement of partners' capital A

statement that shows the changes in owners' equity of a partnership during an accounting period.

statement of retained earnings A financial statement showing the changes in retained earnings during the past year due to net income and dividends.

stock certificate A legal document signifying the number of shares of a particular class of stock an investor owns. The rights attached to the ownership are usually stated on the certificate.

stock dividend A dividend distribution consisting of shares of the corporation's own stock, usually accomplished by a capitalization (transfer) of retained earnings (to Paid-in Capital).

stock split An action taken by the board of directors that increases the number of shares outstanding. It usually involves exchanging the original shares for a larger number of new shares. The par value is reduced, and the market price of the stock is usually reduced proportionately.

stock subscriptions A contract between the corporation and some stockholders to pay for their shares over a period of time. The stock certificate is not issued until the contract is fully paid, but subscribing stockholders do have some of the rights of fully paid holders. The number of rights depend on the various state corporation acts.

straight-line method A method of amortizing bond premiums or discounts that results in a constant *amount* being recorded as interest expense over the life of the bonds.

straight-line method of depreciation A simple method of calculating depreciation whereby it is assumed that equal benefit is received from the asset over its entire useful life. That is, as much benefit is gained from the asset in its first month of life as in its last month of useful life.

subsidiary The corporation in which another corporation, the parent, has a controlling interest.

subsidiary ledgers Separate ledgers that keep a group of homogeneous accounts that correspond to a related control account in the general ledger. Two examples include accounts receivable, accounts payable, and long-term assets ledgers.

sum-of-the-years'-digits depreciation An accelerated method of depreciation that allocates more of the asset's cost in the earlier years of its useful life than the later years. It is a declining rate expressed as a fraction applied to a constant base. The denominator of the fraction is the sum of the years in the useful life, and the numerator is the years of life in reverse order.

T account A form of a general ledger account that is easy to use as a learning tool in the classroom to illustrate the accumulation of financial data.

T-account approach A textbook approach used to gather the information necessary to prepare a statement of cash flows. Since the statement involves accounting for differences in an entity's accounts from the beginning of the year to the end, a T account is set up for each account, showing the change in that account.

tangible long-term assets Long-term assets that have physical substance, such as land, buildings, and equipment.

temporary accounts Accounts that accumulate data for a fiscal year and are closed at the end of the fiscal year; also called *nominal accounts*. All revenue and expense accounts are temporary accounts.

term bonds A bond issue that has only one maturity date for the repayment of the principal. No matter how long the bonds will be outstanding, all of them mature (become due) on the same date.

time-based depreciation Depreciation methods that assign portions of an asset's cost to years rather than to units produced.

times-interest-earned ratio Indicates the ability of the entity to pay the interest on long-term debt, such as bonds; income from operations is divided by interest expense.

trade discount A percentage or dollar amount used to calculate the actual sales or purchase price of merchandise.

trade-in A term used to describe an exchange of one asset for another, either similar or dissimilar.

trade-in allowance A reduction in the cash price when an old asset is exchanged for a new one.

trademark A legal right granted by the federal government to use a symbol or a word to identify a company or one of its products or services.

trading on the equity Utilizing debt as a means of financing when the return on the amount borrowed exceeds the cost of borrowing the funds.

transaction An exchange of assets, obligations, services, or goods.

Transportation In An account used to accumulate freight charges on merchandise purchased for resale; these charges are added to the purchase cost of the merchandise.

treasury stock Shares of the issuing corporation that have been issued and reacquired, but not retired. Treasury stock will normally be reissued at a later time.

trend analysis The comparison of data for several years when analyzing financial statements for evaluation of a company's financial strength and profitability.

trial balance A list of each account together with its individual debit or credit balance; used to establish the equality of debits with credits before the preparation of financial statements.

trustee An intermediary between the corporation issuing the bonds and the bondholders. The trustee represents the bondholders and will often hold title to property securing the bonds, if any.

unappropriated retained earnings See *unrestricted retained earnings*.

uniformity GAAP should be applied consistently within an industry so that the financial statements of one firm in the industry can be compared to another firm in the same industry.

unissued stock The shares of stock that have been authorized to be issued, but have not been at a point in time.

unlimited liability Since a sole proprietorship or a partnership is not considered to be a legal entity, the owners have unlimited liability in that creditors of the business may proceed against the personal assets of the owners.

unrealized holding gains Holding gains on items in inventory that have not been sold during the year, or on depreciable assets held at year-end when current costs are recorded in the accounts.

Unrealized Loss The account title used when the Allowance to Reduce Securities to Market account must be increased when applying LCM to equity securities in the short-term portfolio. The loss is considered unrealized since no sale has taken place. In order for an actual (realized) loss to be recorded, the securities would have to be sold at the lower price.

unrestricted retained earnings That portion of the assets earned by a corporation currently available for dividends. The amount of available cash, however, would dictate cash dividends.

unsecured bonds A bond issue secured only by the good name of the corporation. If the corporation is successful, the bondholders will be paid; if not, they may not receive the interest they are entitled to, or even the principal. These bonds are often referred to as *debenture bonds*.

useful life An estimate of the period of time an asset will be useful to an entity. This will vary depending on the amount of use the asset will have, rather than the type of asset. An automobile for a traveling salesperson will not last as long as one used exclusively to ferry executives visiting a corporate home office.

valuation account An account that is subtracted from the original cost of the asset to arrive at the book value of the asset for balance sheet purposes; often called a *contra-asset account*.

vertical analysis The analysis of the composition of a financial statement through the restating of all items in the statement as percentages; comparison of the percentages between two or more years shows the change in composition of the statement components. Once restated in percentages, the statements are referred to as *common size financial statements*.

weighted average An inventory valuation method that assumes the units in inventory and the units sold came from a mixture of all units purchased at various costs during the year. It is called a *weighted average* since the number of units purchased at each of the various

prices is part of the averaging.

working capital The excess of current assets over current liabilities; also referred to as *net working capital*.

worksheet A multi-column schedule used to organize the many details brought together to facilitate the preparation of financial statements.

worksheet approach A practical approach used to gather the information necessary to prepare a statement of cash flows. Since the statement involves accounting for differences in an entity's accounts from the beginning of the year to the end, the worksheet consists of balance sheets at the beginning and the end of the year. The changes in the various accounts from the beginning to the end of the year are then analyzed and summarized by activity.

year-end The last day of the fiscal year, or of the calendar year.

INDEX

A

Accelerated cost recovery systems, 419
Accelerated depreciation, 415, 420
Account
  Allowance for Doubtful Accounts, 333
  capital—owner, 530
  chart of, 73
  classification, 66–68
  control, 269
  current liability, 115–16
  defined, 55
  Drawing, 530
  ledger, 71–73
  mixed, 115–21
  Purchases, 213–14, 216
  Sales Returns and Allowances, 211
  T account, 55, 71–73, 791
  Transportation In, 217
Accountant, certified public, 54
Account cycle, trial balance, 111
Accounting
  accrual basis, 6, 50
  of bonds, 576–86
  cash basis, 113
  corporate, 461–64
  current cost, 840–43
  debit-credit method, 59–64
  defined, 4
  dividends, 501–2
  double entry, 16–19, 56–58
  financial, 5
  for inflation, 831–43
  international, 824–31
  managerial, 5
  mirror image, 646–48
  organizations, 53–54
  of partnerships, 536–37
  process, 16, 54–58, 170, 172
  for stock dividends, 508–9
  time periods of, 23, 26
Accounting assumptions
  entity, 48
  going-concern, 48
  historical cost, 49
  income determination and matching, 50
  income statements, 51
  periodicity, 49
  revenue recognition, 50
  stable unit of measure, 49
Accounting changes
  in methods, 227
  in principles, 53–54
Accounting cycle
  defined, 73
  general journal, 108–9
  steps, 75, 108–11, 131, 177–78
Accounting equation, 12–13, 58
  example, 13–15
  reviewed, 672–73

Accounting information
  conservatism, 52
  consistency, 51, 52
  limitations on disclosure of, 52
  materiality, 51, 52
  relevance, 51
  reliability, 51
  uniformity, 51
Accounting model, 12–15
Accounting period
  and operating cycle, 100–104
  and salary expense, 128
  sequence of steps, 173
Accounting principles. *See* Accounting
  assumptions; Generally accepted
  accounting principles (GAAP)
Accounting process, fundamentals, 50
Accounting records, updating cash, 331
Accounting systems
  computerized, 290–96
  management uses of computers, 294–96
  relationships among computerized, 295
  use of spreadsheets, 295–96
Accounts payable
  computerized system, 294
  subsidiary ledger, 283
Accounts receivable
  aging schedule of, 336
  collection period, 720
  computerized system, 294
  creation of, 333
  credit balance, 339–40
  defined, 9
  flow through control account, 279
  general ledger, 279
  installment accounts, 339–40
  subsidiary ledger, 281
  turnover, 720–21
  uncollectible accounts estimation, 334
Accrual basis of accounting, 6, 9, 50
  and matching concept, 111–13
Accruals
  defined, 125
  income tax, 130
  interest, 126–27, 129
  recording of, 125
  reversing entries for, 173–76
  salaries, 127
  types, 125
Accrued expenses, 125
  unrecorded, 127
Accrued revenues, 125
  unrecorded, 125
Accumulated depreciation, 118
Acid-test ratio
  adequacy of, 233
  in analyzing short-term solvency, 719
  defined, 233, 719
  relationship to current ratio, 233–34

"Adding apples and oranges," 49
Adjusted trial balance, 131
Adjusting journal entries, 115
  balance sheet accounts, 114–21
  for expenses, 122–24
  posted to ledger, 131
  for prior period, 228–29
  for unearned revenue, 122–24
Allowance, 210
  for doubtful accounts, 333
  to reduce securities to market, 631
American Accounting Association (AAA), 54
American Institute of Certified Public
  Accountants (AICPA), 53
Amortization. *See also* Depreciation, of
  long-term assets
  accrual of bond interest, 592
  bond discount, 589–90, 643, 646–48
  bond premium, 587, 643–45
  of bonds, 577–81, 585
  defined, 413
  effective interest method, 577, 586–92, 643
  investor's books, 646
  straight-line method, 577, 578–81
  table for bonds, 587, 589, 649, 651
Analysis of financial statements. *See*
  Financial statements
Annuity, 582
Arm's length transaction, 8, 49
Assets. *See also* Long-term assets
  costs recorded as, 102
  current, 66, 231–32
  defined, 4, 8
  dissimilar, 426–28
  donated, 472
  intangible, 429–33
  long-term, 67, 729. *See also* Long-term
    assets
  mixed current, 115
  net, 14
  partnership, 532
  partnerships, 546–47
  realization of, 548–49
  relationship to expenses, 103
  return on total, 725
  similar, 426–27
  unmixed current, 116
Auditors
  credibility, 56–57
  report, 54

B

Bad debts. *See also* Uncollectible
  accounts
  estimating, 334
  writing off, 337–39

Balance sheet, 7–9
    account classification, 66–68
    account form, 68, 229, 230
    adjusting journal entries, 114–21
    classification, 229–30
    conversion to adjust to inflation, 833–37
    conversions for exchange rate, 825–27
    and current cost accounting, 842–43
    defined, 5
    estimate of uncollectible accounts, 335–37
    example of retained earnings, 470
    impact of inventory, 373
    need for consistency, 103
    preparation, 69, 165–67
    presentation of bonds, 575–76
    report form, 68, 229
    short-term solvency, 716
    statement of retained earnings, 167
    stockholders' equity, 468
Bank
    certified checks, 325
    deposits in transit, 326
    outstanding checks, 325
    reconciliation, 323, 325–31, 326–31
    relationship of records to books, 327
Bankruptcy classification model, 737–39
Betterment, defined, 410
Board of directors
    defined, 11–12
    relationship to management, 462–63
Bondholders, rights, 568. See also Bonds
Bonds
    accounting process, 576–86
    accrual of interest at year-end, 592
    accrued interest, 584–85
    advantages of financing with, 570–71
    amortization, 577–81, 585, 586–92, 646
    amortization table, 587
    annuity, 582
    authorization, 568
    balance sheet , 575–76
    bearer, 572
    call price, 573
    call provision, 573
    change in value over life, 644
    classification of, 571
    convertible, 573
    debenture, 572
    defined, 568
    disadvantages of financing with, 571
    discounts, 574, 580–81, 585, 589–90, 643, 646–50
    face value, 574–75
    financial statements, 569
    financing with, 569
    future bond analysis, 596–97
    future value tables, 600–601
    indenture, 568
    interest, 577–78
    interest payments, 587
    long-term investments, 642–51, 648–50
    market interest rate, 575
    maturity dates, 568, 573
    premiums, 574, 579–80, 585, 643–45, 645, 650

present value analysis, 592–601
present value tables, 598–599
price, 576
purchase of, 642–43
recording by investor versus issuer, 646–48
redemption, 583
refunding a bond issue, 584
registered, 572
restriction of dividends, 574
sale between interest dates, 584
secured, 572
short-term investments, 632–35
sinking fund, 574, 581
special features of, 572–74
term, 573
trustee, 568
unsecured, 572
versus stock, 570
Bonuses in partnerships
    to current partner, 545
    to new partner, 543–44
Bookkeeping system. See also Double-entry accounting
    double-entry, 12–13
    early forms of, 168
Book of original entry, 268. See also General journal
Book reconciling items, 323–24
Book value
    of common stock, 473
    defined, 118
    of preferred stock, 474–75
Business combinations, 672–74
    defined, 672
    financial statements, 689
    recording the acquisition, 673–74

C

Calendar year, 26
Calendar year-end. See Year-end
Capital, corporate acquisition of, 568–97
Capital expenditures
    building and equipment, 410
    defined, 408
    land, 408–10
    types, 409
Capitalization, of retained earnings, 508
Capitalized, 408
Capital—owner account, 530
Cash
    bank reconciliation, 323, 326–31
    basis of accounting, 113
    book reconciliation, 323
    collections, 323–33
    defined, 66
    dividends, 501
    embezzling, 324–25
    payments, 323–33
    petty cash fund, 332
    updating accounting records, 331
Cash disbursements, posting, 282
Cash disbursements journals, 275
    columns, 277
    example, 276

Cash flow
    analysis of, 763–77
    calculating from operating activities, 767–73
    classification of, 764–65
    statement of, 5, 762–63. See also Statement of cash flows
    T-account approach, 791–99
    worksheet approach, 777–91
Cash receipts journals, 270
    columns, 273
    example, 272
    transactions, 280
Certified public accountant (CPA), 54
Chart of accounts, 73, 74
Checks
    certified, 325
    outstanding, 325
Classification
    advantage of, 223
    defined, 223
Closing the books, 166–70
Closing entries
    defined, 166
    in early forms of bookkeeping, 168
    example of worksheet, 169
    expense accounts, 168
    general journal example, 224
    income summary account, 166–70
    for a merchandiser, 222–23
    posting to ledger, 170–71
    procedure, 166–70
    revenue accounts, 168
Common stock. See also Stock
    book value, 473–75
    defined, 9
Compound journal entry, 70–71
Computers
    management uses, 294–96
    spreadsheets, 295–96
    in the supermarket, 293
    value in accounting systems, 290–96
Conservatism, 52
Consolidated statements, 642. See also Financial statements, consolidated
Constant dollar accounting, 831, 832–39
    balance sheet conversion, 833–37
    defined, 832
    income statement conversion, 838–39
    versus current cost accounting, 838
Consumer Price Index (CPI), 832
Contra-asset account. See Valuation account
Contra revenue account, 210–11
Control account, 269
Controlling interest, 672
Copyrights, 430–31
Corporate organization, 11–12. See also Corporations
Corporate structure, 458–64. See also Corporations
    board of directors, 460–61
    stockholders' rights, 460
Corporations
    accounting terminology, 461, 464
    board of directors, 460–61, 462–63
    bonds. See Bonds

capital needs, 572–73
characteristics, 458–60
combined, 672–74
controlling interest, 672
creation by law, 458
in Delaware, 20–21
dividends, 498–512
donated capital, 472
ease of acquiring capital, 459
financial structure, 14, 712
financing, 569, 572–73
forms of investments, 630
income taxes on earnings, 459–60
limited liability of, 459
paid-in capital transactions, 464–70
parent company, 672
par value, 461
retained earnings restrictions, 470–72
sources of equity, 472–73
stockholders' rights, 460
stock subscriptions, 475–76
stock value, 461
structure, 458–64
subsidiaries, 672
treasury stock, 511–12
unlimited life of, 458–59
versus partnerships, 533
versus sole proprietorships, 531
Cost allocation. *See* Depreciation
Cost of assets, 113
Cost-benefit judgments, 53
Cost flows, in inventory, 367–68,
        370–74. *See also* Flow of costs
Cost of goods, 113
    purchased, 216
    sold, 208, 214
Cost method, 511
Cost outlays
    analysis example, 104–8
    as assets, 102, 103
    as expenses, 102, 103
Costs
    allocation, 413–20, 422
    inventory, 364–70
    research and development, 429
    weighted average, 368–69
Credit
    in double-entry bookkeeping, 55
    memo, 219
Creditors, 12
Current assets, 231–32
    analysis, 232
    cash, 66
    composition of specific items, 232–33,
        718–19
    defined, 66
    liquidity, 66
    nonquick, 719
    notes, 67
    quick, 719
    types, 66–67
Current cost accounting, 831, 840–43
    and balance sheet, 842–43
    defined, 840
    and income statements, 841–42
    versus constant dollar accounting, 838
    versus historical cost, 842
Current liabilities, 231–32

defined, 67–68, 713
types, 67–68
Current market value, of investments,
        631
Current ratio, 231
    analysis, 232
    in calculating working capital, 717–18
    relationship to acid-test ratio, 233–34

D

Debit
    in double-entry bookkeeping, 55
    memo, 219
Debit balance, 64
Debit-credit method, 59–64
    defined, 55
    example, 59–64
    trial balance, 64, 66
    use of, 55
Debt
    long-term, 713–15
    short-term, 713–15
Debt-to-equity ratio, 14, 712
Decision support systems, 295
Declining balance depreciation, 417
Deficit, 499
Delaware, favorable laws for
        corporations in, 20–21
Denomination, 827
Depletion
    defined, 413, 428
    of natural resources, 428–29
    versus depreciation, 428
Deposits in transit, 326
Depreciation
    accelerated cost recovery system, 419
    accelerated method, 420
    comparison of methods, 420
    defined, 118, 412, 422
    double-declining balance method, 417
    expense, 118
    group, 424
    internal revenue code, 418
    of long-term assets, 412–20
    modified accelerated cost recovery
        system, 419
    partial year, 423
    phantom profits, 421
    production method, 413, 420
    revision of charges, 424–25
    straight-line method, 119, 414
    sum-of-the-years'-digits method,
        416–17
    time-based method, 414, 415, 420
    versus depletion, 428
Direct method, 768–70, 787, 791–96
Direct write-off, 339
Disclosure, of long-term assets, 422
Discontinued operations, 225
Discounts. *See* Bonds, discounts
    purchases, 216
    sales, 212
    trade, 220
Dissimilar asset
    defined, 426
    example, 427–28

Dividends
    accounting, 501–2, 508–9
    bond restriction, 574
    cash, 501
    cumulative, 463, 504
    date of payment, 501
    declaration of, 499–500
    defined, 7, 227, 498
    liquidating, 498
    noncumulative, 504
    notice, 501
    participating preferred stock, 504–6
    policy, 499
    preferred stock, 502
    property, 501
    stock, 506–8, 637
    and treasury stock, 512
    types, 503
Dividend-yield ratio, 728
Dollar, 49
Donated capital, 472
Double-declining balance, 417
Double-entry accounting, 12–13, 16–19,
        22, 56–58
    example, 16–19, 22
    system, 64, 66
Drawing account, 530

E

Effective interest method
    of bond amortization, 577, 586–92, 643
    compared to straight-line method, 591
    defined, 586
    long-term investments, 648–51
Efficiency
    measuring, 234
    of operations, 234, 724–30
Embezzling, 324–25
Employee
    individual earnings records, 290
    optional payroll deductions, 286
    records for, 284–85
Entity
    accounting assumptions, 48
    concept of, 4–5
    defined, 4
    evaluation of, 230–31
    financial structure of, 8
Equality of debits and credits, 131
Equipment
    as capital expenditure, 410
    fair market value, 410
Equity
    defined, 9
    in earnings of investee, 641
    method of investments, 631
    owners', 8–9
    partnerships, 9, 11
    proprietorship, 9, 11
    stockholders', 725–27
    trading on, 726
Exchange rate, 825, 828
Expenditures
    asset related, 411
    capital, 411
    revenue, 411

Expenses
 accrual accounting, 113
 accrued, 125
 costs recorded as, 102
 defined, 5, 6
 matching with revenues, 113
 relationship to assets, 103
Extraordinary items, 227
Extraordinary repair, 410

F

Fair market value, 410
Federal income tax. *See* Income tax
Federal Reserve Board, 53
FICA payable, payroll deductions, 286
Fiduciary relationship, 5
FIFO (first in, first out)
 costing in perpetual system, 375–76
 defined, 365
 illustrated, 365
Financial accounting, 5. *See also*
   Financial statements
Financial Accounting Standards Board
   (FASB), 53, 56
 Statement no. 95, 764–65
Financial Executives Institute (FEI), 54
Financial statements, 51–52, 737–39. *See
   also* Operations efficiency
   analysis
 acid-test ratio, 719
 after date of acquisition, 689
 analysis of, 712
 for business combinations, 689
 classification, 4, 4–9, 223
 common size, 733
 consolidated, 642, 672, 675–80, 681–84
 defined, 5
 disclosure of, 422–23
 elements of, 115
 footnotes, 56–57
 interim, 68
 management decisions, 720–21
 for partnerships, 540–41
 preparation of, 68–69, 675–80, 681–84
 preparation from worksheet, 164
 and ratios, 235
 relationship of interim and year-end,
   26, 27
 reporting of, 762
 revenue operating cycle, 723–24
 short-term solvency, 715–24
 for subsidiaries, 675–80, 681–84
 trend analysis, 732–33
 working capital, 717–19
Financial structure
 debt-to-equity ratio, 712
 defined, 712
 of entity, 8
 long-term debt, 713–15
 short-term debt, 713–15
Financial transactions
 analysis, 15–27, 59–69, 104–8
 defined, 4
 posted in ledger, 71–73
 recording in journal, 70–71

Financing activities, 763, 764
Fiscal year, 26
 closing the books, 166
Fiscal year-end. *See* Year-end
Fixed assets. *See* Long-term assets
Flow of costs
 average cost assumption, 368
 FIFO cost assumption, 367
 impact in inventory, 370–74
 LIFO cost assumption, 367–68
 summary in inventory, 374
Flow of goods
 actual, 365
 assumed, 365
 average assumption, 366–67
 FIFO, 365–66
 LIFO, 366
Fob
 defined, 217
 destination, 217
 shipping point, 217
Footing, T accounts, 64, 65
Foreign exchange gains and losses,
   829
Foreign transactions, 827–31
Foreign translations
 balance sheet conversions, 825
 differences caused by GAAP, 824–25
 differences caused by measurement
   unit, 825–27
Franchises, 431
Future value
 analysis, 593
 calculating for bonds, 596
 tables, 600–601

G

GAAP. *See* Generally accepted
   accounting principles
General journal, 70–71
 closing entries, 169, 224
 recording in, 70–71, 108–10
 and special journals, 277
General ledger
 cash receipt journal, 280
 computerized system, 294
 example of transaction posted in, 72
 posting cash disbursements, 282
 posting from payroll journals, 289
 and subsidiary ledgers, 278–84
 updating cash account, 331
Generally accepted accounting
   principles (GAAP), 48–54, 51–52,
   824–25
 development of, 53–54
Going-concern assumption, 48, 101
Goods, 4
Goodwill
 from consolidation, 676–77
 as intangible long-term assets, 431–32
Governmental Accounting Standards
   Board (GASB), 54
Gross profit
 calculation, 208, 381–83
 defined, 208

method of estimating inventory,
   382–83
 usefulness, 208
Group rate, 424

H

Historical cost
 assumption, 49
 versus current cost, 842
Historic rate, 825
Holding gains. *See* Phantom profits
 defined, 841
 net of inflation, 843
 realized, 842
 unrealized, 842
Horizontal analysis
 balance sheet, 733
 defined, 732
 income statements, 734

I

Imprest petty cash system, 332
Income determination and matching
   assumption, 50
Income statements, 6
 accounting assumptions, 51
 adjusting, 122–24
 classification, 224–27
 conversion to adjust for inflation,
   838–39
 and current cost accounting, 841
 defined, 5
 estimate of uncollectible accounts,
   335
 example of adjusting, 122–24
 example of classified, 226
 example of condensed, 227
 horizontal, 734
 impact of inventory, 371–73
 items impacting cash flow, 768–70
 need for consistency, 103
 phantom profits, 373
 preparation of, 68–69
 preparation from worksheet, 164–65
 unmixing, 122–24
 vertical, 734
Income summary, 166
Income tax
 corporate, 459–60
 as expense, 130
 federal, 285
 impact on cash flow, 769
 payable, 130
 recording of, 130
 state, 285
Indirect method, 770–73, 789, 790,
   796–99
Individual employee earnings records
 defined, 290
 payroll journal, 291
Inflation
 accounting for, 831–43
 general, 832

holding gains net, 842–43
rate increase, 834–35
Insolvency, 230, 713–14
Installments accounts receivable, 339–40
Institutional investors, 461
Intangible long-term assets, 429–33
  copyrights, 430–31
  defined, 429
  franchises, 431
  goodwill, 431–32
  leases, 433
  organization costs, 432–33
  patents, 430
  secret processes, 431
  software development, 433
  trademarks, 431
Interest
  accrued on bonds, 584–85
  earned, 126–27
  as expense, 129
  as liability, 129
  payable, 129
  receivable, 126–27
Interim income statements, 69
Internal control, 322–23
Internal revenue code, use in
    depreciation, 418–20
Internal Revenue Service (IRS), 54
International accounting, 824–31
  foreign translations, 824
International Accounting Standards
    Committee (IASC), 54
International Federation of Accountants
    (IFAC), 54
Inventory, 364–85. See also Inventory
    costs
  adequate turnover, 723
  beginning, 215
  computerized control system, 292
  cost determination, 364–70
  ending, 214
  errors, 379–81
  management decisions, 721
  merchandise, 214
  number of days of sales in, 721
  periodic system, 218, 368, 375
  perpetual system, 218–19, 368, 375–79
  in record card, 376, 378
  recording ending inventory, 218
  shrinkage, 370–71
  systems, 375–81
  turnover ratio, 722–23
Inventory costs
  average assumption, 366, 368–69
  comparison of cost-flow assumptions,
    370–74
  costing in the perpetual system,
    376–77
  determination, 364–70
  estimation, 381–85
  FIFO assumption, 365–68, 375–76
  flow assumptions, 374
  flow of costs, 366–67
  flow of goods, 365, 375
  gross profit calculation, 381–83
  impact on balance sheets, 373
  impact on income statements, 371–73

LIFO assumption, 366, 367–68
lower of cost or market, 369
moving average costing, 377
NIFO method, 385
replacement cost, 369
retail inventory method, 383–84
specific identity method, 365
summary of calculation methods, 369
weighted average, 368–69
Investee, 631, 641
Investing activities, 763, 764
Investments. See also Long-term
    investments; Short-term
    investments
  allowance to reduce securities to
    market, 631
  current market value, 631
  equity method, 631
  lower of cost or market (LCM)
    method, 631
  original cost, 631
  into a partnership, 542–43
  security of, 630–31
  valuation methods, 631–32
Investor's books, amortization, 645, 646
Invoice, 15

J

Journal, general, 70–71. See also General
    journal
Journal entry, 70–71
Journalizing
  defined, 70
  steps, 70–71
Journals
  adjusting entries, 115
  cash disbursements, 275–77, 282
  cash receipts, 270–73
  payroll, 287, 288, 291
  purchases, 273, 283
  sales, 269–70, 281
  special, 268–78. See also Special
    journals

L

Land, as capital expenditure, 408–10
Leasehold, 433
Leases, 433
Ledger
  account, 71–73
  adjusting entries, 131
  equality between ledgers, 278
  general, 278–84
  posting the closing entries, 170–71
  subsidiary, 269, 278–84
Legal capital, 466
Leverage, defined, 15
Liabilities
  causing insolvency, 230–31
  current, 67–68, 231–32
  defined, 4, 8
  long-term, 68
  relationship to revenue, 102

LIFO (last in, last out)
  costing in the perpetual system,
    376–77
  defined, 366
  illustrated, 366
Limited liability, of corporations, 459
Liquidation
  of partnerships, 547–51
  values, 49
Long-term assets, 118
  abandonment of, 425–26
  allocation of cost over useful life, 412
  balance sheet value, 422
  betterments versus repairs, 410–11
  building and equipment, 410
  capital expenditures, 408
  cost allocation method, 413–20
    production method, 413
    time-based method, 414
  defined, 67, 408
  depreciation, 412–20
  disclosure, 422–23
  disposal of, 425–28
  dissimilar, 426
  establishing cost of, 408–11
  exchanges and the IRS, 428
  expenditures, 411
  intangible, 429–33
  ratio of sales to, 729, 732
  ratio of stockholders' equity to, 729,
    732
  revisions to useful life of, 424–25
  sale of, 425–26
  similar, 426
  tangible, 412
  trade-in, 426
  types, 67
  useful life, 408
Long-term debt, 713–15
  corporate, 568–97
Long-term investments
  actual control, 642
  in bonds, 642–51
  change in value over life of bond, 644
  effective interest method, 648–51
  equity method, 641
  and lower of cost or market, 640–42
  portfolio, 631–32
  stock, 640–42
Long-term liabilities, 68
Long-term portfolio. See Long-term
    investments
Lower of cost or market (LCM) method,
    369–70, 631, 634, 640–41
  and stock market, 688–89
  where control exists, 688

M

Management
  decisions related to inventory, 721
  decisions related to long-term assets,
    729
  decisions related to receivables, 720–21
  information system (MIS), 295
  uses of computers, 294–96

Managerial accounting, 5
Marketable securities, defined, 632. *See also* Short-term investments
Market interest rate, 575
Market value, in inventory, 369
Matching concept
    and accrual basis of accounting, 111–13
    applied to sales and collection cycle, 333
    and income determination, 50
    in merchandising, 208
    Real World Example, 114–15
Matching principle. *See* Matching concept
Materiality, 51, 52
Maturity date of bond, 568
Memos
    credit, 219
    debit, 219
    purchaser-issued, 220
    seller-issued, 219
Merchandise inventory. *See* Inventory, merchandise
Merchandising
    closing entries, 222, 224
    defined, 208
    income statement for, 224–25
    operations, 206–37
    use of computers, 293
    worksheet, 220–23
Minority interest, in subsidiaries, 681
Mirror image accounting, 646–48
Mixed accounts, 115
    adjustments, in balance sheets, 177
        in income statements, 176–77
    long-term, 118–21
    reversing entries, in balance sheets, 177
        in income statements, 176–77
Mixed income statement accounts. *See* Mixed accounts
Modified accelerated cost recovery system (MACRS), 419
Monetary item, 837
Monetary unit
    defined, 837
    stability, 49
Moving average, 377–378

N

National Association of Accountants (NAA), 54
Natural resources, depletion, 428–29
Natural year, 26
Net assets, 14
Net income
    and accrual accounting, 112
    adjustments to, 770–71
    defined, 5, 7
    and matching concept, 112
Net loss, 5
Net realizable value, 334
NIFO (next in, next out), 385
Noncurrent accounts, changes in, 773–75

Nonmonetary item, 838
No-par no-stated-value stock, 462
No-par value stock, 461–62
Notes
    in financial statements, 230
    receivable, 67

O

One-write system
    defined, 282
    example, 284
Operating activities, 762–63, 764
Operating cycle, 51, 100–104
    illustrated, 100
    overlapping, 101
    problems, 101
    revenue recognition, 101–2
    and special journals, 269
Operating expenses, classification, 225
Operations efficiency analysis, 234–37
    earnings per share, 727, 731
    in financial statements analysis, 724–30
    long-term assets, 729, 731–32
    return-on-sales ratio, 728
    return on stockholders' equity, 725–27, 731
    return on total assets, 725, 730–31
    trend analysis, 732–733
Original cost of investments, 631
Owners' equity, 8–9

P

Pacioli, Luca, 12
Paid-in capital, 458, 464
Parent company, 672
Partner. *See* Partnerships
Partnership, advantages over proprietorships, 11
Partnerships
    accounting of, 536–37
    admitting a new partner, 541–45
    advantages of, 533
    bonus to new partner, 543–44
    break up of, 534–37
    capital accounts, 536–37
    capital balances, 549–50
    characteristics, 532
    co-ownership of assets, 532, 533
    defined, 9, 531
    disadvantages, 533, 534–37
    division of losses, 538–41
    division of profits, 538–41
    equity, 9, 11
    financial statements, 540–41
    gains on sale of assets, 548
    investment in, 542–43
    limited life of, 532, 533
    liquidation of, 547–51
    loss on sale of assets, 548–49
    mutual agency, 532, 533
    payment from partnership assets, 546–47
    purchase of partner's interest, 542

    salary and interest on capital balances, 539
    sale to new partner, 546
    sale to remaining partner, 546
    sharing profits and losses, 533
    statement of partners' capital, 541
    unlimited liability of, 532, 533
    versus corporations, 533
    withdrawal of partner, 545–47
Par value
    of bond, 574
    of stock, 461
Patents, 430
Paycheck, computerized statement of earnings, 292
Payments, recording related to purchase, 219
Payroll accounting, 287, 288
    computerized, 291–92
    deductions, 285
    employee records, 284
Payroll cycle, 284–90
Payroll deductions
    federal income tax, 285
    FICA payable, 286
    optional, 286
    required, 285
    social security tax, 285
    state income tax, 285
    witholding payable, 286
Payroll journals
    defined, 287
    example, 288
    flow through control account, 287
    individual employee earnings records, 291
    individual employee records, 290
    posting to general ledger, 289
    recording payroll related expenses, 287–90
    slow through the subsidiary accounts, 290
Payroll systems, computerized, 291–92
Periodic inventory system, 218, 375
Periodicity assumption. *See* Periodicity concept
Periodicity concept, 26, 48, 49–50, 170
Permanent accounts, defined, 166
Perpetual system
    of inventory, 375–79
    moving average costing, 377–79
Petty cash
    establishing, 332
    fund, defined, 332
    imprest system, 332
    reimbursing, 332–33
    transactions, 332
Phantom profits, 373, 421
Point-in-time financial statement. *See* Balance sheet
Pooling of interests
    defined, 672
    in subsidiaries, 686–87
    versus purchase, 673
Portfolio, investments, 630–51
Post-closing trial balance, 170, 172
Posting, 71–73
    cash disbursements, 282

cash receipts, 280
closing entries, 170–71
to ledger accounts, 109–11
purchases, 283
sales, 281
Preemptive right, 460
Preferred shares. *See* Preferred stock
Preferred stock, 462–63
book value, 474–75
cumulative, 502, 504
dividends, 502
noncumulative, 504
Premium, bonds. *See also* Bonds,
premiums, 650
Prepayments, expenses, 67
Present value
analysis, 592–601
calculating for bonds, 593, 595
of multiple future amounts, 594
of single future amount, 593
tables, 598–99
Price-earnings ratio, 234, 237
Pricing, 210–11
Prior-period adjustments, 228–29
Production depreciation, 413, 420
Profits, phantom, 373, 421
Property dividends, 501
Proprietorships. *See* Sole proprietorships
defined, 9
equity, 9, 11
Purchase cost of subsidiaries, 676, 677,
682, 683
Purchase order, 15
Purchase and payment cycle, 212–20
accounting process, 274
documents for, 273–78
flow through accounts, 280–81
illustrated, 213
Purchase versus pooling of interests, 673
Purchases
account, 213–14
beginning inventory, 215
defined, 672
discounts, 216
merchandise inventory, 214
of partnership interest, 542
posting entries, 283
recording related to payment, 219
recording in subsidiaries, 681
returns and allowances, 216
Transportion In, 217
Purchases journals, 273
columns, 274
example, 275
Purchasing power gain, 836, 837, 839

Q

Quick current assets, 719
Quick ratio. *See* Acid-test ratio

R

Ratio
acid-test, 231, 233–34, 719
analysis, 234, 737–39

calculations of, 730–36
current, 231–32, 717–18
dividend-yield, 728
in evaluating solvency, 231, 717–18
and financial statements, 235
inventory turnover, 722–23
price-to-earnings, 237, 727–28
return-on-sales, 728
sales, 236
of sales to long-term assets, 729, 732
stockholders' equity, 235–36
summary of ratios, 735–36
times-interest-earned, 727
total assets, 234–35
Receipts, 102
Reciprical accounts, in subsidiaries, 675
Reconciliation
bank, 323
book, 323
Redemption of bonds, 583
Refunding a bond issue, 584
Research and development, costs, 429
Retail inventory method, 383–84
Retained earnings, 7, 165–67, 458
balance sheet, 470
restricted (appropriated), 471–72
restrictions, 470–72
statement of, 5, 7, 227
unrestricted (unappropriated), 471–72
Return
on each share/earnings per share, 237
on sales ratio, 728
on stockholders' equity, 725–27
on stockholders' equity ratio, 235–36
Revenue. *See also* Sales
accrued, 125
defined, 5, 6
expenditures, 411
operating cycle, 723–24
relationship to liabilities, 102
Revenue recognition, 101–2
example, 104–8
Revenue recognition assumption, 50
Reverse stock split, 470
Reversing entries, 172–78
for accrual adjustments, 173–76
guidelines, 172
mixed income-statement account
adjustments, 176

S

Salaries, 284
and accounting period, 128
expense, 127–29
payable, 127–29
Sales
account, 208
adjusting revenue, 209
computerized order-entry system,
292
discounts, 212
posting entries, 281
returns and allowances, 210–11
Sales and collection cycle, 208–12
accounting process, 270
accounts receivable, 333–40

completion of, 333–40
documents for, 269–73
flow through account, 279
illustrated, 209
Sales journals, 269–70
example, 271
Sales ratio, return on, 236
Salvage value, 413
Schedule of accounts receivable, 278
Scrap value, 119
Secret process
example of Coca-Cola, 432
as intangible long-term assets, 431
Securities and Exchange Commission
(SEC), 53
Services, 4
Shares. *See* Stock
Short-term debt, 713–15
Short-term investments
in bonds, 632–35
effect of stock dividends, 637
and lower of cost or market (LCM),
634, 635–37
portfolio, 631–32
significant influence, 637
in stock, 635–39
Short-term portfolio. *See* Short-term
investments
Short-term solvency analysis, 231
Similar asset
defined, 426
example, 426–27
Sinking fund, 574, 581
Social security tax, payroll deductions,
285
Software, development, 433
Sole proprietorships
defined, 530
statement of owner's capital, 531
taxation of, 530–31
versus corporations, 531
Solvency
defined, 230, 713
management decisions, 720–23
revenue operating cycle, 723–24
short-term, 231
short-term analysis, 715–24
working capital calculation, 717–19
Source documents, 15
Special journal, cash receipts, 280
Special journals
cash disbursements, 275–77
cash receipts, 270–73
defined, 268
features of, 268
and general journal, 277
and operating cycle, 269
payroll, 287, 288
purchase journals, 273
sales, 269–70
volume of transactions, 268
Specific identification, 365
Spreadsheets, 295, 296
Stable dollar assumption, 421
Stable unit of measure assumption, 49
State Corporation Acts, 461
State income tax, payroll deductions,
285

Statement of cash flows, 9, 23
    analysis of changes in noncurrent
        accounts, 773
    analysis of current accounts, 775
    calculating increase or decrease in
        cash, 764–67
    calculating from operating activities,
        767–73
    defined, 5, 762
    direct method, 768–70, 787, 791–96
        illustrated, 776
    financing activities, 763, 764
    indirect method, 770–73, 789, 790,
        796–99
        illustrated, 778
    investing activities, 763, 764
    noncash financing, 777
    operating activities, 762–63, 764
    preparation of, 764–77
    preparation of formal, 776
    T-account approach, 791–99
    worksheet approach, 777–91
    worksheet for direct method, 787–88,
        791–96
    worksheet for indirect method, 789
Statement of earnings, computerized,
    292
Statement of financial condition. See
    Balance sheet
Statement of financial position. See
    Balance sheet
Statement of owner's capital, 531
Statement of partners' capital, 541
Statement of retained earnings, 7, 227
    defined, 5
    example, 228
    preparation from worksheet, 165–67
Stock
    accounting, 508–9
    actual control, 642
    authorized, 464
    book value, 473–75
    certificate value, 461
    classification of, 465
    converting from bonds, 573
    cumulative dividends, 463
    dividends, 498–512, 503, 506, 637
    issued, 464
    long-term investments, 640–42
    market crash, 688–89
    no-par no-stated-value, 462
    no-par value, 461
    outstanding, 464
    ownership, 672
    par value, 461, 467
    preferred, 462–63, 474, 502–4
    recording transactions, 464–67
    short-term investments, 635–39, 637
    splits, 467–70, 638–39
        Real World Example, 469
        reverse, 470
        versus dividends, 509–11
    subscriptions, 475–76
    treasury, 464, 511–12
    unissued, 464
    unrealized loss, 636
Stock certificate, 9, 10

Stockholders, 11–12
    limited liability, 459
    rights, 460
    unlimited liability, 459
Stockholders' equity. See also
        Corporations
    balance sheet, 468
    bondholder protection, 727
    components, 473, 474, 498–99
    legal capital, 466
    paid-in capital, 464–65
    ratio of long-term assets to, 729, 732
    retained earnings, 464–65
    return on, 725–27
    sources, 472–73
    stock dividend distributions, 506–8
    trading on, 726
Stock subscriptions, 475–76
Straight-line depreciation, 414, 415
Straight-line method
    of bond amortization, 577
    of depreciation, 119
Subsidiaries, 672
    consolidated financial statements,
        675, 681–84
    goodwill from consolidation, 677
    minority interest, 681
    partially owned, 681–86
    reciprical accounts, 675
    recording purchase, 681
    wholly owned, 674–80
Subsidiary account, flow through, 279,
    280
Subsidiary ledger, 269
    accounts payable, 283
    accounts receivable, 281
    and general ledger, 278–84
Sum-of-the-years'-digits depreciation,
    416–17
Supermarket use of computers, 293

T

T account
    approach to solving cash flow
        problems, 791–99
    defined, 55–56
    direct method, 791–96
    footing, 64, 65
    indirect method, 796–99
Tangible long-term assets, 412
Tax. See also Income tax
    double taxation, 530
    internal revenue code, 418–20
Temporary accounts, defined, 166
Theft, 324–25
Time-based depreciation, 414, 415–16,
    420
Times-interest-earned ratio, 727
Total assets ratio, return on, 234–35
Trade discounts, 220
Trademarks, 431
Trading on the equity, 726
Transactions, defined, 4. See also
        Financial transactions
Transportation In account, 217

Treasury stock, 464
    cost method, 511
    and dividends, 512
Trend analysis
    defined, 732
    horizontal, 732–33
    vertical, 733
Trial balance
    adjusted, 131–32
    defined, 64
    example, 66, 111
    post-closing, 170, 172
    preparing balance sheets from, 69
    preparing income statements
        from, 69
    recording on a worksheet, 161–63
    unadjusted, 161
Trustee, 568

U

Unadjusted trial balance, 161
Uncollectible accounts
    balance sheet estimation, 335–37
    collection of amounts written off,
        338–39
    direct write-off method, 339
    estimates related to accounts
        receivable, 334–37
    income statement estimation, 335
    writing off, 337–39
Unlimited liability
    of corporation, 459
    in partnerships, 532
Unrealized loss
    recovery of, 636–37
    in stock, 636
Useful life, of asset, 119, 408

V

Valuation account, 118
Vertical analysis
    balance sheets, 733
    defined, 733
    income statements, 734

W

Wages, 284
Weighted average, 368
Wholly owned subsidiaries. See
        Subsidiaries, wholly owned
Witholding payable, payroll deductions,
    286
Working capital
    calculation, 717
    defined, 229, 717
    use of current ratio, 717
Worksheet, 160–64
    approach to solving cash-flow
        problems, 777–91

balance sheet preparation, 165, 167
balancing of, 163
columns, 160
completion of, 220–23
consolidated, 680
constant dollar accounting, 836, 837, 839
defined, 160
example, 162, 165
function, 161
· income statement preparation, 164–65

merchandising, 220–23
preparation of financial statements, 164
preparation of statement of retained earnings, 165, 167
recording adjustments, 163
recording a trial balance, 161–63
for statement of cash flows, direct method, 787–88, 791–96
  indirect method, 789, 790
steps in preparation, 161
transactions, 23, 24–25

Y

Year-end
  accrual of bond interest, 592
  calendar, 26
  fiscal, 26
  steps in accounting cycle, 178

Z

Z score, calculation of, 737–39

INDEX OF DISCUSSION CASES AND REAL WORLD EXAMPLES

Achilles Corp., 749
A Different Approach to Stock Splits, 638
A Reverse Stock Split, 486
Assessing Corporate Capital Needs, 572
A Tough Call: The Dividend, 500
Ben & Jerry's, 807
Calculating the Z Score, 737
Carpar, 442
Cash on the Balance Sheet, 347
Closing Entries in Early Forms of
        Bookkeeping, 168
Compound Interest, 660
Computers in the Supermarket, 293
Control Data's Fall from Grace, 393
Dividend Choices, 519
Enormous Successful Corporation, 187

Fitz, Inc., and Roy Corp., 748
How Cash Flows Are Classified, 764
If It's Too Complicated, Forget It, 56
Independence of the Board of
        Directors, 462
Inflation Hits 8-Year High, 834
Ivan and Igor, Wheat Growers, 86
Jasmine Technologies, Inc., 611
Joe, the Restaurateur, 249
J.R.'s Ranch, 441
LCM and the October 19, 1987,
        Decline, 688
Making Dough with a PC, 305
Murphy, Inc., 747
Rodolph and Marmaduke, 35
Saguaro Computers, Inc., 852

Surprise! (Discussion Case), 394
Surprise! (Real World Example), 370
The Bottom Line, 141
The Coca-Cola Secret, 432
The Matching Principle: Why It's So Hard
        to Achieve in Practice, 114
The Price Is Right, 210
This Stock Split is 4799 for 1, 469
To Catch a Thief, 324
To Incorporate or Not?, 559
Which Solution?, 697
Why Are So Many Corporations
        Incorporated in Delaware?, 20
Why Partnerships Break Up, 534

P7-3	Bad Debt Expense, (a) $21,000; (b) $7,500; (c) $13,750
P7-4	Bad Debt Expense, Part A, $7,580; Part B, $17,120
AP7-1	Adjusted Balance, $36,700
AP7-2	Adjusted Balance, $1,204
AP7-3	Bad Debt Expense, (a) $56,000; (b) $40,000; (c) $34,000
AP7-4	Bad Debt Expense, Part A, $22,820; Part B, $26,580

Chapter 8

E8-1	LIFO Inventory, $50
E8-2	LIFO Cost of Goods Sold, $600
E8-3	FIFO Inventory, $250
E8-4	FIFO Cost of Goods Sold, $400
E8-5	Average Inventory, $130
E8-6	Average Cost of Goods Sold, $520
E8-7	LIFO Inventory, $250
E8-8	LIFO Cost of Goods Sold, $400
E8-9	FIFO Inventory, $250
E8-10	FIFO Cost of Goods Sold, $400
E8-11	Average Inventory, $250
E8-12	Average Cost of Goods Sold, $400
E8-14	Retail Inventory at Cost, $6,000
E8-15	Estimated Inventory, $6,350
P8-1	FIFO, $1,000; LIFO, $350; Average, $671
P8-2	FIFO, $25; LIFO, $125
P8-3	Gross Profit, FIFO, $176,400; LIFO, $166,300
P8-4	All Methods Inventory, $400
P8-5	Gross Profit, $117,000
P8-6	Inventory Lost, $10,000
AP8-1	FIFO, $1,600; LIFO, $600; Average, $1,127
AP8-2	FIFO, $4,000; LIFO, $4,320; Average, $4,114
AP8-3	FIFO, $276; LIFO, $242; Average, $263
AP8-4	FIFO, $1,500; LIFO, $1,200; Average, $3,910
AP8-5	Estimated Inventory, $72,000
AP8-6	Estimated Inventory at Cost, $28,483; Shortage at Cost, $180

Chapter 9

E9-1	SL, 19X1, $10,000; DDB, 19X2, $17,600
E9-2	Cost of Land, $75,000
E9-3	SYD, 19X1, $7,000; DDB, 19X2, $7,000
E9-5	Cost of Printer, $3,700
E9-6	SL, $22,500; DDB, $35,200
E9-7	(b) Gain, $2,500; (c) Loss, $7,500
E9-8	Simco, Gain, $140,000
E9-10	Depletion on Production, $48,000
E9-11	Amortization Expense, $57,353
E9-12	Amortization Expense, $1,250
P9-1	SL, $1,000 Each Year; SYD, Year 2, $1,200
P9-2	Depreciation Expense, 19X9, $12,400
P9-3	(1) SYD, $3,600; DDB, $5,500; MACRS, $3,667
P9-4	Depreciable Cost, $24,000; Depreciation, 19X7, $4,000
P9-6	Part A, Cost of New Equipment, $205,600; Part B, Loss from Fire, $3,000
AP9-1	SL, $12,000; DDB, Year 3, $444; Usage Year 2, $7,200
AP9-2	Depreciation 19X8, $6,200; Loss from Fire, $7,900
AP9-3	$916, Less Taxes Paid under MACRS vs. SL
AP9-4	Depreciable Cost, $48,000; 19X5 Depreciation, $8,000
AP9-6	Phantom Profit, $4,556

Chapter 10

E10-3	7,000 Shares in the Treasury
E10-5	$304,000 Available for Operations
E10-6	Book Value, $30.40
E10-8	Bool Value, $46.80
P10-1	Total Equity, $416,000
P10-2	Book Value, $11.90; Amount Available for Dividends, $500
P10-3	Stockholders' Equity, Jan. 31, $352,900; June 30, $366,500
P10-4	Total Equity, $99,300
AP10-1	Total Equity, $1,576,000
AP10-2	Book Value, $34; Available for Dividends, $50,000
AP10-3	Stockholders' Equity, Jan. 31, $645,000; June 30, $676,500
AP10-4	Total Equity, $1,409,800

Chapter 11

E11-1	Liquidating Dividend, $86,000
E11-2	Income Dividend, $75,000
E11-4	Preferred, $1,000
E11-6	Preferred, $45,000
P11-3	Total Equity, $28,295
AP11-3	Total Equity, $4,766

Chapter 12

E12-1	Split Equally, $15,000
E12-2	Split Equally, $22,500
E12-3	Split Equally, $22,500
E12-4	$24,000 to A
E12-5	$18,000 to B
E12-6	$25,500 to B
E12-7	$27,000 to A
E12-8	Credit C Capital, $13,000
E12-9	Credit C Capital, $50,000
E12-10	Credit C Capital, $45,000
E12-11	Credit C Capital, $60,000
E12-12	A, $4,000; B and C, $6,000
E12-13	$7,600 to B; $8,400 to C
P12-1	Net Income, $5,400
P12-2	Debit to X Capital, $10,000
P12-3	Credit to H Capital, (1) $16,000; (2) $19,200; (3) $14,400
P12-4	Cash to C, $33,750
AP12-1	Net Income, $19,000
AP12-2	Credit to M Capital, $23,000
AP12-3	Credit to M Capital, (1) $30,000; (2) $22,500; (3) $36,000
AP12-4	Cash to D, $1,200

Chapter 13

E13-2	Premium Amortization, $750
E13-3	Discount Amortization, $650
E13-5	Premium Amortization, $384
E13-6	Discount Amortization, $333
E13-8	Gain on Retirement, $1,500
E13-9	Loss on Retirement, $1,500
E13-10	Selling Price, $100,000
E13-11	Selling Price, $87,550
E13-12	Selling Price, $114,900
E13-13	Annual Contribution, $5,700
P13-1	EPS Bonds, $9.50; Preferred, $8.50; Common, $5.56
P13-2	Discount Amortization, $500
P13-3	Interest Expense, Case A, $12,000; Case B, $11,000; Case C, $14,000
P13-4	Discount Amortization, $4,623; Financing 7.7% Last Interest Period
P13-5	Premium Amortization, SL, $772; Effective Interest, $614 First Interest Payment
P13-6	Issue Price 16% Bonds, $432,800
AP13-1	EPS Bonds, $.64; Common Stock, $1.53
AP13-2	Premium Amortization, $2,000
AP13-3	Interest Expense, Case A, $30,000; Case B, $28,000; Case C, $32,400
AP13-4	Premium Amortization, $1,692; Financing 5.1% Last Interest Period
AP13-5	Discount Amortization, SL, $3,355; Effective Interest, $4,630 Last Interest Period
AP13-6	Issue Price 10% Bonds, $105,056